CHRONOLOGY
OF THE
WAR AT SEA
1939–1945

Chronology of the War at Sea
is published under
the auspices of the
Bibliothek für Zeitgeschichte
(Library of Contemporary History)
Stuttgart

CHRONOLOGY
OF THE
WAR AT SEA
1939–1945

The Naval History of World War Two

J. ROHWER AND G. HUMMELCHEN

Naval Institute Press
Annapolis, MD 21402

Published and distributed in the United States of America
by the Naval Institute Press, 118 Maryland Avenue,
Annapolis, Maryland 21402–5035.

This edition is authorized for sale only in
the United States and its territories and possessions.

First edition 1972, 1974
Second, revised, expanded edition 1992

Library of Congress Catalog Card No. 92–80063

Translated by Derek Masters

ISBN 1–55750–105–X

Quality printing and binding by Butler & Tanner Ltd,
The Selwood Printing Works, Caxton Road
Frome, Somerset BA11 1NF, England.

CONTENTS

Preface

Chronology of the War at Sea 1939–1945 started life in the summer of 1956, when the authors began a monthly column called 'Gedenktage' in the journal of the German Naval Association, *Leinen los!* This continued to late 1963.[1] Meanwhile in September 1959 we began to publish a bi-monthly series 'Vor Zwanzig Jahren' in the naval journal *Marine-Rundschau*; this set out more details of the operations at sea in all oceans.[2] This series was continued to autumn 1965. These two series provided the basis for the first book-edition of the *Chronik des Seekrieges 1939–1945*, which was published in 1968 and reprinted in 1980 and 1981.[3] This German volume was the forerunner of the first English edition, published in a much enlarged and more complete form in two volumes in 1972 and 1974.[4]

Since the publication of these two volumes, a great amount of new information has become available. Most nations opened their archives after thirty years, and many personal contacts with naval experts in many countries on both sides of the 'Iron Curtain' were established. Especially important was the fact that the secrecy around the intelligence background of many operations was lifted after 1975 and that the establishment of 'glasnost' in the countries of the Warsaw Pact allowed experts in the East European countries to answer questions that had been subject to security restriction until this time. Many corrections and additions would be necessary to bring our *Chronology* up to date; by now out of print, it was much sought-after by historians the world over. So the proposal to our publishers, Lionel Leventhal in Great Britain and Tom Epley in the USA, to prepare a new and again enlarged edition was received with enthusiasm.

In the first editions of the chronology we tried to include both important and typical events of the war at sea 1939–1945 in all the oceans of the world. It was not our purpose to provide an historical account in abbreviated form or a simple enumeration of dates recalling certain operations and engagements, but something between the two – an aid to the quick understanding of the many happenings at sea. In so doing, we have tried so far as possible to place the events in their tactical or operational context from both sides. It was, therefore, necessary to lump together the events for certain periods instead of entering them on a purely day-to-day basis. So actions and to some extent, even operations that were important but did not lead to real fighting are recorded in entries giving back-ground to the ensuing successes, losses or damages. But to make it as easy as possible for the reader to find specific events, the first and the last dates of the periods in question are reproduced in bold type followed by the maritime area. The order is chronological. In addition, the detailed indexes of persons and ship names, of units, operational code-names and of convoys will provide further help in a specific quest.

We have quite deliberately given an international basis to the work. Many publications of recent decades limit themselves to describing events essentially from one side, and some authors continue to rely on what are inevitably often one-sided, unreliable or incomplete reports. It has been our aim to give as correct a picture as possible, on the basis of the best available sources, of what actually happened, on both sides and of who participated in the events.

A few figures will show in what detail the navies of all countries engaged in the war have been treated. There are approximately 1,500 German warships and auxiliary warships besides more than 1,200 U-boats. There are more than 1,700 British and about 300 Commonwealth ships, almost 1,700 American, about 800 Soviet, about 700 Japanese and 700 Italian; more than 300 French as well as about 300 warships of the smaller sea powers – Belgium, Brazil, Bulgaria, China, Colombia, Cuba, Denmark, Finland, Greece, Iran, Manchukuo, the Netherlands, Norway, Poland, Rumania, Spain, Sweden, Thailand, Turkey and Yugoslavia. Further, about 2,000 merchant ships of all seafaring states are mentioned (generally more than once).

If, in spite of the more than 11,000 ships and approximately 3,300 persons named, a reader fails to find his own ship or commander, he should bear in mind that in some places another individual or another ship might equally have been mentioned but that, generally speaking, it would have been impossible to include more in the available space. Likewise it was not possible to mention the responsible staffs ashore on both sides in each of the larger operations. We had to confine ourselves to the commanders of forces at sea and the commanding officers of ships and submarines.

In this new edition we have tried to eliminate errors and false claims from the earlier editions. And we made important additions. We have recorded to some extent the influence radio intelligence (not only 'Ultra' but also the efforts of other navies in this field) had on operations. We have added considerably more information on the convoy operations in the North Atlantic, the centre of the Battle of the Atlantic and the U-boat war, to show the efforts of the Allied escort groups and the Allied air forces in the whole campaign. We have tried to provide as complete information as possible on losses of naval ships of all navies from battleships down to minesweepers and submarines (including, for the German

Navy, also most of the auxiliaries). We have corrected the success reports of the Allied, especially the US submarines, according to new sources. And finally we have also included new information from Soviet sources about operations, losses and transfers and have corrected claims on both sides as far as possible. However, this is one field where we shall have to continue comparing sources from both sides with the help of our Russian collegues in the future, because they can only now use the sources openly.

Unfortunately it proved impossible to mention *all* the warships, auxiliary vessels of all navies and the great number of merchant ships in any operation: we had to decide to include ships participating in operations only down to the level of corvettes, minesweepers and submarines, and to omit in most cases the many smaller vessels of the coastal forces and the auxiliaries. And we have to ask the reader to look for merchant ship losses in other, more specialised, books.[5]

Considerable space has been given to submarine warfare, and the defence against it, on both sides, which decisively influenced the course of the war at sea in the Atlantic, the Mediterranean and the Pacific. We have included not only the operations that have so far received almost exclusive attention, (i.e., those in which important results were achieved in attack or defence) but also the 'no result' operations – the abortive and unsuccessful actions that have been largely neglected in the framework of the overall operations. For example, Allied convoys without U-boat contact were the truly successful operations, and we have tried to describe why they were not attacked. So it was necessary to include the convoys of the second half of 1941, when effective convoy-routing based on 'Ultra' prevented contacts, and to include the actions of the last two years the range of which has been greatly underestimated. However, in these cases, we found we could largely omit the names of ships sunk by submarines since they can be found in the publications mentioned in footnote 5.

Mine-warfare operations are new to this edition, and the air war at sea has been, on the basis of the now-available source material, more precisely described than has hitherto been the case. The same is true of the activities of German motor-torpedo boats. We have also tried to pay more attention to the daily war routine of the escort forces and their actions and losses by dealing with typical events in all theatres of war without striving after a completeness that would have exceeded the limits of the book.

The main sources for our work were, first, official and semi-official works on the war at sea, plus specialised studies and the memoirs of commanders and senior officers. We have also made extensive use of unpublished material not only from the German side but also from archives in Great Britain, Canada, the United States, Italy, France and, in the last two years, also the Soviet Union. This was only possible with the great support we got from our colleagues in the archives and researching colleagues in many countries whom we met at the many international conferences and symposia since about 1973, especially during those of the International Commissions on Military History and on the History of the Second World War.

It is not possible to mention here all the sources used and all the relevant literature. We would like to refer the reader to the *Bibliothek für Zeitgeschichte* in Stuttgart (P.O. Box 105441, 7000 Stuttgart 10, Germany) for specific bibliographical information.[6] In what follows, we mention the most important sources for our work.

Germany: We used the central war diaries, for example, the war diaries of the Seekriegsleitung (Naval Staff)[7], of the Befehlshaber der U-Boote (B.d.U.) (Commander U-boats)[8] and of other regional commands as well as situation reports of the C-in-C *Luftwaffe* and operational staffs of the other forces. Of the printed books the most valuable were M. Salewski's *Die deutsche Seekriegsleitung 1939–1945* (3 volumes) and the *Lagevorträge des Oberbefehlshabers der Kriegsmarine vor Hitler 1939–1945*, edited by G. Wagner.[9] A great amount of information on the U-boat war came from the study G. Hessler prepared for the British Admiralty after the war.[10]

Great Britain: The basis of the account is provided by the many volumes of the *History of the Second World War*, especially the four volumes by S. W. Roskill, *The War at Sea*, and the four volumes by F. H. Hinsley and his team, *British Intelligence in the Second World War*, published by H. M. Stationery Office, London. In addition many original archival sources from the Naval Historical Branch, the Air Historical Branch and the Public Records Office were used, especially the 'Pink Lists', the proceedings of convoy commodores and senior officers escort, parts of the war diary of the Naval Staff and volumes of the Air Ministry *The RAF in the Maritime War*. Apart from the relevant literature and a considerable correspondence, particular use was made of the *Secret Naval Notes*, published by the Naval Intelligence Division in London during the war, to clear up many points of detail.

Commonwealth: For Canada, starting with the work by Joseph Schull, *The Far Distant Ships*, published by the Department of National Defence in Ottawa, we used a great amount of archival material on convoys and their escorts from the Directorate of History of the Ministry of Defence in Ottawa, as well as the other publications of this office, especially the works by M. Milner, *North Atlantic Run*, and the volumes of the *Official History of the Royal Canadian Air Force*, edited by W.A.B. Douglas. For Australia and New Zealand, we used relevant volumes of the series *Australia in the War of 1939–1945* from the Australian War Memorial in Canberra and the *Official History of New Zealand in the Second World War 1939–1945*; for South Africa, L.C.F. Turner's, *War in the Southern Oceans 1939–1945*; and for India, *The Royal Indian Navy 1939–1945* by D.J.E. Collins.

USA: Here first use could be made of the very detailed accounts by S.E. Morison, *History of United States Naval Operations in World War II* (fifteen volumes); for amphibious operations the relevant volumes of the official series *United States Army in World War II*, the *Marine Corps Monographs*, the *History of United States Marine Corps Operations in World War II*, and the semi-official volumes of W.F. Craven and J.L. Cate, *The Army Air Forces in World War II*. Also the publications of the Naval Historical Division (later Center of Naval History) were used, especially the *Dictionary of American Naval Fighting Ships*, as well as from the US Naval Institute, particularly, the *US Naval Chronology, World War II*, and the volumes of T. Roscoe, *Destroyers* and *Submarines*, and many individual publications. Later, extensive use was also made of the relevant documents from the Center of Naval History, especially its Operational Archives, the Marine Corps Historical Center, the Center for Military History and the US Air Force Historical Center, as well as the National Archives in Washington.

USSR: Initially the very comprehensive Soviet naval literature on the history of the Second World War was systematically assessed, particularly the memoirs of the most important commanders and accounts by naval historians. During the *détente* period in the early sixties there was also some written exchange of dates with the official naval historian. Thanks to the knowledge gained, it was possible to check, elaborate and clarify many details in the German, Finnish and Swedish documents of the war period. Of great importance also was the exchange of dates with many experts on the Soviet Navy in other countries. For this edition we have begun to make use of new information now made available by the Soviet Military Archives and of new publications such as the volumes of S.S. Berezhnoi *Korabli i Suda VMF SSSR*, of V.I. Dmitriev *Sovetskoe Podvodnoe Korable Stroenie* and *Boevaya Letopis' Voenno-Morskogo Flota 1941–1942*, and many volumes of the series *Sbornik Materialov po Opytu Boevoy Deyatel'nosti Voenno-Morskikh Sil Soyuza SSR*; and finally the series in the journal *Morskoi Sbornik*, which started in June 1991 with detailed monthly diaries. Unfortunately these publications generally became available too late to be completely evaluated for this edition.

Japan: In addition to the Anglo-American literature, it was possible to refer to a number of Japanese works both original and translated. Most important were the naval volumes of the official Japanese series *Senshi-sosho* (War History series, *History of the Second World War in Asia and in the Pacific*, 102 volumes).[11] Of particular value were the *Japanese Monographs*, put together by Japanese officers with the Allied Supreme Command in Tokyo, studies of operations of individual branches of the Japanese Navy and of special battle areas. Special use was made of *The Imperial Japanese Navy in World War II*. In addition there was an extensive exchange of dates and information with Japanese officers and historians.

Italy: The basis for the account of the activities of the Italian Fleet is the very detailed official work of the Ufficio Storico della Marina Militare, *La Marina Italiana nella Seconda Guerra Mondiale* (18 volumes), the exchange of dates with the several chiefs of this office over the years and, later, the volumes of the former archivist of this office, A. Santoni, on the naval-air war in the Mediterranean and the role of 'Ultra' there.

France: For the period up to June 1940 much use was made of the then unpublished volumes of the Service Historique de la Marine about the operations 1939–40.[12] For the subsequent period use was made chiefly of the work by Amiral Auphan and J. Mordal *La Marine Française pendant la Seconde Guerre Mondiale*.

Smaller navies: In addition to relevant, and in some respects extraordinarily detailed, specialist literature, official publications were particularly used, including the following: for Brazil, C.A. Machado da Fonseca, *A Marinha Brasileira e a Segunda Guerra Mundial (1939–1945)* and A.O. Saldanha da Gama's *A Marinha do Brasil na Segunda Guerra Mundial*; for Finland, and official *Suomen Sota 1941–1945* (vol. IX); for Greece, K.A. Alexandre's *To Nautikon Mas Kata ten Polemiken periodon 1941–1945*; for the Netherlands, K.W.L. Bezemer's *Zij vochten op de zeven zeen*; for Norway, E.A. Steen's *Norges Sjökrig 1940–1945* (7 volumes); and for Poland, J. Pertek's *Wiuelkie dni Malej Floty*.

Ships and Ship Losses: For the warships, use was made of the well-known international annual fleet handbooks and of the many reference books that have appeared since the war on individual fleets and their classes of ships, the most important of which is *Conway's All the World's Fighting Ships 1922–1946*. For the merchant ships, use was made of the wartime volumes of *Lloyd's Register of Shipping*, copies of which from the former British Ministry of Transport are now in the collection of the Bibliothek für Zeitgeschichte; also the editions of E. Gröner's *Die Handelsflotten der Welt* as well as much documentation in international naval, maritime and technical periodicals were used.

Apart from the various official national lists of losses of warships and merchant ships that have appeared in the years since the war, two are to be mentioned as exceptionally valuable sources: The list B.R.1337 *British and Foreign Merchant Vessels lost or damaged by Enemy Action during the Second World War* and its supplements for the merchant ships under Allied control; and J.D. Brown's *Warship Losses of World War Two* for losses of warships down to the level of corvettes and minesweepers of all navies.

Appointments: For the German Navy, use was made of Lohmann-Hildebrandt's *Die Deutsche Kriegsmarine 1939–1945* and in the case of foreign navies details were taken from the relevant literature.

Despite these ample sources and extensive use of the international literature, it would not have been possible for us to provide so much detail and to keep it within the permissible framework without the help of numerous correspondents, officers of the German, Axis, Allied and neutral navies and merchant marines and of many naval historians and ship-lovers all over the world. Our thanks are due to all who helped during more than forty years, even if, for reasons of space, they cannot all be named.

In particular, we should like to thank our correspondents and personal friends in the historical departments of the various navies, armies and air forces for their generous help over the years, many of whom are no longer with us.

In *Germany*: Dr M. Kehrig and Dr G. Maierhöfer of the Bundesarchiv-Militärarchiv and Captains Dr F. Forstmeier and Dr W. Rahn of the Militärgeschichtliches Forschungsamt.

In *Great Britain*: Rear-Adm R.M. Bellairs, Commander M.G. Saunders, Lt-Cdr P.K. Kemp, H.C. Beaumont, J.D. Lawson, Rear-Adm P.N. Buckley, Capt D. MacIntyre and J.D. Brown; and especially R. Coppock of the Naval Historical Branch and H. Probert of the RAF Historical Branch. Special thanks go to Mrs M.Z. Pain for her assistance in the Public Record Office.

In *Canada*: Dr G.N. Tucker and E.C. Russell of the former Naval Historical section, Col C.P. Stacey, Prof S.F. Wise and especially Dr W.A.B. Douglas, Dr M. Milner and Dr G. Sarty of the Directorate of History, Ottawa.

In *Australia*: Prof Dr R. O'Neill, then in the Institute for Strategic Studies in Canberra.

In *South Africa*: Prof L.C.F. Turner, J.A.I. Agar-Hamilton and J.E. Betzler of the Union War Histories Section in Pretoria.

In the *USA*: Rear-Adm E.M. Eller, Capt F.K. Loomis, and especially Dr D. Allard, R. Cavalcante and Mrs K. Lloyd of the Center for Naval History; Brig-Gen E. Simmons of the Marine Corps History Division; Dr R. Scheina of the Coast Guard Historical Unit; J.W. Huston and Dr B. Cooling of the office of Air Force History; and Brig-Gen J.L. Collins and Ch. V.P. von Lüttichau of the Center of Military History. In the National Archives we got assistance from Dr R. Wolfe, Mr Taylor and Mr Cunliffe.

In the *Soviet Union/Russia*: First contact was to Capt Dr V.I. Achkasov, long-time head of naval history; and then to Capt I. Amosov of the Institute for Military History and Capt S.S. Berezhnoi from a group of naval experts, as well as to Col I. Venkov and Maj O. Starkov of the Military Archives of the General Staff.

In *Japan*: First we exchanged letters with Col T. Hattori and Capt T. Ohmae, working with the Historical Division of the Allied Supreme Commander in Japan; then with Rear-Adm K. Sakamoto from the Office of War Histories, and finally Maj-Gen Y. Goda and Prof H. Iwashima of the Military History Department of the National Institute for Defense studies in Tokyo, and Rear-Adm Prof Dr S. Toyama of the National Defence Academy helped much.

In *Italy*: Amm di Sq. G. Fioravanzo, Amm di Sq. A. Cocchia, C-Amm V.E. Tognelli, C-Amm P.M. Pollina, C-Amm A. Donato, C-Amm G. Galuppini and Amm di Div R. Sicurezza of the Ufficio Storico della Marina Militare in Rome always gave required assistance.

In *France*: C-Admiral Rostand, Méd-en-chef H. Cras, C-Amirals Brossard, Fliche, Chatelle and Kessler and Prof Ph. Masson of the Service Historique de la Marine in Paris answered many questions.

From the smaller navies, the following were of great help: In *Brazil*, Capt M.J. Guedes of the Serviço de Documentaçâo Geral da Marina in Rio de Janeiro; in *Greece*, Commodores M. Simpas and K. Varfis of the Naval History Department in Athens; in the *Netherlands*, L.L. von Münching and F.C. van Oosten of the Sectie Marine Geschiedenis in Den Haag; in *Norway*, Orlogskapt E.A. Steen of the Forsvarets Krigshistoriske Avdeling in Oslo.

Most helpful were the authors of the histories of the war at sea in Great Britain, Capt S.W. Roskill, and in the United States, Rear-Adm Prof S.E. Morison and his colleagues Dr R. Pineau and Dr J. Bauer.

There were two areas in which we received support from an international group of experts. To clear up many difficult questions about the war in East European waters we could count on the expertise of our friends J. Meister (Barraba, Australia), S. Breyer (Hanau, Germany), C. Huan (Paris), R. Erikson (Phoenix, USA), P. Warneck (Brussels, Belgium), R. Greger (Prague, CSFR) and R.W. Herrick (Washington). And in the area of the most important issue of intelligence we had contact and at many international conferences met D. Kahn (New York), Prof Sir F.H. Hinsley (Cambridge, UK), P. Beesly (Lymington, UK), V-Adm N. Denning (London), Col Dr W. Kozaczuk (Warsaw, Poland), Prof R.V. Jones (Aberdeen, UK), Prof A. Santoni (Rome, Italy), E. Thomas (London), Prof H. Deutsch and Prof M. Handel (both Carlisle, USA), R. Lewin (London), Capt K.A. Knowles (Jacksonville, USA), McDiarmid (Seattle, formerly Ottawa, Canada) and Rear Adm E.T. Layton (USA).

Of the many naval officers, historians and ship-lover correspondents, in addition to the above-mentioned persons, we wish to thank the following.

In *Germany*: Grand-Adm K. Dönitz, V-Adm Prof F. Ruge, R-Adm G. Wagner, R-Adm E. Godt, Capt G. Hessler, Capt H. Meckel, Capt H. Bonatz, and Capt W. Gördes as well as many commanding officers of ships and U-boats; the historians, Prof Dr W. Hubatsch, Prof Dr M. Salewski, Prof Dr J. Dülffer, Prof Dr E. Strohbusch and Dr H.J. Kowark; and the ships experts E. Gröner, Dr D. Jung, M. Maass, H. Bredow, S. Terzibaschitsch, E. Rössler, H. Fock, B. Herzog, W. Harnack, K.V. Kutzleben, J. Brennecke, W. Dinklage, A. Kludas and H.R. Lochner.

In *Great Britain*: Vice-Admirals B.B. Schofield and Sir Peter Gretton, Capt A.B. Sainsbury, Lt-Cdr N.J. Whitley; and the authors A.J. Watts, A. Preston, Dr A. Price, M. Middlebrook, J. Costello, N.L.R. Franks and E.S. Cheek.

In *Canada*: Professors M. Hadley and W. Rodney, Dr G.R. Lindsay and D.G. Harris.

In *Australia*: Lt-Cdr E.M. Stevens.

In the *USA*: Fleet Admiral C.W. Nimitz, Admiral A. Burke, Rear Adm W. Ansel, Capt J. Holmes, Capt J.M. Waters (USCG); Prof E.B. Potter, Prof Ph. K. Lundeberg, Prof J. Kipp, Prof R. Higham, Prof J. Sweetman, Prof M. McGwire, Dr P. Abbazia, Dr M. Vego, F. Uhlig; and the ships experts Dr N. Friedman, N. Polmar, W.H. Garzke, R.O. Dulin and P.H. Silverstone.

In the *Soviet Union/Russia*: The members of the Academy of Sciences, Prof A.M. Samsonov, Prof A.V. Basov and Prof I.M. Moguilevkin assisted in special questions; as did the ships expert B. Lemachko.

In *Japan*: Adm K. Nomura, Rear-Adm N. Fujii, Col Y. Suginoo; the historians Prof Sh. Fujimaki, M. Yamamoto and M. Sekino; and the ships experts Sh. Fukui and H. Fukaya.

In *Italy*: Prof A. Santoni; and the ships experts A. Barilli, A. Fraccaroli and G. Giorgerini.

In *France*: H. le Masson and P. Hervieux.

In *Brazil*: Almirante A.O. Saldanha di Gama.

In *Finland*: Commodore E. Wihtol; Prof Mäkelä; P.O. Ekman.

In *India*: Rear-Adm A.P.S. Bindra.

In *Pakistan*: Commodore T. Majeed.

In *Poland*: J. Pertek and M. Twardowski.

In *Sweden*: Capt K.E. Westerlund.

We express our warm thanks to them all and to many anonymous helpers, not least the members of our own families, without whose cooperation the comprehensive indexes could not have been prepared in time.

Both English editions were revised and in parts considerably amended versions of the old German edition. Best thanks are due to D. Masters, translator, and to A.J. Watts, who was concerned with the illustrations of the first English edition; to R.D. Chesneau, who edited the new, and again much enlarged edition; and not least to our publishers for their splendid assistance in preparing this edition.

Despite all efforts the present work will not answer every question and will contain some mistakes and errors because it has been impossible to fill gaps in the available source material, or to clear up contradictions, or because information has been incorrectly interpreted and printing errors have been overlooked. We shall, therefore, be grateful for any information that may give a truer and more complete picture. We hope that the book will prove to be a useful reference work for all those who use it.

We dedicate this volume to the many thousands of sailors, mariners and airmen who lost their lives during the 73 months of the war at sea.

Stuttgart, 20 January 1992

Jürgen Rohwer
Gerhard Hümmelchen

Please send corrections or amendments to:
Prof Dr Jürgen Rohwer
c/o: Bibliothek für Zeitgeschichte
Postfach 10 54 41
D-7000 Stuttgart 10
Germany

1. Rohwer, Jürgen: 'Gedenktage' in *Leinen los!* Monatszeitschrift des Deutschen Marinebundes. München: Okeanos-Verlag, Nos. 3/1956 to 12/1963.
2. Rohwer, Jürgen and Hümmelchen, Gerhard: 'Vor zwanzig Jahren. Chronik des Seekrieges 1939–1945' in *Marine-Rundschau*. Frankfurt/M: E. S. Mittler and München: J. F. Lehmanns 56(1959) to 62(1965). Total of 259 pages.
3. Rohwer, Jürgen and Hümmelchen, Gerhard: *Chronik des Seekrieges 1939–1945*. Ed. by Arbeitskreis für Wehrforschung and Bibliothek für Zeitgeschichte. Oldenburg/Hamburg: Stalling 1968. 655 pp. Reprints 1980 and 1981.
4. Rohwer, Jürgen and Hümmelchen, Gerhard: *Chronology of the War at Sea 1939–1945*. Translated by Derek Masters. London: Ian Allan, vol. I (1939–1942) 1972, XV, 288 pp., vol. II (1943–1945) 1974, X, 362 pp.
5. Rohwer, Jürgen: *Axis Submarine Successes 1939–1945*. Annapolis: US Naval Institute 1983.
Alden, John D.: *U.S. Submarine Attacks During World War II*. Annapolis: US Naval Institute 1989.
B.R.1337. *British and Foreign Merchant Vessels Lost or Damaged by Enemy Action During Second World War*. London: Naval Staff (Trade Division) Admiralty. 1 October 1945.
6. A bibliographical guide including research reports and bibliographies of 67 nations is: *Neue Forschungen zum Zweiten Weltkrieg. Literaturberichte und Bibliographien*. Hrsg. von Jürgen Rohwer und Hildegard Müller. Schriften der Bibliothek für Zeitgeschichte, Band 28. Koblenz: Bernard & Graefe 1990.
7. *Kriegstagebuch der Seekriegsleitung 1939–1945*. Teil A. Herford: Mittler & Sohn 1987ff. (Planned to be 68 vols.)
8. Available in Microfilm from the National Archives, Washington.
9. English edition without the comments of G. Wagner: *Fuehrer Conferences on Naval Affairs 1939–1945*. London: Greenhill Books 1990.
10. Now Published as *The U-Boat War in the Atlantic 1939–1945* by H.M. Stationery Office, London (1989).
11. Bibliography of this series: Tsuchiya, Ichiro: Das 'National Institute for Defense Studies' und sein 'Military History Department' in Tokyo. In: *Jahresbibliographie der Bibliothek für Zeitgeschichte*. Vol. 59, 1987. Koblenz: Bernard & Graefe 1989. pp. 327–346.
12. Now published by the Service Historique de la Marine.

Abbreviations and Glossary

AA Anti-Aircraft

AF (*Artillerie-Fährprahm*) Gun ferry barge

AK Supply Transport (Auxiliary Kargo)

AKA Attack Supply Transport (Auxiliary Kargo Attack)

AP Troop Transport (Auxiliary Personnel)

APA Attack Troop Transport (Auxiliary Personnel Attack)

APD Fast Transport (Auxiliary Personnel Destroyer)

A/S Anti-submarine

ASV radar Air-to-surface-vessel radar

ATF Tug (Auxiliary Tug Fleet)

Batdiv Battleship Division

BB Battleship

Bde Brigade

BdU Commander of U-boats

BF Base Force

BKA Russian armoured cutter

BLT Battalion Landing Team

Bn Battalion

BO Large Russian submarine-chaser, patrol boat

Bord Fl Gr (*Bordfliegergruppe*) Ship-borne wing, originally earmarked for uncompleted aircraft carrier

BS Bombardment Squadron (USAAF)

Capt 1st Class Russian Captain

Capt 2nd Class Russian Commander* (German *Fregattenkapitän*)

Capt 3rd Class Russian Commander (German *Korvettenkapitän*)

Cdr* Fregattenkapitän (or corresponding rank) in the German, French, Italian, etc, navies

Cdr Korvettenkapitän; Commander

CG Coast Guard (US)

COMINCH Commander-in-Chief (US)

CPO Chief Petty Officer

DD Destroyer

DE Destroyer Escort

Desdiv Destroyer Division (US)

Desron Destroyer Squadron (US)

Div Division

DM (*Drudkdosen*) Oyster Mines

EASTOMP Eastern Ocean Meeting Point

EG Escort Group

EMC German Moored Mine (last letter dcnotcs mark of mine)

ES Escort Squadron

E-torpedo Electric Drive Torpedo

F F1–10 (*Flottenbegleiter*) Fleet Escort Vessel; F100–1200 (*Fährprahm*) Landing Craft Tank; Flagship

FAA Fleet Air Arm

FAGr (*Fern Aufklärungs Gruppe*) Long-range reconnaissance wing

FAT (*Flächen Absuchender* or *Feder Apparat Torpedo*) Pattern running torpedo

FDS Fighter Direction Ship

Fg Off Flying Officer

Fl Div (*Fliegerdivision*) German Air Division. The *Fliegerdivision* was later renamed *Fliegerkorps* and could operate within, or independently of, a *Luftflotte* (Air Fleet)

FK (*Fliegerkorps*) German Air Corps

Frhr Freiherr (Baron)

Front Russian Army Group

FS Fighter Squadron (USAAF)

GB Gunboat

Geschwader German Air Group

Gruppe German Air Wing

(The *Geschwader* was the largest air formation with a nominal fixed strength. It usually comprised 90 aircraft in 3–4 *Gruppen* with each *Gruppe* consisting of 3–4 *Staffeln* or squadrons)

HF/DF High Frequency Direction Finding

Inf Infantry

JG (*Jagdgeschwader*) Fighter Group

KFlGr (*Küstenfliegergruppe*) Coastal Air Wing

KFK (*Kriegsfischkutter*) Naval fishing cutter

KG (*Kampfgeschwader*) Bomber Group

LAT (*Leichter Artillerieträger*) Light aux. gunboat

LCF Landing Craft Flak

LCI Landing Craft Infantry

LCI (G) Landing Craft Infantry Gunboat

LCI (M) Landing Craft Infantry Mortar

LCM Landing Craft Mechanized

LCS Landing Craft Support

LCT Landing Craft Tank

LCVP Landing Craft Vehicle Personnel

LG (*Lehrgeschwader*) Air Trainer Group

LMBC German Ground Mine (Laid by aircraft)

LSD Landing Ship Dock

LSG Landing Ship Gun

LSI Landing Ship Infantry

LSM Landing Ship Medium

LST Landing Ship Tank

LSV Landing Ship Vehicle

Luftwaffe German Air Force

LUT (*Lage Unabhängiger Torpedo*) Pattern running torpedo

M (*Minensucher*) Minesweeper

MAD Magnetic Airborne Detector

MAS Italian Motor Torpedo Boat, originally submarine-chaser

MCMS Mine Countermeasures Ship

MDS Mine Destruction Ship

MFP (*Marine Fährprahm*) Naval ferry barge

MGB Motor Gun Boat

ML Motor Launch

MMS Motor Minesweeper

MO Russian submarine-chaser (small)

MOMP Mid Ocean Meeting Point

MS Minesweeper

Ms Italian motor torpedo boat

MTB Motor Torpedo Boat

OKH (*Oberkommando des Heeres*) Army High Command

OKM (*Oberkommando der Marine*) Naval High Command

OKW (*Oberkommando der Wehrmacht*) Armed Forces Command

OTU Operational Training Unit (RAF)

PB Flotilla (*Vorposten*) Patrol Boat Flotilla

PC Patrol Craft

PCE Patrol Craft Escort

PF Patrol Frigate

P Off Pilot Officer

PT Patrol Torpedo Boat

R (*Räumboot*) Motor Minesweeper

RA (*Räumboot Ausland*) Captured MMS in German Navy

RAAF Royal Australian Air Force

RAN Royal Australian Navy

RCAF Royal Canadian Air Force

RCN Royal Canadian Navy

RCT Regimental Combat Team

Regt Regiment

RIN Royal Indian Navy

RN Royal Navy

RNeN Royal Netherlands Navy

RNoN Royal Norwegian Navy

RNZN Royal New Zealand Navy

RT Trawler

S (*Schnellboot*) Motor Torpedo Boat, E-boat

SAGr (*See Aufklärungs Gruppe*) Sea patrol wing

SAT (*Schwerer Artillerieträger*) Heavy auxiliary gunboat

SC Submarine-chaser

SF (*Siebel Fähre*) Landing craft

SG (*Schnelles Geleitboot*) Fast escort vessel; Support group (Allied)

SGB Steam gunboat

ABBREVIATIONS AND GLOSSARY

SKA Russian patrol boat
SKL (*Seekriegsleitung*) German Navy Staff
SKR Russian patrol ship
SM Submarine
SO Senior Officer
SOE Senior Officer Escort
Sqn Squadron
Stavka Russian supreme headquarters
StG (*Stukageschwader*) Dive Bomber Group
STR Submarine Tracking Room
Supermarina Italian Navy Staff
T (*Torpedoboot*) Torpedo Boat
TA (*Torpedoboot Ausland*) Captured foreign T-boat in German Navy

TB Torpedo Boat
TF Task Force
TG Task Group
TKA Russian motor torpedo boat
TMA, TMB, TMC Ground Mine (torpedo–mine laid by U-boats)
Trägergruppe Air Carrier Wing, originally earmarked for uncompleted aircraft carrier
TU Task Unit
U (*U-Boot*) U-boat
UDT Underwater Demolition Team
UJ (*Unterseebootjäger*) Submarine-chaser
UM Submarine Mine
USAAF US Army Air Forces
USCG US Coast Guard

VP Reconnaissance Squadron (USN)
VPB Patrol Bomber Squadron (USN)
V, Vs (*Vorpostenboot*) Auxiliary patrol vessel, trawler, drifter, etc.
Wehrmacht German Armed Forces
WESTOMP Western Ocean Meeting Point
W/T Wireless telegraphy
YMS Yard Mine Sweeper
Z (*Zerstörer*) Destroyer
ZG (*Zerstörergeschwader*) Heavy Fighter Group
† CO killed

CHRONOLOGY
OF THE
WAR AT SEA
1939–1945

1939

19 Aug   North Atlantic

Owing to the critical international situation, the German Naval Staff (Seekriegsleitung) sends 14 U-boats into the North Atlantic to take up waiting positions there. *U45, U46 U47, U48* and *U52* set out from Kiel and *U28, U29, U33, U34, U37, U38, U39, U40* and *U41* from Wilhelmshaven.

21 Aug   South Atlantic

The pocket-battleship *Admiral Graf Spee* (Capt Langsdorff) sails from Wilhelmshaven towards evening to head for an appointed position in the South Atlantic. The fleet tanker *Altmark* (Capt Dau), whose function is to refuel the pocket-battleship, is sent on 5 Aug to Port Arthur, USA, to take on diesel oil there and then to join *Admiral Graf Spee.*

22–23 Aug   North Atlantic

U30 and *U27* leave Wilhelmshaven for the North Atlantic.

24 Aug   North Atlantic

The pocket-battleship *Deutschland* (Capt Wennecker) sails from Wilhelmshaven to the North Atlantic to take up a waiting position S of Greenland. The fleet tanker *Westerwald* (Cdr Grau), whose function is to refuel the pocket-battleship, puts to sea two days earlier.

25 Aug   General Situation

In the morning, the first warning telegram is sent from Norddeich Radio to German merchant shipping overseas. Hitler revokes the order to start operations against Poland on 26 Aug at 0430 hrs after learning about the British-Polish alliance and the reluctance of Italy to participate.

27 Aug   Baltic

The German torpedo boat *Tiger* is sunk after a collision with the destroyer *Max Schultz* near Bornholm.

27 Aug   General Situation

All German merchant ships overseas are asked by W/T to do everything to reach their home ports 'within the next four days' or to make for ports of friendly or neutral states.

30 Aug   Baltic

The Polish destroyers *Grom, Blyskawica* and *Burza* set out for Britain. They are reported N of Rixhöft by *U31* and *Vorpostenboot 7* and on 31 Aug by the cruiser *Königsberg* near Falsterbo Rev lightvessel.

31 Aug–7 Sept   North Sea

The British Home Fleet (Adm Sir C Forbes), comprising the battleships *Nelson, Ramillies, Rodney, Royal Oak,* and *Royal Sovereign,* the battlecruisers *Hood* and *Repulse,* the carrier *Ark Royal,* 12 cruisers and 16 destroyers of the 6th DD Flotilla (eight 'Tribals') and the 8th DD Flotilla ('F' Class), searches in the waters between Scotland, Iceland and Norway for returning German merchant ships, in particular for the fast Atlantic liner *Bremen.*

1 Sept   Baltic

0445 hrs: start of German attack on Poland. German naval forces consist of Naval Group Command East (Adm Albrecht, Chief of Staff Rear-Adm Schmundt) with overall responsibility. Under its command are Commander Reconnaissance Forces, Vice-Adm Densch, with the light cruisers *Nürnberg, Leipzig* and *Köln;* Officer Commanding Torpedo Boats, Rear-Adm Lütjens, with the destroyers *Leberecht Maass, Georg Thiele, Richard Beitzen, Friedrich Ihn, Erich Steinbrinck, Friedrich Eckoldt, Bruno Heinemann, Wolfgang Zenker, Bernd von Arnim* and the 1st MTB Flotilla with *S11, S12, S18, S19, S20, S21, S22, S23* and the tender *Tsingtau;* Officer Commanding Minesweepers, Capt Ruge, on torpedo boat *T196* with the escort boats *F7, F8, F9, F10,* the 1st MS Flotilla with the minesweepers *M1, M3, M4, M5, M7, M8, M111, M132,* the Experimental Barrage Command with the old minesweepers *Nautilus, Otto Braun, Pelikan, Arkona* and *Sundewall* and the 3rd MMS Flotilla with the tender *Von der Gröben* and *R33, R34, R35, R36, R38, R39, R40;* Officer Commanding U-boats East, Cdr* Schomburg, with *U5, U6, U7, U14, U18, U22, U31, U32, U35* and *U57;* and Officer Commanding Naval Air Forces East, Maj-Gen Coeler, with ten marine air squadrons. In addition, harbour protection flotillas and the old battleship *Schleswig-Holstein* (Capt Kleikamp) in Danzig-Neufahrwasser.
Polish naval forces (C-in-C Rear-Adm Unrug) consist of the destroyer *Wicher,* minelayer *Gryf,* submarines *Sep, Orzel, Wilk, Rys* and *Zbik,* two old torpedo boats, two gunboats and six small minesweepers, as well as auxiliary and training vessels. *Schleswig-Holstein* shells Westerplatte,

whose defenders beat off an attack by a naval assault company. At about 1400 hrs Ju 87s of IV Stuka/LG 1 (Capt Kögl) sink the Polish torpedo boat *Mazur* in the naval harbour of Oksywie (Oxhöft).

2 Sept   Baltic

Commander Reconnaissance Forces and *U31, U32,* and *U35* are transferred to the North Sea. IV/LG 1 sinks the Polish auxiliary ships *Gdynie* (538 tons) and *Gdansk* (538 tons) in the Gulf of Danzig. Polish submarine *Wilk* damaged by depth charges.

3 Sept   General Situation

Great Britain and France declare war on Germany.

3 Sept   Baltic

Early in the morning, Officer Commanding Torpedo Boats makes a sortie towards Hela with the destroyers. Engagement with *Gryf, Wicher,* and 15cm battery. The latter obtains hits on *Leberecht Maass* (four dead). First action by German MTBs in WW2: *S23* (Lt Christiansen) sinks Polish barrage pilot vessel *Lloyd Bydgoski* (133 tons) by gunfire in Gulf of Danzig.

3 Sept   North Atlantic

The British destroyer *Somali* (Capt Nicholson) captures the German merchant ship *Hannah Böge* (2377 tons) 350 miles S of Iceland trying to break the British blockade—the first ship to be captured in WW2.

3 Sept   North Sea

Staff of the General on 'special employment' with Air Fleet 2 becomes 10th F1 Div (Lt-Gen Geisler). Task: Air war against British shipping.

3 Sept   North Atlantic

U30 (Lt Lemp) mistakes British passenger liner *Athenia* (13581 tons) for auxiliary cruiser south of Rockall Bank and torpedoes her. About 1300 survivors from the sinking ship are rescued by the British destroyers *Electra* and *Escort,* the Norwegian motor ship *Knute Nelson,* the American ship *City of Flint* and the Swedish yacht *Southern Cross* which come to the scene; 112 lose their lives. As a result of this first sinking—without warning—the British Admiralty believes that Germany has started unrestricted U-boat warfare. In fact, following the report of the sinking of the *Athenia,* the Germans issue additional instructions curbing mercantile warfare.

3 Sept   North Atlantic

The first U-boat wave, sent into the Atlantic as a precautionary measure from 19 Aug onwards, begins its operations: 2nd U-boat Flotilla W of the British Isles and the Channel with *U27*, *U28*, *U29*, *U30*, *U33* and *U34*. Later also *U26*, *U31*, *U35* and *U53* (mining operations off Portland) and *U32* (mining operations in the Bristol Channel). Successes achieved up to 3 Oct (including those by mines): *U26* (Lt-Cdr Ewerth) sinks three ships of 17414 tons with mines and damages the corvette *Kittiwake* with a mine; *U27* (Lt-Cdr Franz) sinks two ships of 624 tons; *U28* (Lt-Cdr Kuhnke) sinks one ship of 4955 tons; *U29* (Lt-Cdr Schuhart) sinks three ships of 19405 tons (see also 3–17 Sept); *U30* (Lt Lemp) sinks two ships of 9625 tons (excluding *Athenia*); *U31* (Lt-Cdr Habekost) sinks two ships of 8706 tons (see also 16 Sept); *U32* (Lt-Cdr Büchel) sinks two ships of 5738 tons and damages two ships of 17525 tons with mines; *U33* (Lt-Cdr v Dresky) sinks three ships of 5914 tons; *U34* (Lt-Cdr Rollmann) sinks two ships of 11357 tons and takes one ship of 2534 tons as a prize; *U35* (Lt-Cdr Lott) sinks four ships of 7850 tons and damages one ship of 6014 tons; and *U53* (Lt-Cdr Heinicke) sinks two ships of 14018 tons. *U27* is lost on 22 Sept. Of the 7th U-boat Flotilla W of the Bay of Biscay, comprising *U45*, *U46*, *U47*, *U48* and *U52*, and the 6th U-boat Flotilla W of the Iberian peninsula, comprising *U37*, *U38*, *U39*, *U40* and *U41*, *U38* (Lt-Cdr Liebe) sinks two ships of 16698 tons, *U41* (Lt Mugler) brings in two prizes of 2172 tons, *U47* (Lt-Cdr Prien) sinks three ships of 8270 tons and *U48* (Lt-Cdr Schultze) sinks three ships of 14777 tons. The boats are recalled on 7 Sept.

3 Sept   North Sea

54 Blenheims and Wellingtons of RAF Bomber Command are deployed without result against German warships sighted in the North Sea.

3 Sept   Baltic

4/Trägergruppe 186 sinks the Polish destroyer *Wicher*, 3/KFlGr 706 the minelayer *Gryf* and 3/KFlGr 506 some smaller ships and the gunboat *General Haller* in Hela.

3 Sept   North Sea

German cruisers, destroyers, torpedo boats and minelayers begin to lay the 'Westwall' mine barrages in the North Sea. Taking part up to 20 Sept, generally in more than one operation, are Commander Reconnaissance Forces (Vice-Adm Densch) with the cruisers *Nürnberg*, *Leipzig*, *Köln*, *Königsberg* and *Emden*; Officer Commanding Torpedo Boats (Rear-Adm Lütjens) with the 1st DD Flotilla (Capt Meisel), with *Georg Thiele*, *Richard Beitzen*, *Friedrich Ihn*, *Erich Steinbrinck and Friedrich Eckoldt*; the 2nd DD Flotilla (Capt Bonte), with *Theodor Riedel*, *Hermann Schoemann*, *Bruno Heinemann and Leberecht Maass*; the 4th DD Flotilla (Cdr* Bey), with *Bernd von Arnim*, *Hans Lody* and *Erich Giese*; the 5th DD Div (Cdr* H. Hartmann), with *Diether von Roeder*, *Hans Lüdemann*, *Hermann Künne* and *Karl Galster*; the 5th TB Flotilla (Cdr Heyke), with *Greif*, *Möwe*, *Albatros*, *Kondor* and *Falke*; and the 6th TB Flotilla (Cdr Waue), with *Leopard*, *Seeadler*, *Iltis*, *Wolf* and *Luchs* and the minelayers *Cobra*, *Kaiser* and *Roland*.

3 Sept   Baltic

The U-boat *U14* (Lt-Cdr Wellner) attacks the Polish submarine *Zbik* (and reports it sunk) but the torpedo's magnetic pistol fails—a constant problem.

3–5 Sept   South Atlantic

The German merchant ships *Carl Fritzen* (6594 tons) and *Olinda* (4576 tons) are captured or scuttled off the River Plate to avoid capture by the British cruiser *Ajax*. On 5 Sept the British cruiser *Neptune* intercepts the German merchant ship *Inn* (2867 tons), which is sunk.

3–6 Sept   North Sea

U13 (Lt-Cdr Daublebsky v Eichhain), *U15* (Lt-Cdr Buchholz), *U16* (Lt-Cdr Weingaertner) and *U17* (Lt-Cdr v Reiche) lay magnetic mines along the British East Coast off Orfordness, Flamborough, Hartlepool and the Downs. On *U13*'s mine barrage two ships of 11301 tons sink and another of 10902 tons is damaged; on *U15*'s barrage two ships of 4274 tons sink.

3–10 Sept   North Sea

U12, *U56*, *U58* and *U59* are stationed on Great Fisher Bank and *U9* and *U19* off the Scottish East Coast against British naval units. No result. *U20* operates off S Norway.

3–17 Sept   North Atlantic

Aircraft carriers of the Home Fleet are employed against U-boats—*Ark Royal* off the NW Approaches and *Courageous* and *Hermes* off the SW Approaches. On 14 Sept *U39* (Lt-Cdr Glattes) attacks *Ark Royal* but the torpedoes explode prematurely near the ship. *U39* is then sunk by the escorting destroyers *Faulknor*, *Firedrake* and *Foxhound*—the first German submarine loss of the war. The next day two Skua aircraft from *Ark Royal* surprise and attack *U30* (Lt-Cdr Lemp) which is searching a trawler (only light damage, but the two aircraft are lost and two officers are captured). On 17 Sept *U29* (Lt-Cdr Schuhart) sinks the carrier *Courageous* (Capt Makeig-Jones†) W of Ireland; 514 lives are lost. The carriers are then withdrawn from the U-boat search.

3–17 Sept   North Sea

On 3 Sept the British Government announces the blockade of Germany.

First operation to control contraband: submarines are stationed off Hornsriff, the estuaries of the Elbe and Jade and near Terschelling as well as between the Shetlands and Norway, but only German U-boats are sighted and they are attacked without success. On 10 Sept the submarine *Triton* sinks another British submarine, *Oxley*, off Obrestad and on 14 Sept *Sturgeon* only just misses her sister boat *Swordfish*. The submarines are withdrawn from the Shetland narrows on 20 Sept.

From 3 to 6 Sept the Humber Force operates with the cruisers *Glasgow* and *Southampton* and eight destroyers off the Norwegian coast; at the same time, the Home Fleet cruises W of the Hebrides and searches for the *Bremen* (51731 tons), the flagship of the German Merchant Navy, on her way back from New York. But she has already arrived at the North Base near Murmansk. On the basis of a false report that heavy German units have put out to sea, parts of the Home Fleet cruise E of the Orkneys until 6 Sept. From 6 to 10 Sept the Home Fleet (Adm Forbes) with the battleships *Nelson* and *Rodney*, the battlecruiser *Repulse*, the cruisers *Aurora* and *Sheffield* and 10 destroyers operates against German blockade-runners off the Norwegian coast. From 7 to 12 Sept the battlecruisers *Hood* and *Renown*, the cruisers *Belfast* and *Edinburgh* and four destroyers cruise in the waters between Iceland and the Faeroes. The carrier *Ark Royal* provides air cover and reconnaissance.

From 6 Sept the Northern Patrol (Vice-Adm Sir Max Horton) is formed from the cruisers of the 7th and 12th Cruiser Sqns: *Caledon*, *Calypso*, *Diomede*, *Dragon*; and *Effingham*, *Emerald*, *Cardiff* and *Dunedin*. Two cruisers receive orders to operate permanently between the Shetlands and the Faeroes and three between the Faeroes and Iceland. Up to 28 Sept 108 merchant ships are stopped, 28 of which are ordered to Kirkwall for inspection.

4 Sept   North Sea

First attacks by RAF Bomber Command on German warships in the Heligoland Bight: five Blenheims of No 110 Sqn (Flt Lt Doran) get three hits (unexploded) on the pocket-battleship *Admiral Scheer* in the Schillig Roads and lose one machine to AA defence. Four of five Blenheims of No 107 Sqn are destroyed by AA fire. One aircraft, which is shot down, crashes on the side of the light cruiser *Emden* and causes casualties.

14 Wellingtons of Nos 9 and 149 Sqns make an unsuccessful attack on the battlecruisers *Gneisenau* and *Scharnhorst* in Brunsbüttel and lose two aircraft to Me 109s of II/JG 77. Five Blenheims of No 139 Sqn fail to find their targets and have to return.

4 Sept   Baltic
Schleswig-Holstein, *T196* and *Von der Gröben* shell Westerplatte. Officer Commanding Torpedo Boats proceeds to the North Sea with the destroyers.

4 Sept   General Situation
Advance parties of the British Expeditionary Force are transported in destroyers from Portsmouth to Cherbourg.

4 Sept   Baltic
In the early morning, the German minelayers *Hansestadt Danzig* (Cdr* Howaldt) and *Tannenberg* (Capt Leithäuser) and the training ship *Brummer*, escorted by the minesweepers *M75*, *M84* and *M85* and the 5th MMS Flotilla lay the 'Undine' barrage with about 700 mines at the southern entrance to the Sound and the minelayer *Preussen* (Cdr v d Recke) lays 136 mines at the entrance to the Great Belt ('Grosser Bär'). The first loss is the Greek merchant vessel *Kosti* (3933 tons).

4 Sept   General Situation
Following reports about the loss of the *Athenia*, Hitler forbids any attacks on passenger ships for the time being.

4–6 Sept   Baltic
The Polish submarines *Rys*, *Wilk* and *Zbik* lay a total of 50 mines N of the estuary of the Vistula, E of Hela and NE of Heisternest. The first two mine barrages are cleared, but *M85* (Lt Ulrich) is sunk on the last on 1 Oct. The submarines *Rys*, *Sep* and *Wilk* are damaged by depth charges from the 1st MS Flotilla.

4–17 Sept   North Sea
German cruisers, minelayers and destroyers lay the 'Martha' mine barrage as part of the 'Westwall' system: on 4 Sept the minelayers *Cobra* and *Roland* and the destroyers *Erich Giese* and *Theodor Riedel* lay 666 mines; on 5 Sept the same unit lays another 666 mines; on 8 Sept *Cobra*, *Roland* and the destroyer *Friedrich Ihn* lay two barrages with 348 mines and 404 detonators; on 13 Sept the minelayers *Cobra*, *Kaiser*, *Roland* and *Hansestadt Danzig* with the destroyers *Theodor Riedel*, *Friedrich Eckoldt* and *Bernd von Arnim* lay 960 mines; on 15 Sept the same unit in company with the destroyer *Erich Steinbrinck* lays an additional 555 mines; and on 17 Sept *Cobra* and *Hansestadt Danzig* lay 280 mines.

5 Sept   Norway
The British destroyer *Jersey* intercepts the German merchantman *Johannes Mol-*

kenbuhr (5294 tons), whose crew scuttles the ship off Bergen.

5–20 Sept   Baltic
S of the entrance to the Great Belt, German minelayers *Preussen* and *Hansestadt Danzig* (5–6 Sept) and *Preussen* (20 Sept) lay the 'Jade' anti-submarine mine barrage.

6 Sept   North Sea
First convoys along the British East Coast between the Firth of Forth and the Thames estuary.

6–18 Sept   Arctic
The German passenger ship *Bremen* arrives after its breakthrough from the US East Coast on 6 Sept at 'Basis Nord' near Murmansk, followed on 8 Sept by the passenger ship *New York*. The passenger ship *St Louis* and three other vessels arrive on 13 Sept. On 18 Sept the number of German ships there has risen to 18.

7 Sept   Baltic
Surrender of Westerplatte after renewed shelling by *Schleswig-Holstein* and attack by naval assault company with Army engineers. Withdrawal of German U-boats from the Baltic.

New operational area of Polish submarines between Bornholm and the Gulf of Danzig. No successes.

Up to 13 Sept *Schleswig-Holstein* shells Polish positions and batteries near Hochredlau and on Hela daily.

7 Sept   Atlantic
First British Atlantic convoys set out—from the English Channel (OA), from Liverpool (OB) and to Gibraltar (OG).

8 Sept   North Sea
The Dutch Navy loses the minesweeper *Willem von Ewijck* (460 tons) near Terschelling when she runs on her own mine barrage.

9 Sept   General Situation
First troop transport convoy of the British Expeditionary Force sails from Southampton to Cherbourg.

9–10 Sept   North Sea
During the night, the British destroyers *Esk* and *Express* lay the first offensive mine barrage on the suspected German exit channels in the German mine-warning area.

11 Sept   Baltic
Polish submarines receive orders to get through to Britain—*Wilk* actually arrives on 20 Sept—or to allow themselves to be interned in Sweden when they have used up their reserves: *Sep* at Landsort on 17 Sept, *Rys* at Stavnäs on 18 Sept and *Zbik* at Stavnäs on 25 Sept. *Orzel* puts into Reval (Tallinn) on 14 Sept.

11–16 Sept   North Sea
The British minelayers *Adventure* and *Plover* and auxiliary minelayers lay 3000

mines in the Straits of Dover. Escort is provided by the cruiser *Cairo* and the 19th DD Flotilla.

11–29 Sept   North Sea
Unsuccessful operations by six German U-boats against British naval units off the Scottish East Coast. First torpedo failures (premature fuses and depth-keeping defects) in attacks on British destroyers and submarines.

12 Sept   Baltic
The German experimental vessel *Otto Braun* is hit by a Polish battery on Hela.

The Polish minesweepers *Jaskolka*, *Rybitwa* and *Czajka* lay a barrage of 60 mines S of Hela.

12 Sept   Western Atlantic
The US Navy organises neutrality patrols: 'Zero,' with destroyers *Davis*, *Jouett*, *Benham* and *Ellett* between Halifax and Placentia Bay; '1', with destroyers *Hamilton* and *Leary* near the Georges Shoals; '2', with destroyers *Goff*, *Hopkins*, and the Patron 54 with the tender *Owl* working from Newport; '3', with destroyers *Decatur*, *Barry*, *Reuben James* and *Manley* and Patrons 52 and 53 working from Chesapeake Bay; '6', with destroyers *Babbitt* and *Claxton* in the Straits of Florida; '7/8', with cruisers *San Francisco* and *Tuscaloosa*, destroyers *Truxton*, *Sampson*, *Broome* and *Borie* and Patrons 33 and 51 with the tenders *Gannet*, *Lapwing* and *Thrush* in the area of the Caribbean; '9', with cruisers *Quincy* and *Vincennes* off Cape Hatteras. Reserve in Hampton Roads: battleships *New York*, *Texas*, *Arkansas* and *Wyoming* and carrier *Ranger*.

12–14 Sept   Baltic
The German destroyer *Richard Beitzen* and the torpedo boat *T107* conduct an anti-shipping patrol in the Kattegat without results.

13 Sept   Atlantic
The French fast minelayer *La Tour d'Auvergne* (ex-*Pluton*) sinks in Casablanca harbour after an internal explosion.

14 Sept   Baltic
Gdynia is taken by the Kaupisch Korps.

14 Sept   Atlantic
Departure of the first SL convoys from Freetown.

14 Sept–12 Oct   Atlantic
Operations by the French submarines *Agosta*, *Ouessant*, *Persée*, and *Poncelet* against German blockade-runners in the area of the Azores. *Poncelet* (Cdr de Saussine) captures the steamer *Chemnitz* (5522 tons) on 28 Sept near Las Palmas.

15–16 Sept   North Atlantic
For the first time, a U-boat, *U31*, sights a convoy, which is later reported also by *U26*. *U31* (Lt-Cdr Habekost) makes the first

attack on a convoy, OB.4, and sinks the steamer *Aviemore* (4060 tons).

15–23 Sept   Atlantic
First transatlantic convoys. On 15 Sept convoy KJF.1 sets out from Kingston (Jamaica). On 16 Sept convoy HX.1 (18 ships) sets out from Halifax with the destroyers *St Laurent* and *Saguenay* as anti-U-boat screen. On 17 Sept convoy HXF.1 follows with the destroyer *Fraser*. Ocean escort for these convoys is provided by the cruisers *Berwick* and *York*. On 23 Sept convoy HX.2 follows with the destroyer *Skeena*.

15 Sept–4 Oct   North Sea
Off the Norwegian south coast, in mercantile warfare and in accordance with prize regulations, *U3* (Lt-Cdr Schepke) sinks two ships of 2348 tons, *U4* (Lt-Cdr v Klot-Heydenfeldt) three ships of 5133 tons, *U6* (Lt-Cdr Weingaertner) one ship of 3378 tons, *U7* (Lt Heidel) three ships of 5892 tons, and *U36* (Lt-Cdr Fröhlich) two ships of 2813 tons.

18 Sept   Baltic
The Polish submarine *Orzel* (Lt-Cdr Grudzinski) breaks out of Reval. She reaches England on 14 Oct after an adventurous voyage without maps.

19 Sept   Baltic
The Officer Commanding Minesweepers (Capt Ruge), with *M3*, *M4*, *Nautilus*, *Nettelbeck*, *Fuchs*, *Otto Braun*, *Pelikan*, *Arkona*, *Sundewall* and *Drache*, and supported by *Schleswig-Hostein*, shells Polish positions near Oxhöft, Ostrowogrund and Hexengrund.

19–20 Sept   North Atlantic
After two trawlers are sunk by *U27* off the Hebrides, the C-in-C Home Fleet deploys 10 destroyers of the 6th and 8th DD Flotillas to search for U-boats. They are supported by air reconnaissance. On 20 Sept *U27* is found and sunk by *Faulknor*, *Fearless*, *Forester* and *Fortune*. The last-named is able to salvage secret documents with a boarding party shortly before the U-boat goes down.

20 Sept–15 Jan   North Sea
Submarines of the Home Fleet (Rear-Adm Watson) operate against German naval movements in the North Sea and off Norway: large boats of the 2nd Flotilla (*Thames*, *Oberon*, *Triton*, *Triumph*, *Thistle* and later *Triad*, *Trident* and *Truant*) off Norway; medium boats of the 2nd Flotilla (*Swordfish*, *Sturgeon*, *Seahorse*, *Starfish*, *Seawolf*, *Sunfish*, *Spearfish* and *Sterlet*), of the 3rd Flotilla (*Salmon*, *Sealion*, *Shark* and *Snapper*) and of the 6th Flotilla (*Undine*, *Unity*, *Ursula*, *L23*, *L26*, *L27*, and *H49*) off

the Skagerrak, Jutland and Hornsriff, in the Heligoland Bight, off Terschelling and W of the German 'Westwall' minefield. Owing to rare sightings, initial successes are few (cf 20 Nov and 4–14 Dec). From Oct the Polish submarines *Orzel* and *Wilk*, having broken out of the Baltic, also take part.

22–23 Sept   North Sea
Raid by British 2nd Cruiser Sqn, with *Southampton*, *Glasgow*, *Sheffield* and *Aurora* and eight destroyers of the 7th DD Flotilla, is broken off because of collision of two destroyers. The Home Fleet comes out to cover the operation.

22 Sept–3 Nov   Atlantic
The French submarines *Achille*, *Casabianca*, *Pasteur* and *Sfax* are stationed in turn near Cape Ortegal to keep watch on German merchant ships in North Spanish ports.

22 Sept–27 Dec   Atlantic
The French submarines *Agosta*, *Bévéziers*, *Ouessant* and *Sidi-Ferruch* are moved to Martinique to watch for blockade-runners using the passages between the Antilles.

24 Sept   General Situation
The restrictions in the orders relating to mercantile warfare against France are lifted. Permission is given to open fire on merchant ships using W/T.

25–26 Sept   North Sea
The British Home Fleet, with the 2nd Cruiser Sqn (*Southampton*, *Aurora*, *Sheffield* and *Glasgow*) and six destroyers of the 7th DD Flotilla, comes out to recover the submarine *Spearfish* badly damaged in the central North Sea. Cover is provided by the C-in-C (Adm Forbes) with the battleships *Nelson* and *Rodney*, the battlecruisers *Hood* and *Renown*, the carrier *Ark Royal*, the cruisers *Norfolk*, *Newcastle* and *Edinburgh* and destroyers of the 4th and 8th DD Flotillas. The force is located by German air reconnaissance. Four Ju 88s of I/KG 30 attack. One (2nd Lt Storp) has a bomb rebound off *Hood*, another (L/Cpl Francke) gets a near-miss on *Ark Royal* which leads German propaganda to report the sinking of the carrier. Nine He 111s of 1/KG 26 miss the 2nd Cruiser Sqn. First use of air warning radar during air attack by *Rodney* and *Sheffield*.

25–27 Sept   Baltic
Polish artillery positions on Hela are shelled by the old battleships *Schlesien* (Capt Utke) and *Schleswig-Holstein* (Capt Kleikamp).

25 Sept–23 Oct   North Sea
Deep anti-U-boat mine barrages laid in Straits of Dover (3636 mines between Folkestone and Cape Gris Nez). In Oct *U12* (8th), *U40* (13th) and *U16* (15th) are lost.

Passage of U-boats through the Channel is stopped.

26 Sept   North Atlantic
The first convoy sets out from Gibraltar to Britain (HG.1). Permission for operations is given to the pocket-battleships *Admiral Graf Spee* (South Atlantic) and *Deutschland* (North Atlantic).

26 Sept   Baltic
According to Soviet claims, the Soviet freighter *Metallist* (968 tons) is sunk in Narva Bay, ostensibly by a Polish submarine. However, the submarine *Orzel*, having broken out of Tallinn, is on the way to Britain; the boats *Rys*, *Sep* and *Zbik* are interned in Sweden; and *Wilk* is already in the North Sea. According to Finnish information, based on statements made by Soviet prisoners, the *Metallist* was, in fact, sunk by the torpedo boat *Tucha*, on the orders of the Leningrad Party Secretary, Zhdanov, following an unsuccessful attack by the submarine *Shch-303*, in order to provide an excuse to move against Estonia.

26–28 Sept   Baltic/North Sea
The German destroyers *Hans Lody*, *Friedrich Ihn* and *Erich Steinbrinck* and four torpedo boats of the 6th Torpedo Boat Flotilla patrol the Kattegat and Skagerrak: 45 ships are stopped and inspected.

28–30 Sept   North Sea
The destroyers *Wilhelm Heidkamp*, *Bernd von Arnim*, *Erich Giese*, *Diether von Roeder*, *Hans Lüdemann*, *Hermann Künne* and *Karl Galster* patrol the Skagerrak: 58 merchant ships are inspected and nine sent as prizes to Kiel.

29 Sept   North Sea
In a reconnaissance sortie by No 144 Sqn, RAF Bomber Command, over the Heligoland Bight, five out of 11 Hampdens are shot down by German fighters. There is an unsuccessful attack on two German destroyers near Heligoland.

30 Sept   South Atlantic
Admiral Graf Spee achieves her first success, sinking the British steamer *Clement* (5051 tons) off Pernambuco.

30 Sept   North Atlantic
Deutschland begins operations on Bermuda–Azores route. Steamer *Stonegate* (5044 tons) sunk on 5 Oct.

30 Sept–6 Oct   North Sea
German destroyers, torpedo boats and minelayers, employed in mercantile warfare in the Skagerrak and Kattegat, halt another 72 merchant ships and inspect them.

1 Oct   General Situation
British merchant ships receive orders to ram U-boats when they sight them.

1 Oct   Baltic

The German minesweepers *M4*, *M111*, *M132* and *Nettelbeck* shell the Hela peninsula in co-operation with army batteries and a naval railway battery in preparation for the infantry attack. The garrison of Hela (Rear-Adm Unrug) capitulates and the last resistance on the coast is broken.

2 Oct   General Situation

Pan-American Security Zone proclaimed.

2–4 Oct   General Situation

Permission is given for the use of German arms against camouflaged ships in defined areas around Britain and in the Bay of Biscay.

3–5 Oct   Baltic/North Sea

The destroyers *Hermann Schoemann*, *Friedrich Ihn* and *Erich Steinbrinck* and the torpedo boats *Greif*, *Falke* and *Albatros* conduct anti-shipping patrols in the Kattegat and Skagerrak.

4 Oct   General Situation

Permission is given to use all weapons against armed Allied merchant ships.

4 Oct   Western Atlantic

The largest convoy yet, KJ.3 (45 ships), leaves Kingston, escorted by the British cruiser *Berwick* and the Australian *Perth* which, half way to Britain, is relieved by the British cruiser *Effingham*.

5 Oct   Atlantic

Eight British and French hunting groups are formed to search for the German pocket-battleship *Admiral Graf Spee* operating in the South Atlantic: Force F (North America/West Indies) with the British cruisers *Berwick* and *York*; Force G (East Coast of South America) with the British cruisers *Cumberland* and *Exeter* (later *Achilles* and *Ajax*); Force H (Cape of Good Hope) with the British cruisers *Shropshire* and *Sussex*; Force I (Ceylon) with the British carrier *Eagle* and the cruisers *Dorsetshire* and *Cornwall*; Force K (Pernambuco) with the British carrier *Ark Royal* and the battlecruiser *Renown*; Force L (Brest) with the French battleship *Dunkerque*, the carrier *Béarn* and the cruisers *Georges Leygues*, *Gloire* and *Montcalm*; Force M (Dakar) with the French cruisers *Dupleix* and *Foch*; and Force N (West Indies) with the French battleship *Strasbourg*, the British carrier *Hermes* and the British cruiser *Neptune*. From 5 to 12 Oct *Admiral Graf Spee* sinks four ships of 22368 tons on the Cape Town–Freetown route and proceeds to the supply ship *Altmark* for replenishment.

7 Oct   English Channel

So far 161000 troops, 24000 vehicles and 140000 tons of supplies belonging to the British Expeditionary Force have been landed in France without loss.

7–9 Oct   North Sea

The Commander of the German Fleet (Adm Boehm) makes a sortie towards the southern coast of Norway with the battlecruiser *Gneisenau*, the light cruiser *Köln* and nine destroyers (*Max Schultz*, *Paul Jacobi*, *Bernd von Arnim*, *Friedrich Ihn*, *Erich Steinbrinck*, *Friedrich Eckoldt*, *Diether von Roeder*, *Karl Galster* and *Wilhelm Heidkamp*) to draw the Home Fleet across a concentration of four U-boats and within range of the Luftwaffe and, in this way, to take the strain off the pocket-battleships. The German formation is sighted on 8 Oct by a Hudson of No 224 Sqn RAF. Humber Force, comprising light cruisers *Edinburgh*, *Glasgow*, *Southampton* and battlecruiser squadron consisting of *Hood*, *Repulse*, cruisers *Aurora* and *Sheffield* and four destroyers, sets out, as well as the Home Fleet with the battleships *Nelson* and *Rodney*, the carrier *Furious*, the cruiser *Newcastle* and eight destroyers. Twelve Wellington bombers miss their targets. 127 He 111s of KG 26 and of LG 1, as well as 21 Ju 88s of I/KG 30, are deployed, but they achieve no success. The operation ends without result for either side.

7 Oct–28 Jan 1940   Baltic

The German minelayers *Hansestadt Danzig*, *Kaiser*, *Königin Luise*, *Preussen*, *Schiff 23* and *Tannenberg* are used as armed merchant cruisers against merchant traffic in the Baltic W of 20°E. A great number of neutral merchant ships are stopped and after investigation many are directed to sail to German ports.

9 Oct   North Atlantic

The British cruiser *Belfast* of the Northern Patrol captures the German passenger steamer *Cap Norte* (13615 tons). From 29 Sept to 12 Oct another 63 merchant ships are halted, 20 of which are ordered to Kirkwall for inspection.

9–16 Oct   North Atlantic

The pocket-battleship *Deutschland* operates on the HX route. The US freighter *City of Flint* (4963 tons) is captured with contraband and the Norwegian freighter *Lorentz W Hansen* (1918 tons) is sunk.

10–19 Oct   North Atlantic

First attempt to conduct a U-boat group operation with a tactical commander on board (Cdr W Hartmann, on *U37*). Only six boats of the intended nine set out. Of these, *U40* (Lt-Cdr v Schmidt) is sunk in the Channel after hitting a mine and *U42* (Lt-Cdr Dau) and *U45* (Lt-Cdr Gelhaar) are sunk, respectively, by the escorts of convoys OB.17 (destroyers *Ilex* and *Imogen*) on 13 Oct and KJF.3 (destroyers *Icarus*, *Inglefield*, *Intrepid* and *Ivanhoe*) on 14 Oct after

these have been attacked. On 17 Oct an operation is conducted with the remaining three boats—*U37* (Cdr Hartmann), *U46* (Lt-Cdr Sohler) and *U48* (Lt-Cdr Schultze)—against the still unprotected convoy HG.3. Each boat sinks one ship; torpedo failures prevent greater successes. Total sinkings by the boats of this group: *U37* eight ships of 35306 tons; *U45* two ships of 19313 tons; *U46* one ship of 7028 tons; and *U48* five ships of 37153 tons. In addition, *U42* torpedoes one ship of 4803 tons.

12–26 Oct   North Atlantic

The Northern Patrol stops 112 neutral ships and orders 23 of them to Kirkwall. On 19 Oct, in the Iceland–Faeroes gap, the armed merchant cruiser (AMC) *Rawalpindi* intercepts the German merchant ship *Gonzenheim* (4574 tons), which scuttles herself. On the same day the AMC *Scotstoun* captures the German tanker *Biskaya* (6386 tons) near Reykjavik and on 21 Oct the freighter *Poseidon* (5864 tons) which tries to scuttle but is taken in tow and sinks in heavy weather on 27 Oct. On 21 Oct the cruiser *Sheffield* intercepts and captures the freighter *Gloria* (5896 tons) S of Iceland; on 23 Oct the AMC *Transylvania* captures the freighter *Bianca* (1375 tons) in the Denmark Strait; and on 25 Oct the cruiser *Delhi* captures the freighter *Rheingold* (5055 tons) S of Iceland.

14 Oct   North Sea

U47 (Lt-Cdr Prien) penetrates into the Bay of Scapa Flow and in two approaches, despite several torpedo failures, sinks the British battleship *Royal Oak* (Capt Benn†). 833 dead including the Commander of the 2nd Battle Sqn, Rear-Adm Blagrove.

16 Oct   North Sea

Ju 88s of I/KG 30 (Capt Pohlc) attack shipping targets in the Firth of Forth. The light cruisers *Edinburgh* and *Southampton* and the destroyer *Mohawk* are slightly damaged by unexploded bombs. Two aircraft are shot down, including that of the Gruppe commander.

16 Oct   Atlantic

During the searches by the Anglo-French hunting groups in the Atlantic, the German freighter *Halle* (5889 tons) is intercepted by the French cruiser *Duguay-Trouin* on 16 Oct W of Dakar and scuttles herself.

16 Oct–5 Nov   North Sea

U-boats lay magnetic mine barrages off the British East Coast: *U16* (Lt-Cdr Wellner†) in the Straits of Dover—but runs on a mine and sinks; *U19* (Lt-Cdr Meckel) off Inner Dowsing; *U21* (Lt-Cdr Frauenheim) in the Firth of Forth; *U23* (Lt-Cdr Kretschmer) off Cromarty; and *U24* (Lt-Cdr Jeppener-Haltenhoff) off Hartlepool. On the West Coast, *U31* (Lt-Cdr Habekost) lays a barrage in Loch Ewe and *U33* (Lt-Cdr v Dresky) off North Foreland. The following losses occur on these barrages: on *U16*'s, one auxiliary minesweeper (67 tons) sunk; on *U19*'s, three ships of 12344 tons sunk; on *U21*'s, one ship of 2266 tons and the netlayer *Bayonet* sunk and the cruiser *Belfast* damaged (see 21 Nov); on *U24*'s, one ship of 961 tons sunk; on *U31*'s, two auxiliary minesweepers of 160 tons sunk and the battleship *Nelson* damaged (see 4 Dec); and on *U33*'s, two ships of 11929 tons sunk and one ship of 13647 tons damaged.

17 Oct   North Sea
Four Ju 88s of I/KG 30 (Capt Doench) attack ships in Scapa Flow, losing one aircraft. Training ship *Iron Duke* has to be beached after near-misses.

17 Oct   General Situation
The German Naval Staff permits the use of all weapons against all enemy merchant ships, passenger ships excepted.

17–18 Oct   North Sea
Offensive mining operation off the Humber Estuary by the Officer Commanding Torpedo Boats (Rear-Adm Lütjens) with the destroyers *Wilhelm Heidkamp*, *Hermann Künne*, *Friedrich Eckoldt*, *Diether von Roeder*, *Karl Galster* and *Hans Lüdemann*. Total result: seven ships of 25825 tons sunk.

17–19 Oct   North Sea
Anti-shipping patrol by the destroyers *Paul Jacobi*, *Theodor Riedel* and *Hermann Schoemann* and the torpedo boats *Leopard*, *Iltis* and *Wolf* in the Skagerrak.

21 Oct   North Sea
Nine He 115s of 1/KFlGr 406 are intercepted by fighters while approaching a British convoy off the Humber estuary and four are lost.

21–30 Oct   Atlantic
The French Force de Raide (Vice-Adm Gensoul), consisting of the battleship *Dunkerque*, the cruisers *Georges Leygues*, *Gloire* and *Montcalm* and the large destroyers *Mogador*, *Volta*, *L'Indomptable*, *Le Triomphant*, *Le Malin*, *Le Fantasque*, *Le Terrible* and *L'Audacieux*, operates on the Antilles–English Channel route to cover the large convoy KJ.4 against an attack by the pocket-battleship *Deutschland* at sea in the North Atlantic. In this operation the German blockade-runner *Santa Fé* (4627 tons) is captured on 25 Oct by *Le Fantasque* and *Le Terrible* with support from the cruiser *Dupleix*.

22–24 Oct   North Sea
Anti-shipping patrol by the destroyers *Max Schultz*, *Friedrich Ihn*, *Erich Steinbrinck*, *Hans Lody*, *Bernd von Arnim* and *Erich Giese* in the Skagerrak.

23 Oct   Western Atlantic
The German tanker *Emmy Friedrich* (4372 tons) coming from Tampico (Mexico) is reported in the Yucatan Channel by the British cruiser *Orion* and the Canadian destroyer *Saguenay* and scuttles herself on being stopped by the British cruiser *Caradoc*.

23–31 Oct   Norway
British ore convoy from Narvik is escorted by the British cruiser *Aurora* and four destroyers. The Home Fleet (Adm Forbes), consisting of the battleships *Nelson* and *Rodney*, the battlecruiser *Hood* and six destroyers, operates as a covering force.

24 Oct–13 Nov   North Sea
Four German U-boats operate against units of the British Fleet W of the Orkneys. On 30 Oct *U56* (Lt-Cdr Zahn) sights the battleships *Nelson*, *Rodney* and *Hood* with 10 destroyers and attacks the battleship *Nelson* but, owing to torpedo failure, without result. In subsequent operations against merchant ships, *U13* (Lt-Cdr Daublebsky v Eichhain) sinks one ship of 4666 tons and *U59* (Lt Jürst) three ships of 1470 tons.

25 Oct–15 Nov   North Atlantic
A planned sortie by three German U-boats into the Mediterranean fails. *U25* (Cdr Schütze) is damaged after an attack on French convoy 20.K (one ship of 5874 tons sunk); *U53* (Lt-Cdr Heinicke) has to break off the sortie; and only *U26* (Lt-Cdr Ewerth) reaches the Mediterranean after abandoning plans to sow mines off Gibraltar, but she has no success. *U34* (Lt-Cdr Rollmann), which operates on her own further to the N, sinks four ships of 16546 tons, including two on 27 and 29 Oct from the convoy HX.5A.

27 Oct   Pacific
Four Soviet submarines, *M82*, *M84*, *M85* and *M86*, arrive at Vladivostok after their transfer by rail from the Baltic Fleet in July and Aug and are renumbered *M43*, *M44*, *M45* and *M46*, respectively. *M53*, *M56*, and *M57*, from the Black Sea Fleet, are redesignated *M47*, *M48* and *M49* respectively.

27–29 Oct   North Sea
An anti-shipping patrol by destroyers *Hans Lody*, *Bernd von Arnim*, *Karl Galster*, *Max Schultz*, *Friedrich Ihn* and *Erich Steinbrinck* in the Skagerrak has to be cancelled because of a heavy storm which causes some damage to the ships.

28 Oct–6 Nov   Central Atlantic
Whilst British Force K (Rear-Adm Wells), comprising the carrier *Ark Royal*, battlecruiser *Renown* and destroyers *Hardy*, *Hostile*, *Hasty* and *Hereward* operates against German pocket-battleships from Freetown, a carrier aircraft sights the German blockade-runner *Uhenfels* (7603 tons) on 5 Nov. The ship is captured by the destroyer *Hereward*.

29 Oct   General Situation
German warships and U-boats are given permission to attack without warning passenger ships travelling in convoy.

30 Oct–4 Nov   General Situation
A Soviet delegation negotiates in Berlin for support in a naval building programme, wishing to acquire, for example, the cruisers *Seydlitz* and *Lützow* then building in Bremen. The request for *Seydlitz* is turned down but *Lützow* is sold and the carrier 'B' on the slipway is offered. The Soviets order turbines and 15in turrets for their battlecruisers of the *Kronshtadt* class building at Leningrad and Nikolayev.

31 Oct   North Sea/Baltic
So far, of the several hundred ships which have been searched for contraband by German surface naval units, U-boats and aircraft in the North Sea and Baltic, a total of 127, representing 245455 tons, have been brought into German harbours.

4 Nov   General Situation
The American Neutrality Law comes into force, forbidding American ships and citizens to enter clearly defined war zones.

5–15 Nov   North Atlantic
The pocket-battleship *Deutschland* is recalled and returns through the Denmark Strait and the Shetland passage. On 17 Nov the ship anchors in Gotenhafen (Gdynia).

6 Nov–2 Dec   Indian Ocean/South Atlantic
The German pocket-battleship *Admiral Graf Spee* (Capt Langsdorff) operates S of Madagascar. On 15 Nov she sinks the tanker *Africa Shell* (706 tons) and on 16 Nov halts a Dutch steamer. On receipt of this news the British C-in-C East Indies, Vice-Adm Leatham, forms several groups to search for the German ships: battleships *Malaya* and *Ramillies* and carrier *Glorious* in the area of Socotra; carrier *Eagle*, cruisers *Cornwall* and *Dorsetshire* and Australian destroyers *Vendetta* and *Waterhen* in the area of Ceylon; cruisers *Kent* and *Suffren* (French) and Australian destroyers *Vampire* and *Voyager* in the area of Sumatra; Australian cruiser *Hobart* S of the Arabian Sea; cruiser *Gloucester* and French sloop *Rigault de Genouilly* in area N of Madagascar to the Seychelles; and Australian destroyer *Stuart* and one submarine in the area of the Maldives and Chagos Archipelago. Whilst the *Admiral*

Graf Spee returns to the South Atlantic from 17 Nov to 26 Nov to replenish from the supply ship *Altmark*, C-in-C South Atlantic, Vice-Adm d'Oyly Lyon, forms search groups in the South Atlantic too: Force H, comprising the cruisers *Shropshire* and *Sussex*, is reinforced by Force K which is summoned from Freetown and which includes the battlecruiser *Renown*, the carrier *Ark Royal* and the cruiser *Neptune*. On 21 Nov the German blockade-runner *Adolf Woermann* (8577 tons), which has been reported by the British steamer *Waimarama* on 20 Nov, is found by the *Neptune* near Ascension on 22 Nov and scuttles herself. On 2 Dec the blockade-runner *Watussi* (9552 tons) which has been reported by a South African aircraft and intercepted by the cruiser *Sussex*, is sunk by her own crew off South Africa when the *Renown* opens fire. The cruisers of Force G (Commodore Harwood), *Ajax*, *Achilles*, *Exeter* and *Cumberland*, operate in the area off the Falkland Islands and off South America. The submarine *Clyde* and the destroyers *Hardy*, *Hostile*, *Hasty* and *Hereward* patrol on the Freetown–Natal coastal route and the carrier *Hermes* from Dakar with the French cruisers *Dupleix* and *Foch*.

7 Nov   North Sea
First sortie by a torpedo-carrying aircraft of Air Commander West against British destroyers E of Lowestoft. It misses its targets.

9 Nov   North Atlantic
Near Cape Finisterre, the British destroyer *Isis* captures the German merchant vessel *Leander* (989 tons).

10 Nov   North Sea
The German passenger ship *New York* (22337 tons) arrives from Murmansk through Norwegian waters at Kiel-Holtenau.

12–13 Nov   North Sea
Offensive mining operation off the Thames Estuary by the Officer Commanding Destroyers, Capt Bonte, with the destroyers *Karl Galster*, *Wilhelm Heidkamp*, *Hermann Künne* and *Hans Lüdemann*. Successes achieved: the destroyer *Blanche* and 13 merchant ships totalling 48728 tons are sunk and the cruiser-minelayer *Adventure* damaged. The four destroyers are met by the Commander Reconnaissance Forces (Vice-Adm Densch) with the light cruisers *Königsberg* and *Nürnberg* and the 6th TB Flotilla comprising *Leopard*, *Seeadler*, *Iltis* and *Wolf*.

12–17 Nov   Norway
The Home Fleet acts as covering force for a second ore convoy from Narvik (see 23 Oct).

12–23 Nov   North Atlantic
The Northern Patrol intercepts several German merchant vessels trying to break the British blockade. On 12 Nov the cruiser *Newcastle* intercepts the *Parana* (5986 tons) and the cruiser *Delhi* the *Mecklenburg* (7892 tons), both of which scuttle themselves, S of Iceland and near the Faeroes respectively. On 17 Nov the cruiser *Colombo* captures the *Henning Oldendorff* (3986 tons) in the Denmark Strait. On 18 Nov the AMC *California* captures the *Borkum* (3670 tons) near the Orkneys (although this ship is sunk on tow to Kirkwall by the U-boat *U31*), and an AMC captures the *Eilbek* (2185 tons) off Iceland. On 20 Nov, S of Iceland, the AMC *Chitral* stops the *Berta Fisser* (4110 tons), which is scuttled, and on 21 Nov the *Teneriffe* (4996 tons) is scuttled in the Denmark Strait to avoid capture. On 22 Nov the cruiser *Calypso* captures the *Konsul Hendrik Fisser* (4458 tons) off Iceland. On 23 Nov the AMC *Laurentic* intercepts the *Antiochia* (3106 tons), which scuttles herself S of Iceland.

13–15 Nov   North Sea
Anti-shipping patrol by the destroyers *Bruno Heinemann*, *Friedrich Ihn*, *Erich Steinbrinck* and *Friedrich Eckoldt* in the Skagerrak.

14 Nov   Central Atlantic
The French auxiliary cruiser *Koutoubia* captures the German blockade-runner *Trifels* (6198 tons) near the Azores.

15–20 Nov   North Atlantic
Second attempt to conduct U-boat group operations against a convoy. On 15 Nov *U53* (Lt-Cdr Heinicke) sights the French convoy KS.27 W of Gibraltar. Although *U53* is repeatedly driven off by a seaplane, the escorting destroyers *Frondeur* and *Sirocco*, the sloop *Chevreuil* and the large destroyer *Chevalier-Paul*, which is summoned to the scene, she is able to keep in contact until 20 Nov. But the arrival of *U41* (Lt-Cdr Mugler), *U43* (Lt-Cdr Ambrosius) and *U49* (Lt-Cdr v Gossler) brings no success because the boats are partly held up by independents and the approaching convoy OG.7 and because repeated torpedo failures with all the boats frustrate the attacks. In their operations against stragglers and independents, *U41* and *U43* each sink four ships of 12941 tons and 16030 tons respectively.

15–24 Nov   North Sea
In operations off the British East Coast, *U15* (Lt-Cdr Frahm) lays magnetic mines off Lowestoft, *U19* (Lt-Cdr Müller-Arnecke) off Orfordness and *U20* (Lt-Cdr Moehle) near Newarp lightship; *U15* is responsible for one ship of 258 tons sinking on the barrage, *U19* for one ship of 6371 tons and

U20 for two ships of 7929 tons. In simultaneous torpedo operations off the East Coast, *U18* (Lt Mengersen) sinks one ship of 345 tons and *U22* (Lt-Cdr Jenisch) one ship of 500 tons. Near the Noordhinder lightship, *U57* (Lt-Cdr Korth) sinks two ships of 2949 tons.

15 Nov–5 Dec   North Atlantic
In the Bristol Channel, *U28* (Lt-Cdr Kuhnke), on the way to a mining operation, sinks two ships of 10277 tons by torpedo. One ship of 9577 tons sinks on the mine barrage. *U29* (Lt-Cdr Schuhart) has to break off her mining operation because of the strong defences.

17–18 Nov   North Sea
Offensive mining operation by the destroyers *Hermann Künne* (Cdr 5th DD Div, Cdr* H. Hartmann), *Bernd von Arnim* and *Wilhelm Heidkamp* off the central Thames Estuary. Overall result: destroyer *Gipsy*, one trawler and seven ships totalling 27565 tons sunk. The force is met near Terschelling Bank by the Commander Reconnaissance Forces with cruisers *Leipzig* and *Nürnberg* together with *Leopard*, *Seeadler*, and *Iltis* of the 6th TB Flotilla.

18 Nov   Norway
The German supply ship *Westerwald*, having replenished the pocket-battleship *Deutschland* in the North Atlantic, is stopped on its way to Germany in Norwegian territorial waters by Norwegian torpedo boats but after strong protests by the German government is allowed to continue on its way and arrives on 22 Nov at Swinemünde.

18–19 Nov   North Sea
Offensive mining operations by the destroyers *Erich Steinbrinck* (Cdr 4th DD Flotilla, Cdr* Bey), *Friedrich Eckoldt* and *Hans Lody* off the Humber Estuary. Overall result: seven ships totalling 38710 tons sunk including the Polish passenger ship *Pilsudski* (14294 tons) on 26 Nov. The destroyers are met by the cruiser *Leipzig* and the 6th TB Flotilla comprising *Leopard*, *Seeadler*, *Iltis* and *Wolf*.

19 Nov   North Sea
The German minesweeper *M132* is badly damaged off Lister Deep by depth charges from another minesweeper during a submarine hunt and beached as total loss.

20 Nov   Baltic
Incident in the Aaland Sea with the German minelayer *Hansestadt Danzig* and the Swedish torpedo boat *Munin*, which tries to prevent the German ship from stopping a neutral merchant ship for inspection.

20 Nov   North Sea
First British submarine success: *Sturgeon*

(Lt Gregory) sinks the patrol vessel *V209* (428 tons) in the Heligoland Bight.

First use of air mines by seaplanes of the Commander Naval Air Forces (Air Commander West) off the British East Coast: 41 air mines are dropped in three sorties in Nov. On 23 Nov Lt-Cdr Ouvery succeeds in defusing one of these mines off Shoeburyness, where it is discovered on the mud flats.

21 Nov   North Sea
The British cruiser *Belfast* runs on to a mine laid by *U21* (Lt-Cdr Frauenheim) in the Firth of Forth.

21–22 Nov   North Sea
Commander Reconnaissance Forces (Vice-Adm Densch) operates against merchant shipping in the Skagerrak with the pocket-battleship *Lützow* (ex-*Deutschland*), the cruisers *Köln* and *Leipzig* and the 6th TB Flotilla with *Leopard*, *Seeadler* and *Iltis*.

21–27 Nov   North Atlantic
Sortie by the German Fleet Commander (Vice-Adm Marschall) with the battlecruisers *Gneisenau* (Capt Förste) and *Scharnhorst* (Capt Hoffmann) into the North Atlantic against the Northern Patrol, its purpose to relieve pressure on the pocket-battleship *Admiral Graf Spee* in the South Atlantic. On the way out they are accompanied until 22 Nov by the Commander Reconnaissance Forces with the light cruisers *Köln* and *Leipzig* and the destroyers *Bernd von Arnim*, *Erich Giese* and *Karl Galster* which are then dispatched for operations against shipping in the Skagerrak together with the torpedo boats *Leopard*, *Seeadler*, *Iltis* and *Wolf* (until 25 Nov). The battlecruisers make a sortie into the Iceland–Faeroes passage. There on the evening of 23 Nov the auxiliary cruiser *Rawalpindi* (Capt Kennedy†) is surprised and sunk by *Scharnhorst* in a brief gun duel. Whilst rescuing survivors the German force sights the British cruiser *Newcastle* in the vicinity but is able to avoid her in a rain squall and withdraw to a waiting position in the Arctic. In response to *Rawalpindi*'s distress signal and the *Newcastle*'s report, all available ships are deployed in a search: first the old cruiser *Delhi*, which, together with the *Newcastle*, is stationed in the vicinity, then the cruiser *Sheffield* coming from Loch Ewe with three destroyers from Scapa. To cover the Iceland–Faeroes passage, apart from the old cruisers *Calypso* and *Ceres*, which are stationed there, the heavy cruisers *Norfolk* and *Suffolk* are brought up from the Denmark Strait, where the watch is taken over by the battleship *Warspite* detached from an HX convoy. The watch over the Faeroes–Shetland passage, apart from the

old cruisers *Caledon*, *Cardiff* and *Colombo* which are stationed there, is undertaken by the cruisers *Diomede* and *Dunedin* coming from the S. The cruisers *Aurora*, *Edinburgh* and *Southampton* set out with three destroyers from the Firth of Forth to cover the Fair Isle passage and a fourth destroyer guards the Pentland Firth. The convoy ON.3, which has just put to sea, returns and its three destroyers join the cruiser *Glasgow* which is off Norway with two destroyers in the expectation that the German passenger ship *Bremen* will pass there from Murmansk. The C-in-C Home Fleet, Adm Forbes, sets out from the Clyde with the battleships *Nelson* and *Rodney*, the heavy cruiser *Devonshire* and seven destroyers of the 8th DD Flotilla (*Faulknor*). On 24 and 25 Nov the cruisers form a close reconnaissance line W of Bergen, whilst the *Aurora* with the destroyers form the cruiser squadrons stand on the alert off Utsire and the Home Fleet cruises N of the Shetlands until 29 Nov. The submarines *L23*, *Sturgeon*, *Thistle* and *Triad* are stationed off the Skagerrak and all the submarines in the Firth of Forth and Tyne are sent to the area off Lister. Because there is also a danger of the German ships breaking out into the Atlantic, the battlecruiser *Repulse* sets out from Halifax with the carrier *Furious*. On 25 Nov the French Force de Raide (Vice-Adm Gensoul), comprising the battleship *Dunkerque*, the light cruisers *Georges Leygues* and *Montcalm* and the large destroyers *Mogador* and *Volta*, puts to sea from Brest and joins the battlecruiser *Hood* (Vice-Adm Whitworth) coming from Plymouth with the destroyers *Exmouth*, *Echo* and *Eclipse* for a sortie into the area S of Iceland. Many ships suffer considerable damage from a heavy storm beginning on 26 Nov. Taking advantage of the bad weather, the German ships are able to reach the North Sea unnoticed on 26–27 Nov. The French battleship *Strasbourg*, which leaves Dakar on 21 Nov and is escorted from Casablanca by the large destroyers *Guépard*, *Valmy* and *Verdun*, is met on 25 Nov by the large destroyers *Le Malin*, *Le Triomphant* and *L'Indomptable* W of Spain and accompanied to Brest.

21–30 Nov   North Atlantic
The U-boats *U31* (Lt-Cdr Habekost), *U33* (Lt-Cdr v Dresky), *U35* (Lt-Cdr Lott), *U47* (Lt-Cdr Prien) and *U48* (Lt-Cdr Schultze) are stationed near the Orkneys to support Fleet operations. *U33* sinks five trawlers and takes a prize of 5088 tons; *U47* is unsuccessful in attacking the cruiser *Norfolk* on 28 Nov because of a torpedo failure. On 29 Nov *U35* is annihilated by the destroyers

Kingston, *Kashmir* and *Icarus* E of the Shetlands.

21 Nov–4 Dec   Baltic
The German patrol vessels *V701* (21 Nov), *V301* (25 Nov) *V704* (30 Nov) and the submarine-chaser *UJ117* (4 Dec) are lost on the German and Danish defensive mine barrages laid in the Belt and Sound.

24–25 Nov   North Sea
Commander Reconnaissance Forces (BdA), Vice-Adm Densch—on board the pocket-battleship *Lützow* (ex-*Deutschland*)—with the light cruisers *Köln* and *Leipzig*, the destroyers *Bernd von Arnim*, *Bruno Heinemann*, *Friedrich Ihn*, *Erich Steinbrinck* and *Karl Galster* and the torpedo boats *Leopard*, *Seeadler*, *Iltis* and *Wolf* conducts mercantile warfare in the Skagerrak.

27 Nov–7 Dec   North Sea
Off the British East Coast, *U58* (Lt-Cdr Kuppisch) lays magnetic mines off Lowestoft, *U59* (Lt Jürst) off the Cockle lightship and *U61* (Lt-Cdr Oesten) off Newcastle. Two ships of 705 tons sink on *U59*'s barrage and one ship of 4434 tons is damaged on *U61*'s barrage. In torpedo operations off the East Coast, *U21* (Lt-Cdr Frauenheim) sinks one ship of 1277 tons, *U31* (Lt-Cdr Habekost) sinks six of 12338 tons and *U56* (Lt-Cdr Zahn) sinks one of 2119 tons and torpedoes one of 3829 tons.

28 Nov   North Sea
Twelve British Blenheim bombers attack the Borkum seaplane base.

30 Nov–1 Dec   Baltic
Start of Soviet attack on Finland. After an air attack by the air forces of the Baltic Fleet (Bde Cdr Ermachenko), a part of the force of light naval units (Capt 1st Class Ptokhov), consisting of cruiser *Kirov* and two destroyers, shells the Finnish island of Russarö, which returns fire.

30 Nov–2 Dec   Arctic
The Soviet Northern Fleet (Flagman 2nd Class Drozd) attacks Finnish harbours in Petsamo Fjord. Supported by the destroyer *Karl Libknecht*, the patrol ship *Groza*, two NKWD patrol ships and the minesweeping trawlers, elements of the 104th Rifle Div of the 14th Army are landed in the barely defended Liinahamari and at Petsamo. Cover of sea approaches is provided by destroyers *Grozny* and *Kuibyshev*, and N of the Varanger peninsula by submarines *Shch-402* and *Shch-404*.

30 Nov–6 Dec   Baltic
Supported by units of the Soviet Baltic Fleet (Flagman 2nd Class Tributs), Soviet assault forces (Capt 1st Class Ramishvili) land on the islands of Seiskari and Lavansaari (30 Nov–3 Dec), Someri and Narvi (1 Dec), Suur- and Pien-Tytärsaari (4–5 Dec) and

Suursaari (5–6 Dec), lying in the inner Gulf of Finland.

2–13 Dec   South Atlantic
The German pocket-battleship *Admiral Graf Spee* (Capt Langsdorff) sinks the British freighters *Doric Star* (10086 tons) and *Tairoa* (7983 tons) between St Helena and South Africa and on 7 Dec the *Streonshalh* (3895 tons) S of Trinidad. On the first report on 2 Dec, C-in-C South Atlantic (Vice-Adm d'Oyly Lyon) orders Force H with the cruisers *Shropshire* and *Sussex* to proceed to the Cape Town–St Helena route. Force K, comprising the battlecruiser *Renown*, the carrier *Ark Royal* and the cruiser *Neptune*, searches along the route to Freetown from the Central South Atlantic; Force G assembles with the cruisers *Achilles*, *Ajax* and *Exeter* off the River Plate; and the *Cumberland* covers the Falkland Islands. During these movements, the *Shropshire* locates the blockade-runner *Adolf Leonhardt* (2990 tons) on 9 Dec and the *Ajax* and *Cumberland* the *Ussukuma* (7834 tons) on 5 Dec. Both ships scuttle themselves.

2–15 Dec   North Atlantic
In operations W of the English Channel, *U47* (Lt-Cdr Prien) sinks three ships of 23168 tons and *U48* (Lt-Cdr Schultze) four ships of 25618 tons.

3–13 Dec   Norway
In an operation off the Norwegian North Coast, *U38* (Lt-Cdr Liebe) sinks three ships of 13269 tons.

3 Dec   North Sea
Unsuccessful attack on German warships near Heligoland by 24 Wellington bombers of Nos 38, 115 and 149 Sqns RAF.

3–20 Dec   Baltic
Submarines of the Soviet 1st and 2nd SM Brigades (Capt 1st Class Kuznetsov and Capt 1st Class Kosmin) operate in the Gulf of Bothnia (including *S-1*, *Shch-317*, *Shch-319*) and in the Gulf of Finland (including *Shch-322* and *Shch-323*). *S-1* (Lt-Cdr Tripolski) sinks the German steamer *Bolheim* (3324 tons) off Rauma on 10 Dec, *Shch-323* (Lt Ivantsov) the Estonian steamer *Kassari* (379 tons) off Utö on 10 Dec. On 7 Dec the Soviet Union declares the Finnish coast from Tornio to Helsinki a blockade zone. On 17 Dec the Aaland Islands are also included.

4 Dec   North Atlantic
The British battleship *Nelson* runs on to a mine dropped near Loch Ewe by *U31* (Lt-Cdr Habekost).

4–6 Dec   Norway
Mining operation by the cruiser *Nürnberg* (Capt Klüber) off Kristiansand.

4–9 Dec   Baltic
Unsuccessful operations by Finnish submarines: *Vetehinen* against Soviet icebreaker *Ermak* off Libau, *Iku-Turso* against Soviet ships off Stockholm and *Saukko* against Soviet forces shelling off Koivisto.

4–14 Dec   North Sea
In operations by British submarines in the Heligoland Bight, *Salmon* (Lt-Cdr Bickford) sinks the outward-bound German *U36* (Lt-Cdr Fröhlich†). On 12 Dec Bickford tries to halt the passenger liner *Bremen* returning from the Kola Inlet, but has to submerge when a Do 18 flying boat appears. On 13 Dec he fires a salvo at great range against a German naval force (three light cruisers which have met five destroyers returning from a mining operation off Newcastle). *Leipzig* receives a serious hit amidships and *Nürnberg* a hit in the bow. On 14 Dec the submarine *Ursula* (Lt-Cdr Phillips) attacks the force with the damaged *Nürnberg*. The torpedoes are intercepted by the fleet escort vessel *F9* which sinks.

5 Dec   Pacific
The British cruiser *Despatch* captures the German freighter *Düsseldorf* (4930 tons) in Chilean waters off Punta Caldera.

6–7 Dec   North Sea
Naval seaplanes of Air Cdr West (3/KF1Gr 106, 3/506 and 3/906) drop 27 mines in the Humber and Thames estuaries and in the Downs.

6–7 Dec   North Sea
Offensive mining operation by the destroyers *Erich Giese* and *Hans Lody* off Cromer. Results: two ships (5286 tons) sunk, one damaged. As she withdraws, *Erich Giese* torpedoes the British destroyer *Jersey*.

6–27 Dec   North Atlantic
To protect the North Atlantic convoys HXF.11, HX.11 and HX.12 against attacks by German pocket-battleships or battlecruisers, the British and French submarines *Narwhal*, *Seal*, *Sfax*, *Casabianca*, *Pasteur* and *Achille* proceed in the convoys.

7–22 Dec   North Sea
Off the British East Coast, *U13* (Lt-Cdr Scheringer) lays magnetic mines off Dundee, *U22* (Lt-Cdr Jenisch) off Blyth, *U60* (Lt-Cdr Schewe) off Cross Sands and *U61* (Lt-Cdr Oesten) off the Firth of Forth. On *U13*'s barrage one ship of 1421 tons sinks, on *U22*'s four of 4978 tons, on *U61*'s one of 1086 tons and on *U60*'s one of 4373 tons. In torpedo operations off the East Coast and in the southern part of the North Sea, *U20* (Lt-Cdr Moehle) sinks one ship of 1339 tons, *U21* (Lt-Cdr Frauenheim) two of 2827 tons, *U23* (Lt-Cdr Kretschmer) one of 2400 tons, *U57* (Lt-Cdr Korth) one of

1173 tons and *U59* (Lt Jürst) three of 4148 tons.

9–10 Dec   Baltic
The Finnish coastal batteries near Saarenpää on Koivisto carry out a gun duel with a Soviet shelling force consisting of the flotilla leader *Minsk*, the destroyers *Karl Marx* and *Volodarski* and the gunboats *Sestroretsk*, *Kronshtadt* and *Krasnaya Gorka*.

9 Dec–5 Jan   Atlantic
The German tanker *Nordmeer* sails from Curaçao and reaches Vigo in spite of being pursued by the French submarine *Ouessant*.

10–23 Dec   North Atlantic
First Canadian troop convoy TC.1 with 7400 men of the 1st Canadian Div sets out from Halifax with the transports *Aquitania*, *Empress of Australia*, *Empress of Britain*, *Duchess of Bedford* and *Monarch of Bermuda*. Protection against U-Boats in Canadian home waters provided by destroyers *Ottawa*, *Restigouche*, *Fraser* and *St Laurent*. Ocean escort consists of the battlecruiser *Repulse*, the battleship *Resolution* and the carrier *Furious*. At approximately 20°W it is met by an A/S escort comprising twelve destroyers of the 6th and 8th DD Flotillas led by *Faulknor*.

12 Dec   North Sea
Attack by eight Whitley bombers of the RAF against the German seaplane bases at Borkum and Sylt, from where the mine-laying aircraft operating against the British East Coast take off.

12 Dec   Western Approaches
The British destroyer *Duchess* sinks after a collision with the battleship *Barham* off the Mull of Kintyre.

12–13 Dec   North Sea
Offensive mining operation in Newcastle area by the Officer Commanding Destroyers (Commodore Bonte) with destroyers *Hermann Künne*, *Friedrich Ihn*, *Erich Steinbrinck*, *Richard Beitzen* and *Bruno Heinemann*. Result: 11 merchant ships of 18979 tons sunk. After carrying out the operation the destroyers are met by the cruisers *Nürnberg*, *Leipzig* and *Köln*. Attacks by British submarines (see 4–14 Dec).

13–17 Dec   South Atlantic
Battle off the estuary of the River Plate: the pocket-battleship *Admiral Graf Spee* against the cruiser force of the Cdr South American Sqn, Commodore Harwood, with *Exeter* (Capt Bell), *Ajax* (Capt Woodhouse) and *Achilles* (Capt Parry). Heavy cruiser *Exeter* (61 dead and 23 wounded) is put out of action, light cruiser *Ajax* (seven dead and five wounded) severely damaged and *Achilles* (four dead) slightly damaged. *Admiral Graf Spee* (36 dead and 60 wounded) has to

put in to Montevideo because of the damage sustained. C-in-C South Atlantic (Vice-Adm D'Oyly Lyon) summons to the area of the Plate estuary the cruiser *Cumberland* from the Falkland Islands (she arrives 16 Dec) and the cruisers *Dorsetshire* and *Shropshire* from the Cape of Good Hope (they arrive 19 Dec). Force K, comprising the battlecruiser *Renown*, the carrier *Ark Royal* and the cruiser *Neptune*, is ordered to Rio de Janeiro to refuel, where on 17 Dec it joins the destroyers *Hardy*, *Hostile*, *Hasty*, and *Hereward*, which have come from Freetown via Pernambuco (15 Dec), and then proceeds at full speed to the River Plate.

14 Dec   North Sea

The British destroyer *Kelly* is badly damaged after hitting a mine laid by German destroyers off the Tyne.

14 Dec   Baltic

The Soviet destroyers *Gnevny* and *Grozyashchi* shell the Finnish island of Utö, whose battery returns the fire.

14 Dec   North Sea

Twelve Wellington bombers of No 99 Sqn are deployed against a German warship force reported by a submarine in the Heligoland Bight. They are intercepted by Me 109s and lose six of their number.

14–16 Dec   North Sea

The German torpedo boats *Jaguar* and *Seeadler* capture six ships in mercantile warfare in the Skagerrak.

14–19 Dec   Western Atlantic

On 14 Dec the German freighter *Arauca* (4354 tons) and the passenger ship *Columbus* (32581 tons) leave Vera Cruz (Mexico) in an attempt to get home. The Australian cruiser *Perth*, which is employed in watching the Yucatan Channel and is constantly shadowed by the US cruiser *Vincennes* with the destroyers *Evans* and *Twiggs*, does not come up. In the Gulf of Mexico, the Straits of Florida and as far as Cape Hatteras, the *Columbus* is continually escorted by two of the US destroyers *Benham*, *Lang*, *Jouett*, *Bagley*, *Doran*, *Philip*, *Upshur*, *Greer*, *Ellis*, and *Cole*, which relieve each other, and then by the cruiser *Tuscaloosa*. On 19 Dec the British destroyer *Hyperion* comes into sight,

having been directed there by regular position reports passed by the US ships in plain language, with the result that the *Columbus* has to scuttle herself.
The *Arauca* is followed by the destroyers *Benham* and *Truxtun* and is sighted on the same day off Miami by three US naval aircraft which lead the British cruiser *Orion* to the scene. While still in US waters the *Arauca* is able to avoid capture and puts in to Port Everglades.

14–20 Dec   Baltic

Unsuccessful operation by Finnish submarine *Vesikko* against Soviet forces off Koivisto. Finnish submarine *Vesihiisi* lays a mine barrage off Baltischport on which the steamer *Edith Hasseldiek* (?) is said to have been lost.

17 Dec   South Atlantic

Because repairs are impossible in the time allowed by the Uruguayan Government, the German pocket-battleship *Admiral Graf Spee*, which was damaged in the battle off the River Plate (see 13 Dec), is scuttled by the crew. The Commander, Capt Langsdorff, commits suicide on 20 Dec.

17–18 Dec   North Sea

British destroyers *Esk*, *Express*, *Intrepid* and *Ivanhoe* lay 240 mines off the Ems Estuary.

17–19 Dec   North Sea

Bombers of FKX sink 10 vessels, chiefly trawlers, with a total tonnage of 2949 tons off the East Coast of Britain.

18 Dec   North Sea

24 Wellington bombers of Nos 9, 37 and 149 Sqns are intercepted by German fighters when they carry out armed reconnaissance over Wilhelmshaven. They lose 12 machines. No 37 Sqn alone loses five out of six machines taking part and another three damaged bombers are destroyed when they make forced landings.

18–19 Dec   Baltic

Ships of the squadron of the Baltic Fleet (Flagman 2nd Class Nesvitski) shell the Finnish coastal battery at Saarenpää on Koivisto: on 18 Dec battleship *Oktyabrskaya Revolutsiya* (Capt 2nd Class Vdovichenko) with five destroyers and on 19 Dec battleship *Marat* (Capt 1st Class Belousov)

with one flotilla leader, six destroyers, five patrol ships and two gunboats.

19 Dec–22 Jan   North Atlantic

While proceeding to a mining operation, *U30* (Lt-Cdr Lemp) sinks an A/S trawler of 325 tons with a torpedo and also torpedoes the battleship *Barham* (28 Dec). Four ships of 22472 tons sink on the mine barrage laid off Liverpool on 6 Jan and another ship of 5642 tons is damaged. One ship of 959 tons sinks on the mine barrage laid by *U32* (Lt Jenisch) off Ailsa Craig.
U46 (Lt-Cdr Sohler), operating on her own W of Ireland, sinks one ship of 924 tons.

21 Dec   Pacific

The British cruiser *Liverpool* stops the Japanese passenger steamer *Asama Maru* off Japan and takes 21 Germans prisoner.

25 Dec–19 Jan   Baltic

A second group of Soviet submarines forces its way through the Södra–Kvarken passage into the Gulf of Bothnia; it includes *Shch-311* (with the Commander of the 17th Div, Capt 2nd Class Orel, on board), *Shch-309*, *Shch-324* and *S-2*. The last is lost on 2 Jan in the passage on a mine barrage laid by the Finnish minelayer *Louhi*. *Shch-311* (Lt-Cdr Vershinin) sinks the Finnish steamer *Wilpas* (775 tons) on 28 Dec off Vasa and the Swedish steamer *Fenris* (484 tons) on 5 Jan near the Sydosbrottens lightship. *Shch-324* (Lt-Cdr Konyaev) attacks a Finnish convoy in the Aaland waters on 13 Jan; the Finnish yacht *Aura II* (563 tons), part of the escort, is lost because of a leak caused by depth charges.

26 Dec   North Sea

The British submarine *Triumph* is severely damaged by a German mine.

27 Dec   Gibraltar

The British destroyer *Wishart* intercepts the German merchant ship *Glücksburg* (2680 tons), which beaches herself near Chipiona light, SW Spain.

28 Dec–12 Jan   North Sea

U58 (Lt-Cdr Kuppisch) sinks two ships of 4426 tons off the East Coast of Britain. One ship of 1333 tons sinks on a mine barrage laid by *U56* (Lt-Cdr Zahn) on Cross Sand.

1940

1–6 Jan   Baltic

Continuation of mercantile warfare in the eastern Baltic by the minelayer *Hansestadt Danzig* and the training ship *Brummer*. On 4 Jan the cruiser *Karlsruhe* and the minelayer *Schiff 23* are sent out to intercept the Swedish steamer *Kong Oscar* running with Polish refugees from Riga to Sweden. *Karlsruhe* intercepts the vessel and captures 42 Poles. The ship is declared a prize and sent into Memel.

3 Jan   North Atlantic

The American steamer *Mormacsun*, en route to Bergen, is brought into Kirkwall by British blockade forces. Following the sharp reaction of the American press, Churchill gives instructions not to halt any more American merchant ships or bring them into the combat zone.

4 Jan   North Sea

The German special service vessel *Schiff 20* (ex-*Nerissa*, 992 tons) sinks an Estonian merchant vessel, which is darkened, by torpedo and gunfire.

6–7 Jan   North Sea

Offensive mining operation in the Thames Estuary by the 1st DD Flotilla (Cdr* Berger), comprising *Friedrich Eckoldt*, *Erich Steinbrinck* and *Friedrich Ihn*. Results: destroyer *Grenville* and six merchant ships totalling 21617 tons sunk and one ship damaged.

6–9 Jan   North Sea

On 6 Jan, in A/S operations in the Heligoland Bight, the British submarine *Undine* (Lt-Cdr Jackson) unsuccessfully fires torpedoes against the auxiliary minesweepers *M1201*, *M1204* and *M1207* and is counterattacked by German vessels with depth charges and forced to the surface where it surrenders. The crew of 29 is taken prisoner. Lt-Cdr Petzel boards the submarine and confiscates the codebooks from the radio room, but efforts to tow in the submarine fail and it sinks. On 7 Jan the 1st MS Flotilla sinks the British submarine *Seahorse* (Lt Dawson). On 9 Jan the minesweeper *M7* forces the British submarine *Starfish* (Lt Turner) to the surface by depth charges. The submarine is scuttled and the crew is taken prisoner. Following these losses, submarine operations in the Inner Heligoland Bight are halted.

6–16 Jan   North Sea

Off the Scottish East Coast, *U19* (Lt-Cdr Schepke) sinks one ship of 1343 tons, *U20* (Lt-Cdr Moehle) one ship of 1524 tons and *U23* (Lt-Cdr Kretschmer) two ships of 11667 tons. Further successes by *U24* are frustrated by torpedo failures.

6 Jan–12 Feb   Indian Ocean

The first New Zealand and Australian contingents (13500 men) are brought to Suez in the convoy US.1. On 6 Jan the transports *Orion* (23371 tons), *Empress of Canada*, (21517 tons), *Strathaird* (22281 tons) and *Rangitata* (16737 tons) set out from Wellington escorted by the battleship *Ramillies* and the Australian cruiser *Canberra*. In Cook Strait they are joined by the transports *Dunera II* (11162 tons) and *Sobieski* (Polish, 11030 tons) coming from Lyttleton with the New Zealand cruiser *Leander*, and off Sydney on 10 Jan the transports *Orcades* (23456 tons), *Strathnaver* (22283 tons), *Otranto* (20026 tons) and *Orford* (20043 tons) join the convoy and the Australian cruisers *Australia* and *Sydney* (only as far as Jervis Bay) relieve the *Leander*. On 12 Jan the transport *Empress of Japan* (26032 tons), which comes from Melbourne, joins the convoy. On 20 Jan the Australian cruisers are relieved off Fremantle by the British cruiser *Kent* and the French *Suffren*. On 30 Jan these two cruisers are relieved by the Australian *Hobart* and the carrier *Eagle*. The French transport *Athos II* (15276 tons) joins the convoy as far as Djibo ti. On 8 Feb the convoy passes Aden and reaches Suez on 12 Feb, the escort ships having turned away beforehand.

7 Jan–6 Feb   Western Atlantic

The German freighter *Consul Horn* (8384 tons) gets through the Anglo-French blockade at Aruba unnoticed, escapes from the French submarine *Agosta* and deceives US naval reconnaissance aircraft and the British cruiser *Enterprise* as she is disguised as a Soviet ship. She reaches Norwegian waters.

9–30 Jan   North Sea

Bombers of FK X, in attacks on shipping off the British East Coast, sink twelve freighters of 23944 tons and one trawler.

10 Jan   North Atlantic

The German blockade-runner *Bahia Blanca*, en route from Bahia, is lost in the Denmark Strait after hitting an iceberg.

10–11 Jan   North Sea

Offensive mining operations in the Newcastle area by Officer Commanding Destroyers (Commodore Bonte) with *Wilhelm Heidkamp*, *Karl Galster*, *Anton Schmitt*, *Friedrich Eckoldt*, *Richard Beitzen* and *Friedrich Ihn*. Result: one trawler of 251 tons sunk.

At the same time the 4th DD Flotilla (Cdr* Bey), comprising *Bruno Heinemann*, *Wolfgang Zenker* and *Erich Koellner*, drops mines off Cromer causing the sinking of three ships of 11155 tons.

10–17 Jan   Baltic

Mercantile warfare conducted by minelayers *Preussen* and *Königin Luise* in the Eastern Baltic: many ships are stopped and some are sent as prizes into German ports.

13–16 Jan   North Atlantic

The German steamer *Janus* leaves Vigo on 13 Jan but is intercepted by French ships and is scuttled.

15 Jan–13 Feb   North Atlantic

In individual operations in the North Atlantic, *U25* (Cdr Schütze) sinks six ships of 27335 tons, *U44* (Lt-Cdr Matthes) eight ships of 30885 tons and *U51* (Lt-Cdr Knorr) two ships of 3143 tons. *U55* (Lt-Cdr Heidel), having already sunk four vessels of 5742 tons on the way out attacks the convoy OA.80G (OG.16) early on 30 Jan and in two approaches sinks two ships of 10111 tons. She is then damaged by depth charges from the sloop *Fowey* and, after surfacing, is attacked by the Sunderland flying boat 'Y' of No 228 Sqn, which brings up the destroyers *Whitshed* and *Valmy* (French). When they open fire *U55* scuttles herself. On 5 Feb *U41* (Lt-Cdr Mugler), after torpedoing a tanker of 8096 tons and sinking a steamer of 9874 tons from the convoy OA.84, is sunk by depth charges from the British destroyer *Antelope*. *U34* (Lt-Cdr Rollmann) lays a mine barrage off Falmouth, on which one ship of 7807 tons sinks, and she sinks with one torpedo one ship of 5625 tons. A mine barrage laid by *U31* (Lt-Cdr Habekost) off Loch Ewe has no success.

16–17 Jan   North Atlantic

The U-boat *U44* is located by French radio interception stations after reporting a convoy. The German B-Service intercepts the French report and establishes that the reported position is inaccurate by 70 miles.

18 Jan   Baltic
In a Soviet air attack on the Finnish port of Kotka, the icebreaker *Tarmo* is severely damaged.

18–27 Jan   North Sea
In torpedo operations off the British East Coast and in the southern part of the North Sea, *U59* (Lt-Cdr Jürst) sinks one ship of 1296 tons and *U61* (Lt-Cdr Oesten) one ship of 2434 tons; *U9* (Lt Lüth) sinks two ships of 2367 tons, *U22* (Lt-Cdr Jenisch) the destroyer *Exmouth* and one ship of 1469 tons, *U57* (Lt-Cdr Korth) one ship of 1328 tons and also one ship of 8240 tons on a mine barrage, *U18* (Lt Mengersen) one ship of 1085 tons, *U19* (Lt-Cdr Schepke) four ships of 8855 tons, *U23* (Lt-Cdr Kretschmer) one ship of 1000 tons, *U14* (Lt Wohlfarth) one ship of 1752 tons and *U20* (Lt-Cdr v Klot-Heydenfeldt) four ships of 6848 tons. *U15* and *U60* return without success owing to torpedo failures. *U15* (Lt-Cdr Frahm) is sunk on the return voyage in a swept channel following a collision with the torpedo boat *Iltis* on 30 Jan. There are no survivors.

24 Jan   Mediterranean
The Yugoslav destroyer *Ljubljana* is sunk by accident at Kotor. It is later salvaged and repaired.

25–26 Jan   North Sea
A sortie by the German destroyers *Wilhelm Heidkamp, Karl Galster, Anton Schmitt, Paul Jacobi, Richard Beitzen* and *Hermann Schoemann* into the Skagerrak is abandoned owing to heavy weather; most of the vessels sustain some damage.

27 Jan–10 Feb   North Sea
In torpedo operations off the British East Coast and in the southern part of the North Sea, *U13* (Lt Schulte) sinks two ships of 3659 tons, *U21* (Lt Stiebler) two ships of 4900 tons, *U58* (Lt-Cdr Kuppisch) one ship of 815 tons and *U59* (Lt-Cdr Jürst) three ships of 2400 tons; *U56, U24* and *U17* have no success.

29–30 Jan   North Sea
On 29 Jan 18 aircraft from KG 26 and three Ju 88s from KG 30 carry out a strike against shipping off the British East Coast. Result: four ships sunk, four damaged. On 30 Jan 35 He 111s of FK X attack ships, sinking two and damaging a further eight.

Jan–Feb   Arctic
To protect the occupied territory of Petsamo against possible Anglo-French operations, the Soviet minelayers *Pushkin* and *Murman* lay 200 mines in Jan between Vardö and the Fisherman's Peninsula. In Feb *Murman* lays another 170.

3 Feb   North Sea
German air attacks against shipping off the Scottish East Coast. The British minesweeper *Sphinx* is badly damaged and later founders.

4–22 Feb   North Atlantic
In their individual operations in the Atlantic, *U26* (Lt-Cdr Scheringer) sinks three ships of 10580 tons, *U37* (Cdr Hartmann) eight ships of 24539 tons, *U48* (Lt-Cdr Schultze) four ships of 31526 tons (the mine barrage laid off Weymouth has no success) and *U50* (Lt-Cdr Bauer) four ships of 16089 tons; *U53* (Cdr Grosse) sinks five ships of 13298 tons and torpedoes one of 8022 tons. On the return *U53* is sunk by the British destroyer *Gurkha* on 23 Feb.

7 Feb   North Sea
The German minelayer *Cobra* lays an A/S mine barrier off Borkum, notwithstanding thick fog.

9–10 Feb   North Sea
Offensive mining operations by 1st DD Flotilla (Cdr* Berger), comprising *Friedrich Eckoldt, Richard Beitzen* and *Max Schultz* in the Shipwash area. Results: six ships of 28496 tons sunk, one other ship damaged. At the same time the 4th DD Flotilla (Cdr* Bey), consisting of *Bruno Heinemann, Wolfgang Zenker* and *Erich Koellner*, carries out an operation in the area of Haisborough (Cromer Knoll). Three ships of 11855 tons sink on this mine barrage.

10 Feb   North Sea
The British auxiliary minesweepers *Salve* and *Servitor* sweep the first German magnetic mine with LL-sweeping gear off the Sunk Lightvessel.

10 Feb–3 Mar   North Atlantic
To operate against six German merchant ships which have broken out of Vigo, search forces under the C-in-C Western Approaches, Adm Dunbar Nasmith, are formed consisting of ships of the Home Fleet (battlecruiser *Renown*, carrier *Ark Royal*, cruiser *Galatea* and destroyers), of the Western Approaches Command, of the Northern Patrol and of the French Admiral-West. On 11 Feb the French sloop *Elan* captures the *Rostock* (2542 tons) and on 12 Feb the British destroyer *Hasty* seizes the *Morea* (4709 tons). The *Wahehe* (4709 tons) is captured on 21 Feb by the cruiser *Manchester* and the destroyer *Kimberley* of the Northern Patrol. The *Orizaba* (4354 tons), after successfully breaking the blockade, is lost off Skjervöy (Northern Norway) after going aground. The *Wangoni* evades the British submarine *Triton* off Kristiansand on 28 Feb and reaches Kiel. The last ship, the *Arucas* (3359 tons), has to scuttle herself

on 3 Mar when approached by the British cruiser *York* E of Iceland.

10–14 Feb   North Atlantic
Unsuccessful attempt by three U-boats (*U26, U37, U48*) to locate a British force consisting of the aircraft carrier *Ark Royal*, the battlecruiser *Renown* and the heavy cruiser *Exeter* W of the Channel. The force had been identified by radio intelligence.

11–13 Feb   Atlantic
The German freighter *Wakama* (3771 tons), coming from Rio de Janeiro, is stopped by the British cruiser *Dorsetshire* in the area of Cabo Frio and scuttles herself.

12 Feb   North Atlantic/Intelligence
U33 (Lt-Cdr Dresky) is sunk by the British minesweeper *Gleaner* as she tries to lay mines in the shallow waters of the estuary of the Clyde. From some of the 17 prisoners three 'Enigma' rotors are recovered, including nos VI and VII—which are of great importance to Bletchley Park's cryptanalysts because they are two of the three special naval rotors not already reconstructed by Polish codebreakers.

12 Feb   Norway
The British cruiser *Glasgow* captures the German trawler *Herrlichkeit* off Tromsö.

12 Feb   North Atlantic
The British destroyer *Hasty* captures the German merchant vessel *Morea* off NW Spain.

14–16 Feb   Norway
On 14 Feb the German supply ship *Altmark* (Capt Dau), after evading the British Northern Patrol, reaches Norwegian territorial waters near Halten north of Trondheim; on board are 303 prisoners from merchant ships sunk by the pocket-battleship *Admiral Graf Spee*. The ship is twice searched, by the Norwegian torpedo boats *Trygg* and *Snögg*, and then *Garm* (Rear-Adm Tank Nielsen) arrives but her crew is not allowed aboard by Capt Dau. The commanding Adm Diesen allows *Altmark* to continue under escort. When, on 16 Feb near Egersund, the British destroyers *Cossack* (Capt Vian), *Intrepid* and *Ivanhoe* try to stop the German vessel inside Norwegian territorial waters (despite protests by the escorting Norwegian torpedo boats *Skarv* and *Kjell*), *Altmark* enters Jössingfjord. During the night, *Cossack* enters the fjord and goes alongside *Altmark*. A boarding party is sent, shooting ensues, eight German sailors are killed and the prisoners are freed and taken aboard *Cossack*.

17–18 Feb   North Atlantic
Third attempt to conduct a U-boat group operation against convoys with a tactical commander on board (Cdr Hartmann on *U37*). Of the five intended boats, *U54* (Lt-

Cdr Kutschmann) probably ran on to the mine barrage laid by British destroyers on the German exit route and sank (see 22 Feb). When on 17 Feb the B-Service learns of the rendezvous point of the French convoys 10.RS and 65.KS W of Portugal, *U26* and *U50* are still too far away. *U53* (Cdr Grosse) summons *U37* which at first is held up by the convoys OG.18 and independents; but the U-boats are only able to fire successfully at independents and stragglers encountered near the convoy. *U37* sinks three ships and *U53* one ship. Two attacks fail because of torpedo defects and *U53*, on her return, is sunk S of the Faeroes by the British destroyer *Gurkha*.

18–20 Feb   North Sea
Operation 'Nordmark': sortie against convoy traffic between England and Scandinavia by the battlecruisers *Gneisenau* (Capt Netzbandt) and *Scharnhorst* (Capt Hoffmann), the heavy cruiser *Admiral Hipper* (Capt Heye) and two destroyers (*Karl Galster* and *Wilhelm Heidkamp*—*Wolfgang Zenker* returns because of ice damage) under the command of Fleet Cdr (Adm Marschall). The sortie reaches the passage between Shetland and Norway but has no success. The 2nd DD Flotilla, comprising *Paul Jacobi*, *Theodor Riedel*, *Hans Schoemann* and *Leberecht Maass*, and the torpedo boats *Luchs* and *Seeadler*, at first employed as a screen, are sent off on a mercantile warfare mission in the Skagerrak. Of the U-boats employed in the operation, *U9* (Lt Lüth) sinks one ship of 1213 tons, *U14* (Lt Wohlfarth) four ships of 5320 tons, *U61* (Lt-Cdr Oesten) two ships of 5703 tons and *U63* (Lt Lorentz) one ship of 4211 tons. *U57* (Lt-Cdr Korth) sinks one ship of 10191 tons and torpedoes another of 4966 tons; the latter is sunk by *U23* (Lt-Cdr Kretschmer), which also sinks the destroyer *Daring* escorting convoy HN.12. *U10* (Lt Preuss) sinks two ships of 6356 tons in the southern part of the North Sea.

21 Feb   North Atlantic
The British cruiser *Manchester* and the destroyer *Kimberley* of the Northern Patrol capture the German merchant ship *Wahehe* S of Iceland.

22–23 Feb   North Sea
Operation 'Wikinger'. When the Officer Commanding Destroyers (Commodore Bonte) with the 1st DD Flotilla (*Erich Koellner*, *Friedrich Eckoldt*, *Leberecht Maass*, *Max Schultz*, *Richard Beitzen* and *Theodor Riedel*) proceeds towards British trawlers reported by air reconnaissance in the area of the Dogger Bank, the force is attacked in error by He 111s of II/KG 26 (the aircraft crews are not informed about

their own ships in this part of the sea). Three bombs hit *Leberecht Maass*. In taking evasive action *Leberecht Maass* (Cdr Bassenge†) and *Max Schultz* (Cdr Trampedach†) run on to a mine barrage newly laid by two British destroyers in the German mine-free path and sink with the majority of their crews. Only 60 men are rescued from *Leberecht Maass*.

25 Feb   North Sea
When *U63* (Lt Lorentz) tries to attack the Britain–Norway convoy HN.14, she is sighted by the British submarine *Narwhal* and sunk by the escorting destroyers *Escort*, *Imogen* and *Inglefield*.

28 Feb   North Sea
The German minelayers *Roland* and *Cobra* lay an A/S mine barrier off the Ems estuary.

29 Feb–9 Mar   North Sea
In operations off Cross Sand and in the southern part of the North Sea, *U14* (Lt-Cdr Wohlfarth) sinks four ships of 5290 tons, *U17* (Lt-Cdr Behrens) two of 1615 tons and *U20* (Lt-Cdr v Klot-Heydenfeldt) two of 9551 tons.

1–2 Mar   Western Atlantic
The German freighters *Troja* (2390 tons) and *Heidelberg* (6530 tons) try to reach home from Aruba. The *Troja* is encountered on 1 Mar by the British cruiser *Despatch* near Aruba and the *Heidelberg* on 2 Mar by the British cruiser *Dunedin* off the Windward Passage. Both freighters are scuttled.

2 Mar   English Channel
First attack by German aircraft (KG 26) on shipping targets in the southern part of the Channel. Passenger ship *Domala* (8441 tons) is set on fire near the Isle of Wight.

2–6 Mar   North Atlantic
The British heavy cruiser *Berwick* intercepts the German merchant ship *Wolfsburg* (6201 tons) in the Denmark Strait on 2–3 Mar and *Uruguay* (5846 tons) on 6 Mar; also on 6 Mar, the merchantman *Arucas* is intercepted by the heavy cruiser *York* off Iceland. To avoid capture, all the German ships scuttle themselves.

2–11 Mar   North Atlantic/English Channel
U28 (Lt-Cdr Kuhnke), *U29* (Lt-Cdr Schuhart) and *U32* (Lt Jenisch) lay mine barrages off Portsmouth, Newport and Liverpool on the British West and South Coasts. One ship of 710 tons sinks on *U29*'s barrage and one ship of 5068 tons on *U32*'s. In torpedo attacks before and after this, *U28* sinks two ships of 11215 tons and *U29* two ships of 9789 tons. On 1 Mar *U32* misses the Norwegian steamer *Belpamela* but sinks the Swedish *Lagaholm* (2878 tons); both are sent to Kirkwall by British ships. Further attacks are thwarted by torpedo failures.

5 Mar–2 Apr   North Sea
On 5 Mar *U38* and *U52*, which are setting out for the Atlantic, are recalled and with *U30*, *U43*, *U44*, *U46*, *U47*, *U49* and *U51* are concentrated against British naval forces both sides of the Shetlands and Orkneys. In these operations *U38* (Lt-Cdr Liebe) sinks five ships of 14309 tons and *U47* (Lt-Cdr Prien) one ship of 1146 tons. *U44* (Lt-Cdr Mathes), in trying to attack British battle-cruisers, is sunk on 20 Mar by their destroyer screen (*Fortune*, *Faulknor* and *Firedrake*).

5 Mar–8 Apr   Western Atlantic/North Atlantic
On 5–6 Mar the German freighters *Hannover*, *Mimi Horn* and *Seattle* leave Curaçao. The *Hannover* is encountered in the Mona Passage in the night 7–8 Mar by the Canadian destroyer *Assiniboine*. She is prevented from scuttling herself inside Dominican waters by a boarding party from the British cruiser *Dunedin*. During the hunt for the *Hannover*, in which the French cruiser *Jeanne d'Arc* also takes part, the two other ships are able to break out of the Caribbean, but the *Mimi Horn* has to scuttle herself in the Denmark Strait on 28 Mar when approached by the British armed merchant cruiser *Transylvania*. The *Seattle* becomes involved in the beginnings of the Norwegian operation off Kristiansand on 8–9 Apr and is lost. The *Hannover* is later converted into the first escort carrier and renamed *Audacity*.

7–8 Mar   North Sea
The German minelayers *Roland* and *Cobra* lay two A/S mine barriers West of Heligoland.

9 Mar   North Sea
The auxiliary minelayer *Schiff 11* (Cdr Betzendahl) drops barrages E of the North Foreland. Results: five ships of 14152 tons sunk.

11 Mar   North Sea
A Bristol Blenheim of RAF Bomber Command sinks the German U-boat *U31* (Lt-Cdr Habekost†) in Schillig roads. The boat is later raised.

11 Mar–10 Apr   North Atlantic
The heavy French cruiser *Algérie* and the battleship *Bretagne* transport 1179 and 1200 bars of gold respectively from Toulon to Halifax, accompanied by the destroyers *Vauban*, *Aigle* and *Maillé Brézé*. On the return from 29 Mar to 10 Apr the *Aigle* and *Algérie* accompany the freighters *L D Dreyfus* and *Wisconsin* with cargoes of aircraft.

13 Mar   North Atlantic
In the Iceland-Faeroes gap, the British AMC *Maloja* intercepts the German mer-

chant vessel *La Coruña*, which scuttles herself.

13 Mar   General Situation
Peace Treaty signed between the USSR and Finland.

14–29 Mar   North Sea
Unsuccessful operation to hunt down British and French submarines in the North Sea by *U7*, *U9*, *U19*, *U20*, *U23*, *U24*, *U56*, *U57* and off southern Norway by *U1*, *U2*, *U3* and *U4*. When the boats are then ordered to the British East Coast, *U19* (Lt-Cdr Schepke) sinks four ships of 5517 tons and *U57* (Lt-Cdr Korth) two ships of 7009 tons. From 16 Mar there is a large-scale operation by British submarines of the Home Fleet in the North Sea and off Norway. At times there are up to 14 boats in the operational area and up to six coming into and leaving the area. Of these, *Trident* (Lt-Cdr Seale) sinks the steamer *Edmund Hugo Stinnes 4* (2189 tons) and *Ursula* (Lt-Cdr Phillips) the steamer *Heddernheim* (4947 tons) off the Danish coast.

15 Mar–1 Apr   Pacific
In the Sea of Japan, the Australian AMC *Kanimbla* takes the Soviet steamer *Vladimir Mayakovsky* as a prize and escorts her to a rendezvous with the French cruiser *Lamotte-Picgnet*, which in turn escorts her to Indo-China.

16 Mar   North Sea
18 Ju 88s (KG 30) and 16 He 111s (KG 26) of FK X attack units of the British Fleet in Scapa Flow, AA positions and the airfields at Stromness, Barthhouse and Kirkwall. They believe they have hit three battleships and one cruiser; in fact, only the beached old battleship *Iron Duke* and the heavy cruiser *Norfolk* are damaged.

19 Mar   North Sea
30 Whitleys and 20 Hampdens of RAF Bomber Command attack the German seaplane base at Hörnum.

20 Mar   North Sea
The German mine countermeasures vessel *Sperrbecher 12/Altenfels* is sunk off Ameland by torpedo aircraft of RAF Coastal Command

20 Mar   English Channel
In a second attack by German aircraft against shipping off the Isle of Wight, the British freighter *Barn Hill* (5439 tons) is sunk.

22 Mar–20 Apr   North Sea
The first boats of the French 10th SM Flotilla, *Sibylle*, *Antiope* and *Amazone*, arrive in Harwich with their depot ship *Jules Verne* to reinforce the submarines of the Home Fleet. On 14 Apr *Orphée*, *Doris* and *Circé* follow, on 20 Apr *Calypso* and *Thétis*. In addition the 2nd SM Div (*Casabianca*, *Sfax*,

Achille and *Pasteur*) arrives on 17 Apr and the minelaying submarine *Rubis* on 1 May. On 31 Mar *Sibylle* is the first boat to set out on an operation in the North Sea.

23 Mar   North Sea
The German U-boat *U22* is lost in the Skagerrak, either to a mine or in a collision with the Polish submarine *Wilk*.

23 Mar   Indian Ocean
Formation of the British Malaya Force to keep watch on German merchant ships in Dutch East Indies harbours: the destroyers *Stronghold* and *Tenedos* off Sabang (watching *Lindenfels*, *Moni Rickmers*, *Sophie Rickmers*, *Wasgenwald*, *Werdenfels*); the cruiser *Durban* off Padang (*Bitterfeld*, *Franken*, *Rheinland*, *Soneck*, *Wuppertal*), the submarines *Perseus* and *Rainbow* off the Sunda Strait, the cruiser *Dauntless* off Batavia (*Nordmark*, *Rendsburg*, *Vogtland*), the cruiser *Danae* off Surabaya (*Cassel*, *Essen*, *Naumburg*) and the sloop *Falmouth* off Tjilatjap (*Stassfurt*).

28 Mar   North Atlantic
In the Denmark Strait, the British AMC *Transylvania* intercepts the German merchant vessel *Mimi Horn*, which scuttles herself.

31 Mar   North Sea
Schiff 16/Atlantis (Capt Rogge) is the first German auxiliary cruiser of WW2 to receive orders to put to sea.

31 Mar–8 Apr   Norway
The British cruiser *Birmingham* with the destroyers *Fearless* and *Hostile* looks for German fishery vessels along the Norwegian coast up to Vestfjord.

3 Apr   Norway
The first ships of the export echelon for use in Operation 'Weserübung'—seven freighters of 48693 tons—set out from Hamburg for Narvik, Trondheim and Stavanger.

5–8 Apr   Norway
Operation 'Wilfred': British mining operation in Norwegian waters. Force WB simulates minelaying with two destroyers off Bud/Kristiansund-North. Force WS, consisting of minelayer *Teviot Bank* and destroyers *Inglefield*, *Ilex*, *Imogen* and *Isis*, is recalled on 8 Apr before the beginning of the minelaying. Force WV, consisting of minelaying destroyers *Esk*, *Icarus*, *Impulsive* and *Ivanhoe*, escorted by the 2nd DD Flotilla with the destroyers *Hardy*, *Havock*, *Hotspur* and *Hunter*, lays mine barrage near Bodö. The covering force (Vice-Adm Whitworth) comprises the battlecruiser *Renown* and the destroyers *Hyperion*, *Hero*, *Greyhound* and *Glowworm*. The last remains behind in a heavy storm to recover a rating who has fallen overboard and loses contact. On 8 Apr *Glowworm* (Lt-Cdr Roope†) is

encountered by the German Trondheim group and is sunk by the cruiser *Admiral Hipper* after she has previously rammed the cruiser. The landing of troops in Norway (Operation 'R4'), which was intended as an answer to the German counter-moves against Operation 'Wilfred', is called off when the strength of the German forces is recognised and the troops on board are disembarked (see 7 Apr).

6 Apr   North Sea
Schiff 36/Orion (Cdr* Weyher) is the second German auxiliary cruiser to receive orders to put to sea.

7 Apr   North Sea/Norway
The first German naval forces set out for Operation 'Weserübung'. Operational command: Naval Group Command East (Admiral Carls) for the area E of the Skagerrak mine barrage; Naval Group Command West (Adm Saalwächter) for the area W of the Skagerrak mine barrage, under the orders of the Navy staff (Seekriegsleitung). Cover for groups 1 and 2: Vice-Adm Lütjens with the battlecruisers *Scharnhorst* (Capt Hoffmann) and *Gneisenau* (Capt Netzbandt).

Group 1 (Narvik): Commodore Bonte with the destroyers *Wilhelm Heidkamp*, *Georg Thiele*, *Wolfgang Zenker*, *Bernd von Arnim*, *Erich Giese*, *Erich Koellner*, *Diether von Roeder*, *Hans Lüdemann*, *Hermann Künne* and *Anton Schmitt*. Group 2 (Trondheim): Capt Heye with the heavy cruiser *Admiral Hipper* (Heye) and the destroyers *Paul Jacobi*, *Theodor Riedel*, *Bruno Heinemann* and *Friedrich Eckoldt*. Group 3 (Bergen): Rear-Adm Schmundt with the light cruisers *Köln* (Capt Kratzenberg) and *Königsberg* (Capt Ruhfus), the gunnery training ship *Bremse* (Cdr* Förschner), the torpedo boats *Leopard* and *Wolf*, the motor torpedo boat tender *Carl Peters*, the motor torpedo boats *S19*, *S21*, *S22*, *S23* and *S24* and the auxiliary ships *Schiff 9* and *Schiff 18*.

Group 4 (Kristiansand South and Arendal): Capt Rieve) with the light cruiser *Karlsruhe* (Rieve), the torpedo boats *Greif*, *Luchs*, *Seeadler*, the motor torpedo boat tender *Tsingtau* and the motor torpedo boats *S9*, *S14*, *S16*, *S30*, *S31*, *S32* and *S33*.

Group 5 (Oslo): Rear-Adm Kummetz with the heavy cruisers *Blücher* (Capt Woldag) and *Lützow* (Capt Thiele), the light cruiser *Emden* (Capt Lange), the torpedo boats *Albatros*, *Kondor* and *Möwe*, the 1st MMS Flotilla (Lt-Cdr Forstmann) with *R17*, *R18*, *R19*, *R20*, *R21*, *R22*, *R23*, *R24* and the whalers *Rau 7* and *Rau 8*.

Group 6 (Egersund): Cdr Thoma (Cdr of 2nd MS Flotilla) with the minesweepers *M1*, *M2*, *M9* and *M13*.

Group 7 (Nyborg and Korsör): Capt Kleikamp with the old battleship *Schleswig-Holstein* (Kleikamp), the experimental vessels *Claus von Bevern*, *Nautilus* and *Pelikan*, the transports *Campinas* (4541 tons) and *Cordoba* (4611 tons), two tugs and the Training Flotilla of Commander Naval Defence Forces, Baltic (Cdr* Dannenberg) with six trawlers.

Group 8 (Copenhagen): Cdr Schroeder with the minelayer *Hansestadt Danzig* (Schroeder) and the ice-breaker *Stettin* escorted through the Belt by vessels of the 13th Patrol Boat Flotilla (Lt-Cdr Fisher).

Group 9 (Middelfart and Belt Bridge): Capt Leissner (Officer Commanding Patrol Boats East) with the steamer *Rugard* (1358 tons), the minesweepers *Arkona*, *M157* and *Otto Braun*, the motor minesweepers *R6* and *R7*, the patrol vessels *V102* and *V103*, the submarine-chaser *UJ172* and the naval tugs *Monsun* and *Passat*.

Group 10 (Esbjerg and Nordby on Fanö): Commodore Ruge (Officer Commanding Minesweepers West) with command vessel *Königin Luise* (F6), the minesweepers *M4*, *M20*, *M84* and *M102*, the 12th MS Flotilla (Cdr Marguth) with *M1201* to *M1208* (large trawlers) and the 2nd MMS Flotilla (Cdr v Kamptz) with *R25*, *R26*, *R27*, *R28*, *R29*, *R30*, *R31* and *R32*.

Group 11 (Tyborön on Limfjord): Cdr Berger (Cdr of 4th MS Flotilla) with *M61*, *M89*, *M110*, *M111*, *M134* and *M136* and the 3rd MMS Flotilla (Lt-Cdr Küster) with the tender *Von der Gröben* and the motor minesweepers *R33*, *R34*, *R35*, *R36*, *R37*, *R38*, *R39* and *R40*.

In addition, the old battleship *Schiesien* (Capt Horstmann) operates in Danish waters from Kiel.

U-boat groups (individual boats directly under the orders of Commander U-boats, Rear-Adm Dönitz):

1 (Vestfjord): *U25*, *U46*, *U51*, *U64* and *U65*.

2 (Trondheim): *U30* and *U34*.

3 (Bergen): *U9*, *U14*, *U56*, *U60* and *U62*.

4 (Stavanger): *U1* and *U4*.

5 (E of Shetlands): *U47*, *U48*, *U49*, *U50*, *U52* and later *U37*.

6 (Pentland Firth): *U13*, *U19*, *U57*, *U58* and *U59*.

8 (Tindesnes): *U2*, *U3*, *U5* and *U6*.

9 (Shetlands/Orkneys): *U7* and *U10*.

The U-boat operations end as a total failure, despite favourable firing opportunities, because of defects in the depth-keeping mechanisms and in the magnetic fusing of the torpedoes. The only successes: *U4* sinks one submarine and *U13* sinks one transport and torpedoes one tanker. In addition, *U59*

sinks one ship on the outward trip and *U37* three ships while returning from a special operation. Four German U-boats are lost: on 10 Apr *U50* is sunk by the destroyer *Hero* NNE of the Shetlands, on 13 Apr *U64* by an aircraft from the battleship *Warspite* off Narvik, on 15 Apr *U49* by the destroyer *Fearless* off Vaagsfjord and on 16 Apr *U1* by the submarine *Porpoise* off S Norway.

7–8 Apr   Norway

When news is received that a German operation has started, the C-in-C Home Fleet, Adm Forbes, sets out in the evening of 7 Apr from Scapa Flow for the Shetlands–Norway Passage with the battleships *Rodney* and *Valiant*, the battlecruiser *Repulse*, the cruisers *Penelope* and *Sheffield* and the destroyers *Somali*, *Matabele*, *Mashona*, *Bedouin*, *Punjabi*, *Eskimo*, *Kimberley*, *Kelvin*, *Kashmir* and *Jupiter*. They are followed later by the French cruiser *Emile Bertin* (Rear-Adm Derrien) with the destroyers *Maillé-Brézé* and *Tartu*. Vice-Adm Edward-Collins sets out from Rosyth on the afternoon of 7 Apr with the cruisers *Arethusa* and *Galatea* and the destroyers *Codrington*, *Griffin*, *Electra* and *Escapade*; from the escort of convoy HN.24 come the destroyer *Tartar* and the Polish destroyers *Blyskawica*, *Burza* and *Grom*. Convoy ON.25 is recalled and the escort under Vice-Adm Layton, comprising the cruisers *Manchester* and *Southampton* and the destroyers *Janus*, *Javelin*, *Grenade* and *Eclipse*, is ordered to join the Home Fleet. After disembarking the troops on board, Vice-Adm J Cunningham puts to sea from Rosyth on 8 Apr with the cruisers *Devonshire*, *Berwick*, *York* and *Glasgow* and the destroyers *Afridi*, *Gurkha*, *Sikh*, *Mohawk*, *Zulu* and *Cossack*. On 8 Apr, when he receives the *Glowworm*'s distress signal, Adm Forbes detaches *Repulse*, *Penelope* and the destroyers *Bedouin*, *Punjabi*, *Eskimo* and *Kimberley* to join Vice-Adm Whitworth's force, comprising *Renown* and the destroyers *Esk*, *Ivanhoe*, *Icarus*, *Greyhound*, *Hardy*, *Havock*, *Hotspur*, *Hunter* and *Hostile*.

7–29 Apr   North Sea/Norway

The Flag Officer Submarines, Vice-Adm Horton, orders all operational submarines of the British 2nd, 3rd and 6th and the French 10th SM Flotillas to take up positions off the SW and S coasts of Norway, in the Skagerrak and Kattegat and in the North Sea, in order to be able to intercept possible German countermeasures against Operation 'Wilfred'. On 9 Apr the following have taken up their positions: the British submarines *Clyde*, *Sealion*, *Seawolf*, *Shark*, *Severn*, *Snapper*, *Spearfish*, *Sunfish*, *Triad*, *Truant*, *Triton*, *Unity*, *Thistle*, *Ursula*,

Tarpon, *Sterlet* and *Trident*, the Polish *Orzel* and the French *Amazone*, *Antiope* and *Sibylle*. In addition, the British minelaying submarines *Narwhal* and *Porpoise* and later the boats *Swordfish*, *Tetrarch* and the minelaying submarine *Seal* are employed.

At 1200 hrs on 8 Apr *Orzel* sinks the transport *Rio de Janeiro* off the Norwegian coast, at 1330 hrs *Trident* sinks the tanker *Posidonia* and at 1906 hrs *Trident* misses the *Lützow* with ten torpedoes off Skagen. At 1324 hrs on 9 Apr the submarines are given permission to attack transports without warning and at 1956 hrs on 11 Apr to attack all ships without warning within 10 nautical miles of the Norwegian coast. Of the Allied submarines engaged, *Orzel* (Lt-Cdr Grudzinski) sinks one ship of 5261 tons and *Trident* (Lt-Cdr Seale) one ship of 8036 tons; *Truant* (Lt-Cdr Hutchinson) torpedoes the cruiser *Karlsruhe* (eventually sunk by the torpedo boat *Greif*); *Sunfish* (Lt-Cdr Slaughter) sinks three ships of 12034 tons and damages one of 2448 tons; *Triton* (Lt-Cdr Pizey) sinks two ships and *V1507* totalling 9221 tons; *Sealion* (Lt-Cdr Bryant) sinks one ship of 2593 tons and *Triad* (Cdr Oddie) one of 3102 tons; *Snapper* (Lt King) sinks one ship, *M1701* and *M1702*, totalling 1319 tons; and *Porpoise* (Cdr Roberts) sinks the U-boat *U1* (mine?), *Seawolf* (Lt-Cdr Studholme) one ship of 5874 tons and *Sterlet* (Lt Haward) the training ship *Brummer*. In addition, *Spearfish* (Lt-Cdr Forbes) torpedoes the cruiser *Lützow* on her return (11 Apr). *Thistle* (Lt-Cdr Haselfoot) is lost on 10 Apr as a result of a torpedo from *U4*, *Tarpon* (Lt-Cdr Caldwell) on 14 Apr following depth charges from the minesweeper *M6* and *Sterlet* on 18 Apr following depth charges from the submarine-chasers *UJ125*, *UJ126* and *UJ128*. One trawler (709 tons) is lost on the mine barrage laid on 4 Apr by *Narwhal* (Lt-Cdr Burch) off Heligoland and the submarine-chasers and minesweepers *M1101*, *M1302*, *M1703* and *U-Jäger B* (totalling 1625 tons) on the mine barrier laid on 13 Apr near Cape Skagen. The patrol vessel *V403* (432 tons) is damaged.

8–9 Apr   North Sea

The German minelayers *Roland* (Capt Böhmer), *Cobra*, *Preussen* (Capt Bentlage) and *Königin Luise*, escorted by six minesweeps of the 2nd MMS Flotilla, lay Mine Barrages I and II off the Skagerrak.

9 Apr   Norway

The new heavy cruiser *Blücher* is lost with many lives as a result of Norwegian coastal artillery and torpedo hits in the Dröbak Narrows (Oslofjord); 125 sailors and 195 Army personnel are killed. Off Vestfjord there is a brief engagement involving the German battlecruisers *Gneisenau* and *Scharnhorst* and the British battlecruiser *Renown* (Capt Simeon). Both 28cm shells which hit *Renown* fail to explode and do little damage. *Gneisenau* receives three hits, one of them from a 15in shell.

While Adm Forbes cruises with the main body of the Home Fleet (battleships *Rodney* and *Valiant*, cruisers *Galatea*, *Devonshire*, *Berwick*, *York* and *Emile Bertin* and destroyers *Codrington*, *Griffin*, *Jupiter*, *Electra*, *Escapade*, *Tartu* and *Maillé-Brézé*) about 100 nautical miles SW of Bergen, he detaches Vice-Adm Layton to make an attack on Bergen with the cruisers *Manchester*, *Southampton*, *Sheffield* and *Glasgow* and the destroyers *Afridi*, *Gurkha*, *Sikh*, *Mohawk*, *Somali*, *Matabele* and *Mashona* and the approaching cruiser *Aurora*. But the force is compelled to turn away by an attack by 47 Ju 88s of KG 30 and 41 He 111s of KG 26 in which the destroyer *Gurkha* is sunk and the cruisers *Glasgow* and *Southampton* are damaged by near misses. With the main body of the fleet, *Rodney* and *Devonshire* are slightly damaged. Four Ju 88s are shot down. III/KG 4 sinks the Norwegian destroyer *Aeger* in an attack on Stavanger.

As Group 1 comes into Narvik, *Wilhelm Heidkamp* sinks the Norwegian coastal defence ship *Eidsvold* (Cdr* Willoch†) and *Bernd von Arnim* the coastal defence ship *Norge* (Cdr* Askim) with torpedo hits following abortive negotiations; there are 8 and 97 survivors respectively from the Norwegian vessels.

The Norwegian torpedo boat *Aegir* is sunk by German air attack off Stavanger; the Norwegian torpedo boat *Tor* is scuttled at Frederikstad but later raised and recommissioned as *Tiger* in the German Navy. At Horten the Norwegian minelayer *Olav Tryggvason* sinks the German motor minesweeper *R17*. The coast defence ships *Harald Haarfagre* and *Tordenskjold*, the torpedo boats *Balder*, *Odin* and *Gyller* and the minelayer *Olav Tryggvason* are captured by the German occupying forces and later enter German service as *Thetis*, *Nymphe*, *Leopard*, *Panther*, *Löwe* and *Brummer* respectively.

10 Apr   Baltic

The German minelayer *Hansestadt Danzig* lands II Bn Inf Regt 305 at Rönne to occupy the island of Bornholm.

10 Apr   Norway

Fifteen British Skua dive-bombers of Nos 800 and 803 Sqns FAA sink the light cruiser *Königsberg* in Bergen.

10 Apr   Norway

Early in the morning, and in poor visibility, the British 2nd DD Flotilla (Capt Warburton-Lee†), consisting of *Hardy*, *Hunter*, *Hotspur*, *Havock* and *Hostile*, enters Ofotfjord and, in a surprise attack, sinks, in addition to a number of merchant ships caught up in the hostilities there, the German destroyers *Wilhelm Heidkamp* (Officer Commanding Destroyers, Commodore Bonte† on board) and *Anton Schmitt*; *Diether von Roeder* and *Hans Lüdemann* are damaged. In an engagement with the other destroyers of the German Narvik force, *Hardy* and *Hunter* sink while *Havock* and *Hotspur* are damaged. As they withdraw, the German supply transport *Rauenfels* (8460 tons) falls victim to the remaining British destroyers. Two attacks by *U51* (Lt-Cdr Knorr) on the British destroyers entering Vestfjord on 10 Apr, and one attack each by *U51* and *U25* (Cdr Schütze) on the British destroyers as they leave, fail in part because of torpedo defects. The cruiser *Penelope*, which entered Vestfjord to support the destroyers, runs aground at night on 11 Apr and is towed away, badly damaged, by the destroyer *Eskimo*.

10–11 Apr   Norway

Battleship *Warspite* and aircraft carrier *Furious* join the Home Fleet, which continues the unsuccessful search for German forces W of Norway. On 11 Apr the light cruisers and some of the destroyers have to be detached for refuelling. Admiral Forbes makes a sortie towards Trondheim with the battleships *Rodney*, *Valiant* and *Warspite*, the carrier *Furious* and the heavy cruisers *Berwick*, *Devonshire* and *York*. 16 torpedo aircraft from *Furious* attack without success the remaining three German destroyers, after the cruiser *Admiral Hipper* has set out undetected with the destroyer *Friedrich Eckoldt* and escapes to the S.

On 11 Apr the heavy cruisers *Berwick*, *Devonshire* and *York* are ordered to search for German forces off the Norwegian coast between Trondheim and Vestfjord, and later further up to Kirkenes. Two attacks by *U48* (Lt-Cdr Schultze) on the force W of Trondheim fail because of torpedo defects. The cruisers *Glasgow* and *Sheffield* receive orders after refuelling to scour the Inner Leads. One attack by *U37* (Cdr Hartmann) fails on 13 Apr because of torpedo defects.

11–13 Apr   North Sea

The German minelayers *Roland*, *Cobra*, *Preussen* and *Königin Luise* lay two additional mine barrages, III and IV, off the Skagerrak (see 8–9 Apr).

12 Apr   Norway

British air reconnaissance locates the battlecruisers *Gneisenau* and *Scharnhorst* and the cruiser *Admiral Hipper* on their return SW of Stavanger. By taking advantage of the bad weather and with the help of W/T intelligence, they have avoided the forces of the Home Fleet. 92 bombers of RAF Coastal Command and Bomber Command take off to attack but none finds a target.

13 Apr   Norway

In fighting a British naval force (Vice-Adm Whitworth), consisting of the battleship *Warspite* (Capt Crutchley) and the destroyers *Icarus*, *Hero*, *Foxhound*, *Kimberley*, *Forester*, *Bedouin*, *Punjabi*, *Eskimo* and *Cossack*, the remaining eight German destroyers of the Narvik group are lost: *Erich Koellner* is sunk by the *Warspite*, *Bedouin* and *Eskimo*, *Erich Giese* by torpedoes from *Cossack* and *Foxhound* and *Diether von Roeder*, *Hermann Künne*, *Georg Thiele*, *Wolfgang Zenker*, *Bernd von Arnim* and *Hans Lüdemann* are scuttled, the last after being torpedoed by *Hero*. *Punjabi* receives a shell hit, *Eskimo* loses her bow from a torpedo from *Georg Thiele* and *Cossack* is more seriously damaged by shellfire from *Diether von Roeder* and by hitting a wreck. *Warspite*'s aircraft sinks the German U-boat *U64*. Attacks by *U25* on the destroyers of the force as it enters and leaves Ofotfjord on 13 Apr and one attack each by *U25* and *U48* on the battleship *Warspite* in Vestfjord on 14 Apr fail because of torpedo defects.

13–14 Apr   North Sea

First British mining operation with 15 Hampden bombers (No 5 Group RAF Bomber Command, Nos 44, 49, 50, 61 and 144 Sqns) off the Danish coast.

13–15 Apr   Norway

The troop convoy NP.1, which left the Clyde and Scapa Flow for Harstad on 11–12 Apr, is divided on 13 Apr. The transports *Chrobry* and *Empress of Australia* proceed to Namsos with the 146th Infantry Bde, escorted by the cruisers *Manchester* (Vice-Adm Layton), *Birmingham* and *Cairo* and three destroyers (Operation 'Henry'). There, on 14 Apr, advance parties are landed from the cruisers *Glasgow* and *Sheffield* and the destroyers *Afridi*, *Somali*, *Nubian*, *Sikh*, *Matabele* and *Mashona*. There follow on 15 Apr the transports, which at first go further N because of the threat from the air (Operation 'Maurice'). An attack by *U34* (Lt-Cdr Rollmann) on 'Tribal' class destroyers on 15 Apr fails because of torpedo defects.

The remainder of the convoy NP.1, consisting of the troop transports *Batory*,

Monarch of Bermuda and *Reina del Pacifico*, continues its journey to Harstad, where on 14 Apr the cruisers *Southampton*—unsuccessfully attacked by *U38* (Lt-Cdr Liebe) on 14 Apr—and *Aurora* (Admiral of the Fleet Lord Cork and Orrery) arrive. The battleship *Valiant* and nine destroyers cover the convoy. As they proceed *U65* (Lt-Cdr v Stockhausen) misses the *Batory* and *U38* the *Valiant*. Off Vaagsfjord the destroyers *Brazen* and *Fearless* locate *U49* and sink her with depth charges. From the debris coming to the surface, secret documents are recovered, including a map with U-boat positions. The landing of the 24th Guards Bde goes smoothly. In the night of 15–16 Apr *U47* (Lt-Cdr Prien) fires two salvoes of four torpedoes against the troop transports and cruisers lying at anchor, but they are failures. On 15 Apr the C-in-C Home Fleet returns to Scapa Flow with *Rodney* and *Renown* and six destroyers, whilst *Warspite* and *Furious* are ordered to the area W of the Lofotens.

14–16 Apr   Norway

The German destroyers *Bruno Heinemann* and *Friedrich Eckoldt* return from Trondheim to the Jade. A British air attack is unsuccessful.

15 Apr–17 May   Indian Ocean

Second Australian troop convoy, US.2. On 15 Apr the transports *Ettrick*, *Neuralia*, *Strathaird* and *Dunera* set out from Melbourne, escorted by the battleship *Ramillies* and the Australian cruiser *Adelaide*. On 19 Apr the Australian cruiser *Sydney* joins it and on 22 Apr the transport *Nevasa* in Fremantle. There the *Adelaide* remains behind. In the area of the Cocos Islands the French cruiser *Suffren* relieves the *Sydney* on 30 Apr. From 3 to 5 May the convoy is in Colombo; then it continues its journey with *Ramillies*, *Suffren* and the British *cruiser Kent*. It is met off Aden on 12 May by the destroyers *Decoy* and *Defender* and reinforced in the Red Sea by the cruiser *Liverpool* and the sloop *Shoreham*. The convoy reaches Suez on 17 May.

16 Apr   North Atlantic

Landing by British troops on the Faeroe Isles with the agreement of the Danish Governor.

16–18 Apr   Norway

Operation 'Sickle'. On 16 Apr the British sloops *Auckland*, *Bittern*, *Black Swan* and *Flamingo* sail with 700 advance troops who are landed on 17 Apr in Andalsnes. On 18 Apr Vice-Adm Edward-Collins, with the cruisers *Galatea*, *Arethusa*, *Carlisle* and *Curaçoa* and two destroyers, lands the 148th Inf Bde under Maj-Gen Paget in Andalsnes.

With this the German position in Trondheim is threatened from N and S.

17 Apr   Norway

Because of the critical situation which has developed for the defenders in Narvik, Hitler wants to permit Maj-Gen Dietl to cross to Sweden. But at the insistence of Gen Jodl, the order is given in the evening to 'hold on as long as possible'.

The British heavy cruiser *Suffolk* shells the seaplane base at Stavanger. Installations are badly damaged and four seaplanes are destroyed. In attacks by Ju 88s of II/KG 30, *Suffolk* receives heavy bomb hits and can only get back to Scapa Flow with difficulty and with her quarterdeck flooded. The cruiser arrives on the morning of 18 Apr.

17 Apr   North Sea

Aircraft of the 9th Fl Div drop 24 mines in the Downs and in the Edinburgh Channel. Results: two ships of 6417 tons sunk.

18 Apr   Baltic

The German minelayers *Hansestadt Danzig*, *Kaiser*, *Roland*, *Cobra*, *Preussen* and *Königin Luise* lay A/S mine barrages in the Kattegat; escorts comprise the torpedo boats *Greif* (relieved by *Wolf*), *Seeadler* and *Möwe* and the motor minesweepers *R25* and *R27*.

18–20 Apr   Norway

The French auxiliary cruisers *El Djezair*, *El Kantara* and *El Mansour* under Rear-Adm Cadart land the 5th Chasseurs Alpins Demi-Bde in Namsos. Convoy FP.1 is escorted by the destroyers *Bison*, *Epervier* and *Milan*. Supplies are carried on the transport *Ville d'Oran* (Convoy FP.1B) escorted by the destroyers *Chevalier-Paul*, *Maillé-Brézé* and *Tartu*; cruiser escort is provided by *Emile Bertin* (Rear-Adm Derrien) and cover at sea by the battlecruiser *Repulse*. As they approach, there is an attack on the evening of 18 Apr by *U34* on the cruiser and on the morning of 19 Apr an attack by *U46* (Lt-Cdr Sohler) on one of the destroyers, but they fail because of defective torpedoes. During the unloading of the convoy, which is met by the AA cruiser *Cairo*, on the afternoon of 19 Apr, there is an attack by Ju 88s of II/KG 30 when *Emile Bertin* is damaged by bomb hits. On withdrawal an unsuccessful attack is made on the cruiser by *U51* (Lt-Cdr Knorr). On 20 Apr the sloop *Auckland* is damaged by a bomb hit and the trawler *Rutlandshire* driven ashore.

19–20 Apr   Norway

Namsos is almost completely destroyed in a German air attack.

19–21 Apr   Norway

SW of the Lofotens, *U38* (Lt-Cdr Liebe) attacks the cruiser *Effingham* by night and *U47* (Lt-Cdr Prien) the battleship *Warspite* in the afternoon; no success is achieved

owing to torpedo failures. In the evening of 19 Apr an attack by *U65* (Lt-Cdr v Stockhausen) on the cruiser *Enterprise* fails because of a premature fuse. The British destroyers *Faulknor*, *Escapade*, *Jupiter*, *Grenade*, *Fortune*, etc. patrol this area to screen the heavy ships against German U-boat attacks, but they register no successes. On 19 Apr the British destroyer *Escort* sets out from Scapa Flow with the Polish *Grom*, *Blyskawica* and *Burza* as reinforcements for Harstad, but *Burza* has to return because of storm damage. On 20 Apr an attack by *U9* (Lt Lüth) on *Blyskawica* fails because of a premature fuse. On 21 Apr the Polish destroyers and *Bedouin*, *Escort* and *Faulknor* make a sortie into Rombaksfjord.

20 Apr   North Sea

British Hampden and Wellington bombers attack the airfield at Aalborg.

21 Apr   North Sea

The 9th Fl Div drops 26 mines in the sea off Ramsgate/North Foreland and in the King's Channel. Results: three ships of 5540 tons sunk.

21–25 Apr   Norway

Allied supply transports for Andalsnes. On 21 Apr *U26* (Lt-Cdr Scheringer), which is on a supply mission, sinks the transport *Cedarbank* (5139 tons), which is being escorted by two destroyers.

On 22 Apr the cruiser *Arethusa* brings supplies and personnel for an RAF airfield. The ship *Pelican* is damaged in air attack. On 23 Apr the cruisers *Galatea* (Vice-Adm Edward-Collins), *Glasgow*, *Sheffield* and six destroyers land the first part of the 15th Inf Bde, followed by the remainder on 24 Apr on board the cruisers *Birmingham*, *Manchester* and *York* and three destroyers. Air escort comes from the carriers (Vice-Adm Wells) *Ark Royal* and *Glorious*, which fly in Gladiator fighters, and AA cover off Andalsnes and Molde is provided by the AA cruisers *Carlisle* and *Curaçoa* and sloops *Black Swan*, *Flamingo*, *Bittern* and *Fleetwood*. On 24 Apr *Curaçoa* is damaged in a German air attack. On 25 Apr the A/S trawlers *Bradman*, *Hammond* and *Larwood* are lost to air attacks (they are later raised and repaired as the German patrol vessels *Friese*, *Salier* and *Franke*); the Norwegian torpedo boat *Trygg* is also lost. Two attacks by *U25* (Lt-Cdr Beduhn) on the departing cruiser *York* on 25 Apr fail because of defective torpedoes.

22 Apr   North Sea

Another 34 mines are dropped off Harwich and in the Downs. Results: two ships of 2607 tons sunk.

22–23 Apr Norway

The French transport *Ville d'Alger*, led by the cruiser *Birmingham*, the AA cruiser *Calcutta* and the French destroyers *Bison* and *Foudroyant* and met by the British destroyer *Maori* and the sloop *Auckland*, can only land 750 of her 1100 troops in Namsos because of a snowstorm.

23–25 Apr North Sea

The French 8th DD Div (Capt Barthes), comprising the large destroyers *L'Indomptable*, *Le Malin* and *Le Triomphant*, tries to intercept German ships and has a brief action with the German *V702* and *V709* from the 7th Patrol Boat Flotilla (Lt-Cdr G Schulze). The minelayers *Roland* and *Cobra*, on their way from Wilhelmshaven to Kristiansand, pass nearby without being sighted. An attack by German bombers on the French destroyer force on 24 Apr is unsuccessful. On 25 Apr the minelayers lay the Skagerrak V mine barrage.

24 Apr Norway

Admiral of the Fleet Lord Cork shells Narvik using the battleship *Warspite* the cruisers *Effingham* (F), *Aurora* and *Enterprise* and the destroyer *Zulu*, but assault troops held in readiness on the training cruiser *Vindictive* cannot be used. The force is screened against U-boats in Vestfjord and Ofotfjord by the destroyers *Faulknor*, *Encounter*, *Escort*, *Foxhound*, *Havock*, *Hero*, *Hostile*, *Grom* and *Blyskawica*.

24–27 Apr Norway

Troop convoy FP.2, with the French 27th Demi-Bde of Chasseurs-Alpins (Brig-Gen Fleischer) on board the transports *Djenné*, *Flandre*, and *Président Doumer*, sails from Scapa Flow to Harstad. Escort is provided by the destroyers *Chevalier-Paul*, *Milan* and *Tartu* and the British *Codrington* and *Fame*.

Supply convoy FS.2 with the freighters *Brestois*, *Château Pavie* and *Firmin* arrives on 28 Apr.

26 Apr Norway/Intelligence

Outside Romsdalsfjord, the British destroyer *Arrow* intercepts the German special service trawler *Schiff 37* (ex-*Schleswig*, 433 tons) disguised as Dutch vessel, which tries to ram *Arrow* and damages her before being sunk by gunfire from the destroyer and the cruiser *Birmingham*. The destroyers *Griffin*, *Arrow* and *Acheron* are deployed to search for other German ships and intercept the trawler *Schiff 26* (ex-*Julius Pickenpack*, 393 tons) which is boarded by *Griffin* and brought into Scapa Flow. Valuable documents and codebooks are captured.

The Norwegian torpedo boat *Garm* is sunk by German air attack off Sognefjord.

26–27 Apr Norway

Supply convoy FS.1, with the French freighters *Amienois*, *Cap Blanc* and *Saumur*, escorted by the destroyers *Boulonnais*, *Brestois* and the British *Matabele*, arrives in Namsos. The supplies are unloaded and the troops are partly embarked.

27 Apr General Situation

The 'Inter-American Neutrality Committee' in Rio de Janeiro lays before the American Governments proposals to prevent further incidents in the Pan-American Security Zone.

29 Apr Norway

Evacuation of 'Sickle Force' from Andalsnes and Molde. On 29 Apr the cruiser *Glasgow* in Molde takes the Norwegian King and Crown Prince on board and brings them to Tromsö. During the night 30 Apr–1 May the cruisers *Galatea* (Vice-Adm Edward-Collins), *Arethusa*, *Sheffield* and *Southampton*, the transports *Ulster Monarch* and *Ulster Prince* and the destroyers *Tartar*, *Sikh*, *Mashona*, *Walker*, *Westcott* and *Wanderer* take on board 2200 troops in Andalsnes and Molde.

During the night 1–2 May Vice-Adm Layton with the cruisers *Birmingham* and *Manchester* evacuates 1500 troops from Andalsnes; the AA cruiser *Calcutta* and the sloop *Auckland* take nearly 1000 troops of the rearguard on board. The destroyer *Somali* evacuates a battle group from Alesund and the destroyer *Diana* transports the Norwegian C-in-C, Maj-Gen Ruge, to Tromsö.

29–30 Apr North Sea

The minelayers *Roland*, *Cobra*, *Kaiser* and *Preussen*, escorted by the destroyers *Richard Beitzen* and *Bruno Heinemann* and the torpedo boats *Möwe*, *Leopard*, *Wolf* and *Kondor*, lay mine barrage '17' N of the Great Fisherman's Bank. On the way *Leopard* is rammed by *Preussen* and sinks.

29 Apr–20 May Norway

Deployment of the Allied submarines *Severn*, *Porpoise*, *Triton*, *Trident*, *Taku*, *Achille*, *Sfax* and *Casabianca* off the Norwegian SW and W coasts. *Severn* (Lt-Cdr Taylor) sinks one ship of 1786 tons, *Taku* (Lt-Cdr v d Byl) torpedoes the torpedo boat *Möwe* (9 May), *Trident* (Lt-Cdr Seale) torpedoes one ship of 5295 tons and *Narwhal* (Lt-Cdr Burch) lays a mine barrage off Frederikstad (29 Apr) and attacks a convoy on 1 May from which one ship of 6097 tons is sunk and another of 8580 tons torpedoed. One ship of 174 tons sinks on a mine barrage laid on 11 May near Haugesund. The French submarine *Rubis* (Cdr Cabanier) lays a mine barrage near Egersund on 10 May on which one ship of

1706 tons sinks. The British submarine *Seal* lays a mine barrage off Vinga in the southern exit of the Kattegat on which four ships of 6895 tons sink but she herself is damaged by a mine on 4 May and, unable to submerge, has to surrender to German patrol vessels after a seaplane of 1/Bord F1Gr 196 (Sub-Lt Karl Schmidt) has taken her captain, Lt-Cdr Lonsdale, prisoner.

30 Apr North Sea

The British minesweeper *Dunoon* is sunk after striking on mine off Great Yarmouth.

30 Apr Western Approaches

The French destroyer *Maillé-Brézé* is sunk in the Clyde following the explosion of one of her own torpedoes.

30 Apr North Sea

Aircraft of the 9th Fl Div drop 11 mines in the Tyne Estuary, 10 in the Humber Estuary and two in the approach to Dunkirk.

30 Apr–3 May Norway

Evacuation of 'Maurice' Force from Namsos.

In air attacks on 30 Apr, Ju 87s of I/StG 1 damage the AA sloop *Bittern* (mistaken for a cruiser) which is sunk by the cruiser *Carlisle*. On 1 May thick mist sets in, with the result that ships cannot enter. Only Capt Lord Mountbatten with *Kelly*, *Maori* and two other destroyers gets through the mist into the fjord, but he has to return because of air attacks. During the night 2–3 May Capt Vian with the destroyers *Afridi* and *Nubian*, and the cruiser *York*, followed by Rear-Adm Cadart with the French auxiliary cruisers *El Djézair*, *El Kantara* and *El Mansour* and the destroyer *Bison*, enter and take aboard 5400 troops, including 1850 French. The cruisers *Devonshire* (Vice-Adm J H D Cunningham) and *Montcalm* (Rear-Adm Derrien) with the destroyers *Grenade*, *Griffin* and *Imperial* cruise at sea as a covering force. The AA cruiser *Carlisle* (Rear-Adm Vivian) provides AA protection in the harbour.

On its return, the force is attacked several times from the air on 3 May and loses the destroyers *Afridi* (Capt Vian) and *Bison* (Capt Bouan) through Stuka attacks from I/StG 1 (Capt Hozzel).

1 May North Sea

German aircraft drop 42 mines in the Tyne and Humber estuaries and in the harbour approaches to Middlesbrough and Dunkirk. The minelayer *Princess Victoria* sinks on 18 May.

1–6 May Norway

Troop convoy FP.3, with the Foreign Legion Demi-Bde (Col Magrin-Verneret) and the Polish Bde (Gen Bohusz) on board the transports *Ville d'Alger*, *Monarch of Bermuda*, *Colombie*, *Chenonceaux* and

Mexique, escorted by five British and one French destroyers, arrives in Harstad and Tromsö from Scapa Flow on 5 May. Supply convoy FS.3, with the freighters *Albert Leborgne*, *Enseigne Maurice Préchac*, *St Clair* and *Vulcain*, follows on 6 May. On 3 May the battleship *Resolution* and the cruisers *Aurora* and *Effingham* are bombarded off Beisfford, Narvik.

1 May–16 June   Indian Ocean/ Atlantic

Third New Zealand and Australian troop convoy US.3. On 1 May the transports *Aquitania*, *Empress of Britain* and *Empress of Japan* set out from Wellington and the *Andes* from Lyttelton. They reach Sydney on 5 May, escorted by the Australian cruisers *Australia* and *Canberra* and the New Zealand cruiser *Leander*. There the transports *Mauretania* and *Queen Mary* join the convoy, as does the *Empress of Canada* off Melbourne on 6 May. After stopping in Fremantle from 10 to 12 May, the convoy, with the exception of *Leander*, is diverted to the Cape route while on the way to Colombo because it is feared that Italy will enter the war. After the *Canberra* has been relieved by the British cruiser *Shropshire* on 20 May, the convoy skirts the minefield laid by the German auxiliary cruiser *Schiff 16/Atlantis* off Cape Agulhas and discovered on 13 May and reaches Cape Town on 26 May. Leaving the *Empress of Japan* behind, the convoy proceeds to Freetown with the cruisers *Cumberland* and *Shropshire* from 31 May to 7 June. From there it goes N on 8 June. Until 10 June it is additionally escorted by the carrier *Hermes* and from 12 to 14 June it is met W of Gibraltar by a force comprising the battlecruiser *Hood*, the carrier *Argus* and three Canadian (*Restigouche*, *St Laurent* and *Skeena*) and three British (*Brooke*, *Wanderer* and *Westcott*) destroyers. These are reinforced on 15 June by Sunderland flying boats and the destroyers *Warwick* and *Witch*. Following W/T messages decoded by the German B-Service, Cdr U-boats deploys from 12 to 15 June the U-boats *U43*, *U101*, *U29*, *U48* and *U46* as the group 'Rösing' against the convoy, but it is not sighted. It arrives in the Clyde on 16 June.

3 May   North Sea/English Channel

Another 39 mines are dropped by air off Dunkirk, Calais and Boulogne and in the Downs.

3–4 May   North Sea

Unsuccessful sortie by the French destroyers *Chevalier-Paul*, *Milan* and *Tartu* and the British destroyers *Sikh* and *Tartar* into the Skagerrak.

4 May   Norway

An He 111 (Lt Korthals) of KG 100 sinks the Polish destroyer *Grom* off Narvik.

6–28 May   North Sea

Unsuccessful Allied submarine operations off the Dutch coast and in the southern part of the North Sea to cover the eastern entrance to the English Channel by the British submarines *Sturgeon*, *Triad*, *Snapper*, *Seawolf* and *Shark* and the French boats *Orphée*, *Calypso*, *Antiope*, *Circé*, *La Sibylle*, *Thétis* and *Doris*. Of the German U-boats *U7* and *U9* (Lt Lüth), operating in the same area, the latter sinks the *Doris* and two ships of 3838 tons.

On 10 Apr the British minelayer *Princess Victoria* with the destroyers *Esk*, *Express* and *Intrepid* had lain a barrage of 236 mines in the area of Egmond, and this is extended with 60 more mines by *Intrepid* on 15 May. On the same day the destroyers *Esk*, *Express* and *Ivanhoe* lay a barrage of 164 mines off the Hook of Holland. On 26 July the German minesweepers *M61*, *M89* and *M136* sink on these barrages.

7 May   Pacific

President Roosevelt orders the US Pacific Fleet, which is in the Hawaiian area for manoeuvres, to remain in Hawaii until further notice.

9 May   Norway

No 254 Sqn RAF sinks the Germany minesweeper *M134* in Bergen Roads. The vessel is later salvaged and repaired as *M534/Jungingen*.

9–10 May   North Sea

The German minelayers *Roland*, *Cobra*, *Preussen* and *Kaiser*, escorted by the destroyers *Richard Beitzen*, *Hermann Schoemann* and *Bruno Heinemann* and the torpedo boat *Greif*, depart to lay mine barrage '16' west of the Great Fisherman's Bank. A British force comprising the cruiser *Birmingham* and the destroyers *Janus*, *Hyperion*, *Hereward* and *Havock*, supported by the 5th DD Flotilla (Capt Lord Louis Mountbatten) with *Kelly*, *Kandahar* and *Hostile* (*Kimberley* is sent back to Rosyth short of fuel) sorties against the German minelayers; from Scapa Flow a third group of destroyers (Cdr E W B Sim) come to assist. At 56°58′N 05°20′E, the German 1st MTB Flotilla, with *S30*, *S31*, *S32*, *S33* and *S34* report the British force in time for the minelayers to turn round. *S31* attacks the northern group of the British force and hits the *Kelly* with one torpedo amidships; the badly damaged ship is towed with difficulty to Newcastle by the destroyer *Bulldog*. A covering force, consisting of the cruisers *Manchester* and *Sheffield* of the 18th Cruiser Sqn (Vice Adm Layton), arrives when the

main force is ordered south because of the German invasion of the Netherlands, Belgium and France.

10 May   North Sea

Beginning of the German offensive in the W: attack on Belgium, Holland and Luxembourg. In the previous night German aircraft drop 100 mines off Belgian and Dutch ports.

10 May   South Atlantic

The German auxiliary cruiser *Schiff 16/Atlantis* (Capt Rogge) drops 92 mines off Cape Agulhas, South Africa. The barrage is prematurely discovered and causes no shipping losses.

10 May   North Atlantic

British troops land in Iceland.

10–11 May   North Sea

He 111 bombers of KG 4 sink the Dutch passenger ships *Statendam* (28291 tons) and *Veendam* (15450 tons) and the destroyer *Van Galen* in the harbour of Rotterdam.

10–12 May   North Sea

British destroyers land demolition parties in Antwerp (*Brilliant*), Flushing, the Hook of Holland (*Venomous* and *Verity*) and Ijmuiden.

10–15 May   Norway

Advance by German battle group Feurstein from Mosjoen to Mo. To avoid British 'Scissor Force' near Mosjoen, 300 mountain troops are embarked on the Norwegian steamer *Nord Norge* and landed near Hamnesberget before the steamer is sunk by the British cruiser *Carlisle* and the destroyer *Zulu*. 'Scissor Force' has to be evacuated from Sandnessjoen to Bodö by destroyers *Janus* and *Javelin*.

The bulk of the British Guards Bde is ordered to Bodö to block the southern approach to Narvik. Cruisers *Cairo* and *Enterprise*, destroyer *Hesperus*, sloop *Fleetwood* and freighter *Margot* land reinforcements near Mo in spite of air attacks.

On 14–15 May the transport *Chrobry* (11442 tons) takes a battalion to Bodö escorted by the destroyer *Wolverine* and the sloop *Stork* but in the process is hit by Ju 87 bombers of I/StG 1 and has to be abandoned.

12 May   North Sea/English Channel

Another 32 mines are dropped by German aircraft in and outside Dutch and Belgian harbours. The operations are continued during the following nights. From 17 May the French Channel ports (Dunkirk, Calais, Dieppe, Boulogne and Le Havre) are the target of mining operations; from 25 May British harbours (Portsmouth, Dover, Southampton, Folkestone and Newhaven) are also again mined. In all, 575 more mines are dropped.

12–13 May   Norway
Two battalions of the French Foreign Legion land in Bjerkvik (Herjangsfjord-Narvik). The 1500 troops are transported by the cruisers *Effingham* (Adm of the Fleet Lord Cork) and *Aurora* and are disembarked. The battleship *Resolution* puts out two MLC landing boats each with two light tanks. Fire support is provided by the cruiser *Enterprise* and five destroyers, including *Havelock* with a French mountain battery on board.

12–14 May   North Sea/English Channel
The Dutch gunboat *Friso* is scuttled after an air attack in the Ijsselmeer on 12 May. On 14 May the gunboats *Johan Maurits van Nassau* and *Brinio* are sunk by air attacks and the incomplete destroyers *Tjerk Hiddes* and *Gerard Callenburgh* scuttled. The last is later recovered by the Germans and commissioned as *ZH1*.

13 May   North Sea
The British destroyer *Hereward* brings Queen Wilhelmina to Britain from Holland. In the evening the Dutch government follows on the British destroyer *Windsor*.
The Dutch motorvessel *Phrontis* (6181 tons) transports 900 German prisoners of war (Airborne Div) to England; the next morning the Dutch freighter *Texelstroom* (1617 tons) brings a further 300.

14–19 May   North Sea
German bombers sink the Belgian passenger steamer *Ville de Bruges* (13869 tons) in the Scheldt Estuary. Air attack on Rotterdam.

15–19 May   General Situation
Capitulation of the Dutch forces.

15–19 May   North Sea
On 15 May German bombers sink the British destroyer *Valentine* and badly damage the *Winchester* in the Scheldt Estuary. On 19 May the destroyer *Whitley* is beached near Nieuport after bomb damage and sunk by the destroyer *Keith*.

16–17 May   North Sea
The French destroyers *Fougueux*, *Frondeur*, *Cyclone* and *Sirocco*, supported by two squadrons of the naval air force, intervene in the fighting round Zuid Beveland and Walcheren.

16 May–8 June   English Channel
In operations in the Channel, *U9* (Lt Lüth) sinks one ship of 3256 tons and, off Dankirk, *U62* (Lt Michalowski) sinks the British destroyer *Grafton*. Attacks on the destroyers *Blyskawica* and *Vimy* by *U60* (Lt-Cdr Schewe) fail because of torpedo defects. *U13* (Lt-Cdr Schulte) is lost on a mine.

17 May   Norway/Intelligence
During the Norwegian campaign, three intact Army/Air Force 'Enigma' machines are captured; they are usable at Bletchley Park by 17 May.

17 May   Norway
The British cruiser *Effingham*, in trying to bring reinforcements to Bodö, runs on to a shoal and capsizes. Survivors are rescued by the cruisers *Cairo* and *Coventry* and the destroyers *Echo* and *Matabele*.

17 May   Western Atlantic
To prevent further incidents in the Pan-American Security Zone, caused by the seizure of German merchant ships, the Venezuelan Government orders the German freighters *Durazzo* (1153 tons) and *Sesostris* (3987 tons) lying in Maracaibo to be taken over by units of the Navy and their engines to be dismantled.

18 May   Norway
In an attack by Ju 88s of II/KG 30 on shipping targets near Narvik, the battleship *Resolution* is hit by a 1000kg bomb which penetrates three decks. The Norwegian torpedo boat *Troll* is captured at Floro.

18–21 May   Norway
The British aircraft carriers *Furious* and *Glorious* operate off the Lofotens. On 18 May No 701 Sqn FAA, with Walrus amphibious aircraft, is sent to Harstad for reconnaissance and defence against U-boats. On 21 May *Furious* flies 18 Gladiator fighters of No 263 Sqn RAF to Bardufoss. The *Ark Royal*, which is operating off Vestfjord to provide air support, has to go to Scapa on 21 May for replenishment.

19 May–2 June   North Atlantic
U37 (Lt-Cdr Oehrn) is the first U-boat to operate again after a lengthy pause in the area NW of Cape Finisterre. She sinks nine ships of 41207 tons and damages one other of 9494 tons.

20–21 May   English Channel
First German MTB raid against the Belgian coast (1st Flotilla, with *S22*, *S23*, *S24*, *S25*, and 2nd Flotilla, with *S30*, *S31*, *S32*, *S34* and *S13*).

20 May–30 June   Norway
In Allied submarine operations off the Norwegian coast, the French submarine *Rubis* (Cdr Cabanier) lays three mine barrages: near Haugesund (27 May), in Hjeltefjord (9 June) and off Gripholen (26 June) on which, in all, six ships and the submarine-chaser *UJD*, totalling 3772 tons, sink. *Narwhal* (Lt-Cdr Burch) lays a barrage near Utsire on 12 June (on which one ship of 908 tons and the minesweeper *M11* sink). On the way to the Norwegian coast, the Polish submarine *Orzel* runs on to new German mine barrages on either 25 May or 8 June. On 16 June *Tetrach* (Lt-Cdr Mills) sinks one ship of 5978 tons and *Truant* (Lt-Cdr Haggard) sinks one ship of 8230 tons off Northern Norway.

21 May   English Channel
German troops reach the Channel near Abbéville.

22 May–12 June   North Sea
U8, *U56* and *U58* (Lt-Cdr Kuppisch) operate from Bergen W of the Orkneys and in the North Minch. Torpedo defects prevent successes although *U58* sinks one ship of 8401 tons.

23–24 May   English Channel
The British destroyers *Whitshed*, *Vimiera*, *Wild Swan*, *Venomous*, *Venetia* and *Windsor* evacuate 4368 troops under heavy German artillery fire and air attacks; on her second trip alone *Vimiera* takes 1400 from Boulogne. Before this, the large French destroyers *Chacal* and *Jaguar* and the standard destroyers *Fougueux*, *Frondeur*, *L'Adroit* (sunk on 21 May), *Bourrasque*, *Orage*, *Foudroyant*, *Cyclone*, *Sirocco* and *Mistral*, under the command of Capt Urvoy de Porzamparc, intervene and temporararily halt the German advance. *Orage* is sunk by German bombers and *Jaguar* is sunk by the motor torpedo boats *S21* (Lt v Mirbach) and *S23* (Lt Christiansen).

24 May   Norway
Decision by Allied Supreme Command to evacuate Norway. Narvik is first to be occupied in order to destroy its installations.

24–26 May   English Channel
The British cruisers *Arethusa* and *Galatea* and the destroyers *Wessex*, *Vimiera*, *Wolfhound*, *Verity*, *Grafton*, *Greyhound* and *Burza* (Polish) give support to the defenders of Calais from the sea. *Wessex* is sunk by German bombers. The large French destroyer *Chacal* suffers the same fate off Boulogne on 25 May.

26 May   Norway
The carrier *Glorious* brings Hurricane fighters of No 46 Sqn RAF to Skaanland (Northern Norway).

26–28 May   Norway
The AA cruiser *Curlew* (Capt Brooke), which is intended to be the Flagship of Admiral of the Fleet Lord Cork, is sunk on 26 May by German He 111s (P O Wiersbitzky) of KG 100 off Skaanland. For this reason an attack on Narvik in the night 27–28 May is made with the AA cruisers *Cairo* (Lord Cork) and *Coventry* (Rear-Adm Vivian), the destroyers *Whirlwind*, *Fame*, *Havelock*, *Walker* and *Firedrake* and the sloop *Stork*. They support the Foreign Legion's crossing of Rombaksfjord and the advance with light tanks along the ore railway to Narvik, which has to be evacuated by the Germans on 28 May. The cruiser *Southampton* gives fire support to the Polish

Bde W of Narvik; the flagship *Cairo* is damaged by a bomb hit.

28 May   English Channel

King Leopold capitulates with the Belgian Army. Beginning of the Operation 'Dynamo' (return of the British Expeditionary Force). Up to 4 June the following warships participate: British AA cruiser *Calcutta*, destroyers *Anthony*, *Basilisk*, *Blyskawica* (Polish), *Codrington*, *Esk*, *Express*, *Gallant*, *Grafton*, *Grenade*, *Greyhound*, *Harvester*, *Havant*, *Icarus*, *Impulsive*, *Intrepid*, *Ivanhoe*, *Javelin*, *Jaguar*, *Keith*, *Mackay*, *Malcolm*, *Montrose*, *Sabre*, *Saladin*, *Scimitar*, *Shikari*, *Vanquisher*, *Venomous*, *Verity*, *Vimy*, *Vivacious*, *Wakeful*, *Whitehall*, *Whitshed*, *Wild Swan*, *Winchelsea*, *Windsor*, *Wolfhound*, *Wolsey* and *Worcester*, sloops *Bideford*, *Guillemot* and *Kingfisher*, gunboats *Locust* and *Mosquito*, minesweepers *Albury*, *Dundalk*, *Gossamer*, *Halcyon*, *Hebe*, *Leda*, *Lydd*, *Niger*, *Pangbourne*, *Ross*, *Salamander*, *Saltash*, *Skipjack*, *Speedwell*, *Sutton* and *Sharpshooter*, four patrol ships, 53 minesweeping and A/S trawlers, five Q ships, 24 drifters, six MTBs, four MSABs, 28 personnel transports, eight hospital transports and numerous auxiliary and private craft. In addition, the French destroyers *Epervier*, *Léopard*, *Branlebas*, *Bourrasque*, *Cyclone*, *Foudroyant*, *Mistral* and *Sirocco*, the torpedo boats *Bouclier*, *La Flore* and *L'Incomprise* and the sloops *Amiens*, *Amiral Mouchez*, *Arras* and *Belfort*, as well as auxiliary and merchant ships, take part. On the first day 17804 troops are evacuated from the mainland. One small steamer (694 tons) is sunk by the German motor torpedo boat *S34*, the British destroyer *Windsor* is damaged by bombs and other auxiliary ships and transports are sunk or damaged.

28 May–22 June   North Atlantic/ Bay of Biscay

The U-boats *U43*, *U101*, *U29*, *U48* and *U46* operate as the first wave concentrating on the area NW of Cape Finisterre. From 12 to 15 June the boats are concentrated without success to operate as the 'Rösing' group against the troop convoy US.3. On 22 June *U46* attacks the carrier *Ark Royal* which is proceeding with the battlecruiser *Hood* to Gibraltar, but she is unsuccessful owing to torpedo defects. *U43* refuels in Vigo on 18 June and *U29* in El Ferrol on 20 June from German tankers and they continue the operations until 15 June and 4 July respectively. U-boat successes: *U43* (Lt-Cdr Ambrosius) four ships of 29456 tons; *U101* (Lt-Cdr Frauenheim) seven ships of 42022 tons; *U29* (Lt-Cdr Schuhart) four ships of 26638 tons; *U48* (Cdr Rösing) seven ships of 31533 tons and one of 5888 tons

damaged; and *U46* (Lt Endrass) five ships of 35347 tons and one of 8782 tons damaged. Among the ships sunk are the auxiliary cruiser *Carinthia* (20277 tons) by *U46* on 6 June and the refrigerator ships *Wellington Star* (13212 tons) and *Avelona Star* (13376 tons) by *U101* and *U43* on 16 and 30 June respectively.

29 May   Norway

The German patrol vessel *V1109* (*Antares*) is sunk by mine off Norway.

29 May   English Channel

Second day of Operation 'Dynamo': 47310 troops evacuated. The British destroyer *Wakeful* is sunk by *S30* (Lt Zimmermann), *Grenade* by German bombers and *Grafton* by *U62* (Lt Michalowski); *Gallant*, *Jaguar*, *Greyhound*, *Intrepid*, *Saladin*, *Wolfhound* and *Mistral* (French) and the sloop *Bideford* are severely damaged by bombs. The destroyers *Mackay* and *Montrose* are damaged in collision and by running aground. The Luftwaffe also sinks eight auxiliary ships of 6201 tons and seven merchant ships totalling 15830 tons.

30 May   English Channel

Third day of Operation 'Dynamo': 53823 troops evacuated. The French destroyer *Bourrasque* is sunk by German artillery off Nieuport and the destroyers *Anthony*, *Sabre* and *Worcester* are damaged by air attacks. Three large transports and six fishery vessels are sunk.

31 May   English Channel

Fourth day of Operation 'Dynamo': 68014 troops evacuated. The French destroyer *Sirocco* is sunk by the German motor torpedo boats *S23* (Lt Christiansen) and *S26* (Lt Fimmen); the destroyer *Cyclone* loses her bow through a torpedo from *S24* (Lt Detlefsen). The destroyers *Express*, *Harvester*, *Icarus*, *Impulsive*, *Malcolm* and *Scimitar* and the minesweeper *Hebe* are damaged by German bombers.

31 May   North Sea.

The British minesweeper Weston, escorting convoy FN.184, sinks *U13* off Lowestoft.

31 May   North Sea/Norway

The British Home Fleet has the following ships available—2nd BB Sqn: *Resolution*, *Rodney* (F) and *Valiant*; being repaired: *Barham* and *Nelson*. Battlecruiser Sqn: *Renown* (F), *Repulse*; being repaired: *Hood*. Aircraft carriers: *Ark Royal* (F), *Furious* (Clyde), *Glorious*, destroyer *Westcott*; allocated cruisers being repaired: *Cairo* and *Enterprise*. 1st Cruiser Sqn: *Devonshire* (F), *Sussex*; being repaired: *Berwick*, *Norfolk*, *Suffolk*. 2nd Cruiser Sqn: *Galatea* (F), *Arethusa* (both in Sheerness); being repaired: *Aurora*, *Penelope*. 18th Cruiser Sqn: *Southampton* (F), *Birmingham*, Man-

chester and *Sheffield* in the Humber, *York* in Rosyth and *Newcastle* in the Tyne; being repaired: *Glasgow*. 3rd DD Flotilla: *Delight*, *Diana*; being repaired: *Imogen*, *Inglefield*, *Isis*. 5th DD Flotilla: *Jackal*, *Kelvin* in Harwich and *Javelin* in Sheerness; being repaired: *Kelly*, *Kipling*, *Kashmir*, *Jaguar*, *Jersey*, *Jervis*, *Jupiter*. 6th DD Flotilla: *Tartar* (F), *Ashanti*, *Bedouin*, *Mashona*; being repaired: *Somali*, *Matabele*, *Punjabi*, *Eskimo*. 8th DD Flotilla: *Foxhound*, *Fortune*, *Fame*, *Firedrake*; being repaired: *Faulknor*, *Fearless*, *Forester*, *Fury*. 9th DD Flotilla: *Havelock* (F), *Harvester*, *Havant* and *Highlander* in Sheerness; being repaired: *Hesperus*.

1 June   English Channel

Fifth day of Operation 'Dynamo': 64429 troops evacuated. Sunk in heavy German air attacks are the flotilla leader *Keith* (Flagship Rear-Adm Wake-Walker), the destroyers *Basilisk*, *Havant* and *Foudroyant* (French), the minesweeper *Skipjack*, the gunboat *Mosquito* and the transports *British Queen* (807 tons) and *Scotia* (3454 tons) with French troops on board. There are heavy losses of personnel. In a sortie against Dunkirk, *S34* (Lt Obermaier) sinks the British trawlers *Argyllshire* and *Stella Dorado*. The destroyers *Ivanhoe*, *Venomous*, *Vimy*, *Vivacious* and *Whitehall* and the sloops *Bideford* and *Kingfisher* are damaged in air attacks.

1 June   Mediterranean

In a German air attack on Marseilles, the British passenger ship *Orford* (20043 tons) sinks.

2 June   English Channel

Sixth day of Operation 'Dynamo': 26256 troops evacuated. Destroyers *Malcolm* and *Sabre* are again damaged in air attacks.

4 June   English Channel

End of Operation 'Dynamo' (27 May–4 June). In all, 338226 Allied troops, including 123000 French, have been transported from Dunkirk on 848 ships of every kind and size. Eighty five per cent of the British Expeditionary Force is saved, but almost without equipment. Losses: 72 ships including nine destroyers and a large number of small and very small craft, most of them sunk in air attacks. At 0940 hrs, units of the 18th German Army take Dunkirk; 40000 French taken prisoner.

4–10 June   Norway

Allied evacuation of Narvik. In five successive nights up to 7–8 June, 4700, 4900, 5100, 5200 and 4600 men are embarked on troop transports assembled off Harstad under the command of Capt Stevens on *Havelock*, mainly with destroyers. The first convoy, consisting of *Monarch of Bermuda*,

Batory, *Sobieski*, *Franconia*, *Lancastria* and *Georgic*, leaves Harstad on 4 June, accompanied only by the training cruiser *Vindictive*, and reaches Scapa Flow on 8 June without loss. As a result of a false report from the Q-ship *Prunella* about two unidentified ships proceeding towards the Iceland–Faeroes passage, the C-in-C Home Fleet fears a break-out by the German battleships into the Atlantic. Because of this the battlecruisers *Renown* and *Repulse*, the cruisers *Newcastle* and *Sussex* and five escorting destroyers are sent off. Only the battleship *Valiant* remains available to cover the evacuation convoys. On 7 June the second troop transport, consisting of *Oronsay*, *Ormonde*, *Arandora Star*, *Royal Ulsterman*, *Ulster Prince*, *Ulster Monarch* and *Duchess of York* and escorted by the cruisers *Southampton* (Lord Cork, Vice-Adm Layton) and *Coventry* (Rear-Adm Vivian) and the destroyers *Havelock*, *Fame*, *Firedrake*, *Beagle* and *Delight*, leaves Harstad as well as a slow convoy with the transports and tankers *Blackheath*, *Oligarch*, *Harmattan*, *Cromarty Firth*, *Theseus*, *Acrity*, *Cotswold* and *Conch*, escorted by the destroyers *Arrow* and *Veteran*, the sloop *Stork* and ten trawlers. The cruiser *Devonshire* sets out to sea from Tromsö with the Norwegian King. The carrier *Ark Royal* stands by in the area of the troop convoy. The carrier *Glorious*, after taking the last aircraft on board, leaves Bardufoss with her last two destroyers independently for the W, likewise some independents from Vestfjord and the transports *Orama* and *Van Dyck* which were not ordered to Harstad.

4–10 June   Norway

Operation 'Juno': sortie against British evacuation transports in the area W of Harstad by the Fleet Cdr, Adm Marschall, with the battlecruisers *Gneisenau* (Capt Netzbandt) and *Scharnhorst* (Capt Hoffmann), the heavy cruiser *Admiral Hipper* (Capt Heye) and the destroyers *Karl Galster*, *Hans Lody*, *Erich Steinbrinck* and *Hermann Schoemann*. On the way the empty troop transport *Orama* (19840 tons), the tanker *Oil Pioneer* (5666 tons) and the trawler *Juniper* (505 tons) are sunk on 8 June. After detaching themselves from *Admiral Hipper* and the destroyers, the battlecruisers destroy the British aircraft carrier *Glorious* (Capt D'Oyly-Hughes†) and the destroyers *Acasta* (Cdr Glasford†) and *Ardent* (Lt-Cdr Barker†) although *Acasta* is able to obtain a torpedo hit on *Scharnhorst*; 1515 men die and there are only 43 survivors from the carrier and three from both destroyers. But the British evacuation convoys are not found and they reach Scapa

Flow on 10 June. An operation started on 9 June by the Home Fleet with the battleship *Rodney* and the recalled battlecruiser *Renown* is unable to catch the German ships before they sail into Trondheim.

4–21 June   Mediterranean

Beginning on 4 June and continuing until 9 June, 54 Italian submarines set out for positions in the Mediterranean. Except for 26, they return on 14–15 June, and most of the remainder return by 21 June or are relieved: *Veniero*, *Neghelli*, *Gondar*, *Fieramosca* and *Mocenigo* operate along the French Riviera, *H1*, *H4*, *H6* and *H8* in the Gulf of Genoa, *Medusa* off Ajaccio, *Faa'di Bruno*, *Morosini*, *Provana*, *Dandolo* and *Marcello* (not in position owing to breakdown) between Oran and Cartagena, *Barbarigo* and *Nani* N of Algiers, *Axum*, *Turchese*, *Adua* and *Aradam* south of Sardinia, *Alagi* off Bizerta, *Beilul*, *Brin* and *Durbo* in the Sicilian Channel, *Bausan* off Malta, *Uarsciek*, *Balilla*, *Anfitrite* and *Sciesa* off the Greek/Albanian coast, *Salpa*, *Giuliani*, *Bagnolini* and *Tarantini* S of Gaudo (Crete), *Lafolé*, *Diamante*, *Topazio* and *Nereide* N of Sollum, *Galatea* (not in position owing to breakdown), *Fisalia*, *Argonauta*, *Naiade* and *Smeraldo* off Alexandria, *Jantina*, *Jalea*, *Delfino*, *Tricheco*, *Zaffiro* and *Velella* between Crete and Rhodes, *Ametista*, *Gemma* and *Squalo* in the Aegean and *Settimo* and *Uebi Scebeli* N and W of Crete. On 12 June *Bagnolini* (Cdr Tosoni-Pittoni) sinks the British cruiser *Calypso* and *Naiade* (Lt-Cdr Baroni) the Norwegian tanker *Orkanger* (8029 tons). *Dandolo* (Lt-Cdr Boris) attacks a French cruiser force on 13 June and just misses *Jean de Vienne*. *Provana* (Cdr Botta) misses the French convoy IR.2F and is then forced to surface by the sloop *La Curieuse* and sunk by ramming. On 20 June *Diamante* is sunk by the British submarine *Parthian* (Lt-Cdr Rimington). A mine barrage (40 mines) laid off Alexandria on 12 June by *Micca* (Cdr* Meneghini) achieves no success.

5 June–13 July   Central Atlantic

On 5–6 June the Italian submarines *Cappellini* and *Finzi* set out from Cagliari for the Atlantic. *Finzi* passes through the Straits of Gibraltar on 13 June and then operates without success in the area of the Canaries. She passes through the Straits of Gibraltar again (6 July), returning to base on 13 July. *Cappellini* is attacked by the A/S trawler *Arctic Ranger* with depth charges on 14 June off the Straits of Gibraltar; she is then pursued by the destroyer *Vidette* and from 15 to 24 June has to take refuge in Centa, whence she returns.

6–18 June   Norway

The German minesweepers *M11* and *M5* are lost on mines, the first on 6 June off Feiestein and the second on 18 June off Ramsöyfjord.

6 June–10 July   Mediterranean/ Red Sea

Major defensive mine barrages are laid off the Italian Mediterranean coasts. The minelayers *Crotone* and *Fascana* and the auxiliary minelayers *Orlando* and *Sgarallino* lay, in the Gulf of Genoa and in the Elba area, 21 barrages against surface ships and 27 barrages against submarines, involving 1960 mines. In the Naples area the minelayer *Buffoluto* and the steamer *Partenope* lay seven barrages involving 433 mines. Off Sardinia the minelayers *Durazzo* and *Pelagosa*, the auxiliary ship *Deffenu* and the torpedo boats *Papa*, *Cascino*, *Chinotto* and *Montanari* lay 30 barrages consisting of 2196 mines; 12 of the barrages are laid against submarines. In the area of Sicily the auxiliary ships *Adriatico* and *Brioni* and the torpedo boats *Aldebaran*, *Andromeda*, *Alcione*, *Aretusa*, *Ariel*, *Airone*, *Pallade*, *Calliope*, *Circe* and *Clio* lay 28 barrages (12 A/S) consisting of 1375 mines. In the Gulf of Taranto and in the southern part of the Adriatic, including Albania, the minelayer *Vieste*, the auxiliary ship *Barletta*, the cruiser *Taranto* and the destroyers *Mirabello* and *Riboty* lay 37 mine barrages (28 A/S) consisting of 2335 mines. In the Northern Adriatic the minelayers *Albona*, *Azio*, *Laurana* and *Rovigo* and the auxiliary minesweeper *S Guisto* lay 21 barrages (18 A/S) consisting of 769 mines. In the Aegean-Dodecanese area the auxiliary ship *Lero*, the destroyers *Crispi* and *Sella* and the torpedo boats *Libra*, *Lince* and *Lira* lay 28 barrages (4 A/S) consisting of 800 mines. Off Libya the auxiliary ship *Barletta*, and off Tobruk the destroyers *Aquilone*, *Euro*, *Nembo* and *Turbine*, lay 14 barrages consisting of 540 mines. In the Red Sea the minelayer *Ostia* lays eight barrages of 470 mines off Massawa and the destroyer *Pantera* two barrages of 110 mines off Assab on 7 June.

8 June   English Channel

The British destroyers *Vesper* and *Wanderer* bombard the road between Abbéville and Le Tréport.

8–12 June   Mediterranean

Offensive mine barrages are laid by Italian ships in the Sicilian Channel. During the nights 8–9 and 9–10 June the minelayers *Buccari* and *Scilla*, accompanied by the torpedo boat *Altair*, each lay 640 mines between Pantelleria and Sicily. During the night 9–10 June the cruisers *Da Barbiano* (Div Adm Marenco di Moriondo) and

Cadorna, the destroyers *Corazziere* and *Lanciere* and the torpedo boats *Calipso* and *Polluce* lay the barrage 'LK' consisting of 428 mines between Lampedusa and Kerkennah. After an interrupted operation, *Buccari* and *Scilla* with the torpedo boats *Airone* and *Ariel* lay another 800 mines during the night 11–12 June. To cover the operation the cruisers *Pola* (Div Adm Paladini), *Trento*, *Bolzano*, *Eugenio di Savoia* (*Div Adm Sansonetti*), *Attendolo*, *Duca d'Aosta* and *Montecuccoli* put to sea with destroyers on 10–11 June.

9 June   North Sea
The German patrol vessel *V801/Bayern* is sunk by torpedo off Ameland.

9 June–2 July   North Atlantic/Bay of Biscay
The U-boats *U32*, *U47*, *U25*, *U38*, *U28*, *U51* and *U30* operate as second wave concentrating on the area W of the English Channel and in the Bay of Biscay. From 12 to 15 June they are deployed as the group 'Prien' against the convoy HX.48 which is located by the W/T intelligence service (B-Service); some encounter only stragglers but some attack individually—*U48* and *U51* the convoy HGF.34, *U43* the French convoy 65.X and *U30*, *U32*, and *U47* the convoy HX.49. *U30* is replenished in El Ferrol on 25 June and is the first U-boat to enter the new Lorient base on 5 July. In their individual operations, *U32* (Lt-Cdr Jenisch) sinks five ships of 16098 tons, *U47* (Lt-Cdr Prien) eight ships of 51189 tons, *U25* (Lt-Cdr Liebe) six ships of 30353 tons and *U28* (Lt-Cdr Kuhnke) three ships of 10305 tons; *U51* (Lt-Cdr Knorr) sinks three ships of 22146 tons and damages one ship of 3082 tons and *U30* (Lt-Cdr Lemp) sinks six ships of 26329 tons. Among the ships sunk is the unnotified troop transport *Arandora Star* (15501 tons) which is taking German and Italian civilian internees to Canada (sunk by *U47* on 2 July).

10 June   Norway
Capitulation of Norwegian troops (Maj-Gen Ruge) in Northern Norway; this concludes Operation 'Weserübung'. German naval losses: three cruisers, 10 destroyers, one torpedo boat, four submarines, one gunnery training ship, one motor minesweeper and a number of auxiliary ships. Allied losses: one aircraft carrier, two cruisers, nine destroyers, five submarines and many auxiliary ships.

10 June   Mediterranean
Italy enters the war. Strength of the fleet: six battleships (only the two oldest ready for operations), seven heavy cruisers, 12 light cruisers, 59 destroyers, 67 torpedo boats and 116 submarines. A third of the merchant

marine, comprising in all 3.4m tons, is at the moment outside the Mediterranean and so cannot be put to war use. Allied forces comprise the British and French Mediterranean fleets. Eastern Mediterranean (British): four battleships, one aircraft carrier, nine light cruisers, 21 destroyers (four more detached to the Red Sea), six submarines; (French): one battleship, three heavy cruisers, one light cruiser, one destroyer, six submarines. Malta (British): one destroyer, six submarines. Western Mediterranean (French): two modern battleships, two old battleships, four heavy cruisers, six light cruisers, 37 destroyers, six torpedo boats, 36 submarines. Gibraltar: one battleship, one aircraft carrier, one light cruiser, nine destroyers.

10–11 June   Norway
Fifteen Skua aircraft from the British carrier *Ark Royal* attack the German battlecruiser *Scharnhorst* at Trondheim: they score one hit, but the bomb does not explode. Eight Skuas, from Nos 800 and 803 Sqns, are lost.

A sortie by the battlecruiser *Gneisenau* (C-in-C Fleet, Admiral Marschall) and heavy cruiser *Admiral Hipper* with the destroyers *Hans Lody*, *Hermann Schoemann*, *Erich Steinbrinck* and *Karl Galster* sail from Trondheim into the Arctic but without result because air reconnaissance is hampered by bad weather.

10–11 June   English Channel
The taking off of the 51st British Div from St Valéry is only partly successful: 3321 British and French troops are evacuated but the rest are taken prisoner.

10–13 June   English Channel
11059 British troops are evacuated from Le Havre, some to Cherbourg and some to Britain. In the process the transport *Bruges* (2949 tons) sinks after being hit by bombs.

10–25 June   Mediterranean
Allied submarine operations in the Mediterranean. In the Central Mediterranean the British submarines *Odin*, *Osiris*, *Oswald*, *Olympus*, *Orpheus* and *Grampus* operate from Malta off Italian harbours. Of these, *Odin* is sunk by the Italian destroyer *Strale* in the Gulf of Taranto on 13 June, *Grampus* by the Italian torpedo boats *Circe*, *Clio* and *Polluce* off Syracuse on 16 June and *Orpheus* by the destroyer *Turbine* off Tobruk. The French submarines *Le Centaure*, *Pascal*, *Fresnel*, *Vengeur*, *Redoutable*, *Narval*, *Caïman*, *Morse*, *Souffleur*, *Monge*, *Pégase* and *Le Tonnant* operate from Tunisian ports, sometimes repeatedly. *Morse* is lost when she hits a mine off Sfax on 15 June. The British submarines *Parthian*, *Pandora*, *Proteus* and *Phoenix* operate in the Eastern

Mediterranean from Alexandria and *Rorqual* lays a mine barrage off the African coast. The French submarines *Phoque*, *Espadon*, *Protée*, *Achéron* and *Actéon* operate in the Dodecanese area from Beirut; *Iris*, *Vénus*, *Pallas* and *Archimède* operate in the Tyrrhenian Sea from Toulon and *Ariane*, *Eurydice*, *Diane* and *Danaé* off Gibraltar from Oran. The French submarine *Saphir* (Lt-Cdr Caminati) lays a mine barrage off Cagliari (sinking two ships of 1699 tons), *Nautilus* off Tripoli, *Turquoise* off Trapani and *Perlé* off Bastia.

10–26 June   Red Sea/Indian Ocean/Intelligence
First operations by Italian submarines from Massawa (Eritrea). On 10 June *Ferraris* proceeds to Djibouti, *Galilei* to Aden, *Galvani* to the Gulf of Oman and *Macallè* to Port Sudan. On 14 June *Torricelli* relieves *Ferraris*, which returns owing to a breakdown. On 15 June *Macallé* (Lt-Cdr Morone) runs on a shoal and is lost. *Galilei* (Cdr Nardi) sinks the Norwegian tanker *James Stove* (8215 tons) on 16 June. She stops the Yugoslav steamer *Drava* on 18 June but has to release her again and is encountered on 19 June by the A/S trawler *Moonstone* and forced in a gun duel to surrender after the commander becomes a casualty. On the basis of documents captured on board, the sloop *Falmouth* is able to sink *Galvani* (Cdr Spano) off the Persian Gulf on 24 June, the submarine having previously destroyed the Indian sloop *Pathan*. *Torricelli* (Cdr Pelosi) is encountered on 23 June off Perim and is sunk in a gun duel with the British destroyers *Kandahar*, *Khartoum* and *Kingston* and the sloop *Shoreham*. *Torricelli* obtains hits on *Shoreham* and *Khartoum*; the latter is set on fire and sinks after an explosion in a magazine. Of the submarines *Archimede*, *Perla* and *Guglielmotti*, which set out on 19–21 June, the latter runs on to a shoal on 26 June but can be salvaged in spite of severe damage.

10 June–20 Sept   Indian Ocean
The German auxiliary cruiser *Schiff 16/Atlantis* (Capt Rogge) sinks and seizes, respectively, seven Allied merchant ships of 49338 tons and the French passenger ship *Commissaire Ramel* (10061 tons).

11 June   Atlantic
The auxiliary cruiser *Thor* (Capt Kähler) sets out from Sörgulenfjord for her first operation in the Central and South Atlantic, having left Kiel on 6 June.

11 June   Mediterranean
First Italian air attack on Malta. Other bombers attack Toulon.

11 June   Norway
N of Harstad (Norway), German aircraft sink the British auxiliary ship *Van Dyck* (13241 tons).

11–14 June   Mediterranean
First sortie by the British Mediterranean Fleet (Adm Cunningham) against Italian shipping heading for Libya S of Crete and towards Benghazi and Tobruk. Taking part are the battleships *Warspite* (F) and *Malaya*, carrier *Eagle*, 7th Cruiser Sqn (Vice-Adm Tovey) with *Orion, Neptune, Sydney, Liverpool* and *Gloucester*, nine destroyers and old cruisers *Caledon* and *Calypso*; simultaneous sortie by French cruisers (Vice-Adm Godfroy) *Duquesne, Tourville, Suffren* and *Duguay Trouin* and three destroyers into the Aegean and against the Dodecanese. On 12 June *Calypso* is sunk by the Italian submarine *Bagnolini* (Cdr Tosoni-Pittoni). British cruisers *Gloucester* and *Liverpool* with four destroyers shell Tobruk and engage the floating battery *San Giorgio* (ex-armoured cruiser) and four small Italian auxiliary minesweepers, of which *Giovanni Berta* (Chief Petty Officer Paolucci) sinks, firing her only 7.6cm gun. When air reconnaissance reports this British force the Italian 3rd Cruiser Div sets out from Messina with *Pola, Trento* and *Bolzano* together with the 11th and 12th DD Flotillas. In addition, the 1st and 8th Cruiser Divs with *Zara, Fiume, Gorizia, Duca degli Abruzzi* and *Garibaldi* and the 9th and 16th DD Flotillas set out from Taranto. However, no contact results.

11 June–20 Aug   Atlantic
First Southern operation by a German U-boat. *UA* (Lt-Cdr Cohausz) operates on the way out (11–19 June) against the Northern Patrol and, after a miss on 14 June, sinks the auxiliary cruiser *Andania* (13950 tons) on 16 June. On the way S one ship is sunk and another in the first half of the operations in the area of the Canary and Cape Verde Islands. By 10 Aug a fourth ship is sunk, the U-boat having been replenished off Freetown on 19 July from the auxiliary cruiser *Schiff 33*. On the return three more ships are sunk, making a total of seven ships with a tonnage of 40706 tons.

12–20 June   Norway
Climax in the operations of the third British submarine wave off Norway with the boats *Severn, Clyde, Sealion, Spearfish, Porpoise, Narwhal, Trident, Truant, Taku, Tetrarch* and the French *Rubis*. *Narwhal* (Lt-Cdr Burch) lays a mine barrage near Utsire, sinking one ship of 908 tons. *Porpoise* (Lt-Cdr Roberts) lays a barrage off Kristiansand, sinking the minesweeper *M5* on 18 June. *Rubis* (Cdr Cabanier) lays two mine

barrages in the area of Bergen on which four ships of 1898 tons are sunk. *Tetrarch* (Lt-Cdr Mills) sinks the tanker *Samland* (5978 tons) near Lister on 16 June. *Clyde* (Lt-Cdr Ingram) torpedoes the battlecruiser *Gneisenau* in the bows off Trondheim on 20 June. On the way out to Norway the Dutch submarine *O13* is lost, presumably to a mine on 13 June after being attacked in error by the Polish submarine *Wilk*.

12–14 June   Norway
Home Fleet (Adm Forbes) makes a raid on Trondheim with battleship *Rodney*, battlecruiser *Renown* and destroyers to cover the carrier *Ark Royal*. On 13 June 15 Skua dive bombers fly off to attack the German battlecruiser *Scharnhorst*. They get a hit with a 225kg bomb but it does not explode. Eight aircraft are shot down by the defences. On the return the destroyers *Antelope* and *Electra* collide.

13 June   Norway
The German light cruiser *Nürnberg* arrives at Trondheim from Germany.

13 June   Pacific
The auxiliary cruiser *Orion* (Cdr* Weyher) lays 162 mines in Hauraki Bay (New Zealand) and another 60 between Cuvier Island and Great Barrier Island and in the Colville Channel. In Hauraki Bay the British passenger ship *Niagara* (13415 tons) sinks on 18 June.

13 June–13 July   Central Atlantic
The German auxiliary cruiser *Schiff 21/ Widder* (Cdr v Ruckteschell) sinks three Allied freighters of 18552 tons in the western part of the Central Atlantic and seizes the Norwegian motor tanker *Krossfonn* (9323 tons).

14 June   Mediterranean
Sortie by the French 3rd Sqn (Vice-Adm Duplat) with four heavy cruisers and 11 large destroyers from Toulon against the Ligurian coast. The 1st Cruiser Div shells Vado with *Algérie* and *Foch* and the destroyers *Vauban, Lion, Aigle, Tartu, Chevalier-Paul* and *Cassard*; the 2nd Cruiser Div (Rear-Adm Derrien) shells the harbour installations of Genoa with *Colbert* and *Dupleix* and the destroyers *Albatros* and *Vautour*, escorted by the destroyers *Guépard, Valmy* and *Verdun*. A courageous attack by the Italian torpedo boat *Calatafimi* and the 13th MTB Flotilla is not successful. Italian coastal artillery obtains a hit on *Albatros*. The deployment of the Italian submarines *Neghelli* and *Veniero*, which are still at sea, and the submarines *Iride* and *Scire*, coming from La Spezia, achieves nothing.

14 June   Mediterranean
The 1st Italian DD Flotilla (Cdr* Ruggieri),

consisting of *Turbine, Nembo* and *Aquilone*, shells Sollum.

15 June   Baltic
The Lithuanian minesweeper *President Smetona* is seized by the Soviets and commissioned in Aug as *Korall*.

15–18 June   English Channel
British 52nd Div and 'Norman Force', comprising 30630 troops, are evacuated from Cherbourg without loss.

15 June–6 Aug   Arctic
From 15 June to 18 July and from 23 June to 6 Aug the Soviet submarines *K-2* and *K-1* are transferred from the Baltic by way of the White Sea Channel to the Arctic and commissioned in the Northern Fleet.

16–17 June   English Channel
Evacuation of 1st Canadian Div with 21474 troops from St-Malo without loss. Off Brest, 32584 men of the British Army and RAF, as well as Allied troops, are evacuated. The harbour is destroyed on 18–19 June. The French fleet sets out for Casablanca and Oran.

16–18 June   Bay of Biscay
St-Nazaire and Nantes are evacuated. In all, 57235 Allied troops are brought to Britain. Heavy losses – about 3000 men – are sustained when British transport *Lancastria* (16243 tons) is sunk by German bombers.

16 June–2 July   North Atlantic
U61 (Lt-Cdr Oesten) and *U62* (Lt Michalowski) operate from Bergen in the area of the Hebrides. An attack by *U61* on an auxiliary cruiser fails; *U62* misses two ships and sinks a small trawler of 211 tons.

17 June   General Situation
France sues for an Armistice.

17–18 June   General Situation
Evacuation of the British Expeditionary Force from the Continent completed.

17 June–19 July   North Atlantic
U52, U65, U122, U26, U34, U102, U99 and *U30* (which has set out again from Lorient) operate as third wave in the area between the North Channel and Cape Finisterre. Shortly after the first attacks off the North Channel, *U122* (21 June) and *U102* (30 June) are lost from unknown causes (mines?). *U26*, when attacking convoy OA.175 and torpedoing one ship of 4871 tons, on 1 July, is sunk by the corvette *Gladiolus*, supported by a Sunderland flying boat from No 10 Sqn RAAF. This is the first success registered by a Flower class corvette. In their operations, *U52* (Lt-Cdr Salman) sinks four ships of 13542 tons; *U65* (Lt Cdr v Stockhausen) sinks one ship of 1177 tons and damages *Champlain* (see below) and two other ships of 13958 tons; *U122* (Lt Cdr Looff) sinks one ship of 5911 tons but is lost, probably by depth charges

from the corvette *Arabis*, on 23 June; *U26* (Lt-Cdr Scheringer) sinks one ship of 6701 tons and damages one other ship of 4871 tons; *U34* (Lt-Cdr Rollmann) sinks the destroyer *Whirlwind* and seven ships of 21334 tons; *U102* (Lt-Cdr v Klot-Heydenfeldt) sinks two ships of 4505 tons from the convoy SL.35 but is sunk by the destroyer *Vansittart* on 1 July; *U99* (Lt-Cdr Kretschmer) sinks six ships of 20755 tons; and *U30* (Lt-Cdr Lemp) sinks one ship of 712 tons. The troop transport *Champlain* (28124 tons), which hit a mine on 18 June and rested on the bottom, is finished off on 21 June by a torpedo from *U65*.

U30, *U34*, *U52* and *U99* put into Lorient for replenishment.

17–28 June   Gibraltar
From 17 June to 23 June the battlecruiser *Hood*, the carrier *Ark Royal* and the destroyers of the 8th DD Flotilla, *Escapade*, *Faulknor*, *Fearless* and *Foxhound*, move from Scapa Flow to Gibraltar. The ships are attacked on 22 June by *U46* in force 11 winds but *Ark Royal* is missed because of a torpedo failure. In the following days the battleships *Resolution* and *Valiant*, the cruiser *Enterprise* and the destroyers *Escort*, *Foresight* and *Forester* arrive. With the arrival of Vice-Adm Somerville on board the cruiser *Arethusa* on 28 June, Force H is formed. In addition, the 13th DD Flotilla, comprising *Active*, *Wrestler*, *Vidette*, *Douglas*, *Keppel*, *Vortigern*, *Wishart* and *Watchman* (the last returns to Britain in July), is stationed in Gibraltar.

18 June   English Channel/Bay of Biscay
The German 7th Armoured Div occupies Cherbourg; 30630 troops are evacuated beforehand under cover from the battleship *Courbet* (Capt Croiset) and, in the dockyards, five uncompleted submarines, including *Roland-Morillot*, are blown up. Before the occupation of Brest by the German 5th Armoured Div the submarines *Achille*, *Agosta*, *Ouessant* and *Pasteur*, the destroyer *Cyclone* and the sloop *Etourdi*, which are in harbour for repairs, are blown up. The sloop *Vauquois* is sunk off Brest by a mine; at Lorient the sloop *Enseigne Henri* is scuttled.

18 June   Norway
The German auxiliary minesweeper *M1802*/*Friedrich Müller* is sunk by mine off Norway.

18–27 June   Atlantic
On 18 June the incomplete French battleship *Richelieu* (Capt Marzin) sets out from Brest for Dakar with the destroyers *Fougueux* and *Frondeur*. On 19 June the unfinished battleship *Jean Bart* (Capt Ronarch) is towed out of St-Nazaire and, accompanied

by the new destroyers *Le Hardi* (with the Cdr Naval Forces West, Rear-Adm Laborde on board) and *Mameluk*, reaches Casablanca on 22 June. There her movements are observed by the British destroyer *Watchman*. *Richelieu* arrives off Dakar on 23 June. On the same day the cruiser *Dorsetshire* sets out from Freetown to keep watch and meets the carrier *Hermes* off Dakar. On 25 June the British C-in-C South Atlantic, Vice-Adm D'Oyly Lyon, comes from Freetown with the seaplane carrier *Albatross*. But, before she arrives, *Richelieu* sets out at midday on 25 June for Casablanca, followed by the *Dorsetshire*. However, Adm Darlan orders *Richelieu* back to Dakar, where she arrives on 27 June with the auxiliary cruisers *El Djezair*, *El Kantara*, *El Mansour* and *Ville d'Oran* from Brest and the destroyers *Epervier* and *Milan*.

18 June–19 July   Mediterranean
Supply transports from Naples to Leros with the Italian submarine *Atropo*, and to Tobruk with *Bragadino*, *Corridoni* and *Zoea*. The last goes on to Leros.

19 June   English Channel
The German motor torpedo boats *S19* (Lt Töniges) and *S26* (Lt Fimmen) sink the British freighter *Roseburn* (3103 tons) off Dungeness.

19–25 June   Bay of Biscay
Evacuation of some 19000 troops, mainly Polish, from Bayonne and St-Jean-de-Luz. In all, in Operations 'Cycle' (French north coast) and 'Ariel' (Biscay coast)—in addition to 'Dynamo'—144171 British, 18246 French, 24352 Poles, 4938 Czechs and 163 Belgians (total 191870 troops) are evacuated.

On 20 June the destroyer *Beagle* lands a demolition party at Bordeaux.

19–27 June   Mediterranean
A second wave of Italian submarines is stationed in the Eastern Mediterranean: *Bausan* W of Crete, *Manara* and *Menotti* S of Crete, *Sirena* off Sollum, *Rubino* off Alexandria, *Luizzi* off Famagusta and *Delfino*, *Squalo*, *Brin* and *Tricheco* in the approaches to the Aegean. *Sirena* is damaged with depth charges in an Anglo-French cruiser sortie on 21 June and puts in to Tobruk.

19 June–2 July   Mediterranean
A second wave of Italian submarines operates in the Western Mediterranean against French shipping between North Africa and the South of France. Taking part are *H1*, *H4* and *H8* (twice) in the Gulf of Genoa, *Fieramosca* (battery explosion) and *Gondar* off the French Riviera, *Iride*, *Aradam*, *Mocenigo* and *Malachite* in the Gulf of Lyons, *Bandiera*, *Ascianghi*, *Santarosa* and

Nani in the Narrows of the Balearics, *Glauco*, *Tazzoli*, and *Toti* off the Algerian coast, *Medusa* and *Marcello* off Bizerta and *Capponi*, *Da Procida* and *Pisani* in the Sicilian Channel. *Glauco* (Cdr* Corvetti) slightly damages one ship of 3657 tons with gunfire. *Capponi* (Lt-Cdr Romei) sinks the Swedish freighter *Elgö* (1888 tons).

20 June   Baltic
The Latvian minesweeper *Virsaitis* is seized by the Soviets and commissioned on 17 Oct as *T-297*. The small minesweepers *Viesturs* and *Imanta* become *T-298* and *T-299*.

20–21 June   Mediterranean
Last joint Anglo-French operation in the Mediterranean. Vice-Adm Tovey, with the French battleship *Lorraine*, the British cruisers *Neptune*, *Orion* (F) and *Sydney* and the destroyers *Stuart*, *Decoy*, *Dainty* and *Hasty*, sails out to shell Bardia. This is carried out in the night of 20–21 June but causes only slight damage. At the same time, five British destroyers advance along the coast as far as Tobruk without finding targets. As a result of inaccurate air reconnaissance reports about Italian forces, the French cruisers *Duguay-Trouin* and *Suffren* with three British destroyers set out from Alexandria.

20–23 June   Norway
To divert British air reconnaissance from the return of the damaged battlecruiser *Scharnhorst*, the battlecruiser *Gneisenau* and the heavy cruiser *Admiral Hipper* leave Trondheim on 20 June to make a sortie into the Iceland–Faeroes passage. 40 nautical miles NW of Halten the British submarine *Clyde* (Lt-Cdr Ingram) attacks the force and obtains a torpedo hit on the bows of *Gneisenau* with the result that the operation is abandoned. On 21 June *Scharnhorst*, accompanied by the destroyers *Erich Steinbrinck*, *Hans Lody*, *Hermann Schoemann* and *Karl Galster* and joined by the torpedo boats *Greif*, *Kondor*, *Falke* and *Jaguar*, begins the journey to Kiel. Attempted attacks by six Swordfish torpedo aircraft off Utsire are beaten off and two planes are shot down. The ship arrives in Kiel on 23 June.

20–26 June   Mediterranean
Eight Italian merchant ships break through undetected from Leros to Brindisi.

21 June   English Channel
The German MTBs *S21* and *S32* are sunk by mines off Boulogne, 15 miles south of Dungeness. *S21* is salvaged in 1941 and repaired.

22 June   General Situation
Conclusion of the German-French Armistice at Compiègne. Provisions: occupation of France to the line W and N of Geneva–Dôle–Tours–Mont de Marsa–Spanish frontier. Thus the whole of the English Channel

coast and the Atlantic coast are in German hands. Disarming of the French armed forces except for 100000 volunteers; no air force and no army. Disarming of large parts of the Fleet, but no handover. At this point there are in Plymouth and Portsmouth two battleships, two large destroyers, eight ordinary destroyers and torpedo boats, seven submarines and 200 smaller vessels. Continuation of French Government in unoccupied France (transferred to Vichy at the beginning of July). Pierre Laval enters the French Government and becomes leading minister under Pétain.

22 June   Norway
German auxiliary cruiser *Schiff 33/Pinguin* (Capt Krüder) leaves Sörgulenfjord to take part in mercantile warfare. Operational areas: Antarctic and Indian Ocean.

22 June   North Sea
The new Free French corvette *La Bastiaise* is sunk by mine off Hartlepool during trials.

22–24 June   Mediterranean
Sortie by the Italian 7th Cruiser Div (Div Adm Sansonetti) and the 13th DD Flotilla from Cagliari against French convoy traffic between Algiers and Toulon as far as Port Mahon. Operation broken off without result. Met by the 2nd Sqn with 10 cruisers and 12 destroyers.

24 June   English Channel
The German motor torpedo boat *S36* (Lt Babbel) sinks the British tanker *Albuera* (3477 tons) off Dungeness and *S19* a small freighter of 276 tons.

25 June   General Situation
Cease-fire in France from 0135 hrs.

25 June   Bay of Biscay
The Canadian destroyer *Fraser* is sunk in a collision with the cruiser *Calcutta* on the Gironde.

25 June   Norway
The German patrol vessel *M1107 (Portland)* is sunk by mine or torpedo off Norway.

25–27 June   Mediterranean
First Italian supply convoy from Naples to Tripoli: troop transports *Esperia* (11398 tons) and *Victoria* (13098 tons) with 1727 troops on board, escorted by the auxiliary cruiser *Ramb III* and the torpedo boats *Orsa* and *Procione*.

27 June   General Situation
Britain announces the blockade of Europe from the North Cape to Spain.

27–30 June   Mediterranean/ Intelligence
Operations in the Eastern Mediterranean. The British destroyers *Dainty* (Cdr Thomas), *Defender*, *Ilex*, *Decoy* and *Voyager* hunt Italian submarines S of Crete. On the way the submarine *Liuzzi* is sunk on 27

June as she returns from Cyprus by *Dainty*, *Defender* and *Ilex*. On 29 June, out of a patrol line SW of Crete, *Uebi Scebeli* is sunk by *Dainty* and *Ilex*, which recover important cypher materials, including the new general code book with tables for July 1940, and *Salpa* is damaged. In addition *Argonauta* is sunk, very probably by the same two destroyers, as she returns from Tobruk. Sunderland flying boats from No 230 Sqn RAF damage *Anfitrite* as she goes to join the patrol line on 28 June and *Sirena* returning from Tobruk on 29 June. They sink *Rubino* when she returns from Alexandria on 29 June. Only *Ondina* S of Crete and *Gemma* and *Topazio* off Sollum reach their positions.

British convoys from the Dardanelles and Greek harbours to Port Said, escorted by the cruisers *Caledon* and *Capetown* and the destroyers *Garland*, *Nubian*, *Mohawk* and *Vampire*, pass undetected the Italian submarines *Jalea*, *Zaffiro* and *Ametista* in the approaches to the Aegean.

Two British convoys (MA.3) proceed from Alexandria to Malta, covered by Vice-Adm Tovey with the 7th Cruiser Sqn consisting of *Orion*, *Neptune*, *Sydney*, *Liverpool* and *Gloucester* with a covering force comprising the battleships *Ramillies* and *Royal Sovereign*, the carrier *Eagle* and eight destroyers. The Italian destroyers *Espero*, *Ostro* and *Zeffiro* bring supplies from Taranto to Tobruk. British air reconnaissance leads the British 7th Cruiser Sqn to the scene. *Espero* (Flotilla Commander Cdr* Baroni) attacks the British force to cover the withdrawal of the two other destroyers but sinks after hits from the Australian cruiser *Sydney*. Expenditure of ammunition by the British cruisers raises acute logistic problems since there are only 800 rounds of 6in ammunition still available.

28 June   Mediterranean
Italian AA, during a British air attack near Tobruk, inadvertently shoots down the aircraft of Marshal Balbo, the Italian Governor of Libya.

30 June–1 July   English Channel
German occupation of the Channel Islands Jersey, Guernsey and Alderney. 26656 persons are evacuated from the islands to Britain beforehand.

1–2 July   Baltic
RAF bombers, in an attack on German warships in Kiel, use a 2000lb bomb for the first time. The battlecruiser *Scharnhorst* is missed but the heavy cruiser *Prinz Eugen* is hit by two small bombs.

1–13 July   Mediterranean
The Italian submarines *Emor*, *Marconi*, *Dandolo* and *Barbarigo* operate E of Gibral-

tar. On 2 July *Marconi* misses the destroyer *Vortigern* from Force H; on 6 July *Emo* sights the Force with the *Ark Royal*; and on 11 July *Marconi* (Cdr Chialamberto) sinks the destroyer *Escort* from the returning Force H.

1 July–4 Aug   Norway
In Allied submarine operations off Norway, *Snapper* (Lt King) attacks convoys on 3 and 7 July and sinks one ship of 1134 tons; *Swordfish* (Lt Cowell) or *Thames* sink the torpedo boat *Luchs* (26 July) and *Sealion* (Lt-Cdr Bryant) one ship of 3318 tons. Because of the heavy losses—*Shark* is unable to submerge after being hit by bombs off Skudesnes on 5 July and sinks while the minesweepers *M1803*, *M1806* and *M1807* try to take it in tow, *Salmon* (9 July), *Thames* (2–3 Aug) and *Narwhal* (30 July) are all sunk by mines and *Spearfish* is sunk by *U34* on 2 Aug—the operations are broken off near the coast until the situation is clarified.

1–17 July   South Atlantic
The German auxiliary cruiser *Schiff 10/Thor* (Capt Kähler) sinks five Allied merchant ships of 25911 tons in the South Atlantic and captures the Dutch motor ship *Kertosono* (9289 tons).

2 July   General Situation
Directive by OKW: Hitler has decided that 'in certain conditions' a landing in Britain might be considered.

2 July   English Channel
The damaged German MTB *S23* sinks while under tow after hitting a mine east of the Foreland.

2 July–6 Aug   Central Atlantic
Second unsuccessful Atlantic operation by the Italian submarines *Calvi* (Madeira) and *Veniero* (Canary Islands).

3 July   Mediterranean
Operation 'Catapult': attack by a British naval force (Vice-Adm Somerville) on a part of the French fleet in Mers-el-Kebir (near Oran). French forces: battleships *Dunkerque* (Capt Barrois), *Strasbourg* (Capt Collinet), *Provence* (with Cdr of the 2nd BB Div, Rear-Adm Bouxin), *Bretagne* (Capt Le Pivain) and destroyer flotilla (Rear-Adm Lacrois) consisting of the large destroyers *Mogador*, *Volta*, *Tigre*, *Lynx*, *Kersaint* and *Le Terrible*, as well as the aircraft depot ship *Commandant Teste* (Capt Lemaire). The French Cdr, Adm Gensoul, rejects the British ultimatum, whereupon Force H, comprising the battlecruiser *Hood*, the battleships *Resolution* and *Valiant*, the aircraft carrier *Ark Royal*, the light cruisers *Arethusa* and *Enterprise* and the destroyers *Faulknor*, *Foxhound*, *Fearless*, *Forester*, *Foresight*, *Escort*, *Keppel*, *Active*, *Wrestler*, *Vidette* and *Vortigern*, opens fire on the French ships lying at

anchor, some of which are not ready for action. *Bretagne* sinks, after being heavily hit, with 977 of her crew; *Mogador* loses her stern as a result of a direct hit (42 dead); *Dunkerque* (210 dead) and *Provence* are badly damaged. *Strasbourg* and the five remaining large destroyers are able to sail out and escape at high speed in spite of attacks by British carrier aircraft; she reaches Toulon with *Volta*, *Tigre* and *Le Terrible* on the evening of 4 July. Total losses of the French Navy: 1147 dead. On the same day the following units are seized by British forces in Britain: in Portsmouth the French battleship *Courbet*, the large destroyer *Léopard*, the torpedo boats *Branlebas*, *La Cordelière*, *La Flore*, *L'Incomprise* and *La Melpomène*, six sloops and the supply ship *Pollux*; in Plymouth the battleship *Paris*, the destroyers *Mistral* and *Ouragan*, the torpedo boat *Bouclier*, three sloops, the large submarine *Surcouf* and the submarines *Junon* and *Minerve*; in Falmouth the submarines *Ondine* and *Orion*, three sloops and the target ship *L'Impassible*; and in Dundee the submarine *Rubis*. On *Mistral* and *Surcouf* the crews resist with resulting losses on both sides. In addition, three minelayers, sixteen submarine-chasers, seven motor torpedo boats, 98 minesweepers and guard vessels, 42 tugs and harbour craft and 20 trawlers are seized.

3 July   Arctic
The auxiliary cruiser *Schiff 45/Komet* (Capt Eyssen) leaves Gotenhafen. Her operational area is the Pacific and is to be reached with Russian help by way of the Siberian sea route; she sets out from Bergen on 9 July.

3–4 July   Mediterranean
The Italian minelayers *Buccari* and *Scilla*, escorted by the torpedo boats *Alcione*, *Altair*, *Andromeda* and *Aretusa*, lay another 640 mines between Pantelleria and Sicily. The Italian submarine *Zoea* (Cdr Bernabò) lays a mine barrage W of Alexandria.

3–5 July   Mediterranean
The British submarines *Pandora* and *Proteus* receive orders on 3 July off Algiers and Oran to attack all French warships. *Proteus* does not get within range of the aircraft depot ship *Commandant Teste* but *Pandora* sinks the colonial sloop *Rigault de Genouilly* which is part of a force proceeding from Oran to Algiers. On 5 July the order is rescinded.

3–12 July   Mediterranean
The Italian submarine *Tarantini* (Cdr Iaschi), operating off Palestine, sinks one ship of 3040 tons.

4 July   General Situation
The French Pétain Government breaks off diplomatic relations with Great Britain.

4 July   English Channel
Ju 87s of StG 2 (Maj Dinort) sink from the British convoy OA.178 S of Portland the auxiliary AA ship *Foyle Bank* (5582 tons), the freighters *Britsum* (5255 tons), *Dallas City* (4952 tons), *Deucalion* (1796 tons) and *Kolga* (3526 tons) and severely damage nine other ships of 40236 tons. In an attack by German motor torpedo boats, *S20* (Lt v Mirbach) sinks the freighter *Elmcrest* (4343 tons) and *S20* and *S26* torpedo two ships of 12472 tons.

4–5 July   Central Atlantic
As an answer to the British attack on Oran, the submarines stationed in Dakar, *Le Glorieux* and *Le Héros*, and the auxiliary cruisers and destroyers there (see 18–27 June), receive orders to attack British ships. On 5 July the British steamers *Argyll*, *Gambia* and *Takoradian* and the Danish ships sailing under the British flag *Harald*, *Tacoma* and *Ulrich* are seized. *Le Glorieux* is attacked by a British aircraft.

5 July   Mediterranean/Intelligence
The Italian Navy introduces a new code system for submarines.

5 July   Mediterranean
Swordfish torpedo aircraft of No 813 Sqn from the British aircraft carrier *Eagle* sink the destroyer *Zeffiro* and the freighter *Manzoni* (3955 tons) in the harbour at Tobruk. The destroyer *Euro* and two other freighters have to be beached. *Euro* is later salvaged.

6 July   Mediterranean
Torpedo aircraft of No 810 Sqn from the carrier *Ark Royal* attack the French battleship *Dunkerque* at Mers-el-Kebir and sink the auxiliary ship *Terre Neuve* (859 tons) lying alongside her with a cargo of depth charges. As a result of the cargo exploding, the side of the battleship is ripped open. 150 are dead among the crews.

6 July   Mediterranean
The British cruiser *Capetown* and the destroyers *Ilex*, *Imperial*, *Janus* and *Juno* bombard Bardia.

6–10 July   Mediterranean
Battle off Punta Stilo/Calabria. On the evening of 6 July an Italian convoy leaves Naples for Benghazi, consisting of the passenger ship *Esperia* (11398 tons) and the freighters *Calitea* (4013 tons), *Marco Foscarini* (6342 tons) and *Vettor Pisani* (6339 tons). Escort is provided by the 4th TB Div comprising *Orione*, *Orsa*, *Pegaso* and *Procione*. It is joined on 7 July by the freighter *Francesco Barbero* (6343 tons) from Catania with the torpedo boats *Abba* and *Pilo*. On board there are 2200 troops, 300 armoured vehicles and lorries and 16000

tons of supplies. Close escort is provided by the 2nd Div (Div Adm Casardi) comprising the cruisers *Bande Nere* and *Colleoni* and the 10th DD Div consisting of *Maestrale*, *Libeccio*, *Grecale* and *Scirocco*.
On 7 July a British cruiser force is reported to have arrived in Malta. Thereupon Supermarina orders the 2nd Sqn (Sqn Adm Paladini) to set out to cover the convoy: heavy cruiser *Pola* (F) with the 12th DD Div (*Lanciere*, *Carabiniere*, *Corazziere* and *Ascari*); the 1st Div (Div Adm Matteucci), comprising the heavy cruisers *Zara*, *Fiume* and *Gorizia* with the 14th DD Div (*Alfieri Carducci*, *Gioberti* and *Oriani*); the 3rd Div (Div Adm Cattaneo), comprising the heavy cruisers *Bolzano* and *Trento* with the 11th DD Div (*Artigliere*, *Camicia Nera*, *Aviere* and *Geniere*); and the 7th Div (Div Adm Sansonetti), comprising the light cruisers *Eugenio di Savoia*, *Duca d'Aosta*, *Attendolo* and *Montecuccoli* with the 8th DD Div (*Granatiere*, *Fuciliere*, *Bersagliere* and *Alpino*). The Fleet Commander (Sqn Adm Campioni) sets out with the first squadron to cover the operation; he has the 5th Div (Div Adm Brivonesi), comprising the battleships *Cavour* and *Cesare* with the 7th DD Div (*Freccia*, *Saetta*, *Dardo* and *Strale*), the 8th Div (Div Adm Legnani), comprising the DD's light cruisers *Folgore*, *Fulmine*, *Baleno* and *Lampo*, the 4th Div (Div Adm Marenco di Moriondo), comprising the light cruisers *Da Barbiano*, *Di Giussano*, *Cadorna*, and *Diaz* and the 14th DD Div (*Vivaldi*, *Da Noli* and *Pancaldo*), the 15th DD Div (*Pigafetta* and *Zeno*) and the 16th DD Div (*Da Recco*, *Pessagno* and *Usodimare*).
Italian submarine concentrations: E of Gibraltar *Emo*, *Marconi*, *Dandolo* and *Barbarigo*; NW of Sardinia *Argo*, *Iride*, *Scirè* and *Diaspro*; S of Sardinia *Ascianghi*, *Axum*, *Turchese*, *Glauco*, *Manara* and *Menotti*; Sicilian Channel *Santarosa*; Malta *Capponi* and *Durbo*; Ionian Sea *Brin*, *Sciesa*, *Settimo* and *Settembrini*; and between Derna and Gaudo, *Beilul*, *Tricheco*, *Lafolè* and *Smeraldo*.
Shortly before midnight, *Beilul* sights the British Mediterranean Fleet (Adm Cunningham) which has come out to cover two convoys between Malta and Alexandria. It is composed of the following groups: Force A (Vice-Adm Tovey) with the cruisers *Orion*, *Neptune*, *Sydney* (RAN), *Gloucester* and *Liverpool* and the destroyer *Stuart* (RAN); Force B (Cunningham) with the battleship *Warspite* and the destroyers *Nubian*, *Mohawk*, *Hero*, *Hereward* and *Decoy*; and Force C (Vice-Adm Pridham-Wippell) with the battleships *Malaya* and *Royal Sovereign*, the aircraft carrier *Eagle* (with Nos 813 and 824 Sqns FAA) and the

destroyers *Hyperion, Hostile, Hasty, Ilex, Dainty, Defender, Juno, Janus, Vampire* (RAN) and *Voyager* (RAN) as well as the Malta group (Force D) with at first four, and later seven, destroyers.

On the morning of 8 July Force H (Vice-Adm Somerville) puts to sea from Gibraltar with the battlecruiser *Hood*, the battleships *Valiant* and *Resolution*, the aircraft carrier *Ark Royal*, the cruisers *Arethusa, Delhi* and *Enterprise* and the destroyers *Faulknor, Forester, Foresight, Foxhound, Fearless, Keppel, Douglas, Vortigern, Wishart* and *Watchman*. On the same day the Italian convoy reaches Benghazi without loss. The Italian Fleet assembles in the Ionian Sea to make a sortie against the British Mediterranean Fleet in the hope that the Air Force will weaken British fighting strength beforehand. The warding off of Force H is left to the submarines and the Air Force. But Supermarina orders the concentration of boats near to its own coast to prevent the bases being cut off—which is the British aim.

On 9 July British air reconnaissance establishes contact with the Italian Fleet but the Italian Air Force is unable to provide reconnaissance reports. Torpedo attacks by aircraft from *Eagle* are outmanoeuvred. In the afternoon first the cruisers are seen, then also the heavy units. In a battle lasting 105 minutes the British battleship *Warspite* obtains a heavy hit on the Italian battleship *Giulio Cesare* and the heavy cruiser *Bolzano* is slightly damaged by the British cruisers. Adm Campioni then orders his destroyers (the 9th Flotilla comprising *Alfieri, Oriani, Carducci* and *Gioberti*, the 7th Flotilla comprising *Freccia* and *Saetta*, the 11th Flotilla comprising *Artigliere, Camicia Nera, Aviere* and *Geniere*, the 12th Flotilla comprising *Lanciere, Carabiniere, Corazziere* and *Ascari* and the 14th Flotilla comprising *Pancaldo* and *Vivaldi*) to attack and lay smokescreens. Contact is then lost and the British Fleet turns away. The attacks by the Italian Air Force with 126 aircraft achieve only one hit on the British light cruiser *Gloucester*. In numerous attacks on Force H by Italian SM 79 bombers flying at great altitude, many near-misses are registered near *Hood, Resolution* and *Ark Royal* but they only cause splinter damage. The Italian submarine *Marconi* (Cdr Chialamberto) sinks the destroyer *Escort* in the force E of Gibraltar. On 10 July torpedo aircraft from the *Eagle* attack Italian ships in the roads of Augusta and sink the destroyer *Pancaldo* which, however, can later be salvaged.

7 July   Mediterranean
Agreement between the Commander of the French Force X, Vice-Adm Godfroy, and

the C-in-C of the British Mediterranean Fleet, Adm Cunningham, about the internment and demobilisation of the French Squadron at Alexandria. It consists of the battleship *Lorraine*, the heavy cruisers *Duquesne, Suffren* and *Tourville*, the light cruiser *Duguay Trouin*, the destroyers *Basque, Le Fortuné* and *Forbin* and the submarine *Protée*.

7–21   July Mediterranean
Of the British submarines employed in the Mediterranean, two operate off the Gulf of Taranto, one N and one S of the Straits of Messina and one off Cagliari. On 7 July *Olympus* receives considerable damage in Malta during an Italian air attack. *Phoenix* is sunk by the Italian torpedo boat *Albatros* off Augusta on 16 July and *Rorqual* (Cdr Dewhurst) lays a mine barrage on 21 July off Tolmeita (Cyrenaica), on which a ship of 3865 tons sinks.

7–8 July   Central Atlantic
On the morning of 5 July the British carrier *Hermes* (Capt Onslow) and the Australian cruiser *Australia*, coming from Freetown, have joined the cruiser *Dorsetshire* which is observing the movements of the French naval forces off Dakar. On 7 July an order arrives from the Admiralty to give the French Commander an ultimatum similar to the one given at Mers-el-Kebir in order to eliminate *Richelieu*. The French refuse entry to the sloop *Milford* which approaches with an emissary. Following this, a fast British launch from the *Hermes* under the command of Lt-Cdr Bristowe succeeds during the night 7–8 July in getting through the harbour booms unnoticed, dropping depth charges under the stern of the battleship *Richelieu* and escaping. Then six Swordfish aircraft from the *Hermes* attack and get one torpedo hit. The remaining ships, including the cruiser *Primauguet* and the sloop *Bougainville* and destroyers, are undamaged. An attempt by French aircraft to attack the British ships fails, nor are the submarines deployed, *Le Glorieux*, and *Le Héros*, able to attack the ships.

8–9 July   Baltic
Five British aircraft of Bomber Command attack Kiel and secure a hit (unexploded) on the cruiser *Lützow* in the dockyard.

9–30 July   English Channel
Beginning of German air attacks on British convoys in the Channel. In all, 40 Allied merchant ships, totalling 75698 tons, are sunk by German aircraft in July. In addition the sloop *Foxglove* is heavily damaged on 9 July and thereafter used as a depot ship. The destroyer *Brazen* is sunk off Dover escorting convoy CW.7 on 20 July. On 27 July the destroyer *Codrington* is sunk and

the destroyer *Walpole* and the sloop *Sandhurst* are damaged off Dover, while the destroyer *Wren* is sunk and the destroyer *Montrose* damaged off Aldeburgh on 27 July. The destroyer *Delight* is sunk off Portland on 29 July.

10–23 July   North Atlantic
The Type IIC U-boats *U61, U56, U58, U62* and *U57* operate from Bergen between the North Minch and North Channel. In attacks on independents and convoys, *U61* (Lt-Cdr Oesten) sinks two ships of 11531 tons, *U58* (Lt Schonder) one ship of 1591 tons, *U62* (Lt Michalowski) one ship of 4581 tons and *U57* (Lt Topp) two ships of 10612 tons. *U56* (Lt Harms) attacks the transport *Dunera*, which has German and Italian civilian internees on board but is unnotified. Torpedo defects frustrate this and some 10 other attacks made by the five U-boats. *U58* puts in to Lorient for replenishment.

14–16 July   North Sea
German aircraft lay mines in the Thames Estuary and off Harwich.

14–25 July   Mediterranean
The following Italian submarines are operating: E of Gibraltar *Morosini, Nani, Faa' di Bruno* and *Berillo*; in the Sicilian Channel *Bausan*; E of Malta *Brin* and *Pisani*; S of Crete *Bagnolini, Giuliani* and *Toti*; and in the approaches to the Aegean *Atropo* and *Delfino*.

15–25 July   North Sea
The German minelayers *Roland* (Capt Böhmer), *Königin Luise, Kaiser, Preussen* (Capt Bentlage), *Cobra* and *Hansestadt Danzig*, escorted by torpedo boats, leave Wilhelmshaven on 15 July to lay mine barrage '19' N of the 'Westwall' and W of the Skagerrak. When German air reconnaissance reports a British force of two cruisers and seven destroyers E of Scotland, the minelayers return to Wilhelmshaven on 16 July, departing again on 17 July and laying the barrage during the night to 19 July as planned. On the return voyage there is an unsuccessful attack by British aircraft.

The same minelayer force leaves Wilhelmshaven again on 23 July to lay barrage '18' SE of '19', escorted by five torpedo boats and two minesweepers. On 24 July, after an unsuccessful air attack, the barrage is laid. To avoid reported enemy MTBs, the minelayers make for Kristiansand and sail into the Kattegat.

16 July   General Situation
Führer Directive No 16 on preparations for a landing in Britain ('Seelöwe').

16 July   North Sea
The British destroyer *Imogen* is sunk in thick fog off Duncansby Head after colliding with the cruiser *Glasgow*.

17 July Mediterranean/Intelligence
The Italian Navy introduces new cypher tables for the surface fleet.

17–20 July North Sea
German minelayers, escorted by the 2nd and 5th TB Flotillas, lay the mine barrage 'NW 1' in the English Channel.

18 July North Sea
The British submarine *H31* sinks the German submarine-chaser *UJ126* NW of Terschelling.

18 July Mediterranean
All French merchant ships in the Suez Canal are seized by British warships.

19 July General Situation
President Roosevelt signs the 'Two Ocean Navy Expansion Act', which provides for the building of 1325000 tons of warships, 100000 tons of auxiliary ships and 15000 naval aircraft.

Hitler's Reichstag speech: last 'peace appeal' to Britain (rejected by Lord Halifax on 22 July).

19 July Mediterranean
Battle of Cape Spada: the Italian light cruisers *Giovanni delle Bande Nere* and *Bartolomeo Colleoni* (under orders of Div Adm Casardi) are located by British air reconnaissance and are intercepted while proceeding from Tripoli to Leros by the Australian cruiser *Sydney* (Capt Collins) and the destroyers *Havock*, *Hyperion*, *Hasty*, *Ilex* and *Hero*. *Colleoni* receives unlucky hits in the battle with the result that she becomes incapable of manoeuvre. The cruiser sinks after torpedo hits from *Ilex* and *Havock*. *Bande Nere* (Capt Maugeri) continues the engagement until *Sydney* turns away after a hit and reaches Benghazi. The British destroyers rescue 525 crew members from *Colleoni*, including the commander, Capt Novaro (who dies on July 23).

19–20 July North Sea
RAF bombers unsuccessfully attack the battleship *Tirpitz* and the heavy cruiser *Admiral Scheer* in the naval dockyard at Wilhelmshaven.

20 July Mediterranean
Six torpedo aircraft from No 824 Sqn on board the British carrier *Eagle* (Capt Bridge) sink the Italian destroyers *Nembo* and *Ostro* and the freighter *Sereno* (2333 tons) in the Gulf of Bomba near Tobruk.

21–30 July Mediterranean
British convoy operation in the Aegean. On 21 July the cruisers *Capetown* and *Liverpool* and the destroyers *Diamond*, *Stuart*, *Dainty* and *Defender* set out with six merchant ships from Alexandria and Port Said comprising convoy AN.2 for Aegean harbours. On 23 July the cruiser *Orion* and the destroyers

Vampire and *Vendetta* appear off Castellorizo as a diversion. The action is repeated on 26 July before the return of convoy AS.2 when the ocean boarding vessels *Chakla* and *Fiona* are used to simulate a landing. The Mediterranean Fleet, comprising the battleships *Malaya*, *Royal Sovereign* and *Warspite*, the carrier *Eagle* and the cruisers *Neptune* and *Sydney* and ten destroyers, cruises SW of Crete to cover the operations. During the return of the convoy there are several Italian air attacks on 27, 28 and 29 July which, apart from an unexploded hit on *Liverpool*, only obtain near-misses. On 28 July *Neptune* and *Sydney* make a sortie into the Gulf of Athens and sink a small tanker, *Ermioni*, carrying petrol for the Dodecanese.

23 July North Sea
A Do 17 (Lt Karl Müller) of 1/KFlGr 606 bombs and sinks the British submarine *Narwhal* in the northern North Sea.

23–25 July English Channel
The mine barrage 'NW.2' in the Channel is laid out by German minelayers, escorted by torpedo boats.

23–27 July Bay of Biscay
A proposed carrier raid on Bordeaux by Force H, consisting of the carrier *Ark Royal*, the cruiser *Enterprise* and the destroyers *Faulknor*, *Foresight*, *Escapade* and *Forester*, has to be abandoned because of mist. The Force arrives back in Gibraltar on 26 July, followed by the old carrier *Argus* and the destroyers *Encounter*, *Hotspur*, *Gallant* and *Greyhound*.

25 July English Channel
The German MTB *S27* (Lt Klug) sinks the unnotified French repatriation steamer *Meknes* (6127 tons) off the British South Coast. Of the 1100 French troops on board, nearly 400 lose their lives.

25–26 July English Channel
Ju 87s of I/StG 1 (Capt Hozzel) and IV/LG 1 (Capt v Brauchitsch) attack the British convoy CW.8 in the Channel and of the 21 ships in the convoy sink five of 5117 tons. The destroyers *Boreas* and *Brilliant* and five more freighters are damaged. On 26 July the 1st MTB Flotilla (Lt-Cdr Birnbacher), consisting of *S19*, *S20* and *S27*, attacks the same convoy and sinks three ships of 2480 tons.

25–28 July Norway
The battlecruiser *Gneisenau*, having received makeshift repairs after a torpedo hit from a submarine, is transferred from Trondheim to Kiel. She is escorted by the Commander Reconnaissance Forces, Rear-Adm Schmundt, on board the cruiser *Nürnberg*, and the destroyers *Hans Lody*, *Friedrich Ihn*, *Paul Jacobi* and *Karl Galster*

and by the torpedo boats *Luchs*, *Iltis*, *Kondor*, *Jaguar* and *T5* from Utsire onwards. On 26 July the torpedo boat *Luchs* is sunk by the British submarine *Swordfish*.

25 July–9 Aug Arctic
The heavy cruiser *Admiral Hipper* (Capt Heye) conducts mercantile warfare operations in the Arctic between Tromsö and Spitzbergen but she encounters only neutral merchant ships. A small Finnish steamer with contraband is seized as a prize.

26–31 July Red Sea
The Italian submarine *Guglielmotti* searches in vain for two Greek steamers which have sailed S from Suez. The torpedo boats *Battisti* and *Nullo* also return without result.

26 July–5 Aug Mediterranean
The Italian submarines *Alagi*, *Aradam* and *Mocenigo* operate E of Gibraltar without success, *Durbo* operates E of Malta and *Narvalo*, *Speri* and *Mameli* (Cdr Maiorana), which sinks one ship of 1044 tons, between Alexandria and Crete. In addition, *Anfitrite*, *Zaffiro*, *Squalo*, *Ametista* and *Corridoni* operate in the Aegean and its approaches.

26 July–10 Aug North Atlantic
U34, *U52*, *U58* and *U99* operate from Lorient off the North Channel and individually attack outbound and homebound convoys there. On 26–27 July *U34* (Lt-Cdr Rollmann) sinks four ships of 29320 tons from convoy OB.188; *U99* (Lt-Cdr Kretschmer) sinks from 28 to 31 July four ships of 32345 tons and torpedoes on 2 Aug three tankers of 25548 tons from the convoy OB.191; *U52* (Lt-Cdr Salman) sinks on 4 Aug three ships of 17102 tons from the convoy HX.60; *U58* (Lt Schonder) sinks on 4 Aug one ship of 4360 tons; and *U56* (Lt Harms) on 4 Aug sinks one ship each from the convoys SL.40 and OB.193. On her way home on 1 Aug *U34* meets the British submarine *Spearfish* returning from an operation and sinks her near Cape Nose Head.

End of July–20 Aug Bay of Biscay
British submarines begin to patrol the Biscay ports ('Bay Patrol') from the end of July. The first to be employed are *Tribune*, *Tigris* and *Talisman*. The first success is scored by *Cachalot* (Cdr Luce) on 20 Aug when she sinks *U51*.

28 July South Atlantic
In the South Atlantic an engagement takes place between the German auxiliary cruiser *Schiff 10/Thor* (Capt Kähler) and the British auxiliary cruiser *Alcantara* (22209 tons, Capt Ingham). The British ship is badly damaged and has to put in to Rio de Janiero; *Schiff 10*, after repairs to minor damage, is able to continue her mercantile warfare.

28 July–10 Aug   North Atlantic
The Type IIC boats *U59*, *U57* and *U56* operate from Bergen off the North Channel. *U59* goes to Bergen for replenishment, the others to Lorient. The operations again suffer from torpedo failures. *U59* (Lt-Cdr Matz) sinks one ship of 1981 tons, *U57* (Lt Topp) one ship of 2161 tons and *U56* (Lt Harms) the auxiliary cruiser *Transylvania* (16923 tons) on 10 Aug.

28 July–10 Sept   Central Atlantic
Third Atlantic operation by the Italian submarines *Malaspina*, *Barbarigo* and *Dandolo* in the area of the Azores and off Madeira. Subsequently they are moved to the new base at Bordeaux. *Malaspina* (Cdr Leoni) sinks one ship of 8406 tons, *Dandolo* (Cdr Boris) sinks one ship of 5187 tons and damages one ship of 3768 tons and *Barbarigo* (Cdr Ghilieri) secures some shell hits on a ship of 3255 tons.

30 July   General Situation
Extension of British Navicert system to all European ports.

31 July–4 Aug   Mediterranean
Operation 'Hurry': Force H sets out from Gibraltar with the battlecruiser *Hood*, the battleship *Valiant*, the carrier *Ark Royal*, the cruisers *Arethusa*, *Delhi* and *Enterprise* and the destroyers *Faulknor*, *Forester*, *Foresight*, *Foxhound*, *Fearless*, *Escapade*, *Active* and *Wrestler*. On 2 Aug the carrier flies off her 12 Swordfish aircraft to attack Cagliari (Sardinia), where mines are also laid. Simultaneously, the old carrier *Argus* (Capt Bovell), which is proceeding independently of Force H and is escorted by the destroyers *Encounter*, *Gallant*, *Greyhound* and *Hotspur*, flies off SW of Sardinia 12 Hurricane fighters she has on board for transfer to Malta. On the news that Force H has set out, Supermarina concentrates two submarine lines consisting of *Scirè*, *Argo*, *Neghelli*, *Turchese*, *Medusa*, *Axum*, *Diaspro* and *Manara* N of Cape Bougaroni on 1 Aug. But they sight nothing up to 9 Aug. In an attempted attack on an Italian force the British submarine *Oswald* is rammed and sunk by the Italian destroyer *Vivaldi* off Cape Spartivento on 1 Aug.

1 Aug   General Situation
In Directive No 17, Hitler orders the intensification of the sea and air war against Britain.

3–6 Aug   General Situation
Estonia, Latvia and Lithuania become member states of the USSR.

4–10 Aug   North Sea
The German A/S trawler *UJ175/Perseus* is sunk by mine off Ameland.

4–10 Aug   North Atlantic
Force H is transferred from Gibraltar to Britain. On 9 Aug the Force is met W of Ireland by the destroyers *Punjabi*, *Tartar* and *Zulu*, which escort *Hood* and *Ark Royal* to Scapa Flow while *Valiant* and *Argus* and the 8th DD Flotilla proceed to Liverpool.

4–19 Aug   Red Sea/Gulf of Aden
Italian occupation of British Somaliland. On 5 Aug Italian troops occupy Zeila and Hargeisa and on 6 Aug Oodweina. On 11 Aug the attack on the main British position near Tug Argan begins. Between 14 and 19 Aug Berbera is evacuated by British troops: 5690 troops, 1266 civilians and 184 sick are evacuated to Aden with the assistance of the Australian cruiser *Hobart*, the British cruisers *Caledon*, *Carlisle* and *Ceres*, the destroyers *Kandahar* and *Kimberley*, the sloops *Shoreham*, *Parramatta* (RAN) and *Auckland*, the auxiliary cruisers *Chakdina*, *Chantala* and *Laomédon* and the transports *Akbar* and *Vita* (hospital ship). The cruisers and destroyers bombard various positions along the coast by shellfire.

4 Aug–9 Sept   Central Atlantic
The German auxiliary cruiser *Schiff 21* sinks six Allied merchant ships of 30769 tons in the Western part of the Central Atlantic, including the Finnish sailing ship *Killoran* (1817 tons) which is in British service.

5 Aug   General Situation
First preparatory studies drawn up for a campaign against the Soviet Union.

5–16 Aug   Mediterranean
Italian submarines deployed in operations in the Mediterranean: *Ascianghi*, *Gondar* and *Marcello* E of Gibraltar, *Settembrini*, *Dessiè*, *Naiade* and *Balilla* NW to S of Crete, *Jalea* NE of Crete, *Gemma*, *Tricheco* and *Delfino* in the Aegean and *Tembien* off Sollum (1–6 Aug). *Micca* (Cdr* Ginocchio) lays a mine barrage W of Alexandria on 12 Aug and attacks a destroyer two days later. *Sciesa* has to break off a voyage into the Eastern Mediterranean because of engine trouble.

5 Aug–17 Oct   Arctic
The Soviet submarine *Shch-423* (Capt 3rd Class Zaidulin) is the first submarine to be transferred by the northern seaway from Murmansk to Vladivostok, accompanied by ice-breakers and a tanker (the submarine is renamed *Shch-139* in Apr 1942).

6–10 Aug   Mediterranean
Offensive mining operations by the Italians in the Sicilian Channel. On 6 Aug the cruisers *Da Barbiano* (Div Adm Marenco di Moriondo) and *Di Giussano* and the destroyers *Pigafetta* and *Zeno* lay 394 mines (Barrage 7.AN) SSE of Pantelleria; escort comprises the torpedo boats *Cassiopea*, *Cigno*, *Pleiadi* and *Aldebaran*. (The British

destroyer *Gallant* is damaged on this barrage on 10 Jan 1941 and has to be towed to Malta by the destroyer *Mohawk*.) During the nights 8–9 Aug and 9–10 Aug respectively, the minelayer *Scilla* lays 216 and 200 mines W of Pantelleria and the destroyers *Maestrale*, *Grecale*, *Libeccio* and *Scirocco* each night lay 216 mines W of it (Barrages 5.AN and 6.AN); the torpedo boats *Antares* and *Sagittario* provide escort for *Scilla*. The British destroyer *Hostile* is lost on 23 Aug on the mine barrage 5.AN.

7 Aug   Baltic
The German patrol vessel *V1501/Wiking VII* is sunk by mine off Friedrichshaven (but is later raised and repaired).

7–8 Aug   English Channel
The minelayers *Roland* (Cdr* Kutzleben), *Cobra* (Cdr Brill) and *Brummer* (Cdr Koppe), under the orders of Officer Commanding Patrol Boats West (Capt Schiller), lay the offensive mine barrage 'SW.1' in the south-western North Sea; escort is provided by the 5th TB Flotilla (Cdr Henne) comprising *T2*, *T7*, *Falke*, *Kondor* and *Jaguar*.

7 Aug–4 Sept   North Atlantic
The following U-boats operate off the North Channel in varying combinations: *U30* from Lorient and *U37*, *U38*, *U46*, *U48*, *U51*, *U59*, *U60*, *U65* and *U100* from home ports and from Bergen. On the way out, *U25* is lost (on 3 Aug) on a mine barrage laid by British destroyers in the North Sea and *U37* and *U65* have to return prematurely to Lorient because of damage. *U51* is sunk in the Bay of Biscay by the British submarine *Cachalot* (Cdr Luce). The U-boats attack chiefly independents or convoys (OB.197, OB.198 and OA.198) on their own. The attempt to operate with *U38*, *U46* and *U48* from 13 to 16 Aug against convoy HX.62 located by the B-Service does not succeed. *U30* (Lt-Cdr Lemp) sinks two ships of 12407 tons, *U37* (Lt-Cdr Oehrn) one ship of 9130 tons, *U38* (Lt-Cdr Liebe) two ships of 12493 tons, *U60* (Lt Schnee) one ship of 1787 tons and *U59* (Lt-Cdr Matz) one ship of 2339 tons; *U46* (Lt Endrass) sinks six ships of 34499 tons, including the auxiliary cruiser *Dunvegan Castle* (28 Aug), and damages one ship of 6189 tons; *U48* (Cdr Rösing) sinks five ships of 29169 tons and *U51* (Lt-Cdr Knorr) one ship of 5709 tons; and *U100* (Lt-Cdr Schepke) sinks six ships of 25812 tons and damages one of 5498 tons.

8 Aug   English Channel
Attack by the 1st MTB Flotilla (Lt-Cdr Birnbacher), consisting of *S20*, *S21*, *S25* and *S27*, on the British convoy CW.9 off Newhaven. *S21* and *S27* sink two small freighters of 1583 tons and two others are

damaged. One freighter of 1004 tons sinks after a collision in avoiding a torpedo.

8–12 Aug   North Sea

Aircraft of the 9th Fl Div sow mines in the Thames and Humber estuaries and in the harbour entrances of Penzance, Plymouth, Liverpool, Southampton, Falmouth and Belfast.

10 Aug   Pacific

The Japanese Navy extends the blockade of the Chinese coast to South China.

10–20 Aug   Pacific

The German auxiliary cruiser *Schiff 36/ Orion* (Cdr* Weyher) sinks three Allied merchant ships of 16593 tons E of Australia.

13 Aug   Air War/Britain

Beginning of the intensified air war against Britain with the aim of securing air supremacy as a condition of 'Seelöwe'.

13–19 Aug   Red Sea

The British destroyer *Kimberley* and the sloop *Auckland* bombard Italian troops advancing W of Berbera. During Italian air raids on Berbera, the Australian cruiser *Hobart* is slightly damaged by splinters. The Italian submarine *Ferraris* (Cdr Piomarta) tries unsuccessfully to attack the British battleship *Royal Sovereign* which is passing through the Red Sea.

14–15 Aug   English Channel

The minelayers *Tannenberg* (Cdr* v Schönermark), *Cobra* and *Roland*, under the orders of the Chief of Staff of the Commander North Sea Defences, Capt Böhmer, lay the offensive barrage SW.2 in the southwestern part of the North Sea. Escort is provided by the 5th TB Flotilla (Cdr Henne) comprising *Greif*, *Falke*, *Kondor*, *Iltis*, *Jaguar*, *T2* and *T3*. The destroyers *Paul Jacobi* and *Karl Galster* lay mines.
Off Texel the British destroyers *Malcolm* and *Verify* attack a German force and sink two vessels.

15 Aug   Mediterranean

The Greek cruiser *Helli* sinks off Tinos after receiving a torpedo hit from the Italian submarine *Delfino* (Lt Aicardi). Italy rejects responsibility for the incident on 16 Aug.

15–21 Aug   Mediterranean

In the Mediterranean, the British submarines *Pandora* and *Proteus* are used to transport supplies to Malta. On 16 Aug *Rorqual* (Lt-Cdr Dewhurst) lays another mine barrage off Tolmeita (Cyrenaica), on which one ship of 3298 tons, on 5 Dec the torpedo boat *Calipso* and on 23 Dec the torpedo boat *Fratelli Cairoli* sink. An attack on a convoy on 21 Aug fails; *Rorqual* is heavily attacked by the torpedo boat *Papa* with depth charges. Off Durazzo (Albania) *Osiris* (Lt-Cdr Harvey) sinks one ship of 1968 tons on 16 Aug.

16–18 Aug   Mediterranean

The British battleships *Warspite* (Adm Cunningham), *Malaya* and *Ramillies*, the heavy cruiser *Kent* and twelve destroyers of the 2nd, 10th and 14th DD Flotillas shell Bardia and Fort Capuzzo in Cyrenaica on the morning of 17 Aug. On the return to Alexandria an Italian air attack on the Fleet fails to register a hit. Shore-based fighters from the carrier *Eagle* shoot down 12 aircraft.

17 Aug   General Situation

The OKW announces the 'total blockade' of Britain in an operational area around the British Isles. In this area, which is almost identical with the American war zone, forbidden to American ships and citizens, all ships are to be sunk without warning.

17–18 Aug   Red Sea

The British cruisers *Hobart* (RAN), *Carlisle* and *Ceres*, the destroyer *Kimberley* and the sloop *Auckland* (RAN) evacuate 5370 Commonwealth soldiers, 1040 civilians and 175 wounded soldiers from Berbera (British Somali).

17 Aug–7 Sept   Mediterranean

The following Italian submarines operate in the Mediterranean: *Bianchi* off Gibraltar, *Des Geneys* SW of Crete, *Millelire* and *Velella* in the Kaso Strait and *Jantina* in the Aegean. *Dagabur* and *Da Procida* undertake patrols to the Palestine coasts and to Cyprus; *Atropo* and *Foca* act as transports between Taranto and Leros.

18 Aug–2 Sept   Norway

The Dutch submarines *O22* and *O23* operate off Norway. Of the British submarines *Swordfish*, *Snapper*, *Seawolf*, *Sunfish*, *Triumph*, *Taku*, *Tetrarch* and *Sturgeon* (Lt Gregory) operating off Norway up to Sept, *Sturgeon* sinks one ship of 3624 tons in a convoy on 2 Sept.

18 Aug–3 Sept   North Atlantic

U28, *U32*, *U101* and *U124* coming from Germany, and *U37*, *U56*, *U57*, *U59* and *U60* setting out from Lorient, operate against independents and convoys in the area between the Hebrides, the North Channel, Ireland and Rockall Bank. *U57* attacks OB.202 on 24 Aug (sinking two ships and damaging one). *U37*, sent as a weather reporting boat far to the W, attacks SC.1 on 24–25 Aug (sinking the sloop *Penzance* and one ship). *U48* attacks HX.65 on 25 Aug early in the day and *U124* attacks in the evening (the former sinking two ships and the latter sinking two and damaging one with two more sunk on 26 Aug by K Fl Gr 506—see 26 Aug); *U28* again attacks SC.1 on 27 Aug (sinking one ship); *U100* attacks on 29 Aug first HX.66 and then OA.204 (two ships sunk and one torpedoed in the

first and two ships in the second); *U32* attacks HX.66 on 30 Aug (sinking three ships); and *U59*, *U60*, *U59* again and *U38* successively attack OB.205 on 30–31 Aug (sinking one ship and damaging three). Including ships in convoy and independents, *U101* (Lt-Cdr Frauenheim) sinks three ships of 12311 tons, *U28* (Lt-Cdr Kuhnke) sinks four ships of 9945 tons and damages one ship of 4768 tons (inclusive of SC.2), *U32* (Lt Jenisch) sinks three ships of 13093 tons, *U124* (Lt-Cdr Schulz) sinks two ship of 3900 tons, *U57* (Lt Topp) sinks three ships of 24088 tons and torpedoes one ship of 5407 tons, *U37* (Lt-Cdr Oehrn) sinks six ships of 23384 tons and the sloop *Penzance*, *U60* (Lt Schnee) sinks one ship of 1401 tons and torpedoes one ship of 15434 tons and *U59* (Lt-Cdr Matz) sinks two ships of 7451 tons and torpedoes one ship of 8009 tons. On 1 Sept *U32* attacks the convoy which left the Clyde on 31 Aug with the transports for the Dakar operation (Operation 'Menace'—see 23–25 Sept) and which is escorted by a naval force consisting of the cruisers *Devonshire* (Vice-Adm J H D Cunningham) and *Fiji*, the battleship *Barham* and the destroyers *Inglefield*, *Echo*, *Eclipse* and *Escapade*. *Fiji* receives a torpedo hit and has to be replaced by the Australian cruiser *Australia*. An attack by *U56* (Lt Harms) on this ship on 8 Sept is unsuccessful because of a torpedo failure. *Barham* arrives in Gibraltar with the other ships on 3 Sept.

20 Aug   Intelligence

The British Admiralty changes from 'Naval Cypher No 1' and 'Naval Code' to 'Naval Cypher No 2' and 'Naval Code No 2' by distributing new codebooks and long subtractor tables; the circuits are subdivided into smaller ones and the running time of the tables is changed from one a month to two or three. But up to Jan 1941 the German B-Service has solved about 19 per cent of the No 2 ('Köln') codebook and 26 per cent of the 'Code No 2' ('München') codebook, and an increasing proportion of the tables.

20 Aug   General Situation

First operational plan, 'Felix', worked out to capture Gibraltar.
Italy declares the Mediterranean and the African coast an operational area.

20–29 Aug   North Atlantic

A British force comprising the battleship *Valiant*, the new carrier *Illustrious* and the AA cruisers *Calcutta* and *Coventry* is transferred from British ports to Gibraltar. It is accompanied by the cruiser *Sheffield* and the 8th DD Flotilla (*Faulknor*, *Foresight*, *Forester*, *Fury*, *Firedrake*, *Fortune* and *Greyhound*) destined for Force H. The new flagship of Force H, the battlecruiser

Renown, and the carrier *Ark Royal* have already arrived in Gibraltar.

21–31 Aug   Red Sea

The Italian submarines *Guglielmotti* (21–25 Aug) and *Ferraris* (25–31 Aug), the torpedo boats *Nullo* and *Sauro* (24–25 Aug) and *Battisti* and *Manin* (30–31 Aug) and the destroyers *Pantera* and *Tigre* (28–29 Aug) search in vain for Greek ships reported by agents and air reconnaissance in the Red Sea.

22–24 Aug   Mediterranean

Three Swordfish aircraft of No 824 Sqn from the carrier *Eagle* sink the Italian submarine *Iride* and the depot ship *Monte Gargano* (1976 tons) in the Gulf of Bomba near Tobruk while *Iride* is being prepared for the first operation by small battle units (*Maiali* human torpedoes) against Alexandria. Early on 23 Aug the destroyers *Stuart*, *Diamond*, *Juno* and *Ilex* set out from Alexandria to make a raid in the Gulf of Bomba in the night 23–24 Aug while the gunboat *Ladybird*, supported by the destroyer *Waterhen*, penetrates into the harbour of Bardia. On 23 Aug the destroyer *Hostile* is mined off Cape Bon and sunk by *Hero*.

22–25 Aug   North Sea/English Channel

The 9th F1 Div drops mines off Dundee, Newcastle, Middlesbrough, Hartlepool, Dover, Portland and Poole and in Scapa, the Thames Estuary, the Downs and the sea around the Isle of Wight.

23 Aug   North Sea

He 115 torpedo aircraft of KF1Gr 506 from Stavanger attack the British convoy OA. 203 in the Moray Firth and sink the freighters *Llanishen* (5053 tons) and *Makalla* (6677 tons). The motor ship *Beacon Grange* (10119 tons) is badly damaged.

23 Aug   English Channel

The German patrol vessel *V607/Düsseldorf* is beached after hitting a mine near Dieppe.

23–28 Aug   Norway

The British cruiser *Norfolk* and the Australian cruiser *Australia* make an unsuccessful sortie from Scapa Flow to the area of Bear Island to intercept German fishery vessels. An attack by the ships' aircraft on Tromsö has to be abandoned because of the weather.

25 Aug–3 Sept   Central Atlantic

The Vichy French submarine *Sidi-Ferruch*, which has been in the harbour at Duala (Cameroons) since 10 Aug, sets out on 25 Aug. On 27 Aug Capt de Hautecloque, later General Leclerc, takes over power on behalf of the Free French movement; on 28 Aug General de Larminat follows in Brazzaville (Congo). The submarine *Sidi-Ferruch* (Lt-Cdr de Kehror) which is sent to Libreville

on 30 Aug, is able, at first, to stabilise the situation there, in favour of the Vichy Government. On 3 Sept Cdr* Morin sets out to support her from Dakar with the sloop *Bougainville*, the submarine *Poncelet* and the transport *Cap des Palmes*, with 100 Senegalese riflemen and 800 tons of supplies on board; he arrives in Libreville on 10 Sept. On 3 Sept the sloop *D'Entrecasteaux* and the submarine *Ajax* are sent from Casablanca, on 4 Sept the tanker *Tarn* with the cruiser *Primauguet* and the sloop *Gazelle* and on the following days the sloops *D'Iberville*, *Surprise* and *Commandant Rivière*. Before the British cruiser *Delhi* arrives on 6 Sept off Pointe Noire (Congo), three French steamers set out from there. *Jean Laborde* reaches Dakar on 8 Sept; *Touareg* is captured by the British cruiser *Dragon* on 16 Sept and *Cap Padaran* has to put in to Conakry on 23 Sept. *Poitiers* is sunk by the cruiser *Cumberland*.

26 Aug   North Sea

Four He 115s of KF1Gr 506 from Stavanger attack the British convoy HX.65A off Kinnaird Head and sink the freighter *Remuera* (11445 tons) with a torpedo hit. Eight Ju 88s of the same Gruppe also damage the freighter *Cape York* (5027 tons) so badly with bomb hits that she has to be abandoned on 27 Aug.

26–29 Aug   North Sea

German aircraft drop mines in the estuaries of the Thames and Humber, in the Downs and off Harwich.

26 Aug–16 Sept   Indian Ocean

The German auxiliary cruiser *Schiff 33/Pinguin* (Capt Krüder) sinks and captures five Allied merchant ships of 27508 tons in the Indian Ocean.

27 Aug   General Situation

On the basic issue dividing OKH and OKM in connection with 'Seelöwe', Hitler decides in favour of the 'smaller solution' i.e. a landing on a front of approximately 140km on the British South-East Coast (Folkestone to Eastbourne).

27 Aug   North Atlantic

RAF Coastal Command establishes an advance air base on Iceland. The first squadrons stationed there are equipped with old Fairey Battle aircraft.

27 Aug–6 Oct   North Atlantic

A second wave of Italian submarines is moved in two groups from the Mediterranean to Bordeaux. The first group, consisting of *Baracca*, *Emo*, *Faa' di Bruno*, *Giuliani*, *Tarantini*, and *Torelli*, operates in the area between Portugal, the Azores and Madeira and the second, consisting of *Bagnolini* and *Marconi*, off NW Spain. *Emo* (Cdr Liannazza) sinks one ship of 5199 tons;

Baracca (Cdr Bertarelli) one ship of 3687 tons, *Marconi* (Cdr Chialamberto) one trawler of 330 tons and *Bagnolini* (Cdr Tosoni-Pittoni) one ship of 3302 tons. *Faa' di Bruno* makes three unsuccessful attacks.

29 Aug   Pacific

The Japanese Submarine *I-67* is accidentally lost during exercises.

29 Aug–6 Sept   Mediterranean

Operation 'Hats'/MB: a British force, Force F, consisting of the battleship *Valiant*, the carrier *Illustrious* and the AA cruisers *Calcutta* and *Coventry*, proceeds through the Mediterranean to Alexandria. In the Western Mediterranean, Force H (Vice-Adm Somerville), comprising the battle-cruiser *Renown*, the carrier *Ark Royal*, the cruiser *Sheffield* and 12 destroyers, provides cover for the force. On 31 Aug nine Swordfish aircraft from *Ark Royal* attack Port Elmas in Sardinia before Force H turns away. Force F is met S of Sicily by the Mediterranean Fleet (Adm Cunningham) consisting of the battleships *Malaya* and *Warspite*, the carrier *Eagle*, the 3rd Cruiser Sqn (*Gloucester*, *Kent* and *Liverpool*) the 7th Cruiser Sqn (*Orion* and *Sydney*) and 13 destroyers of the 2nd, 10th and 14th DD Flotillas. They simultaneously cover a supply convoy for Malta comprising the transports *Cornwall*, *Plumleaf* and *Volo* and the destroyers *Jervis*, *Juno*, *Dianty* and *Diamond*. On 31 Aug the Polish destroyer *Garland* and the steamer *Cornwall* are damaged in attacks by the Italian Air Force. The Italian Fleet, consisting of five battleships, including the new 35000-ton ships *Littorio* and *Vittorio Veneto*, 13 cruisers and 39 destroyers, which sets out from Taranto and Messina, cannot find the British forces owing to inadequate air reconnaissance and turns back prematurely. Neither the Italian submarines *Corallo* and *Sirena*, stationed S of Crete, nor *Berillo*, *Capponi* and *Durbo*, operating off Malta, sight the British ships; the convoy, plus *Valiant*, *Calcutta* and *Coventry*, arrives in Malta on 2 Sept. Attacks by Italian Ju 87 dive-bombers on *Eagle* and the destroyers *Imperial* and *Janus* are unsuccessful. On the return, Cunningham divides his squadron into Force E (*Malaya*, *Eagle*, *Coventry* and six destroyers) and Force I (*Warspite*, *Valiant*, *Illustrious*, *Calcutta* and seven destroyers). The first proceeds S of Crete and the second N of Crete to the Dodecanese. The cruisers *Gloucester*, *Kent* and *Liverpool* with the destroyers *Mohawk* and *Nubian* are detached to the Gulf of Nauplia to meet a convoy there of five steamers. The cruisers *Orion* and *Sydney* and the destroyers *Decoy* and *Ilex* shell Scarpanto during the night 3–4 Sept. When the

Italian *MAS 536* and *MAS 537* try to attack, the latter is sunk by *Ilex* in the Kaso Strait. Swordfish aircraft from *Eagle* and *Illustrious* attack the Italian airfields of Kalatho and Maritza on Rhodes; four aircraft are shot down by Italian CR.42 fighters. An attack by the British submarine *Parthian* on an Italian cruiser force is not successful.

30 Aug   General Situation
Vichy France is forced to allow Japan to undertake the military occupation of harbours, airfields and railways in Northern Indo-China.

OKM reports that the Navy's preparation for 'Seelöwe' cannot be completed by 15 Sept; the earliest possible date is 20 Sept.

30 Aug–9 Sept   North Atlantic
First successful group operation with U-boats against convoy SC.2 (53 ships). On 30 Aug the B-Service decodes the route instructions and the escort meeting point for 6 Sept. On 2 Sept *U124*, *U65*, *U47* and *U101* are accordingly deployed, but *U124* has to proceed far to the W to provide weather reports for 'Seelöwe'. Shortly after SC.2 is met by the escort group—sloops *Lowestoft* (Cdr Knapp) and *Scarborough*, destroyers *Skeena* (RCN) and *Westcott*, corvette *Periwinkle* and A/S trawlers *Apollo* and *Berkshire*)—*U65* (Lt-Cdr v Stockhausen) sights the convoy but is driven off by the *Skeena* and *Periwinkle*. Towards midnight on 6–7 Sept, *U65* again approaches and leads *U47* (Lt-Cdr Prien) to the scene; the latter sinks three ships in succession. Flying-boats drive the U-boats off on 7 Sept and only in the late evening of 8 Sept do *U65* and *U47* again approach. The latter sinks a fourth steamer. Towards morning on 9 Sept *U28* (Lt-Cdr Kuhnke) and *U99* (Lt-Cdr Kretschmer) approach and attack simultaneously. *U28* sinks a fifth ship. When light, *U99* is driven away from the North Channel. The surface night attacks by the U-boats cannot be prevented by the escorts which rely only on visual sightings and asdic detection. Total result: five ships of 20943 tons sunk.

31 Aug   English Channel
Result so far of Battle of Britain: 4779 German aircraft employed and 4447 tons of HE and 191 tons of incendiary bombs dropped; German losses are 252 fighters and 215 bombers, British losses are 359 aircraft.

31 Aug–1 Sept   North Sea
At sea NW of Texel, the 20th British DD Flotilla, trying to intercept a German convoy, runs into a German minefield and loses the destroyers *Esk* and *Ivanhoe*; *Express* is severely damaged. — — —

31 Aug–2 Sept   English Channel
The Officer Commanding Minelayers (Capt Bentlage), with the minelayers *Tannenberg*, *Roland* and *Cobra*, lays the offensive mine barrage SW.3 in the south-western North Sea; escort is provided by the 5th DD Flotilla (Cdr* F Berger) with the destroyers *Erich Steinbrinck*, *Karl Galster* and *Paul Jacobi*, the 2nd TB Flotilla (Cdr Riede) with *T8*, *T5*, *T6* and *T7* and the 5th TB Flotilla (Cdr Henne) with *Falke*, *Iltis*, *Jaguar* and *Greif*.

31 Aug–13 Sept   North and Central Atlantic
Preparations for the British and Free French operation 'Menace'. On 31 Aug a convoy consisting of two troop transports, four freighters and one tanker (with 4200 British and 2700 Free French troops on board), three French sloops and one trawler sets out from the Clyde. Cover and escort are provided by Vice-Adm JHD Cunningham with the battleship *Barham* the cruisers *Devonshire* (F) and *Fiji* and the destroyers *Inglefield*, *Eclipse*, *Echo* and *Escapade*. On 1 Sept the force is attacked W of the Hebrides by *U32* (Lt Jenisch). *Fiji* is hit by a torpedo and has to return. On 6 Sept the Australian cruiser *Australia* sets out as a replacement; an attack on her by *U56* (Lt Harms) on 8 Sept fails because of torpedo defects. In the meantime, Force H has set out on 6 Sept from Gibraltar with the battleship *Resolution*, the carrier *Ark Royal* and the destroyers *Faulknor*, *Foresight*, *Forester*, *Fortune*, *Fury* and *Greyhound* in order to meet, on 13 Sept, the convoy and the cruisers *Cornwall* and *Cumberland* and the sloops *Bridgewater* and *Milford* summoned from the South Atlantic and then to proceed together to Freetown (see 9–22 Sept for continuation).

1 Sept   Bay of Biscay
Formation of the Italian submarine command BETASOM (Rear-Adm Parona) in Bordeaux. For operational purposes it is placed under the orders of the German Commander U-boats (Vice-Adm Dönitz).

1–24 Sept   Bay of Biscay
The British Bay Patrol submarines in the Bay of Biscay are from time to time reinforced by submarines on the way to the Mediterranean. Off Brest *Tigris* (Lt-Cdr Bone) sinks a French trawler of 168 tons on 1 Sept and *Truant* (Lt-Cdr Haggard) encounters in the Bay of Biscay on 2 Sept the prize ship *Tropic Sea* (5781 tons) captured by the German auxiliary cruiser *Orion*: the ship is sunk by the prize crew. On 22 Sept *Tuna* (Lt-Cdr Cavanagh-Mainwaring) sinks the prize *Tirranna* (7230 tons) captured by the auxiliary cruiser *Atlantis*

and, two days later, the catapult ship *Ostmark* (1281 tons).

2 Sept   General Situation
Destroyer/Naval Base Deal between Britain and the USA signed: the USA makes over 50 old destroyers to Britain in return for the use of bases in the Bahamas, Jamaica, Santa Lucia, Trinidad, Bermuda and British Guiana and in Argentia in Newfoundland.

2 Sept   North Sea
The German 9th Fl Div drops mines in the Thames Estuary, in Scapa, in the Moray Firth and off Aberdeen, Middlesbrough and Newcastle.

2 Sept   North Sea
The German A/S Whaler *UJ121/Jochen* is sunk by mine off the Dutch coast.

3 Sept   General Situation
Hitler accepts 21 Sept as the possible date for the beginning of the landing in Britain ('Seelöwe').

4 Sept   English Channel
In an attack by the 1st MTB Flotilla (Lt-Cdr Birnbacher) on a British convoy NE of Great Yarmouth, *S21* (Lt Klug) sinks the freighters *Corbrook* (1729 tons) and *New Lambton* (2709 tons), *S18* (Lt Christiansen) the freighters *Joseph Swan* (1571 tons) and *Nieuwland* (1075 tons) and *S22* (Lt Grund) the freighter *Fulham V* (1562 tons). *S54* torpedoes another steamer of 1350 tons.

5 Sept   North Sea
The German patrol vessel *V403/Deutschland* is sunk by mine off the Wester Schelde.

5 Sept   English Channel
The German patrol vessel *V201/Gebr Kähler* is sunk by mine on Dunkirk roads.

5–6 Sept   Mediterranean
The Italian torpedo boats *Altair*, *Alcione*, *Ariel* and *Aretusa*, under Cdr* Del Cima, lay the offensive mine barrages M.1 and M.2, consisting of 112 mines, NE and SE of Malta.

5–6 Sept   English Channel
German minelayers, escorted by the 2nd TB Flotilla (Cdr Riede) comprising *T5*, *T6*, *T7* and *T8*, carry out the mining operation 'Walter' in the Straits of Dover.

5–7 Sept   Red Sea
During the night 5–6 Sept the Italian torpedo boats *Battisti*, *Manin* and *Sauro*, and during the night 6–7 Sept the destroyers *Leone* and *Tigre* and the torpedo boats *Battisti* and *Sauro*, are deployed against a convoy from Aden to Suez located by air reconnaissance. They do not find the target. The submarines *Ferraris* and *Guglielmotti*, stationed to the N, do not sight the convoy but *Guglielmotti* (Cdr Tucci) sinks the Greek tanker *Atlas* (4008 tons) sailing as an independent.

6 Sept General Situation
First invasion warning in Britain. America hands over the first eight of its old destroyers to the Royal Navy.

6 Sept North Atlantic
The British corvette *Godetia* is sunk in collision with the SS *Marsa* off the Irish coast.

6–7 Sept English Channel
Offensive mining operation SW.0. The minelayers *Togo* (Capt Böhmer) and *Kaiser*, with 405 EMB mines, and the 5th TB Flotilla (Cdr Henne) with *Greif*, *Falke*, *Iltis* and *Jaguar* carrying 1000 detonator-buoys and escorted by the destroyer *Karl Galster* and the 1st TB flotilla (Cdr v Rennenkampff) with the torpedo boats *Kondor T1*, *T2* and *T3*, lay the barrage and return to den Helder.

6–8 Sept Norway
Unsuccessful sortie by the British aircraft carrier *Furious* against shipping targets off the Central Norwegian coasts.

6–9 Sept Mediterranean
The Italian Fleet sets out with five battleships, six cruisers and 19 destroyers to intercept Force H from Gibraltar S of Sardinia. The Force returns when it is learned that Force H has passed Gibraltar on a westerly course.

7 Sept North Sea
In an attack by the German MTBs *S33* and *S36* on the British convoy FS.273, *S33* (Lt Popp) sinks the Dutch freighter *Stad Almaer* (5750 tons) E of Lowestoft.

7 Sept Mediterranean
The Vichy Government orders a first 'trial convoy', consisting of the tug *Pescagel*, accompanied by the sloop *Elan*, to proceed from Casablanca to Oran through the Straits of Gibraltar. Up to Nov 1942 540 Vichy French convoys comprising 1750 ships pass through the Straits of Gibraltar in both directions.

7–8 Sept English Channel
British aircraft attack German assault craft in the Channel ports.

8–9 Sept English Channel
Offensive mining operation 'Hannelore' in the Straits of Dover by the 2nd TB Flotilla (Cdr Riede) comprising *T5*, *T6*, *T7* and *T8*.

8–11 Sept English Channel
Transfer of the minelaying forces for Operation 'Seelöwe' to western ports. On 8 Sept the minelayers *Schiff 23* (Capt Bentlage), *Königin Luise*, *Schwerin*, *Preussen*, *Hansestadt Danzig* and *Grille* depart from German North Sea ports, escorted by four torpedo boats; on 9 Sept they are joined off Rotterdam by the minelayers *Tannenberg*, *Cobra*, *Kaiser*, *Roland* and *Togo* and two torpedo boats. *Hansestadt Danzig* and *Kaiser* enter Antwerp. When *Grille*, *Königin Luise*, *Preussen* and *Roland* enter Ostend they are attacked by aircraft but suffer only splinter damage. The western group with *Schiff 23*, *Tannenberg*, *Cobra*, *Togo* and *Schwerin* continues its way on 10 Sept from Calais, the task of escort now taken over by the destroyers *Hans Lody* (Capt Bey), *Karl Galster*, *Theodor Riedel*, *Friedrich Eckoldt* and *Friedrich Ihn*, which had departed on 9 Sept from Wilhelmshaven. They arrive on 11 Sept at Cherbourg.

8–23 Sept North Sea
In the North Sea, the Allied submarine *Rubis* (French) operates on the Dogger Bank, the Dutch *O22* off SW Norway and *O23* off the Skagerrak.

9 Sept General Situation
The US Navy gives building orders for 210 warships, including seven battleships and 12 aircraft carriers.

9 Sept Baltic
The German mine countermeasures vessel *Sperrbecher 11*/*Zeus* is heavily damaged by a mine off Korsor but is towed into Kiel and later repaired.

9–22 Sept North Atlantic
After the SC.2 operation, *U47* acts as the weather boat. *U28*, *U65* and *U99* remain W of the Hebrides and off the North Channel where also the newly dispatched *U48*, *U61*, *U59*, *U58*, *U100* and *U138* are stationed. They operate individually against independents and convoys. *U28* (Lt-Cdr Kuhnke) successfully attacks OA.210 on 11 Sept, *U48* SC.3 (escort sloop *Dundee*) on 15 Sept and *U138* OB.216 (escorted by the sloop *Scarborough*, the destroyer *Vanquisher* and the corvette *Arabis*) on 20–21 Sept. On 20 Sept the weather boat *U47* (Lt-Cdr Prien) sights the convoy HX.72 (41 ships) shortly after the ocean escort auxiliary cruiser *Jervis Bay* has turned away. With only one torpedo left, *U47* maintains contact for *U29*, *U65*, *U48*, *U46* and *U43*, which have been ordered to the scene in spite of the convoy's efforts to escape. Before the convoy is met by the escort group, *U99* (Lt-Cdr Kretschmer) comes up in the evening and torpedoes three ships in succession, one of which sinks and two of which are finished off on 21 Sept by torpedoes and gunfire with the help of *U47*. In the morning of 21 Sept *U48* (Lt-Cdr Bleichrodt) sinks one ship. From the escort group which arrives soon after—the sloop *Lowestoft* (Cdr Knapp) and the corvettes *La Malouine*, *Calendula* and *Heartsease*—the only destroyer *Shikari* is sent to help the torpedoed ships. In the evening of 21 Sept *U100* (Lt-Cdr Schepke) reaches the convoy and, in the course of several approaches lasting four hours, sinks seven ships without being detected by the four escorts present. In the morning the destroyers *Scimitar* and *Skate* meet the ships of the scattered convoy and, together with *Lowestoft*, drive off *U32* (Lt Jenisch), which attacks a steamer of the convoy with gunfire. Total result in operating against HX.72: 12 ships of 77863 tons. In all, *U46* (Lt Endrass) sinks three ships, *U47* (Lt-Cdr Prien) sinks five ships of 27544 tons and one of 5156 tons with *U99*, *U99* (Lt-Cdr Kretschmer) sinks six ships of 20063 tons, *U48* (Lt-Cdr Bleichrodt) sinks seven ships of 35138 tons and the sloop *Dundee* from SC.3 and damages, in addition, one ship of 5136 tons, *U65* (Lt-Cdr v Stockhausen) sinks two ships of 10192 tons, *U138* (Lt Lüth) sinks four ships of 34644 tons and *U100* (Lt-Cdr Schepke) sinks seven ships of 50340 tons.

9–22 Sept Central Atlantic
Expedition by a French naval force (Rear-Adm Bourragué), consisting of the light cruisers *Georges Leygues*, *Gloire* and *Montcalm* and the large destroyers *L'Audacieux*, *Le Fantasque* and *Le Malin*, to re-establish the authority of the Vichy Government in the colony of Gabon which has gone over to De Gaulle. The squadron leaves Toulon on 9 Sept; it is first reported early on 11 Sept 50 nautical miles E of Gibraltar by the British destroyer *Hotspur* and it passes through the Straits of Gibraltar in the morning at high speed. On the way to Dakar it puts in to Casablanca to refuel on 12–13 Sept. The remaining British units of Force H in Gibraltar (see 31 Aug–13 Sept) receive orders too late to stop the French ships. On 14 Sept Vice-Adm Cunningham, approaching Freetown with the British forces for Operation 'Menace', receives orders to prevent the French ships getting to Dakar. A reconnaissance patrol undertaken 75 nautical miles NW of Dakar during the night 14–15 Sept by the 1st Cruiser Sqn, comprising *Devonshire*, *Cumberland* and *Australia*, as well as the *Ark Royal*, is unable to find the ships, whose entry into Dakar is reported by reconnaissance aircraft on 15 Sept. However, on 16 Sept *Cumberland* intercepts and sinks the French merchantman *Poitiers* (4185 tons) sailing for the Ivory Coast with ammunition. On 18 Sept the three French cruisers leave Dakar, after the older light cruiser *Primauguet* has been sent in advance to Libreville with the tanker *Tarn* to provide fuel supplies. But the latter are intercepted by the British cruisers *Cornwall* and *Delhi* and escorted to Casablanca. The cruiser force is at once shadowed by the heavy cruisers *Australia* and *Cumberland* patrolling in the area S of

Dakar. When *Gloire* has to remain behind because of engine trouble, the British escort this ship, too, to Casablanca. The operation against Gabon is then abandoned and the two remaining French cruisers return to Dakar.

10–20 Sept   Mediterranean
The Italian Expeditionary Corps for a campaign against Greece is brought from Brindisi to Albania without loss: 40310 troops, 7728 horses, 701 vehicles and 33535 tons of supplies.

12–14 Sept   English Channel
The minelayers *Stralsund* (Capt Brinkmeier), *Skagerrak* and *Brummer* transfer from German ports to the west, escorted by four torpedo boats. *Brummer* goes to Antwerp, the two others to Le Havre after defending themselves against an air attack off Zeebrugge.

13 Sept   North Sea
The Royal Navy transfers the battlecruiser *Hood*, the battleships *Nelson* and *Rodney*, two cruisers and eight destroyers from Scapa Flow to Rosyth in order to be able to intervene in any German attempt to invade in the Channel.

13 Sept   Baltic
The German auxiliary minesweeper *M1306/ Hermann Krone* is lost on a mine off Hanstholm.

14 Sept   North Sea
The 9th Fl Div drops mines in the estuary of the Thames. The mining is continued on 15, 17, 18, 23 and 30 Sept.

14–15 Sept   English Channel
The RAF attacks shipping targets in French and Belgian harbours between Boulogne and Antwerp, causing appreciable damage to the transport fleet assembled for 'Seelöwe'.

15–16 Sept   English Channel
Offensive mining operation 'Bernhard' by the 2nd TB Flotilla, comprising *T5*, *T6*, *T7* and *T8*, in the Straits of Dover.

15–19 Sept   Mediterranean
British attack on Benghazi. On 15 Sept the battleship *Valiant*, the carrier *Illustrious* (Rear-Adm Lyster), the cruiser *Kent* and seven destroyers set out from Alexandria. On 16 Sept they join the 3rd Cruiser Sqn, comprising the AA cruisers *Calcutta* and *Coventry*, W of Crete and proceed to the take-off position for the aircraft of the *Illustrious* which mine the harbour of Benghazi and attack ships with torpedoes during the night 16–17 Sept. The destroyer *Aquilone* is lost on a mine, and the destroyer *Borea* (later salvaged) and the freighters *Gloria Stella* (5490 tons) and *Maria Eugenia* (4702 tons) are lost as a result of torpedoes from No 815 Sqn FAA. On the return the cruiser *Kent* and two destroyers are detached to shell

Bardia. The cruiser receives a heavy torpedo hit in the stern in an attack by Italian torpedo aircraft and is, with great difficulty, towed on 15 Sept by the destroyers to Alexandria. An attack by the Italian submarine *Corallo* (Cdr Albanese) on the *Illustrious* and *Valiant* fails. Of the submarines *Ondina*, *Uarsciek* and *Settimo* stationed off Tobruk, the last misses two destroyers. On 17 Sept the destroyers *Janus* and *Juno* bombard Sidi Barrani and *Juno* and the gunboat *Ladybird* in addition bombard Sollum.

16 Sept   General Situation
No progress is made in the exploratory talks about Spain's participation in the war and in the conquest of Gibraltar when the Spanish Foreign Minister Serrano Suñer visits Berlin.

16–25 Sept   South Pacific
The Free French Governor of the New Hebrides, Sautot, is brought by the Australian cruiser *Adelaide* (16–19 Sept) from Vila to Nouméa (New Caledonia) to take over the area for De Gaulle. The plan is at first frustrated by the Vichy French sloop *Dumont d'Urville* (Cdr de Quièvrecourt), in whose support the sloop *Amiral Charner* sets out from Saigon on 20 Sept. But on 25 Sept *Dumont d'Urville* has to withdraw and returns to Saigon with *Amiral Charner*. Nouméa goes over to De Gaulle.

17 Sept   General Situation
Hitler postpones Operation 'Seelöwe' although the preparations for a landing in Britain are to be continued.

17 Sept   Indian Ocean
The auxiliary cruiser *Schiff 16* (Capt Rogge) sinks the French passenger ship *Commissaire Ramel* (10061 tons) sailing in British service.

17–18 Sept   Air War/Britain
In an air attack on Glasgow, the British heavy cruiser *Sussex* is severely damaged.

17–18 Sept   English Channel
In a British air attack against Cherbourg, the Freighter *Johann Blumenthal* is sunk and the minelayer *Schiff 23* and torpedo boat *T11* are damaged by bomb hits.

Off Le Havre, the torpedo boat *T3* capsizes after a bomb hit but is later salvaged and recommissioned.

17–25 Sept   Mediterranean
The Italian submarines *Beilul*, *Delfino*, *Narvalo* and *Squalo* operate in the area N and NW of Crete.

18 Sept   North Africa
The Italian North African offensive (10th Army), which began on 13 Sept, comes to a halt as a result of supply difficulties after crossing the Egyptian/Libyan frontier and capturing Sidi Barrani (16 Sept).

19–20 Sept   English Channel
The Führer der Zerstörer, Capt Bey, departs from Cherbourg with the destroyers *Hans Lody*, *Friedrich Eckoldt*, *Karl Galster*, *Theodor Riedel* and *Friedrich Ihn* for a strike against the area between the Lizard and Start Point but, owing to the weather, the operation has to be cancelled.

19–21 Sept   English Channel/Bay of Biscay
The minelayers of the western group, *Schiff 23*, *Tannenberg*, *Schwerin*, *Togo* and *Cobra*, transfer from Cherbourg to St-Nazaire, escorted by the 5th TB Flotilla.

19–21 Sept   Red Sea
The Italian destroyers *Leone* and *Pantera* and the torpedo boats *Battisti* and *Manin*, together with the submarines *Archimede* and *Guglielmotti*, search in vain for a convoy of 23 ships reported by air reconnaissance. The steamer *Bhima* (5280 tons) is damaged by near-miss bombs and has to be beached. The escort for the British convoy includes the Australian sloops *Parramatta* and *Yarra*.

21 Sept   English Channel
So far 51 barges, nine steamers and one tug have been destroyed by British air attacks on channel ports. In all, 155 transports (approximately 700000 tons), 1277 barges and lighters, 471 tugs and 1161 motor boats have been assembled for 'Seelöwe' between Le Havre and Antwerp.

22 Sept   General Situation
Following an agreement with the Vichy government, Japanese troops occupy bases in Northern Indo-China.

22 Sept   English Channel
The German mine counter measures vessel *Sperrbrecher 2* (*Athen*) is heavily damaged by a mine in the harbour entrance at Boulogne and beached; the wreck is later repaired and recommissioned as a merchant ship.

22–23 Sept   English Channel
The destroyers *Erich Steinbrinck* and *Paul Jacobi* are transferred from Wilhelmshaven to Brest.

22–25 Sept   Mediterranean
The British destroyers *Jervis* (D14), *Janus*, *Juno* and *Mohawk* bombard an airfield and troop concentrations at Sidi Barrani, which is bombarded again by the gunboat *Ladybird* on 23 Sept. On 25 Sept the bombardment is continued by the destroyers *Hereward*, *Hyperion*, *Juno* and *Mohawk*.

22–28 Sept   Mediterranean
In British submarine operations in the Mediterranean, *Osiris* (Lt-Cdr Harvey) attacks an Italian convoy off Durazzo (Albania) and sinks the escorting torpedo boat *Palestro*. The submarines *Regent*,

Triton and *Truant*, newly transferred to the Mediterranean, report successes: *Truant* (Lt-Cdr Haggard) sinks one ship of 8459 tons off Ischia and *Triton* (Lt-Cdr Watkins) sinks one ship of 1434 tons off Genoa and shells installations in Vado and Savona. Off Benghazi, *Pandora* (Lt-Cdr Linton) sinks one ship of 813 tons and is heavily attacked by depth charges from the escorting torpedo boat *Cosenz*.

22 Sept–16 Oct   North Atlantic

The U-boats *U29*, *U43*, *U31*, *U32*, *U46*, *U37*, *U38*, *U137*, *U103* and *U123* arrive successively in the North Atlantic between the North Channel and Rockall Bank. The boats operate in varying concentrations against independents and convoys. An attempt to catch a convoy on 9 Oct with a reconnaissance line consisting of *U123*, *U103*, *U37*, *U38* and *U48* W of Rockall fails. There are only individual attacks in which the boats score the following successes (*U38* and *U123* include their successes against HX.79 and SC.7): *U29* (Lt-Cdr Schuhart) sinks one ship of 6223 tons and *U31* (Lt-Cdr Prellberg) two ships of 4400 tons; *U32* (Lt Jenisch) sinks eight ships of 42645 tons and damages one of 7886 tons; *U37* (Lt-Cdr Oehrn) sinks five ships of 23237 tons; *U38* (Lt-Cdr Liebe) sinks four ships of 30345 tons and damages one of 3670 tons; *U43* (Lt-Cdr Ambrosius) sinks one ship of 5802 tons and *U46* (Lt Endrass) two of 43920 tons; *U103* (Cdr Schütze) sinks five ships of 20279 tons and one of 3697 tons with *U123*, three of them from SC.6 (sloop *Enchantress*); *U123* (Lt-Cdr Moehle) sinks four ships of 14589 tons and one of 3697 tons with *U103*, one of 5458 tons with *U101* and *U100*, one of 3106 tons with *U99*; and *U137* (Lt Wohlfarth) sinks three ships of 12103 tons and damages one of 4917 tons. The missions undertaken by *U60* (Lt Schnee) off the Pentland Firth and by *U61* (Lt-Cdr Stiebler) off the North Minch have no success.

23 Sept   Bay of Biscay

The German auxiliary minesweeper *M1604/ Österreich* is sunk by two mines off Penmarch.

23–25 Sept   Central Atlantic

Operation 'Menace': British naval forces attack Dakar to prepare a landing by Free French troops. The British force under Vice-Adm J H D Cunningham consists of the battleships *Barham* and *Resolution*, the carrier *Ark Royal*, the heavy cruisers *Devonshire*, *Cumberland* and *Australia* (RAN), the light cruiser *Delhi* and the destroyers *Faulknor*, *Foresight*, *Forester*, *Fortune*, *Fury* and *Greyhound* (from Force H) and *Inglefield*, *Eclipse*, *Echo* and *Escapade* as well as the

sloops *Bridgewater* and *Milford*; in addition, there are the Free French sloops *Savorgnan de Brazza*, *Commandant Duboc* and *Commandant Dominé*. 3670 Free French troops are embarked on the troop transports *Pennland* (16381 tons) and *Westernland* (16479 tons) and four freighters; 4270 British troops on four more troop transports and one freighter are only to be landed in an emergency. One tanker and one Free French armed tug accompany the force. In Dakar the following pro-Vichy units are stationed: the unfinished battleship *Richelieu*, the cruisers *Georges Leygues* and *Montcalm*, the large destroyers *Le Fantasque*, *L'Audacieux* and *Le Malin*, the destroyer *Le Hardi*, the sloops *D'Entrecasteaux*, *D'Iberville*, *Calais*, *Commandant Rivière*, *Le Surprise* and *Gazelle*, five auxiliary cruisers and the submarines *Bévéziers*, *Persée* and *Ajax*. Attempts by De Gaulle, through an emissary and wireless messages, to persuade the French naval forces (Rear-Adm Landriau) to transfer their allegiance are rejected by Governor Boisson, whereupon the French coastal batteries open fire on the assault fleet. In the process, the cruiser *Cumberland* and the destroyers *Foresight* and *Inglefield* are hit.

The French submarine *Persée* (C C Lapierre) is lost in a surface attack on the cruiser *Dragon* by the destroyers *Inglefield* and *Foresight* and the large destroyer *L'Audacieux* receives heavy hits from the cruiser *Australia* and is beached on fire (80 dead). An attempt at landing by De Gaulle's troops in Rufisque Bay is beaten off.

On 24 Sept, in trying to attack, the French submarine *Ajax* (C C Guimont) is sunk by the destroyer *Fortune*. After that *Barham*, *Resolution*, *Devonshire* and *Australia* shell coastal batteries and French ships lying in harbour. The French defence obtains four hits on *Resolution*; attacks by carrier aircraft from *Ark Royal* achieve no results and they lose six of their number.

On 25 Sept there is renewed shelling of the harbour by the British battleships. *Richelieu* gets a 38cm (15in) hit on *Barham* and the submarine *Bévéziers* (Lt-Cdr Lancelot) torpedoes the *Resolution*, whereupon Churchill orders the operation to be abandoned. The French armed forces suffer 100 dead and 182 wounded, the civilian population 84 dead and 197 injured.

23 Sept–6 Oct   Norway

Of the Dutch submarines *O21* and *O24* operating off Norway, *O21* just misses the German *U61* near Bergen.

23 Sept–5 Nov   Central and North Atlantic

A third wave of Italian submarines is trans-

ferred to the Atlantic. The first group, consisting of *Da Vinci*, *Otaria*, *Glauco*, *Veniero*, *Nani* and *Cappellini*, operates in the area of the Azores and Madeira, the second, consisting of *Argo*, *Calvi* and *Tazzoli*, off the Spanish/Portuguese coast. *Nani* (Cdr Polizzi) sinks the A/S trawler *Kingston Sapphire* in the Straits of Gibraltar and one other ship together totalling 1939 tons, *Cappellini* (Cdr Todaro) sinks one ship of 5186 tons and *Tazzoli* (Cdr Raccanelli) sinks one ship of 5135 tons.

24–25 Sept   Mediterranean

As a reprisal for the British attack on Dakar, 60 Vichy French aircraft from Morocco bomb Gibraltar on 24 Sept and drop 45 tons of bombs; on 25 Sept 81 aircraft make a second attack with 60 tons of bombs. The trawler *Stella Sirius* is sunk and two aircraft are lost. The French destroyers *Epée*, *Fleuret*, *Fougueux* and *Frondeur* from Casablanca sortie off Gibraltar during the night 24–25 Sept when *Epée* opens fire on the British destroyer keeping watch before she continues the journey to Oran.

24–27 Sept   North Sea

In operations off Terschelling, the British submarine *H49* (Lt Coltart) attacks two German convoys and sinks one ship of 2186 tons.

24–30 Sept   North Atlantic

The heavy cruiser *Admiral Hipper* (Capt Meisel) leaves Kiel to carry out mercantile warfare in the Atlantic. On 27 Sept serious engine trouble develops W of Stavanger which compels the ship to return. The cruiser reaches Kiel on 30 Sept.

25 Sept   Mediterranean

During a French air raid against Gibraltar, the patrol vessel *Stella Sirius* is sunk.

26 Sept   Pacific

The Canadian auxiliary cruiser *Prince Robert* captures the German motor ship *Weser* (9179 tons) off Manzanillo (Peru).

27 Sept   General Situation

Conclusion of the Three-Power Pact between Germany, Italy and Japan in Berlin. Purpose: to prevent the USA intervening by threatening a two-front war in the Atlantic and the Pacific. The relations of the three powers with the USSR are to remain unaffected.

27 Sept   Mediterranean

First Vichy French convoy to pass through the Straits of Gibraltar from Casablanca since Operation 'Menace'. It consists of three merchant ships accompanied by the sloop *La Gracieuse*.

28–29 Sept   English Channel

Offensive mining operation in Falmouth Bay by the Officer Commanding Destroyers (Capt Bey) with the destroyers *Hans Lody*,

Karl Galster, Paul Jacobi, Erich Steinbrinck and *Friedrich Ihn.* Covering group: *Frieddrich Eckoldt* and *Theodor Riedel*. Results: five ships of 2026 tons sunk.

The minelayers *Stralsund* and *Skagerrak*, escorted by the torpedo boat *Wolf*, transfer from Le Havre to Brest.

28 Sept–3 Oct   Mediterranean

The British cruisers *Gloucester* and *Liverpool* leave Alexandria for Malta with 1200 troop reinforcements. Escort is provided by the Mediterranean Fleet (Adm Cunningham) with the battleships *Valiant* and *Warspite*, the carrier *Illustrious*, the cruisers *Orion*, *Sydney* and *York* and 11 destroyers of the 2nd and 14th DD Flotillas (Operation MB.5). Italian air reconnaissance locates the Force, whereupon the Italian Fleet sets out with the battleships *Littorio* and *Vittorio Veneto* (9th Div), *Cavour*, *Cesare* and *Duilio* (5th Div), the heavy cruisers *Pola*, *Zara*, *Gorizia* and *Fiume* (1st Div) and *Bolzano*, *Trento* and *Trieste* (3rd Div), the light cruisers *Duca degli Abruzzi* and *Garibaldi* (8th Div) and *Eugenio di Savoia* and *Duca d'Aosta* (7th Div) and 23 destroyers from Taranto and Messina. In the afternoon of 29 Sept many Italian air attacks (28 Savoia SM 79s) have no success.

When reconnaissance aircraft from *Illustrious* report the Italian Fleet, only nine Swordfish aircraft are available, but they cannot be employed because of Italian air superiority. In consequence, the Italian Fleet returns on 30 Sept unmolested. *Gloucester* and *Liverpool* are detached on 30 Sept, disembark their troops in Malta and rejoin the British Fleet on 1 Oct which then sets out for base. On 2 Oct *Orion* and *Sydney* shell Stampalia when they make a sortie into the Aegean. The Italian submarine operations become known to the British by the decyphering of radio orders from Rome to Rhodes, coded in the Italian 'Enigma' variant 'Alfa'. *Ambra* and *Serpente* are stationed S of Crete and *Mameli*, *Tembien*, *Colonna* and *Berillo*, which are standing off the coast of Cyrenaica, do not approach the British forces; the last is sunk on 2 Oct by the British destroyers *Hasty* and *Havock*. The submarine *Gondar*, which has set out to make a *Maiali* human torpedo attack on Alexandria, is sunk on 30 Sept W of its target by the Australian destroyer *Stuart* and a Sunderland flying boat of No 230 Sqn RAF.

29 Sept   Mediterranean

The Italian submarine *Scirè* (Cdr Borghese), on her way to make a human torpedo attack on Gibraltar, is ordered back because Force H has set out for the Atlantic (Dakar operation).

29 Sept   Central Atlantic

The German auxiliary cruiser *Schiff 10* sinks the Norwegian whale-oil factory ship *Kosmos* (17801 tons) in the Central Atlantic.

29 Sept–4 Oct   Central Atlantic

Force H, with the battlecruiser *Renown* and destroyers, is deployed against the French battleship *Richelieu* which, it is feared, is to be transferred from Dakar to a harbour in the Bay of Biscay. On 1 Oct the ships operate in the area of the Azores against a possible German assault on the Canaries. On 4 Oct Force H returns to Gibraltar.

30 Sept   English Channel

The British monitor *Erebus* and the destroyers *Garth* and *Vesper* bombard Calais.

30 Sept–1 Oct   English Channel

Offensive mining operation 'Werner' by the 5th TB Flotilla (Cdr Henne) comprising *Greif*, *Kondor*, *Falke* and *Seeadler* off Dover.

1 Oct   Mediterranean/ Intelligence

The Italian Navy introduces a top-secret code with a new codebook and new tables.

1 Oct   General Situation

Conclusion of a German-Finnish agreement on German arms deliveries to Finland. In return, Finland gives Germany the entire right to buy up all ore concessions (nickel mines near Petsamo).

1–8 Oct   Mediterranean

The Italian submarines *Ametista*, *Gemma* and *Tricheco* operate in the SE approaches to the Aegean. On 6 Oct *Tricheco* sinks *Gemma* in error. *Zaffiro* operates in the Aegean.

1–30 Oct   North Sea/English Channel

In many sorties off British ports and river estuaries, the 9th Fl Div drops 715 air mines, 317 of them in the Thames Estuary, 81 in the Humber Estuary, 46 in the Tees Estuary, 40 off Liverpool and 39 in the Firth of Forth. The remaining mines are dropped off Hartlepool, Cardiff, Sunderland, Plymouth and Swansea.

On 16 Oct the British minesweeper *Dundalk* is sunk off Harwich; on 19 Oct the destroyer *Venetia* is lost off the Thames Estuary.

2 Oct   Mediterranean

The British cruisers *Orion* and Sydney (RAN) bombard the Maltezana area near Stampalia.

2–9 Oct   Central Atlantic

To protect the French Cameroons, 1564 troops of a British brigade are sent on 2 Oct from Freetown to Duala on board the transport *Westernland*, escorted by the cruiser *Devonshire*, the destroyers *Escapade*, *Faulknor*, *Foresight* and *Fury* and the Free

French sloops *Savorgnan de Brazza*, *Commandant Dominé* and *Commandant Duboc*. The troops are landed there from 7 to 9 Oct.

4–9 Oct   Mediterranean

In the Gulf of Genoa, the British submarine *Triton* (Lt-Cdr Watkins) sinks one ship of 1860 tons and off Durazzo *Regent* (Lt-Cdr Browne) sinks two ships of 6088 tons.

5–16 Oct   North Atlantic

In operations against independents and convoys in and just off the North Channel, the Type II U-boats have the following successes: *U58* (Lt Schonder) sinks one straggler from HX.76 of 4956 tons, *U59* (Lt-Cdr Matz) sinks two ships of 12706 tons and *U137* (Lt Wohlfarth) torpedoes the auxiliary cruiser *Cheshire* (10552 tons); *U138* (Lt Lüth) sinks one ship of 5327 tons and torpedoes two ships of 11555 tons, some from HX.77.

7–10 Oct   Mediterranean

The Italian 14th DD Flotilla (Capt Galati), comprising *Vivaldi*, *Da Noli* and *Tarigo* (*Malocello* is out of action because of engine trouble), lays during the night 7–8 Oct the mine barrage 4.AN with 176 mines E of Cape Bon and in the night 9–10 Oct the mine barrage M.3 with 174 mines S of Malta. The British destroyer *Hyperion* sinks on the first mine barrage on 22 Dec and the British destroyer *Imperial* ~~sinks~~ on the second on 11 Oct. DAMAGED

7–19 Oct   Norway

The Dutch submarines *O22* and *O23* and the French *Rubis* operate off Norway. The British submarines *Snapper*, *Seawolf*, *Sunfish*, *Triumph*, *Tetrarch* and *Cachalot* continue to be employed off Norway.

8 Oct   Bay of Biscay

In the Bay of Biscay the British submarine *Trident* misses the German *U31* with a torpedo and has a gun duel with the German boat.

8–9 Oct   English Channel

The 5th TB Flotilla (Cdr Henne), comprising *Greif*, *Seeadler*, *Kondor*, *Falke*, *Wolf* and *Jaguar*, makes a sortie off the Isle of Wight.

8–14 Oct   Mediterranean

Operation 'MB.6', a British supply convoy of four steamers, escorted by the AA cruisers *Calcutta* and *Coventry* and four destroyers, from Alexandria to Malta with cover from the Mediterranean Fleet (Adm Cunningham) comprising the battleships *Warspite*, *Valiant*, *Malaya* and *Ramillies*, the carriers *Eagle* and *Illustrious*, the cruisers *York*, *Gloucester* and *Liverpool* (3rd Cruiser Sqn), *Ajax*, *Orion* and *Sydney* (7th Cruiser Sqn) and 16 destroyers. The convoy reaches Malta undetected in stormy weather on 11

Oct but the destroyer *Imperial* is damaged on a mine. When an Italian civilian aircraft reports sighting the returning force, Supermarina tries to lay an ambush in the Ionian Sea. The 1st TB Flotilla (Cdr Banfi), comprising *Airone*, *Alcione* and *Ariel*, makes a surprise but unsuccessful attack on the cruiser *Ajax* (Capt McCarthy) during the night 11–12 Oct. *Airone* and *Ariel* sink in the defensive fire; *Alcione* rescues the crew of the sinking *Airone* and escapes. The 11th DD Flotilla (Capt Margottini), comprising *Artigliere*, *Aviere*, *Camicia Nera* and *Geniere*, which arrives at the scene of the fighting, is likewise caught in the defensive fire of *Ajax* as it approaches. *Artigliere* receives heavy, and *Aviere* light, hits. *Camicia Nera* takes *Artigliere* in tow; she is located on the morning of 13 Oct by a Sunderland flying boat which leads three Swordfish from the *Illustrious* to her but they do not hit her. When the British cruiser *York* (Capt Portal) approaches, *Camicia Nera* cuts loose and *Artigliere* is sunk after the crew have disembarked. The 3rd Cruiser Div, consisting of *Trieste*, *Trento* and *Bolzano*, and three destroyers of the 14th Flotilla, set out to help from Messina but arrive too late. 225 survivors are recovered by the hospital ship *Aquileja*. On the return, Swordfish bombers from the British carriers *Eagle* and *Illustrious* attack Leros (13–14 Oct) and on the evening of 14 Oct the cruiser *Liverpool* is hit in the bows by a torpedo from an Italian aircraft.

9 Oct   North Atlantic
The Italian submarine *Malaspina* (Cdr Leoni) is the first to proceed to the North Atlantic from Bordeaux. In the course of Oct, *Dandolo*, *Otaria*, *Barbarigo*, *Finzi*, *Baracca*, *Bagnolini*, *Marconi* and *Faa' di Bruno* follow. At the end of Oct and the beginning of Nov there are more Italian submarines than German U-boats in the operational area.

9 Oct   Central Atlantic
Gen de Gaulle lands in Duala (Cameroons) from the minesweeper *Commandant Duboc* and hoists the Free French flag for the first time on French territory.

9–20 Oct   North Atlantic
Whilst *U47* and *U124* take up weather positions far to the W, *U48*, *U101*, *U93*, *U100*, *U46*, *U99* and *U28* operate with *U123* and *U38* (which have already been longer at sea) in varying concentrations in the area round the Rockall Bank and off the North Channel. On 11–12 Oct *U48* sinks three ships from the convoy HX.77. On 15 Oct *U93* sinks one ship from OB.227 and on 16 Oct she establishes contact with OB.228 from which *U138* has torpedoed two ships the day

before. She shadows the convoy, which makes a wide detour to the N, until 20 Oct and sinks two ships on 17 Oct, but the other boats are too far off. On 17 Oct *U48* sights the convoy SC.7 with 30 ships (four stragglers) shortly after it has been met by the sloops *Scarborough* and *Fowey* and the corvette *Bluebell*; she sinks two ships but is then driven off by flying boats. *Scarborough* remains behind. On receipt of *U48*'s report, the Commander U-boats forms a patrol line with *U101*, *U46*, *U123*, *U99* and *U100*. During the night 17–18 Oct *U38* attacks the convoy twice and torpedoes one ship but she is driven off by the corvette *Heartsease* which has arrived with the sloop *Leith*. In the evening the convoy runs into the patrol line. The escorts with the convoy, *Leith* (Cdr Allen), *Fowey* and *Bluebell*, are powerless with their asdics against *U101*, *U46*, *U99* (which fires whilst moving in the convoy), *U123* and *U100* as they attack in the night in quick succession and sometimes more than once. 16 ships are sunk, one other ship is torpedoed and the convoy is completely scattered. *U101* sinks three ships and torpedoes two, *U46* sinks two ships, *U99* sinks six ships and torpedoes one, *U100* sinks one straggler and again torpedoes two ships disabled by *U101* and *U123* sinks two ships as well as two previously disabled by *U101* and *U100* and by *U99*. *U99*, *U101* and *U123* have to return, having fired all their torpedoes. *U100*, *U46*, *U28*, which failed to get to the scene, and *U38* and *U48*, which are further to the N, encounter on 19 Oct the convoy HX.79 located far to the W by *U47*. The convoy's ocean escort, the auxiliary cruisers *Alaunia* and *Montclare*, has already turned away and its escort group has only come up on the morning of 19 Oct, after releasing the westbound OB.229. In spite of its unusual strength—the destroyers *Whitehall* (Lt-Cdr Russell) and *Sturdy*, the minesweeper *Jason*, the corvettes *Hibiscus*, *Heliotrope*, *Coreopsis* and *Arabis*, the A/S trawlers *Lady Elsa*, *Blackfly* and *Angle* and submarine *O21*—*U47* maintains contact and guides the other boats to HX.79 with its 49 ships. During the night 19–20 Oct the U-boats attack in succession and sometimes more than once: *U38* sinks two ships and *U46* sinks two ships and one ship hit by *U47*, *U47*, moving partly in the convoy, sinks three ships and torpedoes three others, *U48* sinks one ship previously disabled by *U47* and *U100* sinks three ships. Only *U28* does not reach the scene before daylight. The boats taking part have fired all their torpedoes and have to return. In the W, in the meantime, *U124* attacks OB.229 and sinks two ships but fails to get the Italian

submarine *Malaspina* to the convoy. Overall results (inclusive of some scattered ships and stragglers): *U48* (Lt-Cdr Bleichrodt) sinks six ships of 37083 tons and one of 6023 tons with *U47*; *U101* (Lt-Cdr Frauenheim) sinks three ships of 10645 tons and one of 5458 tons with *U100* and *U123* and torpedoes one ship of 4155 tons with *U100*; *U93* (Lt-Cdr Korth) sinks three ships of 13214 tons; *U124* (Lt-Cdr Schulz) sinks five ships of 20061 tons; *U46* (Lt Endrass) sinks four ships of 20426 tons and one of 4947 tons with *U47*; *U99* (Lt-Cdr Kretschmer) sinks six ships of 28066 tons and one of 3106 tons with *U123*; *U100* (Lt-Cdr Schepke) sinks four ships of 24715 tons and one of 5458 tons with *U101* and *U123* and torpedoes one ship of 4155 tons with *U101*; and *U47* (Lt-Cdr Prien) sinks three ships of 17067 tons, one ship of 6023 tons with *U48* and one ship of 4947 tons with *U46* and torpedoes one tanker of 8995 tons. From the convoy SC.7, in all, 21 ships of 79592 tons (including four stragglers) are sunk and two more are torpedoed; from HX.79 12 ships of 75069 tons are sunk and one tanker torpedoed.

10–11 Oct   Bay of Biscay
Heavy British air attacks are carried out against the German destroyers in Brest but only splinter damage and some losses of personnel result.

11 Oct   English Channel
MTB22, *MTB31* and *MTB32* sink two German trawlers off Calais.

Operation 'Medium'. The British battleship *Revenge*, escorted by the 5th DD Flotilla with *Javelin*, *Jupiter*, *Kelvin*, *Kipling*, *Jackal*, *Jaguar* and *Kashmir* and the 3rd MGB Flotilla with MGB Nos *46*, *40*, *42*, *43* and *44*, fires 120 rounds of 15in and the destroyers 801 rounds of 4.7in on harbour installations in Cherbourg.

11 Oct   Air War/Britain
In a heavy air attack on Liverpool, four ships of 34744 tons are badly damaged in the harbour.

11–12 Oct   English Channel
Second sortie by the 5th TB Flotilla (Cdr Henne), comprising *Falke*, *Greif*, *Kondor*, *Seeadler* and *Wolf*, into the area off the Isle of Wight. In engagements with light forces the Free French submarine-chasers *Ch6* and *Ch7* and the trawlers *Listrac* (778 tons) and *Warwick Deeping* are sunk.

11–16 Oct   Central Atlantic
The Vichy French submarine *Vengeur* moves from Toulon to Oran (11–13 Oct) and from there proceeds with the submarines *Monge*, *Pégase* and *L'Espoir* to Casablanca (16–18 Oct) and on to Dakar (23–26 Oct).

12 Oct   North Sea
The German MTB *S37* is sunk by mine 40 miles E of Orfordness.

12–20 Oct   Mediterranean
Two Italian submarines operate E of Gibraltar and fall victim to the British submarine hunt. *Durbo* is sunk on 18 Oct by the destroyers *Firedrake* and *Wrestler*, with support from two London flying boats of No 202 Sqn RAF; a boarding party captures cypher and operating documents, which lead to the sinking of *Lafolé* on 20 Oct by the destroyers *Gallant*, *Griffin* and *Hotspur*.

13–14 Oct   Norway
A British destroyer force (Capt Vian) comprising *Cossack*, *Ashanti*, *Maori* and *Sikh* attacks a group of ships in German service near Egersund and sinks two of them in a confused engagement by night.

13–14 Oct   Mediterranean
In mining operations by the Italian submarines *Foca* (Cdr Giliberto) on 13 Oct off Haifa and *Zoea* (Cdr Bernabo) on 14 Oct off Jaffa, the first is lost through an unknown cause.

14 Oct   Norway
The German netlayer *Genua* is torpedoed and sunk by the British destroyer *Cossack* off Egersund.

15 Oct   General Situation
The plan to attack Greece is decided on by the Italian War Council in Rome. Finland gives a treaty undertaking to the Soviet Union not to fortify the Aaland Islands.

15–18 Oct   North Sea/English Channel
In operations by British submarines in the Channel, *L27* attacks a convoy on 15 Oct. On 18 Oct *H49* is sunk near Terschelling by the German submarine-chasers *UJ116* and *UJ118* under Lt-Cdr Kaden.

15–21 Oct   Mediterranean
An Italian submarine group consisting of *Bandiera*, *Santarosa*, *Speri*, *Ascianghi*, *Topazio* and *Anfitrite* is stationed between Crete and Alexandria but has no success. The submarine *Toti* (Cdr Bandini), which is returning because of a breakdown and cannot submerge, encounters on 15 Oct off Calabria the British submarine *Rainbow* which is sunk in a gun duel. On about 20 Oct the submarine *Triad* is lost on a mine barrage in the Gulf of Taranto.

16 Oct   Air War/Britain
The 9th Fl Div (Lt-Gen Coeler), which since the spring has flown mining sorties against British ports, is transformed into FK IX without there being any reinforcement of the flying formations.

16 Oct   Norway
Eleven Swordfish and three Skua aircraft of Nos 816 and 801 Sqns from the carrier *Furious* bomb oil tanks and a seaplane base near Tromsö.

16–17 Oct   Air War/Germany
British bombers attack Bremen, Cuxhaven, Hamburg and Kiel by night.

17–18 Oct   North Sea
In a sortie by German motor torpedo boats against the British SE coast, *S18* (Lt Christiansen) sinks the British freighter *Hauxley* (1595 tons), and *S24* and *S27* torpedo two freighters totalling 6726 tons.

17–18 Oct   English Channel
Sortie by the Officer Commanding Destroyers (Bey) with the destroyers *Hans Lody*, *Karl Galster*, *Friedrich Ihn* and *Erich Steinbrinck* towards the western exit of the Bristol Channel. There is an engagement with British cruisers and destroyers. *Steinbrinck* reports a so far unconfirmed torpedo hit on a cruiser. The 5th TB Flotilla operates as a support group with *Greif*, *Seeadler*, *Kondor*, *Falke*, *Wolf* and *Jaguar*.

18 Oct–1 Nov   Norway
The Dutch submarine *O24* operates off Holmangrund/Norway.

19 Oct   Soviet Union
The Soviet government decides on its warship building programme for 1941. No more new battleships and battlecruisers are to be laid down; it had been planned to build up to the end of 1945 no fewer than 15 battleships, 16 battlecruisers, two aircraft carriers of 10000 tons, 26 new cruisers (Project 68), 36 flotilla leaders, 162 destroyers, 88 large, 225 medium and 120 small submarines and 166 patrol ships. Of the 59150-ton battleships already building, *Sovetskij Sojuz* at Leningrad and *Sovetskaya Ukraina* at Nikolaev are to be completed in June 1943, and *Sovetskaya Rossiya* at Molotovsk is to be launched in the third quarter of 1943; *Sovetskaya Belorussiya*, due to be laid down in Nov 1940, is cancelled and instead four Type 30 destroyers are to be laid down in 1941. Of the 35240-ton battlecruisers, *Kronshtadt* in Leningrad and *Sevastopol* in Nikolaev are to be launched in the third quarter of 1942. Of the Project 26b cruisers (8177 tons), the building of *Kalinin* and *Kaganovich* at Komsomolsk is to be continued. Of the Project 68 cruisers (11300 tons), *Zheleznyakov*, *Chapayev* and *Chkalov* at Leningrad and *Frunze*, *Kujbyshev*, *Ordzhonikidze* and *Sverdlov* at Nikolaev are to be continued and in 1941 three additional cruisers at Leningrad and one at Komsomolsk are to be laid down. The former German cruiser *Petropavlovsk* (ex-*Lützow*) is to be completed.
Of the flotilla leaders of Project 38 (2890 tons), *Kiev* and *Erevan* at Nikolaev are to

be completed in the third and fourth quarters of 1942 and *Ochakov* and *Perekop* are to be continued. Work on No 542 at Leningrad is to be discontinued. After the completion of the last destroyers of Project 7 and 7u, 10 destroyers of Project 30 (1800 tons) are to be launched up to the end of 1941; in that year nine are to be laid down at Leningrad, eight at Molotovsk (including the four taking the place of the cancelled battleship) four at Nikolayev and two at Komsomolsk.
Of the patrol ships of Project 29 (995 tons), about 13 vessels are to laid down by the end of 1940 and an additional 11 in 1941, 11 in 1942 and eight in 1943. In addition to seven diesel-powered minesweepers (Project 53) to be laid down in 1941, and in addition to the fast turbine minesweepers of Project 59 (879 tons) already building, six more are to be laid down in 1941, 12 in 1942 and two in 1943.
Instead of the planned 21 Type S-IXbis submarines and two icebreaker-guardships for the NKVD, the People's Commissar of the Navy asks for a new submarine building programme in 1941: four Type K-XIV (1487 tons), six Type L-XIII (1123 tons), 11 Type S-IXbis (837 tons), four Type Shch-Xbis (584 tons), 12 Type M-XII (203 tons) and three Type M-XV (283 tons) in addition to the vessels already building.

20–21 Oct   Red Sea
Unsuccessful attempt by the Italian destroyers *Pantera*, *Leone*, *Sauro* and *Nullo* to attack the British convoy BN.7 in the Red Sea (32 ships escorted by the RNZN cruiser *Leander*, the destroyer *Kimberley*, the sloops *Auckland*, *Indus* and *Yarra* and the minesweepers *Derby* and *Huntley*). The attackers are driven off by the escort. *Nullo* (Cdr Borsini) has to be beached near Massawa after the engagement. The destroyer *Kimberley* is hit by coastal guns and has to be towed to Port Sudan. *Nullo* is destroyed on 21 Oct by three Blenheim bombers of No 45 Sqn. The Italian submarines *Ferraris* and *Guglielmotti*, stationed further to the N, do not assist.

20–22 Oct   English Channel
The destroyer *Richard Beitzen* sails from Wilhelmshaven to Brest.

20 Oct–5 Nov   North Atlantic
After the great convoy attacks only *U28* and *U124* remain for the present in the operational area. Some days later *U29*, *U31* and *U32*, which have recently set out, arrive. On 26 Oct *U28* (Lt-Cdr Kuhnke) torpedoes the freighter *Matina* (5389 tons), the wreck of which is sunk on 29 Oct by *U31* (Lt-Cdr Prellberg). On 26 Oct an Fw 200 (Lt Jope) of 2/KG 40 obtains a bomb hit on the British

passenger ship *Empress of Britain* (42348 tons) about 110km NW of Donegal Bay (Ireland). The ship catches fire but is taken in tow by escort vessels. *U28*, *U31* and *U32* (Lt Jenisch) are ordered to pursue: the last reaches the ship on 28 Oct and sinks her with two torpedoes whilst she is escorted by two destroyers. In an attack on a convoy on 30 Oct, *U32* is sunk by the British destroyers *Harvester* and *Highlander*. *U31* is likewise sunk in an attack on convoy OB.237 on 2 Nov by the destroyer *Antelope* with aircraft support. *U99* (Lt-Cdr Kretschmer), which arrives shortly afterwards in the operational area, encounters the British auxiliary cruisers *Laurentic* (18724 tons) and *Patroclus* (11314 tons) W of Ireland, after sinking a steamer on 3 Nov. The *Laurentic* is first hit by a torpedo and then hit again half an hour later in an attempt to finish her off. She is brought to a standstill and is sunk in the morning with a torpedo, the *Patroclus* having been hit and reduced to a wreck with three torpedoes. The *Patroclus* only sinks after two more hits. *U99* returns having sunk, in all, four ships of 42407 tons.

The first group of Italian submarines to be stationed in the North Atlantic W of the German U-boats, *Malaspina*, *Dandolo*, *Otaria* and *Barbarigo*, sights several ships and convoys but achieves no successes.

The British destroyer *Sturdy*, escorting convoy SC.8, is wrecked in a storm on the West Coast of Scotland on 30 Oct.

21 Oct   Mediterranean
Formation of the Italian Command 'Maritrafalba' (Capt Polacchini) in Brindisi to carry out, and escort, troop and supply transportation to Albania. Under command are the destroyers *Mirabello* and *Riboty*, the torpedo boats *Calatafimi*, *Castelfidardo*, *Curtatone*, *Monsambano*, *Confienza*, *Solferino*, *Prestinari*, *Cantore*, *Fabrizi*, *Medici* and *Stocco*, the escort ships *Ramb III*, *Capit*, *Cecchi*, *Lago Tana* and *Lago Zuai* and the 13th MAS Flotilla with four boats. In addition, the 12th TB Flotilla, consisting of *Antares*, *Altair*, *Andromeda* and *Aretusa*, is allotted as a fighting force.

22 Oct   North Atlantic
Escorting the convoy OL.8, the Canadian destroyer *Margaree* is sunk after colliding with the merchant vessel *Port Fairy*.

23 Oct   General Situation
Hitler meets General Franco in Hendaye on the Franco-Spanish frontier. The talks on Spain's entry into the war and the conquest of Gibraltar lead to no result.

23 Oct   Atlantic
The heavy cruiser *Admiral Scheer* (Capt Krancke) leaves Gotenhafen for mercantile warfare operations in the Atlantic. On 27

Oct the cruiser receives orders in Brunsbüttel to set out and reaches Stavanger on 28 Oct. From 31 Oct to 1 Nov the ship passes through the Denmark Strait undetected.

24–25 Oct   Mediterranean
Fourteen aircraft from Nos 815, 819 and 824 Sqns FAA, disembarked from the carriers *Illustrious* and *Eagle*, bombard Tobruk and mine the harbour entrance.

On 25 Oct the gunboat *Aphis* bombards a concentration 15 miles E of Sidi Barrani.

24 Oct–30 Nov   Atlantic
The German freighter *Helgoland* breaks out of the Colombian port of Puerto Colombia, eludes pursuit by the US destroyers *Bainbridge*, *Overton* and *Sturtevant*, passes the Antilles chain near St Thomas on 3 Nov and reaches St-Nazaire.

25–28 Oct   Mediterranean
British sortie into the Aegean to cover a convoy operation between Alexandria and Greece. The operation is covered by the 2nd Sqn of the Mediterranean Fleet, comprising the battleships *Malaya* and *Ramillies* and the carrier *Eagle*, as far as the Kaso Strait. Carrier aircraft attack the airfield at Maltezana. The cruisers *Orion* and *Sydney* with the destroyers *Jervis* and *Juno* make a sortie as far as the Dardanelles for contraband control.

25 Oct–2 Dec   Central and North Atlantic
The fourth group of Italian submarines is transferred to Bordeaux. *Marcello* and *Morosini* operate at first without success between Vigo and the Azores. *Bianchi* and *Brin* have to put in to Tangiers on 4 Nov after *Bianchi* has been bombed by a London flying boat of No 202 Sqn RAF and attacked by the destroyer *Greyhound* with depth charges and damaged.

27–30 Oct   Mediterranean
After three attempts have been abandoned because of the defence, the Italian submarine *Scirè* (Cdr Borghese) launches three *Maiali* human torpedoes off Gibraltar but these do not reach their targets.

28 Oct   Mediterranean
Italian troops cross the Greek/Albanian frontier and invade Greece.

28 Oct–6 Nov   Mediterranean
The Italian submarines *Zaffiro*, *Narvalo* and *Corridoni* (after a transport mission from Taranto to Rhodes and Leros) operate in the south-eastern approaches to the Aegean. *Delfino* and *Jantina* cruise in the Aegean. *Atropo* (Cdr Manca) has to break off a mining operation off Zante on 29 Oct while actually laying mines; *Bragadino* (Cdr Vannutelli) lays 24 mines off Navarino on 30 Oct.

29–30 Oct   English Channel
Offensive mining operation 'Alfred' by the torpedo boats *Iltis* and *Jaguar* off Dover.

29 Oct–2 Nov   Mediterranean
Sortie by the British Mediterranean Fleet (Adm Cunningham) with four battleships, two carriers, four cruisers and destroyers into the Ionian Sea to cover convoys to Greece. No opposition. The Italian submarines *Menotti*, *Settembrini*, *Dessiè* and *Tricheco*, operating S of Crete from 28 Oct to 5 Nov, do not establish contact.

31 Oct   Mediterranean
British Army and Air Force units land on Crete.

31 Oct–1 Nov   Mediterranean
Sortie by Force H, comprising the battlecruiser *Renown*, the battleship *Barham* and the destroyers *Forester*, *Fortune*, *Firedrake*, *Gallant*, *Greyhound* and *Griffin*, along the Moroccan West Coast against suspected movements by Vichy French warships.

1–20 Nov   Norway
Of the Allied submarines operating off Norway, the French *Rubis* (Cdr Cabanier) lands agents in Korsfjord. The British *Sturgeon* (Lt Gregory) attacks two German convoys on 3 and 6 Nov off Obrestad and sinks two ships of 2631 tons. She is relieved by the Dutch submarine *O23*. *O22* is sunk on 8 Nov off SW Norway by depth charges from the German submarine-chasers *UJ177* and *UJ1104*.

2–12 Nov   Bay of Biscay
In the Bay of Biscay, the British submarine *Taku* (Lt-Cdr van der Byl) sinks the tanker *Gedania* (8923 tons). The submarine *Swordfish*, which relieves the *Usk* off Brest, is lost (on a mine?) about 10 Nov. *Tigris* (Lt-Cdr Bone) sinks one trawler of 301 tons.

3 Nov   North Sea
An Fw 200 of I/KG 40 severely damages the British passenger ship *Windsor Castle* (19141 tons) with a bomb hit W of Ireland.

4 Nov   Mediterranean
The British submarine *Tetrarch* (Lt-Cdr Mills) torpedoes one ship of 2532 tons in a convoy off Benghazi.

4–14 Nov   Mediterranean
British naval operations in the Mediterranean with carrier attacks on Taranto. On 4 Nov the convoys AN.6 and MW.3 set out from Port Said and Alexandria for the Aegean and Malta, accompanied by the AA cruisers *Calcutta* and *Coventry* and the destroyers *Dainty*, *Vampire*, *Waterhen* and *Voyager*. After bringing AN.6 into Suda Bay these ships, with the exception of the last, proceed westwards with MW.3. The cruisers *Ajax* and *Sydney* set out from Alexandria on 5 Nov, land supplies in Suda Bay

on 6 Nov, and then join the Mediterranean Fleet at sea on the same day.

Operation MB.8. Convoy MW.3 with five supply ships proceeds to Malta. It is covered by the Mediterranean Fleet (Adm Cunningham,) comprising the battleships *Warspite*, *Valiant*, *Malaya* and *Ramillies*, the carrier *Illustrious* (Rear-Adm Lyster), the cruisers *Gloucester* and *York* (3rd Cruiser Sqn), the *Orion* (and later *Ajax* and *Sydney*) (7th Cruiser Sqn, Vice-Adm Pridham-Wippell) and 13 destroyers: *Nubian* (14th Flotilla), *Mohawk*, *Jervis*, *Janus*, *Juno*, *Hyperion* (2nd Flotilla) *Hasty*, *Hero*, *Hereward*, *Havock*, *Ilex* and, detached from the 2nd Flotilla, *Decoy* and *Defender*.

Operation 'Coat'. On 7 Nov Force H (Vice-Adm Somerville) goes to sea from Gibraltar with the carrier *Ark Royal*, the cruiser *Sheffield* and the destroyers *Faulknor* (8th Flotilla), *Duncan*, *Firedrake*, *Forester*, *Fortune* and *Fury*, in order to cover Force F (reinforcements for the Mediterranean Fleet comprising the battleship *Barham*, the cruisers *Berwick* and *Glasgow* and the destroyers *Encounter*, *Gallant*, *Greyhound* and *Griffin*), as far as S of Sardinia. On 9 Nov Swordfish aircraft of Nos 810, 818 and 820 Sqns make an attack on Cagliari. Italian bombers attack the force which is located on 9 Nov but only near misses are obtained near *Ark Royal*, *Barham* and *Duncan*. An Italian submarine group, comprising *Alagi*, *Axum*, *Aradam*, *Medusa* and *Diaspro*, is stationed SW of Sardinia on 9 Nov but is unable to find either force. The 14th DD Sqn (*Vivaldi*, *Da Noli*, *Pancaldo* and *Malocello*) which is sent to the Sicilian Channel passes by Force F (now detached from Force H) during the night 9–10 Nov. Force F joins the Mediterranean Fleet coming from the E on the morning of 10 Nov when S of Malta and then enters Malta to land 2150 troop reinforcements. Of the Italian submarines *Mameli*, *Corallo*, *Bandiera*, *Topazio* and *Capponi* (Cdr Romei), stationed E of Malta, only the last is able to fire—unsuccessfully—at *Ramillies* as she comes into Malta with *Coventry* and the destroyers and convoy MW.3. On 10 Nov the convoy ME.3 with four empty ships (unsuccessfully attacked on 11 Nov by the Italian submarine *Topazio*, Cdr Berengan) and the escort of MW.3 and *Ramillies* sets out eastwards, followed by the destroyer *Vendetta* (repaired in Malta) and the monitor *Terror*, which arrives in Suda Bay on 13 Nov. The destroyers *Faulknor*, *Fortune* and *Fury*, which have led Force F as minesweepers to Malta, return to Force H, S of Sardinia. The latter proceeds back to Gibraltar after the *Ark Royal* has flown off another three

Fulmars to Malta. After meeting the units coming from the W on 10 Nov, the forces of the Mediterranean Fleet at first proceed eastwards. The Italian aircraft, seeking to keep contact, suffer losses from the Fulmar fighters from *Illustrious*. On 11 Nov *Illustrious* (Capt Boyd), with the cruisers *Gloucester*, *Berwick*, *Glasgow* and *York* and the destroyers *Hasty*, *Havock*, *Hyperion* and *Ilex*, turns to attack Taranto; the cruisers *Orion*, *Sydney* and *Ajax* and the destroyers *Mohawk* and *Nubian* turn to the N to make a raid on the Strait of Otranto.

Operation 'Judgement'. A force composed of 12 and nine Swordfish aircraft from Nos 813, 815, 819 and 824 Sqns from the *Illustrious* attacks the Italian Fleet lying in the harbour of Taranto during the night 11–12 Nov. In two waves under Lt-Cdr Williamson and Lt-Cdr Hale, the Swordfish aircraft obtain three hits on the modern battleship *Littorio* and one each on the older *Caio Duilio* and *Conte di Cavour*. *Cavour* sinks on the bottom; she is later salvaged but not put into service. The heavy cruiser *Trento* and the destroyer *Libeccio* are slightly damaged by bomb hits (unexploded). Two of the attacking aircraft are shot down by AA fire.

In the night the cruisers under Vice-Adm Pridham-Wippell find a convoy of four ships in the Strait of Otranto proceeding from Valona to Brindisi and escorted by the auxiliary cruiser *Ramb III* and the old torpedo boat *Fabrizi*. These escape while the steamers *Antonio Locatelli* (5691 tons), *Capo Vado* (4391 tons), *Catalani* (2429 tons) and *Premuda* (4427 tons) are sunk. Apart from a bomb hit on the destroyer *Decoy* on 13 Nov, the forces of the British Mediterranean Fleet return to Alexandria without further losses.

5–8 Nov   English Channel
The destroyers *Paul Jacobi*, *Theodor Riedel*, *Friedrich Eckoldt*, *Friedrich Ihn* and *Erich Steinbrinck* are transferred from Brest to Wilhelmshaven and disperse to different German yards for repairs.

5–8 Nov   Mediterranean
The temporarily repaired French battleship *Provence* is transferred from Oran to Toulon, accompanied by the destroyers *Epée*, *Fleuret*, *Le Hardi*, *Lansquenet* and *Mameluck*. The force is met by the battleship *Strasbourg*, the cruisers *Algérie*, *Dupleix*, *Foch*, *La Galissonnière* and *Marseillaise* and five destroyers.

5–17 Nov   North Atlantic
The German heavy cruiser *Admiral Scheer* (Capt Krancke), after sinking an independent of 5389 tons, attacks on 5 Nov E of Newfoundland the convoy HX.84 (37 ships)

proceeding from Halifax to Britain. The escorting auxiliary cruiser *Jervis Bay* (Capt Fegen†, 14164 tons) at once gives orders for the convoy to scatter under a smokescreen, while she tries to tie down the German ship in order to gain time. After she goes down, *Scheer* is able to sink five steamers of 33331 tons before dark and to damage three ships, including the tanker *San Demetrio*, totalling 27853 tons. On receipt of *Jervis Bay*'s distress signal, the Home Fleet deploys the battleships *Nelson* and *Rodney* with destroyer escorts to block the Iceland–Faeroes passage and the battlecruisers *Hood*, *Repulse* and *Renown* (the last recalled from Force H) and the cruisers *Dido*, *Naiad* and *Phoebe* of the 15th Cruiser Sqn to block the approaches to the Bay of Biscay. Two HX convoys are recalled. Normal convoy traffic is not resumed until 17 Nov with HX.89. *Admiral Scheer*, however, proceeds to the South Atlantic.

6–7 Nov   North Sea
Sortie by the 1st and 2nd TB Flotillas (Cdr v Rennenkampff and Cdr Riede), comprising *T1*, *T4*, *T6*, *T7*, *T8*, *T9* and *T10*, against the Scottish East Coast. *T6* (Lt-Cdr Wolfram) is lost when she hits a mine, whereupon the operation is abandoned.

7–8 Nov   Pacific
The British freighter *Cambridge* (10846 tons) and an American freighter (5883 tons) sink, on 7 and 8 Nov respectively, on the mine barrage laid from 29 Oct to 2 Nov in the Bass Strait (Australia) by the German auxiliary minelayer *Passat* (Lt-Cdr Warning).

7–9 Nov   Central Atlantic
Free French attack on Libreville. The transports *Fort Lamy*, *Nevada* and *Casamaoce* land troops of the Foreign Legion under Col Leclerc on 7 Nov in the Bay of Mondah, N of Libreville (Gabon). Escort is provided by the Free French sloops *Commandant Dominé* and *Savorgnan de Brazza* (Cdr* d'Argenlieu); British forces, including the cruisers *Delhi* and *Devonshire*, confine themselves to blockading the coast of Gabon. The Vichy French submarine *Poncelet* (Cdr de Saussine), which tries to attack the British sloop *Milford*, is forced to surface by depth charges from the latter and has to scuttle herself. On 9 Nov, after several attacks by Free French aircraft on the French sloop *Bougainville* (Cdr* Morin) lying in Libreville, there is an engagement between this ship and *Savorgnan de Brazza* in which *Bougainville* is set on fire and sinks. By 14 Nov the whole of French Equatorial Africa has fallen into De Gaulle's hands.

8 Nov   North Sea

The German MTB *S38* is sunk in a gun battle in the Thames Estuary with two British destroyers after being rammed by one of the destroyers.

8–30 Nov   North Atlantic

U137, U138, U93, U100, U103, U123 and *U104* operate in the area W of the North Channel; and further to the W are weather boats *U29* and *U47*, as well as the Italian boats *Baracca, Finzi* and *Marconi. Faa' di Bruno* is sunk when setting out by the destroyer *Havelock* on 8 Nov. Also on 8 Nov, *Marconi* (Cdr Chialamberto), in attempting to maintain contact with HX.84, which has been attacked by an Fw 200 of KG 40, is able on the following day to finish off the Swedish freighter *Vingaland* (2734 tons), set on fire by an Fw 200 of I/KG 40. On 16–17 Nov *U137* sinks three ships of an outbound convoy; following her report, *U47* and *U100* approach the convoy on 18–19 Nov but have no success. One of the two boats is located by a Sunderland flying boat of the RAF with ASV-I radar equipment—the first radar location of a U-boat by an aircraft. *U93, U103, Finzi* and *Marconi* are too far off. On 20 Nov *U103* sights OB.244 and sinks two of its ships but is driven off in a depth-charge pursuit by the British corvette *Rhododendron*. On 23 Nov *U123* establishes contact with the dispersing convoy and sinks five ships. From the homebound SC.11 (escort sloop *Enchantress*), *U100* sinks seven ships during the night 22–23 Nov; *U93* does not approach nor are *U29, U43* and *Finzi* able to get to OB.244. In all, *U137* (Lt Wohlfarth) sinks four ships of 13341 tons, *U100* (Lt-Cdr Schepke) sinks seven of 24601 tons, *U103* (Cdr Schütze) sinks seven of 38465 tons, *U123* (Lt-Cdr Moehle) sinks six of 27895 tons, *U104* (Lt-Cdr Jürst) sinks one of 8240 tons and torpedoes one of 10516 tons, *Baracca* (Cdr Bertarelli) sinks one of 4866 tons and *Marconi* (Cdr Chialamberto) sinks one of 2734 tons, disabled by bombing from I/KG 40. *U104* must have sunk from unknown causes on 27 Nov during an attack against convoy HX.87 (the report of the sinking of this boat by the corvette *Rhododendron* with convoy OB.244 on 21 Nov must be in error).

9 Nov   North Sea/North Atlantic

German aircraft drop mines in the estuaries of the Thames and Humber and off Liverpool. An Fw 200 of I/KG 40 damages the British passenger ship *Empress of Japan* (26032 tons) in the North Atlantic.

10 Nov–2 Jan   Central Atlantic

From 15 to 19 Nov, *U65* (Cdr v Stockhausen), which set out on 15 Oct, operates off Freetown, after being replenished from

the supply ship *Nordmark*, and sinks four ships. After being replenished on 29 Nov the U-boat sinks four more ships and torpedoes one tanker by 2 Jan. Total result: eight ships of 47785 tons sunk and one ship of 8532 tons torpedoed.

12 Nov   North Sea

He 115s of 3/KFlGr 906 torpedo three freighters of 6604 tons in a British convoy off Middlesbrough.

14–16 Nov   Mediterranean

The British cruisers *Berwick, Glasgow, Sydney* and *York* transport 3400 troops from Alexandria to Piraeus.

14–22 Nov   Mediterranean

After the British raid of 11–12 Nov, the Italian submarines *Jalea* and *Millelire* operate in the Strait of Otranto to cover their own convoys. Cruisers and destroyers are sent to Brindisi as a precautionary move.

15 Nov   Western Atlantic

Flying boats of US Navy Patron 54, based on the tender *George E Badger*, begin reconnaissance flights from Bermuda.

15–20 Nov   Mediterranean

Operation 'White': British Force H (Vice-Adm Somerville), with the battlecruiser *Renown*, the aircraft carrier *Ark Royal*, the cruisers *Despatch* and *Sheffield* and the destroyers *Faulknor, Fortune, Fury, Wishart, Forester, Firedrake, Duncan* and *Foxhound*, accompanies the carrier *Argus* to the area SW of Sardinia where 12 Hurricane fighters and two Skua bombers are flown off to Malta. But because of the strong contrary winds only four Hurricanes and one Skua reach Malta. A raid by *Ark Royal* on the airfield at Alghero (Sardinia) planned for 17 Nov has to be abandoned because of the weather. The Italian submarines *Alagi, Aradam* and *Diaspro* are deployed but they are unable to find Force H.

On 17 Nov the cruiser *Newcastle* sets out for Malta with 200 RAF personnel and important spare parts and arrives on 19 Nov. From 15 to 20 Nov the cruisers *Gloucester, York, Orion, Ajax* and *Sydney* bring 4000 troops from Alexandria to Piraeus and return without incident.

16–17 Nov   Air War/Germany

127 British bombers attack Hamburg.

16–18 Nov   Western Atlantic

The German freighters *Phrygia, Idarwald, Orinoco* and *Rhein* try to break through from Tampico (Mexico) to Western France. At once escorted by the US destroyers *Plunkett, McCormick* and *Broome, Phrygia* scuttles herself in the belief that she has been found by the enemy; the other three return after unsuccessful attempts to shake off the pursuers.

16–29 Nov   Norway

The Dutch submarine *O24* operates off Egersund.

18–28 Nov   Indian Ocean

On 18 Nov the British cruiser *Dorsetshire* bombards Zante in Italian Somaliland. The German auxiliary cruiser *Schiff 33* sinks four Allied freighters of 35083 tons, including the British refrigerator ship *Maimoa* (10123 tons), in the Indian Ocean.

19–20 Nov   North Sea

Raid by the 3rd German MTB Flotilla (Lt-Cdr Kemnade) with *S54, S57* and *S38* (from the 1st Flotilla) E of Lowestoft. In a surprise attack, the boats are engaged by British destroyers. *S38* (Lt Detlefsen) sinks after being rammed—the first loss of a German MTB in action.

20 Nov   Mediterranean

The Italian torpedo boat *Confienza* is lost off Brindisi after a collision with the patrol vessel *Cecchi*.

20–30 Nov   Mediterranean

In the Eastern Mediterranean, the Italian submarine *Onice* operates NW of Alexandria (only until 24 Nov), *Narvalo* in the Kaso Strait and *Delfino* in the Northern Aegean; *Atropo* carries out a supply operation from Taranto to Leros.

22–28 Nov   Red Sea

The Italian submarines *Archimede* and *Ferraris* search in vain for a reported British convoy.

23–24 Nov   Air War/Britain

Heavy German air attack on Southampton. Among other ships, the passenger steamer *Llandovery Castle* (10640 tons) is badly damaged.

23–28 Nov   North Sea/English Channel

German aircraft drop mines in the estuaries of the Thames and Humber and off Newcastle, Pembroke, Plymouth, Falmouth and Bristol.

23 Nov–1 Dec   Mediterranean

The Italian submarines *Nereide* and *Sirena* operate in the Strait of Otranto.

23 Nov–13 Dec   North Atlantic

The U-boats *U43, U47* and *U103* (weather boats) and *U52, U94, U95, U101* and *U140* operate in the North Atlantic, W of the North Channel, as do, further to the W, the Italian boats *Argo, Giuliani* and *Tarantini*. On 1 Dec *Argo* (Lt-Cdr Crepas) torpedoes the Canadian destroyer *Saguenay* belonging to the escort of the convoy HG.47. On the afternoon of 1 Dec *U101*, which is stationed the furthest W, sights the convoy HX.90, whose ocean escort, the auxiliary cruiser *Laconia*, soon afterwards leaves the convoy. Before the arrival of the escort group, *U101, U52* and *U47* approach and continually attack the convoy during the night 1–2 Dec. In four approaches, *U101* sinks two ships and damages one, *U47* sinks one ship and torpedoes one other ship and the tanker *Conch* and *U52*, in two approaches, sinks two ships and torpedoes one. In the evening of 1 Dec, *U99* hits with one torpedo, a little to the N, the auxiliary cruiser *Forfar* proceeding westwards and finishes her off with four torpedoes. The escorting destroyer HMCS *St Laurent* has been detached to HX.90. An attack by *Argo* fails. After the arrival of the escort group, comprising the sloop *Folkestone*, the corvette *Gentian* and the destroyer *Viscount*, *Tarantini* is attacked with depth charges. Contact is lost in the morning and air reconnaissance, made with three machines, produces no result. While *U95* and *U99* finish off and sink the disabled *Conch* from the rear, *U99* sinks another independent and *U43* attacks an outbound convoy making a detour to the N and sinks two ships. *U94* finds HX.90 again in the afternoon of 2 Dec and in two approaches sinks two ships. The convoy is scattered. On receipt of a B-Service report, *U43*, *U52*, *U94*, *U99* and *U103* are ordered on 3 Dec to look for convoy SC.13, but they do not find it. *Argo* sinks one of its ships.

In the convoy operation and in individual attacks, *U43* (Lt Lüth) sinks three ships of 21262 tons and torpedoes one of 10350 tons, *U47* (Lt-Cdr Prien) sinks one ship of 7555 tons, torpedoes one of 3862 tons and sinks one of 8376 tons with *U95* and *U99*, *U52* (Lt-Cdr Salman) sinks two ships of 4368 tons and torpedoes one of 5448 tons, *U94* (Lt-Cdr Kuppisch) sinks three ships of 13617 tons, *U95* (Lt-Cdr Schreiber) sinks one ship of 5448 tons and one of 8376 tons with *U47* and *U99* and torpedoes one of 1296 tons, *U99* (Lt-Cdr Kretschmer) sinks three ships of 25915 tons and one of 8376 tons with *U47* and *U95*, *U101* (Lt-Cdr Mengersen) sinks five ships of 28505 tons and *U140* (Lt Hinsch) sinks three ships of 12386 tons; *Argo* (Lt-Cdr Crepas) sinks one ship of 5066 tons and torpedoes the destroyer *Saguenay*.

On the return, *Tarantini*, after being met by the German minesweeper escort, is lost on 15 Dec in the Bay of Biscay as a result of an attack by the British submarine *Thunderbolt* (Lt Crouch).

In all, nine ships of 52817 tons belonging to HX.90 are sunk.

24–25 Nov   English Channel
Sortie by the Officer Commanding Destroyers (Capt Bey) with the destroyers *Karl Galster*, *Hans Lody* and *Richard Beitzen* into the area off Plymouth. Two ships of 2156 tons are sunk.

24–29 Nov   Mediterranean
Operation 'Collar': battle off Cape Teulada (Sardinia). On 24 Nov Force D, consisting of the battleship *Ramillies* and the cruisers *Berwick* and *Newcastle*, leaves Alexandria for Gibraltar and the cruiser *Coventry* and the destroyers *Defender*, *Gallant*, *Greyhound*, *Griffin* and *Hereward* go to meet a convoy coming from Gibraltar S of Sardinia. They are accompanied until S of Malta by a covering group (Force C) consisting of the battleships *Barham* and *Malaya* and the carrier *Eagle* (which carries out a raid on Tripoli on 26 Nov). On 25 Nov the Mediterranean Fleet (Force A, Admiral Cunningham) leaves Alexandria with the battleships *Valiant* and *Warspite*, the carrier *Illustrious*, the 7th Cruiser Sqn with *Ajax*, *Orion* and *Sydney* and destroyers to cover a convoy to Suda Bay (Crete). In the process *Illustrious* makes a raid on Rhodes on 26 Nov. In addition, a supply convoy to Malta puts to sea with the 3rd Cruiser Sqn (Force E) consisting of *Glasgow*, *Gloucester* and *York*. On 25 Nov the convoy, which is to go E (Force F) with the cruisers *Manchester* (Vice-Adm Holland) and *Southampton* (each with 700 men on board), the destroyer *Hotspur*, the corvettes *Peony*, *Salvia*, *Gloxinia* and *Hyacinth* and the transports *Clan Forbes*, *Clan Fraser* and *New Zealand Star*, is met off Gibraltar by the covering group (Force B) consisting of the battlecruiser *Renown* (Vice-Adm Somerville), the carrier *Ark Royal*, the cruisers *Despatch* and *Sheffield* and the destroyers *Faulknor*, *Firedrake*, *Forester*, *Fury*, *Encounter*, *Duncan*, *Wishart*, *Kelvin* and *Jaguar*.

On a report that Force B has left Gibraltar and on the sighting of Force D, S of Malta, by an Italian civilian aircraft on 25 Nov, the Italian submarines *Alagi*, *Aradam*, *Axum* and *Diaspro* are stationed S of Sardinia and *Dessiè* and *Tembien* off Malta. On 26 Nov the Italian Fleet Commander, Sqn Adm Campioni, with the battleships *Giulio Cesare* and *Vittorio Veneto*, the 13th DD Flotilla (comprising *Granatiere*, *Fuciliere*, *Bersagliere* and *Alpino*), the 7th DD Flotilla (comprising *Freccia*, *Saetta* and *Dardo*) and the Commander of the 2nd Sqn, Sqn Adm Iachino, with the 1st Cruiser Div, consisting of *Pola* (F), *Fiume* (Div Adm Matteucci), *Gorizia* and the 9th DD Flotilla (comprising *Alfieri*, *Carducci*, *Gioberti* and *Oriani*), sets out from Naples; and the 3rd Cruiser Div (Div Adm Sansonetti), consisting of *Trieste*, *Trento*, *Bolzano* and the 12th DD Flotilla (comprising *Lanciere*, *Ascari* and *Carabinieri*) from Messina to intercept the forces coming from the W. Of the boats of the 10th TB Flotilla, *Alcione*, *Vega*, *Sagittario* and

Sirio, sent into the Sicilian Channel from Trapani, the last fires unnoticed torpedoes at Force D during the night 26–27 Nov.

After reconnaissance aircraft from *Ark Royal* have sighted elements of the Italian Fleet in the morning of 27 Nov, Admiral Somerville joins up two hours later with Force D approaching from the E. He orders the convoy with the three transports, the four corvettes and the destroyers *Duncan* and *Wishart*, as well as the cruiser *Coventry* coming from Force D and its destroyers, to proceed to the SE whilst he himself sails to meet the Italian Fleet with *Ramillies* and *Renown*, the cruisers *Manchester*, *Sheffield*, *Newcastle* and *Berwick* and destroyers. Attacks by torpedo aircraft from *Ark Royal*, escorted by the destroyers *Jaguar* and *Kelvin*, on *Vittorio Veneto* and *Pola* are outmanoeuvred. In an engagement of about one hour between the cruisers and battleships, the Italians obtain a hit on *Berwick* and the Italian destroyer *Lanciere*, having received a heavy hit, is taken in tow. Then Admiral Campioni breaks off the battle because he believes, on the basis of inadequate air reconnaissance, that he faces superior enemy forces.

Two attempted attacks by the Italian submarines *Dessiè* and *Tembien* during the night of 27–28 Nov on the 3rd Cruiser Sqn sent to the Sicilian Channel to support the convoy are unsuccessful.

24 Nov–26 Dec   North Atlantic
The two last Italian submarines, *Mocenigo* and *Velella*, are transferred to the Atlantic. In operations between the Portuguese coast and the Azores, *Mocenigo* (Cdr Agostini) attacks the convoy OG.47 and sinks one ship of 1253 tons on 21 Dec. A gun attack on a scattered ship on 22 Dec has no great effect.

25 Nov–18 Dec   Norway
In operations off Norway, the British submarine *Sunfish* attacks convoys on 25 Nov and 5 Dec and sinks the Finnish steamer *Oscar Midling* (2182 tons) from the second. The Dutch submarine *O21* operates in the northern North Sea and the French *Rubis* off Norway.

26 Nov   Mediterranean
Fifteen Swordfish aircraft of Nos 815 and 819 Sqns from the carrier *Illustrious* bomb Port Laki on Leros.

26 Nov   Pacific
The auxiliary cruisers *Schiff 45/Komet* (Capt Eyssen) and *Schiff 36/Orion* (Cdr* Weyher) sink the British passenger ship *Rangitane* (16712 tons) NE of Auckland, New Zealand.

28 Nov   Mediterranean
The Italian 15th DD Flotilla, consisting of *Pigafetta*, *Da Recco*, *Pessagno* and *Riboty*

and the attached torpedo boats *Bassini* and *Prestinari*, shells Greek positions NE of Corfu with some 1600 rounds of 12cm and 10.2cm.

28–29 Nov   English Channel
Second sortie by the Officer Commanding Destroyers (Capt Bey) with the destroyers *Karl Galster*, *Hans Lody* and *Richard Beitzen* off Plymouth. Two small ships of 424 tons are sunk and in a gun and torpedo action with the British 5th DD Flotilla (*Javelin*, *Jupiter*, *Kashmir*, *Jackal* and *Jersey*), *Javelin* is torpedoed fore and aft and loses her bow and stern.

30 Nov–1 Dec   Air War/Britain
Heavy German air attack on Southampton by 128 bombers.

1 Dec   North Sea
The Norwegian passenger ship *Oslofjord* (18673 tons) and a British tanker (6990 tons) sink on German aircraft mines off the Tyne Estuary.

1 Dec   South Atlantic
The British auxiliary cruiser *Calvin Castle* stops the Brazilian steamer *Itape* off the Brazilian coast and takes off 22 German citizens.

1–11 Dec   Mediterranean
The Italian submarines *Da Procida* and *Jalea* operate SW of Corfu. *Ametista*, *Jantina* and *Zaffiro* are employed in the Aegean.

1–19 Dec   Central Atlantic
In a southern operation, *U37* (Lt-Cdr Clausen) sinks four small ships of 6814 tons W of Spain from 1 to 4 Dec, one trawler of 223 tons W of Morocco on 16 Dec and, in error, the Vichy French submarine *Sfax* and the naval tanker *Lot* (2785 tons) on 19 Dec. Because of her high expenditure of torpedoes, the boat receives orders to return.

2 Dec   English Channel
The minelayers *Schiff 23* and *Togo* depart from Brest for a minelaying operation off Land's End and the Scilly Isles but are recalled because of superior enemy forces in the area.

2 Dec   North Sea
Admiral Sir C Forbes is succeeded as C-in-C Home Fleet by Admiral Sir J C Tovey. At this time the Home Fleet has at its disposal the battleships *King George V*, *Nelson* and *Rodney*, the battlecruisers *Hood* and *Repulse* and 11 cruisers.

2–3 Dec   English Channel
Offensive mining operation 'Oskar' by the torpedo boats *Iltis* and *Jaguar* off Dover.

3 Dec   North Atlantic
Auxiliary cruiser *Schiff 41/Kormoran* (Cdr Detmers) leaves Gotenhafen on a mercantile warfare sortie. Operational areas: Atlantic and Indian Oceans. The ship passes through

the Denmark Strait unobserved by the enemy on 12–13 Dec.

3 Dec   Mediterranean
In an attack by Italian torpedo aircraft on Suda Bay, the British cruiser *Glasgow* is badly damaged by two hits but can be brought back to Alexandria.

3–4 Dec   English Channel
Offensive mining operation 'Marianne' off Dover by the 5th TB Flotilla (Cdr Henne) consisting of the boats *Greif*, *Kondor*, *Falke* and *Seeadler*.

3–5 Dec   Red Sea
The Italian destroyers *Tigre*, *Leone*, *Manin* and *Sauro* and the submarine *Ferraris* search in vain for a British convoy.

3–11 Dec   Western Atlantic
The freighters *Idarwald* (5033 tons) and *Rhein* (6031 tons) try again to break out of Tampico. *Idarwald* is pursued by the US destroyer *Broome*, on whose reports the British cruiser *Diomede* comes up on 5 Dec. A prize crew cannot save the ship, which is set on fire and sinks on 9 Dec on the Cuban South Coast while the US destroyer *Sturtevant* looks on. *Rhein* is accompanied by the US destroyer *Simpson* which, with her relief, the destroyers *McCormick* and *MacLeish*, also brings up the Dutch gunboat *Van Kinsbergen* in the Straits of Florida. The Dutch boat makes an unsuccessful effort to board. The wreck of the *Rhein*, set on fire by the crew, is sunk by the British cruiser *Caradoc* on 11 Dec.

5 Dec   English Channel
The British destroyer *Cameron* is struck by German bombers at Portsmouth and capsizes on 15 Dec at Portland.

5 Dec   South Atlantic
The German auxiliary cruiser *Schiff 10/Thor* (Capt Kähler) damages the British auxiliary cruiser *Carnarvon Castle* (20122 tons, Capt Hardy) in an engagement SE of Rio de Janeiro. A search for *Schiff 10*, started immediately by the British cruisers *Cumberland*, *Enterprise* and *Newcastle*, is unsuccessful.

5–9 Dec   English Channel
The destroyers *Karl Galster* and *Hans Lody* are transferred from Brest to Germany, stopping on 6–8 Dec at Vlissingen because of heavy weather.

6–7 Dec   North Atlantic
The heavy cruiser *Admiral Hipper* (Capt Meisel) passes unobserved through the Denmark Strait into the North Atlantic.

6–8 Dec   Pacific
The auxiliary cruisers *Schiff 45/Komet* (Capt Eyssen) and *Schiff 36/Orion* (Cdr* Weyher) sink, in the area of the British island of Nauru (Pacific), five ships of 25904 tons, including three special ships for the

transport of phosphates. The proposed disembarkation of a landing party of 185 men made up of the crews of both auxiliary cruisers has to be abandoned because of unfavourable weather.

6–18 Dec   Mediterranean
In operations in the Ionian Sea and off Durazzo (Albania), the British submarine *Triton* (Lt-Cdr Watkins) torpedoes one ship of 6040 tons but is sunk in the Strait of Otranto, probably by a mine, on 18 Dec. On 6 Dec the British submarine *Regulus* is lost off Taranto, probably on a mine barrage. *Truant* (Lt-Cdr Haggard) sinks two ships of 9723 tons off Albania.

8–26 Dec   North Atlantic
The U-boats *U96* and *U100* operate in the area W of the North Channel and mainly S of Rockall and the Italian boats *Calvi*, *Emo* and *Veniero* between 15° and 20°W. On 11–12 Dec *U96* sinks four ships from the convoy HX.92 and on 18 Dec with her last torpedo hits one tanker from OB.259 but *U52* and *U100*, which are ordered to the scene, do not come up. Otherwise the U-boats only attack stragglers and independents. *U96* (Lt-Cdr Lehmann-Willenbrock) sinks five ships of 37037 tons and torpedoes two of 15864 tons, *U100* (Lt-Cdr Schepke) sinks three of 17166 tons, *Calvi* (Cdr Caridi) sinks one of 5162 tons and *Veniero* (Cdr Petroni) sinks one of 2883 tons.

9–11 Dec   Mediterranean
Reorganisation of the Italian Fleet. Admiral Riccardi replaces Admiral Cavagnari as Under-Secretary of State and Head of Supermarina and the former Cdr of the 2nd Sqn, Sqn Adm Iachino, replaces Admiral Campioni as Fleet Cdr. Reorganisation of the Squadrons: Flagship *Vittorio Veneto*; 5th Div (Div Adm Bruto Brivonesi)—old battleships *Andrea Doria* and *Giulio Cesare* and one destroyer flotilla; 1st Div (Div Adm Cattaneo)—heavy cruisers *Zara*, *Pola*, *Gorizia*, *Fiume* and two destroyer flotillas; 3rd Div (Div Adm Sansonetti)—heavy cruisers *Trieste*, *Trento*, *Bolzano* and one destroyer flotilla; 7th Div (Div Adm Casardi)—light cruisers *Duca d'Aosta*, *Eugenio di Savoia*, *Montecuccoli* and two destroyer flotillas; 8th Div (Div Adm Legnani)—light cruisers *Attendolo*, *Duca degli Abruzzi*, *Garibaldi* and one destroyer flotilla; 4th Div (Div Adm Marenco)—light cruisers *Bande Nere*, *Diaz* and two destroyer flotillas (4th Div directly under command of Supermarina).

9–17 Dec   Mediterranean
A support force under Rear-Adm Rawlings is formed to aid the Western Desert Force in its offensive against the Italian Army in

Cyrenaica. It is composed of four groups: Force A—monitor *Terror*, gunboats *Ladybird*, *Aphis* and *Gnat*; Force B—destroyers *Vampire*, *Vendetta*, *Voyager* and *Waterhen*; Force C—battleships *Barham* and *Malaya*, one cruiser and seven destroyers. Force D—carrier *Eagle*, three cruisers and three destroyers. These units, particularly Forces A and B, carry out many shellings of Italian positions and supply routes on the coast. From 13 Dec the Italian submarines *Naiade*, *Narvalo* and *Neghelli* are employed against them. On 13 Dec *Neghelli* (Lt-Cdr Ferracuti) torpedoes the cruiser *Coventry*. On 14 Dec *Naiade* is sunk by the British destroyers *Hereward* and *Hyperion*.

10 Dec   Mediterranean
OKW directive to transfer German Air Force units (FK X) to Southern Italy and Sicily.

11 Dec   General Situation
Operation 'Felix' (Conquest of Gibraltar) is played down by OKW directive after an attempt to persuade Spain to enter the war has failed.

12 Dec   Mediterranean
The British monitor *Terror* and the gunboats *Aphis* and *Ladybird* bombard Italian positions on the Egyptian frontier (repeated by *Aphis* on 17 Dec).

12–19 Dec   North Sea
Large mining operation by German Air Force in the Thames Estuary. 93 aircraft drop 183 mines on 12–13 Dec, 45 aircraft drop 89 mines on 13–14 Dec, and another 28 are dropped up to 19 Dec. 12 ships of 20675 tons sink on these barrages up to the end of Dec 1940.

12–21 Dec   Mediterranean
The Italian submarines *Ambra* and *Sciesa* operate SW of Corfu.

12–22 Dec   Red Sea
The Italian submarine *Archimede* operates twice without result against reported ship movements in the Red Sea.

13–18 Dec   North Atlantic
The Italian submarines *Bianchi* and *Brin* are transferred from Tangier to Bordeaux.

14 Dec   English Channel
The Free French torpedo boat *Branlebas* founders in heavy weather. The destroyer *Mistral* rescues three survivors.

14 Dec   Mediterranean
British air attack on Naples. The heavy cruiser *Pola* is damaged.

15 Dec   English Channel
The destroyer *Cameron* is damaged beyond repair in an air raid on Portsmonth.

15–16 Dec   North Sea
The German motor torpedo boat *S58* (Sub-Lt Geiger) sinks the Danish freighter *N C*

Monberg (2301 tons) in a British convoy E of Yarmouth.

16–24 Dec   Mediterranean
Operations MC.2 (bringing a convoy through to Malta) and MC.3 (attack in the Strait of Otranto) by the Mediterranean Fleet (Adm Cunningham). While the battleship *Malaya* with three destroyers forms the close escort for the four freighters of convoy MW.5, the Fleet sets out from Alexandria on 16 Dec with the battleships *Valiant* and *Warspite*, the carrier *Illustrious*, the cruisers *Gloucester* and *York* and 11 destroyers. It joins up with the cruisers operating in the Aegean and carries out attacks with aircraft from *Illustrious* on Italian airfields on Rhodes and Stampalia. During the night 18–19 Dec, *Valiant* and *Warspite* shell the Albanian port of Valona, while Vice-Adm Pridham-Wippell with the 7th Cruiser Sqn (cruisers *Ajax*, *Orion* and *Sydney* and destroyers *Janus*, *Jervis* and *Juno*) makes a sortie into the Strait of Otranto. On 20–22 Dec, Admiral Cunningham enters Malta with *Warspite*. *Malaya* proceeds westwards with three destroyers through the Sicilian Channel. Here the destroyer *Hyperion* is torpedoed by the Italian submarine *Serpente* (Lt Dotta) off Cape Bon on 22 Dec; an attempt by the destroyer *Ilex* to take her in tow fails and the ship has to be abandoned and sunk by the destroyer *Janus*. The force, to which two empty freighters from Malta also belong, is met S of Sardinia by Force H, comprising the battlecruiser *Renown*, the carrier *Ark Royal*, the cruiser *Sheffield* and six destroyers, which have set out from Gibraltar on 10 Dec. The carrier *Illustrious* attacks with her aircraft two convoys escorted by the Italian torpedo boats *Clio* and *Vega* on 21 Dec and sinks two steamers of 7437 tons from the second convoy. Of the Italian submarines *Dessiè*, *Serpente* and *Bandiera* operating in the Malta area, *Serpente* misses a destroyer of the *Malaya* force on 20 Dec.

17 Dec   English Channel
The British destroyer *Acheron* is sunk by minc off the Islc of Wight.

18 Dec   Mediterranean
The Italian cruisers *Eugenio di Savoia* and *Montecuccoli*, with the destroyers *Pigafetta*, *Da Recco*, *Pessagno* and *Riboty*, shell Greek positions and coastal batteries near Lukova, 30km N of the Corfu Channel.

18 Dec   South Atlantic
The heavy cruiser *Admiral Scheer* (Capt Krancke) captures the British refrigerator ship *Duquesa* (8651 tons) in the South Atlantic. On receipt of the distress signal, which is deliberately not interfered with, three British squadrons are deployed against the

cruiser: the cruisers *Dorsetshire* and *Neptune* from Freetown; the aircraft carrier *Hermes* with the cruiser *Dragon* and the auxiliary cruiser *Pretoria Castle* from St Helena; and Force K with the new aircraft carrier *Formidable* and the heavy cruiser *Norfolk* which is on the way to Freetown from Britain. The British search operations produce no results.

18–25 Dec   Mediterranean
Off the Cyrenaican coast, the Italian submarines *Malachite*, *Settembrini* and *Smeraldo* operate without success against the 'inshore fire support ships'.

18 Dec–1 Jan   Norway
The Dutch submarine *O23* operates off Korsfjord.

18 Dec–16 Jan   South Atlantic
The Vichy French submarines *Vengeur*, *Monge*, *Pégase* and *L'Espoir* are transferred from Dakar to Tamatave (Madagascar).

19 Dec–18 Jan   North Atlantic
The U-boats *U95*, *U124* and *U38* operate W of the North Channel, the Italian *Bagnolini* and *Tazzoli* further to the W. They encounter only independents. *U38* (Lt-Cdr Liebe) sinks with *Tazzoli* (Cdr Raccanelli) one ship of 4980 tons and on her own one of 3760 tons, *U95* (Lt-Cdr Schreiber) sinks one ship of 12823 tons, *U124* (Lt-Cdr Schulz) sinks one ship of 5965 tons and *Bagnolini* (Cdr Tosoni-Pittoni) sinks one ship of 3660 tons and misses the A/S trawler *Northern Pride* on 1 Jan.

20–22 Dec   Air War/Britain
Two night attacks by the Luftwaffe with about 200 aircraft on Liverpool. In the harbour 19 merchant ships totalling 121678 tons are badly damaged and one ship of 1293 tons is sunk.

21–22 Dec   English Channel
The minelayers *Roland* (Capt Bentlage), *Cobra*, *Kaiser* and *Skagerrak*, escorted by the 5th TB Flotilla (Lt-Cdr Neuss) with the torpedo boats *Greif*, *Falke* and *Seeadler*, depart from Rotterdam to lay the mine barrage 'SWa Wagner' in the Channel.

21–30 Dec   Mediterranean
The Italian submarines *Da Procida*, *Jalea* and *Salpa* are stationed in the Strait of Otranto against British raids. *Onice* and *Zaffiro* operate in the Aegean. *Zoea* carries out a transport mission from Taranto to Leros.

22–29 Dec   Mediterranean
Greek submarines are employed against Italian supply traffic to Albania. *Papanicolis* (Lt Iatrides) unsuccessfully attacks a convoy on 22 Dec and sinks one ship of 3952 tons on 24 Dec. *Proteus* (Lt-Cdr Hazikostantis) sinks the Italian transport *Sardegna* (11452 tons) in a convoy on 29 Dec but, in a counter-attack, is rammed and sunk by the

Italian torpedo boat *Antares*. The Greek submarine *Katsonis* (Sub-Lt Spanides) torpedoes on 31 Dec one small ship of 531 tons which becomes a total loss.

23–24 Dec English Channel

In an attack on the convoy FN.366, escorted by the destroyers *Wolsey* and *Verdun* and the corvette *Shearwater*, off the British South Coast by the 1st, 2nd and 3rd MTB Flotillas, consisting of *S26*, *S28*, *S29*, *S34*, *S54*, *S56*, *S57*, *S58*, *S59* and *S101*, *S59* (Lt Albert Müller) sinks the Dutch freighter *Stad Maastricht* (6552 tons) and *S28* (Lt Klug) the British trawler *Pelton* (358 tons).

23–30 Dec Red Sea

The Italian submarine *Ferraris* operates off Port Sudan.

24–28 Dec North Atlantic

The German heavy cruiser *Admiral Hipper* (Capt Meisel) encounters, about 700 nautical miles W of Cape Finisterre, the British troop convoy WS.5A (20 ships, including five provided for the Operation 'Excess') proceeding southwards. The convoy is escorted by the cruisers *Berwick*, *Bonaventure* and *Dunedin* and accompanied by the carriers *Argus* and *Furious* destined for Takoradi with aircraft cargoes. On the morning of 25 Dec there is a brief engagement between *Hipper* and *Berwick*, which receives two hits. In an attack on the convoy, the transport *Empire Trooper* (13994 tons) and another ship are damaged. Because of the strong escort and the state of *Hipper*'s engines, Meisel breaks off the engagement and heads for Brest. As he withdraws, one independent (6078 tons) is sunk. On 27 Dec the cruiser arrives in Brest. On the British side, the cruiser *Naiad*, relieved by the *Berwick* on 23 Dec, is again sent to the convoy, while the cruiser *Kenya* covers the two SL convoys and the battlecruiser *Repulse* with the cruiser *Nigeria* covers the North Atlantic convoys. Force H puts to sea from Gibraltar with the battlecruiser *Renown*, the carrier *Ark Royal*, the cruiser *Sheffield* and destroyers but suffers considerable damage in a heavy storm.

On 28 Dec *Bonaventure* intercepts the German blockade-runner *Baden* (8204 tons) coming from Tenerife and sinks her by torpedo as the weather is unsuitable for boarding.

27 Dec Pacific

The auxiliary cruiser *Schiff 45/Komet* (Capt Eyssen) shells the British island of Nauru (Pacific): phosphate loading equipment, oil tanks, etc are destroyed.

28 Dec–2 Jan Arctic

First attempt by the German battlecruisers *Gneisenau* and *Scharnhorst*, under the orders of the Fleet Cdr, Admiral Lütjens, to break out into the North Atlantic to undertake mercantile warfare operations there. The operation has to be abandoned off Norway because of storm damage to *Gneisenau*.

31 Dec–7 Jan Mediterranean

The Italian submarine *Dagabur* operates off the Cyrenaican coast.

1941

1 Jan   Mediterranean
Five British destroyers stop a French convoy of four ships escorted by an armed trawler off Oran, after it has previously passed through the Straits of Gibraltar. The ships are captured. The destroyers *Jaguar* and *Duncan* fire a machine-gun burst near the passenger ship *Chantilly*, which, in the cross-fire, sustains two dead and four wounded.

1–12 Jan   Mediterranean
In the Eastern Mediterranean, the Italian submarines *Turchese*, *Ambra* and *Corridoni* operate in the Strait of Otranto, *Galatea* and *Tembien* off Derna and *Beilul* and *Delfino* in the Aegean. None of the boats meets with any success.

1–18 Jan   North Atlantic
The German U-boats *U38* and *U124* operate W of the North Channel and the Italian *Nani*, *Da Vinci* and *Glauco* W of that. In trying to attack a convoy on 7 Jan, *Nani* is sunk by the British corvette *Anemone* escorting convoy HX.99.

1–20 Jan   Central Atlantic
In operations in the area of the Azores and Canaries, the Italian submarine *Cappellini* (Cdr Todaro) sinks two ships of 14051 tons in gun engagements.

2–3 Jan   Mediterranean
British attack on Bardia, which is encircled. After harassing fire from the British monitor *Terror* and several gunboats on 2 Jan, Admiral Cunningham carries out a heavy coastal bombardment early on 3 Jan with the battleships *Warspite*, *Valiant* and *Barham* and seven destroyers, while aircraft from the *Illustrious* act as artillery spotters. On 5 Jan the remains of the Italian garrison capitulate.

4–5 Jan   Air War/Western Europe
54 aircraft of RAF Bomber Command attack German warships in Brest.

5 Jan   North Sea
The German patrol vessel *V306/Fritz Hinke* is sunk by mine near Ymuiden.

5–15 Jan   Mediterranean
The large British submarines of the 1st SM Flotilla (Capt Raw) stationed in Alexandria, operate, sometimes with short stays in Malta, in the Western and Central Medi-

terranean and against the Italian supply route between Tripoli and Benghazi. The Greek submarines operate off the Albanian/Greek coast in the Ionian Sea.
On 7 Jan the Free French submarine *Narval* is sunk off Tobruk by the Italian torpedo boat *Clio*. On 9 Jan *Pandora* (Lt-Cdr Linton) sinks two ships of 8115 tons off Sardinia and *Parthian* (Lt-Cdr Rimington) one of 4208 tons off Calabria. On 15 Jan *Regent* (Lt-Cdr Browne) sinks the steamer *Città di Messina* (2472 tons), accompanied by the torpedo boat *Centauro*, off Benghazi. The first missions of the newly formed 10th SM Flotilla (Cdr Simpson) with *Upright* and *Ursula*, operating from Malta on the Trapani–Tripoli route, prove to be unsuccessful.

6 Jan   Mediterranean
The Italian 9th DD Flotilla, consisting of *Alfieri*, *Carducci*, *Fulmine* and *Gioberti*, and the 14th TB Flotilla, comprising *Partenope*, *Pallade*, *Andromeda* and *Altair*, shell Greek positions on the front in Albania.

6–13 Jan   Mediterranean
Operation 'Excess': convoy operations to Malta and Piraeus. On 6 Jan the convoy 'Excess' (Operation MC.4), with the motor ship *Essex* (11063 tons), carrying 4000 tons of ammunition, 3000 tons of seed potatoes and 12 Hurricane fighters for Malta and the freighters *Clan Cumming*, *Clan MacDonald* and *Empire Song* for Piraeus, set out from Gibraltar. Escort is provided by Force F comprising the cruiser *Bonaventure* and the destroyers *Jaguar*, *Hereward*, *Hasty* and *Hero*. Cover as far as the Skerki Channel is provided by Force H, consisting of *Malaya* and *Renown*, the carrier *Ark Royal*, the cruiser *Sheffield* and the destroyers *Faulknor*, *Fury*, *Forester*, *Fortune* and *Firedrake* which set out on 7 Jan.
Force B (Rear-Adm Renouf) puts to sea from the Aegean on 7 Jan with the cruisers *Gloucester* and *Southampton* (with 500 troops for Malta on board) and the destroyers *Ilex* and *Janus* which are to meet the convoy. In addition, Force A (Adm Cunningham), comprising the battleships *Valiant* and *Warspite*, the carrier *Illustrious* and the destroyers *Jervis*, *Nubian*, *Mohawk*, *Dainty*, *Greyhound*, *Griffin* and *Gallant* (and later *Juno*), puts to sea from Alexandria to cover the operation. The cruisers *Orion* and

York with the tanker *Brambleleaf* and the corvettes *Peony*, *Gloxinia*, *Hyacinth* and *Salvia*, coming from Alexandria, join the cruisers *Ajax* and *Perth* (RAN) in Suda Bay to form Force D (Vice-Adm Pridham-Wippell). The convoy MW.5, with the freighters *Breconshire* (9776 tons) and *Clan Macaulay* (10492 tons), sets out from Alexandria, escorted by Force C, comprising the AA cruiser *Calcutta* and the destroyers *Defender* and *Diamond*, joined later by the four corvettes. Force A is located in the afternoon of 7 Jan by Italian air reconnaissance. The submarines *Aradam* and *Axum* do not approach.

On 8 Jan Force B lands the embarked troops in Malta and proceeds to sea westwards to meet the convoy 'Excess.' The Australian cruiser *Sydney* sets out with the destroyer *Stuart* in an eastward direction.

On 9 Jan Force A and Force D and *Sydney* meet 210 nautical miles SE of Malta. Force H and the 'Excess' convoy are discovered by Italian reconnaissance aircraft 100 nautical miles SW of Cape Spartivento. Attacks by 10 Italian SM 79 bombers are not successful. In the afternoon Force H leaves the 'Excess' convoy with Force F and Force B to proceed through the Central Mediterranean and then turns off to the W. The Italian submarines *Bandiera* and *Santarosa* do not approach.

On 10 Jan the Italian torpedo boats *Circe* (Cdr Caputi) and *Vega* (Cdr Fontana) attack 'Excess' with torpedoes S of Pantelleria but are repulsed. *Vega* is sunk by the fire of the cruiser *Bonaventure* and finished off by a torpedo from the destroyer *Hereward*. The Italian submarine *Settimo* misses the British ships with a salvo of torpedoes. The destroyer *Gallant* of Force A runs on a mine and is towed to Malta by the destroyer *Mohawk*. In heavy German and Italian air attacks on Force A, Ju 87s of I/StG 1 (Capt Hozzel) and II/StG 2 (Maj Enneccerus) obtain six heavy bomb hits on the carrier *Illustrious* and one light hit on the battleship *Warspite*. *Illustrious* has to put into Malta badly damaged.

On 11 Jan Force B leaves Malta again and then runs into new air attacks. Ju 87s of II/StG 2 obtain a hit on the *Gloucester* (unexploded) and damage *Southampton* so severely that she has to be abandoned in the evening. Force H reaches Gibraltar.

On 12 Jan the cruisers *Orion*, *Perth* and *Gloucester* with their destroyers meet Force A, W of Crete, and another force (Rear-Adm Rawlings) which has set out from Alexandria and consists of the battleship *Barham*, the carrier *Eagle*, the cruiser *Ajax* and destroyers. Rear-Adm Rawling's group is to carry out a raid in the Dodecanese but abandons this plan owing to bad weather. Between 14 and 18 Jan the units of the British Mediterranean Fleet return to Alexandria.

6–29 Jan South Atlantic
On her way through the Atlantic, the auxiliary cruiser *Schiff 41/Kormoran* (Cdr Detmers) sinks four ships of 28399 tons including an aircraft transport and the refrigerator ship *Afric Star* (11900 tons). Search operations by the heavy cruisers *Devonshire* and *Norfolk* and the auxiliary cruiser *Arawa* have no success.

7–8 Jan English Channel
Unsuccessful sortie by German motor torpedo boats against a British convoy off the Thames Estuary. Offensive mining operation 'Renate' by the torpedo boats *Kondor* and *Wolf* off Dover; on the return *Wolf* (Lt Peters†) is sunk by a mine, laid by RN motor launches, off Dunkirk.

7–8 Jan Mediterranean
During the night 7–8 Jan the Italian destroyers *Vivaldi*, *Malocello*, *Da Noli* and *Tarigo* and the torpedo boats *Sagittario* and *Vega* lay the mine barrages X2 and X3 each with 180 mines N of Cape Bon.

7 Jan–4 Feb North Atlantic
On 7 Jan I/KG 40, with Fw 200 Condor long-range reconnaissance aircraft, is put under the operational command of the Commander U-boats, the first joint operations by U-boats and air reconnaissance. *U105*, *U94*, *U96* and *U93* operate W of the North Channel and Ireland; *U106* is detached as a weather boat; and W of the German boats are the Italian *Malaspina*, *Marcello* and *Torelli*. An Fw 200 sinks one ship on 8 Jan while on a reconnaissance flight. On 11 Jan an Fw 200 sights an OG convoy but the U-boats are unfavourably placed for action and only one steamer is sunk. On 14 Jan *U105* sights an outbound convoy but the attempt to direct two Fw 200s to the scene with D/F bearings fails. However, on 15–16 Jan *Torelli* approaches the convoy and sinks three ships. On 16 Jan an Fw 200 sights an outbound convoy: two steamers are sunk with bombs. *U96*, *U94*, *U106* and *U93* are deployed but do not come up; *U96* sinks the large passenger steamers *Oropesa* and *Almeda Star* sailing on their own and *U106*

sinks the passenger motor ship *Zealandic*. On 20 Jan Fw 200s sight two homebound convoys and the only U-boat in the area, *U105*, sights an outbound convoy, but no successes are achieved. From 21 to 23 Jan the Fw 200s engaged in air reconnaissance sink seven ships. On 28 Jan a large reconnaissance operation is undertaken with five machines when an outbound convoy is found, from which each Fw 200 sinks or damages two ships. Of the U-boats *U94*, *U103*, *U52*, *U93*, *U101* and *U106* engaged, *U93* sights the convoy SC.19 on 29 Jan and sinks three of its ships; of the U-boats which are directed at once to the target, *U94* and *U106* come up and each sinks one ship.

In all, the following ships, inclusive of independents, are sunk in these operations: I/KG 40 sinks 15 ships of 57770 tons, damages two which are sunk by U-boats and also damages three of 11593 tons. *U105* (Lt-Cdr Schewe) sinks one ship of 4843 tons and sinks one of 6516 tons damaged from the air, *U94* (Lt-Cdr Kuppisch) sinks three ships of 12652 tons, *U96* (Lt-Cdr Lehmann-Willenbrock) sinks two ships of 29053 tons, *U106* (Lt-Cdr Oesten) sinks two ships of 13540 tons, *U93* (Lt-Cdr Korth) sinks three ships of 20283 tons and one ship of 2660 tons damaged from the air, *Torelli* (Cdr* Langobardo) sinks four ships of 17489 tons and *Marcello* (Cdr Teppati) sinks one ship of 1550 tons.

8–9 Jan Mediterranean
British Wellington bombers attack Naples. The battleship *Giulio Cesare*, which is lying in harbour, springs leaks after three near-misses. Then *Cesare* and the last undamaged battleship, *Vittorio Veneto*, sail to La Spezia.

9 Jan General Situation
Final abandonment of proposed operation 'Felix' (capture of Gibraltar).

9 Jan Mediterranean
Renewed shelling of Porto Palermo (Albania) by the Italian destroyers *Ascari*, *Carabiniere*, *Folgore* and *Fulmine*.

10–11 Jan Air War/Britain
Heavy German air attack on Portsmouth Harbour.

11 Jan General Situation
Hitler's directive No 22: German forces are to help in the fighting in the Mediterranean. *Inter alia*, it orders the establishment of a German armoured defence force for Libya and its transportation to Tripoli from about 20 Feb.

12 Jan North Atlantic
A troop convoy (WS.5B) leaves Britain for North Africa: 21 passenger ships of 418000 tons with 40000 troops on board, escorted by the battleship *Ramillies*, the cruisers

Australia, *Naiad* and *Phoebe* and 12 destroyers.

12–20 Jan Mediterranean
In the Eastern Mediterranean, the Italian submarine *Smeraldo* operates E of Malta, *Menotti* and *Speri* off the Strait of Otranto, *Serpente* off Derna and *Narvalo* and *Neghelli* (Lt-Cdr Ferracuti) in the Aegean. The last torpedoes on 19 Jan the transport *Clan Cumming* (7264 tons) in a British Piraeus convoy and is then sunk with depth charges from the escorting destroyer *Greyhound*.

12–30 Jan Norway
Among other boats in the British 9th SM Flotilla to operate off Norway are the Dutch *O21* and *O23*.

14–15 Jan South Atlantic
The auxiliary cruiser *Schiff 33/Pinguin* captures in the Antarctic the Norwegian whale-oil factory ships *Ole Wegger* (12201 tons), *Pelagos* (12083 tons) and *Solglimt* (12246 tons) and 11 whalers of 3417 tons. Except for three whalers, all ships reach Western France in Mar 1941, the factory ships with 22200 tons of whale oil on board.

15–16 Jan Air War/Germany
76 bombers of the RAF attack Wilhelmshaven.

16 Jan Mediterranean
Air attack by FK X on Malta: the cruiser *Perth* and a freighter are damaged and the aircraft carrier *Illustrious* is again hit several times.

16 Jan–22 Feb North Atlantic
Unsuccessful operation by the Italian submarines *Glauco* and *Marconi* off Portugal.

17 Jan South China Sea
As a reprisal against Thai actions against Cambodia, a French naval force of the naval C-in-C Indo-China, Rear-Adm Terraux, comprising the light cruiser *Lamotte-Picquet* (Capt Béranger) and the gunboats *Dumont-d'Urville*, *Amiral Charner*, *Marne* and *Tahure*, attacks Thai warships in the roads of Koh-Chang in the Gulf of Siam. On the Thai side the small coastal defence ships *Dhonburi* and *Sri Ayuthia* and the torpedo boats *Trat*, *Cholbury* and *Songkhla*, with, in all, eight 20.3cm, eight 8cm and nine 7.6cm guns, engage the eight 15.5cm, eight 13.8cm, four 10cm, five 7.5cm and two 6.5cm guns on the French side. In a two-hour engagement the French squadron destroys, without loss to itself, *Cholbury*, *Dhonburi* and *Songkhla* and severely damages the remaining ships.

18 Jan Western Atlantic
The British auxiliary cruiser *Asturias* captures the Vichy French steamer *Mendoza* (8199 tons) NE of Puerto Rico.

18–20 Jan   South Atlantic
The heavy cruiser *Admiral Scheer* (Capt Krancke) captures three British merchant ships of 18738 tons in the South Atlantic.

19 Jan   Mediterranean
In a new attack by FK X on Malta, further hits are secured on the carrier *Illustrious*.

19 Jan   East Africa
Indian troops take Kassala and begin an offensive in Eritrea and Abyssinia.

21–22 Jan   Mediterranean
After the shelling of Tobruk and its military installations by the British monitor *Terror*, the gunboats *Aphis* and *Ladybird* and the Australian destroyers *Stuart*, *Vampire* and *Voyager*, the 6th Australian Div breaks into the fortress which is occupied on 22 Jan; 25000 Italian troops are taken prisoner. In the harbour the old cruiser *San Giorgio* is scuttled.

21–31 Jan   Mediterranean
The Italian submarines *Corallo* and *Diaspro* operate N of the Tunisian coast, *Colonna* and *Settimo* in the Eastern Mediterranean E of Malta, *Jalea* and *Millelire* off the Strait of Otranto and *Dessiè* and *Salpa* off Derna. No success.

22–30 Jan   North Atlantic
New attempt by the battlecruisers *Gneisenau* and *Scharnhorst* to break out into the Atlantic to take part in mercantile warfare (Operation 'Berlin'). On 22 Jan they leave Kiel. The report of their passing the Belt reaches London the next day. On 25–26 Jan the Home Fleet (Adm Tovey) sets out from Scapa with the battleships *Nelson* and *Rodney*, the battlecruiser *Repulse*, eight cruisers and 11 destroyers and takes up a position to intercept S of Iceland. On 27 Jan part of the Home Fleet leaves to refuel. On 28 Jan the German ships, in trying to break through S of Iceland, encounter two British cruisers of the watch line and turn away in time to the Arctic for replenishment. They are sighted briefly by the cruiser *Naiad* as they turn off but immediately afterwards she loses contact again.

23 Jan   North Sea
The Norwegian freighters lying in Gotenburg (Sweden), *Elizabeth Bakke* (5450 tons), *John Bakke* (4718 tons), *Tai Shan* (6962 tons) and *Taurus* (4767 tons), and the tanker *Ranja* (6355 tons), break through the German mine barrages in the Skagerrak under the leadership of Capt Binney and are met by cruisers of the Home Fleet. The ships only just avoid a chance meeting in the Kattegat with the German battlecruisers setting out for the operation 'Berlin'.

23–24 Jan   English Channel
Offensive mining operation 'SWb Wagner' off the northern entrance to the Channel in the latitude of Orfordness and Scheveningen with the minelayers *Roland*, (Capt Bentlage), *Cobra*, *Kaiser* and *Skagerrak*, escorted by the destroyer *Richard Beitzen* (Cdr v Davidson) and the torpedo boats *Iltis* (Lt-Cdr Jacobson) and *Seeadler* (Lt-Cdr Kohlauf).

23–25 Jan   Mediterranean
The aircraft carrier *Illustrious* (Capt Boyd), which has been hit several times in air attacks, gets away from Malta to Alexandria after the dockyards in Malta have done emergency repairs sufficient to allow the ship to do 24 knots again. The ship then goes to Norfolk, USA, for repairs.

24 Jan–2 Feb   Indian Ocean
The auxiliary cruiser *Schiff 16/Atlantis* (Capt Rogge), off the Seychelles, sinks one freighter and captures two other ships totalling 17329 tons. The troop transport *Strathaird* (22281 tons), which is sighted, is not attacked and the freighter *Troilus* (7422 tons) escapes.

25 Jan–18 Feb   North Atlantic
The German U-boats *U103*, *U52*, *U101*, *U48*, *U107* and *U96* operate W of the North Channel and Ireland; *U123* is detached to the W as a weather boat; and further to the W are the Italian boats *Baracca*, *Dandolo* and *Morosini*. These last are relieved in the middle of Feb by a new group consisting of *Bianchi*, *Otaria*, *Marcello* and *Barbarigo*. On 3 Feb *U107* sights the convoy OB.279 but *U123*, *U52*, *U96* and *U103*, which are ordered to the scene, do not get there; *U107* sinks one ship from the convoy and one straggler. Up to 18 Feb the Fw 200s of I/KG 40, which are sent on reconnaissance, and the U-boats attack only independents and stragglers from convoys. The following ships are sunk: I/KG 40 (Maj Petersen) sinks three ships of 8793 tons and damages two of 15489 tons, *U123* (Lt-Cdr Moehle) sinks four ships of 22186 tons, *U103* (Cdr Schütze) sinks three ships of 22948 tons and one of 10516 tons together with *U96*, *U52* (Lt-Cdr Salman) sinks two ships of 4662 tons, *U101* (Lt-Cdr Mengersen) sinks two ships of 10699 tons, *U48* (Lt-Cdr Schultze) sinks two ships of 8640 tons, *U96* (Lt-Cdr Lehmann-Willenbrock) sinks five ships of 31975 tons, one of 10516 tons with *U103* and one of 6999 tons with KG 40 and *U107* (Lt-Cdr Hessler) sinks four ships of 18482 tons including the ocean boarding vessel *Manistee* with the participation of *Bianchi* which does not, however, secure a torpedo hit. *Bianchi* (Cdr Giovannini) sinks three ships of 14705 tons and slightly damages one ship of 7603 tons with gunfire (see *U107* above; see also 19–26 Feb).

26–30 Jan   Norway
Minelaying group 'Nord' (Cdr* v Schönermark, comprising the minelayers *Tannenberg*, *Brummer*, *Königin Luise* and *Hansestadt Danzig*, carries out defensive mining operation '20 Pommern' from Stavanger, escorted by the torpedo boats *T12* and *Falke* and the minesweepers *M15* and *M22*, in the night of 26/27 Jan. During the next night the minelayers, escorted by the same ships but by the torpedo boat *T5* and *T9* instead of *Falke*, lay the barrage '21 Oder'.

27 Jan–3 Feb   Mediterranean
In operations by the first four boats of the 10th SM Flotilla against the Italian Trapani–Tripoli supply line, *Upholder* (Lt-Cdr Wanklyn) sinks one ship of 3950 tons on 27–28 Jan and torpedoes one steamer of 7389 tons from a convoy. On 30 Jan *Unique*, when attacking a convoy, is herself attacked by the escorting torpedo boat *Aldebaran* with depth charges.
The minelaying submarine *Rorqual* (Lt-Cdr Dewhurst) lays a barrage off Ancona on 28 Jan. In the Gulf of Sirte *Truant* sinks one ship of 1130 tons on 3 Feb and misses a convoy.

29 Jan   General Situation
Beginning of secret Anglo-American talks in Washington on joint conduct of war in the event of American entry.

29 Jan   Mediterranean
Seven He 111s of 2/KG 4 (Capt Kühl) drop mines in the Suez Canal.

31 Jan   General Situation
First preparatory directive drawn up by OKH for 'Barbarossa'.

31 Jan   Mediterranean
An He 111 of II/KG 26 (Maj Bertram) sinks off Marsa Matruk the British minesweeper *Huntley* (710 tons) and near Sidi Barrani the Egyptian transport *Solloum* (1290 tons) with 250 Italian prisoners of war.

31 Jan–4 Feb   Mediterranean
Unsuccessful operation by the British Gibraltar Squadron (Force H) against Sardinia. The Force, consisting of the battlecruiser *Renown* (flagship of Adm Somerville), the battleship *Malaya*, the aircraft carrier *Ark Royal*, the light cruiser *Sheffield* and ten destroyers, departs on 31 Jan. On 2 Feb torpedo aircraft from the carrier unsuccessfully attack the dam at Tirso (Sardinia) against a strong defence. A proposed attack on Genoa does not take place because of bad weather. On 4 Feb Force H returns to Gibraltar. The British Mediterranean Fleet sets out for a diversionary operation.
The submarines *Corallo*, *Manara*, *Santarosa* and *Tembien*, stationed S of Sardinia

49

and in the Malta area against a British sortie in the Central Mediterranean, do not find any targets.

1 Feb   North Atlantic

The heavy cruiser *Admiral Hipper* (Capt Meisel) leaves Brest for her second Atlantic operation.

1–10 Feb   Mediterranean

The Italian submarines *Turchese* and *Uarsciek* operate without success on the Greek/Albanian coast.

1–15 Feb   Norway

Operating off the Norwegian coast are the British *Sealion* (Cdr Bryant) of the British 9th SM Flotilla, which sinks the Norwegian coaster *Ryfylke* (1151 tons) on 5 Feb, and the Dutch *O21* and *O23* and the Free French *Minerve*.

1 Feb–15 Mar   Bay of Biscay

In operations in the Bay of Biscay, *Tigris* (Lt-Cdr Bone) sinks two ships of 3704 tons and *Snapper* is lost on a mine barrage. Among others, the submarines *Unbeaten*, *O21* and *O23* operate in the Bay of Biscay in the course of being transferred to Gibraltar.

2 Feb   Indian Ocean

The carrier *Formidable*, which is on the way to the Mediterranean to relieve the damaged *Illustrious*, mounts a raid on the harbour at Mogadishu (Italian Somaliland) together with the cruiser *Hawkins* (Force K). After mines are laid by aircraft, nine Albacore aircraft attack shore installations (Operation 'Breach'). At the same time the cruisers *Shropshire*, *Ceres* and *Colombo* blockade Kisimayu.

2–3 Feb   Red Sea

Unsuccessful attack on a British convoy in the Red Sea by the Italian destroyers *Pantera*, *Tigre* and *Leone* based on Massawa.

3–4 Feb   Norway

Mining operation '23 Rügen' by the mine-laying force, with *Tannenberg* and *Brummer*, off the Norwegian coast. Escort is provided by the 1st and 2nd TB Flotillas and *Falke*.

3–4 Feb   North Atlantic

The battlecruisers *Gneisenau* (Capt Fein) and *Scharnhorst* (Capt Hoffmann) pass through the Denmark Strait undetected by the enemy.

3–4 Feb   Mediterranean

Air mining operation by 2/KG 4 against Tobruk.

3–15 Feb   Mediterranean

Relatively unsuccessful activity by British submarines off the North African coast. On 3 Feb *Truant* (Lt-Cdr Haggard) sinks one freighter of 1130 tons from a convoy off Benghazi and on the following day unsuccessfully attacks an independent, on 11–12 Feb *Utmost* (Lt Cayley) attacks two outbound convoys off Tripoli and torpedoes

one steamer on 12 Feb and on 15 Feb *Upholder* (Lt-Cdr Wanklyn) unsuccessfully attacks an Italian convoy proceeding to Tripoli near Buerat.

5–6 Jan   North Sea

In a sortie by *S30*, *S54*, *S58* and *S59* of the 2nd MTB Flotilla, *S30* (Lt Feldt) sinks one British freighter (501 tons) between Ipswich and Newcastle.

5–7 Feb   Mediterranean

Large Italian convoys from Naples to Tripoli with the passenger ships *Esperia* (11398 tons), *Conte Rosso* (17879 tons), *Marco Polo* (12272 tons) and *Calitea* (4013 tons); escort is provided by the destroyers *Freccia*, *Saetta* and *Tarigo* and from 6 Feb by the light cruiser *Giovanni delle Bande Nere*. On 9–11 Feb the convoy returns with 5000 refugees on board.

6 Feb   General Situation

Hitler issues Directive No 23, covering principles guiding the conduct of operations against the British war economy.

6–11 Feb   Mediterranean

Attack on Genoa by Force H (Vice-Adm Somerville). On 6 Feb the Squadron leaves in three groups. Group 1: battlecruiser *Renown*, battleship *Malaya*, aircraft carrier *Ark Royal* and light cruiser *Sheffield*. Group 2: destroyers *Fearless*, *Foxhound*, *Foresight*, *Fury*, *Encounter* and *Jersey*. Group 3: destroyers *Duncan*, *Isis*, *Firedrake* and *Jupiter*. Groups 1 and 2 leave Gibraltar shortly after the convoy HG.53 on a westerly course, but they turn round in the night and pass eastwards through the Straits of Gibraltar. Group 3 carries out a submarine search E of the Straits and then joins the other two groups. On 8 Feb, on receipt of a report about British carrier aircraft S of the Balearics, Supermarina thinks a new supply convoy for Malta is under way, whereupon a strong Italian naval force sets out under Adm Iachino. This consists of the battleships *Vittorio Veneto*, *Andrea Doria* and *Giulio Cesare* and eight destroyers from La Spezia and the heavy cruisers *Trieste*, *Trento* and *Bolzano* and two destroyers from Messina to meet up on the morning of 9 Feb SW of Sardinia. Simultaneously, Genoa is shelled by *Renown*, *Malaya* and *Sheffield* with 273 15in, 782 6in and 400 4.5in shells. Of 55 ships in the harbour, four freighters and an old training vessel are sunk; 18 others receive slight damage from splinters and near misses and there are 144 dead. Severe damage in the city. The damaged battleship *Caio Duilio*, which is in dock, is not hit. The defensive fire of the Italian coastal batteries is unsuccessful because of poor visibility. The Italian fleet turns N when near the Straits of Bonifacio to intercept Force H.

Thick mist impedes visibility, with the result that the air reconnaissance provided cannot keep contact with the withdrawing British force. In addition, the reconnaissance aircraft are misled by a French convoy of six ships proceeding to Corsica, with the result that the Italian fleet misses the enemy. *Ark Royal* makes a raid on Livorno with four destroyers; her aircraft mine the harbour entrance of La Spezia.

On 11 Feb Force H returns to Gibraltar.

7–8 Feb   Mediterranean

German air attack on Malta.

8 Feb   North Atlantic

The battlecruisers *Gneisenau* and *Scharnhorst* sight the British convoy HX.106 E of Newfoundland but the Fleet Cdr, Adm Lütjens, does not attack when it is established that the convoy is escorted by the battleship *Ramillies*.

8–11 Feb   Mediterranean

First convoy of troops and supplies for the German Afrika Korps proceeds from Naples to Tripoli; it comprises the German freighters *Ankara* (4768 tons), *Arcturus* (2596 tons) and *Alicante* (2140 tons), escorted by the Italian destroyer *Turbine* and the torpedo boats *Orsa*, *Cantore* and *Missori*. From 8 to 10 Feb the convoy remains in Palermo because of Force H. On the return, an unsuccessful attack is made by British torpedo aircraft from Malta on 14 Feb.

8–12 Feb   North Atlantic

Operations against the convoys HG.53 and SLS.64. On the evening of 8 Feb *U37* (Lt-Cdr Clausen) sights HG.53 with 16 ships SW of Cape St Vincent. *U37* sinks two ships on 9 Feb and then, in accordance with orders, maintains contact and by providing bearings helps 2/KG 40 (Capt Fliegel) to approach. Around midday on 9 Feb it attacks with five Fw 200s and sinks five ships of 9201 tons. In a second approach, *U37* sinks a third ship on 10 Feb. The heavy cruiser *Admiral Hipper* (Capt Meisel) is directed to the scene by the reports from the contact-keeper, but on 11 Feb she finds only one straggler from the convoy, which has been meanwhile dispersed, and sinks her. In all, nine freighters of 15218 tons are sunk out of HG.53's 16 ships. During the night 11–12 Feb *Admiral Hipper* makes contact with the convoy SLS.64, consisting of 19 ships and still unescorted; in the morning of 12 Feb she sinks seven ships of 32806 tons and severely damages two more. On 15 Feb *Admiral Hipper* arrives in Brest.

9–18 Feb   Mediterranean

In the Eastern Mediterranean the Italian submarines *Speri* and *Topazio* operate off the Greek/Albanian coast, *Malachite* off

Cyrenaica and *Beilul* and *Sirena* in the Aegean—without success.

10–25 Feb   Indian Ocean

To support the British offensive against Italian Somaliland from Kenya, the C-in-C East Indies, Vice-Adm Leatham, forms Force T with the cruiser *Shropshire* (Capt Edelsten), the carrier *Hermes*, the old cruisers *Hawkins*, *Capetown* and *Ceres* and the destroyer *Kandahar*. They support the advance on land with their fire.

The German supply ship *Tannenfels* sets out from Kisimayu on 31 Jan. On 10–11 Feb eight Italian and two German merchant ships set out in an attempt to reach Mogadishu or Vichy French Diego Suarez. Three Italian ships of 16758 tons have to scuttle themselves on 12 Feb when British troops approach and occupy the town on 14 Feb with fire support from *Shropshire*. Of the ships which set out, five Italian vessels of 28055 tons are reported by *Hermes'* aircraft and are captured by *Hawkins*, the German *Uckermark* (7021 tons) scuttles herself and the German *Askari* (590 tons) and the Italian *Pensilvania* (6861 tons) are found off Mogadishu and destroyed by bombs and gunfire. Only the Italian *Duca degli Abruzzi* (2315 tons) and *Somalia* (2699 tons) reach Diego Suarez. On 25 Feb Mogadishu is occupied.

11–17 Feb   Mediterranean

In operations by the British 10th SM Flotilla E of the Tunisian coast, *Unique* misses a convoy escorted by the torpedo boat *Missori* on 11 Feb. *Utmost* (Lt-Cdr Cayley) torpedoes one ship of 5463 tons from a convoy escorted by the torpedo boat *Centauro*. *Upholder* misses on 16–17 Feb a convoy escorted by the torpedo boats *Cascino* and *Pilo*. From the 1st SM Flotilla, *Rover* torpedoes one ship of 6161 tons and *Triumph* (Lt-Cdr Wards) lands a commando unit on the Apulian Coast which is to destroy an important water main near Foggia.

12–13 Feb   General Situation

Mussolini and Franco meet in Bordighera and Franco and Pétain in Montpellier.

12–14 Feb   Mediterranean

Second convoy of the Afrika Korps from Naples to Tripoli with the German freighters *Adana* (4205 tons), *Aegina* (2447 tons), *Kybfels* (7764 tons) and *Ruhr* (5954 tons). Escort consists of the Italian destroyer *Camicia Nera* and torpedo boat *Procione*.

13 Feb–1 Mar   Red Sea

Operation 'Composition': raid on Massawa by the British carrier *Formidable* which is on the way to the Mediterranean. On 13 Feb 14 Albacore aircraft attack the harbour and destroy the Italian steamer *Moncalieri* (5723

tons). Slight damage is caused to warships and other merchant ships. On 21 Feb there is a second raid with seven Albacores used as dive-bombers but they do little damage. Because the Suez Canal is closed by German air mines, *Formidable* makes another raid from Port Sudan with five Albacores on 1 Mar. Slight damage.

14 Feb   Baltic

The Danish torpedo boat *Dragen* is lost, probably to a mine, in the Danish Narrows.

14 Feb–3 Mar   Indian Ocean

From 14 to 17 Feb the German pocket-battleship *Admiral Scheer*, the auxiliary cruiser *Schiff 16/Atlantis* with her prizes *Ketty Brovig* and *Speybank* and the supply ship *Tannenfels* meet some 1000 nautical miles E of Madagascar for replenishment and exchange of information. On 15 Feb the convoy WS.5B (20 troop transports, including 11 of 17000 to 27000 tons) sets out from Durban with the cruisers *Australia* and *Emerald*. On 21 Feb it is joined off Mombasa by the cruiser *Hawkins*, while *Emerald* turns off with four transports to Bombay. *Admiral Scheer* (Capt Krancke) has, in the meantime, advanced to the area of the Seychelles. There on 20 Feb she locates two merchant ships with her aircraft, takes the *British Advocate* (6994 tons) as a prize—she arrives in the Gironde on 29 Apr—and sinks the Greek *Grigorios C II* (2546 tons). The third ship, *Canadian Cruiser* (7178 tons), is able to transmit a distress signal before being sunk on 21 Feb. This is received by the cruiser *Glasgow*, stationed in the area, which also receives a signal from the Dutch steamer *Rantaupandjang* (2542 tons) sunk by *Scheer* on 22 Feb. When *Admiral Scheer* is sighted on 22 Feb by an aircraft from *Glasgow*, the British C-in-C East Indies, Vice-Adm Leatham, deploys from Mombasa the carrier *Hermes* and the cruiser *Capetown*, the cruisers *Emerald* and *Hawkins*, which are relieved by the *Enterprise*, from the convoy WS.5B and the cruiser *Shropshire* from the Somali coast. The Australian cruiser *Canberra*, relieved on 20 Feb off Colombo by the New Zealand cruiser *Leander* whilst with the convoy US.9 (three troop transports which left Fremantle on 12 Feb), is sent from the Maldives. Until 26 Feb the ships search in vain for *Admiral Scheer*, which turns away to the SE and reaches the South Atlantic again on 3 Mar. In the meantime, on 20–21 Feb the Italian auxiliary cruiser *Ramb I* (3667 tons) and the German supply ship *Coburg* (7400 tons) break out of Massawa. After being detached from the convoy US.9 off Bombay, the cruiser *Leander* (Capt Bevan) sights, on 27 Feb W of the Maldives, *Ramb I* (Lt-Cdr

Bonezzi) which, after a short engagement, explodes; 103 survivors are rescued. On 4 Mar an aircraft from *Canberra* (Capt Farncomb) sights, SE of the Seychelles, the *Coburg* with the prize tanker *Ketty Brovig* (7031 tons). Both ships scuttle themselves when approached by *Canberra* and *Leander*. The Italian colonial sloop *Eritrea* and auxiliary cruiser *Ramb II*, which set out from Massawa on 18 and 22 Feb respectively, reach Kobe on 22 Mar. The motor ship *Himalaya* (6240 tons), which sets out on 1 Mar, reaches Rio de Janeiro on 4 Apr.

18 Feb   Mediterranean

4/KG 4 drops mines in the Suez Canal. There is another mining operation during the night 22–23 Feb. Because of these and other mining operations, the canal has to be closed several times for a number of days. This leads to heavy delays in shipping traffic. Among other ships, the aircraft carrier *Formidable*, which is to replace the damaged *Illustrious* (see 6–13 Jan) is affected.

19 Feb   North Sea

Sortie by the 1st MTB Flotilla, consisting of *S28*, *S101* and *S102*, to the Thames Estuary. *S102* (Lt Töniges) sinks the British freighter *Algarve* (1355 tons).

19–22 Feb   North Atlantic

Operations against the convoy OB.287. On 19 Feb the convoy is sighted by an Fw 200 of I/KG 40, which sinks two ships of 11201 tons. *U73*, *U107*, *U48*, *U96*, *U69*, *Bianchi*, *Marcello* and *Barbarigo* are ordered to the reported position. On 20 Feb two Fw 200s again find the convoy and damage four ships, including a large tanker, totalling 18532 tons. But, because of inexact reports of the location, the submarines are unable to get to the convoy on this day. On 21 Feb an Fw 200 damages a tanker of 6999 tons which, later in the day, is sunk by *U96*. The submarine operation is then broken off. On 22 Feb an Fw 200 again succeeds in finding the convoy and in hitting an already damaged steamer. Total result: two ships of 18200 tons sunk and four ships of 18694 tons damaged. On 22 Feb *Marcello* is sunk by the escorting vessels, probably by the British destroyer *Montgomery*. The destroyer *Hurricane* and the corvette *Periwinkle* attack another submarine.

19–23 Feb   Mediterranean

The British Mediterranean Fleet brings the convoy MC.8 from Alexandria to Malta; at the same time there are convoys to Greece. The Italian submarine *Dagabur*, stationed SE of Malta, does not see the forces.

19 Feb–6 Mar   Mediterranean

In the Eastern Mediterreanean, the Italian submarines *Menotti* and *Turchese* operate off the Greek/Albanian coast; *Settimo* E of Malta and *Ambra* off Cyrenaica, but without success. The submarines *Micca* and *Zoea* bring supplies from Tobruk to Leros.

21–22 Feb   Air War/Germany
RAF Bomber Command attacks Wilhelmshaven.

21–25 Feb   Mediterranean
The British submarine *Regent* (Lt-Cdr Browne) torpedoes one steamer of 5609 tons in a convoy of two German steamers and the Italian destroyers *Freccia*, *Saetta* and *Turbine*. The torpedoed ship is taken in tow by *Saetta*. On the next day a convoy with two Italian steamers and the torpedo boat *Montanari* approaching from the N is attacked near Kerkennah by the British submarine *Ursula* (Lt Ward), which torpedoes one ship of 5788 tons. The second ship is later sunk off Tripoli by *Regent*. On 24–25 Feb *Unique* and *Upright* miss convoys. On the Greek/Albanian coast the Greek submarines *Nereus* (Lt-Cdr Rotas) and *Papanicolis* (Lt Iatrides) report successes.

22 Feb   Mediterranean
Ju 88s of II/LG 1 damage with bomb hits the British monitor *Terror* in Benghazi harbour. She sinks off Derna on 23 Feb in the course of an attempt to tow her to Alexandria.

22 Feb   North Atlantic
About 500 nautical miles E of Newfoundland, the battlecruisers *Gneisenau* and *Scharnhorst* sink five merchant ships totalling 25784 from a westbound convoy which has dispersed.

22–23 Feb   Norway
From Bergen, the minelayer group 'Nord', with *Brummer* (Cdr* v Schönermark), *Cobra* and *Königin Luise*, escorted by the 5th MS/Flotilla, lays the '23 Swine' barrage between the Shetlands and Korsfjord.

22–24 Feb   North Atlantic
Operations against the convoy OB.288. On 22 Feb an Fw 200 of I/KG 40 sights the convoy W of Ireland and damages two ships of 11249 tons. From a favourably situated patrol line consisting of *U73*, *U69*, *U96*, *U107*, *U552*, *U97*, *Barbarigo* and *Bianchi*, *U73* establishes contact a little later. After losing contact in the evening, a new patrol line, consisting of *U73*, *U96*, *U69*, *U123*, *Barbarigo* and *Bianchi*, is ordered. By day on 23 Feb *U96*, *U73* and *U69* approach. The convoy turns away to the N and the Fw 200s fly past. At midnight on 23–24 Feb *U96*, *U69* and *U95* attack at short intervals and sink first one and then two ships. In the morning of 24 Feb the convoy scatters: *U95*, *U96*, *Bianchi* and *U73* each sink one ship and *U96* and *U123* each another independent. In all, 10 ships of 52875 tons are

sunk. The following sinkings are made by these U-boats returning from this operation, apart from those already listed (see 25 Jan–18 Feb); *U73* (Lt-Cdr Rosenbaum) one ship of 4260 tons, *U69* (Lt-Cdr Metzler) three ships of 18576 tons and *U95* (Lt-Cdr Schreiber) five ships of 24910 tons, including two while she is employed later as a weather boat.

22 Feb–25 Apr   Central Atlantic
Southward move and first chapter in operations of a U-boat group in the area of Freetown. During the nights from 3 to 6 Mar the U-boats *U105*, *U106* and *U124* refuel in Las Palmas from the German tanker *Charlotte Schliemann*. From 7 to 8 Mar *U105* and *U124* operate against convoy SL.67 (qv), and then the three of them proceed in line abreast to Freetown. While *U105* and *U106* from 15 to 22 Mar locate the next convoy SL.68 and pursue it (qv), *U124* is replenished from the auxiliary cruiser *Schiff 41/Kormoran* (18 Mar) and then operates for about four weeks off Freetown, when seven ships are sunk. After the convoy operation, *U105* and *U106* go for replenishment from the supply ship *Nordmark* (28 Mar) but, before they can start their operations off Freetown, they are detached, after taking further replenishment from the *Nordmark* (7 Apr) in order to go to Rio de Janeiro, to meet the German blockade-runner *Lech* and to escort her through the Pan-American Security Zone. After two weeks *U105* is relieved of this task and goes to Freetown: *U106* meets the *Lech*. These two boats only operate off Freetown with the second wave (see 26 Apr). *U124* (Lt-Cdr Schulz) begins her return on 20 Apr, having expended all her torpedoes. Total result (inclusive of SL.67): 11 ships of 52397 tons sunk. An operation by the Italian submarine *Finzi* in the area of the Canaries (23 Mar–7 Apr) produces no result.

23 Feb–2 Mar   North Atlantic
Operations against the convoy OB.289. On 23 Feb *U552* sights the convoy and keeps contact for *U95*, *U97* and *U108* which are ordered to the scene. While *U552*, as a result of torpedo defects, has no success in two attacks, *U97* sinks three ships in three approaches during the night 23–24 Feb and torpedoes one tanker. *U552* maintains contact until 25 Feb, but *U95* does not come up before the convoy is dispersed.
Sinkings by the U-boats (some of which latter remain in the operational area until Mar), apart from those already mentioned: *U552* (Lt-Cdr Topp) sinks two ships of 12749 tons (one from convoy HX.109), *U97* (Lt-Cdr Heilmann) sinks three ships of

16761 tons and damages one of 9718 tons from convoy OB.289, *U108* (Lt-Cdr Scholtz) sinks two ships of 8078 tons, one from HX.109, and *U95* (Lt-Cdr Schreiber) sinks one ship of 6034 tons from HX.109.
At the same time *U147* (Lt-Cdr Hardegen) and *U46* (Lt Endrass) operate between the North Minch and the Faeroes. The former sinks one ship of 4811 tons from the convoy HX.109 on 2 Mar.

24 Feb   Mediterranean
Ju 88s of II/LG 1 sink the British destroyer *Dainty* off Tobruk.

24–26 Feb   North Atlantic
Operation against convoy OB.290. In the afternoon of 25 Feb *U47* (Lt-Cdr Prien), newly arrived in the operational area, sights the convoy but is driven off by an aircraft. She again comes up shortly before dark. In the night *U47* sinks three ships in three approaches and torpedoes a tanker. As a result of her contact reports, *U73*, *U97*, *Barbarigo* and *Bianchi* are ordered to the scene and, on 26 Feb, *U99* as well; but they do not come up. With the aid of bearings, *U47* leads one Fw 200 of I/KG 40 to the area at mid-day on 26 Feb, and five Fw 200s in the afternoon. They sink seven ships of 36250 tons from the dispersing convoy and damage another four of 20755 tons. This is the greatest single success registered by KG 40. A straggler of 6803 tons is sunk by *Bianchi*. On 28 Feb *U99* misses another straggler from the convoy OB.290 which *U47* then sinks. Total result: *U47* sinks four ships of 16310 tons and damages one of 8106 tons.

24–26 Feb   Mediterranean
Large convoy from Naples to Tripoli with the passenger ships *Esperia*, *Conte Rosso*, *Marco Polo* and *Victoria* (13098 tons). Escort is provided by the destroyers *Baleno* and *Camicia Nera* and the torpedo boat *Aldebaran*, with a covering force consisting of the light cruisers *Bande Nere* and *Diaz* with the destroyers *Ascari* and *Corazziere*. The British submarine *Upright* (Lt Norman) sinks the cruiser *Diaz* (Capt Mazzola) on 25 Feb.

25 Feb   North Sea
S30 (Lt Feldt) sinks the British escort destroyer *Exmoor* off Lowestoft.

25–26 Feb   English Channel
The torpedo boats *Iltis* (Lt-Cdr Jacobsen) and *Jaguar* (Lt-Cdr Hartenstein) carry out the mining operation 'Augsburg A' off Eastbourne.

25–26 Feb   Air War/Western Europe
RAF attack on Brest, in which Avro Manchester bombers are used for the first time.

25–27 Feb Mediterranean

The British destroyers *Decoy* and *Hereward* land 200 commando troops and navy personnel on the island of Castelorizo (East of Rhodes). The gunboat *Ladybird* puts a detachment of Royal Marines in the harbour. Slight Italian resistance. *Ladybird* is damaged by air attack. On the two following days the Italian destroyers *Crispi* and *Sella* and the torpedo boats *Lince* and *Lupo* are able to land reinforcements from Rhodes and with their gunfire are able with the garrison to overwhelm the British landing party. Elements get away in the night. The deployment of the submarine *Galatea* produces no result.

26–27 Feb North Sea

In a sortie by the 1st MTB Flotilla, *S28* (Lt-Cdr Klug) sinks the British freighter *Minorca* (1123 tons) off Cromer.

28 Feb Mediterranean

Air mining sortie by 2/KG 4 against Tobruk.

28 Feb–1 Mar Air War/Germany

British air attack on Wilhelmshaven.

1 Mar General Situation

Bulgaria joins the Three Power Pact.

1 Mar Atlantic

The US Navy forms a Support Force Atlantic Fleet (Rear-Adm Bristol Jr) consisting of three destroyer flotillas and flying boat squadrons for convoy protection in the North Atlantic: Desron 7 (Capt Kauffman)—destroyers *Plunkett*, *Niblack*, *Benson*, *Gleaves*, *Mayo*, *Madison*, *Lansdale*, *Hilary P Jones* and *Charles F Hughes*; Desron 30 (Capt Cohen)—*Dallas*, *Ellis*, *Cole*, *Bernadou*, *Dupont*, *Greer*, *Tarbell*, *Upshur* and *Lea*; and Desron 31 (Capt Baker)—*Macleish*, *Bainbridge*, *Overton*, *Sturtevant*, *Reuben James*, *McCormick*, *Broome*, *Simpson* and *Truxton*.

1–3 Mar Mediterranean

Supply convoy for the Afrika Korps from Naples to Tripoli comprising four steamers escorted by three torpedo boats, and, at the same time, a return convoy of five steamers with a destroyer and three torpedo boats. No losses.

1–4 Mar Indian Ocean/Atlantic

The last Italian submarines in the Red Sea set out from Massawa for Bordeaux via the Cape of Good Hope: *Perla* (Lt-Cdr Napp), *Archimede* (Cdr Salvatori), *Guglielmotti* (Cdr Spagone) and *Ferraris* (Cdr Piomarta). *Perla* is supplied in the Indian Ocean on 29 Mar by the German auxiliary cruiser *Schiff 16/Atlantis* (Capt Rogge), the other boats in the South Atlantic on 16 and 17 Apr by the fleet tanker *Nordmark*. All four boats reach Bordeaux between 7 and 20 May.

2–5 Mar North Atlantic

Operations against the convoy OB.292. An Fw 200 of I/KG 40 locates the convoy OB.292 and sinks one ship of 6533 tons. A patrol line consisting of the submarines *U70*, *U108*, *U552*, *U95*, *U99*, *U47*, *Barbarigo* and *Velella* is formed for 3 Mar and three Fw 200s are deployed, but the convoy is not found again. On 4 Mar an Fw 200 sights the convoy and a new patrol line consisting of *UA*, *U70*, *U47*, *U99*, *U95*, *U108*, *U552* and *Velella* is formed for 5 Mar; but the convoy avoids the line, which has been located by W/T interception.

2–17 Mar Mediterranean

The Italian submarines *Topazio* and *Uarsciek* operate off the Greek/Albanian coast and *Serpente* off Cyrenaica.

3–4 Mar Norway/Intelligence

Operation 'Claymore', a successful British raid on the Lofotens, organised partly to capture important cryptographic material. Taking part are the destroyers *Somali* (Capt Caslon), *Eskimo*, *Tartar*, *Legion* and *Bedouin* and the assault ships *Princess Beatrix* and *Queen Emma* with 500 commando troops on board; covering forces consist of the light cruisers *Edinburgh* and *Nigeria*. The fishery processing installations at Stamsund, Henningsvaer, Svolvaer and Brettesnes are destroyed and the merchant ships *Hamburg* (5470 tons), *Felix Neumann* (2468 tons), *Pasajes* (1996 tons), *Eilenau* (1404 tons), *Bernhard Schulte* (1058 tons), *Gumbinnen* (1381 tons) and *Mira* (1152 tons) are sunk, The Norwegian fishery vessel *Myrland* (321 tons) joins the British force. 213 Germans and 12 Norwegians are taken prisoner; 314 move voluntarily to Britain, providing a good cover story for the more important success—*Somali* puts the patrol vessel *NN04 Krebs* out of action and boards her, capturing codes which enable Bletchley Park to read the German 'Enigma-Heimische Gewässer' radio traffic for 13 to 23 Feb and for various dates from 20 Mar.

3–6 Mar Mediterranean

Supply convoy for the Afrika Korps from Naples to Tripoli: four freighters escorted by two destroyers and one torpedo boat. No losses.

5 Mar Mediterranean

The British submarine *Triumph* (Lt-Cdr Wards) sinks two ships of 1855 tons off Calabria.

5–6 Mar English Channel

Offensive mining operation 'Augsburg' by the torpedo boats *Iltis* and *Jaguar* off Eastbourne.

5–7 Mar Mediterranean

Return convoy from Tripoli to Naples: three freighters escorted by the auxiliary cruiser *Ramb III* and two torpedo boats. No losses.

5 Mar–2 Apr Mediterranean

Operation 'Lustre': transport of four British divisions from Alexandria to Greece. By 2 Apr 58000 are transported without significant loss. Air protection for the convoys is provided principally by the AA cruisers *Coventry*, *Calcutta* and *Carlisle*. In all, 25 ships of 115026 tons are lost in the operation, but mainly after unloading (only seven ships in convoys). The Italian submarines *Anfitrite*, *Ondina*, *Beilul*, *Galatea*, *Malachite*, *Smeraldo*, *Nereide*, *Ascianghi*, *Ambra*, *Dagabur* and *Onice*, which take their turns in the passage both sides of Crete and SE of the island, have no success against the convoys. *Anfitrite* is sunk on 6 Mar by the escorting destroyer *Greyhound* when she tries to attack the convoy GA.8 E of Crete. On 30 Mar *Dagabur* attacks a British cruiser force from which *Ambra* (Lt-Cdr Arillo) sinks the cruiser *Bonaventure* on 31 Mar.

6–7 Mar Norway

The minelayer group 'Nord', with *Brummer* (Cdr* v Schönermark), *Cobra* and *Königin Luise*, escorted by the 5th MS flotilla, lays the '24 Wollin' mine barrage 45 miles E of the Outer Skerries (Shetlands).

6–9 Mar North Atlantic

Operation against the convoy OB.293. In the evening of 6 Mar *U47* locates the convoy and leads *U70* and *U99* to it during the night 6–7 Mar but she is herself temporarily driven off. *U70* (Lt-Cdr Matz) torpedoes two ships of 13916 tons in the convoy but is then sunk by the corvettes *Arbutus* and *Camellia*. Shortly afterwards *U99* (Lt-Cdr Kretschmer) sinks one tanker of 6568 tons and torpedoes the whaling ship *Terje Viken* (20638 tons) which, later in the day, is finished off with further hits; but she survives as a wreck and only sinks finally on 14 Mar. In the evening of 7 Mar *UA* (Cdr Eckermann) makes contact but, after an attack which fails because of torpedo defects, is badly damaged by depth charges from escort vessels. *U37* does not approach. During the night 7–8 Mar *U47* (Cdr Prien†) again approaches but is surprised in a heavy squall by the destroyer *Wolverine* (Cdr Rowland) and is sunk with depth charges. During the night 8–9 Mar *U74* (Lt-Cdr Kentrat) sights, further to the N, a homebound convoy but has no success. *U99* and the Italian submarines *Emo*, *Mocenigo* and *Veniero*, which are ordered to the scene, do not come up on 9 Mar.

7–8 Mar North Sea

The 1st MTB Flotilla (Lt-Cdr Birnbacher), consisting of *S26*, *S39*, *S101* and *S102*, and the 3rd MTB Flotilla (Lt-Cdr Kemnade), consisting of *S31*, *S57*, *S59*, *S60* and *S61*, attack the British convoys FN.26 and FS.29, escorted by the corvettes *Sheldrake* and *Puffin*, off Cromer and Southwold. The 1st MTB Flotilla sinks five freighters of 7282 tons and the 3rd MTB Flotilla two freighters of 5852 tons, including *Boulderpool* (4805 tons) sunk by *S61* (Lt v Gernet).

7–10 Mar   Central Atlantic
Operations against convoy SL.67. In the morning of 7 Mar the German battlecruisers *Gneisenau* (Capt Fein) and *Scharnhorst* (Capt Hoffmann) sight the convoy some 300 nautical miles NE of the Cape Verde Islands. It is accompanied by the battleship *Malaya* and screened by the destroyers *Faulknor* and *Forester* and the corvette *Cecilia*. When he ascertains the presence of the battleship, Admiral Lütjens breaks off the attack on the convoy. On receipt of the contact report, the Commander U-boats orders *U105* (Lt-Cdr Schewe) and *U124* (Lt-Cdr Schulz), which are in the vicinity, to the scene. During the night 7–8 Mar they attack in turn and sink one ship of 5229 tons and four of 23259 tons respectively without, however, sighting *Malaya* which is sailing with the convoy. *U105* is forced to submerge by a depth charge pursuit until the afternoon of 8 Mar and *U124* is driven off, with the result that the battleships have to break off their operation. On 10 Mar the convoy is met by Force H.

8–12 Mar   Mediterranean
A German supply convoy (four freighters, escorted by three destroyers) from Naples to Tripoli and a return convoy experience no attacks.

9–10 Mar   Mediterranean
A German supply convoy for the Afrika Korps (four freighters, escorted by five destroyers and two torpedo boats), which had temporarily put in to Palermo, reaches Tripoli unmolested. An Italian convoy from Trapani to Tripoli, consisting of five ships and the torpedo boat *Papa*, is attacked off the Tunisian coast by the British submarines *Utmost* (Lt-Cdr Cayley) and *Unique* (Lt Collett), which each sink one ship of 5683 and 2584 tons respectively.

10–11 Mar   Air War/Western Europe
First operation by four-engined British Handley Page Halifax bombers against Le Havre (six aircraft of No 35 Sqn).

10–11 Mar   Norway
The minelayers *Königin Luise* and *Cobra*, escorted by the 5th MS flotilla, lay the '17a Pregel' mine barrage to finish the lengthening of the 'Westwall' barrages to the N.

10–17 Mar   North Atlantic
U99, *U37*, *U74*, *U110* and *U100*, as well as the Italian submarines *Velella*, *Brin*, *Argo*, *Mocenigo*, *Emo* and *Veniero*, operate NW of the North Channel.

In the evening of 15 Mar *U110* (Lt-Cdr Lemp) sights the homebound convoy HX.112, with 41 ships escorted by the 5th EG (Cdr Macintyre) consisting of the destroyers *Walker*, *Vanoc*, *Volunteer*, *Sardonyx* and *Scimitar* and the corvettes *Bluebell* and *Hydrangea*. *U99*, *U37*, *U100* and *U74* are ordered to the scene. During the night 15–16 Mar *U100* attacks twice and torpedoes one tanker of 6207 tons but is driven off towards morning. At mid-day on 16 Mar, *U37* (Lt-Cdr Clausen) approaches but is driven off in the evening, whilst *U100* (Lt-Cdr Schepke) and *U110* have also to withdraw in face of the destroyers *Scimitar*, *Vanoc* and *Walker*. During the night *U99* (Lt-Cdr Kretschmer) is able to penetrate the convoy and to sink, in several approaches, three tankers and two steamers of 34505 tons and to torpedo one tanker of 9314 tons. Whilst *U99* withdraws, having expended her torpedoes, *U100* approaches from the stern but is located by *Vanoc* at a distance of 1000m with the aid of radar (the first successful location with Type 286 equipment) and is rammed when she submerges. *Vanoc*, damaged in the bows, takes the survivors screened by *Walker*. *U99* observes the two destroyers and submerges, but she is located by asdic and is compelled to surface as a result of six depth charges from *Walker*. Six men from *U100* and Lt-Cdr Kretschmer and 39 men from *U99* are taken prisoner.
U110 follows the convoy until the next day but is not able to attack.

10–20 Mar   Norway
Among other boats, *Sturgeon*, *Sealion* and *Sunfish* of the 9th British SM Flotilla and also *Undaunted* and *Urchin* in 'working-up patrols' operate off Norway. They achieve no success.

11 Mar   General Situation
The American Lend-Lease Law comes into force on its signing by President Roosevelt.

11–12 Mar   Air War/Germany
The RAF attacks Kiel and Bremerhaven.

12–13 Mar   Air War/Germany
RAF Bomber Command attacks Hamburg and Bremen.

12–13 Mar   Mediterranean
Italian troop convoy from Naples to Tripoli, consisting of the passenger ships *Conte Rosso*, *Marco Polo* and *Victoria*. Close escort is provided by three destroyers, distant escort by the heavy cruisers *Trieste*, *Trento* and *Bolzano* with three destroyers and one

torpedo boat. No losses. At the same time a convoy pair for the Afrika Korps comes to Tripoli and returns to Italy without loss.

12–15 Mar   North Sea
S28 (Lt-Cdr Klug) sinks the British motor ship *Trevethoe* (5257 tons), from convoy FS.32, E of Orford Ness. Off Southwold, the destroyer *Worcester* drives off some E-boats approaching convoy FS.37. On 14–15 Mar the destroyer *Versatile*, with FS.35, avoids two E-boat torpedoes and the destroyers *Holderness* and *Vanessa* drive off the intruders.

13 Mar   Air War/Britain
Heavy German air attack on Liverpool: one ship of 5644 tons sunk and seven others of 45114 tons severely damaged.

15 Mar   South-West Pacific
First troop transport convoy from Australia to New Guinea and to the Bismarck Archipelago. On 15 Mar the convoy ZK.1 sets out with two coastal steamers and the escort ship *Manoora* from Brisbane to Port Moresby and Rabaul. In Apr, and from July to Sept, three more convoys follow, transporting 3373 troops.

15–16 Mar   North Atlantic
The battlecruisers *Gneisenau* (Capt Fein) and *Scharnhorst* (Capt Hoffmann) encounter in the Central North Atlantic the scattered ships of a dispersed convoy from Britain to America. *Gneisenau* sinks seven ships totalling 26693 tons and captures three tankers of 20139 tons, of which, however, only one is able to reach the Gironde on 24 Mar. At the same time *Scharnhorst* sinks six ships of 35080 tons. In rescuing the survivors of her last victim, *Gneisenau* is surprised by the British battleship *Rodney* employed in escorting the convoy HX.114, but, by skilful feinting, is able to avoid an engagement with the slower but better-armed opponent.

15–19 Mar   Mediterranean
In operations by the British 1st SM Flotilla, *Parthian* (Lt-Cdr Rimington) torpedoes one ship of 3141 tons on 16 Mar near Palmi and *Truant* (Lt-Cdr Haggard) penetrates the harbour of Buerat on 19 Mar but her torpedoes detonate by the pier behind the tanker *Labor*.

15–21 Mar   Central Atlantic
U-boat operations against the British convoy SL.68 off the West African coast. *U106* (Lt-Cdr Oesten) sights the convoy and leads *U105* (Lt-Cdr Schewe) to the scene. Taking turns to attack and maintain contact, the boats remain with the convoy for a week. *U105* sinks five ships of 27890 tons; *U106* sinks two ships of 10113 tons and, without herself at first noticing it, torpedoes during the night 19–20 Mar the

battleship *Malaya* employed in escorting the convoy.

15–28 Mar North Atlantic
The heavy cruiser *Admiral Hipper* (Capt Meisel) returns to Kiel from Brest. On 23 Mar she passes through the Denmark Strait unnoticed and on 28 Mar she arrives in Kiel. The cruiser's movements are unknown to the British Admiralty which, therefore, takes no special measures in the area of the Denmark Strait.

16 Mar Mediterranean
Two He 111 torpedo aircraft of FK X, in an armed reconnaissance flight, attack elements of the British Mediterranean Fleet 30 nautical miles W of Crete. They report torpedo hits on two large units, 'probably battleships'. This false report has serious consequences for Italian naval operations.

16 Mar Red Sea/East Africa
Operation 'Appearance': two Indian battalions and one Somali commando detachment are landed both sides of Berbera/Somaliland by Force D, comprising the cruisers *Glasgow* (Capt Hickling) and *Caledon*, the destroyers *Kandahar* and *Kipling*, the auxiliary cruisers *Chakdina* and *Chantala*, the Indian trawlers *Netravati* and *Parvati*, two transports and *ML109*. The town is taken against only slight Italian resistance, which is broken by naval gunfire.

16 Mar–9 Apr Mediterranean
The Italian submarines *Fisalia* and *Adua* relieve each other off the Greek/Albanian coast.

17 Mar North Sea
Action by escorts of convoy FN.33 off Lowestoft: the destroyers *Vesper*, *Cottesmore* and *Cattistock* drive off E-boats.

17–18 Mar Air War/Germany
The RAF attacks Bremen and Wilhelmshaven.

17–29 Mar North Atlantic
British operations against the German battlecruisers reported by *Rodney*. The Home Fleet tries to bring up *Rodney*, from the convoy HX.114, and *King George V*, sent to Newfoundland to cover HX.115, to *Nelson*, which is stationed with the cruiser *Nigeria* and two destroyers to cover the Iceland passages, where they patrol from 17 to 20 Mar. Force H sets out from Gibraltar with *Renown*, *Ark Royal*, *Sheffield* and destroyers. On 20 Mar reconnaissance aircraft from *Ark Royal* sight two of the tankers captured by *Gneisenau*—*Bianca* and *San Casimiro*—which have to scuttle themselves when they come within sight of Swordfish aircraft from *Ark Royal* and surface ships of Force H. In the afternoon on 20 Mar a Swordfish sights the two German battlecruisers but is only able to transmit its

report after some delay, with the result that an interception is no longer possible. *Gneisenau* and *Scharnhorst* are met on 22 Mar by the torpedo boats *Iltis* and *Jaguar* and by mine destructor ships and reach Brest. Force H continues to search after contact is lost and, after brief refuelling in Gibraltar on 24 Mar, returns to the waters SW of the Bay of Biscay until 28 Mar. British air reconnaissance does not report the German battlecruisers back in Brest before 28 Mar. Total result of mercantile warfare operation 'Berlin': 22 ships of 115622 tons sunk.

18 Mar Mediterranean
The Italian torpedo boat *Aldebaran* is sunk by British torpedo aircraft (No 815 Sqn FAA) off Valona.

18 Mar North Sea
Sortie by the 1st MTB Flotilla, comprising *S26*, *S29*, *S39*, *S55*, *S101* and *S102*, into the estuary of the Humber. *S102* (Lt Töniges) sinks the French freighter *Daphne II* (1970 tons) from convoy FN.34.

18–19 Mar Air War/Germany
Air attacks by the RAF on Kiel and Wilhelmshaven.

19–20 Mar Air War/Britain
370 German bombers attack London—the heaviest raid since 29 Dec 1940.

19–24 Mar North Atlantic
On 19 Mar an Fw 200 of I/KG 40 reports an outbound convoy W of Ireland, to which are directed *U46* and the Italian submarines *Brin*, *Mocenigo* and *Giuliani* (which is on the way to Gotenhafen). *U46* establishes contact and tries unsuccessfully to direct several Fw 200s to the scene but these, instead, find a homebound convoy in the area and sink one ship of 5193 tons and damage one tanker of 8245 tons. In addition, they sight NW of the Hebrides an outbound convoy, to which two Fw 200s from Bordeaux and one from Stavanger, as well as the U-boats *U110*, *U74* and *U98*, are unsuccessfully directed for 20 Mar. At mid-day on 21 Mar *U69* sights W of Southern Ireland a homebound convoy, against which *U48*, *Argo* and *Mocenigo* are deployed without success. On 23 Mar *U97* sights in the area the outbound convoy OG.56 and sinks one tanker; on the next day *U97* and *Veniero* each sink one ship from the dispersed convoy. On the way out on 23 Mar, *U551* is sunk by the British trawler *Vizalma* in the Iceland–Faeroes passage. Of the returning Italian submarines, *Emo* (Lt-Cdr Roselli-Lorenzini) has sunk one ship of 5759 tons and *Veniero* (Cdr Petroni) one ship of 2104 tons.

19–24 Mar Mediterranean
With distant escort from the British Mediterranean Fleet (three battleships, one air-

craft carrier and destroyers), the supply convoy MC.9 is brought to Malta without German and Italian air reconnaissance locating the forces. The Italian submarines *Malachite* and *Smeraldo*, stationed SE of Crete, do not sight the British forces.

22 Mar Bay of Biscay
Beginning of the massive British submarine concentrations off Brest to provide against a break-out by the German battlecruisers *Gneisenau* and *Scharnhorst*. In the following months *L27*, *Torbay*, *Tuna*, *Taku*, *L26*, *H31*, *H32*, *H33*, *H44*, *H50*, *O9* (Dutch), *O10* (Dutch), *Undaunted*, *Sokol* (Polish), *Sealion*, *Sturgeon*, *Sunfish* and *O24* (Dutch) participate.

23–31 Mar Mediterranean
Off Valona, the Greek submarine *Triton* (Lt Zepos) sinks one ship of 5451 tons in an Italian convoy accompanied by the torpedo boat *Castelfidardo*.

On 25 Mar the British minelaying submarine *Rorqual* (Lt-Cdr Dewhurst) lays a barrage near Capo Gallo W of Sicily, on which on 26 Mar two ships of 2902 tons from a convoy sink and on 28 Mar the torpedo boat *Chinotto*. *Rorqual* sinks with torpedoes one ship of 3645 tons on 30 Mar and the Italian submarine *Capponi* on 31 Mar. On 28 Mar *Utmost* (Lt-Cdr Cayley) attacks a Naples–Tripoli convoy of five ships, escorted by the destroyers *Folgore*, *Dardo* and *Strale*; she sinks one ship of 1927 tons and torpedoes one of 5954 tons.

23 Mar–1 Apr Red Sea
On 23 Mar the German-Italian steamers *Oder* (8516 tons) and *India* (6366 tons) set out from Massawa. The former is found by the British sloop *Shoreham* in the Straits of Perim and has to scuttle herself; the latter then puts in to Assab. In another attempt, *Bertrand Rickmers* (4188 tons), which sets out on 29 Mar, has to scuttle herself on 1 Apr in the presence of the destroyer *Kandahar*. *Piave*, which sets out on 30 Mar, also goes to Assab; and *Lichtenfels*, which puts to sea on 1 Apr, has to return.

25 Mar–5 Apr North Atlantic
On 25 Mar the submarines *U48*, *U98*, *U69*, *U46*, *U74* and *U97* are gathered in a new concentration S of Iceland to operate with air reconnaissance on convoys, but the Fw 200s of I/KG 40 only find single ships, and no convoys, up to 28 Mar. They sink three ships totalling 19982 tons and damage the passenger motor ship *Staffordshire* (10683 tons). *U98* sinks an independent. On 29 Mar *U48* sights the homebound convoy HX.115 with eight escort vessels and sinks two of the ships. *U98* does not approach. An Fw 200 sights an outbound convoy, which is found again on 30 Mar, but *U73* and *U97*

do not come up. The convoy OB.302, sighted by *U69*, is shadowed on 29–30 Mar by *U46* and *U69*, each of which sink one ship. The attempt to direct *U73*, *U97* and *U101* also to the convoy OB.302, located on 31 Mar by two Fw 200s, fails. *U46* sinks one tanker. A patrol line is formed for 2 Apr consisting of *U46*, *U98*, *U101*, *U69*, *U73*, *U97*, *U74* and *U76* against an outbound convoy reported by *U76* S of Iceland on 1 Apr. SC.26 runs into this patrol line in the evening. *U74* leads *U46*, *U69* and *U73* to the scene in the night and by morning they sink six ships of 33615 tons and damage the auxiliary cruiser *Worcestershire* (11402 tons)—the latter effected by *U74*. One of the partly scattered ships is sunk by day on 3 Apr by *U76*. In the evening *U94* re-establishes contact with the main body of the convoy and directs *U98* to the scene. Together they sink three more ships in the night totalling 13303 tons. On 4 Apr *U98*, *U101* and *U76* continue the operation but only the latter fires another torpedo in the afternoon and sinks one ship. She is, however, herself sunk towards the morning of 5 Apr by the destroyer *Wolverine* (Cdr Rowland) and the sloop *Scarborough*. In their operations since the HX.112 convoy, the U-boats have made the following sinkings: *U110* (Lt-Cdr Lemp) damages two ships of 8675 tons, *U98* (Lt-Cdr Gysae) sinks four ships of 15588 tons, *U48* (Lt-Cdr Schultze) sinks five ships of 27256 tons, *U97* (Lt-Cdr Heilmann) sinks three ships of 20510 tons, *U94* (Lt-Cdr Kuppisch) sinks two ships of 10994 tons; *U76* (Lt v Hippel) sinks two ships of 7290 tons and *U74* (Lt-Cdr Kentrat) sinks three ships of 15407 tons with *U73* (Lt-Cdr Rosenbaum) in a simultaneous attack on SC.26. *U73* also sinks one tanker of 6895 tons with *U69* (Lt-Cdr Metzler) and one ship of 4313 tons with *U46* (Lt Endrass); in addition, *U46* sinks on her own one tanker of 7000 tons and *U69* one ship of 3759 tons.

26 Mar   Mediterranean
The Italian destroyers *Crispi* and *Sella*, coming from Leros, disembark six explosive boats (Lt-Cdr Faggioni) off Suda Bay (Crete). The boats penetrate unseen into the bay, sink the Norwegian tanker *Pericles* (8324 tons) and put the British heavy cruiser *York* out of action.

26–27 Mar   North Atlantic
The pocket-battleship *Admiral Scheer* (Capt Krancke) breaks through the Denmark Strait on her way home and, unnoticed by the enemy, evades the British light cruisers *Fiji* and *Nigeria*. On 30 Mar *Scheer* reaches the area off Bergen, anchors for a day in Grimstadfjord and, with destroyer escort,

reaches Kiel on 1 Apr. Total result of the mercantile warfare operation: 17 ships of 113233 tons.

26–29 Mar   Mediterranean
Battle of Cape Matapan. On 26 Mar, at the wish of the Germans and on the basis of a faulty appreciation of the situation (see 16 Mar), the Italian Fleet puts to sea in order to attack British convoys to Greece under air cover to be provided by the German Fliegerkorps X. Taking part are the battleship *Vittorio Veneto* (Capt Sparzani), as flagship of the Fleet with Adm Iachino on board, and 13th DD Flotilla with the destroyers *Alpino*, *Bersagliere*, *Fuciliere* and *Granatiere* from Naples; the 1st Div (Div Adm Cattaneo), comprising the heavy cruisers *Zara*, *Pola* and *Fiume* and the 9th DD Flotilla with the destroyers *Gioberti*, *Alfieri*, *Oriani* and *Carducci* from Taranto; the 8th Div (Div Adm Legnani), comprising the light cruisers *Duca degli Abruzzi* and *Garibaldi* and the 16th DD Flotilla with the destroyers *Da Recco* and *Pessagno* from Brindisi; and the 3rd Div (Div Adm Sansonetti), comprising the heavy cruisers *Trieste*, *Trento* and *Bolzano* and the 12th DD Flotilla with the destroyers *Corazziere*, *Carabiniere* and *Ascari* from Messina.

At Bletchley Park, the British decode two Italian messages from Rome to Rhodes, transmitted in the Italian 'Alfa' version of 'Enigma', and a German signal to Fliegerkorps X, transmitted in the 'Light Blue' code, indicating an operation in the area of Crete. This leads Cunningham to dispose his forces accordingly in great secrecy. On 27 Mar, the Italian divisions meet S of the Straits of Messina. The British cruiser squadron (Vice-Adm Pridham-Wippell) sets out as Force B, consisting of the light cruisers *Orion*, *Ajax*, *Perth* and *Gloucester* and the 2nd DD Flotilla (Capt Nicolson) comprising *Ilex*, *Hasty*, *Vendetta* and *Hereward* from Piraeus; and Force A (Adm Cunningham), consisting of the battleships *Warspite*, *Barham* (with the Commander 1st BB Sqn, Rear-Adm Rawlings) and *Valiant*, the aircraft carrier *Formidable* with the Commander Mediterranean Carriers (Rear-Adm Boyd) on board and the 14th DD Flotilla (Capt Mack) comprising *Jervis*, *Janus*, *Mohawk* and *Nubian*. Detached later is Force C, consisting of the 14th DD Flotilla (Capt Waller RAN) with *Stuart*, *Greyhound*, *Griffin*, *Hotspur* and *Havock* from Alexandria.

Around mid-day British reconnaissance planes locate the Italian fleet. There is no sign of the German air cover. Adm Iachino, therefore, abandons his plans to force his way into the Aegean because he can no

longer count on the enemy being surprised. In the morning of 28 Mar, Italian naval aircraft locate Force B. A pursuit engagement which starts between the British cruiser squadron and the 3rd Div is broken off on the orders of the Fleet Commander. The British cruisers now take up the pursuit themselves and come between the 3rd Div and *Vittorio Veneto*, but they are able, with the support of six torpedo aircraft from *Formidable*, to break loose from the enemy. At mid-day the Italian Fleet returns and makes for Taranto. In the afternoon Swordfish torpedo aircraft from *Formidable* and bombers stationed on Crete attack the Italians and score a torpedo hit on both *Vittorio Veneto* and *Pola*. The battleship is able to continue on her course, but the cruiser is brought to a standstill and is rendered unmanoeuvrable. In the evening Iachino sends the remaining ships of the 1st Div to support *Pola*. This group and Force A arrive almost simultaneously in the vicinity of *Pola*. Here the British locate the Italian ships by optical means but in the action, thanks to the radar location of *Ajax* and *Warspite*, obtain a clearer picture of the situation than the Italians, who can hardly see in the dark. In the ensuing engagement, the British battleships annihilate the Italian division at short range. *Fiume* (Capt Giorgis†), *Zara* (Capt Corsi†) and the destroyers *Alfieri* and *Carducci* sink; *Oriani* gets away damaged and only *Gioberti* is not hit. The half-abandoned cruiser *Pola* (Capt Pisa), after the remaining 22 officers and 236 men have been taken off, is finished off with torpedoes and sunk by *Jervis* and *Nubian*.
On 29 Mar, attacks by 16 Ju 88s of III/KG 30 on Force A are not successful.
The Italian losses are about 3000 men, including the Division Commander, Adm Cattaneo. British and Greek ships rescue 55 officers and 850 men, the Italian hospital ship *Gradisca* another 13 officers and 147 men.

27 Mar   General Situation
The Anglo-American staff talks in Washington lead to the drawing up of a basic strategic plan in the event of American entry into the war—the 'ABC-I Staff Agreement'.

30 Mar   General Situation
German, Italian and Danish merchant ships are seized in American harbours.

30–31 Mar   Air War/Western Europe
Unsuccessful attack by 109 RAF bombers on the battlecruisers *Gneisenau* and *Scharnhorst* lying in Brest.

30–31 Mar   Gibraltar/ Mediterranean
A French convoy of six steamers, escorted

by one destroyer, sets out from Casablanca through the Straits of Gibraltar, for North Africa and Marseilles. Because it is believed that 3000 tons of rubber are on the steamer *Bangkok*, coming from Indo-China (it has, in fact, already been unloaded in Casablanca), Force H sends the cruiser *Sheffield* and four destroyers to seize the steamer. The French convoy is able to escape to the cover of the 15.5cm guns of the coastal battery near Nemours with the result that the destroyer *Fearless*, which has instructions to attempt to board, has to turn away.

Apr   Mediterranean/Intelligence
For the German naval forces in the Mediterranean and the Black Sea, a new code, 'Süd', is introduced. The U-boats use this code only from 5 Nov to 12 Dec 1941; after that, 'Triton' is used, up to the introduction of 'Medusa' in June 1943. 'Süd' is broken in Aug 1942.

1 Apr   English Channel
Aircraft of KG 27 (Maj Ulbricht) attack a British convoy in the southern exit of the Bristol Channel and sink the tanker *San Conrado* (7982 tons) and *Hidlefjord* (7639 tons). Three more tankers totalling 26002 tons are severely damaged.

1–2 Apr   Mediterranean
Italian troop transport from Naples to Tripoli: the passenger ships *Esperia* (11398 tons), *Conte Rosso* (17879 tons), *Marco Polo* (12272 tons) and *Victoria* (13098 tons), escorted by three destroyers and two torpedo boats. No attacks.

1–8 Apr   East Africa/Red Sea
Final battle for the Italian base of Massawa (Eritrea). After the destroyer *Leone*, which went aground on 31 Mar, is destroyed by her crew, the remaining seaworthy destroyers, *Pantera*, *Tigre*, *Manin*, *Sauro* and *Battisti*, put to sea on 2 Apr to attack Port Sudan. Cap Gasparini is in command of the operation. *Battisti* has soon to remain behind because of engine trouble and scuttles herself the next day off the Arabian Coast. On the same day aircraft from the British carrier *Eagle*, taking off from shore bases, attack the remaining force about 10 nautical miles off Port Sudan and sink *Manin* and *Sauro*. The two other destroyers are able to get away, and they scuttle themselves off the Arabian Coast. After the defenders of Massawa have beaten off some attacks, the enemy begins his big attack on 6 Apr, following sea and air bombardment. This leads, two days later, to the fall of the town. The last operational motor torpedo boat, *MAS 213* (Sub-Lt Valenza), torpedoes the British light cruiser *Capetown* off the harbour on 6 Apr. The motor torpedo boat is scuttled on 8 Apr with the torpedo boat

Orsini and the MTBs *MAS 204*, *MAS 206*, *MAS 210* and *MAS 216* and many merchant ships shortly before the British enter the town. Among the merchantmen, in addition to many small vessels, there are 11 Italian and six German ships totalling 89870 tons, including the passenger ship *Colombo* (11760 tons). Apart from two Italian ships bombed beforehand, five other Italian steamers totalling 38125 tons scuttle themselves near the Island of Dalac and three others of 23765 tons in Assab on 10 Apr.

2 Apr   Pacific
The German motor ships *München* (5619 tons) and *Hermonthis* (4833 tons) scuttle themselves off Callao (Peru) to avoid capture by the Canadian auxiliary cruiser *Prince Henry*.

2–3 Apr   Mediterranean
German aircraft of FK X attack the convoys AS.23 and AFN.23 destined for Greece and sink three ships of 21155 tons, including the motor ship *Northern Prince* (10917 tons).

2–5 Apr   Mediterranean
Operation 'Winch': 12 Hurricane fighters brought by the carrier *Argus* from Britain to Gibraltar are taken on board the carrier *Ark Royal* on 2 Apr. On 3 Apr, with three Skua bombers, they are flown off at a distance of 400 nautical miles to Malta, where they all arrive safely. Escort is provided by Force H, comprising the battlecruiser *Renown*, the cruiser *Sheffield* and the destroyers *Faulknor*, *Fearless*, *Foresight*, *Fortune* and *Fury*. On 3 Apr one Cant reconnaissance aircraft is shot down by Fulmar fighters from *Ark Royal*. The Italian submarines *Corallo*, *Santarosa* and *Turchese*, stationed N of the Tunisian coast and W of Malta to cope with a British sortie into the Central Mediterranean, sight no ships.
Supply convoy for the German Afrika Korps from Naples to Tripoli: five freighters escorted by the Italian destroyers *Saetta* and *Turbine* and the torpedo boat *Orsa*. No attacks.

2–15 Apr   Mediterranean
The Italian submarines *Aradam* and *Onice* operate off the Cyrenaican coast.

2–18 Apr   Bay of Biscay
The British submarine *Tigris* sinks the tanker *Thorn* (5486 tons) off St-Nazaire on 2 Apr. The submarine *Urge* (Lt Tomkinson), on the way to the Mediterranean, sinks on 18 Apr the Italian blockade-running tanker *Franco Martelli* (10535 tons), coming from Brazil.

3–4 Apr   Air War/Western Europe
RAF Bomber Command attacks the German battlecruisers *Gneisenau* and *Scharnhorst* lying in Brest. At the same time

there are continual air mining sorties against the approaches to Brest. In addition to the mine barrages (approximately 300 mines) laid at the end of Mar by the minelayer *Abdiel*, 106 air mines are dropped in Apr. On 4 Apr the Free French sloops *Conquerante* and *Suippe* are sunk by German air attack at Falmouth.

4 Apr   Central Atlantic
The auxiliary cruiser *Schiff 10/Thor* (Capt Kähler) sinks the British auxiliary cruiser *Voltaire* (Capt Blackburn, 13301 tons) in a gun duel in the Central Atlantic and rescues 197 survivors.

5–16 Apr   North Atlantic
Operation by Force H (Adm Somerville), comprising the battlecruiser *Renown*, the carrier *Ark Royal*, the cruisers *Fiji* and *Sheffield* and the destroyers *Faulknor*, *Fearless*, *Foresight*, *Fury* and *Highlander* in the area W of the Bay of Biscay to blockade the German heavy ships in Brest.

6 Apr   Bay of Biscay
A Bristol Beaufort of No 22 Sqn RAF obtains a torpedo hit on the battlecruiser *Gneisenau*.

6 Apr   North Atlantic
The British AMC *Comorin* is damaged in an accidental fire and is sunk by the destroyer *Broke*. The destroyer *Lincoln* and SS *Glenartney* rescue 405 of 425 crew members in a gale.

6–7 Apr   Mediterranean
Eleven He 111s of 2/KG 4 (Capt Kühl) carry out a mining operation in the Bay of Piraeus and secure a bomb hit on the British ammunition freighter *Clan Fraser* (7529 tons) lying in the harbour. As a result of the explosion on the ship, heavy damage is done to harbour installations. Thirteen ships of 41942 tons, 60 lighters and 25 motor sailing ships are sunk.

6–17 Apr   Mediterranean
Balkan campaign against Yugoslavia. The Yugoslav Navy, which consists of the training cruiser *Dalmacija*, the destroyers *Dubrovnik*, *Beograd*, *Zagreb* and *Ljubljana*, the submarines *Smeli*, *Osvetnik*, *Hrabi*, and *Nebojša*, two torpedo boats, the minesweepers *Kobac*, *Galeb*, *Jastreb*, *Labud*, *Orao* and *Sokol* and three minelayers in Cattaro, four torpedo boats, ten motor torpedo boats, two minesweepers and three minelayers in Sibenik and the aircraft depot ship *Zmaj* in Split, remains in harbour. On 10 Apr the minesweeper *Kobac* is captured at Sebenico. In Italian air attacks (186 bomber sorties), the minesweeper *Malinska* and the minelayers *Orao*, *Sokol* and *Kobac* are damaged. On 16 Apr the submarine *Nebojša* and the motor torpedo boats *Kajmakčalan* and *Durmitor* (Capt Kern) set out, break through

the Strait of Otranto and reach Suda Bay on 22–24 Apr. On the day of the surrender (17 Apr), *Zagreb* (Lt-Cdrs Masara† and Spasié†) is blown up; the remaining ships leave and are taken over by the Italians by 25 Apr.

The Italian submarines *Salpa*, *Medusa* and *Jalea*, detailed to guard the harbours, sight no targets.

6–29 Apr Mediterranean

Balkan campaign against Greece and the British Expeditionary Force.

7–8 Apr Air War/Germany

RAF Bomber Command makes a heavy air raid on Kiel.

7–30 Apr North Atlantic

From 7 to 16 Apr the U-boats stationed SW of Iceland find hardly any targets or convoys. *U108* (Lt-Cdr Scholtz), ordered to watch the Denmark Strait, sinks the auxiliary cruiser *Rajputana* (16444 tons) on 13 Apr; the destroyer *Legion* rescues 277 of 314 crew. *U52* sinks two independents. On 16 Apr, an attempt to operate against a convoy sighted by I/KG 40 SW of the Faeroes and by *U96* W of Ireland fails. It is suspected that the enemy recognises the U-boat concentrations and avoids them. To obtain a better picture, a patrol line, consisting of *U65*, *U95*, *U96*, *U123* and *U552*, is formed S of Iceland from 18 Apr and one consisting of *Da Vinci*, *Cappellini*, *U110*, *U101*, *U73*, *Torelli* and *Malaspina* W of Ireland, while *U147* is stationed near the Faeroes. On 22 Apr *Torelli* sights a homebound convoy but is unable to bring *U101* and *U110* to the scene; the same happens with an outbound convoy on 23 Apr. Air reconnaissance with Fw 200s does not sight any convoys. On 28 Apr *U123* sights the convoy HX.121, to which the five northern boats are directed. When *U123* is driven off, *U96* establishes contact and brings up *U552* in the evening. This sinks one steamer and torpedoes one tanker, the wreck of which is sunk by *U201* on 2 May. *U96* sinks two tankers and a steamer. Later, on 28 Apr, *U65* comes up but is herself sunk by the corvette *Gladiolus*. The patrol lines formed on 29 and 30 Apr by the remaining four boats are avoided by the convoy, which air reconnaissance also fails to find. In the S, *U75* sinks the large steamer *City of Nagpur* on 29 Apr. The successes of the boats in this period are fewer. *U108* (Lt-Cdr Scholtz) sinks one auxiliary cruiser of 16444 tons, *U52* (Lt-Cdr Salman) two ships of 13993 tons, *U552* (Lt-Cdr Topp) three ships of 15970 tons and one of 8190 tons with *U201*, *U123* (Lt-Cdr Moehle) one ship of 6991 tons, *U110* (Lt-Cdr Lemp) one ship of 2564 tons, *U65* (Lt-Cdr Hoppe) one ship of 8897 tons, *U75*

(Lt-Cdr Ringelmann) one ship of 10146 tons, *U95* (Lt-Cdr Schreiber) one ship of 4873 tons, *U96* (Lt-Cdr Lehmann-Willenbrock) three ships of 27305 tons and *U147* (Lt-Cdr Hardegen) one ship of 1334 tons.

7 Apr–10 June Western and North Atlantic

On 7 Apr the US naval base in Bermuda is put into service. On 8 Apr US TG.7.3. (Rear-Adm Cook) arrives to operate from here as the Central Atlantic Neutrality Patrol; it comprises the carrier *Ranger*, the cruisers *Tuscaloosa* and *Wichita* and the destroyers *Kearny* and *Livermoore*. On 18 Apr the boundary of the Western Hemisphere is advanced to 30°W. On 15 May TG.7.3 is joined by the cruisers *Quincy* and *Vincennes*. In addition, the new destroyers of Desron 11, which are in the process of joining the fleet, are allocated to it. These are the leader *Sampson* (Capt Deyo), with *Eberle*, *Gwin*, *Grayson*, *Meredith*, *Monssen* and *Ericsson* and also the carrier *Wasp*.

After a directive on 7 Apr, the following ships are transferred from the US Pacific Fleet to the Atlantic: the carrier *Yorktown* with the destroyers *Mayrant*, *Trippe*, *Rhind*, *Mustin* and *Russell*. From 19 to 23 May the following ships set out in three groups from Pearl Harbor: the battleships *Mississippi*, *Idaho* and *New Mexico* (Batdiv 3), the cruisers *Savannah*, *Brooklyn*, *Nashville* and *Philadelphia* (Crudiv 8) and the destroyers *Lang*, *Sterett*, *Wilson*, *Winslow*, *Wainwright*, *Stack*, *Morris*, *Buck* and *Roe*; and from San Diego on 29 May the destroyers *Sims*, *Anderson*, *Hughes* and *Hammann*. They pass through the Panama Canal from 2 to 8 June.

8–10 Apr Mediterranean

Supply convoy for the Afrika Korps from Naples to Tripoli: five freighters escorted by three torpedo boats. At the same time, there is a return convoy (see 2–5 Apr). No attacks.

8–14 Apr Norway

The Norwegian destroyer *Mansfield* (Cdr Ulstrup) sails from Lerwick (Shetland) into Lopphavet (Northern Norway) and destroys a fish factory in Öksfjord on 11–12 Apr.

9–11 Apr Mediterranean

Italian supply convoy from Naples to Tripoli: five transports escorted by one destroyer and two torpedo boats. No attacks.

9–30 Apr North Atlantic

Unsuccessful operation by the Italian submarines *Baracca* and *Dandolo* W of Gibraltar.

10 Apr North Atlantic

On the way to Iceland, the US destroyer *Niblack* (Lt-Cdr Durgin) attacks a suspected submarine contact with depth charges.

10–11 Apr Air War/Western Europe

RAF Bomber Command, in an attack on Brest, registers four bomb hits on *Gneisenau* lying in dock.

10–12 Apr Mediterranean

An Italian supply convoy consisting of two steamers and two tankers, escorted by the torpedo boats *Missori*, *Montanari* and *Perseo*, from Palermo to Tripoli is unsuccessfully attacked by the British submarine *Upholder* off the Tunisian coast on 11 Apr. *Tetrarch* (Lt-Cdr Greenway) sinks one tanker of 2474 tons off Tripoli on 12 Apr.

10–20 Apr Mediterranean

Units of the Mediterranean Fleet are employed to cover and support the withdrawal of the British 8th Army in Cyrenaica between Tobruk and the Egyptian frontier. During the nights 9–10 and 10–11 Apr the gunboats *Aphis* and *Gnat* shell Bomba and Gazala. On 12 Apr six destroyers, covered by *Ajax*, *Orion* and *Perth*, make a sortie along the coast as far as Ras et Tin. On 13 Apr the destroyers *Griffin* and *Stuart* and the gunboat *Gnat* support operations near Sollum. On 15 Apr the British cruiser *Gloucester* and the destroyer *Hasty* bombard targets between Fort Capuzzo and Bardia and the gunboat *Ladybird* bombards the airfield at Gazala. On 18 Apr *Gloucester* and *Ladybird* again shell targets near Bardia and Sollum. On 19 Apr the destroyers *Stuart*, *Voyager* and *Waterhen* and the AA cruiser *Coventry* set out from Alexandria with the transport *Glengyle* and carry out a commando raid against Bardia on the morning of 20 Apr.

The Italian submarines *Malachite* and *Topazio* operate off the Cyrenaican coast without success.

12–13 Apr Air War/Western Europe

Renewed attacks by RAF Bomber Command on the German battlecruisers at Brest and on the U-boat base at Lorient and the Merignac airfield near Bordeaux, the base of I/KG 40 of Air Commander Atlantic (Col Harlinghausen) which is equipped with long-range Fw 200 bombers.

12–29 Apr Persian Gulf

After Rashid El-Gailani's coup in Iraq on 3–4 Apr, the convoy BM.7 (eight transports with one Indian brigade and one artillery group for Malaya), which is in Karachi, receives orders to proceed to Basra in the company of the Australian sloop *Yarra*. On the way the escort is strengthened by the sloops *Falmouth* and *Lawrence* (RIN). It is off Basra on 18 Apr where, in the meantime, the cruisers *Emerald* and *Leander* (C-in-C East Indies, Vice-Adm Leatham on board), the trawler *Seabelle*, the gunboat *Cockchafer* and 400 airborne troops have arrived. On 19 Apr the troops land. On 28 Apr a second troop convoy, BP.1, arrives, while in the Persian Gulf the carrier *Hermes* and the cruiser *Enterprise* are held on alert. On 29 Apr the troops of the second convoy land.

13–16 Apr   Mediterranean
A convoy for the German Afrika Korps consisting of the freighters *Adana* (4205 tons), *Aegina* (2447 tons), *Arta* (2452 tons), *Iserlohn* (3704 tons) and *Sabaudia* (1590 tons), escorted by the Italian destroyers *Baleno*, *Lampo* and *Tarigo*, is intercepted on the evening of 16 Apr near the island of Kerkennah by British Force K (Capt Mack), comprising the destroyers *Jervis*, *Nubian*, *Mohawk* and *Janus*. The convoy is completely destroyed. *Tarigo* (Cdr* de Cristofaro) sinks *Mohawk* by torpedo. On the next day seven Italian destroyers and torpedo boats, two hospital ships and sea rescue aircraft are able to save 1248 troops from the approximately 3000 embarked on the five freighters.

16–17 Apr   Air War/Britain
681 German bombers attack London.

17 Apr   General Situation
General Wavell receives permission from the British Government to make preparations for the withdrawal from Greece. The surrender of the Yugoslav armed forces is signed in Belgrade.

17 Apr   North Sea
In an attack on a British convoy off Great Yarmouth by the 2nd MTB Flotilla (Lt-Cdr Feldt), consisting of *S41*, *S42*, *S43*, *S55* and *S104*, two freighters of 2744 tons are sunk and a third freighter of 5673 tons is torpedoed.

17 Apr   South Atlantic
The auxiliary cruiser *Schiff 16/Atlantis* (Capt Rogge) sinks the Egyptian passenger ship *Zamzam* (8299 tons) in the South Atlantic and takes the whole crew, together with 138 American passengers, aboard.

17 Apr   Mediterranean
The British submarine *Truant* (Lt-Cdr Haggard) sinks two ships of 2753 tons and one sailing ship off the Cyrenaican coast. The submarine *Regent* (Lt-Cdr Browne) enters the Bay of Cattaro to take on board the British Minister in Yugoslavia.

18 Apr   Western Atlantic
Formation of the US Navy's Caribbean Patrol: the destroyers *Barney* and *Blakely*, Patron 51, with the tender *Lapwing*.

18–20 Apr   Mediterranean
Supply convoy from Palermo to Tripoli for the Afrika Korps (four freighters escorted by four destroyers and one torpedo boat). At the same time an Italian convoy (three freighters and two tankers escorted by five torpedo boats) from Trapani and Palermo to Tripoli.

18–23 Apr   Mediterranean
Operation by the British Mediterranean Fleet (Adm Cunningham). On 18 Apr the battleships *Warspite*, *Barham* and *Valiant*, the aircraft carrier *Formidable* and the light cruisers *Calcutta* and *Phoebe* and destroyers leave Alexandria. The force accompanies the transport *Breconshire* (9776 tons) to Malta. In the evening of 20 Apr the battleships, with the light cruiser *Gloucester* which has just joined the force, proceed to Tripoli, which is heavily shelled during the night 20–21 Apr. In the harbour, six freighters and one destroyer are hit and oil installations are set on fire. On the return, *Valiant* is slightly damaged by a detonating mine. On 23 Apr the squadron enters Alexandria.

19 Apr   Norway
The Free French submarine *Minerve* (Lt Sonneville) attacks a convoy off Stavanger and is herself then attacked with depth charges.

19–20 Apr   Air War/Britain
712 German bombers attack London.

19–23 Apr   Mediterranean
The Italian 7th Cruiser Div (Div Adm Casardi), consisting of the cruisers *Eugenio di Savoia*, *Duca d'Aosta*, *Montecuccoli* and *Attendolo* and the destroyers *Pigafetta*, *Zeno*, *Da Mosto*, *Da Verazzano*, *Da Recco* and *Pessagno*, lays E of Cape Bon the first part of the mine barrages S.11, S.12 and S.13 (321 mines and 492 explosive floats). The second part, consisting of 740 mines, is laid on 23–24 Apr.

20–24 Apr   Mediterranean
In attacks by Air Fleet 4 on shipping targets in Greek waters on 20 Apr, the destroyer *Psara* is sunk near Megara and the new destroyer *Vasilefs Georgios I* is damaged; on 22 Apr the destroyers *Hydra* and *Leon* and the torpedo boat *Thyella* are sunk in Piraeus, as are, on 23 Apr, the decommissioned old battleships *Kilkis* and *Lemnos*. In, addition, the torpedo boats *Kios*, *Alkioni*, *Doris* and *Aigli*, three minelayers, one survey ship and 43 merchant ships, totalling together 63975 tons, are sunk.

Supply convoy for the Afrika Korps from Naples and Palermo to Tripoli (five transports with close escort from four destroyers and distant escort from the light cruisers *Bande Nere*, *Cadorna* and two destroyers). After the convoy is located by British air

reconnaissance, the destroyers *Jervis* (Capt Mack), *Jaguar*, *Janus* and *Juno* put to sea from Malta. They encounter, on 23 Apr, the armed motor ship *Egeo* (3311 tons) which is sunk after a lengthy engagement. The convoy is able to evade the enemy.

20–30 Apr   Mediterranean
The Italian submarines *Settembrini*, *Fisalia* and *Ondina* operate off the Cyrenaican coast and *Nereide* and *Turchese* off Alexandria.

21 Apr   General Situation
Field-Marshal List receives the Greek surrender in Larissa.

21–22 Apr   Air War/Britain
Heavy German air attack on Plymouth.

21 Apr–10 May   Intelligence
Bletchley Park, using the materials captured from *Krebs* (see 3–4 Mar), decodes the daily 'Enigma/Heimische Gewässer' keys for nine days in Apr.

23 Apr   Atlantic
The auxiliary cruiser *Schiff 10/Thor* (Capt Kähler) reaches the Bay of Biscay after 322 days of raiding and arrives in Hamburg on 30 Apr. Total results: 11 merchant ships and one auxiliary cruiser (totalling 96602 tons) sunk and two more large auxiliary cruisers damaged.

24 Apr   Mediterranean
The Italian torpedo boat *Simone Schiaffino* is lost on an Italian minefield near Cape Bon.

24–25 Apr   Air War/Germany
RAF Bomber Command attacks Kiel and Wilhelmshaven.

24–28 Apr   Mediterranean
Operation 'Dunlop': Force H (Vice-Adm Somerville), comprising the battlecruiser *Renown*, the carrier *Ark Royal*, the cruisers *Fiji* and *Sheffield*, and the 8th DD Flotilla with *Faulknor* and four destroyers, enters the Western Mediterranean in order to fly off, to Malta, 20 Hurricane fighters (brought to Gibraltar in the carrier *Argus*) with three Fulmar fighters from the *Ark Royal*. Because of the weather the take-off cannot take place until 27 Apr. On the same day reinforcements for the Mediterranean Fleet, consisting of the cruiser *Dido*, the minelayer *Abdiel* and the 5th DD Flotilla (Capt Lord Mountbatten) with *Kelly*, *Kashmir*, *Kipling*, *Kelvin*, *Jackal* and *Jersey* are dispatched to land reinforcements and to relieve the 14th DD Flotilla (Capt Mack). The cruiser *Gloucester* arrives in Malta on 24 Apr to reinforce Force K. On 28 Apr the reinforcements arrive. After unloading, *Dido*, *Abdiel* and the destroyers *Janus*, *Jervis* and *Nubian* and the empty transport *Breconshire* put to sea in the evening for Alexandria. The Italian submarines, stationed both sides of

Malta, *Mameli*, *Manara*, *Settimo* and *San-tarosa*, do not attack.

24–29 Apr Mediterranean

Operation 'Demon', the evacuation from Greece by the British Fleet. In all, 50672 troops are embarked and brought to Crete and Egypt. The evacuation is carried out by Vice-Adm Pridham-Wippell with the light cruisers *Orion*, *Ajax*, *Phoebe*, *Calcutta*, *Carlisle* and *Coventry*, together with the destroyers *Stuart*, *Voyager*, *Vendetta*, *Waterhen*, *Vampire*, *Wryneck*, *Diamond*, *Decoy*, *Defender*, *Griffin*, *Hasty*, *Havock*, *Hero*, *Hotspur*, *Hereward*, *Isis*, *Nubian*, *Kandahar*, *Kingston* and *Kimberley*, the sloops *Grimsby*, *Flamingo* and *Auckland*, the corvettes *Hyacinth* and *Salvia*, the assault ships *Glenearn* and *Glengyle*, 19 transports and many smaller vessels. The British forces are mostly embarked on the open beach (near Raftina and Raftis) in Attica, at Nauplia, at Monemvasia and at Kalamata in the Peloponnese. The following are sunk by bombers of German FK VIII: the destroyers *Diamond* and *Wryneck* and the transports *Costa Rica* (8672 tons), *Pennland* (16381 tons), *Slamat* (11636 tons) and *Ulster Prince* (3791 tons).

The Italian submarines *Settembrini*, *Fisalia*, *Ondina*, *Nereide* and *Turchese*, stationed between Crete and Greece, have no successes.

25 Apr–15 June Central Atlantic

Climax of the submarine operations off Freetown. *U105* and *U106*, still belonging to the first wave, and *U107*, *Calvi*, *U103*, *Tazzoli*, *U38*, *UA* and *U69* (out on 5 May), which set out as the second wave from 29 Mar, operate in the area between the Canaries and Freetown. The operations of the German boats are, in some cases, considerably extended by fuel and torpedo replenishment from supply ships. *U105* and *U107*, having sunk three ships from convoy OG.57 on 8–9 Apr, obtain replenishment from the supply ship *Nordmark* on 3 May, *U107* from the *Egerland* on 10 May, *U38*, *U103* and *U106* from the same source on 17 May, *UA* on 28 May and *U38* on 6 June. In their torpedo and gun attacks, the submarines sink the following ships (inclusive of the operations against the convoys SL.67, SL.68 and SL.76): *U105* (Lt-Cdr Schewe) sinks twelve ships of 71450 tons, *U106* (Lt-Cdr Oesten) sinks eight ships of 44730 tons and torpedoes the battleship *Malaya*, *U107* (Lt-Cdr Hessler) sinks 14 ships of 86699 tons (the most successful patrol of World War II), *U103* (Cdr Schütze) sinks 12 ships of 58553 tons, *Tazzoli* (Cdr Fecia di Cossato) sinks three ships of 17860 tons, *U38* (Lt-Cdr Liebe) sinks eight ships of

47279 tons and *U69* sinks (Lt-Cdr Metzler) five ships of 25544 tons and one of 2879 tons with a mine, as well as damaging one of 5445 tons. *U69* sinks, *inter alia*, the American steamer *Robin Moor*, in accordance with prize regulations, on 21 May, and lays seven mines each in the harbours of Lagos and Takoradi, on 25–26 May and 26–27 May respectively. *Calvi* and *UA* have no success. Owing to the loss of supply ships in connection with Operation 'Rheinübung'—it is planned to supply *U103*, *U107*, *UA* and *U69* from the tanker *Lothringen* on 18 June—the remaining boats have to return. In the process, *U69* and *U103* get involved from 25 to 27 June in the operation against the convoy SL.76 (qv).

27 Apr General Situation

Conclusion of an Anglo-Australian-Dutch planning conference in Singapore for the defence of the Malayan and Indonesian area with the participation of American observers.

27 Apr Mediterranean

German troops occupy Athens.

29 Apr North Sea

In a sortie by the 1st MTB Flotilla, consisting of *S26*, *S27*, *S29* and *S55*, in the area NW of Cromer, *S29* (Lt v Mirbach) sinks the British freighter *Ambrose Fleming* (1555 tons).

30 Apr General Situation

Completion of the Axis occupation of the Greek mainland, including the Peloponnese.

30 Apr–1 May Mediterranean

Supply convoy for the Afrika Korps from Messina and Augusta to Tripoli, consisting of three German and two Italian steamers. Close escort is provided by the Italian destroyers *Euro* and *Fulmine* and torpedo boats *Castore*, *Orione* and *Procione* and distant escort by the cruisers *Trieste*, *Bolzano* and *Eugenio di Savoia* and the destroyers *Ascari*, *Carabiniere* and *Gioberti*. On 1 May there are many unsuccessful British air and submarine attacks. At the same time there is a return convoy consisting of four German and one Italian freighters escorted by the Italian destroyers *Folgore*, *Saetta*, *Strale* and *Turbine*. It loses two ships in two attacks by the British submarine *Upholder* (Lt-Cdr Wanklyn). Total loss, including a ship sunk on 25 Apr 15410 tons.

30 Apr–12 May Mediterranean

The Italian submarine *Ascianghi* operates in the area of Mersa Matruh and *Galatea* and *Sirena* in the Aegean.

1 May Mediterranean

The Italian 7th Div (Div Adm Casardi), consisting of the cruisers *Eugenio di Savoia*, *Duca d'Aosta* and *Attendolo* and the

destroyers *Pigafetta*, *Zeno*, *Da Mosto*, *Da Verazzano*, *Da Recco* and *Pessagno*, lays N of Tripoli the mine barrage 'T' to protect the harbour from shelling by British heavy ships (see 18–23 Apr).

1–7 May Air War/Britain

In heavy air attacks on port installations in Liverpool, 18 British merchant ships of 35605 tons are sunk and 25 others of 92964 tons are badly damaged; 69 out of 144 cargo docks are destroyed and the turnover capacity of the port is reduced to one quarter.

1–11 May North Atlantic/Intelligence

U123, *U95* and *U96* are directed to an outbound convoy sighted by an Fw 200 of I/KG 40 on 1 May SW of the Faeroes. But neither they nor three Fw 200s find it on 2 May. On 3 May *U143* sights a south-bound convoy S of the Faeroes, but *U141* and *U147* and I/KG 40 do not come up on 3–4 May. On 4/5 May *U96* keeps contact with a home-bound convoy S of Iceland, but no U-boats or aircraft approach. On 6 May the Commander U-boats decides to search with submarines further to the SW, to forgo direct co-operation with air reconnaissance and to use the Italian submarines in their own operational area separately from the German boats. On 6 May *U97* sinks, W of the Bay of Biscay, the British ocean boarding vessel *Camito* and the captured Italian tanker *Sangro*.

On 7 May an Fw 200 sights the convoy HX.122 W of the Faeroes. *U95* sights SC.29 off the North Channel and, in the evening, *U94* the outbound OB.318 S of Iceland, when the 3rd EG (Cdr Baker-Cresswell), with the destroyers *Bulldog*, *Amazon*, *Broadway* and the attached auxiliary cruiser *Ranpura*, coming from Reykjavik/Hvalfjord, meets the convoy and relieves the 7th EG (Cdr Bockett-Pugh) with the destroyers *Westcott*, *Newmarket* and *Campbeltown*. But its sloop *Rochester* and the corvettes *Primrose*, *Nasturtium*, *Marigold*, *Dianthus* and *Auricula* stay with the convoy. *U94* (Lt-Cdr Kuppisch) attacks, sinks two ships of 15901 tons and is then damaged by depth charges from *Amazon*, *Bulldog* and *Rochester*. On 8 May the corvettes of the 3rd EG, *Aubrietia*, *Hollyhock* and *Nigella*, and the trawlers *Angle*, *Daneman* and *St Apollo* come to provide escort and to relieve the corvettes of the 7th EG, which proceed to convoy HX.123. In the evening of 8 May *U110* (Lt-Cdr Lemp) makes contact with the convoy and in the morning directs *U201* (Lt Schnee) to the scene. Towards mid-day on 9 May *U110* attacks and sinks two ships of 7585 tons but is immediately forced to surface by *Aubrietia*'s depth charges, and a boarding party (Lt Balme) from the *Bulldog* is able to take over the boat abandoned by the crew before she sinks. *Broadway* is damaged in the manoeuvring by the hydroplane. Secret papers, a code machine and documents are recovered from *U110* and these materials, together with those captured from *München* (see 7 May), allow the German 'Enigma/Heimische Gewässer' signals for the month of June to be read. But the boat, which is taken in tow by *Bulldog*, sinks on 11 May on the way to Iceland. While *U110* is taken over, *U201* attacks the convoy, which is still escorted by *Amazon*, *Nigella*, *Hollyhock* and *Daneman*, and sinks one ship of 5802 tons and torpedoes one of 5969 tons. Damage is caused by depth-charge attacks from *Nigella* and *St Apollo*.

On the morning of 10 May, *U556* (Lt-Cdr Wohlfarth) attacks the convoy, which is still escorted by *Daneman* and *Hollyhock*, and torpedoes one ship. Later she sinks two more ships of 9947 tons from the convoy as it disperses. The deployment of the Italian submarines *Cappellini* and *Torelli* against a convoy sighted by an Fw 200 W of Iceland on 9 May meets with no success.

2 May   North Sea
The German patrol vessel *V808/Hindenburg* is sunk by bomb hits NW of Borkum.

2 May   Near East
British Forces in Iraq start operations against the Iraqi Army and an open conflict between Great Britain and the Iraqi Government of Rashid Ali El Ghailani ensues.

2–4 May   Mediterranean
In returning from an operation by Force K (5th DD Flotilla, Capt Lord Mountbatten), the destroyers *Kelly*, *Jackal* and *Kelvin* put into harbour but the destroyer *Jersey*, which follows, runs on to a mine and sinks. The result is that the cruiser *Gloucester* with the destroyers *Kashmir* and *Kipling* go W and join Force H. The minesweeper *Fermoy*, in drydock at Malta, is destroyed by bombs.
The Italian torpedo boat *Canopo* is sunk in an RAF raid on Tripoli on 3 May. On 4 May the torpedo boat *Giuseppe la Farina* is lost on a mine near Kerkennah.

4–7 May   Air War/Western Europe
93 British bombers attack the German battlecruisers in Brest.

4–5 May   Mediterranean
Large Italian convoy to North Africa consisting of seven ships, including the motor ship *Victoria* (13098 tons), escorted by the destroyers *Vivaldi*, *Da Noli* and *Malocello* and the torpedo boats *Pegaso*, *Orione* and

Cassiopea. Distant escort is provided by the cruisers *Eugenio di Savoia*, *Duca d'Aosta* and *Attendolo* and the destroyers *Pigafetta*, *Zeno*, *Da Recco*, *Da Mosto* and *Da Verazzano*. On the way, *Pigafetta* and *Zeno* of the covering force sink the British submarine *Usk* W of Sicily. British air attacks on 5 May have no success. On the return, the distant escort covers a German convoy to Italy consisting of five steamers, the destroyers *Euro* and *Fulmine* and the torpedo boats *Procione*, *Orsa*, *Centauro*, *Cigno* and *Perseo*.

5–7 May   Mediterranean
British and Australian destroyers and sloops begin to supply the beleaguered British fortress of Tobruk in night missions. The first trip is made with the Australian destroyers *Voyager* and *Waterhen*. The supply missions, briefly interrupted during the Crete operation, continue until the fortress is relieved.
On 7 May the minesweeper *Stoke* is sunk in a German air attack on Tobruk.

5–12 May   Mediterranean
Operation 'Tiger': a convoy is brought through the Mediterranean. On the evening of 5 May Force H (Vice-Adm Somerville) sets out from Gibraltar for the W with the battlecruiser *Renown*, the carrier *Ark Royal*, the cruisers *Fiji* and *Sheffield* and the destroyers *Wrestler*, *Kashmir* and *Kipling*, in order to meet the convoy with the 15kt transports *Clan Campbell*, *Clan Chattan*, *Clan Lamont*, *Empire Song* and *New Zealand Star* and naval reinforcements comprising the battleship *Queen Elizabeth*, the cruisers *Naiad* (Rear-Adm King) and *Gloucester* and the destroyers *Fearless*, *Foresight*, *Fortune* and *Velox* (the last have gone out ahead from Gibraltar.) The groups pass through the Straits of Gibraltar during the night 5–6 May. On 6 May the destroyers *Faulknor*, *Forester* and *Fury* follow them, as well as the newly arrived destroyers *Harvester*, *Havelock* and *Hesperus* with the battlecruiser *Repulse*, left behind because of her inadequate AA protection.
On 6 May a slow convoy of two tankers and a fast convoy of four transports set out from Alexandria for Malta. They are escorted by the AA cruisers *Dido*, *Phoebe*, *Calcutta*, *Coventry* and *Carlisle* as well as three destroyers and two corvettes. The operation is covered by the Mediterranean Fleet (Adm Cunningham), comprising the battleships *Warspite*, *Barham* and *Valiant*, the carrier *Formidable*, the 7th Cruiser Sqn (Vice-Adm Pridham-Wippell) with *Ajax*, *Orion* and *Perth*, the fast minelayer *Abdiel*, the transport *Breconshire* and the remaining operational destroyers of the Mediterranean

Fleet, *Isis*, *Imperial*, *Ilex*, *Havock*, *Hotspur*, *Hero*, *Hereward*, *Hasty*, *Greyhound*, *Griffin*, *Jervis*, *Janus*, *Juno*, *Jaguar*, *Nubian*, *Kandahar*, *Kingston*, *Kimberley* and *Nizam* (RAN). During the night 7–8 May the cruiser *Ajax* (Capt McCarthy) and the destroyers *Imperial*, *Havock* and *Hotspur* are detached. They shell the harbour of Benghazi and sink two steamers of 3463 tons to the S.
On 8 May both groups are located by German and Italian air reconnaissance. Several attacks by Italian SM 79 bomber and torpedo squadrons with CR42 fighter protection are unsuccessful: *Renown* and *Ark Royal* evade the torpedoes. Attacks by Ju 87 units with Me 110 fighter protection are intercepted by the Fulmar fighters from the *Ark Royal*. In the E there are air engagements between *Formidable*'s fighters and the oncoming Italian and German aircraft. No damage is done to the ships. The deployment of an Italian cruiser force consisting of *Duca degli Abruzzi*, *Garibaldi*, *Bande Nere* and *Cadorna* and five destroyers from Palermo comes too late. In the meantime Force H and the convoy with its covering forces—*Queen Elizabeth*, *Naiad*, *Fiji*, *Gloucester*, *Kashmir*, *Kipling*, *Faulknor* (8th DD Flotilla), *Forester*, *Fury*, *Foresight*, *Fortune* and *Fearless*—have separated near the Skerki Bank and proceed to Malta. In spite of the use by the 'F' class destroyers of minesweeping equipment, the transport *Empire Song* (9228 tons) is lost on two mines on 9 May and the *New Zealand Star* is damaged. *Queen Elizabeth* is just able to avoid a torpedo attack. In the morning of 9 May the corvette *Gloxinia*, which has made a mine-free channel by the use of depth charges, escorts the two convoys from the E into the harbour of Valetta. The destroyers of the 5th DD Flotilla (Capt Lord Mountbatten), *Kelly*, *Jackal* and *Kelvin*, blockaded until then, are able to go out to the 'Tiger' convoy and meet it with the cruisers *Orion*, *Ajax*, *Perth*, *Dido* and *Phoebe* and escort it to the rendezvous with the Mediterranean Fleet, while the 8th DD Flotilla takes on oil in Malta and follows Force H. Bad visibility impedes German and Italian air attacks.
The Italian submarines *Santarosa* and *Settimo* W of Malta and *Corallo* off the Tunisian coast do not fire their torpedoes.
On 10 May visibility does not permit attacks by German and Italian aircraft until the afternoon. Then *Fortune* of the 8th DD Flotilla, which is closing up on Force H, receives a heavy hit. No losses are sustained by the Mediterranean Fleet nor by the convoy. During night 10–11 May the

destroyers *Kelly*, *Jackal*, *Kelvin*, *Kashmir* and *Kipling* of the 5th DD Flotilla again shell Benghazi. There is an unsuccessful night dive-bomber attack by Ju 87s of a squadron (Lt Rieger) from II/StG 2. On 12 May the British forces reach Gibraltar and Alexandria respectively. Only 57 of 295 tanks and 10 out of 53 Hurricane fighters have been lost.

6 May   North Atlantic
The convoy HX.125 leaves Halifax and gets an ocean escort comprising the battleship *Revenge*, the AMC *Ascania*, and the sloops *Aberdeen*, *Hartland*, *Culver*, *Fishguard* and *Banff*.

6 May   Mediterranean
Of the boats of the British 1st SM Flotilla, *Taku* (Lt-Cdr v d Byl) sinks one ship of 2322 tons off Calabria, *Truant* (Lt-Cdr Haggard) sinks one ship of 1716 tons near Sardinia and *Triumph* unsuccessfully attacks a small convoy off Buerat and is hunted by the torpedo boat *Climene*.

6-7 May   Air War/Britain
Heavy German air raid on harbour installations in the Clyde.

7 May   Arctic/Intelligence
After intercepting 'Enigma' traffic from a weather observation ship located by British D/F stations, a British force, consisting of the cruisers *Edinburgh* (Vice-Adm Holland) *Manchester* and *Birmingham* and the destroyers *Nestor*, *Bedouin*, *Eskimo* and *Somali* is directed to the position of the *München* (*WBS-6*, 306 tons) near Jan Mayen. In poor visibility *München* is surprised and the destroyer *Somali* (Capt Caslon) goes alongside and captures important cypher equipment, notably the 'Wetter-Kurzschlüssel 1940', the most valuable source for 'cribs'. The material is sent to Scapa Flow aboard the destroyer *Nestor* and allows the British to read immediately the German 'Enigma/Heimische Gewässer' traffic in June. However, the newly introduced 'Kernflotte' circuit, used for Fleet operations, is never broken because of its infrequent use by the Germans.

8 May   Indian Ocean
The British heavy cruiser *Cornwall* (Capt Manwaring) sinks the German auxiliary cruiser *Schiff 33/Pinguin* (Capt Krüder†) in an engagement near the Seychelles; 18 officers and 323 men and about 200 prisoners are lost with the German ship which, on her mission as a raider, has sunk or captured (inclusive of mine successes) a total of 32 ships amounting to 154619 tons in all. *Cornwall* rescues three officers, 57 seamen and 22 prisoners.

8-9 May   Air War/Germany
RAF Bomber Command, with 359 aircraft, carried out its heaviest night attack so far on Germany. The main targets are Hamburg and Bremen, which are attacked by 317 bombers.

9-29 May   Mediterranean
The Italian submarines *Atropo* and *Zoea* each conduct two transport operations, carrying petrol and ammunition from Taranto to Derna.

10-11 May   Air War/Britain
Heavy German air raid on London (last major attack for three years). Approximately 2000 fires; five docks and 71 installations connected with the war effort, including 35 factories, destroyed or badly damaged. 110 British bombers attack Hamburg.

10-24 May   Intelligence
Bletchley Park breaks the 'Enigma/Heimische Gewässer' signals of 7 and 8 May on 10 and 11 May, those of 9 and 10 May on 13 and 14 May, those of 11 and 12 May on 22 May and those of 13 and 14 May on 20 and 21 May.

11 May   Mediterranean
The British submarine *Rorqual* (Lt-Cdr Dewhurst) lays a mine barrage in the Gulf of Salonica.

11-14 May   Mediterranean
German-Italian supply convoy for North Africa, consisting of six ships escorted by the destroyers *Aviere*, *Geniere*, *Grecale*, *Camicia Nera* and *Dardo* with distant escort from the cruisers *Bande Nere*, *Cadorna*, *Duca degli Abruzzi* and *Garibaldi* and the destroyers *Alpino*, *Bersagliere*, *Fuciliere*, *Maestrale*, *Scirocco*, *Da Recco*, *Usodimare*, *Pessagno* and *Pancaldo*. This convoy, like two returning ones, reaches its destination without incident.

In an attempt to attack a steamer escorted to Benghazi by the torpedo boat *Pleiadi*, the British submarine *Undaunted* is destroyed by depth charges off Tripoli on 13 May.

On 12 May the British gunboat *Ladybird* is sunk in a German air attack off the Libyan coast.

11-22 May   North Atlantic
After the OB.318 operation, *U93*, *U94*, *U98* and *U556* are formed into a 'West' group, to which are added on 13 May *U111*, *U97*, *U74* and *U109*. It proceeds to the area SSE of Cape Farewell, Greenland. In the process, *U98* (Lt-Cdr Gysae) sinks on 13 May the auxiliary cruiser *Salopian* (10549 tons), which belongs to the convoy SC.30. On 19 May *U94* sights the convoy HX.126, escorted by the AMC *Aurania* and the submarine *Tribune*, and, before losing contact, sinks two ships; on 20 May, at mid-day, *U556* finds the convoy again and in two

approaches sinks two ships and torpedoes one tanker. In addition, by evening *U111*, *U98* and *U94* arrive one after the other and *U93* comes up towards morning on 21 May. They each sink one ship. On 22 May *U46*, *U66*, *U557*, *U94* and *U74* also operate against the convoy. *U74* is damaged by depth charges. Only *U111* sights the convoy but her one success is against an independent. Then contact is lost.

Of the boats operating with the 'West' group, the following make sinkings in the period 1-22 May (inclusive of convoys OB.318 and HX.126): *U97* (Lt-Cdr Heilmann) sinks three ships of 17852 tons, *U556* (Lt-Cdr Wohlfarth) sinks five ships of 23557 tons and damages two of 18023 tons, *U94* (Lt-Cdr Kuppisch) sinks five ships of 31940 tons, *U110* (Lt-Cdr Lempt†) sinks two ships of 7585 tons; *U201* (Lt Schnee) sinks one ship of 5802 tons and damages one of 5969 tons, *U111* (Lt-Cdr Kleinschmidt) sinks three ships of 15978 tons, *U98* (Lt-Cdr Gysae) sinks two ships of 15905 tons, *U109* (Cdr Fischer) sinks one ship of 7402 tons and *U93* (Lt-Cdr Korth) sinks one ship of 6235 tons.

In the eastern part of the North Atlantic, I/KG 40 sights a convoy on 11 May, from which one ship of 8790 tons is sunk, but to which no U-boat comes. On 14 May a convoy is again sighted, and one ship of 1843 tons is sunk. Of the Italian submarines deployed, *Bianchi* and *Malaspina* sight the convoy but, like *Barbarigo*, *Morosini* and *Otaria*, have no success. On 19 May *Otaria* (Lt-Cdr Vocaturo) sinks one ship of 4662 tons in the convoy SL.73.

Of the U-boats operating in the area of the North Channel and the Faeroes, *U96* (Lt-Cdr Lehmann-Willenbrock) sinks one ship of 2922 tons and *U138* (Lt Gramitzky) one of 8593 tons.

12-20 May   Mediterranean
In the Eastern Mediterranean, the Italian submarine *Ambra* operates SE of Malta, *Beilul* and *Salpa* NW of Alexandria and *Onice* and *Galatea* in the Kaso Strait.

13 May   Air War/Germany
Daylight attack by British bombers on Heligoland.

13-29 May   Norway
Among others, the British submarine *P31/Uproar* and the French *Minerve* operate off Norway,

14-23 May   North Atlantic
On 14 May the Italian submarine *Cappellini* reports the French sailing vessel *Notre Dame du Chatelet* (488 tons), which is sunk by gunfire from *U43* (Lt-Cdr Lüth). Two survivors are rescued on 23 May by the Italian submarine *Otaria*.

18 May   South Atlantic
In the South Atlantic, the auxiliary cruiser *Schiff 16/Atlantis* (Capt Rogge) passes unnoticed the British battleship *Nelson* and the aircraft carrier *Eagle* at a distance of only 7000m.

18 May   Mediterranean
The British submarine *Tetrarch* (Lt-Cdr Greenway) sinks a ship of 2362 tons, escorted by the torpedo boat *Polluce*, off Benghazi.

18–27 May   Intelligence
Bletchley Park suffers from delays in breaking the daily 'Enigma/Heimische Gewässer' key and is not able to decode signals concerning Operation 'Rheinübung' in time for operational or tactical use.

18–27 May   North Atlantic
Operation 'Rheinübung': Atlantic operation by the battleship *Bismarck* (Capt Lindemann) and the heavy cruiser *Prinz Eugen* (Capt Brinkmann) under the orders of the Fleet Cdr, Adm Lütjens.

On 18 May the battle squadron leaves Gotenhafen (Gdynia). To supply the squadron, the escort tankers *Heide* and *Weissenburg* are stationed in the European Arctic and from France the supply ship *Spichern* and the escort tankers *Belchen*, *Esso Hamburg*, *Friedrich Breme* and *Lothringen* set out for positions in the North and Central Atlantic. In support, the patrol ships *Gonzenheim* and *Kota Pinang* put to sea on 17–18 May and the weather observation ships *August Wriedt*, *Freese* and *Lauenburg* have taken up positions in the Arctic and Atlantic (the *München* has already been lost).

On 19 May the squadron is escorted from Cape Arkona by *Sperrbrecher 13* and *Sperrbrecher 31* and the destroyers *Friedrich Eckoldt* and *Z23*; off the Belt there is also the destroyer *Hans Lody* and an escort from the 5th MS Flotilla. On 20 May the force is reported in the Kattegat by the Swedish cruiser *Gotland*; British intelligence receives the news. On 21 May the force is discovered by British air reconnaissance when it is refuelling in Korsfjord near Bergen, but it is able to leave in the evening undetected. The submarines *Minerve* (French) and *P31*, which are sent N, cannot find the force. The commander of the Battle Cruiser Sqn, Vice-Adm Holland, puts to sea from Scapa Flow in the direction of the area S of Iceland with the battlecruiser *Hood*, the battleship *Prince of Wales* and the destroyers *Electra*, *Anthony*, *Echo*, *Icarus*, *Achates* and *Antelope*.

On 22 May British air reconnaissance establishes the departure of the German ships. The British Home Fleet (Adm Tovey) then puts to sea from Scapa Flow with the battleship *King George V* (Capt Patterson), the carrier *Victorious* (Capt Bovell), the 2nd Cruiser Sqn (Rear-Adm Curteis), comprising *Galatea*, *Aurora*, *Kenya* and *Hermione*, and the available destroyers *Active*, *Punjabi*, *Nestor*, *Inglefield*, *Intrepid* and *Lance* (the last returns because of damage). It is joined by the battlecruiser *Repulse* (Capt Tennant), earmarked to cover convoy WS.8B, with three Western Approaches destroyers. The light cruisers *Manchester*, *Birmingham* and *Arethusa*, five trawlers and flying boats watch the Iceland–Faeroes passage and the heavy cruisers *Norfolk* (with the Cdr 1st Cruiser Sqn, Rear-Adm Wake-Walker) and *Suffolk* the Denmark Strait.

On 23 May the German ships are sighted in the evening in the Denmark Strait by *Norfolk* (Capt Philipps) and *Suffolk* (Capt Ellis), whereupon Adm Holland's force comes up to intercept the German units south of the Denmark Strait.

In the morning of 24 May there is a brief engagement between the two forces, in which *Hood* (Capt Kerr†) is sunk in five minutes by *Bismarck* and *Prinz Eugen* and the *Prince of Wales* (Capt Leach) is damaged and forced to turn away. 95 officers and 1323 men, including Vice-Adm Holland, are lost with *Hood*; only three seamen can be rescued. On the *Bismarck* two heavy and one light hits cause a reduction in speed and a clearly visible trail of oil. *Prinz Eugen* is undamaged. The British cruisers are able to maintain contact.

The convoys HX.126, SC.31, HX.127, OB.323 and OB.324, which are particularly threatened, are ordered to make detours. The battleship *Ramillies* with HX.127, the battleship *Rodney* and the destroyers *Somali*, *Tartar* and *Mashona* (the destroyer *Eskimo* remains with the transport *Britannic*) from a force proceeding to the US and the cruiser *Edinburgh* (with the Cdr of the 18th Cruiser Sqn, Commodore Blackman) from the area W of Cape Finisterre are all deployed, while the ships of the Home Fleet try to close in, but the destroyers have to be detached because of shortage of fuel. Force H (Vice-Adm Somerville), comprising the battlecruiser *Renown* (Capt McGrigor), the carrier *Ark Royal* (Capt Maund), the cruiser *Sheffield* (Capt Larcom) and the destroyers *Faulknor*, *Foresight*, *Forester*, *Foxhound*, *Fury* and *Hesperus*, sets out from Gibraltar. The battleship *Revenge* is sent from Halifax to the convoy HX.128.

The Commander U-boats stations the 'West' group, comprising *U94*, *U43*, *U46*, *U557*, *U66* and *U93*, in a patrol line over which the *Bismarck* is to draw her pursuers

on 25 May. The submarines *U73*, *U556*, *U97*, *U98*, *U74*, *U48* and *Barbarigo* are stationed in the western part of the Bay of Biscay as a precautionary measure to meet the *Bismarck*.

During the night 24–25 May nine aircraft from the carrier *Victorious* attack *Bismarck* and register an insignificant hit. Thanks to a brief attack by *Bismarck*, *Prinz Eugen* is able to get away, unnoticed by the enemy, to pursue mercantile warfare on her own. Shortly afterwards the British cruisers, which are keeping contact by radar, lose touch when *Bismarck* turns away and makes for Brest behind the withdrawing cruisers.

On 25 May *Bismarck* proceeds to the SE behind the British ships which are searching in fan formation towards the SW and she sends long W/T messages assuming that the enemy is still in contact. Bearings are at once taken on the W/T messages, although at first they are incorrect.

In the morning of 26 May a Catalina flying boat (Fg Off Briggs) of No 209 Sqn finds the *Bismarck* again. Force H is deployed, but its destroyers have to remain behind. Also deployed are *King George V* and *Rodney* (Capt Dalrymple-Hamilton) with the destroyers *Mashona*, *Somali* and *Tartar* and the cruiser *Norfolk* which follows. The destroyers *Cossack* (4th DD Flotilla, Capt Vian), *Sikh*, *Zulu*, *Maori* and *Piorun* (Polish) are withdrawn from convoy WS.8B: it continues with the cruisers *Cairo* and *Exeter* and three destroyers. The convoys OB.325 and OB.326 are re-routed and from the convoys SL.74 and SL.75, coming from the S, the cruisers *Dorsetshire* and *London* are put on the trail, as is the battleship *Nelson* with the carrier *Eagle* from Freetown. At mid-day aircraft from *Ark Royal* establish contact and, soon afterwards, the cruiser *Sheffield* is attacked in error by the first wave of the carrier's torpedo aircraft but is able to avoid all the torpedoes. Despite unfavourable weather, a second wave of 15 Swordfish of Nos 810, 818 and 828 Sqns takes off under Lt-Cdr Coode in the afternoon. *Bismarck* is hit twice. A torpedo hit destroys the steering gear and renders the battleship unmanoeuvrable. Shortly before, *U556* (Lt-Cdr Wohlfarth) sights Force H but, although in a certain firing position, has to let it pass because the boat is returning to her base after expending all her torpedoes.

During the night 26–27 May *Bismarck* beats off attacks by the 4th British DD Flotilla (Capt Vian) consisting of *Zulu*, *Sikh*, *Cossack*, *Maori* and the Polish *Piorun*.

On 27 May the battleships *King George V* and *Rodney* come up in the morning and shell *Bismarck* to pieces although the latter defends herself to the last gun. The battle-ships then return because of fuel shortage and the cruiser *Dorsetshire* (Capt Martin) and *Norfolk* shell the wreck and torpedo her twice. At about 1035 hrs *Bismarck* sinks after the detonation of scuttling charges. *Dorsetshire* and *Maori* rescue 110 survivors, including two officers, and *U74* and the weather observation ship *Sachsenwald* rescue another five later, but 2106 men, including the entire Fleet staff, perish. A search for survivors made by the Spanish cruiser *Canarias* has no result.

Attempts by the German Air Force—Air Cdr Atlantic (Col Harlinghausen)—reinforced by II/KG 1, II/KG 54 and I/KG 77 to help *Bismarck* lead to many misses on British warships. On 28 May Ju 88s of I/KG 77 sink the British destroyer *Mashona* W of Ireland and He 111s of KG 100 badly damage *Maori*.

19–21 May   Mediterranean

German-Italian supply convoy from Palermo to Sicily, consisting of seven ships, escorted by the destroyers *Euro*, *Folgore*, *Fulmine*, *Strale* and *Turbine*; distant escort comprises the cruisers *Duca degli Abruzzi* and *Garibaldi* and the destroyers *Granatiere*, *Alpino* and *Bersagliere*. On 19 May two ships collide trying to avoid an attack by the British submarine *Urge* (Lt-Cdr Tomkinson) which, on the following day, sinks a single steamer of 5165 tons and on 21 May misses *Duca degli Abruzzi*. Two returning convoys with eight ships arrive: an attack by *Upholder* fails.

19–22 May   Mediterranean

Operation 'Splice': British Force H, consisting of the battlecruiser *Renown* (Vice-Adm Somerville), the carriers *Ark Royal* and *Furious*, the cruiser *Sheffield* and six destroyers, proceeds to the area S of Sardinia and flies off, on 21 May, 48 Hurricane fighters, bound for Malta, from the carriers; all the aircraft arrive. The Italian submarines *Corallo* and *Diaspro*, stationed S of Sardinia, do not approach the force.

19 May–2 June   Mediterranean

During the battle for Crete, the Italian submarines *Tricheco*, *Uarsciek*, *Fisalia*, *Topazio*, *Adua*, *Dessiè*, *Malachite*, *Squalo*, *Smeraldo* and *Sirena* operate between Crete, Alexandria and Sollum and *Nereide* N of Crete. Their operations have no success.

20 May–1 June   Mediterranean

Operation 'Merkur': German airborne landing on Crete. On 20 May attacks by FK VIII (General of the Air Force v Richthofen) and airborne landings (by FK XI) in the area of Maleme, Heraklion, Canea and Retimo begin against strong opposition from the British garrison. In the morning

the minesweeper *Widnes* is sunk in Suda Bay (she is later refloated and commissioned by the Germans as *UJ2109*). The Italian torpedo boat *Curtatone* sinks on a Greek minefield off Piraeus. During the night 20–21 May an attack by six Italian motor torpedo boats on British Force C (Rear-Adm King), comprising the cruisers *Naiad* and *Perth* (RAN) and the destroyers *Kandahar*, *Nubian*, *Kingston* and *Juno*, achieves no success. The destroyers *Jervis* (Capt Mack), *Ilex* and *Nizam* shell the airfield at Scarpanto.

On 21 May 17 Ju 87s of III/StG 2 (Capt Heinrich Brüker) hit the cruiser *Ajax* and five Cant Z.1007bis of the 50th Italian Bomber Group (Lt Morassuti) sink the destroyer *Juno*. Both ships belong to the British Mediterranean Fleet, elements of which have been at sea since 15 May in the expectation of German action. It has the following units at its disposal: the battle-ships *Queen Elizabeth*, *Barham*, *Warspite* and *Valiant*, the aircraft carrier *Formidable*, the cruisers *Gloucester*, *Fiji*, *Ajax*, *Dido*, *Orion*, *Perth*, *Naiad*, *Phoebe*, *Calcutta* and *Carlisle*, the fast minelayer *Abdiel*, the destroyers *Napier*, *Nizam*, *Kandahar*, *Kelvin*, *Kipling*, *Kingston*, *Kimberley*, *Kelly*, *Nubian*, *Juno*, *Janus*, *Jervis*, *Jackal*, *Isis*, *Imperial*, *Ilex*, *Hero*, *Hotspur*, *Hereward*, *Hasty*, *Havock*, *Griffin*, *Greyhound*, *Decoy*, *Defender*, *Stuart*, *Voyager*, *Vendetta* and *Waterhen*, the sloops *Auckland* and *Flamingo* and the netlayer *Protector*. In the course of the fighting all ships are involved.

On 21 May the first German motor sailing flotilla (Lt Oesterlin), some 20 craft, departs, escorted by the Italian torpedo boat *Lupo* (Cdr* Mimbelli); towards midnight the British Force D (Rear-Adm Glennie), consisting of the cruisers *Dido*, *Orion* and *Ajax* and the destroyers *Janus*, *Kimberley*, *Hasty* and *Hereward*, attacks the German convoy 18 nautical miles N of Canea and scatters it. Thanks to the courageous action of *Lupo*, only 10 motor sailing vessels are lost while of the 2331 troops embarked only 297 are lost.

On 22 May Force C (Rear-Adm King), consisting of the cruisers *Naiad*, *Perth*, *Calcutta* and *Carlisle* as well the destroyers *Kandahar*, *Nubian* and *Kingston*, attacks the second motor sailing flotilla. As a result of the skilful action of the escorting Italian torpedo boat *Sagittario* (Cdr* Cigala-Fulgosi) and constant air attacks by Ju 88s of I/LG 1 (Capt Cuno Hoffmann) and III/KG 30, as well as by Do 17s of KG 2 (Col Rieckhoff), the convoy loses only two craft. *Carlisle* (Capt Hampton†) and *Naiad* are damaged by bomb hits. Force C then turns away to join

the powerful covering group (Rear-Adm Rawlings) which in the course of the after-noon is also the target of strong air attacks by Ju 87s of StG 2 (Lt-Col Dinort), Ju 88s of I/LG 1 and II/LG 1 (Capt Kollewe) and Me 109 fighter-bombers. I/LG 1 and a fighter-bomber detachment (Lt Huy) of III/JG 77 secure several hits on the battle-ship *Warspite* (Capt Crutchley), Ju 87s sink the destroyer *Greyhound* and Ju 88s and Ju 87s sink the cruiser *Gloucester* (Capt Rowley†), which is lost with 45 officers and 648 members of the crew. Two single Me 109 fighter-bombers of I/LG 2 (Capt Ihle-feld) hit the cruiser *Fiji* (Capt William Powlett) so heavily in the evening that she has to be abandoned. *Kandahar* and *Kingston* rescue 523 survivors. In the air attacks, *Carlisle* and *Naiad* are again hit and the battleship *Valiant* (Capt Morgan) is more lightly damaged. During the night 22–23 May *Kashmir*, *Kelly* and *Kipling* shell the airfield at Maleme. *Decoy* and *Hero* take the Greek king and his party on board.

On 23 May I/StG 2 (Capt Hitschhold) locates *Kashmir* and *Kelly* as they return in the evening and sinks them. *Kipling* rescues 279 survivors. Fighter-bombers of III/JG 77 (Maj v Winterfeldt) sink in Suda Bay the boats *MTB67*, *MTB213*, *MTB214*, *MTB216* and *MTB217* of the British 10th MTB Flotilla.

On 25 May Vice-Adm Pridham-Wippell puts to sea from Alexandria with the battle-ships *Barham* and *Queen Elizabeth*, the carrier *Formidable* and nine destroyers in order to attack the air base of III/StG 2 (Capt Brücker) at Scarpanto. On 26 May carrier aircraft from *Formidable* bombard Scarpanto. On return, *Formidable* and destroyer *Nubian* are badly damaged by II/StG 2 (Maj Ennerccerus). The ~~mine-sweeper~~ *sloop* *Grimsby* is sunk in an air attack 40 miles N of Tobruk.

On 27 May Ju 88s of LG 1 damage the battleship *Barham*. Because, in the mean-time, the situation on Crete has developed in a way favourable to the German invading forces, all British attempts to bring reinforcements to the island are stopped. The evacuation is begun.

On 28 May on the way to the evacuation, the cruiser *Ajax* and the destroyer *Imperial* are damaged by bombs. During the night 28–29 May 4700 troops are embarked in Sphakia and Heraklion; *Imperial* is aban-doned when her rudder is disabled and scuttled by *Hotspur*.

On 29 May the destroyer *Hereward* is sunk by III/StG 2; *Decoy* is hit and *Ajax* is again hit. The cruisers *Dido* and *Orion* (Capt Back†) are badly damaged. There are 260 dead and 280 wounded among the 1100 troops embarked on *Orion*. During the night 29–30 May another 6000 are evacuated.

On 30 May the cruiser *Perth* and the destroyer *Kelvin* are damaged by LG 1. 700 troops are evacuated during the night 30–31 May.

On 31 May the destroyer *Napier* receives bomb hits. During the night 31 May–1 June Rear-Adm King makes a last effort with *Phoebe*, *Abdiel*, *Jackal*, *Kimberley* and *Hotspur* to evacuate troops from Sphakia, where there are still approximately 6000 men left behind. 4000 troops can be taken off. The Italian torpedo boat *Pleiadi* is damaged in error by an Italian aircraft and beached near Tobruk.

On 1 June the AA cruisers *Calcutta* and *Coventry*, sent out from Alexandria to meet Adm King's force, are located by two Ju 88s some 100 nautical miles N of Alexandria and *Calcutta* (Capt Leese) is sunk by Lt Sauer of II/LG 1. *Coventry* rescues 255 survivors out of 372. 17000 troops in all are evacuated from Crete. Losses: 15743 men and, in addition, 2011 in the Navy. German losses: 6580 dead, missing and wounded.

21 May   Mediterranean

The British fast minelayer *Abdiel* lays 150 mines E of Cape Dukato. Within 24hr the Italian destroyer *Mirabello*, the gunboat *Matteucci* and the German transports *Marburg* (7564 tons) and *Kybfels* (7764 tons) sink on this barrage.

22–25 May   Mediterranean

The British submarines *Urge* and *Upholder* each torpedo one ship of 4856 tons and 4854 tons respectively off Tunis and Messina on 22 and 24 May.

On 24 May an Italian troop convoy, consisting of the passenger ships *Esperia* (11398 tons), *Conte Rosso* (17879 tons), *Marco Polo* (12272 tons) and *Victoria* (13098 tons), proceeds to Tripoli. Close escort is provided by the destroyers *Camicia Nera* and *Freccia* and the torpedo boats *Procione*, *Orsa* and *Pegaso* with distant escort by the cruisers *Bolzano* and *Trieste* and the destroyers *Ascari*, *Corazziere* and *Lanciere*. E of Sicily, *Conte Rosso* is sunk by the British submarine *Upholder* (Lt-Cdr Wanklyn); of the 2500 troops on board, 1680 are saved.

25 May   Mediterranean

The French sloop *Menlière* is lost by stranding at Corsica.

25 May–16 June   North Atlantic

Operation by an Italian submarine group consisting of *Argo*, *Veniero*, *Mocenigo*, *Emo*, *Marconi*, *Brin* and *Velella* against convoys W of Gibraltar. Early in the morning of 30 May *Veniero* sights the carrier *Ark Royal* from Force H returning from the hunt for

the *Bismarck* and she misses one destroyer of a convoy escort. In subsequent attacks, *Mocenigo* misses a tanker and *Marconi* (Lt-Cdr Pollina) sinks the British fleet tanker *Cairndale* and, later, an small unmarked Portuguese trawler, totalling 8447 tons. On 31 May submarines are heavily attacked with depth charges from the convoy escort, consisting of the corvettes *Coreopsis* and *Fleur de Lys*, and the destroyers *Faulknor*, *Forester* and *Fury* sent as reinforcements, as well as by the French corvette *Alysse*, the sloop *Bideford*, the trawler *Imperialist* and the destroyer *Wrestler*. They are able to evade the attacks.

On 5 June *Velella* (Lt-Cdr Terra) sights the homebound convoy OG.63 and brings up *Marconi* which attacks during the night 5–6 June and observes four hits. She is followed by *Velella* which obtains two hits. Two ships of 4787 tons sink. In the afternoon of 6 June *Emo* (Cdr Roselli-Lorenzini) also attacks OG.63 and reports two unconfirmed hits. During the night 5–6 June *Veniero* (Cdr Petroni) sights the approaching HG.64 S of OG.63 and reports two unconfirmed hits. In the morning of 7 June *Brin* sights the convoy NE of Madeira but is not able to fire. *Mocenigo* does not find the convoy.

On 12 June *Brin* (Cdr Longanesi-Cattani) sights the convoy SL.76 E of the Azores and on 13 June sinks two of its ships totalling 7241 tons. But *Velella* and *Veniero* do not find the convoy, nor do the German U-boats *U204*, *U43*, *U73* and *U201*, stationed further to the N and known as the 'Kurfürst' group.

26 May   Western Atlantic

The Dutch gunboat *Van Kinsbergen* captures the Vichy French steamer *Winnepeg* (8379 tons) E of Martinique.

26–27 May   Mediterranean

The Italian 13th TB Flotilla (Cdr Unger di Lowenberg), consisting of the torpedo boats *Circe*, *Calliope*, *Clio* and *Perseo*, lays the mine barrages M.4 and M.4A E of Malta. An Italian supply convoy to Tripoli (six freighters, escorted by two destroyers and three torpedo boats with a distant escort of one cruiser and two destroyers) is attacked by British aircraft from Malta and two ships are hit.

27 May   North Atlantic

The convoy HX.129 is the first British convoy from Halifax to be escorted the whole way across the Atlantic against submarines.

27 May–20 June   North Atlantic

For 1 June a new 'West' group is formed from the U-boats stationed in the Western Atlantic: *U111* (replenished on 25–26 May

from the tanker *Belchen* in the Davis Strait), *U43*, *U46* and *U66*. These are to be joined, after being replenished from *Belchen*, by *U557* (1–2 June) and *U93*. *Belchen* is sunk on 3 June, when replenishing *U93*, by the cruisers *Aurora* and *Kenya*; *U93* rescues 49 survivors. By 20 June the boats *U108*, *U101*, *U75*, *U48*, *U73*, *U204* (previously south of Iceland), *U553*, *U77*, *U558* and *U751* also join the 'West' group. They encounter only independents. *U557* (Lt Paulshen) sinks one ship of 7290 tons, *U46* (Lt Endrass) sinks two of 10893 tons and damages one of 6207 tons, *U108* (Lt-Cdr Scholtz) sinks six of 24445 tons, *U48* (Lt-Cdr Schultze) sinks five of 38462 tons, *U75* (Lt-Cdr Ringelmann) sinks one of 4801 tons, *U101* (Lt-Cdr Mengersen) sinks two of 11644 tons, *U43* (Lt-Cdr Lüth) sinks two of 7529 tons, *U204* (Lt-Cdr Kell) sinks two of 7902 tons, *U553* (Lt-Cdr Thurmann) sinks two of 7945 tons, *U77* (Lt-Cdr Schonder) sinks three of 11725 tons and *U751* (Lt-Cdr Bigalk) sinks one of 5370 tons. A sortie by *U111* into the area of the Belle Isle Strait and as far as Cape Race is not successful owing to mist. Off the North Channel, *U147* (Lt Wetjen) sinks one ship of 2491 tons and, after torpedoing a steamer of 4996 tons in convoy OB.239 on 2 June, is sunk by the British destroyer *Wanderer* and the corvette *Periwinkle* of the escort. *U552* (Lt-Cdr Topp) sinks three ships of 24401 tons in the North Channel and *U141* (Lt Schüler) sinks one of 1277 tons W of Ireland. Of the U-boats *U559* and *U79* (Lt-Cdr Kaufmann), stationed in the Denmark Strait to support the proposed break-out of the heavy cruiser *Lützow*, the latter sinks one ship of 1524 tons.

28 May   General Situation

Franco-German negotiations in Paris. Agreement provides for, *inter alia*, support for German naval operations in the Central Atlantic from Dakar (planned from 15 July). In view of the scant German accommodation shown by Hitler, however, the French Government returns to its policy of *attentisme* in its Note of 14 July.

30 May   Mediterranean

The British submarine *Triumph* (Lt-Cdr Wards) torpedoes the Italian auxiliary cruiser *Ramb III* (3667 tons) off Benghazi. A further attack on 30–31 May on a small convoy is outmanoeuvred.

1 June   North Atlantic

The US Coast Guard organises the South Greenland Patrol: four ships operate between Cape Brewster, Cape Farewell and Upernivik.

1–13 June Mediterranean
In operations by the British 8th SM Flotilla (Gibraltar), *Clyde* (Cdr Ingram) sinks two ships of 4271 tons in the Western Mediterranean and the Dutch *O24* (Lt-Cdr De Booy) two ships of 6803 tons. In the area of Lampedusa, *Unique* (Lt Collett) sinks one small ship of 736 tons. In the area of the Aegean, *Parthian* (Cdr Rimington) sinks one Italian ship of 5232 tons off the Dardanelles and *Torbay* (Lt-Cdr Miers) sinks two ships and a sailing ship totalling 7114 tons and torpedoes one Rumanian passenger ship of 5700 tons.

In the area of Buerat, *Taku* (Lt-Cdr v d Byl) attacks a small Italian convoy and, in a gun engagement, sinks on 5 June the Italian gunboat *Valoroso* (340 tons, armed with one 7.6cm gun) and two small freighters totalling 489 tons; on 11–12 June she sinks two more ships of 2967 tons and evades the Italian torpedo boats *Pallade* and *Polluce*.

2 June Air War/Germany
RAF Bomber Command attacks the Kaiser Wilhelm Canal.

3 June Mediterranean
An Italian convoy (six ships with four destroyers and a distant escort of two cruisers and four destroyers) is attacked off the Tunisian coast by British Maryland bombers. The freighters *Beatrice C* (6132 tons) and *Montello* (6117 tons) are lost.

3 June Mediterranean
The Italian 7th Div (Div Adm Casardi), comprising the cruisers *Eugenio di Savoia*, *Duca d'Aosta* and *Attendolo*, and the 4th Div (Div Adm Giovanola), comprising the cruisers *Bande Nere* and *Di Giussano* and the destroyers *Pigafetta*, *Da Mosto*, *Da Verazzano*, *Da Recco*, *Usodimare*, *Gioberti* and *Scirocco*, lay two mine barrages NE of Tripoli against British coastal shelling. On 19 Dec the British Force K runs on to the barrages (qv).

3–23 June Atlantic
In connection with Operation 'Rheinübung' (see 18–25 May), units of the British Fleet begin a systematic search for the ships of the German supply organisation during which German and Italian blockade-runners at sea are also lost. The process is facilitated by the capture of codes when the weather observation ship *München* (7 May) and the U-boat *U110* (10 May) are seized and later the supply ships *Gedania* and *Lothringen* (qv). This makes it possible to decode and read current German W/T traffic in 'Enigma/Heimische Gerwässer' in June.

On 28 May the blockade-runner *Lech* (3290 tons), coming from Rio de Janeiro, has to scuttle herself in the South Atlantic when a British warship comes into sight. Then on 29 May the weather observation ship *August Wriedt*, and probably also the weather observation ship *Hinrich Freese*, become victims of the British search operations.

On 3 June the tanker *Belchen* (6367 tons), after replenishing *U111* and *U557* in the Davis Strait, is sunk by the British cruisers *Aurora* and *Kenya* between Greenland and Labrador. *U93* rescues the survivors.

On 4 June the tanker *Gedania* (8923 tons) is abandoned in a panic when the auxiliary warship *Marsdale* comes into sight and is captured by her. An aircraft from the carrier *Victorious*, which is proceeding to Gibraltar with the cruiser *Hermione*, sights the patrol ship *Gonzenheim* (4000 tons) N of the Azores. The latter is able to escape from the auxiliary cruiser *Esperance Bay* (14204 tons) but has to scuttle herself when the battleship *Nelson* and the cruiser *Neptune*, which are summoned to the scene, come into view. *Neptune* torpedoes the burning wreck.

On 4 and 5 June respectively the tankers *Esso Hamburg* (9849 tons) and *Egerland* (9798 tons) scuttle themselves in the supply area of the Freetown–Natal route when approached by the heavy cruiser *London* and the destroyer *Brilliant*.

On 6 June the blockade-runner *Elbe* (9179 tons), coming from East Asia, is sunk by aircraft from the carrier *Eagle* near the Azores.

On 8 June Force H, comprising the battlecruiser *Renown*, the carrier *Ark Royal*, the cruiser *Sheffield* and six destroyers, sets out from Gibraltar for the W to avoid the anticipated Vichy French air attacks (in reprisal for the operation against Syria) and at the same time to intercept enemy supply ships and blockade-runners. On 9 June the carrier *Victorious*, coming from the N with the cruiser *Hermione*, is met. *Sheffield* returns to Britain: on 12 June she encounters the homebound *Friedrich Breme* (10397 tons) in the North Atlantic WNW of Cape Finisterre; the tanker scuttles herself. Force H arrives in Gibraltar on 11 June to carry out a new Malta operation (see 13–15 June). On 15 June the supply ship *Lothringen*, earmarked to replenish the U-boats operating off Freetown, is sighted in the Central Atlantic by an aircraft from the carrier *Eagle* and is captured by the cruiser *Dunedin*. When, at this time, the British search groups are replenishing and Force H is operating in the Mediterranean, the patrol ship *Kota Pinang*, the supply ships *Ermland* and *Spichern*, the Italian blockade-runners *Atlanta* and *Todaro* (coming from the Canaries) and the German *Regensburg* (from East Asia) pass through the blockade and reach western French ports.

On reports that ships have been sighted, Force H again sets out for the Atlantic on 16 June with *Renown*, *Ark Royal*, *Hermione* and five destroyers. It is then that *U138* (Lt Gramitzky), the only U-boat deployed in the area, falls victim to the destroyers *Faulknor*, *Fearless*, *Forester*, *Foresight* and *Foxhound*, which are sent to Gibraltar on 18 June to refuel.

After another unsuccessful search, Force H returns to Gibraltar on 21 June, but in the afternoon of 22 June British air reconnaissance sights the supply ship *Alstertor* (3039 tons) returning from the Indian Ocean. The auxiliary ship *Marsdale* and the destroyers *Faulknor*, *Fearless*, *Forester*, *Foxhound* and *Fury* are deployed in the search. When they come into view, *Alstertor* has to scuttle herself on 23 June off Cape Finisterre. With the crew, 78 British prisoners from the auxiliary cruiser *Atlantis* are rescued. On the return the destroyers meet the carrier *Furious*, which is proceeding to Gibraltar with the destroyers *Lance* and *Legion*, and they reach harbour again on 25 June.

In the meantime the cruiser *London* has compelled the German blockade-runner *Babitonga* (4422 tons), coming from Brazil, to scuttle herself in the South Atlantic.

5–7 June Mediterranean
Operation 'Rocket': British Force H, with the battlecruiser *Renown*, the carriers *Ark Royal* and *Furious* and six destroyers, leaves Gibraltar for the western Mediterranean and flies off on 6 June 35 Hurricane fighters which, led by Blenheim bombers from Gibraltar, reach Malta. On the return one machine makes a reconnaissance by moonlight over Mers-el-Kebir in order to establish the state of the Vichy French battleship *Dunkerque* before the operation in Syria.

On the Italian side, the submarines *Colonna* and *Da Procida* are stationed to counter a sortie by Force H towards Genoa and, to the W, *Bandiera*, *Diaspro* and *Manara* to prevent the passage through the Sicilian Channel.

6 June General Situation
Law enables the US Government to take over ships of foreign states laid up in American harbours.

7–9 June Mediterranean
An Italian convoy with three troop transports and a strong escort reaches Tripoli without loss.

7 June–14 July Mediterranean
British and Gaullist troops occupy Syria against strong French resistance. Sea operations are under the command of Vice-Adm King (15th Cruiser Sqn). The French naval commander in Syria, Rear Adm Gouton, has at his disposal the flotilla leaders

Guépard (Commander, Capt Gervais de Lafond) and *Valmy*, the sloop *Elan* and the submarines *Caiman*, *Marsouin* and *Souffleur*, as well as some smaller units unsuitable for action. On the 6 June British assault ship *Glengyle* sets out from Alexandria with the destroyers *Isis* and *Hotspur*. A commando operation N of Tyre on 7–8 June is abandoned because of the swell. The operation is covered by a force consisting of the cruisers *Phoebe* (F) and *Ajax* and the destroyers *Kandahar*, *Kimberley*, *Janus* and *Jackal*.

On 8 June *Kimberley* shells French positions near Tyre.

On 9 June a commando party from *Glengyle* lands behind French troops to capture an important bridge. Air cover is provided by the AA cruiser *Coventry*. The French submarine *Caiman* just misses *Ajax* with a torpedo. The large French destroyers *Guépard* and *Valmy* shell the forward troops of an Australian unit as they advance along the coast. In the pursuit there is an engagement off Sidon in which the British destroyer *Janus* receives five heavy hits. When the British destroyers *Jackal* (also hit), *Isis* and *Hotspur* come up, the French ships turn off and return to Beirut.

On 10 June the Australian destroyer *Stuart* and on 13 June the New Zealand cruiser *Leander* arrive as reinforcements. On 14 June there is unsuccessful sortie by the French destroyers which have a brief encounter with British units.

On 15 June Ju 88s of II/LG 1 (Capt Kollewe) damage the British destroyer *Isis* off Sidon and aircraft of the French 4th Naval Air Group badly damage *Ilex* with bombs.

On 16 June British torpedo aircraft of No 815 Sqn sink the French flotilla leader *Chevalier Paul*, employed as an ammunition transport, 50 nautical miles off the Syrian coast. *Guépard* and *Valmy* rescue the crew. The second ammunition transport, the flotilla leader *Vauquelin*, coming from Toulon, reaches Beirut but is damaged there on 17 June by British bombers.

On 17 June British forces are reinforced or relieved by the cruiser *Naiad* (F) with the destroyers *Nizam*, *Jaguar* and *Kingston*.

On 23 June *Guépard* tries to break through the British blockade of Beirut. In a night engagement with the cruisers *Leander* and *Naiad* and the destroyers *Jaguar*, *Kingston* and *Nizam*, she receives one hit but is able to get away because of her superior speed. The British destroyers *Jervis*, *Havock*, *Hotspur* and *Decoy*, engaged in submarine hunting in the area, do not approach.

On 25 June the British submarine *Parthian*

(Cdr Rimington) sinks the French submarine *Souffleur* in the Bay of Djounieh.

On 2 July the French 4th Naval Air Group (Lt-Cdr Hubert†) attacks Haifa. The Australian cruiser *Perth*, with *Naiad*, *Kandahar*, *Kingston*, *Havock* and *Griffin*, shells French positions on the coast.

The coast is shelled on 4 July by *Naiad*, *Ajax*, *Jackal*, *Nizam*, *Kimberley*, *Havock* and *Hasty*. Continuation of operations on 5, 6 and 7 July near Damour, the last fortified position before Beirut.

On 4 July Albacore torpedo aircraft from No 829 Sqn sinks the French supply steamer *St Didier* (2778 tons) off the Anatolian coast. The second ship, *Château Yquem* (2536 tons), which is en route with supplies for Syria, is later recalled when it is clear that it is impossible to break the British blockade. On 9–12 July the French flotilla leaders *Guépard*, *Valmy* and *Vauquelin* proceed from Syria to Salonica to take on a French infantry battalion which has arrived by the land route. The force is located by British air reconnaissance 200 nautical miles off the Syrian coast and goes, in accordance with instructions, to Toulon.

On 12 July there is an Armistice in Syria after General Dentz accepts the British conditions. The submarines *Caiman* and *Morse* go to Bizerta. The signing of an Armistice takes place on 14 July.

10 June   North Sea
The British corvette *Pintail* is mined and sunk off the Humber.

10 June   Red Sea
Operation 'Chronometer': the landing of an Indian battalion in Assab, the last Italian harbour in the Red Sea, by a force (Rear-Adm Hallifax) comprising the cruiser *Dido*, the auxiliary cruiser *Chakdina*, the Indian sloops *Clive* and *Indus* and one transport.

12 June   General Situation
The US Navy calls up its non-exempted reservists.

12–13 June   North Sea
Attempt by the heavy cruiser *Lützow* (Capt Kreisch) to break out into the Atlantic to take part in mercantile warfare. Shortly before midnight on 12 June British air reconnaissance locates the cruiser with her five escort destroyers off Lindesnes. Two hours later Bristol Beaufort torpedo aircraft of No 42 Sqn Coastal Command attack the force. Flt Sgt Loveitt secures one torpedo hit on *Lützow* amidships. With partly disabled engines and a heavy list, the cruiser returns to the Baltic and reaches Kiel in the afternoon of 14 June where she has to remain in dock until Jan 1942.

13–14 June   Air War/Western Europe
110 British bombers attack the German battlecruisers in Brest.

13–15 June   Mediterranean
Operation 'Tracer': Force H, with the battlecruiser *Renown*, the carriers *Ark Royal* and *Victorious* and six destroyers. On 14 June 47 Hurricane fighters are flown off to Malta S of the Balearics; 43 of them, led by four Hudson bombers, reach their destination. The Italian submarines *Corallo* and *Santarosa*, stationed S of Sardinia, do not sight the force.

13 June–18 Nov   Arctic
Transfer of Soviet submarines from the Baltic Fleet to the Northern Fleet by way of the White Sea Channel: *K-23* 13 June–30 Sept, *K-21* 15 July–24 Oct, *S-101*, *S-102*, *L-20* and *L-22* 5 Aug–8 Sept, *K-22* 22 Aug–30 Oct and *K-3* 23 Aug–8 Nov.

June   Intelligence
Because the US Navy is not willing to provide the Royal Navy with its ECM Mark I code machine, the Admiralty introduces 'Naval Cypher No 3' for inter-Allied communications and for the direction of the North Atlantic convoys. The German B-Service concentrates its efforts against this new code. Success is slow to come, but finally from Dec 1942 to May 1943 up to about 80 per cent of the intercepted signals are decoded (though only 10 per cent of them in time to take effective action).

14 June–11 Sept   North Atlantic
On 14 June the boundary of the Western Hemisphere is moved forward from 30°W to 26°W. The following battleships patrol in the Central North Atlantic in 7–14 day sorties in co-operation with destroyer groups: *Texas* (19–27 June and 17–25 July) and *Arkansas* (7–15 Aug and 2–11 Sept) with *Rhind* and *Mayrant*; *New Mexico* (26 June–4 July, 25 July–2 Aug and 14 Aug–23 Aug) with *Hughes* and *Russell*; *Mississippi* (3–11 July, 1–16 Aug and 27 Aug–11 Sept) with *O'Brien* and *Walke* and *Stack*, *Sterett* and *Rowan*; and *Idaho* (10–18 July) with *Morris* and *Sims*.

With the Central Atlantic Neutrality Patrol (see 7 Apr–10 June), Crudiv 7 is relieved from 15 July by Crudiv 8 comprising the cruisers *Savannah*, *Brooklyn*, *Nashville* and *Philadelphia* and from the beginning of Sept Desron II is withdrawn for convoy service and operations from Iceland.

On 15 June US TF.3 (Rear-Adm Ingram), with the cruisers *Memphis*, *Milwaukee*, *Cincinnati* and *Omaha* (Crudiv 2) and the destroyers *Somers*, *Winslow*, *Moffett*, *Davis* and *Jouett*, begins its patrols in the Neutrality Zone, extended to 20° S from the Brazilian bases of Recife and Bahia.

16 June Atlantic/Intelligence

The BdU starts to send, in radio signals, the positions by distance and direction from secret reference points instead of using the probably compromised grid positions.

17 June Western Atlantic

The British auxiliary cruiser *Pretoria Castle* captures the Vichy French steamer *Desirade* (9645 tons) E of the Antilles.

19–21 June General Situation

As a result of information received about German preparations to attack the Soviet Union, the People's Commissar for the Soviet Navy, Adm N G Kuznetsov, issues a Grade 2 Alert for the subordinate fleet commanders on 19 June and a Grade 1 Alert at 23.37 hrs on 21 June. Strict instructions are issued to avoid any provocations which would give the Germans an excuse to attack.

19–21 June Baltic

During the nights 18–19, 19–20 and 20–21 June the German minelayers *Preussen*, *Grille*, *Skagerrak* and *Versailles*, together with six boats of the 6th MS Flotilla, under the command of the Officer Commanding Minelayers Capt Bentlage, lay between Memel and Öland the mine barrages 'Wartburg I–III' (1150 EMCs and 1800 explosive floats). In the process the Soviet cruiser *Kirov* is observed in the evening of 18 June W of Libau. Finnish minelayers lay mine barrages on 21 June near Manni and Jussarö.

19 June–11 July Mediterranean

The British-Australian 10th DD Flotilla, comprising *Stuart*, *Vendetta*, *Waterhen*, *Voyager*, *Vampire*, *Defender*, *Decoy* and *Dainty* and the sloops *Flamingo*, *Auckland* and *Parramatta*, suffers losses in the frequent German and Italian dive-bomber attacks on their supply missions between Alexandria, Mersa Matruh and the beleaguered fortress of Tobruk. On 24 June *Auckland* sinks, as does, on 29 June, *Waterhen*, both off Bardia and, on 11 July, *Defender* off Sidi Barani.

20–29 June North Atlantic

Because it is suspected that the 'West' group is being avoided, the U-boats *U71*, *U96*, *U203*, *U79*, *U651*, *U371*, *U108*, *U553*, *U556*, *U562*, *U201*, *U751*, *U75*, *U558*, *U557*, *U77*, *U101*, *U111*, *U43*, *U559*, *U202* and *U564* are distributed in a loose formation over the Central North Atlantic.

On 20 June *U203* (Lt-Cdr Mützelburg) sights the US battleship *Texas* inside the operational area announced by Germany and shadows her for several hours. On her reporting this, orders are issued forbidding attacks on US ships even when they are in the operational area. The British decode this

signal and Churchill informs President Roosevelt. On 23 June *U203* sights the convoy HX.133, escorted by the Canadian destroyer *Ottawa* and the corvettes *Chambly*, *Collingwood* and *Orillia*, and sinks one ship during the night 23–24 June but then loses contact. At mid-day she comes across the approaching OB.336, from which one ship of 9358 tons is sunk. On 24 June *U79* directs to the scene in turn *U71*, which is driven off, *U371* (Lt-Cdr Driver) and *U651* (Lt-Cdr Lohmeyer) which each sink one ship, of 4765 tons and 5297 tons respectively. *U111* has to break off the pursuit. *U108*, *U553*, *U101*, *U77* and *U558* shadow OB.336 without success. On 25 June *U75* (Lt-Cdr Ringelmann) sinks one ship of 1967 tons. On 26 June *U556*, *U564* and *U201* establish contact with HX.133. *U564* (Lt Suhren) sinks two ships of 17463 tons during the night 26–27 June and torpedoes one other of 9467 tons. On 27 June *U556* (Lt-Cdr Wohlfarth) is sunk by the escorting corvettes *Nasturtium*, *Celandine* and *Gladiolus*. *U651*, *U79*, *U562*, and *U201* do not fire their torpedoes. On 28 June only *U651* is able to maintain contact; *U201* is driven off. Shortly after midnight on 29 June *U651* sinks one ship of 6342 tons but is then sunk by the destroyers *Malcolm* and *Scimitar*, the corvettes *Arabis* and *Violet* and the minesweeper *Speedwell*. The sighting of the convoy by an Fw 200 of I/KG 40 on 29 June does not result in any more U-boats coming to the scene. Total results: eleven ships of 57215 tons sunk and two ships damaged. On 28 June *U146* (Lt Ites), operating NW of the Hebrides, sinks one ship of 3496 tons. *U137* has no success.

W of Gibraltar, the Italian submarine *Glauco* is sunk by the destroyer *Wishart* on 27 June.

June Baltic/Intelligence

The German forces in the eastern Baltic are allocated a separate cypher circuit for operations against the Soviet Union—'Östliche Ostsee', used up to Nov 1941, and again from May 1942 to Jan 1943. 'Potsdam' is used from Apr 1943 up to the end of the war, now encompassing the whole of the Baltic, the Kattegat and the Skagerrak. (It is broken only in Jan 1944 as 'Plaice'/'Whelk'.)

21–22 June Baltic

Minelayer Group North (Cdr* v. Schönermark), comprising the minelayers *Tannenberg*, *Brummer* and *Hansestadt Danzig* and escorted by four boats of the 2nd MTB Flotilla and five boats of the 5th MMS Flotilla, lays the 'Apolda' barrage (500 EMCs and 700 explosive floats) between Fanöfjord and Dagö. The operation is carried out according to plan despite an attack by two

Soviet aircraft and despite being sighted by destroyers and guard vessels.

At the same time the 'Cobra' Group (Cdr Dr Brill), comprising *Cobra*, *Kaiser* and *Königin Luise* and escorted by six boats of the 1st MTB Flotilla and five minesweepers of the 5th MMS Flotilla, lays the 'Corbetha' barrage (400 EMCs and 700 explosive floats) between Kallbada-Grund and Pakerort. This force sights a Soviet battleship and a number of other vessels.

The 2nd MTB Flotilla lays 12 TMB mines in both the Soelo and Moon Sound exits ('Coburg' and 'Gotha' barrages); the 5th MTB Flotilla lays 12 TMBs in the western approaches to the Irben Strait ('Eisenach') and the 3rd MTB Flotilla lays 12 TMBs in both the approaches to Libau and Windau ('Weimar' and 'Erfurt'). A few minutes after the opening of hostilities, at 0300 hrs, *S59* (Lt Albert Müller) and *S60* (Lt Wuppermann) sink the Latvian steamer *Gaisma* (3077 tons) off Windau. The 1st MTB Flotilla captures the Estonian steamer *Estonia* (1181 tons).

21–23 June Mediterranean

German/Italian return convoy from Tripoli is continually attacked by British aircraft based on Malta. All ships, including two damaged freighters, reach Trapani and Naples under the protection of four destroyers and five torpedo boats.

22 June General Situation

Beginning of the German attack on the Soviet Union.

Strength of the Soviet Fleets: the Baltic Fleet (Vice-Adm Tributs) comprises two battleships, two heavy cruisers, two flotilla leaders, seven old and 12 modern destroyers, seven patrol ships (torpedo boats), 65 submarines, six minelayers, 32 minesweepers, one gunboat, 48 torpedo cutters (motor torpedo boats) and 656 aircraft; the Northern Fleet (Vice-Adm Golovko) has three old and five modern destroyers, seven patrol ships (including three torpedo boats), 15 submarines, two minesweepers, 15 patrol cutters, two torpedo cutters, auxiliary ships and 116 aircraft; and the Black Sea Fleet (Vice-Adm Oktyabrski) consists of one battleship, two modern, three old and one training cruiser, three flotilla leaders, five old and eight modern destroyers, two patrol ships (torpedo boats), 47 submarines, 84 torpedo cutters, 15 minesweepers and 625 aircraft.

22 June Arctic

Soviet Northern Fleet (Vice-Adm A G Golovko) begins operations. The submarine brigade (Capt 1st Class N I Vinogradov) sends the submarines *K-1*, *D-3*, *Shch-421* and *Shch-401* on operations against German supply traffic in Söröy-Sund, to the North Cape and Nordkyn and off Syltefjord. *M-176*, *M-175* and *M-173* are stationed in defensive positions in the area of the Fisherman's Peninsula.

On orders of the People's Commissar, the submarines *Shch-403* and *Shch-404* are employed defensively off the Kola coast and the destroyers *Grozny* and *Sokrushitelny* in the entrance to the White Sea. The evacuation to the east of women and children in transports from Murmansk begins.

22 June Black Sea

The Black Sea Fleet, in accordance with plans, begins to lay out defensive mine barrages off its own bases at Sevastopol, Odessa, Kerch, Novorossisk, Tuapse and Batum. The cruisers *Krasny Kavkaz* and *Chervona Ukraina*, the flotilla leader *Kharkov*, the destroyers *Boiki*, *Besposhchadny* and *Bezuprechny*, the minelayer *Ostrovski* and the training cruiser *Komintern* take part off Sevastopol and the destroyer *Dzerzshinski* off Batum. In all, 3453 mines and 509 barrage protection devices are laid off Sevastopol in 1941. Aircraft of the German FK IV attack Sevastopol. Rumanian coastal batteries shell the Soviet monitors *Rostovtsev*, *Zheleznyakov* and *Zhemchuzhin* in the Danube Estuary near Reni.

22 June North Atlantic

U48 returns to Kiel after making her twelfth and last mission into enemy waters. On these missions, under the command of Lt-Cdr Herbert Schultze (eight missions), Cdr Hans Rösing (two missions) and Lt-Cdr Heinrich Bleichrodt (two missions), she has, in all, sunk one sloop and 54 ships of 322378 tons and damaged two ships of 11024 tons. She is therefore the most successful submarine of the Second World War.

22–23 June Baltic

Ju 88s of K F1 Gr 806 drop 27 mines in the area of Kronstadt, on which the Estonian steamer *Ruhno* (499 tons) sinks on 22 June, and they attack ships. The Soviet steamer *Luga* (2329 tons) is sunk.

The Finnish submarines *Iku-Turso* (Lt-Cdr Pekkanen) and *Vetehinen* (Lt-Cdr Pakkala) lay 20 mines each on 22 June in the Gulf of Finland, E of Ekholm and N of Kunda Bay respectively; and *Vesihiisi* (Lt-Cdr Kijanen) lays 20 mines N of Ekholm on 23 June (mine barrages F.4, 5 and 3).

In a sortie into the area off Hangö, the 3rd MTB Flotilla attacks one steamer and *S44* (Lt Opdenhoff) sinks the Soviet patrol boat *MO-238*.

The 3rd MTB Flotilla lays 18 TMB mines in the Irben Strait.

At 1822 hrs on 22 June a force (Capt 2nd Class I G Svyatov) comprising the cruiser

Maksim Gorki and the destroyers *Gnevny*, *Gordy* and *Steregushchi* leaves Ust-Dvinsk to go through the Irben Strait and take up a position off the western exit of the Gulf of Finland to cover mining operations. To carry out these operations (under the orders of the Cdr of the Sqn, Rear-Adm D D Vdovichenko), the minelayers *Marti* and *Ural*, the flotilla leaders *Leningrad* and *Minsk* and the destroyers *Karl Marx*, *Artem* and *Volodarsky* set out from Tallinn. Three BT Shchs and some MOs and the destroyer *Smely* form the anti-mine and submarine escorts. On 23 June at 0340 hrs the covering force runs into the German 'Apolda' mine barrage in the area of the Oleg Bank; the destroyer *Gnevny* has her bow blown off by a detonating mine and sinks. *Gordy* is damaged by mines detonating in her bow paravanes. *Maksim Gorki*, as a result of hitting a mine, loses her bow up to her 60th frame. *Steregushchi* detonates two mines with her bow paravanes but she brings the disabled cruiser to Worms. From there minesweepers and torpedo cutters bring her to Tallinn. On 24 June the minesweeper *T-208* is lost on a mine.

22–27 June Baltic

Defence of Soviet naval base at Libau (Commandant: Capt 1st Class M S Klevenski) by the 67th Rifle Div (Maj-Gen Dedaev). In the harbour are 15 submarines of the 1st SM Bde, one destroyer, six torpedo cutters, 12 patrol cutters and one minesweeper.

The submarines *Kalev*, *Lembit*, *S-7*, *S-8*, *M-77*, *M-78* and *S-9* are moved with a steamer to Dünamünde and on the way *M-78* is lost off Windau to a torpedo hit from *U144*. The submarines *Kalev* and *Lembit* and the transport *Zheleznodorozhnik*, with the patrol boat *MO-218*, are transferred to Windau, followed by eight steamers. The mine-sweeper *Fugas* (Lt Gillerman) lays several barrages with 207 mines on 22–23 June, on which the minesweeper *M3134* sinks on 1 July, the submarine-chaser *UJ113* on 10 July, the patrol vessel *V309* on 28 Oct and the minesweepers *M1708* on 31 Oct and *M1706* on 22 Nov.

On 23 June the submarine *S-3*, with very many personnel on board, is transferred from Libau to Dünamünde, but off Steinort, after several torpedo misses from the motor torpedo boat *S35* (Sub-Lt H. Weber), is sunk by depth charges and hand grenades. Attacks by *S27* and *S60* on the force of 12 patrol boats and one auxiliary warship, which is transferred at the same time, fail. On 24 June the non-operational ships in Libau, the destroyer *Lenin*, the submarines *S-1*, *M-71*, *M-80*, *Ronis* and *Spidola*, the ice-breaker *Silach* (541 tons) and the auxili-

ary gunboat *Tunguska* (947 tons), are scuttled. The torpedo cutter *TKA-27* is lost.

On 25 June the returning *M-83* scuttles herself off Libau; the other submarines are diverted at sea to Dünamünde. During the night 25–26 June *Fugas* (see above) lays another barrage and then leaves for the N. During the night 26–27 June the torpedo cutters *TKA-37*, *TKA-57* and *TKA-67* proceed to Dünamünde and, finally, *TKA-17* (Lt Osipov with Capt Klevenski on board) and *TKA-47*. The last is captured off Backofen after an engagement with the 2nd MTB Flotilla. Units of the German 291st Inf Div, supported by the Naval Assault Detachment Bigler, enter Libau on 27–29 June and occupy the town.

22–30 June Mediterranean

In British submarine operations in the Western Mediterranean, *Severn* (Lt-Cdr Campbell) sinks two ships of 4192 tons and the Dutch *O23* (Lt-Cdr v Erkel) one ship of 5317 tons. In the Central Mediterranean, *Union* (Lt Galloway) and *Utmost* (Lt-Cdr Cayley) each sink one ship, of 1004 tons and 4080 tons respectively. *Triumph* (Lt-Cdr Wards) sinks the Italian submarine *Salpa* off Sollum. In the middle of the year the British submarine flotillas in the Mediterranean consist of the 8th SM Flotilla (Gibraltar), with *Clyde* and *Severn* and the Dutch *O21*, *O23*, *O24* and other boats proceeding E to form the 10th and 1st SM Flotillas; the 10th SM Flotilla (Malta), comprising *Ursula*, *Utmost*, *Upright*, *Unique*, *Upholder*, *Unbeaten*, *Urge*, *Union*, *P32* and *P33*; and the 1st SM Flotilla (Alexandria), consisting of *Truant*, *Triumph*, *Taku*, *Tetrarch*, *Torbay*, *Regent*, *Rover*, *Otus*, *Rorqual*, *Cachalot*, *Parthian* and *Pandora* and the Greek *Katsonis*, *Papanicolis*, *Nereus*, *Triton* and *Glavkos*.

22–30 June Baltic

The German U-boats *U140*, *U142*, *U144*, *U145* and *U149* operate W of Memel, S of Gotland, W of Windau, W of Ösel-Dagö and off the Gulf of Finland. During the night 22–23 June *U144* (Lt-Cdr v Mittelstaedt) sinks the Soviet submarine *M-78*, on 24 June *U140* misses a large submarine and on 26 June *U149* (Lt-Cdr Höltring) sinks *M-99* off Utö.

First climax of the Soviet submarine effort. At the beginning of the war, *S-4* is off Memel, *S-5* and *S-6* off the Pomeranian Coast, *S-10* in the Gulf of Danzig, *S-7* and *S-101* off Gotland for reconnaissance, *Shch-309*, *Shch-310* and *Shch-311* further to the E and *Shch-322*, *Shch-323* and *Shch-324* in defensive positions off the Gulf of Finland—and, similarly, *M-94*, *M-96*, *M-99* and *M-102* in the area Bengtskär-Utö.

Of the 1st Bde (Capt 1st Class Egipko), *M-79*, *M-81* and *M-83* take up defensive positions off Libau and *L-3* (Capt 3rd Class Grishchenko) sets out for a mining operation off Memel (mines laid on 27 June). On 23 June six boats go to sea from Tallinn from the 2nd Bde (Capt 2nd Class Orel); on 25 June there are 16 boats and on 27 June 20 boats stationed mainly in defensive positions. Apart from the boats named, some of which have come in to port, *S-5*, *S-8* and *S-102* operate from Riga and *M-89*, *M-90*, *M-95*, *M-97*, *M-98*, *Shch-309*, *Shch-310* and *Shch-311* from Tallinn. On 24, 25 and 28 June *S-10*, *S-4* and *L-3* make unsuccessful attacks. On 27 June the boats of the 1st Bde, which are not yet on the way back, are recalled to Tallinn. On the return through the Irben Strait, *S-7* is narrowly missed by the 3rd MTB Flotilla on 25 June. *S-10* is probably involved in an engagement on 27 June and is lost.

22–30 June   Black Sea

First air attacks by the air force of the Soviet Black Sea Fleet on Constanza. On 22 June six SB-2s and three DB-3s of the 63rd Air Bde (Col Khotiashvili) attack. Up to the end of the month there are 38 attacks in 285 sorties with the participation of the 2nd and 4th Air Regts of the 62nd Fighter Bde.

22 June–4 July   Black Sea

The German II/KG 4, operating from Zilista, drops 120 mines in on and off Sevastopol and 50 mines in the area of Nikolaev. On 22–23 June there sink on these mines the tug *SP-12*, the barge *Dnepr*, one floating crane and the destroyer *Bystry* which is later salvaged and dismantled to repair damaged sister-ships. The destroyer *Bditelny* is badly damaged and the flotilla leader *Kharkov* slightly damaged on 12 July.

22 June–17 July   Black Sea

Submarines of the Soviet 1st SM Bde (Capt 1st Class P I Boltunov) operate from Sevastopol in defined areas off Constanza, Mangalia and Varna; some of the boats of the 2nd Bde (Capt 1st Class M G Solovev) operate in the area of the Danube estuary and the remainder in defensive formations off the Caucasian coast. The first wave consists of *M-33*, *M-34*, *Shch-205*, *Shch-206* and *Shch-209*. *Shch-206* does not return: she is probably sunk on one of the flanking mine barrages laid off the Rumanian coast.

23 June   Black Sea

The Soviet destroyer *Shaumyan* and the minesweeper *T-413/No 27* lay a mine barrage of 70 mines off the Kilia estuary.

23–25 June   Black Sea

On a report by the Danube Flotilla that six enemy destroyers and torpedo boats have been sighted, the flotilla leader *Kharkov* and the destroyers *Besposhchadny* and *Smyshleny* proceed to the area of Fidonisi Island but sight no enemy ships.

24–26 June   Baltic

On 24 June the Finnish submarines *Vesihiisi* and *Iku-Turso* lay 18 and 20 mines respectively E and SE of Rodskär in the Gulf of Finland. The German 2nd MTB Flotilla lays 36 TMB mines (barrage 'D.1') N of Cape Takhkona.

During the night 25–26 June the German minelayer *Brummer* (Cdr Dr Tobias) lays 100 EMC mines and 50 explosive floats ('D.2') north of Moon Sound. In escorting her, boats of the 2nd and 5th MTB Flotillas run on to the Soviet barrages laid out at the beginning of the war and *S43* and *S106* sink. On returning from a minelaying operation W of the Irben Strait, the boats of the 3rd MTB Flotilla encounter the Estonian steamer *Lidaza*, which is torpedoed by *S34* (Sub-Lt Lüders). *S54*, *S60* and *S61* fire torpedoes in the harbour of Windau and obtain three hits on the mole and one on a steamer.

The Finnish minelayers *Riilahti* and *Ruotsinsalmi* lay the 'Kipinola' barrage with 200 mines during the night 25–26 June. On 26 June the Finnish submarines *Vesihiisi* and *Iku-Turso* lay two more barrages, of 20 and 18 mines respectively S of Stenskär and S of Suur-Tytärsaari.

24–26 June   Indian Ocean

The German auxiliary cruiser *Schiff 41/Kormoran*, coming up to mine Madras, encounters the British auxiliary cruiser *Canton* (15784 tons). *Schiff 41* is able to escape undetected but has to abandon the proposed operation. On 26 June she sinks two freighters of 7625 tons in the Bay of Bengal.

24–27 June   Baltic

The Soviet group of light naval forces (Rear-Adm V P Drozd) based Dünamünde begins with the laying of mine barrages in the western half of the Irben Strait. Taking part are the destroyers *Storozhevoi*, *Silny*, *Serdity*, *Strashny*, *Stoiki*, *Grozyashchi* and *Smetlivy* and, for support, the cruiser *Kirov* and minesweepers. In all, some 500 mines are laid during the nights 24–25 and 26–27 June. In the second operation there is an engagement with the 3rd MTB Flotilla which is likewise out on a mining sortie. At first *S59* (Lt Müller) and *S31* (Sub-Lt Haag) attack and obtain one hit in the bow of *Storozhevoi*. Then *S59* and *S60* (Lt Wuppermann) get hits on a vessel to the rear, possibly the submarine *S-10* which has just joined. In a third attack, *S35* (Sub-Lt

Weber) and *S60* probably sink the Soviet minesweeper *T-208/Shkiv*.

On the barrages laid out, the motor minesweeper *R205* sinks, the minesweepers *M201* and *R203* are badly damaged and *R53*, *R63* and *R202* slightly damaged.

24–30 June   Mediterranean

The British sloop *Auckland* is dive-bombed NE of Tobruk by German aircraft. The RAN sloop *Parramatta* rescues 162 survivors. On 29 June the destroyer *Waterhen* is damaged in a German air attack off Tobruk and sinks while under tow by the destroyer *Defender* on 30 May. The gunboat *Cricket* is damaged by dive-bombers; towed to Alexandria, it becomes a constructive total loss.

24 June–8 July   Black Sea

Soviet-Danube Flotilla (Rear-Adm N O Abramov) with the Reni group—the monitors *Rostovtsev*, *Zheleznyakov* and *Zhemchuzhin* and four armoured cutters (BKAs)—holds up attempts by Rumanian monitors to advance down the Danube across the Pruth Estuary. From Ismailia, the monitors *Udarny* and *Martynov* with 12 BKAs support small landings of units of the 25th Rifle Div on the S bank of the Kilia arm.

24 June–17 July   North Atlantic

Operations by an Italian submarine group against convoys W of Gibraltar. On 24 June *Da Vinci* (Cdr Calda) sinks one tanker of 8030 tons sailing on her own. *Bianchi*, which is setting out to join the group, is sunk when still in the Bay of Biscay by the British submarine *Tigris* (Cdr Bone) on 5 July. On 5 July *Torelli* (Cdr de Giacomo) sights one small convoy proceeding westward, to which *Da Vinci*, *Baracca*, *Malaspina* and *Morosini* are directed. Only *Torelli* is able to make an unsuccessful attack on one destroyer. On 7 July *Torelli* sights another outbound convoy (possibly HG.66), to which *Morosini*, *Da Vinci* and *Baracca*, as well as *U103*, are directed. But they do not find the convoy. From 14 to 17 July *Morosini* (Cdr Fraternale) and *Malaspina* (Lt-Cdr Prini) each sink two ships, of 13552 tons and 7978 tons respectively.

25–26 June   Arctic

Covered by destroyers and submarine-chasers of the Northern Fleet, the Soviet transport *Mossovet* brings troop reinforcements to the Titovka sector. German air attacks are unsuccessful.

25–27 June   Black Sea

Soviet sortie against Constanza. On the evening of 25 June the assault group (Capt 2nd Class M F Romanov) leaves Sevastopol with the flotilla leaders *Kharkov* and *Moskva*, followed by a covering force (Rear-

Adm T A Novikov) comprising the cruiser *Voroshilov* and the destroyers *Smyshleny* and *Soobrazitelny*. Simultaneously with a diversionary attack by aircraft of the 63rd Naval Air Bde, *Kharkov* and *Moskva* shell oil tanks and railway installations near Constanza on 26 June, resulting in fires and the blowing up of an ammunition train. The fire is answered from a railway battery to the N and from the 28cm battery 'Tirpitz' to the S of Constanza. In avoiding the salvos, *Moskva* runs on to one of the flanking mine barrages laid before the war and sinks. As a result of a mine being detonated by the bow paravanes of *Soobrazitelny*, there is temporary damage to *Voroshilov*. *Kharkov* becomes unmanoeuvrable for a short time because of near-miss bombs and the two other destroyers are sent to provide help in the form of additional AA cover. The destroyers *Besposhchadny* and *Bodry*, which have sailed from Sevastopol, meet *Voroshilov*.

25–28 June Arctic/Intelligence
The British cruiser *Nigeria*, with three destroyers, is directed to the weather signals from the weather observation ship *Lauenburg* (*WBS 2*, 344 tons), located by D/F. In spite of mist, it is possible to find the *Lauenburg* near Jan Mayen on 28 June after another D/F location by the destroyer *Bedouin*. She is abandoned by the crew in the fire of the British ships; the destroyer *Tartar* goes alongside at once and is able to recover valuable code materials which enable Bletchley Park to read the 'Enigma/Heimische Gewässer' messages for the month of July. For fear of revealing the secret of 'Ultra', further similar operations are strictly forbidden.

25–29 June Mediterranean
Italian convoy with four large troop transports from Naples to Tripoli via Taranto; close escort is provided by four destroyers and distant escort by two cruisers and three destroyers. Slight damage is sustained by the passenger ship *Esperia* during British air attacks.

26 June Baltic
A Soviet force including the minelayer *Marti* (Capt 1st Class N I Meshcherski) lays further parts of a mine barrage in the western part of the Gulf of Finland between Odensholm and Hangö.

26–27 June Baltic
The minelayer *Brummer*, escorted by the MTBs *S43*, *S106*, *S42*, *S105*, *S44* and *S104* of the 2nd MTB Flotilla and *S47*, *S28* and *S46* of the 5th Flotilla, lays a minefield between the 'Apolda' and 'Corbetha' barrages.

26 June–1 July Mediterranean
Operation 'Railway': Force H, with the battlecruiser *Renown*, the carrier *Ark Royal*, the cruiser *Hermione* and six destroyers, sets out from Gibraltar on 26 June for the area S of the Balearics where, in spite of bad weather, 22 of the Hurricane fighters received from *Furious* are flown off. They all reach Malta with their Blenheim guide aircraft. Force H returns on 28 June but puts to sea on 29 June with the carrier *Furious* for a second operation. On 30 June 26 Hurricanes fly off from *Ark Royal* and nine from *Furious* and they all reach Malta. Then a take-off accident on *Furious* makes it impossible for the remaining eight machines to fly off and Force H returns on 1 July.

27 June Baltic
The Finnish minelayers *Riilahti* and *Ruotsinsalmi* lay the 'Kulemajärvi' barrage (200 S/40s) NE of Odensholm.

27 June Manchukuo/Western France
The blockade-runner *Regensburg* (8068 tons, Capt Harder) reaches Bordeaux from Dairen.

27–28 June Air War/Germany
British bombers attack Bremen, Cuxhaven, Emden and Wilhelmshaven.

27–30 June Arctic
Some 150 Soviet civilian ships, boats and fishery vessels are evacuated to the White Sea from the Kola Inlet. The operation suffers no losses.

27 June–4 July Central Atlantic
Operations against the convoy SL.76 in the area of the Cape Verde Islands. The returning *U69* (Lt-Cdr Metzler) sights the convoy as the U-boat is proceeding to Las Palmas to refuel from the German tanker *Charlotte Schliemann* and sinks two ships of 13026 tons. On the same day *U123* (Lt-Cdr Hardegen), which is outbound and coming from Las Palmas, establishes contact and sinks two more ships of 7642 tons. On 29 June she approaches again and sinks one steamer of 4088 tons, while the outbound *U66* (Cdr Zapp) sinks two scattered ships of 10031 tons and the returning *U103* (Cdr Schütze), which is in the area, sinks the Italian blockade-runner *Ernani* 6619 tons) in error. The U-boats *UA*, *U95*, *U97* and *U98*, which are directed to SL.76 from the N, do not get to the scene.

28 June Mediterranean
Mine barrage S.2 (442 mines and barrage protection devices) is laid in the Sicilian Channel by the Italian 7th Div (Div Adm

Casardi), comprising the cruisers *Attendolo* and *Duca d'Aosta* and the destroyers *Pigafetta*, *Pessagno*, *Da Mosto*, *Da Verazzano* and *Da Recco*.

28 June Baltic
The Finnish submarine *Vetehinen* lays the mine barrage F.6 (17 S/36s) between Suursaari and Klein Tütters.

29 June Baltic
The Finnish minelayers *Riilahti* and *Ruotsinsalmi* lay the 'Valkjärvi' mine barrage (200 S/40s) N of Cape Purikari.

29 June–4 July Arctic
On 29 June the German XIX Mountain Corps (Gen Dietl), with the 2nd Mountain Div from the Petsamo area and the 3rd Mountain Div from the Yläluostari area, starts to attack in the direction of Murmansk. Early on 1 July the 136th Mountain Regt has, with two battalions, blocked the approach to the Small Fisherman's Peninsula and forms with one battalion a bridgehead across the Titovka. To support the hard-pressed defending forces of the Soviet 14th Rifle Div, a Soviet formation (Capt 2nd Class E M Simonov), consisting of the destroyers *Kuibyshev* and *Uritski* and the submarine-chasers *MO-121* and *MO-123*, lands reinforcements on 30 June on the narrow neck of the Fisherman's Peninsula and shells German advance troops. Attacks by Ju 87s of IV/LG 1 miss the Soviet ships, in particular the submarine-chaser *MO-121*. By 4 July the German Mountain Divs push the Soviet 14th and 52nd Rifle Divs back over the Litsa and form several bridgeheads. The Soviet troops are repeatedly supported by gunfire from the patrol ships *Groza* and *Smerch* from Motovski Bay.

29 June–15 July North Atlantic
The U-boats *U201*, *U562*, *U564*, *U561*, *U559*, *U557*, *U553*, *U202*, *U111*, *U108*, *U98*, *U96* and *U77* operate in a wide, loose formation in the Central Atlantic with very little success. On 29 June a convoy, probably OG.66, is sighted by I/KG 40. On 30 June and 1 July Fw 200s again report the convoy and their bearings are received by U-boats. The cryptography service also gives positions of the convoy but, of the boats directed to the scene, only *U108* comes briefly into the area and she is driven off again. *U77*, *U79*, *U96* and *U557* do not come up. On 3 July the operation is abandoned. The following sinkings of single ships are made: *U564* (Lt Suhren) sinks one ship of 1215 tons, *U108* (Lt-Cdr Scholtz) one of 2486 tons, *U98* (Lt-Cdr Gysac) two of 10842 tons and *U96* (Lt-Cdr Lehmann-

Willenbrock) one of 5954 tons. *U143* operates in the North Channel without success.

30 June   South Atlantic

The British cruiser *Dunedin* captures, E of St Paul, the Vichy French steamer *Ville de Tamatave* (4993 tons).

30 June–2 July   Baltic

The Soviets evacuate Riga and Dünamünde. The cruiser *Kirov*, which cannot pass through the Irben Strait because of the mines, is lightened and brought with the destroyers *Grozyashchi*, *Smetlivy* and *Stoiki* through the shallow waters of the Moon Sound to Tallinn. In the move from Dünamünde to Tallinn, the submarines *M-77* and *M-79* run on to German mine barrages and are damaged. *M-81* is lost on 1 July.

30 June–10 July   Mediterranean

In the Aegean the British submarine *Torbay* (Lt-Cdr Miers) sinks one ship of 2933 tons and six sailing ships, as well as the Italian submarine *Jantina* (5 July). She also torpedoes one ship of 5232 tons. In the Central Mediterranean *Urge* (Lt-Cdr Tomkinson) and *Upholder* (Lt-Cdr Wanklyn) each sink one ship, of 6996 tons and 5867 tons respectively.

1–5 July   Baltic

The 5th and 31st MS Flotillas make a channel in the mine barrage to Libau. In doing so, *M3134* sinks on 2 July. There are mining operations N of Cape Takhkona (1 July), E of the 'Apolda' barrage (2 July) and S of 'Corbetha' and W of Soelo Sound (5 July). The minelayer *Brummer*, the 5th MMS Flotilla and the 1st, 2nd and 3rd MTB Flotillas drop, in all, 196 mines and 130 explosive floats.

1 July   North Atlantic

Patrol Wing 7 of the US Navy starts reconnaissance over the North West Atlantic from Argentia (Newfoundland).

1–19 July   North Atlantic

American occupation of Iceland. On 1 July TF.19 (Rear-Adm McD Le Breton) sets out from Argentia with the battleships *Arkansas* and *New York*, the cruisers *Brooklyn* and *Nashville* and the destroyers *Plunkett*, *Niblack*, *Benson*, *Gleaves*, *Mayo*, *Charles F Hughes*, *Lansdale*, *Hilary P Jones* (Desron 7, Capt Kauffman), *Ellis*, *Bernadou*, *Upshur*, *Lea* (Desdiv 60) and *Buck*, the tanker *Salamonie* and the tug *Cherokee*. Its purpose is to land in Reykjavik, on 7 July, the 1st Marine Bde (Brig-Gen Marston), embarked on the troop transports *William P Biddle*, *Fuller*, *Heywood* and *Orizaba* and the freighters *Arcturus* and *Hamul*, to relieve the British forces stationed there. After the operation has been carried out according to plan, TF.19 returns to Argentia from 12 to 19 July.

1–30 July   Arctic

The Soviet submarines *M-174*, *Shch-422*, *Shch-402*, *Shch-401*, *M-172* and *D-3* operate off the Norwegian polar coast. On 14 July *Shch-402* (Lt-Cdr N G Stolbov) unsuccessfully attacks the steamer *Hanau* off Porsangerfjord and on the same day *Shch-401* (Lt-Cdr A E Moiseev) the submarine-chasers *UJ177* and *UJ178* off Vardö.

2–6 July   Baltic

The remaining destroyers of Rear-Adm Drozd's force carry out mining operations in the Irben Strait from Moon Sound. In the process, *Strashny* is badly damaged on a mine on 2 July. On 6 July *Serdity* and *Silny* encounter, when dropping mines, the German *Minenräumschiff 11* and the minesweeper *M31*: they have hurriedly to throw the remaining mines overboard and make off while firing. *Silny* is lightly hit. The two German ships reach Dünamünde undamaged after four unsuccessful air attacks.

2–27 July   Mediterranean

In transport operations by the Italian submarines *Zoea* (two), *Corridoni* (two) and *Atropo* (one), 268 tons of supplies are brought to Bardia.

3–4 July   Baltic

The minelayer *Brummer*, escorted by the 2nd MTB Flotilla and the 5th MMS Flotilla, with five vessels each, lays a minefield between the 'Apolda' and 'Corbetha' barrage.

3–17 July   Mediterranean

Of the Italian submarines *Malachite*, *Ametista*, *Settembrini* and *Dagabur* operating off the coasts of Cyrenaica and Egypt, *Malachite* is the only one to fire her torpedoes, which she does on 3 July. But she misses the cruiser *Phoebe* with two destroyers.

4 July   Air War/Germany

British bombers carry out a daylight raid on Bremen.

4 July   Baltic

The Finnish submarine *Vesikko* (Lt-Cdr Aittola) sinks the Soviet steamer *Viborg* S of Someri after unsuccessful attacks by *Saukko* and *Vetehinen*.

4–6 July   Baltic

The 5th German MS Flotilla creates a channel through the mine barrages from Libau to Windau. Soviet air attacks are beaten off: there is slight damage to *Sperrbrecher 6* and *11*.

4–10 July   Mediterranean

The submarines *Corallo* and *Diaspro* are stationed between the Balearics and the Algerian coast to act against sorties by British Force H.

5–15 July   Arctic

First operations by the German U-boats

U81 and *U652* off the Kola Coast. On 6 July *U652* (Lt Fraatz) sinks the Soviet patrol ship *SKR-11/No 70* (ex-*RT-66*, 1107 tons) off Cape Teriberski. On 12 July the Soviet patrol ship *SKR-29/Brilliant* attacks *U81* unsuccessfully off Svyatoy Nos.

5 July–6 Aug   Baltic

The Soviet submarines *S-7* and *S-9* cruise off Libau and Stolpmünde, followed by *S-11* and *S-8*. *L-3* lays a mine barrage off Memel and *S-11* misses one ship off Polangen on 19 July. *K-3* and *Kalev* have to cancel a mine operation. The returning *S-9* is damaged by air attack on 20 July and *S-11* sinks on 2 Aug on a mine barrage off Soelo Sund. From mid-July *Shch-322*, *Shch-323*, *Shch-406*, *Shch-308*, *Shch-405*, *Shch-307* and *Shch-324* relieve each other in the Central and Southern Baltic and *M-90*, *M-94*, *M-97* and *M-98* off the Finnish Gulf, where *M-94* is sunk on 22 July by *U140* (Lt Hellriegel).

6 July   Mediterranean

Off Benghazi, the British submarine *Triumph* sinks the Italian freighter *Ninfea* (607 tons) and the escorting gunboat *De Lutti* after a lengthy surface engagement. The submarine is also hit and has to put in to Malta.

6–8 July   Arctic

On 6 July the German 2nd and 3rd Mountain Divs start their attack across the Litsa. To support the hard-pressed Soviet 14th and 52nd Rifle Divs, a landing force (Capt 1st Class V I Platonov) is formed consisting of the patrol ships *Groza*, *Musson* and *Tuman*, the minesweepers *T-890* and *T-891* and the submarine-chasers *MO-131*, *MO-132* and *MO-133*. It lands a naval battalion on 6 July and again on 7 July, making in all 1029 troops. Their attack leads to regrouping on the German side and to the interruption of the attack across the Litsa.

7 July   Mediterranean

Mine barrages S.31 and S.32 are laid out in the Sicilian Channel (292 mines and 444 barrage protection devices) by the Italian 7th Cruiser Div (Div-Adm Casardi), comprising the cruisers *Attendolo* and *Duca d'Aosta*, and the 4th Cruiser Div (Div Adm Giavanola), comprising the cruisers *Bande Nere* and *Di Giussano* and the destroyers *Pigafetta*, *Pessagno*, *Da Recco*, *Da Mosto*, *Da Verazzano*, *Maestrale*, *Grecale* and *Scirocco*.

8 July   Baltic

Pernau is taken by German troops.

8–9 July   Black Sea

The Reni group of the Soviet Danube Flotilla breaks through to Ismailia with three monitors and four armoured cutters (*BKA-114* is sunk).

9 July Baltic

First German convoy with six coastal motorships and four drifters, escorted by five minesweepers, leaves Libau for Riga. Returning from Finland to Swinemünde, the minelayers *Tannenberg* (Cdr* v Schönermark), *Preussen* (Cdr Barthel) and *Hansestadt Danzig* (Cdr Schroeder) sink on a Swedish mine barrage E of the southern tip of Öland, which has been laid at German request.

9 July Black Sea

Unsuccessful sortie by the Soviet 2nd DD Div (flotilla leader *Tashkent*, destroyers *Bodry*, *Boiki*, *Besposhchadny* and *Bezuprechny*) to attack enemy shipping in the Fidonisi area.

9–11 July Baltic

The Finnish submarines *Iku-Turso* (Lt-Cdr Pekkanen) and *Vetehinen* (Lt-Cdr Pakkala) lay mine barrages E of Ekholm.

10 July Baltic

The 1st MTB Flotilla, comprising *S28*, *S26*, *S101*, *S40* and *S39*, attacks a Soviet force in the Gulf of Finland near Ekholm. But they only encounter the Latvian steamer *Rasma* (3204 tons), beached after hitting a mine on 5 July on the barrage laid by the Finnish submarine *Vesihiisi* (Lt-Cdr Kijanen).

10 July South Atlantic

When the British auxiliary cruiser *Canton* approaches, the German motor ship *Hermes* (7209 tons) scuttles herself NW of St Paul.

10–11 July Baltic

The German *Minenräumschiff 11*, with the minesweepers *M201* and *M23*, proceeds through the Irben Strait, where *M201* hits a mine and sinks, and the Gulf of Riga to Pernau, where also *M23* has to be beached after hitting a mine. Both minesweepers are salvaged and recommissioned after repairs in 1942–43.

10–12 July Arctic

The German 6th DD Flotilla (Capt Schulze-Hinrichs), comprising *Hans Lody*, *Karl Galster*, *Hermann Schoemann*, *Friedrich Eckoldt* and *Richard Beitzen*, arrives in Kirkenes on 10 July and makes a sortie along the Kola Coast on 12 July. In doing so, a group of three destroyers encounters, near Cape Teriberski, a small Soviet convoy with the patrol ship *SKR-22/Passat* (Lt Okunevich) and two trawlers. *Passat* and the trawler *RT-67/Molotov* sink and *RT-32/Kumzha* gets away. The other destroyers find no targets near Iokanga.

10 July–10 Aug Central Atlantic

After the conclusion of the operation against SL.76 (27 June), *U66* and *U123* proceed to the area off Freetown but their only successes are on the way out, up to 10 July.

Inclusive of the ships of SL.76, *U66* (Cdr Zapp) sinks four ships of 19078 tons and *U123* (Lt-Cdr Hardegen) five of 21507 tons. From 10 to 25 July they operate without success off Freetown. *U109* is likewise unsuccessful off NW Africa from 6 July. She replenishes on 27 June from a tanker in Cadiz and then operates W of Gibraltar. From 23 to 29 July *U93*, *U94* and *U124* proceed in line abreast to the S and are then stationed with *U123* in the area W of Morocco. With other boats they are directed on 10 Aug to the convoy HG.69 (qv). The boats do not have any success.

11 July Baltic

The Finnish submarine *Iko-Tursu* (Lt-Cdr Pekkanen) lays mine barrage F.15 (18 mines) E of Ekholm.

11 July Black Sea

In attempts by Soviet forces to land on the Kilia arm of the Danube estuary, the armoured cutters *BKA-111* and *BKA-134* are lost. The monitors *Zhemchuzhin*, *Rostovtsev* and *Martynov* are transferred to the Danube estuary.

11–12 July Mediterranean

In the nightly supply missions to Tobruk, the British destroyer *Defender* is badly damaged by German bombers and sinks when being towed by the destroyer *Vendetta*; the sloop *Flamingo* is damaged. About 30 German aircraft attack Port Said and Ismailia on the Suez Canal during the night 11–12 July.

11–20 July Baltic

The 5th MMS Flotilla sows 90 mines in the area N of 'Juminda' (11, 13 and 20 July).

12–13 July Baltic

The German Baltic Experimental Force proceeds from Libau to Riga with naval barges, Siebel ferries, lighters, floating gun carriers, coastal motor ships and assault boats. Cape Domesnäs is passed on 12 July with an escort from the 2nd MMS Flotilla. There is ineffectual shelling from Russian coastal batteries on Svorbe. On 13 July there are attacks by Soviet motor torpedo boats under Lt Gumanenko and by aircraft. One assault ship is sunk and two larger and three small craft receive splinter damage. An attack by a Soviet destroyer formation (Rear-Adm Drozd) consisting of *Engels*, *Gordy*, *Grozyashchi*, *Stoiki*, *Silny*, *Steregushchi* and *Serdity* and the torpedo boats *Sneg* and *Tucha*, off the Dvina estuary, has no result. Attempts by the Soviet submarine *S-102*, operating in the Gulf of Riga, to fire her torpedoes fail because the water is too shallow.

13–16 July Arctic

The second German attack by the reinforced 2nd Mountain Div from the

widened Litsa bridgehead begins on 13 July. The Soviet defence is supported by the patrol ship *Smerch* in the bay of Litsa. On 14 July a Soviet force (Capt 1st Class V I Platonov), consisting of three patrol ships, three minesweepers and 10 submarine-chasers, lands the 325th Rifle Regt and a naval battalion totalling 1600 troops on the western bank of the Bay of Litsa. Their counter-attack is supported by gunfire from the destroyer *Kuibyshev*, the patrol ship *Groza* and four submarine-chasers. The operation is covered towards the sea by the destroyers *Gremyashchi*, *Gromki* and *Stremitelny*. Once again the German attack comes to a standstill. On 16 July three patrol ships land another battalion in the Bay of Litsa, supported by the destroyer *Kuibyshev* and the patrol ships *Groza*, *Priliv*, *Smerch* and four submarine-chasers.

14 July Baltic

The 1st MTB Flotilla, comprising *S28*, *S27*, *S40*, *S101* and *S26*, attacks a Soviet convoy near Ekholm without success.

14 July Mediterranean

Ju 88s of LG 1 attack Suez from Crete. The troop transport *Georgic* (27751 tons) is set on fire and becomes a total loss.

14–18 July Mediterranean

Italian supply convoys to North Africa. From 14 to 16 July a convoy of five freighters, escorted by the destroyers *Malocello*, *Fuciliere* and *Alpino* and the motor torpedo boats *Procione*, *Pegaso* and *Orsa*, proceeds to Tripoli. In the area of Pantelleria, the British submarine *P33* (Lt Whiteway-Wilkinson) attacks and sinks the motor ship *Barbarigo* (5293 tons). This is the first success attributable to 'Ultra', by which details about the movement of the convoy have been discovered.

From 16 to 18 July the second convoy proceeds; it consists of the large troop transports *Marco Polo*, *Neptunia* and *Oceania*, escorted by the destroyers *Geniere*, *Gioberti*, *Lanciere*, *Oriani* and the torpedo boat *Centauro*, with distant escort by the cruisers *Bolzano* and *Trieste* and destroyers *Ascari*, *Carabiniere* and *Corazziere*. The British submarine *Unbeaten* (Lt Woodward) just misses the *Oceania*.

15 July Baltic

S54, *S47*, *S58* and *S57* of the 3rd MTB Flotilla try, in groups, to make a pincer attack on a Soviet destroyer in the Bay of Riga. Only one torpedo, from *S57* (Lt Erdmann), explodes near the target.

15–20 July North Atlantic

Because of the absence of sightings, the U-boats operating in the Central Atlantic, *U372*, *U431*, *U401*, *U68*, *U565*, *U331*, *U74*, *U126*, *U562*, *U561*, *U561*, *U97*, *U98*, *U203* and *U95*, are concentrated in a more compact formation. On 17 July I/KG 40 sights an outbound convoy NW of the North Channel about which several reports are also received from the W/T cryptographic service. Air reconnaissance again finds the convoy on 18 and 19 July, but the convoy avoids the patrol line formed on 19 July with five boats and on 20 July with *U431, U401, U68, U565, U331, U74, U562, U561, U564, U97, U203, U126* and *U95*. Only *U203* (Lt-Cdr Mützelburg) and *U95* (Lt-Cdr Schreiber) damage one ship each, of 8293 tons and 5419 tons respectively, in gun attacks on 20 July.

16 July Baltic
Minenräumschiff 11 clears a channel through a mine barrage newly laid by Soviet destroyers off Dünamünde.

17 July Mediterranean
The Italian petrol tanker *Panuco* (6212 tons) receives an air torpedo hit in the harbour of Tripoli which makes it impossible to unload parts of the ship. After emergency repairs she has to go to Italy on 19 July with 6000 tons of petrol still on board.

17-18 July Mediterranean
The Italian submarines *Alagi* and *Diaspro* are stationed N of Cape Bougaroni against a sortie by Force H eastwards from Gibraltar.

18 July Baltic
Unsuccessful sortie by the 3rd MTB Flotilla against Kübassare (Ösel). The Soviet destroyers *Serdity* and *Steregushchi* try to attack a German supply convoy off Dünamünde. The convoy reaches the Dvina estuary without loss. On the return on 19 July *Serdity* is damaged by a bomb hit (from a Ju 88 of K Fl Gr 806) in Moon Sound and, after vain attempts to salvage her, she has to be abandoned and scuttled on 22 July.

18-19 July Black Sea
The Soviet Danube Flotilla evacuates the Kilia arm as part of the withdrawal of Soviet XIV Rifle Corps from the Danube and breaks through the Rumanian defensive positions near Periprava. Off the estuary, the monitors, armoured cutters and minesweepers are met by a detachment coming from Odessa consisting of the cruiser *Komintern*, the gunboats *Krasnaya Armeniya* and *Krasnaya Gruziya*, 10 torpedo cutters and six patrol cutters as well as the destroyers *Bodry*, *Kharkov* and *Shaumyan*.

18-30 July North Atlantic
German-Italian operations against Gibraltar convoys. On 18 July it is reported that agents have observed the departure of HG.67 from Gibraltar. The Italian submarines *Malaspina*, *Morosini*, *Torelli*, *Bagnolini* and *Barbarigo* are concentrated against the convoy, which avoids them. After *Torelli* (Cdr de Giacomo) has sunk a single tanker of 8913 tons, *Barbarigo* sights HG.67 on 22 July but soon loses contact, with the result that the Italians and the German *U93*, *U94*, *U124* and *U203*, which are ordered to the scene, do not find the convoy. *Bagnolini* (Cdr Chialamberto), which has briefly sighted a homebound convoy on 19 July, attacks OG.68 on 23 July and hears three detonations which are not, however, caused by hits. *Barbarigo* (Cdr Murzi) sinks two independents of 13407 tons on 25–26 July. On 24 July the B-Service locates the positions of the convoys OG.69 and SL.80. *U79*, *U126*, *U331*, *U68*, *U561*, *U562*, *U564* (only briefly) and *U203* are directed to OG.69 and *U431*, *U565*, *U401*, *U74*, *U94* and *U97* to SL.80. On 25 July SL.80 is reported once and OG.69 twice by Fw 200s of I/KG 40—up to 15 boats receive the bearings from the aircraft establishing contact. On 26 July contact is not re-established with SL.80 and the operation is abandoned. On the same day *U141* (Lt Schüler) attacks off Northern Ireland the outbound convoy OS.1 (escorted by the 5th EG, Cdr Macintyre on board the destroyer *Walker*), sinks one ship of 5106 tons and torpedoes one more of 5133 tons. She is pursued for 20 hours with depth charges. Fw 200s again establish contact twice with OG.69 and with the aid of bearings bring *U68* up in the afternoon. In addition to the seven German boats, *Barbarigo* and *Calvi* are also directed to the convoy. During the night 26–27 July *U79* (Lt-Cdr Kaufmann) and *U203* (Lt-Cdr Mützelburg) each sink one ship, of 2475 tons and 1459 tons respectively. *U561*, *U126*, *U79* and *U331* have no successes. On 27 July *U371* (Lt-Cdr Driver) establishes contact with OS.1 to the west and, with interruptions, maintains contact until 30 July, when two ships of 13984 tons are sunk.

Two Fw 200s again keep contact with OG.69 and *U68*, *U562* and *U126* come up; but only the last (Lt-Cdr Bauer) is able to sink two ships of 2639 tons towards midnight. During the night 27–28 July *U561* (Lt Bartels) also sinks one ship of 1884 tons. On 28 July Fw 200s, *U68*, *U79*, *U561*, *U331* and *U126* are in temporary contact and in the evening *U203* sinks two ships of 2846 tons. An agent's report about the departure of HG.68 from Gibraltar is received. During the night 28–29 July *U331* is driven off from OG.69. A concentration with the boats *U79*, *U126*, *U66*, *Calvi*, *Bagnolini* and *Barbarigo* on 29–30 July against both convoys, OG.69 and HG.68, meets

with no success. Total sinkings among OG.69: seven ships of 11303 tons.

18 July-6 Aug Arctic
Operation by the German U-boats *U81* and *U652* off the Kola Coast. On 24 July *U652* misses the Soviet patrol ship *SKR-23/Musson* off Kildin Island.

19-31 July Mediterranean
The Italian submarines *Axum*, *Squalo* and *Uarsciek* operate off the Egyptian coast.

19 July-13 Sept North Atlantic
On 19 July the US Atlantic Fleet forms TF.1 for the defence of Iceland and to conduct convoys to and from Iceland. A Task Group consisting of the carrier *Wasp*, the cruisers *Quincy* and *Vincennes* and the destroyers *O'Brien* and *Walke* brings P-40 fighters to Iceland which are flown off without loss at sea and reach their destination.

Among the units employed in convoy service to Iceland are Desron 7 (Capt Kauffman) with the destroyers *Benson*, *Niblack*, *Hilary P Jones*, *Plunkett*, *Mayo*, *Madison*, *Gleaves*, *Charles F Hughes* and *Lansdale*, Desron 11 with *Grayson*, *Roe*, *Sampson*, Desron 30 (Capt Cohen) with *Dallas*, *Greer*, *Tarbell*, *Cole*, *Bernadou*, *Lea*, *Ellis* and *Upshur* and Desdiv 62 with *McCormick*, *Sturtevant*, *Reuben James* and *Bainbridge*. From 6 Aug the Catalina flying boats of Patron 73 and the Mariner flying boats of Patron 74 operate from Reykjavik and Hvalfjord respectively.

19-20 July Arctic
In attacks by Ju 87s of 12/LG 1 (Lt J Pfeiffer) on Soviet ships in Ekaterinski Gavan in the Kola Inlet, the patrol vessel *SKR-20/Shtil* and the destroyer *Stremitelny* (Capt 2nd Class A D Vinogradov) is hit and sunk.

20-29 July Mediterranean
On 20 July the British submarine *Union* is sunk by the Italian torpedo boat *Circe* in an attack on a convoy off Cape Bon.

On 24 July *Upright* misses a floating dock under tow near Capo dell'Armi and *Upholder* (Lt-Cdr Wanklyn) torpedoes one ship (4964 tons) E of Sicily.

On 28 July *Utmost* (Lt-Cdr Cayley) sinks one ship of 11466 tons and *Upholder* attacks, near Marettimo, the distant escort of an Italian return convoy from North Africa consisting of the cruisers *Garibaldi* and *Montecuccoli* and the destroyers *Granatiere*, *Bersagliere*, *Fuciliere* and *Alpino*. She torpedoes *Garibaldi*. In the Western Mediterranean, *Olympus* (Lt-Cdr Dymott) sinks one ship of 747 tons and there are transport operations to Malta with submarines of the 1st SM Flotilla (see 30 June).

21 July   Baltic
Finnish minelayers lay the mine barrage F.16 (85 mines and 15 explosive floats) E of the 'Valkjärvi' barrage.

21–23 July   Mediterranean
The Italian motor tanker *Brarena* (6996 tons) is sunk by British aircraft when accompanied by the destroyer *Fuciliere* on the way from Palermo to Tripoli.

Supply convoy from Naples to Tripoli: five large freighters, escorted by six destroyers and one torpedo boat. On 22 July the German steamer *Preussen* (8203 tons) is hit in a British air attack and explodes.

21–27 July   Mediterranean
Operation 'Substance': supply convoy from Gibraltar to Malta with the troop transport *Leinster* and the freighters *Melbourne Star*, *Sydney Star*, *City of Pretoria*, *Port Chalmers*, *Durham* and *Deucalion*. The operation is escorted by Force H (Vice-Adm Somerville), comprising the battlecruiser *Renown*, the carrier *Ark Royal*, the cruiser *Hermione* and the destroyers *Faulknor*, *Fearless*, *Foxhound*, *Firedrake*, *Foresight*, *Fury*, *Forester* and *Duncan*. They are reinforced by ships of the Home Fleet: the battleship *Nelson*, the cruisers *Arethusa*, *Edinburgh* and *Manchester*, the fast mine-layer *Manxman* and the destroyers *Cossack*, *Maori*, *Sikh*, *Nestor*, *Lightning*, *Farndale*, *Avon Vale* and *Eridge*. The Mediterranean Fleet carries out a diversion in the Eastern Mediterranean. Eight submarines are stationed off Cagliari, Naples, N of Sicily and both sides of the Straits of Messina.

On 21 July, in setting out from Gibraltar, the troop transport *Leinster* (4302 tons) goes aground and has to return.

On 22 July, the force is located S of the Balearics by Italian air reconnaissance. Because it is thought that aircraft are being transferred to Malta, the Italian Fleet does not set out. Of the Italian submarines *Alagi* and *Diaspro* (Lt-Cdr Dotta), stationed N of Bougaroni, the latter just misses *Renown* and *Nestor* (RAN).

On 23 July, Italian air reconnaissance again locates the force in the area of Bône, but it is now too late for the Fleet to go into action. Italian aircraft secure hits on the cruiser *Manchester* and the destroyer *Fearless*. The latter has to be abandoned. The destroyer *Firedrake* receives a bomb hit and has to return. In the evening Force H returns to Gibraltar. The Italian submarines *Bandiera*, *Dessiè*, *Manara* and *Settimo*, stationed between Pantelleria and Malta from 23 July, do not fire their torpedoes.

On 24 July the convoy continues its journey with *Edinburgh* (Rear-Adm Syfret), *Arethusa*, *Manxman* and destroyers. In the area of Pantelleria, the Italian motor torpedo boats *MAS 532* and *MAS 533* attack the convoy and torpedo the transport *Sydney Star* (12696 tons). On the same day the force enters Malta. From Malta, seven empty ships proceed to the W, of which the tanker *Hoëgh Hood* (9351 tons) receives a hit from an air torpedo S of Sardinia. On 25 July Force H meets the returning cruisers and the empty convoy. The ships reach Gibraltar on 27 July.

22 July   South Atlantic
The British cruiser *Dunedin* captures the Vichy French steamer *Ville de Rouen* (5383 tons) E of Natal.

22 July   Baltic
Sortie by the 3rd MTB Flotilla towards the area E of Arensburg (Ösel); the torpedo cutter *TKA-71* and one tug are sunk.

22–24 July   Arctic
The 6th DD Flotilla, comprising *Karl Galster*, *Hermann Schoemann*, *Friedrich Eckoldt* and *Richard Beitzen*, sinks the Soviet survey ship *Meridian* in the Polar Sea between Iokanga and Teriberka.

22 July–4 Aug   Arctic
British carrier raid on Kirkenes and Petsamo. From 22 to 25 July the ships ear-marked for the operation are assembled in Seidisfjord (Iceland). In the process the destroyer *Achates* is severely damaged on a mine.

On 26 July the minelaying cruiser *Adventure*, used as a transport to Murmansk, leaves with the destroyer *Anthony*. There follows later Force P (Rear-Adm Wake-Walker), consisting of the aircraft carriers *Furious* and *Victorious*, the heavy cruisers *Devonshire* and *Suffolk* and the destroyers *Echo*, *Eclipse*, *Escapade* and *Intrepid*.

On 28 July the destroyers take on oil from the cruisers and from the tanker *Black Ranger*, which is escorted by the destroyers *Icarus* and *Inglefield* and which is waiting at a rendezvous.

On 30 July *Adventure* is released and the force is divided into two groups each having a carrier as its main element. The force is located by German air reconnaissance. 20 Albacore torpedo aircraft and nine Fulmar fighters take off from *Victorious* to attack the German gunnery training ship *Bremse* and other ships lying in Kirkenes. 11 torpedo aircraft and two fighters are shot down by AA fire and aircraft of 6/JG 5. Only slight damage is sustained by the ships under attack. 18 Albacore aircraft, four Hurricane fighters and six Fulmars take off from *Furious* to attack Petsamo. Because no ships have arrived in the harbour, the force attacks land targets. One fighter and one torpedo aircraft are lost.

On 31 July *Furious* hands over her oper-ational aircraft to *Victorious* and returns because of fuel shortage. On 4 Aug three Fulmars take off from *Victorious* to attack Tromsö and one aircraft is lost. Then this force also returns.

23 July   Baltic
M3131 is sunk in clearing mines off the Dvina Estuary.

23 July   English Channel
The German patrol vessel *V1508* (*Rau III*) is sunk SW of Boulogne in a British MTB attack with torpedoes.

23–24 July   Arctic
The Soviet destroyers *Grozny* and *Sokru-shitelny* and the minelayer *Kanin* lay a defensive barrage of 275 mines in the entrance to the White Sea.

24 July   Air War/Western Europe
Heaviest daylight attack so far by RAF with 149 bombers on the German battlecruisers *Gneisenau* (Brest) and *Scharnhorst* (La Pallice). The latter receives five hits which cause serious damage to the ship's electric cables.

25 July   South Atlantic
The German steamer *Erlangen* (6101 tons) scuttles herself SE of the River Plate when approached by the British cruiser *Newcastle*.

25–26 July   Mediterranean
Attempt by the Italian 10th MAS Flotilla to attack the supply ships which have arrived in Malta. The frigate *Diana* with eight explosive boats and *MAS 451* and *MAS 452*, each with a human torpedo team, reach Malta, but are detected by British radar as they approach. Nevertheless, the torpedo rider, Maj Tesei, the inventor of the *Maiali*, and two explosive boats are able to blow up the harbour boom, but, as a result of the detonation, the St Elmo bridge collapses and bars the way to the other six explosive boats. They are destroyed by coastal batter-ies. The next morning fighter-bombers locate the withdrawing *MAS 451* and *MAS 452* and sink them.

25–26 July   Baltic
Aircraft of KG 4 drop 40 mines E of Moon Island.

25–26 July   Baltic
Attacks by the Soviet Naval Air Force and a TKA group on the 2nd MMS Flotilla detailed to look for mines in the Irben Strait. On 25 July *R53* and *R63* are slightly damaged by mine detonations and on 26 July *R169* is sunk by a bomb hit. TKA attacks are unsuccessful.

26 July   General Situation
President Roosevelt puts the 'Western Hemisphere Defence Plan 4' (WPL-51) into effect.

26–27 July Baltic
In a sortie by the 3rd MTB Flotilla (Lt-Cdr Kemnade) into the northern part of the Gulf of Riga, the command boat *S55* and *S54* (Sub-Lt Wagner) locate a single Soviet destroyer. After an unsuccessful approach, *S54* sinks the destroyer, probably *Smely*. *S57* and *S58* miss two minesweepers lying at anchor off Arensburg (Ösel). On 28 July the 3rd MTB Flotilla sinks the ice-breaker *Lachplesis* (253 tons) in a gun engagement off Arensburg.

27 July–6 Aug Arctic
British Force K (Vice-Adm Vian), comprising the cruisers *Aurora* and *Nigeria* and the destroyers *Punjabi* and *Tartar*, leaves Scapa Flow for Spitzbergen to investigate Norwegian and Russian settlements there; they arrive on 31 July. On the return the Norwegian weather station on Bear Island is evacuated and destroyed. A sortie against the Norwegian coast is detected in time by German air reconnaissance.

28 July Baltic
The Soviet submarine *Shch-307* (Lt-Cdr Petrov) sinks *U144* off the Gulf of Finland.

29 July Arctic
Sortie by the 6th DD Flotilla with four destroyers (as on 22 July) towards Yugor and Kara Straits; it is abandoned in the area of Kolguev when the British carrier force is located (see 22 July–4 Aug).

29 July Mediterranean
The British submarine *Thrasher* (Lt-Cdr Cowell) arrives in Alexandria with 78 British troops who had remained hidden in Crete since the end of the fighting.

30 July Mediterranean
The Italian torpedo boat *Papa* (Lt Rosica) attacks with gunfire the British submarine *Cachalot* as she proceeds on the surface and rams her. The submarine surrenders but sinks shortly after the crew of 70 have been taken off.

30 July China
Japanese bombers attack the US gunboat *Tutuila* lying in Chungking.

30 July–4 Aug Mediterranean
The Italian submarine *Delfino*, operating off Mersa Matruh, is attacked by a British Sunderland flying boat but is able to shoot it down and take four prisoners.

30 July–10 Aug North Atlantic
The U-boats which are ordered on 30 July to form a new concentration in the Central North Atlantic are directed to convoy SL.81, detected on 1 Aug by the B-Service. The convoy's escort comprises the destroyers *Wanderer*, *Campbeltown* and *St Albans* (Norwegian) and the corvettes *La Malouine*, *Zinnia*, *Campanula*, *Bluebell*,

Wallflower, *Carnation*, *Heliotrope* and *Hydrangea*. On 2 Aug *U204* establishes contact and brings up *U559*. On 3 Aug *U204* brings up in turn *U431*, *U205*, *U558*, *U75*, *U372*, *U401*, *U565* and *U559*. An Fw 200 of I/KG 40 is shot down by a Hurricane flown off from the catapult ship *Maplin*. On 4 Aug *U558*, *U431*, *U559*, *U75*, *U83* and *U74* come up again but they are all prevented from attacking by the defences. On 3 Aug *U401* is sunk by the destroyers *Wanderer* and *St Albans* and the corvette *Hydrangea* of the 7th EG. Fw 200s sight the convoy on 3 and 4 Aug and sink one ship of 4337 tons. *U372* (Lt-Cdr Neumann), *U204* (Lt-Cdr Kell), *U75* (Lt-Cdr Ringelmann) and *U74* (Lt-Cdr Kentrat) are not able to fire their torpedoes until the night 4–5 Aug, when they do so in turn. They sink two ships, two ships, one ship and one ship respectively, totalling 23190 tons. By day the boats are finally driven off by the air and sea escort.

The U-boats, *U71*, *U77*, *U96*, *U751* and *U43* are directed to a homebound convoy sighted by *U565* on 4 Aug but they have no success. On 6–7 Aug *U43*, *U71*, *U96*, *U751*, *U83*, *U75*, *U46*, *U205*, *U559*, *U204* and *U372* operate without result against the convoy HG.68 reported by the B-Service, likewise from 8 to 10 Aug the same boats move against a southbound convoy without sighting anything.

31 July–1 Aug Baltic
Aircraft of KG 4 drop 38 LMB mines on the roads of Triigi. The 2nd MTB Flotilla lays 24 TMB mines near Dagerort.

31 July–4 Aug Mediterranean
Operation 'Style': Force X brings 1750 troops and RAF personnel and 130 tons of supplies from the disabled transport *Leinster* (see Operation 'Substance') on board the cruiser *Arethusa*, the fast minelayer *Manxman* and three destroyers from Gibraltar to Malta. They arrive on 2 Aug, are unloaded and return. The Italian submarines stationed in the Malta area, *Bandiera*, *Manara*, *Settimo* and *Zaffiro*, and those positioned near Galita and Cape Bougaroni, *Serpente*, *Alagi* and *Diaspro*, do not attack. British Force H, comprising the British battlecruiser *Renown*, the battleship *Nelson*, the carrier *Ark Royal*, the cruiser *Hermione* and the destroyers *Cossack*, *Maori*, *Nestor*, *Faulknor*, *Fury*, *Foresight*, *Forester*, *Foxhound*, *Encounter*, *Sikh* and *Lightning*, operates as a covering group in the Western Mediterranean. During the night 31 July–1 Aug the destroyers *Cossack* and *Maori* are detached to shell the harbour of Alghero (Sardinia), whose airfield is attacked early in the morning by nine Swordfish aircraft

from *Ark Royal*. On the way, *Hermione* rams and sinks the Italian submarine *Tembien* in the area of Tunis. After returning to Gibraltar, the battlecruiser *Renown* proceeds to Britain for an refit. Vice-Adm Somerville hoists his flag on the battleship *Nelson*.

1 Aug General Situation
President Roosevelt forbids the export of oil and aviation spirit to countries outside British control and outside the Western Hemisphere. The substantial Japanese imports are particularly affected by this measure.

1 Aug Baltic
Near Cape Domesnäs, German 1st MS Flotilla beats off an attack by four Soviet motor torpedo boats which are covered at some distance by two Soviet destroyers. *TKA-122* is sunk.

1 Aug Black Sea
Soviet bombers attack Constanza.

1–2 Aug Baltic
Aircraft of KG 4 drop 15 LMBs in the area E of Moon, 22 LMBs N of Moon Island and 18 LMBs W of Worms Island.

1–20 Aug Arctic
The German U-boats *U451* and *U566* operate off the entrance to the White Sea and off the Kola Coast respectively. *U451* (Lt-Cdr Hoffmann) misses one guard boat on 7 Aug but sinks the Soviet patrol ship *SKR-27/Zhemchug* off Svyatoy Nos on 10 Aug.

2 Aug Baltic
The Finnish submarine *Vesihiisi* (Lt-Cdr Kijanen) lays the mine barrage F.17 (18 mines) E of Odensholm. Unsuccessful attack by the motor torpedo boats *S55* and *S58* on the Soviet destroyer *Artem* in the Gulf of Riga.

2 Aug General Situation
Beginning of the American Lend-Lease deliveries to the USSR.

2–3 Aug Air War/Germany
British bombers attack Hamburg and Kiel.

2–3 Aug Arctic
The Soviet reinforced 325th Rifle Regt, which is still on the west bank of Litsa Bay, cannot hold out against the attack of the German 136th Mountain Regt. What is left of it is evacuated on 3 Aug by ships of the Northern Fleet.

2–28 Aug Black Sea
The Soviet submarines *L-4* and *L-5* each lay three mine barrages off the Axis coast.

3–7 Aug Mediterranean
In the Western Mediterranean, the Dutch submarines *O21* (Lt-Cdr v Dulm) and *O24* (Lt-Cdr de Booy) sink one sailing ship and two small ships of 909 tons respectively. In the area of Rhodes the Greek submarine

Nereus (Lt-Cdr Rotas) reports one steamer and one sailing ship sunk.

4 Aug   North Atlantic
U126 sinks a trawler of 172 tons.

4–5 Aug   Baltic
Aircraft of KG 4 drop 16 LMBs S of Zerel in the Irben Strait and 16 LMBs in the roads of Triigi (Kassarwik).

5 Aug   Intelligence
Bletchley Park succeeds in breaking the 'Enigma/Heimische Gewässer'/'Dolphin' circuit for 1 Aug. The transmissions are decyphered almost daily, at first with some delay but later within 36 hours.

5–16 Aug   North Atlantic
The Allied convoys HX.142 (ocean escort AMC *Ausonia*, destroyer *Chesterfield* and corvettes *Hepatica*, *Windflower* and *Trillium*) and SC.39 (ocean escort AMC *Maloja*, destroyer *Churchill* and corvettes *Arrowhead*, *Camellia* and *Eyebright*) are routed clear of the U-boat group forming up S of Iceland by using decoded German radio signals.
The following convoy, HX.143, with 57 ships and escorted from Halifax to WESTOMP by the destroyers *Niagara* and *Annapolis* (ocean escort AMC Wolfe, destroyer *Burnham* and corvettes *Sunflower* and *Agassiz*), is also led round the German U-boats and on 16 Aug meets its Eastern ocean escort, the British 8th EG with the destroyers *Malcolm*, *Watchman*, *Sardonyx* and *Scimitar* and the corvettes *Arabis*, *Verbena* and *Violet*; it reaches the Western Approaches without being sighted.

5–28 Aug   North Atlantic
Formation of a new U-boat group in a loose concentration SW of Iceland with *U563*, *U568*, *U129*, *U567*, *U206*, *U84*, *U501*, *U71*, *U553*, *U77*, *U43*, *U96*, *U101*, *U38*, *U73*, *U105*, *U751*, *U202*, *U82*, *U569* and *U652*. On 9 Aug *U206* (Lt Opitz) sinks one trawler. On 11 Aug *U501* sights the outbound convoy ON(S).4, from which *U568* (Lt-Cdr Preuss) sinks the corvette *Picotee* on 12 Aug. On 12 Aug *U129* sights a westbound convoy but *U563*, *U567* and *U206*, which are directed to it, find nothing up to 13 Aug. On 18 Aug *U38* (Cdr Schuch) sinks one independent of 1700 tons. As a consequence of convoy re-routing by the Submarine Tracking Room (Cdr Winn) thanks to the decoded 'Ultra' messages, the convoys ON.6(F), ON.7(S), ON.8(F), ON.9(S), HX.144, HX.145 and SC.40 evade the U-boat disposition to the N made on 22 Aug. The outbound *U452* is sunk on 25 Aug by Catalina 'J' of No 209 Sqn and the trawler *Vascama*. *U570*, *U38*, *U82*, *U202*, *U652*, *U501*, *U569*, *U84*, *U567*, *U553* and *U207* are unsuccessfully directed S of Iceland to

the convoy HX.145 located on 27 Aug in a B-Service report. *U570* (Lt Rahmlow) is attacked in bad weather by Hudson bomber 'S' of No 269 Sqn RAF (Sqn Ldr Thompson) and slightly damaged, with the result that the commander surrenders. The U-boat spends several hours on the surface with the bomber circling overhead. Supported by a Catalina of No 209 Sqn RAF, the trawler *Northern Chief* (Lt Knight) arrives in the evening of 27 Aug and the trawler *Kingston Agathe*, the destroyers *Burwell* and *Niagara* and the trawlers *Westwater* and *Windermere* the next morning. After taking off the crew, two of the trawlers tow the boat to Iceland. On 19 Sept she is put into service as HMS *Graph* (Lt Colvin).

6 Aug   Mediterranean
Off the Tunisian coast, British torpedo aircraft attack a convoy (six ships with five escorting destroyers and one torpedo boat) proceeding from Naples to Tripoli and sink the freighter *Nita* (6813 tons).

6–8 Aug   Baltic
The Soviet destroyers *Surovy* and *Statny* shell the German coastal battery 'Hainasch' in Moon Sound on 6 Aug and the battery 'Markgraf' on 8 Aug.
In the Gulf of Finland, Ju 88s of K Fl Gr 806 destroy the Soviet destroyer *Karl Marks* in Loksa Bay near Tallinn.

6–16 Aug   North Atlantic
U331, *U126*, *U94*, *U124*, *U79*, *U109*, *U93* and *U371* assemble in the area between Gibraltar and the Azores to operate against the convoy HG.69, whose departure is reported by agents on 9 Aug. The Italian boats *Finzi*, *Marconi* and *Veniero* are included in the formation. On 10 Aug *U79* sights the convoy but is driven off. On 11 Aug *U93* and *U94* establish temporary contact and *Marconi* (Lt-Cdr Pollina) misses the sloop *Deptford* and the corvette *Convolvulus* which are part of the escort. On 12 Aug *U331*, *Finzi* and *U123*, which is returning, and in the night of 12–13 Aug also *U124*, *Veniero* and *U331*, are all in turn driven off. *Marconi* continues to send contact reports with interruptions until 14 Aug, when she is driven off with *Finzi*. *Marconi* destroys an independent of 2589 tons with gunfire and the wreck is finished off by a torpedo from *U126* (Lt-Cdr Bauer). A patrol line consisting of *U123*, *U124*, *U126*, *Marconi* and *Finzi* has no success on 15 Aug. On 11 Aug one freighter of 2852 tons is sunk by Fw 200s of I/KG 40 which have been ordered to undertake air reconnaissance and a report is sent on 12 Aug. On 16 Aug the operation has to be broken off.

6–20 Aug   Mediterranean
The Italian submarines *Zoea*, *Corridoni* and *Atropo* transport 192 tons of supplies and fuel to Bardia. On the way *Zoea* is attacked by aircraft.

6–30 Aug   Arctic
The Soviet submarines *Shch-421*, *M-175*, *Shch-401*, *Shch-402* and *K-2* (Capt 3rd Class V P Utkin) operate off the Norwegian polar coast. The last misses the steamers *Hans* and *Lübeck* off Tanafjord on 13 Aug. *M-173* undertakes a reconnaissance sortie off Petsamo Fjord. Then *M-172* (Lt-Cdr I I Fisanovich), with the Div Cdr, Capt 2nd Class I A Kolyshkin on board, penetrates the fjord on 21 Aug but misses a ship lying alongside the pier in Liinahamari. On 22 Aug she misses the hospital ship *Alexander von Humboldt* off Petsamo Fjord.

On 11 and 16 Aug respectively the British submarines *Tigris* and *Trident*, which have been transferred to Murmansk, proceed on operations in Svaerholt and Lopphavet. *Tigris* (Cdr Bone) sinks the Norwegian coaster *Haakon Jarl* (1482 tons) on 17 Aug; *Trident* (Cdr Sladen) damages the steamer *Levante* (4769 tons) by gunfire on 19 Aug and sinks from convoys the steamer *Ostpreussen* (3030 tons) on 22 Aug and the steamers *Donau* (2931 tons) and *Bahia Laura* (8561 tons) on 30 Aug.

6–30 Aug   Baltic
The Soviet submarines *S-4*, *S-5*, *S-6* and *Shch-301* operate in the central Baltic. Only *S-4* (Lt-Cdr Abrosimov) attacks a vessel on 10 Aug off Libau. *Kalev* and *Lembit* lay mines on 13 and 18 Aug. *M-103* does not return from a sortie in the Gulf of Finland.

8 Aug   Black Sea
A naval force of the North-West Command is formed under Rear-Adm D D Vdovichenko to support the coastal army. It consists of the cruiser *Komintern*, the destroyers *Nezamozhnik* and *Shaumyan*, the minelayer *Lukomski*, a gunboat division with the gunboats *Krasnaya Abkhaziya*, *Krasny Adzharistan*, *Krasnaya Armeniya* and *Krasnaya Gruziya*, the 2nd Torpedo Cutter Bde (three divisions of 12, 18 and 10 boats) and the 5th MS Div (seven auxiliary minesweepers). The force, which is based at Odessa and Ochakov, is under the command of the Commandant, Naval Base, Odessa, Rear-Adm G V Zhukov.

8–12 Aug   Black Sea
Units of the Soviet Danube Flotilla support the withdrawal of troops over the Bug Estuary.

8–26 Aug   Baltic
The 'Juminda' mine barrages are laid out. The German minelayers *Cobra* (Cdr Dr

Brill), *Kaiser* (Cdr Bohm) and *Königin Luise* (Lt-Cdr Wünning), supported by the 5th MMS Flotilla (Lt-Cdr Dobberstein) and the 1st MTB Flotilla (Lt-Cdr Birnbacher), lay the mine barrages D.10 to D.30 with, in all, 673 EMC mines and 636 explosive floats. The Finnish minelayers *Riilahti* (Sub-Lt Kivilinna) and *Ruotsinsalmi* (Lt-Cdr Arho) lay the mine barrages F.18-F.22 with a total of 696 mines and 100 explosive floats.

9-10 Aug Arctic
Sortie by the German 6th DD Flotilla, comprising *Hans Lody*, *Friedrich Eckoldt* and *Richard Beitzen*, towards Kildin Island and the mouth of the Kola Inlet. During this, the Soviet patrol ship *SKR-12/Tuman* (Sub-Lt Shestakov) is surprised and sunk after courageous resistance. The German force is shelled by coastal guns and attacked by aircraft as it withdraws. *Richard Beitzen* is damaged by near-misses.

9-12 Aug General Situation
President Roosevelt and Churchill meet on board the British battleship *Prince of Wales* and the heavy US cruiser *Augusta* in Argentia Bay (Newfoundland). Proclamation of the Atlantic Charter.

10 Aug Norway
The German auxiliary minesweeper *M 1102/ H A W Müller* is sunk in an air attack off Lindesnes.

10-11 Aug Baltic
Soviet convoy from Tallinn to Suursaari and Kronstadt with the transport *Vyacheslav Molotov* (7494 tons) with 3500 wounded on board, escorted by the destroyer *Steregushchi*, *BTShch* (Fugas) minesweepers and MO submarine-chasers. The minesweeper *T-201/Zaryad* is sunk after hitting a mine (possibly as early as 3 Aug); *V Molotov* is damaged off Suursaari by a mine. Boats of the German 2nd MTB Flotilla lay the mine barrage 'Allirahu' with 24 TMB mines in the Gulf of Riga. Boats of the 5th MS Flotilla lay the flanking mine barrages 'Pinnass I-IV' with 47 EMC mines off Cape Domesnäs.

10-23 Aug North Atlantic
After the SL.81 operation, *U75*, *U559*, *U204* and *U83*, and *U106*, *U201*, *U564* and *U552* (which have recently set out) assemble in the area W of the North Channel. On 17 Aug they are directed to convoy OG.71— escorted by the sloop *Leith*, the destroyer *Bath* (RNoN), the corvettes *Campanula*, *Hydrangea*, *Bluebell*, *Campion*, *Wallflower* and *Zinnia* and the A/S trawler *Lord Nuffield*—reported by an Fw 200 of I/KG 40. *U201* (Lt Schnee) establishes contact late in the evening and maintains it, with several interruptions, until 19 Aug. On 18 and 19 Aug Ju 88s of Air Commander Atlan-

tic, which have taken off for operations, only find the convoy individually. Guided by reports from aircraft and from *U201*, the boats *U559* (Lt Heidtmann), *U201* and *U204* (Lt-Cdr Kell) fire their torpedoes during the night 18-19 Aug. *U204* sinks *Bath* (Lt-Cdr Melsom) belonging to the 5th EG and one ship of 1809 tons; *U559* and *U201* sink one ship of 1584 tons and two ships of 5064 tons respectively. In the evening *U106* takes over contact but is driven off. On 20 Aug the destroyers *Gurkha* and *Legion* arrive as support, as does, on 21 Aug, the destroyer *Boreas*. Contact is lost until the afternoon of 21 Aug but is then regained by an Fw 200. However, *U201*, *U108*, *U564*, *U106* and *U552*, which are directed to the scene, do not find the convoy. As a result of several aircraft reports, *U564* (Lt Suhren) establishes contact in the afternoon of 22 Aug and brings *U201* up again. During the night 22-23 Aug *U564* sinks two ships of 1687 tons and *U201* two ships of 2761 tons. Another ship (2129 tons), torpedoed by *U564*, is sunk by *U552* (Lt Topp). In the morning of 23 Aug *U564* sinks the corvette *Zinnia* belonging to the escort. Total result: two escorts and nine ships of 13225 tons sunk.

11 Aug North Sea
In an attack by boats of the 4th MTB Flotilla on a convoy off Dungeness, *S49* (Sub-Lt Günther) sinks the British freighter *Sir Russell* (1548 tons).

11 Aug Mediterranean
In a British air torpedo attack on ships in the harbour of Syracuse, the Italian hospital ship *California* (13060 tons) sinks.

12-13 Aug Baltic
Boats of the 2nd MTB Flotilla lay the mine barrage 'Mona I' (18 TMBs) in the southern entrance to Moon Sound. Boats of the 5th MS Flotilla lay the flanking mine barrages 'Pinnas V-VI' with 28 EMC mines off Cape Domesnäs. In engagements in the Gulf of Finland, motor torpedo boats of the 1st MTB Flotilla sink the Soviet motor minesweeper (Rybintsi) *R-101* and a minesweeper near Great Wrangel on 13 Aug.

12-16 Aug Black Sea
Soviet Danube Flotilla supports withdrawal over the Lower Dnieper. It arrives in Kherson on 12 Aug.
Unsuccessful operation by the Rumanian submarine *Delfinul* and the MTBs *Viscolul*, *Vijelia* and *Viforul* against Soviet supplies between Sevastopol and Odessa.

12-18 Aug Mediterranean
The British fast minelayers *Abdiel* and *Latona* and destroyers bring 6000 troops to the beleaguered fortress of Tobruk to relieve the battle-weary Australian units. 5000

troops are evacuated. In this operation and others from 12 Sept and 12 Oct the Australian cruiser *Hobart* and the destroyers *Napier* and *Nizam* also take part.

12-23 Aug Mediterranean
The mine barrages S.41, S.42, S.43 and S.44 are laid out on 12, 16, 19 and 23 Aug respectively in the Sicilian channel by the Italian auxiliary minelayers (ferry ships) *Aspromonte* and *Reggio* with a total of 1125 mines. In addition, 3202 barrage protection devices are laid by the destroyers *Zeno*, *Da Verazzano*, *Pigafetta*, *Da Mosto*, *Da Noli* and *Pessagno*.

13 Aug Black Sea
The Soviet destroyers *Nezamozhnik* and *Shaumyan*, together with the gunboat *Krasny Adzharistan* and the coastal batteries Nos 412 and 726, support the counter-attack of the 1st Naval Rifle Regt near Grigorevka.

13-20 Aug Black Sea
The destroyers *Shaumyan*, *Nezamozhnik*, *Frunze* and *Dzerzhinski* operate in turns in shelling Rumanian positions in the area of Odessa and Ochakov.

13 Aug-4 Sept Norway
In the British 9th SM Flotilla operating off Western Norway there are, *inter alia*, the French *Minerve* and *Rubis* (Lt-Cdr Rousselot), the Dutch *O14* and various British submarines. *Rubis* sinks one ship of 4360 tons.

14-15 Aug Baltic
Soviet convoy from Tallinn to Suursaari-Kronstadt. The motor ship *Sibir* (3767 tons), with 2500 wounded on board, is sunk in an air attack. The minesweeper *T-202/Buy* is sunk near Suursaari on 15 Aug after hitting two mines.

14-17 Aug Black Sea
Evacuation of the Soviet naval base at Nikolaev (Rear-Adm Kuleshov). Ships on the stocks in the Marti South yard (the 59150-ton battleship *Sovetskaya Ukraina*, the 11300-ton cruiser *Ordzhonikidze*, the Types S-IXbis submarines *S-36*, *S-37* and *S-38* and two gunboats) and in the Kommunar 61 North yard (the 35240-ton battlecruiser *Sevastopol*, the 11300-ton cruiser *Sverdlov*, the flotilla leaders *Perekop* and *Ochakov*, the destroyer *Opashny* and one other destroyer) are blown up. The ships which are fitting out, including the 11300-ton cruisers *Frunze* and *Kujbyshev*, the flotilla leaders *Kiev* and *Erevan*, the destroyers *Svobodny*, *Ognevoi* and *Ozornoi*, the submarines *L-23*, *L-24*, *L-25* and *S-35* and the ice-breaker *Mikoyan*, are towed away. These operations are screened by the destroyers *Bodry*, *Boiki*, *Besposhchadny*, *Bezuprechny*, *Dzerzhinski*, *Frunze*, *Nezamozhnik* and *Shaumyan*.

Mid-Aug Black Sea

Soviet submarines continue to operate off the Rumanian and Bulgarian coasts. Participating from late June to early July have been *Shch-204*, *Shch-202*, *M-35*, *M-62* and *M-31*, in mid-July *D-5*, *Shch-201*, *Shch-210*, *Shch-211*, *S-33*, *M-51*, *M-52* (damaged in collision 14 July), *M-58*, *M-33*, *M-34*, *M-62*, *M-32* and *M-36* and from late July *S-31*, *S-34*, *Shch-203*, *Shch-209*, *Shch-208*, *Shch-204*, *M-31*, *M-36*, *A-3*, *M-58* and *M-62*. None of these boats has met with any success.

L-4 (Lt-Cdr Polyakov) and *L-5* (Lt-Cdr Zhdanov) each lay three mine barrages, off Cape Olinka and off Mangalia. *Shch-212*, *Shch-215* and *Shch-211* (Lt-Cdr Devyatko) operate in the SW. *Shch-211* disembarks agents near Varna on 11 Aug and, after an unsuccessful attack by *Shch-216*, sinks the Rumanian steamer *Peles* (5708 tons) near Cape Emine. The small boats are in the NW: *M-33*, *M-36*, *M-34*, *M-32*, *M-35*, *M-31*, *M-62* and again *M-33* (Lt Surov), the last-mentioned missing on 19 Aug the returning Rumanian submarine *Delfinul*. Up to 14 Sept *L-4* and *L-5* each lay one mine barrage, off Georgi and Varna respectively, *S-31*, *S-32*, *S-33*, *S-34*, *Shch-213*, *Shch-208* and *Shch-214* operate off the W and SW coasts and *M-31*, *M-32*, *M-34*, *M-35*, *M-58*, *M-62*, *M-33*, *M-51* and *M-111* operate off the W and NW coasts.

14–19 Aug Pacific

The auxiliary cruiser *Schiff 45/Komet* (Rear-Adm Eyssen) sinks or captures three ships totalling 27178 tons in the area of the Galapagos Islands.

15 Aug South Atlantic

The German steamer *Norderney* (3667 tons) scuttles herself NE of the Amazon estuary when approached by the British cruiser *Despatch* and the auxiliary cruiser *Pretoria Castle*.

15–16 Aug Black Sea

The Soviet gunboats *Krasnaya Armeniya* and *Krasnaya Gruziya* give fire support to Soviet troops near Grigorevka and Spiridovka (Odessa).

16 Aug Baltic

A Soviet convoy from Suursaari to Tallinn, led by the ice-breaker *Oktyabr*, loses several ships on the 'Juminda' mine barrage.

17 Aug Baltic

Unsuccessful attack by four Soviet TKAs on German ships off Cape Domesnäs.
Off Arensburg-Ösel, the German auxiliary minesweeper *M1707* is lost on a mine.

18–19 Aug Baltic

In an operation in the Gulf of Riga, the Soviet destroyer *Statny* runs on a mine in Moon Sound on 18 Aug and sinks. During the night 18–19 Aug the German motor torpedo boat *S58* (Lt Geiger) sinks the Soviet minesweeper *T-51/Pirmunas* lying at anchor off the southern entrance of Moon Sound.

18 Aug–8 Sept North Atlantic

The Italian submarines *Marconi*, *Finzi*, *Cappellini* and, from 23 Aug, *Calvi*, are directed from 20–24 Aug to convoy HG.71 (EG.36 with the sloop *Deptford*, corvettes *Samphire*, *Convolvulus*, *Marigold* and *Auricula* and, from 23 Aug, support destroyers *Wild Swan* and *Vimy*) reported to have left Gibraltar on 18 Aug, but they do not find it. Neither is HG.72 (escort destroyers *Faulknor*, *Boreas*, *Wild Swan*, *Avon Vale*, *Encounter* and *Nestor*) found: this sets out on 2 Sept and against it *Calvi*, *Baracca*, *Cappellini* and *Da Vinci* operate from 4 to 6 Sept. On 8 Sept *Baracca*, in taking up a new patrol line, is compelled to surface W of Gibraltar by depth charges from the British destroyer *Croome* and, after a short gun engagement, she is sunk by ramming.

19 Aug Black Sea

Shelling of German-Rumanian transports near Meshchanka, Mikhailovka and Visarka in the Odessa area by the 2nd DD Division consisting of the flotilla leader *Tashkent* and the destroyers *Bodry*, *Besposhchadny* and *Bezuprechny* with 450 rounds of 13cm.

19–23 Aug Mediterranean

Italian supply convoy to Tripoli. On 19 Aug the British submarine *P32*, in trying to attack a convoy coming into Tripoli and comprising four steamers and the destroyers *Freccia*, *Euro* and *Dardo* and the torpedo boats *Procione*, *Pegaso* and *Sirtori*, runs on to a mine and sinks.
The submarine *Unique* (Lt-Cdr Hezlet) makes an attack 11 nautical miles N of Tripoli on a subsequent convoy comprising the troop transports *Esperia*, *Marco Polo*, *Neptunia* and *Oceania* and the destroyers *Vivaldi*, *Da Recco*, *Gioberti*, *Oriani*, *Maestrale*, *Grecale* and *Scirocco* and the torpedo boat *Dezza*. She sinks *Esperia* (11398 tons) with three hits. Of 1170 troops, 1139 are rescued.
On 22 Aug *Upholder* (Lt-Cdr Wanklyn) sinks one ship of 3988 tons from a small convoy near Sicily, escorted by the torpedo boats *Cigno* and *Pegaso*.
On 23 Aug the submarine *P33*, in an attempted attack off Pantelleria, is sunk by the Italian torpedo boat *Partenope*.

19 Aug–10 Sept Arctic

British operations in the Arctic. On 19 Aug Force K (Rear-Adm Vian), comprising the cruisers *Aurora* and *Nigeria*, the destroyers *Icarus*, *Antelope* and *Anthony* and the troop transport *Empress of Canada*, leaves Scapa Flow for Spitzbergen in order to evacuate the Norwegian and Soviet colonies there and to destroy installations. *Empress of Canada* and *Nigeria* transport the Russian colony to Archangel and rejoin *Aurora* on 1 Sept off Barentsburg. Together with three colliers coming from Norway, one ice-breaker, one whaler, one tug and two fishing boats, the force returns to England on 3 Sept. On 21 Aug the first experimental convoy 'Dervish' (Capt Dowding) leaves Hvalfjord (Iceland) with seven merchant ships and arrives in Archangel on 31 Aug without any contact with the enemy; escort is provided by a force, under Rear-Adm Wake-Walker, consisting of the cruisers *Devonshire* and *Suffolk* and the carrier *Victorious*. The carrier *Argus* with six destroyers flies off, just N of the Kola Inlet, 24 Hurricane fighters of the 151st Fighter Wing to be stationed at Vaenga near Murmansk; 24 more aircraft are moved by steamer to Archangel, from where they are sent to Vaenga on 11 Sept. The minelaying cruiser *Adventure* brings a cargo of mines to Murmansk. On the return, the covering force makes two raids with aircraft from *Victorious* on 3 and 7 Sept on German shipping in the Tromsö area. They meet with little success.
Rear-Adm Vian makes a sortie with *Aurora* and *Nigeria* on 6–7 Sept to the Polar Coast and, in the course of it, meets a small convoy off Porsanger Fjord. The cruisers destroy the gunnery training ship *Bremse* (Cdr von Brosy-Steinberg†). The two transports *Barcelona* (3101 tons) and *Trautenfels* (6418 tons) with about 1500 troops of the 6th Mountain Div on board escape into the fjord in bad visibility. On 10 Sept the British forces arrive back in Scapa Flow.

20 Aug North Sea

In an attack by boats of the 4th MTB Flotilla on a British convoy off Cromer, *S48* (Lt v Mirbach) sinks the Polish freighter *Czenstochowa* (1971 tons) and torpedoes a second of 2774 tons.

21 Aug Baltic

The third wave of the German ferry battalion of Army engineers is attacked several times by Soviet aircraft after passing through the Irben Strait. Little damage is done. An unsuccessful attack is made by the Soviet destroyers *Artem* and *Surovy* in the Gulf of Riga.
On the way from Suursaari to Tallinn, a Soviet convoy has losses on the 'Juminda' mine barrage.

21 Aug Black Sea

German troops take Kherson. The Military Council of the Black Sea Fleet decides to keep the cruisers *Chervona Ukraina*, *Krasny*

Krym and *Krasny Kavkaz*, the auxiliary cruiser *Mikoyan*, the flotilla leaders *Kharkov* and *Tashkent* and the destroyers *Bodry*, *Bezuprechny*, *Besposhchandny*, *Sposobny*, *Smyshleny* and *Soobrazitelny* on the alert to support the coastal army in the Odessa area.

21–22 Aug Black Sea
The cruiser *Krasny Krym*, the destroyers *Dzerzhinski* and *Frunze* and the gunboat *Krasnaya Armeniya* shell Rumanian positions near Sverdlovka and Chebanka.

22–26 Aug Mediterranean
Operation 'Mincemeat'. On 22 Aug Force H (Vice-Adm Somerville), consisting of the battleship *Nelson*, the carrier *Ark Royal*, the cruiser *Hermione* and the destroyers *Nestor*, *Fury*, *Forester*, *Foresight* and *Encounter*, is reported by Italian agents as it leaves Gibraltar. The intention of the force is to mine Livorno with the fast minelayer *Manxman* disguised as a large French destroyer and, simultaneously, to make a carrier attack on North Sardinia. The Italian 9th Div (Adm Iachino) sets out with the battleships *Littorio* and *Vittorio Veneto* and five destroyers and, on 23 Sept E of Sardinia, joins the 3rd Div coming from Messina with the heavy cruisers *Trieste*, *Trento*, *Bolzano* and *Gorizia*, four destroyers and other groups of 10 destroyers in all. On 24 Aug they make a sortie to the area S of Sardinia to bring to battle, within range of their own air force, the covering force for the suspected Malta operation. The Malta convoy is to be found by the 8th Div setting out from Palermo for the area N of Tunisia and consisting of the light cruisers *Duca degli Abruzzi*, *Attendolo* and *Montecuccoli* and five destroyers. The submarines *Alagi*, *Serpente*, *Aradam* and *Diaspro* are stationed SW of Sardinia; the Sicilian Channel, apart from the mine barrages (see 12–23 Aug), is barred by the submarines *Squalo*, *Bandiera*, *Tricheco*, *Topazio* and *Zaffiro* and thirteen MAS boats. But the deployment is not effective: the reconnaissance aircraft flown off by the ships find nothing because Force H is proceeding northwards to the E of the Balearics. Of the British submarines stationed between Sicily and Sardinia and off the Straits of Messina, *Upholder* reports the Italian fleet on 24 Sept. On the same day *Manxman* lays, undetected, 70 magnetic and 70 moored mines off Livorno, while 10 Swordfish aircraft attack the airfield at Tempio in North Sardinia. The returning British force is not found by Italian reconnaissance. Adm Iachino waits in vain for the convoy and has to set out for home on 25 Aug. Before reaching harbour, the cruiser *Bolzano* is torpedoed by the British submarine *Triumph* (Lt-Cdr Woods).

22–30 Aug North Atlantic
The U-boats *U143*, *U83*, *U101*, *U751*, *U561*, *U557*, *U95* and *U141* are stationed in the area W of the North Channel. Of them, *U143* (Lt Gelhaus) sinks one ship of 1418 tons in a convoy on 23 Aug. On 26 Aug *U141* (Lt Schüler) sights the outbound convoy OS.4 W of Ireland but is forced to submerge by an aircraft. In the afternoon *U557* (Lt Paulshen) comes up and during the night 26–27 Aug attacks in three approaches. Four ships of 20407 tons are sunk. On 27 Aug *U557* leads *U751*, and on 28 Aug *U71* and *U558* (Lt-Cdr Krech), to the scene: the last sinks the motor ship *Otaio* (10298 tons). No operation is possible against convoy HG.71 located SW of Ireland by air reconnaissance on 29 Aug. *U143* sights the outbound convoy ON.12 on 30 Aug off the North Channel but is forced to submerge by the 3rd EG (destroyer leader *Bulldog*). At the beginning of Sept *U141* sinks two fishery vessels.

23–27 Aug Baltic
The Soviet cruiser *Kirov*, the flotilla leaders *Leningrad* and *Minsk* and several destroyers, including *Gordy*, support the fighting by the defenders of Tallinn.

23–28 Aug Mediterranean
Several small Italian convoys between Tripoli and Benghazi are attacked by British aircraft which, on 23 and 24 Aug, sink one vessel and one auxiliary gunboat. In the Gulf of Sirte the British submarine *Tetrarch* (Lt-Cdr Greenway) sinks two small ships of 808 tons. *Rorqual* (Lt Napier) lays a mine barrage on 25 Aug near Cape Skinari (Aegean) and on 28 Aug sinks with a torpedo one ship of 2747 tons escorted by the torpedo boat *Antares*. One more ship from this convoy is damaged by bombs from British aircraft and has to return to Morea. In the Central Mediterranean, *Urge* (Lt-Cdr Tomkinson) torpedoes one ship of 4971 tons in a Tripoli convoy consisting of four steamers, the destroyers *Euro* and *Oriani* and the torpedo boats *Procione*, *Orsa*, *Clio* and *Pegaso*. *Unbeaten* (Lt Woodward) sinks one ship of 373 tons off Augusta.

23 Aug–1 Sept Atlantic
Following indications from 'Ultra' intelligence and air reconnaissance, the British auxiliary cruiser *Circassia* from Freetown and the Canadian auxiliary cruiser *Prince David* from Halifax are ordered to intercept at the suspected meeting point a German auxiliary cruiser and a blockade-runner in the Central Atlantic SE of Bermuda. On its way, on 27 Aug, *Prince David* sights an unknown vessel and reports it as a possible cruiser of the *Admiral Hipper* class. This leads to a big search operation.

From Bermuda the British battleship *Rodney* departs, followed by the US Task Group 2.6 with the carrier *Wasp*, the cruiser *Savannah* and the destroyers *Gwin*, *Monssen* and *Meredith* on 27 Aug. In the morning of 28 Aug aircraft from *Wasp* report several merchant vessels and a warship, possibly of the *Hipper* class, whereupon *Rodney* is ordered to join the *Wasp* group. The British cruiser *Diomede*, the auxiliary cruisers *Circassia* and *Ascania* and the battleship *Revenge* at sea in the area are re-routed accordingly. From Bermuda, on 28–29 Aug, the US Task Group 2.7 with the escort carrier *Long Island*, the cruiser *Nashville* and the destroyers *Livermore* and *Kearny* and the replenished Task Group 2.5 with the carrier *Yorktown*, the cruiser *Brooklyn* and the destroyers *Roe*, *Eberle* and *Grayson* fan out to contact the suspected vessel. Merchant ships are ordered to take cover west of the Antilles and Bahamas. From Freetown the British Force F sets out with the carrier *Eagle*, the cruisers *Dorsetshire* and *Newcastle* and the oiler *Echodale* to search and cover the troop transport *Durban Castle*, escorted by the auxiliary cruiser *Queen of Bermuda*. From Trinidad the US task groups of Force 3 with the cruisers *Memphis*, *Milwaukee* and *Omaha* and the destroyers *Somers*, *Warrington*, *Davis* and *Jouett* cover the Caribbean exits and the NE coast of Brazil and Guiana. Even when good aerial photographs of Brest show the German capital ships *Scharnhorst* and *Gneisenau* and the *Hipper*-class *Prinz Eugen* in dock on 29 Aug, new fears are raised by a report from the US Coast Guard cutter *Alexander Hamilton* on 30 Aug about a *Hipper*-class cruiser being sighted between Bermuda and Newfoundland. To prevent clashes with such a ship, the convoys HX.147 and ON.9(F) with British escorts and SC.41 with Canadian escorts and the US Task Units 1.1.7 and 1.1.4, escorting shipping between Newfoundland and Iceland, are warned, and the US Task Group 1.2.2 with the battleship *New Mexico*, the cruiser *Quincy* and the destroyers *Sims*, *Hughes* and *Russell* sails to block the Denmark Strait from Hvalfjord. However, the German auxiliary cruiser *Schiff 36/Orion* (Cdr Weyher) has already been met by *U75* and *U205* on 20–21 Aug and has entered the Gironde on 23 Aug after a raiding operation lasting 510 days in the Atlantic, Pacific and Indian Oceans. Success: 10 ships of 62915 tons sunk and two of 21125 tons in co-operation with *Schiff 45/Komet*. The Italian blockade-runners *Himalaya* and *Africana* from Brazil enter the Gironde on 29 Aug. The German blockade-runner

Anneliese Essberger (5173 tons, Capt Bahl) from Japan is not found by the searching Allied forces and reaches Bordeaux on 10 Sept.

23 Aug–17 Sept Arctic

The German U-boats *U571*, *U752*, *U451* and *U566* operate off the Kola Coast. *U752* (Lt Schroeter) sinks the Soviet trawler *T-898/Nenets* (1050 tons) on 25 Aug and torpedoes a guard ship off Svyatoy Nos on 27 Aug. *U571* (Lt-Cdr Möhlmann) torpedoes the Soviet transport *Mariya Ulyanova* (3870 tons) off Cape Teriberski on 26 Aug. On 3 Sept *U566* misses the British submarine *Trident* returning to Polyarnoe and *U451* avoids a submarine torpedo.

24–25 Aug Baltic

Soviet convoy with the ice-breaker *Oktyabr* and nine transports from Tallinn to Suursaari-Kronstadt. On 24 Aug the destroyer *Engels*, the minesweepers *T-209/Knecht*, *T-212/Shtag* and *T-213/Krambol* and three transports are lost on the 'Juminda' mine barrage. Two other transports are lost on 25 Aug through air attacks W of Suursaari. Among the sunken transports are probably *Daugava* (1430 tons) and *Lunacharski* (3618 tons) and the tanker *Zheleznodorozhnik* (2029 tons).

The German minelayers *Brummer* and *Roland* and boats of the 3rd MTB Flotilla lay the 'Rusto' mine barrage with 170 EMCs and 30 TMBs N of Cape Ristna (Dagö).

25 Aug Iran

Soviet and British-Indian troops move into Iran. Weak resistance by the Iranian Army is quickly broken. British naval forces carry out landing operations in Abadan, Khorramshahr and Bandar Shapur (Operation 'Countenance'). Taking part are the auxiliary cruiser *Kanimbla* (Capt Adams), the sloops *Falmouth*, *Shoreham* and *Yarra* (RAN), the river gunboat *Cockchafer*, the corvette *Snapdragon* and some small auxiliary vessels. In Abadan, *Shoreham* sinks the Iranian gunboat *Palang* (950 tons). *Yarra* seizes the gunboats *Chahbaaz* and *Karkass* (331 tons each) in the Karun estuary and sinks the gunboat *Babr* (950 tons) in Khorramshahr. In the defence of the naval base there, the C-in-C Iranian Navy, Rear-Adm Bayendor, is killed. In Bandar Shapur the Royal Navy seizes the German freighters *Hohenfels* (7862 tons), *Marienfels* (7575 tons), *Sturmfels* (6288 tons) and *Wildenfels* (6224 tons), the Italian tanker *Bronte* (4769 tons) and the freighters *Barbara* (3065 tons) and *Caboto* (5225 tons) and, on 27 Aug in Bandar Abbas, the Italian freighter *Hilda* (4901 tons). The German freighter *Weissenfels* (7861 tons) is set on fire and destroyed by her crew.

27 Aug Baltic

Attack by four Soviet TKAs on a German coastal motor boat convoy near Cape Domesnäs. Two coastal motor boats are slightly damaged.

28–29 Aug Baltic

Withdrawal of the Soviet Baltic Fleet and the remainder of X Rifle Corps from Tallinn to Kronstadt. After embarking the units during the night 27–28 Aug, the convoys and covering forces assemble in the course of 28 Aug in the roads of Tallinn.

1st convoy (Capt 2nd Class N G Bogdanov): six transports, one ice-breaker, one repair ship, one training ship and submarines *Shch-308*, *Shch-307* and *M-97*. Escort: destroyer *Surovy*, patrol ships *Ametist*, *Kasatka* and *Saturn*, five old minesweepers, two MO-IV submarine-chasers, five patrol cutters and one tug.

2nd convoy (Capt 2nd Class N V Antonov): six transports, two netlayers, one survey ship and one schooner. Escort: gunboat *Moskva*, patrol ship *Chapaev*, four old minesweepers, nine motor minesweepers and two MO-IV submarine-chasers.

3rd convoy (Capt 2nd Class Y F Yanson): eight transports and one tanker. Escort: gunboat *Amgun*, patrol ships *Kolyvan* and *Ural*, four old minesweepers, four motor minesweepers and two MO-IV submarine-chasers.

4th convoy (Capt 3rd Class S A Gikhorovtsev): nine various small craft. Escort: patrol ship *Razvedchik*, gunboat *I-8*, nine motor minesweepers and two magnetic minesweepers.

Main forces (Vice-Adm V F Tributs): cruiser *Kirov* (F), flotilla leader *Leningrad*, destroyers *Gordy*, *Smetlivy* and *Yakov Sverdlov*, submarines *S-4*, *S-5*, *Shch-301* and *Kalev*, minesweepers *T-204*, *T-205*, *T-206*, *T-207* and *T-217*, torpedo cutters *TKA-73*, *TKA-74*, *TKA-94*, *TKA-103* and *MO-131*, *MO-133*, *MO-142* and *MO-202*, tender *Pikker* and ice-breaker *Suur-Töll*.

Covering detachment (Rear-Adm Y A Panteleev): flotilla leader *Minsk* (F), destroyers *Skory* and *Slavny*, submarines *Shch-322*, *M-98*, *M-95* and *M-102*, minesweepers *T-210*, *T-214*, *T-215*, *T-216* and *T-218*, submarine-chasers *MO-207*, *MO-212*, *MO-213* and *MO-510*, four torpedo cutters and patrol ship *Neptun*. Rearguard (Rear-Adm Y F Rall): destroyers *Kalinin* (F), *Artem* and *Volodarski*, patrol ships *Burya*, *Sneg* and *Tsiklon*, two torpedo cutters, five MO-IV submarine-chasers and minelayer *Vaindlo*. After the departure of the ships, *Burya*, *Sneg*, *Tsiklon* and *Vaindlo* lay mine barrages

in the harbour and in the approaches. The old minelayer *Amur*, the steamer *Gamma* (696 tons) and three tugs are sunk as blockships. The withdrawing forces are attacked in the afternoon of 28 Aug W of the mine barrages by Ju 88s of 2/KG 77 and of K F1 Gr 806, when the ice-breaker *Krisyanis Valdemars* (2250 tons), the transports *Skrunda* (2414 tons), *Lake Lucerne* (2317 tons) and *Atis Kronvalds* (1423 tons) are sunk and the staff ship *Vironia* (2026 tons) is damaged and later sinks on mines. In breaking through the 'Juminda' mine barrages during the night 28–29 Aug, the following are sunk: the destroyers *Sverdlov*, *Skory*, *Kalinin*, *Artem* and *Volodarski*, the patrol ships *Sneg*, *Tsiklon* and *Saturn*, the minesweepers *T-214*, *T-216* and *Krab*, the submarines *Shch-301*, *S-5* and *S-6*, the gunboats *I-8*, *Amgun* (?) and *Moskva* (?), the netlayers *Onega* and *Vyatka*, the torpedo cutter *TKA-103*, the submarine-chaser *MO-202* and the transports *Alev* (1446 tons), *Tobol* (2758 tons), *Yärvamaa* (1363 tons), *Everita* (3251 tons), *Luga* (2329 tons), *Kumari* (237 tons), *Balkhash* (2191 tons), *Yana* (2917 tons), *Naissaar* (1839 tons), *Ergonautis* (206 tons), *Ella* (1522 tons), *Ausma* (1791 tons) and *Tanker 2* (1700 tons). Heavy damage is sustained by the flotilla leader *Minsk*, the destroyers *Gordy* and *Slavny*, the minesweeper *T-205* and other transports. On 29 Aug the remaining transports are again attacked in the area of Suursaari by the Ju 88s of 2/KG 77 and of K F1 Gr 806, after the fast warships have gone on to Kronstadt in accordance with orders. In this action the transports *Kalpaks* (2190 tons) and *Vtoraya Pyatiletka* (3974 tons) and the training ship *Leningradsovet* (1270 tons), are sunk; the transports *Ivan Papanin* (3974 tons) and *Saule* (1207 tons) and the repair ship *Serp i Molot* (5920 tons) are severely damaged and have to be beached near Suursaari. Only the transport *Kazakhstan*, having disembarked 2300 of her 5000 troops on Steinskär, reaches Kronstadt badly damaged by bombs. A special covering and salvage force (Capt 2nd Class I G Svyatov) is sent out from Suursaari, consisting of 12 old minesweepers, one patrol ship division, six torpedo cutters, eight submarine-chasers, two tugs, four motor boats, two cutters and the rescue ship *Meteor*. In the following days this force rescues 12160 troops in all, including some from the islands of the Gulf of Finland.

The submarine *Shch-322*, employed in covering the operation, does not return.

28 Aug–14 Sept North Atlantic

Operations by the U-boat 'Markgraf' group, formed from *U652*, *U105*, *U432*, *U38*, *U84*,

U501, U43, U202, U82, U207, U569, U433, U85 and *U81* which assemble SW of Iceland. *U202* (Lt-Cdr Linder) has sunk one fishing steamer of 230 tons south of Iceland on 27 Aug.

On 1 Sept the BdU signals for 28, 30 and 31 Aug are decoded at Bletchley Park and the STR re-routes convoys ON.10S and ON.11F, going W, and HX.146 (escorted by EG.17 with the British destroyer *Broadway*, the corvette *Polyanthus* and the Canadian corvettes *Cobalt* and *Trail*) and SC.41 (escorted by EG.21 with the destroyer *St Croix* and the corvettes *Pictou*, *Buctouche* and *Galt*), going E, to the N of group 'Markgraf'.

While the US Task Units 1.1.5 (with the destroyers *Bernadou* and *Lea*, escorting one US and one Icelandic ship from Reykjavik to Argentia) and 1.1.7 (with the destroyers *Lansdale*, *Gleaves*, *Madison* and *C F Hughes*, escorting two US ships from Argentia to Iceland) are routed clear, on 4 Sept a British aircraft informs the US destroyer *Greer* (Lt-Cdr Frost, with Com Desdiv Cdr Johnson on board), which is on the way to Iceland, about a German U-boat located in the area. *Greer* proceeds to the position given and herself locates the submerged U-boat. The British aircraft attacks the U-boat—*U652* (Lt Fraatz)—with depth charges. *U652* suspects that *Greer* is the attacker and tries to sink her. *Greer* takes evasive action and unsuccessfully attacks the U-boat with depth charges.

On 4 Sept 'Markgraf' is ordered 150 miles to the W just after TU.1.1.5 and convoy ON.10S have passed the area. When this order is decoded on 6 Sept TU.1.1.7 and convoy HX.147, escorted by EG.20 with the destroyer *Columbia* and the corvettes *Wetaskiwin* (RCN), *Mimose* (FFN) and *Gladiolus*, are re-routed sharply to the N and just evade the new patrol line. On 5 Sept *U501* (Cdr Förster) sinks one independent of 2000 tons.

On 6 Sept the BdU decides, after waiting in vain for sighting reports, to distribute the 'Markgraf' group over a larger area to the SE of Greenland to cover a greater part of the possible convoy routes. When this order is decoded on 8 Sept by Bletchley Park, there are difficulties in identifying the reference points exactly but the STR tries to steer the convoys round the possible danger area. Convoys ON.12S, HX.148 (escorted by EG.22 with the destroyer *Richmond* and the corvettes *Candytuft*, *Bittersweet* and *Fennel*) and SC.43 (escorted by EG.18 with the destroyers *Churchill* and *Chesterfield* and the corvettes *Arrowhead*, *Camellia*, *Eyebright* and *Celandine*) have to make a wide detour to the S, as has the US Task Force 15, consisting of the battleship *Idaho*, the cruisers *Tuscaloosa* and *Vincennes* and the destroyers *Winslow*, *Sampson*, *Anderson*, *Mustin*, *O'Brien*, *Walke*, *Morris*, *Benson*, *Niblack*, *H P Jones*, *MacLeish*, *Truxtun*, *Overton*, *Reuben James* and *Bainbridge*, escorting nine transports with an Army brigade to relieve the Marines on Iceland (Operation 'Indigo III'). The escorting destroyers attack eight different assumed U-boat contacts which were in reality false.

Convoy SC.42 (64 ships, Commodore Mackenzie), escorted by the Canadian EG.24 (Lt-Cdr Hibbard) with the destroyer *Skeena* and the corvettes *Alberni*, *Kenogami* and *Orillia*, has no chance of turning round to the S owing to the very heavy storm raging and is directed close to the Greeland ice barrier.

Early on 9 Sept *U81* (Lt Guggenberger) sinks one straggler from SC.41 of 5591 tons. In the afternoon *U85* (Lt Greger) intercepts the convoy close to Cape Farewell. Its first attack fails, but on its contact reports the following U-boats close in and attack during the night 9–10 Sept: *U432* (Lt Schultze) sinks one ship of 5229 tons, *U81* fails, *U652* torpedoes two ships of 4318 tons (one is towed back to harbour by the corvette *Orillia*, the other is sunk later by *U372* under Lt-Cdr Neumann), *U81* sinks one ship of 3252 tons and *U82* (Lt Rollmann) sinks one catapult ship of 7465 tons and fires a spread against *Skeena* which misses. The fact that the corvettes remain behind to recover survivors facilitates the U-boats' attacks.

By day on 10 Sept *U432* maintains contact and *U85* attacks twice and sinks one ship of 4748 tons but is herself damaged by depth charges from *Skeena* and *Alberni*. The first air escort, a Catalina of No 209 Sqn RAF from Iceland forces *U501* down. The Canadian corvettes *Chambly* (Cdr Prentice) and *Moosejaw*, sent N from St John's to support the convoy in greatest danger, are sent to SC.42. Coming up from the rear, they surprise and sink *U501*.

During the night 10–11 Sept several U-boats again attack. *U82* sinks two ships of 11434 tons, *U432* one ship of 1231 tons, *U433* (Lt Ey) one straggler of 2215 tons, *U207* (Lt Meyer) two ships of 9739 tons and damages one more and *U82* hits two more ships, one of 5463 tons sinking and one of 1980 tons being finished off the next day by *U202* (Lt-Cdr Linder), which has attacked before unsuccessfully.

During the morning of 11 Sept, first the corvettes *Wetaskiwin*, *Mimose* and *Gladiolus* and the trawler *Buttermere*, diverted from convoy HX.147, join, and later the British EG.2 (Cdr Banks) with the destroyers *Douglas*, *Veteran*, *Leamington*, *Skate* and *Saladin*, refuelled at Hvalfjord after leaving the convoy ON.13F, which is now escorted only by the corvettes *Anemone*, *Veronica* and *Abelia* and the trawlers *Vizalma* and *St Zeno* and has been re-routed north of SC.42. The US Task Unit 1.1.6 with the destroyers *Ellis*, *Cole*, *Broome* and *Simpson*, escorting four ships from Reykjavik to Argentia, is diverted to the S.

During daytime on 11 Sept aircraft from Nos 209 and 269 Sqns RAF from Iceland provide air cover. *Veteran* and *Leamington* sight and sink *U207*. *U432* continues to maintain contact. *U652* attacks unsuccessfully and *U105* (Lt-Cdr Schewe) sinks one independent of 1549 tons.

During the night 11–12 Sept the escort, now numbering 14 units under Cdr Banks, augmented by the trawler *Windermere* escorting a straggler, prevents successful attacks, *U84* (Lt Uphoff) and *U43* (Lt-Cdr Lüth) both firing but both missing.

By day on 12 Sept *Skeena*, *Kenogami* and *Alberni* leave to refuel at Hvalfjord, while the Canadian destroyers *St Croix* from SC.41 and *Columbia* from HX.147, being refuelled, join. *U432*, *U373* and *U433* keep contact but are held off by the strong sea and air escort.

After a quiet night on 13 Sept, the US destroyers *Sims*, *Hughes* and *Russell* join, allowing the five destroyers of EG.2 to refuel again. In the rising fog, *U433*, *U572*, *U552*, *U373* and *U575*, which are still operating against the convoy, cannot find it because of poor visibility. Later *Skeena*, with five merchant vessels from Iceland to Great Britain, joins again.

On 14 Sept *Chambly* leaves for Hvalfjord and the three US destroyers are recalled, but only *U552* (Lt Topp) has a short contact with escorts before the operation is broken off by the BdU. Total result: 16 ships of 65409 tons sunk, one tanker of 6508 tons torpedoed. Two U-boats are lost.

On 15 Sept a US task unit is sent out from Hvalfjord against the U-boats behind SC.44 with the destroyers *Gleaves*, *Madison*, *Lansdale* and *Charles F Hughes*.

28 Aug–24 Sept   Central Atlantic

From 28 Aug *U108*, *U111* and *U125* proceed in line abreast from the area W of the Azores to the area around St Paul. Only *U111* (Lt-Cdr Kleinschmidt) sinks one ship on both 10 and 20 Sept, totalling 14193 tons. On 24 Sept the boats are brought into the area of the Cape Verde Islands and W of Freetown in order to operate with boats of the following wave (see 21 Sept).

29–31 Aug Baltic
A Finnish minelayer sows 24 more mines at the N end of the 'Juminda' barrage during the night 28–29 Aug. Boats of the 5th MMS Flotilla lay 96 mines during the nights 28–29, 29–30 and 30–31 Aug between the old Finnish 'Valkjärvi' and the 'Juminda' barrage. In addition, a new barrage section of 36 EMC mines and 40 explosive floats is laid on 31 Aug on the Russian route in the 'Juminda' barrage.

29 Aug–4 Sept Mediterranean
On 29 Aug an Italian convoy with the large transports *Neptunia*, *Oceania* and *Victoria*, escorted by the destroyers *Aviere*, *Da Noli*, *Camicia Nera*, *Gioberti*, *Usodimare* and *Pessagno*, departs from Naples for Tripoli, while from there another convoy with five cargo vessels and one mine vessel, escorted by the destroyers *Oriani* and *Euro* and the torpedo boats *Pegaso*, *Orsa* and *Calliope*, returns to Naples. Neither convoy makes contact with the enemy. The return voyage of the *Neptunia* convoy from 31 Aug to 2 Sept is also uneventful.

A new convoy of five cargo ships from Naples to Tripoli from 1–4 Sept, escorted by the destroyers *Da Recco*, *Dardo*, *Folgore* and *Strale*, later augmented by *Ascari* and *Lanciere*, is attacked in the evening of 3 Sept by torpedo aircraft from Malta which sink one ship of 6338 tons and damage one more, the latter being towed back to Messina by *Dardo*.

30 Aug Baltic
The ships of the squadron of the Baltic Fleet are concentrated to form an artillery support force for the Leningrad Front under Rear-Adm I I Gren. The first group is on the Neva consisting of the destroyers *Opytny* (provisionally completed) and *Strogi*, *Stroiny* and the gunboats *Zeya*, *Sestroretsk* and *Oka* to support the 42nd and 55th Armies SE of Leningrad. The second group is in the Leningrad area as far as the eastern part of the Sea Canal with the cruiser *Maksim Gorki*, which has been provisionally repaired, the cruiser *Petropavlovsk* (Capt 1st Class Vanifatev), which is still being fitted out and which has two turrets capable of firing, the flotilla leader *Leningrad*, the destroyers *Svirepy*, *Grozyashchi*, *Silny*, *Stoiki* and *Storozhevoi* (being repaired) and probably the minelayer *Marti*. The third group is in the area Kronstadt-Oranienbaum with the battleships *Oktyabrskaya Revolutsiya* (Rear-Adm M S Moskalenko) and *Marat* (Capt 1st Class M G Ivanov), the cruiser *Kirov* (Capt 1st Class M G Sukhoruchenko), the flotilla leader *Minsk*, the destroyers *Surovy*, *Gordy*, *Smetlivy*, *Slavny*, *Steregushchi* and *Strashny* (the last

two are being repaired) and the gunboat *Volga*.

1 Sept Intelligence
The British introduce new indicator tables for the long subtractor tables but because of an error in the method the work of the German B-Service in solving the 'Naval Cypher No 3', used for convoys, is eased.

1 Sept North Atlantic
Reorganisation of the Canadian ocean escort forces as follows: EG.14—destroyers *Assiniboine*, *Havelock* (RN), *Harvester* (RN), *Ripley* (RN) and *St Laurent*; EG.15—destroyers *Burwell (RN)* and *Saguenay*, corvettes *Dianthus*, *Honeysuckle* and *Snowberry* (all RN); EG.16—destroyer *Broadwater* (RN), corvettes *Chilliwack*, *Rimouski* and *Spikenard*; EG.17—destroyer *Broadway*, corvettes *Polyanthus*, *Cobalt*, and *Trail*; EG.18—destroyer *Churchill*, corvettes *Camellia*, *Arrowhead* and *Eyebright*; EG.19—destroyer *Burnham*, corvettes *Mayflower*, *Agassiz*, and *Levis*; EG.20—destroyer *Columbia*, corvettes *Gladiolus*, *Mimose* and *Wetaskiwin*; EG.21—destroyer *St Croix*, corvettes *Chambly*, *Pictou*, *Buctouche* and *Galt*; EG.22—destroyer *Ramsey*, corvettes *Candytuft*, *Bittersweet* and *Fennel*; EG.23—destroyer *Chesterfield*, corvettes *Reading*, *Hepatica* and *Prescott*; EG.24—destroyer *Skeena*, corvettes *Alberni*, *Orillia*, *Kenogami*; EG.25—destroyer *Niagara*, corvettes *Alysse*, *Celandine* and *Collingwood*.

1–2 Sept Black Sea
The cruisers *Chervona Ukraina* and *Komintern* and the destroyers *Soobrazitelny*, *Besposhchadny*, *Boiki*, *Nezamozhnik* and *Shaumyan* are used to support the coastal army, especially near Dofinovka and Ilyichevka. Smokescreen floats are used for cover against the Rumanian coastal battery near Fontanka.

1–18 Sept North Atlantic
The 'Kurfürst' group is formed on 1 Sept from *U77*, *U568*, *U553*, *U206*, *U567*, *U563* and *U96* in the area W of the North Channel and the 'Bosemüller' group from *U71*, *U557*, *U561*, *U95*, *U751*, *U83*, *U562* and *U558* W to SW of Ireland. On 1 Sept the 'Bosemüller' group is directed to the convoy SL.84 sighted by the returning *U73*, but it finds nothing in the poor visibility. The 'Kurfürst' group is directed to OG.73 sighted by an Fw 200 of I/KG 40. On 2 Sept *U557* comes across OG.73 in the mist; *U83* sights a corvette of the escort and the convoy is also reported by air reconnaissance. In consequence, the 'Kurfürst' and 'Bosemüller' groups are combined to form 'Seewolf' and are directed to this convoy. But they find neither this convoy nor one sighted by *U98* on 3 Sept. *U567* (Lt-Cdr

Fahr) sinks one independent of 3485 tons. The Italian submarines *Da Vinci*, *Morosini*, *Torelli* and *Malaspina*, operating W of Gibraltar, are driven off from convoy HG.72, which has set out on 10 Sept, by the escort—in particular, by the destroyers *Faulknor* (SOE Capt de Salis), *Avon Vale*, *Encounter* and *Nestor* and EG.36 with the sloop *Deptford* and five corvettes, to which are added on 12 Sept the destroyers *Boreas* and *Wild Swan* from Plymouth. On 11 Sept 'Seewolf' is sent with the remaining boats, *U69*, *U94*, *U557*, *U561*, *U565*, *U95* and *U98*, to the area NW of the Hebrides. On 14, 15 and 18 Sept convoys are sighted by air reconnaissance and also by *U565* on 14 Sept but no other boats come up and *U561* and *U95* are attacked by aircraft. Only *U98* (Lt-Cdr Gysae) is able to sink one ship of 4392 tons from the convoy SC.42 on 16 Sept.

1 Sept–30 Nov South Atlantic
The US Task Force 3 (Rear-Adm Ingram) carries out regular overlapping patrols of about three weeks from Trinidad to Recife (Brazil), then to a point SW of the Cape Verde Islands, back to Recife and on to Trinidad again. There are four task groups, each consisting of one cruiser and one destroyer: 3.6(A) with *Milwaukee* and *Warrington* 1–21 Sept and 7–27 Oct; 3.5(B) with *Omaha* and *Somers* 23 Sept–11 Oct and 20 Oct–15 Nov; 3.7(C) with *Memphis* and *Davis* 1–19 Oct and 5–23 Nov; and 3.8 with *Cincinnati* and *Jouett* 9–27 Oct and 4–30 Nov (broken off because *Cincinnati* and *Warrington* return to Yorktown).

2–3 Sept Baltic
A Finnish minelayer lays 84 new mines W of the 'Juminda' barrage. The German minelayer *Kaiser* protects the barrage with 120 explosive floats. In a sortie into the Koivisto narrows, the Finnish motor torpedo boat *Syöksy* sinks the Soviet-Estonian steamer *Meero* (1866 tons).

3–17 Sept Arctic
Among others, the Soviet submarines *K-1*, *K-2*, *Shch-422*, *M-174*, *M-176*, *M-171*, *M-173* and *M-172* operate off the Norwegian polar coast. *K-1* (Capt 3rd Class M P Avgustinovich) operates for 28 days without success in the area of Vestfjord. *K-2* (Capt 3rd Class V P Utkin) lays on 10 Sept the first Soviet submarine mine barrage in the Arctic off Vardö (later cleared) and attacks on 12 Sept the steamer *Lofoten* (1517 tons) with gunfire off Persfjord, but the ship gets away. On board the submarine is the Cdr of the 1st SM Division, Capt 2nd Class M I Gadzhiev. *Shch-422* (Lt-Cdr Malyshev) achieves the first success with the sinking of the Norwegian steamer *Ottar Jarl* (1459

tons) off Tanafjord on 12 Sept. On 13 and 14 Sept *M-171* and *M-172* miss targets with torpedoes off Liinahamari and Bokfjord respectively. *M-173* (Lt-Cdr I A Kunets) disembarks 13 agents on the coast of the Varanger Peninsula. Off Breisund, the British submarine *Tigris* (Cdr Bone) sinks the steamer *Richard With* (905 tons) and misses on 15 and 17 Sept two convoys in Lopphavet.

4–8 Sept   Norway
The pocket-battleship *Admiral Scheer* is transferred temporarily to Oslo. B-17 bombers of No 2 Group RAF Bomber Command try unsuccessfully to attack the ship on 5 and 8 Sept. She returns to Swine-münde.

5 Sept   Black Sea
The Soviet cruiser *Komintern* engages the Rumanian coastal battery near Fontanka.

5–14 Sept   Mediterranean
In operations in the Western Mediterranean, the Dutch submarines *O21* (Lt-Cdr v Dulm) and *O24* (Lt-Cdr de Booy) sink one ship of 5738 tons and two ships of 5469 tons respectively. Off the Dardanelles, the British submarine *Perseus* (Lt-Cdr Nicolay) sinks one ship of 3867 tons escorted by the torpedo boat *Sirio*. In the area of Sirte the British submarine *Thunderbolt* (Lt-Cdr Crouch) sinks three ships of 3191 tons from several small convoys escorted by the Italian torpedo boats *Centauro* and *Polluce*. An Italian convoy with six ships from Naples to Tripoli, escorted by the destroyers *Oriani* and *Fulmine* and the torpedo boats *Procione*, *Pegaso*, *Orsa*, *Circe* and *Perseo* from 10 to 13 Sept is attacked several times on 12 and 13 Sept by British aircraft from Malta, which bomb and sink three ships of 15538 tons.

6–14 Sept   Mediterranean
The Italian submarine *Dagabur* reconnoitres the Egyptian coast between Tobruk and Port Said and *Topazio* (Cdr Berengan) sinks one ship of 691 tons on the Syrian coast.

7 Sept   North Sea
In an attack by the 4th MTB Flotilla (Lt-Cdr Bätge), comprising *S48*, *S49*, *S50*, *S52* and *S107*, on a British convoy off the Norfolk coast, two freighters of 1914 tons are sunk.

7 Sept   Black Sea
The Soviet flotilla leader *Kharkov*, with the destroyers *Boiki* and *Sposobny*, brings the C-in-C Black Sea Fleet, Vice-Adm F S Oktyabrski, to Odessa for inspections and conferences. During their stay, the ships, together with the destroyer *Dzerzhinski*, shell Rumanian positions. The destroyer *Sposobny* is damaged by a near-miss bomb in the second engine compartment.

7–8 Sept   Baltic
On 7 Sept the cruiser *Maksim Gorki*, from the Leningrad merchant harbour, and the battleship *Marat*, from the Sea Canal, fire on attacking outposts of the German 18th Army S of Leningrad. On 8 Sept the gunboat *Krasnoe Znamya* supports, from Cape Shepelev, the right wing of the Soviet 8th Army in the Oranienbaum cauldron and the battleship *Oktyabrskaya Revolutsiya* and the cruiser *Kirov* shell German assembly areas near Krasnoe Selo and Peterhof.
Boats of the German 5th MTB Flotilla lay a barrage of 48 EMC mines NE of Seiskari and the 1st MTB Flotilla protects it with 40 explosive floats. On the next day, on the way to another mining operation, the motor minesweeper *R58* hits a mine and is towed to harbour badly damaged.

8 Sept–Nov   Baltic
In transport operations from Suursaari to Hangö, submarines of the Baltic Fleet are used. *P-1* (17 Sept), *L-2* and *Kalev* are lost through mines.

8–14 Sept   Mediterranean
Operation 'Status' (8–10 Sept): *Ark Royal* proceeds with the cruiser *Hermione* and six destroyers to the area S of the Balearics and flies off 14 Hurricane fighters. In a second sortie, the battleship *Nelson* and another destroyer take part. On 13 Sept the carriers *Ark Royal* and *Furious* fly off another 45 Hurricane fighters to Malta. The Italian submarines *Alagi* and *Serpente*, stationed N of the Algerian coast, do not approach. The concentration of the submarines *Axum*, *Adua*, *Aradam* and *Settembrini* near Cape Bon is ineffective.

8–19 Sept   Arctic
New attack by the German XIX Mountain Corps across the Litsa has to be broken off after initial, small ground gains against the tough defence of the Soviet 14th Army.

10–13 Sept   General Situation
Military exercise by the Japanese Navy under the command of the C-in-C of the Combined Fleet, Adm Yamamoto.

10–15 Sept   Arctic
The Soviet 1st DD Div of the Northern Fleet, consisting of the destroyers *Gremyashchi*, *Gromki*, *Grozny* and *Sokrushitelny*, lays two mine barrages in the area of the Fisherman's Peninsula using the mines brought to Murmansk by the British minelaying cruiser *Adventure*.

11 Sept   Atlantic/Intelligence
Because of the difficulties in establishing positions by means of the reference point system, the BdU introduces random superencyphering for the first two letters of the grid map in order to confuse enemy radio intelligence.

11 Sept   Baltic
During the night the 5th MMS Flotilla lays a barrage of 36 EMC mines E of Suursaari and the 1st MTB Flotilla lays 40 explosive floats.

11 Sept   General Situation
President Roosevelt announces, as an answer to the *Greer* incident (see 28 Aug–14 Sept 1941), the so-called 'shoot on sight' order against all ships of the Axis Powers which dare to sail into seas 'the protection of which is necessary for American defence'.

11–12 Sept   Arctic
The Soviet torpedo cutters *TKA-11* (Lt-Cdr G K Svetlov) and *TKA-12* (Sub-Lt A O Shabalin) attack a German convoy for the first time off Petsamofjord. The convoy is escorted by the patrol vessel *NT05/Togo* (ex-Norwegian minesweeper *Otra*). No hit is recorded.

11–12 Sept   Black Sea
Off Odessa, the Soviet cruiser *Krasny Kavkaz* shells Rumanian positions near Ilinka and Krasny Pereselnets. On 12 Sept she is attacked several times by German aircraft but suffers no damage.

12–18 Sept   Baltic
The Soviet submarine *M-77* occupies a position near Someri, *M-99* near Tallinn and *M-98* and *M-102* near Helsinki as a defence against German-Finnish operations. *M-97* (Lt-Cdr A I Mylnikov) makes an unsuccessful attack on 17 Sept.

12–22 Sept   Mediterranean
The British fast minelayers *Abdiel* and *Latona* and some destroyers transport 6300 troops and 2100 tons of supplies to Tobruk and bring 6000 Australians back to Alexandria.

13 Sept   Baltic
The German patrol vessel *V308* (*Oscar Neynaber*) is sunk by a torpedo from a Soviet MTB off Porkkala.

13–14 Sept   Air War/Western Europe
Heavy attack by RAF Bomber Command on the German battlecruisers at Brest.

13 Sept–5 Oct   Baltic
Ösel Island is captured. On 13–14 Sept Feint operations ('Nordwind') take place with the Finnish Armoured Ship Division (Capt Rahola) comprising the coastal defence vessels *Ilmarinen* (Cdr* Göransson) and *Väinämöinen* (Cdr* Koivisto) escorted by a patrol boat force (Lt-Cdr Peuranheimo) with *VMV1*, *VMV14*, *VMV15* and *VMV16*, the German minelayer *Brummer* (Cdr Dr Tobias), five boats of the 3rd Patrol Boat Flotilla, two ocean tugs, eight smaller craft and the Finnish ice-breakers *Tarmo* and *Yääkarhu*; similarly 'Westwind', with

the torpedo boats *T11*, *T2*, *T5*, *T8*, the 2nd and 3rd MTB Flotillas and nine smaller craft, is conducted against the western side of the island. A third operation, 'Südwind', consisting of three groups with approximately 50 small craft, is directed against the S coast from Riga to distract the Soviet garrison. *Ilmarinen* sinks with 13 officers and 258 men after being hit by a drifting mine. The patrol boats rescue 132 survivors. On 14 Sept the first wave of the 61st Inf Div lands on Moon Island. On 16 Sept a bridgehead on Dagö is formed. On 16–17 Sept Soviet defenders forced back on the Sworbe Peninsula are shelled by the light cruisers *Emden* (Capt Mirow) and *Leipzig* (Capt Stichling) with *T-7*, *T-8* and *T-11*. Unsuccessful attack by four Soviet motor torpedo boats. The Soviet submarine *Shch-317* fails to hit *Leipzig*.

14 Sept Baltic
In the Helsinki dockyards, the German motor minesweepers *R60*, *R61* and *R62* and the tug *Pellworm* are destroyed by sabotage and two tugs are damaged.

14–15 Sept Arctic
The Soviet torpedo cutters *TKA-13* (Sub-Lt Polyakov) and *TKA-15* (Lt P I Chapilin) attack the Norwegian coaster *Mittnattsol* on the Petsamo–Kirkenes route and sink her. On 15 Sept *TKA-14* (Lt Zhilyaev) sinks the coaster *Renöy*.

15–16 Sept Air War/Germany
Attacks by RAF Bomber Command on Hamburg, Bremen, Cuxhaven and Wilhelmshaven.

15–18 Sept Baltic
After the breakthrough by German Army units into Kronstadt Bay near Peterhof, German Army coastal batteries shell Soviet warships. On 16 Sept *Marat* and *Petropavlovsk* receive the first 15cm hits without, however, much effect. On 18 Sept *Maksim Gorki* is lightly and *Petropavlovsk* is severely hit.

15–18 Sept Mediterranean
Following the decoding of German and Italian signals to Africa by 'Ultra' on 15 Sept, Malta is warned about a large new Italian convoy consisting of the troop transports *Vulcania*, *Oceania* and *Neptunia*, escorted by the destroyers *Da Recco*, *Da Noli*, *Pessagno*, *Usodimare* and *Gioberti*, from Taranto to Tripoli. Early on 17 Sept British air reconnaissance locates the ships E of Calabria. The British submarines *Upright*, *Upholder* and *Unbeaten* are deployed in a patrol line NE of Tripoli and *Ursula* off the harbour. *Upholder* (Lt-Cdr Wanklyn), led to the scene by *Unbeaten* (Lt Woodward), sinks *Neptunia* (19475 tons) and *Oceania* (19507 tons). *Upright* (Lt

Wraith) is driven off by the destroyers; a salvo from *Ursula* (Lt-Cdr Hezlet) against *Vulcania* is evaded. 6500 men are rescued and 384 drown. The Italian submarine *Smeraldo* is lost to an unknown cause on 16 Sept.

15–29 Sept Black Sea
In the W Black Sea, the Soviet submarines *D-5*, *Shch-211*, *Shch-209* and *S-31* operate in the S and *M-60*, *M-112*, *M-51*, *M-59*, *M-34*, *M-36*, *M-35*, *M-111*, *M-58* and *M-62* in the N. *M-34* misses the Italian steamer *Tampico* on 21 Sept but *Shch-211* (Lt-Cdr Devyatko) sinks the Italian tanker *Superga* (6154 tons) S of Varna on 29 Sept. *L-4* (Lt-Cdr Polyakov) and *L-5* (Lt-Cdr Zhdanov) lay mine barrages off the Bulgarian and Rumanian coasts respectively. On the first, the Rumanian minelayer *Regele Carol I* (2369 tons) sinks on 10 Oct and the Bulgarian steamer *Chipka* founders (2304 tons) on 15 Sept; on the second, the escort ship *Theresia Wallner* and the tugs *Brüsterort* and *Drossel* sink on 24–25 Oct.

15 Sept–2 Oct North Atlantic
Operations by the U-boat 'Brandenburg' group in the area SE of Greenland. On the way to assembling in a patrol line SE of Cape Farewell, *U94* (Lt Ites) sinks three stragglers of 14447 tons from the convoy ON.14. From 18–19 Sept *U74*, *U94*, *U575*, *U372*, *U373*, *U552*, *U69*, *U562* and *U572* take up their positions. Before the BdU order is decrypted at Bletchley Park on 18 Sept, *U74* (Lt-Cdr Kentrat) sights the convoy SC.44 (56 ships, Commodore Robinson), escorted by the Canadian EG.23 with the destroyer *Chesterfield* (RN) and the corvettes *Mayflower*, *Levis*, *Honeysuckle* (RN) and *Agassiz*. Owing to radio interference, no co-ordinated attack operation is possible: in addition to *U74*, only *U373*, *U94*, *U552* and *U562* operate. During the night 18–19 Sept *U74* attacks and sinks the corvette *Levis*. During the night 19–20 Sept *U74* attacks again and sinks one ship of 6956 tons; *U552* (Lt-Cdr Topp) in its first attack sinks two ships of 12361 tons and in its second torpedoes one tanker of 6325 tons, which is finished off in daylight by *U69* (Lt-Cdr Zahn). The escort is strengthened on 20 Sept by the arrival of the Free French corvette *Alysse* and on 21 Sept by the Canadian corvettes *Arrowhead* and *Eyebright*, detached from other convoys. Also on 20 Sept a US destroyer unit consisting of *Winslow*, *Overton*, *Truxtun*, *Bainbridge* and *Reuben James* is sent in for support. Further attacks by *U74* and *U562* (Lt Hamm) fail but the latter sinks one independent of 1590 tons on 22 Sept. On the same day the escort of SC.44 is taken over by the British EG.3

with the destroyers *Bulldog*, *Amazon*, *Richmond* and *Georgetown*, the corvettes *Heartsease* and *Aconit* (FFN) and four trawlers. The remaining 'Brandenburg' boats, *U94*, *U372*, *U562*, *U431*, *U564*, *U575*, *U69*, *U373* and *U572*, are ordered to proceed to a new patrol line SE of Cape Farewell. After some boats have started to return, the formation is further dispersed on 26 Sept. On 30 Sept–1 Oct *U372* shadows a convoy without success. On 2 Oct *U94* sinks the tanker *San Florentino* (12842 tons), *U562* the catapult ship *Empire Wave* (7463 tons) of convoy ON(S).19 and *U575* (Lt-Cdr Heydemann) and *U431* (Lt-Cdr Dommes) one ship each, of 4652 tons and 3198 tons respectively.

15 Sept–6 Oct North Atlantic
The reorganisation of the North Atlantic convoy operations, decided upon at the Atlantic Conference (see 9–12 Aug 1941) is implemented. Control of operations W of 22°W is transferred to US COMINCH in Washington; operations E of 22°W remain under the control of the Admiralty in London.

The US Navy's TF.4 (Rear-Adm Bristol) takes over from Argentia (Newfoundland) and Hvalfjord (Iceland) the escorting of the HX and ON convoys on the North Atlantic route in the area between Newfoundland and Iceland. The slow SC and ONS convoys in the same area are escorted by the Canadian Newfoundland Escort Force (Rear-Adm Murray). E of approximately 22°W, the British escort groups take over.
On 17 Sept TG.4.1.1 (Capt Deyo), comprising the destroyers *Ericsson*, *Eberle*, *Upshur*, *Ellis* and *Dallas*, escorts the convoy HX.150 (Commodore: Rear-Adm Manners RN) consisting of 50 ships and hands it over to a British *ad hoc* escort group with the destroyers *Churchill*, *Chesterfield* and *Broadwater* and the corvettes *Camellia*, *Celandine*, *Alysse* (FFN) and *Honeysuckle* on 25 Sept, to arrive in the North Channel on 28 Sept. From 18 Sept the Canadian EG.4.1.11, with the destroyer *St Laurent* and the corvettes *Pictou*, *Bittersweet*, *Collingwood*, *Chilliwack*, *Spikenard*, *Dianthus* (RN), *Snowberry* and *Trail*, escorts convoy SC.45 (60 ships) from the Western Ocean Meeting Point (WESTOMP) to the Mid Ocean Meeting Point (MOMP), where on 29 Sept the British EG.2 takes over after escorting ON.18 (25 ships) from the Eastern Ocean Meeting Point (EASTOMP) to MOMP with the destroyers *Veteran*, *Skate*, *Saladin* and *Leamington*, the corvettes *Abelia*, *Anemone* and *Veronica* and the trawlers *Vizalma*, *St Edelsten* and *St Heenan*. ON.18 is taken over at MOMP on 24 Sept

by the US TG.4.1.2 (Capt Kirtland) with the destroyers *Madison*, *Gleaves*, *Lansdale*, *Charles F Hughes* and *Simpson*, to be delivered to the Western Local Escort at WOMP on 1 Oct.

From 20 Sept the British EG.4 with the destroyers *Beagle*, *Salisbury*, *Roxborough* and *Montgomery* and the corvettes *Heather*, *Narcissus*, *Lobelia* (FFN) and *Kenogami* (RCN) and four minesweepers escorts the convoy ON(S).19 (33 ships) to MOMP, where the Canadian EG.4.1.13 takes over with the corvettes *Kamloops*, *Sorel*, *Camrose*, *Mimose* (FFN) and *Rosthern*, to arrive at MOMP on 6 Oct.

All four convoys are routed clear of German U-boat dispositions by the Submarine Tracking Room using 'Ultra' data.

16–21 Sept   Black Sea

The Russian 157th Rifle Div is transported from Novorossisk to Odessa in five groups each with two to three transports, escorted by the cruisers *Chervona Ukraina*, *Komintern* and *Krasny Krym* and the destroyers *Bodry*, *Boiki*, *Besposhchadny*, *Bezuprechny*, *Sposobny*, *Soobrazitelny* and *Frunze*. On 17 Sept German bombers and torpedo aircraft attack the group comprising the transports *Abkhaziya*, *Dnepr* and *Gruziya* and escorted by the cruiser *Chervona Ukraina* and the destroyers *Bezuprechny*, *Boiki* and *Nezamozhnik*, but the convoy reaches Odessa without loss.

16 Sept–5 Oct   North Atlantic/Mediterranean

The first group of German U-boats proceeds to the Mediterranean—'Goeben', consisting of *U371*, *U559*, *U97*, *U331*, *U75* and *U79*. Between 24 Sept and 5 Oct they pass through the Straits of Gibraltar and go to the Eastern Mediterranean.

17 Sept   North Sea

S50, *S51* and *S52* of the 4th MTB Flotilla sink the freighter *Teddington* (4762 tons) in a British convoy E of Cromer and torpedo one ship of 5389 tons.

17 Sept   Baltic

The Swedish destroyers *Göteborg*, *Klas Horn* and *Klas Uggla* are severely damaged by an explosion: *Göteborg* is damaged beyond repair but components from the other two are combined to produce a rebuilt *Klas Horn*.

17–19 Sept   Black Sea

The destroyer *Dzerzhinski* and the cruiser *Voroshilov* shell, on 17 and 19 Sept respectively, German troops on the coast near Alexeevka, Khorli and Skadovsk (Odessa).

17–25 Sept   Baltic

The 'Juminda' mine barrages are reinforced against a possible break-out by the Soviet Baltic Fleet towards Sweden in the event

of the fall of Leningrad. On 17 Sept the minelayers *Cobra* and *Kaiser* lay barrages near Cape Purikari (36 EMCs and 100 explosive floats) and W of 'Juminda' (136 EMCs and 200 explosive floats). On 21 Sept *Kaiser* lays another barrage (86 EMCs and 100 explosive floats) N of 'Juminda' and on 22 Sept *Cobra* a barrage near Kallbadagrund (126 EMCs and 100 explosive floats). On 25 Sept the minelayer *Königin Luise* (Lt-Cdr Wünning) lays a further barrage (86 EMCs) but is lost, when returning, on a mine barrage laid by Soviet torpedo cutters off Helsinki.

18–27 Sept   Mediterranean

In British submarine operations, *Triumph* (Lt-Cdr Woods) sinks one ship of 2373 tons and torpedoes two others of 15573 tons in the Adriatic. *Tetrarch* (Lt-Cdr Greenway) sinks one ship of 2499 tons from a Piraeus-Candia convoy in the Aegean escorted by the torpedo boats *Sella* and *Libra*. *Upright* (Lt Wraith) sinks the Italian torpedo boat *Albatros* off Sicily and the Dutch submarine *O21* (Lt-Cdr v Dulm) sinks one sailing ship in the Western Mediterranean.

18–28 Sept   North Atlantic

Operations on the Gibraltar convoy route. On 20 Sept the outbound *U124* (Lt-Cdr Mohr) reports the convoy OG.74 SW of Ireland. It consists of 27 ships, the ocean boarding vessel *Corinthian* and EG.36 (Lt-Cdr White) with the sloop *Deptford* and the corvettes *Arbutus*, *Pentstemon*, *Marigold*, *Periwinkle* and one other. For the first time there is an escort carrier, *Audacity* (Cdr Mackendrick), with the convoy. The only U-boat in the area, the outbound *U201* (Lt Schnee), is directed to it but is forced to submerge by a Martlet aircraft, *Deptford* and *Arbutus*. *U124* continues to keep contact and sinks two ships of 4225 tons during the night 20–21 Sept. On 21 Sept one Fw 200 of I/KG 40 sinks the rescue ship *Walmer Castle* (906 tons) which has stayed behind; another Fw 200 is shot down by a Martlet fighter. While the main group continues its journey with *Pentstemon*, both *Deptford* and *Marigold* turn back to support a scattered group of four steamers with which *U124* and *U201* are in contact. *U201* sinks three of them totalling 4467 tons during the night 21–22 Sept. After losing contact, the two boats are directed to the oncoming convoy HG.73. The Italian submarines *Torelli*, *Morosini* and *Da Vinci*, which are stationed in the waiting areas W of Gibraltar, are directed towards this convoy for 18 Sept. The convoy, which set out in the afternoon of 17 Sept, consists of 25 ships (Commodore: Rear-Adm Creighton), the catapult ship *Springbank* and an escort comprising

the destroyer *Vimy*, two sloops and eight corvettes. *Malaspina* is sunk from an unknown cause on the way out after 7 Sept. On 19 Sept *U371*, which is on the way to the Mediterranean, *Morosini* and *Torelli* successively establish brief contact. In the evening of 20 Sept *Torelli* again establishes contact but is damaged by depth charges from the British destroyer *Vimy* during the night 21–22 Sept. On 23 Sept *Da Vinci* maintains contact for some time. On 24 Sept an Fw 200, in contact with the convoy, is driven off by the Fulmar fighter from *Springbank*. During the night 24–25 Sept *U124* first comes up and sinks one ship of 2922 tons, then *U203* also comes up. During the night 25–26 Sept *U203* (Lt-Cdr Mützelburg) sinks three ships of 7658 tons, including that of the convoy Commodore (who is rescued by the corvette *Periwinkle*), and *U124* sinks two ships of 2702 tons. Aircraft in contact bring up *U124*, *U203* and *U205* by day on 26 Sept; in the night *U124* sinks one ship of 1810 tons and *U201* two ships of 7623 tons, including *Springbank*. On 27 Sept *U203*, *U205* and aircraft keep contact but *U205* is bombed by a British air escort taking off from Cornwall and is damaged. In the evening of 27 Sept *U201* sinks one more ship of 3103 tons SW of Ireland. On 28 Sept the operation has to be broken off because all the operational U-boats have expended their torpedoes. Total result with OG.74 is six ships of 9598 tons sunk and with HG.73 nine ships of 25818 tons.

19 Sept   Black Sea

The Soviet monitor *Udarny* is sunk by German aircraft near Tendra Island.

19–20 Sept   Air War/Germany

Attack by RAF Bomber Command on Stettin.

20 Sept   Mediterranean

The Italian submarine *Scirè* (Cdr Prince Borghese) penetrates the Bay of Gibraltar by night and launches three human torpedo teams which sink a freighter of 2444 tons in the roads and naval base and severely damage the motor ship *Durham* (10893 tons). In addition, the naval tanker *Denbydale* (8145 tons) sinks (but is later raised and repaired).

20 Sept–21 Oct   Baltic

The Soviet Submarines *Shch-317*, *Shch-319* and *Shch-320* (Lt-Cdr I M Vishnevski) set out for operations in the Baltic. The last is said to have sunk the steamer *Holland* (991 tons) off the Gulf of Danzig on 26 Sept. *Shch-319* does not return. *S-7* (Capt 3rd Class S P Lisin) operates off the Swedish coast and sinks one ship of 343 tons which, however, is salvaged.

20–27 Sept   Pacific

Replenishment meeting 'Romulus' involving German raiders and blockade-runners E of the Tuamotu Archipelago in the South-East Pacific. First, on 20 Sept, the auxiliary cruiser *Schiff 16/Atlantis* (Capt Rogge) meets the replenishment ship *Münsterland* coming from Japan, then on 24 Sept the auxiliary cruiser *Schiff 45/Komet* (Rear-Adm Eyssen) and its prize *Kota Nopan* join. On 27 Sept *Schiff 16* goes to a meeting with its prize *Silvaplana*. Both the prizes and *Komet* then disperse to round Cape Horn for the Atlantic, to be followed by the *Atlantis* on 29 Oct.

21 Sept   Norway

The German motor minesweeper *R158* is heavily damaged in a collision with the patrol vessel *NT05/Togo* (the former Norwegian minelayer *Otra*) and is beached. It sinks on 5 Nov during an attempt to take it in tow.

21–22 Sept   Black Sea

Soviet landing near Grigorevka, in order to place the 3rd Naval Rifle Regt behind the 13th and 15th Rumanian Inf Divs to facilitate the attack by the 157th and 421st Rifle Divs designed to remove the Rumanian coastal batteries near Fontanka and Dofinovka. On 21 Sept the cruisers *Krasny Kavkaz* and *Krasny Krym* take one and two battalions respectively of the 3rd Marine Rifle Regt on board in Sevastopol and set out, escorted by the destroyers *Besposhchadny*, *Bezuprechny* and *Boiki* under the orders of the Commander of the Cruiser Bde, Capt 1st Class S G Gorshkov. They are preceded by the destroyer *Frunze* with the Commander of the Sqn, Rear-Adm L A Vladimirski, on board, who is to co-ordinate the landing operation with the forces coming from Odessa—the gunboat *Krasnaya Gruziya*, one tug and 22 cutters, plus 10 barges with which to disembark the troops. In the afternoon of 21 Sept *Frunze*, en route, turns off to help the gunboat *Krasnaya Armeniya* which has been attacked by Ju 87s of StG 77 off the Tendra Peninsula. Both ships are sunk by the Stukas together with the tug *OP-8* which is summoned to the scene. In spite of this loss, the disembarkation and landing succeeds during the night 21–22 Sept and the heights near Fontanka and Dofinovka are re-taken. On 22 Sept Ju 87s of StG 77 attack the destroyers *Besposhchadny*, *Bezuprechny* and *Boiki*, which are still cruising off the coast to give fire support to the troops already landed. *Bezuprechny* is damaged by a near-miss and *Besposhchadny* receives heavy hits in the bow and is towed into Odessa, stern first, by

the tug *SP-14*. The destroyer *Soobrazitelny* takes over the escort.

21–24 Sept   Baltic

Attacks by I and III Gruppen of StG 2 (Lt-Col Dinort) on ships of the Soviet Baltic Fleet. On 21 Sept a Ju 87 of III/StG 2 under Lt Rudel hits the battleship *Marat* with a 1000kg bomb. Its bow demolished, *Marat* settles on the bottom off the harbour mole of Kronstadt but the 30.5cm turrets C and D, and later also B, are again made operational. In the dive-bombing attack on the cruiser *Kirov* in Kronstadt harbour, the Ju 87 of the Commander of III/StG 2, Capt Steen, is hit by AA fire and falls into the sea near the ship, which is damaged by the explosion. In the area of the Sea Canal, *Oktyabrskaya Revolutsiya* evades many attacks but is hit by six medium bombs. The destroyer *Steregushchi* capsizes after a direct hit (she is later salvaged) and the destroyers *Gordy*, *Grozyashchi* and *Silny*, the submarine depot ship *Smolny* and the submarine *Shch-306* are damaged. On 23 Sept the cruiser *Maksim Gorki* is again damaged in Leningrad, as are *Kirov* and the destroyer *Grozyashchi* off Kronstadt. The submarine *P-2* is destroyed in the dockyards and in the harbour the flotilla leader *Minsk* sinks after a direct hit (she is later salvaged). The patrol ship *Taifun* is destroyed and the submarine *Shch-302* damaged.

21–28 Sept   Mediterranean

The Italian submarine *Ascianghi* (Lt-Cdr di Derio) sinks one ship of 389 tons off the coast of Palestine and *Fisalia* is sunk by the British corvette *Hyacinth* off Haifa on 28 Sept. The Italian submarines *Malachite* and *Tricheco* operate N of Cyrenaica.

21 Sept–5 Nov   Central Atlantic Intelligence

Of the U-boats proceeding in line abreast to a southern operation, *U107* (Cdr Hessler) sights the convoy SL.87 with 11 ships, escorted by EG.40 with the sloops *Bideford*, *Lulworth* and *Gorleston*, the corvette *Gardenia* and the Free French sloop *Commandant Duboc*. In the evening of 21 Sept *U68* (Cdr Merten) comes up and, after an unsuccessful attack, sinks one ship of 5302 tons. *U107* makes two unsuccessful approaches. On 22 Sept *U103* (Lt-Cdr Winter) also comes up and, after a miss by *U68* on an escort, sinks two ships of 10594 tons in the night. *U68* misses an isolated tanker. The convoy divides into two groups. From the first, *U67* (Lt-Cdr Müller-Stöckheim) sinks one ship of 3753 tons by day on 23 Sept and from the second *U107* sinks three out of four ships totalling 13641 tons on the morning of 24 Sept. Total result: seven ships of 33290 tons sunk. At the end

of this operation, *U66*, *U103*, *U107*, and *U125* head for the area W of Freetown, *U108* for the line Cape Verde Islands–St Paul and *U68* for Ascension and St Helena. *U111*, which is to provide *U67* and *U68* with supplies in Tarafal Bay in the Cape Verde Islands, is surprised by the British submarine *Clyde* (sent following the deciphering of the signal for the meeting) on 27–28 Sept, but the torpedoes explode prematurely. (This incident leads to the separation of U-boat radio traffic on 5 Oct.) *U67* and *U111* return and *U111* gets involved on 4 Oct near Madeira in an engagement with the British A/S trawler *Lady Shirley* and is lost. Of the remaining U-boats, only *U66* (Cdr Zapp) sinks a tanker of 7052 tons. On 16 Oct *U66*, *U103*, *U107* and *U125* start the delayed return in line abreast without, however, finding more targets. *U126* (Lt-Cdr Bauer), new to the operational area, sinks one ship en route and two ships on 19–20 Oct off Freetown totalling 16905 tons, including the US steamer *Lehigh*. She continues operations with *U68* in the South Atlantic (see 12 Oct).

22 Sept   Baltic

In an attack by the Finnish motor torpedo boats *Vinha* and *Syöksy* on the harbour of Suursaari, the latter (Chief Petty Officer Ovaskainen) sinks the incoming minesweeper *T-41/Sergey Kirov* (400 tons).

22 Sept   North Atlantic

The area for the Mid Ocean Meeting Point (MOMP) to exchange the ocean escort groups for the transatlantic convoys is moved from about 26°W to 22°W.

22–23 Sept   Mediterranean

The mine barrages M6 and M6A are laid out SE of Malta by the Italian 12th DD Flotilla (Capt Melodia), consisting of the destroyers *Corazziere*, *Ascari*, *Carabiniere* and *Lanciere* escorted by the destroyers *Aviere* and *Camicia Nera*.

22–27 Sept   Arctic

The British cruiser *London* brings an Anglo-American delegation with Lord Beaverbrook and Averell Harriman from Scapa Flow to Archangel for a meeting with the Soviet Government in Moscow.

23–29 Sept   Baltic

The German 'Baltic Fleet' (Vice-Adm Ciliax) is transferred to the Aaland Sea to prevent a possible break-out by the Soviet Fleet into the Baltic. Northern Group: the battleships *Tirpitz* (Capt Topp) and *Admiral Scheer* (Capt Meendsen-Bohlken), the cruisers *Köln* (Capt Hüffmeier) and *Nürnberg* (Capt v Studnitz), the destroyers *Z25*, *Z26* and *Z27*, the torpedo boats *T2*, *T5*, *T7*, *T8*, *T11* and some motor torpedo boats in the Aaland Sea. Southern Group: the cruisers

Emden (Capt Mirow) and *Leipzig* (Capt Stichling) and motor torpedo boats in Libau. On 23 Sept the Fleet leaves Swinemünde; on 24 Sept, after heavy air attacks on the Soviet warships (see 21–24 Sept), *Tirpitz*, *Admiral Scheer* and two torpedo boats are recalled and three torpedo boats join the Southern Group. On 29 Sept the remaining units return to Gotenhafen.

Against the expected entry of these ships into the Gulf of Finland, the Soviet Baltic Fleet Command concentrates the Soviet submarines *M-95*, *M-98*, *S-4*, *Shch-303*, *Shch-311* and *Lembit* in the western part of the Gulf of Finland; *L-3* remains in the area W of Suursaari. In the eastern part of the Gulf of Finland, near Suursaari, the minelayer *Marti* lays a barrage on 24 Sept to cover Kronstadt Bay.

23 Sept–3 Oct   North Atlantic
U-boats escort outbound blockade-runners through the Bay of Biscay into the Atlantic. From 23 Sept *U204* goes with the *Rio Grande* (6062 tons), destined for Japan, and from 27/28 Sept *U79* and *U129* are ordered to escort the U-boat supply ship *Kota Pinang* (7277 tons), destined for the South Atlantic. Based on 'Ultra' data, the British cruisers *Sheffield* and *Kenya* are sent to intercept. While the *Rio Grande* escapes and reaches Osaka on 6 Dec, the *Kota Pinang* is sunk W of Cape Finisterre by *Kenya* with gunfire. *U129* is unable to attack but rescues 119 survivors and hands them over to a Spanish naval tug on 6 Oct. *U204* proceeds to the area off Gibraltar (and is sunk there on 19 Oct), *U79* enters the Mediterranean and *U129* goes for the South Atlantic.

23 Sept–11 Oct   Arctic
In submarine operations off the Norwegian Polar Coast, the British submarine *Trident* (Cdr Sladen) misses the steamer *Weser* off Rolvsöy on 23 Sept and the hospital ship *Birka* on 30 Sept. On 27 Sept the submarine-chaser *UJ1201* is sunk in a convoy. The Soviet submarine *Shch-401* cruises for four weeks off Svaerholt without success. The submarine *D-3* (Lt-Cdr F V Konstantinov, with the Commander of the 2nd SM Division, Capt 2nd Class I A Kolyshkin, on board) attacks ships and convoys off Tanafjord on 26, 27 and 30 Sept and 1 and 11 Oct but the torpedoes miss or explode on the cliffs. All six small submarines *M-171*, *M-172*, *M-173*, *M-174*, *M-175* and *M-176* carry out patrols of 6–8 days in the Varangerfjord area. On 26 Sept the Soviet submarine *M-174* (Lt-Cdr N E Egorov) and on 2 Oct *M-171* (Lt-Cdr V G Starikov) penetrate Petsamofjord as far as Liinahamaari but the torpedoes which are fired damage only the pier. In a similar attempt to penetrate Bökfjord (Kirkenes), *M-176* runs into a net on 30 Sept and has to return. On 3 and 8 Oct *M-176* and *M-175* miss ships in Varangerfjord. On 25 Sept the submarines *K-3*, *S-101* and *S-102* arrive in Molotovsk from the Baltic, having come via the White Sea Canal. They are transferred in Oct and Nov to Polyarnoe. *L-20* and *L-22*, which are not yet ready for operations, remain at present in the White Sea.

23 Sept–14 Oct   North Atlantic
When indications in 'Ultra' from the Baltic stimulate fears of a break-out by the German battleship *Tirpitz* into the Atlantic, the US Atlantic Fleet transfers the carrier *Yorktown*, the cruisers *Brooklyn* and *Savannah* and some destroyers from Bermuda to Argentia to join there the old battleships *Arkansas* and *New York*. On 23 Sept a task group with the battleship *Mississippi*, the carrier *Wasp*, the cruiser *Wichita* and the destroyers *Gwin*, *Meredith*, *Grayson* and *Monssen* is transferred from Argentia to Hvalfjord, arriving there on 28 Sept, to strengthen the 'White Patrol' covering the Denmark Strait, consisting then of the battleship *New Mexico*, the cruisers *Vincennes* and *Quincy* and the destroyers *Moffett*, *McDougal*, *Sims*, *Hughes* and *Russell*.

From 25 Sept to 4 Oct the rest of TF.15 (see 28 Aug–14 Sept), with the battleship *Idaho*, the cruiser *Tuscaloosa*, nine transports and oilers and nine destroyers, returns from Hvalfjord to Argentia.

Because of the bad flying conditions, the carrier *Wasp*, with the cruiser *Vincennes* and four destroyers, is recalled from Hvalfjord to Argentia on 6 Oct, arriving on 11 Oct.

24 Sept   General Situation
Fifteen governments of Allied countries, including the USSR, endorse the aims of the Atlantic Charter.

24–30 Sept   Mediterranean
Operation 'Halberd': supply convoy from Gibraltar to Malta consisting of the transports *Breconshire*, *Clan Macdonald*, *Clan Ferguson*, *Ajax*, *Imperial Star*, *City of Lincoln*, *Rowallan Castle*, *Dunedin Star* and *City of Calcutta*. Close escort for the convoy is provided by Group II (Vice-Adm Curteis), comprising the battleships *Prince of Wales* and *Rodney*, the cruisers *Kenya* (10th Cruiser Sqn), *Edinburgh* (18th Cruiser Sqn), *Sheffield* and *Euryalus* and the destroyers *Duncan* (13th DD Flotilla), *Gurkha*, *Legion*, *Lance*, *Lively*, *Oribi*, *Isaac Sweeres* (Dutch), *Piorun* (Polish), *Garland* (Polish), *Fury*, *Farndale* and *Heythrop*. Covering Group (I) is Force H (Vice-Adm Somerville), with the battleship *Nelson*, the carrier *Ark Royal*, the cruiser *Hermione* and the destroyers *Cossack* (4th DD Flotilla), *Zulu*, *Foresight*, *Forester*, *Laforey* (19th DD Flotilla) and *Lightning*. The tanker *Brown Ranger* is sent on ahead with the corvette *Fleur de Lys* to refuel the destroyers.

On 26 Sept Italian air reconnaissance locates parts of the British forces S of the Balearics. The submarines *Adua*, *Dandolo* and *Turchese* are stationed N of Cape Ferrat, *Axum*, *Serpente*, *Aradam* and *Diaspro* N of Cape Bougaroni and *Squalo*, *Bandiera* and *Delfino* N of Cape de Fer, with *Narvalo* near Cape Bon. Motor torpedo boats are stationed near Pantelleria. In the evening the Italian Fleet (Adm Iachino), comprising the battleships *Littorio* and *Vittorio Veneto*, the heavy cruisers *Trento*, *Trieste* and *Gorizia*, the light cruisers *Attendolo* and *Duca degli Abruzzi* and 14 destroyers, sets out for the area SE of Sardinia, so as to be able to attack from there the British forces (whose strength is underestimated) within range of Italian air escort. Other Italian units cannot put to sea because of a shortage of oil. On 27 Sept neither side is able to form a clear picture of the situation from reports from reconnaissance aircraft. Italian aircraft torpedo the British battleship *Nelson* S of Sardinia. Admiral Curteis and Admiral Iachino cruise between Sardinia and the Skerki Bank, keeping an even distance between each other, and start the return journey in the evening. The transports separate in the area of the Skerki Bank in the evening of 27 Sept and go on to Malta with Force X (five cruisers and the destroyers *Cossack*, *Zulu*, *Laforey*, *Oribi*, *Heythrop* and *Farndale*, as well as *Forester*, *Foresight* and *Fury* which are equipped as minesweepers). In the evening they lose the *Imperial Star* (12427 tons) to Italian torpedo aircraft in the area of Cape Bon. Motor torpedo boats are unable to find the convoy during the night 27–28 Sept. On 28 Sept *Hermione* shells Pantelleria without effect. On 29 Sept *Diaspro* and *Serpente* and on 30 Sept *Adua* unsuccessfully attack the returning British forces off the Algerian coast. *Adua* is sunk by the British destroyers *Gurkha* and *Legion*. During the operation four unescorted empty transports proceed from Malta to Gibraltar. Of the Allied submarines *Utmost*, *Upright*, *Urge*, *Sokol* (Polish), *Trusty* and *Upholder* stationed N of Sicily, only *Utmost* is able to attack the three homebound Italian heavy cruisers—unsuccessfully. *Unbeaten* and *Ursula*, stationed S of the Straits of Messina, and *O21* (Dutch), stationed off Cagliari, sight no ships.

24 Sept–14 Oct North Atlantic
From 24 Sept to 1 Oct the US TG.4.1.4 (Capt Thebaud), with the destroyers *Plun-

kett, *Livermore*, *Kearny*, *Decatur* and *Greer*, escorts the convoy HX.151 (44 ships) from WESTOMP to MOMP, there to be taken over by the British EG.4, with the destroyers *Beagle*, *Salisbury*, *Roxborough* and *Montgomery* and the corvettes *Lobelia* (FFN), *Heather* and *Narcissus* and three trawlers, arriving at EASTOMP on 7 Oct.

From 24 Sept to 5 Oct the Canadian EG.4.1.12, with the destroyers *Ottawa*, *Broadway* (RN) and *Burwell* (RN) and the corvettes *Brandon*, *Cobalt*, *Buctouche* and *Galt*, later augmented by the corvettes *Algoma* and *Ployanthus* (RN), escorts the convoy SC.46 (61 ships) from WESTOMP to MOMP, to be relieved by the British EG.5, with the destroyers *Walker*, *Vanoc*, *Volunteer* and *Caldwell*, the corvette *Hydrangea* and the trawler *St Cathan* which had escorted convoy ON.20 (51 ships) from EASTOMP since 26 Sept, there to be taken over by the US TU.4.1.3 (Cdr Webb), with the destroyers *Winslow*, *Benson*, *Niblack*, *Hilary P Jones* and *Reuben James*, for WESTOMP, arriving there on 9 Oct.

From 27 Sept to 5 Oct the British EG.1, with the destroyers *Keppel*, *Venomous* and *Sabre*, the corvettes *Sunflower* and *Dianella* and the trawlers *Lady Elsa*, *Man O' War* and *Northern Dawn*, escorts convoy ON(S).21 (30 ships) from EASTOMP to MOMP, to be taken over there by the Canadian EG.4.1.11 with the corvettes *Collingwood*, *Dianthus* (RN), *Snowberry*, *Bittersweet*, *Chilliwack*, *Spikenard* and *Pictou* for WESTOMP, arriving on 14 Oct. After the operation against the convoy SC.44 there are only homebound and outbound German U-boats near the convoy routes. *U562* (Lt Hamm) sinks one ship of 4652 tons from SC.46.

27 Sept General Situation
The first 14 Liberty Ships are launched in American yards. Another 312 merchant ships of this type, amounting to 2200000 tons, have already been ordered.

27 Sept–5 Oct Artic
The German U-boats *U132* and *U576* operate in the entrance to the White Sea. On 18 Oct *U132* (Lt-Cdr Vogelsang) attacks a small coastal convoy near Cape Gorodetski and sinks the steamer *Argun* (3487 tons) and, later, an unknown ship.

28 Sept–9 Oct Arctic
The British convoy QP.1, with 14 merchant ships, accompanied by the cruiser *London*, returns from Archangel to Scapa Flow.

29–30 Sept Air War/Germany
Air attacks by RAF Bomber Command on Stettin and Hamburg (repeated during the night 30 Sept–1 Oct).

29 Sept–1 Oct Black Sea
Owing to the unfavourable situation of the 51st Army, which is defending the approaches to the Crimea, the Military Council of the Black Sea Fleet proposes to the Stavka on 29 Sept that the coastal army should be evacuated from Odessa and moved to the Crimea. On 30 Sept the Stavka agrees to this proposal and on 1 Oct the Deputy People's Commissar of the Navy, Vice-Adm E I Levchenko, arrives in Odessa in order to work out evacuation plans with the Military Council of the Odessa Defence District.

29 Sept–11 Oct Arctic
The British convoy PQ.1, with ten merchant ships, escorted by the cruiser *Suffolk* and two destroyers, proceeds from Hvalfjord to Archangel without making contact with the enemy.

29 Sept–19 Oct North Atlantic
The Canadian EG.4.1.14, with the destroyers *Richmond* (RN) and *Ramsey* (RN) and the corvettes *Sherbrooke*, *Chicoutimi*, *Chambly*, *Matapedia* and *Napanee*, escorts convoy SC.47 from WESTOMP to MOMP, where the British EG.6 takes over with the destroyers *Broke*, *Richmond*, *Mansfield*, *St Albans* and *Wolverine* and the corvettes *Eglantine* (RNoN) and *Kingcup* on 7 Oct, after delivering ON.22 (48 ships) at MOMP to the US TU.4.1.1, with the destroyers *Ericsson*, *Eberle*, *Dallas*, *Ellis* and *Upshur*. These convoys are delivered to local escorts on 17 and 14 Oct.

On 30 Sept the US TU.4.1.5, with the destroyers *Mayo*, *Schenck*, *Leary*, *Babbitt* and *Broome*, picks up convoy HX.152 (60 ships) at WOMP and is relieved at MOMP on 6 Oct by the British EG.1 with the destroyers *Keppel*, *Venomous*, *Sabre* and *Shikari*, the corvette *Dianella* and three trawlers after this group has taken ON(S).21 to MOMP.

From 4 Oct ON(S).23 (31 ships) is escorted by the British EG.8, with the destroyers *Malcolm*, *Sardonyx* and *Watchman*, the corvettes *Arabis*, *Dahlia*, *Monkshood*, *Petunia*, *Violet* and *Verbena* and three trawlers to MOMP, where the Canadian EG.4.1.12, with the destroyers *Ottawa*, *Broadway* (RN) and *Burwell* (RN) and the corvettes *Cobalt*, *Galt*, *Buctouche* and *Algoma*, takes over on 10 Oct to arrive at WESTOMP on 19 Oct.

To avoid a German U-boat group building up SE of Cape Farewell, which is noted from 'Ultra' data on 9 Oct, the convoys are diverted south slightly. Only the straggler *Svend Foyn* (a whale factory ship of 14795 tons) of HX.152 is torpedoed, by *U502* (Lt-Cdr v Rosenstiel).

1 Oct North Atlantic
British Ocean Escort Groups Organisation (ships under refit are shown in parentheses):
1st EG, based at Londonderry: destroyers *Keppel*, *Rockingham*, *Sabre*, *Venomous*, (*Lincoln*), (*Shikari*); corvettes *Alisma*, *Kingcup*, *Sunflower*, (*Dianella*).
2nd EG, Londonderry: destroyers *Douglas*, *Leamington*, *Saladin*, *Sherwood*, *Skate*, *Veteran*; corvettes *Abelia*, *Anemone*, *Veronica*.
3rd EG, Greenock: destroyers *Amazon*, *Belmont*, *Georgetown*, (*Ambuscade*), (*Bulldog*); corvettes *Heartsease*, *Aconit*/FFN, *Roselys*/FFN, (*Aubrietia*), (*Renoncule*/FFN).
4th EG, Greenock: destroyers *Beagle*, *Montgomery*, *Roxborough*, (*Boadicea*), (*Salisbury*); corvettes *Commandant Détroyat*/FFN, *Heather*, *Lobélia*/FFN, *Narcissus*, *Orchis*, *Snowdrop*.
5th EG, Liverpool: destroyers *Caldwell*, *Vanoc*, *Volunteer*, (*Walker*); corvettes *Calendula*, *Campanula*, *Gentian*, *Honeysuckle*, *Sweetbriar*.
6th EG, Liverpool: destroyers *Broke*, *Buxton*, *Chelsea*, *Verity*, *Wolverine*, (*Mansfield*); corvettes *Begonia*, *Camellia*, *Clematis*, *Columbine*, *Larkspur*, (*Jasmine*).
7th EG, Liverpool: destroyers *Campbeltown*, *St Albans*, *Westcott*, (*Wanderer*); corvettes *Acanthus* (*Eglantine*/RNoN), (*Montbretia*/RNoN), *Hibiscus*, *Periwinkle*, (*Gardenia*).
8th EG, Londonderry: destroyers *Malcolm*, *Beverley*, *Sardonyx*, *Scimitar*, *Watchman*, (*Newmarket*); corvettes *Arabis*, *Dahlia*, *Monkshood*, *Petunia*, *Violet*, *Verbena*.
9th EG, Liverpool: destroyers *Harvester*, *Havelock*, *Hesperus*, *Highlander*.
10th EG, Liverpool: destroyers *Vanquisher*, *Witch*, *Whitehall*.
11th EG, Greenock: destroyers *Garland*/Pol, *Piorun*/Pol.
12th EG, Londonderry: destroyers *Badsworth*, *Blankney*, *Croome*, *Exmoor*, *Lamerton*.
36th EG, Liverpool: sloops *Deptford*, *Stork*; corvettes *Arbutus*, *Cowslip*, *Convolvulus*, *Marigold*, *Pentstemon*, *Rhododendron*, *Samphire*, *Vetch*.
37th EG, Liverpool: sloops *Black Swan*, *Fowey*; corvettes *Bluebell*, *Campion*, *Carnation*, *Heliotrope*, *La Malouine*, *Mallow*, *Myosotis*, *Stonecrop*.
40th EG, Londonderry: sloops *Landguard*, *Bideford*, *Culver*, *Gorleston*, *Lulworth*; destroyer *Stanley*.
41st EG, Londonderry: sloops *Ibis*, *Aberdeen*, *Enchantress*, *Hartland*, *Walney*; destroyer *Clare*.
42nd EG, Londonderry: sloops *Weston*, *Fol-*

kestone, Londonderry, Wellington, Sennen, Totland.

43rd EG, Londonderry: sloops *Rochester, Hastings, Leith, Sandwich,* (*Philante*); destroyer *Newport.*

44th EG, Londonderry: sloops *Egret, Fleetwood, Scarborough, Banff, Fishguard*; destroyer *Bradford.*

1 Oct Baltic

The German A/S trawler *UJ117* (*II, Gustav Kröner*) is sunk W of Hanko by a mine laid by the Soviet minelayer *Marti.*

1–4 Oct Norway

The Norwegian torpedo boat *Draug* tows the Norwegian *MTB56* from Scapa Flow to a point 120 nautical miles off the Norwegian coast. During the night 3–4 Oct *MTB56* (Sub-Lt Danielsen) attacks a German convoy in Korsfjord consisting of *M1101, V5505/Seeteufel* and the Norwegian tanker *Borgny* (3015 tons); the last is sunk by a torpedo hit. *MTB56* is met by *Draug* and towed back.

2–8 Oct Mediterranean

On 2 Oct the British submarine *Perseus* (Lt-Cdr Nicolay) sinks one ship of 2086 tons off Benghazi belonging to a convoy from Naples escorted by the torpedo boats *Calliope* and *Pegaso.*

From 2 to 5 Oct an Italian convoy comprising six ships, escorted by the destroyers *Da Noli, Usodimare, Gioberti* and *Euro* and the torpedo boats *Calliope* and *Partenope* coming out to support them from Tripoli, sails from Naples. On 5 Oct the convoy is attacked by torpedo aircraft from Malta and the cargo *Rialto* (6099 tons) is sunk.

In the Aegean, *Tetrarch* (Lt-Cdr Greenway) sinks one ship of 3751 tons in a convoy accompanied by the torpedo boats *Monzambano, Calatafimi* and *Aldebaran*; *Talisman* (Lt-Cdr Willmott) sinks one other ship of 8194 tons. *Rorqual* (Lt Napier) lays a mine barrage (8 Oct) in the Gulf of Athens on which the Italian torpedo boats *Aldebaran* and *Altair* sink on 20–21 Oct. *Thunderbolt* (Lt-Cdr Crouch) sinks a small sailing ship. In the Western Mediterranean, the Dutch submarine *O21* (Lt-Cdr v Dulm) sinks one ship of 1369 tons.

2–14 Oct North Atlantic

Operation by the 'Breslau' group against convoy OG.75 escorts. On 2 Oct two Fw 200s of I/KG 40 successively sight the convoy W of the North Channel. On 3 and 4 Oct the convoy, which consists of 25 steamers and nine escort vessels, is located by air reconnaissance but the outbound U-boats *U71, U83, U206* and *U563* and the homebound *U204* and the *U564* (released from escorting the outward-bound blockade-runner *Rio Grande*), all of which are

directed to the convoy, do not come up. On 5, 6 and 7 Oct the air reconnaissance which is provided finds only a small steamer of 744 tons. This is sunk. Only on 8 Oct does an Fw 200 report the convoy in the area of Cape Finisterre. *U83* comes up by day and *U71* briefly in the night, but on 9 Oct contact is again lost in bad weather. A single tanker of 9158 tons is probably sunk by *U204* (Lt-Cdr Kell). On 10 Oct an Fw 200 again reports the convoy, but the U-boats fall astern because the speed of the convoy is underestimated. *U83* (Lt Kraus) sinks a large floating crane and on 12 Oct a Portuguese steamer of 2044 tons in accordance with prize regulations. *U563*, which again gets near the convoy on 12 Oct, is forced to submerge by an aircraft and *U206* (Lt Opitz) sinks the corvette *Fleur de Lys* off the Straits of Gibraltar just before she comes into harbour. *U204* and *U564* put into Cadiz at night to take on fuel from a German tanker.

3–6 Oct Black Sea

Evacuation of the Soviet 157th Rifle Div from Odessa to Sevastopol in several convoys comprising the transports *Armeniya, Kotovski, Bolshevik, Zhan Zhores, Volga* and *Belostok* and the tankers *Moskva* and *Sergo* (3 Oct); the transports *Egurtsa* and *Uralets* and the tug *SP-14* with lighter (4 Oct); and the transports *Abkhaziya, Dnepr* and *Kalinin*, the patrol ships *SKR-113/Bug* and *SKR-114/Dnestr*, the gunboat *Krasny Adzharistan* and the minesweepers *TShch-38/Raikomvod, TShch-39/Doroteya* and *TShch-41/Khenkin* (5 Oct). Escort and cover are provided by the cruisers *Chervona Ukraina, Krasny Kavkaz* and *Krasny Krym* and the destroyers *Bodry, Boiki, Nezamozhnik, Shaumyan* and *Dzerzhinski.*

4 Oct South Atlantic

The Argentine destroyer *Corrientes* is sunk in a collision with the cruiser *Almirante Brown* off Tierra del Fuego.

4–25 Oct Mediterranean

The first group of German U-boats operates on the British supply routes between Alexandria and Tobruk. *U559* (Lt-Cdr Heidtmann) misses supply steamers on 4 and 10 Oct and an escort vessel and three A-lighters on 18 Oct. *U331* (Lt v Tiesenhausen) damages *A18* in a gun engagement with three A-lighters on 10 Oct; *U75* (Lt-Cdr Ringelmann) sinks the lighters *A2* and *A7* on 12 Oct and misses a destroyer on 25 Oct; *U97* (Lt-Cdr Heilmann) sinks two transports of 1966 tons from a supply convoy on 17 Oct and sinks a steamer on 23 Oct; *U79* (Lt-Cdr Kaufmann) sinks an A-lighter on 18 Oct and torpedoes the gunboat *Gnat* on 21 Oct which has to be beached in Bardia

as a total loss; and *U371* (Lt-Cdr Driver) is damaged by depth charges on 20 Oct.

5 Oct Atlantic/Intelligence

Separation of the U-boat radio traffic in the Atlantic from 'Enigma/Heimische Gewässer' into a new circuit, 'Triton'. However, because, first, the same 'M-3' machine and then the same 'Kurzsignalheft' and 'Wetterkurzschlüssel' are used, Bletchley Park is able to break into this key and to decode the signals with delays of two to four days during Oct and Nov.

5–6 Oct Arctic

Under Lt-Cdr S G Korshunevich, the Soviet torpedo cutters *TKA-12, TKA-14* and *TKA-15* attack ships between Kirkenes and Petsamo and *TKA-12* (Sub-Lt A O Shabalin) sinks the Norwegian cutter *Björnungen* (163 tons).

5–11 Oct Arctic

Operation by the Home Fleet off the Norwegian coast. On 8 Oct aircraft from the carrier *Victorious* carry out a raid on shipping in the area of Vestfjord. Two steamers are hit.

6 Oct and 8 Oct Mediterranean

German He 111 bombers sink the freighters *Thistlegorm* (4898 tons) and *Rosalie Moller* (3963 tons) and damage the MV *Salamaua* (6676 tons) off Suez.

7–16 Oct Black Sea

Flanking mine barrages are laid out to protect Axis Sea traffic off the Bulgarian coast. Participating are the Rumanian mine-layers *Dacia, Regele Carol I* and *Amiral Murgescu* (Cdr Niculescu, German adviser Cdr v Davidson). Escort is provided by the Rumanian torpedo boats *Naluca, Sborul* and *Smeul*, and the gunboats *Dumitrescu* and *Ghigulescu*, for a time by the Bulgarian torpedo boats *Smeli, Derzky* and *Khabri* and, in the approach and the departure, also by Rumanian destroyers. Four mine barrages and one partial barrage are laid. Shortly after setting out from Varna on 10 Oct, *Regele Carol I* (Lt-Cdr Popovici), with 150 mines on board, sinks on a Soviet submarine mine barrage.

7–18 Oct North Atlantic

On 7 Oct the US TU.4.1.6, with the destroyers *Sampson, Lea, Bernadou, Dupont* and *MacLeish*, picks up at MOMP convoy HX.153 (59 ships); the Candian EG.4.1.15, (Lt-Cdr Davis), with the destroyer *Columbia* and the corvettes *Wetaskiwin, Mimose* (FFN), *Baddeck, Shediac, Rosthern, Camrose* and *Gladiolus* (RN), takes the convoy SC.48 (52 ships, Commodore Elliott) off the Belle Isle Strait.

On 9 Oct 'Ultra' data show that the BdU intends to form a new group SE of Cape Farewell with *U374, U573, U208* and *U109.*

On 10 Oct, in addition, the BdU sends *U502*, *U568* and *U553* to the area. The convoys ON(S).23 (see 29 Sept–14 Oct) and ON.24 with the British EG.3 (Cdr Baker-Cresswell), comprising the destroyers *Bulldog* and *Amazon* and the corvettes *Heartsease*, *Aconit* (FFN) and *Dianthus*, are re-routed S of the German concentration, as is SC.48 and the following troop convoy TC.14, escorted by the Canadian destroyers *Restigouche*, *Ottawa* and *Skeena* and the British *Havelock*, *Harvester* and *Buxton*.

On 12 Oct it becomes clear, thanks to 'Ultra', that in addition *U558*, *U432*, *U101*, *U77*, *U751* and *U73* are coming from France to lengthen the patrol line to the SE, making necessary a more extensive re-routing to the S for the convoys ON(S).23, ON.24, SC.48 and TC.14. On 13 Oct convoy ON(S).25 (32 ships) with the British EG.2 (comprising the destroyers *Douglas*, *Veteran*, *Saladin* and *Skate*, the corvettes *Abelia*, *Veronica*, *Arvida* and *Dauphin* and two trawlers) is redirected to a more southerly MOMP.

During the night 14–15 Oct, while *U558* (Lt-Cdr Krech) sinks the independent *Vancouver Island* (9472 tons), *U553* (Lt-Cdr Thurmann) sights SC.48, still comprising 49 ships (11 stragglers), escorted at the time by the corvettes *Wetaskiwin*, *Gladiolus*, *Mimose* and *Baddeck*, and sinks two ships of 5937 tons at once. On her report, first the oncoming *U568*, *U432*, *U558* and *U502* and then the following *U101*, *U77*, *U751* and *U73* are directed to attack the convoy. At midday *U553* is driven off by the returning destroyer *Columbia*, which avoids a torpedo salvo. *U568* (Lt-Cdr Preuss) takes over contact, sinks one ship of 6023 tons and is driven off by *Gladiolus* in the evening.

Meantime the Admiralty takes measures to strengthen the escort. The British EG.3 with the destroyer *Bulldog* (Cdr Cresswell-Baker), *Amazon*, *Richmond*, *Georgetown* and *Belmont*, the corvette *Heartsease*, the trawlers *Angle*, *St Apollo* and *Cape Warwick* and the rescue ship *Zaafaran*, which after refuelling at Reykjavik coming from ON.24 had to relieve EG.4.1.15 with SC.48 on 17 Oct, is ordered to depart earlier. EG.2, escorting ON(S).25, is instructed to detach the corvettes *Veronica* and *Abelia*. The British destroyers *Highlander* (Cdr Voucher) and *Broadwater*, sent from Reykjavik with the destroyer *Sherwood* to relieve the three Canadian destroyers with TC.14, are redirected to SC.48, as is the Canadian corvette *Pictou*, straggling from convoy ON(S).21. But all these vessels can arrive only from daylight on 17 Oct, so the only way to augment SC.48's escort is to disperse

convoy ON.24 outside the danger area (according to 'Ultra') and to send its escort, the US TU.4.1.4 (Capt Thebaud), with the destroyers *Plunkett*, *Livermore*, *Kearny*, *Decatur* and *Greer*, at high speed to SC.48, where the group arrives at noon on 16 Oct; Capt Thebaud becomes OTC of the now five US, three RCN, one RN and one FFN units. Notwithstanding several depth-charge attacks, aggressive patrolling and a drastic course change, the U-boats cannot be shaken off and they attack during the night: *U553* sinks one ship of 6595 tons, and probably the missing corvette *Gladiolus*, *U558* sinks three of 17516 tons and *U432* (Lt-Cdr Schultze) sinks two of 15022 tons. Finally, in the morning of 17 Oct *U568* torpedoes and damages *Kearny* (Lt-Cdr Danis), assumed to be a British 'Tribal' class destroyer. In the early hours of 17 Oct the additional escorts arrive and Cdr Voucher takes over as OTC; the US destroyers leave for Hvalfjord. While the arriving air escort, comprising the US VP-73 and 74 with Catalinas, puts down the contact-holding U-boats, the last four, *U101*, *U77*, *U751* and *U73*, come to the scene and during the next night *U101* (Lt-Cdr Mengersen) sinks the destroyer *Broadwater*. By daylight the operation is broken off.

8 Oct   Black Sea
German troops occupy Mariupol on the Sea of Azov.

8–10 Oct   Black Sea
Evacuation of heavy equipment and weapons, rear services, party organisations and labour force from Odessa to Sevastopol on board the transports *Chekhov* and *Kalinin*, the tanker *Moskva*, the minelayer *Syzran* and the minesweeper *TSch-32/Zemlyak*, escorted by the cruiser *Komintern*, the destroyer *Shaumyan* and three SKA patrol cutters (8 Oct) and the transports *Armeniya* and *Sergo* on 9 Oct.

8–15 Oct   Mediterranean
First regular decoding from the Italian 'C38' transmissions for the North African supply convoys by Bletchley Park. From 8 Oct a number of intercepts reveal the composition, the escort and the departure and arrival times of convoy 'Giulia', which leaves Naples in the late evening of 8 Oct with the cargo vessels *Giulia*, *Casaregis*, *Zena* and *Bainsizza* and the oiler *Proserpina*, escorted by the destroyers *Granatiere* (Capt Capponi), *Bersagliere*, *Fuciliere* and *Alpino* and a strong air escort during daylight. To cover the source of the intelligence, Malta sends out air reconnaissance which reports the convoy at noon on 10 Oct south of Pantellaria. In the evening of 11 Oct two waves of torpedo aircraft from Malta attack

and sink *Zena* (5219 tons) and *Casaregis* (6485 tons). *Bainsizza*, 7933 tons, having returned to Trapani after some machinery problems, is included in a convoy of two ships and one German tug which leaves Trapani on 12 Oct, escorted by the destroyers *Da Recco* and *Sebenico* and the torpedo boat *Cascino*. Attacked on 14 Oct several times by aircraft with bombs and torpedoes, *Bainsizza* sinks on 15 Oct.

10 Oct–10 Nov   Baltic
In an operation E of the Swedish coast, the Soviet submarine *Shch-323* (Capt 3rd Class Ivantsev) unsuccessfully attacks the German cruiser *Köln* as she sets out on 13 Oct N of Dagö. From 15 Oct to 5 Nov the submarine makes seven attacks on merchant ships, but she sinks only the steamer *Baltenland* (3724 tons). The submarines *S-8* and *Shch-322* are lost on mines. *M-97* makes one unsuccessful attack off Tallin on 24 Oct.

10–26 Oct   Mediterranean
The Italian submarines *Saint Bon* and *Cagni* (both large new boats), together with *Atropo*, manage to transport 354 tons of fuel and supplies from Taranto to Bardia in spite of various air attacks.

11–12 Oct   Air War/Germany
RAF Bomber Command attacks Emden.

11–26 Oct   North Atlantic
On 11 Oct, at WESTOMP, the convoys HX.154 (47 ships and five more for Iceland) and SC.49 are taken over by the US TU.4.1.2 with the destroyers *Charles F Hughes*, *Madison*, *Gleaves*, *Lansdale* and *Simpson* or by the Canadian EG.4.1.16 with the destroyer *St Francis* and the corvettes *Mayflower*, *Kenogami*, *Amherst*, *Eyebright*, *Nanaimo*, *Prescott* and *Lethbridge*. They are re-routed a little N of the SC.48 battle, now free of U-boats according to 'Ultra'. On 19 Oct TU.4.1.2, with HX.154, is relieved by the British EG.2, with the destroyers *Douglas*, *Veteran*, *Saladin* and *Skate*, the corvettes *Arvida* (RCN) and *Dauphin* (RCN), two trawlers and one rescue ship, coming from ON(S).25. On the same day the British EG.4, with the destroyers *Beagle*, *Salisbury* and *Roxborough*, the corvettes *Heather*, *Narcissus* and *Lobelia* (FFN) and the attached destroyer *Sherwood* as well as the trawlers *Lady Madelaine*, *Norwich City* and *Arab*, is relieved at MOMP as the escort for convoy ON.26 (32 ships) by the US TU.4.1.5 with the destroyers *Mayo*, *Schenck*, *Leary*, *Broome* and *Babbitt*, later to be supported by the attached US destroyers *Badger* and *Greer* and re-routed N of the forming U-boat group 'Reissewolf' detected via 'Ultra' on 21 Oct. On 22 Oct the refuelled British EG.4 relieves the Canadian

EG.4.1.16 with SC.49 at MOMP. There are no contacts with U-boats.

12 Oct   North Sea

Attack by the 2nd MTB Flotilla (Lt-Cdr Feldt), comprising *S41*, *S47*, *S53*, *S62*, *S104* and *S105*, on a British convoy N of Cromer. The British freighter *Chevington* (1537 tons) and the Norwegian freighter *Roy* (1768 tons) are sunk.

12–13 Oct   Air War/Germany

RAF Bomber Command attacks Bremen.

12–13 Oct   Mediterranean

Proposed Italian mining operation 'B' to protect Benghazi, with the cruisers *Duca d'Aosta*, *Eugenio di Savoia* and *Montecuccoli* and the destroyers *Vivaldi*, *Malocello*, *Pigafetta*, *Da Verazzano*, *Aviere* and *Camicia Nera*, is abandoned because reconnaissance reports that the British Mediterranean Fleet has set out.

On 13 Oct the torpedo boat *Pleiadi* is hit by bombs during salvage operations at Tripoli and becomes a constructive total loss.

12–21 Oct   Baltic

Capture of Dagö, 12–13 Oct. By means of feint operations 'Westfalen', with the cruiser *Köln* (Capt Hüffmeier), the torpedo boats *T2*, *T5*, *T7*, *T8* and seven minesweeping boats of the 1st and 2nd MS Flotillas near Cape Ristna, and 'Ostpreussen', with the 2nd MMS Flotilla against the East Coast near the Kertel battery, the Soviet forces are misled and tied down. A landing is made with craft of the experimental force on the South Coast. Support is provided by the 5th MS Flotilla against Soviet coastal batteries. On 14 Oct *Köln* again shells Cape Ristna. On 16–21 Oct the Soviets evacuate part of the island garrison to Odensholm and Hangö. Soviet resistance at Cape Takhkona ends on 21 Oct. In all, 3388 prisoners are taken.

12–26 Oct   Mediterranean

The fast British minelayers *Abdiel* and *Latona* transport 7138 troops and supplies to Tobruk to relieve 7234 Australians and 727 wounded. On the last journey, *Latona* (2650 tons) is destroyed by Ju 87s of I/StG 1 (Maj Sorge) off Bardia during the night 25–26 Oct. Among the escorting destroyers, *Hero* is damaged by a near-miss from Lt Steinhagen; *Encounter* and *Hotspur* escape.

12 Oct–20 Nov   South Atlantic

U68 (Cdr Merten) operates in the area of Ascension from 12 to 18 Oct and on 22 Oct sinks the British naval tanker *Darkdale* (8145 tons) in the roads of St Helena, and then, on the way to the Walfish Bay area, sinks another two steamers of 10250 tons. On 13 Nov she meets, S of St Helena, the German auxiliary cruiser *Schiff 16*/*Atlantis* (Capt Rogge) for replenishment. *U126* (Lt-

Cdr Bauer), which on 13 Nov sinks one steamer of 6961 tons off the Guinea coast, is to be replenished from *Schiff 16* on 22 Nov (qv). The U-boats *U124* and *U129*, which set out from Western France with the supply ship *Python*, go off into their operational areas after refuelling from the supply ship on 20 Nov SW of the Cape Verde Islands. *UA* operates off Freetown from 9 Nov.

13–16 Oct   Black Sea

On 13 Oct the Military Council of the Black Sea Fleet gives approval for an early evacuation, requested by the Odessa Defence District, to take place during the night 15–16 Oct. On 14 Oct the transports *Ukraina*, *Gruziya*, *Abkhaziya*, *Armenia*, *Kotovski*, *Zhan Zhores*, *Vostok*, *Kalinin*, *Bolshevik*, *Kursk* and *Chapaev*, the minelayers *Lukomski* and *Syzran* and the survey ships *Chernomorets* and *Tsenit* arrive. The warships to assemble are the cruisers *Chervona Ukraina* and *Krasny Kavkaz*, the destroyers *Smyshleny*, *Bodry*, *Nezamozhnik* and *Shaumyan*, the patrol ships *SKR-102*/*Petrash*, *SKR-113*/*Bug* and *SKR-114*/*Dnestr*, the fast minesweepers *T-404*/*Shchit*, *T-405*/*Vzryvatel*, *T-406*/*Iskatel* and *T-408*/*Yakor*, the auxiliary minesweeper *T-39*/*Doroteya* and many patrol boats, tugs and other base craft. On 14 Oct *Gruziya* receives a hit in a German air attack. During a heavy bombardment by guns and warships combined with simulated attacks, the forces of the coastal army begin quickly to withdraw from their positions to the harbour at 1900 hrs on 15 Oct. From 2300 hrs until 0300 hrs on 16 Oct some 35000 men of the 421st and 95th Rifle Divs and of the 2nd Cavalry Div are embarked and the transports proceed to the roads. Towards 0600 hrs the cruisers and destroyers, which have taken the rear guard and defence battalions on board, put out to sea.

The patrol ship *SKR-101*/*Kuban* takes 1200 men from demolition parties and rearguard on board. At 0900 hrs the last patrol boat departs and the minesweeper *T-405*/*Vzryvatel* lays magnetic ground mines in the harbour and approach. The evacuation is accomplished in one night without any enemy counter-action. Not before the afternoon of 16 Oct do German aircraft begin to attack the evacuation transports, but only the transport *Bolshevik* (1412 tons) is sunk, all the other ships, including the damaged *Gruziya*, reaching Sevastopol.

During the embarkation, the destroyers *Bodry* and *Smyshleny* lay a mine barrage in the area of Ilyichevka. Part of it, consisting of 32 mines, is cleared on 21 Oct by boats of the German Danube Flotilla. The Hung-

arian steamer *Ungvar* (Commander of the German Danube Flotilla, Cdr Petzel†) and the Rumanian motor torpedo boats *Viforul* and *Vijelia* on 9 Nov, and the German steamer *Cordelia* (1357 tons) and the Rumanian steamer *Cavarna* (3495 tons) on 2 Dec, run on to another part of it and are lost.

14 Oct   Mediterranean

A Commando unit (Lt-Col Keyes†), landed from the British submarines *Talisman* and *Torbay*, makes an unsuccessful raid on the headquarters of the German C-in-C in North Africa, Gen Rommel.

14–19 Oct   Mediterranean

British Force H (Vice-Adm Somerville), consisting of the battleship *Rodney*, the carrier *Ark Royal*, the cruiser *Hermione* and seven destroyers, proceeds eastwards and on 18 Oct flies off 11 Albacores and two Swordfish torpedo bombers to Malta from the carrier when 450 nautical miles away. At the same time Force K (Capt Agnew) goes with the cruisers *Aurora* and *Penelope* and the destroyers *Lance* and *Lively* to Malta, where it arrives on 21 Oct.

On the news that Force H has set out, apart from the Italian submarines *Bandiera* and *Aradam* already stationed near Galita and Cape Bougaroni, a patrol line is concentrated from 17 Oct with *Turchese*, *Serpente*, *Diaspro* and *Alagi* N of Cape de Fer, *Narvalo* and *Squalo* near Cape Bon and *Settembrini* and *Delfino* near Pantelleria. But they do not sight any ships.

14–20 Oct   Arctic

Off the Norwegian polar coast, there operate, *inter alia*, the British submarine *Tigris* and the Soviet *K-2*, *Shch-402*, *M-172* and *M-174*. *Tigris* misses convoys in Svaerholthavet on 11 and 14 Oct and, after a short stay in Polyarnoe, begins the return trip to England on 20 Oct. *Shch-402* (Lt-Cdr N G Stolbov) sinks the Norwegian coaster *Vesteraalen* (682 tons) on 17 Oct in Söröysund.

15–22 Oct   Mediterranean

The Italian submarines *Dagabur*, *Topazio* and *Zaffiro* operate off Mersin Bay E of Cyprus and W of Haifa and *Uarsciek* operates off Cyrenaica.

16 Oct–13 Nov   North Atlantic

U573, *U374*, *U208* and *U109*, which did not take part in the operations against SC.48, are sent from 16 Oct as the 'Mordbrenner' group to reconnoitre in the area off the Strait of Belle Isle, but when they arrive on 20 Oct there is no traffic and after intercepts of their position on 23 Oct the convoys are routed S in order to avoid attack. From 28 Oct they proceed to the area SW of Newfoundland and from 31 Oct they are directed to convoy ON.28, shadowed by the 'Reissewolf' group since 27 Oct. *U374* (Lt v Fischel) sinks one independent of 5120 tons and sights the convoy SC.52 on 1 Nov (qv). The other three boats start the return on 3 Nov after *U208* (Lt Schlieper) has sunk one more independent of 3872 tons on 2 Nov.

17–29 Oct   North Atlantic
Operation by the 'Breslau' group against convoy HG.75. From 17 Oct *U206*, *U563* and *U564* are stationed near Cape Trafalgar for the expected departure of convoy HG.75 from Gibraltar, *U204*, *U71* and *U83* are stationed near Cape Spartel and, further W, the Italian boats *Archimede*, *Ferraris* and *Marconi* are deployed. On 19 Oct *U206* (Lt Cdr Opitz) and *U204* (Lt-Cdr Kell) each sink one ship, of 3081 tons and 9158 tons respectively, but the latter is then sunk in the U-boat search undertaken by the sloop *Rochester* and the corvette *Mallow*. *U71* (Lt-Cdr Flachsenberg) misses a destroyer. HG.75, escorted by EG.37 with the sloop *Rochester* and the corvettes *Campion*, *Carnation*, *Heliotrope*, *La Malouine* (FFN), *Mallow* and *Commandant Duboc* (FFN) and a support group with the destroyers *Cossack*, *Legion*, *Lamerton*, *Duncan* and *Vidette*, only sets out in the afternoon of 22 Oct and is reported shortly after midnight on 23 Oct by *U71*. Two attacks by *U206* and *U564* (Lt Suhren) fail, but the boats are able to maintain contact in spite of the strong escort. During the night 23–24 Oct *U563* (Lt Bargsten) sinks one ship of 1352 tons and torpedoes the destroyer *Cossack*, which sinks on 26 Oct; *U564* sinks two ships of 5846 tons. The lost contact is regained in the afternoon of 24 Oct by I/KG 40 and in the evening by *U71*. On 25 Oct *U71*, *U83*, *U206* and *Archimede* are driven off, partly by aircraft and partly by the naval escort. *Ferraris* springs a leak in an oil tank as a result of bombing by a Catalina flying boat; Lt-Cdr Flores remains on top when the destroyer *Lamerton* approaches and sinks the boat after a long gun duel. During the night 25–26 Oct *U83* and *U563* come up and *U83* (Lt Kraus) torpedoes the catapult ship *Ariguani* (6746 tons). By day *U71* and *U564* maintain contact, but the attacks by *U563* and *U564* in the night 26–27 Oct have no success. At this period *Marconi* must have been lost from an unknown cause. *U564* and *U563* maintain contact until 28 Oct and bring up the returning *U432* (Lt Schultze), which sinks one more ship of 1574 tons. On 29 Oct the three boats, having fired all their torpedoes, begin the return journey.

17–30 Oct   Arctic
Convoy PQ.2 proceeds with six ships from Scapa Flow to Archangel.

18–27 Oct   Black Sea
On 18 Oct German troops occupy Taganrog. Of the Soviet submarines *Shch-215*, *S-33*, *Shch-216*, *S-34*, *Shch-212* and *Shch-207*, only *Shch-210* attacks on 18 Oct the tanker *Le Progrès*, but the torpedo is a premature. *Shch-212* (Lt-Cdr Burnashev) is heavily damaged by a mine but is brought in with great difficulty. Off the Rumanian coast, *M-62*, *M-35*, *M-58*, *D-5*, *M-33* and *M-36* have no success and *M-35* (Lt Greshilov) misses on 26–27 Oct one steamer and the submarine-chaser *Schiff 19/Lola*. *M-58* is lost on a mine.

18–30 Oct   Mediterranean
In operations in the Central Mediterranean, the British submarine *Ursula* (Lt-Cdr Hezlet) torpedoes on 18 Oct one ship of 4859 tons near Lampedusa which is in a convoy of five steamers with the destroyers *Folgore*, *Fulmine*, *Usodimare*, *Gioberti*, *Da Recco* and *Sebenico* and the torpedo boat *Calliope*. On 22 Oct *Urge* (Lt-Cdr Tomkinson) misses one ship but the next day torpedoes one of 5996 tons, which is sunk by *Utmost* (Lt-Cdr Cayley) on 28 Oct. On the Petrasso–Brindisi route, *Truant* (Lt-Cdr Haggard) sinks two ships of 5570 tons, including one in a convoy, and torpedoes one other of 1589 tons. *Triumph* (Lt-Cdr Woods) sinks one ship of 6703 tons in the Aegean and *Thrasher* (Lt Mackenzie) one of 384 tons off Benghazi. *Rorqual* (Lt Napier) lays a mine barrage off Sardinia on 21–22 Oct.

18 Oct–2 Nov   North Atlantic
After the conclusion of the SC.48 operation, *U568*, *U502*, *U432*, *U77*, *U751*, *U73* and *U101* form the 'Reissewolf' group in the Central North Atlantic on 22 Oct. New boats coming from France, *U569*, *U123*, *U38*, *U82*, *U202*, *U84*, *U203*, *U93* and *U85*, are ordered to form the 'Schlagetot' group on 28 Oct NW of 'Reissewolf'. En route on 20 Oct *U84* (Lt Uphoff) sights parts of convoy SL.89 and attacks unsuccessfully on 21 Oct. *U123* (Lt-Cdr Hardegen) comes up and torpedoes the armed merchant cruiser *Aurania* (13984 tons). In the evening *U123* directs *U203* and *U82* to the convoy and the last (Lt Rollmann) sinks two ships of 9317 tons. On 22 Oct the convoy, escorted by the sloops *Wellington* and *Stork*, the destroyer *Beverley* and the corvettes *Asphodel* and *Clematis*, is located by German air reconnaissance but *U85*, *U202* and *U203* are driven off on 23 Oct and the group is sent to its new line again. *U123* is ordered to the Belle Isle Strait.

In the meantime the STR estimates from 'Ultra' signals received since 21 Oct that at least ten U-boats are in the area of the 'Reissewolf' line and orders nearby convoys to take wide detours: HX.155 (59 ships) with the US TU.4.1.7 comprising the destroyers *Roe*, *Bainbridge*, *Sturtevant*, *Overton* and *Truxtun*, to be relieved at MOMP on 25 Oct by the British EG.5 with the destroyers *Vanoc* and *Volunteer* and the corvettes *Sweetbriar*, *Periwinkle*, *Honeysuckle*, *Hibiscus*, *Gentian* and *Myosotis* and two trawlers coming from ON(S).27 (62 ships), to be taken over in turn by the Canadian EG.4.1.15, with the destroyers *Skeena* and *Columbia* and the corvettes *Camrose*, *Brandon*, *Shediac*, *Wetaskiwin* and *Mimose* (FFN). Also re-routed is the fast troop convoy CT.4 and the convoy SC.50 (36 ships) with the Canadian EG.4.1.13 comprising the destroyers *St Croix* and *Restigouche* and the corvettes *Collingwood*, *Alysse* (FFN), *Alberni*, *Bittersweet* and *Mayflower*, to be relieved at MOMP on 28 Oct by the British EG.1 with the destroyers *Venomous*, *Sabre* and *Rockingham*, the corvette *Alisma*, five trawlers and one rescue ship coming with convoy ON.28 (40 ships).

On 25 Oct SC.50 passes just S of 'Reissewolf' and ON.26 (see 11–26 Oct) between the forming 'Schlagetot' group and the four 'Mordbrenner' boats off the Belle Isle Strait. The convoy ON(S). 27 is routed N along the route taken by ON.26.

On 25 Oct ON.28 is picked up by the US TU.4.1.6 with the destroyers *Sampson*, *Bernadou*, *Dupont*, *Lea* and *MacLeish*, accompanied by the oiler *Salinas*, coming from Iceland at MOMP, and ON.28 is routed S. The MOMP for SC.50 with EG.1 is to be postponed and transferred to the S, to take place on 31 Oct.

On 27 Oct the outbound *U74* (Lt-Cdr Kentrat) sights convoy ON.28, to which the 'Reissewolf' group is directed. *U106* (Lt Rasch), which is also outbound, sinks an unidentified independent. On 28, 29 and 30 Oct *U568*, *U77*, *U73*, *U751* and *U106* successively maintain contact but are continually driven off by the attacks of the five US destroyers and, apart from *U77* and *U74* on one occasion each, are unable to attack. Because of the fuel situation, *U568*, *U751*, *U77* and *U502* have to break off; they join the 'Stosstrupp' group; only *U73*, *U74*, and *U106* continue to shadow. On 31 Oct *U106* torpedoes the US Navy oiler *Salinas* but fails to sink the ship with a *coup de grâce* because of counter-attacks from *Dupont* and *Lea*, later supported by the US Coast Guard cutter *Campbell* and the Navy tug *Cherokee*. The boats of the 'Mordbrenner' group, which are directed to the scene, do not approach the convoy, whose escort is strengthened by the US destroyers *Leary*, *Babbitt* and *Schenck*, just arrived at St Johns after leaving convoy ON.26, and *Buck* and *Ludlow*, waiting for the next HX convoy. The fruitless search is broken off on 1 Nov after *U74* has maintained contact for over 1600 nautical miles.

20–21 Oct   Air War/Germany
RAF Bomber Command attacks Wilhelmshaven, Bremen and Emden.

20–21 Oct   Mediterranean
On 20 Oct the Italian torpedo boat *Altair* hits a mine in the Gulf of Athens and, although taken in tow by the torpedo boat *Lupo*, sinks on 21 Oct. On the same day the assisting torpedo boat *Aldebaran* runs on to a minefield laid by the British submarine *Rorqual* on 8 Oct and sinks.

20 Oct–15 Nov   Baltic
In operations by Soviet submarines, *L-3* (Capt 3rd Class P D Grishchenko) lays a mine barrage at the end of Oct in the area of the Gulf of Danzig, as does *Lembit* (Lt A M Matiyasevich) off Koivisto Sound. *S-4* operates on the Tallinn–Helsinki route and misses the transport *Hohenhörn* on 21 Oct; *S-7* disembarks agents in Narva Bay; and *Shch-324*, *L-2* and *M-98* run on to mines W of Suursaari and sink.

21–25 Oct   Black Sea
Creation of a mine-free passage from the Kilia estuary to the Dnieper estuary by the Danube Flotilla (Cdr Petzel), comprising the depot ship *Theresia Wallner*, three river minesweepers and three Rumanian auxiliary minesweepers. On 21 Oct a passage is made through a mine barrage near Ilyichevka S of Odessa. On 23 Oct Ochakov is reached, on 24 Oct the journey continued to Kherson and on 25 Oct the lower course of the Dnieper is checked.

21 Oct–17 Nov   Arctic
The Soviet submarine *Shch-421* has three misses and *K-1* and *K-23* lay mine barrages off the North Cape and Kirkenes respectively.

23 Oct   Biscay
The German minesweeper *M6* is lost to a mine S of the Lorient.

23–27 Oct   Baltic
A Soviet force of three fast minesweepers and two submarine-chasers (Capt 3rd Class V P Likholetov) proceeds from Kronstadt to Hangö. *T-203/Patron* is lost on a mine when she sets out on 25 Oct. The remaining vessels go with 499 troops and the equipment of a rifle brigade to Oranienbaum.

24 Oct–2 Nov   Mediterranean
The Italian submarines *Alagi*, *Axum*, *Diaspro* and *Santarosa* are concentrated off the Algerian/Tunisian coast to operate against British traffic expected between Gibraltar and Malta.

24 Oct–4 Nov   North Atlantic
On 24–25 Oct, at WESTOMP, the convoys HX.156 (44 ships) and SC.51 (37 ships) are taken over by the US TU.4.1.3 (Cdr Webb) with the destroyers *Benson*, *Hilary P Jones*, *Niblack*, *Reuben James* and *Tarbell* or by the Canadian EG.4.1.11 with the destroyer *St Laurent* and the corvettes *Trail*, *Primrose* (RN), *Nasturtium* (RN), *Polyanthus* (RN), *Arrowhead*, *Chilliwack* and *Snowberry*. Because on 25–26 Oct 'Ultra' shows four U-boats off the Belle Isle Strait and up to 20 U-boats in the Central North Atlantic, both convoys are re-routed to the S of the U-boat areas. When, on 27 Oct, the 'Reissewolf' group makes contact with ON.28, convoys HX.156 and SC.51 are detoured more to the S.

Convoy ON(S).29 (34 ships) is escorted from 26 Oct by the British EG.6 with the destroyers *Broke*, *Wolverine* and *Buxton* and the corvettes *Montbretia* (RNoN), *Larkspur*, *Begonia*, *Camellia*, *Eglantine* (RNoN) and *Moosejaw* and two trawlers and relieved on 28 Oct by the Canadian EG.4.1.16 with the destroyer *Broadway* (RN) and the corvettes *Mayflower*, *Eyebright*, *Lethbridge*, *Prescott* and *Kenogami*. The convoy is routed north of the German 'Schlagetot' group between Cape Farewell and the Belle Isle Strait. New outbound boats receive orders on 30 Oct to form the 'Stosstrupp' group E of the Newfoundland Bank: they are *U571*, *U577*, *U133*, *U567*, *U552* and *U96*. En route, *U552* (Lt-Cdr Topp) sights in the morning of 31 Oct in the Central North Atlantic convoy HX.156 with a US escort group (Cdr Webb) comprising five destroyers. *U552* attacks at once and sinks the destroyer *Reuben James*. *U552* is driven off in the afternoon but *U567* (Lt-Cdr Endrass) comes up. On 1 Nov the US TU.4.1.3 is relieved by the British EG.6 (qv) but *U552* and *U567* continually take turns in maintaining contact up to 3 Nov. Two attacks on 1 Nov fail.

In looking for HX.156, *U96* (Lt-Cdr Lehmann-Willenbrock) encounters the convoy OS.10—escorted by EG.40 with the sloops *Bideford*, *Lulworth* and *Gorleston* and the corvettes *Gardenia* and *Commandant Duboc* (FFN)—on 31 Oct and sinks one ship of 5998 tons. The returning and outbound *U568*, *U502*, *U77*, *U571* and *Barbarigo* are directed to it and, because *U96* is in contact, also *U572*, *U201*, *U98*, *U373*, *U103*, *U107* and *U66* from 1 Nov. Air reconnaissance again reports the convoy on 2 Nov. *U98*

comes up briefly; then contact is lost and is not re-established by air reconnaissance on 4 Nov.

Meanwhile, on 1 Nov, convoy ON.30 (42 ships), with the British EG.8 consisting of the destroyers *Malcolm*, *Watchman* and *Sardonyx* and the corvettes *Dahlia*, *Monkshood* and *Arabis* and two trawlers, is delivered to the US TU.4.1.2 with the destroyers *Charles F Hughes*, *Lansdale*, *Gleaves*, *Madison* and *Simpson*, routed from a northerly position for a wide detour to the S to evade the German U-boat concentration off Newfoundland.

After its long detour to the S, convoy SC.51's escort group 4.1.11 is relieved only on 4 Nov by the British EG.8, coming down from the MOMP with ON.30 and TU 4.1.2.

25 Oct–2 Dec   Atlantic/Indian Oceans
On 25 Oct Force G (Adm Phillips) sets out from the Clyde for the Far East with the battleship *Prince of Wales* and the destroyers *Electra* and *Express*. On 5 Nov the ships arrive in Freetown, on 16 Nov in Simonstown and on 28 Nov in Colombo, where they are joined by the battlecruiser *Repulse* from the Atlantic and the destroyers *Encounter* and *Jupiter* from the Mediterranean. On 2 Dec the Force arrives in Singapore.

26–27 Oct   Air War/Germany
RAF Bombers attack Hamburg.

28 Oct–7 Nov   North Atlantic
Following a request by Prime Minister Churchill and a decision of President Roosevelt in Sept, six US cargo ships and six transports are made available to the British. The six cargo vessels—*Empire Pintail* (ex-*Howell Lykes*), *Empire Egret* (ex-*Nithingale*), *Empire Fulmar* (ex-*Hawaiian Shipper*), *Empire Widgeon* (ex-*Exemplar*), *Empire Peregrine* (ex-*China Mail*) and *Empire Oriole* (ex-*Extania*)—are transferred to the British registry. They are formed into a fast convoy under escort by the US Task Force 14 (Rear-Adm Hewitt) with the battleship *New Mexico*, the carrier *Yorktown*, the cruisers *Philadelphia* and *Savannah* and Desron 2 with the destroyers *Morris*, *Sims*, *Hughes*, *Hammann*, *Anderson*, *Mustin*, *Russell*, *O'Brien* and *Walke*, leaving Halifax on 28 Oct. Routed south of the German U-boat 'Schlagetot' and 'Stosstrupp' groups, the escort attacks several suspected (but false) U-boat contacts. On 2 Nov the outbound troop convoy CT.5, with the equivalent of one British division for the Middle East aboard the transports *Duchess of Atholl*, *Orcades*, *Sobieski*, *Warwick Castle*, *Andes*, *Durban Castle*, *Oronsay* and *Reina del Pacifico*, escorted by the AA cruiser *Cairo* and

five destroyers, is met. The escorts change, the ex-US cargo vessels continuing under British escort as convoy 'Tango' for the North Channel, the British transports under US escort as convoy CT.5 for Halifax. From 3 to 7 Nov the destroyers of Desron 2, low on fuel, are relieved by TG.14.9 with Desron 8 (destroyers *Wainwright, Mayrant, Trippe, Rhind, Rowan, McDougal, Moffett* and *Winslow*). At Halifax the British troops are transferred to the US Navy transports of convoy WS.124 (see 10 Nov–27 Dec).

29–31 Oct   Black Sea
After the German break-through near Ishun on the Perekop Isthmus (26 Oct), the main fleet base at Sevastopol is put in a state of alert. Vice-Adm F S Oktyabrski becomes the Commander of the Sevastopol Defence District (SOR). The German advance drives the 51st Army on to the Kerch Peninsula and the Coastal Army to the Yaila Mountains and passes the 7th Naval Infantry Bde stationed on the W coast.

On 29–30 Oct the cruiser *Krasny Kavkaz* transports the 8th Naval Infantry Bde from Novorossisk to Sevastopol and there the 16th, 17th, 18th and 19th Naval Inf Bns are formed out of ships' crews.

By a decision of the Military Council, the battleship *Parizhskaya Kommuna*, the cruiser *Molotov*, the flotilla leader *Tashkent* and the destroyer *Soobrazitelny* leave Sevastopol and are brought to Caucasian ports. An air attack on the force has no result. There remain in Sevastopol the cruisers *Chervona Ukraina* and *Krasny Krym* and the destroyers *Bodry, Nezamozhnik* and *Shaumyan*, forming an artillery support unit under the Chief of Staff of the Squadron, Capt 1st Class V A Andreev; added on 31 Oct are the cruiser *Krasny Kavkaz* and the destroyers *Dzerzhinski* and *Zheleznyakov*. Of the ships still being repaired, the destroyers *Bditelny* and *Boiki* are also allotted to the artillery support force.

On 31 Oct the destroyer *Bodry* shells German forward tank units in the area of Nikolaevka. In an attack by Ju 87s StG 77, 50 men, including the commander, arc wounded by aircraft gunfire.

31 Oct–1 Nov   Air War/Germany
Air attacks by RAF Bomber Command on Hamburg and Bremen.

31 Oct–4 Nov   Baltic
First evacuation convoy leaves Kronstadt on 31 Oct under the Commander of the Sqn of the Baltic Fleet, Vice-Adm V P Drozd, and goes on 1 Nov from Suursaari to Hangö. Taking part are the destroyers *Slavny* and *Stoiki*, the fast minelayer *Marti* (Capt 1st Class N I Meshcherski), the minesweepers *T-207/Shpil, T-210/Gak, T-215* and *T-217*

and five MO-IV submarine-chasers. On the return, 16 mines explode in the ships' bow paravanes and *Marti* and *T-210* are damaged. There are 4230 men on board. The submarines *S-9* and *Shch-324* are stationed in the western entrance to the Gulf of Finland and *S-7* off Tallinn to cover the operation.

1–2 Nov   Mediterranean
The British submarine *Utmost* (Lt-Cdr Cayley) sinks the Italian freighters *Balilla* (2469 tons) and *Marigola* (5996 tons) in surface engagements in the Mediterranean.

1–7 Nov   Indian Ocean
British naval forces comprising the heavy cruiser *Devonshire*, the light cruiser *Colombo* and the auxiliary cruisers *Carnarvon Castle* and *Carthage* capture a French convoy coming from Madagascar off South Africa. It consists of the freighters *Bangkok* (8056 tons) and *Commandant Dorise* (5529 tons) and the passenger ships *Compiègne* (9986 tons), *Cap Touraine* (8009 tons) and *Cap Padaran* (8009 tons). The only escort vessel for the convoy, the sloop *D'Iberville*, is able to withdraw unmolested. As a reprisal, the French Admiralty orders the submarines *Le Glorieux* and *Le Héros*, which are en route to Madagascar, to attack British ships on the way. *Le Héros* sinks the Norwegian freighter *Thode Fagelund* (5757 tons) on 17 Nov.

1–9 Nov   Black Sea
The cruisers *Krasny Krym, Krasny Kavkaz* and *Chervona Ukraina*, the flotilla leader *Kharkov* and the destroyers *Bodry, Boiki, Bditelny, Bezuprechny, Nezamozhnik, Shaumyan* and *Zheleznyakov* evacuate troops which are cut off and dispersed from the Tendra Peninsula and from the Crimean ports of Chernomorsk, Yalta, Evpatoria and Feodosia and transport them to Sevastopol. By 9 Nov 8000 troops have arrived by this means. The cruisers also transport 15000 troops from the Caucasus ports to Sevastopol. The flotilla leader *Tashkent* and the destroyers *Sposobny, Smyshleny* and *Soobrazitelny*, as well as the patrol ships *Shtorm* and *Shkval*, escort the supply convoys between Caucasus ports and Sevastopol.

1–8 Nov   North Atlantic
On 1 Nov the convoy HX.157 (44 ships) is taken over by the US TU.4.1.1 with the destroyers *Dallas, Ericsson, Eberle, Ellis* and *Upshur* at WESTOMP; the convoy SC.52, after evading the suspected U-boat group off Newfoundland, which in reality was sent as 'Mordbrenner' against the oncoming ON.28, is taken over by the Canadian EG.4.1.12 with the destroyers *Broadway* (RN) and *Burwell* (RN) and the corvettes *Cobalt, Galt, Buctouche, Aconit* (FFN), *Nasturtium* (RN) and *Windflower*. Both convoys

are directed N to the entrance of the Davis Strait and Cape Farewell to go round the 'Schlagetot' and the forming 'Stosstrupp' groups, identified by 'Ultra' data. Near the WESTOMP on 1 Nov *U374* (Lt v Fischel) sights and reports SC.52. After having sunk one straggler of 5720 tons off the Belle Isle Strait, *U123* (Lt-Cdr Hardegen) and the 'Schlagetot' group with *U569, U38, U82, U202, U84, U203, U93* and *U85*, as well as *U74* and *U106* from ON.28, are deployed as the 'Raubritter' group against the convoy SC.52. *U374* keeps contact and brings up first *U123* and later also *U38, U569, U82* and *U202*. During the night 3–4 Nov first *U569* (Lt-Cdr Hinsch) and then *U202* (Lt-Cdr Linder) in two attacks sink one or two ships of 9957 tons. The next evening *U203* (Lt-Cdr Mützelburg) sinks two more ships of 10456 tons. The operation is much impeded by radio interference and by mist. Contact is lost during the night to 4–5 Nov and not re-established because the convoy is ordered to take shelter for a while in the Belle Isle Strait.

The oncoming convoy ON(S).29 (see 24 Oct–4 Nov) is routed close to the coast of Labrador and evades the 'Raubritter' boats, of which *U123, U38, U577, U106, U571, U133, U82* and *U85* are ordered to form a new patrol line SE of Cape Farewell from 8 Nov after fruitless searches for SC.52.

While the convoy ON.30 (see 24 Oct–4 Nov) is re-routed SE to evade the submarine-infested waters between Greenland and Newfoundland, the following convoys ON.31 (33 ships), with the British EG.3 comprising the destroyers *Amazon* and *Georgetown*, the corvettes *Renoncule* (FFN), *Roselys* (FFN) and *Heartsease* and three trawlers, and ON(S).32 (49 ships), with the British EG.2 comprising the destroyers *Douglas, Leamington* and *Skate*, the corvettes *Anemone* and *Abelia* and three trawlers, are relieved at MOMP on 4 or 6 Nov by the US TU.4.1.7 with the destroyers *Roe, Bainbridge, Sturtevant, Overton* and *Truxton* or the Canadian EG.4.1.13 with the destroyers *St Croix* and *Restigouche* and the corvettes *Alysse* (FFN), *Alberni, Agassiz, Bittersweet* and *Amherst*. They are sent on a southerly route for WESTOMP.

1–11 Nov   North Atlantic
The 'Störtebecker' group, consisting of *U96, U98, U69, U201, U103, U107, U373* and *U572*, is concentrated for 5 Nov W of Spain to operate against convoy HG.76 which is expected to leave Gibraltar on 1 Nov. However, the convoy is not located by four Fw 200s of I/KG 40 sent out to reconnoitre, nor is it reported on 6 Nov by six aircraft and a patrol line. From 7 Nov

the 'Störtebecker' group—without *U103* and *U107*—is directed to convoy SL.91 located by the B-Service, but up to 11 Nov it is not found either by the air reconnaissance sent out or by the U-boats.

2 Nov   Black Sea
In an attack by three Ju 88s of KG 51, the Soviet cruiser *Voroshilov* (Capt 1st Class F S Markov) receives two bomb hits. The cruiser is towed to Poti, where she remains for repairs until Feb 1942.

2–5 Nov   Baltic
Second evacuation convoy sets out for Hangö under Capt 2nd Class V N Narykov from Kronstadt on 2 Nov and Suursaari on 3 Nov. Participating are the destroyers *Smetlivy* and *Surovy*, the mine-sweepers *T-205/Gafel*, *T-206/Verp*, *T-207/Shpil* and *T-211/Rym*, four MO-IV submarine-chasers and four TKAs. During the stay in Hangö, *Smetlivy*, while loading, receives one hit from Finnish artillery. In the evening of 4 Nov the convoy leaves Hangö. *Smetlivy* (Capt 2nd Class V I Maslov†) runs on to two mines in the channel through the 'Corbetha' barrage and sinks. *T-205* returns to Hangö with 350 survivors. The remainder of the force reaches Suursaari with 1200 men from Hangö.

3 Nov–2 Dec   Baltic
Off Kolberg the German minesweepers *M511* and *M529* are lost on a 'friendly' harbour defence mine barrage.

2–5 Nov   Arctic/North Atlantic
Indications in 'Ultra' signals from the Western Baltic and Norwegian areas show the danger of a new German attempt to send a big ship, possibly the new battleship *Tirpitz*, out into the Atlantic for a raiding operation. In reality, the intended break-out of the pocket-battleship *Admiral Scheer* from Norway has had to be cancelled owing to machinery problems.

Against this awaited attempt, the C-in-C Home Fleet, Adm Tovey, with the battle-ship *King George V*, the carrier *Victorious*, heavy cruisers, light cruisers and destroyers, takes up covering positions S of Iceland while the US TG.1.3 (Rear-Adm Giffen), with the battleships *Idaho* and *Mississippi*, the heavy cruisers *Tuscaloosa* and *Wichita* and the destroyers *Gwin*, *Meredith* and *Monssen*, is sent from Hvalfjord to cover the Denmark Strait against the break-out.

2–8 Nov   Mediterranean
In several sorties, the British fast minelayer *Abdiel·*and destroyers relieve the Cyprus garrison by transporting 14000 troops to and from Alexandria.

The Italian submarine *Dandolo* (Lt-Cdr Auconi) torpedoes the French tanker *Tarn* (4220 tons) off Algiers on 4 Nov in a sortie

towards the Straits of Gibraltar and on 8 Nov she sinks the Spanish steamer *Castillo Oropesa* (6600 tons) off Melilla.

2–12 Nov   Arctic
Off the Norwegian polar coast, the Soviet submarine *K-22* operates in Vestfjord and *Shch-421* (Lt-Cdr N A Lunin) in Lopphavet; they make three unsuccessful attacks, on 2, 10 and 11 Nov. *K-1* (Capt 3rd Class M P Avgustinovich) lays two mine barrages in Mageroysund and Breisund. *K-21* (Capt 3rd Class A·A Zhukov) lays mine barrages in Söröysund and off Hammerfest. On the latter, the steamer *Bessheim* (1774 tons) sinks on 21 Nov. An attack on a convoy misses the patrol boat *Nordwind* on 12 Nov. The British submarine *Trident* (Cdr Sladen) sinks the submarine-chaser *UJ1213* on 3 Nov in Svaerholthavet and the steamer *Flottbek* (1930 tons) on 7 Nov from convoys. The Soviet submarine *K-23* (Capt 3rd Class I S Potapov) lays a mine barrage in Bökfjord (Kirkenes), on to which the minesweeper *M22* runs on 5 Nov and is seriously damaged. In addition, the Soviet submarines *Shch-401*, *M-172* and *S-102* are among others at sea.

2–17 Nov   Arctic
The British convoy QP.2, with 12 merchant ships, returns to Kirkwall from Archangel without making contact with the enemy.

2–25 Nov   Black Sea
Of the Soviet submarines *S-31*, *D-4*, *Shch-214*, *Shch-213*, *Shch-215*, *M-59*, *M-60* and *M-34*, *Shch-214* (Lt-Cdr Vlasov) sinks on 2 and 4 Nov the Turkish sailing vessel *Koraltepe* and the Italian tanker *Torcello* (3336 tons) respectively and *Shch-215* (Lt-Cdr Apostolov) sinks on 18 Nov the Turkish freighter *Yenice* (300 tons). *M-59* and *S-34* are lost on mine barrages. *L-6* and *L-5* each lay a mine barrage.

3 Nov   Baltic
The German minelayer *Kaiser* (Cdr Bohm) lays a new barrage with 150 EMC mines on the Russian route W of 'Juminda'.

3 Nov   Western Atlantic
The British aircraft carrier *Indomitable* is damaged off Kingston (Jamaica) when she runs aground.

3–10 Nov   Mediterranean
The British submarines *Proteus* and *Olympus* and the Greek *Glavkos* (Cdr Aslanoglu) each torpedo one ship, of 4958 tons, 1049 tons and 2392 tons respectively, in the Aegean. *Proteus* also sinks one ship of 1773 tons off Milos.

4–17 Nov   South Atlantic
In regular patrols, from Trinidad and Recife to the area of the Cape Verde Islands, US Task Force 3 (Rear-Adm Ingram) covers the routes of German and Italian blockade-

runners. On 4 Nov the British navy oiler *Olwen* sends a raider warning; in reality, the auxiliary cruiser *Schiff 45/Komet* is in the area, returning to France, as are the blockade-runners *Burgenland* outbound and the *Portland* returning as well as the prizes *Silvaplana* and *Kota Nopan*. The US TG.3.6, with the cruiser *Milwaukee* and the destroyer *Warrington*, returns from San Juan to Yorktown and is too far to the W to act; TG.3.7, with the cruiser *Memphis* and the destroyers *Davis* and *Jouett*, returning from an escort mission with British ships for Lagos (Nigeria), and TG.3.5, with the cruiser *Omaha* (Capt Chandler) and the destroyer *Somers*, are sent to search for the German raider or blockade-runner reported by *Olwen*. On 6 Nov TG.3.5 captures off the Brazilian coast the German blockade-runner *Odenwald* (5098 tons), carrying rubber and disguised as the American *Willmoto*. *Silvaplana* and *Kota Nopan* reach Bordeaux on 17 Nov, *Schiff 45* on 24 Nov and *Burgenland* on 10 Dec; *Portland* arrives at Osaka on 1 Jan.

5–16 Nov   North Atlantic
On 5 and 6 Nov, at WESTOMP, the convoys SC.53 (35 ships) and HX.158 (40 ships) are taken over by their respective ocean escort groups—SC.53 by the Canadian EG.4.1.14, with the destroyer *Ottawa* and the corvettes *Dauphin*, *Arvida*, *Algoma* and *Orillia*, later strengthened by a support group with the destroyer *Burnham* (RN) and the corvettes *Chambly*, *Matapedia* and *Napanee*; and HX.158 by the US TU.4.1.8, with the destroyers *Buck*, *Ludlow*, *Swanson*, *McCormick* and *Greer*, supported by the destroyers *Woolsey* and *Wilkes*—to screen the convoys against the newly forming German U-boat group detected by 'Ultra'. On 8 Nov *U123*, *U38*, *U577*, *U106*, *U571*, *U133*, *U82* and *U85* form a new concentration as the 'Raubritter' group SE of Greenland, but the convoys are routed S of it, so besides SC.53 and HX.158 there are now the convoys ON(S).33 (54 ships) with the British EG.4, comprising the destroyer *Roxborough*, the corvettes *Lobelia* (FFN), *Narcissus*, *Heather* and *Commandant Détroyat* (FFN) and five trawlers, to be relieved at MOMP on 9 Nov by the Canadian EG.4.1.11, consisting of the destroyer *St Laurent* and the corvettes *Polyanthus* (RN), *Primrose* (RN), *Chilliwack*, *Arrowhead*, *Snowberry* and *Trail*, and ON.34 (46 ships) with the British EG.5, consisting of the destroyers *Vanoc*, *Volunteer* and *Caldwell*, the corvettes *Periwinkle*, *Gentian*, *Myosotis*, *Sweetbriar*, *Honeysuckle* and *Hibiscus* and the attached Canadian corvettes *Chicoutimi* and *Sherbrooke*, to be relieved

on 12 Nov by the US TU.4.1.3 with the destroyers *Benson*, *Niblack*, *Hilary P Jones*, *Tarbell* and *Edison*.

When the German B-Service locates ON(S).33, the 'Raubritter' group is deployed against it from 12 to 15 Nov, but the U-boats do not find the convoy and begin to return.

U577, *U571*, *U85* and *U133* operate, still unsuccessfully, against the convoy OS.11 on 16 Nov. During their return voyages, *U74* (Lt-Cdr Kentrat) sinks one independent of 8532 tons and *U561* (Lt Bartels) two stragglers from SC.53 of 8531 tons.

On 13 Nov HX.158 is taken over by the British EG.4 at MOMP and on 15 Nov SC.53 by EG.5.

5–20 Nov   North Atlantic/Mediterranean

U205, *U81*, *U433* and *U565* set out from France for the Mediterranean as the 'Arnauld' group. They pass through the Straits of Gibraltar between 11 and 16 Nov and operate at first E of Gibraltar. Early on 13 Nov, and in the afternoon of that day, *U205* (Lt-Cdr Reschke) and *U81* (Lt-Cdr Guggenberger) respectively are able to fire their torpedoes at British Force H, reported on 12 Nov by Italian air reconnaissance. The latter torpedoes the carrier *Ark Royal* (see 10–14 Nov). On 16 Nov *U433* (Lt-Cdr Ey) tries to attack a convoy setting out eastwards but is then herself sunk by the corvette *Marigold*. From 18 Nov the boats move off to the Eastern Mediterranean.

7–9 Nov   Mediterranean

The Italian convoy 'Beta' with seven ships, escorted by the destroyers *Maestrale* (Capt Bisciani), *Fulmine*, *Euro*, *Grecale*, *Libeccio* and *Oriani* and by a distant covering group consisting of the heavy cruisers *Trieste* and *Trento* (Div Adm Brivonesi) and the 13th DD Flotilla (Capt Capponi) with *Granatiere*, *Fuciliere*, *Bersagliere* and *Alpino*, from Naples through the Messina Strait to Tripoli, is detected, after 'Ultra' intercepts of German Air Force 'Enigma' transmissions, by a Maryland from No 69 Sqn RAF from Malta in the afternoon of 8 Nov. The British Force K (Capt Agnew), with the cruisers *Aurora* and *Penelope* (Capt Nicholl) and the destroyers *Lance* and *Lively*, is sent out from Malta to intercept. It sinks all seven transports—*Duisburg* (7389 tons), *San Marco* (3113 tons), *Maria* (6339 tons), *Sagitta* (5153 tons), *Rina Corrado* (5180 tons) and the tankers *Conte di Misurata* (5014 tons) and *Minatitlan* (7599 tons)— and also *Fulmine*, one of six escorting destroyers. Two other destroyers, *Euro* and *Grecale* of the close escort, are damaged. Force K is able, with the help of radar, to

manoeuvre itself unnoticed into a favourable position to attack and destroy the convoy without the Italian covering force, which has no radar, being able to intervene effectively. The next morning the British submarine *Upholder* (Lt-Cdr Wanklyn) torpedoes the destroyer *Libeccio*, engaged in recovering the survivors, which sinks shortly afterwards when being towed by the damaged *Euro*. The destroyers *Maestrale*, *Euro*, *Oriani*, *Alpino*, *Fuciliere* and *Bersagliere* rescue, in all, 704 survivors of the sunken ships. The Italian submarines *Beilul*, *Corallo*, *Delfino* and *Settembrini*, stationed to protect the convoy, do not fire their torpedoes.

The success of Force K is a result of work with 'Ultra'. The Italian Div Adm Brivonesi and the escort leader in *Maestrale* lose their commands after this disaster.

9 Nov   Black Sea

The cruiser *Molotov* (Capt 1st Class Y K Zinovev) shells German troop concentrations in the area Feodosia–Cape Chauda to support the hard-pressed units of the 51st Army. An attack by torpedo aircraft and bombers on 10 Nov off Tuapse is repulsed.

9–10 Nov   Air War/Germany

Attacks by RAF on Hamburg, Cuxhaven and Emden.

9–12 Nov   Baltic

Third evacuation convoy to Hangö under Rear-Adm M S Moskalenko leaves Kronstadt on 9 Nov and Suursaari on 10 Nov. Participants are the flotilla leader *Leningrad*, the destroyer *Stoiki*, the minelayer *Ural* (Capt 2nd Class I G Karpov), the transport *Andrei Zhdanov* (Capt 1st Class N I Meshcherski), the minesweepers *T-201*/*Zaryad*, *T-211*/*Rym*, *T-215*, *T-217* and *T-218* and four MO-IV submarine-chasers. On the way out, in the evening of 10 Nov, *T-217* and *T-218* collide in poor visibility and have to return. Because of the weather, the force turns back to Suursaari in the morning of 11 Nov and sets out again in the evening of the same day. During the night *Leningrad* (Capt 3rd Class G M Gorbachev) is brought to a standstill after two near-misses from mines and then returns with two minesweepers and *Zhdanov* which, however, runs on to a mine and sinks. In the morning of 12 Nov the remainder of the force turns round and goes back to Suursaari.

9–28 Nov   Arctic

British convoy PQ.3, with eight merchant ships, proceeds from Hvalfjord to Archangel without making contact with the enemy. One ship returns because of damage from ice. *K-21* lays three mine barrages.

The convoy PQ.4 (eight merchant ships) follows on 17 Nov and arrives with PQ.3.

10–12 Nov   Black Sea

The Soviet cruisers *Chervona Ukraina* (Capt 2nd Class N E Basisty) and *Krasny Krym* (Capt 2nd Class A I Zubkov) and the destroyers *Nezamozhnik* and *Shaumyan* support with their guns the defence against German attacks on the N and E fronts of the Sevastopol fortress. At mid-day on 12 Nov aircraft from FK IV attack the ships. Ju 87s of II/StG 77 (Capt Orthofer) obtain three bomb hits on *Chervona Ukraina* which, in spite of measures to save her, slowly fills with water and sinks to the bottom. The guns are later dismantled and taken ashore. In these attacks the destroyer *Sovershenny*, lying in the south dock of the navy yard waiting to be fitted out, and the destroyer *Besposhchadny*, having only left dock on 11 Nov after repairs to the damage sustained on 22 Sept, are heavily hit. The latter is towed by the destroyer *Shaumyan* to Poti for repairs on 17 Nov.

10–14 Nov   Mediterranean

Operation 'Perpetual': British Force H (Vice-Adm Somerville) proceeds from Gibraltar to the Western Mediterranean with the battleship *Malaya*, the carriers *Argus* and *Ark Royal*, the light cruiser *Hermione* and seven destroyers including *Laforey*, *Legion*, *Sikh* and the Dutch *Isaac Sweers*. In the afternoon of 12 Nov seven Blenheim bombers, flown off as escort aircraft from Gibraltar, arrive in Malta, as do 34 out of 37 Hurricane fighters flown off from the carriers. On the return, early on 13 Nov, *U205* (Lt-Cdr Reschke) first attacks the force with a salvo of three torpedoes, one of which explodes in the wake of *Legion*. Although six radar-equipped Swordfish are flown off, neither *U81* nor *U205* are found. At mid-day *U81* (Lt-Cdr Guggenberger) hits *Ark Royal* (Capt Maund) with one torpedo from a salvo of four. The carrier sinks while under tow the next day after the crew has been rescued (one life lost), only 25 nautical miles from Gibraltar. The Italian submarines *Aradam*, *Squalo*, *Turchese*, *Bandiera*, *Onice* and *Narvalo* are stationed too far to the E.

10 Nov–27 Dec   Atlantic/Indian Oceans

On 10 Nov the convoy WS.24 puts to sea from Halifax to proceed to the Near East via the Cape of Good Hope. It has more than 20000 British troops, on board the US troop transports *Wakefield*, *Mount Vernon*, *West Point*, *Leonard Wood*, *Joseph T Dickman* and *Orizaba* with the tanker *Cimarron*. The escort comprises TG.14.4 (Rear-Adm Cook) with the carrier *Ranger*, the cruisers *Quincy* and *Vincennes* and the destroyers (Capt Kinkaid) *Wainwright*, *Moffett*, *McDougal*, *Winslow*, *Mayrant*, *Trippe*, *Rhind* and *Rowan*. At 17°S, *Ranger* returns to Trinidad with *Rhind* and *Trippe*. The convoy is ordered to Bombay instead of Basra. It arrives in Cape Town on 9 Dec and then sets out with the British cruiser *Dorsetshire* and arrives in Bombay on 27 Dec. *Mount Vernon* goes direct to Singapore.

11–15 Nov   Baltic

The German U-boat *U580* is sunk during exercises off Memel following a collision with the SS *Angelburg* on 11 Nov. On 15 Nov *U583* is lost after a collision with *U153* off Danzig.

11 Nov–2 Dec   North Atlantic

The U-boats *U431*, *U402*, *U332* and *U105*, stationed in the area of the Denmark Strait from 4 to 10 Nov in anticipation of the intended sortie of the pocket-battleship *Admiral Scheer*, are sent from 13 Nov to the area of Cape Race.

The convoy HX.159 (33 ships), with its ocean escort US TU.4.1.4, comprising the destroyers *Plunkett*, *Decatur*, *Livermore*, *Badger* and *Cole* and the Coast Guard cutter *Campbell*, and the convoy SC.54, with its ocean escort Canadian TU 4.1.15, comprising the destroyers *Columbia* and *Skeena* and the corvettes *Wetaskiwin*, *Camrose*, *Shediac*, *Brandon*, *Mimose* (FFN), *Aconit* (FFN) and *Orillia* going E, are successfully routed round the U-boats, as are ON.34, taken on 12 Nov from the British EG.5 by the US TU.4.1.3, comprising the destroyers *Benson*, *Niblack*, *H P Jones*, *Tarbell* and *Edison* and the Canadian corvette *Chicoutimi*, and ON.35, taken on 15 Nov from the British EG.1 by the US TU.4.1.1, comprising the destroyers *Ericsson*, *Dallas*, *Eberle*, *Ellis* and *Upshur*.

On 15 Nov the 'Störtebecker' group, consisting of *U552*, *U567*, *U98*, *U96*, *U572*, *U69*, *U373*, *U201* and *U77* organised in the Central North Atlantic, is sent against the convoy OS.11 located by the B-Service. *U332* and *U402* reinforce the patrol line on 17 and 18 Nov but the convoy is routed clear. On 19 Nov the boats are formed in three loose lines to meet the expected convoy OG.77: the 'Gödecke' group, with *U98*, *U69*, *U201* and *U572*, the 'Beneke' group with *U332*, *U402*, *U96* and *U552* and the 'Störtebecker' group with *U85*, *U133*, *U571* and *U577*. *U43* and *U575* form a new group 'Steuben' off Newfoundland, to be joined there by *U105*, *U434*, *U574* and *U372*, but on 22 and 23 Nov all boats with enough fuel are ordered to the area W of Gibraltar and

into the Mediterranean to counter the developments in the African campaign.

Meanwhile the following convoys are also routed clear of the U-boats: HX.160 (62 ships), escorted by US TU.4.1.5 with the destroyers *Mayo*, *Nicholson*, *Leary*, *Schenck* and *Babbitt*, relieved on 15 Nov by the British EG.8 with the destroyers *Sardonyx*, *Watchman*, *Beverley* and *Scimitar* and the corvettes *Dahlia* and *Monkshood*; SC.55, escorted by Canadian TU.4.1.16 with the corvettes *Sorel*, *Mayflower*, *Kenogami*, *Nanaimo*, *Prescott* and *Eyebright*, going E; ONS.36 (39 ships), whose escort, the British EG.6, is relieved on 18 Nov by the Canadian TU.4.1.12 with the destroyer *Broadway* (RN) and the corvettes *Arrowhead*, *Nasturtium*, *Cobalt*, *Buctouche*, *Galt*, *Pictou*, *Moosejaw* and *Windflower*); and ON.37 (46 ships), whose escort, the British EG.8, is relieved by the US TU.4.1.8 with the destroyers *Swanson*, *Greer*, *Buck*, *Ludlow* and *McCormick*, going W.

On the way to the area W of Gibraltar, *U43* (Lt-Cdr Lüth) first sights, on 28 Nov, the convoy OS.12 (escorted by the 42nd EG with the sloops *Weston*, *Sennen*, *Totland*, *Londonderry* and *Wellington*) and then sinks, on 29 Nov, one ship of 5569 tons; on 30 Nov *U43* sinks one more ship, of 4868 tons, from the troop convoy WS.13. *U105*, *U372*, *U434*, *U575* and *U574* and directed to the reports and although some boats reach the convoys they cannot achieve any success. On 2 Dec *U43* in addition sinks the US tanker *Astral* (7541 tons), sailing on her own. The convoys ONS.38 (34 ships), escorted up to 24 Nov by the British EG.3 and then the Canadian TU.4.1.14, and ON.39 (38 ships), escorted up to 25 Nov by the British EG.2 and then the US TU.4.1.4, are routed clear of the German U-boats.

12–28 Nov   Arctic

The U-boats *U578* and *U752* operate in the entrance to the White Sea. On 15 Nov *U752* (Lt Schroeter) attacks a small convoy near Cape Gorodetski and torpedoes a timber freighter and an escort ship. On 27 Nov the Soviet patrol ship *SKR-25/Briz* attacks *U578* near Kanin Nos and slightly damages her by ramming.

12 Nov–7 Dec   Arctic

Soviet MO-IV submarine-chasers, operating from the bays of the Fisherman's Peninsula, lay 34, 20 and 14 mines off Petsamo, Kirkenes and Vardö respectively in several operations.

12–13 Nov   Baltic

The Finnish minelayers *Riilahti* and *Ruotsinsalmi* lay a new barrage with 141 EMC mines NW of 'Juminda'.

13 Nov   General Situation

A change in the American Neutrality Law allows American merchant ships to enter the war zone and provides for the arming of merchant ships. It comes into force on 18 Nov.

13–25 Nov   Baltic

Fourth evacuation convoy to Hangö under Capt 2nd Class V N Narykov sets out from Suursaari on 13 Nov. Participating are the destroyers *Gordy* and *Surovy*, the minelayer *Ural* the minesweepers *T-206/Verp*, *T-207/Shpil*, *T-211/Rym* and *T-215* and four MO-IV submarine-chasers. During the night 13–14 Nov the submarine-chaser *MO-301*, the minesweeper *T-206* and the destroyer *Surovy* (Capt 3rd Class M T Ustinov) run on to mines of the newly laid Finnish barrage and sink. In the evening of 14 Nov *Gordy* (Capt 3rd Class E B Efet) runs on to mines of the 'Corbetha' barrage and also sinks. Only *T-215*, *Ural* and three submarine-chasers reach Hangö on 14 Nov. Because of the losses, the movements of the larger ships are temporarily halted. Only after some small convoys have made the passage does the force return, reinforced by *T-205/Gafel*, *T-217*, *T-218* and three submarine-chasers. On 25 Nov it lands 4588 men in Kronstadt.

13–26 Nov   Mediterranean

The Italian submarines *Atropo*, *Saint Bon*, *Cagni* and *Millo* carry out transport operations from Taranto to Bardia.

14–15 Nov   Mediterranean

Off the Tunisian coast, Italian torpedo aircraft sink the British transports *Empire Defender* (5649 tons) and *Empire Pelican* (6463 tons), which are trying to break through from Gibraltar to Malta.

14–18 Nov   Mediterranean

Successful attempts by the Italians to bring supplies to North Africa with small fast convoys and warships: on both 16 and 18 Nov two ships reach Benghazi.

15–24 Nov   Mediterranean

Unsuccessful sortie by the Italian submarine *Ascianghi* to the Palestinian coast.

15 Nov–1 Dec   Black Sea

Strong elements of the Soviet Black Sea Fleet, including the battleship *Parizhskaya Kommuna*, the cruisers *Krasny Kavkaz* and *Krasny Krym* and the destroyers *Besposhchadny*, *Boiki*, *Smyshleny*, *Soobrazitelny*, and *Zheleznyakov*, support the defenders of Sevastopol with their gunfire on 15, 23, 25, 28 and 29 Nov and on 1 Dec.

15 Nov–11 Dec   Baltic

The Soviet submarines *S-9* and *Shch-309* operate in the western part of the Gulf of Finland.

16 Nov   Black Sea

Capture of Kerch. With it the whole of the Crimea, with the exception of Sevastopol, is in the hands of the German 11th Army.

17–21 Nov   North Atlantic

After the U-boats *U561* (Lt Bartels) and *U652* have served as an escort for the home-bound auxiliary cruiser *Schiff 45/Komet*, *U561* sinks two stragglers from the convoy SC.53 totalling 8514 tons.

17–24 Nov   Arctic

In submarine operations off the Norwegian polar coast, the Soviet *M-171* (Lt-Cdr V G Starikov) unsuccessfully attacks a tanker. The British submarines *Sealion* (Lt-Cdr Colvin) and *Seawolf* (Lt Raikes), recently transferred to the Arctic, sink, respectively, the tanker *Vesco* (331 tons) on 18 Nov in Svaerholthavet and, after an unsuccessful firing on 22 Nov, the steamer *Bahia* (4117 tons) on 24 Nov off Syltefjord. In addition, *M-172* and *Shch-403* are among the submarines at sea. *K-23* lays mines.

17 Nov–2 Dec   Black Sea

A counter-attack by the Soviet 9th and 37th Armies against the flank of the German 1st Panzer Army advancing on Rostov begins on 17 Nov. German forward troops actually take Rostov on 21 Nov but have to evacuate it again on 24 Nov because of the threatening situation in the rear. The 1st Panzer Army withdraws to the Mius sector by 2 Dec.

18–27 Nov   Mediterranean

The British 8th Army (Gen Cunningham) starts a counter-offensive in North Africa on 18 Nov to relieve Tobruk (Operation 'Crusader'). On 21 Nov the Tobruk garrison breaks out to the E to meet the advancing 8th Army. To supply Tobruk, the Australian sloops *Parramatta* and *Yarra* bring a slow convoy to the fortress (18–23 Nov). To relieve the shortage of ammunition, *Parramatta* and the destroyer *Avon Vale* escort the ammunition transport *Hanne* (1360 tons) to Tobruk. *U559* (Lt-Cdr Heidtmann) sinks *Parramatta* near Tobruk on 27 Nov.

18 Nov–7 Dec   Pacific

The Japanese SM flotillas 1 (Rear-Adm Sato) and 2 (Rear-Adm Yamazaki) leave Yokosuka on 18–19 Nov for the waters round Hawaii. *I-26* (Cdr* M Yokota) reconnoitres the Aleutian island of Kiska on 25 Nov, Dutch Harbor with her aircraft on 27–28 Nov and Adak and Kodiak on 30 Nov. *I-10* (Cdr* Kayahara) reconnoitres with her aircraft over Suva (Samoa) on 29 Nov and by periscope off Pago-Pago on 4 Dec. From 3 Dec *I-9*, *I-15*, *I-17* and *I-25* form a patrol line N of Oahu; *I-7* is stationed N of Oahu, with *I-1*, *I-2*, *I-3* W and *I-4*, *I-5*, *I-6* E of Oahu. The 3rd SM Flotilla (Rear-Adm Miwa), coming from Kwajalein, consisting of *I-8*, *I-68*, *I-69*, *I-70*, *I-71*, *I-72*, *I-73*, *I-74* and *I-75*, takes up positions in a semi-circle S of Oahu.

During the night 6–7 Dec the midget submarine transports *I-16*, *I-18*, *I-20*, *I-22* and *I-24* put out their craft. One of them is sunk in the night by the destroyer *Ward* (Lt-Cdr Outerbridge) off the harbour (the first shot in the Pacific War), two are sunk penetrating the harbour and two are sunk in the harbour before they are able to fire. On the return, *I-16* and *I-22* shell Johnston on 16 Dec.

19 Nov   Indian Ocean

The Australian light cruiser *Sydney* (Capt Burnett†) encounters the German auxiliary cruiser *Schiff 41/Kormoran* (Cdr* Detmers) about 170 nautical miles W of Shark Bay (Western Australia). Detmers is able to prolong the signal exchanges until *Sydney* has approached within 900m and come alongside the German ship. The latter has no choice but to drop the disguise and to open fire with all her guns. *Sydney* is badly hit by the first salvos and receives a torpedo hit in the bow, then, on fire, disappears from view and is never seen again. *Schiff 41* has to be abandoned when a fire caused by burning oil cannot be extinguished because the auxiliary engines are out of action; the majority of the crew reaches the Australian coast and is taken aboard Allied ships. Total result of the auxiliary cruiser's activities: 11 merchant ships of 68274 tons sunk.

19 Nov   Bay of Biscay

The British submarine *Rorqual* (Lt Napier) lays a mine barrage off La Rochelle. A French trawler of 600 tons is lost on it.

19–20 Nov   North Sea

Attack by the 2nd MTB Flotilla with four boats on a British convoy off Great Yarmouth. *S104* (Lt Rebensburg) sinks the British naval tanker *War Mehtar* (5502 tons), *S105* the freighter *Aruba* (1159 tons) and *S41* the freighter *Waldinge* (2462 tons). *S41* (Lt Popp) is damaged in a collision in an engagement with the convoy escort and, on the return, has to be abandoned while under tow.

19–25 Nov   Baltic

After the losses on 14 Nov, several small Soviet convoys proceed from Suursaari to Hangö and back.

On 19–20 Nov Capt 3rd Class D M Belkov goes to Hangö with the netlayer *Azimut*, the patrol ship *T-297/Virsaitis* and the minesweepers *T-58*, *T-35*, *T-42* and *T-54/Klyuz*. On the return on 21–22 Nov, *Azimut* and *T-35/Menzhinski* are lost on mines.

On 20–21 Nov the minesweepers *T-205*, *T-217* and *T-218* go to Hangö; the transport *No 548/Minna* and two submarine-chasers have to turn back. The minesweepers return with the fourth convoy.

On 21–22 Nov the transport *No 10* goes with five motor minesweepers to Hangö. On 22–23 Nov Lt-Cdr G S Dus goes with the transport *No 548/Minna*, the patrol ship *Tsh-26/Korall*, the minesweeper *Tsh-53/Udarnik* and two submarine-chasers to Hangö. On 23–24 Nov Capt 3rd Class Belkov follows with *T-42*, *Klyuz*, *Virsaitis*, and two submarine-chasers. On 24 Nov the force, comprising *No 548/Minna*, *Klyuz*, *Udarnik* and *Virsaitis*, starts the return journey. *Klyuz* is lost on mines and *Udarnik* is slightly damaged. In all, 4424 men, 18 tanks, 720 tons of rations and 250 tons of ammunition are evacuated by these convoys.

19–28 Nov   Mediterranean

In operations in the Western Mediterranean, the Dutch submarine *O21* (Lt-Cdr v Dulm) sinks two sailing ships and the U-boat *U95*. On 19 Nov the Polish submarine *Sokol* (Cdr Karnicki) attacks the harbour at Navarino and damages the destroyer *Aviere*.

Thrasher (Lt Mackenzie) sinks one ship of 3510 tons from a Patrasso/Brindisi convoy. In the Aegean *Triumph* (Lt-Cdr Woods) sinks one ship of 632 tons.

20–22 Nov   Mediterranean

The critical supply situation of the German/Italian Army forces the Italian Fleet to make further efforts to bring through supply transports. On 21 Nov two convoys each with two transports set out, escorted by seven destroyers and torpedo boats and the 3rd Div (Div Adm Parona) comprising the heavy cruisers *Gorizia*, *Trento* and *Trieste*.

On 21 Nov British air reconnaissance and a submarine locate the convoys. As it passes through the Straits of Messina, the 8th Div (Div Adm Lombardi), comprising the light cruisers *Duca degli Abruzzi* and *Garibaldi*, joins the covering group. From both Taranto and Brindisi two further transports set out, as does, from Brindisi, the cruiser *Cadorna* as a fuel transport. A ship from the Taranto convoy has to return because of engine trouble; the other three and *Cadorna* reach Benghazi on 22 Nov.

The rest of the force is attacked shortly before midnight on 21–22 Nov by the British submarine *Utmost* (Lt-Cdr Cayley). *Trieste* (Capt Rouselle) receives a torpedo hit and only reaches Messina with difficulty. A little later the force is attacked by British aircraft from Malta and *Duca degli Abruzzi* (Capt Zannoni) is hit by a torpedo. Meanwhile, the B-service has learnt of the departure of the British Force K from Malta but the Italian submarines *Delfino*, *Squalo*, *Tricheco*, *Settembrini* and *Corallo*, stationed E of Malta as a cover, do not sight it. The

3rd Div receives orders to put into Taranto with the transports. *Garibaldi* and the destroyers *Vivaldi, Da Noli, Granatiere, Fuciliere, Alpino, Corazziere, Carabiniere* and *Turbine* and the torpedo boat *Perseo* take over the task of escorting the badly damaged *Duca degli Abruzzi*. The Mediterranean Fleet, which has put to sea to support Force K, returns.

21 Nov–15 Dec   Arctic

The Soviet submarines *K-3* (Capt 3rd Class K I Malofeyev, with the Commander 1st SM Division, Capt 2nd Class M I Gadzhiev, on board) and *K-23* (Capt 3rd Class I S Potapov) set out on 16 Nov and lay mine barrages on 20 and 22 Nov off Hammerfest and in Kvaenangenfjord respectively. The Norwegian coasters *Ingar Nielsen* and *Kong Ring* (1994 tons) run on to the second barrage on 26 Dec and have to be beached. The submarine-chaser *UJ1110* is lost, possibly on the first on 9 July 1942. On 26 Nov *K-23* unsuccessfully attacks a minesweeper and on 3 Dec *K-3* attacks a convoy with the steamer *Altkirch* off Rolvsöy. The submarine-chasers *UJ1403, UJ1416* and *UJ1708* attack the submarine with depth charges. Capt Gadzhiev orders the submarine to surface because of the resulting damage and in a gun engagement scores a direct hit on *UJ1708* (470 tons), which sinks. The two other submarine-chasers, which are only armed with 2cm AA guns, have to withdraw in face of the better-armed submarine (two 10cm and two 4.5cm guns), which escapes. Off Porsangerfjord, *D-3* (Lt-Cdr N A Bibeev, with the Commander 2nd SM Division, Capt 2nd Class I A Kolyshkin, on board) attacks steamers on 28 Nov, 5 Dec and 6 Dec, but the torpedoes explode on the cliffs. Off Tanafjord, the British submarine *Sealion* (Lt-Cdr Colvin) sinks the small Norwegian steamer *Island* (638 tons); the Soviet *M-171* misses a tanker in Varangerfjord; *M-174* lands agents on the Varanger coast; and *M-176* operates without result. *Shch-421* has one miss.

K-22 (Capt 3rd Class V N Kotelnikov), which sets out on 6 Dec with the Commander of the Submarine Bde, Capt 1st Class N I Vinogradov, lays a mine barrage in Rolvsöy Sound on 9 Dec, attacks with gunfire a Norwegian cutter (which, however, escapes) and sinks a convoy of vessels under tow on 11 Dec near Mylingen.

21 Nov–30 Dec   North Atlantic

While the North Atlantic U-boats are moved to the area W of Gibraltar and the new U-boats, coming from Germany, are transferred to French ports in preparation for operations in the Western Atlantic after the American entry into the war, there is no operation against the Allied North Atlantic convoys. Based on information from 'Ultra', the latter are routed more directly.

From 23 Nov to 28 Dec the American and Canadian ocean escort groups escort eastbound convoys from the WESTOMP to the MOMP and take westbound convoys there back to WESTOMP: US TU.4.1.6, with the destroyers *Woolsey, Roe, Lea, MacLeish, Dupont* and *Bernadou*, escorts HX.161 and ON.43; Canadian TU.4.1.13, with the destroyer *Restigouche* and the corvettes *Alysse, Agassiz, Bittersweet, Amherst, Chicoutimi, Orillia* and *Morden*, escorts SC.56 and ONS.44; US TU.4.1.2, with the destroyers *Charles F Hughes, Wilkes, Lansdale, Madison* and *Sturtevant*, escorts HX.162 and ON.45; Canadian TU.4.1.11, with the destroyer *Ottawa* and the corvettes *Primrose, Trail, Polyanthus* (RN), *Fennel, Battleford, Arvida* and *Sherbrooke*, escorts SC.57 and ONS.46; US TU.4.1.3, with the destroyers *Niblack, Hilary P Jones, Benson, Edison* and *Tarbell*, escorts HX.163 and ON.47; and Canadian TU.4.1.12, with the destroyer *St Laurent* and the corvettes *Nasturtium, Hepatica, Moosejaw, Windflower, Pictou* and *Buctouche*, escorts SC.58 and ONS.48.

From 21 Nov to 30 Dec, in the Eastern Atlantic, the British EGs escort convoys from EASTOMP to MOMP and take over there the eastbound convoys: EG.3, with the destroyers *Foxhound* and *Amazon* and the corvettes *Heartsease, Roselys* and *Renoncule* (FFN), escorts ON.38 and SC.55; EG.2, with the destroyers *Douglas, Veteran* and *Leamington*, the corvette *Anemone*, the minesweeper *Thyme* and four A/S trawlers, escorts ON.39 and HX.161 (*Veronica* and *Alisma* replace *Thyme* for the latter); EG.4, with the destroyers *Beagle* and *Boadicea* and the corvettes *Heather, Narcissus* and *Commandant Détrayer* (FFN) and four A/S trawlers, escorts ONS.40 and SC.56; EG.5, with the destroyers *Vanoc* and *Caldwell* and the corvettes *Honeysuckle, Calendula, Gentian* and *Celandine*, escorts ON.41 and HX.162; EG.1, with the destroyers *Sabre* and *Skate* and the corvettes *Sunflower, Alisma* and *Kingcup* and three A/S trawlers, escorts ONS.42 and SC.57—this convoy is met by chance by the outgoing *U130* (Cdr Kals), which sinks three ships of 14971 tons, the only success against a North Atlantic convoy in Dec; EG.6, with the destroyers *Havelock* and *Newport* and the corvettes *Camellia, Hibiscus* and *Begonia*, escorts ON.43 and with the destroyers *Broke, Newport* and *Verity* and the corvettes *Camellia, Begonia, Hibiscus* and *Rosthern* escorts HX.163; EG.8, with the destroyers *Watchman* and *Newmarket* and the corvettes *Arabis, Dahlia, Montbretia* (RNoN) and *Rose* (RNoN), escorts ONS.44 and SC.58; EG.3, with the destroyer *Wanderer* and the corvettes *Aubrietia, Heartsease* and *Roselys* and two A/S trawlers, escorts ON.45 and HX.164; EG.2, with the destroyers *Douglas* and *Leamington* and the corvette *Sweetbriar*, escorts ONS.46 and SC.59; and EG.4, with the destroyers *Boadicea* and *Roxborough* and the corvettes *Narcissus, Lobélia* (FFN), *Heather* and *Commandant Détroyat* (FFN), escorts ON.47 and HX.165.

22 Nov–30 Nov   South Atlantic

Even without being able to break into the 'Ausserheimische Gewässer' codes which are used by the German auxiliary cruisers, Bletchley Park is able to pinpoint the area where U-boats are to be replenished by an auxiliary cruiser by means of intercepting radio messages to the U-boats sent in 'Triton' code.

On 22 Nov the German auxiliary cruiser *Schiff 16/Atlantis* (Capt Rogge) is surprised by the British heavy cruiser *Devonshire* (Capt Oliver) N of Ascension when she is replenishing *U126* (Lt-Cdr Bauer). She has to scuttle herself. *U126* submerges near *Schiff 16* under the impression that the cruiser will approach closer. After the sinking of the auxiliary cruiser and the departure of *Devonshire*, she tows the crew in their boats and takes the wounded below until on 24 Nov they can be handed over to the submarine supply ship *Python*, which has been summoned to the scene.

On her way to support *U126, U124* (Lt-Cdr Mohr) encounters the British cruiser *Dunedin* proceeding on her own and sinks her. There are only 67 survivors. For the period 30 Nov–4 Dec, it is proposed to supply a U-boat group consisting of *U68, UA, U129* and *U124* 780 nautical miles S of St Helena for an operation off Cape Town. On the way, *U124* sinks the American steamer *Sagadahoc* (6275 tons) on 3 Dec (see also 1 Dec).

22 Nov–3 Dec   North Atlantic/ Mediterranean

The situation in North Africa necessitates the transfer of more German U-boats to the Mediterranean and the concentration of the remaining boats in the Gibraltar area. *U431* and *U95*, which are proceeding to the Atlantic, are ordered to the Mediterranean and pass through the Straits of Gibraltar on 24 and 26 Nov respectively. *U95* (Lt-Cdr Schreiber) is sunk on 28 Nov by the Dutch submarine *O21* (Lt-Cdr v Dulm). After taking supplies in Spanish harbours, *U557* and *U562* first take up their positions in the Western Mediterranean from 27 to 29 Nov and then from 2 Dec proceed with *U431* to the Eastern Mediterranean. Of the boats supplied from German tankers in Cadiz, *U562* passes through the Straits of Gibraltar on 28 Nov and remains just E of there until 7 Dec. *U96* and *U558* are located on 1 and 3 Dec respectively with ASV radar by the Swordfish aircraft of No 812 Sqn from *Ark Royal* operating from the airfield at Gibraltar. The submarines are damaged by bombs and have to return. On 2 Dec *U562* (Lt Hamm) and *U557* (Lt-Cdr Paulshen) each sink one ship, of 4274 tons and 4033 tons respectively.

23–25 Nov   Mediterranean

Further attempts by the Italian Navy to bring small convoys through to North Africa. The ship movements are detected by British air reconnaissance, whereupon Force K, comprising the cruisers *Aurora* (Capt Agnew) and *Penelope* and the destroyers *Lance* and *Lively*, sets out from Malta. But it is reported by the Italian submarine *Settembrini* and all convoys receive orders to put into the nearest harbour. A convoy (two freighters and two torpedo boats) from the Aegean, and destined for Benghazi, does not receive the orders and is attacked by Force K 100 nautical miles W of Crete. The German transports *Maritza* (2910 tons) and *Procida* (1842 tons) are sunk by *Penelope* and *Lively*, although the Cdr of the escort (Cdr* Mimbelli), which consists of the torpedo boats *Cassiopea* and *Lupo*, does everything to prevent their loss.

At Churchill's insistence, Adm Cunningham has gone to sea with the bulk of the Mediterranean Fleet—the battleships *Queen Elizabeth*, *Barham* and *Valiant* and eight destroyers (Force A) and the cruisers *Ajax*, *Neptune*, *Naiad*, *Euryalus* and *Galatea* and four destroyers (Force B, Rear-Adm Rawlings) as support for Force K. At this time the Italian submarines *Beilul*, *Dagabur* and *Zaffiro* are operating as escorts off the Cyrenaican coast and the German U-boats *U79*, *U331* and *U559* on the supply route to Tobruk. The British troop transport *Glenearn* (784 tons) receives an air torpedo hit on 23 Nov and is beached near Tobruk. On 25 Nov *U331* (Lt v Tiesenhausen) penetrates the screen of the battleship force of the Mediterranean Fleet N of Bardia and, at short range, obtains three hits from a salvo of four torpedoes on *Barham*, which capsizes and explodes. The destroyers *Jervis*, *Jackal*, *Nizam* (RAN) and *Hotspur* rescue the Cdr of the 1st Battle Sqn, Vice-Adm Pridham-Wippell, and 450 survivors; the ship's commander, Capt Cooke, and 861 men perish.

23 Nov–2 Dec   Baltic

The Soviet gunboat *Laine* evacuates, during the nights 22–23, 24–25 and 28–29 Nov, 165, 70 and 206 men respectively from the island of Odensholm (Capt Verbizki) to Hangö. During the night 1–2 Dec she takes 543 men on board and brings them direct to Suursaari. The last demolition parties (17 men) are brought by torpedo cutters to Suursaari.

24 Nov   Arctic

A British force (Rear-Adm Burrough), consisting of the cruiser *Kenya* and the destroyers *Bedouin* and *Intrepid* and the attached Soviet destroyers *Gremyashchi* and *Gromki*, searches unsuccessfully for German ships off the Norwegian polar coast between Nordkyn and Vardö and shells Vardö.

24 Nov   North Sea

Attack by the 4th MTB Flotilla (Lt-Cdr Bätge), comprising *S50*, *S51*, *S52*, *S109* and *S110*, on a British convoy E of Orfordness. *S109* (Sub-Lt Bosse) sinks the British tanker *Virgilia* (5723 tons) and *S52* (Lt Karl Müller) the Dutch freighter *Groenlo* (1984 tons). *S51* torpedoes the freighter *Blairnevis* (4155 tons).

25 Nov   Pacific

The US Navy introduces compulsory convoys for merchant ships in the Pacific.

25 Nov   General Situation

President Roosevelt decides to break off negotiations with Japan and on 26 Nov hands the Japanese Ambassador, through Secretary of State Hull, a 10-point note which is unacceptable to Japan. A breach between the two states has, therefore, become inevitable.

25 Nov   English Channel

The German patrol vessel *V412* (*Nordland*) is sunk by a torpedo from a British MTB off Dunkirk.

25 Nov   Mediterranean

The Italian minesweeper *Zirona* (ex-Yugoslav *Jastreb*) is damaged in an air raid on Benghazi and beached.

25 Nov–30 Nov   Black Sea

The tankers *Avanesov*, *Tuapse* and *Sakhalin* and the ice-breaker *Mikoyan* (a former auxiliary cruiser) leave Batum on 25 Nov, escorted by the flotilla leader *Tashkent* (Rear-Adm L A Vladimirski) and the destroyers *Soobrazitelny* and *Sposobny*, for the Bosphorus, which they enter on 28 Nov when the warships return. On the subsequent journey to the Far East, *Avanesov* is sunk on 19 Dec by *U652* (Lt-Cdr Fraatz) off the Turkish coast near Cape Baba.

25 Nov   North Atlantic

After the withdrawal of all fully operational U-boats to the Gibraltar area, there remain,

for the time being, in the North Atlantic the U-boats which have small reserves of fuel: *U69*, *U201* and *U402*. They form the 'Letzte Ritter' group. They are directed to convoy OG.77, which sets out on 26 Nov and is located by air reconnaissance on 28 Nov but which is not found again on 29 Nov, 30 Nov and 1 Dec.

26 Nov   Pacific

The Japanese Striking Force, which is to attack Pearl Harbor and which is assembled in Hittokappu Bay, sets out. The Cdr is the Officer Commanding the 1st Naval Air Fleet, Vice-Adm Nagumo, with the aircraft carrier Sqns 1, 2 and 5 (*Akagi* and *Kaga*, *Hiryu* and *Soryu*, *Shokaku* and *Zuikaku*, with a total of 423 aircraft). Escort is provided by the 1st DD Flotilla with the light cruiser *Abukuma* (Rear-Adm Omori) and the destroyers *Tanikaze*, *Urakaze*, *Isokaze*, *Hamakaze*, *Kasumi*, *Arare*, *Kagero*, *Shiranuhi* and *Akigumo*. The support force (Vice-Adm Mikawa) consists of 3rd BB Sqn with the battleships *Hiei* and *Kirishima* and the 8th Cruiser Sqn comprising the heavy cruisers *Chikuma* and *Tone*. In addition, the submarines *I-19*, *I-21* and *I-23* and eight tankers and supply ships, as well as a destroyer force (Capt Konishi) consisting of *Akebono* and *Ushio*, intended for the shelling of Midway Island, belong to the group. The force proceeds for eleven days under conditions of complete radio silence, at first on easterly courses in storm and mist, then to the SE and better weather.

27 Nov   General Situation

'War Warning' to the overseas commanders of the US armed forces.

27–29 Nov   Mediterranean

Rear-Adm Rawlings moves from Alexandria to Malta with the cruisers *Ajax* (Capt McCarthy) and *Neptune* and the destroyers *Kimberley* and *Kingston* to reinforce Force K. On the first part of the journey they are accompanied by the cruisers *Naiad* (Rear-Adm Vian) and *Euryalus* and two destroyers.

The Italian submarines *Delfino* and *Squalo*, which are stationed SE of Sicily to cover Italian operations, and *Alagi* and *Aradam*, stationed on the Tunisian coast, sight no targets. SE of Malta, *Tricheco* unsuccessfully attacks the advancing cruiser force.

27 Nov–12 Dec   Arctic

The British convoy QP.3, with 10 merchant ships, proceeds from Archangel to Seidisfjord (Iceland) without making contact with the enemy. Two ships have to return because of storm damage.

The British convoy PQ.5, with seven merchant ships, goes from Hvalfjord to Archangel without making contact with the enemy.

28–29 Nov   Black Sea

The battleship *Parizhskaya Kommuna* (Capt 1st Class Kravchenko) and the destroyer *Smyshleny* from Cape Feolent shell German and Rumanian positions S of Sevastopol with 146 rounds of 305mm, 120 rounds of 130mm and 299 rounds of 120mm. On 29 Nov the cruiser *Krasny Kavkaz* (Capt 2nd Class A M Gushchin) and the destroyer *Zheleznyakov* shell German positions near Kutschuk.

28 Nov–7 Dec   Mediterranean

The German U-boats *U81*, *U205* and *U565* arrive from 28 Nov in the operational area between Alexandria and Tobruk from the Western Mediterranean and reinforce *U79*, *U331* and *U559*. Their attacks on supply ships, sailing ships, destroyers and warship formations, including one on 6 Dec by *U79* (Lt-Cdr Kaufmann) on the battleship *Queen Elizabeth*, are unsuccessful. On 5 Dec the transport *Chakdina* (3033 tons) is lost to a torpedo hit from an Italian aircraft and *Chantala* (3129 tons) to a mine off Tobruk. Both are engaged in the Tobruk supply traffic. The sloop *Flamingo* is damaged by bomb hits.

28 Nov–31 Dec   Mediterranean

Major deployment of Italian submarines as supply transports: to Bardia (13 transports), Derna (2), Benghazi (4) and Tripoli (2). The following boats participate: *Millo* (3), *Menotti* (2), *Cagni* (2), *Settimo* (1), *Caracciolo* (1), *Saint Bon* (1), *Mocenigo* (2), *Dandolo* (2), *Otaria* (1), *Bragadino* (1), *Veniero* (1) and *Emo* (1). On 11 Dec *Caracciolo* is encountered on the return by the British destroyer *Farndale*, escorting convoy TA.2, and sunk. The submarines transport, in all, 1757.6 tons of material and fuel.

29 Nov   North Sea

In an attack by the 4th MTB Flotilla on a British convoy NW of Cromer, *S51* (Lt Hans-Jürgen Meyer) sinks the freighter *Cormarsh* (2848 tons), *S52* (Lt Karl Müller) the *Empire Newcomen* (2840 tons) and *S64* (Lt Wilcke) the tanker *Asperity* (699 tons).

29 Nov–2 Dec   Mediterranean

New Italian convoy operations to North Africa. From Brindisi the freighters *Capo Faro* (3476 tons) and *Iseo* (2366 tons) set out with the torpedo boat *Procione*, from Taranto the motor ship *Sebastiano Venier* (6311 tons) with the destroyer *Da Verazzano*, from Navarino the tanker *Volturno* (3363 tons) with two destroyers and from Argostoli the passenger ship *Adriatico* (1976 tons). All ships are destined for Benghazi. From Trapani to Tripoli there set out the motor tanker *Irido Mantovani* (10540 tons)

and the destroyer *Da Mosto* and, in addition, two covering groups: the 7th Div (Div Adm de Courten), comprising the light cruisers *Attendolo*, *Duca d'Aosta* and *Montecuccoli*, the destroyers *Aviere*, *Camicia Nera* and *Geniere* and the battleship *Caio Duilio* (Div Adm Giovanola), the cruiser *Garibaldi* and the destroyers *Granatiere*, *Alpino*, *Bersagliere*, *Fuciliere*, *Corazziere* and *Carabiniere*. The Italian movements are again detected by British air reconnaissance. *Volturno* again receives bomb hits and has to return. On 30 Nov Force K, comprising *Aurora*, *Penelope*, *Ajax*, *Neptune* and the destroyers *Lively*, *Kimberley* and *Kingston*, leaves Malta, whereupon the Italian cruisers join the *Venier* convoy, which is the most threatened. The *Duilio* group is held up by engine trouble on *Garibaldi* and cannot arrive on time. Supermarina therefore orders the other cruisers to avoid the superior Force K and the convoys to go off eastwards. Bombers from Malta sink the *Capo Faro*, and the *Iseo* has to return to Argostoli after a bomb hit. During the night 30 Nov–1 Dec Force K sinks the solitary *Adriatico* but *Venier* is able to avoid it and reaches Benghazi on 2 Dec. About 70 nautical miles N of Tripoli, *Mantovani* is hit by an air torpedo and, some hours later, is sunk by bombs. *Da Mosto* (Cdr dell'Anno) sights the advancing British cruiser *Penelope* while rescuing the survivors from the large tanker and attacks her with torpedoes. But she is destroyed by the fire of the British ships and sinks.

29 Nov–4 Dec   Baltic

Evacuation of the rest of the Hangö garrison (Lt-Gen S I Kabanov). On 29 Nov Vice-Adm V P Drozd leaves Kronstadt with the destroyers *Slavny* and *Stoiki*, the transport *Josif Stalin*, the minesweepers *T-205/Gafel*, *T-207/Shpil*, *T-211/Rym*, *T-215*, *T-217* and *T-218* (Capt 2nd Class N A Mamontov), seven submarine-chasers and four torpedo-cutters. On the way to Suursaari, the ice-breaker *Oktyabr* is lost in an air attack. The force arrives in Hangö on 30 Nov. On 30 Nov–1 Dec another force proceeds to Hangö under Lt-Cdr P B Shevtsov with the transport *No 539/Maya*, the minesweeper *T-210/Gak*, the gunboat *Volga*, the minesweepers *Udarnik* and *Virsaitis* and the submarine-chasers *MO-405* and *MO-406*. An attempted attack by the Finnish gunboats *Hämeenmaa* and *Uusimaa* two boats of the 3rd Patrol Boat Flotilla and four other patrol boats, is unsuccessful.

On 2 Dec the Soviet troops leave and are embarked. In the evening Lt-Cdr Shevtsov leaves first, his force strengthened by the gunboat *Laine* and four tugs. *Virsaitis* is lost

to a mine en route and *Maya* and *Volga* are damaged.

In the late evening Vice-Adm Drozd follows with the minesweepers *T-205*, *T-207*, *T-211*, *T-215*, *T-217* and *T-218*, *Josif Stalin*, *Slavny* and *Stoiki* and submarine protection consisting of seven submarine-chasers and four torpedo cutters. The remaining demolition parties and command staffs are taken on board fourteen other torpedo cutters. On 3 Dec the force runs on to the 'Corbetha' mine barrage: *T-211*, *T-215* and *T-218* lose their minesweeping equipment on explosive floats. *Josif Stalin* (7500 tons) drifts into the barrage and is hit by four mines in succession. The last causes the magazine to explode, bringing about heavy loss of life (some 4000 men?); 650 men are recovered by *T-217*, 160 by *T-205* (damaged on a mine), 120 by *T-207*, 500 by *T-211* and *T-215* and 400 by the submarine-chasers *MO-106*, *MO-210*, *MO-307* and *MO-407*. About 2000 men remain on the drifting wreck.

Capt 2nd Class Svyatov sets out from Suursaari with the destroyer *Svirepy* and the rescue ship *Neptun* but has to return when *T-207* loses her minesweeping equipment. A second attempt to set out on 4 Dec with four minesweepers is abandoned on the orders of the Fleet Command because, in the meantime, German boats of the 3rd Patrol Boat Flotilla have taken the wreck of *Josif Stalin* in tow. Only half of the last 12000 men reach Suursaari. From there the ships are brought to Kronstadt with the help of the ice-breaker *Ermak*.

30 Nov   North Sea

The auxiliary cruiser *Schiff 45/Komet* (Rear-Adm Eyssen) comes into Hamburg after 516 days in enemy waters. Results: 6 ships of 31005 tons sunk and two other ships totalling 21125 tons in co-operation with the auxiliary cruiser *Schiff 36/Orion*.

30 Nov   Indian Ocean

The Free French destroyer *Léopard* (Cdr* Evenou) occupies the island of Réunion after an engagement with the Vichy French battery at Point des Galets and breaking the local resistance.

30 Nov–18 Dec   Black Sea

In Soviet submarine operations off the Rumanian/Bulgarian coast, *Shch-204*, *Shch-211* and, probably, *M-34* are lost on flanking mine barrages (though one is sunk possibly as a result of a depth charge attack) following an unsuccessful assault on the Rumanian destroyer *Regele Ferdinand I*. *Shch-205* (Lt-Cdr T D Sukhomlinov) runs on to a flanking barrage on 4 Dec near Varna and reaches Sevastopol only with difficulty. Near Cape Emine, the Rumanian steamer

Oituz (2686 tons) is damaged, probably by one of the submarines that were lost.

1 Dec   Pacific

The blockade-runner *Portland* (7132 tons, Capt Tünemann) reaches Osaka from Bordeaux.

1–3 Dec   Black Sea

The destroyer *Boiki* shells assembly positions near Kalych Kiap on 1 Dec, the destroyer *Zheleznyakov* shells the area E of Inkerman from Severnaya Bay on 1 and 2 Dec and the cruiser *Krasny Krym* bombards the area of Balaklava on 1 Dec. On 3 Dec the cruiser *Krasny Kavkaz* brings 1000 troops, shells German positions from Severnaya Bay and returns to Novorossisk with 600 wounded. On the way the Balaklava area is shelled.

1–7 Dec   Arctic

The British cruiser *Kent* brings the British Foreign Secretary, Eden, from Scapa Flow to Murmansk, from where he travels to Moscow for a conference with Stalin.

1–12 Dec   Pacific

The US submarines *Tambor* and *Triton* are stationed off Wake and *Argonaut* and *Trout* off Midway for reconnaissance purposes.

1–13 Dec   Mediterranean

New Italian convoy operations to North Africa are greatly impeded by stormy weather. On 9–10 Dec the light cruiser *Luigi Cadorna* brings petrol to Benghazi and returns with 900 prisoners of war on board. From 9 to 12 Dec the British submarine *Porpoise* (Cdr Pizey) damages the motor ship *Sebastiano Venier* (6311 tons) which is returning from Benghazi with 2000 prisoners of war, then on 15 Dec *Torbay* sinks her. In spite of bad weather, the hospital ship *Arno* is able to rescue 1800 of those on board but 309 British and 11 Italian soldiers lose their lives. On 11 Dec the cruiser *Cadorna* again brings petrol to Benghazi. The British submarine *Talisman* (Lt-Cdr Willmott) sinks the Italian motor ship *Calitea* (4013 tons) S of Cape Matapan. On 13 Dec the 4th Div (Div Adm Toscano), comprising the cruisers *Da Barbiano* (Capt Rodocannacchi) and *Di Giussano* (Capt Marabotto), sets out as petrol transports with the torpedo boat *Cigno* from Palermo but turns back shortly after passing Cape Bon when located by British air reconnaissance. On the return both cruisers are sunk by torpedoes, from the British destroyers *Sikh* (Cdr Stokes), *Legion* and *Maori*, and by the Dutch *Isaac Sweers*, proceeding from Gibraltar to Alexandria. Div Adm Toscano and over 900 members of the crews of both cruisers perish but *Cigno* is able to get away. 'Ultra' has given the British full details of the convoys.

1–29 Dec   South Atlantic

The British heavy cruiser *Dorsetshire* (Capt Agar), led by 'Ultra' intercepts about U-boat replenishment rendezvous, surprises the German U-boat supply ship *Python* (Lt-Cdr Lueders) while the latter is providing *UA* (Cdr Eckermann) and *U68* (Cdr Merten) with oil at 27°53′S 03°55′W. Both U-boats submerge at once; *UA* attacks the cruiser with five torpedoes, but these miss. With that the fate of *Python* is sealed. When *Dorsetshire* fires a salvo to halt her, the crew of *Python* leave the ship, which sinks after being blown up. The crews of *Schiff 16* (see 22 Nov) and *Python*, in all 414 men, are towed on the following days in boats and floats by *UA* and *U68*, and then on 3 Dec *U129* (Lt-Cdr Clausen) comes up and takes the entire *Python* crew on board. On 5 Dec *U124* (Lt-Cdr Mohr) also comes up. Between 14 and 18 Dec the Italian submarines *Torelli* (Cdr Giacomo), *Tazzoli* (Cdr Fecia di Cossato), *Finzi* (Cdr Giudice) and *Calvi* (Cdr Olivieri) take part of the crew of *Schiff 16* and bring them to St-Nazaire, where the crews of the two German ships are landed between 23 and 29 Dec.

1–31 Dec   Intelligence

The decoding of 'Dolphin' is delayed for part of the month by up to 80 hrs.

2 Dec   Indian Ocean

The British battleship *Prince of Wales*, the battlecruiser *Repulse* and four destroyers arrive in Singapore.

2 Dec   Southern Asia

The submarines of the Dutch East Indies Fleet, which are ready for operations, take up their positions: *K-XII* and *O16* on the E coast of the Malayan peninsula, *K-XI*, *K-XIII* and *O19* in the Karimata Strait and *K-XIV*, *K-XV*, *K-XVI* and *K-XVII* off Kuching.

2–5 Dec   Mediterranean

The Italian submarine *Ametista* operates S of Crete.

4–11 Dec   Mediterranean

In operations in the area of the Peloponnese, the British submarine *Trusty* (Lt-Cdr Batstone) sinks one ship of 3586 tons on 4 Dec, *Talisman* (Lt-Cdr Willmott) sinks one ship of 4013 tons in a Brindisi–Benghazi convoy on 11 Dec and *Truant* (Lt-Cdr Haggard) torpedoes, also on 11 Dec, the torpedo boat *Alcione*, which is beached. The British submarine *Perseus* is lost, probably on a mine, in this area.

4–7 Dec   Southern Asia

On the morning of 4 Dec the Japanese Malaya landing group sets out from Samah (Hainan) with 18 transports; on board are 26640 troops of the 5th Inf Div (Lt-Gen Matsui) and the 56th Inf Regt of the 18th

Inf Div. The escort consists of the 3rd DD Flotilla with the cruiser *Sendai* and the destroyers of the 12th DD Div (*Murakumo*, *Shinonome*, *Shirakumo* and *Usugumo*), the 19th (*Isonami*, *Uranami*, *Shikinami* and *Ayanami*) and the 20th (*Amagiri*, *Asagiri* and *Yugiri*). Vice-Adm Ozawa's flagship, the heavy cruiser *Chokai*, accompanies the convoy with the destroyer *Sagiri*.

At the same time, the 7th Cruiser Sqn (Rear-Adm Kurita), comprising the heavy cruisers *Kumano*, *Mikuma*, *Mogami* and *Suzuya*, and the 11th DD Div (destroyers *Fubuki*, *Hatsuyuki* and *Shirayuki*), sets out as a covering force. On 4 Dec Vice-Adm Kondo puts to sea from the Pescadores with the 1st Div of the 4th Cruiser Sqn, comprising the heavy cruisers *Atago* and *Takao*, and the 2nd Div of the 3rd BB Sqn with the battleships *Haruna* and *Kongo*, as a distant escort force for the Malaya and Luzon landings. The plan is to take up a position in the South China Sea. The heavy ships are screened by the destroyers of the 4th DD Div (*Arashi*, *Hagikaze*, *Maikaze* and *Nowake*), the 2nd Group of the 6th DD Div (*Ikazuchi* and *Inazuma*) and the 8th DD Div (*Asashio*, *Oshio*, *Michishio* and *Arashio*). On 5 Dec the convoy is joined by the minesweepers (Sokaitei) *W2*, *3* and *4* from Camranh Bay and by the minesweepers (Sokaitei) *W1*, *5* and *6*, a submarine-chaser division, the minelayer *Hatsutaka* and two transports from the Poulo Condore Islands. In the afternoon the Southern Expeditionary Fleet sets out from Saigon with the cruiser *Kashii* and four transports and the frigate *Shimushu* with three transports carrying units of the 143rd Inf Regt of the 55th Div. They join the convoy S of Cape Camao on 6 Dec. In this area the Japanese forces are, in part, located and reported by British air reconnaissance on 6 Dec, but contact is lost owing to bad weather. An RAF Catalina flying boat is shot down by Japanese fighters at mid-day on 7 Dec (in point of time the first military action in the 'Greater East Asian War').

To cover the operation, the submarines *I-121* and *I-122* have laid barrages each containing 42 mines off the NE exits from Singapore during the night 6–7 Dec. The auxiliary minelayer *Tatsumiya Maru* lays a barrage of 456 mines between the islands of Tioman and Anamba, and, N of that, the submarines *I-54* and *I-55* take up positions NE of Kuantan and *I-53* N of Anamba. In the area of Trengganu, *I-57*, *I-58*, *I-62*, *I-64* and *I-66* form a patrol line and *I-57* is stationed NE of Redang. At mid-day on 7 Dec the convoy divides up into its attack groups. From the Southern Expeditionary

Fleet one transport proceeds to Prachuab, two to Jumbhorn, one with *Kashii* to Bandon and three with *Shimushu* to Nakhorn to block the Kra Isthmus. The main force, of 17 transports, the 20th and 12th DD Divs, four minesweepers, the submarine-chaser division and nine assault vessels, proceeds to Singora and Patani, while *Sendai*, with the 19th DD Div, the minesweepers *Sokaitei W2* and *3*, submarine-chasers and three transports, goes to Khota Bharu. The flagship *Chokai* and the *Sagiri* join the Kurita group S of Cape Camao.

6–15 Dec   Southern Asia
Operation by the Japanese South Philippines Force from Palau. On 6 Dec a force consisting of the 5th Cruiser Sqn (Rear-Adm Takagi) with *Haguro*, *Myoko* and *Nachi*, the 4th Carrier Sqn with *Ryujo* and the destroyer *Shiokaze* and the 2nd DD Flotilla with the cruiser *Jintsu*, the 15th DD Div (*Kuroshio*, *Oyashio*, *Hayashio* and *Natsushio*) and the 16th DD Div (*Hatsukaze*, *Amatsukaze*, *Yukikaze* and *Tokitsukaze*) sets out from Palau. While the cruisers take up a covering position W of Mindanao, *Ryujo* flies off 13 bombers with nine fighters to make a raid on Davao in the morning of 8 Dec. At the same time the 15th DD Div enters the Gulf of Davao and the remainder of the 2nd DD Flotilla provides a rendezvous off the approach. On the same day (8 Dec) an assault force (Rear-Adm Kubo) sets out from Palau with the cruiser *Nagara*, the 22nd DD Div (*Umikaze*, *Yamakaze*, *Kawakaze* and *Suzukaze*), the 11th Carrier Sqn with the seaplane carriers *Chitose* and *Mizuho*, the minelayers *Itsukushima* and *Yaeyama* (17th ML Div) and seven transports. On the way to the NW it joins up on 9 and 10 Dec with Takagi's force. During the night 10–11 Dec Rear-Adm Kobayashi, with the minelayer *Itsukushima*, escorted by the destroyers *Kuroshio* and *Oyashio*, lays 300 mines in the San Bernardino Strait and the minelayer *Yaeyama* with the cruiser *Jintsu* and the destroyers *Hayashio* and *Natsushio* 133 mines in the Surigao Strait. The destroyers frustrate with depth charges an attack by the American submarine *S39*. During the night 11–12 Dec the assault force (Attack Force 4) lands a battalion of 2500 men of the 16th Inf Div near Legaspi.

6–16 Dec   Mediterranean
The U-boats *U431* and *U557* arrive in the operational area between Alexandria and Tobruk from the Western Mediterranean. On 6 and 10 Dec *U431* misses one destroyer and one steamer and on 13 Dec torpedoes the water tanker *Myriel* (3560 tons). *U557*

is rammed and sunk in error by the Italian torpedo boat *Orione* in the Aegean on her return to Salamina.

6–23 Dec   North Atlantic
More German U-boats are transferred to the Mediterranean. After *U206*, which was to have sailed there, has been sunk in the Bay of Biscay on 30 Nov by Whitley 'B' of No 502 Sqn RAF, *U208*, *U372* and *U375*, which are operating W of Gibraltar, are detached on 6 Dec for transfer to the Eastern Mediterranean; *U568*, *U374*, *U573* and *U453* follow on 7 Dec. *U372*, *U375* and *U453* pass through the Straits of Gibraltar on 9 Dec and *U568*, *U374* and *U208* on 11 Dec. In the process, *U374* (Lt v Fischel) sinks the British A/S trawlers *Rosabelle* and *Lady Shirley* and *U208* is sunk by the British corvette *Bluebell*. On 13 Dec *U453* (Lt-Cdr v Schlippenbach) sinks one Spanish ship of 4202 tons E of Gibraltar. After several attempts, *U573* (Lt-Cdr Heinsohn) breaks through the Straits of Gibraltar on 21 Dec and sinks one ship of 5289 tons. On 11 Dec *U74*, *U77*, *U569*, *U83* and *U432* receive orders to proceed to the Eastern Mediterranean. They pass through the Straits of Gibraltar on 16–17 Dec but *U432* and *U569* are damaged by Swordfish aircraft and have to return. Of the boats ordered into the Eastern Mediterranean on 18–19 Dec, *U451* is sunk by Swordfish 'A' of No 812 Sqn FAA and *U202* is damaged and compelled to return. *U133* and *U577* come through on 23 and 21 Dec respectively.

7 Dec   North Atlantic
The Canadian corvette *Windflower* sinks during convoy operations following a collision in fog with the SS *Zypenberg*.

7 Dec   Pacific
Japanese attack on Pearl Harbor. The Japanese Force (see 26 Nov for its composition) reaches the take-off point N of Oahu and flies off the first wave (Cdr* Fuchida) at 0600 hrs. It consists of 50 high-level bombers, 40 torpedo bombers, 51 dive-bombers and 43 fighters. Shortly afterwards, the second wave takes off with 54 high-level bombers, 81 dive-bombers and 36 fighters. In a surprise strike, they knock out the American air defence and sink the battleships *Arizona* (flagship Rear-Adm Kidd†, Capt v Valkenburgh†) with 47 officers and 1056 men, *California* (flagship Vice-Adm Pye, Capt Bunkley) with six officers and 92 men, *Nevada*, *Oklahoma* (Capt Bode) with 20 officers and 395 men, *West Virginia* (Capt Bennion†) with two officers and 103 men, the minelayer *Oglala* and the target ship *Utah*; heavily damaged are the battleships *Maryland* (Capt

Godwin), *Pennsylvania* (Capt Cooke) and *Tennessee* (Capt Reordan), the light cruisers *Helena*, *Honolulu* and *Raleigh*, the flying boat tender *Curtiss*, the destroyers *Cassin*, *Downes* and *Shaw* and the repair ship *Vestal*. 92 naval and 96 army aircraft are destroyed. Losses in personnel are 2403 dead and 1178 wounded. The Japanese lose five torpedo bombers, 15 dive-bombers and nine fighters with 55 men, and five midget submarines. Among the ships undamaged are the heavy cruisers *New Orleans* and *San Francisco*, the light cruisers *Detroit*, *Phoenix* and *St Louis*, the destroyers *Selfridge*, *Case*, *Tucker*, *Reid*, *Conyngham*, *Monaghan*, *Farragut*, *Dale*, *Aylwin*, *Phelps*, *MacDonough*, *Worden*, *Dewey*, *Hull*, *Henley*, *Patterson*, *Ralph Talbot*, *Jarvis*, *Mugford*, *Helm*, *Cummings*, *Blue*, *Bagley* and *Schley*, the destroyer-minelayers *Preble*, *Pruitt*, *Sicard* and *Tracy*, the fast minesweepers *Ramsay*, *Gamble*, *Montgomery*, *Trever*, *Breese*, *Zane*, *Perry* and *Wasmuth*, the submarines *Cachalot*, *Narwhal*, *Gudgeon*, *Dolphin* and *Tautog* and numerous other auxiliary ships. There are at sea in the area of Oahu the cruiser *Minneapolis*, the destroyer *Litchfield* and the submarines *Thresher*, *Plunger*, *Pollack* and *Pompano*. En route to Midway is TF.11 (Rear-Adm Newton), with the carrier *Lexington*, whose mission has been to bring aircraft of the Marine Corps to Midway, the cruisers *Astoria*, *Chicago* and *Portland* and the destroyers *Porter*, *Flusser*, *Drayton*, *Lamson* and *Mahan*. The submarine *Trout* is stationed near Midway. The Japanese destroyers *Akebono* and *Ushio* are not, however, impeded in their shelling of Midway.

TF.8 (Vice-Adm Halsey), which set out from Pearl Harbor on 24 Nov with the carrier *Enterprise*, the cruisers *Chester*, *Northampton* and *Salt Lake City* and the destroyers *Balch*, *Gridley*, *Craven*, *McCall*, *Maury*, *Dunlap*, *Fanning*, *Benham* and *Ellett*, is returning to Oahu after flying off aircraft to Wake on 4 Dec. The aircraft from *Enterprise* run into the Japanese attack as they arrive over Ford Island.

7–10 Dec   Mediterranean
The sloops *Flamingo* and *Yarra* escort the last supply convoy to Tobruk. In an air attack on 7 Dec, *Flamingo* is rendered unmanoeuvrable as a result of several near misses and has to be taken in tow by *Yarra*. The Australian cruiser *Hobart*, which is escorting the transport *Breconshire* on her way back from Malta, is summoned to the scene and provides cover. On 8 Dec the British 8th Army re-establishes land communications with the beleaguered garrison in Tobruk. Units of the British Mediterranean Fleet

and transports have brought, during the siege of Tobruk from 12 Apr, 32667 troops and 33946 tons of supplies to the garrison and have evacuated 34115 troops, 7516 wounded and 7097 prisoners. In the process, two destroyers, three sloops, seven submarine-chasers and minesweepers, one gunboat, one minelaying cruiser, seven supply ships and six A-lighters have been sunk and seven destroyers, one sloop, 11 submarine-chasers and minesweepers, three gunboats, three A-lighters, one schooner, one troop transport and six merchant ships have been damaged.

7–12 Dec   Southern Asia

Attack by the Japanese North Philippines Force on North Luzon. At first light on 8 Dec, 192 aircraft of the 21st and 23rd Naval Air Flotillas of the 11th Air Fleet (Vice-Adm Tsukahara) attack from Formosa the US air bases at Clark and Iba Fields and destroy 12 B-17 bombers and 30 fighters while losing seven of their own number. Aircraft of the 5th Army Air Div attack from Formosa, Tuguegarao and Baguio. A surprise force (Rear-Adm Hirose), which set out from Takao (Formosa) on 7 Dec, comprising the destroyer *Yamagumo*, the torpedo boats *Chidori*, *Hatsukari*, *Monadzuru* and *Tomodzuru*, two minesweepers, two gunboats, two patrol boats, nine submarine-chasers and two transports, lands in the morning of 8 Dec an assault group on the island of Bataan, where an immediate start is made in establishing an airfield. A second force (Rear-Adm Hara), with the cruiser *Natori*, the destroyers *Fumitsuki*, *Satsuki*, *Nagatsuki*, *Minatsuki*, *Harukaze* and *Hatakaze*, three minesweepers, nine submarine-chasers and six transports, sets out on 7 Dec from Mako (Pescadores) and lands 2000 troops of an advanced detachment of the 14th Army near Aparri on the N coast of Luzon early on 10 Dec. In an attack by P-40 fighters and B-17 bombers of the US Far East Air Force, the minesweeper (Sokaitei) *W19* is hit and has to be beached. A third force (Rear-Adm Nishimura), comprising the cruiser *Naka*, the destroyers *Murasame*, *Yudachi*, *Harusame* and *Samidare* (2nd DD Div) and *Asagumo*, *Minegumo* and *Natsugumo* (4th DD Div), six minesweepers, nine submarine-chasers and six transports, which has also set out from Mako, tries on 10 Dec to land some 2000 troops near Padan on the NW tip of Luzon. But it has to abandon the plan because of the weather. The minesweeper *W10* is lost as a result of action by US aircraft and two transports are damaged. On 11 Dec a landing further S near Vingan succeeds.

The operation is covered by the Commander of the 3rd Fleet, Vice-Adm Takahashi, with the cruisers *Ashigara*, *Kuma* and *Maya*, the destroyers *Asakaze* and *Matsukaze* and the aircraft depot ships *Sanuki Maru* and *Sanyo Maru*. The latter is hit on 14 Dec by an unexploded torpedo from the US submarine *Seawolf*. After successfully carrying out the landings, the air units of the 11th Naval Air Fleet and the 5th Army Air Div make new heavy attacks on the US air bases on Luzon (12 Dec) and eliminate the US Far East Air Force. What is left withdraws to Mindanao and Australia.

7–13 Dec   Black Sea

Five transports and the cruisers *Krasny Kavkaz* and *Krasny Krym*, the flotilla leader *Kharkov* and the destroyers *Bodry* and *Nezamozhnik* transport the 388th Rifle Div (10582 troops) from Novorossisk and Tuapse to Sevastopol.

7–18 Dec   Pacific

The Japanese 3rd SM Flotilla operates in the area S of Hawaii. On 8 Dec *I-68* and *I-69* are attacked with depth charges S of Pearl Harbor. On 10 Dec an aircraft of the US carrier *Enterprise* sinks *I-70*. *I-75* (Cdr* Inouc) and *I-72* (Cdr Togami) each sink one ship, of 3253 tons and 5113 tons respectively. On the return, on 22 Dec, *I-68* shells Johnston and *I-71* and *I-72* Palmyra.

7–27 Dec   Pacific

In the pursuit of a US carrier sighted by a submarine, the Japanese 1st SM Flotilla makes a sortie on 10 Dec to the US West Coast and takes up positions between Vancouver and Los Angeles. On the way and in the operational area the submarines have the following successes: *I-26* (Cdr* M. Yokota) sinks one ship of 2140 tons, *I-10* (Cdr* Kayahara) sinks one ship of 4473 tons, *I-9* (Cdr* Fujii) sinks one ship of 5645 tons, *I-17* (Cdr* Nishino) sinks one ship of 6912 tons and damages one ship of 7038 tons, *I-23* (Cdr* Shibata) damages two ships of 8890 tons, *I-19* (Cdr* Narahara) damages two ships of 16458 tons, *I-21* (Cdr* Matsumura) sinks one ship of 8272 tons and damages one ship of 6418 tons and *I-25* (Cdr* Tabata) damages one ship of 8684 tons. On 27 Dec the boats start the return journey. *I-19* reconnoitres over Pearl Harbor with her aircraft on 8 Jan.

7 Dec–31 Jan   Pacific

The submarine cruisers of the Japanese 2nd SM Flotilla operate in the area S of Hawaii. Many ships are sighted but only *I-4* (Cdr* Nakagawa) sinks one ship, of 4858 tons. On 17 Dec the command boat *I-7* reconnoitres over Pearl Harbor with her aircraft. *I-1* shells the island of Hilo on 30–31 Dec. On

11 Jan *I-6* (Cdr* Inaba) torpedoes the US carrier *Saratoga*.

8 Dec   China

Japanese Army and Navy units, supported by the old armoured cruiser *Izumo*, occupy the international settlement in Shanghai. The British gunboat *Peterel* sinks after a short engagement and the US gunboat *Wake* surrenders. In addition, the Japanese seize 13 British, US and Panamanian merchant ships totalling 15586 tons and four other ships of 18744 tons, including the US freighter *President Harrison* (10509 tons) on the Wangpo.

8–10 Dec   Pacific

After several air attacks, in which the US minesweeper *Penguin* is sunk, transports with BF 5 (7th GB Div, 15th MS Div and 59th and 60th SC Divs) land parts of the South Sea Detachment of the Army and some 700 naval assault troops on Guam. The operation is under the command of Rear-Adm Goto, who supports the action with the 6th Cruiser Sqn, comprising *Aoba*, *Kinugasa*, *Kako* and *Furutaka* and the destroyers *Kikuzuki*, *Uzuki* and *Yuzuki*. The American garrison is overwhelmed after brief resistance.

8–10 Dec   Central Pacific

The 19th ML Div of the Japanese 4th Fleet (Vice-Adm Inoue), with the minelayers *Okinoshima*, *Tokiwa* and *Tsugaru* and two transports, proceeds from Kwajalein and makes landings on the Gilbert Islands of Tarawa and Makin (Butaritari) on 9 and 10 Dec.

8–11 Dec   Mediterranean

The British destroyers *Jervis* (Capt Mack), *Jackal* and *Javelin*, supported by the light cruisers *Naiad* (Rear-Adm Vian), *Euryalus* and *Galatea* and the destroyers *Griffin* and *Hotspur*, make a sortie against German and Italian supply traffic to North Africa and shell Derna. Italian torpedo aircraft severely damage *Jackal* with air torpedoes.

8–12 Dec   South Asia

The Japanese transports of the Malaya Force (see 4–7 Dec), which have arrived on the evening of 7 Dec off their assault areas, begin in the night 7–8 Dec the first landings of the Pacific War. In the N they are impeded by the sea swell but encounter no resistance from the Thai forces; in the S they meet resistance at Kota Bharu. In attacks by British aircraft, one transport of 9749 tons is destroyed and the two others are damaged. In the afternoon of 8 Dec Force Z (Adm Phillips) sets out from Singapore with the battleship *Prince of Wales*, the battlecruiser *Repulse* and the destroyers *Electra*, *Express*, *Tenedos* and *Vampire* to attack the Japanese invasion fleet. After passing E of the

Anamba Island, the Force is reported in the afternoon of 9 Dec by the most easterly submarine *I-65* of the patrol line. Because of the inaccuracy of the position given, the air reconnaissance which is provided, and the submarines operating on the report, do not find the targets. Force Z, after dismissing the destroyer *Tenedos*, proceeds northwards in order to attack the invasion fleet in the morning at Kota Bharu. But, as a result of a new and false reconnaissance report, it turns away to the SW on the evening of 9 Dec to attack a Japanese landing near Kuantan on the morning of 10 Dec.

On the Japanese side, Vice-Adm Kondo, who with his force (cruisers *Atago* and *Takao*, battleships *Haruna* and *Kongo* and destroyers *Arashi*, *Hagikaze*, *Nowake*, *Maikaze*, *Ikazuchi*, *Inazuma*, *Asashio*, *Oshio*, *Michishio* and *Arashio*) is proceeding S from Poulo Condore, orders Rear-Adm Kurita in the night to join him with the cruisers *Kumano*, *Mikuma*, *Mogami* and *Suzuya* and the destroyers *Fubuki*, *Hatsuyuki* and *Shirayuki* and Vice-Adm Ozawa with the cruiser *Chokai* and the destroyer *Sagiri*. From the assault area the cruiser *Sendai* with the destroyers *Asagiri*, *Murakumo*, *Shinonome*, *Shirakumo*, *Usugumo*, *Amagiri* and *Yugiri*, and *Ayanami*, *Isonami*, *Shikinami* and *Uranami* receive orders to close up, as do the cruisers *Kinu* and *Yura* stationed between Poulo Condore and Kurita.

During its advance to Kuantan, Force Z is sighted shortly after midnight by the Japanese submarine *I-59* (Lt-Cdr Ohashi), is unsuccessfully attacked with torpedoes and is shadowed for five and a half hours. Air reconnaissance by ten aircraft of the 22nd Naval Air Flotilla (Rear-Adm Matsunaga), provided as a result of the submarine's reports, finds Force Z and leads 27 bombers and 61 torpedo aircraft from the flotilla (which have already taken off) to the scene. They sink *Repulse* (Capt Tennant) and *Prince of Wales* (Capt Leach†, Adm Phillips†) in perfectly co-ordinated torpedo and bomb attacks. The destroyers rescue 1285 and 796 members, respectively, of the crews of the two ships.

8–13 Dec   Central Pacific
First Japanese attack on Wake. The 6th DD Flotilla (Rear-Adm Kajioka) sets out from Kwajalein with the cruiser *Yubari* and the destroyers *Hayate* and *Oite* (29th DD Div) and *Mutsuki*, *Yayoi*, *Mochizuki* and *Kisaragi* (30th DD Div), the fast transports *P32* and *P33* and two transports with naval assault troops on board. Shore-based air formations attack Wake from Kwajalein on 8, 9 and 10 Dec. The operation is supported

by the cruisers *Tatsuta* and *Tenryu* (18th Cruiser Sqn) and the submarines *Ro-60* and *Ro-61* off Wake.

During the night 10–11 Dec the invasion force arives off Wake but the attempted landing, which is supported by the cruisers and destroyers, is repulsed by the island's garrison (450 marines under Maj Devereux) and an air squadron. The destroyers *Hayate* and *Kisaragi* are lost as a result of the shelling by the American coastal batteries and air attack. On 13 Dec the remainder of the force returns to Kwajalein.

8–15 Dec   South Asia
The minelaying submarines of the 6th Flotilla (Rear-Adm Kono) lay barrages on 8–9 Dec: *I-121* (Cdr Yendo) and *I-122* (Cdr Utsuki) off Singapore, *I-123* (Cdr Ueno) off Balabac and *I-124* (Cdr Kishigami) off Manila. One ship is lost on the Manila barrage and *I-124* sinks another ship with a torpedo, making 3404 tons sunk in all.

8–23 Dec   Arctic
The British convoy PQ.6, with seven ships, proceeds from Hvalfjord to Murmansk without making contact with the enemy. Two ships remain there on 20 Dec; the other five go on with a Soviet ice-breaker but on 23 Dec they get stuck in the ice in Molotovsk and have to spend the winter there.

8–31 Dec   South West Pacific
The submarines of the US Asiatic Fleet are stationed from 8 to 9 Dec partly in defensive positions round the Philippines, e.g. *Seal* near Vingan and *S-36*, *Saury* and *Seawolf* near the San Bernardino Strait, and partly in offensive positions, e.g. *S-38*, *S-37*, *S-41* near Mindoro, *Sculpin* E of Luzon, *S-39*, *S-40*, *Tarpon*, *Shark*, *Sailfish*, and *Stingray* off Lingayen Gulf, *Perch* and *Permit* W of Luzon, *Searaven* and *Sturgeon* near Formosa, *Pike*, *Snapper* and *Swordfish* near Hainan, *Spearfish* off Camranh, *Sargo* in the Gulf of Siam and *Skipjack* near Palau. The operations of the boats, which make numerous attacks on Japanese ships and formations, are restricted by torpedo failures (depth-keeping and magnetic fusing—see German/Norwegian operation). The only successes are by *Swordfish* (Cdr Smith), which sinks two ships of 11391 tons and damages one of 8407 tons, *Seal* (Lt-Cdr Hurd) which sinks one of 856 tons and *S-38* (Lt Chappell) which sinks one of 5445 tons off Lingayen Gulf; in addition, *Seawolf* damages one ship of 8360 tons, *Perch* damages one of 7190 tons and *Sailfish* and *S-39* each miss one ship in one attack.

9 Dec   Arctic
On the way to Kirkenes, the German U-boat *U134* (Lt-Cdr Schendel) sinks in error

the German steamer *Steinbek* (2184 tons) off Tanafjord.

10 Dec   Japan/Western France
The German blockade-runner *Burgenland* (7320 tons, Capt Schütz) reaches Bordeaux from Kobe.

10 Dec–15 Jan 1942   North Atlantic
While there are only very few U-boats in the North Atlantic returning or transferring to France, the convoys are running almost undisturbed, directed according to 'Ultra' information. US and Canadian escort groups cover the following convoys: US TU.4.1.1, with the destroyers *Dallas*, *Ellis*, *Gleaves* and *Upshur* and the Coast Guard cutter *Ingham*, escorts HX.164 and ON.49; Canadian TU.4.1.1, with the destroyer *Burnham* (RN) and the corvettes *Chilliwack*, *Napanee*, *Trillium*, *Summerside*, *Algoma* and *Drumheller*, escorts SC.59 and ONS.50; US TU.4.1.8, with the destroyers *Swanson*, *Buck*, *McCormick*, *Greer* and *Herbert*, escorts HX.165 and ON.51; and Canadian TU.4.1.15, with the destroyer *Saguenay* and the corvettes *Shediac*, *Camrose*, *Spikenard* and *Wetaskiwin*, escorts SC.60 and ONS.52. After the dispersal of ONS.52 from 17 to 19 Jan, the U-boats on the way to Newfoundland, *U553* (Lt-Cdr Thurmann) and *U87* (Lt Berger), each sink a ship, of 8106 and 8087 tons respectively, and *U86* (Lt-Cdr Schug) torpedoes one of 8627 tons.

US TU.4.1.4, with the destroyers *Plunkett*, *Decatur*, *Cole* and *Badger* and the Coast Guard cutter *Campbell* escorts HX.166 and ON.53; and Canadian TU.4.1.16, with the destroyer *Niagara* and the corvettes *Lethbridge*, *Dianthus*, *Nanaimo*, *Galt*, and *Matapedia*, escorts SC.61 and ONS.54 (*Niagara* and *Lethbridge* have to return owing to weather damage).

The British escort groups accompany the convoys from EASTOMP to MOMP and take the eastbound convoys there: EG.5, with the destroyer *Caldwell* and the corvettes *Honeysuckle*, *Gentian* and *Alisma*, escorts ONS.48 and SC.60; EG.1, with the destroyers *Sabre* and *Scimitar* and the corvettes *Sunflower* and *Alisma*, escorts ON.49 and HX.166; EG.6, with the destroyers *Broke* and *Chelsea* and the corvettes *Columbine*, *Camellia*, *Pimpernel* and *Barrie*, escorts ONS.50 and SC.61; EG.8, with the destroyer *Watchman* and the corvettes *Arabis*, *Monkshood* and *Snowflake* and one A/S trawler, escorts ON.51 and HX.167; and EG.7, with the destroyer *St Albans* and the corvettes *Hibiscus*, *Montbretia* (RNoN), *Rose* (RNoN) and *Kiwi* (RNZN), escorts ON.52 and HX.168. One of the three U-boats operating in the North Atlantic, *U43*

(Lt-Cdr Lüth), sinks one straggler from HX.168 of 5246 tons.

11 Dec General Situation
Declaration of war on America by Germany and Italy.

11–14 Dec Pacific
The first US submarines *Gudgeon*, *Plunger* and *Pollack* leave Pearl Harbor for operations in Japanese home waters.

12 Dec South Asia
The Allied ships left in Singapore—the British cruisers *Danae*, *Dragon* and *Durban*, the British destroyers *Encounter*, *Stronghold* and *Tenedos*, the Dutch cruiser *Java* with the destroyer *Evertsen* and the Australian minesweepers *Burnie*, *Bendigo*, *Goulburn* and *Maryborough*—are employed on escort duties between Singapore and Sunda Strait. They are joined on 8 Dec by the British destroyers *Scout* and *Thanet*, which have broken out of Hong Kong, by the destroyers *Electra*, *Express* and *Jupiter*, which have returned from the operation with Force Z, and by the Australian *Vampire*.

13 Dec South Asia
British forces evacuate Kowloon, the suburb of Hong Kong on the Chinese mainland, before the attack by the Japanese 38th Inf Div.

13–19 Dec Mediterranean
Italian convoy operation M41 to North Africa. The intention is to bring eight transports in three convoys with seven destroyers and two torpedo boats to Benghazi, covered by the whole operational part of the Italian Fleet comprising four battleships, five cruisers and eighteen destroyers. Of the British submarines *Unbeaten*, *Utmost* and *Upright* (Lt Wraith) stationed off the Gulf of Taranto, the last sinks the motor ships *Fabio Filzi* and *Carlo del Greco* (each 6836 tons) in the morning of 13 Dec as they proceed with the destroyers *Da Recco* and *Usodimare* to the Taranto assembly point.

In the afternoon of 13 Dec the motor ships *Monginevro*, *Napoli* and *Vettor Pisani* put to sea with three destroyers and the German freighter *Ankara* sails with two destroyers as two groups. In addition, two freighters put to sea with two destroyers from Argostoli. From Taranto there set out as close covering forces Sqn Adm Bergamini with the battleship *Duilio*, the cruisers *Garibaldi*, *Gorizia* and *Montecuccoli* and three destroyers, and Div Adm De Courten with the battleship *Doria*, the cruisers *Duca d'Aosta* (F) and *Attendolo* and three destroyers. Two groups of destroyers follow, one of three and one of four; the latter is to join the distant covering force from Naples to which the battleships *Littorio* and *Vittorio Veneto* and four

destroyers, under Adm Iachino, belong. When British submarines report the movements of Italian forces in the Ionian Sea, Rear-Adm Vian puts to sea in the evening of 13 Dec with the cruisers *Euryalus*, *Galatea* and *Naiad* and destroyers (Force B) in order to attack the Italian convoys, after joining up with Force K consisting of the cruisers *Aurora*, *Neptune* and *Penelope* and destroyers. In the evening of 14 Dec the British submarine *Urge* (Lt-Cdr Tomkinson), stationed off the Straits of Messina, torpedoes *Vittorio Veneto*. The latter reaches Taranto, but the Italian operation is then abandoned and the convoys and covering forces return. In the process the two freighters of the Argostoli convoy, *Capo Orsam* and *Iseo* (accompanied by the destroyers *Strale* and *Turbine*), collide and drop out. British Force K, against which the Italian submarines *Santarosa*, *Narvalo*, *Squalo*, *Veniero* and *Topazio* are stationed E of Malta, remains in Malta. Force B is recalled. The Italian boats *Ascianghi*, *Dagabur* and *Galatea*, stationed S of Crete, are too far N; the last misses the returning British submarine *Talisman*. On 15 Dec the German U-boat *U557* (Lt-Cdr Paulshen) sinks, off Alexandria, the cruiser *Galatea* (Capt Sims†) from the returning Force B. The returning U-boat is lost in the Aegean after a collision with the Italian torpedo boat *Orione*.

British convoy operation to Malta. On 15 Dec British Force B (Rear-Adm Vian), with the cruisers *Naiad*, *Euryalus* and *Carlisle* and the destroyers *Jervis*, *Kimberley*, *Kingston*, *Kipling*, *Nizam* (RAN), *Havock*, *Hasty* and *Decoy*, sets out to bring the transport *Breconshire* (9776 tons) from Alexandria to Malta. On 16 Dec Force K (Capt Agnew) sets out from Malta with the cruisers *Aurora* and *Penelope* and the destroyers *Lance* and *Lively*, as well as the destroyer division (Capt Stokes), comprising *Sikh*, *Legion*, *Maori* and *Isaac Sweers* (Dutch), to meet the transport on 17 Dec. The cruiser *Neptune* is to follow with the destroyers *Jaguar* and *Kandahar*.

Italian convoy operation M42. In the afternoon of 16 Dec one convoy sets out from Taranto with the motor ships *Monginevro*, *Napoli* and *Vettor Pisani*, escorted by the destroyers *Vivaldi*, *Da Noli*, *Da Recco*, *Malocello*, *Pessagno* and *Zeno* and a second with the freighter *Ankara*, the destroyer *Saetta* and the torpedo boat *Pegaso*. Adm Bergamini provides a close covering force with the battleship *Duilio*, the cruisers (7th Div, Div Adm de Courten) *Duca d'Aosta*, *Attendolo* and *Montecuccoli* and the destroyers *Ascari*, *Aviere* and *Camicia Nera*.

The distant covering force, which sets out at the same time, is formed by Adm Iachino with the battleships *Doria*, *Cesare* and *Littorio*, the heavy cruisers (3rd Div, Div Adm Parona) *Gorizia* and *Trento* and the destroyers *Granatiere*, *Bersagliere*, *Alpino*, *Fuciliere*, *Corazziere*, *Carabiniere*, *Usodimare*, *Maestrale*, *Oriani* and *Gioberti*.

First Battle of Sirte. On 17 Dec British Forces B and K join up. Italian air attacks are unsuccessful. As a result of reports from his reconnaissance aircraft, Adm Iachino turns towards the British force and engages it shortly after dark. No results are achieved by either side because both forces try to cover their convoys without knowing about the worthwhile targets on the other side.

On 18 Dec Rear-Adm Vian returns to Alexandria and *Breconshire* arrives in Malta with Force K. The Italian convoy then continues its journey to Tripoli. Off Tripoli, Force K, with the cruisers *Aurora*, *Neptune* and *Penelope* and the destroyers *Havock*, *Kandahar*, *Lance*, and *Lively*, is directed to the convoy but soon runs into the Italian mine barrage 'T' (see 3 June 1941). *Neptune* (Capt O'Connor†) sinks with about 550 members of her crew after hitting four mines. Only one survivor can be rescued. *Kandahar* also has to be abandoned after hitting a mine. *Aurora* (Capt Agnew) is severely and *Penelope* (Capt Nicholl) lightly damaged. During the night 18–19 Dec the Vian force returns to Alexandria and is unsuccessfully attacked by *U371* (Lt-Cdr Driver).

Through the harbour boom gap opened for the ships to come in, three Italian human torpedo teams (Lt-Cdr Durand de la Penne with Sgt-Maj Bianchi, Capt Marceglia with L/Cpl Schergat and Capt Martellotta with Sgt-Maj Marino), launched from the Italian submarine *Scirè* (Cdr* Borghese), enter the harbour and lay their explosive charges under the battleships *Queen Elizabeth* (Capt Barry) and *Valiant* (Capt Morgan) and the Norwegian tanker *Sagona* (7554 tons). All ships come to rest on the bottom badly damaged. The destroyer *Jervis*, lying alongside the *Sagona*, is also damaged.

13–26 Dec South Asia
Landing by the second wave of the Malaya Force. On 13 Dec the second wave sets out from Camranh Bay with the bulk of the 5th Inf Div and the supporting troops of the Japanese 25th Army (Gen Yamashita) on 39 transports. It is accompanied by the cruiser *Kashii*, the frigate *Shimushu*, the minesweeper *W4* and the 3rd DD Flotilla with the cruiser *Sendai* and the destroyers *Isonami*, *Uranami*, *Shikinami* and *Ayanami* (19th DD Div), *Arashi*, *Hagikaze*, *Maikaze* and *Nowake* (4th DD Div) and *Amagiri*,

Asagiri and *Yugiri* (20th DD Div). Vice-Adm Ozawa provides a covering force with the heavy cruiser *Chokai* and the light cruiser *Kinu*, to which are added the 2nd Div of the 7th Cruiser Sqn (*Mikuma* and *Mogami*) and the destroyers *Hatsuyuki* and *Shirayuki* from Poulo Condore on 14 Dec. They take up a covering position NE of Kuantan by 17 Dec. During the night 16–17 Dec the submarines *I-58*, *I-57*, *I-56* (which has sunk one ship on 11 Dec) and *I-55* take up a patrol line N of the Anamba Islands and *I-53* and *I-54* W of Natoma Island. During the night 16–17 Dec one transport arrives off Bandon, two off Nakhorn, 31 with the aircraft depot ship *Sagara Maru* flying air cover, the mine-sweeper *W2* and the 11th SC Div off Singora and Patani and five off Kota Bharu. Dutch submarines are deployed from Singapore against the Japanese landings. *K-XII* (Lt-Cdr Coumou) sinks a transport off Kota Bharu on 12 Dec and a tanker on 13 Dec totalling 5457 tons. *O16* (Lt-Cdr Bussemaker) torpedoes four transports of 33953 tons off Patani on 16 Dec but is lost on a British minefield when returning to Singapore. *O20* is sunk on 20 Dec by the Japanese destroyer *Uranami* and *K-XVII* on 24 Dec by other Japanese destroyers in the landing area. Off Camranh Bay, the American submarines *Sargo* and *Swordfish* attempt several attacks on 14 Dec but only the latter sinks one ship of 8663 tons.

Japanese landing on Borneo. Simultaneously with the Malaya convoy, a convoy sets out for Miri (North Borneo) on 13 Dec from Camranh Bay. It consists of 10 transports with the 124th Inf Regt (16th Inf Div) and the 2nd Yokosuka Special Landing Force. Escort for the convoy is provided by the cruiser *Yura* (Rear-Adm Hashimoto) with the destroyers of the 12th DD Div (*Murakumo*, *Shinonome*, *Shirakumo* and *Usugumo*), the submarine-chaser *Ch7* and the aircraft depot ship *Kamikawa Maru*. The support force consists of Rear-Adm Kurita with the cruisers *Kumano* and *Suzuya* and the destroyers *Fubuki* and *Sagiri*. Distant cover for the Malaya and Borneo operations NE of Natoma Island from 15 to 17 Dec is provided by Vice-Adm Kondo with the heavy cruisers *Atago* and *Takao*, the battleships *Haruna* and *Kongo* and the destroyers *Ikazuchi*, *Inazuma*, *Asashio*, *Oshio*, *Michishio* and *Arashio*. To provide cover westwards, the submarines *I-62*, *I-64*, *I-65* and *I-66* are stationed in the passage between Natoma Island and NW Borneo.

Before daylight on 16 Dec the troops are

landed at Miri, Seria and Lutong in N Borneo, where the oilfields are set on fire by the withdrawing Dutch and British forces. On 17 Dec the destroyer *Shinonome* is sunk by the Dutch flying boat 'X-32' with a torpedo, while 'X-33' damages a transport.

On 22 Dec six of the transports leave again with two battalions re-embarked in order to land these troops in Kuching (Sarawak) on 23 Dec. The convoy is accompanied by the cruiser *Yura*, the destroyers *Murakumo*, *Shirakumo* and *Usugumo*, the minesweepers (Sokaitei), *W3* and *W6* and the *Kamikawa Maru*. The cruisers *Kinu*, *Kumano* and *Suzuya*, with the destroyers *Fubuki* and *Sagiri*, form the covering force. W of it the 2nd Div of the 7th Cruiser Sqn (*Mikuma* and *Mogami*) cruises with the attached destroyer *Hatsuyuki*. The approaching convoy is attacked by the Dutch submarine *K-XIV* (Lt-Cdr v Well Groeneveld). One transport of 9849 tons sinks and three more of 19862 tons are damaged. During the night 23–24 Dec *K-XVI* (Lt-Cdr Jarman) sinks the destroyer *Sagiri* but is herself sunk on the return by the Japanese submarine *I-66* (Cdr Yoshitome.) Dutch Martin bombers sink the Japanese minesweeper (Sokaitei) *W6* and one transport of 2827 tons on 26 Dec.

14–17 Dec   South Asia
On 14 Dec 'Gull Force' puts to sea from Port Darwin with 1090 Australian troops on board three Dutch freighters escorted by the Australian cruiser *Adelaide* and the minesweeper *Ballarat*. On 17 Dec the troops are landed in Ambon.

On 16–17 Dec 650 Dutch and Australian troops ('Sparrow Force') are brought from Koepang to Dili in Portuguese Timor by the Dutch coastal defence ship *Soerabaja* with one transport.

14–23 Dec   North Atlantic
Operation by the 'Seeräuber' group against the convoy HG.76. On 14 Dec the convoy of 32 ships (Commodore Fitzmaurice) sets out, escorted by the 36th EG (Cdr Walker) consisting of the sloops *Deptford* and *Stork* and the corvettes *Rhododendron*, *Marigold*, *Convolvulus*, *Pentstemon*, *Gardenia*, *Samphire* and *Vetch*. The support group consists of the escort destroyers *Blankney*, *Exmoor* and *Stanley*, as well as the escort carrier *Audacity* (Cdr MacKendrick). At the same time a U-boat hunter group from Force H, comprising the destroyers *Croome*, *Gurkha*, *Foxhound* and *Nestor* (RAN), sets out. The last sinks *U127* (Lt-Cdr Hansmann) with depth charges on 15 Dec. In addition, a Near East convoy of four ships goes to sea escorted by one destroyer and three

corvettes. Following agents' reports, the 'Seeräuber' group, comprising *U434*, *U131*, *U67*, *U108* and *U107*, is directed to the scene. *U108* (Lt-Cdr Scholtz) sinks an independent Portuguese ship of 4751 tons. Shortly before midnight on 14–15 Dec *U74*, which is on the way to the Mediterranean, sights the Near East convoy, from which *U77* (Lt-Cdr Schonder) sinks one ship of 4972 tons in the night. On 15 Dec air reconnaissance has no success because the convoy goes S along the Moroccan coast. On 16 Dec an Fw 200 of I/KG 40 sights HG.76 at mid-day. But *U67* and *U108*, which approach the area, are driven off. Likewise *U131* is driven off in the night. *U574* is ordered to the area. On 17 Dec the convoy is sighted by *U107*, *U108* and *U131* (Cdr Baumann). The last, after several air attacks and the shooting down of a Swordfish from *Audacity*, is unable to submerge and has to scuttle herself when *Stork*, *Blankney*, *Exmoor* and *Stanley* approach. *U434* (Lt-Cdr Heyda), which has had contact since the evening of 17 Dec, is detected in the morning of 18 Dec and forced to surface by depth charges from the destroyers *Blankney* and *Stanley* and the crew has to abandon the boat. Two of the Fw 200s keeping contact with the convoy are shot down by Martlet fighters from *Audacity*. In the evening *Pentstemon* forces *U107* to submerge and *U67*, after a miss, is driven off by *Convolvulus*. Towards morning on 19 Dec *U574* (Lt Gengelbach) establishes contact and sinks the destroyer *Stanley* shadowing her but is rammed by Cdr Walker in a counter-attack by *Stork* and sinks. *U108*, in the meantime, shells one ship of 2869 tons out of the convoy. In the afternoon Martlets from *Audacity* shoot down two Fw 200s keeping contact, but *U107* (Lt-Cdr Gelhaus) is able to maintain contact and, in the course of 20 and 21 Dec, to bring up *U108*, *U67*, *U567*, *U751* and *U71* (the last pair newly deployed since 20 Dec). *U67* is driven off by an aircraft, and other U-boats by depth charges from *Marigold* and *Samphire*. During the night 21–22 Dec *U567* (Lt-Cdr Endrass) and *U751* (Lt-Cdr Bigalk) attack in quick succession and respectively sink one freighter of 3324 tons and the carrier *Audacity*. *U567* then falls victim to a depth-charge attack by *Deptford*. *U67* (Lt-Cdr Müller-Stöckheim) just misses a catapult ship in the convoy. On 22 Dec *U71* and *U125* (which is on the way to America), and, early on 23 Dec, *U751*, are in contact but they are driven off by the corvette *Vetch* and the destroyers *Vanquisher* and *Witch* which have come up as reinforcements.

14–23 Dec   Central Pacific

Second battle for Wake: American attempt to relieve the island.

On 14 Dec TF.11 (Rear Adm Brown) sets out from Pearl Harbor with the carrier *Lexington*, the cruisers *Chicago*, *Indianapolis* and *Portland* and the destroyers of Desron 1, comprising *Phelps*, *Dewey*, *Hull*, *MacDonough* and *Worden* (Desdiv 1) and *Aylwin*, *Dale* and *Drayton* (Desdiv 2), and the tanker *Neosho* in order to carry out a diversionary raid on Jaluit. On 16 Dec TF.14 (Rear-Adm Fletcher) follows with the carrier *Saratoga* (Rear-Adm Fitch, with 18 Buffalo fighters for Wake), the cruisers *Minneapolis* (F), *Astoria* and *San Francisco* and the destroyers of Desron 4 comprising *Selfridge*, *Henley*, *Blue* and *Helm* (Desdiv 7) and *Jarvis*, *Mugford*, *Patterson* and *Ralph Talbot* (Desdiv 8), with the aircraft depot ship *Tangier* (with supplies for Wake) and the tanker *Neches*. To support the operation and for cover from Hawaii, TF.8 (Vice-Adm Halsey) sets out from Pearl Harbor on 20 Dec with the carrier *Enterprise*, the cruisers *Northampton* (Rear-Adm Spruance), *Chester* and *Salt Lake City* and the Desron 6 destroyers *Balch*, *Craven*, *Gridley*, *McCall* and *Maury* (Desdiv 11) and *Fanning*, *Dunlap*, *Benham* and *Ellet* (Desdiv 12) for the area between Midway and Johnston. On 20 Dec TF.11 is turned away to the N to support the Wake operation and the raid on Jaluit is abandoned.

Japanese attack on Wake. On 20 Dec Rear-Adm Kajioka's Force again sets out from Kwajalein with the cruisers *Tatsuta*, *Tenryu* and *Yubari*, the destroyers *Asanagi*, *Oite* and *Yunagi* (29th DD Div) and *Mochizuki*, *Mutsuki* and *Yayoi* (30th DD Div), with the fast transports *P32* and *P33*, three transports, one minelayer and one aircraft tender to attack Wake. The support force is the 6th Cruiser Sqn (Rear-Adm Goto), comprising the cruisers *Aoba*, *Furutaka*, *Kinugasa* and *Kako* and the 23rd DD Div with *Kikuzuki*, *Uzuki* and *Yuzuki* from Truk. A force from the returning 1st Air Fleet under Rear-Adm Abe, comprising the carriers *Hiryu* and *Soryu*, the heavy cruisers *Chikuma* and *Tone* and the destroyers *Tanikaze* and *Urakaze*, is detached to support the operation. After shore-based aircraft have made attacks on Wake on 12, 14, 15, 16, 17 and 19 Dec, 47 and 39 aircraft from the Japanese carriers make attacks on the island on 21 and 22 Dec respectively. On 22 Dec some 2000 troops from the 2nd Maizuru Special Landing Force are able to land on the island. By 23 Dec they have captured the island with support from the ships. The two fast transports *P32* and *P33* are sunk by American defensive fire.

Because of the difficulty in refuelling at sea, the US Task Forces do not arrive in time and they are recalled on 23 Dec. On the same day Wake surrenders.

15–28 Dec   South West Pacific

On 15 Dec the Australian cruisers *Canberra* and *Perth* leave Sydney to meet, with the New Zealand cruiser *Achilles*, the American cruiser *Pensacola* (which has set out with eight transports for the Philippines from San Francisco on 21 Nov) and to bring her to Brisbane. At the same time, the New Zealand cruiser *Leander* and the large Free French destroyer *Le Triomphant* escort reinforcements from New Zealand to the Fiji Islands and from Sydney to New Caledonia respectively.

On 28 Dec convoy ZK.5, with three large transports (4250 troops and 10000 tons of supplies), sets out from Brisbane for Port Moresby, escorted by the cruisers *Achilles*, *Australia*, *Canberra* and *Perth*, while *Pensacola* proceeds to Darwin with seven of her transports. On 28 Dec US TF.5, comprising the cruiser *Houston* and the destroyers *Alden*, *Edsall* and *Whipple*, bring three important supply ships of the Asiatic Fleet from Surabaya to Port Darwin.

15–29 Dec   Arctic

The Soviet submarines *M-172*, *M-174*, *S-101*, *S-102*, *Shch-401*, *Shch-403* and *Shch-404* operate off the Norwegian polar coast. On 17 Dec *K-1* lays two mine barrages. On 18 Dec there is an indecisive engagement between a submarine (*S-101?*) and the submarine-chaser *UJ1214* off Kvaenangenfjord. On 22 Dec *Shch-403* misses the coaster *Ingöy* off Porsangerfjord and on 21 Dec *M-174* (Lt-Cdr N E Egorov) sinks the steamer *Emshörn* (4301 tons) off Vardö. On 28–29 Dec *K-1*, *Shch-401* and *Shch-404* miss targets.

16–20 Dec   South Asia

Japanese landing on Mindanao. The Japanese South Philippines Force sets out from Palau on 16 Dec with the minelayer *Shirataka* and 14 transports with some 5000 troops of the 56th Independent Mixed Bde, escorted by the 2nd DD Flotilla (Rear-Adm Tanaka) with the cruiser *Jintsu* and the destroyers *Kuroshio*, *Oyashio*, *Hayashio* and *Natsushio* (15th Div) and *Amatsukaze* and *Hatsukaze* (16th Div); the covering force (Rear-Adm Tagaki) is the 5th Cruiser Sqn comprising *Myoko* (F), *Haguro* and *Nachi*, the carrier *Ryujo*, the destroyer *Shiokaze* and the seaplane carrier *Chitose*. During the night 19–20 Dec the Japanese land their troops on both sides of Davao against slight resistance and occupy the town; they establish a seaplane base on 20 Dec. At the begin-

ning of Jan 1942 the 21st Naval Air Flotilla is transferred to Davao.

16–30 Dec   Bay of Biscay

All available Allied submarines are stationed in the area W of Brest because it is feared that the heavy German ships in Brest are about to leave (see 22 Mar). Boats include the Free French *Junon*. In these operations *H31* is lost, probably on a mine.

16–31 Dec   Mediterranean

During the nights 15–16, 21–22, 22–23 and 30–31 Dec the German 3rd MTB Flotilla (Lt-Cdr Kemnade), comprising *S-55*, *S-35*, *S-61*, *S-31* and *S-34*, carries out MT 1–4, the first mining operations off Valetta, Malta. 73 TMA mines are laid.

17 Dec   Arctic

In a sortie to the Kola Coast, the German 8th DD Flotilla (Capt Pönitz), comprising *Z23*, *Z24*, *Z25* and *Z27*, encounter, about 14 nautical miles N of Cape Gorodetski, the British minesweepers *Hazard* and *Speedy*, which have come out to meet the convoy PQ.6. They are taken in error for Russian destroyers of the 'G' class. *Speedy* receives four hits but *Hazard* is undamaged. The British heavy cruiser *Kent* puts to sea with the Soviet destroyers *Grozny* and *Sokrushitelny* from the Kola Inlet to intercept the German force but has no success.

17 Dec   General Situation

Adm Chester W Nimitz relieves Adm Husband E Kimmel as C-in-C US Pacific Fleet. Adm Pye assumes command until the arrival of the new C-in-C.

17 Dec   Central Pacific

The Japanese submarine *Ro-66* is lost following a collision in the Mandate Islands.

17–24 Dec   South Asia

Japanese landing in Lingayen Gulf and in Lamon Bay (Luzon). On 17 Dec the 3rd Attack Force (Rear-Adm Hirose), consisting of the 2nd BF with the destroyer *Yamagumo*, the torpedo boats *Chidori*, *Hatsukari*, *Manazuru* and *Tomozuru* and eight smaller and auxiliary warships as well as 21 transports, sets out from Keelung (Formosa). On 18 Dec there follow from Takao (Formosa) the 1st Force (Rear-Adm Hara) with the cruiser *Natori*, the destroyers *Fumitsuki*, *Satsuki*, *Nagatsuki*, *Minatsuki*, *Harukaze* and *Hatakaze*, two minesweepers and auxiliary warships and 27 transports; and the 2nd Force (Rear-Adm Nishimura) with the cruiser *Naka*, the destroyers *Murasame*, *Yudachi*, *Harusame*, *Samidare*, *Asagumo*, *Minegumo* and *Natsugumo*, five minesweepers, six submarine-chasers and 28 transports. During the night 21–22 Dec Forces 1 and 2 arrive, and the following night Force 3, off Lingayen Gulf, where they land, with the reinforced 48th Inf Div, the bulk of the 14th Army (Lt-Gen Homma) on the NE side of the bay. Air support for the landing is provided from the advanced fighter bases won on 8–10 Dec and from Formosa with units of Naval Air Flotillas 21 and 23, as well as from the 5th Army Air Div. To cover the operation, Vice-Adm Takahashi takes up a position 250 nautical miles W of Luzon with the heavy cruisers *Ashigara* and *Maya* and the light cruiser *Kuma*. Vice-Adm Kondo stands by to provide a heavy covering force in the western part of the South China Sea (simultaneously to assist the Borneo operation) with the heavy cruisers *Atago* and *Takao* and the battleships *Haruna* and *Kongo*.

The C-in-C Asiatic Fleet, Adm Hart, deploys against the invasion the US submarines *S38*, *S40*, *Stingray*, *Saury* and *Salmon*. *S-38* (Lt Chappell) sinks the converted minelayer *Hayo Maru* (5446 tons) and *Seal* (Lt-Cdr Hurd) one ship of 836 tons. All other attacks fail because of torpedo defects.

On 24 Dec a 4th Attack Force (Rear-Adm Kubo), comprising the cruiser *Nagara*, the destroyers *Yamakaze*, *Suzukaze*, *Kawakaze* and *Umikaze* (24th DD Div) and *Tokitsukaze* and *Yukikaze* (16th Div) and smaller units of the 1st BF with 24 transports, which have set out from Amami Oshima (Ryukyu Islands) on 17 Dec, lands some 7000 troops of the 16th Inf Div in Lamon Bay on the SE side of Luzon.

18–25 Dec   South Asia

Final battle for Hong Kong. The Japanese 38th Inf Div has, by 25 Dec, driven the defenders into a small area of the western part of the island with the result that they have to capitulate. In the harbour, the Japanese capture 26 more or less damaged British, Soviet, Panamanian and Norwegian merchant ships totalling 52604 tons. During the fighting there sink, or are scuttled before the capitulation, the British destroyer *Thracian*, the minelayer *Redstart* the gunboats *Cicala*, *Moth*, *Robin*, and *Tern*, the motor torpedo boats *MTB7*, *MTB8*, *MTB9*, *MTB10*, *MTB11*, *MTB12*, *MTB26* and *MTB27* and four auxiliary ships.

18–27 Dec   Baltic

The attempt by the large Soviet submarine *K-51* to reach the Baltic from Kronstadt and to operate for three months there has to be abandoned because of the ice W of Lavansaari.

18–28 Dec   Mediterranean

The German U-boats coming from Salamis, *U371*, *U559*, *U562*, *U79* and *U75*, as well as the U-boats newly transferred from the W, *U652*, *U374*, *U568*, *U74*, *U77*, *U83*, *U573* and *U577* and *U133*, operate off the coast

of Egypt and Cyrenaica. Of them, *U371* (Lt-Cdr Driver) misses a cruiser of Force B off Alexandria on 18 Dec and a destroyer force on 20 Dec. In attacks on a convoy on 23 Dec, *U559* (Lt-Cdr Heidtmann) sinks one ship of 3059 tons and with *U562* misses escort vessels, among which *Hasty* and *Hotspur* sink *U79* with depth charges. On 24 Dec *U568* (Lt-Cdr Preuss) sinks the corvette *Salvia* from a convoy escort and *U562* misses one ship. On 26 Dec *U559* sinks one more ship of 2486 tons. In an attack on a convoy on 28 Dec, *U559* and *U652* miss their targets; *U75* (Lt-Cdr Ringelmann) sinks one ship of 1587 tons but is then sunk by the destroyer *Kipling*.

18–29 Dec   South Asia

The Japanese 6th SM Flotilla, comprising *I-123*, *I-124*, *I-121* and *I-122*, operates in the area W of Mindanao. *I-123* lays a mine barrage off Surabaya.

18 Dec–1 Feb   Pacific

First reconnaissance operations by US submarines: *Dolphin* on Arno, Maloelap, Wotje, Kwajalein and Jaluit and *Pompano* on Wake, Ujelang, Ponape, Rongelau and Bikini.

19–20 Dec   Black Sea

The Soviet cruisers *Krasny Kavkaz* and *Krasny Krym*, the flotilla leader *Kharkov* and the destroyers *Bodry* and *Nezamozhnik* transport the 79th Naval Infantry Bde (3500 men) to Sevastopol.

19–24 Dec   Mediterranean

The Italian submarines *Axum* and *Turchese* are stationed near Cape Bougaroni and *Alagi* and *Aradam* E of that to counter an expected operation by Force H.

20 Dec–16 Jan   Arctic

The British convoy QP.4 with eleven merchant ships leaves Archangel for Seidisfjord; two other ships remain in Murmansk.

21–27 Dec   Black Sea

In operations to bring the 345th Rifle Div (10600 men) and ammunition transports to Sevastopol, the following ships of the squadron shell German positions and assembly areas on the Sevastopol front: on 21 Dec *Krasny Krym*, *Kharkov*, *Bodry*; on 22 Dec *Krasny Kavkaz*, *Krasny Krym*, *Tashkent*, *Kharkov*, *Bodry*, *Smyshleny*, *Nezamozhnik* (1,938 rounds fired); on 23 Dec *Smyshleny*, *Tashkent*; on 24 Dec *Boiki*, *Smyshleny*, *Tashkent*; on 25 Dec *Tashkent*, *Smyshleny*, *Boiki*, *Bezuprechny*; on 26 Dec *Bezuprechny*; on 27 Dec *Smyshleny*, *Tashkent*. From 23 to 27 Dec 1299 rounds are fired. On 22 Dec the cruisers *Krasny Kavkaz* and *Krasny Krym*, the flotilla leader *Kharkov* and the destroyer *Bodry* are withdrawn in preparation for the Kerch-Feodosia landing.

22 Dec   Mediterranean

The British submarine *Umbra* sinks one ship of 1010 tons from a convoy off Misurata (Tripolitania).

22–25 Dec   South Asia

Part of the Japanese South Philippines Force, comprising nine transports with a part of the 56th Bde on board, proceeds from Davao to Jolo and lands there on 24 Dec. On 25 Dec the island is captured. Escort for the operation is provided by Rear-Adm Tanaka with the cruiser *Jintsu*, the 15th DD Div (see 17 Dec), the carrier *Ryujo* with the destroyer *Shiokaze* and the seaplane carrier *Chitose*.

At the beginning of Jan 1942 the 23rd Naval Air Flotilla is stationed in Jolo.

22–29 Dec   Mediterranean

The British cruiser *Dido*, with the destroyers *Gurkha* and *Nestor*, sets out from Gibraltar for the E and reaches Malta on 24 Dec. From there the ships proceed with convoy ME.8, which consists of returning empty ships, to Alexandria, where they arrive on 29 Dec.

22 Dec–1 Jan   Arctic

British raid on the Lofotens: Operation 'Anklet'. On 22 Dec Rear-Adm Hamilton sets out from Scapa Flow with the cruiser *Arethusa*, the destroyers *Somali*, *Ashanti*, *Bedouin* and *Eskimo*, the escort destroyers *Wheatland*, *Lamerton*, *Krakowiak* (Polish) and *Kujawiak* (Polish), the Norwegian corvettes *Acanthus* and *Eglantine*, the minesweepers *Speedwell*, *Harrier*, and *Halcyon*, the landing ships *Prince Albert* and *Princess Charlotte* (Belgian), the tankers *Black Ranger* and *Grey Ranger*, the auxiliary ships *Gudrun Maersk* (Danish) and *Scott* and the tug *Jaunty*. The force is led into Vestfjord on 26 Dec by the marker submarine *Sealion* (*Princess Charlotte* returns with *Wheatland* because of disablement). *Prince Albert*, with *Lamerton*, *Eglantine* and *Acanthus*, lands 260 commando troops to destroy the fish-oil factory in Moskenesöy and the wireless station in Tind. *Bedouin* destroys the Napp wireless station on Flakstadöy on the N side. *Arethusa*, *Somali*, *Ashanti* and *Eskimo* penetrate into Vestfjord in a search for ships. The Norwegian coasters *Kong Harald* and *Nordland* (1125 tons and 725 tons respectively) are captured and the German patrol boat *V5904*/*Geier* (145 tons) is sunk by *Ashanti* after the crew has been taken off. In German air attacks, *Arethusa* is damaged by near-misses; the operation is broken off and on 28 Dec the return journey is begun. Operation 'Archery'. On 24 Dec Rear-Adm Burrough sets out from Scapa Flow with the cruiser *Kenya*, the destroyers *Offa*, *Onslow* and *Oribi*, the escort destroyer *Chid-*

dingfold and the landing ships *Prince Charles* and *Prince Leopold*. The force is piloted into Vaagsfjord by the marker submarine *Tuna* on 27 Dec. Commandos, numbering 585 men, are landed in five groups in the area of Vaagsö and Maalöy and they destroy the local fish-processing and telecommunication installations. In Maalöy Sound, *Onslow* and *Oribi* sink the patrol boat *V5108/Föhn* (207 tons) and drive the freighters *Reimar Edzard Fritzen* (2935 tons), *Norma* (2258 tons), *Eismeer* (1003 tons) and, a little later, *Anita L M Russ* (1712 tons) on to the beach. Near Vaagsöy, *Offa* and *Chiddingfold* sink the patrol boat *V5102/Donner* (223 tons) and the freighter *Anhalt* (5870 tons). *Kenya* receives several hits in an engagement with the Rugsundöy coastal battery. Attacks by some German aircraft on 27 and 28 Dec meet with no success. On 1 Jan the Allied forces arrive back at Scapa Flow and bring with them 343 Norwegian volunteers.

23 Dec   Mediterranean
Axis troops evacuate Benghazi.

23 Dec   Baltic
The German minesweeper *M557* is sunk in a snowstorm near Rügen.

24 Dec   Western Atlantic
Vice-Adm Muselier, with the Free French corvettes *Mimose*, *Alysse* and *Aconit* and the large submarine *Surcouf*, occupies the islands of St Pierre and Miquelon off Newfoundland which have been loyal to Vichy France.

24 Dec–2 Jan   Indian Ocean
The British convoy BM.9A (troop transports *Devonshire*, *Ethiopia*, *Lancashire*, *Rajula* and *Varsova*), escorted by the Australian cruiser *Hobart*, proceeds from Colombo to Singapore.

25 Dec–25 Jan   Arctic
First deployment of German U-boat group 'Ulan', comprising *U134*, *U454* and *U584*, in the passage S of Bear Island against British Murmansk convoys. Attacks on the convoys PQ.7A and PQ.8 (qv).

26–31 Dec   Black Sea
Soviet landing on the Kerch Peninsula. On 26 Dec formations of the Azov Flotilla (Rear-Adm S G Gorshkov) from Temryuk and Kuchugury land the 244th Rifle Div and the 83rd Naval Infantry Bde of the 51st Army (Lt-Gen Lvov) on the N coast of the Kerch Peninsula; simultaneously units of the Kerch base (Rear-Adm Frolov) from Taman land the 302nd Rifle Div on both sides of Kerch with the object of pinning the forces of the German XLII Corps to the coast in the N and E. Of the five groups of the Azov Flotilla, at first only Groups 1 and 2 reach land near Cape Zyuk and Group 4 near Cape Khroni because of bad weather

and enemy resistance. Groups 3 and 5 are later brought to these assault areas. By 29 Dec 5870 men and nine tanks are landed from lighters, fishing cutters and patrol boats, with support from the gunboats *Dnestr* and *Don*, but are forced on to the defensive until 29 Dec by the German 72nd Inf Regt. Adm Frolov's forces (three groups with eight TKAs, 41 fishing cutters and three towed convoys of barges) are able to land 2175 men at four points near Kamysh-Burun on 26 Dec and, in spite of the bad weather, to bring up 9050 men by 29 Dec and to hold the bridgehead against the attacks of the 42nd Inf Regt. The landing of Group B (Rear-Adm N O Abramov) with the 122nd and 143rd Rifle Bdes from Anapa near Cape Opok on 27 Dec has to be postponed because of the stormy weather. The troops land on 29 Dec near Kamysh-Burun. The support group consists of the gunboats *Krasny Adzharistan*, *Krasnaya Gruziya*, the patrol ship *Shtorm*, a TKA detachment and patrol boats.

On 29 Dec the main landing of the 44th Army (Maj-Gen Pervukhin) is effected by the squadron (Capt 1st Class Basisty) in Feodosia with the object of cutting off the German forces on the Kerch Peninsula from the rear and encircling them and, by advancing into the Crimea, to relieve beleaguered Sevastopol. During the night 28–29 Dec 300 naval infantry are at first landed from an advance party of 12 patrol boats and two motor minesweepers (Lt-Cdr A P Ivanov). They occupy the moles and the lighthouse. Shortly afterwards, the support force (Capt 1st Class V A Andreev) begins to disembark some 4200 troops. The cruiser *Krasny Krym* anchors 300m from the mole; *Krasny Kavkaz* lies alongside the mole; and the destroyers *Zheleznyakov*, *Shaumyan* and *Nezamozhnik* go into the harbour after being led to it by the marker submarines *M-51* and *Shch-201*. During the day on 29 Dec the ships support the disembarked troops with their guns against what is, at first, a weak German and Rumanian defence. On news of the landing in Feodosia, the Commander of the German troops on the Kerch Peninsula, Lt-Gen Count Sponeck, orders, on his own responsibility, the 46th Inf Div to withdraw quickly from Kerch to form a defensive position in the west. In the following days a new defence line is constructed with troops which are quickly brought up by the commander of the 11th Army, Col-Gen v Manstein. But the current attack on Sevastopol has to stop. During the night 29–30 Dec the transport detachment (Capt 2nd Class N A Zaruba), with the 63rd Rifle Div (11270 troops) on the transports

Kuban, *Azov*, *Shakhter*, *Zyryanin*, *Krasny Profintern*, *Tashkent*, *Nogin*, *Zhan Zhores* and *Serov*, arrives with the escort group (Capt 3rd Class N P Negoda) comprising the destroyers *Bodry* and *Boiki*; the following night the 2nd Transport Detachment (Capt 2nd Class A M Filipov), with the 157th Rifle Div (6395 troops) on the transports *Kalinin*, *Kursk*, *Dmitrov*, *Fabritsius* and *Krasnogvardeets*, arrives with the escort group (Capt 2nd Class M F Romanov) comprising the destroyers *Soobrazitelny* and *Sposobny*. In the roads of Feodosia, *Krasny Kavkaz* receives 17 hits, *Krasny Krym* 11, *Shaumyan* and *Zhelezynakov* four each and *Nezamozhnik* one from artillery and mortar fire. The patrol boat *SKA-063* sinks, as does the minesweeper *T-402/Minrep*, after an air attack.

27 Dec–29 Jan   North Atlantic
While the German U-boats sail for their operations off the US East Coast (Operation 'Paukenschlag') with *U123*, *U109*, *U66*, *U125* and *U130*, followed by *U103*, *U106*, *U107*, *U108* and *U126*, and at the Newfoundland Bank with *U87*, *U135*, *U552*, *U84*, *U86*, *U203*, *U582*, *U654*, *U754*, *U701*, *U553*, *U85*, *U333* and *U82*, the convoys are still routed according to 'Ultra' data on straight courses as follows: US TU.4.1.5, with the destroyers *Mayo*, *Simpson*, *Babbitt* and *Schenck*, escorts HX.167 and, together with *Leary*, ON.55 (on 24 Jan *U333* sinks one ship of 4765 tons from ON.55); Canadian TU.4.1.13, with the destroyer *Assiniboine* and the corvettes *Chicoutimi*, *Kenogami* and *Aconit* (FFN), escorts SC.62 and ONS.56 (*U82*, Lt-Cdr Rollmann, sinks one ship of 6118 tons on 23 Jan and *U582*, Lt-Cdr Schulte, one ship of 5.189 tons on 26 Jan, both victims being from ONS.56); US TU.4.1.6, with the destroyers *Bainbridge*, *Woolsey*, *Truxton*, *Broome* and *Dickerson*, escorts HX.168 and ON.57; and Canadian TU.4.1.11, with the corvettes *Polyanthus* (RN), *Celandine* (RN), *Amherst* and *Fennel* escorts SC.63 but has to return because of heavy weather before taking over ONS.58.

The British groups escort the convoys between EASTOMP and MOMP as follows: EG.3, with the destroyer *Wanderer* and the corvettes *Renoncule* (FFN), *Roselys* (FFN), *Vervain* and *Aubrietia*, escorts ON.53 and SC.62; EG.4, with the destroyer *Boadicea* and the corvettes *Heather*, *Narcissus*, *Commandant Détroyat* (FFN) and *Lobélia* (FFN), escorts ONS.54 and SC.63; EG.2, with the destroyers *Douglas* and *Leamington* and the corvettes *Sunflower*, *Kingcup*, *Alisma* and *Loosestrife*, escorts ON.55 and HX.169 (from ON.55, *U43* sinks first one straggler and then two ships of 16061 tons on 14 Jan); EG.5, with the destroyer *Caldwell* and the corvettes *Honeysuckle*, *Gentian*, *Loosestrife*, *Thyme* and *Fennel*, escorts ONS.56 and SC.64; EG.6, with the destroyer *Chelsea* and the corvettes *Pimpernel*, *Columbine*, *Camellia*, *Eglantine* (RNoN), *Mignonette*, *Snowdrop* and *Arbutus*, escorts ON.57 and HX.170; and EG.7, with the destroyers *Newport* and *St Albans* and the corvettes *Acanthus*, *Montbretia* (RNoN), *Rose* (RNoN) and *Hibiscus*, escorts ONS.58 and HX.172

28 Dec   South West Pacific
The convoy ZK.5, with 4250 Australian troops and 10000 tons of supplies on board the transports *Aquitania*, *Herstein* and *Sarpedon*, puts to sea from Sydney for Port Moresby. It is escorted by the cruisers *Achilles*, *Australia*, *Canberra* and *Perth*. The US cruiser *Pensacola* proceeds to sea with a convoy of seven ships from Brisbane to Port Darwin. On the same day the US cruiser *Houston* and the destroyers *Alden*, *Edsall* and *Whipple* and three auxiliary ships arrive in Port Darwin from Surabaya.

29 Dec   Central Pacific
The Japanese Submarine *Ro–60* is grounded and lost on a reef in the Mandate Islands.

29 Dec–30 Dec   Black Sea
The battleship *Parizhskaya Kommuna* arrives in Sevastopol, having been met in the evening of 27 Dec by the flotilla leader *Tashkent* and the destroyer *Smyshleny* off Poti. She is followed by the cruiser *Molotov* with the destroyer *Bezuprechny*. The ships support with their gunfire the defence against German attacks in the areas of Belbek, Kamyshly and Verkhne on 29 and 30 Dec. When they return, the battleship takes 1025 wounded on board and the cruiser 600.

30 Dec   Mediterranean
In the area of the Peloponnese, the British submarine *Thorn* (Lt-Cdr Norfolk) sinks one ship of 3032 tons and *Proteus* torpedoes another of 2480 tons.

31 Dec   Mediterranean
Bombardment of Bardia with the participation of the destroyers of the 7th DD Flotilla, including the Australian *Napier* (F), *Nestor* and *Nizam*.

31 Dec   Black Sea
The Soviet submarine *Shch–214* (Lt-Cdr Vlasov) sinks the Turkish sailing ship *Kaynakdere* on the Turkish/Bulgarian frontier.

31 Dec–10 Jan   South Asia
On 31 Dec a convoy sets out from Formosa with the third wave of the Japanese 25th Army for Malaya on board 56 transports. Escort is provided by the 5th DD Flotilla with the cruiser *Natori* and the destroyers *Asakaze*, *Harukaze*, *Hatakaze* and *Matsukaze* (5th DD Div), *Satsuki*, *Minazuki*, *Fumitsuki* and *Nagatsuki* (22nd DD Div), and *Asashio*, *Oshio*, *Michishio*, and *Arashio* (8th DD Div), together with the cruiser *Kashii*, the frigate *Shimushu* and the destroyers *Ayanami* and *Isonami*. The heavy cruiser *Maya*, with the destroyers *Ikazuchi* and *Inazuma*, operates as a covering force until 2 Jan in the South China Sea. On 3 Jan *Arashi* and *Hagikaze* from the 4th DD Div together with *Fubuki* take the place of the first two destroyers of the 8th DD Div. *Kashii*, *Shimushu*, *Ayanami*, *Isonami* and *Fubuki*, with 11 transports, proceed off Cape Camao to Bangkok to unload supplies for the Guards Division. The remainder go to Patani and Singora where, on 8 Jan, transports arrive. From 5 to 10 Jan the 1st Div of the 7th Cruiser Sqn operates as a covering force with *Kumano* and *Suzuya* and the destroyers *Hatsuyuki* and *Shirayuki* SW of Saigon. From 8 to 10 Jan elements of the 18th Inf Div are transferred from Canton to Camranh Bay in a convoy of 11 transports. Escort for the convoy is provided by the cruiser *Sendai* with the destroyers *Amagiri*, *Asagiri* and *Yugiri* and (20th DD Div) and *Shikinami*. The US submarine *Stingray* (Lt-Cdr Moore) sinks one ship of 5100 tons from the convoy as it comes in.

During these operations, small battle groups of the Japanese 16th Inf Div proceed from Miri in Sarawak in small vessels to Labuan in Brunei Bay (1 Jan) and Jesselton/North Borneo (8 Jan).

1942

1 Jan   General Situation

United Nations Pact: 26 nations declare in Washington that they will not conclude a separate peace with Germany and Japan. The principles of the Atlantic Charter are accepted.

1 Jan   Intelligence

The British Admiralty changes from 'Naval Cypher No 2' to 'Naval Cypher No 4' and raises the number of circuits in the cypher to 16 and in the code to 26.

1–5 Jan   Black Sea

The Soviet cruiser *Molotov*, the flotilla leader *Tashkent* and the transports *Abkhaziya* and *Belostok* bring elements of the 386th Rifle Div from Novorossisk to Sevastopol. Before the return on 2 Jan *Molotov* and *Tashkent*, with the destroyers *Bezuprechny* and *Smyshleny*, repeatedly shell German positions near Sevastopol. *Smyshleny* brings the transport *Pestel* with 690 reserve troops and 185 tons of ammunition to Sevastopol on 3 Jan. Supplies for the 44th Army are brought on 1 Jan by the destroyer *Sposobny* with the transport *Kalinin* from Novorossisk and by the cruisers *Komintern* and *Krasny Krym* from Tuapse to Feodosia. On 2 Jan the destroyers *Boiki* and *Shaumyan* follow with the minesweeper *T-401/Tral* and five transports from Novorossisk. On 3 Jan the cruiser *Krasny Kavkaz* with the 224th AA Div (22 8.5cm AA guns) on board, *Krasny Krym* and the destroyers *Soobrazitelny* and *Sposobny* shell land targets near Feodosia before they return. On the return *Krasny Kavkaz* is attacked on 4 Jan off Tuapse by six Ju 87s of StG 77 and badly damaged by four near-misses close to the stern (her repairs continue until Oct 1942).

From 3 to 5 Jan the destroyers *Boiki* and *Soobrazitelny* accompany the transports *Kuban* and *Krasnogvardeets* to the Bosphorus.

1–18 Jan   Mediterranean

In British submarine operations in the Central Mediterranean, *Upholder* (Lt-Cdr Wanklyn) sinks the Italian submarine *St Bon*, which is being used as a petrol transport, on 5 Jan, *Unbeaten* (Lt Woodward) the German *U374* on 12 Jan and *P35/Umbra* (Lt Maydon) a small ship of 301 tons. On the western side of Cephalonia, *Thunderbolt*

(Lt-Cdr Crouch) sinks a caique of 32 tons and *Proteus* and *Thrasher* (Lt Mackenzie) each sink one ship, of 5413 tons and 5016 tons respectively, near Cape Ducato. *Porpoise* (Cdr Pizey) lays a barrage of 50 mines off Crete on 11 Jan and sinks one ship of 2471 tons with a torpedo. *Triumph* is lost, probably to a mine, on 14 Jan in the southern Aegean and in Malta *P31/Uproar* is damaged in an air attack on the same day.

1 Jan–15 Feb   North Atlantic

While the German U-boats are being sent from France directly to the area off Newfoundland and the US East Coast, the Allied convoys in the North Atlantic are sent by the Admiralty's OIC and the OPNAV's routing section mostly along the great circle route. 'Ultra' shows no U-boat concentrations in this area. When the U-boat 'Ultra' blackout starts on 1 Feb (qv), there is no great change with the North Atlantic convoy routing and only some chance meetings with inbound and outbound U-boats lead to sinkings.

US and Canadian escort groups accompany the HX and SC convoys from WESTOMP to MOMP, where they are taken over by British groups, while the US and Canadian groups take over the ON and ONS convoys, escorted by the British groups to MOMP and from there to WESTOMP; Canadian Western Local Escort Groups accompany the convoys between WESTOMP and Halifax and Sydney.

The following Mid Ocean Escort Groups are directed by TF.4 (Rear-Adm Le Bristol USN): TU.4.1.1, with the US destroyers *Gleaves*, *Dallas* and *Upshur* and the US Coast Guard cutter *Ingham*; TU.4.1.2, with the US destroyers *Wilkes*, *Madison*, *Roper*, *Sturtevant* and *Jacob Jones*; TU.4.1.3, with the US destroyers *Niblack*, *Overton* and *Tarbell* and the USCG *Alexander Hamilton*; TU.4.1.4, with the US destroyers *Plunkett*, *Badger*, *Decatur* and *Cole* and the USCG *Campbell*; TU 4.1.5, with the US destroyers *Mayo*, *Simpson*, *Babbitt*, *Schenck* and *Leary* (redesignated TU.4.1.7 in Feb; new TU.4.1.5 comprises *Edison*, *Nicholson*, *MacLeish*, *Lea* and *Bernadou*); TU.4.1.6, with the US destroyers *Woolsey*, *Bainbridge*, *Truxtun*, *Broome* and *Dickerson*;

TU.4.1.8, with the US destroyers *Swanson*, *Buck*, *McCormick*, *Greer* and *Herbert*; TU.4.1.11, with the Canadian destroyer *Ottawa* (in refit) and the corvettes *Polyanthus* (RN), *Celandine* (RN), *Amherst* and *Fennel*; TU.4.1.12, with the Canadian destroyer *St Laurent* and the corvettes *Hepatica*, *Pictou*, *Buctouche*, *Moosejaw* and *Battleford*; TU.4.1.13, with the Canadian destroyer *Restigouche* and the corvettes *Bittersweet*, *Chicoutimi*, *Orillia* and *Agassiz*; TU.4.1.14, with the RN destroyer *Burnham* and the Canadian corvettes *Chilliwack*, *Napanee*, *Trillium*, *Summerside*, *Algoma* and *Drumheller*; TU.4.1.15, with the Canadian destroyer *Saguenay* and the corvettes *Shediac*, *Camrose*, *Spikenard*, *Wetaskiwin* and *Dauphin*; TU.4.1.16, with the Canadian destroyer *Niagara* and the corvettes *Lethbridge*, *Dianthus* (RN), *Nanaimo*, *Galt* and *Matapedia*; TU.4.1.17, with the Canadian destroyer *Assiniboine* and the corvettes *Kenogami*, *Aconit* (FFN), *Alysse* (FFN), *Sorel* and *Cowichan*; EG.B.1, with the RN destroyers *Keppel*, *Shikari* (in Feb in addition the Norwegian destroyer *St Albans*) and the Norwegian corvettes *Acanthus* and *Rose*; EG.B2, with the RN destroyers *Douglas* and *Leamington* and the corvettes *Sunflower*, *Kingcup*, *Alisma* and *Loosestrife*; EG.B3, with the RN destroyers *Wanderer* and *Scimitar* and the corvettes *Renoncule* (FFN), *Roselys* (FFN), *Vervain*, *Aubrietia*, *Dianella* and *Asphodel*; EG.B4, with the RN destroyer *Boadicea* and the corvettes *Heather*, *Narcissus*, *Commandant Détroyat* (FFN) and *Lobélia* (FFN); EG.B5, with the RN destroyer *Caldwell* and the corvettes *Honeysuckle*, *Gentian*, and *Thyme*; EG.B6, with the RN destroyers *Broke* (in refit in Jan) and *Chelsea* and the corvettes *Camellia*, *Pimpernel* and *Columbine* and, in addition, the corvettes *Eglantine* (RNoN), *Mignonette*, *Snowdrop* and *Arbutus*; EG.B7, with the Norwegian destroyer *St Albans* (Jan only, then Norwegian destroyer *Newport*) and the corvettes *Hibiscus*, *Montbretia* (RNoN) and *Kiwi* (RNZN; Jan only); and EG.B8, with the RN destroyer *Watchman* and the corvettes *Arabis*, *Monkshood* and *Snowflake*.

The following convoy pairs are running (for HX and SC, dates of WESTOMP/ EG/MOMP/EG/EASTOMP; for ON and ONS, EASTOMP/EG/MOMP/EG/ WESTOMP): HX.167: 29 Dec/4.1.5/7 Jan/B8/9 Jan; SC.62: 29 Dec/4.1.17/11 Jan/B7/13 Jan; ON.51: 27 Dec/B8/2 Jan/4.1.8/11 Jan; ONS.52: 30 Dec/B7/5 Jan/4.1.15/16 Jan (during and after dispersal, one ship each sunk or torpedoed by *U553*, Lt-Cdr Thurmann; *U86*, Lt Schug; *U87*, Lt Berger; and *U751*, Lt-Cdr Bigalk); HX.168: 4 Jan/4.1.6/11 Jan/B3/14 Jan (one straggler sunk by *U43*, Lt-Cdr Lüth); SC.63: 8 Jan/4.1.11/18 Jan/B4/21 Jan (one straggler sunk by *U86*; one ship sunk by *U333*, Lt-Cdr Cremer); ON.53: 4 Jan/B3/9 Jan/4.1.4/22 Jan (after dispersal, one ship each sunk by *U333*; *U106*, Lt-Cdr Rasch; and *U754*, Lt-Cdr Oestermann); ONS.54: 6 Jan/B4/10 Jan/4.1.16/21 Jan (after dispersal, one ship sunk by *U135*, Lt-Cdr Praetorius); HX.169: 11 Jan/4.1.2/18 Jan/B2/22 Jan; SC.64: 12 Jan/4.1.12 through 24 Jan; ON.55: 8 Jan/B2/15 Jan/4.1.5/24 Jan (on 14 Jan, three stragglers sunk by *U43*; after dispersal, one ship sunk by *U333*); ONS.56: 12 Jan/B5/17 Jan/4.1.17/28 Jan (two ships sunk in convoy by *U82*, Lt Rollmann; and *U582*, Lt Schulte); HX.170: 15 Jan/4.1.3/23 Jan/B6/26 Jan (from Iceland section, USCG *Alexander Hamilton* sunk by *U132*, Lt-Cdr Vogelsang); SC.65: 17 Jan/4.1.14/28 Jan/B5/1 Feb; ON.57: 18 Jan/B6/23 Jan/4.1.6/7 Feb; ONS.58: 20 Jan/B7/25 Jan/4.1.11/10 Feb; HX.171: 22 Jan/4.1.1/27 Jan/B7/1 Feb; SC.66: 23 Jan/4.1.15/4 Feb/B8/6 Feb; ON.59: 23 Jan/B3/28 Jan/4.1.2/11 Feb; ONS.60: 26 Jan/B4/31 Jan/4.1.12/12 Feb (after dispersal, one ship sunk by *U566*, Lt-Cdr Borchert); HX.172: 28 Jan/4.1.8./4 Feb/B3/6 Feb; SC.67: 30 Jan/4.1.16/9 Feb/B2/12 Feb (corvette *Spikenard* sunk by *U136* and one ship sunk by *U591*, Lt-Cdr Zetzsche); ON.61: 29 Jan/B1/3 Feb/4.1.3/12 Feb; ONS.62: 1 Feb/B2/6 Feb/4.1.14/17 Feb; HX.173: 4 Feb/4.1.4/10 Feb/B4/13 Feb (one ship torpedoed by *U751*); SC.68: 6 Feb/4.1.17/15 Feb/B7/18 Feb (FFN corvette *Alysse* sunk by *U654*, Lt Forster); ON.63: 4 Feb/B5/10 Feb/4.1.1/19 Feb (corvette *Arbutus* sunk by *U136*); ONS.64: 7 Feb/B6/12 Feb/4.1.15/23 Feb; HX.174: 9 Feb/4.1.7/16 Feb/B1/19 Feb (one straggler sunk by *U136*); SC.69: 11 Feb/4.1.11/21 Feb/B3/24 Feb; ON.65: 10 Feb/B7/15 Feb/4.1.8/24 Feb (one ship torpedoed by *U107*, Lt-Cdr Gelhaus); ONS.66: 13 Feb/B3/18 Feb/4.1.16/1 Mar; HX.175: 15 Feb/4.1.5/23 Feb/B6/26 Feb (one ship sunk by *U752*, Lt Schroeter); and ON.67: 16 Feb/B4/21 Feb/4.1.6/2 Mar (chance convoy battle, with eight ships sunk and one damaged; see 21–25 Feb).

2 Jan   Arctic
U134 (Lt-Cdr Schendel) sinks the British freighter *Waziristan* (5135 tons) belonging to the Murmansk convoy PQ.7A (two ships; PQ.7B nine ships).

3 Jan   General Situation
Formation of the Allied ABDA Command (American, British, Dutch, Australian) under General Wavell in the Dutch East Indies.

3–6 Jan   Mediterranean
Italian operation M.43. Three Italian supply convoys set out on 3 Jan: three transports with the destroyers *Vivaldi*, *Da Recco*, *Usodimare*, *Bersagliere* and *Fuciliere* from Messina; two transports with the torpedo boats *Orsa*, *Aretusa*, *Castore* and *Antares* from Taranto; and one transport with the destroyer *Freccia* and the torpedo boat *Procione* from Messina. The convoys join up on 4 Jan. A close escort force (Div-Adm Bergamini), comprising the battleship *Duilio*, the cruisers *Garibaldi*, *Montecuccoli*, *Duca d'Aosta* and *Attendolo* and the destroyers *Maestrale*, *Gioberti*, *Oriani*, *Scirocco* and *Malocello*, is added and a distant covering force (Adm Iachino), consisting of the battleships *Littorio*, *Doria* and *Cesare*, the cruisers *Gorizia* and *Trento* and the destroyers *Carabiniere*, *Alpino*, *Pigafetta*, *Da Noli*, *Ascari*, *Aviere*, *Geniere* and *Camicia Nera*, sets out. The operation is covered E of Malta by the submarines *Pisani*, *Onice*, *Dandolo*, *Alagi*, *Aradam*, *Tricheco* and *Axum* and between Crete and Cyrenaica by *Beilul*, *Dessiè*, *Galatea* and *Zaffiro*. Although the convoy is sighted by the British submarine *P34*/*Ultimatum* and the covering force by *Unique* and aircraft, this does not lead to successful attacks. On 5 Jan the transports arrive in Tripoli. The *Littorio* force returns on 5 Jan and the *Duilio* force on 6 Jan to Taranto.

4–9 Jan   Dutch East Indies
Of the Japanese 4th SM Flotilla (Rear-Adm Yoshitome), *I-57* (Cdr Nakashima) sinks one ship of 3077 tons and *I-56* (Cdr Ohashi) sinks three ships of 7957 tons and torpedoes two more of 5065 tons S of Java. In the Java Sea, *I-58* (Cdr Kitamura) sinks one ship of 2380 tons, while *I-55*, like *Ro-33* and *Ro-34*, has no success in the area of the Anambas Islands.

4–18 Jan   Pacific
Off the Japanese East Coast, the US submarine *Gudgeon* (Lt-Cdr Grenfell) misses one ship, *Plunger* (Lt-Cdr White) sinks one of 4702 tons and *Pollack* (Lt-Cdr Mosely) sinks two of 7612 tons and damages one of 2700 tons.

5–8 Jan   Black Sea
Soviet offensive to relieve Sevastopol. During the night 4–5 Jan a Soviet force (Capt 2nd Class Buslaev), consisting of the minesweeper *T-405*/*Vrzyvatel*, the tug *SP-14* and seven SKA cutters, lands a naval infantry battalion in Evpatoria, where at the same time partisan units have assembled. *Vrzyvatel* is damaged in an air attack and by gunfire from the shore, goes aground and is lost. During the night 5–6 Jan a second force, consisting of the destroyer *Smyshleny*, the minesweeper *T-408*/*Yakor* and four SKAs, lands another battalion. A third wave, with the flotilla leader *Tashkent*, the *Yakor* and two SKAs, is not able to land in the evening of 6 Jan because of the defensive fire. The main body of the disembarked troops is destroyed by the German defenders (which includes Reconnaissance Detachment 22, Lt-Col v Boddien); 203 prisoners are brought in. The remainder embark in the evening of 6 Jan. The cruiser *Molotov*, which comes to Sevastopol with supplies on 5 Jan, and *Tashkent* support with their gunfire Soviet attacks on the north front of the fortress on 5, 6 and 7 Jan. The battleship *Parizhskaya Kommuna* (Commander of the Squadron, Rear-Adm Vladimirski, on board) and the destroyer *Boiki* shell German positions near Stary Krym (Feodosia) during the night 5–6 Jan. Simultaneously the destroyer *Sposobny*, with the patrol cutter *SKA-0111*, lands 218 men of the 226th Mountain Regt near Sudak. On the return, *Sposobny* evades attacks by Ju 88s off Feodosia. During the night 7–8 Jan the destroyer *Boiki* lands a battalion (450 men) in Dvuyakornoy Bay W of Feodosia instead of in Feodosia because of the danger of air attack. *Sposobny*, which has set out to land a second battalion, is badly damaged by ground mines off Cape Myskhako and is towed to Novorossisk by the destroyer *Nezamozhnik*.

5–9 Jan   Mediterranean
British supply operation MF.2 to Malta. On 5 Jan the transport *Glengyle* sets out from Alexandria with Force B (Rear-Adm Vian), comprising the cruisers *Dido*, *Euryalus* and *Naiad* and the destroyers *Gurkha*, *Sikh*, *Kipling*, *Kingston* and *Foxhound*. On 6 Jan the empty transport *Breconshire* puts to sea from Malta with Force C, consisting of the destroyers *Lance*, *Lively*, *Jaguar* and *Havock*. On 7 Jan the two forces meet: they exchange the transports and the destroyers *Sikh* and *Havock* and arrive in Malta and Alexandria respectively on 8–9 Jan. The Italian submarines (see 3–6 Jan) do not approach.

5–15 Jan Arctic

The Soviet submarines *Shch-401* and *Shch-404* have only misses. *K-23* (Capt 3rd Class Potapov) lays a minefield off Porsanger Fjord on 7 Jan on which a Norwegian coaster of 327 tons sinks on 30 Jan. *M-175* is sunk NW of the Fisherman's Pensinsula on 10 Jan by *U584* (Lt-Cdr Deecke). *S-102* (Capt 3rd Class Gorodnichi) has one miss on 10 Jan; on 14 Jan she sinks the steamer *Türkheim* (1904 tons) from a convoy off Sylte Fjord and escapes attacks by *UJ1205*, *UJ1403* and *V5903*, which expend 198 depth charges. *K-21* has one miss on 13 Jan and sinks one fishing vessel on 21 Jan.

6–10 Jan Norway

The German minelayer *Cobra* lays a mine barrage between the northerly Norwegian islands of Arnöy and Fuglöy
The minelayers *Ulm*, *Brummer* and *Roland* lay several barrages off the Skagerrak, escorted by six vessels of the 17th Patrol Flotilla. Two Swedish ships and a Norwegian blockade-runner are lost on the barrages.

7–13 Jan Dutch East Indies

Japanese landing on Tarakan. On 7–8 Jan the units of the Central Force (Vice-Adm Hirose) with the 2nd BF as an advance party set out from Davao (Mindanao) and Jolo. They comprise the minelayers *Imizu Maru*, *Itsukushima* and *Wakataka*, the submarine-chasers (Kusentai) *Ch10*, *11* and *12*, the minesweepers (Sokaitei) *W13*, *W14*, *W15*, *W16* (17th MS Div) and *W17* and *W18* (30th MS Div), the fast assault boats (Ishokaitei) *P36*, *P37*, *P38* and *P39* and a convoy of sixteen transports with the 56th Regimental Combat Group and the 2nd Kure Special Landing Force on board. As escort they have the 4th DD Flotilla (Rear-Adm Nishimura) with the cruiser *Naka* and the destroyers *Yudachi*, *Harusame*, *Samidare* and *Murasame* (2nd DD Div), *Asagumo*, *Minegumo* and *Natsugumo* (9th DD Div) and *Kamakaze*. Air escort is provided by the 23rd Naval Air Flotilla (Jolo) and seaplanes from the depot ships *Sanuki Maru* and *Sanyo Maru*. On 10 Jan the invasion fleet arrives off Tarakan. During the night 10–11 Jan the landing succeeds in the face of slight resistance and the Dutch commander surrenders after setting the oil wells on fire. On 11 Jan the Dutch minelayer *Prins van Oranje* is sunk south of Tarakan by gunfire from the destroyer *Yamakaze* and from *P38*. On 12 Jan the Karoengan battery, not informed about the capitulation, sinks the mine-sweepers *W13* and *W14*. As a reprisal the Japanese execute 84 artillery men from the battery. On 16 Jan the airfield is operational. *Asagumo* is put out of action when she goes around.

Japanese landing near Menado and Kema (Celebes). On 9 Jan the Eastern Force (Rear-Adm Kubo) puts to sea from Davao with the 1st BF. It consists of the cruiser *Nagara*, the minelayer *Aotaka*, the freighter *Tsukushi Maru*, the fast transports (Ishokaitei) *P1*, *P2* and *P34*, the minesweepers (Sokaitei) *W7*, *W8*, *W9*, *W11* and *W12* (21st MS Div) and the submarine-chasers (Kusentai) *Ch1* and *Ch3* with six transports (1st Sasebo Special Landing Force on board), escorted by the 2nd DD Flotilla (Rear-Adm Tanaka) with the cruiser *Jintsu* and the destroyers *Kuroshio*, *Oyashio*, *Natsushio* and *Hayashio* (15th DD Div) and *Yukikaze*, *Tokitsukaze*, *Amatsukaze* and *Hatsukaze* (16th DD Div); air escort is provided by the 21st Naval Air Flotilla from Davao and seaplanes from the 11th Carrier Sqn, consisting of the seaplane carriers *Chitose* and *Mizuho* (Rear-Adm Fujita). On 11 Jan 334 men of the Yokosuka Naval Air Landing Force are dropped by parachute near Menado; there follows a landing from the sea near Menado and Kema. Slight resistance is met. Both operations are covered to the S by the 5th SM Flotilla comprising *I-59*, *I-60*, *I-62*, *I-64*, *I-65* and *I-66* and to the N by Rear-Adm Takagi with the heavy cruisers *Haguro* and *Nachi* (*Myoko* is damaged on 4 Jan in an air attack in Davao) and the destroyers *Inazuma* and *Ikazuchi* in the Celebes Sea.

8–13 Jan Mediterranean

The British gunboat *Aphis* supports the 8th Army by bombarding the Halfaya Pass.

8 Jan–12 Feb Western Atlantic

A first wave of 12 Type VIIC boats ('Ziethen' group) arrives one after the other in the area of the Newfoundland Bank and operates singly as far S as Nova Scotia. Many ships are sunk. *U135* (Lt-Cdr Praetorius) sinks one ship of 9626 tons, *U87* (Lt-Cdr Berger) sinks two of 16324 tons (including one on 31 Dec while en route), *U552* (Lt-Cdr Topp) sinks two of 6722 tons, *U86* (Lt-Cdr Schug) sinks one of 4271 tons and damages one of 8627 tons, *U203* (Lt-Cdr Mützelburg) sinks three of 2341 tons and damages one of 888 tons and *U582* (Lt-Cdr Schulte) sinks one of 5189 tons; *U654* (Lt Forster) sinks the Free French corvette *Alysse*; and *U701* (Lt-Cdr Degen) sinks one ship of 3657 tons, *U333* (Lt-Cdr Cremer) three of 14045 tons, *U553* (Lt-Cdr Thurmann) two of 16366 tons and *U754* (Lt-Cdr Oestermann) four of 11386 tons. *U84* (Lt Uphoff) returns without success.

9 Jan North Sea

The British destroyer *Vimiera* is lost to a mine in the Thames estuary while escorting convoy FS.693.

9–17 Jan Mediterranean

In operations against British supplies for Tobruk, *U77* (Lt-Cdr Schonder) torpedoes on 12 Jan the British destroyer *Kimberley*, which has to be towed to Alexandria with a blown-off stern. *U205* has no success and *U577* is sunk by Sunderland 'X' of No 230 Sqn RAF on 9 Jan.

9–20 Jan Pacific

The Japanese 3rd SM Div with *I-16*, *I-20*, *I-22* and *I-24* and the 2nd SM Flotilla still operating in the area of Hawaii with *I-7*, *I-1*, *I-2*, *I-3*, *I-4*, *I-5* and *I-6* (Cdr* Inaba) are directed to US TF.14 with the carrier *Saratoga* which has been reported by the Japanese submarine *I-18*. *I-6* torpedoes the carrier on 11 Jan. On the return, *I-18* and *I-24* shell Midway without success.

9 Jan–3 Feb Indian Ocean

I-65 (Lt-Cdr Harada) and *I-66* (Cdr Yoshitome) of the Japanese 5th SM Flotilla operate at first in the Java Sea and later off Rangoon. They sink two and three ships, of 6105 and 10530 tons, respectively. *I-59* (Cdr Yoshimatsu) sinks W of Sumatra one ship of 4184 tons and one further unidentified ship in Sabang. In proceeding through the Sunda Strait, *I-60* is sunk by the British destroyer *Jupiter* on 17 Jan. In the Bay of Bengal, *I-64* (Cdr Ogawa) sinks four ships of 16244 tons and damages one of 391 tons. *I-62* (Lt-Cdr Kinashi) torpedoes two tankers of 16865 tons.

10 Jan South Asia

In Allied submarine operations, the US submarine *Pickerel* (Lt-Cdr Bacon) sinks one ship of 2929 tons off Davao. The Dutch *O19* (Lt-Cdr Knoops) to sinks one ship of 3817 tons and damages one of 4944 tons in the Gulf of Siam. The US submarines *Stingray* (Lt-Cdr Moore) sinks one ship of 5167 tons and *Sculpin* misses one off Hainan and off Lamon Bay respectively.

10–18 Jan South Asia

Japanese forces are transferred in the South China Sea. The heavy covering force under Vice-Adm Kondo returns to the Pescadores on 11 Jan and is transferred to Palau by 16 Jan. It comprises the heavy cruisers *Atago*, *Maya* and *Takao* (4th Cruiser Sqn), the battleships *Haruna* and *Kongo* (3rd BB Sqn) and the destroyers *Arashi*, *Hagikaze*, *Maikaze* and *Nowake* (4th DD Div) and *Akatsuki* and *Hibiki* (6th DD Div). The 2nd Carrier Sqn (Rear-Adm Yamaguchi) arrives there from Kure on 17 Jan with the carriers *Hiryu* and *Soryu*, the cruiser *Tone* and the destroyers *Tanikaze* and *Urakaze*.

From 12 to 18 Jan the 8th DD Div, consisting of the destroyers *Asashio*, *Oshio*,

Michishio and *Arashio*, is transferred from Hong Kong to Davao. While light craft transport elements of the Japanese 16th Inf Div from Brunei and Jesselton to Sandakan (North Borneo) on 17 Jan, the Western Force under Vice-Adm Ozawa cruises in the South China Sea from Camranh Bay from 16 to 19 Jan. It consists of the heavy cruiser *Chokai* (F), the 7th Cruiser Sqn (Rear-Adm Kurita) with the heavy cruisers *Kumano*, *Suzuya*, *Mikuma* and *Mogami*, the 4th Carrier Sqn (Rear-Adm Kakuta) with the carrier *Ryujo* and the destroyer *Shikinami*, the 3rd DD Flotilla with the cruiser *Sendai* and the destroyers *Fubuki*, *Hatsuyuki* and *Shirayuki* (11th DD Div), *Murakumo*, *Shirakumo* and *Usugumo* (12th Div) *Ayanami*, *Isonami* and *Uranami* (19th DD Div) and *Amagiri*, *Asagiri* and *Yugiri* (20th DD Div), and the light cruisers *Kinu* and *Yura*.

10–23 Jan   North Atlantic

First US troop convoy, NA.1, of two transports, escorted by two British destroyers, from Halifax to Londonderry. There follow in Jan convoys NA.2–NA.7.

11 Jan   English Channel

The German MMS *R42* runs on to a wreck off Ambleteuse and sinks.

11–16 Jan   North Atlantic

The three German U-boats *U71*, *U93* and *U571*, operating off Gibraltar and the Azores ('Seydlitz' group), try to attack convoy HG.78 but are driven off by the escort group, whose leading destroyer *Hesperus* sinks *U93* on 15 Jan.

11 Jan–7 Feb   Western Atlantic

The first five U-boats to arrive off the American East Coast open the attack on American coastal shipping (Operation 'Paukenschlag'). *U123* (Lt-Cdr Hardegen) sinks nine ships of 53173 tons and torpedoes one of 8206 tons, *U130* (Cdr Kals) sinks six ships of 36993 tons and torpedoes one of 6986 tons, *U66* (Cdr Zapp) sinks five of 33456 tons, *U109* (Lt-Cdr Bleichrodt) sinks five of 33733 tons and *U125* (Lt-Cdr Folkers) sinks one of 5666 tons.

12 Jan   Black Sea

The Soviet battleship *Parizhskaya Kommuna*, escorted by the destroyers *Bodry* and *Zheleznyakov*, shells German positions near Isyumovki and Stary Krym.

12–14 Jan   North Atlantic

U43 (Lt-Cdr Lüth), which is returning home from France, sinks a straggler from convoy HX.168 in the North Atlantic and, in a heavy storm, three ships from convoy ON.55 totalling 21307 tons.

12–25 Jan   South Asia

The Japanese 6th SM Flotilla lays mine

barrages: *I-121* and *I-122* in the Clarence Strait on 12 and 16 Jan respectively and *I-123* in the Bundas Strait. In a mining operation off Port Darwin, *I-124* is sunk on 20 Jan by the US destroyer *Edsall* and the Australian minesweepers *Deloraine*, *Lithgow* and *Katoomba*.

13 Jan   Arctic

The German 8th DD Flotilla (Capt Pönitz), comprising *Z25*, *Z23* and *Z24*, lays four barrages with 100 EMC mines in the western channel of the White Sea near Cape Kachovski.

13–24 Jan   Arctic

The Allied convoy QP.5 leaves Murmansk for Reykjavik with four ships.

14–17 Jan   Norway

The German battleship *Tirpitz* is transferred from Wilhelmshaven to Trondheim, escorted by the destroyers *Richard Beitzen*, *Bruno Heinemann*, *Paul Jacobi* and *Z29* (Operation 'Polarnacht').

14–25 Jan   North Atlantic

Twelve Type VII U-boats setting out from Germany ('Schlei' group) are halted, on Hitler's instructions, in the area W of the Hebrides and Faeroes, so as to be ready, if necessary, to repel an invasion of Norway. The operation leads to no result. Only *U588* (Lt-Cdr Vogel) reports the sinking of a so-far unidentified ship. On 24 Jan the U-boats receive orders to continue their journey to France.

14–25 Jan   South West Pacific

Japanese landings at Rabaul and Kavieng. On 14 Jan the 19th ML Div (Rear-Adm Shima) sets out from Guam for Rabaul with the minelayers *Okinoshima*, *Tenyo Maru* and *Tsugaru*, the destroyers *Mochizuki* and *Mutsuki* (30th DD Div), the auxiliary gunboats *Kongo Maru* and *Nikkai Maru* and Army transports with the 144th Inf Regt of the South Sea Detachment. On 17 Jan Rear-Adm Kajioka comes out from Truk to meet the force with the cruiser *Yunagi*, the destroyers *Asanagi*, *Oite* and *Yunagi* (29th DD Div) and *Yayoi* (30th DD Div) and one auxiliary ship and two transports with elements of the Maizuru Naval Landing Force and the aircraft depot ship *Hijirigawa Maru*.

To cover and support the operation the 1st Carrier Air Fleet (Vice-Adm Nagumo), with the carriers *Akagi* and *Kaga* (1st Carrier Sqn) and *Shokaku* and *Zuikaku* (5th Carrier Sqn), the battleships *Hiyei* and *Kirishima* (1/3rd BB Sqn), the cruiser *Chikuma* (8th Cruiser Sqn) and the 1st DD Flotilla with the cruiser *Abukuma* and the destroyers *Isokaze*, *Hamakaze*, *Kasumi*, *Arare*, *Kagero*,

Shiranuhi and *Akigumo*, puts to sea from Truk on 17 Jan for the area N of New Ireland. On 18 Jan the 6th Cruiser Sqn (Rear-Adm Goto) follows with the cruisers *Aoba*, *Kinugasa*, *Kako* and *Furutaka* and on 20 Jan the invasion force for Kavieng with the 18th Cruiser Sqn (Rear-Adm Matsuyama) with the cruisers *Tatsuta* and *Tenryu*, the destroyers *Kikuzuki*, *Uzuki* and *Yuzuki* (23rd DD Div) and, on board several transports, the rest of the Maizuru and the Kashima Naval Landing Forces.

On 20 Jan the carrier force makes a heavy attack on Rabaul. While the 1st Carrier Sqn remains in the area N of New Ireland, the 5th Carrier Sqn proceeds with *Chikuma* and three destroyers on 21 Jan into the Bismarck Sea where the 6th Cruiser Sqn is also taking up a covering position for the landings. The 7th SM Flotilla (Flagship *Jingei*, Rear-Adm Onishi) takes up a patrol line in the area off St George's Channel to cover the Rabaul operation with the submarines *Ro-61*, *Ro-62*, *Ro-63*, *Ro-64*, *Ro-65*, *Ro-67* and *Ro-68*. After the destroyers have been refuelled on 21 Jan, and with air support from the carriers, the assault forces arrive off their targets on the evening of 22 Jan and land their troops during the night 22–23 Jan. By 24 Jan they have occupied all key points and have begun to establish airfields.

The covering forces start the return journey on 23 Jan and reach Truk again on 25 Jan.

14 Jan–2 Feb   Indian Ocean

The British carrier *Indomitable* proceeds with the Australian destroyers *Napier*, *Nestor* and *Nizam* from Port Sudan on 14 Jan to the area S of Java via Addu Atoll (21 Jan) and Cocos Islands (25 Jan, for refuelling). The purpose is to fly off 48 Hurrican fighters on 27–28 Jan to reinforce the air defence of Java. The force arrives in Trincomalee (Ceylon) on 2 Feb.

15 Jan   Mediterranean

The German 3rd TB Flotilla (Lt-Cdr Kemnade) lays the barrage MT.5 E of Valetta (Malta) with 24 TMA mines and four protection and eight explosive floats.

15–16 Jan   Black Sea

A Soviet landing force (Capt 1st Class Andreev), comprising the cruiser *Krasny Krym*, the gunboat *Krasny Adzharistan* and six SKA patrol cutters, lands the bulk of the 226th Mountain Regt in Sudak; the destroyers *Shaumyan* and *Soobrazitelny* land diversionary groups at three other coastal points numbering in all 750 men. Covering fire is provided by a force (Rear-Adm Vladimirski) consisting of the battleship *Parizhskaya Kommuna* and the destroyers *Bezuprechny* and *Zheleznyakov*. As a diversion the destroyer *Smyshleny* simultaneously shells Evpatoria. The destroyer *Boiki* brings supplies to Sevastopol.

15–26 Jan   North Atlantic
First US troop transport to the United Kingdom. Embarked on the transports *Chateau Thierry* and HMS *Strathard*, 3900 US Army troops of the 34th US Div go to Northern Ireland, with the transport *Munargo* proceeding to Iceland. Task Force 15, with the battleship *Texas*, the carrier *Wasp* (first part only), the cruiser *Quincy* and Desdiv 16 with *Mayrant*, *Trippe*, *Rhind* and *Rowan*, acts as escort.

16–20 Jan   Mediterranean
British supply operation MF.3 to Malta. On 16 Jan there set out from Alexandria the convoys MW.8A (the transports *Ajax* and *Thermopylae* with the AA cruiser *Carlisle* and the destroyers *Arrow*, *Griffin*, *Hasty* and *Hero*) and MW.8B (the transports *City of Calcutta* and *Clan Fergusson* with the destroyers *Gurkha*, *Isaac Sweers*, *Legion* and *Maori*) which later join up. They are followed by the covering group, Force B (Rear-Adm Vian), with the cruisers *Naiad*, *Dido* and *Euryalus* and the destroyers *Kelvin*, *Kipling*, *Havock*, *Foxhound* and *Hotspur*. On 17 Jan the German U-boat *U133* (Cdr Hesse) torpedoes *Gurkha*. *Isaac Sweers* tows the sinking ship out of the burning oil and rescues the crew. On 18 Jan *Thermopylae*, because of engine trouble, has to be sent to Benghazi with *Carlisle*, *Foxhound* and *Hotspur*. They are harassed by air attacks on 19 Jan as they continue their journey. The convoy is met on 18 Jan by Force K, coming from Malta with the cruiser *Penelope* and the destroyers *Sikh*, *Zulu*, *Lance*, *Lively* and *Jaguar*, and brought to Malta on 19 Jan. After exchanging the destroyers *Legion* and *Maori* for *Jaguar*, Force B returns to Alexandria on 20 Jan.

16 Jan–4 Feb   North Atlantic
The outbound *U402* and *U581* locate a troop transport convoy from which *U402* (Lt-Cdr S Freiherr v Forstner) torpedoes the *Llangibby Castle* (12053 tons), which is brought into Punta Delgada. When news is received that the repaired ship is about to sail, *U402*, *U572* and *U581*, which are operating between Gibraltar and the Azores, are directed to her (1–4 Feb) but they have no success. The British destroyer *Westcott*, belonging to the escort, sinks *U581* on 2 Feb.
Of the Italian submarines operating at this time in the area of the Azores, *Bagnolini* and *Barbarigo*, the latter sinks on 23 Jan the Spanish steamer *Navemar* (5473 tons), which is returning empty after a journey

with Jewish refugees from Cadiz to New York.

17 Jan   Arctic
For the first time a U-boat group ('Ulan'), consisting of *U134*, *U454* and *U584*, operates against an Arctic convoy. After the torpedoing of the Soviet trawler *RT-68* from a Soviet coastal convoy, *U454* (Lt-Cdr Hackländer) attacks in several approaches the convoy PQ.8 (eight steamers). She torpedoes the convoy commodore's ship, *Harmatris* (5395 tons), and sinks the destroyer *Matabele*. The C-in-C Home Fleet sends Rear-Adm Burrough with the cruiser *Nigeria* to Murmansk to persuade the Command of the Soviet Northern Fleet to play a larger part in bringing in the convoys.

18 Jan   Black Sea
Troops of the German 11th Army recapture Feodosia.

19 Jan–9 Feb   Arctic
On 19 Jan, on the Norwegian polar coast, the Soviet submarines *K-23* (Capt 3rd Class Potapov) and *K-22* (Capt 3rd Class Kotelnikov, with the Div Cdr, Capt 2nd Class Gadzhiev, on board) attack the fishing harbours of Svaerholthavet (Porsangerfjord) and Berlevaag (Tanafjord) and each sink with their guns one small ship, of 506 tons and 106 tons respectively. Three attacks by *Shch-422* (Lt-Cdr Malyshev with the Div Cdr, Capt 2nd Class Kolyshkin, on board) are unsuccessful, as are one each by *S-101*, *Shch-401* and *M-171*. *Shch-421* (Lt-Cdr Lunin) sinks, after two abortive attacks, the steamer *Konsul Schulte* (2975 tons) from a convoy in Porsangerfjord on 5 Feb.

20 Jan   Dutch East Indies
Formation of the 'China Force' (Commodore Collins) for convoy duties between Singapore, Sunda Strait and Java, consisting of the cruisers *Danae*, *Dragon* and *Durban*, the destroyers *Jupiter*, *Encounter*, *Express*, *Electra*, *Stronghold* and *Vampire* (RAN) and the sloops *Jumna* (RIN) and *Yarra* (RAN). The US submarine *S36* is lost by grounding in the Strait of Macassar.

20–26 Jan   South Asia
On 20 Jan a Japanese convoy of 11 transports with the 18th Inf Div on board sets out from Camranh Bay for Singora and Patani. The convoy is escorted by the destroyers *Amagiri*, *Asagiri*, *Fubuki* and *Yugiri*. The troops are disembarked on 24 Jan. From there two transports, escorted by the above destroyers, proceed to Kuantan and disembark troops there on 26 Jan. From 25 Jan support is also provided by the cruiser *Sendai* and destroyers *Hatsuyuki* and *Shirayuki*, coming from Poulo Condore, as well as by the 1st MS Div, comprising the minesweepers (Sokaitei) *W1*, *W2*, *W3*, *W4*, *W5*

and the 11th A/S Div, consisting of the submarine-chasers (Kusentai) *Ch7*, *Ch8* and *Ch9*. To cover the operation, the cruisers *Kumano*, *Suzuya* and *Yura*, with the destroyers *Ayanami* and *Isonami*, cruise NW of Natoma; further off, the carrier *Ryujo* provides air cover with the destroyer *Shikinami*. The cruisers *Mikuma* and *Mogami*, which also set out originally, proceed on 22 Jan to Saigon with the destroyer *Uranami*. After an unsuccessful attack by 68 British aircraft from Singapore (13 planes lost), the destroyers *Thanet* (RN) and *Vampire* (RAN) are deployed during the night 26–27 Jan to attack the Japanese transports reported off Endau. *Vampire* misses with her three torpedoes *W4* and *Shirayuki*; *Thanet* is sunk in an engagement with *Yugiri*, *W1*, *Sendai*, *Fubuki* and *Asagiri*.

20 Jan–20 Feb   Pacific
Operation by the Japanese 3rd SM Flotilla (Rear-Adm Miwa) in the Pacific. The Command Boat *I-8* (Cdr* Emi) reconnoitres the American West Coast between San Francisco and Seattle; *I-71* (Cdr Kawasaki) and *I-72* (Cdr Togami) operate in the area of Hawaii. *I-72* sinks the fleet tanker *Neches* (7383 tons). *I-73* (Cdr* Isobe) shells Midway on 25 Jan, sinks a small transport of 244 tons near Oahu and is herself sunk on 27 Jan by the submarine *Gudgeon*. *I-69* (Cdr Watanabe) shells Midway on 8 and 10 Feb. *I-74* (Cdr* Ikezawa) and *I-75* (Cdr Inoue) operate without success in the area of the Aleutians.

21–25 Jan   Dutch East Indies
Japanese landing at Kendari (Celebes). On 21 Jan the Eastern Force (Rear-Adm Kubo) sets out from Bangka Roads near Menado with the 1st BF (the cruiser *Nagara*, the minelayer *Aotaka*, the freighter *Tsukushi Maru*, the fast transports *P1*, *P2* and *P34*, the minesweepers *W7*, *W8*, *W9*, *W11* and *W12*, the submarine-chasers *Ch1*, *Ch2* and *Ch3* and six transports (with the 1st Sasebo Special Landing Force on board). It is escorted by the destroyers of the 15th and 16th DD Divs, *Kuroshio*, *Oyashio*, *Hatsushio*, *Hayashio*, *Yukikaze*, *Tokitsukaze*, *Amatsukaze* and *Hatsukaze*. The purpose is to land at Kendari on 24 Jan, which they do without encountering strong resistance. Air escort and support is provided by the 23rd Naval Air Flotilla and the 11th Carrier Sqn with the seaplane carriers *Chitose* and *Mizuho*.
On 24 Jan one transport of 4124 tons is sunk by the US submarine *Swordfish* (Lt-Cdr Smith) and another of 8035 tons is damaged. The 21st DD Div, consisting of the destroyers *Nenohi*, *Hatsushimo*, *Wakaba* and *Hatsuharu*, arrives off Kendari on 25 Jan as

reinforcement. *Hatsuharu* is damaged in an attack by US bombers.

To cover the operation, the submarines *I-59*, *I-62*, *I-64*, *I-65* and *I-66* form a patrol line in the Ambon Sea. In the Celebes Sea, Rear-Adm Takagi cruises with the heavy cruisers *Haguro* and *Nachi* and the destroyers *Akebono* (a replacement for *Inazuma*, damaged when she goes aground) and *Ikazuchi*. The Allied base at Ambon, after a heavy attack on 24–25 Jan by the 23rd Naval Air Flotilla, is repeatedly attacked by the aircraft of a carrier force (Rear-Adm Yamaguchi) consisting of *Hiryu* and *Soryu* with the cruiser *Tone* and the destroyers *Tanikaze* and *Urakaze* which is operating in the Banda Sea. As additional covering groups there operate, E of Mindanao, the battleship *Haruna* with the heavy cruiser *Maya* and the destroyers *Akatsuki* and *Hibiki* and, S of Palau, the heavy cruisers *Atago* and *Takao*, the battleship *Kongo* and the destroyers *Arashi*, *Hagikaze*, *Maikaze* and *Nowake*.

21–27 Jan   Dutch East Indies

Japanese landing at Balikpapan (Borneo). On 21 Jan the Central Force sets out from Tarakan with 13 transports. Close escort is provided by the fast assault boats (APD) *P36*, *P37* and *P38*, the minesweepers *W15*, *W16*, *W17*, *W18* and the submarine-chasers *Ch10*, *Ch11*, and *Ch12*, the covering force by Rear-Adm Nishimura with the cruiser *Naka* and the destroyers *Yudachi*, *Harusame*, *Samidare*, *Murasame*, *Natsugumo*, *Minegumo*, *Yamakaze* and *Suzukaze*; the advance detachment consists of one transport with the destroyers *Kawakaze* and *Umikaze*. Allied air reconnaissance locates the force and in the Makassar Strait the American submarines *S40*, *Pickerel*, *Porpoise*, *Saury*, *Spearfish*, and *Sturgeon*, as well as the Dutch *K-XIV* and *K-XVIII*, are deployed against it. Allied TF.5 (Rear-Adm Glassford, USN), comprising the cruisers *Boise* and *Marblehead* and the destroyers *John D Ford*, *Parrott*, *Paul Jones* and *Pope*, is directed to it from Koepang Bay, but *Boise* drops out in Sape Strait when she goes aground and *Marblehead*, because of engine trouble, can only take up a position to meet the destroyers.

On the evening of 23 Jan the Japanese invasion force arrives off Balikpapan with the 56th RCT on board. In the meantime it has also been reported by *Sturgeon*, which has made an abortive attack owing to torpedo failures. Before the bulk of the embarked troops can be landed, the four US destroyers (Cdr Talbot) arrive during the night 23–24 Jan. This happens immediately after the Dutch submarine *K-XVIII* (Lt-

Cdr v Well Groen.eld), having missed *Naka*, has sunk the patrol essel *P37*/*Hishi* and the transport *Tsuruga Maru* (6987 tons) and therefore diverted the Japanese destroyers to sea in a submarine hunt. With the oilfields ablaze in the background, the destroyers can easily recognise the transports lying at anchor, but in several approaches at short ranges, when 48 torpedoes are fired against initially little resistance, they are only able to sink the three transports *Kuretake Maru* (5175 tons), *Sumanoura Maru* (3519 tons), and *Tatsukami Maru* (7064 tons) and to damage two other ships. *Naka* and the Japanese destroyers *Minegumo* and *Natsugumo*, which come up first, are not able to catch the US destroyers as they withdraw. In the morning of 24 Jan the Japanese troops are landed and they occupy Balikpapan. On 25 Jan the aircraft depot ships *Sanuki Maru* and *Sanyo Maru* arrive, followed on 26 Jan by reinforcements consisting of the minelayers *Imizu Maru*, *Itsukushima* and *Wakataka* and transports. *Sanuki Maru* (9246 tons) is lost in an air attack on 26 Jan. On 28 Jan the Japanese 23rd Naval Air Flotilla has Balikpapan in operation.

21 Jan–19 Feb   Western Atlantic

A second wave of eight Type VII U-boats makes the following sinkings in the area between the Newfoundland Bank and Nova Scotia: *U85* (Lt Greger) sinks one ship of 5408 tons, *U82* (Lt-Cdr Rollmann) sinks two of 18117 tons and the destroyer *Belmont*, *U566* (Lt-Cdr Borchert) sinks one of 4181 tons, *U751* (Lt-Cdr Bigalk) sinks two of 11487 tons and damages one of 8096 tons, *U98* (Lt-Cdr Gysae) sinks one of 5298 tons, *U564* (Lt-Cdr Suhren) sinks one of 11410 tons and torpedoes one of 6195 tons and *U576* (Lt-Cdr Heinicke) sinks one of 6946 tons. *U575* (Lt-Cdr Heydemann), held up by special duties, returns without success. Two operational ventures against escorted convoys are not successful. *U564*, which had gone furthest to the S, takes on fuel supplies from *U107* on 16 Feb for the return.

21 Jan–6 Mar   Western Atlantic

A second wave of five Type IX U-boats operates off the US East Coast. *U103* (Lt-Cdr Winter) sinks four ships of 26539 tons, *U106* (Lt-Cdr Rasch) five of 42139 tons, *U107* (Lt-Cdr Gelhaus) two of 10850 tons, *U108* (Cdr Scholtz) five of 20082 tons and *U128* (Lt-Cdr Heyse) three of 27312 tons.

22 Jan   Black Sea

The cruiser *Molotov* and the destroyers *Boiki* and *Smyshleny* are damaged in a storm in Tuapse.

22–24 Jan   Central Pacific

US TF.11 (Rear-Adm Brown) sets out from Pearl Harbor on 22 Jan to make a raid on Wake. It consists of the carrier *Lexington*, the cruisers *Minneapolis*, *Indianapolis*, *Pensacola* and *San Francisco* and Desron 1 comprising the destroyers *Phelps*, *Dewey*, *MacDonough*, *Hull*, *Aylwin*, *Dale*, *Clark*, *Patterson*, *Bagley* and *Drayton*. When on 23 Jan the Japanese submarine *I-72* (Cdr Togami) sinks the escort tanker *Neches* (7383 tons), the sortie has to be abandoned because it cannot be carried out without the destroyers being refuelled.

22–25 Jan   Mediterranean

Italian supply operation T.18 to Tripoli. On 22 Jan five transports set out from Taranto and Messina and join up under the escort of the destroyers *Vivaldi*, *Malocello*, *Da Noli*, *Aviere*, *Camicia Nera* and *Geniere* and the torpedo boats *Orsa* and *Castore*. A close escort force (Div-Adm de Courten), comprising the cruisers *Duca d' Aosta*, *Attendolo* and *Montecuccoli* and the destroyers *Alpino*, *Bersagliere*, *Carabiniere* and *Fuciliere*, also joins it. Further away, a distant covering force (Div-Adm Bergamini) comprising the battleship *Duilio* and the destroyers *Pigafetta*, *Oriani*, *Scirocco* and *Ascari*, is at sea. In spite of air escort from German Ju 88s, four British Swordfish torpedo aircraft from No 830 Sqn on Malta sink the transport *Victoria* (13098 tons) NE of Tripoli on 24 Jan. The convoy and the covering forces arrive in Tripoli on 24 Jan and Taranto on 25 Jan respectively.

23–24 Jan   Black Sea

A Soviet landing force (Capt 1st Class Andreev), comprising the cruiser *Krasny Krym*, the destroyer *Shaumyan*, the minesweeper *T-412*/*Arseni Rasskin* and six SKA patrol cutters, lands 1576 troops of the 544th Rifle Regt in Sudak. Fire support is provided by the destroyers *Bezuprechny* and *Soobrazitelny*. The cruiser *Komintern* brings supplies to Sevastopol.

23 Jan–11 Feb   Dutch East Indies

In Allied submarine operations, the US submarine *Sturgeon* (Lt-Cdr Wright) torpedoes two ships of 15803 tons which are beached, and *Seadragon* (Lt-Cdr Ferrall) torpedoes three ships of 19689 tons, one of which sinks. On 11 Feb *Shark* is sunk by the Japanese destroyer *Amatsukaze* off Menado.

24 Jan   Pacific

The US submarine *S-26* is lost in a collision with *PC460* off Panama.

24–28 Jan   Mediterranean

British supply operation MF.4 to Malta. On 24 Jan the transport *Breconshire* sets out from Alexandria with Force B (Rear-Adm Vian), consisting of the cruisers *Naiad*,

Euryalus, *Dido* and *Carlisle* and the destroyers *Griffin*, *Kelvin*, *Kipling*, *Arrow*, *Kingston*, *Jaguar*, *Hasty* and *Isaac Sweers* (Dutch). On 25 Jan Force K—the cruiser *Penelope* (Capt Nicholl) and the destroyers *Zulu*, *Lance*, *Legion*, *Lively* and *Maori*—puts to sea from Malta with the empty transports *Glengyle* and *Rowallan Castle*. On 26 Jan the two convoys meet. The covering forces exchange the destroyers *Kingston* and *Lance* and the transports and return to Malta on 27 Jan and Alexandria on 28 Jan respectively. Attempted air attacks lead to no result.

24 Jan–2 Feb   Arctic
Allied convoy QP.6 proceeds with six ships from Murmansk to Britain.

24 Jan–4 Feb   Norway
The German minelayers *Cobra* and *Ulm*, escorted by *M1502*, *UJ1707 UJ1708 UJ1211 UJ1212* and *R160*, lay four and one mine barrage respectively between Harslad and Mageroy to cover the coastal route against submarines.

25 Jan   English Channel
The effective mining of the German coastal routes by British MLs forces the Germans to use the outer channels which are in turn mined by the minelayer *Plover*. On 25 Jan the German destroyer *Bruno Heinemann* is lost on one of the mines.

25 Jan–7 Feb   Central Pacific
US carrier raid on Marshall and Gilbert Islands. On 25 Jan TF.8 (Vice-Adm Halsey) and TF.17 (Vice-Adm Fletcher) join up off Samoa to proceed northwards. When the submarine *Dolphin* reports the light defence of the Marshall Islands, Halsey deploys his Task Force on 27 Jan in three groups to attack on 1 Feb. TG.8.5, comprising the carrier *Enterprise* and the destroyers *Ralph Talbot*, *Blue* and *McCall*, carries out raids in two waves on the islands of Wotje, Maloelap and Kwajalein with a total of 18 torpedo aircraft and 46 dive-bombers. Six of its aircraft are lost. The Japanese minelayer *Tokiwa*, the cruiser *Katori* and five auxiliary and transport ships are damaged; only one small auxiliary gunboat sinks. In counter-attacks by Japanese aircraft, *Enterprise* is slightly damaged. TG.8.1 (Rear-Adm Spruance), comprising the cruisers *Northampton* and *Salt Lake City* and the destroyer *Dunlap*, shells Wotje; and TG.8.3 (Capt Shock), comprising the cruiser *Chester* and the destroyers *Balch* and *Maury*, shells the island of Taroa in the Maloelap Atoll. *Chester* is slightly damaged. TF.17, comprising the carrier *Yorktown*, the cruisers *Louisville* and *St Louis* and the destroyers *Hughes*, *Mahan*, *Russell*, *Sims* and *Walke*, carries out raids on Jaluit, Mili and Makin

with 37 aircraft in all, losing six. The tankers *Platte* and *Sabine* refuel the ships.

As a counter-move against the US raid, the submarine cruisers *I-9*, *I-15*, *I-17*, *I-25*, *I-19*, *I-23* (sustains slight damage in an attack) and *I-26* are deployed from Kwajalein, and *I-71* and *I-72* from the boats stationed in the area of Hawaii, but they do not approach. The 1st Carrier Air Fleet (Vice-Adm Nagumo) puts to sea from Truk with the carriers *Akagi*, *Kaga*, *Shokaku* and *Zuikaku*, the battleships *Hiyei* and *Kirishima*, the cruisers *Abukuma* and *Chikuma* and destroyers (see 14–25 Jan), but it is recalled on 4 Feb. *Shokaku* and *Zuikaku* are ordered to home waters to stand on alert for possible US raids; the remainder of the force arrives in Palau on 8 Feb.

26 Jan–3 Feb   Mediterranean
In British submarine operations in the Central Mediterranean, *P34/Ultimatum* (Lt Harrison) and *P35/Umbra* (Lt Maydon) each sink one ship, of 3320 tons and 6142 tons respectively. In the Adriatic, *Thorn* (Lt-Cdr Norfolk) sinks one ship of 4583 tons and the Italian submarine *Medusa* on 30 Jan, and *Thunderbolt* (Lt-Cdr Crouch) sinks two ships of 5156 tons W of Greece.

26 Jan–26 Mar   North Atlantic
On Hitler's orders, six U-boats remain temporarily stationed in the area W of the Hebrides and Faeroes (see 14–24 Jan). In Feb *U653*, *U213*, *U136*, *U591*, *U455*, *U352* and *U752* participate and in Mar *U135*, *U553*, *U87*, *U753*, *U701*, *U569* and *U593*. Occasionally convoys are located, eg ON.63 on 4 Feb near the Rockall Bank, against which *U136*, *U213* and *U591* operate. Only *U136* (Lt-Cdr Zimmermann) is able to attack. She sinks the British corvette *Arbutus* on 5 Feb and misses a destroyer of the escort on 7 Feb. On 10 Feb *U591* (Lt-Cdr Zetzsche) sights the convoy SC.67 (21 ships and an escort consisting of the destroyer *St Albans* (RNoN) the corvettes *Honeysuckle* and *Gentian* and the Canadian corvettes *Spikenard*, *Dauphin*, *Louisbourg*, *Chilliwack*, *Shediac*, *Lethbridge* and *Pictou*). She sinks one ship of 4028 tons and brings up *U136* which sinks *Spikenard* on 11 Feb. On 22 Feb *U154* (Cdr Kölle), which is on the way to France, reports convoy HX.175 (26 ships and the US TU.4.14 with the destroyers *Mayo*, *Decatur*, *Leary* and *Simpson*, relieved on 23 Feb by the British corvettes *Camellia*, *Pimpernel* and *Columbine*). In the morning of 23 Jan she makes four approaches and in the morning of 24 Jan two, but 14 torpedoes miss because of a failure in the range equipment. One destroyer and one steamer and, in the second

case, several ships are missed by *U136* and *U752*, which are directed to the scene, because of the ships' defensive manoeuvring. In individual operations, *U569* (Lt Hinsch) sinks one ship of 984 tons and *U701* (Lt-Cdr Degen) three ships of 1253 tons and one unidentified vessel.

27 Jan–3 Feb   Dutch East Indies
Japanese landing on Ambon. On 27 Jan five transports set out from Davao with one Japanese infantry regt, escorted by the destroyers *Arashio* and *Michishio* (8th DD Div) and the submarine-chasers *Ch1* and *Ch2*. On 28 Jan Rear-Adm Tanaka, coming from Menado with the cruiser *Jintsu*, the destroyers *Hatsushio* and *Hayashio* (2/15th DD Div) and *Yukikaze*, *Tokitsukaze*, *Amatsukaze* and *Hatsukaze* (16th DD Div) and six transports with a Kure Naval Landing Force, joins it. On 29 Jan Rear-Adm Fujita comes from Kendari with the seaplane carriers *Chitose* and *Mizuho*, the destroyers *Kuroshio* and *Oyashio* (1/15th DD Div), the minesweepers *W7*, *W8*, *W9*, *W11* and *W12* and the assault boats (ex-torpedo boats) *P34* and *P39*. The operation is covered in the Celebes Sea by Vice-Adm Takagi with the cruisers *Haguro* and *Nachi* and the destroyers *Akebono* and *Ikazuchi*. Whilst Rear-Adm Tanaka takes up a covering position in the SW with *Jintsu*, *Tokitsukaze* and *Yukikaze*, six transports with *Amatsukaze*, *Hatsukaze*, *W9* and *W11* land troops in the N on 31 Jan. The 15th DD Div makes a demonstration in the W and the remaining ships land the army units in the S of the island of Ambon. By 2 Feb the island is occupied despite resistance by a Dutch/Australian battle group. *W9* sinks on mines laid by the Dutch minelayer *Gouden Leeuw* at the end of Dec, and *W11* and *W12* are damaged.

27 Jan–20 Feb   South Asia
The US submarines *Seawolf*, *Seadragon*, *Sargo*, *Trout*, *Swordfish*, *Permit* and others are used for transport operations to Corregidor. The supplying by submarines is continued until the island falls on 8 May. *Swordfish* sinks one ship of 4124 tons.

28 Jan–9 Feb   Black Sea
During the night 28–29 Jan the Soviet destroyer *Bezuprechny* shells German positions near Feodosia. The Soviet flotilla leaders *Kharkov* and *Tashkent* transport supplies to Sevastopol from 31 Jan to 2 Feb and from 3 to 4 Feb in co-operation with *Bezuprechny*. Before returning, they repeatedly shell land targets on the fronts near Sevastopol and on 4 Feb also near Feodosia. *Kharkov* carries out a further operation from 7 to 9 Feb.

28 Jan   English Channel
During an air raid on Rotterdam the German auxiliary minesweeper *M4014* is sunk.

29 Jan   North Atlantic
U132 (Lt-Cdr Vogelsang) attacks the US transport *Yukon* under tow by the US Coast Guard cutter *Alexander Hamilton* escorted by the US destroyer *Gwin* off Reykjavik. *Yukon* is missed, but *Hamilton* is hit and sunk.

29 Jan–4 Feb   Mediterranean
The German U-boats *U431*, *U375*, *U73* and *U561*, despite many attacks, operate without success against British supply traffic to Tobruk.

31 Jan–3 Feb   North Atlantic
On 31 Jan the outbound *U105* (Cdr Schuch) encounters the convoy SL.98 (26 ships, escorted by EG.40 comprising the sloops *Londonderry*, *Landguard*, *Lulworth*, *Bideford* and *Culver*) W of the Bay of Biscay; *Culver*, the first ship to be equipped with automatic HF/DF, is sunk, though *U105* has to turn back damaged.

On 31 Jan *U82* (Lt-Cdr Rollmann) sights convoy NA.2 consisting of two transports and two destroyers and sinks the British destroyer *Belmont*. *U566*, *U86* and *U575*, which are in the area, cannot come up by 3 Feb because of the high speed of the convoy.

31 Jan–6 Mar   South West Pacific
On 31 Jan TF.11 (Rear-Adm Brown) sets out from Pearl Harbor with the carrier *Lexington*, the cruisers *Indianapolis*, *Minneapolis*, *Pensocola* and *San Francisco* and Desron 1 with the destroyers *Phelps*, *Clark*, *Patterson*, *Dewey*, *MacDonough*, *Hull*, *Aylwin*, *Dale*, *Bagley* and *Drayton* to cover the journey of the two convoys from the Panama Canal into the SW Pacific. They consist of six transports with 4500 troops and supplies for Bora Bora, escorted by the cruisers *Concord* and *Trenton* with two destroyers; and eight transports with 20000 troops for Christmas, Canton and Nouméa. After completing this assignment, TF.11 is allocated to the ANZAC forces (Vice-Adm Leary USN).

From 17 Feb TF.11 proceeds to the NW from the area of the New Hebrides in order to carry out a heavy carrier raid on Rabaul. But the force is reported on 20 Feb some 300 nautical miles ENE of Rabaul by Japanese Emily four-engined flying boats; two of the latter are shot down by the fighter cover. An attack by two squadrons each with nine carrier aircraft of the Japanese 25th Naval Air Flotilla from Rabaul is intercepted by *Lexington*'s fighter cover: Lt O'Hare alone shoots down five planes. Rear-Adm Brown abandons the plan to attack and makes for

the rendezvous with the tanker *Platte* on 23 Feb. She is accompanied by the ANZAC Force (Rear Adm Crace RAN), comprising the cruisers *Achilles* (RNZN), *Australia* (RAN), *Chicago* (USN) and *Leander* (RNZN) and the destroyers *Flusser* and *Perkins* (USN). The combined forces make a sortie into the Coral Sea from 27 Feb to 4 Mar and join up with the newly-arrived TF.17 on 6 Mar near the New Hebrides.

1 Feb   Atlantic/Intelligence
Introduction into service of the new 'M-4' cypher machine for Atlantic U-boats. This machine has, instead of three rotors inside, the left one divided into a new small reflector 'B' and a 'Greek' rotor 'Beta', forcing Bletchley Park to use 26 times more bomb runs to break the daily key. However, at the same time a new 'Wetterkurzschlüssel' is introduced, and there are few convoy operations with many contact signals, so Bletchley Park experiences an 11-month 'black-out' regarding U-boat signals; information on U-boats now comes only from decoded 'Heimisch' signals from vessels escorting U-boats out from or into the Biscay ports.

1–10 Feb   Arctic
The Allied convoys PQ.9 and PQ.10 with ten ships together leave Reykjavik for Murmansk. The escort comprises the destroyers *Faulknor* and *Intrepid* and several trawlers. Cover is provided by the cruiser *Nigeria*.

3–6 Feb   Dutch East Indies
On 3 Feb 26 bombers of the Japanese 23rd Naval Air Flotilla, based on Kendari, make an attack on Soerabaya for the first time with fighter protection. Following a reconnaissance report by an Allied aircraft about the concentration of a Japanese landing force off Balikpapan, ABDAFLOAT (Adm Hart) orders an Allied Force under the Dutch Rear-Adm Doorman to make a sortie towards the Makassar Strait. It sets out from Madoera during the night 3–4 Feb with the cruisers *De Ruyter* (F, Dutch), *Houston*, *Marblehead* (US), *Tromp* (Dutch) and the destroyers *Barker*, *Bulmer*, *Edwards* and *Stewart* (US) and *Banckert*, *Piet Hein* and *Van Ghent* (Dutch). The force is sighted on the morning of 4 Feb N of Bali by a Japanese formation of 37 bombers with fighter protection as it flies to Soerabaya and it is attacked. *Marblehead* (Capt Robinson) is badly damaged by hits and many near-misses and only reaches Tjilatjap by steering with her propellers. *Houston* loses her third 8in turret. The other ships are unharmed despite near-misses but they turn back and reach port on 5–6 Feb.

The US submarine *Salmon* (Lt Mc-Kinney) torpedoes the Japanese destroyer *Suzukaze* off Kendari on 4 Feb.

4–18 Feb   Dutch East Indies
Of the Japanese 4th SM Flotilla, *I-55* (Cdr Nakajima) sinks two ships of 6456 tons in the area of Makassar and the Java Sea and two more sinkings are unconfirmed. *I-56* (Cdr Ohashi) sinks one ship of 979 tons and one other unidentified vessel in Sunda Strait.

5–7 Feb   Dutch East Indies
To cover a Dutch reinforcement mission with two transports, escorted by the cruiser *Java* from Batavia to Palembang, a British force comprising the cruiser *Exeter* and the destroyers *Encounter* and *Jupiter*, strengthened by the Australian cruiser *Hobart*, makes a sortie from Sunda Strait through Banka Strait. On the return the force is unsuccessfully attacked NW of Sunda Strait by the Japanese submarine *Ro-34* (Lt-Cdr Ota) which also misses a Dutch destroyer.

At this time the cruisers *Canberra*, *Cornwall*, *Danae*, *Dragon* and *Durban*, the destroyer *Electra* and the sloops *Sutlej* and *Yarra* operate in convoy service between Ceylon and Sunda Strait.

5–15 Feb   Mediterranean
In British submarine operations, *Upholder* (Lt-Cdr Wanklyn) sinks one ship of 2710 tons E of Sardinia, *Una* (Lt Norman) one of 8106 tons off Cotrone and *P38* (Lt Hemingway) one of 4116 tons in a convoy escorted by the Italian destroyer *Premuda* and the torpedo boat *Polluce* off the Tunisian coast. In an attempt to attack a convoy off Cephalonia, *Proteus* is damaged by the Italian torpedo boat *Sagittario*. On 13 Feb *Tempest* (Lt-Cdr Cavaye) is forced to surface in the Gulf of Taranto by the Italian torpedo boat *Circe* (Cdr Palmas) and sinks when an attempt is made to take her in tow; 39 men are lost.

6 Feb   North Atlantic
The U-boat *U82*, which is on her way from the US coast, encounters the convoy OS.18 and is sunk by depth charges from the sloop *Rochester* and the corvette *Tamarisk*.

6–9 Feb   Dutch East Indies
Japanese landing near Makassar (Celebes). On 6 Feb Rear-Adm Kubo sets out from Kendari with the cruiser *Nagara*, three fast assault boats and two submarine-chasers of the 1st BF and six transports with the Sasebo Special Landing Force on board; escort is provided by the minesweepers *W7* and *W8*, the destroyers *Asashio*, *Oshio*, *Michishio* and *Arashio* (8th DD Div), *Kuroshio*, *Oyashio*, *Hayashio* and *Natsushio* (15th DD Div) and *Hatsushimo*, *Nenohi* and *Wakaba* (21st DD Div). On 8 Feb the force arrives off Makassar, where the US submarine *S37* (Lt Dempsey) sinks the

destroyer *Natsushio*. In addition, the destroyers *Kawakaze*, *Umikaze* (1/24th DD Div), *Minegumo* and *Natsugumo* (9th DD Div) and the minesweepers *W15*, *W16*, *W17* and *W18* under Rear-Adm Hirose come from Balikpapan to support the landing. Air escort for the operation is provided by the 11th Carrier Sqn (Rear-Adm Fujita) with the seaplane carriers *Chitose* and *Mizuho* and the depot ship *Sanyo Maru*. A covering force is provided (by Vice-Adm Takagi) with the cruisers *Haguro* and *Nachi* and the destroyers *Akebono* and *Ikazuchi*. The landing succeeds against slight resistance. A sortie made by the Dutch Rear-Adm Doorman with the cruisers *De Ruyter* and *Tromp* and two destroyers is abandoned on 8 Feb shortly after the ships set out.

6–23 Feb   Arctic
The Allied convoy PQ.11 with 13 ships leaves Loch Ewe for Murmansk.

7–8 Feb   Mediterranean
The British destroyers *Lively* and *Zulu* sink two small Italian independents of 816 tons in a sortie W of Sicily.

7–15 Feb   South Asia
Final battle for Singapore. During the night 7–8 Feb a battle group of the Japanese Guards Div lands on the island of Ubin in the eastern part of the Johore Strait.
On 8 Feb the artillery of the 25th Army begins to shell Singapore, while bombers of the 3rd Air Div simultaneously attack the British positions. In the night of 9 Feb the Japanese 5th and 18th Inf Divs cross the Johore Strait and they are followed the next night by the Guards Div from Johore-Bharu. On 9 Feb the British survey sloop *Herald* is damaged in an air raid and is scuttled, (though is later salvaged by the Japanese and commissioned as the escort vessel *Heiyo*). Supported by two armoured regiments, the Japanese force the British back into the city of Singapore by 15 Feb. In the evening of the same day Lt-Gen Percival, who is responsible for the defence, surrenders to the Commander of the 25th Army, Lt-Gen Yamashita.

8–10 Feb   North Atlantic
U85 and *U654* (Lt Forster) attack the convoy ONS.61 off Newfoundland. *U654* torpedoes the Free French corvette *Alysse* after leaving convoy ONS.60. She is taken in tow but founders on 10 Feb.

8 Feb–8 Mar   Pacific
The Japanese submarines *I-9*, *I-17* and *I-23* operate from 8 to 15 Feb S of Oahu. *I-17* (Cdr* Nishino) then proceeds to the American West Coast. On 20 Feb she observes San Diego; on 23–24 Feb she shells Elwood in California; and on 1 Mar she unsuccessfully attacks the tanker *William H*

Berg (8298 tons) off San Francisco. *I-23* disappears after 14 Feb. *I-9* (Cdr* Fujii) reconnoitres Pearl Harbor with her aircraft on 24 Feb. On 26 Feb *I-15*, *I-19* and *I-26*, after being equipped as flying boat suppliers, set out from Kwajalein to the French Frigate Shoals and supply there on 3–4 Mar two four-engined flying boats on their flight from Wotje to attack Pearl Harbor. The bombs miss. On 7 Mar *I-15* (Cdr* Ishikawa) sights US TF.8 with the carrier *Enterprise* returning from the raid on Marcus, but the other boats do not come up.

9 Feb   Western Atlantic
The US troop transport *Lafayette* (ex-*Normandie*, 83423 tons) is burnt out and capsizes in New York harbour.

9 Feb   Mediterranean
German bombers badly damage the British destroyer *Farndale* W of Mersa Matruh.

9–11 Feb   Mediterranean
The British cruiser *Cleopatra* is transferred with the destroyer *Fortune* from Gibraltar to Malta.

9–17 Feb   Dutch East Indies
Japanese landings near Palembang. On 9 Feb an advance detachement of the Japanese 38th Inf Div on board eight transports sets out from Camranh Bay. It is escorted by Rear-Adm Hashimoto with the cruiser *Sendai*, the destroyers *Fubuki*, *Amagiri*, *Yugiri* and *Asagiri*, the minesweepers *W1*, *W2*, *W3*, *W4*, *W5* and the submarine-chasers *Ch7* and *Ch8*. On 10 Feb Vice-Adm Ozawa follows with the covering group of the Western Force, comprising the cruisers *Chokai*, *Kumano*, *Mikuma*, *Mogami* and *Suzuya*, the destroyers *Uranami*, *Isonami*, *Ayanami*, the cruiser *Yura* and the carrier *Ryujo* with the destroyer *Shikinami*. On 11 Feb the bulk of the 229th Inf Regt and one battalion of the 230th Inf Regt put to sea on board 13 smaller transports, escorted by the cruiser *Kashii* (Capt Kojima), the frigate *Shimushu*, the destroyers *Shirayuki*, *Hatsuyuki*, *Murakumo* and *Shirakumo* and the submarine-chaser *Ch9*.
The Dutch submarines *K-XI*, *K-XII*, *K-XIII* and *K-XIV*, which have been stationed both sides of the Anambas against such operations, do not approach. On 11 Feb an Allied reconnaissance aircraft sights the invasion fleet. At this point many small craft as well as 13 larger merchant ships, the transports *Empire Star* and *Gorgon*, the auxiliary ship *Kedah* and the British cruiser *Durban* and the destroyers *Jupiter* and *Stronghold*, loaded with refugees from Singapore, now threatened from the mainland, are proceeding to Sumatra and Java. On 11–12 Feb two auxiliary ships, 12 steamers and

a convoy with six large tankers, coming from Palembang, join the convoys. They are accompanied by the Australian mine-sweeping corvettes *Wollongong*, *Bendigo*, *Toowoomba* and *Ballarat*.
Carrier aircraft from *Ryujo* and shore-based bombers with fighter protection from the Genzan Air Corps are deployed by the Japanese against the shipping concentrations. On 13 Feb the large tankers *Manvantara* (8237 tons) and *Merula* (8277 tons), the steamer *Subadar* (5424 tons) and many smaller ships fall victim. The transport *Anglo-Indian* (5609 tons), the *Empire Star* (12656 tons) and the tanker *Seirstad* (9916 tons) are badly damaged. From the Japanese submarines of the 4th Flotilla deployed against the evacuations and as cover, *I-55* (Lt-Cdr Nakajima) sinks the ammunition transport *Derrymore* (4799 tons) N of Sunda Strait and *I-56* (Cdr Ohashi) torpedoes a ship from the convoys JS.1 and SJ.1 escorted by the cruisers *Exeter*, *Hobart* and *Java*, the destroyer *Electra* and the sloop *Jumna* S of Sunda Strait.
While, during the night 13–14 Feb, the Japanese advance detachment enters the Banka Strait sinking the British gunboat *Scorpion*, an Allied Striking Force (Rear-Adm Doorman), comprising the cruisers *De Ruyter*, *Java*, *Tromp* (Dutch), *Exeter* (British) and *Hobart* (Australian) and the destroyers *Banckert*, *Kortenaer*, *Piet Hein* and *Van Ghent* (Dutch) and *Barker*, *Bulmer*, *John D Edwards*, *Parrott*, *Pillsbury* and *Stewart* (US), puts to sea from Batavia to attack. It is located in the morning of 14 Feb by Japanese air reconnaissance and throughout the day attacked by carrier aircraft from *Ryujo* and shore-based aircraft S of Banka Island, where the British gunboats *Dragonfly* and *Grasshopper* are sunk but no significant hits are obtained on bigger ships; only *Barker* and *Bulmer* drop out because of numerous near-misses. *Van Ghent* is lost on the way out when she goes aground. Because of the threat from the Allied squadron, Adm Ozawa orders the advance detachment to anchor off Muntok (Banka) and the main body to withdraw to the NE. At the same time he tries with all his operational ships to close in on the Allied squadron which, however, gets away. But many of the smaller evacuation transports fall victim to his ships and aircraft.
Early on 14 Feb Japanese transport aircraft land 460 parachute troops to capture the airfield N of Palembang and the refinery and oilfields of Pladjoe to the E of it. Against tough resistance the Japanese can only just hold on with their remaining forces. Air attacks by 36 Hudson and Blenheim

bombers with 22 Hurricane fighters on the invasion force off Muntok on 14 Feb sink the transport *Inabasan Maru* (989 tons) and hold up the advance of the Japanese assault boats on the Moesie River on the way to Palembang on 15 Feb. After the Allied Striking Force has gone away, the main Japanese force arrives and lands with the result that Palembang has to be evacuated on 16 Feb.

9–20 Feb   Indian Ocean
Off Ceylon the Japanese submarines *I-65* (Lt-Cdr Harada) and *I-66* (Cdr Yoshitome) sink two ships of 9960 tons (and probably one more unknown ship) and one of 2076 tons respectively.

9–28 Feb   Pacific
Off the east coast of Japan, the US submarine *Trout* (Lt-Cdr Fennon) sinks three ships of 9507 tons, *Triton* (Lt-Cdr Lent) sinks two of 5984 tons and *Cuttlefish* (Lt-Cdr Hottel) damages one of 6515 tons.

10 Feb–20 Mar   Western Atlantic
A third wave of 15 U-boats operates singly in the area between Newfoundland and Cape Hatteras, including the six boats which participate in the operation against the convoy ONS.67 (21–25 Feb). The following are the results achieved solely on the American East Coast: *U432* (Lt-Cdr Schultze) sinks five ships of 24987 tons, *U504* (Cdr Poske) sinks four ships of 26561 tons, *U96* (Cdr Lehmann-Willenbrock) sinks five ships of 25464 tons, *U69* (Lt-Cdr Zahn) has no success, *U578* (Cdr Rehwinkel) sinks two ships of 10540 tons and the destroyer *Jacob Jones*, *U653* (Lt-Cdr Feiler) sinks one ship of 1582 tons, *U656* (Lt-Cdr Kröning) is lost on 1 Mar (to a Hudson of VP-82) having achieved no success, *U404* (Lt-Cdr v Bülow) sinks four ships of 22653 tons, *U94* (Lt Ites) sinks four ships of 14442 tons, *U558* (Lt-Cdr Krech) has successes only with convoy ONS.67, *U587* (Lt-Cdr Borcherdt) sinks two ships of 6619 tons, *U155* (Lt-Cdr Piening) sinks one ship of 7874 tons and *U158* (Lt-Cdr Rostin) sinks three ships of 21202 tons and torpedoes one of 7118 tons.

10–25 Feb   Mediterranean
The German U-boats *U652*, *U83*, *U81* and *U559*, despite many attacks, operate without success against British supply traffic for Tobruk.

11 Feb   Western Atlantic
American troops occupy Curaçao and Aruba (Dutch West Indies).

11–12 Feb   Norway
The German minelayers *Ulm* and *Brummer* lay flanking mine barrages off Arnöy and the Bökfjord.

12 Feb   English Channel
Operation 'Cerberus'. After several weeks of minesweeping work by the 1st, 2nd, 4th, 5th and 12th MS Flotillas and the 2nd, 3rd and 4th MMS Flotillas in the Channel and in the southern North Sea, in which *M1208* is lost during the night 10–11 Feb off Barfleur, the battlecruisers *Scharnhorst* (Capt Hoffmann with the Cdr Battleships, Vice-Adm Ciliax on board) and *Gneisenau* (Capt Fein) and the heavy cruiser *Prinz Eugen* (Capt Brinkmann) set out from Brest during the night of 11–12 Feb. Escort is provided by the destroyers *Z29* (with the Officer Commanding Destroyers, Rear-Adm Bey, on board), *Richard Beitzen* (with the Cdr 5th DD Flotilla, Capt Berger, on board), *Z25*, *Paul Jacobi*, *Friedrich Ihn* and *Hermann Schoemann*. Later the 2nd TB Flotilla (Cdr Erdmann), comprising *T2*, *T4*, *T5*, *T11* and *T12* from Le Havre and the 3rd TB Flotilla (Cdr Wilcke), comprising *T13*, *T15*, *T16* and *T17* from Dunkirk, join the force. In addition, the 5th TB Flotilla (Cdr* Schmidt), consisting of *Seeadler*, *Falke*, *Kondor*, *Iltis* and *Jaguar*, joins them in the area of Cape Gris Nez. Beyond this, units of Cdr Naval Defence Forces West and, later, Commander Naval Forces North and the MTB Flotillas 2 (Lt-Cdr Feldt), 4 (Lt-Cdr Bätge) and 6 (Lt-Cdr Obermaier) form part of the Force's escort. Luftflotte 3 (Field Marshal Sperrle) makes 176 heavy bombers and fighter aircraft available (chiefly JG 2 and 26 and later JG 1) for air protection, of which at least 16 machines are able to fly constantly over the naval force.

The German force is first discovered in the area of Le Touquet and unsuccessfully shelled by British coastal batteries. From Dover five MTBs (Cdr Pumphrey) and from Ramsgate three MTBs (Lt-Cdr Long) put to sea. Their torpedo attacks are unsuccessful. Three boats are damaged. The Swordfish from No 825 Sqn (Cdr Esmonde†), which are on the spot, attack the German ships in the area of Gravelines; all six aircraft are shot down. Many bombers and torpedo aircraft which are later sent in fail to find their targets. They sink the patrol ship *V1302* and damage the torpedo boats *T13* and *Jaguar*. Finally, a destroyer force from Harwich (21st DD Flotilla, Capt Pizey), comprising *Campbell* and *Vivacious*, and, under command, the 16th DD Flotilla (Capt Wright), comprising *Worcester*, *Whitshed* and *Walpole*, succeeds in approaching the German force; but these destroyer attacks also fail in the heavy defensive fire. *Worcester* is set on fire and reaches harbour with difficulty. On the way *Scharnhorst* hits two mines and *Gneisenau* one, but they are

able to reach Wilhelmshaven and the Elbe estuary respectively under their own steam.

12 Feb   South West Pacific
Formation of the ANZAC Squadron (Rear-Adm Crace), consisting of the cruisers *Australia* (Australian), *Chicago* (US) and *Achilles* and *Leander* (New Zealand) and the destroyers *Lamson* and *Perkins* (US) in Suva (Fiji).

12–16 Feb   Mediterranean
British supply operation MF.5 to Malta. On 12 Dec the convoys MW.9A (transports *Clan Campbell* and *Clan Chattan*, escorted by the cruiser *Carlisle* and the destroyers *Lance*, *Heythrop*, *Avon Vale* and *Eridge*) and MW.9B (transport *Rowallan Castle*, escorted by the destroyers *Beaufort*, *Dulverton*, *Hurworth* and *Southwold*) set out from Alexandria with a small interval between them. They are followed by the covering group Force B (Rear-Adm Vian), comprising the cruisers *Naiad*, *Dido* and *Euryalus* and the destroyers *Jervis*, *Kipling*, *Kelvin*, *Jaguar*, *Griffin*, *Havock*, *Hasty* and *Arrow*. In a German air attack on Malta the destroyer *Maori* blows up after bomb hits, damaging the destroyer *Decoy*. On 13 Feb Force K, consisting of the cruiser *Penelope* and the destroyers *Zulu*, *Sikh*, *Legion*, *Lively*, *Fortune* and *Decoy*, puts to sea from Malta with convoy ME.10 (the transports *Ajax*, *Breconshire*, *Clan Fergusson* and *City of Calcutta*). On 13 Feb German and Italian air reconnaissance locates the westbound forces and the *Clan Campbell* (7255 tons) has to put into Tobruk after being hit by a bomb. Shortly before the convoys MW.9 and ME.10 join up on 14 Feb, the first is again attacked by German bombers of LG 1: *Clan Chattan* (7262 tons) is so badly hit that she has to be scuttled. After the convoys have joined up, *Rowallan Castle* (7798 tons) also sinks after bomb hits. The covering forces, after exchanging the destroyer *Lance* for *Decoy* and *Fortune*, start the return journey. Div-Adm Bergamini sets out to sea to search for the British forces from Taranto with the battleship *Duilio*, the cruisers *Duca d'Aosta* and *Montecuccoli* and the destroyers *Folgore*, *Fulmine*, *Saetta*, *Alpino*, *Carabiniere*, *Fuciliere* and *Bersagliere* and Div-Adm Parona from Messina with the heavy cruisers *Gorizia* and *Trento* and the destroyers *Aviere*, *Geniere*, *Camicia Nera* and *Ascari*. But the search produces no results on 15 Feb. Force K, with *Penelope*, *Lance* and *Legion*, reaches Malta on this day and *Zulu*, *Sikh* and *Lively* proceed with Force B to Alexandria, where they arrive on 16 Feb. The British submarine *P36* (Lt Edmonds) torpedoes the destroyer *Cara-*

biniere from the returning Italian forces off Taranto; the ship is taken in tow.

12–22 Feb   Arctic
The Allied convoy QP.7 proceeds with eight ships from Murmansk to Seidisfjord, escorted by the destroyers *Faulknor* and *Intrepid*. Cover is provided by the cruiser *Nigeria*.

13–14 Feb   Black Sea
On 13 and 14 Feb respectively the Soviet cruisers *Komintern* and *Krasny Krym*, accompanied by the destroyers *Dzerzhinski* and *Shaumyan* respectively, bring 2109 reserve troops to Sevastopol.

14 Feb–10 Mar   Central Pacific
US carrier raids on Wake and Marcus. On 14 Feb TF.8 (Vice-Adm Halsey) sets out from Pearl Harbor with the carrier *Enterprise*, the cruisers *Northhampton* (Rear-Adm Spruance) and *Salt Lake City* and Desron 6, comprising the destroyers *Balch, Maury, Craven, Dunlap, Blue* and *Ralph Talbot*, and the escort tanker *Sabine*. On 24 Feb 36 bombers, accompanied by six fighters, make a raid on Wake (one plane lost); then the island is shelled by *Northampton, Salt Lake City, Balch* and *Maury*. On 4 Mar *Enterprise* makes a similar raid on the island of Marcus, lying further to the W (one plane lost). TF.17 (Vice-Adm Fletcher), which sets out on 16 Feb to make a raid on Eniwetok Atoll (Carolines) and which consists of the carrier *Yorktown*, the cruisers *Astoria* and *Louisville*, the destroyers *Sims, Hughes, Walke, Russell, Anderson* and *Hammann* and the escort tanker *Guadeloupe*, has to be recalled to undertake very urgent convoy covering duties on the route to the SW Pacific. From 17 Feb it proceeds via the Phoenix Islands (21–28 Feb) to the New Hebrides, where on 6 Mar it joins up with TF.11.

15–24 Feb   Dutch East Indies
Japanese attacks on Port Darwin, Timor and Bali. To counter the growing threat to Timor, an Allied convoy of four transports, escorted by the US cruiser *Houston*, the US destroyer *Peary* and the Australian sloops *Swan* and *Warrego*, tries on 15 Feb to bring reinforcements from Port Darwin to Timor. After an air attack by 36 Japanese naval bombers from Kendari (Celebes) on the force on 16 Feb, it is recalled and arrives back in Port Darwin on 17 Feb. The Dutch Vice-Adm Helfrich, who is appointed ABDAFLOAT in place of the US Adm Hart on 16 Feb, takes those ships which are still operational and are being used to cover the evacuation from Southern Sumatra in the area of the Sunda Strait to the E. *Houston* is ordered to proceed at high speed to Tji-latjap to join Rear-Adm Doorman's forces.

Japanese carrier raid on Port Darwin. On 15 Feb the 1st Carrier Air Fleet (Vice-Adm Nagumo) sets out from Palau with the carriers *Akagi* and *Kaga* (1st Carrier Sqn) and *Hiryu* and *Soryu* (2nd Carrier Sqn), the battleships *Kirishima* and *Hiyei* (1/3rd BB Sqn), the heavy cruisers *Chikuma* and *Tone* (8th Cruiser Sqn) and the 1st DD Flotilla with the cruiser *Abukuma* and the destroyers *Urakaze, Isokaze, Tanikaze* and *Hamakaze* (17th DD Div), *Kasumi, Arare, Kagero* and *Shiranuhi* (18th DD Div) and *Akigumo*. It proceeds westwards past Halmahera and Ambon into the Banda Sea. There, early on 19 Feb, it flies off 71 dive-bombers and 81 torpedo bombers with 36 fighters to attack the North Australian harbour of Port Darwin. The US destroyer *Peary* and seven large transports and merchant ships of 43429 tons are destroyed and, in addition, four small defence and harbour craft. The Australian sloop *Swan*, the US aircraft tender *William B Preston* and six large transports and merchant ships are damaged. On 21 Feb the Japanese force returns to Kendari (Celebes). On the same day Vice-Adm Kondo, who sets out from Palau on 18 Feb, arrives there with the Japanese Main Force. He has in his force the heavy cruisers *Atago, Maya* and *Takao* (4th Cruiser Sqn), the battleships *Haruna* and *Kongo* (2/3rd BB Sqn) and the destroyers *Nowake, Hagikaze, Maikaze* and *Arashi* (4th DD Div) and *Akatsuki* and *Hibiki* (1/6th DD Div).

Landing on Bali and battle in the Bandoeng Strait. On 17 Feb a Japanese advance detachment sets out from Makassar, comprising the transports *Sagami Maru* (7189 tons) and *Sasago Maru* (8260 tons) with one battalion of the 48th Inf Div on board, escorted by the destroyers *Oshio, Asashio, Michishio* and *Arashio* (8th DD Div). N of Bali Rear-Adm Kubo, with the cruiser *Nagara* and the destroyers *Wakaba, Hatsushimo* and *Nenohi* (21st DD Div), acts as a covering force. The invasion force arrives in the evening of 18 Feb and lands the troops early on 19 Feb without resistance. In an air attack by Dutch planes, both transports are slightly damaged. Torpedo attacks by the submarine *Seawolf* (US) and *Truant* (British) fail as a result of defects and misses. When air reconnaissance reports the force, Doorman sets out in the evening of 18 Feb from Tjilatjap (South Java) with the cruisers *De Ruyter* and *Java* and the destroyers *Kortenaer* and *Piet Hein* (Dutch) and *Ford* and *Pope* (US) to attack the invasion fleet; in addition, the Dutch cruiser *Tromp* sets out from Soerabaya with the US destroyers *Stewart, Parrott, John D Edwards* and *Pillsbury*. Doorman's force, which arrives

first in the late evening of 19 Feb after the withdrawal of the remaining Japanese ships in the Bandoeng Strait, only encounters the *Sasago Maru*, which is hit several times by gunfire from *Java*. *Asashio* and *Oshio* sink *Piet Hein* in a confused engagement. Shortly after midnight on 20 Feb the second Allied force attacks but all 20 torpedoes fired by the US destroyers miss. In the gun engagement, *Stewart* and *Tromp*, as well as *Oshio*, sustain damage. One hour later the Japanese destroyers *Asashio* and *Michishio*, which are recalled, again find the withdrawing Allied force. In a fierce engagement, *Michishio* is shelled and becomes unmanoeuvrable and *Tromp* receives heavy hits from *Arashio*. Five Dutch motor torpedo boats, directed to the Japanese force, do not find their targets. In attacks by shore-based Japanese naval air units, the Dutch destroyer *Van Nes* is destroyed on 18 Feb in the Sunda Strait and the coast defence ship *Soerabaja* and the submarine *K-XII* in Soerabaya.

Japanese landing on Timor. On 17 Feb the seaplane carrier *Mizuho* sets out from Kendari with a submarine-chaser for the Flores Sea to reconnoitre for the Timor and Port Darwin operations. On the same day nine transports with the 228th Inf Regt and the 3rd Yokosuka Special Air Landing Force put to sea from Ambon, escorted by Rear-Adm Tanaka with the cruiser *Jintsu* and the destroyers *Yukikaze, Tokitsukaze, Amatsukaze* and *Hatsukaze* (16th DD Div), *Kuroshio, Oyashio* and *Hayashio* (15th DD Div) and *Umikaze*. On 18 Feb a second force of five transports follows, escorted by the destroyers *Kawakaze* and *Yamakaze* (1/24th DD Div), the minesweepers W7 and W8, the fast transports P1, P2 and P34 and submarine-chasers. Rear-Adm Takagi provides cover for the operation in the Timor Sea with the heavy cruisers *Haguro* and *Nachi* (5th Cruiser Sqn) and the destroyers *Akebono* and *Ikazuchi*. Early on 20 Feb the landings succeed in Dili (Portuguese Timor) and Koepang (Dutch Timor). An attack by the US submarine *Pike* on the minesweeper W7 fails. On 24 Feb all key points in Timor are occupied and the Japanese forces return to Makassar, Ambon and Kendari.

15 Feb–3 Mar   Arctic
Off Tanafjord on 15 Feb the Soviet submarine *S-101* (Capt 3rd Class Vekke with the Div Cdr, Capt 3rd Class Khomyakov, on board) sinks the Norwegian steamer *Mimona* (1147 tons) from a convoy and *K-1* lays mines there. On the way to laying out the first flanking mine barrages off the Varanger peninsula, to protect German supplies from Soviet submarine attacks, the

minelayer *Brummer* (Cdr* Dr Tobias) sights in the mist off Porsangerfjord on 18 Feb the surfaced Soviet submarine *Shch-403* (Lt-Cdr Kovalenko), which narrowly evades being rammed by the minelayer but is then lightly rammed by *M1503* (Sub-Lt Abel). The Cdr is rescued from the sinking conning tower of the submarine. But the crew save the submarine and bring her back to Murmansk. On 19 Feb *M-171* (Lt-Cdr Starikov) attacks a convoy, misses two steamers and is attacked by depth charges from the submarine-chasers *UJ1205* and *UJ1214*. *Shch-402* (Capt 3rd Class Stolbov), which has come into Porsangerfjord as a relief, sinks the patrol boat *NM01/Vandale* on 27 Feb, misses a convoy on 1 Mar and is severely damaged by the submarine-chasers *UJ1102* and *UJ1105* on 3 Mar. Because the submarine-chasers withdraw with the minesweeping ship *Paris*, *K-21* (Capt 3rd Class Lunin), which is sent to give help, is able to meet the disabled *Shch-402* and bring her to Polyarnoe.

16 Feb–18 Mar   Western Atlantic
Operation 'Neuland': a simultaneous attack on the oil terminal ports at Aruba (*U156*), Curaçao (*U67*) and Maracaibo/Venezuela (*U502*) on 16 Feb. On 19 Feb *U161* enters Port of Spain (Trinidad) and on 10 Mar Port Castries (St Lucia) and torpedoes ships lying along the pier. *U129* operates off the Guiana coast and the other boats, after their attacks, in the Caribbean. Their total successes: *U67* (Lt-Cdr Müller-Stöckheim) sinks one ship of 8436 tons and damages two of 12210 tons, *U156* (Cdr Hartenstein) sinks five ships of 22723 tons and damages two of 10769 tons, *U502* (Lt-Cdr v Rosenstiel) sinks five ships of 25232 tons, damages one of 9002 tons and has one more certain but unidentified success, *U129* (Lt-Cdr Clausen) sinks seven ships of 25613 tons and *U161* (Lt-Cdr Achilles) sinks four ships of 26903 tons and the US Coast Guard ship *Acacia* and torpedoes four ships of 30511 tons in harbour.

16 Feb–19 Apr   North Atlantic
The progressive withdrawal of US destroyers from the Mid Ocean Escort Force in the North Atlantic, for use in the Pacific or for escorting troop convoys from the US to the UK and as fleet escorts, forces a change in the escort operations for the HX, SC, ON and ONS convoys. The WESTOMP is changed to 45° W and EASTOMP to 22° W to allow the MOEF groups a through escort without change at MOMP: Canadian Western Local Escort Groups escort the convoys between Halifax and WESTOMP and British groups between EASTOMP and Londonderry.

The 'short leg' destroyers are assigned to the Local Escort Groups.

The EGs of the MOEF change their composition between round trips, but the general assignment is as follows:

A1/24.1.1: US destroyers *Benson*, *Broome* and *MacLeish* or *McCormick*, RCN corvettes *Alberni*, *Collingwood*, *Hepatica*; A2/24.1.2: US destroyer *Niblack*, US Coast Guard cutter *Ingham*, RCN corvettes *Mayflower*, *Rosthern*, *Agassiz*, *Chambly* and *Barrie*, FFN corvette *Aconit*; A3/24.1.3: US destroyer *Gleaves*, US Coast Guard cutter *Spencer*, RCN corvettes *Bittersweet*, *Chilliwack*, *Shediac* and *Algome*; A4/24.1.4: US destroyers *Mayo* and *Simpson*, US corvettes *Impulsive* and *Ready*, RNoN corvettes *Acanthus*, *Eglantine*, *Rose* and *Potentilla*, RN corvette *Mignonette*; A5/24.1.5: US destroyers *Bristol* and *Buck*, RN corvettes *Kingcup*, *Loosestrife* and *Dianella*, FFN corvette *Roselys*; C1/24.1.11: RCN destroyers *Assiniboine* and *St Croix*, RCN corvettes *Buctouche* and *Chambly*, RN corvettes *Dianthus* and *Nasturtium*; C2/24.1.12: RCN destroyer *St Laurent*, RN destroyer *Broadway*, RCN corvettes *Brandon*, *Drumheller* and *Morden*, RN corvette *Polyanthus*; C3/24.1.13: RCN destroyers *Saguenay* and *Skeena*, RCN corvettes *Wetaskiwin*, *Sackville*, *Galt* and *Camrose*; C4/24.1.14: RCN destroyers *Ottawa*, *Restigouche* and *St Francis*, RCN corvettes *Lethbridge*, *Prescott*, *Eyebright* and *Arvida*; B1/24.1.15: RN destroyers *Hurricane*, *Rockingham* and *Venomous*, RN corvettes *Anchusa*, *Dahlia* and *Monkshood*; B2/24.1.16: RN destroyers *Hesperus*, *Leamington* and *Veteran*, RN corvettes *Clematis*, *Gentian*, *Sweetbriar* and *Vervain*; B3/24.1.17: RN destroyers *Harvester*, *Georgetown* and *Bulldog*, RN corvettes *Heartsease* and *Narcissus*, FFN corvettes *Lobélia* and *Renoncule*; B4/24.1.18: RN destroyers *Highlander*, *Roxborough* and *Winchelsea*, RN corvettes *Anemone*, *Pennywort* and *Asphodel*; B5/24.1.19: RN destroyers *Havelock*, *Caldwell*, *Vanoc* and *Walker*, RN corvettes *Pimpernel*, *Godetia* and *Saxifrage* (most of this group is transferred to the Caribbean in late Feb/early Mar).

The convoys SC.70–SC.80, HX.176–HX.185, ONS.68–ONS.93 and ON.68–ON.95 are escorted by these groups. There are only very few chance contacts with individual U-boats running to and from the US East Coast and only from ONS.68 and ON.77 are ships sunk (one from each), by *U587* (Lt-Cdr Borcherdt) and *U94* (Lt Ites) respectively. *U507* (Lt-Cdr Schacht) attacks ONS.76 but all the torpedoes either fail to

detonate or explode at distances from the targets on 19 Mar.

17 Feb–23 Mar   Pacific
Reconnaissance operation by the Japanese submarine *I-25* (Cdr* Tagami) in the South Pacific. With her aircraft (CPO Fujita) she reconnoitres over Sydney (17 Feb), Melbourne (26 Feb), Hobart (1 Mar), Wellington (8 Mar), Suva/Samoa (19 Mar) and, with periscope, Pago Pago (23 Mar).

17–24 Feb   Dutch East Indies
Japanese forces prepare to attack Java.

Eastern Force: From 17 to 18 Feb light escort forces are transferred from Jolo to Balikpapan. From 19 to 22 Feb the main body with the 48th Inf Div on 41 transports proceeds from Jolo to Balikpapan. Escort is provided by the 4th DD Flotilla (Rear-Adm Nishimura—see 25 Feb–9 Mar for composition of forces). On 21 Feb they are reported by a US submarine. In Balikpapan the 56th Regimental Combat Group is embarked.

Western Force: On 8 Feb Vice-Adm Ozawa puts to sea from Camranh Bay with the main force—HQ 16th Army, the 2nd Inf Div and the 230th Inf Regt of the 38th Inf Div—on board 56 transports. Escort consists of the 5th DD Flotilla (Rear-Adm Hara). On 21 Feb the 3rd DD Flotilla (Rear-Adm Hashimoto) and the 1st MS Div come up from the Anamba Islands. On 22 Feb the invasion, fixed for 26 Feb, is postponed for two days when Allied naval forces are sighted by Japanese air reconnaissance. The Western Force cruises in the area of the Anamba Islands (flagship cruiser *Chokai*, the destroyer *Ayanami* out of action on going ashore) and the Eastern Force off Balikpapan. On 24 Feb the Western Force is reported by the US submarine *Saury*.

18 Feb   Western Atlantic
The large French submarine *Surcouf* (2880/4300 tons) sinks near the Antilles after a collision with an American freighter.

The US destroyer *Truxtun* runs aground in the entrance to Placentia Bay, Newfoundland, in a blizzard and is lost. The transport *Pollux* is wrecked and the destroyer *Wilkes* damaged.

19 Feb–2 Mar   North Atlantic
Troop convoy AT-12, with 13 ships and 14688 men, escorted by TF.32 with the battleship *New York*, the cruiser *Philadelphia* and the destroyers *Rhind*, *Rowan*, *Mayrant*, *Roe*, *Trippe*, *Hilary P Jones*, *Ludlow*, *Charles F Hughes*, *Lansdale* and *Ingraham*, from Casco Bay to MOMP. From there, 9646 men go for Belfast escorted by British destroyers. The rest, with escort by TF.32, relieve the US Marines in Iceland.

20 Feb   English Channel
The German mine destructor ship (MDS) *Sperrbrecher 171/Jason* is sunk by mine off Calais.

20 Feb–24 Mar   Western Atlantic
Five Italian submarines ('Da Vinci' group) operate E of the Antilles and make the following sinkings: *Torelli* (Cdr de Giacomo) two ships of 16469 tons, *Finzi* (Cdr Giudice) three ships of 21496 tons, *Tazzoli* (Cdr Fecia di Cossato) six ships of 29198 tons, *Morosini* (Cdr Fraternale) three ships of 22048 tons and *Da Vinci* (Cdr Longanesi) two ships of 7201 tons.

21–23 Feb   Norway
The pocket-battleship *Admiral Scheer* and heavy cruiser *Prinz Eugen*, escorted by the destroyers *Richard Beitzen*, *Paul Jacobi*, *Z25*, *Hermann Schoemann* and *Friedrich Ihn*, are transferred from Brunsbüttelkoog to Norway. British reconnaissance aircraft locate the ships in the southern North Sea, but an aircraft, maintaining contact, is shot down by fighters. Of the British aircraft which are then deployed, only one bomber finds the force. It drops its bombs near *Prinz Eugen* and is shot down by the ship's AA guns. On 22 Feb British reconnaissance aircraft again locate the force as it enters and anchors in Grimstadfjord, from where it sets out again on the same evening. *Beitzen*, *Ihn* and *Jacobi* return to Bergen owing to heavy weather. On 23 Feb, from a British submarine group (four boats) stationed off Trondheim, *Trident* (Cdr Sladen) approaches the force in the morning and scores a heavy torpedo hit on the stern of *Prinz Eugen*. An attempt by the British Home Fleet (Adm Tovey) with the aircraft carrier *Victorious*, the heavy cruiser *Berwick* and four destroyers—and the battleship *King George V* as cover—to intercept the German ships on their way N fails. The British force had put to sea to attack German shipping off Tromsö.

21–23 Feb   Mediterranean
Italian operation K.7, with two convoys from Messina and Corfu to Tripoli: one convoy of three ships escorted by the destroyers *Vivaldi*, *Malocello*, *Premuda*, *Zeno* and *Strale* and the torpedo boat *Pallade* and one of three ships escorted by the destroyers *Pigafetta*, *Pessagno*, *Usodimare*, *Maestrale*, and *Scirocco* and the torpedo boat *Circe*; distant cover is provided by the cruisers *Bande Nere*, *Gorizia* and *Trento*, the destroyers *Alpino*, *Da Noli*, *Oriani* and the battleship *Duilio* with the destroyers *Ascari*, *Aviere*, *Camicia Nera* and *Geniere*. Air attacks are repelled on 22 Feb by German fighter protection. An attempted attack by the British submarine *P38* ends

with her sinking by *Circe* and *Usodimare*.

21–25 Feb   North Atlantic
U155 (Lt-Cdr Piening) locates on 21 Feb, some 600 nautical miles NE of Cape Race, the convoy ON.67 which consists of 36 ships and is escorted by the US EG.A6 (Cdr Murdaugh), comprising the destroyers *Edison*, *Nicholson*, *Lea* and *Bernadou* and the Canadian corvette *Algoma*. For the first time contact signals are located by the rescue ship *Toward* fitted with a short wave D/F. But *U155* is able to evade the search by *Lea*, which is not yet equipped with radar, and during the night 21–22 Feb evades *Bernadou* and sinks two ships of 9783 tons. On the basis of her reports, the outbound U-boats *U69*, *U587*, *U558*, *U69*, *U588* and *U158* are directed to the convoy. In the morning of 24 Feb *U558* (Lt-Cdr Krech), after missing *Edison*, in three approaches torpedoes four ships of 27508 tons, of which two sink at once and the other two later. *U158* (Lt-Cdr Rostin) torpedoes two stray tankers, of which one (8032 tons) is sunk as a wreck on 26 Feb by *U587* and the other (8146 tons) is taken in tow. *U587* (Lt-Cdr Borcherdt) torpedoes one tanker of 9432 tons which *U558* later finishes off.

22 Feb   Black Sea
The Soviet cruiser *Krasny Krym* and destroyer *Boiki* bring supplies to Sevastopol and shell land targets.

22 Feb–11 Mar   Indian Ocean
In operations against the evacuation from Java, Japanese submarines sink twelve ships south of the Dutch East Indies Archipelago: *I-58* (Cdr Kitamura) sinks two ships of 10117 tons and torpedoes one other of 6735 tons, *I-53* (Cdr Nakamura) sinks three ships of 11002 tons, *I-54* (Cdr Kobayashi) sinks one ship of 8806 tons, *I-7* (Cdr* Koizumi) sinks one ship of 3271 tons, *I-1* (Cdr* Ankyu) sinks one ship of 8667 tons, *I-2* (Cdr* Inada) sinks one ship of 4360 tons, *I-3* (Cdr* Tonozuka) sinks one unknown medium-sized ship, *I-4* (Cdr* Nakagawa) sinks one ship of 1693 tons and *I-59* (Cdr Yoshimatsu) sinks one ship of 1035 tons. *I-121* operates in the Timor Sea, *I-121* in the Arafura Sea and *Ro-33* and *Ro-34* S of Java without success. *I-123* lays a mine barrage in the Torres Strait.

23 Feb   South Asia
General MacArthur, C-in-C in the Philippines, receives orders from President Roosevelt to proceed to Australia and to take over the command of Allied forces there. General Wainwright becomes the new C-in-C in the Philippines.

23–24 Feb   Black Sea
In operations against Axis shipping off the Bosphorus, the Soviet submarine *Shch-213*

(Lt D M Denezhko), after a torpedo miss, sinks the Turkish vessel *Çankaya* (454 tons) by gunfire at night. By day the Bulgarian *Struma*, sailing under the Panamanian flag and with 764 Jewish refugees on board, is sunk by torpedo; only one survivor is rescued. *Struma* had set out from Constanza on 12 Dec with 769 refugees, arriving at Istanbul on 16 Dec. Neither the disembarkation of the refugees nor their continued journey had been permitted by the Turkish authorities since the British mandatory government in Palestine had not granted immigration visas, and only five passengers had been allowed to land.

25 Feb–9 Mar   Dutch East Indies
Japanese invasion of Java. On 25 Feb the Japanese forces start their advance from the assembly areas. The Western Force consists of 56 transports, escorted by the 5th DD Flotilla (Rear-Adm Hara) comprising the cruiser *Natori* and the destroyers *Asakaze*, *Harukaze*, *Hatakaze* and *Matsukaze* (5th DD Div) and *Satsuki*, *Minatsuki*, *Fumitsuki* and *Nagatsuki* (22nd DD Div) and the 3rd DD Flotilla (Rear-Adm Hashimoto) comprising the cruiser *Sendai* and the destroyers *Fubuki*, *Hatsuyuki* and *Shirayuki* (11th DD Div) and *Murakumo* and *Shirakumo* (12th DD Div) and other units of the 9th BF including the cruiser *Yura* and the minelayer *Shirataka*, the minesweepers *W1*, *W2*, *W3* and *W4* (1st MS Div) and submarine-chasers. Cover is provided by the 7th Cruiser Sqn (Rear-Adm Kurita, also in overall command) with the cruisers *Kumano*, *Mikuma*, *Mogami* and *Suzuya* and the destroyers *Isonami*, *Shikinami* and *Uranami* (19th DD Div). Air support comes from the 4th Carrier Sqn (Rear-Adm Kakuta) with the carrier *Ryujo*, the 22nd Carrier Sqn with the seaplane carrier *Chiyoda*, the depot ship *Kamikawa Maru* and the destroyers *Amagiri*, *Asagiri* and *Yugiri* (20th DD Div).

The Eastern Force consists of 41 transports, escorted by the 4th DD Flotilla (Rear-Adm Nishimura) comprising the cruiser *Naka* and the destroyers *Asagumo*, *Minegumo* and *Natsugumo* (9th DD Div), *Murasame*, *Harusame*, *Samidare* and *Yudachi* (2nd DD Div) and *Umikaze*; in addition, units of the 2nd BF including the cruiser *Kinu*, the minelayer *Wakataka*, the minesweepers *W15* and *W16* and the submarine-chasers *Ch4*, *Ch5*, *Ch6*, *Ch16*, *Ch17* and *Ch18*. The 2nd DD Flotilla (Rear-Adm Tanaka), comprising the cruiser *Jintsu* and the destroyers *Yukikaze*, *Tokitsukaze*, *Amatsukaze* and *Hatsukaze* (16th DD Div), sets out from Koepang (Timor) on 24 Feb and joins the force. The 5th Cruiser Sqn (Rear-Adm

Takagi), comprising the cruisers *Haguro* and *Nachi* and the destroyers *Sazanami* and *Ushio* (1/7th DD Div) and *Kawakaze Yamakaze* (from the 24th DD Div), operates in the eastern part of the Java Sea as a covering force. In addition, the Commander of the 3rd Fleet (Vice-Adm Takashashi) comes up from Kendari (Celebes) with the 16th Cruiser Sqn, the cruisers *Ashigara* and *Myoko* and the destroyers *Akebono* and *Inazuma*. Apart from shore-based aircraft, air escort is provided by the 24th Carrier Sqn with the seaplane carrier *Mizuho* and the depot ship *Sanyo Maru*.

On 25 Feb the 1st Carrier Air Fleet (Vice-Adm Nagumo) sets out from Kendari (Celebes) through the Sape Strait to the area S of Java. It consists of the carriers *Akagi* and *Kaga* (1st Carrier Sqn) and *Hiryu* and *Soryu* (2nd Carrier Sqn), the battleships *Hiyei* and *Kirishima* (1/3rd BB Sqn), the heavy cruisers *Chikuma* and *Tone* (8th Cruiser Sqn) and the 1st DD Flotilla comprising the cruiser *Abukuma* and the destroyers *Tanikaze*, *Isokaze*, *Hamakaze* and *Urakaze* (17th DD Div) and *Shiranuhi*, *Kasumi*, *Ariake* and *Yugure* (18th DD Div) and six tankers. It is followed by the main force under Vice-Adm Kondo with the cruisers *Atago*, *Maya* and *Takao* (4th Cruiser Sqn), the battleships *Haruna* and *Kongo* (2/3rd BB Sqn) and the destroyers *Arashi*, *Hayashio* and *Nowake* (4th DD Div).

Of the Allied submarines *S37*, *S38*, *S39*, *Perch*, *Seal*, *Saury* and *Sailfish* (US) and *K-XIV*, *K-XV*, *K-X* and *O19* (Dutch) stationed in anticipation of Japanese movements, *S38* and *Seal* report elements of the Eastern Force on 24–25 Feb and *Saury* elements of the Western Force, but they do not attack. Further reports are received from air reconnaissance. The Allied Naval Commander, Vice-Adm Helfrich, then orders up the British cruiser *Exeter*, which is on escort duty with the destroyers *Electra*, *Encounter* and *Jupiter*, from Batavia to Soerabaya to reinforce Rear-Adm Doorman's battle squadron as well as the Australian cruiser *Perth*, the US cruiser *Houston* and the destroyers *Paul Jones*, *Alden* and *John D Ford*. The old British cruisers *Danae* and *Dragon* are ordered to Tandjok Priok (Batavia) with the destroyers *Scout* and *Tenedos* and also the Australian cruiser *Hobart* which cannot be refuelled in time. When Japanese air reconnaissance reports the Allied shipping movements off Java, the Japanese invasion forces are again halted on 26 Feb and forced to retire. A sortie made by the Allied Western Force (Capt Howden) with the cruisers *Danae*, *Dragon* and *Hobart* and the destroyers *Scout* and *Tenedos* from

Batavia to the area of Banka and Biliton on 26–27 Feb finds nothing. However, attacks by Japanese aircraft from *Ryujo*, *Chiyoda* and *Kamikawa Maru* are also unsuccessful. A sortie by the Eastern Force (Rear-Adm Doorman) with the cruisers *De Ruyter*, *Java*, *Houston*, *Exeter* and *Perth* and nine destroyers (see below) from Soerabaya against Japanese forces reported by reconnaissance in the night 26–27 Feb likewise leads to no result, as does a US air attack on the Japanese Eastern Force.

Battle of the Java Sea. Directly after returning to harbour at mid-day on 27 Feb, Doorman receives new reports and sets out again at once. He sends out the British destroyers *Electra*, *Encounter* and *Jupiter* ahead and to the port side the Dutch destroyers *Kortenaer* and *Witte de With*, in line the cruisers *De Ruyter*, *Exeter*, *Houston* and *Java*, followed by the US destroyers *Alden*, *John D Edwards*, *John D Ford* and *Paul Jones*. As a result of air reconnaissance reports from aircraft from the Japanese ships, the advancing eastern convoy is turned away to the W with the destroyers *Natsugumo* and *Umikaze* early in the afternoon when W of Bawean Island. The covering forces proceed at high speed to meet the Allied force. Shortly after 1600 hrs Rear-Adm Takagi opens fire with the cruisers *Haguro* and *Nachi* at a range of 26km. In the E *Jintsu* with the destroyers *Yukikaze*, *Tokitsukaze*, *Amatsukaze* and *Hatsukaze*, followed by *Ushio*, *Sazanami*, *Yamakaze* and *Kawakaze*, and in the W *Naka* with *Murasame*, *Samidare*, *Harukaze*, *Yudachi*, *Asagumo* and *Minegumo* approach to make torpedo attacks. Of the 34 and 86 torpedoes fired, only one from *Haguro* hits *Kortenaer*, which sinks. A heavy shell hit compels *Exeter* to turn away. Escorted by *Witte de With*, she proceeds to Soerabaya whilst Doorman orders the British destroyers to attack in order to cover this manoeuvre. In poor visibility caused by smokescreens, the destroyers become involved in engagements at short range with *Naka*'s destroyers, in which *Electra* is sunk by *Agagumo*. Before Takagi breaks off this phase of the battle because of the proximity of suspected Dutch mine barrages, *Perth* obtains a heavy hit on *Asagumo*. An attack by four US destroyers fails, as do 24 Japanese torpedoes. After reforming his force with four cruisers and six destroyers Doorman makes a sortie to the NW, when there is another brief engagement with *Haguro* and *Nachi* and four torpedoes miss from the *Jintsu* before contact is lost. Owing to fuel shortage, Doorman has to dismiss the four US destroyers and, off the coast when proceeding westwards,

Jupiter is lost following an explosion caused by a mine from the field laid by the Dutch minelayer *Gouden Leeuw*. *Encounter* shortly afterwards remains behind to rescue the survivors from *Kortenaer* and goes to Soerabaya. At the same time Doorman makes another sortie to the N with his four cruisers, in the course of which there is an engagement during the night 27–28 Feb with the cruisers *Haguro* and *Nachi*. They respectively fire four and eight torpedoes and hit and sink the *De Ruyter* (Cdr Lacomblé) and *Java* (Capt v Stralen). The two remaining cruisers, *Houston* and *Perth*, get away to Batavia. A sortie by the Western Force, which has just been joined by the Dutch destroyer *Evertsen*, leads to no result in the night 27–28 Feb. The force then goes through the Sunda Strait; only *Evertsen* returns to Batavia. On the Japanese side, *Asagumo* and *Minegumo* are damaged.

Of the surviving Allied ships, the US destroyers *Alden*, *John D Edwards*, *John D Ford* and *Paul Jones* proceed early in the morning of 28 Feb from Soerabaya through the Bali Strait to Australia, which they reach after a short, indecisive engagement with three Japanese ships.

In the afternoon of 28 Feb the cruisers *Houston* and *Perth*, followed later by *Evertsen*, put to sea from Batavia/Tandjok and *Exeter* with the destroyers *Encounter* and *Pope* (US) from Soerabaya, in order to reach Tjilatjap through the Sunda Strait. In the meantime the Japanese invasion forces have resumed their advance. In the evening the Eastern Force (41 transports), covered by the 2nd and 4th DD Flotillas (see above), reaches the area of Kragan some 100 nautical miles W of Soerabaya and, in spite of Allied air attacks, in which the cruiser *Kinu* and one transport are damaged, begins to disembark troops. To the N, Rear-Adm Takagi cruises to provide cover with the cruisers *Haguro* and *Nachi* and the destroyers *Kawakaze* and *Yamakaze*, as does, further to the NW, Vice-Adm Takahashi with the cruisers *Ashigara* and *Myoko* and the destroyers *Akebono* and *Inazuma*. S of Borneo, *Exeter* (Capt Gordon) with her destroyers comes between both forces and is sunk on 1 Mar with *Encounter* by gunfire and torpedoes from *Inazuma*. *Pope* at first gets away but is then rendered unmanoeuvrable by six dive-bombers from *Ryujo* and sunk by gunfire from *Myoko* and *Ashigara*. Some 800 survivors are rescued by the Japanese.

Battle of the Sunda Strait. The Japanese Western Force (56 transports) divides up early on 28 Feb. Two smaller groups (each consisting of about 10 transports) land

126

troops during the night 28 Feb–1 Mar. The first comprises the cruiser *Yura* and the 22nd DD Div (see above) and lands near Anjer Lor on the NW extremity of Java in the entrance to the Sunda Strait; the second consists of *Sendai* and the 20th DD Div and lands near Semarang in Central Java. The main force arrives in Banten Bay N of Serang in NW Java in the evening of 28 Feb and begins to disembark. Shortly after midnight the destroyer *Fubuki*, which is providing a screen to the NE, sights the Allied cruisers *Houston* (Capt Rooks) and *Perth* (Capt Waller) approaching from Batavia. Taking advantage of the mutual surprise, the two cruisers try to attack the Japanese invasion fleet. The transports *Horai Maru* (9192 tons) and *Sakura Maru* (7167 tons) sink and the minesweeper *W2* and the destroyer *Harukaze*, which comes up from the S, are damaged. After a torpedo attack by *Fubuki*, the covering forces, summoned from the W, attack: they consist of the destroyers *Asakaze* and *Hatakaze*, the cruiser *Natori* with the destroyers *Hatsuyuki* and *Shirayuki*, the minelayer *Shirataka* and, finally, from the N, the covering group with the cruisers *Mikuma* and *Mogami* and the destroyer *Shikinami*. In the fierce gun and torpedo duels that ensue, *Houston* and *Perth* sink and, on the Japanese side, *Shikinami* and *Shirakumo* suffer damage. 368 survivors are rescued from the Allied cruisers. The Dutch destroyer *Evertsen*, which is behind the two cruisers, runs into the Japanese forces, is set on fire by shelling from the destroyers *Shirakumo* and *Murakomo* and has to be beached in the Sunda Strait.

Operations in the Indian Ocean S of Java. When the US aircraft depot ship *Langley* is sunk on 27 Feb by Japanese bombers of the 21st and 23rd Naval Air Flotillas as she brings fighter planes to Java after the attack on Java begins, the remaining Allied ships try to get away. The cruisers *Danae*, *Dragon* and *Hobart* with the destroyers *Scout* and *Tenedos* set out from the Sunda Strait for Colombo on 28 Feb and, on the way, take on board refugees in Padang. Some of the ships which set out on 28 Feb–2 Mar from Tjilatjap, however, run into the operations being carried out by the Japanese Task Forces under Vice-Adms Nagumo and Kondo from the S of Java to the S of Christmas Island. On 1 Mar the battleships *Hiyei* and *Kirishima*, supported by the cruisers *Chikuma* and *Tone*, sink the US destroyer *Edsall* and aircraft from the carrier *Soryu* sink the tanker *Pecos* (14800 tons). Five merchant ships are sunk and one is captured. On 2 Mar the cruiser *Maya* with the destroyers *Arashi* and *Nowake* sink the British

destroyer *Stronghold* in a one-hour engagement and the cruisers *Atago* and *Takao* the US destroyer *Pillsbury*. One merchant ship is sunk and one captured. On 2 Mar the damaged Dutch destroyers *Banckert* and *Witte de With* and the US destroyer *Stewart* are scuttled in drydock in Soerabaja (*Banckert* and *Stewart* are rebuilt by the Japanese as the escort vessels *106* and *102*). On 3 Mar units of Kondo's force sink the US gunboat *Asheville*. On 4 Mar the last-named Japanese cruisers and destroyers sink a whole convoy with the Australian sloop *Yarra*, the minesweeper *MMS51*, the auxiliary ship *Anking* and the tanker *Francol*; one more ship is captured. On 5 Mar the carriers of the Nagumo force, *Akagi*, *Hiryu*, *Kaga* and *Soryu*, make a raid on Tjilatjap which is already being demolished and evacuated: two merchant ships are destroyed and 15 more are scuttled or blown up. On 6 Mar the Dutch minesweepers *Ian van Amstel*, *Pieter de Bitter* and *Eland Dubois* are scuttled in Java. On 7 Mar *Hiyei* and *Kirishima*, with the destroyers *Tanikaze*, *Isokaze*, *Hamakaze* and *Urakaze*, shell Christmas Island and sink one merchant ship. Further successes are obtained by the Japanese submarines deployed from 22 Feb (qv).

Of the Allied ships, apart from merchantmen, the Indian sloop *Jumna* escapes to Colombo, as do the US destroyers *Parrott* and *Whipple*, the gunboats *Isabel* and *Tulsa* and the Australian minesweepers *Maryborough*, *Toowoomba*, *Ballarat*, *Bendigo*, *Goulburn*, *Burnie* and *Wollongong* of the 21st Div. Likewise, the Allied troop transports and convoys proceeding 400 to 800 nautical miles W to S of Christmas Island are not caught by the Japanese Forces, eg the convoy MS.5 handed over by the US cruiser *Phoenix* to the British *Enterprise*, the troop transport *Mount Vernon* (with 4668 troops on board) proceeding on her own to Australia and the convoy SU.1 with 12 transports and 10,090 troops on board, escorted by the battleship *Royal Sovereign*, the cruiser *Cornwall*, the destroyers *Express*, *Nizam* and *Vampire*, the corvette *Hollyhock* and the Australian auxiliary cruiser *Manoora*.

During the fighting for Java, the US submarine *Seal* misses a cruiser of the Japanese Eastern Force on 1 Mar, *Sailfish* (Lt-Cdr Voge) sinks one ship of 6440 tons and *Perch* is sunk by the destroyers *Amatsukaze* and *Hatsukaze* when she tries to attack the advancing Japanese eastern invasion force. *Seawolf* torpedoes one ship of 4466 tons and has four torpedo failures. The Japanese naval tanker *Tsurumi*, belonging to the Western Force, is torpedoed by the US sub-

marine *S39* (Lt-Cdr Coe) and the Dutch submarine *K-XV* (Lt-Cdr v Boetzelaer). In Soerabaya, the non-operational submarines *K-XII*, *K-XVIII* and *K-IX*, the US destroyer *Stewart* and many other warships and merchant ships are blown up.

On 9 Mar the Allied forces on Java capitulate; 60000 prisoners are taken.

25 Feb–13 June   Central Atlantic

Off the West African coast, the submarine *Da Vinci* (Cdr Longanesi-Cattani) sinks four ships of 19997 tons, *U68* (Cdr Merten) seven of 39350 tons and *U505* (Lt-Cdr Loewe) four of 25041 tons.

26–27 Feb   Air War/Germany

In an attack by RAF Bomber Command on Kiel, the battlecruiser *Gneisenau* receives a heavy bomb hit in the bows. The passenger ship *Monte Sarmiento* (13625 tons), lying alongside, is burnt out. *Gneisenau* remains in Kiel unfit for operations until 4 Apr and is then brought to Gotenhafen to be lengthened and equipped with 38cm guns. The work is however suspended at the beginning of 1943 and the ship is laid up.

26–28 Feb   Black Sea

In support of an offensive by the Soviet 44th Army on the Kerch Peninsula, units of the Squadron (Rear-Adm Vladimirski) of the Black Sea Fleet shell positions and troop concentrations W and N of Feodosia: the flotilla leader *Tashkent* and destroyers *Bditelny* and *Boiki* during the night 25–26 Feb, the battleship *Parizhskaya Kommuna*, the cruiser *Molotov* and the destroyers *Bezuprechny* and *Smyshleny* during the nights 26–27 and 27–28 Feb. The cruiser *Krasny Krym* supports the defenders of Sevastopol on 26 and 28 Feb and on 27 Feb, with the flotilla leaders *Kharkov* and *Tashkent* and the destroyers *Boiki*, *Shaumyan* and *Zheleznyakov*, shells the harbours on the S coast of the Crimea as a diversionary move. In all, 1590 rounds—10.2cm to 30.5cm—are fired.

27–28 Feb   Air War/Germany

RAF Bomber Command attacks Kiel and Wilhelmshaven.

27–28 Feb   Mediterranean

An attempt by Force H (Vice-Adm Syfret), comprising the battleship *Malaya*, the carriers *Argus* and *Eagle*, the cruiser *Hermione* and the destroyers *Laforey*, *Lightning*, *Active*, *Anthony*, *Duncan*, *Whitehall*, *Wishart*, *Blankney* and *Croome*, to fly off fighter aircraft for Malta S of the Balearics has to be broken off because of trouble with the supplementary tanks of the aircraft.

27 Feb–5 Mar   Mediterranean

In British submarine operations, *Upholder* (Lt-Cdr Wanklyn) sinks a steamer of 5584 tons escorted by the destroyer *Strale* off Tripoli and *Torbay* (Cdr Miers) torpedoes two ships of 6455 tons off Corfu. E of Tunisia, *Unbeaten* (Lt-Cdr Woodward) and *P31/Uproar* (Lt Kershaw) each sink one ship, of 5417 tons and 5081 tons respectively.

1–30 Mar Pacific

In operations by US submarines off Japan, in the East China Sea and in the area of the Mandate Islands, *Narwhal* (Lt-Cdr Wilkins) sinks one ship of 1243 tons and damages one of 6515 tons, *Pollack* (Lt-Cdr Mosely) sinks two of 6720 tons, *Gar* (Lt-Cdr McGregor) sinks one of 1462 tons, *Grayback* (Lt-Cdr Saunders) sinks one of 3291 tons, *Gudgeon* (Lt-Cdr Grenfell) sinks one of 6526 tons, *Tuna* (Lt-Cdr De Tar) damages one, *Grenadier* damages one of 4551 tons and *Tambor* (Lt-Cdr Murphy) sinks one of 394 tons and damages one of 6334 tons. *Grampus* (Lt-Cdr Hutchinson) sinks one ship of 8632 tons near Truk.

2–23 Mar Western Atlantic

Off the American East Coast, *U332* (Lt-Cdr Liebe) sinks four ships of 25125 tons and *U124* (Lt-Cdr Mohr) sinks seven of 42048 tons and torpedoes three of 26167 tons. *U503* (Lt-Cdr Gericke) is sunk on 15 Mar by a Hudson of VP-82 belonging to the escort of convoy ON.72.

3 Mar Mediterranean

Sixteen Wellington bombers from Malta attack Palermo. In the harbour the ammunition ship *Cuma* (8260 tons) explodes after being hit and four other steamers, four auxiliary ships and five destroyers and torpedo boats are damaged.

5–13 Mar Arctic

Operations in connection with the convoys PQ.12 (16 ships) and QP.8 (15 ships) which set out on 1 Mar from Reykjavik and the Kola Inlet respectively. On 5 Mar an Fw 200 locates PQ.12 about 70 nautical miles S of Jan Mayen. *U134*, *U377*, *U403* and *U584* then form a patrol line. On 6 Mar the battleship *Tirpitz* (Capt Topp, with Vice-Adm Ciliax) and the destroyers *Paul Jacobi*, *Friedrich Ihn*, *Hermann Schoemann* and *Z25* put to sea from Trondheim in an attempt to attack the convoy. 'Ultra' intercepts disclose the German departure, helping British countermeasures, and one of the five British submarines stationed there, *Seawolf* (Lt Raikes), reports that the force is setting out. In the meantime the covering force (Vice-Adm Curteis), consisting of the battleship *Duke of York*, the battlecruiser *Renown*, the cruiser *Kenya* and the destroyers *Faulknor*, *Eskimo*, *Punjabi*, *Fury*, *Echo* and *Eclipse*, and the main body of the Home Fleet (Adm Tovey), comprising the battleship *King George V*, the carrier *Victorious*, the cruiser *Berwick* and the destroyers *Onslow*, *Ashanti*,

Intrepid, *Icarus*, *Lookout* and *Bedouin*, join up. *Kenya* is detached as close escort to PQ.12. The cruiser *Sheffield*, which has come out to relieve *Berwick* (left behind with engine trouble), is damaged on a mine and has to return. In the prevailing poor visibility the Home Fleet does not find *Tirpitz*. The German ships just miss the convoy QP.8, which is escorted only by two minesweepers and two corvettes, and the destroyers only find a straggler, the Soviet freighter *Izhora* (2815 tons), which *Friedrich Ihn* sinks. On 9 Mar *Tirpitz* is unsuccessfully attacked off Vestfjord by 12 Albacore torpedo aircraft of Nos 817 and 832 Sqns from *Victorious*, escorted by *Faulknor*, *Eskimo*, *Bedouin* and *Tartar*, and two aircraft are shot down. An attempt by three Ju 88s to attack the British carrier on 9 Mar is unsuccessful.

Tirpitz enters Narvik. On 11–12 Mar the destroyers *Faulknor*, *Fury*, *Intrepid*, *Icarus*, *Bedouin*, *Eskimo*, *Tartar* and *Punjabi* try to intercept the expected *Tirpitz* off Bodö, but the battleship is transferred again to Trondheim on 12–13 Mar.

The Soviet submarines *D-3*, *K-21*, *K-23*, *S-102* and *Shch-422*, which were stationed to cover the convoys S of the convoy routes, proceed to the Norwegian polar coast on the conclusion of the operation on 13 Mar. Here *D-3* (Capt 3rd Class Bibeev) misses on 14 Mar the German minelayer *Brummer*, which is on the way to laying out a flanking mine barrage, and *M1504*. She is attacked with depth charges by the submarine-chaser *UJ1109*. The Soviet submarines *M-171* and *M173* make unsuccessful attacks in Varangerfjord.

5–18 Mar South Pacific

Elements of the Japanese 4th Fleet (Vice-Adm Inoue)—transports, minelayers, minesweepers and other small craft—which set out from Rabaul on 5 Mar land a battalion of the South Sea Detachment of the Army in Salamaua and a naval landing unit in Lae in Huon Gulf on 8 Mar. Escort and support for the landings is provided by the 6th DD Flotilla with the cruiser *Yubari* and the destroyers *Oite*, *Asanagi*, *Yunagi*, *Mutsuki*, *Yayoi* and *Mochizuki*, as well as by the 24th Naval Air Flotilla with the depot ship *Kiyokawa Maru*. The covering force consists of the 6th Cruiser Sqn, comprising the cruisers *Aoba*, *Kinugasa*, *Kako* and *Furutaka*, and the 18th Cruiser Sqn, with the light cruisers *Tatsuta* and *Tenryu*, which investigate Buka N of Bougainville on 8 Mar.

From 7 to 12 Mar convoy ZK.7, escorted by the US cruisers *Honolulu* and *New Orleans* and the destroyer *Mugford*, trans-

ports the US Americal Div from Melbourne to Noumea. TF.11 (Rear-Adm Brown), consisting of the carrier *Lexington*, the cruisers *Indianapolis*, *Minneapolis*, *Pensacola* and *San Francisco* and the destroyers (Desron 1) *Phelps*, *Clark*, *Patterson*, *Dewey*, *MacDonough*, *Hull*, *Aylwin*, *Dale*, *Bagley* and *Drayton*, joins TF.17 (Rear-Adm Fletcher), which comprises the carrier *Yorktown* and the destroyers *Russell* and *Walke* (on 6 Mar), to make a raid on Japanese landing points from S of the Papuan peninsula. On 10 Mar the two carriers fly off 104 aircraft which attack the harbours over the Owen Stanley Mountains: the armed merchant cruiser *Kongo Maru* and the transport *Yokohama Maru* (6143 tons) are sunk and the cruiser *Yubari*, the minelayer *Tsugaru*, the destroyers *Asanagi* and *Yunagi*, two transports and two auxiliary ships are damaged. The transport *Tenryu Maru* (6843 tons) has to be beached after being hit.

The ANZAC Force (Rear-Adm Crace), comprising the cruisers *Australia* (RAN) and *Chicago* and the destroyers *Lamson* and *Perkins*, as well as the cruisers *Astoria* and *Louisville* and the destroyers *Anderson*, *Hammann*, *Hughes* and *Sims* detached from TF.17, operates as a covering group SE of Papua.

From 16 to 18 Mar the Australian auxiliary cruiser *Westralia* brings one battalion of the US Americal Div from Noumea to Efate (New Hebrides). Escort is provided by the New Zealand cruisers *Achilles* and *Leander*.

6–8 Mar Mediterranean

The British Force H (Vice-Adm Syfret) flies off 15 Spitfire fighters for Malta from the carriers *Argus* and *Eagle* S of the Balearics. They arrive there together with seven Blenheim bombers from Gibraltar. Escort for the operation consists of the battleship *Malaya*, the cruiser *Hermione* and the destroyers *Laforey*, *Lightning*, *Active*, *Anthony*, *Whitehall*, *Wishart*, *Blankney*, *Exmoor* and *Croome*. The Italian submarine *Brin* reports Force H on 6 and 8 Mar.

6–8 Mar Indian Ocean

Because of the advance made by the Japanese 33rd Inf Div on Rangoon from the N, reinforcement convoys for the Allied defenders have to turn back on 6 Mar. On 7 Mar Rangoon is evacuated on the orders of Gen Alexander. Light craft evacuate 3500 troops with cover from the US destroyer *Allen* and the Indian sloop *Hindustan*. The last demolition parties are taken aboard the freighter *Heinrich Jensen*. On 8 Mar the Japanese enter Rangoon.

6–20 Mar Black Sea

Soviet supply transports to Sevastopol: on 6–7 Mar with the cruiser *Komintern*; on 11–

12 Mar with the cruiser *Krasny Krym*, the destroyers *Shaumyan* and *Svobodny* and the transport *Lvov* (several air attacks beaten off); on 12–13 Mar with the destroyer *Dzerzhinski* (shelling of land targets); on 13–14 Mar with the cruiser *Molotov* and destroyers *Bditelny* and *Boiki* (shelling of land targets near Feodosia and Sevastopol); on 15–16 Mar with the destroyers *Bditelny* and *Svobodny* (shelling of land targets); and from 18 to 20 Mar with the cruiser *Krasny Krym*, the destroyer *Nezamozhnik* and the tankers *Peredovik* and *Sergo* and also the destroyers *Bditelny* and the transport *Abkhaziya*. Several air attacks are beaten off.

7–18 Mar   Mediterranean
Italian supply operation V.5 to North Africa. From 7 to 9 Mar three Italian convoys with four transports, escorted by the destroyers *Pigafetta*, *Da Noli*, *Bersagliere*, *Vivaldi* and *Fuciliere* and the torpedo boats *Aretusa* and *Castore*, set out from Brindisi, Messina and Naples for Tripoli. The covering force is provided by Div-Adm De Courten with the cruisers *Eugenio di Savoia*, *Garibaldi* and *Montecuccoli* and the destroyers *Ascari*, *Aviere*, *Geniere*, *Oriani* and *Scirocco*. A return convoy with four transports puts to sea from Tripoli on 8 Mar, escorted by the destroyer *Strale* and the torpedo boats *Cigno* and *Procione*, which are joined by *Pigafetta* and *Scirocco* on 9 Mar. On that day a second convoy with two steamers and one tug, escorted by the destroyers *Bersagliere* and *Da Noli* and the torpedo boats *Castore* and *Pallade*, follows. Another operation, 'Sirio', with two transports (and a close escort of six destroyers and one torpedo boat and a distant escort of one cruiser and two destroyers) is also undertaken, without loss. The Italian submarines *Corallo*, *Millo*, *Veniero*, *Uarsciek* and *Onice* are in covering positions E of Malta.
In British submarine operations in the Central Mediterranean, *P34/Ultimatum* (Lt Harrison), *Unbeaten* (Lt-Cdr Woodward) and *Upholder* (Lt-Cdr Wanklyn) sink the Italian submarines *Millo* on 14 Mar, *Guglielmotti* on 17 Mar and *Tricheco* on 18 Mar. *Una* (Lt Norman) sinks one sailing ship (248 tons) in a gun duel.
As a result of a false report about the torpedoing of an Italian cruiser, British Force B (Rear-Adm Vian) sets out from Alexandria on 9 Mar with the cruisers *Naiad*, *Dido* and *Euryalus* and the destroyers *Jervis*, *Kipling*, *Kelvin*, *Lively*, *Sikh*, *Zulu*, *Hasty*, *Havock* and *Hero* to intercept the ship and to meet the cruiser *Cleopatra* and the destroyer *Kingston* coming from Malta. Italian torpedo aircraft and German bombers

attack the force unsuccessfully. On 11 Mar *U565* (Lt Jebsen) sinks Vian's flagship, *Naiad* (Capt Grantham), from the returning force N of Sollum. All except 82 of the crew are rescued.

8–12 Mar   Indian Ocean
Japanese landing in Northern Sumatra. On 8 Mar a Japanese force, comprising the cruiser *Kashii* (flagship of the 1st Southern Expeditionary Fleet), the cruiser *Yura*, the destroyers *Shirakumo*, *Yugiri*, *Asagiri*, *Amagiri*, *Uranami*, *Isonami* and *Ayanami* and transports, sets out from Singapore to land troops on 12 Mar in Sabang and Iri in Northern Sumatra. Cover for the operation is provided by Vice-Adm Ozawa with the cruisers *Chokai*, *Kumano*, *Suzuya*, *Mikuma* and *Mogami* and the destroyers *Hatsuyuki*, *Fubuki*, *Shirakumo* and *Murakumo* and by the aircraft depot ship *Soya Maru* in the area of the Nicobars.

10–22 Mar   Indian Ocean
Off the Indian East Coast, *I-62* (Lt-Cdr Kinashi) and *I-64* (Cdr Ogawa) sink two ships and one ship, of 1100 tons and 1513 tons, respectively. *I-62* also torpedoes two larger ships but of these only one tanker of 8012 tons is identified.

11 Mar   English Channel
In an attack by boats of the German 2nd MTB Flotilla on a British convoy in the Channel, *S70* (Lt Klose) sinks one freighter of 951 tons.

11–16 Mar   North Atlantic
The British EG.7 escorts the convoy PQ.13 from Liverpool to Hvalfjord. Participating are the destroyers *Blyskawica* (Polish, SOE), *Saladin*, *Sardonyx*, *Lamerton* and *Newport* (RNoN).

11–26 Mar   Mediterranean
In operations against the British supply traffic for Tobruk, *U83* (Lt-Cdr Kraus) torpedoes one ship of 2590 tons, *U652* (Lt-Cdr Fraatz) sinks on 20 Mar the destroyer *Jaguar* and *U205* (Lt-Cdr Reschke) sinks the tanker *Slavol* (2623 tons) from a convoy; *U371*, *U559*, *U568* and the Italian *Onice* miss their targets. *U133* is lost on one of her own mines. Of the Italian submarines, *Ametista* and *Galatea* off Palestine, the latter sinks one sailing vessel. In the Western Mediterranean the Italian submarine *Mocenigo* (Lt-Cdr Monechi) sinks a Vichy French ship of 1518 tons.

12–13 Mar   South Atlantic
The German auxiliary minelayer *Schiff 53/Doggerbank* (Lt-Cdr Schneidewind) lays 60 mines off Cape Town and 15 off Cape Agulhas on which one freighter of 4534 tons sinks and two others of 13015 tons are damaged.

13/14 Mar–24 Apr   English Channel
The German auxiliary cruiser *Schiff 28/Michel* (Cdr* v Ruckteschell) passes through the Channel, escorted by the 5th TB Flotilla (Cdr* Schmidt) comprising *Seeadler*, *Iltis*, *Jaguar*, *Falke* and *Kondor* and nine minesweepers. In fierce engagements with British MTBs, motor gunboats and destroyers, the destroyers *Fernie* and *Walpole* are damaged without German loss. *Schiff 28* reaches Le Havre on 14 Mar, St-Malo on 15 Mar and La Pallice on 17 Mar, from where she sets out for the Atlantic on 20 Mar.

14/15 Mar–24 Apr   English Channel
In mining operations by German motor torpedo boats in the Channel and off the British south-east coast, *S53* is lost on a mine. *S104* (Lt Roeder) sinks the British destroyer *Vortigern* from convoy FS.749 on 15 Mar. On her return, *S111* is badly damaged in an engagement with the motor gunboats *MGB87*, *MGB88* and *MGB91* and sinks while being towed away.

14–25 Mar   North Atlantic
The rest of the US First Marine Bde is embarked on four transports and departs on 14 Mar from Reykjavik, escorted by TF.32 with the battleship *New York*, the cruisers *Quincy* and *Philadelphia* and the destroyers *Rhind*, *Rowan*, *Mayrant*, *Roe*, *Trippe*, *Hilary P Jones*, *Ludlow*, *Charles F Hughes*, *Lansdale* and *Ingraham*. On 17 Mar the convoy meets two escorts and seven transports with 3000 RAF and US Army personnel and returns to New York on 25 Mar. From 14 to 19 Mar the US destroyers *Swanson* and *Nicholson* escort two transports with 5000 British and Canadian troops, which are taken over on 19 Mar by British escorts, while the US destroyers take over two transports from the UK with 5000 British and Canadian soldiers going west to Halifax on 6 Apr.

14 Mar–20 Apr   Western Atlantic
The 11 U-boats of a fourth wave which arrive successively sink many ships off the US East Coast in individual operations. *U373* (Lt Loeser) sinks two ships of 9867 tons, *U71* (Lt-Cdr Flachsenberg) sinks five of 38894 tons, *U202* (Lt-Cdr Linder) sinks one of 5249 tons and torpedoes one of 8882 tons, *U160* (Lt Lassen) sinks five of 36731 tons and torpedoes one of 6837 tons, *U105* (Cdr Schuch) sinks two of 18005 tons, *U123* (Lt-Cdr Hardegen) sinks eight of 39917 tons and torpedoes three of 24310 tons, *U552* (Lt-Cdr Topp) sinks seven of 45731 tons,

U754 (Lt-Cdr Oestermann) sinks seven of 31578 tons and damages one tug of 490 tons, *U203* (Lt-Cdr Mützelburg) sinks two ships of 14232 tons and torpedoes two of 16164 tons, *U571* (Lt-Cdr Möhlmann) sinks three of 24319 tons, and *U572* (Lt-Cdr Hirsacker) sinks two of 9532 tons and torpedoes one of 6207 tons.

15 Mar   Mediterranean
The British cruisers *Dido* and *Euryalus* and six destroyers shell Rhodes (Operation 'MF.8').

15–19 Mar   Mediterranean
The German 3rd MTB Flotilla (Lt-Cdr Kemnade) lays in four nights E and W of Valetta/Malta the barrages MT.6–9 with 48 TMA and 45 UMB mines, 18 protection floats and 54 explosive floats.

15 Mar–3 Apr   North Atlantic
US TF.39 (Rear-Adm Wilcox*) transfers from Casco Bay to Scapa Flow with the battleship *Washington*, the carrier *Wasp*, the cruisers *Wichita* and *Tuscaloosa* and the destroyers *Wainwright*, *Plunkett*, *Madison*, *Sterett*, *Lang* and *Wilson*.

15–20 Mar   Norway
On 16–17 Mar the German minelayer *Ulm* lays a flanking barrage off Helnes. A mine operation, 'Karin', has to be postponed owing to weather; instead of this, a barrage is laid off the Porsanger Fjord on 18 Mar. 'Karin' takes place on 19 Mar. On 20 Mar the minelayers *Cobra* and *Brummer* lay barrage 'Bantos A', escorted by *UJ1108*, *UJ1109*, *M1506*, the patrol vessel *Polarkreis* and the E-boats *S42*, *S44*, *S45* and *S46*.

18–20 Mar   North Atlantic
U507 (Cdr Schacht), which is on the way to France, sights the convoy ONS.76 (28 ships) but cannot maintain contact until *U506*, *U593* and *U753*, which are ordered to the scene, arrive. An attack made on 19 Feb at too great range is unsuccessful.

19–20 Mar   Norway
The heavy cruiser *Admiral Hipper* (Capt Meisel) moves to Trondheim with the destroyers *Z24*, *Z26* and *Z30* and the torpedo boats *T15*, *T16* and *T17*.

19–25 Mar   Indian Ocean
A Japanese transport fleet brings troops of the Japanese 56th Inf Div from Singapore to Rangoon from 19 to 25 Mar. In these operations, Japanese detachments establish seaplane bases and emergency fleet bases at Pukhet on 21 Mar and Mergui on 23 Mar. On 20 Mar a force sets out from Penang with a battalion of the 18th Inf Div which on 23 Mar occupies Port Blair on the Andaman

Islands. Apart from transports, the flag cruiser *Kashii* of the 1st Southern Expeditionary Fleet and the 9th and 12th Special BF are employed on these operations. The operations are escorted and covered by the Malaya Force (Vice-Adm Ozawa), comprising the cruisers *Chokai*, *Kumano*, *Suzuya*, *Mikuma* and *Mogami*, the carrier *Ryujo*, the light cruisers *Sendai* and *Yura* and 11 destroyers (see 8–12 Mar).

20–26 Mar   Mediterranean
Second battle of Sirte. On 20 Mar the British 5th DD Flotilla, comprising *Southwold*, *Beaufort*, *Dulverton*, *Hurworth*, *Avon Vale*, *Eridge* and *Heythrop*, sets out from Alexandria for Tobruk on a submarine-hunting operation. *Heythrop* is torpedoed N of Sollum by *U652* (Lt Fraatz) and has to be scuttled by *Eridge*.
Supply convoy MW.10 for Malta sets out from Alexandria. It consists of the transports *Breconshire* (9776 tons), *Clan Campbell* (7255 tons), *Pampas* (5415 tons) and *Talabot* (6798 tons), escorted by the AA cruiser *Carlisle* and the 22nd DD Flotilla consisting of *Sikh*, *Zulu*, *Lively*, *Hero*, *Havock* and *Hasty*; the covering force is provided by Rear-Adm Vian with the cruisers *Cleopatra*, *Dido*, *Euryalus* and the 14th DD Flotilla consisting of *Jervis*, *Kelvin*, *Kingston* and *Kipling*. Six British submarines take up flanking positions in the Gulf of Taranto and off Messina. On 21 Mar Force H (composition as on 6 Mar) puts to sea from Gibraltar to fly in more Spitfire fighters to Malta. The Italian submarines *Mocenigo* and *Dandolo* sight the force and *Mocenigo* attacks *Argus* without success.
The Italian submarines *Onice* and *Platino* report MW.10. To deal with it, Supermarina sends out from Messina Div-Adm Parona with the cruisers *Bande Nere*, *Gorizia* and *Trento* and the destroyers *Alpino*, *Bersagliere*, *Fuciliere* and *Lanciere* and from Taranto the battleship *Littorio* (Adm Iachino) with the destroyers *Ascari*, *Aviere*, *Grecale* and *Oriani*, followed later by *Geniere* and *Scirocco*. In addition, the submarines *Perla*, *Acciaio*, *Galatea*, *U73*, *U205* and *U431* are deployed and bombers and torpedo aircraft of the German FK II and the Italian 4th Air Fleet act together. The British submarine *P36* reports the *Littorio* force. The cruiser *Penelope* and the destroyer *Legion* set out from Malta to escort MW.10 and they join it on 22 Mar. At 1424 hrs the Italian Messina force sights British covering force and tries in vain to entice it towards *Littorio*. At 1618 hrs *Littorio* has come up in a strong freshening wind and deteriorating visibility and tries to get between the convoy and Malta. Rough

seas and skilful operating by Adm Vian in the use of smoke impede the Italian gunnery to such an extent that only *Havock* and *Kingston* are severely damaged by near-hits or direct hits by the 38cm shells. *Cleopatra* receives a hit from a 15cm shell whilst on *Euryalus* and *Lively* only slight splinter damage is sustained. Torpedo attacks by destroyers on both sides are unsuccessful. At 1858 hrs Iachino breaks off the engagement as darkness begins to fall and MW.10 resumes its course to Malta. On the return, the Italian force loses *Lanciere* and *Scirocco* in the storm and the cruiser *Trento* has to break off her attempts to help because of severe storm damage. Almost all other Italian and British ships suffer more or less heavy storm damage on the return.

The evasive movements in the engagement result in MW.10 arriving off Malta only after daybreak on 23 Mar. There the ships are attacked by bombers of FK II. *Clan Campbell* sinks, *Breconshire* is badly damaged and beached and later capsizes when attempts are made to salvage her after further hits and *Southwold* sinks on a mine barrage. On 24 Mar *Legion* is beached after a near-miss and is destroyed on 26 Mar. On the same day *Pampas* and *Talabot* also sink after bomb hits, so that only 5000 tons of the 25900 tons of cargo come ashore; the submarine *P39* is also lost and the cruiser *Penelope* is damaged. The covering force reaches Alexandria on 24 Mar; the already badly damaged *Kingston* has received a bomb hit on 23 Mar and reaches Malta. On 25 Mar *Carlisle*, *Hurworth*, *Dulverton*, *Eridge* and *Beaufort* set out from Malta and reach Alexandria on 27 Mar without incident.

20–30 Mar   Mediterranean
The British Force H (Vice-Adm Syfret), comprising the battleship *Malaya*, the carriers *Argus* and *Eagle*, the cruiser *Hermione* and the destroyers *Laforey*, *Duncan*, *Active*, *Anthony*, *Whitehall*, *Wishart*, *Blankney*, *Exmoor* and *Croome*, sets out from Gibraltar on 20 Mar to make a new attempt to fly aircraft into Malta. But the force has to break off the attempt and return on 23 Mar. The operation is repeated from 27 to 30 Mar with the same force and sixteen Spitfire fighters reach Malta.

On 29 Mar the cruiser *Aurora*, repaired after hitting a mine in Dec 1941, proceeds with *Avon Vale* from Malta to Gibraltar. On the way the ships are sighted by the Italian submarine *Narvalo* and unsuccessfully attacked by torpedo aircraft S of Sardinia. The Italian submarines *Aradam*, *Santarosa* and *Turchese* report no contacts.

21–22 Mar   Black Sea
The Soviet battleship *Parizhskaya Kommuna* (Rear-Adm Vladimirski), together with the flotilla leader *Tashkent* and the destroyers *Boiki* and *Zheleznyakov*, shell land targets in the area of Feodosia during the nights 20–21 and 21–22 Mar. After returning on 23 Mar the battleship goes into the dockyard at Poti to change her heavy guns and for repairs.

23 Mar–early Apr   Western Atlantic
First use of U-boat decoys (Q-ships) off the American East Coast fails: the USS *Asterion* and *Eagle*, disguised respectively as a freighter and as a fishing steamer, sight no U-boats. *Atik* (Lt-Cdr Hicks) is attacked by *U123* (Lt-Cdr Hardegen) on 26 Mar and sunk after a violent gun duel.

23 Mar–9 Apr   South Atlantic
The German auxiliary cruiser *Schiff 10/Thor* (Capt Gumprich) sinks five ships totalling 23626 tons.

23 Mar–22 Apr   Atlantic
Preparatory naval movements for Allied Operation 'Ironclad' (Madagascar). On 23 Mar a convoy leaves Britain with troops of the British 5th Inf Div earmarked for the operation. On 25 Mar US TF.39 (Rear-Adm Wilcox†—lost overboard in a storm—then Rear-Adm Giffen) sets out from Casco Bay (USA) for Scapa Flow with the battleship *Washington*, the carrier *Wasp*, the heavy cruisers *Tuscaloosa* and *Wichita* and Desron 8 with the destroyers *Wainwright*, *Lang*, *Sterett*, *Wilson*, *Plunkett*, *Madison*, *Livermoore* and *Ellyson*. Its role is to relieve units of the Home Fleet as a replacement for Force H earmarked for 'Ironclad'. The US force is met on 3 Apr by the British cruiser *Edinburgh* and four destroyers and reaches Scapa Flow on 5 Apr. The 'Ironclad' convoy joins Force H (Rear-Adm Syfret), comprising the battleship *Malaya*, the cruiser *Hermione* and destroyers and the carrier *Illustrious* with destroyers in Freetown on 6 Apr. On 9 Apr the entire force sets out. On 19 Apr the warships put in to Cape Town; *Malaya* then returns and the other ships arrive in Durban on 22 Apr.

24 Mar   English Channel
Near Vissingen, the German auxiliary minesweeper *M3625* is lost to a mine.

24–25 Mar   North Atlantic
The newly replenished *U203* (Lt-Cdr Mützelburg) sights the convoy ON.77 and directs the returning *U94* (Lt Ites) to it; the latter torpedoes a tanker of 8022 tons.

24 Mar–3 Apr   North Atlantic
The U-boat *UA* (Cdr Cohausz), which is equipped as a supply boat, carries out for the first time the refuelling of *U84* and *U203*, which are proceeding to the American coast, and of the returning *U202*.

24 Mar–9 Apr   Arctic
Operations in connection with the convoys QP.9 and PQ.13. QP.9 (19 ships), which leaves the Kola Inlet on 21 Mar, passes, without incident, the concentration of the German U-boats *U209*, *U376*, *U378* and *U655*. The last is sunk on 24 Mar after being rammed by the escorting minesweeper *Sharpshooter*. Vice-Adm Curteis, with the battleship *Duke of York*, the battlecruiser *Renown*, the carrier *Victorious*, the cruiser *Nigeria* and destroyers, acts as a covering force NE of Iceland. From 24 to 27 Mar PQ.13 (19 ships with an escort consisting of the cruiser *Trinidad*, the destroyers *Eclipse* and *Fury*, the A/S trawlers *Blackfly* and *Paynter* and the three Norwegian M/S whalers *Silja*, *Sulla* and *Sumba* being transferred to the Soviet Northern Fleet) is scattered in a heavy storm. On the morning of 27 Mar a Bv 138 of 2/KFlGr 406 sights ships of PQ.13. Then on 28 Mar the U-boats *U435*, *U436*, *U454*, *U456*, *U585* and *U589* and the 8th DD Flotilla (Capt Pönitz) comprising *Z26*, *Z24* and *Z25* are ordered to it. Ju 88s of III/KG 30 sink the scattered freighters *Raceland* (4815 tons) and *Empire Ranger* (7007 tons). On 29 Mar the British destroyer *Oribi* and the Soviet *Gremyashchi* and *Sokrushitelny* arrive from the Kola Inlet. Of the 8th DD Flotilla, *Z26* (Cdr v Berger) sinks the scattered freighter *Bateau* (4687 tons) and then the three destroyers encounter *Trinidad* running ahead of the convoy with *Fury*. In confused engagements impeded by a heavy snowstorm, *Trinidad* renders *Z26* unmanoeuvrable but is hit by one of her own torpedoes dispatched to finish the destroyer off. In the mêlée, *Z24* and *Z25* rescue 88 men from the sinking *Z26*, hit *Eclipse* heavily and escape following a short exchange with *Oribi* and *Sokrushitelny*; eight more survivors from *Z26* are rescued by *U378*. *U585* (Lt-Cdr Lohse) is attacked by *Fury* as she moves in on the disabled *Trinidad* but is lost later in the German 'Bantos' minefield. On 30 Mar the British 6th MS Flotilla (Cdr Jay), comprising *Harrier*, *Gossamer*, *Speedwell* and *Hussar*, which sets out from Murmansk on 28 Mar, reaches the convoy. *U209* (Lt-Cdr Brodda) and *U456* (Lt-Cdr Teichert) miss ships of the convoy groups. *U376* (Lt-Cdr Marks) and *U435* (Lt-Cdr Strelow) sink the stragglers *Induna* (5086 tons) and *Effingham* (6421 tons). On 1 Apr *U436* (Lt-Cdr Seibicke) sinks a single ship, probably the missing *Sulla*, and *U589* (Lt-Cdr Horrer) misses a destroyer. The Soviet submarines *K-21*, *K-22*, *Shch-404* and *Shch-421*, which were formed in a flanking concentration S of the convoy as a screen against surface attacks, leave for the polar coast on 1 Apr, where *Shch-404* (Capt 2nd Class Ivanov) sinks the steamer *Michael* (2318 tons) off Tanafjord. In Svaerholthavet, *K-22* misses a minesweeping force consisting of *M1505*, *M1506* and *M1508* on 3 Apr. Further attacks by *K-21*, *Shch-404* and *Shch-421*, and by *M-171* deployed in Varangerfjord, are unsuccessful. Shortly after the German Minelayer Group 'Nord' (Capt Schönermark), consisting of the minelayers *Ulm*, *Brummer* and *Cobra*, has laid a flanking mine barrage to protect German traffic in Svaerhollthavet, the Soviet submarine *Shch-421* (Lt-Cdr Vidyaev with the Div Cdr, Capt 2nd Class Kolyshkin, on board) runs on this barrage, is badly damaged and is sunk on 9 Apr by *K-22* after the crew has been taken off. *K-1* lays mines 6–8 Apr.

25–26 Mar   Black Sea
The Soviet flotilla leader *Kharkov* and destroyer *Svobodny* bring supplies to Sevastopol on 25 Mar. The destroyers *Bditelny* and *Boiki* shell German positions on the edge of the fortress on 26 Mar.

25 Mar–12 Apr   South Atlantic
The Italian submarine *Calvi* (Cdr Olivieri) sinks five ships of 29031 tons off the Brazilian NE coast.

26 Mar–8 Apr   Baltic
The Finnish Group P, consisting of three infantry battalions of the 18th Inf Div, advances on skis over the ice from Kotka to Suursaari and, helped by a snowstorm, overwhelms the Soviet defenders, the remainder of whom withdraw to Suur-Tytärsaari. Finnish units, and German ones coming over the ice from the S, destroy the Soviet garrison of this island on 3–4 Apr. A Soviet relief sortie on 5 and 7–8 Apr, consisting of a total of 10 battalions, is driven off.

26 Mar–11 Apr   Indian Ocean
Japanese raid on Ceylon. On 26 Mar the Japanese 1st Carrier Fleet (Vice-Adm Nagumo) sets out from Staring Bay (South Celebes). It comprises the carriers *Akagi* (1st Carrier Sqn), *Hiryu* (Rear-Adm Yamaguchi, 2nd Carrier Sqn), *Soryu* and *Zuikaku* (Rear-Adm Hara, 5th Carrier Sqn) and *Shokaku*, the battleships *Kongo* (3rd BB Sqn, Rear-Adm Mikawa) and *Haruna*, *Hiyei* and *Kirishima*, the heavy cruisers *Tone* (8th Cruiser Sqn, Rear-Adm Abe) and *Chikuma* and the 1st DD Flotilla (Rear-Adm Omori) with the cruiser *Abukuma* and the destroyers *Urakaze*, *Tanikaze*, *Isokaze* and *Hamakaze* (17th DD Div) and *Kasumi*, *Arare*, *Kagero* and *Shiranuhi* (18th DD Div) and *Akigumo*. The force proceeds W of

Timor to the area S of Java, where it is replenished by a tanker force from 1 Apr. The 1st SM Flotilla, with *I-7, I-2, I-3, I-4, I-5* and *I-6*, leaves Penang from 27 Mar to take up covering positions W of India. Adm Somerville, who took over command as C-in-C Eastern Fleet on 27 Mar, receives reports on 29 Mar of an impending Japanese attack on Ceylon. He concentrates his available naval forces in two groups S of Ceylon by 31 Mar: Force A (fast group), comprising the battleship *Warspite* (F), the carriers (Rear-Adm Boyd) *Indomitable* and *Formidable*, the cruisers *Cornwall, Dorsetshire, Emerald* and *Enterprise*, the destroyers *Napier* (RAN), *Nestor* (RAN), *Paladin, Panther, Hotspur* and *Foxhound*; and Force B (Vice-Adm Willis), with the battleships *Resolution, Ramillies, Royal Sovereign* and *Revenge*, the carrier *Hermes*, the cruisers *Caledon, Dragon* and *Jacob van Heemskerck* (Dutch) and the destroyers *Griffin, Norman* (RAN), *Arrow, Vampire* (RAN), *Decoy, Fortune, Scout* and *Isaac Sweers* (Dutch). The Eastern Fleet cruises S of Ceylon without sighting the enemy until the evening of 2 Apr and then proceeds to Addu Atoll for replenishment (arrives 4 Apr). *Cornwall* and *Dorsetshire* are detached to Colombo and *Hermes* and *Vampire* to Trincomalee. On 1 Apr the Japanese destroyer *Ayanami* proceeds from Penang to Port Blair (arrives on 4 Apr) with the transport *Tatekawa Maru* and reinforcements for the Andaman Islands. On the same day the Malaya Force (Vice-Adm Ozawa) with the heavy cruisers *Chokai* and *Kumano* (7th Cruiser Sqn, Rear-Adm Kurita) and *Mikuma, Mogami* and *Suzuya*, the carrier *Ryujo* (4th Carrier Sqn, Rear-Adm Kakuta), the light cruiser *Yura* and the destroyers *Fubuki, Shirayuki, Hatsuyuki* and *Murakumo* (11th DD Div), sets out to sea from Mergui to make a raid in the Bay of Bengal. On 3–4 Apr the force waits S of the Andamans and in the process exchanges the 11th DD Div, which goes to Port Blair, for the 20th DD Div, comprising *Amagiri, Asagiri, Shirakumo* and *Yugiri*.

On 2 Apr a Japanese convoy with 46 transports puts to sea from Singapore for Rangoon with the 18th Inf Div on board. It is escorted by the cruiser *Kashii*, the destroyers *Hatakaze* and *Shikinami* and the submarine-chaser *Ch8*. On 4 Apr *Kashii* and *Shikinami* turn away and are replaced by an escort force from Penang consisting of the minelayer *Hatsutaka* and the destroyers *Asakaze, Harukaze* and *Matsukaze* (5th DD Div). The convoy arrives in Rangoon on 7 Apr without incident. On the evening of 4 Apr the 3rd DD Flotilla, comprising the cruiser *Sendai* and the destroyers *Fubuki, Hatsuyuki, Murakumo* and *Shirayuki* (11th DD Div) and *Isonami, Uranami* and *Ayanami* (19th DD Div), leaves Port Blair to take up a covering position W of the Andamans until 8 Apr.

The Japanese carrier fleet, advancing from the S, is reported on the afternoon of 4 Apr by one of the six British Catalina flying boats stationed in Ceylon before it is shot down by the fighter cover. Then all operational ships leave the harbour of Colombo, including the cruisers *Cornwall* and *Dorsetshire* which receive orders to join up with Force A. The latter, after hurried refuelling, sets out from Addu Atoll shortly after midnight on 5 Apr. Force B follows in the morning. Early on 5 Apr a Catalina again reports the Japanese carrier fleet. At the same time Nagumo flies off 53 high-level and 38 dive-bombers with 36 fighters 300 nautical miles SE of Ceylon to attack Colombo. In heavy air engagements, the Japanese fighters shoot down 19 out of 42 Hurricane and Fulmar fighters and six Swordfish torpedo aircraft, whilst losing seven of their own. The attack causes heavy damage. The auxiliary cruiser *Hector* (11198 tons) and the destroyer *Tenedos* sink in the harbour. At mid-day a reconnaissance plane from *Tone* sights the British cruisers *Cornwall* (Capt Manwaring) and *Dorsetshire* (Capt Agar); 53 dive-bombers under Lt-Cdr Egusa, which are immediately flown off from the Japanese carriers, sink the ships with many hits. 1122 men from a total of 1546 are later rescued by *Enterprise* and two destroyers. Although the distance between British Force A and the Japanese carrier fleet on the afternoon of 5 Apr is at times no more than 200 nautical miles, the Japanese reconnaissance aircraft do not find the British forces and Adm Somerville is able to keep out of Japanese range during the day. From 5 to 8 Apr the Japanese carrier fleet withdraws to the SE. On the evening of 5 Apr Vice-Adm Ozawa divides his force in order to attack shipping off the Indian Coast. On 6 Apr a Northern Group (Rear-Adm Kurita) with the cruisers *Kumano* and *Suzuya* and the destroyer *Shirakumo* sinks nine ships off Puri (Orissa); a Central Group (Vice-Adm Ozawa) with *Chokai, Yura, Asagiri* and *Yugiri* sinks four ships; and a Southern Group (Capt Sakiyama) with the cruisers *Mikuma* and *Mogami* and the destroyer *Amagiri* sinks three ships and damages two more. The carrier *Ryujo*, operating with the Central Group, carries out raids with her aircraft on Vizagapatam and Cocanada and sinks three ships and damages one more. In all, 92000 tons of shipping are sunk.

On 8 Apr a Catalina flying boat again reports the advancing Japanese carrier fleet but, in the meantime, Adm Somerville has returned with his two battle squadrons to Addu Atoll. The ships in Trincomalee receive orders to withdraw to the S. Early on 9 Apr 91 Japanese high-level bombers and dive-bombers with 38 fighters attack Trincomalee. Nine of the 23 British Hurricane and Fulmar fighters which are sent up to defend the harbour are shot down. The Japanese fighter escort over the carriers intercepts a force of nine Blenheim bombers and shoots five down. Only a few near-misses are obtained. Japanese reconnaissance aircraft again locate the British ships withdrawing southwards along the coast. 80 dive-bombers with fighter escort destroy *Hermes* (Capt Onslow†), the destroyer *Vampire*, the corvette *Hollyhock* and two tankers; the hospital ship *Vita* is respected. The Japanese forces, which, apart from the above mentioned warships, have sunk, in all, 23 merchant ships of 112312 tons, start the return journey. Adm Ozawa, reinforced by the 3rd DD Flotilla, passes through the Straits of Malacca on 9–10 Apr, followed by Vice-Adm Nagumo on 12–13 Apr. Of the British formations, Force A proceeds on 9 Apr to Bombay and Force B to Kilindini on the East African coast.

Of the Japanese submarines operating W of India in the Maldive and Laccadive passages and W of Ceylon, *I-6* (Cdr* Inaba) sinks two ships of 11321 tons and two sailing ships, *I-7* (Cdr* Koizumi) sinks one ship of 9415 tons, *I-5* (Cdr* Utsuki) sinks one ship of 6617 tons and one sailing ship, *I-3* (Cdr* Tonozuka) sinks one ship of 5051 tons and torpedoes one of 4872 tons and *I-2* (Cdr* Inada) sinks one unidentified ship.

27 Mar   North Atlantic

U587 (Lt-Cdr Borcherdt), which is returning from the American East Coast, hears and sights the fast troop transport convoy WS.17. Her contact report is located by HF/DF. The escort destroyer *Leamington*, which is sent to the scene, at first goes past her but, on her return, sights the U-boat which has just sent off a second report and is now sunk by the destroyers *Aldenham, Grove, Leamington* and *Volunteer*. This is the first success with shipboard HF/DF.

27 Mar   Arctic

The German 8th Destroyer Flotilla, with *Z24, Z25* and *Z26*, returns to Kirkenes.

27 Mar   English Channel

The German MDS *Sperrbrecher 147/Koert* is sunk by mine off the Hook of Holland.

27–28 Mar Arctic
Off Petsamo, the German auxiliary mine-sweepers *M5607* and *M5608* are sunk on mines; the first is salvaged.

27–28 Mar Bay of Biscay
British raid on St-Nazaire (Operation 'Chariot'), with the object of destroying the giant drydock capable of taking the battle-ship *Tirpitz*. The following ships are deployed: the destroyer *Campbeltown* (Lt-Cdr Beattie), *MGB314*, *MTB74* and 16 motor launches (*ML156, 160, 177, 192, 262, 267, 268, 270, 298, 306, 307, 341, 443, 446, 447* and *457*) with, in all, crews of 353 and 268 commandos (Lt-Col Newman). They are to be supported and met by the destroyers *Atherstone, Tynedale, Cleveland* and *Brocklesby*. *Campbeltown*, in spite of strong defensive fire which takes a heavy toll, particularly of the small craft of the force as they approach, succeeds in ramming the dock gate and setting the time fuses for the explosive charge. The commandos are unable to overcome the defences and are wiped out. When the 5th TB Flotilla (strength as on 13–14 Mar) intervenes from the sea, only five launches—*ML160* and *443* (returned) and *ML156, 270* and *446* (sunk by own forces)—are able to break through to the destroyers waiting to meet them.

27 Mar–9 Apr Mediterranean
The German U-boats *U205, U431* and *U453* (Lt-Cdr Frhr v Schlippenbach) operate against British supply traffic to and from Tobruk. *U453* torpedoes the hospital ship *Somersetshire* (9716 tons), which is not recognised as such by the submarine.

28 Mar–1 Apr South Asia
The US submarine *Sturgeon* (Lt-Cdr Wright) sinks two ships of 1592 tons off Makassar and damages one of 5100 tons. In several attacks on a Japanese landing force off Christmas Island on 31 Mar and 1 Apr, the US submarine *Seawolf* (Lt-Cdr Warder) torpedoes the Japanese cruiser *Naka*. The British *Truant* (Lt-Cdr Haggard) sinks two ships of 11719 tons off Penang.

29 Mar–5 Apr Black Sea
The Soviet flotilla leader *Tashkent* and destroyer *Shaumyan* bring supplies to Seva-stopol on 29 Mar and the destroyers *Bditelny* and *Soobrazitelny* shell land targets. On 2 Apr the damaged and beached cruiser *Chervona Ukraina* is destroyed by fresh bomb hits. On 2 Apr the flotilla leader *Kharkov* and the destroyer *Svobodny*, and on 5 Apr the destroyer *Boiki*, arrive in Seva-stopol with supplies. *Shaumyan* runs aground near Gelendzhik in Apr and is lost.

29 Mar–5 Apr Mediterranean
The British submarine *Proteus* sinks on 29 Mar off Brindisi one ship from a convoy of seven ships, escorted by the destroyer *Sebenico* and the torpedo boats *Bassini, Castelfidardo* and *Mosto*, and on 31 Mar a second ship escorted by the destroyer *Strale*. Together they amount to 11688 tons. On 1 Apr *Urge* (Cdr Tomkinson) sinks the Italian cruiser *Bande Nere* off Stromboli.

From 2 to 4 Apr three Italian convoys (Operation 'Lupo') proceed to Tripoli without incident. They consist of six ships escorted by seven destroyers and two torpedo boats, distant escort being provided by the cruiser *Eugenio di Savoia* and two destroyers.

On 5 Apr the British submarine *Una* (Lt Norman) sinks one ship of 5335 tons off Calabria.

30 Mar Norway
33 Halifaxes of No 4 Group RAF Bomber Command unsuccessfully attack the battle ship *Tirpitz* lying in Föttenfjord off Trond-heim. Five aircraft are shot down.

30 Mar–4 Apr North Atlantic
U702 is lost to an unknown cause going out into the Atlantic, probably in the Ice-land/Faeroes area.

31 Mar–1 Apr Norway
In the evening of 31 Mar ten Norwegian merchant ships (54681 tons) try to break through the Kattegat and Skagerrak from Göteborg to England. The destroyers *Faulknor, Escapade, Eskimo, Wallace, Vanity* and *Valorous* are on the way to escort them but only the tankers *B P Newton* (10324 tons) and *Lind* (461 tons) reach their destination; the whaling depot ship *Skytteren* (12358 tons), the tanker *Buccaneer* (6222 tons) and the freighters *Gudvang* (1470 tons) and *Charente* (1282 tons) are either sunk by German warships (*V908, 1604, 1609, 1612, 1613*) or scuttle themselves, while the tanker *Rigmor* (6305 tons) is sunk by German torpedo planes and the tanker *Storsten* (5343 tons) hits a mine. The remaining freighters *Lionel* (5653 tons) and *Dicto* (5263 tons) return to Göteborg.

Apr 1942 Mediterranean
The British Admiralty allows Italy to fetch colonists from East Africa in the passenger ships *Vulcania* (24469 tons), *Saturnia* (24470 tons), *Duilio* (23635 tons) and *Giulio Cesare* (21900 tons). They arrive back in Italy in July 1942.

1 Apr Baltic
The German A/S trawler *UJ1203* is sunk by a mine in the Gulf of Finland.

1–11 Apr Mediterranean
Heavy air attacks by FK II (Gen Loerzer) and Italian formations on Malta. In them the British destroyers *Lance, Gallant* and *Kingston*, the minesweeper *Abingdon*, the submarines *P36, Glavkos* and *Pandora*, the naval tanker *Plumleaf* (5916 tons) and several smaller ships are sunk and the cruiser *Penelope* is damaged. In the middle of the month the remaining boats of the British 10th SM Flotilla have to leave Malta.

In Apr 1942 comes the climax of the air attacks on Malta: German bombers fly 4082 day and 256 night sorties against the island.

1–14 Apr Bay of Biscay
On 1 Apr, during patrols over the U-boat routes, an RAF Whitley, 'F' of No 502 Sqn, damages the returning *U129* and on 14 Apr another Whitley, 'M' of No 502 Sqn, damages *U590* on the latter's voyage from Kiel to France.

2–25 Apr Central Pacific
US raid on Tokyo. On 2 Apr the carrier *Hornet*, escorted by the cruisers *Nashville* and *Vincennes* and the destroyers *Grayson, Gwin, Meredith* and *Monssen* (Desdiv 22) and the tanker *Cimarron*, sets out from San Francisco. On 8 Apr Vice-Adm Halsey with the carrier *Enterprise*, the cruisers *Northampton* (Rear-Adm Spruance) and *Salt Lake City* and the destroyers *Balch* (Desron 6) and *Benham, Ellet* and *Fanning* (Desdiv 12) and the tanker *Sabine* put to sea from Pearl Harbor. The two groups join up to form TF.16 on 13 Apr. On the way they are located early on 18 Apr by the Japanese picket boat line stationed 700 nautical miles E of Japan; two boats are sunk by aircraft from *Enterprise* and two others are damaged; one is captured by *Nashville*. Halsey decides to fly off the 16 B-25 bombers (Lt-Col Doolittle) embarked on *Hornet* to make a daylight attack on Tokyo when still 668 nautical miles away. The damage done in Tokyo (13 aircraft), Nagoya (two) and Kobe (one) is slight. Apart from one bomber which makes an emergency landing near Vladivostok, all aircraft are lost making forced landings in China. The crews of two are taken prisoner. On the basis of the picket boats' reports, the Japanese 1st Carrier Fleet (Vice-Adm Nagumo), comprising five carriers, four battleships, two heavy and one light cruiser and nine destroyers (see 26 Mar–11 Apr), which is in the area E of Formosa on its return to Japan from the raid on Ceylon, is put on the trail. But it has to abandon the sortie on 22 Apr as hopeless. Likewise, the submarines *I-21, I-22, I-24, I-27, I-28* and *I-29*, which are E of the Bonin Islands on their way from Japan to Truk, and the 3rd SM Flotilla, comprising *I-8, I-74, I-75, I-68, I-69, I-71* and *I-72*, do not get to TF.16, which withdraws at high speed and reaches Pearl Harbor on 25 Apr.

3 Apr Arctic
German bombers sink in Murmansk the British freighter *Empire Starlight* (6850

tons) and *New Westminster City* (4747 tons) belonging to PQ.13.

4–24 Apr   Western Atlantic

U154 (Cdr Kölle) sinks five ships of 28715 tons in the Greater Antilles.

4–30 Apr   Baltic

The German FK I (Gen Förster) attacks the large units of the Baltic Fleet in Leningrad to prevent their deployment after the spring thaw.

Operation 'Eisstoss'. On 4 Apr 62 Ju 87s of StG 1 (Lt-Col Hagen) with III/StG 1, I and II/StG 2 and 33 Ju 88s of KG 1 (Maj-Gen Angerstein) attack the ships and 37 He 111s of KG 4 (Col Rath) attack the AA positions with fighter protection from JG 54 (Maj Trautloft) comprising 59 Me 109s. During the night 4–5 Apr 31 He 111s of KG 4 again attack the ships. The battleship *Oktyabrskaya Revolutsiya* receives four hits, the cruiser *Maksim Gorki* seven medium calibre hits, the cruisers *Kirov* and *Petropavlovsk* and the destroyer *Silny* one serious hit each and the destroyer *Grozyashchi*, the minelayer *Marti* and the training ship *Svir* less serious hits.

Operation 'Götz von Berlichingen'. In the continuation of the attacks on 24, 25 and 30 Apr, one hit, *inter alia*, is scored on *Kirov*. In all, FK I flies 596 sorties against Leningrad in Apr and Luftflotte 1 in the same period a total of 9047 sorties in support of Army Group North. Altogether, 29 aircraft are lost.

5 Apr   Mediterranean

The British destroyer *Havock*, in attempting to break through from Malta to Gibraltar, runs aground near Kelibia and is destroyed there by a torpedo from the Italian submarine *Aradam*.

6 Apr   Indian Ocean

The Indian sloop *Indus* is sunk by Japanese Aircraft near Akyab.

7–19 Apr   Mediterranean

In British submarine operations, *Turbulent* (Cdr Linton) sinks two ships of 5677 tons off Brindisi, *Thrasher* (Lt-Cdr Mackenzie) two ships of 2326 tons off the Cyrenaican coast (from a convoy escorted by the torpedo boats *Pallade* and *Perseo* and four German motor minesweepers) and *Torbay* (Cdr Miers) two ships of 1434 tons off Corfu and Taranto. Off Sfax *P35/Umbra* (Lt Maydon) sinks a ship of 4219 tons which is setting out and has just been met by the torpedo boat *Castore*.

8–25 Apl   Arctic

Operations against the convoys PQ.14 and QP.10. On 8 Apr PQ.14 sets out from Iceland with 24 ships, escorted by five destroyers, four corvettes, two minesweepers and four A/S trawlers; close escort

consists of the cruisers *Edinburgh* (Rear-Adm Bonham-Carter) and *Norfolk* and two destroyers. Near Jan Mayen the convoy runs into pack ice: 16 ships and two minesweepers have to return after being damaged by ice. On 10 Apr QP.10 sets out from the Kola Inlet with 16 ships, escorted by the cruiser *Liverpool*, the destroyers *Oribi*, *Punjabi*, *Marne*, *Fury* and *Eclipse*, the minesweeper *Speedwell* and the A/S trawlers *Blackfly* and *Paynter*. Between Iceland and Norway a covering force operates, comprising the battleships *Duke of York* and *King George V*, the carrier *Victorious*, the cruisers *Kent* and *Nigeria* and eight destroyers. On 11 Apr the Soviet Air Force attacks the German airfield at Kirkenes with little success. Ju 88s of III/KG 30 sink the freighter *Empire Cowper* (7164 tons) from QP.10. The destroyer *Hermann Schoemann*, *Z24* and *Z25* search without success for the convoy. During the night 12–13 Apr *U435* (Lt-Cdr Strelow) misses *Punjabi* and sinks in turn the freighters *El Occidente* (6008 tons) and *Kiev* (5823 tons). Towards morning an attack by *U209* fails and Ju 88s of III/KG 30 sink the freighter *Harpalion* (5486 tons). German air reconnaissance locates PQ.14 but isolated air attacks on the convoy from 15 to 17 Apr fail and the escort of QP.10 (Cdr McBeath on *Oribi*) counters attacks by *U376*, *U377* and *U456*. *U376* narrowly misses *Edinburgh* on 17 Apr E of Bear Island. *U403* (Lt-Cdr Clausen) sinks the freighter *Empire Howard* (6985 tons) from PQ.14 and the convoy's Commodore Rees is lost. Attempts by the German 8th DD Flotilla to find the two convoys fail in the prevailing bad weather. Seven freighters arrive in Murmansk and 11 in Iceland. The Soviet submarines, including *K-21*, *S-101* and *Shch-401*, which were stationed as a flank screen, go to the polar coast. On 19 Apr the German minesweepers *M154* and *M251* prevent an attack by *Shch-401* (Capt 3rd Class Moiseev) on a convoy off Tanafjord. *K-2* lays mines on 11 Apr.

Shch-401 sinks the steamer *Stensaas* (1359 tons) from another convoy on 24 Apr and is then attacked with depth charges from the submarine-chasers *UJ1101* and *UJ1110*. After that the boat is missing but it is possible that she has been sunk in error by two Soviet torpedo cutters on her return on 25 Apr.

8 Apr–11 May   Western Atlantic

Twelve U-boats arrive one after the other off the American East Coast as the fifth wave. In individual operations they sink many ships: *U84* (Lt Uphoff) sinks two of 8240 tons, *U654* (Lt Forster) sinks three of 17755 tons, *U85* (Lt Greger) sinks one of

4904 tons, *U575* (Lt-Cdr Heydemann) sinks one of 6887 tons, *U201* (Lt-Cdr Schnee) sinks three of 15313 tons and torpedoes one of 7417 tons, *U576* (Lt-Cdr Heinicke) sinks two of 6441 tons, *U109* (Lt-Cdr Bleichrodt) sinks three of 12099 tons and torpedoes one of 6548 tons, *U136* (Lt-Cdr Zimmermann) sinks three of 12707 tons and torpedoes one of 8955 tons, *U402* (Lt-Cdr Freiherr v Forstner) sinks three of 11135 tons and *U752* (Lt-Cdr Schroeter) sinks three of 15506 tons. Attacks made by *U86* (Lt-Cdr Schug) and *U582* (Lt-Cdr Schulte) fail. *U85* is sunk on 14 Apr by the US destroyer *Roper*.

9–15 Apr   Black Sea

In German air attacks on Novorossisk and Tuapse, the cruiser *Voroshilov* and the destroyers *Nezamozhnik* and *Sposobny* are damaged; 30 crew die. On 10 Apr the flotilla leader *Kharkov* and the destroyer *Svobodny* bring supplies to Sevastopol. On 13 Apr the destroyers *Boiki* and *Nezamozhnik* follow, while *Bditelny* and *Soobrazitelny* shell land targets. *Nezamozhnik* makes another supply voyage on 15 Apr.

10 Apr–4 June   Pacific

US submarines sink the following ships off Japan: *Thresher* (Lt-Cdr Anderson) sinks one ship of 3039 tons, *Trout* (Lt-Cdr Fenno) sinks two ships of 7138 tons and damages two of 23322 tons, *Drum* (Lt-Cdr Rice) sinks the seaplane-carrier *Mizuho* and two ships of 7736 tons, *Grenadier* (Lt-Cdr Lent) sinks one ship of 14457 tons, *Silversides* (Lt-Cdr Burlingame) damages three ships of 16400 tons, *Tuna* (Lt-Cdr de Tar) sinks one ship of 805 tons, *Pollack* (Lt-Cdr Mosely) sinks two guard boats of 123 tons and two fishing vessels and *Pompano* (Lt-Cdr Parks) sinks two ships of 8885 tons. Near Truk, *Greenling* (Lt-Cdr Bruton) sinks one ship of 3262 tons and damages one of 6659 tons, *Tautog* (Lt-Cdr Willingham) sinks one ship of 4467 tons and the submarine *I-28* and damages two ships of 13930 tons and *Triton* (Lt-Cdr Kirkpatrick) sinks three ships of 18549 tons and the submarine *I-164*.

10 Apr–9 June   South Asia

Elements of the Japanese South-West Area Fleet land army units on the west and east coast of Cebu on 10 Apr; by 14 Apr they have broken the resistance of the American forces. 4160 troops are landed on 16 Apr near Ho Ho on Panay and two days later near San José (Panay). By 20 Apr this island is also occupied.

4852 troops are embarked on 26 Apr in Cebu to be landed on 29 Apr in Cotabato and Parang (Mindanao). On 3 May further Japanese forces from Panay are landed in Macajalar Bay on Mindanao. After General Wainwright on Corregidor has officially offered the capitulation of the American forces on the Philippines, many of the remaining battle groups are dissolved in order to carry out partisan warfare with the Filipinos.

The Japanese land on Leyte and Samar, from Panay on 21 May and from Cebu on 25 May.

11–13 Apr Mediterranean
The Italian destroyers *Vivaldi* and *Malocello* lay in two nights SW of Marettimo (Western Sicily) the barrages S.51 and S.52, each with 180 EMC mines. The German 3rd MTB Flotilla (Lt-Cdr Kemnade) lays in three nights E of Malta the barrages MT.10–12 with eight EMF and 72 UMB mines as well as 16 protection floats and 48 explosive floats.

12 Apr–19 May Western Atlantic
In the Caribbean and near Trinidad, *U130* (Cdr Kals) sinks two ships of 13092 tons and *U66* (Cdr Zapp) sinks six of 43956 tons and torpedoes one of 12502 tons. On 19 Apr *U130* shells the oil installations of Curaçao.

12 Apr–28 May Arctic
Intensive deployment of the Soviet 3rd SM Division (Capt 3rd Class Morosov) against convoy traffic on both sides of the Varanger Peninsula. In up to five operations, *M-171* (Lt-Cdr Starikov) makes four attacks and torpedoes the steamer *Curityba* (4,969 tons), *M-172* (Lt-Cdr Fisanovich) makes five attacks with no success, *M-173* (Lt-Cdr Terekhin) makes three attacks and sinks the steamer *Blankenese* (3263 tons) and *M176* (Lt-Cdr Bondarevich) makes five attacks with no success. The submarines avoid the depth charge pursuits by the German submarine-chasers (eg *M-172*) on 15 May after an 8hr pursuit in which *UJ1104* and *UJ1108* drop depth charges but then have to turn away when under fire from the Soviet coastal batteries on the Fisherman's Peninsula.

13–26 Apr Mediterranean
From 13 to 16 Apr the U-boats *U562* (Lt Hamm), *U331* (Lt-Cdr v Tiesenhausen), *U81* (Lt-Cdr Guggenberger) and *U561* (Lt-Cdr Bartels) lay mine barrages off Famagusta (two ships of 238 tons sunk) and off Beirut, Haifa and Port Said (two ships of 11754 tons sunk and one of 4043 tons damaged). Later *U331* sinks three sailing ships and *U81* sinks one tanker of 6018 tons and nine sailing ships. *U97* has no success off Tobruk.

14 Apr Mediterranean
In an attempt to attack an Italian convoy off Tripoli, Britain's most successful submarine, *Upholder* (Lt-Cdr Wanklyn†), is sunk, probably by the German motor minesweepers *R9*, *R12* and *R15*, on her 25th mission.

14 Apr North Atlantic
After disembarking agents in Iceland (8 Apr) and a still unconfirmed attack on a small ship on 11 Apr, *U252* (Lt-Cdr Lerchen) encounters during the night 13–14 Apr the convoy OG.82 which is escorted by the 36th EG (Cdr Walker). The submarine is located by the corvette *Vetch* with radar at a distance of 7,000m (first success with the 10cm Type 271 radar), which evades a torpedo salvo and, together with the command boat, the sloop *Stork*, sinks the U-boat by gunfire and depth charges.

14–26 Apr Mediterranean
Operation 'Calendar'. Anglo-American Force W (Commodore Daniell) sets out from Greenock on 14 Apr with the British battlecruiser *Renown*, the US carrier *Wasp* and the destroyers *Inglefield*, *Echo*, *Partridge* and *Ithuriel* (British) and *Lang* and *Madison* (US). It is reinforced off Gibraltar on 19 Apr by the British cruisers *Cairo* and *Charybdis* and flies off 47 British Spitfire fighters for Malta on 20 Apr; 46 of them arrive. Force W returns to Scapa Flow on 26 Apr. The Italian submarines *Brin*, *Veniero*, *Argo* and *Velella* operate S of the Balearics but only *Velella* attacks a destroyer, which is missed.

16 Apr South Atlantic
Schiff 53/Doggerbank (Lt-Cdr Schneidewind) drops 80 EMC mines in five sections off Cape Agulhas. The British freighter *Soudan* (6,677 tons) sinks, and the depot ship *Hecla* (10850 tons) is damaged, on the barrages.

16 Apr Mediterranean
Operation 'Lighter'. Royal Marines from the destroyers *Kelvin* and *Kipling* land on Kuphorisi (Crete) to destroy a W/T station.

17–26 Apr South West Pacific
The US submarine *Tambor* (Lt-Cdr Murphy) sinks one ship of 394 tons off Kavieng, *Spearfish* (Lt-Cdr Dempsey) sinks one of 5402 tons and torpedoes two others of 13990 tons off Lingayen Gulf and *Pickerel* (Lt-Cdr Bacon) torpedoes one of 9347 tons off Ambon.

18–19 Apr Mediterranean
The Italian destroyers *Malocello* and *Vivaldi* lay S of Malta the barrage M.5, consisting of 156 mines. The sowing of the M.7 barrage planned for the following night SE of Malta has to be abandoned because the minelaying formation is prematurely sighted.

19–22 Apr South Atlantic
The German auxiliary cruiser *Schiff 28/Michel* (Cdr* v Ruckteschell) sinks two tankers of 16152 tons in the South Atlantic.

20 Apr Norway
The British submarine *Trident* (Cdr Sladen) sinks one ship of 5386 tons NW of Namsos.

Off Trondheim, the German minelayers *Ulm*, *Kaiser*, *Brummer* and *Roland* lay flanking mine barrages.

20 Apr Black Sea
After the thawing of the ice, German and Rumanian convoy traffic begins between Constanza and Ochakov. The merchant ships used are *Zar Ferdinand* (1994 tons), *Kolozsvar* (1200), *Kassa* (1022), *Danubius* (1489), *Oituz* (2686), *Sulina* (3495), *Tisza* (961), *Budapest* (485), *Carpati* (4336), *Salzburg* (1742), *Arkadia* (1756), *Ardeal* (5695), *Suceava* (6876) and *Le Progrès* (311). Escort is provided by the Danube Flotilla and Rumanian warships (destroyers *Marasesti*, *Maresti*, *Regina Maria*, torpedo boat *Smeul* and gunboat *Dumitrescu*).

The Soviet destroyers *Bditelny* and *Soobrazitelny* bring supplies to Sevastopol.

20–28 Apr Mediterranean
The German 3rd MTB Flotilla (Lt-Cdr Kemnade) lays W and NE of Valetta and E of Malta the mine barrages MT.13–18 with 19 UMB and 84 EMC mines, 36 protection floats and 108 explosive floats.

20 Apr–9 May South Pacific
The Japanese submarines *Ro-33* and *Ro-34* each undertake two patrols off Port Moresby.

20 Apr–14 June North Atlantic
First rota with 11 regularly established ocean escort groups for the Allied North Atlantic convoys HX, SC, ON and ONS from WESTOMP to EASTOMP. HX.186 leaves Halifax on 20 Apr with 21 ships; EG.B7, with destroyers *Churchill* and *Firedrake* and corvettes *Dianella*, *Kingcup*, *Loosestrife* and *Roselys* (FFN), returns with ONS.94. SC.81 leaves Halifax on 23 Apr with 70 ships; EG.B2, with destroyers *Hesperus* and *Piorun* (Polish) and corvettes *Clematis*, *Gentian*, *Sweetbriar* and *Vervain*, returns with ON.97. HX.187 leaves Halifax on 27 Apr with 26 ships; EG.B1, with destroyers *Hurricane* and *Rockingham* and corvettes *Anchusa*, *Dahlia* and *Monkshood*, returns with ONS.96. SC.82 leaves Halifax on 30 Apr with 32 ships; EG.B4, with destroyers *Highlander* and *Winchelsea* and corvettes *Anemone*, *Asphodel* and *Pennywort*, returns with ON.99. HX.188 leaves Halifax on 3 May with 28 ships; EG.B3, with destroyer *Harvester* and corvettes *Mignonette*, *Narcissus*, and *Lobélia* and *Renoncule* (FFN), returns with ONS.98. SC.83 leaves Halifax on 7 May with 63 ships; EG.B6, with destroyer *Viscount* and corvettes *Acanthus* (Norwegian), *Eglantine*, *Potentilla* and *Rose*, returns with ON.101. HX.189 leaves Halifax on 10 May with 21 ships; EG.C1, with destroyers *Assiniboine* and *St Croix* and corvettes *Buctouche*, and

Chambly, Dianthus and *Nasturtium* (RN) and *Mimose* and *Aconit* (FFN), returns with ONS.100. SC.84 leaves Halifax on 14 May with 46 ships; EG.C2, with destroyers *Broadway* (RN) and corvettes *Brandon, Drumheller, Dunvegan* and *Morden* and *Polyanthus* (RN), returns with ON.103. HX.190 leaves Halifax on 17 May with 18 ships; EG.A3, with US Coast Guard cutters *Campbell* and *Ingham* and corvettes *Rosthern, Agassiz, Mayflower* and *Collingwood* (RCN), returns with ONS.102. HX.191 leaves Halifax on 24 May with 26 ships; EG.C3, with destroyers *Saguenay* and *Skeena* and corvettes *Westaskiwin, Sackville, Galt* and *Camrose*, returns with ONS.104. SC.85 leaves Halifax on 29 May with 62 ships; EG.C4, with destroyers *Ottawa* and *St Francis* and corvettes *Lethbridge, Prescott, Eyebright* and *Arvida*, arrives in Britain on 14 June and returns with ON.105.

These ocean escort groups meet an ON or ONS convoy at EASTOMP and return with it to WESTOMP. Between the convoy journeys they take on supplies in St Johns (Newfoundland) and Londonderry (Northern Ireland). In later operations the composition of the escort groups changes depending on the availability of the vessels. Of these convoys, only ONS.94, ONS.96, ONS.100 and ONS.102 are intercepted by U-boat group 'Hecht' (see 11 May–21 June).

23 Apr–4 May   Mediterranean
In operations against the British Tobruk supply traffic, *U565* (Lt-Cdr Franken) sinks one ship of 1301 tons and *U372* misses two guard ships. On 1 May, NW of Cape Tenes, *U573* (Lt-Cdr Heinsohn) is heavily damaged by Hudson 'M' of No 233 Sqn but is able to limp into Cartagena. The boat is paid off, sold to Spain and later recommissioned as *G7*. *U74* is lost on 2 May as a result of action by the British destroyers *Wishart* and *Wrestler* with air support by Catalina 'C' of No 202 Sqn. The Italian submarine *Corallo* (Cdr Andreani) sinks two sailing vessels off the Tunisian coast.

23 Apr–5 May   North Atlantic
The first U-boat tanker, *U459* (Lt-Cdr v Wilamowitz-Moellendorf), refuels 14 outgoing and homebound U-boats 500 nautical miles NE of Bermuda.

24 Apr–24 May   Western Atlantic
Between the Bahamas and the Greater Antilles, *U108* (Cdr Scholtz) sinks five ships of 31340 tons; in the Gulf of Mexico, *U506* (Lt-Cdr Würdemann) sinks eight ships of 39906 tons and damages three of 23354 tons and *U507* (Cdr Schacht) sinks nine ships of 44782 tons; off Cuba and Yucatan, *U125* (Lt-Cdr Folkers) sinks nine ships of 47055

tons; and, off Guinea, *U162* (Cdr* Wattenberg) sinks nine ships of 47181 tons.

25 Apr   Baltic
Beginning of the transfer of German forces to the Gulf of Finland for the summer of 1942. Taking part are Officer Commanding Minesweepers East, Capt Böhmer, the 3rd MS Flotilla (seven Type 35 minesweepers), the 1st MMS Flotilla (one tender and nine R-boats), the 17th MS Flotilla (five converted trawlers—only until May 1942), the 18th MS Flotilla (seven converted trawlers), the 12th SC Flotilla (ten converted trawlers and whalers), the 3rd Patrol Boat Flotilla (11 converted trawlers), the 31st MS Flotilla (one R-boat and 13 converted fishing drifters), the 34th MS Flotilla (14 converted fishing drifters), the 27th Landing Flotilla (five large gun carriers, 15 minelaying barges and nine transport barges), two minesweeping depot ships (each with 16 sweeper long-boats), one mine destructor ship and the minelayers *Kaiser* and *Roland*. In addition, auxiliary vessels and the coastal defence flotilla Ostland participate.

25 Apr–8 May   Indian Ocean
Operation 'Ironclad': British landing near Diego Suarez (Madagascar). On 25 Apr the slow convoy Y with two special landing ships, six supply transports, one fleet tanker and one hospital ship sets out from Durban, escorted by the cruiser *Devonshire* and three destroyers, the 14th MS Flotilla and the 3rd EG. On 28 Apr the fast convoy Z with five attack transports and three troop transports follows with the covering force (Rear-Adm Syfret) consisting of the battleship *Ramillies*, the carrier *Illustrious*, the cruiser *Hermione* and six destroyers. On 3 May the convoys and reinforcements detached from the Eastern Fleet, comprising the carrier *Indomitable* (Rear-Adm Boyd) and two destroyers, join up. From there the invasion fleet (Capt Oliver) reaches the area NW of the island. It comprises *Devonshire*, the destroyers *Active, Anthony, Duncan, Inconstant, Javelin, Laforey, Lightning,Lookout, Pakenham, Paladin* and *Panther*, the corvettes *Freesia, Auricula, Nigella, Fritillary, Genista, Cyclamen, Thyme* and *Jasmine* and the minesweepers *Cromer, Poole, Romney* and *Cromarty*, as well as the transports. The covering force operates with *Ramillies*, the carriers *Illustrious* and *Indomitable* and the destroyers *Active, Duncan, Javelin, Lookout, Inconstant, Paladin* and *Panther* further off. *Hermione* carries out a diversionary sortie.

On 5 May an attack is carried out by British carrier aircraft on the French airfields and ships. The auxiliary cruiser *Bougainville* is sunk by aircraft from *Illustrious* and the

submarine *Bévéziers* is sunk by depth charges (but later raised). The British landing in Courrier Bay, where the corvette *Auricula* runs on a mine, takes place without resistance; but the further advance of the British landing troops is held up on 5 and 6 May by the French defenders. The landing of British marine commandos by the destroyer *Anthony* and the capture of important central installations lead, however, to the rapid collapse of French resistance. The gunboat *D'Entrecasteaux*, which has supported the defenders with her guns, has to be beached after being hit by bombs from aircraft from *Indomitable* and by gunfire from the destroyer *Laforey*. On 7 May the French submarine *Le Héros* is sunk by a corvette and aircraft from *Illustrious* when attempting to attack the British main force. On 8 May the submarine *Monge* unsuccessfully attacks *Indomitable* and is then sunk by the destroyers *Active* and *Panther*. The French submarine *Le Glorieux* and the gunboat *D'Iberville* escape to South Madagascar and, later, from there to Toulon.

26 Apr   Western Atlantic
The US destroyer *Sturtevant* is mined and sunk near Key West; later three merchant vessels founder on a friendly minefield.

26 Apr–1 May   Black Sea
On 26 Apr the Soviet cruiser *Krasny Krym* and the destroyers *Bditelny* and *Boiki* with 3487 relief troops and the transport *Serov*, escorted by the destroyers *Soobrazitelny* and *Zheleznyakov* and carrying equipment and ammunition, arrive in Sevastopol. On 28 Apr *Krasny Krym, Bditelny* and *Soobrazitelny* with 2000 relief troops for Sevastopol have to return because of an air attack: they reach Sevastopol on 29 Apr, when the flotilla leader *Tashkent* takes the place of *Bditelny*. On 1 May the flotilla leader *Kharkov* brings supplies to Sevastopol and shells land targets.

26 Apr–12 May   Arctic
Operations against the convoys PQ.15 and QP.11. On 26 Apr PQ.15 sets out from Iceland with 50 ships, escorted by the destroyers *Somali, Matchless, Boadicea, Venomous, Badsworth* and *St Albans* (RNoN), four minesweepers, four A/S trawlers, the AA ship *Ulster Queen* and the catapult ship *Empire Morn*. Senior officer of the escort is Capt Crombie on the minesweeper *Bramble*. Close support is provided by the cruisers *Nigeria* (Rear-Adm Burrough) and *London* and two destroyers and the covering force between Iceland and Norway consists of the battleships *King George V* (Adm Tovey) and *Washington* (Rear-Adm Giffen), the carrier *Victorious*, the cruisers *Tuscaloosa, Wichita* and *Kenya* and four British

and four US destroyers. On 28 Apr QP.11 sets out from Murmansk with 13 ships, escorted by the destroyers *Bulldog* (Cdr Richmond), *Amazon*, *Beagle* and *Beverley*, four corvettes and one A/S trawler. Close escort is provided by the cruiser *Edinburgh* (Rear-Adm Bonham-Carter), the destroyers *Foresight* and *Forester* and, until 29 Apr, one British minesweeper and the Soviet destroyers *Kuibyshev* and *Sokrushitelny* and there is a flanking concentration of four British submarines and the Soviet submarines *D-3*, *K-2*, *K-22* and *K-23* against German surface ships. U-boats assembled are *U88*, *U251*, *U405*, *U436*, *U456*, *U589* and *U703*.

On 29 Apr German air reconnaissance and U-boats establish contact with QP.11. On 30 Apr *U88* misses the convoy and *U436* (Lt-Cdr Seibicke) misses *Edinburgh* ahead of the convoy, but the cruiser is later hit by two torpedoes from *U456* (Lt-Cdr Teichert). The German destroyers *Hermann Schoemann* (Capt Schulze-Hinrichs), *Z24* and *Z25* are deployed against QP.11 but they are impeded by ice and are repeatedly driven off by the four British destroyers and the corvette *Snowflake*: they are only able to sink the Soviet freighter *Tsiolkovski* (2847 tons) and to damage *Amazon*. They operate against the disabled *Edinburgh* where, in the meantime, the Soviet patrol ship *Rubin*, one tug and the British minesweepers *Harrier*, *Niger*, *Gossamer* and *Hussar* have arrived. In the attack on 1 May *Hermann Schoemann* is badly hit by *Edinburgh* (Capt Faulknor). In heavy engagements impeded by a snow shower and a smokescreen, *Z24* (Cdr Saltzwedel) and *Z25* (Cdr* Peters) badly damage *Forester* (Lt-Cdr Huddart†) and *Foresight* (Cdr Salter) and hit *Edinburgh* with another torpedo with the result that the cruiser has to be abandoned and sunk by a torpedo from *Foresight*. *Z24* and later *U88* rescue the majority of the crew from *Hermann Schoemann*. In attacks on QP.11, *U589* misses one steamer and *U251* one destroyer. With PQ.15 the Norwegian destroyer *St Albans* and the minesweeper *Seagull* sink the Polish submarine *P551/Jastrzab* which has wandered from her position in the flanking concentration. In the case of the covering force, *King George V* runs into the destroyer *Punjabi*, whose exploding depth charges damage the battleship as she sinks, with the result that the battleship has to be relieved by *Duke of York* (Vice-Adm Curteis). Attacks by German torpedo aircraft and bombers on QP.11 are unsuccessful. On 2 May torpedo aircraft of I/KG 26 sink the British freighters *Botavon* (5848 tons, convoy commodore Capt

Anchor†) and *Cape Corso* (3807 tons) and damage the *Jutland* (6153 tons), which is sunk on 3 May by *U251* (Lt-Cdr Timm). 22 ships of PQ.15 arrive in Murmansk on 5 May and 12 ships of QP.11 in Iceland on 7 May. After the operations the Soviet submarines go to the polar coast, where *D-3* and *K-2* attack several convoys without success. On 12 May *K-23* (Capt 3rd Class Potapov with Capt 2nd Class Gadzhiev on board) misses off Nordkyn a convoy with two steamers, the patrol boats *V6106*, *V6107*, *V6108* and the submarine-chaser group *UJ1101*, *UJ1109* and *UJ1110*, from which the submarine tries to escape with her superior speed on the surface. She is forced to submerge by an aircraft called to the scene and is sunk by the submarine-chasers in a group depth charge attack.

26 Apr–23 May   Western Atlantic
Thirteen U-boats arrive in turn on the American East Coast and in Canadian coastal waters and they operate individually against the still largely unorganised coastal traffic. The following ships are sunk by this sixth wave: *U564* (Lt-Cdr Suhren) sinks four ships of 24390 tons and torpedoes two of 13245 tons, *U333* (Lt-Cdr Cremer) sinks three ships of 13596 tons and torpedoes one of 8327 tons, *U455* (Lt-Cdr Giessler) sinks one ship of 6994 tons, *U553* (Lt-Cdr Thurmann) sinks three ships of 16995 tons, *U588* (Lt-Cdr Vogel) sinks four ships of 13975 tons and torpedoes one of 7460 tons, *U593* (Lt-Cdr Kelbling) sinks one ship of 8426 tons and torpedoes one of 4853 tons, *U653* (Lt-Cdr Feiler) sinks one ship of 6225 tons, *U135* (Lt-Cdr Praetorius) sinks one ship of 7127 tons and *U432* (Lt-Cdr H O Schultze) sinks five ships of 6110 tons and torpedoes one of 7073 tons. *U352* (Lt-Cdr Rathke) is lost on 9 May after an unsuccessful attack on the US Coast Guard cutter *Icarus* which then counter-attacks. *U98* and *U566* return without success. *U213* (Lt v Varendorff) lays an unsuccessful mine barrage near St Johns on 14 May.

27 Apr   North Sea
The British minesweeper *Fitzroy* is lost, probably on a British mine ENE of Great Yarmouth.

27–28 Apr   Norway
Thirty-one Halifax and 12 Lancaster bombers attack, without result, the German battleship *Tirpitz* lying off Trondheim. Five aircraft are shot down. Another attack the following night by 23 Halifax and 11 Lancaster bombers is also unsuccessful. Two aircraft are lost.

28 Apr   Mediterranean
The British submarine *Urge* is sunk off Malta by a mine on its way to Alexandria.

30 Apr–14 May   North Atlantic
First combined troop convoy, AT.15 from New York and NA.8 from Halifax, of 17 transports (one to Argentia, four to Iceland), escorted by TF.32 with the battleship *New York*, the cruiser *Brooklyn* and 12 US destroyers to Londonderry.

1 May   South Atlantic
The British turbine ship *Menelaus* (10307 tons, Capt J H Blyth) escapes in the South Atlantic from an attack by the auxiliary cruiser *Schiff 28/Michel* (Cdr* v Ruckteschell) and her motor torpedo boat.

2–9 May   Mediterranean
In British submarine operations, *Proteus* torpedoes one ship of 3682 tons off the Albanian coast. Two attacks on 2 and 7 May on Italian convoys off Benghazi are repelled by the escort ships *Cantore* and *Vivaldi*, and *Turbine*, respectively. On a supply journey to Malta, *Olympus* sinks on one of the mines laid by the German 3rd MTB Flotilla. *Upright* (Lt Wraith) attacks a towed convoy with a dock off Calabria.

3–8 May   South Pacific
Carrier air battle in the Coral Sea. The Japanese plan is to make an amphibious landing near Port Moresby (New Guinea) on 10 May and to establish an air base on the South Solomons Island of Tulagi. Vice-Adm Inoue is in overall command.

The Tulagi Force (Rear-Adm Shima) comprises the minelayer *Okinoshima*, the destroyers *Kikutsuki* and *Yuzuki*, eight auxiliary minesweepers, some smaller vessels and one transport with parts of the 3rd Kure Special Landing Force. The Port Moresby Force (Rear-Adm Kajioka) comprises the cruiser *Yubari*, the minelayer *Tsugaru*, the destroyers *Oite*, *Asanagi*, *Uzuki*, *Mutsuki*, *Mochitsuki* and *Yayoi*, some smaller units and 11 transports with the bulk of the 3rd Kure Special Landing Force and the South Sea Detachment (Maj-Gen Horii). The Support Force (Rear-Adm Marumo) comprises the cruisers *Tatsuta* and *Tenryu*, one aircraft depot ship and three gunboats, the Covering Force (Rear-Adm Goto) the cruisers *Aoba*, *Furutaka*, *Kako* and *Kinugasa*, the aircraft carrier *Shoho* and the destroyer *Sazanami* and the Carrier Force (Rear-Adm Hara) *Shokaku* and *Zuikaku*, escorted by Vice-Adm Takagi with the cruisers *Haguro* and *Myoko* and the destroyers *Ushio*, *Akebono*, *Ariake*, *Yugure*, *Shiratsuyu* and *Shigure* and a tanker.

US TF.17 (Rear-Adm Fletcher), comprising the carrier *Yorktown*, the cruisers (Rear-Adm Smith) *Astoria*, *Chester* and *Portland* and the destroyers *Morris*, *Anderson*, *Hammann* and *Russell*, has joined up with TF.11 (Rear-Adm Fitch) on 1 May.

The latter consists of the carrier *Lexington*, the cruisers (Rear-Adm Kinkaid) *Minneapolis* and *New Orleans* and the destroyers *Phelps, Dewey, Farragut, Aylwin* and *Monaghan*. A support force (Rear-Adm Crace), TF.44, comprises the Australian cruisers *Australia* and *Hobart* and the US cruiser *Chicago* and destroyers *Perkins* and *Walke*; it operates to the SW and joins up on 4 May. Tankers deployed are the *Neosho* and *Tippecanoe* with the destroyers *Sims* and *Worden*, while submarines operating in the area are *S37, S38, S39, S40, S41, S42, S43, S44, S45, S46* and *S47*.

On 3 May the Japanese land on Tulagi. On 4 May 99 carrier aircraft from *Yorktown* attack the Japanese Tulagi Force and sink the destroyer *Kikutsuki* and three minesweepers and damage four other ships. On 5 May the US carriers and cruisers refuel and then make a sortie in the direction of the expected Japanese landing fleet for Port Moresby. Simultaneously, the Japanese Carrier Force enters the Coral Sea from the E. On 6 May both forces look for each other in vain in poor visibility, although at times they are only 70 nautical miles apart. On 7 May 93 US carrier aircraft attack the Japanese covering force and Japanese aircraft attack the US supply force. The Japanese carrier *Shoho* (Capt Izawa†) and the US tanker *Neosho* and destroyer *Sims* are sunk. The Japanese destroyer *Sazanami* rescues 100 survivors from the carrier. In the morning of 8 May the two carrier forces sight each other and fly off their aircraft (90 Japanese and 78 American) to attack. *Shokaku* receives three bomb hits while *Lexington* (Capt F C Sherman) has to be abandoned after bomb and torpedo hits. *Yorktown* is damaged. The Japanese abandon the Port Moresby landing, although they have achieved a tactical success. Thus the American fleet achieves its strategic aim.

3–15 May   Mediterranean
Operation 'Bowery'. The Anglo-American Force W (Commodore Daniell), comprising the battlecruiser *Renown*, the US carrier *Wasp*, the British cruiser *Charybdis* and the destroyers *Lang* and *Sterett* (US) and *Echo* and *Intrepid* (RN), sets out from Scapa Flow on 3 May. During the night 7–8 May it joins up with the British carrier *Eagle* coming from Gibraltar with the destroyers *Partridge, Ithuriel, Antelope, Wishart, Wrestler, Westcott, Vidette, Georgetown* and *Salisbury*. On 9 May it flies off 47 and 17 Spitfires respectively from each carrier. Three aircraft are lost but the remainder reach Malta. Force W returns to Scapa Flow on 16 May. During the operation the fast

minelayer *Welshman* sets out from Gibraltar on 8 May with important supplies and reaches Malta on 10 May. After unloading she puts to sea at once and arrives in Gibraltar on 12 May.

3 May–20 June   South Pacific
B Group of the Japanese 8th SM Flotilla (Capt Sasaki) operates in the South Pacific. From 5 to 11 May *I-22, I-24, I-27* and *I-28* form a patrol line to cover the Port Moresby operation against US carrier forces. After the battle of the Coral Sea they return to Truk to take on board midget submarines. In the process, *I-28* is sunk by the US submarine *Tautog* (Lt-Cdr Willingham) S of Truk. *I-21* (Cdr* Matsumura) reconnoitres in the area of New Caledonia and sinks two ships of 11821 tons. On 19–20 May her aircraft reconnoitres Suva (Fiji) and on 23–24 May Auckland. *I-29* (Cdr* Izu) scours the Australian coast, damages one ship of 5135 tons and reconnoitres Sydney with her aircraft on 22–23 May. After renewed air reconnaissance over Sydney on 29 May, *I-22, I-24* and *I-27* put out their midget submarines on 31 May, some of which penetrate the bay of Sydney. But they only sink the accommodation ship *Kuttabul* there and just miss the cruiser *Chicago*. After an unsuccessful search for the midget submarines, *I-21* shells Newcastle and *I-24* (Cdr* Hanabusa) Sydney on 8 June. While *I-22* carries out a periscope reconnaissance of Wellington, Auckland and Suva and *I-29* makes a sortie towards Brisbane, *I-21* pursues mercantile warfare off Newcastle, *I-24* off Sydney and *I-27* (Cdr* Yoshimura) off Tasmania. In the course of this *I-21* sinks one ship of 5527 tons, *I-24* sinks one of 4312 tons and lightly damages three of 15844 tons and *I-27* sinks one of 3353 tons and damages one of 4239 tons.

4 May   General Situation
OKW directive to capture Malta (Operation 'Herkules').

4–5 May   Black Sea
German positions on the SE coast of the Crimea are shelled at night by the Soviet flotilla leader *Kharkov* and destroyers *Bditelny, Bezuprechny* and *Smyshleny*.

4–6 May   Philippines
On 4 May Japanese forces land on Corregidor after three days of preparatory bombardment. From 4 to 6 May the minesweepers *Tanager, Pigeon, Finch* and *Quail* and the gunboats *Mindanao, Luzon* and *Oahu* are destroyed by gunfire, bombs or scuttling. On 6 May the last organised resistance by US forces ends.

5 May–22 June   Western Atlantic
A wave of seven U-boats proceeds singly from Cape Hatteras to the Straits of Florida

and to the area of the Greater Antilles, Cuba, Yucatan and the Eastern Caribbean. In their operations they sink many ships: *U106* (Lt-Cdr Rasch) sinks five of 29154 tons and damages one of 4639 tons, *U753* (Cdr v Mannstein) sinks two of 13769 tons and damages two of 6908 tons, *U751* (Lt-Cdr Bigalk) sinks two of 4555 tons, *U558* (Lt-Cdr Krech) sinks seven of 19002 tons and damages one of 7061 tons, *U103* (Lt-Cdr Winter) sinks nine of 42169 tons and *U107* (Lt-Cdr Gelhaus) sinks six ships of 26983 tons.

6–19 May   South West Pacific
In operations in the South China Sea the US submarine *Skipjack* (Lt-Cdr Coe) sinks three ships of 12848 tons, *Swordfish* (Lt-Cdr Smith) sinks two of 6531 tons and *Pickerel* (Lt-Cdr Bacon) torpedoes one of 9347 tons. In the South Pacific *S42* (Lt Kirk) sinks the Japanese minelayer *Okinoshima* and *S44* (Lt Moore) one ship of 5144 tons.

7–17 May   Mediterranean
The German 3rd MTB Flotilla (Lt-Cdr Kemnade) lays NE of, and off, Valetta, as well as E of Malta, the barrages MT.19–24 with 108 FMC mines, 16 protection floats and 46 explosive floats. On 10 May *S31* is lost on a mine off La Valetta and on 17 May *S34* is sunk by a coastal battery off Malta.

7 May–28 June   Western Atlantic
In individual operations in the area of the Caribbean, *U69* (Lt Gräf) sinks four ships of 12030 tons and one unidentified tug, *U155* (Lt-Cdr Piening) sinks seven ships of 32392 tons, *U502* (Lt-Cdr v Rosenstiel) sinks eight ships of 44855 tons and *U156* (Cdr Hartenstein) sinks eleven ships of 44086 tons and torpedoes the US destroyer *Blakeley* and one ship of 8042 tons.

7 May–2 July   Black Sea
77 missions in all by submarines of the Soviet Black Sea Fleet to supply Sevastopol: from 7 May *D-4* (five), *L-4* (seven); from 15 May *L-5* (six), *L-23* (seven); from 30 May *S-31* (five), *S-32* (seven); from the beginning of June *D-5* (three), *L-24* (four); and from the middle of June *Shch-205* (two), *Shch-208* (two), *Shch-209* (two), *Shch-212* (two), *Shch-213* (two), *Shch-214* (one), *A-2* (two), *A-4* (three), *M-31* (three), *M-32* (one), *M-33* (three), *M-52* (one), *M-60* (one), *M-112* (two), *M-117* (two) and *M-118* (three). In these missions the following boats are lost: *Shch-212* to a petrol explosion, *Shch-214* when hit by a torpedo from the Italian *MAS 571* on 19 June and *S-32* by a bomb hit on 26 June. Another submarine is claimed by the Italian midget submarine *CB-2* on 18 June.

8–16 May   Black Sea

The German 11th Army (Col-Gen v Manstein) attacks the Soviet Crimean Front on the Kerch Peninsula consisting of the 47th, 51st and 44th Armies, breaks through the front in the S and destroys the main body of the Soviet forces W of Kerch. The remainder escape by sea from Kerch to the Taman Peninsula. From 10 to 16 May the Soviet cruiser *Voroshilov*, the flotilla leaders *Kharkov* and *Tashkent* and the destroyers *Bditelny* and *Soobrazitelny* intervene in the fighting from the S but with little success. On 9 May the two destroyers escort the transport *Serov* to Sevastopol and on 12 May they themselves bring further supplies. From 12 to 14 May the cruiser *Krasny Krym* and the destroyers *Dzerzhinski* and *Nezamozhnik* bring 2250 relief troops to Sevastopol. On 14 May *Dzerzhinski* runs on an air-laid mine and sinks, whilst *Nezamozhnik* shells land targets.

9 May   English Channel

The German minesweeper *M533* is lost NW of Boulogne in a collision with the motor minesweeper *R45* which also sinks.

9 May   North Sea

The German MDS *Sperrbrecher 36/Eider* is damaged by a mine off Heligoland; she is towed in but, as she is damaged beyond repair, is decommissioned.

9–10 May   Norway

The pocket-battleship *Admiral Scheer* is transferred from Trondheim to Narvik with the fleet tanker *Dithmarschen* and the torpedo boats *T5* and *T7*.

9–15 May   Baltic

The German minelayers *Kaiser* and *Roland* lay the 'Nashorn 1–5' mine barrages between Porkkala and Naissaari. They are later supplemented by nine more sections. In all, 1915 mines are laid.

10 May   South Atlantic

The US carrier *Ranger* flies off 40 P-40 fighters for Accra off the Gold Coast. They are transferred from there via Africa and the Near East to India.

10 May–17 June   Arctic

Transfer of the Soviet submarine *M-121* from the Caspian Flotilla to the Northern Fleet.

11 May   Mediterranean

The British destroyers *Jervis* (Capt Poland), *Jackal*, *Kipling* and *Lively* make a sortie from Alexandria against a German-Italian convoy reported to be on the way to Benghazi. In the process the force is located by German reconnaissance aircraft S of Crete and returns in accordance with orders. In the afternoon the destroyers are attacked by 14 Ju 88s of I/LG 1 (Capt Helbig) from Heraklion (Crete), when *Lively* sinks. An attack by II/LG 1 (Capt Kollewe) from Eleusis, near Athens, is unsuccessful. In a second attack by I/LG 1 at sunset, *Kipling* and *Jackal* (sunk on 12 May) are destroyed. Only *Jervis* is able to escape, after rescuing 650 survivors.

11–14 May   North Atlantic

The outbound U-boats *U126*, *U161* and *U128* (Lt-Cdr Heyse) operate against the convoy SL.109, located by chance. *U128* sinks one ship of 3491 tons.

11 May–21 June   North Atlantic

First attempt to carry out a planned group operation ('Hecht') in the North Atlantic, with *U124*, *U94*, *U569*, *U406*, *U96* and *U590*. On the way to the first patrol line, *U569* (Lt-Cdr Hinsch) sights on 11 May the convoy ONS.92 consisting of 41 ships escorted by EG.A3 (Cdr Hefferman) with the US destroyer *Gleaves*, the Coast Guard cutter *Ingham*, the Canadian corvettes *Algoma*, *Arvida*, *Bittersweet* and *Shediac* and the rescue ship *Bury* (HF/DF). During the night 11–12 May *U124* (Lt-Cdr Mohr) fires torpedoes in two approaches and sinks four ships of 21784 tons, *U569* possibly gets one hit on a disabled ship and *U94* (Lt Ites) sinks one ship of 5630 tons. The next night *U406* (Lt Dieterichs) misses a corvette as a result of torpedo failure and *U94* sinks two ships of 8870 tons in two approaches. Then contact is lost in bad weather. The failure of the escorts is in part due to their failure to use the HF/DF bearings supplied by *Bury*. In the afternoon of 20 May *U406* sights the convoy ONS.94 escorted by the British group B7 with the destroyers *Churchill* and *Firedrake* and the corvettes *Dianella*, *Kingcup*, *Loosestrife* and *Roselys* (FFN), but she is driven off after four hours by a destroyer and aircraft and the other boats do not come up in the mist of the Newfoundland Bank. After being supplied from *U116* (Cdr v Schmidt) from 25 to 27 May, the boats of the 'Hecht' group again take up a patrol line in the area of the Newfoundland Bank. On 1 June *U590* (Lt-Cdr Müller Edzards) sights the convoy ONS.96, escorted by British group B1 with the destroyers *Hurricane* and *Rockingham* and the corvettes *Anchusa*, *Dahlia* and *Monkshood*, in a heavy westerly storm and on a moonlit night. Because of the weather and the proximity to Newfoundland the operation is broken off on 2 June. In the evening of 8 June *U124* sights the convoy ONS.100, consisting of 37 ships with EG.C1 comprising the Canadian destroyers *Assiniboine* (Lt-Cdr Stubbs) and the British corvettes *Dianthus* and *Nasturtium* and the French *Aconit* and *Mimose* and the rescue ship *Gothland*. *U124* sinks *Mimose* in the first attack. On 9 June all six U-boats of the 'Hecht' group establish contact but *U96*, *U406* and *U590* remain behind because of diesel trouble. *U94* sinks two ships of 11002 tons during the night 9–10 June. Contact is lost in the mist. On 11 June *U96* (Lt Hellriegel) again sights the convoy; *U94* and *U569* are held up by a straggler (4458 tons) which they sink in several approaches The escorts are strengthened by the Canadian corvettes *Chambly* (Cdr Prentice) and *Orillia*. On 13 June the corvettes *Bittersweet* and *Primrose* arrive. In the morning of 12 June *U124* again comes up and sinks one ship of 4093 tons. In the morning of 16 June *U94* sights the convoy ONS.102, which comprises 48 ships with EG.A3 (Cdr Heineman USN) comprising the US Coast Guard cutters *Campbell* and *Ingham*, the destroyers *Leary* and *Restigouche* and the Canadian corvettes *Collingwood*, *Rosthern*, *Mayflower* and *Agassiz*. The contact signals from *U94*, *U406*, *U96*, *U124* and *U569* are located by *Restigouche*, which is equipped with HF/DF, and the escorts drive the U-boats off. *U94* and *U590* are damaged by depth charges. *U406* misses *Leary* with five torpedoes in the morning of 17 June. After breaking off the operation on 18 June, *U124* meets the convoy again and sinks one ship of 5627 tons in an underwater attack. By 21 June the 'Hecht' group has begun the return journey. In all, 12 ships of 61464 tons and one corvette have been sunk without loss.

12–19 May   English Channel

The German auxiliary cruiser *Schiff 23/Stier* (Cdr* Gerlach) breaks through the Channel. On 12 May she leaves Rotterdam escorted by the 5th TB Flotilla (Cdr* M Schmidt) comprising *Kondor*, *Falke*, *Iltis* and *Seeadler* and 16 motor minesweepers. In the early hours of 13 May, after shelling from British coastal batteries in the Straits of Dover, there is an attack by British MTBs. *Iltis* (Lt-Cdr W Jacobsen†) and *Seeadler* (Lt-Cdr Strecker) sink after torpedo hits from *MTB221* and *MTB219*; 118 men are lost. The British force loses *MTB220*. The auxiliary cruiser continues her journey in the following nights by small stages without further contact with the enemy. On 19 May she enters the Gironde Estuary. From here the ship breaks out into the Atlantic undetected on 10–21 May.

On 14 May a German convoy is attacked by British aircraft and loses the minesweeper *M26* off Cap de la Hague. *M256* is heavily damaged and sinks in Cherbourg (though she is later salvaged and restored to service).

13–18 May   Arctic

The British cruiser *Trinidad* (Capt Saunders), having received emergency repairs after being hit by a torpedo on 29 Mar, sets out from Murmansk with the destroyers *Somali*, *Matchless*, *Foresight* and *Forester*. W of Bear Island there is a force of cruisers—*Nigeria* (Rear-Adm Burrough), *Kent*, *Liverpool* and *Norfolk*—and four destroyers to meet them. Of the promised Soviet long-range fighter cover up to 200 nautical miles from the coast, only a few aircraft arrive. On 14 May the force is located by German reconnaissance about 100 nautical miles from the coast. There follow several unsuccessful attacks by torpedo aircraft of I/KG 26 and bombers of III/KG 30. Then a Ju 88 of III/KG 30 hits the cruiser in a dive-bombing attack and the ship is set on fire. On 15 May the fire can no longer be brought under control, with the result that *Trinidad* has to be sunk by *Matchless*. The Home Fleet sets out from Scapa Flow to cover the returning ships.

In German air attacks against the Lokanga Roads from 12 to 18 May, the patrol ships *SKR-29/Brilliant* and *SKR-21/Kuibyshev* are sunk and *SKR-15*, *SKR-22* and *SKR-25/Briz* and the minesweepers *T-911* and *T-904* are damaged. *SKR-29* is later raised and recommissioned.

13 May–2 June   Mediterranean

In operations against the British Tobruk supply traffic, *U431* (Lt-Cdr Dommes) sinks one ship of 4216 tons, *U83* misses a convoy and *U81*, *U205* and *U565* are unsuccessful. *U568* (Lt-Cdr Preuss) is sunk on 28 May off Sollum after a 15hr pursuit by the British destroyers *Hero*, *Hurworth* and *Eridge*. On 2 June *U652* is so badly damaged by a Blenheim of No 203 Sqn RAF and a Swordfish of No 815 Sqn FAA that *U81* has to sink the boat by torpedo after taking off the crew. Operations by the Italian submarines *Galatea*, *Nereide*, *Asteria*, *Platino* and *Beilul* off the Cyrenaican coast are unsuccessful.

14 May   Western Atlantic

The pro-Vichy French aircraft carrier *Béarn* and cruisers *Emile Bertin* and *Jeanne d'Arc*, which have been stationed in Martinique and Guadeloupe since June 1940, are demilitarized under American pressure.

14 May   North Sea

Off Esbjerg, the German minesweeping trawler *M1307* is lost to a mine.

14–19 May   Western Atlantic

Introduction of through-convoy traffic on the American East Coast. On 14 May the first convoy proceeds from Hampton Roads to Key West (NK) and on 15 May from Key West to Hampton Roads (KN); on 19 May the first feeder convoy sails from New York for Halifax (BX). The grouping of the ships in convoys leads to a sharp decline in the number of merchant ships being sighted by U-boats.

14–31 May   Mediterranean

In operations against Italian supply traffic to Benghazi, the British submarine *Turbulent* (Cdr Linton) attacks convoys with destroyer and torpedo boat escort on 14, 18, 20, 24, 25 and 29 May. Three ships of 5799 tons and the destroyer *Pessagno* are sunk. Off Bari, *Thrasher* (Lt-Cdr Mackenzie) sinks one ship of 1160 tons and on 30–31 May *Proteus* sinks two ships of 8407 tons from two convoys.

15 May   North Sea

A Hudson of No 407 Sqn RAF sinks the patrol trawler *V2002* in the southern North Sea.

15 May   Arctic

Ju 87s of I/StG 5 attack Murmansk. The Soviet submarine *Shch-403* and the US freighter *Yaka* (6187 tons) are badly damaged.

15–20 May   Norway

From 15 to 17 May the heavy cruiser *Lützow*, escorted by the destroyers *Richard Beitzen*, *Hans Lody*, *Z27* and *Z29* and the escort *F1*, deploys from Swineminde to Kristiansand (Operation 'Walzertraum'). The destroyers lay on 17–18 May a minefield W of the Skagerrak to cover the operation.

On 16 May the heavy cruiser *Prinz Eugen* (Capt Brinkmann), which has received emergency repairs after being hit by a torpedo on 23 Feb, leaves Trondheim with the destroyers *Z25* and *Paul Jacobi* and the torpedo boats *T11* and *T12* on transfer to Kiel (Operation 'Zauberflöte'). On 17 May 12 Beauforts, six Blenheims and four Beaufighters of No 42 (TB) Sqn RAF (Wg Cdr Williams) attack without success. Three aircraft are lost to AA fire and Me 109s of III/JG 1. Attacks by 30 more aircraft are intercepted by Me 109s, which shoot down another four aircraft while losing a total of three. On 18 May *Prinz Eugen* arrives in Kiel. From 18 to 20 May the heavy cruiser *Lützow* (Capt Stange) moves in stages with her four destroyers and *T15* from Kristiansand to Trondheim.

16–25 May   Black Sea

Soviet supply transports to Sevastopol and some shelling of land targets: on 16 May the destroyer *Bditelny*, on 17 May the cruiser *Krasny Krym* and flotilla leader *Tashkent*, on 19 May the flotilla leader *Kharkov*, on 21 May the destroyer *Svobodny*, on 22 May *Krasny Krym*, *Tashkent* and the destroyers *Nezamozhnik* and *Zheleznyakov*, on 23 May the destroyer *Boiki*, on 24 May the destroyer *Bezuprechny* and on 25 May the *Krasny Krym* and *Tashkent*.

17–20 May   Mediterranean

British Force H sets out from Gibraltar with the carriers *Argus* and *Eagle*, the cruiser *Charybdis* and the destroyers *Partridge*, *Ithuriel*, *Antelope*, *Wishart*, *Westcott*, *Wrestler* and *Vidette* on 17 May. It flies off 17 Spitfire fighters on 18 May, all of which arrive in Malta. But six Albacore torpedo aircraft have to turn back. Force H returns to Gibraltar on 20 May. Of the Italian submarines *Mocenigo*, *Otaria* and *Dessiè*, only *Mocenigo* fires a salvo of three torpedoes on a cruiser without success.

18 May–11 June   Black Sea

In Soviet submarine operations, *Shch-205* (Lt-Cdr Sukhomlinov) sinks the small Turkish steamers *Duatape* and *Safak* of 628 tons off the Turkish-Bulgarian border. *Shch-214* (Capt 3rd Class Vlasov) sinks three small Turkish schooners. In the bay of Odessa, *A-3* (Lt-Cdr Tsurikov) sinks the Rumanian transport *Sulina* (3495 tons) and *A-5* (Lt Kukuy) torpedoes the Rumanian transport *Ardeal* (5695 tons), which is beached.

20–31 May   Baltic/Norway

From 20 to 24 May the German minelayers *Kaiser* (Cdr Bohm) and *Roland* (Capt v Kutzleben), the 3rd MS Flotilla (Cdr* Knuth) and the 27th Landing Flotilla (Capt Masberg) lay the mine barrages 'Seeigel 1–8' SE of Suursaari with 2522 mines; these are later extended to 41 sections with 5779 mines, 1450 protection floats and 200 explosive floats. *Kaiser* and *Roland* then transfer to Norway and, with the minelayers *Cobra*, *Ulm*, *Brummer*, *Ostmark* and *Skagerrak*, lay various barrages along the coast.

20 May–30 June   Western Atlantic

In the Gulf of Mexico, off Cuba and Yucatan, *U158* (Lt-Cdr Rostin) sinks 12 ships of 62536 tons and *U504* (Cdr Poske) sinks six of 19418 tons. On the return, *U158* is lost in the area of Bermuda, after being located by HF/DF, as a result of an attack by an American Mariner flying boat from VP-74.

21 May   North Atlantic

U159 (Lt-Cdr Witte) attacks convoy OS.28 and sinks two ships from it of 9175 tons. Then the boat continues her journey out to the Caribbean.

21 May–27 June   North Pacific

Reconnaissance operation with their aircraft by the Japanese 1st SM Flotilla (Rear-Adm Yamazaki) in the area of the Aleutians: *I-9* (Cdr* Fujii) reconnoitres Kiska and Amchitka on 25 May and Kiska on 26 May, *I-26* (Cdr* Yokota) Kodiak on 24 May, Sitkinak on 26 May and Seattle on 1 June and *I-25* (Cdr* Tagami) Kodiak on 27 May. *I-19*

(Cdr* Narahara) is surprised when flying off her aircraft near Bogorlov Island on 27 May and is damaged by depth charges: she reconnoitres Dutch Harbor by periscope on 4 June. In June *I-25* operates in the area of Seattle, torpedoes one ship of 7100 tons and shells Port Stevens (Oregon) on 24 June. *I-26* sinks one ship of 3286 tons and shells Port Estevan (Vancouver) on 20 June.

23 May   English Channel
The German patrol trawler *V1808* is lost to a mine at the Hoofden.

23–27 May   Western Atlantic
Because of the absence of sightings (the result of the through-convoy traffic), the six U-boats operating off the American coast are concentrated in a new formation, 'Pfadfinder', away from the coast in which two newly arrived boats participate. But the formation has no success and the boats are sent back to the coast.

24–25 May   Norway
The heavy cruiser *Lützow* is moved with the tanker *Dithmarschen*, *Lody* and *T-7* from Trondheim to Narvik and joins the pocket-battleship *Admiral Scheer* which was transferred from Trondheim to Narvik on 9–10 May.

25 May   Arctic
The Soviet submarine *S-101* (Capt 3rd Class Vekke) is attacked for 22hr off Tanafjord by the submarine-chasers *UJ1102*, *UJ1105*, *UJ1108* and *UJ1109* with depth charges but is able to escape despite severe damage. *Shch-402* misses a target on 2 June.

25 May–8 July   Western Atlantic
After the attack on SL.109, three U-boats proceed to the area of the Brazilian N coast but they find little traffic there and then go into the Caribbean. There *U126* (Lt-Cdr Bauer) sinks seven ships of 41803 tons and damages one of 7104 tons, *U128* (Lt-Cdr Heyse) sinks four of 32129 tons and *U161* (Lt-Cdr Achilles) sinks three of 8802 tons and torpedoes one of 3305 tons in the harbour of Santa Lucia.

25 May–1 June   Arctic
Operations against the Allied convoys QP.12 and PQ.16. QP.12 (15 ships, one of which turns back) sets out from the Kola Inlet on 21 May but is not engaged. An aircraft keeping contact is shot down on 25 May by the Hurricane from the catapult ship *Empire Morn* sailing in the convoy. 14 ships arrive in Reykjavik on 29 May. PQ.16 (35 ships and the AA ship *Alynbank*), which sets out from Reykjavik on 21 May with the minesweeper *Hazard* and the A/S trawlers *St Elstan*, *Lady Madeleine*, *Northern Spray* and (only until 23 May) *Retriever*, is met early on 24 May by the escort group consisting of the destroyers *Ashanti* (Cdr

Onslow), *Martin*, *Achates*, *Volunteer* and *Garland* (Polish) and on 23 May by the corvettes *Honeysuckle*, *Starwort*, *Hyderabad* (RIN) and *Roselys* (French). A little later, on 25 May, the close escort force, consisting of the cruisers *Nigeria* (Rear-Adm Burrough), *Kent*, *Liverpool* and *Norfolk* and the destroyers *Onslow*, *Oribi*, and *Marne*, takes up positions with the convoy. The Home Fleet cruises as a covering force between Iceland and Norway. Two British submarines sail with PQ.16 to operate against German surface ships and five British and three Soviet submarines form a flanking screen. On 25 May German air reconnaissance locates PQ.16, which has evaded a German U-boat formation. In two air attacks by III/KG 26 (air torpedoes) and III/KG 30 with 19 He 111s and six Ju 88s, two bombers are lost through massive AA fire and one torpedo aircraft falls victim to the Hurricane from the catapult ship *Empire Lawrence* travelling with the convoy. The freighter *Carlton* (5127 tons) is damaged by near-misses and towed back to Iceland by *Northern Spray*. During the night 25–26 May *U703* (Lt-Cdr Bielfeld) sinks the freighter *Syros* (6191 tons). On 26 May the close escort force leaves the convoy because of the U-boat danger. But *U436* misses a steamer and a corvette and *U591* misses *Ashanti*. Weak air attacks have no success. SE of Bear Island, seven He 111s of I/KG 26 and 11 Ju 88s of KG 30 attack in several waves on 27 May and, while losing three of their number, sink the freighters *Alamar*, *Mormacsul*, *Empire Lawrence* and *Empire Purcell* with bombs and the *Lowther Castle* by torpedo, making in all 30796 tons. *Stari Bolshevik*, *Ocean Voice* (convoy commodore Capt Gale), *Empire Baffin*, *City of Joliet* and the destroyer *Garland* are damaged; on 28 May *City of Joliet* (6167 tons) has to be abandoned. The Soviet destroyers *Grozny*, *Kuibyshev* and *Sokrushitelny* reinforce the escort. Because of poor visibility there are only a few unsuccessful single attacks by German bombers. During the night 28–29 May *U586* attacks the convoy unsuccessfully and by day the attacks of KG 30 achieve nothing. The British minesweepers *Bramble*, *Seagull*, *Harrier*, *Niger*, *Gossamer* and *Hussar* come out from the Kola Inlet to the convoy and six steamers are detached for Archangel with *Alynbank*, *Martin* and two minesweepers. On 30 May bombers of KG 30 attack both parts of the convoy but are driven off by AA fire and Soviet fighters. In air combats over the convoy, the most successful pilot of the Soviet Northern Fleet, Lt-Col Safonov, is killed. On 31 May the Murmansk part of the convoy arrives

and on 1 June the Archangel part. Total convoy losses: 43205 tons with a cargo of 32400 tons including 147 tanks, 77 aircraft and 770 vehicles.

25 May–2 June   Central Pacific
Preparatory movements for the Midway operation. The Japanese plan is, after making a diversionary sortie against the Aleutians (see 21 May), to carry out an air attack and an invasion of Midway with all available units of the Combined Fleet (Adm Yamamoto) and then to seek a decisive battle with the American fleet as it approaches to relieve the island. American naval W/T intelligence learns of the operation from the radio picture and Cdr Rochefort in Hawaii is able to identify its target as Midway so that countermeasures are promptly set in train.

On 25 May the 2nd Carrier Force (Rear-Adm Kakuta) sets out from Ominato (Hokkaido) with the carriers *Junyo* and *Ryujo* (4th Carrier Sqn), the heavy cruisers *Maya* and *Takao* (2/4th Cruiser Sqn), the destroyers *Akebono*, *Sazanami* and *Ushio* (7th DD Div) and the tanker *Teiyo Maru* to carry out a diversionary raid on Dutch Harbor (Aleutians).

On 26 May US TF.16 (see below) arrives in Pearl Harbor, having been recalled from the South Pacific. On 27 May TF.17 follows with the damaged carrier *Yorktown*, which is repaired in 48 hours. On 26 May the Japanese 1st Carrier Fleet (Vice-Adm Nagumo) sets out from Hashirajima Bay (Inland Sea) to attack Midway. It comprises the carriers *Akagi* and *Kaga* (1st Carrier Sqn) and *Hiryu* and *Soryu* (2nd Carrier Sqn, Rear-Adm Yamaguchi), the battleships *Haruna* and *Kirishima* (2/3rd BB Sqn), the heavy cruisers *Chikuma* and *Tone* (8th Cruiser Sqn, Rear-Adm Abe), the 10th DD Flotilla (Rear-Adm Kimura) with the light cruiser *Nagara* and the destroyers *Nowake*, *Arashi*, *Hagikaze* and *Maikaze* (4th DD Div), *Kazegumo*, *Makigumo* and *Yugumo* (10th DD Div) and *Urakaze*, *Isokaze*, *Tanikaze* and *Hamakaze* (17th DD Div) and five tankers with the destroyer *Akigumo*.

On 27 May the Japanese forces earmarked for the operation against the Aleutians set out from Ominato. They consist of the Attu/Adak Force (Rear-Adm Omori) with the light cruiser *Abukuma* and the destroyers *Wakaba*, *Nenohi*, *Hatsuharu* and *Hatsushimo* (21st DD Div) with one auxiliary minelayer and one transport with 1200 army troops; the Kiska Force (Capt Ohno) with the light cruisers *Kiso* and *Tama* and the auxiliary cruiser *Asaka Maru* (21st Cruiser Sqn), the destroyers *Akatsuki*, *Hibiki* and *Hokaze* (6th DD Div), two transports with 1250 troops and three auxiliary minesweepers; and the covering force (Vice-Adm Hosogaya) comprising the heavy cruiser *Nachi*, the destroyers *Ikazuchi* and *Inazuma*, two tankers and three freighters. On 27 May the Japanese invasion fleet earmarked for Midway puts to sea from Saipan (Marianas). It comprises 12 transports with 5000 army and naval landing troops, one tanker, the fast assault boats *P1*, *P2* and *P34* escorted by the 2nd DD Flotilla (Rear-Adm Tanaka), consisting of the light cruiser *Jintsu*, the destroyers *Kuroshio* and *Oyashio* (15th DD Div), *Yukikaze*, *Amatsukaze*, *Tokitsukaze* and *Hatsukaze* (16 DD Div) and *Shiranuhi*, *Kasumi*, *Arare* and *Kagero* (18th DD Div); a seaplane force (Rear-Adm Fujita) with the seaplane carrier *Chitose*, the depot ship *Kamikawa Maru* (11th Carrier Sqn), the destroyer *Hayashio* and the APD *P35*; and a minesweeping force with four minesweepers, the submarine-chasers *Ch16*, *Ch17*, *Ch18*, one supply ship and two freighters. At the same time the 7th Cruiser Sqn (Rear-Adm Kurita) puts to sea from Guam as a covering force with the heavy cruisers *Kumano*, *Suzuya*, *Mikuma* and *Mogami*, the destroyers *Arashio* and *Asashio* (8th DD Div) and one tanker.

On 28 May the main force of the invasion fleet (Vice-Adm Kondo) puts to sea from Hashirajima Bay with the heavy cruisers *Atago* and *Chokai* (4th Cruiser Sqn) and *Haguro* and *Myoko* (5th Cruiser Sqn, Vice-Adm Takagi), the battleships *Hiyei* and *Kongo* (3rd BB Sqn, Rear-Adm Mikawa) and the 4th DD Flotilla (Rear-Adm Nishimura) with the light cruiser *Yura* and the destroyers *Murasame*, *Harusame*, *Samidare* and *Yudachi* (2nd DD Div) and *Asagumo*, *Minegumo* and *Natsugumo* (9th DD Div) and the carrier *Zuiho* with the destroyer *Mikazuki*. In addition, the bulk of the fleet puts to sea. This consists of the Midway Support Group (Adm Yamamoto) with the battleships *Yamato*, *Nagato* and *Mutsu* (1st BB Sqn), the carrier *Hosho* with the destroyer *Yukaze*, the seaplane carrier *Chiyoda* (*Mizuho* is sunk), used as a midget submarine transport, the 3rd DD Flotilla (Rear-Adm Hashimoto) with the light cruiser *Sendai* and the destroyers *Fubuki*, *Hatsuyuki*, *Murakumo* and *Shirayuki* (11th DD Div) and *Isonami*, *Uranami*, *Shikinami* and *Ayanami* (12th DD Div) and two tankers; and the Aleutian Support Group (Vice-Adm Takasu) with the battleships *Fuso*, *Hyuga*, *Ise* and *Yamashiro* (2nd BB Sqn) the light cruisers *Kitakami* and *Oi* (9th Cruiser Sqn, Rear-Adm Kishi) and the destroyers *Asagiri*, *Yugiri*, *Shirakumo* and *Amagiri* (20th DD Div), *Umikaze*, *Yamak-*

aze, *Kawakaze* and *Suzukaze* (24th DD Div) and *Ariake*, *Shigure*, *Shiratsuyu* and *Yugure* (27th DD Div) and two tankers.

On the US side, TF.16 (Rear-Adm Spruance) puts to sea from Pearl Harbor on 28 May with the carriers *Enterprise* and *Hornet*, the heavy cruisers (Rear-Adm Kinkaid) *Minneapolis*, *New Orleans*, *Northampton*, *Pensacola* and *Vincennes*, the AA cruiser *Atlanta*, the destroyers (Desron 1) *Phelps*, *Worden*, *Monaghan*, *Aylwin*, *Balch*, *Conyngham*, *Benham*, *Ellet* and *Maury* and the tanker force comprising *Cimarron* and *Platte* with the destroyers *Dewey* and *Monssen*. On 28 May TF.17 (Rear-Adm Fletcher) follows with the repaired carrier *Yorktown*, the cruisers (Rear-Adm Smith) *Astoria* and *Portland* and the destroyers (Desron 2) *Hammann*, *Hughes*, *Morris*, *Anderson*, *Russell* and *Gwin*. On 2 June the Task Forces meet. From the Central Pacific forces, the cruisers *Louisville*, *St Louis*, *Indianapolis* and *Honolulu* and nine more destroyers are sent to join TF.8 (Rear-Adm Theobald) formed in the Aleutians area on 21 May with the cruiser *Nashville* and five destroyers. They join up on 3 June S of the Aleutian island of Kodiak. From the US West Coast, Rear-Adm Anderson puts to sea from San Francisco on 31 May with the battleships *Colorado* and *Maryland* and three destroyers and Rear-Adm Fitch sets out from San Diego on 1 June with the carrier *Saratoga*.

25 May–21 June   South West Pacific

In operations in the South China Sea, the US submarine *Salmon* (Lt-Cdr McKinney) sinks the repair ship *Asahi* (an ex-battleship of 11441 tons) and one ship of 4382 tons, *Permit* (Lt Chapple) damages one ship of 4472 tons, *Seal* (Lt-Cdr Hurd) and *Swordfish* (Lt-Cdr Smith) together sink one ship of 1946 tons and the latter one more of 4585 tons and *Seawolf* (Lt-Cdr Warder) sinks one ship of 1206 tons. In the South Pacific, *S44* (Lt Moore) sinks one ship of 2626 tons. Off Penang the British submarine *Trusty* (Lt Cdr King) sinks two ships of 12853 tons.

27 May–7 June   Black Sea

Soviet supply transports to Sevastopol. On 27–28 May Rear-Adm Basisty with the cruiser *Voroshilov* (Capt 1st Class Markov) and the destroyers *Soobrazitelny* (Capt 3rd Class Vorkov) and *Svobodny* (Lt-Cdr Shevchenko) brings the 9th Naval Infantry Bde (3017 men and 340 tons of supplies) from Batumi to Sevastopol. On the way out and back, air attacks by He 111s are outmanoeuvred. *Svobodny* shells land targets. On 28 May the destroyer *Bezuprechny* (Lt-Cdr Burnyak), on 30 May *Bezuprechny* and *Svobodny*, on 1 June *Svobodny* and on 2

June *Tashkent* and *Bezuprechny* bring supplies and from time to time shell land targets. On 3 June the cruiser *Krasny Krym* (Capt 2nd Class Zubkov) with *Soobrazitelny* and *Svobodny* brings 1759 relief troops and evacuates 1998 wounded and 275 civilians. On 5 and 6 June the flotilla leaders *Kharkov* (Capt 3rd Class Melnikov) and *Tashkent* (Capt 3rd Class Eroshenko) put in to Sevastopol with *Bezuprechny* in spite of bomb and torpedo attacks. On 7 June the destroyer *Nezamozhnik* (Lt-Cdr Bobrovnikov) brings supplies.

27 May–26 June   Western Atlantic

Nine U-boats of the 'Pfadfinder' group operate in changing positions off the American East Coast against ships increasingly travelling in convoys. They make the following sinkings: *U404* (Lt-Cdr v Bülow) sinks seven ships of 31051 tons and *U578* (Cdr Rehwinkel) two of 13095 tons, while of the boats still left of the sixth wave *U135* (Lt-Cdr Praetorius) sinks one ship of 4549 tons, *U566* (Lt-Cdr Borchert) sinks one ship of 8967 tons and *U653* (Lt-Cdr Feiler) sinks the flying boat tender *Gannet*; *U553*, *U432* and *U213* return without success, and *U455* sinks a ship of 6914 tons on the return journey.

28 May   English Channel

The German MDS *Sperrbrecher 174/Tindefjell* is sunk by mines off Dunkirk.

29 May   North Sea

The German MDS *Sperrbrecher 150/Viriato* and the patrol trawler *V1103* are sunk by mine and air attack off Ameland.

29 May–6 June   Baltic

First operation by the Soviet submarine *M-97* (Lt-Cdr Dyakov) to reconnoitre the German 'Seeigel' mine barrage.

30 May–15 June   Pacific

From 30 May the Japanese submarines *I-174*, *I-175*, *I-169* and *I-171* take up positions off Oahu; *I-121* and *I-123* go as flying boat suppliers to the French Frigate Shoals and *I-122* to Lisianski Island. *I-168* operates in the Midway area on 1 June. From 4 June *I-156*, *I-157*, *I-158*, *I-159*, *I-162*, *I-165* and *I-166* take up patrol lines as Group B—*I-164* is sunk on the way out by the US submarine *Triton* (Lt-Cdr Kirkpatrick)—and *I-174*, *I-175*, *I-169*, *I-171*, *I-121*, *I-122* and *I-123* as Group C between Oahu and Midway against advancing US carrier forces but they sight no targets.

The submarines of the US Pacific Fleet (Rear-Adm Lockwood) are concentrated against the Japanese operation against Midway as established by W/T intelligence: *Gudgeon*, *Grouper*, *Nautilus*, *Grenadier*,

Grayling, *Gato*, *Trout*, *Dolphin*, *Tambor*, *Flying Fish* and *Cachalot* against a landing NW of the island, *Narwhal*, *Plunger* and *Trigger* NE of Midway and *Finback*, *Growler*, *Pike* and *Tarpon* N of Oahu. *Cuttlefish* is stationed 700 nautical miles W of Midway for reconnaissance and the returning *Greenling*, *Drum*, *Pollack*, *Tuna*, *Pompano* and *Porpoise* are appropriately deployed. Later on, some of the submarines operate in Japanese waters, where *Nautilus* sinks the destroyer *Yamakaze* off Yokosuka on 25 June.

30 May–26 July Indian Ocean

Group A of the Japanese 8th SM Flotilla (Rear-Adm Ishizaki) operates in the area of Madagascar. *I-30* (Cdr* Endo), which set out on 20 Apr with two auxiliary cruisers after refuelling from the *Aikoku Maru* on 25 Apr, reconnoitres Aden on 7 May with her aircraft in a search for the British Eastern Fleet, followed by Djibouti on 8 May, Zanzibar and Dar-es-Salaam on 19 May and Mombasa on 20 May by periscope. *I-10*, *I-16*, *I-18* and *I-20*, which set out from Penang on 29–30 Apr, refuel from the *Hokoku Maru* on 5 May. *I-10* reconnoitres over Durban with her aircraft on 20 May and on the following days observes East London, Port Elizabeth and Simonstown. After finding British naval forces in Diego Suarez, *I-10* reconnoitres with her aircraft over the bay during the night 29–30 May; *I-16* and *I-20* put out their midget submarines which during the night 30–31 May torpedo the battleship *Ramillies* and the tanker *British Loyalty* (6993 tons). The midget submarine from *I-18* falls out with motor trouble. In two more flights, the aircraft of *I-10* tries to establish the result of the attack. While *I-30* again reconnoitres Durban, the other four submarines go from 5 to 12 June to carry out mercantile warfare in the Mozambique Channel. After being refuelled from the auxiliary cruisers, *I-30* proceeds to Western France (she arrives in Lorient on 5 Aug); the other submarines operate again from 28 June to 9 July against merchant ships on the African coast and off Madagascar. On the return, *I-10* reconnoitres Réunion and Mauritius with her aircraft on 15 and 16 July and *I-16* and *I-18* carry out periscope observations of Mahé (Seychelles), the Rodriguez Islands and Diego Garcia. On 10 Aug *I-16* is the last boat to return to Penang. They have made the following sinkings: *I-10* (Cdr* Kayahara) eight ships of 34536 tons, *I-16* (Cdr* K Yamada) four of 17727 tons, *I-18* (Cdr Otani) three of 11304 tons, *I-20* (Cdr* T Yamada) seven of 35501 tons and the auxiliary cruisers three of 21051 tons.

1–2 June Arctic

Ju 87s of I/StG 5 sink the British freighter *Empire Starlight* (6850 tons) and damage the submarine *Shch-404* in Murmansk. In the course of the month German aircraft repeatedly drop mines in the Kola Inlet, on which the American freighter *Steel Worker* (5686 tons) sinks on 3 June and the steamer *Alcoa Cadet* (4823 tons) on 21 June.

1 June–24 July Western Atlantic

In operations in the area of the Greater Antilles, in the Gulf of Mexico and in the Gulf of Campeche, *U157* (Cdr Henne) sinks one ship of 6401 tons, *U129* (Lt-Cdr Witt) sinks 11 of 41571 tons and *U67* (Lt-Cdr Müller-Stöckheim) sinks six of 30015 tons and damages two of 14831 tons. *U157* is sunk off Cuba on 13 June by the US Coast Guard cutter *Thetis*.

June Intelligence

The American ECM Mark I cypher machine is made compatible by an adaptor to the British 'Typex' machine.

2 June English Channel

Off Dieppe, the German patrol trawler *V1510* runs on to a wreck and sinks.

2–4 June Mediterranean

Operation 'Style'. British Force H, comprising the carrier *Eagle*, the cruiser *Charybdis* and the destroyers *Ithuriel*, *Antelope*, *Wishart*, *Wrestler* and *Westcott*, sails from Gibraltar on 2 June and flies off 31 Spitfire fighters on 3 June S of the Balearics; 27 of them reach Malta. Force H returns on 4 June to Gibraltar. The Italian submarines *Brin* and *Malachite*, off Algiers, sight nothing. Off Tunisia, *Corallo* (Cdr Andreani) sinks one sailing vessel.

3–7 June Pacific

Battle of Midway. On 3 June an attack by the diversionary force (Rear-Adm Kakuta) with the carriers *Junyo* and *Ryujo* on Dutch Harbor has little effect because it is anticipated. The diversion, therefore, fails. In the morning American air reconnaissance locates parts of the Japanese invasion force (Vice-Adm Kondo) with a total of two battleships, one aircraft carrier, eight heavy and two light cruisers, 21 destroyers, two aircraft depot ships, six tankers, 20 transports and seven small escort vessels. In the afternoon nine B-17s attack the transports unsuccessfully; in the night four Catalinas torpedo the tanker *Akebono Maru*.

In the morning of 4 June there is an attack on Midway by 108 aircraft of the Japanese carrier force (Vice-Adm Nagumo), comprising the carriers *Akagi*, *Kaga*, *Hiryu* and *Soryu*, the battleships *Haruna* and *Kirishima*, the heavy cruisers *Chikuma* and *Tone*, the light cruiser *Nagara* and the destroyers *Nowake*, *Arashi*, *Hagikaze*, *Maikaze*,

Kazegumo, *Yugumo*, *Makigumo*, *Urakaze*, *Isokaze*, *Tanikaze* and *Hamakaze*. Thanks to prompt radar reporting, there are no aircraft on the ground. In air combat the American fighters are wiped out, but only limited damage is sustained on the ground. Simultaneously attacks are made on the Japanese carrier force by US aircraft based on Midway (four B-26s with torpedoes, six Avengers with torpedoes, 27 dive-bombers and 15 B-17s): they lose 17 aircraft and secure no hit. Japanese air reconnaissance locates parts of the US carrier forces, which are advancing to the attack (Rear-Adms Fletcher and Spruance) and which comprise the carriers *Enterprise*, *Hornet* and *Yorktown*, the cruisers *Astoria*, *Portland*, *New Orleans*, *Minneapolis*, *Vincennes*, *Northampton*, *Pensacola* and *Atlanta* and the destroyers *Hammann*, *Hughes*, *Morris*, *Anderson*, *Russell*, *Gwin*, *Phelps*, *Worden*, *Monaghan*, *Aylwin*, *Balch*, *Conyngham*, *Benham*, *Ellet* and *Maury*. As a result of confusing reports, Nagumo decides too late to deploy his aircraft against this carrier force. The US carrier aircraft (156 machines), however, divide themselves up as they approach. The torpedo squadrons from *Enterprise*, *Hornet* and *Yorktown* reach the Japanese carriers successively and without fighter protection: 35 of the 41 aircraft are shot down by Japanese fighters and AA fire. They secure no hits and all the squadron commanders (Lt-Cdrs Lindsey, Massey and Waldron) are killed. Simultaneously, after a wide detour, the dive-bombers from *Enterprise* and those from *Yorktown* (which flew off later), under Lt-Cdrs McClusky and Leslie respectively, reach the Japanese carriers whose defence is still busy dealing with the torpedo aircraft. Within five minutes *Akagi* (Capt Aoki†), *Kaga* (Capt Akada†) and *Soryu* (Capt Yanagimoto†) are hit by 2–4 bombs which detonate between the aircraft on deck ready for take-off and cause serious fires and explosions. The three carriers sink later in the day or during the night. At midday and in the afternoon *Hiryu* flies off her aircraft in two waves (Lt-Cdr Tomonaga). They obtain two torpedo and three bomb hits on *Yorktown*. In the late afternoon air groups from *Enterprise* and *Hornet* concentrate their attacks on *Hiryu* (Capt Kaku†, Rear-Adm Yamaguchi†, Cdr of the 2nd Carrier Sqn) which, likewise, is set on fire and has to be abandoned in the morning.

During the night 4–5 June Adm Yamamoto, who with the bulk of his forces is far to the NW (two groups with a total of seven battleships, one carrier, three light cruisers, 21 destroyers and two midget submarine-carriers), has to break off the operation. In a sortie by four cruisers against Midway, *Mikuma* and *Mogami* collide trying to avoid the US submarine *Tambor* with the result that the sortie is abandoned.

On 5 June the Japanese Fleet concentrates NW of Midway for the return. US carriers take up the pursuit but are unable to catch the Japanese when they attack in the afternoon. The destroyer *Tanikaze*, which arrives independently, escapes the attack of 58 dive-bombers. Attacks by B-17 bombers on the damaged cruisers *Mikuma* and *Mogami* have no result. The Japanese submarine *I-168* shells Midway.

On 6 June the US carriers *Enterprise* and *Yorktown* attack in three waves the damaged cruisers: *Mikuma* (Capt Sakiyama) finally sinks, while *Mogami* (Capt Sato) escapes, badly damaged, with the destroyers *Arashio* and *Asashio*.

On 7 June *I-168* (Cdr Tanabe) sinks the damaged *Yorktown* (Capt Buckmaster) and the destroyer *Hammann* lying alongside. A sortie by a fast Japanese task force against the US carriers finds nothing because, in the meantime, the latter have started the journey to their supply ships. During the battle of Midway, Japanese troops land on the Aleutian Islands of Attu and Kiska. Japanese losses total 3500 dead and 253 aircraft; the US Navy loses 307 men and 150 aircraft.

3 June–2 Aug   Western Atlantic
In operations in the Caribbean, *U68* (Cdr Merten) sinks seven ships of 50898 tons, *U159* (Lt-Cdr Witte) sinks eight ships of 41197 tons and two unidentified sailing ships and *U172* (Lt-Cdr Emmermann) sinks ten ships of 40745 tons.

3 June–15 Oct   North Atlantic
The Allied Mid Ocean Escort Groups escort the following convoys (convoys attacked by U-boat groups are denoted thus*—see later entries): B1: HX.193, ONS.108, SC.92, ON.119/HX.201, ONS.124, HX.206, ONS.134. B2: SC.86, ON.107, HX.198, ONS.118, HX.203, ONS.128, HX.208. B3: HX.194, ONS.110, SC.93, ON.121/HX.202, ONS.126, HX.207, ONS.136*. B4: SC.87, ON.109, HX.199, ONS.120, HX.204, ONS.130, HX.209*. B6: SC.88, ON.111, HX.200, ONS.122*, HX.205, ONS.132, SC.104*. B7: HX.192, ONS.106, SC.91, ON.117, SC.103. C1: HX.195, ONS.112, SC.94*, ON.123, SC.99, ON.133, HX.211. C2: ON.103, SC.89, ON.113*, HX.201/ON.119, SC.97*, ON.129*, SC.102. C3: ONS.104, SC.90, ON.115*, HX.202/ON.121; SC.98, ON.131*, HX.210. C4: ON.105, HX.197, ONS.116, SC.96, ON.127*, SC.101*. A3: HX.196, ONS.114, SC.95*, ON.125,

SC.100*, ON.135. B5 is in the Caribbean on loan.

4–6 June   Central Atlantic
The German auxiliary cruiser *Schiff 23/Stier* (Capt Gerlach) sinks the British freighter *Gemstone* (4986 tons) and the Panamanian turbine tanker *Stanvac Calcutta* (10170 tons) in the Central Atlantic.

4–16 June   Mediterranean
In operations against the British Tobruk supply traffic, *U431* (Lt-Cdr Dommes) sinks one ship of 2073 tons and *U77* (Lt-Cdr Schonder) the British destroyer *Grove* on 12 June. *U331*, *U453* and *U205* have no success. Off Alexandria *U559* (Lt-Cdr Heidtmann) sinks one ship of 4681 tons and torpedoes one ship of 5917 tons. *U81* misses a target. Off the coast of Palestine, *U83* (Lt-Cdr Kraus) sinks five and *U97* (Lt Bürgel) two small vessels. The Italian submarines *Ondina*, *Sirena*, *Galatea* and *Beilul* have no success.

4–23 June   Bay of Biscay
During air operations against U-boat transit routes, Wellington 'F' of No 172 Sqn (Sqn Ldr Greswell) damages on 4 June the Italian submarine *Torelli* (Ten Vasc Migliorini), which is again attacked on 7 June by Sunderlands 'X' and 'A' of No 10 Sqn RAAF and has to be beached with heavy damage at Santander; it is later repaired. On 5 June Sunderland 'U' of No 10 Sqn damages *U71*, forcing it to return, and on 11 June Sunderland 'W' of No 10 Sqn damages *U105*, also forcing it to return. On 23 June Whitley 'C' of No 58 Sqn damages *U753* returning from a cruise.

7–9 June   Mediterranean
The Catalinas 'M' and 'J' of No 202 Sqn sink on 7 and 9 June E of Gibraltar the Italian submarines *Veniero* and *Zaffiro* respectively. On 8 June the Italian destroyer *Usodimare* is torpedoed and sunk in error off Cape Bon by the submarine *Alagi*.

British Force H, comprising the carrier *Eagle*, the cruisers *Cairo* and *Charybdis* and the destroyers *Partridge*, *Ithuriel*, *Antelope*, *Wishart*, *Wrestler* and *Westcott*, flies off 32 Spitfire fighters for Malta from S of the Balearics on 9 June. They all arrive.

8 June   North Sea
The German MDS *Sperrbrecher 15/Taronga* is heavily damaged by air attack off Scharhörn; it is towed to Hamburg but is considered beyond repair and decommissioned.

8–10 June   Arctic
The German minelayers *Ostmark* (Capt v Schönermark), *Ulm* and *Brummer*, escorted by the 5th MS Flotilla, lay flanking mine barrages off Varangerfjord.

8–30 June   Black Sea
Major attack by the German 11th Army (Col-Gen v Manstein) on the Soviet fortress of Sevastopol with strong support from the heaviest artillery and FK VIII (Col-Gen v Richthofen). The Soviet Black Sea Fleet (Vice-Adm Oktyabrski) is fully committed to supplying the fortress and taking off the wounded. Air Force units of the Air Cdr South, from 10 June Italian small battle units (Cdr* Mimbelli) and from 17 June the German 1st MTB Flotilla (Lt-Cdr Birnbacher) are deployed against Soviet shipping traffic. On 10 June the Soviet destroyers *Bditelny* and *Svobodny* escort with two minesweepers and three patrol cutters the transport *Abkhaziya* to Sevastopol. On the way, there is an attack by the Italian *MAS573* and destroyers shell land targets. There is a German air attack while unloading and *Abkhaziya* (4727 tons), the minesweeper *T-413* and *Svobodny* are sunk by Ju 88s in the Southern Bay. On 12 June the cruiser *Molotov* (Capt 1st Class Romanov) and the destroyer *Bditelny* bring 3300 men of the 138th Rifle Bde to Sevastopol and shell land targets. Air attacks are outmanoeuvred. The return journey is made shortly after the departure of the German motor torpedo boats *S28*, *S72* and *S102*. The Italian midget submarine *CB3* misses. On 13 June the transport *Gruziya* (4857 tons) is attacked by Italian motor boats in the night on the way to Sevastopol. In the morning she is sunk by the mine pier in Sevastopol in an air attack. On 15–16 June *Molotov* and *Bezuprechny* bring 3855 troops as relief, shell land targets and evacuate 3000 wounded and civilians. Located by air reconnaissance, motor torpedo boats, MAS boats and midget submarines cannot approach. The flotilla leader *Kharkov* is rendered unmanoeuvrable on 18 June by near-misses from German bombers when proceeding to Sevastopol. She is towed away by Rear-Adm Vladimirski in *Tashkent*. Attacks are made on 19 June by the German motor torpedo boats *S27*, *S72* and *S102* (Lt-Cdr Töniges), of which the last sinks an evacuation transport. On 20 June *Bditelny*, *Bezuprechny* and the patrol ship *Shkval* bring 845 men and 293 tons of ammunition into the southern bay of Sevastopol. On 23 June *Tashkent* and *Bezuprechny* bring supplies into Kamyshov Bay. On the way there are unsuccessful torpedo attacks by the German motor torpedo boats *S28*, *S72* and *S102*. The destroyer *Smyshlenny* is sunk by a mine S of the Strait of Kerch. *Bditelny* and *Bezuprechny* bring supplies to Sevastopol on 24 June. Unsuccessful attacks are made by the motor torpedo boats *S27*, *S28*,

S40, S72 and S102. On 25 June *Tashkent* and *Bditelny* bring supplies to Sevastopol and there is an unsuccessful attack by *S28* and *S40*. On 26 June *Bezuprechny* brings supplies to Sevastopol but while returning she is sunk S of the Crimea by Ju 88s of the Air Cdr South. On 27 June *Tashkent* (Capt 3rd Class Eroshenko) brings 944 relief troops to Sevastopol and evacuates 2300 wounded and civilians. There are many air attacks on the return and many leaks caused by splinters from near-misses and aircraft fire: 1900 tons of water are taken aboard the ship. The destroyer *Bditelny* with seven TKAs and the rescue ship *Jupiter* sets out from Novorossisk to help; the Sqn Cdr, Rear-Adm Vladimirski, is on one of the TKAs. *Soobrazitelny* takes on 1975 wounded and *Bditelny* tows *Tashkent* to Novorossisk, where she sinks on the bottom.

10–15 June Pacific
Reinforcement and reorganisation of the US Pacific Fleet. On 10 June the carrier *Wasp*, returning from the Home Fleet Force with the destroyers *Lang*, *Sterett*, *Stack*, and *Wilson* (Desdiv 15), the heavy cruiser *Quincy* and the new ships, the battleship *North Carolina* and the destroyers *Farenholt*, *Aaron Ward*, *Laffey* and *Buchanan* (Desdiv 23), passes through the Panama Canal.

On 15 June the new organisation comes into force: TF.1 (Vice Adm-Pye), with the old battleships *Pennsylvania*, *Colorado*, *Maryland*, *Tennessee*, *Idaho*, *Mississippi* and *New Mexico* and eight to ten destroyers at San Francisco up to 1 Aug and then at Pearl Harbor; TF.8 (Rear-Adm Theobald), with the cruisers *Louisville*, *Indianapolis*, *Nashville*, *Honolulu* and *St Louis* and the destroyers *Reid*, *Case*, *Gridley*, *McCall* and *Elliot* (DMS) in the Aleutians; TF.11 (Rear-Adm Fitch), with the carrier *Saratoga*, the cruisers *Astoria*, *Minneapolis* and *New Orleans* and the destroyers (Desron 1) *Phelps*, *Farragut*, *MacDonough*, *Worden*, *Dale*, *Dewey* and *Hull* on the way to Hawaii; TF.16 (Rear-Adm Fletcher), with the carrier *Enterprise*, the cruisers *Portland*, *Chester* and *Atlanta* and the destroyers (Desron 6) *Balch*, *Maury*, *Benham*, *Ellet*, *Gwin*, *Grayson* and *Monssen* at Pearl Harbor; TF.17 (Rear-Adm Mitscher), with the carrier *Hornet*, the cruisers *Northampton*, *Salt Lake City*, *Pensacola* and *San Diego* and the destroyers (Desron 2) *Morris*, *Hughes*, *Anderson*, *Russell*, *O'Brien*, *Walke* and *Mustin* at Pearl Harbor; TF.18 (Rear-Adm Noyes), with the carrier *Wasp*, the battleship *North Carolina*, the cruisers *Quincy*, *Vincennes*, *San Francisco* and *San Juan* and destroyers of Desdivs 15 and 23 (see above) at San Diego; and TF.44 (Rear Adm Crutch-

chley RN), with the cruisers *Australia*, *Canberra*, *Hobart* (RAN) and *Chicago* and the destroyers (Desron 4) *Selfridge*, *Patterson*, *Ralph Talbot*, *Mugford*, *Jarvis*, *Blue*, *Helm*, *Henley* and *Bagley* in Australian and New Zealand waters. Other ships do convoy service between the USA, Hawaii, the South Seas and Australia.

11–16 June North Atlantic
The departure of convoy HG.84—23 ships, escorted by the 36th EG (Cdr Walker) comprising the sloop *Stork* and the corvettes *Convolvulus*, *Gardenia* and *Marigold*—is reported by agents on 9 June. I/KG 40 is ordered to reconnoitre, and an Fw 200 reports the convoy on 11 June and escapes from the Hurricane of the catapult ship *Empire Moon*. The outbound U-boats *U132*, *U89*, *U552*, *U84*, *U437*, *U575*, *U134* and *U571* are ordered to operate as the 'Endrass' group for 14 June. In the afternoon of 14 June an Fw 200 sights the convoy and first leads *U552* (Lt-Cdr Topp) to it and then *U89* and *U132* which are, however, driven off by *Stork*, *Gardenia* and *Marigold*. As *Stork* must soon follow the convoy again, *U552* is able to operate on the reports of *U437* which has, in the meantime, come up but then been driven off by *Convolvulus*. During the night 14–15 June she sinks first three and then two ships totalling 15858 tons in two approaches. By day on 15 June *U71*, *U84* and *U575* are driven off by the air escort. In the night *Stork*, *Marigold* and *Convolvulus* drive off *U84*, *U71*, and *U552*. *U575* (Lt-Cdr Heydemann) misses the convoy with five torpedoes fired at great range. Although in the morning of 16 June *U571* and two Fw 200s establish contact, the operation is broken off because of the weather (wind and sea Force 0 with good visibility). The Support Group sent to assist the escort, consisting of the British destroyers *Beagle* and *Wild Swan*, the frigate *Spey* and the Polish Hunt class destroyer *Krakowiak*, is attacked in the evening of 17 June by a squadron from KF1Gr 106, which damages *Wild Swan*; the latter is subsequently lost following a collision with a Spanish trawler.

11 June–19 July Western Atlantic
German U-boats lay mines off the American East Coast: *U87* (Lt-Cdr Berger) near the Ambrose lightship off Boston (no success but later sinks two ships of 14298 tons), *U373* (Lt-Loeser) off Delaware (sinks one tug of 396 tons and later fails with two torpedo attacks) and *U701* (Lt-Cdr Degen) off Chesapeake Bay (on which one A/S trawler and one ship totalling 7565 tons are sunk and the destroyer *Bainbridge* and two tankers of 22852 tons are damaged). The

harbour defence boat *YP-389* is sunk by gunfire, two tankers of 23364 tons are sunk by torpedo and two ships of 14241 tons are damaged. *U701* is sunk by a USAAF bomber from the 396th BS on 7 July. *U584* (Lt-Cdr Deecke) and *U202* (Lt-Cdr Linder) disembark agents on the American East Coast and then *U202* sinks two ships of 10725 tons. *U332* (Lt-Cdr Liebe) sinks two ships of 10738 tons in a torpedo operation off the American East Coast.

12 June Bay of Biscay
The German auxiliary minesweeper *M4212* sinks on a mine NW of Bayonne.

12–16 June Mediterranean
Double convoy operation 'Harpoon' and 'Vigorous' from Gibraltar and Alexandria to supply Malta.

The western convoy (Force X) comprises the freighters *Troilus*, *Burdwan*, *Chant*, *Tanimbar* and *Orari* and the tanker *Kentucky* with an escort provided by the AA cruiser *Cairo* (Capt Hardy), the destroyers *Bedouin*, *Marne*, *Matchless*, *Ithuriel*, *Partridge*, *Blankney*, *Middleton*, *Badsworth* and *Kujawiak* (Polish), the minesweepers *Hebe*, *Speedy*, *Rye* and *Hythe* and six motor gunboats. The covering force (Force W) consists of the battleship *Malaya*, the aircraft carriers *Argus* and *Eagle*, the cruisers *Kenya* (Vice-Adm Curteis), *Charybdis* and *Liverpool* and the destroyers *Onslow*, *Icarus*, *Escapade*, *Wishart*, *Westcott*, *Wrestler*, *Vidette* and *Antelope*. The tanker force (Force Y) consists of the tanker *Brown Ranger* with the corvette *Coltsfoot* and one other corvette. The fast minelayer *Welshman*, with supplies on board, operates with Force X.

On signs of a British operation, two Italian submarine groups, *Malachite*, *Velella*, *Bronzo* and *Emo* and *Uarsciek*, *Giada*, *Acciaio*, *Otaria* and *Alagi* are stationed N of the Algerian coast, a third group, consisting of *Corallo*, *Dessiè*, *Onice*, *Ascianghi* and *Aradam*, in the area Malta–Lampedusa and a fourth group, consisting of *Axum*, *Platino*, *Micca*, *Zoea* and *Atropo*, in the Ionian Sea. *Galatea*, *Sirena* and the German *U77*, *U81*, *U205*, *U431*, *U453* and *U559* operate further to the E. On 12 June the western convoy passes through the Straits of Gibraltar and is met by Force W. German reconnaisance aircraft locate the convoy S of the Balearics.

The eastern convoy, MW.11 (Commodore Rear-Adm England), sets out from Alexandria, Port Said and Haifa with the freighters *City of Pretoria*, *City of Calcutta*, *Bhutan*, *Potaro*, *Bulkoil*, *Rembrandt*, *Aagtekerk*, *City of Edinburgh*, *City of Lincoln*, *Elizabeth Bakke* and *Ajax*, the dummy battleship *Centurion* and the rescue ships

Antwerp and *Malines*. With the convoy as close escort are the corvettes *Delphinium*, *Primula*, *Erica* and *Snapdragon* and the minesweepers *Boston* and *Seaham* in addition to the 2nd DD Flotilla with *Fortune*, *Griffin* and *Hotspur* and the 5th DD Flotilla with *Dulverton*, *Exmoor*, *Croome*, *Eridge*, *Airedale*, *Beaufort*, *Hurworth*, *Tetcott* and *Aldenham*. The covering force (Rear-Adm Vian) is provided by the 15th Cruiser Sqn with *Cleopatra*, *Dido*, *Hermione*, *Euryalus*, *Arethusa* and *Coventry*, the 4th Cruiser Sqn (Rear-Adm Tennant) with *Birmingham* and *Newcastle*, the 7th DD Flotilla with *Napier*, *Nestor*, *Nizam* and *Norman* (RAN), the 14th DD Flotilla with *Jervis*, *Kelvin* and *Javelin*, the 12th DD Flotilla with *Pakenham*, *Paladin* and *Inconstant* and the 22nd DD Flotilla with *Sikh*, *Zulu*, *Hasty* and *Hero*. Four MTBs towed by merchant ships have to return because of the stormy weather. *MTB259* is lost on the way back to Alexandria. The British submarines *Proteus*, *Thorn*, *Taku*, *Thrasher*, *Porpoise*, *Una*, *P31*, *P34* and *P35* are stationed off Taranto and S of the Straits of Messina and *P211*, *P42*, *P43* and *P46* between Sicily and Sardinia.

The convoy MW.11 is located by German air reconnaissance on 12 June and attacked S of Crete by Ju 88s of I/KG 54 (Maj Linke). The transport *City of Calcutta* (8063 tons) is damaged and has to put in to Tobruk. On 13 June German and Italian air reconnaissance again locate the western convoy but Italian torpedo aircraft from Sardinia cannot find it. The 7th Italian Div (the cruisers *Eugenio di Savoia* and *Montecuccoli* and the destroyers *Oriani*, *Ascari* and *Gioberti*) goes to sea from Cagliari to attack the convoy in the area of Cape Bon, but puts in to Palermo after being reported by two British submarines. The British forces join up N of Mersa Matruh. During the night 13–14 June a raid is made on the airfield of Maleme (Crete), used by the German LG 1, by a British commando party landed from the Greek submarines *Papanicolis* and *Triton*. The Italian submarines *Giada* and *Uarsciek* attack the western convoy unsuccessfully.

In the morning of 14 June there are attacks by Italian torpedo aircraft (Savoia SM 79s) on the western convoy: *Tanimbar* (8619 tons) is sunk and *Liverpool*, after a hit in the engine room, has to be towed back to Gibraltar. Other attacks by German and Italian bombers are unsuccessful. Force W turns off to the W. The 7th Italian Div (Div-Adm da Zara), reinforced by the destroyers *Vivaldi*, *Malocello* and *Premuda* (two others, *Zeno* and *Gioberti*, have to return because of

engine trouble), sets out from Palermo to attack. The freighter *Aagtekerk* (6811 tons) from the eastern convoy has to be sent off to Tobruk, escorted by the corvettes *Erica* and *Primula*, because of engine trouble. This group is attacked a few nautical miles from the harbour by approximately 40 Ju 87s and Ju 88s: *Aagtekerk* is sunk and *Primula* is damaged. In the afternoon Ju 88s of LG 1 from Crete attack the main convoy and sink the freighter *Bhutan* (6104 tons) and damage *Potaro* (5410 tons). In the evening the German 3rd MTB Flotilla (Lt Wuppermann), comprising *S54*, *S55*, *S56*, *S58*, *S59* and *S60*, operates from Derna against the eastern convoy: *S56* (Lt Wuppermann) torpedoes the British cruiser *Newcastle* and *S55* (Lt Horst Weber) sinks the destroyer *Hasty*. The Italian fleet sets out with the battleships *Littorio* (Adm Iachino) and *Vittorio Veneto* (9th Div, Div-Adm Fioravanzo), the heavy cruisers *Gorizia* and *Trento* (3rd Div, Div-Adm Parona), the light cruisers *Garibaldi* (Commander 8th Div, Div-Adm de Courten) and *Duca d'Aosta* and the destroyers *Legionario*, *Folgore*, *Freccia* and *Saetta* (7th Flotilla) *Alpino*, *Bersagliere*, *Pigafetta* and *Mitragliere* (13th Flotilla) and *Aviere*, *Geniere*, *Camicia Nera* and *Corazziere* (11th Flotilla). On 15 June the Italian 7th Div attacks the western convoy, sinks the British destroyer *Bedouin* and badly damages *Partridge* but cannot penetrate the strong convoy escort and is driven off. Simultaneously, the German StG 3 (Lt-Col Siegel) attacks: the freighters *Burdwan* (5601 tons) and *Chant* (5601 tons) and the tanker *Kentucky* (9308 tons) are so badly damaged that they have later to be abandoned. Further losses are avoided by AA fire from the escort vessels and from the fast minelayer *Welshman* which joins the convoy. But the convoy runs into a newly laid minefield off Malta: the destroyer *Kujawiak* is sunk and *Badsworth*, *Matchless*, *Hebe* and *Orari* (10350 tons) are damaged. During the night and early morning British Beaufort torpedo aircraft from No 217 Sqn RAF on Malta attack the Italian fleet. *Trento* (Capt Esposito) is torpedoed by a Beaufort and later sunk by the British submarine *Umbra* (Lt Maydon). In the morning an American Liberator bomber scores a hit on *Littorio*. In the afternoon Ju 87s of StG 3 and Italian Cant 1007s damage the British cruiser *Birmingham* with near-misses and damage the destroyers *Airedale* and *Nestor* so badly that the latter has to be sunk by *Aldenham* and *Hurworth* the following day. As the Italian fleet at first continues its sortie, the British convoy turns away and then the Italians also start to

return to Taranto. In the process, five Wellington torpedo aircraft from No 38 Sqn find the force again and P Off O L Hawes scores a torpedo hit on *Littorio*. On 16 June *U205* (Lt-Cdr Reschke) sinks S of Crete the cruiser *Hermione* from the returning British Eastern Force and the Polish destroyer *Kujawiak* sinks on a mine off Grand Harbour, Malta. *Cairo*, *Welshman*, *Marne*, *Ithuriel*, *Blankney* and *Middleton* start the return journey from Malta to Gibraltar.

12–19 June   Baltic

The Soviet submarines *M-95*, *S-4*, *Shch-304*, *Shch-317* and *Shch-320* break through the 'Seeigel' mine barrage from Lavansaari. They set out at one-day intervals supported by sorties by Soviet torpedo cutters and patrol boats and by operations of the Soviet naval air force against the mine barrage guard. During the night 12–13 June there is an engagement off Suursaari involving the Finnish minelayers *Ruotsinsalmi* and *Riilahti*, the gunboats *Hämeenmaa* and *Uusimaa* and three VMV boats (patrol boats) and Soviet minesweeper vessels (Capt Pakholchuk) which try to bring the submarines through the barrages. In the following days there are more engagements. On 15 June *M-95* is lost on a mine E of Suursaari.

14 June–4 July   Indian Ocean

The German auxiliary cruiser *Schiff 10/ Thor* (Capt Gumprich) sinks the Dutch tanker *Olivia* (6307 tons) in the Indian Ocean and captures the Norwegian tankers *Herborg* (7892 tons) and *Madrono* (5894 tons). Both later reach Japan.

15–18 June   North Sea

The German minelayers *Roland* and *Cobra*, escorted by the gunboat *K1* and the 8th R (MMS) Flotilla with 12 R-boats, lay in two nights additional minefields to strengthen the northern 'Westwall' barrages.

15 June–5 Aug   Baltic

In the second half of June Finnish minelayers lay the 'Rukajärvi A–C' (559 mines) barrages N of Suursaari. Later these are extended to 18 sections with 1326 mines and 221 protection floats. Of the Soviet submarines of the first wave which broke into the Baltic, *Shch-303* and *Shch-304* operate near Porkkala-Utö, *Shch-317* and *Shch-320* off Sweden, *Shch-320* off the Baltic coast and near Rixhöft and *S-7* off Sweden and then the Baltic coast. Results: *Shch-304* (Capt 3rd Class Y P Afanasev) misses the minelayer *Kaiser*; *Shch-317* (Lt-Cdr Mokhov) sinks four ships of 8283 tons and misses one and is sunk by Finnish VMV boats on 19 July; *Shch-320* (Capt 3rd Class Vishnevski) sinks one ship of 676 tons and misses two; *Shch-406* (Capt 3rd Class

Osipov) damages one ship of 545 tons and misses four; *Shch-303* (Capt 3rd Class Travkin) damages one ship of 7891 tons and misses one; and *S-7* (Capt 3rd Class Lisin) sinks four ships of 9164 tons and misses one. Amongst the sunken ships are three Swedish vessels.

16 June–14 July   North Sea
The German minelayers *Cobra*, *Roland*, *Brummer*, *Ostmark* and *Ulm* lay several new mine barrages W of the Skagerrak and in the northern North Sea.

17 June–20 July   North Pacific
Deployment of the Japanese 2nd SM Flotilla (Rear-Adm Ichioka) in the area of the Aleutians with *I-1*, *I-2*, *I-3*, *I-4*, *I-7* and later (until 15 Aug) also *I-6*. Only *I-7* (Cdr* Koizumi) has any success, sinking one ship of 2722 tons.

18 June   English Channel
During an attack on a German convoy (two ships with an escort of one torpedo boat flotilla) by the destroyer *Albrighton* and gunboats *SGB6*, *SGB7* and *SGB8*, one German transport and *SGB7* are sunk.

19 June   North Pacific
The US submarine *S27* is lost when she goes aground off Amchitka.

20–21 June   Mediterranean
On 20 June Tobruk is taken by the German Afrika Korps and the 3rd MTB Flotilla (Lt-Cdr Kemnade), consisting of *S36*, *S54*, *S55*, *S56*, *S58* and *S59*, operates from Derna against British ships fleeing from Tobruk. On 21 June, in an engagement, the South African auxiliary minesweeper *Parktown* (250 tons) is sunk and *S58* (Lt Geiger†) badly damaged. In addition, one motor yacht, six LCs and two motor launches are sunk or captured. *S55* (Lt Weber) captures *LCT150* (296 tons).

20 June–6 July   Mediterranean
U561 (Lt Schomburg) lays a mine barrage off Port Said (20 June). *U97* (Lt Bürgel) sinks three ships of 3974 tons off the Palestine coast, *U372* (Lt-Cdr Neumann) sinks the British submarine depot ship *Medway* (14600 tons) off Port Said on 30 June and *U375* (Lt-Cdr Könenkamp) sinks one ship of 1376 tons. *U77* and *U562* have no success. The Italian submarines *Atropo*, *Micca*, *Zoea* and *Corridoni* transport fuel to Cyrenaican ports.

20 June–19 July   Western Atlantic
The last seven U-boats deployed on the American East Coast find no further worthwhile targets apart from convoys. After the loss of two boats (*U215* and *U576*), the rest receive orders on 19 July to leave. *U402* starts the return journey having achieved no

results and *U89*, *U132*, *U458* and *U754* go to the area SE of Nova Scotia.

20 June–28 July   Arctic
Convoy operations QP.13 and PQ.17 in the Arctic. On 26 June 12 ships of QP.13 set out from Archangel and on 27 June 23 ships of QP.13 set out from Murmansk. The escort for the whole convoy comprises five destroyers, three corvettes, one AA ship, three minesweepers, two trawlers and one submarine. Convoy PQ.17 (Commodore Dowding) leaves Reykjavik with 36 ships, one fleet tanker and three rescue ships; three ships return because they run aground or suffer damage from ice. Close escort is provided by Cdr Broome with the destroyers *Keppel* (F), *Offa*, *Fury*, *Leamington*, *Ledbury* and *Wilton*, the corvettes *Lotus*, *Poppy*, *Dianella* and *La Malouine*, the minesweepers *Britomart*, *Halcyon* and *Salamander* and the trawlers *Lord Austin*, *Ayrshire*, *Northern Gem* and *Lord Middleton*, AA ships *Palomares* and *Pozarica* and submarines *P614* and *P615*. On 28–29 June the distant covering force (Adm Tovey), comprising the battleships *Duke of York* and *Washington*, the carrier *Victorious*, the cruisers *Cumberland* and *Nigeria* and nine (later 14) destroyers, leaves Scapa Flow for the area between Iceland and Bear Island.

On 30 June QP.13 is located in the Barents Sea by German air reconnaissance but is not pursued because the target of the German operation is convoy PQ.17. The close covering force (Rear-Adm Hamilton), consisting of the cruisers *London*, *Norfolk*, *Tuscaloosa* and *Wichita* and the destroyers *Somali*, *Rowan* and *Wainwright*, leaves Seidisfjord (Iceland) for a position N of PQ.17. On 1 July the German B-Service locates PQ.17, which is also sighted in the morning by *U255* (Lt-Cdr Reche) and *U408* (Lt-Cdr v Hymmen) about 60 nautical miles E of Jan Mayen. *U334* (Lt Siemon) and *U456* (Lt-Cdr Teichert) are directed to it at once and *U251* (Lt-Cdr Timm), *U355* (Lt-Cdr La Baume), *U657* (Lt Göllnitz), *U88* (Lt-Cdr Bohmann), *U457* (Cdr Brandenburg) and *U376* (Lt-Cdr Marks) form a patrol line further to the E as the 'Eisteufel' group. PQ.17 and distant covering force are located by German air reconnaissance in the afternoon.

On 2 July German air reconnaissance and *U88* locate QP.13, but there is no additional operation since the target is PQ.17, which passes QP.13 in the afternoon. The sighting of both convoys and the mistaken reporting of the close covering force as the distant escort by German air reconnaissance leads to confusion. *U456* keeps contact with PQ.17 and *U457*, *U657*, *U376* and *U255* are partly driven off in attacks. In the afternoon

Force I (Adm Schniewind), comprising the battleship *Tirpitz*, the cruiser *Admiral Hipper*, the destroyers *Karl Galster*, *Friedrich Ihn*, *Hans Lody* and *Theodor Riedel* and the torpedo boats *T7* and *T15*, leaves Trondheim for northern Norway as a base for the operation 'Rösselsprung'. In the afternoon an attack by seven He 115s of 1/KF1Gr 906 has no success.

On 3 July Force II (Vice-Adm Kummetz), comprising the pocket-battleships *Lützow* and *Admiral Scheer* and the destroyers *Z24*, *Z27*, *Z28*, *Z29*, *Z30* and *Richard Beitzen*, proceeds from Narvik to Altafjord to join up with Force I which has arrived there together with the destroyers *Erich Steinbrinck* and *Friedrich Eckoldt*. But *Lützow*, *Hans Lody*, *Karl Galster* and *Theodor Riedel* are put out of action by going aground in Grimsöystraumen. Air contact is lost in poor visibility. *U88* attacks destroyers unsuccessfully and *U456*, *U255*, *U657*, *U703* (Lt-Cdr Bielfeld) and *U334* generally establish only brief contact. British air reconnaissance establishes the departure of the German surface forces northwards. The British submarines *P212/Sahib*, *Sturgeon*, *Minerve* (FFN), *P45/Unrivalled* and *P54/Unshaken* and *Ursula*, *Tribune*, *Seawolf* and *Trident* are stationed in two lines S of Bear Island to cover the convoy. In addition, there are the Soviet submarines *D-3*, *K-2*, *K-22*, *K-21*, *Shch-402* and *Shch-403*. Inter alia, *M-176* is off Varangerfjord. In these operations, *D-3* and *M-176* are lost, probably on German flanking mine barrages. The cruiser *Manchester* and the destroyer *Eclipse* come from Spitzbergen to join the distant covering force.

On 4 July a single He 115 torpedo aircraft from 1/KF1Gr 906 obtains hits on the steamer *Christopher Newport* (7191 tons), which is later finished off and sunk by the British submarine *P614* and the German *U457*. *U88*, *U225* and *U334* are in temporary contact with the convoy and *U457* with the cruiser force. Two attacks by *U88* fail. The Germans are unclear about the position of the British heavy forces with the result that the fleet receives no order to sail. In the evening a squadron of KG 30 attacks without success. Torpedo aircraft of I/KG 26 (Capt Eicke) sink the freighter *Navarino* (4841 tons); the freighter *William Hooper* (7177) tons is damaged and finished off by *U334*; and the Soviet tanker *Azerbaidzhan* (6114 tons) is torpedoed. Of 25 attacking He 111s three are shot down. In the evening the First Sea Lord (Adm Pound), knowing generally about the German intentions from information transmitted by the naval attaché in Stockholm based on details of the

German operational order which was decoded by Swedish intelligence from an intercepted T-52c teleprinter message—and not convinced by the purely 'negative' intelligence of the OIC about the German force and therefore expecting a German surface attack in superior strength—orders the cruiser force and the destroyers of the escort to turn back to the W and has the convoy scattered.

On 5 July German air reconnaissance and U-boats report the breaking up of the convoy and the departure of the cruisers westwards. Then *Tirpitz* (Capt Karl Topp), *Admiral Hipper* (Capt Meisel), *Admiral Scheer* (Capt Meendsen-Bohlken), seven destroyers and two torpedo boats put to sea. Off Ingöy the Soviet submarine *K-21* (Capt 2nd Class Lunin) makes an unsuccessful attack on *Tirpitz*. In the course of the day all three Gruppen (Capts Kahl, Stoffregen and Herrmann) of KG 30 (Maj Bloedorn) attack the transports of the convoy as they sail singly or in groups and sink the freighters *Washington* (5564 tons), *Bolton Castle* (5203 tons), *Pan Kraft* (5644 tons), *Peter Kerr* (6476 tons) and *Fairfield City* (5686 tons) and the rescue ship *Zaafaran* (1559 tons) and damage *Paulus Potter* (7168 tons), *Earlston* (7195 tons—finished off by *U334*), *Empire Byron* (6645 tons—finished off by *U703*) and the fleet tanker *Aldersdale*. *U88* sinks *Carlton* (5127 tons) and *Daniel Morgan* (7177 tons), *U456 Honomu* (6977 tons) and *U703* the *River Afton* (5479 tons). A Catalina flying boat of No 210 Sqn RAF and the British submarine *Unshaken* sight and report the German naval force. After the early and intercepted reports by the submarines and the aircraft, the C-in-C of the Navy, in accordance with the Führer's directive not to take risks, orders the naval operation to be broken off. The destruction of the remaining ships in the convoy is to be left to U-boats and aircraft. Convoy QP.13 runs into one of its own minefields in the Denmark Strait in the mist and storms and loses the minesweeper *Niger* and the steamers *Heffron*, *Hybert*, *John Randolph*, *Massmar* and *Rodina* totalling 30909 tons.

On 6 July the German naval force arrives in the Kaafjord. The British cruiser force joins up with the distant covering force. Aircraft of KG 30 sink the tanker *Pan Atlantic* (5411 tons) and *U255* the *John Witherspoon* (7191 tons). On 7 July, of the U-boats deployed to hunt the single ships, *U255* sinks the *Alcoa Ranger* (5116 tons), *U355* the *Hartlebury* (5082 tons) and *U457* the abandoned tanker wreck *Aldersdale* (8402 tons). Five ships and some escort vessels of the convoy arrive in the Matochkin Strait.

On 8 July *U255* sinks the steamer *Olopana* (6069 tons) off Novaya Zemlya. Commodore Dowding forms a convoy in the Matochkin Strait consisting of five steamers, three minesweepers, three corvettes and three trawlers, the AA ships *Palomares* and *Pozarica* and the rescue ship *Zamalek* and this proceeds southwards along the west coast of Novaya Zemlya and the ice barrier. The Soviet destroyers *Gremyashchi* and *Grozny* reinforce the escort.

On 9 July part of the convoy, comprising the rescue ship *Rathlin* and the motor tanker *Donbass* and steamer *Bellingham*, arrives in Archangel. *U255* establishes contact with the rest of the convoy, against which *U457*, *U703*, *U376* and *U251* operate. On 10 July, in attacks by II/KG 30 against the rest of the convoy off the entrance to the White Sea, the *Hoosier* (5060 tons) and *El Capitan* (5255 tons) are damaged and then finished off by *U376* and *U251* respectively. The steamer *Samuel Chase* is damaged by bomb hits.

On 11 July the rest of the convoy, comprising *Zamalek*, the steamers *Ocean Freedom* and *Samuel Chase*, arrives in Archangel. Another group of ships with the trawler *Ayrshire* arrives in the Matochkin Strait. On 12 July *U376* attacks a trawler off Kanin Noss without success and the next day, from the homebound U-boats, *U255* sinks the abandoned wreck of the steamer *Paulus Potter*. The German U-boats put into harbour on 15 July. Commodore Dowding sets out on 16 July with the corvettes *Poppy*, *Lotus* and *La Malouine*, accompanied by the Soviet destroyer *Gremyashchi*, to fetch the ships anchored off the coast of Novaya Zemlya. From 20 to 24 July the second remnant of the convoy, comprising the above-named escort vessels and the steamers *Benjamin Harrison*, *Silver Sword*, *Troubadour*, *Ironclad* and *Azerbaidzhan*, led by the Soviet ice-breaker *Murman* (Commodore Dowding) and the trawler *Kerov*, proceeds from the Matochkin Strait to Archangel. The steamer *Empire Tide* is met on the way in Moller Bay. On 28 July the steamer *Winston Salem*, which was temporarily beached, is the last straggler to arrive in Molotovsk.

Total losses sustained by PQ.17 amount to 24 ships of 142695 tons; German losses are five aircraft in 202 sorties. Eight ships of 48218 tons have been sunk by U-boats and eight ships of 40376 tons by the Luftwaffe; in addition, eight ships of 54093 tons, damaged by air attack, have been finished off by U-boat torpedoes. In all, 3350 vehicles, 430 tanks, 210 aircraft and 99316 tons of other war equipment have been lost.

20 June–4 Aug   Western Atlantic

Of the U-boats operating in the area of Cuba, the Gulf of Mexico and off the Greater Antilles, *U84* (Lt-Cdr Uphoff) sinks three ships of 14206 tons and torpedoes one of 7176 tons, *U154* (Cdr Kölle) sinks one ship of 2160 tons and one unidentified ship, *U571* (Lt-Cdr Möhlmann) sinks three ships of 18980 tons and torpedoes one of 11394 tons and *U134* and *U437* have no success with their attacks. Of the U-boats operating in the area of Trinidad, in the Caribbean and off Panama, *U153* (Cdr Reichmann) sinks three ships of 16166 tons, *U203* (Lt-Cdr Mützelburg) sinks five ships of 32985 tons, *U505* (Lt-Cdr Loewe) sinks three ships of 12748 tons and *U575* (Lt-Cdr Heydemann) sinks four ships of 8274 tons and torpedoes one of 12910 tons. *U153*, after an unsuccessful attack on a netlayer off the Panama Canal, is forced to submerge by the submarine-chaser *PC458* and is jointly damaged by USN and USAAF aircraft. She is sunk on 13 July by the destroyer *Lansdowne* (Lt-Cdr Smedberg).

21 June   Western Atlantic

The British submarine *P514* (ex-US *R19*) is sunk in a collision with the minesweeper *Georgian*, escorting convoy CL.43 off Cape Race.

22 June   Bay of Biscay

The German MDS *Sperrbrecher 14/Bockenheim* is heavily damaged by a mine off Royan. Laid up, she is scuttled as a blockship on 25 Aug 44.

22 June–2 July   North Sea

The German minelayers *Ostmark* and *Brummer*, escorted by the gunboat *K1* and four R-boats of the 8th MMS Flotilla, lay in four nights the 'Herzog', 'Coral', 'Grossfürst' and 'Erika' mine barrages W of the Skagerrak.

23 June   Baltic

Soviet motor minesweepers enter the 'Seeigel' mine barrage while torpedo cutters attack German submarine-chasers W of Suursaari in order to bring the submarine *Shch-406* through the barrages.

23–29 June   Mediterranean

In the Gulf of Sirte on 23 and 24 June, the British submarines *Thrasher* (Lt-Cdr Mackenzie) and *Turbulent* (Cdr Linton) attack an Italian convoy of three ships, escorted by the torpedo boat *Perseo* on the way from Tripoli to Benghazi, and each sink one ship, of 1480 tons and 1085 tons respectively. On 29 June *Thrasher* also sinks the Italian fast sloop *Diana*.

24 June   Arctic

I/StG 5 (Ju 87s) sinks the British minesweeper *Gossamer* in the Kola Inlet.

24–27 June   Black Sea

Strong flanking mine barrages to protect Odessa Bay against Soviet submarines are laid out by the Rumanian minelayers *Amiral Murgescu* and *Dacia* with an escort from the destroyers *Regele Ferdinand*, *Regina Maria* and *Marasesti*, the gunboats *Dumitrescu*, *Ghigulescu* and *Stihi*, the torpedo boat *Smeul* and motor minesweepers of the Danube Flotilla. In Aug/Sept the Soviet submarines *M-33* and *M-60* are lost on these barrages.

25 June–9 July   Pacific

In the area of Truk, the US submarine *Grouper* (Lt-Cdr Duke) torpedoes the Japanese whale factory ship *Tonan Maru No 2* (19262 tons) and *Thresher* (Lt-Cdr Millican) sinks one ship of 4836 tons. *Plunger* (Lt-Cdr White) sinks two ships of 6259 tons off Japan. On 25 June *Nautilus* (Cdr Brockman) sinks the destroyer *Yamakaze*.

26 June   Western Atlantic

Germany announces the extension of the blockade area to the American East Coast.

28 June–27 July   South West Pacific

In operations in the South China Sea, the US submarine *Sturgeon* (Lt-Cdr Nimitz) sinks one ship of 7266 tons and damages one of 7268 tons, *Sailfish* (Lt-Cdr Voge) damages one ship of 8811 tons and *Seadragon* (Lt-Cdr Ferrall) sinks three ships of 15637 tons. *Spearfish* (Lt-Cdr Dempsey) torpedoes one ship of 9627 tons. *Stingray* (Lt-Cdr Lamb) sinks one ship of 1292 tons E of the Philippines and *S37* one ship of 2775 tons off Rabaul. In the Malacca Straits the British submarine *Truant* (Lt-Cdr Haggard) sinks one ship of 3019 tons.

29–30 June   North Atlantic

On the way to the American coast, *U458* (Lt-Cdr Diggins) and *U754* (Lt-Cdr Oestermann) each sink an independent, of 2714 tons and 12435 tons respectively, in the North Atlantic.

30 June   Black Sea

The Soviet Command gives orders to evacuate Sevastopol. But the evacuation can only be carried out on a small scale with small units and submarines before the last attempts at resistance are wiped out.

30 June–15 July   Baltic

Soviet minesweeper forces and torpedo cutters support the return of the submarine *Shch-304* (30 June) and the break-out of *S-7* and *Shch-303* through the mine barrages (4 and 8 July). The returning *Shch-317* (with the Div Cdr, Capt 3rd Class Egorov, on board) is attacked repeatedly from 12 to 15 July by Finnish and German submarine-chasers between the 'Nashorn' and 'Seeigel'

mine barrages and is sunk by the Finnish minelayers *Ruotsinsalmi* and *VMV16*.

1 July   Black Sea

The German *Sperrbrecher 191/Motor I* sinks on a Soviet mine barrage on the Odessa–Ochakov route.

1–20 July   South Pacific

Forces are assembled for the operation 'Watchtower' (landing on Guadalcanal). On 1 July a convoy, consisting of six transports with the last additional troops of the Marine Corps, sets out from San Diego, accompanied by the newly formed TF.18 (see 10–15 June). On 7 July TF.11 and 16 put to sea from Pearl Harbor to join up with the other forces in the area of the Fiji Islands on 20 July.

2 July   Black Sea

Air attack by I/KG 76 (Capt Heise) on Novorossisk. The wreck of the Soviet flotilla leader *Tashkent* is destroyed, the destroyer *Bditelny* is sunk and the training cruiser *Komintern* is damaged.

3 July   Western Atlantic

U215 (Lt-Cdr Hoeckner) sinks one ship of 7191 tons from convoy BA.2 S of Nova Scotia and is then destroyed by the escort, the Free French *Le Tigre*.

4 July   North Sea

The German MDS *Sperrbrecher 61/Iris* is sunk by mine off Schiermonnikoog.

5–30 July   North Pacific

Off Kiska, the US submarine *Growler* (Lt-Cdr Gilmore) sinks the Japanese destroyer *Arare* and torpedoes the destroyers *Kasumi* and *Shiranui*. The destroyer *Nenohi* is sunk by the submarine *Triton* (Lt Cdr-Kirkpatrick); *Finback* misses another. On 15 July *Grunion* (Lt-Cdr Abele) sinks the Japanese submarine-chasers *Kusentai Ch25* and *Ch27* and one ship of 8572 tons; the submarine is lost on 30 July.

6 July   Black Sea

II/KG 26 sinks a Soviet submarine-chaser S of the Crimea.

6–7 July   North Sea

The German minelayers *Roland* and *Ulm* and the minesweepers *M82* and *M102*, escorted first by *Sperrbrecher 173* and the AA whaler *FJ22*, and then by the minesweepers *M301*, *M321*, *M322* and *M382* of the 22nd MS Flotilla, lay the 'Thusnelda' barrage in the 'Westwall' area.

6–20 July   Western Atlantic

U132 (Lt-Cdr Vogelsang), which has penetrated the Gulf of St Lawrence, sinks three ships of 10249 tons from the convoy QS.15 (escorted by the minesweepers *Bangor* and *Drummondville*) on 6 July and one ship of 4367 tons from the convoy QS.19 (escorted by the corvettes *Weyburn* and *Chedabucto*

and the MLs *Q074*, *Q059* and *Q064* on 20 July.

6–27 July   Bay of Biscay

During air operations against the U-boat transit routes on 6 July, Wellington 'M' of No 172 Sqn (P Off Howell—USA), aided by radar and Leigh Light, sinks *U502* and, on 12 July, damages *U159*; both boats are returning from patrols. On 17 July Whitley 'H' of No 502 Sqn and Lancaster 'F' of No 61 Sqn in two attacks sink *U751* outbound. On 27 July Wellington 'A' of No 311 (Czech) Sqn damages the outgoing *U106*, which has to return.

7–9 July   English Channel

On 9 July the German 2nd MTB Flotilla (Lt-Cdr Feldt), comprising *S48*, *S50*, *S63*, *S67*, *S70*, *S104* and *S109*, attacks the British convoy WP.183 off Lyme Bay. *S67* (Lt-Cdr Zymalkowski) sinks the British tanker *Pomella* (6766 tons) and the others four freighters totalling 5426 tons and the trawler *Manor*.

On 8 July aircraft sink one more ship of 1109 tons from WP.183 off Portland Bill.

7–11 July   Baltic

During the night 7–8 July, after a preparatory air attack, some 30 Soviet craft, chiefly torpedo cutters (TKAs) and patrol boats (MOs), attack the island of Someri in the inner Gulf of Finland which is occupied by weak Finnish forces. At first they are able to land some 80 men and to take the base of Itäpää and later to bring up some reinforcements. But the Finnish defenders hold out until the Finnish gunboats *Hämeenmaa* and *Uusimaa* and the patrol boats *VMV8*, *VMV9*, *VMV10*, *VMV12* and *VMV17* and the motor torpedo boat *Vasama* come up before dawn. Together with the coastal guns the latter sink the Soviet *TKA-83*, *TKA-113* and *TKA-123*. Simultaneously with the arrival of Soviet reinforcements, which are landed by MO cutters, the Finnish gunboat *Turunmaa* with eight motor boats brings a Finnish company whose counter-attack is supported by the fire of the German minesweeper *M18* as well as of the Finnish minelayers *Riilahti* and *Ruotsinsalmi*, the German minesweeper *M37*, the auxiliary gunboat *SAT27/Ostsee* and the motor minesweeper tender *Nettelbeck* which arrive in the afternoon. They also prevent a Soviet gunboat, two patrol ships and several Fugas minesweepers from effectively intervening. By midday on 9 July the Soviet forces which landed are defeated: 149 men surrender and 126 dead are counted. At sea the Soviets, in gun engagements with the German and Finnish ships on 9 July, also lose *TKA-101*, *TKA-31* and *TKA-72*. The gunboat *Kama* sinks after being hit by a bomb from the

149

Finnish aircraft Le R4. The Soviets continue their efforts to establish contact with the forces landed up to 11 July.

9 July   Arctic Ocean
The German A/S trawler *UJ1110* is sunk by an explosion, possibly caused by a mine laid by the Soviet submarine *K-1*.

9–23 July   Mediterranean
U561 (Lt Schomburg) lays another mine barrage off Port Said. *U562* (Lt Hamm) torpedoes one ship of 3359 tons and *U375* (Lt-Cdr Könenkamp) sinks a guard ship off Famagusta. Off the Syrian coast, the Italian submarine *Perla* misses a large transport and is captured on 9 July off Beirut by the corvette *Hyacinth*; it is later commissioned as *P712*. *Alagi* (Lt-Cdr Puccini) sinks one Turkish ship of 3723 tons. *Ondina*, *Nereide* and *Asteria* have no success. *Ondina* is sunk on 11 July by the South African A/S trawlers *Southern Maid* and *Protea*, supported by a Walrus of No 700 Sqn FAA.

10 July   Bay of Biscay
NW of Arcachon, the German auxiliary minesweeper *M4401* sinks after striking a mine.

10 July–10 Sept   Western Atlantic
In the area of Trinidad and to the SE of it, *U160* (Lt Lassen) sinks six ships of 29281 tons and *U66* (Lt-Cdr Markworth) nine ships of 48896 tons. *U66* lays mines on 20 July off Port Castries (St Lucia) on which one US Coast Guard cutter and the British *MTB339* and *MTB342* are damaged. *U160* also torpedoes the Norwegian tanker *Havsten* (6161 tons), which is later sunk by the Italian submarine *Tazzoli* (Cdr Fecia di Cossato).

11 July   Mediterranean
The British destroyers *Beaufort*, *Dulverton*, *Eridge* and *Hurworth* bombard Mersa Matruh and sink one ship driven out to sea by Albacores of No 820 Sqn FAA.

11–15 July   Central Atlantic
From the 'Hai' group proceeding S, the U-tanker *U116* (Cdr v Schmidt) locates convoy OS.33 (41 ships), after a part (six ships) has been detached for South America. In a simultaneous attack by *U116* and *U201* (Lt-Cdr Schnee) one ship of 7093 tons is sunk, while *U582* (Lt-Cdr Schulte) sinks one ship of 8826 tons. *U136* (Lt-Cdr Zimmermann) is sunk by the frigate *Spey*, the sloop *Pelican* and the Free French destroyer *Léopard*. *U572* (Lt-Cdr Hirsacker) and *U752* (Lt-Cdr Schroeter) keep contact with the main convoy, with interruptions, until the evening of 13 July. *U582* sinks a straggler of 7524 tons on 15 July. In shadowing the western part of the convoy, *U116* sinks one

ship of 4284 tons and *U201*(Lt-Cdr Schnee) two ships of 11965 tons.

11 July–21 Sept   Western Atlantic
U166 lays a mine barrage on 25 July off the estuary of the Mississippi which remains undetected. In the Gulf of Mexico, *U166* (Lt Kuhlmann) sinks four ships of 7593 tons and *U171* (Lt-Cdr Pfeffer) three of 17641 tons. Operations by *U173* (Cdr* Beucke) off the Greater Antilles and by *U509* (Cdr Wolff) in the Gulf of Mexico have no success. *U166* is sunk by a US Coast Guard aircraft off the Mississippi estuary on 1 Aug. *U171* is lost (9 Oct) on a mine off Lorient.

12–15 July   Mediterranean
The British submarine *P211/Safari* (Cdr Bryant) sinks one ship and damages one totalling 2094 tons off the coast of Sardinia.

13–29 July   North Atlantic
Resumption of convoy operations on the North Atlantic route by the U-boat 'Wolf' group (*U454*, *U704*, *U597*, *U71*, *U552*, *U43*, *U379*, *U86*, *U90* and, from 25 July, *U607*). On 13 July *U71* (Lt Rodler v Roithberg) sights the convoy ON.111 (EG.B6) S of Iceland but, as a result of an obscure report, the boats search in the wrong direction. *U704* and *U552* are driven off by the escort on 14 July. The group proceeds to the SW without sighting anything until 23 July and is directed to ON.113 which is identified by the B-Service. *U552* (Cdr Topp) locates it on 24 July according to plan. The convoy consists of 33 ships and is escorted by the Canadian EG.C2 with the destroyers *Burnham* (RN; Cdr Taylor) and *St Croix* (RCN), and the corvettes *Brandon*, *Dauphin*, *Drumheller* (RCN) and *Polyanthus* (RN). *St Croix* (Lt-Cdr Dobson) sinks *U90* (Lt-Cdr Öldorp) with depth charges as she keeps contact. During the first night only *U552* attacks: she sinks one ship of 5136 tons and torpedoes a tanker of 8093 tons. In poor visibility and bad weather only a few boats get near the convoy on 25 July. Attacks by *U43* and *U597* in the night fail; only *U607* (Lt-Cdr Mengersen) torpedoes one ship of 6942 tons which is later sunk by *U704* (Lt-Cdr Kessler). On 26 July contact is lost and a search on 27 July yields no results. The 'Wolf' group splits up and goes to the supply boat *U461* (29–30 July). One more ship (6734 tons) of ON.113, now escorted by the Western Local Escort group, is sunk by *U132* (Lt-Cdr Vogelsang), operating independently off the Canadian coast on 29 July.

13 July–7 Aug   South Pacific
Of the Japanese 3rd SM Flotilla (Rear-Adm Kono), *I-11*, *I-174* and *I-175* operate off Sydney, *I-169* off New Caledonia and *I-171* off Fiji. They have the following results: *I-*

11 (Cdr* Hichiji) sinks three ships of 15301 tons and lightly damages one, *I-175* (Cdr Uno) sinks two of 3023 tons and damages one of 3279 tons and *I-169* (Cdr* Watanabe) sinks one of 9227 tons.

14 July   Central Atlantic
The German U-boats on the way to Freetown on 14 July report convoy SL.115 escorted by EG.42 with the sloops *Londonderry*, *Lulworth*, *Bideford* and *Hastings*. The summoned Italian submarine *Calvi* (Cdr* Longobardo) is located by *Lulworth* and forced to surface by a depth charge attack. In a gun duel *Calvi*, which misses *Lulworth* with two torpedoes, is heavily damaged and sinks later, after the German *U130* (Cdr* Kals) unsuccessfully attacks *Lulworth*, which then tries to attack *U130* and leaves *Calvi*. 35 of the latter's survivors are rescued 4hr later.

14 July   Pacific
Reorganisation of the Japanese Combined Fleet as a result of Midway. The Combined Fleet (Adm Yamamoto) now comprises the battleship *Yamato*, the escort carriers *Taiyo* and *Unyo*, the seaplane carriers *Chiyoda* and *Nisshin* and the destroyers *Akebono*, *Ushio* and *Sazanami* (7th Destroyer Div).
The 1st Fleet (Adm Yamamoto) comprises the battleships *Nagato*, *Mutsu*, *Fuso* and *Yamashiro* (2nd BB Sqn, Vice-Adm Takasu) and, from 5 Aug, *Musashi* and *Yamato* (1st BB Sqn); the cruisers *Kitakami* and *Oi* (9th Cruiser Sqn), *Abukuma* (1st DD Flotilla, Rear-Adm Omori), the destroyers *Akatsuki*, *Ikazuchi* and *Inazuma* (6th DD Div—detached to the Aleutians); *Hatsuharu*, *Hatsushimo* and *Wakaba* (21st DD Div—detached to the Aleutians); the cruiser *Sendai* (3rd DD Flotilla, Rear-Adm Hashimoto) with the destroyers *Fubuki*, *Hatsuyuki*, *Murakumo* and *Shirayuki* (11th DD Div), *Ayanami*, *Isonami*, *Shikinami* and *Uranami* (19th DD Div) and *Amagiri*, *Asagiri*, *Shirakumo* and *Yugiri* (20th DD Div).
The 2nd Fleet (Vice-Adm Kondo) comprises the heavy cruisers *Atago*, *Maya* and *Takao* (4th Cruiser Sqn) and *Haguro* and *Myoko* (5th Cruiser Sqn, Vice-Adm Takagi), the battleships *Haruna* and *Kongo* (3rd BB Sqn, Rear-Adm Kurita) and the 2nd DD Flotilla (Rear-Adm Tanaka) with the cruiser *Jintsu* and destroyers *Kagero*, *Kuroshio*, *Oyashio* and *Hayashio* (15th DD Div), *Umikaze*, *Kawakaze* and *Suzukaze* (24th DD Div); and the 4th DD Flotilla (Rear-Adm Takama) with the cruiser *Yura* and destroyers *Murasame*, *Yudachi*, *Harusame* and *Samidare* (2nd DD Div), *Asagumo*, *Minegumo* and *Natsugumo* (9th DD Div) and *Ariake*, *Yugure*, *Shiratsuyu* and *Shigure*

(27th DD Div). Also under command is the 11th Carrier Sqn with the seaplane carriers and tenders *Chitose*, *Kamikawa Maru* and *Kamikaze Maru*.

The 3rd Fleet (Vice-Adm Nagumo) comprises the carriers *Shokaku*, *Zuikaku* and *Zuiho* (1st Carrier Sqn) and, from 31 July, *Ryujo*, *Junyo* and *Hiyo* (2nd Carrier Sqn, Rear-Adm Kakuta), the battleships *Hiyei* and *Kirishima* (11th BB Sqn, Rear-Adm Abe), the heavy cruisers *Kumano* and *Suzuya* (7th Cruiser Sqn, Rear-Adm Nishimura) and *Chikuma* and *Tone* (8th Cruiser Sqn, Rear-Adm T Hara) and the 10th DD Flotilla (Rear-Adm Kimura) with the cruiser *Nagara* and the destroyers *Arashi*, *Hagikaze*, *Maikaze* and *Nowake* (4th DD Div), *Akigumo*, *Yugumo*, *Makigumo* and *Kazegumo* (10th DD Div), *Hatsukaze*, *Yukikaze*, *Amatsukaze* and *Tokitsukaze* (16th DD Div) and *Urakaze*, *Isokaze*, *Tanikaze* and *Hamakaze* (17th DD Div).

The 4th Fleet (Vice-Adm Inoue), in Truk, has the cruiser *Kashima* (F), the minelayer *Tokiwa*, the 2nd ES with the cruiser *Yubari* and the destroyers *Yuzuki*, *Oite*, *Asanagi* and *Yunagi* (29th DD Div), two auxiliary gunboats and the 4th, 5th and 6th BF with light vessels and auxiliary ships in the Mandate territories.

The 5th Fleet (Vice-Adm Hosogaya) consists of the heavy cruiser *Nachi*, the cruisers *Kiso* and *Tama*, the destroyers *Oboro*, *Usugumo*, *Hokaze* and *Shiokaze* with further units detached from the 1st Fleet, three auxiliary cruisers, three picket boat divisions and the 7th BF in the area of the Kuriles and Aleutians and, in addition, the 7th SM Flotilla.

The 6th Fleet (Vice-Adm Komatsu) comprises the cruiser *Katori* and the 1st, 2nd, 3rd and 8th SM Flotillas. The 8th Fleet (Vice-Adm Mikawa) comprises the heavy cruisers *Chokai* (F), *Aoba*, *Kinugasa*, *Furutaka* and *Kako* (6th Cruiser Sqn, Rear-Adm Goto), the light cruisers *Tatsuta* and *Tenryu* (18th Cruiser Sqn, Rear-Adm Matsuyama), the destroyers *Mutsuki*, *Yayoi*, *Mochizuki* and *Uzuki* (30th DD Div), the minelayers *Shirataka* and *Tsugaru* and light vessels of the 8th BF and 6th SM Flotilla.

14–19 July   Mediterranean

Operation 'Pinpoint'. Part of British Force H leaves Gibraltar with the carrier *Eagle*, the cruisers *Cairo* and *Charybdis* and five destroyers to fly off 31 Spitfire fighters for Malta S of the Balearics. The Italian submarines *Emo* and *Otaria* sight nothing. The fast minelayer *Welshman*, with supplies, continues the journey to Malta. On the way there are unsuccessful attacks by 28 Italian bombers and 16 Ju 87s and by the submarine

Axum. The British ship arrives in Malta on 16 July and returns on 18–19 July. Italian attempts to intercept her with surface forces, submarines (*Cobalto*, *Dessiè*, *Velella*, *Malachite*, *Dagabur* and *Bronzo* off Cape Bon) and aircraft fail. The British submarines *Parthian*, *Regent*, *Rorqual* and *Porpoise* bring supplies to Malta. The Italian submarines *Bragadino*, *Sciesa*, *Toti*, *Santarosa*, *Atropo*, *Narvalo*, *Micca*, *Zoea* and *Corridoni* transport 1105 tons of supplies to North Africa (15 missions).

15 July   Western Atlantic

U576 (Lt-Cdr Heinicke), which has previously torpedoed a tanker of 11147 tons, attacks a convoy on the American East Coast and sinks two ships of 10373 tons. She is then attacked by an aircraft of VS-9, rammed by the steamer *Unicoi* in the convoy and lost.

15 July–23 Aug   Central Atlantic

After the operation against OS.33, the 'Hai' group proceeds in line abreast to the Freetown area. The following additional sinkings are made (some of the boats have in the meantime taken oil from *U116*): *U201* (Lt-Cdr Schnee) the A/S trawler *Laertes* and two ships totalling 21963 tons, *U572* (Lt-Cdr Hirsacker) one ship of 5281 tons, *U752* (Lt-Cdr Schroeter) four ships of 21624 tons and *U582* (Lt-Cdr Schulte) two ships of 14294 tons.

15 July–14 Oct   Arctic

Operation EON.18. A Soviet destroyer force is transferred by the Northern seaway from the Pacific to the Arctic. On 15 July the flotilla leader *Baku* and the destroyers *Razumny*, *Razyarenny* and *Revnostny* leave Vladivostok. The last collides on 18 July with the freighter *Terney* in the Tatar Sound and has to remain behind. The other ships go through the Kurile Passage on 22 July and put into Petropavlovsk on 26 July. They pass through the Bering Strait on 30 July and reach Tiksi on 14 Aug accompanied by the ice-breaker *Mikoyan*. On 19 Aug the journey is continued; on 24 Sept Dikson is reached and on 9 Oct the Yugor Strait. On 14 Oct the ships are met by the Northern Fleet off the Kola Inlet.

16 July   South Atlantic

The German auxiliary cruiser *Schiff 28* (Capt Ruckteschell) sinks the US tanker *William F Humphrey* (7983 tons) in the South Atlantic.

16 July   Black Sea

In an air attack on Poti, the Soviet cruiser *Komintern* receives such heavy hits that she has to have her armament dismantled. The destroyer *Bodry* is badly damaged. A large ship has a near-miss.

17–20 July   Central Atlantic

The returning *U202* (Lt-Cdr Linder) sights the convoy OS.34 (35 ships) but is driven off during the night 17–18 July by a corvette. On the morning of 18 July the returning *U126* (Lt-Cdr Bauer), which has expended her torpedoes, sights the convoy and brings up the outbound *U564* (Lt-Cdr Suhren), *U108* (Cdr Scholtz) and *U654* (Lt Forster), which, even during darkness, are repeatedly forced to submerge by aircraft. During the night 18–19 July *U564* sinks two ships of 11096 tons and *U108*, after an unsuccessful attack, is attacked with depth charges. At mid-day on 19 July *U108* and *U126* are finally driven off and on 20 July, after a fruitless search, the operation is stopped. The outbound boats continue their journey to the Caribbean.

19 Jul   Mediterranean

The British cruisers *Dido* and *Euryalus* and destroyers *Jervis*, *Javelin*, *Pakenham* and *Paladin* bombard Mersa Matruh. The destroyers *Aldenham* and *Dulverton* engage German E-boats.

19 July   South Atlantic

The US carrier *Ranger* flies off 60 USAAF P-40 fighters for Accra off the Gold Coast. From there they are transferred across Africa to the Near East and India and Burma.

20 July   Indian Ocean

The German auxiliary cruiser *Schiff 10/Thor* (Capt Gumprich) sinks the British freighter *Indus* (5187 tons) in the Indian Ocean.

20–22 July   English Channel

The 3rd TB Flotilla (Cdr Wilcke), comprising *T13*, *T4*, *T10* and *T14*, carries out two defensive mining operations, 'Rhein' and 'Stein', in the Channel.

20–22 July   Mediterranean

Operation 'Insect'. British Force H with the carrier *Eagle*, the cruisers *Cairo* and *Charybdis* and five destroyers proceeds to the area S of the Balearics from Gibraltar and flies off 28 Spitfire fighters for Malta. On 20 July the Italian submarine *Dandolo* misses *Eagle* with four torpedoes. *Platino* sights nothing.

20–24 July   Arctic

The British destroyers *Blankney*, *Marne*, *Martin* and *Middleton* proceed to Murmansk with supplies and ammunition for escort vessels of convoy QP.14.

20 July–5 Aug   Western Atlantic

The four U-boats withdrawn from the American East Coast operate SE of Nova Scotia. Here *U89* (Lt-Cdr Lohmann) sinks one sailing ship of 54 tons, *U754* (Lt-Cdr Oestermann) one fishery vessel of 260 tons and *U158* (Lt-Cdr Diggins) one ship of 4870 tons. On 29 July *U132* (Lt-Cdr Vogelsang) sights the convoy ON.113 (escorted by the WLEF group) and sinks one ship of 6734 tons from it on 30 July. *U754* and *U458* are not able to attack; the former is sunk on 31 July by an RCAF Hudson of No 113 Sqn and the latter is attacked twice on 2 Aug by Hudsons from No 113 Sqn and damaged.

20 July–7 Aug   South Pacific

A Japanese force with three transports, escorted by the light cruisers *Tatsuta* and *Tenryu* (18th Cruiser Sqn), the destroyers *Asanagi*, *Uzuki* and *Yuzuki*, the minelayer *Tsugaru* and submarine-chasers and other light vessels, sets out from Rabaul on 20 July. In the afternoon of 21 July it lands naval troops and units of the South Sea Detachment of the Army near Buna (New Guinea) which are to advance over land in the direction of Port Moresby. Allied air attacks on 22 July damage the transport *Ayatosan Maru* (9788 tons) and *Uzuki*, but all the ships get back to Rabaul by 24 July. On 26 and 29–30 July the Japanese bring more troops to Buna with these ships and also the destroyer *Yunagi*. On 29 July a transport, *Kotoku Maru* (6701 tons), is lost in an air attack. On 30 July Vice-Adm Mikawa arrives in Rabaul on board the cruiser *Chokai* as the new Commander of the 8th Fleet. On 31 July another Japanese convoy for Buna, comprising *Tsugaru*, one transport and submarine-chasers, has to return because of air attacks. A convoy which sets out on 5 Aug with three transports, *Tatsuta*, *Uzuki* and *Yuzuki*, is recalled on 7 Aug when news is received of the Allied landing on Guadalcanal.

22 July–19 Aug   North Atlantic

On 22 July the outbound *U609* (Lt Rudloff) sights a UR convoy and shadows it with *U254* (Lt-Cdr Gilardone) to the neighbourhood of Reykjavik. Then the boats are stationed in the area W of Iceland but attempts to attack US task groups on 28 July and 1 Aug fail. On 2 Aug *U609* sinks one ship of 1218 tons. In the area of the Faeroes, the outbound *U605* (Lt-Cdr Schütze) sinks one trawler of 239 tons on 3 Aug.

24–25 July   Mediterranean

After an attack by the British submarine *Unbeaten* (Lt-Cdr Woodward), British torpedo aircraft and bombers sink near Argostoli the Italian transport *Vettor Pisani* (6339 tons), escorted by the torpedo boats *Antares*, *Calliope* and *Orsa*. On 26 July the British submarine *Thrasher* is damaged off Port Said in an attack by a British Swordfish aircraft.

24 July–17 Aug   Pacific

Off the South Kuriles, the US submarine *Narwhal* (Lt-Cdr Wilkins) sinks six ships of 6905 tons and torpedoes one other ship of 6040 tons. Off Japan, *Silversides* (Lt-Cdr Burlingame) sinks one ship of 5783 tons; off Truk, *Greenling* (Lt-Cdr Bruton) sinks two ships of 17228 tons, *Gudgeon* (Lt-Cdr Stovall) sinks one ship of 4853 tons and torpedoes two tankers of 20040 tons and off Wotje *Tambor* sinks two ships of 5819 tons.

26 July–1 Aug   Arctic

In the search for the remaining ships from PQ.17 sighted by German reconnaissance off the west coast of Novaya Zemlaya, *U601* (Lt-Cdr Grau) shells on 26 July the Soviet polar station Karmakuly and destroys two aircraft and sinks the steamer *Krestyanin* (2513 tons) off the Kostin Strait on 1 Aug.

26 July–10 Sept   Western Atlantic

In the area SE of Trinidad, *U108* (Cdr Scholtz) sinks three ships of 17495 tons, *U155* (Lt-Cdr Piening) sinks ten of 43892 tons and *U510* (Cdr Neitzel) sinks two of 10256 tons and torpedoes one of 8016 tons.

27–28 July   Baltic

The returning Soviet submarine *S-4* is damaged by a mine on the 'Seeigel' barrage: the Commander (Capt 3rd Class Abrosimov) is blown overboard but the boat reaches Lavansaari. On 28 July the minesweeper *T-58* is damaged by a German coastal battery when *Shch-320* is transferred to Kronstadt.

27 July–11 Sept   South West Pacific

In the Malacca Straits, the Dutch submarine *O23* (Lt-Cdr Valkenburg) sinks two ships of 12313 tons and torpedoes one of 729 tons. In the South China Sea, the US submarine *Saury* (Lt-Cdr Mewhinney) sinks one ship of 8606 tons and torpedoes one of 9024 tons, *Seal* (Lt-Cdr Hurd) torpedoes two ships of 14634 tons, *Skipjack* torpedoes one of 14050 tons and *Seawolf* (Lt-Cdr Warder) sinks two of 4462 tons. Off Bougainville *Tautog* (Lt-Cdr Willingham) sinks one ship of 5873 tons.

28 July   English Channel

Off Cape de la Hague, the German patrol trawler *V202* is sunk in an engagement with British destroyers.

29 July–3 Aug   North Atlantic

The outbound *U210* (Lt-Cdr Lemcke) sights in the North Atlantic the convoy ON.115, consisting of 41 ships and the Canadian EG.C3 (Lt-Cdr Wallace) including the destroyers *Saguenay* and *Skeena* and the corvettes *Galt*, *Sackville*, *Wetaskiwin*, *Agassiz* and *Louisburg* (in addition there is the destroyer HMCS *Hamilton*). On 30 and 31 July the escort repeatedly drives off the

U-boats which make contact—*U164*, *U210*, *U511*, *U553* and *U217*. *U588* is sunk by depth charges from *Skeena* (Lt Dyer) and *Wetaskiwin* (Lt-Cdr Windeyer). On 1 Aug a patrol line 'Pirat' is formed with *U210*, *U217*, *U553*, *U511* and *U164* which the replenished 'Wolf' boats *U607*, *U454*, *U704*, *U597*, *U71*, *U552* and *U43* join on 2 Aug. In the night *Saguenay* and *Skeena* have to leave because of fuel shortage. Only *Louisburg*, *Sackville* and *Agassiz* remain with the convoy after *Wetaskiwin* fails to return after a hunt. In the afternoon the destroyers *Witch* (RN) and *Hamilton* arrive from WLEF. On 2 Aug *U552* (Cdr Topp) sights the convoy and brings up *U71*, *U704*, *U217*, *U597* and *U553*. *U552* torpedoes two ships, one of 10627 tons and another of 7176 tons: the latter is sunk by *U607* (Lt-Cdr Mengersen). *U553* (Cdr Thurmann) sinks one ship of 9419 tons. Further attacks by *U71*, *U217* and *U552* on the convoy and by *U597* on a straggler fail. On 3 Aug the operation has to be broken off in the mist.

30 July   English Channel

Near Le Havre, the German auxiliary minesweeper *M4008* is lost in an air attack.

30 July–9 Aug   Mediterranean

In operations off the Palestine coast, *U77* (Lt-Cdr Schonder) sinks nine sailing ships and *U565* (Lt-Cdr Franken) one sailing ship. *U372* is found and sunk by a British patrol consisting of the destroyers *Zulu*, *Sikh*, *Croome* and *Tetcott* with air support from Wellington 'M' of No 203 Sqn RAF on 4 Aug. In attempting to launch torpedo riders to attack the port of Haifa, the Italian submarine *Scirè* is sunk by the British A/S trawler *Islay* on 10 Aug.

31 July   North Atlantic

The outbound *U213* (Lt v Varendorff†) encounters a convoy W of the Bay of Biscay and is sunk by the sloops *Erne*, *Rochester* and *Sandwich*, belonging to EG. 43.

31 July–6 Aug   South Pacific

Preparations for Operation 'Watchtower' (landing on Guadalcanal). After final landing exercises the South Pacific Amphibious Force, TF.62 (Rear-Adm Turner), advances from the area of the Fiji Islands. It consists of the convoy (TG.62.1) divided into six sections, comprising 19 troop and supply transports, four fast transports, TG.62.2 (Rear-Adm Crutchley) with the cruisers *Australia*, *Canberra* and *Hobart* (RAN) and *Chicago* and the destroyers (Desron 4) *Selfridge*, *Patterson*, *Ralph Talbot*, *Mugford*, *Jarvis*, *Blue*, *Helm*, *Henley* and *Bagley*, the Fire Support Groups 62.3 (Capt Riefkohl) with the cruisers *Vincennes*, *Quincy* and *Astoria* and the destroyers *Dewey*, *Ellet*, *Hull* and *Wilson* and 62.4

(Rear-Adm Scott) with the cruiser *San Juan* and the destroyers *Buchanan* and *Monssen* and also the Minesweeper Force 62.5 with five fast minesweepers.

Cover is provided by the Air Support Force, TF.61 (Vice-Adm Fletcher, Air Operations Rear-Adm Noyes) with Units 1 (Fletcher), comprising the carrier *Saratoga*, the cruisers *Minneapolis* and *New Orleans*, the destroyers *Phelps*, *Farragut*, *Worden*, *Mac-Donough* and *Dale*; 2 (Rear-Adm Kinkaid) with the carrier *Enterprise*, the battleship *North Carolina*, the cruisers *Portland* (Rear-Adm Tisdale) and *Atlanta*, the destroyers *Balch*, *Maury*, *Gwin*, *Benham* and *Grayson*; and 3 (Noyes) with the carrier *Wasp*, the cruisers *San Francisco* and *Salt Lake City*, the destroyers *Lang*, *Sterett*, *Aaron Ward*, *Stack*, *Laffey* and *Farenholt*. The Tanker Force consists of the fleet tankers *Platte*, *Cimarron*, *Kaskaskia*, *Sabine* and *Kanawha*. For preparatory air action and support, the shore-based aircraft in TF.63 (Rear-Adm McCain) are assembled. To cover the operation, the submarines (TF.42, Capt Christie) *S38*, *S39*, *S41*, *S43*, *S44* and *S46* are deployed from Brisbane in the area of Kavieng and Rabaul and the submarines *Drum* and *Greenling* from the Pacific Fleet in the area of Truk. Overall command of the operation is in the hands of Vice-Adm Ghormley (at Nouméa).

Protected by a weather front, the advance is undetected by the enemy until 6 Aug.

31 July–12 Aug   South Pacific
From Rabaul, *Ro-34* (Cdr Morinaga) and *Ro-33* (Cdr Kuriyama) of the Japanese 7th SM Flotilla (Rear-Adm Yoshitomi) operate in the area of the Gulf of Papua. They torpedo one transport of 9424 tons and sink one fishery vessel of 300 tons respectively. After the US landing on Guadalcanal, *I-121*, *I-122*, *I-123*, *Ro-33* and *Ro-34* are ordered to Indispensable Strait.

1 Aug   Black Sea
The Soviet TKAs *D-3* and *SM-3* sink the store ferry *F334* by torpedo in the Bay of Ivan Baba.

1–2 Aug   English Channel
The German 3rd TB Flotilla (Cdr Wilcke), comprising *T13*, *T10* and *T14*, lays the 'Masuren' defensive mine barrage.

1–10 Aug   Indian Ocean
Operation 'Stab'. Force A of the British Eastern Fleet (Vice-Adm Somerville), which was transferred from Kilindini (East Africa) to Colombo at the end of July and which comprises the battleship *Warspite*, the carriers *Formidable* and *Illustrious*, the 4th Cruiser Sqn and destroyers, simulates an intended invasion of the Andamans to divert the attention of the Japanese from

Operation 'Watchtower', the landing on Guadalcanal. It employs three decoy convoys on the east coast of India and in the Bay of Bengal.

1 Aug–16 Sept   Western Atlantic
In individual operations in the Caribbean, *U164* (Cdr Fechner) sinks one ship of 1745 tons, *U217* (Lt Reichenbach) sinks a sailing ship of 75 tons and *U558* (Lt-Cdr Krech) sinks one ship of 2606 tons. *U511* and *U94* have no individual successes. (For operations against convoys, see below.)

Aug   Mediterranean/Intelligence
Bletchley Park breaks into the German naval 'Süd' code, used since Apr 1941 for communications in the Mediterranean and the Black Sea. It is named 'Porpoise'.

2 Aug   North Atlantic
Beginning of the troop transports from the USA to England and Northern Ireland with the large passenger ships *Queen Elizabeth* (83673 tons), *Queen Mary* (81235 tons), *Pasteur* (29253 tons), *Empress of Scotland* (26313 tons), *Wakefield* (24289 tons), *Mariposa* (18017 tons) and others.

2–3 Aug   Black Sea
The commander of the Soviet Cruiser Bde, Rear-Adm N E Basisty, goes to sea on 2 Aug with the cruiser *Molotov* (Capt M F Romanov) and the flotilla leader *Kharkov* (Cdr P I Shevshenko) and shells targets in the Bay of Feodosia during the night 2–3 Aug. The submarine *M-62* is sent in as a marker. On the return there are attacks by German torpedo aircraft (6/KG 26, Lt Wilhelm Kleemann) and the Italian MTBs *MAS 568* and *MAS 573*. *Molotov* receives a torpedo hit in the stern and 20m of the ship are blown off. The ship is repaired using the stern of the incomplete cruiser *Frunze* and is back in service in 1944.

3–7 Aug   Mediterranean
Off the Libyan coast, the British submarine *Thorn* (Lt-Cdr Norfolk) sinks on 3 Aug the Italian transport *Monviso* (5322 tons), already slightly damaged by an air torpedo on 28 July, when escorted by the destroyers *Alpino* and *Corazziere*. After two unsuccessful attacks on a tanker escorted by the destroyers *Turbine* and *Graecale*, *Thorn* is sunk on 7 Aug by the Italian torpedo boat *Pegaso*. *Turbulent* (Lt-Cdr Linton) destroys on 6 Aug the wreck of the destroyer *Strale* which went aground on 21 June near Cape Bon. In the Aegean, the Greek submarine *Nereus* sinks two small ships. The British *Proteus* sinks the German steamer *Wachtfels* (8467 tons) on 7 Aug.

3–11 Aug   North Atlantic
After the ON.115 operation, the U-boats

U210, *U607*, *U454*, *U704*, *U597*, *U71*, *U379* and *U593* form the 'Steinbrinck' group E of the Newfoundland Bank. After the sighting of an ON convoy by *U704* (Lt-Cdr Kessler), which is not shadowed, *U593* (Lt-Cdr Kelbling) reports on 5 Aug the convoy SC.94 consisting of 36 ships escorted by the Canadian EG.C1 with the destroyer *Assiniboine*, the corvettes *Chilliwack* and *Orillia* and the British *Primrose* (Lt-Cdr Ayer, SOE), *Nasturtium* and *Dianthus*. *U593* at once attacks and sinks one ship of 3616 tons from an isolated group, but is driven off with *U595* by *Nasturtium* and *Orillia*. On 6 Aug *U595* is damaged by gunfire and depth charges from *Chilliwack* and *Primrose* and *U454* by depth charges from *Dianthus*; they have to break off. *U210* (Lt-Cdr Lemcke) is forced to surface by *Assiniboine* (Lt-Cdr Stubbs) and in a gun duel at close range is sunk by ramming. Apart from *U595*, the outbound *U176*, *U660*, *U256*, *U174*, *U438* and *U705* also operate against SC.94 from 7 Aug. In the afternoon of 7 Aug *U607* (Lt-Cdr Mengersen) misses a group of stragglers and during the night 7–8 Aug *U704*, and in the morning of 8 Aug *U660* (Lt Baur), miss the convoy. At mid-day attempts by *U597* and *U605* to attack stragglers fail. In the afternoon of 8 Aug *U176* (Lt-Cdr Dierksen) and *U379* (Lt-Cdr Kettner) attack almost simultaneously and sink three ships and two ships, respectively, of 16687 tons and 8910 tons. Three other undamaged ships are abandoned in a panic, one of which (3201 tons) is later finished off by *U176*. An attack by *U704* fails. In the evening of 8 Aug the British destroyer *Broke* (Lt-Cdr Layard) joins the convoy and, later in the night, also the Polish destroyer *Blyskawica*, but *Dianthus*, which has sunk *U379* with depth charges and by ramming, drops out. All escorts, apart from *Primrose*, remain behind in the night fighting U-boats, supported by the HF/DF on the destroyers. *Broke* is just missed by torpedoes from *U595* (Lt-Cdr Quaet Faslem). All attempts at attack are thwarted; only *U607* is able to fire—unsuccessfully—and then keeps contact. In spite of the deployment of air protection with Liberators of No 120 Sqn RAF from Northern Ireland in the afternoon of 9 Aug, *U254*, *U174*, *U704*, *U256* in the afternoon and evening and *U597* in the morning of 10 Aug are able to fire, but no hits are scored. The fact that some escorts remain behind to deal with the located U-boats makes it possible for *U438* (Lt-Cdr Franzius) and *U660* to make a simultaneous attack at mid-day. They sink three ships of 16074 tons and one of 4439 tons respectively.

3–12 Aug   Norway
In operations off the Norwegian coast, the British submarine *P213/Saracen* (Lt Lumby) sinks the German *U335* on 3 Aug and *P54/Unshaken* (Lt Oxborrow) and *Sturgeon* (Lt Wingfield) each sink one ship, of 2890 tons and 3335 tons respectively, on 12 Aug.

3–26 Aug   Western Atlantic
Off the American East Coast, *U98* (Cdr Schulze) lays a mine barrage on 8 Aug off Jacksonville, which is swept without loss. S of Cape Hatteras this boat, like *U86* (Lt-Cdr Schug), which, because of damage, is at the time cruising away from the coast, has no success.

4 Aug   South Pacific
The US destroyer *Tucker* is lost in an Allied minefield off Esperitu Santo.

4 Aug   Black Sea
Beginning of German supply operations by sea in the Sea of Azov.

4–24 Aug   Arctic
The Soviet submarine *K-1* lays on 6 Aug a mine barrage off Porsanger Fjord and is herself damaged by a mine on 11 Aug. *Shch-403* (Lt-Cdr Shuyski) misses two convoys off Vardö and is attacked on 11 Aug with 110 depth charges by *UJ1104*, *UJ1108* and *UJ1101*. On 14 Aug the CO, Capt 3rd Class Stolbov, and 17 men are killed in an internal explosion on board *Shch-402*; the boat is taken back from Tanafjord to Polyarnoe. *K-21* (Capt 3rd Class Lunin) lays a mine barrage on 16 Aug in Lopphavet and misses a convoy on 19 Aug. *M-173* has not returned by 18 Aug. On 22–23 Aug *Shch-422* (Lt-Cdr Vidyaev) misses two convoys in Varangerfjord; *V6105*, *UJ1101*, *UJ1108* and *UJ1112* attack the submarine on 24 Aug but it escapes.

5–23 Aug   Black Sea
On 5 Aug the Soviet submarine *Shch-205* (Capt 3rd Class Sukhomlonov) misses a convoy off Olinka. *L-5* and *L-4* lay minefields off Feolent and Sarych. *M-118* (Lt Savin), *M-62* (Lt-Cdr Malyshev), *M-31* Lt-Cdr Rastochil), *M-111* (Lt-Cdr Iosseliani) and *M-36* (Lt-Cdr Komarov) attack ships in Odessa Bay but only the last has any success, sinking the German tug *Ankara* on 23 Aug. *M-33* is lost on a flanking mine barrage.

6 Aug   Baltic
U612 is lost in a collision with *U444* off Warnemünde.

6–10 Aug   Baltic
Soviet ground-attack air formations attack the German minesweepers and submarine-chasers stationed in the A/S positions W of the 'Seeigel' mine barrages, and Soviet motor minesweepers penetrate the 'Seeigel' barrages on 6 Aug in order to meet the returning submarines *Shch-303* and *Shch-406*. In pursuing one of the boats between Suur- and Pien-Tytärsaari on 7 Aug, *UJ1211* runs on to an old Soviet mine barrage and sinks. On 11 Aug *S-7* arrives in Lavansaari.

7 Aug   English Channel
The German MDS *Sperrbrecher 170/M M Müller* is sunk by mine off Ostend.

7 Aug   Black Sea
The Soviet cruiser *Krasny Krym* and the destroyer *Nezamozhnik* evacuate 2895 men and 100 tons of supplies from Novorossisk to Batum.

7–9 Aug   South Pacific
Operation 'Watchtower': US landing on Guadalcanal. On 7 Aug, after preparatory fire by aircraft from the carriers *Enterprise*, *Saratoga* and *Wasp* and from the guns of the cruisers and destroyers of the Support Force, the Amphibious Force (Rear-Adm Turner) lands the reinforced 1st Marine Div from 15 transports on the N side of Guadalcanal and parts of the division from four transports and four fast transports on Tulagi. The nearly completed Japanese airfield on Guadalcanal is seized and there is stiff resistance on Tulagi. In the afternoon two attacks by 27 bombers and 16 dive-bombers of the Japanese 25th Flotilla are intercepted by fighters from *Enterprise* and *Saratoga*: 12 US and 16 Japanese aircraft are shot down and the US destroyer *Mugford* is slightly damaged. The Japanese 8th Fleet (Vice-Adm Mikawa), comprising five heavy and two light cruisers and one destroyer, sets out from Rabaul: it is sighted by the US submarine *S38*.

On 8 Aug there is an attack by 26 Japanese torpedo aircraft; 17 are shot down by AA fire and fighters, but the US destroyer *Jarvis* is sunk by the Japanese destroyer *Yunagi* and torpedo aircraft. In the following attack by dive-bombers and fighter-bombers, a crashing aircraft hits the US transport *G F Elliott* (8378 tons) which catches fire and later has to be abandoned. *S38* (Lt-Cdr Munson) sinks the Japanese supply transport *Meiyo Maru* (5628 tons) S of Rabaul. There is now a gap in signal intelligence following a change in the Japanese codes from JN.25C to 25D and reconnaissance reports from Australian aircraft about the Japanese cruiser force are tardily transmitted. Thus faulty intelligence leds to poor ship dispositions and, ultimately, disaster.

On 9 Aug, by night, the Japanese force, comprising the cruisers *Chokai, Aoba, Kinugasa, Furutaka, Kako, Tenryu* and *Yubari* and the destroyer *Yunagi*, enters the narrows between Savo Island and Guadalcanal and passes the US radar picket destroyers *Blue* and *R Talbot* undetected. There the Southern covering force, comprising the cruisers *Canberra* (RAN) and *Chicago* and the destroyers *Bagley* and *Patterson*, is surprised.

Canberra (Capt Getting†) is set on fire and reduced to a wreck (84 men are lost); *Chicago* is damaged by a torpedo hit and *Patterson* by gunfire. Then Mikawa, thanks to serious deficiencies in the Allied command organisation, is also able to surprise the Northern covering force, comprising the cruisers *Vincennes, Quincy* and *Astoria* and the destroyers *Helm* and *Wilson*, and to destroy the cruisers with concentrated torpedo salvoes and gunfire. *Quincy* (Capt S N Moore) and *Vincennes* (Capt Riefkohl) sink at once; *Astoria* (Capt Greenman) and *Canberra* have to be abandoned in the morning, the former losing 1203 men. On the Japanese side only *Chokai* and *Kinugasa* suffer slight damage The northern picket destroyer *R Talbot* is badly hit by the retiring Japanese. As a result of the obscure situation and faulty command, the cruisers *Australia* (RAN), *Hobart* (RAN) and *San Juan* and seven destroyers, which are stationed in the area, are not deployed. The carrier force (Vice-Adm Fletcher), operating S of Guadalcanal, after 48hr of operations, has turned away in the evening of 8 Aug from fear of torpedo aircraft and submarines and can no longer catch the retiring Japanese. Adm Turner decides to withdraw with his remaining warships and transports. The 1st Marine Div (Maj-Gen Vandergrift) is left on its own. From the returning Japanese force, the US submarine *S44* (Lt-Cdr Moore) sinks the cruiser *Kako* off Kavieng on 10 Aug. Total Allied losses: 1270 dead and 709 wounded.

7 Aug–8 Oct   Central Atlantic
Off West Africa, *U109* (Lt-Cdr Bleichrodt) sinks five ships of 35601 tons, *U125* (Lt-Cdr Folkers) six of 22846 tons and *U506* (Lt-Cdr Würdemann) five of 28023 tons.

9 Aug   South Atlantic
The auxiliary cruiser *Schiff 23/Stier* (Cdr Gerlach) sinks the British freighter *Dalhousie* (7072 tons) in the South Atlantic.

9–11 Aug   Black Sea
The Soviet cruiser *Krasny Krym* and the destroyer *Nezamozhnik* evacuate 2000 men from Novorossisk to Batum. The German *S102* (Lt-Cdr Töniges) sinks a Soviet steamer off Tuapse on 10 Aug; on 11 Aug she makes an unsuccessful attack with *S28* (Lt-Cdr Künzel) on tankers between Novorossisk and Tuapse.

10–11 Aug Bay of Biscay

During air operations against the U-boat transit routes, the Czech Wellington 'H' (Fg Off Nyult) of No 311 Sqn sinks *U578* outbound on 10 Aug. The Italian submarine *Morosini*, returning from the Antilles, is lost, probably during an air attack on 11 Aug in the Bay of Biscay.

10–15 Aug Mediterranean

Operation 'Pedestal'. On 10 Aug, in anticipation of a large supply convoy for Malta, Supermarina stations the submarines *Brin*, *Dagabur*, *Giada*, *Uarsciek*, *Volframio*, *U73* and *U331* between Algiers and the Balearics. In the area N of Tunisia and off Cape Bon, another submarine group is formed with *Granito*, *Emo*, *Otaria*, *Dandolo*, *Avorio*, *Cobalto*, *Alagi*, *Ascianghi*, *Axum*, *Bronzo* and *Dessié* and W of Malta *Asteria*. The British convoy, consisting of 13 transports and one tanker, escorted by Rear-Adm Burrough with the cruisers *Nigeria*, *Kenya*, *Manchester* and *Cairo* and the destroyers *Ashanti*, *Intrepid*, *Icarus*, *Foresight*, *Fury*, *Pathfinder*, *Penn*, *Derwent*, *Bramham*, *Bicester* and *Ledbury*, passes through the Straits of Gibraltar together with the covering force (Vice-Adm Syfret), consisting of the battleships *Nelson* and *Rodney*, the carriers *Victorious* (Rear-Adm Lyster), *Indomitable*, *Eagle* and *Furious*, the cruisers *Phoebe*, *Sirius* and *Charybdis* and the destroyers *Laforey*, *Lightning*, *Lookout*, *Quentin*, *Eskimo*, *Tartar*, *Ithuriel*, *Antelope*, *Wishart*, *Vansittart*, *Westcott*, *Zetland* and *Wilton*. An empty convoy, consisting of the transports *Orari* and *Troilus*, accompanied by the destroyers *Badsworth* and *Matchless*, sets out from Malta. There is a brief engagement with the Italian destroyer *Malocello* near Cape Bon which is laying a mine barrage there.

On 11 Aug there is an unsuccessful attack by the Italian submarine *Uarsciek* on carriers of the covering force. The 24 British destroyers and cruiser *Cairo* take on fuel from the supply force, consisting of the tankers *Brown Ranger* and *Derwentdale*. German and Italian air reconnaissance locates the British forces. *Furious* flies off S of the Balearics 37 Spitfire fighters for Malta and is then met by the reserve destroyers *Keppel*, *Malcolm*, *Venomous*, *Wolverine* and *Wrestler* for the return journey to Gibraltar. *U73* (Lt-Cdr Rosenbaum) sinks with a salvo of four torpedoes the carrier *Eagle* (Capt L D Mackintosh); 260 of the crew perish. Ten British Beaufighter and 16 Hurricane aircraft attack Italian air bases in Sardinia. In the evening an attack by 36 German Ju 88s and He 111s is frustrated by fighter and AA defence.

On 12 Aug, in attempting to attack the returning *Furious*, the Italian submarine *Dagabur* is rammed and sunk by the destroyer *Wolverine* (Lt-Cdr Gretton). The Italian submarine *Giada* is bombed and damaged by a Sunderland flying boat. In the morning there is an unsuccessful attack by 19 Ju 88s in which six planes are lost. At mid-day there are attacks by ten SM 84, eight G 42 and 33 SM 79 bombers and ten SM 84 torpedo aircraft of the Italian Air Force and 37 German Ju 88s with fighter protection. The transport *Deucalion* is damaged and left behind with the destroyer *Bramham*. Two Italian Re 2001 fighter-bombers attack the carrier *Victorious* with armour-piercing bombs but the latter rebound from the armoured flight deck. In the afternoon the submarines are repeatedly driven off by the destroyers *Tartar*, *Zetland* and *Pathfinder*. *Emo* fires a salvo of four torpedoes at the destroyer *Lookout* and *Cobalto* is rammed by the destroyer *Ithuriel* which is herself badly damaged. In the late afternoon there is an attack by 29 Ju 87s of I/StG 3 (Capt Mossdorf) with fighter protection—they score three heavy hits on the carrier *Indomitable* which is then no longer able to operate aircraft—and by 14 SM 79 torpedo aircraft of 132 Gruppo (Capt U Rivoli) which torpedo the destroyer *Foresight* with the result that she later has to be sunk by *Tartar*. The covering force turns away to the W. In the evening the submarines *Dessié* and *Axum* (Lt-Cdr Ferrini) attack in turn: *Axum* scores one hit each on the cruisers *Cairo* and *Nigeria* and the tanker *Ohio*. *Cairo* has to be abandoned and *Nigeria* starts the return journey with the destroyers *Bicester*, *Derwent* and *Wilton*. There follows an attack by 30 Ju 88s with bombs, to which the transports *Empire Hope* (12688 tons) and *Glenorchy* (8982 tons) fall victim, and by seven He 111s with torpedoes which cause the *Brisbane Star* (12791 tons) to stop. In an attack by the Italian submarine *Alagi* (Lt-Cdr Puccini), the cruiser *Kenya* and the transport *Clan Ferguson* are torpedoed and damaged. Shortly before midnight the submarine *Bronzo* (Lt-Cdr Buldrini) sinks the wreck of the *Empire Hope*.

On 13 Aug, to distract attention from 'Pedestal', the Mediterranean Fleet conducts operation MG.4 in which the cruisers *Arethusa* and *Cleopatra* and the destroyers *Javelin*, *Kelvin*, *Sikh* and *Zulu* bombard Rhodes. Back at the convoy, in 15 successive motor torpedo attacks in four hours, *Ms 16* (Cdr Manuti) and *Ms 22* (Lt Mezzarda) score hits on the cruiser *Manchester*, which is later abandoned; *Ms 31* (Lt-Cdr Calvani) on the wreck of the *Glenorchy*, which sinks;

and *S30* (Lt Weber), *S36* (Lt Brauns), *MAS 554* (Lt Calcagno) and *MAS 557* (Sub-Lt Cafiero) on the transports *Rochester Castle*, *Santa Elisa* (8379 tons), *Almeria Lykes* (7773 tons) and *Wairangi* (12436 tons), the last three of which sink at once. The attacks by *S59*, *Ms 26*, *Ms 25*, *Ms 23*, *MAS 552*, *MAS 564* and *MAS 553* are not successful. In the night the cruiser *Charybdis* and the destroyers *Eskimo* and *Somali* reach the convoy as reinforcements. The two destroyers are sent off to *Manchester* and then start the return journey after taking on the survivors. In the morning there are continuous air attacks: six He 111s have no success; 12 Ju 88s of II/LG 1 sink the transport *Waimarama* (12843 tons); eight Italian Ju 87s score hits on the transports *Dorset* and *Port Chalmers* and the tanker *Ohio*; 20 Ju 88s and Ju 87s again hit *Ohio*, *Rochester Castle* and *Dorset* with bombs; and five SM 79 torpedo aircraft have no success. In the evening 14 Ju 87s sink the damaged *Dorset* (10624 tons). The minesweepers *Hebe*, *Speedy*, *Hythe* and *Rye* from Malta meet the convoy with seven motor minesweepers and accompany the remaining transports *Melbourne Star*, *Port Chalmers* and *Rochester Castle* to Malta. Later, the badly damaged *Ohio* arrives, accompanied by the destroyers *Penn*, *Ledbury* and *Bramham*; the *Brisbane Star*, which remains temporarily behind near Sousse, follows on 14 Aug. The intervention of the Italian surface ships, the cruisers *Gorizia*, *Trieste*, *Bolzano*, *Eugenio di Savoia*, *Montecuccoli* and *Attendolo* and 11 destroyers (*Aviere*, *Geniere*, *Camicia Nera*, *Legionario*, *Ascari*, *Corsaro*, *Grecale*, *Maestrale*, *Gioberti*, *Oriani* and *Fuciliere*), planned for 13 Aug, has to be abandoned because insufficient air escort is available. On the return, the British submarine *Unbroken* (Lt Mars) torpedoes the cruisers *Attendolo* and *Bolzano* near the Aeolian Islands.

On 14 Aug, on the return, the British escort forces, comprising the cruisers *Kenya* and *Charybdis* and the destroyers *Ashanti*, *Intrepid*, *Icarus*, *Fury* and *Pathfinder*, are successively attacked by *MAS556*, the submarine *Granito*, 26 Ju 88s, 13 Ju 87s, 15 SM 84s and 20 SM 79s, but without result. In the afternoon the force joins the covering group which has returned to meet it N of Algiers. An attack by *U73* on the damaged *Nigeria* and four destroyers is unsuccessful. By 15 Aug all the ships have reached Gibraltar.

10 Aug–1 Sept Western Atlantic

The U-boats *U658*, *U598*, *U600*, *U553* and *U163* operate in the area of the Greater Antilles. Only *U600* (Lt-Cdr Zurmühlen) sinks a sailing ship of 130 tons. Otherwise the boats only attack convoys. On 13 Aug they attack WAT.13, on 13–14 Aug TAW.12 and on 17–18 Aug TAW.13 and PG.6 (see below).

11–21 Aug   Baltic
The first part of the second wave of Soviet submarines, *L-3*, *M-96*, *M-97* (sunk on the 'Seeigel' barrage on 14 Aug), *Shch-407*, *Shch-309* and *Lembit*, breaks through the mine barrages of the Gulf of Finland. On the way to Lavansaari, *Shch-405* sinks on an old Soviet barrage near Seiskari. The operation is supported by Soviet ground-attack aircraft, which sink the German motor minesweeper *R106* off Hungerburg on 16 Aug. The Soviet submarines are brought into the mine barrages by sweeper cutters and are at first covered by *MO* patrol cutters. Torpedo cutters attack the German-Finnish guard forces W of the barrages.

11–22 Aug   South Pacific
When news is received of the American landing on Guadalcanal, elements of the Combined Fleet are moved on 11 Aug from the Inland Sea to Truk. They include Adm Yamamoto with the battleship *Yamato* (F), the escort carrier *Taiyo* and the destroyers *Akebono*, *Sazanami* and *Ushio*; the 2nd Fleet (Vice-Adm Kondo); and the 3rd Fleet (Vice-Adm Nagumo). (For composition see 14 July 1942.) The 2nd DD Flotilla (Rear-Adm Tanaka) with the cruiser *Jintsu* and the destroyers *Kagero*, *Hagikaze*, *Maikaze*, *Urakaze*, *Isokaze* and *Hamakaze* is put under the command of the 8th Fleet in Rabaul.

On 16 Aug Capt Sato puts to sea from Truk with the above six destroyers and 916 men of the Ichiki Detachment of the Army on board. He lands them during the night 18–19 Aug E of the US bridgehead on Guadalcanal. But the force is annihilated when it attacks the positions of the much under-estimated 1st US Marine Div. The remainder of the Ichiki detachment with supplies follows on 16 Aug with two transports, escorted by *Jintsu* and the APDs *P34* and *P35* which are then joined by the destroyers *Umikaze*, *Kawakaze* and *Suzukaze*. They are followed by the fast convoys with the transport *Kinryu Maru* and the APDs *P1* and *P2* which have the 5th Yokosuka Special Landing Force on board. This is to be landed on 21 Aug. The three ships of the 17th DD Div return to Rabaul but *Kagero*, *Hagikaze* and *Maikaze* (4th DD Div), which remain behind, are attacked on 19 Aug by B-17 bombers coming from Espiritu Santo. *Hagikaze* is damaged by bomb hits and has to return with *Maikaze*.

On 20 Aug the US escort carrier *Long Island* flies off S of Guadalcanal the first 31 US Marine Corps fighters for Henderson Airfield. When *Kagero* reports attacks by carrier aircraft and air reconnaissance reports a US carrier force, the Japanese landing force is temporarily turned away so that the elements of the 2nd and 3rd Fleets, which have in the meantime put to sea, can come up to support the landing now postponed until 23 Aug. *Kagero* withdraws.

On 21–22 Aug the US transports *Alhena* and *Fomalhaut* with the destroyers *Blue*, *Helm* and *Henley* bring supplies to Guadalcanal. In screening the unloading, *Blue* is torpedoed in Savo Sound by the Japanese destroyer *Kawakaze* which comes up from a reconnaissance sortie S of Guadalcanal to relieve *Kagero*. She has to be abandoned on the following day.

11–30 Aug   Arctic
Operation 'Wunderland'. From 11 to 17 Aug, to prepare for this German operation against the Siberian sea route, *U255* (Lt-Cdr Reche) reconnoitres Spitzbergen together with a Bv 138 flying boat equipped with additional fuel tanks and *U435* (Lt-Cdr Strelow) disembarks there the weather observation detachment 'Knospe'.

On 16 Aug the pocket-battleship *Admiral Scheer* (Capt Meendsen-Bohlken) sets out from Narvik to the Barents Sea and, following ice reconnaissance by *U601* (Lt-Cdr Grau) and *U251* (Lt-Cdr Timm), passes Cape Zhelania on 19 Aug and proceeds eastwards through the Kara Sea. The ship's aircraft reports parts of three convoys with the ice-breakers *Krassin* and *Lenin* on 20 Aug near the island of Krakovka and on 23 Aug in the Vilkitski Strait. Mist and ice prevent an approach. On 25 Aug *Scheer* encounters NW of the Nordenskjöld Archipelago the Soviet ice-breaker *Sibiryakov* (Capt Kacharev), which is sunk after a courageous defence. On 27 Aug *Scheer* attacks the main base of Dikson and badly damages the shore installations and the patrol ship *SKR-19/Dezhnev* and the steamer *Revolutsioner*. On 30 Aug *Scheer* returns to Narvik. Of the two U-boats operating in the Kara Sea, *U601* sinks one ship E of Dikson on 24 Aug; and of the boats stationed W of Novaya Zemlya, *U209* (Lt-Cdr Brodda) sinks the tugs *Nord* and *Komsomolets* with the lighters *B-III* and *P-IV* W of the Yugor Strait on 17 Aug and *U456* (Lt-Cdr Teichert) tries in vain to torpedo the ice-breaker *SKR-18/Fedor Litke* off Belusha on 20 Aug. *U255* and *U209* shell the wireless stations at Cape Zhelania and Khodovarikha on 25 and 28 Aug respectively.

From 13 to 23 Aug the US cruiser *Tuscaloosa* with the destroyers *Rodman*, *Emmons* and *Onslaught* (British) proceeds to Murmansk with ground personnel, supplies and torpedoes for two squadrons of Hampdens of RAF Bomber Command which are being transferred to Northern Russia. They are met by the British destroyers *Marne* and *Martin* off Kola.

Operation 'Zar'. The German minelayer *Ulm* (Lt-Cdr Biet) is to lay mines in the area N of Cape Zhelania after the return of *Scheer*. After unloading, *Tuscaloosa*, *Emmons* and *Rodman* set out from Murmansk to return to Scapa Flow on 24 Aug. *Marne*, *Martin* and *Onslaught* are detached to make a sortie to the Norwegian polar coast. In the course of this sortie they encounter *Ulm* on 25 Aug S of Bear Island and sink her.

Of the simultaneously planned mining operations 'Peter' with *U589* (Lt-Cdr Horrer) off the Matochkin Strait and 'Paul' with *U591* off the Yugor Strait, only 'Peter' can be carried out (28 Aug). The Soviet patrol ship *SKR-23/Musson* is lost on the mines.

11 Aug–3 Sept   Western Atlantic
After refuelling from *U463* (Cdr Wolfbauer), *U564* (Lt-Cdr Suhren) and *U654* (Lt Forster) arrive in the Caribbean with *U162* (Cdr* Wattenberg). *U654* falls victim on 22 Aug to a USAAF aircraft off the Panama Canal. After the operation against the convoy TAW(S) on 19 Aug, *U162* sinks three ships of 24759 tons and *U564* one of 8176 tons.

12 Aug   Western Atlantic
U508 (Lt-Cdr Staats), which operates off Cuba from the end of July to 18 Aug, attacks a Key West–Havana convoy and sinks two ships of 2710 tons.

12 Aug   Mediterranean
The Italian destroyer *Malocello* (Cdr* Tona) lays the mine barrage St.1 with 104 mines in two sections off Cape Bon. Escort is provided by the torpedo boat *Climene*. *Malocello* meets British Force Y—destroyers *Matchless* and *Badsworth* and transports *Troilus* and *Orari*—on the way from Malta to Gibraltar, each thinking the other to be Vichy French.

12–13 Aug   Black Sea
The Soviet cruiser *Krasny Krym* and the destroyer *Nezamozhnik* evacuate a regiment of the 32nd Guards Rifle Div from Novorossisk to Batum.

12–18 Aug   Mediterranean
The British submarine *Porpoise* (Cdr Bennington) lays a mine barrage on 12 Aug

off the Cyrenaican coast on which the Italian torpedo boat *Cantore* is lost on 22 Aug. In attacks on 12 Aug on a steamer escorted by the torpedo boat *Montanari* and on 16 Aug on a convoy with the destroyers *Mitragliere* and *Bersagliere* and the torpedo boats *Calliope* and *Castore*, *Porpoise* sinks two ships of 10623 tons. In a further attack on 19 Aug, the submarine is assailed by depth charges from the torpedo boats *Lince* and *Sagittario*. On 17 Aug *Turbulent* (Cdr Linton) torpedoes near Navarino the transport *Nino Bixio* (7137 tons), escorted by the destroyers *Da Recco* and *Saetta* and the torpedo boats *Castore*, *Orione* and *Polluce*. The transport has 2000 prisoners on board, of whom 336 perish.

Near Pantelleria *P44/United* (Lt Roxburgh) torpedoes the transport *Rosolino Pilo* (8326 tons) escorted by the destroyers *Maestrale* and *Gioberti*. The transport is later sunk by torpedo aircraft from Malta. Off Sardinia *P211/Safari* (Cdr Bryant) sinks two ships of 5075 tons.

12–19 Aug   South Pacific
Japanese reinforcement convoys from Rabaul to Buna. On 12–13 Aug three transports with the cruiser *Tatsuta*, the destroyers *Yunagi* and *Yuzuki* and submarine-chasers land the Nankai Detachment. On 16–17 Aug the same force brings elements of the South Sea Detachment of the Army and of the 25th Naval Air Flotilla ashore. On 19 Aug a third convoy, comprising two transports, suffers slight damage from US air attacks. The Japanese make air attacks on Milne Bay to cover the operations.

13–14 Aug   Western Atlantic
In the Windward Passage, *U658* (Lt-Cdr Senkel) sights two convoys meeting each other. From convoy WAT.13 (Escort Commander on the British destroyer *Havelock*), she sinks one ship of 1311 tons but then operates on the northbound TAW.12, which comprises 47 ships escorted by the destroyer HMS *Churchill* (Lt-Cdr Fitzgerald RN) with the trawler HMS *Ruby*, the US Coast Guard cutter *Lemaire*, the corvette *Agassiz*, the submarine-chasers *PC475* and *PC505* and the minesweeper *YMS50*. From this convoy *U600* (Lt-Cdr Zurmühlen) sinks two ships of 9552 tons on 14 Aug. Despite reinforcement of the escort by the new US destroyers *Fletcher* and *O'Bannon*, *U598* (Lt-Cdr Holtorf) is able to sink two more ships of 9295 tons on 14 Aug and to torpedo one tanker of 6197 tons.

13–27 Aug   North Atlantic
On 13 Aug *U755*, *U438*, *U705*, *U373*, *U660*, *U569*, *U596*, *U176*, *U256*, *U174* and

U605 (coming from the SC.94 operation as well as new outbound boats), and later *U135* and *U432*, take up a new patrol line 'Lohs' to search for convoy SC.95 located by the B-Service. On 15 Aug *U256* (Lt-Cdr Loewe) sights the convoy SC.95—27 ships with EG.A3 comprising the destroyer *Schenck*, the Coast Guard cutter *Spencer*, the Canadian corvettes *Bittersweet*, *Collingwood*, *Mayflower* and *Trillium* and the RN corvettes *Snowflake* and *Wallflower*—but contact is soon lost because an ON convoy had been expected. Attacks by *U256* and *U605* fail. *U705* (Lt-Cdr Horn) sinks one ship of 3279 tons. On 16 Aug *U596* (Lt-Cdr Jahn) sinks a straggler of 4966 tons. On 22 Aug *U135* (Lt-Cdr Praetorius) sights by chance the convoy ONS.122 routed by C-in-C Western Approaches S of the 'Lohs' group. It includes 36 ships and has with it EG.B6 with the destroyer HMS *Viscount* (Lt-Cdr Waterhouse)—equipped with HF/DF, radar Type 271 and 'Hedgehog'—the Norwegian corvettes *Potentilla*, *Montbretia*, *Eglantine* and *Acanthus* and the rescue ship *Stockport*. *U135* and *U660*, which are in contact, are located by HF/DF on 23 Aug and on 24 Aug are driven off. In rainy weather, nine U-boats come into the area of the convoy during the night 24–25 Aug. *U605* (Lt-Cdr Schütze) sinks two ships of 8180 tons and is then damaged by depth charges from *Eglantine*. *U176* (Lt-Cdr Dierksen) and *U438* (Lt-Cdr Franzius), which shortly afterwards attack simultaneously, each sink one ship of 7454 tons and 1598 tons respectively. Mist impedes the operation and causes contact to be lost. *U256*, which has suffered damage in a depth charge attack by *Potentilla* and *Viscount*, is heavily bombed on 31 Aug (see 31 Aug–2 Sept) in the Bay of Biscay when she returns and is out of action for more than a year. *U705* is sunk in the Bay of Biscay on 3 Sept. The 'Lohs' group proceeds southwards to refuel from *U174* (three boats) and *U462* (six).

14 Aug   South Atlantic
The auxiliary cruiser *Schiff 28/Michel* sinks the British freighter *Arabistan* (5874 tons) in the South Atlantic.

14 Aug   South Pacific
The US submarine *S39* is lost by grounding off Russell Island.

14 Aug–28 Sept   Baltic
Of the Soviet submarines of the second wave which have broken through the German mine barrages, *L-3* (Capt 3rd Class Grishchenko) sinks the steamer *C F Liljevalch* (5492 tons) from a Swedish convoy W of Gotland and lays a mine barrage on 23 Aug

off the Bay of Pomerania, on which one ship of 5798 tons probably sinks. Further torpedo attacks have no success. Of the remaining boats, *M-96* (Lt-Cdr Marinesko) operates near Porkkala (one miss), *Shch-407* (Capt 3rd Class Afanasev) on the Baltic Coast (one miss), *Shch-309* and *Shch-308* in the Aaland Sea, *S-13* in the Gulf of Bothnia and *Lembit* off Utö. *Shch-309* (Capt 3rd Class Kabo) sinks one ship of 695 tons and misses two, *S-13* (Lt-Cdr Malanchenko) sinks two of 3704 tons and misses one and *Lembit* (Capt 3rd Class Matiyasevich) damages one of 2302 tons and misses two.

During operations to support submarines forcing the mine barrages on 24 Aug, the torpedo boat *Burya* and the minesweeper *T-204 Fugas* are sunk by mines near Suursaari.

15 Aug   South Pacific
The US fast transports *Colhoun*, *Gregory*, *Little* and *McKean* bring supplies for the first time to Guadalcanal.

15 Aug–26 Sept   Indian Ocean
In the Arabian Sea, the Japanese submarine *I-29* (Cdr* Izu) reconnoitres with her aircraft over the Seychelles on 19 Aug and then up to 22 Sept sinks four ships of 23303 tons. *I-27* cruises without success off East Africa and *I-162* in the Bay of Bengal. In the area off Ceylon, *I-165* (Cdr Torisu) sinks one ship of 5237 tons and *I-166* has no success.

16 Aug   English Channel
The German 10th MMS Flotilla lays a flanking mine barrage off Calais and is attacked by the British *MGB330*, *MGB331*, *MGB609*, *MGB6* and *MGB10*. All boats are heavily damaged but *MGB330* sinks the German motor minesweeper *R184* by ramming.

The German MDS *Sperrbrecher 60/Elster* is beached after hitting a mine off Den Helder.

16–17 Aug   Black Sea
The Soviet cruiser *Krasny Krym* and destroyer *Nezamozhnik* evacuate 1850 men and 60 tons of supplies from Novorossisk to Batum.

16–18 Aug   Mediterranean
Operation 'Baritone'. British Force H, comprising the carrier *Furious*, the cruiser *Charybdis* and 12 destroyers, sets out from Gibraltar for the area S of the Balearics and flies off 32 Spitfire fighters to Malta. All except three land safely. The British submarines *Otus*, *Rorqual* and *Clyde* bring aviation petrol, torpedoes and ammunition to Malta. The Italian submarines *Alagi*, *Asci-*

anghi, *Asteria*, *Avorio*, *Bronzo* and *Porfido* report no contacts.

16–20 Aug   Central Atlantic
U653 (Lt-Cdr Feiler) of the 'Blücher' group, which is assembling to proceed to Freetown, reports the convoy SL.118. *U566*, *U214*, *U406*, *U594*, *U333* and *U590* are directed to it. On 17 Aug *U566* (Lt Remus) sinks one ship of 6607 tons; *U214* (Lt-Cdr G Reeder) sinks two ships of 13840 tons on 18 Aug and torpedoes the auxiliary cruiser *Cheshire* belonging to the escort. The U-boats are driven off by the air escort provided by Liberator bombers from Cornwall on 18 Aug and *U653* is damaged by Liberator 'F' of No 120 Sqn (Sqn Ldr Bulloch) which has already damaged the returning *U89* on 16 Aug. On 19 Aug only *U406* (Lt-Cdr Dieterichs) is able to attack, sinking one ship of 7452 tons. *U333* (Lt-Cdr Cremer) is damaged by depth charges from a corvette. The operation is broken off when contact is lost.

17 Aug   Mediterranean
U83 (Lt-Cdr Kraus) sinks a British transport (5875 tons) off Port Said.

17 Aug   Pacific
The 2nd Raider Battalion, landed by the US submarines *Argonaut* and *Nautilus*, carries out a raid on the Gilbert Island of Makin.

17–20 Aug   Western Atlantic
On 17 Aug *U658* (Lt-Cdr Senkel) sights S of Cuba the convoy PG.6 (23 ships escorted by the US destroyers *Goff* and *Tattnall* and the submarine-chasers *SC497* and *SC530*) and sinks two ships of 10835 tons and torpedoes one of 6466 tons. That evening PG.6 joins up with convoy TAW.13 off Guantanamo and then consists of 36 ships with the destroyers USS *Breckinridge* and *Goff*, the corvettes HMS *Pimpernel* and USS *Spry*, the submarine-chasers USS *PC431*, *PC460*, *PY20* and later the *Tattnall* and *SC530*. From the combined convoy, *U553* (Cdr Thurmann) sinks three ships of 16980 tons in two approaches. *U163* (Cdr Engelmann) shadows the convoy into the Yucatan Strait but is unable to attack.

18 Aug   Bay of Biscay
The German patrol trawler *V406* sinks on a mine SW of the Gironde estuary.

18 Aug–3 Sept   Western Atlantic
Off Trinidad, *U564* (Lt-Cdr Suhren) sights the convoy TAW(S) with 15 ships escorted by the corvettes HMS *Clarkia* and USS *Courage*, the US Coast Guard cutters *Antietam* and *Marion* and the submarine-chasers *PC482*, *PC492*, *SC504* and *SC514*. After an attack by *U162* (Cdr* Wattenberg) on 19 Aug in the area of Grenada (one ship of 5722 tons sunk), *U564* attacks and sinks two ships of 12909 tons. Further attempts to

attack are frustrated. On 3 Sept *U162* is sunk by the destroyers *Vimy*, *Pathfinder* and *Quentin* escorting a convoy.

19 Aug   English Channel
Operation 'Jubilee': British raid on Dieppe. Landing of 6100 men, in all, of the 4th and 6th Bdes of the 2nd Canadian Div (Maj-Gen Roberts) and the 3rd and 4th Commandos of the Royal Navy with tanks and strong air support both sides of Dieppe, transported on the infantry landing ships *Prins Albert*, *Princess Beatrix*, *Invicta*, *Queen Emma*, *Princess Astrid*, *Glengyle*, *Prince Charles*, *Prince Leopold* and *Duke of Wellington* and covered by the destroyers *Calpe*, *Garth*, *Berkeley*, *Albrighton*, *Bleasdale*, *Brocklesby*, *Slazak* (Polish) and *Fernie*, the minesweepers *Alresford*, *Bangor*, *Blackpool*, *Bridlington*, *Bridport*, *Rhyl*, *Sidmouth* and *Tenby* (9th MS Flotilla) and *Blyth*, *Clacton*, *Eastbourne*, *Felixtowe*, *Ilfracombe*, *Polruan* and *Stornoway* (13th MS Flotilla), the gunboat *Locust* and many SGBs, MGBs, MLs etc—in all 252 ships, including landing craft. In approaching, the eastern landing group encounters a German coastal convoy in the dark and in the engagement the landing craft of the group are scattered, the leading boat *SGB5* is set on fire and the German *UJ1404* is sunk. Inf Regt 71 (Lt-Col Bartel) of the 302nd Inf Div, coastal artillery and fighter-bombers of the Air Cdrs 2 and 3 (Cols Huth and Ibel) are deployed against the forces which have gone ashore. By mid-day the remnants of the raiding party begin to re-embark, having sustained heavy losses. Thanks to fighter-bombers of 10/JG 2 (Lt Fritz Schröter) and of 10/JG 26 (Lt Paul Keller), the destroyer *Berkeley* is hit and, her back broken, has to be scuttled by *Albrighton*; *Calpe* is damaged. *Brocklesby* and *Fernie* are hit by gunfire and, in addition, 33 landing craft and small vessels, 106 aircraft and all 30 tanks are lost. Losses in personnel are 4350, including 1179 dead and 2190 taken prisoner. German losses are 48 aircraft and 591 men, including 311 dead and missing.

20 Aug   North Atlantic
The tanker U-boat *U464* is sunk on its maiden patrol SE of Iceland by the Catalina 'R' of VP-73 near convoy SN.73.

20 Aug–10 Oct   Western Atlantic
From 20 to 31 Aug *U165*, *U513* and *U517* operate off the Belle Isle Strait when *U517* (Lt-Cdr Hartwig) sights on 27 Aug the convoy SG.6F with the transport *Chatham* (5649 tons) and the US Coast Guard cutters *Mojave* and sinks *Chatham*. On 28 Aug *U165* (Cdr Hoffmann) attacks the following convoy SG.6S (five steamers and the US Coast Guard cutters *Algonquin*

and *Mohawk*) and sinks one steamer of 3304 tons and torpedoes one of 7252 tons. The wreck of the first is finished off by *U517*. On 31 Aug both boats enter the St Lawrence River and there *U517* sights on 3 Sept the convoys NL.6, escorted by the Canadian corvette *Weyburn* and the minesweeper *Clayoquot*, and LN.7, with the corvettes *Shawinigan* and *Trail*. *U517* outmanoeuvres *Weyburn* and sinks one ship of 1781 tons. On 6 Sept *U517* sights the convoy QS.33 (eight ships) escorted by the Canadian corvette *Arrowhead* and the minesweeper *Truro*, the MLs *Q.083* and *Q.065* and the yacht *Raccoon*. Whilst *Arrowhead* follows the U-boat, *U165* sinks one ship of 4729 tons and two hours later *Raccoon* (358 tons), which has stayed behind to save the crew. On 7 Sept *U517* sinks three ships of 10742 tons from the convoy, which is now strengthened by the minesweeper *Vegreville*. On 11 Sept *U517* attacks the corvette *Charlottetown* steaming on her own with the minesweeper *Clayoquot* and sinks the first. On 15 Sept *U517* sinks two ships of 4907 tons from the homebound convoy SQ.36 (escorted by the British destroyer *Salisbury*, *Arrowhead*, *Vegreville* and 3 MLs) and brings up *U165* which sinks two ships of 10292 tons in the morning of 16 Sept and torpedoes one of 4570 tons. *U165* then starts the homeward journey. *U517* has no success in two further attacks on convoys in the Gulf of St Lawrence and evades a ramming attack by the minesweeper *Georgian* from convoy SQ.38 on 21 Sept. *U513* (Cdr Rüggeberg) in the meantime continues to operate in the waters around Newfoundland, enters the roads of St Johns on 5 Sept, sinks two ships of 12789 tons and torpedoes another of 7174 tons on 29 Sept. *U165* is lost, probably on a British mine, off her own base.

21–25 Aug   North Sea
The German minelayers *Roland*, *Kaiser* and *Skagerrak* and the minesweepers *M82*, *M102* and *M20* lay two mine barrages, 'Eleanor' and '5.Kolonne' in the 'Westwall' area.

21 Aug–17 Sept   Pacific
Off North East Honshu, the US submarine *Guardfish* (Lt-Cdr Klakring) sinks five ships of 16708 tons and two fishery vessels. Off Japan, *Cuttlefish* (Lt-Cdr Hottel) torpedoes one ship of 6534 tons and near Formosa *Haddock* (Lt-Cdr Taylor) sinks two ships of 8585 tons, *Growler* (Lt-Cdr Gilmore) the naval transport *Kashino* (10360 tons), three steamers and one patrol boat of 10974 tons and *Grouper* (Lt-Cdr McGregor) two ships of 11123 tons, including the transport *Lisbon Maru* with 1800 British prisoners of whom only a few are rescued.

22 Aug West Atlantic
In thick fog off Nova Scotia, while accompanying a troop convoy, the US destroyer *Buck* is damaged in a collision with a troopship and the destroyer *Ingraham* is lost in a collision with the oiler *Chemungo*.

23 Aug English Channel
Off the Schelde estuary, the auxiliary minesweeper *M3206* is mined and beached; it is a total loss.

23–26 Aug Central Pacific
A Japanese force, consisting of the cruiser *Yubari*, the destroyers *Yuzuki*, *Oite*, *Asanagi* and *Yunagi* and other auxiliary ships, shells the island of Nauru on 23 Aug, which is then occupied. On 26 Aug the same force occupies Ocean Island.

23–31 Aug South Pacific
Sea and air battle E of the Solomons. The Japanese plan (Operation 'KA') is to land 1500 men on Guadalcanal under cover of the Combined Fleet. On 23 Aug two Japanese forces are to intercept the US carrier groups E of the Solomons after they have been diverted by a special force. The main body (Vice-Adm Kondo) comprises the cruisers *Atago*, *Takao*, *Maya*, *Myoko*, *Haguro* and *Yura* and the destroyers *Asagumo*, *Yamagumo*, *Kuroshio*, *Oyashio* and *Hayashio* and a support force with the battleship *Mutsu*, the seaplane carrier *Chitose* and the destroyers *Natsugumo*, *Murasame*, *Harusame* and *Samidare*. The carrier force (Vice-Adm Nagumo) comprises the carriers *Shokaku* and *Zuikaku* and the destroyers *Akigumo*, *Yugumo*, *Makigumo*, *Kazegumo*, *Shikinami* and *Uranami* and a covering force with the battleships *Hiyei* and *Kirishima*, the cruisers *Kumano*, *Suzuya*, *Chikuma* and *Nagara* and the destroyers *Akizuki*, *Hatsukaze*, *Maikaze*, *Nowake*, *Tanikaze* and *Yukikaze*. The diversionary force (Rear-Adm Hara) comprises the cruiser *Tone*, the carrier *Ryujo* and the destroyers *Amatsukaze* and *Tokitsukaze*. The US carrier groups of TF.61 (Vice-Adm Fletcher) are 61.1, comprising the carrier *Saratoga*, the cruisers *Australia* (Rear-Adm Crutchley), *Hobart*, *Minneapolis* and *New Orleans* and the destroyers *Phelps*, *Farragut*, *Worden*, *MacDonough* and *Dale*; 61.2 (Rear-Adm Kinkaid), comprising the carrier *Enterprise*, the battleship *North Carolina*, the cruisers *Portland* (Rear-Adm Tisdale) and *Atlanta* and the destroyers *Balch*, *Benham*, *Maury*, *Ellet*, *Grayson* and *Monssen*; and 61.3 (Rear-Adm Noyes), comprising the carrier *Wasp*, the cruisers *San Juan* (Rear-Adm Scott) *San Francisco* and *Salt Lake City* and the destroyers *Farenholt*, *Aaron Ward*, *Buchanan*, *Lang*, *Stack*, *Sterett* and *Selfridge*.
Under cover of the operations of the

Japanese forces mentioned against the US carrier groups, the Japanese landing force (Rear-Adm Tanaka), with the cruiser *Jintsu*, the destroyers *Suzukaze*, *Umikaze* and *Uzuki*, the APDs *P1*, *P2*, *P34* and three transports, is to put the troops ashore on Guadalcanal after the island has been shelled during the night 23–24 Aug by the destroyers *Kagero*, *Isokaze*, *Kawakaze*, *Mutsuki* and *Yayoi* whilst the cruisers *Chokai*, *Aoba*, *Kinugasa* and *Furutaka* take up a covering position in the NW. Simultaneously the submarines *I-121*, *I-123* and *Ro-34* occupy the approaches to Guadalcanal (*I-121* is damaged by carrier aircraft in the process). From the 3rd SM Flotilla, *I-11*, *I-174* and *I-175* take up a patrol line W of the Solomons and the 1st SM Flotilla (Rear-Adm Yamazaki), comprising *I-9*, *I-15*, *I-17*, *I-19*, *I-26* and *I-31*, E of Santa Cruz.
On 23 Aug US air reconnaissance from Ndeni locates the Japanese landing force. The attack force from *Saratoga* flies off and, after unsuccessful attempts, lands on Henderson Field. TG.61.3, because of fuel shortage, has to retire to the S for replenishment. During the night 23–24 Aug the Japanese destroyer *Kagero* shells Henderson with little result. *Saratoga*'s aircraft return to the carrier in the morning.
On 24 Aug US air reconnaissance locates the *Ryujo* force. *Saratoga* flies off her attack force, which sinks *Ryujo* with bombs and torpedoes and damages *Tone*. In the meantime Japanese air reconnaissance sights the US carrier groups. *Shokaku* and *Zuikaku* fly off their attack forces. They secure three hits on *Enterprise* in spite of strong US fighter cover over the carriers. *Enterprise*'s attack force does not find the enemy. The aircraft from *Saratoga* damage the seaplane carrier *Chitose*.
During the night 24–25 Aug the Japanese destroyers *Isokaze*, *Kagero*, *Kawakaze*, *Mutsuki* and *Yayoi* shell Henderson Field and then join the Tanaka force. This is attacked in the morning of 25 Aug by US Marine Corps aircraft from Henderson and *Kinryu Maru* is sunk and *Jintsu* damaged. *Mutsuki* is sunk 40m N of Santa Isabel by a USAAF B-17 bomber (the first such success during the Solomons campaign). The Japanese break off the operation without seeking a decision. Of the Japanese submarines, *I-17* (Cdr* Nishino) is damaged on 27 Aug by an aircraft from *Wasp*. On 30 Aug the aircraft from *I-19* (Cdr Kinashi) reconnoitres over Santa Cruz and on 31 Aug *I-26* (Cdr* Yokota) attacks TG.61.1 and torpedoes *Saratoga*.
The Japanese 2nd DD Flotilla continues to

dispatch supply transports to Guadalcanal. On 26 Aug the destroyers *Suzukaze*, *Umikaze* and *Isokaze* set out with 390 men from Shortland but are recalled on 27 Aug in order to land them jointly with the newly arrived 20th DD Div (Capt Arita) which has elements of the Kawaguchi Detachment from Borneo on board. Owing to inadequate co-ordination, the 20th DD Div is attacked by US Marine Corps dive-bombers from *Enterprise* and shore-based aircraft N of Guadalcanal when on its own on 28 Aug. *Asagiri* is sunk, *Shirakumo* and *Yugiri* severely damaged and *Amagiri* slightly damaged. On 28 Aug *Umikaze*, *Kawakaze*, *Suzukaze* and *Isokaze* (Capt Murakami), which have returned, again set out, followed by *Fubuki*, *Hatsuyuki* and *Murakumo*, and land their troops near Cape Taivu during the night 28–29 Aug. Japanese aircraft sink the APD *Colhoun* from a small US supply force comprising one transport and the APDs *Little* and *Colhoun*. During the night 29–30 Aug *Yudachi*, *P1* and *P34* land troops. During the night 31 Aug–1 Sept 1000 men of the Kawaguchi Detachment are landed from the destroyers *Kagero*, *Fubuki*, *Hatsuyuki*, *Murakumo*, *Umikaze*, *Kawakaze*, *Suzukaze* and *Amagiri*. In trying to attack a US reinforcement convoy, the Japanese submarine *I-123* is sunk on 29 Aug by the US destroyer-minesweeper *Gamble*.

24 Aug–11 Sept South Pacific
Battle for Milne Bay. During the night 24–25 Aug seven Japanese assault boats from Buna land 1318 men of the 5th Sasebo Special Landing Force on Goodenough Island off the Papuan Peninsula. The next night two transports land 1171 men of the 5th Kure and 5th Sasebo Special Landing Forces in the eastern part of Milne Bay at the southern extremity of the Papuan Peninsula. Escort is provided by Rear-Adm Matsuyama with the cruisers *Tatsuta* and *Tenryu* and by the destroyers *Tanikaze*, *Urakaze* and *Hamakaze* and the submarine-chasers *Ch22* and *Ch24*. On 27 Aug 775 men of the 3rd Kure Special Landing Force arrive on board the destroyers *Arashi*, *Murakumo* and *Yayoi* and three submarine-chasers, escorted by Matsuyama's force. After initial successes, the Japanese forces are unable to overcome the strong resistance put up by Australian and American units. A Japanese cruiser sortie on 29 Aug cannot prevent them being repulsed. On 31 Aug the C-in-C of the 17th Army, Lt-Gen Hyakutake, orders that the army operations be concentrated against Guadalcanal and that Milne Bay be evacuated. Whilst the Australian destroyer *Arunta* and the sloop *Swan* bring reinforcements from Port

Moresby into Milne Bay and *Arunta* sinks (on 29 Aug) the Japanese submarine *Ro-33* after the torpedoing of a ship of 3310 tons, the Japanese cruisers and destroyers evacuate troops which have been landed. In the process *Tenryu* and the destroyer *Arashi* sink an Allied transport on 5 Sept. TF.44 (Rear-Adm Crutchley), which comprises the cruisers *Australia*, *Hobart* and *Phoenix* and the destroyers *Selfridge*, *Bagley*, *Henley*, *Helm* and *Patterson* and which sets out from Brisbane on 7 Sept to support the operations, is not able on 11 Sept to intercept the Japanese destroyers *Isokaze* and *Yayoi*, which have come up to help the evacuation of the Trobriand Islands. But the latter ship falls victim to the two US air attacks.

24 Aug–14 Oct   Indian Ocean
The Japanese *I-30* (Cdr* Endo) proceeds from Lorient as the first transport submarine to Penang without incident. She arrives there on 9 Sept but on her further journey she is lost with her cargo on a mine off Singapore on 14 Oct.

25 Aug   Western Atlantic
U558 (Lt-Cdr Krech) and *U164* (Cdr Fechner) each sink a straggler, of 1987 tons and 3780 tons respectively, from the convoy WAT.15 in the Caribbean.

25–29 Aug   Mediterranean
The British destroyers *Aldenham* and *Eridge* bombard the Daba area on the Egyptian coast. On 29 Aug *Eridge* is torpedoed by a German E-boat; though towed by *Aldenham* to Alexandria, she is a constructive total loss.

25–29 Aug   Central Atlantic
The convoy SL.119 is located by *U214* (Lt-Cdr G Reeder) of the 'Iltis' group which is proceeding southwards. The other three U-boats, *U566*, *U406* and *U107*, are directed to the convoy and also the favourably situated four boats of the 'Eisbär' group, *U68*, *U156*, *U172* and *U504*, which are proceeding to South Africa. On 26 Aug *U156* (Cdr Hartenstein) sinks a straggler (5941 tons). On orders from the Skl, the 'Eisbär' group continues its journey. *U566* (Lt Remus) sinks two ships of 14085 tons on 28 Aug and is then damaged by a depth charge pursuit. *U107* is driven off. On 29 Aug the other boats have to turn away.

26 Aug   Baltic
Off Vikalla Flat, the German A/S whaler *UJ1216* is sunk in an engagement with Soviet torpedo cutters.

26 Aug–15 Sept   Mediterranean
In the Eastern Mediterranean, *U375* (Lt-Cdr Könenkamp) destroys two ships of 6846 tons and two sailing ships. *U205*, *U371* and *U331* have no success.

27 Aug   Western Atlantic
In the Windward Passage, the convoy TAW.15, consisting of 21 ships escorted by the destroyer *Lea* (Cdr Walsh), the minelayer *Jan van Brakel*, the Canadian corvettes *Halifax*, *Oakville* and *Snowberry*, one PC and three SC submarine-chasers, is sighted by *U94* (Lt-Cdr Ites). The U-boat is damaged by depth charges dropped from a US Catalina of VP-92 and three times rammed by the corvette *Oakville* and sunk. In the meantime *U511* (Lt-Cdr Steinhoff) attacks the convoy, sinks two ships of 21999 tons and torpedoes a third ship of 8773 tons.

27 Aug   North Atlantic
From the outbound U-boats, the 'Vorwärts' group is formed on 27 Aug on the eastern side of the North Atlantic. To it belong *U609*, coming from Iceland, and *U407*, *U91*, *U411*, *U92*, *U659*, *U756*, *U409*, *U211* and *U604* (Lt-Cdr Höltring); the last has been stationed since 15 Aug in a waiting area and has sunk one ship of 7906 tons there. On 31 Aug *U609* (Lt Rudloff) sights the convoy SC.97—58 ships, escorted by EG.C2 comprising the RN destroyers *Burnham* (Lt-Cdr Taylor SOE) and Broadway and the corvettes *Brandon*, *Dauphin* *Drumbeller* and *Morden*—in the N of the patrol line. She attacks immediately and sinks two ships of 10228 tons but is then driven off. In the morning of 1 Sept there are six U-boats in the neighbourhood of the convoy, but attacks by *U604* and *U756* fail. By day the U-boats are driven off by Catalina flying boat 'B' (Lt Odell) of VP-73 from Iceland which damages *U91* slightly. *U756* (Lt-Cdr Harney) is sunk by the Canadian corvette *Morden*. During the night 1–2 Sept only *U91* is able to attack—unsuccessfully. By day the operation has to be broken off because of the strong air escort.

27 Aug–5 Sept   Mediterranean
The British submarine *P35/Umbra* (Lt-Cdr Maydon) sinks near Cape Spada the transport *Manfredo Campiero* (5463 tons) which is proceeding to Tobruk, accompanied by the destroyer *Da Recco* and the torpedo boats *Climene* and *Polluce*. *Rorqual* (Lt-Cdr Napier) lays a mine barrage near Corfu on 30 Aug and sinks by torpedo one ship of 5311 tons. On 4 Sept a convoy from Piraeus to Tobruk with the torpedo boats *Castore*, *Lupo* and *Polluce* is attacked by torpedo aircraft and the British submarine *Thrasher* (Lt-Cdr Mackenzie); the latter sinks one ship of 1589 tons and the aircraft one more steamer and *Polluce*. Off the Cyrenaican coast, the British submarine *Traveller* (Lt-Cdr St John) sinks a ship of 1245 tons escorted by the torpedo boat *Montanari*.

28 Aug–11 Oct   Pacific
The Japanese submarine *I-25* (Cdr* Tagami) carries out a reconnaissance operation to the American West Coast, and on 28–29 Aug and 9–10 Sept her aircraft drops incendiary bombs in the forests of Oregon. At the beginning of Oct the boat sinks two ships of 13691 tons and on 11 Oct attacks with her last torpedo the Soviet submarines *L-15* and *L-16* which are proceeding from Dutch Harbor to San Francisco. She sinks *L-16*.

29 Aug   English Channel
Off Ostend, the German auxiliary minesweeper *M3606* is sunk by air attack.

29 Aug–24 Sept   North Atlantic
After the operation against convoy SL.119, *U107*, *U214*, *U406*, *U590*, *U87* and *U333* assemble W of Lisbon. Only *U107* (Lt-Cdr Gelhaus) is successful, sinking two ships of 8565 tons. On 8 Sept the boats proceed in line abreast to the area of the Cape Verde Islands but they find no targets. From 25 to 27 Sept they are refuelled from *U460* (Lt-Cdr Schnoor) and four boats then occupy operational areas off Freetown.

30 Aug–25 Sept   North Pacific
On the news of a US landing on the Aleutian island of Adak, the Japanese submarines *Ro-61*, *Ro-62* and *Ro-64* are directed there. *Ro-61* (Lt-Cdr Tokutomi) torpedoes on 30 Aug the aircraft tender *Casco* but is sunk on 31 Aug by the US destroyer *Reid* supported by a Catalina from VP-43. In the following weeks the submarines *Ro-62*, *Ro-63*, *Ro-64*, *Ro-68* and, from the middle of Sept, *Ro-62*, *Ro-65* and *Ro-67* operate in turns in the area of the Aleutians.

31 Aug   Black Sea
Off Novorossisk, *S102* (Lt-Cdr Töniges) sinks a tanker of 3000 tons and *S28* (Lt-Cdr Künzel) the Soviet freighter *Zhan-Tomp* (1988 tons).

31 Aug–3 Sept   Bay of Biscay
During air operations against the U-boat transit routes on 31 Aug, the Whitleys 'B' and 'O', of Nos 502 and 51 Sqns respectively, damage *U256* on its way to France. The U-boat is so heavily damaged that it is rebuilt as an AA submarine. On 1 Sept Sunderlands 'U' and 'R' of No 10 Sqn RAAF damage the Italian submarine *Giuliani*, whose captain, Cdr Raccanelli, is killed; after being further damaged on 2 Sept by Polish Wellington 'A' (Fg Off Kucharski) from No 304 Sqn, *Giuliani* enters the Spanish port of Santander. On 3 Sept Whitley 'P' of No 77 Sqn sinks *U705* on its first patrol.

31 Aug–14 Sept   North Atlantic

From the 'Stier' group, formed from out bound boats during the SC.97 operation and the boats coming from the SC.97 operation, a new 'Vorwärts' group is formed from 4 Sept consisting of *U96*, *U594*, *U608*, *U380*, *U404*, *U584*, *U211*, *U218*, *U407*, *U91*, *U411*, *U92* and *U659*. In the evening of 9 Sept *U584* (Lt-Cdr Deecke) reports the convoy ON.127, comprising 32 ships escorted by EG.C4 with the Canadian destroyers *St Croix* (Lt-Cdr Dobson) and *Ottawa* and the corvettes *Amherst*, *Arvida*, *Sherbrooke* and *Celandine* (RN). Contact is lost in the night and is only regained at midday on 10 Sept. *U96* (Lt Hellriegel) sinks two ships of 10554 tons in an underwater attack and torpedoes one more of 12190 tons. During the night 10–11 Sept successive attacks are made: *U659* (Lt-Cdr Stock) torpedoes one ship of 8029 tons (later sunk by *U584*), *U404* (Lt-Cdr v Bülow) torpedoes one ship of 7147 tons, *U608* (Lt Struckmeier) misses, *U218* (Lt-Cdr Becker) torpedoes one ship of 7361 tons, *U92* (Lt Oelrich) misses and *U594* (Lt Mumm) misses. The escort is greatly impeded by the failure of all radar equipment. By day on 11 Sept *U96* sinks one trawler of 415 tons with gunfire in the area of the convoy. During 11–12 Sept the U-boats attack successively: *U584* sinks one ship of 4885 tons, *U380* (Lt-Cdr Röther) misses, *U211* (Lt-Cdr Hause) torpedoes two ships of 20646 tons (both later finished off by *U608*), *U92* misses *Ottawa* and *U404* torpedoes one ship of 9272 tons. The escort, which has damaged *U659* on 11 Sept, is able to drive off the U-boats throughout the day on 12 Sept, but in the darkness they come up again. The attacks by *U407* (Lt Brüller) and *U594* the night 12–13 Sept fail. By day one straggler of 6131 tons falls victim to *U594*. Air escort sent from Newfoundland drives some of the U-boats off. During the night 13–14 Sept the destroyers *Witch* (RN) and *Annapolis* from the WLEF arrive and *U91* (Lt-Cdr Walkerling) sinks the destroyer *Ottawa* (Lt-Cdr Rutherford) in two attacks. *U92* misses the convoy and *U411* (Lt Litterscheid) one corvette. Because of the proximity of air bases in Newfoundland, the operation has to be ended on 14 Sept. It is the only instance in 1942–43 when all the U-boats deployed against a North Atlantic convoy fire their torpedoes.

1 Sept   Baltic

On Lake Ladoga, the Soviet torpedo boat *Purga* is sunk in shallow water by German air attack. The machinery is salved and installed in the damaged sister-ship *Vikhr*.

1–9 Sept   Black Sea

Battle for the Taman Peninsula. The breakthrough of the Rumanian Cavalry Div to Anapa on 31 Aug has prevented parts of the Soviet 47th Army from withdrawing from the Taman Peninsula, into which the Rumanian 5th and 6th Cavalry Divs penetrate. On 2 Sept the German 46th Inf Div is landed on the N and W side of the Taman Peninsula (Operation 'Blücher') in 24 MFPs (naval store ferries) of the 1st Landing Flotilla (Lt-Cdr Giele), Siebel ferries and engineers' landing and assault boats under the protection of the 3rd MMS Flotilla (Cdr Hölzerkopf) and the Luftwaffe. The Rumanian 3rd Div follows. From 2 to 5 Sept Soviet warships and transports, under the commander of the Azov Flotilla (Rear-Adm S G Gorshkov), including the patrol ship *Shtorm* and the gunboats *Oktyabr* and *Rostov-Don*, evacuate the bulk of the Army and naval forces from the south coast of the Taman Peninsula to Novorossisk. During the nights of 2, 3 and 5 Sept the 1st MTB Flotilla (Lt-Cdr Christiansen), comprising *S102* (Lt-Cdr Töniges), *S28* (Lt-Cdr Künzel), *S27* (Lt-Cdr Büchting) and *S72* (Lt Schneider), attacks the loading points and reports 19 successes. *S27* is sunk by her own torpedo. There follows the battle for Novorossisk, which is defended against the attack of the German V Army Corps (125th, 73rd and 9th Inf Divs) by the Soviet 77th Rifle Div and the 14th, 142nd, 83rd and 2nd Naval Infantry Bdes under Rear-Adm Kholostyakov. Despite fire support for the defenders from the Soviet flotilla leader *Kharkov* (Capt 2nd Class Melnikov) and the destroyer *Soobrazitelny* (Capt 3rd Class Vorkov) on 1, 2 and 4 Sept, German units enter the outskirts of Novorossisk on 5 Sept, capture the centre of the city on 6 Sept and occupy the harbour area on 9 Sept. The elements of the Soviet forces driven to the W are evacuated to Gelendzhik by sea.

1–9 Sept   South Pacific

Continuation of Japanese attempts to supply and reinforce Guadalcanal. In this the following units are deployed as fast transports: the aircraft depot ships *Akitsushima* and *Nisshin*, the minelayer *Tsugaru* and the 3rd DD Flotilla (Rear-Adm Hashimoto) with the cruiser *Sendai* and the destroyers *Isonami*, *Uranami*, *Shikinami* and *Ayanami* (19th DD Div), *Fubuki*, *Hatsuyuki* and *Murakumo* (11th DD Div) and *Amagiri* (from 20th DD Div) and the 4th DD Flotilla (Rear-Adm Takama) with the cruiser *Yura* and the destroyers *Yudachi*, *Harusame*, *Murasame* and *Samidare* (2nd DD Div), *Akatsuki*, *Ikazuchi* and *Inazuma* (6th DD Div) and *Ariake*, *Yugure*, *Shiratsuyu* and *Shigure* (27th DD Div) and also the 34th DD Div with *Akikaze*, *Hakaze* and *Tachikaze*.

In attacks by US B-17 bombers, *Akitsushima* and *Akikaze* are slightly damaged on 1 Sept and *Tsugaru* on 3 Sept. During the nights 4–5 Sept the 4th DD Flotilla brings the last elements of the Kawaguchi Detachment to Guadalcanal. Off Lunga Point, the covering force, consisting of the destroyers *Yudachi*, *Hatsuyuki* and *Murakumo*, encounters the patrolling US APDs *Gregory* and *Little* and sinks them after a brief engagement.

On 7 Sept the US APDs *McKean* and *Manley* land 600 men from Tulagi on Guadalcanal E of the Japanese landing area near Cape Taivu. They make a sortie in the rear of the Kawaguchi Detachment, which is preparing for an attack on 12 Sept, and by their raid upset the Japanese preparations. At the same time the transports *Bellatrix* and *Fuller* land supplies near Lunga Point. Japanese bombers from Rabaul are deployed without success against the transports on 8 Sept. In addition, the 3rd DD Flotilla with *Sendai* and eight destroyers sets out but is unable to find the transports during the night 8–9 Sept and, instead, shells Tulagi.

From the 1st Japanese SM Flotilla (see 23–31 Aug), operating further E of the Solomons, *I-9* reconnoitres over Nouméa with her aircraft on 4 Sept. On 6 Sept *I-11* (Cdr* Hichiji), command boat of the 3rd Flotilla, attacks US TF.18 (Rear-Adm Murray; see 9–23 Sept) which has arrived to relieve the *Saratoga* group and just misses the flagship, the carrier *Hornet*, whose aircraft are covering supply transports to Guadalcanal (see above). On 8 Sept *I-31* shells the island of Graciosa.

1 Sept–25 Oct   Western Atlantic

After unsuccessful mining operations off Chesapeake Bay (10 Sept) and off Charleston (18 Sept), *U69* (Lt Gräf) and *U455* (Lt-Cdr Giessler) operate S of Novia Scotia and near Cape Race, as well as in the Gulf of St Lawrence, where *U69* after several misses sinks on 9 Oct one ship of 2245 tons and on 13 Oct the ferry *Caribou* (2222 tons) from convoy NL.9 (escorted by the Canadian corvettes *Trail*, *Arrowhead* and *Shawinigan*; *U455* returns without success.

SE of Trinidad, *U175* (Lt-Cdr Bruns) sinks nine ships of 33426 tons and damages one of 2400 tons, *U512* (Lt-Cdr Wolfgang Schultze) sinks two of 14585 tons, *U514* (Lt-Cdr Auffermann) sinks five of 17354 tons and torpedoes one of 5458 tons, *U515* (Lt-Cdr Henke) sinks nine of 46782 tons and *U516* (Cdr Wiebe) sinks five of 29357 tons; in addition, *U512* and *U515* jointly sink one ship of 6034 tons. On 2 Oct *U512* is sunk by a USAAF B-18A bomber of the 99th BG from Trinidad.

2 Sept   North Sea
The German MDS *Sperrbrecher 64/Bitsch* is sunk by mine off Schiermonnikoog.

2 Sept   Baltic
The U-boat *U222* is sunk in the Danzig Bight following a collision with *U626* during training exercises.

4 Sept   Mediterranean
The Italian torpedo boat *Polluce* is damaged in an air attack 50 nautical miles N of Tobruk and sinks after a munitions explosion.

4–8 Sept   Arctic
Offensive mining operation with the destroyers *Richard Beitzen*, *Z29* and *Z30* off the Kara Strait.

5–8 Sept   Baltic
Break-out of the last part of the second wave of Soviet submarines, *S-13*, *Shch-308* and *Shch-323*, through the mine barrages. The last runs on to a mine and returns to Lavansaari with severe damage. *L-3* is met on return by patrol and minesweeping cutters. *S-13* (Lt-Cdr Malanchenko) sinks two ships of 3704 tons in the Botten Sea; *Shch-308* (Capt 3rd Class Kostylev) sinks one of 1467 tons and misses two off Utö.

6–25 Sept   North Atlantic
The boats of the 'Lohs' group, *U755*, *U373*, *U569*, *U176*, *U135* and *U432*, having refuelled from *U462* (Lt Vowe), form a new patrol line on 6 Sept on the western side of the North Atlantic. On 9 Sept *U755* (Lt-Cdr Göing) sinks the US weather observation ship *Muskeget* (1827 tons). From 13 Sept the boats *U410*, *U599* and *U259* also join the 'Lohs' group. Following a decoded course instruction, the group locates on 18 Sept the convoy SC.100 comprising 24 ships escorted by EG.A3 (Cdr Heineman US) with the US Coast Guard cutters *Campbell* and *Spencer*, and, among others, the corvettes *Bittersweet*, *Mayflower*, *Trillium* and *Rosthern* (RCN) and the *Lunenburg*, *Nasturtium* (RN) and *Weyburn* on transfer for Operation 'Torch'. As a result of a skilful evasive movement, the submarine in contact is shaken off on 18 Sept. On 19 Sept only individual boats get close to the convoy in deteriorating weather, mist and rain. To find the convoy again, the 'Pfeil' group, stationed to the SE and comprising *U615*, *U258*, *U221*, *U617*, *U216*, *U356*, *U595* and *U607*, is deployed. *U569* and *U373* miss escort vessels when they try to approach on 20 Sept. *U596* (Lt-Cdr Jahn) sinks one ship of 5676 tons. The storm prevents both sides on 21 Sept from using their weapons and

the operation is broken off on 22 Sept but on 23 Sept the favourably stationed boats are directed to RB.1 located by the 'Vorwärts' group whilst others follow SC.100. *U617* (Lt-Cdr Brandi) sinks one ship from the convoy during the night 22–23 Sept and two stragglers the following day totalling 14787 tons and *U432* (Lt-Cdr H O Schultze) sinks one ship of 5868 tons. Attacks by *U258*, *U221* and *U755* fail. On 25 Sept the pursuit of SC.100 has finally to be broken off.

7–28 Sept   Black Sea
Of the Soviet submarines operating off the Bosphorus, Constanza, Odessa and the Crimea, *Shch-208* and *M-60* are lost on mines on 8 and 23–26 Sept respectively. *L-5* and *L-4* lay mines in the area of Burnas on 16 and 19 Sept. On 20–21 Sept *M-35* (Lt Greshilov) attacks two convoys without result. *S-31* (Lt-Cdr Belorukov) claims two landing barges off Yalta on 21–22 Sept and *M-111* has one miss.

8–11 Sept   Black Sea
The Soviet cruiser *Krasny Krym*, the flotilla leader *Kharkov*, the destroyers *Soobrazitelny* and *Zheleznyakov* and the patrol ship *Shtorm* bring elements of the 137th and 145th Rifle Regts and the 3rd Naval Infantry Bde with supplies from Poti to Tuapse and Gelendzhik.

9 Sept   Baltic
U446 is sunk in the Danzig Bight by a British air-laid mine. The boat is salvaged but decommissioned.

9–10 Sept   Mediterranean
British torpedo aircraft sink the Italian hospital ship *Arno* (8024 tons) N of Tobruk.

9–23 Sept   South Pacific
Both sides carry out naval operations to reinforce their positions on Guadalcanal. On 9 Sept there set out from Truk the Japanese 2nd Fleet (Vice-Adm Kondo), comprising the heavy cruisers *Atago*, *Takao*, *Maya*, *Myoko* and *Haguro*, the battleships *Haruna* and *Kongo* and the 2nd DD Flotilla (Rear-Adm Tanaka) with the destroyers *Hayashio*, *Kagero*, *Kuroshio* and *Oyashio* (15th DD Div) and *Asagumo*, *Minegumo* and *Natsugumo* (9th DD Div); and the 3rd Fleet (Vice-Adm Nagumo), comprising the carriers *Shokaku*, *Zuiho* and *Zuikaku*, the cruisers *Kumano*, *Suzuya* and *Chikuma*, the battleships *Hiyei* and *Kirishima* and the 10th DD Flotilla with the cruiser *Nagara* and the destroyers *Arashi*, *Nowake*, *Maikaze*, *Akigumo*, *Yugumo*, *Makigumo*, *Kazegumo*, *Hatsukaze*, *Yukikaze*, *Amatsukaze* and *Tokitsukaze*. Their purpose is to escort, and cover against US naval forces and reinforcements, new troop movements carried out by the 3rd and 4th DD Flotillas from Rabaul

(see 1–9 Sept) and to cover the attack on Guadalcanal planned for 12 Sept by the Kawaguchi Detachment which has already been landed. But the attack by the Detachment fails. The Japanese forces which make a sortie on 13 Sept as far as Ndeni do not find targets and withdraw to the N for supplies. After US TF.18 (Rear-Adm Noyes), comprising the carrier *Wasp*, the cruisers *San Francisco* (Rear-Adm Scott), *Salt Lake City*, *San Juan* and *Juneau* and the destroyers (Desron 12) *Farenholt*, *Aaron Ward*, *Buchanan*, *Laffey*, *Lansdowne* and *Lardner*, has flown off on 12 Sept from S of Guadalcanal aircraft to reinforce the US Marine Corps air strength on Henderson Field, it joins up S of the Solomons on 14 Sept with TF.17 (Rear-Adm Murray). The latter comprises the carrier *Hornet*, the battleship *North Carolina*, the cruisers *Northampton*, *Pensacola* and *San Diego* and the destroyers (Desron 2) *Morris*, *Anderson*, *Hughes*, *Mustin*, *O'Brien*, *Russell* and *Barton*. Their function is to cover a convoy which sets out on the same day from Espiritu Santo with six transports (7th US Marine Corps Regt) and cruiser and destroyer escort for Guadalcanal (TF.65, Rear-Adm Turner.)

On 14 Sept US B-17 bombers attack the Japanese forces and slightly damage *Myoko*. When many reports are received about the Japanese forces the US convoy turns back temporarily. The US carrier groups run into the Japanese submarine concentration of the 1st Flotilla (see 23 Aug–1 Sept) on 15 Sept. *I-19* (Cdr Kinashi) fires a salvo of six of her 'Long Lance' torpedoes. Three hit *Wasp* (Capt Sherman), one just misses *Lansdowne* (which later has to finish off the abandoned *Wasp* with torpedoes) and two more torpedoes reach TF.17 some five nautical miles away and hit *North Carolina* and *O'Brien*. The latter sinks on 19 Oct on the way back to the US. *I-15*, stationed in the vicinity, observes the successful attack but is not herself able to fire.

After replenishing from 15 to 17 Sept, the Japanese 2nd and 3rd Fleets make another sortie to the S, but they are recalled on 20 Sept and arrive back in Truk on 23 Sept. When no further air reconnaissance reports are received, Adm Turner orders the convoy to turn back to Guadalcanal on 16 Sept. On 18 Sept the transports, supported by the cruisers *Minneapolis*, *Boise* and *Leander* (RNZN) and the destroyers *Phelps*, *Farragut*, *Worden*, *MacDonough*, *Dale*, *Grayson* and *Monssen*, land their troops near Lunga Point.

10 Sept   English Channel
A British force comprising *MTB234*, *MTB230*, *MGB91*, *MGB82* and *MGB84*

attacks a German convoy off Texel and damages two ships.

The British *MGB35* is damaged by fire in an engagement with the 2nd S-boat Flotilla, is captured and is towed into Den Helder.

10–27 Sept Mediterranean

In British submarine operations, *Una* misses a convoy W of Crete on 10 Sept. On 12 Sept *P212/Sahib* (Lt Bromage) sinks one sailing ship of 24 tons near Marettimo. On 17 Sept two small independents of 419 tons fall victim to *P44/United* (Lt Roxburgh) off Sliten, while *Talisman* is lost on 6 Sept in the Sicilian Channel, having probably run on to a mine. *Taku* attacks convoys off Tobruk on 18 and 20 Sept, but the torpedoes are outmanoeuvred, as is an attack by *Thrasher* on 22 Sept in the same area. *P46/Unruffled* (Lt Stevens) sinks from 20 to 22 Sept three ships of 5305 tons off the Tunisian coast. Near Rhodes the Greek *Nereus* sinks one small ship of 622 tons on 24 Sept. *P35/Umbra* (Lt-Cdr Maydon) attacks a convoy with the destroyers *Da Verazzano* and *Lampo* and the torpedo boats *Partenope*, *Clio*, *Aretusa* and *Lince* near Navarino and sinks one ship of 6343 tons.

10 Sept–5 Nov Indian Ocean

British operations to occupy Madagascar: Operation 'Stream'. A force under Rear-Adm Tennant, comprising the cruisers *Birmingham*, *Gambia* and *Jacob van Heemskerck* (Dutch) and the destroyers (7th DD Flotilla) *Napier*, *Nizam*, *Nestor*, *Norman* (RAN), *Van Galen*, *Tjerk Hiddes* (Dutch) and *Nepal*, brings a transport force to Majunga (west coast) where on 10 Sept the 29th Inf Bde is landed. *Napier* lands commando troops in Morandova. Air escort is provided by the carrier *Illustrious* and aircraft depot ship *Albatross* with the destroyers *Hotspur*, *Express*, *Fortune* and *Inconstant*.

While some forces make a sortie over land, to the capital Tananarive, Operation 'Jane' is carried out on 18 Sept. The 29th Inf Bde is re-embarked and landed near Tamatave. The transports are escorted and supported by a force consisting of the carrier *Illustrious*, the battleship *Warspite* and *Jacob van Heemskerck*, *Van Galen*, *Tjerk Hiddes*, *Napier*, *Norman*, *Nizam*, *Nestor* and *Hotspur*. On 23 Sept Tananarive is occupied and the Vichy French Governor withdraws. After landing a South African regiment in Thelar on 29 Sept, the French troops are pursued until they surrender in Ihosy on 5 Nov. *Nizam* captures two French transports S of Madagascar on 24 and 30 Sept which are sunk.

12–17 Sept South Atlantic

Laconia incident. On 12 Sept *U156* (Cdr Hartenstein) sinks the British transport

Laconia (19695 tons) with 1800 Italian prisoners of war on board NE of Ascension. *U156* begins at once with the rescue and in W/T plain language appeals to all ships in the area for help. The Commander U-boats orders *U506* (Lt-Cdr Würdemann) and *U507* (Cdr Schacht) and the Italian submarine *Cappellini* (Lt-Cdr Revedin) to the scene and they arrive on 15 and 16 Sept respectively; he also requests, through diplomatic channels, the French Navy in West Africa to assist. When the report is picked up in Freetown, the British merchant ship *Empire Haven* and the auxiliary cruiser *Corinthian* from Takoradi are ordered to the spot. The US 1st Composite Air Sqn on Ascension, which has received the *U156*'s W/T message in garbled form and is not informed of the rescue action by the U-boats, is asked to provide air escort for the British ships. In the meantime, the U-boats have taken aboard a large number of British, Polish and Italian survivors and taken the rest in tow in lifeboats in order to proceed to the rendezvous with the French ships. A Liberator bomber of the USAAF's 343rd BS (Lt Harden), which happens to be in Ascension on the way to Africa, sees the U-boats when escorting the British ships and, after referring to the Commander of the 1st Composite Sqn, Capt Richardson, receives an order to attack. It attacks *U156* with bombs in spite of the clear Red Cross flags. Thereupon the Commander U-boats gives orders on 17 Sept to all German U-boats that the rescue of survivors from sunken ships is forbidden ('Laconia' Order). On 17 Sept the cruiser *Gloire*, the sloop *Dumont D'Urville* and the minesweeper *Annamite* arrive, having been sent to sea on the instructions of the Vichy government by Adm Collinet, the naval commander in French Equatorial Africa. They take on 1041 survivors from the German U-boats and lifeboats and on 18 Sept *Dumont D'Urville* takes on another 42 from *Cappellini*.

12–18 Sept Arctic

Operation against Allied supply convoy PQ.18 in the Arctic. On 12 Sept German reconnaissance aircraft locate the convoy consisting of 39 freighters, one rescue ship, one tanker, three minesweepers and two fleet tankers. Escort is provided by the destroyers *Achates* and *Malcolm*, the AA ships *Alynbank* and *Ulster Queen*, two submarines, four corvettes, three minesweepers and four trawlers and, in addition, the escort carrier *Avenger* with two destroyers. As close support, divided into two groups, there are the light cruiser *Scylla* (Rear-Adm Burnett) with the destroyers *Onslow*, *Onslaught*, *Opportune*, *Offa*, *Ashanti*,

Eskimo, *Somali*, *Tartar*, *Milne*, *Marne*, *Martin*, *Meteor*, *Faulknor*, *Intrepid*, *Impulsive* and *Fury* while the covering force comprises the heavy cruisers *Norfolk* (Vice-Adm Bonham-Carter), *London* and *Suffolk* and distant cover is provided by the battleships *Anson* (Vice-Adm Fraser) and *Duke of York*, the light cruiser *Jamaica* and five Hunt class destroyers. The rescue ship *Copeland* is part of the convoy.

On 12 Sept the destroyer *Faulknor* sinks *U88* (Lt-Cdr Bohmann) near Bear Island. On 13 Sept *U405* (Cdr Hopmann) and *U589* (Lt-Cdr Horrer) sink the US freighter *Oliver Ellsworth* (7191 tons) and the Soviet steamer *Stalingrad* (3559 tons). Bombers from KG 30 (Maj Bloedorn) and torpedo from aircraft from I/KG 26 (Maj Klümper) and elements of III/KG 26 (Capt Nocken) destroy in several attacks the freighters *Wacosta* (5432 tons), *Oregonian* (4826 tons), *Macbeth* (6131 tons), *Africander* (5441 tons), *Empire Stevenson* (6209 tons) and *Empire Beaumont* (7044 tons) and the Soviet steamer *Sukhona* (3124 tons). On 13–14 Sept Sea Hurricanes from *Avenger* shoot down five German aircraft and four Hurricanes are lost. On 14 Sept, in the night, *U457* (Cdr Brandenburg) torpedoes the British tanker *Atheltemplar* (8992 tons) which later has to be abandoned. In the afternoon, in a renewed attack, I/KG 26 loses 12 aircraft and seven crews and III/KG 26 eight aircraft and seven crews. The destroyer *Onslow*, supported by a Swordfish from *Avenger*, sinks *U589*.

On 16 Sept bad weather prevents further air attacks. The next day the convoy is again located, but an attack by KG 26 is broken off. *U457* is sunk by the destroyer *Impulsive*. On 18 Sept there is a further attack by KG 26 and KG 30 in poor visibility. KG 26 has many torpedo failures. A Hurricane from the catapult ship *Empire Morn* shoots down two He 115s. The convoy, whose escort the Soviet destroyers *Gremyashchi*, *Kuibyshev*, *Sokrushitelny* and *Uritski* have now joined, loses the freighter *Kentucky* (5446 tons). The freighter *Troubador* (6458 tons) is damaged by bombs and beached in the Kola Inlet. She is later dismantled. In all, PQ.18 loses three ships of 19742 tons to U-boats and ten ships of 55915 tons to air attack.

On 18 Sept the Soviet submarine *K-2* sinks after striking a mine off Tanafjord.

12–27 Sept Indonesia

After several journeys, since May, by the small vessels *Kuru* and *Vigilant* from Port Darwin to supply the Dutch and Australian troops left on Timor, the Australian corvette *Kalgoorlie* brings reinforcements from 12 to 17 Sept. The transportation of a relief company in the Australian destroyer *Voyager* fails because the ship runs on a reef off Timor on 23 Sept and has to be blown up. The corvettes *Kalgoorlie* and *Warnambool* rescue the survivors.

12–30 Sept Norway
The German minelayers *Roland*, *Kaiser* and *Skagerrak*, escorted by the 17th A/S Flotilla, lay three anti-submarine mine barrages, 'Rigel I-III', off the south-west coast of Norway.

13 Sept Western Atlantic
From the convoy TAG.5, *U558* (Lt-Cdr Krech) sinks in two approaches three ships of 21828 tons.

13–14 Sept Mediterranean
Operation 'Agreement': British raid on Tobruk. On 13 Sept the destroyers *Sikh* (Capt Micklewait) and *Zulu* with 350 Marines on board set out from Alexandria and meet at sea the AA cruiser *Coventry* and the 5th DD Flotilla (Hunt class) with *Belvoir*, *Dulverton*, *Hursley* and *Croome*; in addition, 18 MTBs and three launches arrive with 150 landing troops. During the night 13–14 Sept there are heavy attacks by the RAF on Tobruk. On 14 Sept an attempt is made to land but only a few soldiers are able to get ashore. *Sikh* is damaged in the fire of the AA battery I/43 (Maj Wegener) near the coast and sinks while under tow by *Zulu*. Most of the crew and the surviving Marines are taken prisoner.

Ju 87s (Lt Goebel) of 8/StG 3 and Ju 88s of I/LG 1 (Capt Hoffman) damage *Coventry*, which has to be scuttled by *Zulu*. MC.200s of the 13th Italian Fighter Bomber Group (Maj Renzo Viale) sink. *MTB308*, *ML352* and *ML353* and 19 Ju 87s of III/StG 3 (Capt Kurt Walter) damage *Zulu* and sink *MTB310*; the destroyer sinks while under tow by *Hursley*. Twenty Ju 88s from II/LG 1 on Crete sink *MTB312*, and *MTB314* is brought in by boats of the 6th MMS Flotilla (Lt-Cdr Reischauer) with 117 men on board. A simultaneous Commando operation from the landward side (Col Haselden†) also fails. The German and Italian defenders of Tobruk take, in all, 576 prisoners and important code and cypher equipment is captured.

14 Sept Mediterranean
Off Algiers, Sunderland 'R' of No 202 Sqn sinks the Italian submarine *Alabastro*.

The British cruiser *Dido* and the destroyers *Jervis*, *Javelin*, *Pakenham* and *Paladin* bombard the Daba area in Egypt.

14 Sept English Channel
The German MDS *Sperrbrecher 142/Westerbroek* is sunk by mine off Ostend.

13–20 Sept North Atlantic
On the way to a patrol line, 'Pfeil', planned for 14 Sept, *U216* (Lt-Cdr Schultz) sights on 13 Sept convoy SC.99 (61 ships with EG.C1 comprising the destroyer *St Francis* and the corvettes *Battleford*, *Chambly*, *Chilliwack*, *Eyebright*, *Napanee*, *Orillia* and *Rosthern*) but is at once driven off. Of the boats *U615*, *U258*, *U221*, *U617* (Lt-Cdr Brandi; sinks one trawler on the way out), *U618*, *U356* and *U440*—all of which are ordered to the scene—only *U440* comes up on 14 Sept but is attacked by escort vessels with depth charges and severely damaged. On 15 Sept Whitley 'Q' of No 58 Sqn sinks NW off the Butt of Lewis the outgoing *U261*. Before a new patrol line can be taken up on 16 Sept, *U221* (Lt Trojer) sights on 15 Sept convoy ON.129, consisting of 30 ships with EG.C2 comprising the destroyers *Burnham* (RN) and *Winchelsea* (RN) and the corvettes *Drumheller*, *Dauphin*, *Morden* and *Polyanthus* (RN), but loses contact in the mist. On 16 Sept the boats which approach are driven off by the escort which makes skilful use of smoke. With the exception of *U440*, the boats are ordered to take part in a new patrol line and are directed to SC.100 (EG.A3) on 18 Sept.

15 Sept Baltic
The German MMS *R66* is lost on a Soviet mine off the island of Halli in the Gulf of Finland.

15 Sept Gibraltar
Italian frogmen sink the British freighter *Ravens Point* (1787 tons) in Gibraltar.

17–19 Sept North Atlantic
The convoy terminals in the Western Atlantic are changed to New York. The first convoys departing from New York are HX.208 on 17 Sept and SC.102 on 19 Sept. The Boston–Halifax convoys are discontinued after BX.37. The North Atlantic convoy cycle is opened from 7 to 8 days. WESTOMP is moved again from 52° W to 46° N. The Western Local Escort Force is composed of five destroyers, 22 corvettes and seven Bangor class minesweepers.

18–30 Sept Baltic
Break-out of the first group of the third wave of Soviet submarines—*S-9*, *Shch-310*, *S-12*, *M-102*, *D-2* and *Shch-307*—through the mine barrages. In spite of some detonations close to several boats, the operations are continued. The returning *Shch-407* runs on to a mine near Porkkala on 25 Sept but is brought in heavily damaged.

19 Sept–14 Oct South West Pacific
In the Indonesian area, the US submarines *Sargo* (Lt-Cdr Gregory) and *Seadragon* (Lt-Cdr Ferrall) each sink one ship, of 4472 tons and 1579 tons respectively. *Searaven* (Lt-

Cdr Cassedy) sinks one ship of 833 tons and torpedoes the German blockade-runner *Regensburg* (8068 tons) off Sunda Strait. In the area of the Bismarck Islands and N of the Solomons, *Amberjack* (Lt-Cdr Bole) sinks two ships of 5231 tons and torpedoes two of 24120 tons including the large whaler *Tonan Maru*. *Sculpin* (Lt-Cdr Chappell) sinks two ships of 6652 tons and torpedoes the seaplane carrier *Nisshin* and *Sturgeon* (Lt-Cdr Piaczentkowski) sinks one ship of 8033 tons.

20 Sept Bay of Biscay
Off Bayonne, the German auxiliary minesweeper *M4448* is lost on a mine.

20–22 Sept Arctic
The German U-boats *U251*, *U255*, *U403*, *U408*, *U435*, *U592* and *U703* operate in the Arctic against the convoy QP.14. The convoy consists of 15 merchant ships, escorted by two AA ships, 11 corvettes, minesweepers and trawlers together with the rescue ships *Rathlin* and *Zamalek*. They set out from Archangel on 13 Sept. Close escort is provided by Rear-Adm Burnett's force (see PQ.18). On 20 Sept *U435* (Lt-Cdr Strelow) sinks the minesweeper *Leda*, *U255* (Lt-Cdr Reche) sinks the freighter *Silver Sword* (4937 tons) and *U703* (Lt-Cdr Bielfeld) torpedoes the destroyer *Somali*; the last is taken in tow by her sister *Ashanti* but sinks in a gale on 24 Sept. On 22 Sept, although the convoy is still escorted by 11 destroyers and nine smaller units after the withdrawal of a part of Adm Burnett's force, *U435* is able to come up to attack again and to sink the freighters *Bellingham* (5345 tons) and *Ocean Voice* (7174 tons) and the tanker *Grey Ranger* (3313 tons).

20–26 Sept North Atlantic
Of the 10 boats of the 'Vorwärts' group refuelled from *U461* (Lt-Cdr Stiegler) from 16 to 18 Sept, *U380*, *U404*, *U584*, *U211*, *U407*, *U91* and *U96* form a new patrol line E of the Newfoundland Bank on 20 Sept and they are joined by *U260*, *U582* and *U619* over the next few days. From 18 to 24 Sept the boats sink independents or stragglers: *U380* (Lt-Cdr Röther) one of 2994 tons, *U211* (Lt-Cdr Hause) one of 11237 tons, *U582* (Lt-Cdr Schulte) one of 2993 tons and *U619* (Lt Makowski) one of 7176 tons.

On 23 Sept *U404* (Lt-Cdr v Bülow) sights the convoy RB.1 (eight passenger steamers from the Great Lakes escorted by the British destroyers *Vanoc* and *Veteran*) whose steamers are taken for large troop transports. Apart from the 'Vorwärts' group, the 'Pfeil' group comprising *U618*, *U216*, *U356*, *U595*, *U607*, *U410* and *U617*, is accordingly ordered to the scene from the E on completion of the operation against SC.100. But because of the high speed of the convoy, the boats have difficulty in getting to it. During the night 24–25 Sept *U211* and *U260* attack unsuccessfully. In the afternoon of 25 Sept *U216* (Lt-Cdr Karl-Otto Schultz) sinks one ship of 4989 tons and in the evening *U96* (Lt Hellriegel) sinks one also of 4989 tons. Attacks by *U410* (Cdr Sturm; twice), *U91* and *U356* fail. In the morning of 26 Sept *U404* sinks the destroyer *Veteran* and in the evening *U619* one straggler of 1547 tons.

20 Sept–6 Oct   Mediterranean
In the Eastern Mediterranean, *U431* (Lt-Cdr Dommes) and *U561* (Lt Schomburg) sink four sailing ships. The Italian submarines *Ametista* and *Nereide* operate SE of Crete, *Argo*, *Argente* and *Nichelio* off Algeria.

24 Sept   Mediterranean
P.108s of the Italian 274th Long-Range Bomber Sqn attack Gibraltar. The attack is repeated during the nights 19–20 and 20–21 Oct.

24–28 Sept   Arctic
Offensive mining operation 'Zarin' by the heavy cruiser *Admiral Hipper* (Rear-Adm Meisel) and the destroyers *Z23*, *Z28*, *Z29*, *Z30* and *Richard Beitzen*, off the NW coast of Novaya Zemlya.

22 Sept   North Atlantic
The first Support Group is formed: EG.20 (Cdr Walker) with ten ships. Some of the vessels sail on 23 Oct to support convoy ONS.132 (EG.B6). The convoy is accompanied by an oiler with rubber hose equipment for refuelling the escorts. In Oct EG.20 is disbanded because of the needs of Operation 'Torch'.

24 Sept–9 Oct   South Pacific
Both sides continue to try to supply Guadalcanal. From 24 to 27 Sept US Marine Corps companies brought by sea in assault boats try to prevent a Japanese concentration on the Matanikau River but have to retire again under cover from the APD *Ballard*. The Japanese 3rd and 4th DD Flotillas (see 1–9 Sept) continue their night missions to Guadalcanal. On 24 Sept the destroyers *Kawakaze* and *Umikaze*, whilst thus engaged, are slightly damaged by divebombers from Henderson Field and on 25 Sept the cruiser *Yura* suffers the same fate from B-17 bombers from Espiritu Santo. In a raid on Rabaul on 2 Oct, the cruiser *Tenryu* is damaged.

To prevent Allied supplies, the Japanese submarine group A, comprising *I-4*, *I-5*, *I-7*, *I-8*, *I-22* and *I-176*, is deployed in the

area of Guadalcanal. *I-5* is damaged on 25 Sept when she tries to attack. *I-4* (Cdr Kawasaki) torpedoes the US transport *Alhena* (7440 tons) off Lunga Point on 29 Sept. *I-22* misses a convoy on 29 Sept and is lost on 1 Oct after reporting a further convoy.

To cover and support the US operations, TF.17 (Rear-Adm Murray) sets out on 2 Oct from Nouméa with the carrier *Hornet*, the cruisers *Northampton*, *Pensacola*, *San Diego* and *Juneau* and the destroyers *Morris*, *Anderson*, *Hughes*, *Mustin*, *Russell* and *Barton* and carries out two raids on Japanese shipping in the roads of Shortland on 5 Oct. But because of the weather they are not pressed home. US Marine Corps bombers from Henderson Field, however, damage the destroyers *Minegumo* and *Murasame* in the area.

On 9 Oct a Japanese force comprising the cruiser *Tatsuta* and five destroyers brings the C-in-C of the 17th Army (Lt-Gen Hyakutake) to Tassafaronga on Guadalcanal. In addition, elements of the Japanese 2nd Inf Div (Lt-Gen Matsuyama) are landed.

24 Sept–15 Oct   Indian Ocean
Off the coasts of India and Ceylon, the Japanese submarine *I-162* (Cdr Shimose) sinks two ships of 7929 tons and damages one more of 4161 tons, *I-165* (Cdr Torisu) sinks one ship of 5549 tons and one unidentified ship and *I-166* (Cdr Tanaka) sinks one ship of 1201 tons and damages one unidentified ship. In addition, the last lands agents on the coast of Calicut.

26 Sept   North Atlantic
The outgoing *U262* is damaged in attacks by two Hudsons ('A' and 'Z') of No 48 Sqn near the Facrocs and has to return.

26–30 Sept   North Atlantic
On 26 Sept *U617* (Lt-Cdr Brandi), which has been directed to SC.100, sights the convoy ON.131, escorted by EG.C3 comprising the destroyers *Saguenay* (Lt Cdr Wallace SOE) and *Skeena* and the corvettes *Agassiz*, *Anemone* (RN), *Galt*, *Sackville* and *Wetaskiwin*. However, the submarine's immediate attack fails because of torpedo defects and skilful use of HF/DF by the commodore's vessel SS *Cairnesk*. From the boats which were widely scattered after the operations against RB.1 and SC.100, *U615*, *U258*, *U221*, *U617*, *U618*, *U216*, *U356*, *U595*, *U607*, *U410*, *U599*, *U755*, *U373*, *U569* and *U176* are ordered to the scene as the 'Tiger' group. After losing contact, a systematic search is impossible because of the uncertain position of the boats and an

incipient storm. The operation has to be broken off. Eight boats go S to refuel, four with *U118* and four with *U116*.

26 Sept–24 Oct   Pacific
On the Japanese east coast, the US submarine *Nautilus* (Lt-Cdr Brockman) sinks three ships of 72069 tons and three sailing vessels, *Kingfish* (Lt-Cdr Lowrance) sinks two ships of 5468 tons, *Greenling* (Lt-Cdr Bruton) sinks four ships of 20180 tons, *Trigger* (Lt-Cdr Lewis) sinks one ship of 5870 tons and damages two of 14517 tons and *Drum* (Lt-Cdr Rice) sinks three ships of 13808 tons; in addition, *Greenling* lightly hits the Japanese carrier *Hiyo* on 20 Oct. Off Formosa, *Guardfish* (Lt-Cdr Klakring) sinks one ship of 6362 tons and *Finback* (Lt-Cdr Hull) three of 21842 tons. Near Truk, *Trout* (Lt-Cdr Ramage) torpedoes the Japanese escort carrier *Taiyo* on 28 Sept and sinks one ship of 863 tons. Off the Kuriles, *S31* (Lt Sellars) sinks one ship of 2864 tons.

26 Sept–20 May   Pacific/Arctic
Soviet submarines of the Pacific Fleet are transferred to the Northern Fleet via the Panama Canal. On 26 Sept *L-15* and *L-16* and on 15 and 18 Oct *S-51*, *S-54*, *S-55* and *S-56* set out from Petropavlovsk and proceed under Capt 1st Class Tripolski via Dutch Harbor, San Francisco and the Panama Canal to Halifax (*L-16* is sunk on 11 Oct). *S-51* goes from there via Iceland direct to Polyarnoe, where she arrives on 24 Jan 1943. *S-55*, *S-56* and *S-54*, after stops at Rosyth, proceed to the Kola Inlet, where they arrive in Mar 1943. *L-15* follows in May after being repaired at Greenock.

27 Sept   Bay of Biscay
U165, returning from the Gulf of St Lawrence, is lost in the Bay of Biscay, probably on a mine.

27 Sept   South Atlantic
In the South Atlantic, the German auxiliary cruiser *Schiff 23/Stier* (Capt Gerlach) comes unexpectedly in poor visibility across the US freighter *Stephen Hopkins* (Capt Paul Buck, 7181 tons), sinks her but receives such heavy damage in the engagement that she has to be abandoned. The crew reach the Gironde estuary in the blockade-runner *Tannenfels* on 2 Nov. Sinkings by *Schiff 23* amount to four ships of 29409 tons.

27 Sept–5 Nov   Baltic
Of the Soviet submarines of the third wave which have broken through the mine barrages, *S-9* operates in the Gulf of Bothnia, *D-2*, *Shch-310* and *Shch-406* between Rixhöft and Bornholm, *S-12* off the Baltic coast, *Shch-307*, *S-7*, *Shch-305* and *Shch-306* in the Aaland Sea, *Shch-303* in Swedish

waters and *M-102* in the western part of the Gulf of Finland. *L-3* (Capt 2nd Class Grishchenko) lays mine barrages off Utö, Libau and the Irben Strait on which three ships of 11789 tons are probably lost. Of the other boats, *S-9* (Lt-Cdr Mylnikov with the Div Commander, Capt 2nd Class Yunakov, on board) sinks one ship of 290 tons, torpedoes one of 6370 tons and misses one; *Shch-310* (Capt 3rd Class Yarosevich) sinks one ship of 1419 tons and misses one; *S-12* (Capt 3rd Class Turaev) damages two ships of 12326 tons; *M-102* (Lt-Cdr Gladilin) misses one; *D-2* (Capt 2nd Class Lindenberg) sinks one ship of 4090 tons and damages one of 2972 tons; *Shch-307* (Capt 3rd Class Momot) sinks one ship of 2478 tons and misses three; *Shch-406* (Capt 3rd Class Osipov) sinks two ships of 3855 tons and misses one; and *Shch-303* (Capt 3rd Class Travkin) misses four. *Inter alia*, *Shch-406* sinks the Swedish steamer *Bengt Sture* during the night 28–29 Oct and takes six prisoners.

28 Sept–28 Nov   Western Atlantic
SE of Trinidad, *U202* (Lt Poser) sinks one ship of 1815 tons, *U201* (Lt Rosenberg) sinks two of 8505 tons and *U201* and *U202* jointly sink one of 7191 tons, *U332* (Lt-Cdr Liebe) sinks two of 11004 tons, and *U67* (Lt-Cdr Müller-Stöckheim) sinks four of 20467 tons and damages two of 11781 tons.

28–30 Sept   Black Sea
The Soviet destroyer *Nezamozhnik* and the patrol ship *Shtorm* transport 8000 men of the 408th Rifle Div to Tuapse.

29 Sept–6 Oct   North Atlantic
It is proposed to form a new large patrol line, 'Luchs', for 1 Oct on the E side of the Atlantic from outbound boats. The first outbound boats, *U620*, *U610* and *U253*, are temporarily stationed in the Denmark Strait from 20 Sept and here *U253* (Lt-Cdr A Friedrichs†) is lost on about 25 Sept after striking a mine off Iceland. On 23 Sept Catalina 'U' of No 210 Sqn damages *U255*. *U610* (Lt-Cdr Frhr v Freyberg) sinks one straggler of 1774 tons from the convoy SC.101 (EG.C4 with the destroyers *Restigouche* and *St Croix* and the corvettes *Amherst*, *Arvida* and *Celandine*). On the way, *U442* (Cdr Hesse) sinks one ship of 1774 tons from a small convoy and *U382* (Lt-Cdr Juli) one independent of 1324 tons. On 29 Sept the outbound U-tanker *U118* (Cdr Czygan) sights an ON convoy with the result that the line of the 'Luchs' group is moved to the N on 1 Oct. It consists of *U437*, *U597*, *U442*, *U254*, *U382*, *U620*, *U610*, *U706*, *U260*, *U582*, *U619*, *U753*, *U755*, *U257*, *U602*, *U183* and *U757*. Whilst the U-boats proceed slowly to the SW, the

most northerly boat, *U260* (Lt-Cdr Purkhold), sights the convoy HX.209 (31 ships, EG.B4). Storms, rain and hail squalls delay the approach of the other boats from an unfavourable stern position but *U254* (Lt-Cdr Loewe) finds an abandoned drifting tanker of 11651 tons and sinks her. Atmospheric interference prevents the reception of a contact signal on 4 Oct from *U437* (Lt-Cdr Lamby) with the substantially better situated ON convoy. Most of the boats continue the pursuit of HX.209 despite the air escort that it gets on 4 Oct. But on 5–6 Oct *U582* (Lt-Cdr Schulte) and *U619* (Lt Makowski) are lost in air attacks by Catalina 'I' of VP-73 and Hudson 'N' of No 269 Sqn RAF and *U257* (Lt-Cdr Rahe) is damaged. On 6 Oct the operation has to be broken off.

30 Sept   English Channel
A German convoy is attacked by British coastal forces off Terschelling. Escorts sink one MGB and four MTBs against only one loss, that of the freighter *Thule*.

1–3 Oct   Black Sea
The Soviet patrol ship *Shtorm* shells Anapa on 1 Oct. The destroyer *Boiki* (with the Commander of the Sqn, Vice-Adm L A Vladimirski, on board) and *Soobrazitelny* shell Yalta during the night 2–3 Oct, firing 406 rounds.

1 Oct   North Sea
The German patrol trawler *V2003* is torpedoed and sunk off Den Helder.

1–20 Oct   Central Atlantic
In operations by Italian submarines in the area SW of Freetown and in the Gulf of Guinea, *Barbarigo* (Cdr Grossi) attacks the British corvette *Petunia* on 6 Oct which she mistakes for a US battleship and thinks depth detonations are hits. On 9 Oct *Archimede* (Lt-Cdr Saccardo) sinks the British troop transport *Oronsay* (20043 tons) and on 10 Oct attacks the transport *Nea Hellas* (16991 tons) which, however, is hardly damaged. *Bagnolini* has no success.

1–26 Oct   Black Sea
In Soviet submarine operations, *M-118* (Lt-Cdr Savin) sinks on 1 Oct the German transport *Salzburg* (1742 tons) but is herself sunk by the gunboat *Ghigulescu* in an attack on a Rumanian convoy. *M-31* sinks the Rumanian tug *Oituz*, *Shch-216* (Capt 3rd Class Karbovski) the Rumanian steamer *Carpati* (4336 tons) and *M-35* (Capt 3rd Class Greshilov) the tanker *Le Progrès* (511 tons). Among others, *M-32* and *Shch-207* make unsuccessful attacks and *L-24*, *L-23* and *L-5* lay mines.

1–30 Oct   Central Atlantic
Of the U-boats *U87*, *U107*, *U590* and *U333* which have just been refuelled and deployed off Freetown, only *U107* (Lt-Cdr Gelhaus)

and *U87* (Lt-Cdr Berger) have any success, each sinking one ship, of 14943 tons and 7392 tons respectively. *U333* (Lt-Cdr Cremer) has a gun duel at short range with the British corvette *Crocus* on 6 Oct in which both ships suffer damage and loss of personnel.

U156, stationed W of Freetown since the *Laconia* affair, has no success at first in this phase, like the newcomers *U552*, *U128* and *UD5*, but on 29 Oct *UD5* (Cdr* Mahn) sinks one ship of 7628 tons.

2 Oct   English Channel
In an attack by the 5th MTB Flotilla, consisting of *S65*, *S77*, *S82* and *S112*, on a British convoy off Eddystone, *S112* (Lt Karl Müller) sinks the British trawler *Lord Stonehaven*.

2 Oct   North Atlantic
Off the British south-west coast the AA cruiser *Curaçoa* sinks with 338 members of the crew after a collision with the troop transport *Queen Mary* (81236 tons).

2–3 Oct   Mediterranean
The Italian tankers *Scrivia*, *Sesia* and *Tirso*, which are equipped as auxiliary minelayers, lay with the destroyers *Ascari* and *Mitragliere* the mine barrage S.61 (400 mines) S of Marettimo (Western Sicily). Simultaneously, the destroyer *Da Verazzano* lays near Cape Bon 194 protection and explosive floats in two sections.

2–10 Oct   Mediterranean
In the Adriatic, the British submarine *P211/Safari* (Cdr Bryant) attacks four ships and torpedoes two of 1052 tons. On 8 and 9 Oct, off the Cyrenaican coast, *Turbulent* (Cdr Linton) sinks one ship of 853 tons and *P37/Unbending* (Lt Stanley) two of 2230 tons and a small sailing ship. *P43/Unison* (Lt Halliday) sinks on 10 Oct W of the Peloponnese a ship of 4652 tons escorted by the torpedo boat *Bassini*. *Porpoise* (Cdr Bennington) lays a mine barrage on 3 Oct near Tobruk.

5–27 Oct   Baltic
Break-out of the last group of the third wave of Soviet submarines through the mine barrages: *Shch-320*, *Shch-303*, *Shch-302*, *Shch-311*, *Shch-303*, *Shch-306*, *S-7*, *Shch-406*, *Shch-304*, *L-3* and *Shch-305*. On the way out *Shch-320*, *Shch-302* and *Shch-304* run on to mines and are lost and *Shch-311* is sunk by Finnish VMV-boats. Of the Finnish submarines deployed in hunting areas in the Aaland Sea, *Vesihiisi* (Lt-Cdr Aittola) sinks *S-7* near Söderarm on 21 Oct and takes four prisoners including the CO, Capt 3rd Class Lisin. On 26 Oct *Iku-Turso* (Lt-Cdr Pakkala) sinks the returning *Shch-308* and on 5 Nov *Vetehinen* (Lt-Cdr Leino) *Shch-305*. Of the returning boats, *Shch-310*

is badly damaged by a mine on 9 Oct and *S-13* escapes attacks by the Finnish *VMV-123* and *VMV-15* near Vaidlo on 15 Oct. In operations to guard the mine barrages, the German *UJ1204* runs on to a Soviet-laid mine near Pien-Tytärsaari and sinks.

6 Oct–3 Dec   Western Atlantic
In Oct *U43* operates in the Gulf of St Lawrence, *U183* and *U518* off the Belle Isle Strait and *U106* (Lt-Cdr Rasch) off Cabot Strait where she sinks one ship of 2140 tons. On 2 Nov *U518* (Lt Wissmann) enters Conception Bay and sinks two ore ships of 13336 tons. An attack by *U183* (Cdr Schäfer) remains unclarified. On 18 Nov *U43* (Lt Schwantke), NE of the Newfoundland Bank, torpedoes from the convoy SC.109 (EG.C3, with the rescue ship *Bury* equipped with effective HF/DF) a tanker of 9132 tons which is at first taken in tow but then sinks on 25 Jan 1943 on the way to the repair yard. From the convoy ON.145 (EG.A3), *U518* sinks off Newfoundland on 21 Nov a ship of 6140 tons and torpedoes two of 15440 tons. On 3 Dec *U183* sinks one ship of 6089 tons from the convoy ONS.146 off Nova Scotia.

7–8 Oct   English Channel/North Sea
Sortie by the 2nd MTB Flotilla, comprising *S101*, *S46*, *S62*, *S80*, *S105* and *S108*, as well as *S63*, *S79* and *S117* of the 4th MTB Flotilla, against a British convoy off Cromer: three British freighters of 7576 tons, one RN tug (444 tons) and the launch *ML339* are sunk. The German auxiliary cruiser *Schiff 45/Komet*, escorted by the 2nd MMS Flotilla, runs on a newly laid minefield off Dunkirk and loses *R77*, *R78*, *R82* and *R86*.

7 Oct–13 Nov   South Atlantic
The 'Eisbär' group operates off South Africa. After *U68* has sunk two ships of 12157 tons on 12–15 Sept in the Central Atlantic on the outward journey and all boats have refuelled from *U459* (Cdr v Wilamowitz-Moellendorf) on 24–25 Sept S of Ascension, the four boats simultaneously attack the traffic off South Africa on 7–8 Oct. Up to 3 Nov *U172* (Lt-Cdr Emmermann) sinks six ships of 48054 tons, *U159* (Lt-Cdr Witte) eight of 47233 tons, *U68* (Cdr Merten) seven of 44173 tons and *U504* (Cdr Poske) six of 36156 tons. In addition, *U179* (Cdr* Sobe) of the second wave of IXD2 boats, which arrives on 8 Oct, sinks one ship of 6558 tons but is then sunk by depth charges and ramming from the British destroyer *Active*.

8–16 Oct   North Atlantic
On the E side of the Atlantic, the 'Panther' group is formed from 8 Oct from the boats coming from the HX.209 convoy and from

new arrivals. It consists of *U84*, *U454*, *U353*, *U437*, *U597*, *U442*, *U254*, *U706*, *U260*, *U753*, *U575*, *U602* and *U757*, to which in the following days are added *U662*, *U382*, *U620*, *U610*, *U301*, *U443*, *U563*, *U621* and *U441*. *U254* (Lt-Cdr Loewe) sinks an independent of 6098 tons. In the evening of 11 Oct *U620* (Lt-Cdr Stein) sights the convoy ONS.136 (36 ships, EG.B3). *U353*, *U662*, *U437*, *U597*, *U442*, *U254*, *U382* and *U620* are directed to it as the 'Leopard' group. With winds of Force 8–10, only *U597* (Lt-Cdr Bopst) is able to fire (twice unsuccessfully) but she is sunk on 12 Oct by a Liberator bomber from No 120 Sqn RAF (Sqn Ldr Bulloch). After that only independents and stragglers are sighted. *U382* (Lt-Cdr Juli) misses a destroyer and *U706* (Lt-Cdr v Zitzewitz) sinks one ship of 4265 tons. On 14 Oct the operation is broken off and the 'Leopard' group is directed to the oncoming SC.104. With the boats *U615*, *U258*, *U221*, *U618*, *U356*, *U607*, *U410* and *U599*, which have been refuelled from *U116*, which is lost from an unknown cause around 15 Oct, and *U118*, the 'Wotan' group is formed E of Newfoundland on 8 Oct and to this are added by 12 Oct *U216* and *U661*, replenished by the newly arrived *U463*. On 11 Oct *U615* (Lt-Cdr Kapitzky) sinks one independent of 4219 tons. On the same day *U258* (Lt-Cdr v Mässenhausen) sights a corvette from the convoy SC.104. The latter consists of 48 ships and EG.B6 (Cdr Heathcote) with the British destroyers *Fame* and *Viscount*, the Norwegian corvettes *Potentilla*, *Eglantine*, *Montbretia* and *Acanthus* and the rescue ship *Goathland* with HF/DF. Radio atmospherics prevent the contact report from coming through before 12 Oct and the deployment of the 'Wotan' group is delayed by the sighting of convoy ON.135 (EG.A3) by *U356*. Only during the night 12–13 Oct, therefore, does *U221* (Lt Trojer) approach SC.104 and in three skilfully executed approaches sink three ships of 11354 tons. By day on 13 Oct *U221* keeps contact and brings up *U599*, *U216*, *U607* and *U258*, but they are driven off by *Viscount*, *Potentilla* and *Eglantine*, the last of which shells *U258*. During the night 13–14 Oct *U221* attacks again whilst three escorts remain astern, sinks one ship of 5929 tons and torpedoes the whale factory ship *Southern Empress* (12398 tons) which is later finished off. A little later *U607* (Lt-Cdr Mengersen) and *U661* (Lt v Lilienfeld) attack almost simultaneously and each sinks one ship, of 4826 tons and 3672 tons respectively. *U607* is attacked by *Viscount* and damaged with depth charges. Towards morning *U618* (Lt

Baberg) sinks one ship of 5791 tons. *Montbretia* drives off *U615*, which has been located with radar. At mid-day on 14 Oct contact is re-established by *U216* but before dark the escorts drive off *U661*, *U258* and *U599* which are found by HF/DF near the convoy. The 'Leopard' group is directed from ONS.136 to SC.104. In the night first *Montbretia* (Lt-Cdr Söiland) drives off *U661*, then *U607* is forced to submerge and is damaged by *Acanthus* (Lt-Cdr Bruun). *Viscount* (Lt-Cdr Waterhouse) locates *U661* by radar and rams the boat at 26kt. *Potentilla* (Lt-Cdr Monssen) forces *U254* to submerge and *Eglantine* (Lt-Cdr Voltersvik) damages the boat with depth charges. By day on 15 Oct *U410* (Cdr Sturm) sinks an unknown disabled ship; *Fame* and *Acanthus* drive off *U258* and *U599* and in the afternoon *Acanthus* attacks *U442* with depth charges. Liberator 'H' of No 120 Sqn RAF bombs *U615* and forces *U437* underwater. Contact is only re-established by *U258* in the morning of 16 Oct but further Liberators and Catalinas of No 120 Sqn and VP-84 drive off all boats. At mid-day *U353* is located by asdic by *Fame* when she attempts an underwater attack: she is compelled by depth charges to surface and is sunk by ramming. In the evening *U571*, which has just arrived in the operational area, approaches the convoy, now only escorted by the four Norwegian corvettes, but she is slightly damaged by gunfire and depth charges from *Potentilla*. Before *U258* once again sights the convoy on the morning of 16 Oct, the 'Wotan' group is directed to the nearby convoy ON.137 (EG.C4), which has been reported by *U704*.

9 Oct   Bay of Biscay
U171 (Lt-Cdr Pfeffer), returning from a long patrol in the Gulf of Mexico, is lost on a mine in the Bay of Biscay.

9 Oct   English Channel
The German MDS *Sperrbrecher 143/Lola* is sunk after striking a mine off Nieuport.

9–13 Oct   South Pacific
Naval battle off Cape Esperance. On 9 Oct a US convoy (Rear Adm Turner), comprising the transports *McCawley* and *Zeilin* and eight fast transports (APDs) with the 164th Inf Regt, sets out from Nouméa for Guadalcanal. It is escorted by destroyers. Covering the operation are TF.17 (Rear-Adm Murray), with the carrier *Hornet*, four cruisers and six destroyers (see below) 180 nautical miles S of Guadalcanal, a force (Rear-Adm Lee) comprising the battleship *Washington*, two cruisers and five destroyers 50 nautical miles E of Malaita and TF.64 (Rear-Adm Scott) with the cruisers *San*

Francisco, Salt Lake City, Boise and *Helena* and the destroyers *Farenholt, Duncan, Laffey, Buchanan* and *McCalla* near Rennell Island.

On 11 Oct a Japanese transport force (Rear-Adm Joshima) approaches Tassafaronga from Rabaul with the seaplane carriers *Chitose* and *Nisshin* and the destroyers *Akizuki* (Rear-Adm Takama, 4th DD Flotilla), *Asagumo, Natsugumo, Yamagumo, Murakumo* and *Shirayuki* with 728 men of the 2nd Inf Div and heavy artillery and tanks on board. The uneventful disembarkation is to be covered by the 6th Cruiser Sqn (Rear-Adm Goto†) with the cruisers *Aoba, Furutaka* and *Kinugasa* and the destroyers *Fubuki* and *Hatsuyuki* with orders to shell Henderson Field. But this force is located on 11 Oct by US air reconnaissance and Rear-Adm Scott is able to bar its way. Shortly before midnight he attacks the Japanese force with the help of radar from a 'crossing the T' position: *Fubuki* is sunk by gunfire from the four US cruisers and *Furataka* sinks after a torpedo hit from the destroyer *Duncan*, which is in turn sunk by gunfire from *Furutaka* and *Hatsuyuki*. *Aoba* and *Hatsuyuki* are hit and Adm Goto is killed. *Boise* is severely and *Salt Lake City* and *Farenholt* are lightly damaged. An attack by the Japanese submarine *I-2* on the destroyer *McCalla*, which rescues survivors from *Duncan*, fails in the morning. In the morning of 12 Oct the Japanese destroyers *Murakumo* and *Shirayuki* rescue 400 survivors but the returning destroyers *Murakumo* and *Natsugumo* are sunk by dive-bombers from Henderson Field.

In the course of 12 Oct the APDs *Hovey* and *Southard* tow four motor torpedo boats to Tulagi and on 13 Oct some 3000 troops of the convoy are landed near Lunga Point. The destroyers *Gwin, Nicholas* and *Sterett* of the escort shell Japanese artillery positions in the NW of the island where on the day before disembarked guns were brought into position. A Japanese attack with 24 and 15 bombers on the ships has no success. In the evening of 13 Oct Turner sets out again.

10 Oct–31 Dec   Black Sea
Soviet ships transport 14527 troops and 3000–4000 tons of supplies and ammunition off the Caucasian coast.

11–20 Oct   Mediterranean
The British submarine *P46/Unruffled* (Lt Stevens) sinks two ships of 2452 tons off Capri and *Utmost* (Lt Coombe) one of 2070 tons off Sardinia. In the Aegean, *Thrasher* (Lt-Cdr Mackenzie) sinks two ships of 2110 tons and two sailing ships. The Italian submarines *Dandolo* and *Mocenigo* operate S of the Balearics.

11–22 Oct   South Pacific
Naval operations off Guadalcanal (cf 9–13 Oct). On 11 Oct the Japanese Combined Fleet leaves Truk to cover and support the major attack on Guadalcanal planned for 21 Oct. The 2nd Fleet (Vice-Adm Kondo) comprises the heavy cruisers *Atago* and *Takao* (4th Cruiser Sqn) and *Maya* and *Myoko* (5th Cruiser Sqn, Rear-Adm Omori), the battleships *Haruna* and *Kongo* (3rd BB Sqn, Rear-Adm Kurita), the carriers *Hiyo* and *Junyo* (2nd Carrier Sqn, Rear-Adm Kakuta) and the 2nd DD Flotilla (Rear-Adm Tanaka) with the cruiser *Isuzu* and the destroyers *Naganami, Makinami, Takanami* and *Isonami* (31st DD Div), *Umikaze, Kawakaze* and *Suzukaze* (24th DD Div), *Kagero, Oyashio, Hayashio* and *Kuroshio* (15th DD Div) and *Inazuma*. The 3rd Fleet (Vice-Adm Nagumo) comprises the carriers *Shokaku, Zuiho* and *Zuikaku* (1st Carrier Sqn), the battleships *Hiyei* and *Kirishima* (11th BB Sqn, Rear-Adm Abe), the cruisers *Kumano* and *Suzuya* (7th Cruiser Sqn, Rear-Adm Nishimura) and *Chikuma* and *Tone* (8th Cruiser Sqn, Rear-Adm Hara) and the 10th DD Flotilla (Rear-Adm Kimura) with the cruiser *Nagara* and the destroyers *Kazegumo, Makigumo, Yugumo* and *Akigumo* (10th DD Div), *Amatsukaze, Tokitsukaze, Yukikaze* and *Hatsukaze*, (16th DD Div), *Isokaze, Tanikaze* and *Urakaze* (17th DD Div) and the attached *Arashi, Maikaze* and *Nowake* (4th DD Div), *Hamakaze* and *Terutsuki* and a supply force of four tankers and three freighters. A submarine line, B, with the 1st SM Flotilla, comprising *I-9, I-15, I-21, I-24, I-174* and *I-175*, operates as a vanguard whilst the submarine group A (see 24 Sept–9 Oct) remains in the Guadalcanal area. *I-7* has reconnoitered Espiritu Santo on 7 Oct with her aircraft and shells of the island on 14 and 23 Oct.

After the battle of Cape Esperance (see 9–13 Oct), the forces of the Japanese fleet reach the area E of the Solomons on 13 Oct. On 13 Oct Japanese air reconnaissance reports US forces S of Guadalcanal.

During the night 13–14 Oct Rear-Adm Kurita makes a sortie towards Guadalcanal with the battleships *Haruna* and *Kongo*, the cruiser *Isuzu* (Rear-Adm Tanaka) and the destroyers *Takanami, Makinami, Naganami, Hayashio, Oyashio, Kuroshio* and *Kagero* and bombards Henderson Field with 918 rounds of 35.6cm shells including about 300 with HE fuses. Of 90 aircraft, 48 are destroyed; all but one of the remainder are damaged. The attempt by the four US motor torpedo boats *PT46, PT48, PT60* and *PT38* to attack the force from Tulagi is

frustrated by *Naganami*. The Japanese 2nd and 3rd Fleets reach the area of Ndeni on 14 Oct. Japanese air reconnaissance reports US convoys S of Guadalcanal and US air reconnaissance sights Japanese naval forces NE of the Solomons.

In the night 14–15 Oct Vice-Adm Mikawa again bombards Henderson Field with 752 rounds of 20.3cm shells from the cruisers *Chokai* and *Kinugasa* but to much less effect. At the same time Rear-Adm Takama (4th DD Flotilla) brings six transports with 11 destroyers to Tassafaronga and lands some 4500 men of the 2nd and 38th Inf Divs there. In the morning of 15 Oct the *Azumasan Maru, Kyushu Maru* and *Sasago Maru* from among the transports have to be beached after US air attacks and are lost; the destroyer *Samidare* is slightly damaged. In order to bring petrol to Guadalcanal for the aircraft at Henderson Field, the US transports *Alchiba, Bellatrix* and *Jamestown* and the tug *Vireo* each set out with a lighter in tow, escorted by the destroyers *Meredith* and *Nicholas*. They are recalled when reports are received of Japanese forces in the NE. Only *Meredith* and *Vireo* proceed: they fall victim to an attack force from the Japanese carrier *Zuikaku* on 15 Oct.

During the night 15–16 Oct Rear-Adm Omori makes a sortie towards Guadalcanal with the cruisers *Maya* and *Myoko* and Rear-Adm Tanaka does likewise with the *Isuzu* and the above-mentioned destroyers. They bombard Henderson Field with nearly 1500 rounds of 20.3cm shells.

Whilst the Japanese 2nd and 3rd Fleets replenish from the tanker force N of the Equator on 17–18 Oct, the 3rd and 4th DD Flotillas continue their night supply missions to Guadalcanal. In the process the cruiser *Yura* is slightly damaged on 18 Oct in an attack by the US submarine *Grampus*. On 19 Oct the destroyer *Ayanami* suffers the same fate in an air attack. In US supply operations the destroyers *Aaron Ward* and *Lardner* shell Japanese concentrations on 21 Oct. The Japanese submarine *I-176* (Lt-Cdr Tanabe) torpedoes on 20 Oct the heavy cruiser *Chester* from US TF.64 (Rear-Adm Lee) operating in the area S of Rennell Island. On 23 Oct *I-7* again shells Espiritu Santo.

On the Allied side, Vice-Adm Halsey relieves Vice-Adm Ghormley as C-in-C South Pacific on 18 Oct.

11 Oct–10 Dec   Western Atlantic
U-boats operate against convoys and independents both sides of Trinidad. *U516* (Cdr Wiebe) and *U160* (Lt-Cdr Lassen) shadow an eastbound convoy on 16 Oct and also

U67 (Lt-Cdr Müller-Stöckheim) and U332 (Lt-Cdr Liebe (J)) on 17 and 18 Oct but only U160 sinks one ship of 730 tons and torpedoes one of 6197 tons. From 1 to 4 Nov U160 shadows the convoy TAG.18 and in three approaches sinks four ships of 25855 tons. On 5 Nov U129 (Lt-Cdr Witt) establishes contact with TAG.18 near Aruba and sinks two ships of 14622 tons. At the same time U160 sinks one ship of 5431 tons from an approaching GAT convoy. Further E U508 (Lt-Cdr Staats) locates the convoy TAG.19 (?) during the night 5–6 Nov and sinks in two approaches two ships of 12424 tons on 7 Nov. On 12 Nov U129 misses near Aruba a feeder convoy for TAG.20 which U163 (Cdr Engelmann) attacks a little later. The first approach is beaten off but in the second the US gunboat Erie is hit. She has to be beached and is burnt out. In attacks on independents, U160 also sinks two ships of 12849 tons, U129 sinks three of 17991 tons, U154 (Cdr Schuch) sinks three of 17936 tons, U505 (Lt-Cdr Zschech) sinks one of 7173 tons, U508 sinks seven of 37841 tons and U163 sinks three of 15011 tons and damages one of 7127 tons. U505 is unexpectedly attacked on 10 Nov by an aircraft from Trinidad: a bomb explodes on the barrel of the 3.7cm AA gun and causes heavy damage and losses on the boat. The aircraft crashes in the explosion.

12–31 Oct Indian Ocean
In the Gulf of Oman, the Japanese submarine I-27 (Cdr Kitamura) sinks one ship of 7174 tons.

13–14 Oct English Channel
Unsuccessful attempt to bring the auxiliary cruiser Schiff 45/Komet (Capt Brocksien†) through the Channel from Le Havre. In spite of a strong escort of minesweepers and the 3rd TB Flotilla (Cdr Wilcke), comprising T4, T10, T14 and T19, a British force of eight MTBs, MTB49, MTB55, MTB56, MTB84, MTB95, MTB203, MTB229 and MTB236, and the escort destroyers Cottesmore, Quorn, Glaisdale, Eskdale and Albrighton, is able to intercept the German force near Cape de la Hague, where Schiff 45 is sunk in the morning of 14 Oct by two torpedoes from MTB236 (Sub-Lt Drayson). None of the crew can be rescued. The German torpedo boats and coastal batteries later damage the destroyer Brocklesby from a second group which also includes the destroyers Fernie, Tynedale and Krakowiak (Polish).

13–14 Oct Mediterranean
The Italian 15th DD Flotilla (Capt Mirti della Valle), comprising Pigafetta, Zeno, Da Noli and Da Verazzano, lays N of Cape Bon the S.71 mine barrage with 258 mines and 286 explosive floats.

13–15 Oct Arctic
Offensive mining operation by the destroyers Richard Beitzen, Friedrich Eckoldt, Z27 and Z30 off Kanin Nos. The Soviet ice-breaker Mikoyan runs on this barrage. On 13 Oct U592 (Lt-Cdr Borm) lays the 'Paul' barrage off the Yugor Strait; the Soviet steamer Shchors (3770 tons) strikes one of its mines and is damaged. Whilst U212 and U586 reconnoitre near Jan Mayen, U377 (Lt-Cdr Köhler) disembarks the weather detachment 'Nussbaum' on Spitzbergen.

13–14 Oct Black Sea
The Soviet destroyer Nezamozhnik and the patrol ship Shkval shell land targets near Sarygol and Kiik-Atlama (121 rounds) during the night 13–14 Oct.

13–28 Oct Arctic
The British cruiser Argonaut and the destroyers Intrepid and Obdurate proceed from Scapa Flow to Murmansk to take hospital equipment and medical personnel and to bring back survivors from PQ.18.

14 Oct North Sea
The German 6th MTB Flotilla, comprising S69, S71, S74 and S75, attacks a British convoy off Cromer and torpedoes two freighters of 2905 tons.

15–19 Oct Norway
In operations by Allied submarines off Norway, the Norwegian Uredd (Lt Rören) sinks the transport Libau (3663 tons). The French Junon (Lt Querville) attacks two convoys without success. A Norwegian steamer (726 tons) sinks on a mine barrage laid on 19 Sept by the French Rubis (Lt-Cdr Rousselot).

16 Oct North Pacific
The Japanese destroyer Oboro is sunk N of Kiska in an attack by USAAF aircraft.

16–29 Oct North Atlantic
On 16 Oct U704 (Lt-Cdr Kessler) sights in the southern half of the 'Panther' patrol line (see 8–18 Oct) the convoy ON.137 consisting of 40 ships escorted by EG.C4 (Lt-Cdr Piers) with the Canadian destroyers Restigouche (HF/DF) and St Croix (HF/DF), the Canadian corvettes Amherst, Arvida and Orillia and the British corvette Celandine (radar Type 271) together with the rescue ship Bury (HF/DF). From the 'Panther' group U609, U658, U132, U71, U571, U438, U402, U89, U381, U84 and U454 and from the 'Wotan' group (see 8–16 Oct) from convoy SC.104, U615, U258, U618, U216, U356, U410, U599, U662, U437 and U442 are ordered to attack. U704 sinks one straggler of 4212 tons. U609 (Lt Rudloff) in bad visibility comes up against

Celandine in trying to attack, submerges and is heavily bombarded by depth charges set shallow but is able to escape. In a westerly wind the boats do not get up to the convoy on 17–18 Oct. The 'Wotan' group has to start the journey home on 18 Oct and on 19 Oct the operation is broken off. On its way back to France U216 (Lt-Cdr K O Schultz) is sunk by Liberator 'H' from No 224 Sqn (Fg Off Sleep) on 20 Oct and U599 (Lt-Cdr Breithaupt) is sunk near convoy KX.2 off Cape Finisterre on 24 Oct.

The boats of the 'Panther' group go either to refuel from U463 or to the new 'Veilchen' patrol line NE of Newfoundland. On the way the boats encounter independents: U610 (Lt-Cdr Frhr v Freyberg-Eisenberg-Allmendingen) sinks one ship of 5718 tons, U615 (Lt-Cdr Kapitzky) the large motor ship Empire Star of 12656 tons and U618 (Lt Baberg) one ship of 4772 tons.

On 16 Oct the 'Puma' group is formed from U441, U621, U602, U563, U757, U753, U301 and U443, which were not directed to ON.137 (see 8–16 Oct). It is sent S to the convoy ONS.138 reported by the B-Service and escorted by EG.B2 (Cdr MacIntyre) with the destroyers Hesperus, Whitehall and Vanessa and the corvettes Gentian, Clematis and Heather. On 22 Oct U443 (Lt v Puttkamer), the most southerly boat, sights convoy ON.139, escorted by EG.C2 (Lt-Cdr Chavasse RN) with the RN destroyers Broadway, Sherwood and Winchelsea, the RCN corvettes Drumheller, Morden and Pictou and the RN corvettes Polyanthus and Primrose. Since an attack by the other boats from the stern is impossible, she receives permission to engage and sinks two ships of 17843 tons. Together with U301, she tries to keep contact in order to bring up U260, U706, U620 and U662 which are advancing after refuelling from U463. But on 25 Oct contact is lost after the boats have shadowed convoy OS.42 instead of ON.139 from 23 Oct.

After U441 and U621 (Lt-Cdr Schünemann) have sighted independents on 22 Oct, of which U621 sinks one ship of 6113 tons, the 'Puma' group, reinforced up to 26 Oct by U436, U624, U606, U383 and U224, proceeds westwards. On 26 Oct convoy HX.212—comprising 45 ships escorted by EG.A3 (Cdr Lewis USCG) with the US Coast Guard cutter Campbell, the US destroyer Badger, the RCN corvettes Rosthern and Trillium and the RN corvette Dianthus, supported by the RCN corvettes Alberni, Summerside and Ville de Quebec on transfer for Operation 'Torch'—runs into the patrol line and is reported by U436 (Lt-Cdr Seibicke) which keeps contact until the next day, while several other boats of the group are driven off. During the night 26–27 Oct *U436* attacks and with five hits sinks one ship of 10107 tons and damages two others, of 7350 tons and 8225 tons respectively; the last is finished off later by *U606* (Lt Döhler), which has beforehand torpedoed the whale factory ship *Kosmos II* of 16966 tons which is later finished off by *U606* and *U624*. Attacks by *U621* and *U563* fail. In the course of 28 Oct *U443*, *U606*, *U624*, *U441* and *U436* come up but are repeatedly forced to submerge by the air escort of No 120 Sqn RAF sent out from Iceland. During the night 28–29 Oct *U224* (Lt Kosbadt) sinks one straggler of 4000 tons and *U624* (Lt Count Soden-Fraunhofen) one ship of 7700 tons from the convoy. On 29 Oct the boats are again driven off by the air escort. On the way to a new station *U436* sinks one ship of 4998 tons and *U575* (Lt-Cdr Heydemann) the transport *Abosso* of 11330 tons.

On 27 Oct the outgoing *U627* (Lt Kindelbacher) is sunk S of Iceland near convoy SC.105 (EG.B1, with the destroyers *Hurricane*, *Watchman* and *Rockingham* and the corvettes *Dahlia*, *Wallflower*, *Meadowsweet* and *Monkshood*) by the escorting Fortress 'F' of No 206 Sqn (P Off Cowey). The outgoing *U664* (Lt-Cdr Gräf) is sunk by Catalina 'A' of VP-84 (Lt Millard), escorting HX.212 on 1 Nov.

In the meantime convoy ONS.140 (32 ships escorted by EG.B4 with the destroyers *Highlander* and *Beverley*, and the corvettes *Anemone*, *Clover*, *Abelia*, *Pennywort* and *Borage*) passes unobserved N of HX.212. The convoy following HX.212, SC.106 (22 ships escorted by EG.B3 with the destroyer *Harvester* and the Polish *Garland*, the RN corvettes *Orchis* and *Narcissus*, and the FFN corvettes *Lobélia*, *Aconit* and *Roselys*, supported by the RCN corvettes *Camrose*, *Calgary* and *Kitchener*, on transfer to Operation 'Torch') is routed N to evade the U-boats following HX.212.

Convoy ON.141 (59 ships with EG.C3 comprising the RCN destroyers *Saguenay* and *Skeena*, the RCN corvettes *Sackville*, *Agassiz*, *Galt* and *Wetaskiwin* and the supporting RN destroyer *Witherington*) passes S of HX.212. Convoy ONS.142 (51 ships with EG.B7 comprising the destroyers *Firedrake* and *Ripley* and the corvettes *Sunflower*, *Loosestrife*, *Alisma* and *Pink*) is routed N of HX.212.

16–30 Oct   Central Atlantic

A sortie by *U161* and *U126* to the Congo estuary is unsuccessful apart from the torpedoing of the British cruiser *Phoebe* on 23 Oct by *U161* (Lt-Cdr Achilles).

18 Oct–8 Nov   South West Pacific

In the Malacca Straits, the Dutch submarine *O23* (Lt-Cdr Valkenburg) torpedoes one ship of 4621 tons. On the coast of Indo-China and in the Gulf of Siam the US submarines *Thresher* (Lt-Cdr Millican), *Gar* (Lt-Cdr Mc-Gregor), *Grenadier* (Lt-Cdr Charr), *Tambor* (Lt-Cdr Ambruster), *Whale* (Lt-Cdr Azer) and *Tautog* (Lt-Cdr Willingham) lay mine barrages. *Tautog* sinks one guard boat of 33 tons by gunfire and *Tambor* one ship of 2461 tons by torpedo. In the area of Davao, *Seawolf* (Lt-Cdr Warder) sinks three ships of 13051 tons. Off the Bismarck Archipelago *Gudgeon* (Lt-Cdr Stovall) sinks one ship of 6783 tons and *Grayback* (Lt-Cdr Stephan) torpedoes one of 7191 tons. *Grampus* (Lt-Cdr Craig) torpedoes on 18 Oct the Japanese cruiser *Yura*, which is slightly damaged. *Whale* sinks one ship of 5959 tons.

19–26 Oct   Mediterranean

An Italian convoy of four steamers from Naples to Tripoli, which is escorted by the destroyers *Pigafetta*, *Da Verazzano*, *Oriani*, *Gioberti*, *Da Noli* and *Ascari* and the torpedo boats *Centauro* and *Sagittario*, is located by a British submarine formation. On 19 Oct *P37/Unbending* (Lt Stanley) sinks one ship of 4459 tons and *Da Verazzano*. On 20 Oct *P42/Unbroken* (Lt Mars) torpedoes one ship of 5397 tons, which is sunk by *P211/Safari* (Cdr Bryant) when being towed by *Ascari*. *P35/Umbra* (Lt-Cdr Maydon) destroys on 23 Oct one ship of 8670 tons beached after an air torpedo hit and sinks one small vessel of 182 tons. In the Aegean *Taku* sinks one ship of 2238 tons.

19–28 Oct   Black Sea

The Soviet cruisers *Krasny Krym* and *Krasny Kavkaz*, the flotilla leader *Kharkov* and the destroyers *Besposhchadny* and *Soobrazitelny* transport the 8th, 9th and 10th Guards Rifle Bdes (12600 troops, 50 guns, 65 mortars and 100 tons of ammunition) from Poti to Tuapse from 20 to 23 Oct. During the night 22–23 Oct four motor torpedo boats of the 1st MTB Flotilla (Lt-Cdr Christiansen) attack the incoming force: two torpedoes explode on the mole, the others go ashore. From 24 to 28 Oct the destroyers *Nezamozhnik*, *Boiki* and *Besposhchadny*, the patrol ships *Shkval* and *Shtorm* and transports bring more troops and supplies from Sochi to Tuapse.

19 Oct–6 Nov   North Atlantic

After the conclusion of the ON.137 operation, *U71*, *U438*, *U84*, *U89*, *U704*, *U381*, *U658*, *U402*, *U571*, *U454* and *U132* receive orders to form the 'Veilchen' group E of Newfoundland from 24 Oct. From 27 Oct it is reinforced in the S by *U437* and *U442*.

On 28 Oct *U437* reports convoy ON.140 (see 16–29 Oct) but no operation is ordered: waiting continues for eastgoing convoys. *U522*, *U520* and *U521* are stationed S of Newfoundland and *U183* and *U518* on the north-east coast. On 30 Oct *U658* is sunk in the patrol line by a Hudson of No 145 Sqn RCAF. A little later *U522* (Lt-Cdr Schneider) sights the convoy SC.107 with the Western Local Escort North (the British destroyer *Walker* and the Canadian corvettes *Fennel*, *Cowichan* and *Timmins*) SW of Cape Race which has just joined up with the feeder convoys from Halifax and Sydney and is met by EG.C4 (Lt-Cdr Piers). The convoy (Commodore Vice-Adm Watson) consists of 42 ships with an escort of the Canadian destroyer *Restigouche*, the Canadian corvettes *Algoma*, *Amherst* and *Arvida* and the British *Celandine* and, initially, the destroyers of the Western Local Escort Group *Walker* (RN) and *Columbia* (RCN). There is also the rescue ship *Stockport* with HF/DF. An attack by *U522* on *Columbia* fails. *U520* is sunk in the area of the convoy by a Digby bomber of No 10 Sqn RCAF. On 31 Oct *U522* is driven off by a destroyer and *U521* by a Hudson of No 145 Sqn RCAF. As a result of a B-Service report, the Commander U-boats has moved the 'Veilchen' patrol line to the S with the result that SC.107 is sighted on 1 Nov by *U381* (Lt-Cdr Count v Pückler und Limpurg). Located by HF/DF, the first boats to approach, *U381*, *U704*, *U402*, are driven off by *Celandine* and *Restigouche*. Shortly after sunset *U71* is located by radar and forced to submerge. *U89* passes by. After midnight *U402* (Lt-Cdr Frhr v Forstner) attacks for the first time and torpedoes one ship of 7459 tons which is later finished off by *U84* (Lt-Cdr Uphoff). An attack by *U381* on *Restigouche* is outmanoeuvred. In the night *U402* and *U522* with a 3hr interval each attack the convoy twice—almost simultaneously. *U402* sinks three ships of 15270 tons and torpedoes one of 4558 tons which is later sunk by *U438* (Lt-Cdr Franzius). *U522* sinks two ships of 11466 tons and torpedoes one of 5496 tons which *U521* (Lt-Cdr Bargsten) later sinks. An attack by *U442* (Cdr Hesse) misses the convoy. By day on 2 Nov *U132*, *U402* and *U522* keep contact with SC.107, whose escort is reinforced by the Canadian corvette *Moosejaw*. In an underwater attack by day *U522* sinks one ship of 3189 tons. In the evening mist sets in, contact is lost and the convoy falls into disorder. The destroyer *Vanessa* is detached from convoy HX.213 and joins SC.107. When visibility improves, *U438*, *U402*, *U84*, *U381*, *U571*, *U71*, *U704*, *U521* and

U522 in turn establish contact by day on 3 Nov, because the convoy, after several zigzag moves, again proceeds on its general course. An attempt to attack by the boat in contact, *U438*, fails and *Celandine* and *Vanessa* drive off other U-boats detected by HF/DF. Only at mid-day does *U521* attack, when she sinks one tanker of 6855 tons. *U522* misses *Restigouche*. Until evening the escorts drive off all U-boats: only *U438* attacks the detached rescue ship *Stockport*—unsuccessfully. After dark on 4 Nov *U89* (Lt-Cdr Lohmann) comes up and sinks the ship of the convoy commodore, *Jeypore* (5318 tons). Later in the night *U132* (Lt-Cdr Vogelsang) sinks two ships of 11886 tons and torpedoes one of 6690 tons which is later sunk by *U442*. *U132* is lost, probably in this attack as a result of a tremendous explosion aboard the ammunition steamer *Hatimura*. (The incident led many crews to assume that their ship was hit; *U132* might have been within lethal range of this explosion.) Further attacks by *U71*, *U438* and *U442* have no success. By day on 4 Nov the tugs *Uncas* and *Pessacus* (overcrowded with 240 survivors), the rescue ship *Stockport* (likewise overcrowded), one tanker and the corvettes *Arvida* and *Celandine* are detached to Iceland. The US destroyers *Schenck* and *Leary* and the US Coast Guard cutter *Ingham* arrive in the late evening from Iceland shortly after *U89* has sunk one more ship of 4640 tons. In the morning of 5 Nov *U84*, *U381*, *U571*, *U454*, *U442*, *U522* and *U521*, which are still operating against the convoy, are driven off by Liberators from No 120 Sqn RAF which are directed by the HF/DF beams of the command boat *Restigouche*. On 5 Nov *U89* is damaged by Liberator 'H' of No 120 Sqn (Sqn Ldr Bulloch). The operation is broken off on 6 Nov.

21–23 Oct Lake Ladoga
A German attempt to land on the island of Suho in the southern part of Lake Ladoga fails.

22 Oct North Atlantic
During a patrol N of the Shetlands, Wellington 'B' of No 179 Sqn (Flt Sgt Martin), aided by the radar and Leigh Light, sinks the outgoing *U412* (Lt-Cdr Jahrmärker).

22–23 Oct South Pacific
The Australian destroyers *Arunta* and *Stuart* land an assault team of one battalion numbering 640 men on Goodenough Island, which has been evacuated by the Japanese.

22–27 Oct South Pacific
Carrier air battle near the Santa Cruz Islands and battle for Guadalcanal. Because of the difficulties in concentrating the Japanese troops of the 17th Army (Lt-Gen Hyakutake) brought to Guadalcanal, the original aim to take Henderson by 21 Oct is postponed more than once until 24 Oct. On 22 Oct the Japanese Army units make an attack but this repeatedly comes to a halt thanks to the resistance of the US Marines. When the airfield is prematurely reported to be taken during the night 24–25 Oct, the Combined Fleet, which has been at sea since 11 Oct and which has been partly able to replenish its destroyers again on 24 Oct, makes a sortie E of the Solomons to the S in several groups.

NE of Malaita there is the Advance Force (Vice-Adm Kondo) with the heavy cruisers *Atago*, *Takao*, *Myoko* and *Maya*, the battleships *Haruna* and *Kongo* and the 2nd DD Flotilla with the cruiser *Isuzu* and the destroyers *Takanami*, *Makinami*, *Naganami*, *Umikaze*, *Kawakaze*, *Suzukaze*, *Oyashio* and *Kagero*; the 2nd Carrier Sqn (Rear-Adm Kakuta) with the carrier *Junyo* and the destroyers *Hayashio* and *Kuroshio* is stationed further to the W. The second carrier, *Hiyo*, has had to return to Truk with engine trouble on 22 Oct, escorted by the destroyers *Inazuma* and *Isonami*.

SE of the Kondo Force is the Striking Force (Vice-Adm Nagumo) with the carriers *Shokaku*, *Zuikaku* and *Zuiho*, the heavy cruiser *Kumano* and the destroyers *Amatsukaze*, *Tokitsukaze*, *Hatsukaze*, *Yukikaze*, *Arashi*, *Maikaze*, *Hamakaze* and *Teruzuki*, and stationed to the S is the Vanguard Group (Rear-Adm Abe) with the battleships *Hiyei* and *Kirishima*, the heavy cruisers *Tone*, *Chikuma* and *Suzuya* and the 10th DD Flotilla with the cruiser *Nagara* and the destroyers *Akigumo*, *Yugumo*, *Makigumo*, *Kazegumo*, *Tanikaze*, *Urakaze* and *Isokaze*. In addition, the 4th DD Flotilla (Rear-Adm Takama) sets out from Shortland with the transport force, taking the cruiser *Yura*, the new destroyer leader *Akizuki* and the destroyers *Harusame*, *Yudachi*, *Murasame* and *Samidare* (2nd DD Div) and a bombardment force with the destroyers *Akatsuki*, *Ikazuchi* and *Shiratsuyu*. The latter, as they advance to a first daylight bombardment of Lunga Point, encounter the US APDs *Trever* and *Zane* coming from Tulagi. The APDs escape through the Sealark Channel after a short engagement but the Japanese destroyers then sink the tug *Seminole* and the harbour craft *YP-284* off Lunga. In the process *Akatsuki* is hit by a coastal battery. Dive-bombers from Henderson Field obtain hits on the cruiser *Yura*, which is coming up to shell, and on *Akatsuki*. The former has to be abandoned in the afternoon after further attacks by B-17 bombers and dive-bombers and is scuttled by the *Harusame* and *Yudachi*. The four Japanese carriers have 87 fighters, 68 dive-bombers and 57 torpedo aircraft. The 11th Air Fleet (Vice-Adm Kusaka), stationed on land on the Solomons and in the area of Rabaul, has about 220 aircraft at the beginning of the operations, but during the period 16–25 Oct these sustain considerable losses at the hands of the new fighters flown into Henderson Field. Japanese shore-based reconnaissance repeatedly locates on 21, 23 and 24 Oct US TF.64 (Rear-Adm Lee), comprising the battleship *Washington*, the cruisers *San Francisco* (Rear-Adm Scott), *Atlanta* and *Helena* and the destroyers *Aaron Ward*, *Lansdowne*, *Lardner*, *McCalla*, *Benham* and *Fletcher*. But it is not able to find the US carriers.

TF.61 (Rear-Adm Kinkaid), which sets out from Pearl Harbor on 16 Oct with the carrier *Enterprise*, the battleship *South Dakota*, the cruisers *Portland* (Rear-Adm Tisdale) and *San Juan* and Desron 5 with the destroyers *Porter*, *Mahan*, *Cushing*, *Preston*, *Smith*, *Maury* and *Conyngham*, joins up on 24 Oct 273 nautical miles NE of Espiritu Santo with TF.17 (Rear-Adm Murray), comprising the carrier *Hornet*, the cruisers *Northampton* (Rear-Adm Good), *Pensacola*, *San Diego* and *Juneau* and the destroyers *Morris*, *Anderson*, *Hughes*, *Mustin*, *Russell* and *Barton*. Both groups go to meet the Japanese Vanguard Group reported on 23 Oct by a Catalina flying boat of TF.63 (Rear-Adm Fitch—shore-based air units). On 25 Oct Catalinas report, in addition to the Vanguard Group, the Japanese carrier force behind it. Rear-Adm Fitch deploys against them B-17 bombers and Catalinas temporarily equipped as torpedo carriers. They secure near-misses by *Kirishima*, *Zuikaku* and *Isokaze*. Nevertheless, reconnaissance aircraft from *Enterprise* and the Japanese carriers do not find their targets. Aircraft from *Junyo* carry out a raid on US positions near Lunga Point.

Early on 26 Oct a reconnaissance aircraft from the Japanese cruiser *Tone* sights the US carrier forces. The carriers *Shokaku*, *Zuiho* and *Zuikaku* fly off 65 and 44 aircraft in two waves, followed by 29 planes from *Junyo*, which tries to close up to the Nagumo force. About the same time several of the 16 dive-bombers from *Enterprise*, flown off for armed reconnaissance, sight the Abe and Nagumo forces and obtain two hits on *Zuiho* which can no longer operate aircraft but which remains manoeuvrable. When this is reported, *Enterprise* and *Hornet* fly off three attack groups totalling 73 aircraft. Although the 38 aircraft of the US carriers' fighter cover shoot down almost half the

Japanese attackers, the latter, operating in several waves, obtain four bomb and two torpedo hits on *Hornet* (Capt Moran). Two other aircraft crash on to the ship, which is halted. The second wave concentrates on the *Enterprise* group, as does the *Junyo* force. They obtain two hits and one near-miss on the *Enterprise*, but the ship avoids all the torpedoes and, despite damage, remains substantially operational. *South Dakota*, *San Juan* and *Smith* are damaged by bomb hits and their own AA fire. *Portland* remains operational in spite of three torpedoes which hit but fail to detonate. *Hornet* is damaged by another torpedo from the last Japanese aircraft and *Hughes* is slightly damaged.

Of the two attack groups from *Hornet*, the first meanwhile attacks the Japanese carrier force and obtains three bomb hits on *Shokaku* (Adm Nagumo has later to transfer to the destroyer *Arashi*). *Suzuya* outmanoeuvres torpedoes. The second group, with the *Enterprise* group, attacks the Abe force and obtains five heavy hits on *Chikuma*. *Tone* and *Kirishima* just avoid torpedo and bomb hits respectively.

In the evening the Abe force (without *Chikuma*) and Kondo force make a sortie to the SE in the direction of the stricken US ships, while the carriers retire to the N. The US forces have to retire to the SE in face of the advancing Japanese heavy ships. The destroyers *Mustin* and *Anderson*, each using eight torpedoes with three and six hits respectively and 430 rounds of 5in shells, are unable to sink the wreck of the abandoned *Hornet*. Because it is impossible to tow her away, the Japanese destroyers *Akigumo* and *Makigumo* finish the ship off with torpedoes. At night a Catalina torpedo flying boat damages the destroyer *Teruzuki*.

Of the Japanese submarine groups A and B (see 24 Sept–9 Oct) deployed in support of the operations, *I-21* (Cdr* Matsumura) attacks the *Hornet* group during the carrier air battle and torpedoes the destroyer *Porter*, which has to be sunk by the destroyer *Shaw*. On 27 Oct *I-15* (Cdr* Ishikawa) just misses Adm Lee's flagship, the battleship *Washington*. On the same day the battleship *South Dakota* and the destroyer *Mahan* suffer damage in a collision while trying to avoid an attack by another Japanese submarine. *I-15* is lost on 2 Nov N of San Cristobal following a depth charge attack by the destroyer *McCalla*.

The battle of Santa Cruz ends with a tactical victory for the Japanese, but they are unable to exploit it because the Army's offensive by land on Guadalcanal has failed. The remaining carrier aircraft are no longer sufficient to eliminate Henderson Field; in addition,

the fleet has to return to Truk because of fuel shortages. It is therefore not possible to free the route for the transports from Rabaul to Guadalcanal.

23 Oct Mediterranean
Beginning of a British offensive on the Alamein front by the 8th Army (Gen Montgomery).

23 Oct North Sea
The German MDS *Sperrbrecher 11/ Belgrano* hits a mine off Ameland and breaks in two having swept her 100th mine. The after part of the ship is towed to Hamburg and repaired.

23 Oct North Atlantic
The British submarine *Unique*, on its way from the UK to the Mediterranean, is lost W of Gibraltar to an unknown cause.

23–31 Oct North Atlantic
From 23 Oct *U510*, *U509*, *U572*, *U134*, *U409*, *U203*, *U604* and *U659* proceed, as the 'Streitaxt' group, in line abreast to the S, west of Africa. On 25 Oct *U510* sights one steamer, *U659* two escorts and *U203* one escorted tanker (7705 tons); the last is shadowed by *U134* on 27 Oct and sunk by *U604* (Lt-Cdr Höltring). In the morning of 27 Oct *U409* (Lt Massmann) reports the convoy SL.125 (37 ships and four corvettes including the British *Petunia* (Lt-Cdr Rayner)). In the evening *U203*, *U509* and *U659* are brought up. They attack, but only *U509* (Lt Witte) sinks two ships of 14099 tons. On 28 Oct *U203* (Lt Kottmann) keeps contact and brings up *U409*, *U659*, *U509*, *U510* and *U604*. *U103* and *U440*, coming from the N, are also directed to the scene. After a miss in the morning, *U509* torpedoes in the evening one ship of 5283 tons which is later sunk by *U203*. On 29 Oct *U134* (Lt-Cdr Schendel) keeps contact from mid-day and brings up *U103*, *U510*, *U509* and *U604*. In the night *U509* attacks twice and each time torpedoes one ship of 4772 tons and 7131 tons respectively. Both victims receive finishing-off hits from *U659* (Lt-Cdr Stock); the second ship is sunk by torpedo and gunfire from *U203*. *U409* sinks one ship of 7519 tons and in the morning *U509* misses one of the corvettes. On 30 Oct *U509* and *U604* continually keep contact and bring all except three boats up. In the night *U604* in two attacks sinks the transport *President Doumer* (11898 tons) and one ship of 3642 tons, *U659* sinks one ship of 6373 tons, *U409* sinks one ship of 6405 tons and *U510* (Cdr Neitzel) torpedoes one ship of 5681 tons. *U103* (Lt Janssen) misses one corvette and two ships of the scattered convoy. *U659* is damaged by depth charges. On 31 Oct *U509* and *U604* keep contact

with the remainder but towards evening all boats are driven off when air escort is provided and there is reinforced sea escort. As this operation involves the U-boats in the area W of Morocco and Gibraltar, the simultaneous 'Torch' convoys reach their destinations unmolested by U-boats.

23 Oct–7 Nov Central Atlantic
Crossing of the US 'Torch' invasion force for French North Africa—Task Force 34 (Rear-Adm Hewitt): TG.34.1/Covering Group (Rear-Adm Giffen), with the battleship *Massachusetts*, the cruisers *Wichita* and *Tuscaloosa*, the destroyers *Wainwright*, *Mayrant*, *Rhind* and *Jenkins* and the tanker *Chemungo* (sailed from Casco Bay to rendezvous point on 28 Oct 450 nautical miles SE of Cape Race): TG.34.8/Northern Attack Group (Rear-Adm Kelly) with the battleship *Texas*, the cruiser *Savannah*, the destroyers *Roe*, *Livermore*, *Kearny*, *Ericsson* and *Parker*, the submarine *Shad*, the escort carriers *Sangamon* and *Chenango* with the destroyers *Hambleton*, *Macomb*, *Dallas* and *Eberle*, six transports, two freighters, one tanker, two minesweepers and the seaplane tender *Barnegat*; TG.34.9/Centre Attack Group (Capt Emmet) with the cruisers *Augusta* and *Brooklyn*, the destroyers *Wilkes*, *Swanson*, *Ludlow* and *Murphy*, 112 transports, three freighters with the destroyers *Bristol*, *Woolsey*, *Edison*, *Tillman*, *Boyle* and *Rowan*, three fast minesweepers, two minelayers, one minesweeper, the carriers *Ranger* and *Suwanee*, the destroyers *Ellyson*, *Forrest*, *Fitch*, *Corry* and *Hobson*, the submarines *Gunnel* and *Herring* and one tanker; and TG.34.10/Southern Attack Group (Rear-Adm Davidson) with the battleship *New York*, the cruiser *Philadelphia*, the destroyers *Mervine*, *Knight* and *Beatty*, five transports, one freighter with the destroyers *Cowie*, *Quick*, *Doran*, *Cole* and *Bernadou*, one minelayer, two fast minesweepers, two tankers, the submarine *Barb*, the carrier *Santee* with the destroyers *Rodman* and *Emmons* and one tug. The transports and freighters constitute convoy UGF.1.

25 Oct–14 Nov South Atlantic
The Italian submarines *Da Vinci* (Lt-Cdr Gazzana-Priaroggia) operates until 30 Oct W of the Cape Verde Islands and then off the NE coast of Brazil. She sinks four ships of 26042 tons from 2 to 11 Nov. On 3 Nov the Dutch steamer *Frans Hals* escapes when she forces the submarine to submerge with gunfire after a torpedo miss.

26 Oct Baltic
The German A/S trawler *UJ1204* sinks after hitting a mine in a gale off Tysmersaari.

26 Oct–8 Jan   North Atlantic

The Allied Mid Ocean Escort Groups escort the following convoys on the North Atlantic route (convoys attacked by U-boat groups are denoted thus *): B1: SC. 105, HX.215, ON.151, SC.114. B2: HX.213, ONS.148, HX.219. B3: SC.106, ONS.146*, HX.218, ON.157. B4: HX.214, ONS.150, HX.220. B6: ONS.144*, HX.217*, ON.155. B7: ONS.142, HX.216, ON.153*. C1: ON.143*, SC.110, ONS.154*. C2: SC.108, ON.149, SC.113. C3: ON.141, SC.109*, ONS.152*. C4: SC.107, ON.147, SC.112. A3: ON.145*, SC.111, ONS.156. B5 is on loan in the Caribbean.

28–30 Oct   Mediterranean

British Force H, with the carrier *Furious*, the cruisers *Aurora* and *Charybdis* and eight destroyers, proceeds from Gibraltar into the area S of the Balearics and flies off 29 Spitfire fighters to Malta. The Italian submarines *Emo*, *Brin*, *Corallo*, *Turchese*, *Topazio* and *Axum* S of the Balearics and *Porfido*, *Nichelio*, *Asteria* and *Argo* off Cape Bon sight nothing. At the end of Oct and the beginning of Nov, the fast minelayer *Welshman* and the submarines *Parthian*, *Clyde*, *Traveller* and *Thrasher* have again to be employed to bring aviation fuel, food and ammunition to Malta. The Italian submarines *Micca*, *Sciesa*, *Bragadino*, *Narvalo*, *Atropo* and *Zoea* transport fuel and ammunition to North Africa. On 7 Nov *Sciesa* is sunk off Derna in a USAAF air attack.

28 Oct–8 Nov   South Pacific

Continuation of the supply operations for Guadalcanal.

The Japanese 8th Fleet (Vice-Adm Mikawa) continues the transport of supplies at first with the 3rd DD Flotilla (Rear-Adm Hashimoto) comprising the cruiser *Sendai* and the destroyers *Shirayuki*, *Hatsuyuki*, *Uranami*, *Shikinami* and *Ayanami* and the 4th DD Flotilla (Rear-Adm Takama) comprising the destroyers *Murasame*, *Yudachi*, *Harusame*, *Samidare*, *Asagumo*, *Yugure*, *Shiratsuyu* and *Shigure*. From 5 Nov they are relieved by the 2nd DD Flotilla (Rear-Adm Tanaka) comprising the cruiser *Isuzu* and the destroyers *Hayashio*, *Oyashio*, *Kagero*, *Umikaze*, *Kawakaze*, *Suzukaze*, *Naganami*, *Makinami* and *Takanami*. These ships, together with the cruiser *Tenryu* and the destroyers *Arashio*, *Asashio*, *Michishio*, *Amagiri* and *Mochizuki*, which are with the 8th Fleet, undertake, in all, two cruiser and 65 destroyer missions, in the course of which there are repeated air attacks and engagements with US PT boats from Tulagi. US TG. 62.4 (Rear-Adm Scott) with the cruiser *Atlanta* and the destroyers *Aaron Ward*, *Benham*, *Fletcher* and *Lardner* brings the

transports *Alchiba* and *Fuller* with two 155mm batteries to Guadalcanal and from 30 to 31 Oct supports the attack of the 1st Marine Div over the Matanikau River to the W. On 2–3 Nov the attack is supported by the destroyers *Conyngham* and *Shaw* with 803 rounds of 5in shell and reaches Point Cruz on 3 Nov. But the same night a Japanese force of one cruiser, three destroyers and one transport lands 1500 men of the 230th Inf Regt near Koli Point, E of the US bridgehead, while other units of the 'Tokyo Express' land elements of the 228th Inf Regt in the W near Kokumbona. The 1st Marine Div temporarily halts its attack towards the W and regroups forces for a counter-attack in the E. Simultaneously, TG.67.4 (Rear-Adm Callaghan) arrives off Lunga Point on 4 Nov and disembarks the 8th Marine Inf Regt (2nd Div) as reinforcement. The cruisers *Helena* and *San Francisco* with the destroyer *Sterett* from the covering forces shell the Japanese troops which have landed near Koli Point. The latter are wiped out by 9 Nov in the counter-attack.

A second US group, consisting of the transports *Neville*, *Heywood* and *Fomalhaut* and the destroyer transports *McKean* and *Manley*, lands on 4 Nov near Aola Bay on the E coast of Guadalcanal 1700 men of the 147th Inf Regt and a Marine Raider Battalion, as well as 500 Seabees to construct an airfield. But this proves impossible because of the difficulties of the terrain.

On 7 Nov the Japanese 2nd DD Flotilla under Capt Sato with the destroyers *Oyashio*, *Kagero*, *Umikaze*, *Kawakaze*, *Suzukaze*, *Naganami*, *Makinami* and *Takanami*, plus *Yugumo*, *Makigumo* and *Kazegumo* from the 10th DD Div, sets out from Shortland for Guadalcanal with an advance party of 1300 men from the 38th Inf Div. On the way they are attacked by dive-bombers from Henderson Field which damage *Naganami* and *Takanami*. A successful disembarkation is made during the night 7–8 Nov. The following night (8–9 Nov) the destroyers *Asashio*, *Arashio*, *Michishio*, *Amagiri* and *Mochizuki* also arrive with reinforcements and supplies. The US motor torpedo boats *PT61*, *PT39* and *PT37* attack from Tulagi and obtain a light torpedo hit on *Mochizuki*.

The Japanese deploy the SM Group A (*I-16*, *I-20* and *I-24*) against the US supply transports. *I-20* (Cdr* Yoshimura) torpedoes the transport *Majaba* (2227 tons) on 7 Nov and evades pursuit by the destroyers *Lansdowne* and *Lardner*, the first of which has landed 90 tons of ammunition.

29 Oct–4 Nov   Mediterranean

During the nights 29–30 Oct and 3–4 Nov the Italian destroyers *Pigafetta* (Captain Del Minio), *Da Noli* and *Zeno* and the torpedo boat *Castelfidardo* lay the mine barrages S.72 and S.73, with 388 and 338 mines respectively, N of Cape Bon.

29 Oct–9 Nov   Arctic

At the wish of the Russians, 13 single freighters sail on 29 Oct from Reykjavik to Murmansk and Archangel with 200 nautical miles between them and five independents return from Soviet harbours to Iceland. Of the eastbound ships, six are lost. On 2 Nov *U586* (Lt-Cdr v d Esch) sinks the *Empire Gilbert* (6640 tons). On 4 Nov the first ships are located by KF1Gr 406. The Soviet *Dekabrist* (7363 tons) is sunk by Ju 88s of I/KG 30 sent to the scene, while II/KG 30 damages two ships. Of them, the *William Clark* (7176 tons) is finished off by *U354* (Lt-Cdr Herbschleb) and the *Chulmleigh* (5445 tons) by one torpedo from *U625* (Lt Benker) on 16 Nov, the latter victim having been beached by another bomb hit on 5 Nov on the S Cape of Spitzbergen. *U625* also sinks the *Empire Sky* (7455 tons). The heavy cruiser *Admiral Hipper* (Capt Hartmann, with the Commander Cruisers, Vice-Adm Kummetz, on board) and the 5th DD Flotilla (Capt Schemmel), comprising *Z27*, *Z30*, *Friedrich Eckoldt* and *Richard Beitzen*, are also used against the traffic on 5 Nov. KG 30 flies reconnaissance flights. On 7 Nov the westbound Soviet tanker *Donbass* (7925 tons) is located and sunk by *Z27*, as is the Soviet auxiliary escort *SKR-23/Musson*.

30 Oct–12 Dec   Mediterranean/ Intelligence

In the eastern Mediterranean, the British destroyers *Pakenham*, *Petard*, *Hero*, *Dulverton* and *Hurworth*, supported by a Wellesley aircraft from No 47 Sqn RAF, force *U559* (Lt-Cdr Heidtmann) to the surface and a specially trained boarding party from *Petard* enters the submarine and recovers the codebooks and the new 'Wetterkurzschlüssel'. However, two men, Lt F A B Fasson and Able Seaman C Grazier, go down with the U-boat while trying to recover the 'M-4' cypher machine. The documents arrive at Bletchley Park on 24 Nov. Using the 'Wetterkurzschlüssel' and Norddeich meteorological broadcasts as broken by Hut 10 at Bletchley Park, Hut 8 succeeds in penetrating 'Triton' on 13 Dec.

30 Oct–15 Dec   South Atlantic

Between St Paul and the Brazilian coast, *U174* (Cdr Thilo) sinks five ships of 30813 tons, *U128* (Lt-Cdr Heyse) three ships of 15571 tons and *U172* (Lt-Cdr Emmermann) and *U159* (Lt-Cdr Witte), which are returning from South Africa, two ships of 11994 tons and three ships of 16497 tons respectively.

1–8 Nov North Atlantic

The 'Natter' group is formed W of Ireland from the U-boats *U224*, *U383*, *U436*, *U606*, *U624* coming from HX.212 and from the newly arrived *U98*. By 4 Nov *U566*, *U613*, *U92*, *U564*, *U563* and the newly replenished *U753* are added to it. On 4 Nov *U92* (Lt Oelrich) sights the convoy ON.143 (EG.C1) but contact is soon lost and is not re-established until 6 Nov because most of the boats have not yet reached their position. On 7 Nov *U566* (Lt Remus) and *U613* (Lt-Cdr Köppe) each sink a straggler of 4252 tons. On 8 Nov the boats with adequate fuel supplies are sent to the area W of Gibraltar; those short of fuel go to the 'Kreuzotter' group.

1 Nov–16 Dec South Africa

After *U178* has sunk the transport *Duchess of Atholl* (20119 tons) on the way on 10 Oct, three Type IXD2 boats operate as a second wave off South Africa. *U178* (Capt Ibbeken) sinks five ships of 26978 tons and damages one of 6348 tons, *U177* (Lt-Cdr Gysae) sinks eight of 49371 tons and *U181* (Lt-Cdr Lüth) sinks twelve of 58431 tons. In addition, the Italian submarine *Cagni* (Cdr* Liannazza), coming from the Mediterranean, sinks one ship on the way out and another off South Africa, totalling 5840 tons.

2–18 Nov Central Atlantic

Convoy UGF.2 from New York to Casablanca, escorted by TF.38 with the battleship *Arkansas* and the destroyers *Plunkett*, *Gleaves*, *Benson*, *Mayo*, *Taylor*, *La Valette*, *Chevalier* and *Strong*.

3–7 Nov Mediterranean

The German 3rd MTB Flotilla (Lt-Cdr Kemnade) lays off Malta the barrages MT.25–27 with 108 UMB mines, 18 protection and 29 explosive floats.

4–6 Nov Mediterranean

During RAF air attacks on Benghazi, the Italian torpedo boat *Centauro* (4 Nov) and the minesweeper *Selve* (ex-Yugoslav *Galeb*) are destroyed.

4 Nov North Pacific

The Japanese submarine *Ro-65* is lost in an air attack on Kiska harbour.

4–8 Nov Atlantic

In preparation for Operation 'Torch', the US submarines *Shad*, *Gunnel*, *Herring*, *Barb* and *Blackfish* reconnoitre off the Moroccan harbours of Rabat, Fedala, Casablanca, Safi and off Dakar. *Herring* (Lt-Cdr Johnson) sinks the French steamer *Ville du Havre* (5083 tons) on 8 Nov. The submarines are then deployed in the Bay of Biscay from

British bases. The first operation with *Gurnard* takes place in early Dec.

4–19 Nov Western Atlantic

U608 (Lt Struckmeier), operating off New York, sinks one ship of 5621 tons and lays an unsuccessful mine barrage on 10 Nov.

5 Nov Arctic

Catalina 'H' of VP-84 (Lt Millard), on patrol N of Iceland, sinks *U408* (Lt-Cdr v Hymmen).

5–15 Nov Mediterranean

All available German U-boats are stationed in the area W of the line Balearics–Algiers in the western Mediterranean as a precaution against the heavy concentrations of ships observed in Gibraltar. They include *U73*, *U77*, *U81*, *U205*, *U331*, *U431*, *U458*, *U561*, *U565*, *U593*, *U605* and *U660* from the Mediterranean boats as well as *U595*, *U407*, *U617*, *U596*, *U755*, *U259* and *U380* which have just come from the Atlantic. In the area of Algiers and to the E, the Italian boats *Axum*, *Topazio*, *Argo*, *Platino*, *Mocenigo*, *Emo*, *Nichelio*, *Asteria*, *Porfido*, *Velella*, *Brin*, *Dandolo*, *Argento*, *Acciaio*, *Bronzo*, *Turchese*, *Corallo*, *Aradam*, *Diaspro*, *Alagi* and *Avorio* are deployed. On 7 Nov *U205* (Lt-Cdr Reschke) probably torpedoes the US transport *Thomas Stone* (9255 tons), which is later beached off Algiers; on 10 Nov *U431* (Lt-Cdr Dommes) sinks the British destroyer *Martin* and *U81* (Lt-Cdr Guggenberger) the transport *Garlinge* (2012 tons); and on 11 Nov *U380* (Lt-Cdr Röther) sinks the transport *Nieuw Zeeland* (11069 tons), *U407* (Lt-Cdr Brüller) the transport *Viceroy of India* (19627 tons) and *U595* (Lt-Cdr J Quaet-Faslem) the transport *Browning* (5332 tons). On 12 Nov *U77* (Lt-Cdr Otto Hartmann) torpedoes the British sloop *Stork* and the Italian submarine *Argo* (Lt-Cdr Gigli) attacks in the roads of Bougie the transports *Awatea* and *Cathay*, respectively damaged by mines and air attacks, and hits them again. The damaged AA ship *Tynwald* is torpedoed and sunk. On 13 Nov *U431* sinks the Dutch destroyer *Isaac Sweers* and *U73* (Lt-Deckert) the transport *Lalande* (7453 tons). The Italian submarine *Platino* (Lt-Cdr Rigoli) torpedoes the British transport *Narkunda* (16632 tons), already damaged in an air attack. On 14 Nov *U81* sinks the transport *Maron* (6487 tons) and on 15 Nov the Italian submarine *Ascianghi* (Lt-Cdr Erler) sinks the minesweeper *Algerine* off Bougie. On 10 Nov *Emo* is sunk by the trawler *Lord Nuffield* and on 12 Nov *U660* is sunk by the corvettes *Lotus* and *Starwort* from convoy TE.3. On 13 Nov *U458* (Lt-Cdr Diggins) is damaged by Hudson 'S' of No 500 Sqn (Lt M A Ensor) but manages to limp back to La Spezia.

On 14 Nov *U595* (Lt-Cdr Quaet-Faslam) is damaged by Hudsons 'C' and 'D' of No 608 Sqn W of Cap Tenes and has to be beached during attacks by Hudsons 'X', 'J', 'F', 'K' and 'W' of No 500 Sqn while damaging some of the aircraft with AA fire; the crew is rescued by the French. On the same day *U605* (Lt-Cdr H V Schütze) is sunk by Hudson 'B' of No 233 Sqn. On 15 Nov *U259* (Lt-Cdr Köpke) is sunk by Hudson 'S' of No 500 Sqn (Fg Off M A Ensor) N of Algies but shoots down the aircraft. On 17 Nov *U331* (Lt-Cdr v Tiesenhausen) is sunk by an Albacore of No 820 Sqn FAA from the carrier *Formidable* and Hudsons 'Z' 'L' and 'C' of No 500 Sqn RAF. On 17 Nov *U566* (Lt-Cdr Hornkohl) is damaged by Hudson 'U' of No 233 Sqn (Sgt Smith).

5–17 Nov Pacific

The US submarine *Haddock* (Lt-Cdr Taylor) sinks three ships of 14324 tons off Japan and torpedoes one more of 2732 tons.

5–20 Nov Baltic

Because it begins to ice up, the Soviet submarines have to return from the Baltic to Lavansaari through the mine barrages of the Gulf of Finland. *D-2*, *Shch-406*, *Shch-307*, *Shch-303*, *S-12* and *L-3* are in turn met by minesweeper forces, patrol cutters and torpedo cutters with air support. *M-96* operates in Nov in the Gulf of Finland as the last boat to set out. In the escort operations and submarine escorts the following Soviet vessels are lost between May and Nov 1942: the minesweepers *T-204*/*Fugas*, *Udarnik* and *T-48* and the patrol cutters *MO-211*, *MO-212*, *MO-308* and *MO-225*.

7–9 Nov Mediterranean

During the night 7–8 Nov the new Italian cruiser *Attilio Regolo* with the destroyers *Pigafetta* (Rear-Adm Gasparri), *Ascari*, *Da Noli*, *Mitragliere* and *Zeno* lay the barrage S.8 with 241 mines E of Cape Bon, whilst, at the same time, the destroyer *Corazziere* lays the explosive float barrage St. 2. On the return the cruiser *Regolo* is torpedoed by the British submarine *Unruffled* (Lt Stevens) W of Sicily but is taken in tow by the tug *Polifemo*, escorted by the torpedo boats *Cigno*, *Lince* and *Abba*. An attack by the British submarine *United* misses the towing convoy.

8 Nov North Africa

Operation 'Torch': Allied landing in French North Africa. The Western Task Force (landing on the W coast of Morocco between Safi and Mehedia with the main target Casablanca) is commanded by Rear Adm-Hewitt (USN) and Maj-Gen Patton (US Army). Naval forces comprise the battleships *Massachusetts* and *Texas*, the aircraft carrier *Ranger*, the escort carriers *Sangamon*, *Chen-*

ango, *Suwanee* and *Santee*, the heavy cruisers *Wichita*, *Tuscaloosa* and *Augusta*, the light cruisers *Savannah*, *Brooklyn*, *Cleveland* and *Philadelphia*, 38 destroyers, three minelayers, eight minesweepers, one flying boat tender, four submarines, 23 troop transports, eight supply transports and five tankers. Land forces consist of the 2nd US Armoured Div, the 3rd US Inf Div and two-thirds of the US 9th Inf Div, comprising 34305 troops, 54 medium and 198 light tanks.

The Centre Task Force (landing in the area of Oran) is under Commodore Troubridge (RN) and Maj-Gen Fredendall (US Army). Naval forces consist of the headquarters ship *Largs*, the escort carriers *Biter* and *Dasher*, the light cruisers *Aurora* and *Jamaica*, the AA cruiser *Delhi*, one AA ship, 13 destroyers, four sloops, six corvettes, eight minesweepers, eight trawlers, ten launches, two submarines, 19 landing ships and 28 supply transports. Land forces comprise the 1st US Inf Div and half of the US Armoured Div, comprising 39000 troops.

The Eastern Task Force (landings in the area of Algiers) is commanded by Rear-Adm Burrough (RN) and Maj-Gen Ryder (US Army). Naval forces consist of the headquarters ship *Bulolo*, the monitor *Roberts*, three AA ships, eight destroyers, three sloops, six corvettes, seven minesweepers, eight trawlers, eight launches, three submarines, 17 landing ships, 16 supply transports and Force O (Rear-Adm Harcourt) with the carrier *Argus*, the escort carrier *Avenger*, the light cruisers *Sheffield*, *Scylla* and *Charybdis* and five destroyers. Land forces are made up by the 34th US Inf Div, one-third of the 9th US Inf Div, one-half of the 1st US Armoured Div and the 78th British Inf Div, comprising 33000 troops.

The operations in the Mediterranean are covered by Force H (Vice-Adm Syfret) with the battleships *Duke of York*, *Nelson* and *Rodney*, the battlecruiser *Renown*, the carriers *Victorious* (Rear-Adm Lyster), *Formidable* and *Furious*, the light cruisers *Argonaut*, *Bermuda* and *Sirius* and 17 destroyers.

The French forces put up considerable resistance in places to the Allied landing fleets. Attempts by the sloops *Walney* and *Hartland* to enter the harbour of Oran (Naval Commander Vice-Adm Rioult) to prevent the French ships scuttling themselves fail, as does a similar operation in Algiers (HQ Adm Darlan; Naval Commander Vice-Adm Leclerc) with the destroyers *Broke* and *Malcolm*. Apart from *Malcolm* the participating ships are sunk by

French coastal artillery and *Hartland* by the destroyer *Typhon*. The submarines *Caïman* and *Marsouin* break out of Algiers for Toulon.

In the fighting for Oran, the French Navy loses the flotilla leader *Epervier* (Cdr* Laurin), the destroyers *Tornade*, *Tramontane* and *Typhon*, the minesweeper *La Surprise* (to gunfire from the cruiser *Aurora* and the destroyer *Brilliant*) and, in addition to smaller vessels, the submarines *Ariane*, *Cérès*, *Diane* and *Pallas*. The submarines *Actéon* (Cdr Clavières) and *Argonaute* (Lt-Cdr Veron) try to attack but are sunk by the destroyers *Achates* and *Westcott*; the submarine *Fresnel* attacks the cruiser *Sheffield* without success and is able to escape to Toulon. In Casablanca (Naval Commander Vice-Adm Michelier), too, the French Navy resists strongly. The unfinished battleship *Jean Bart* is severely damaged by shelling and air attacks. Attempts by Rear-Adm de Lafond to attack the Western Task Force with the cruiser *Primauguet* (Capt Mercier†), the flotilla leaders *Albatros* and *Milan* and the destroyers *Boulonnais*, *Brestois*, *Fougueux* and *Frondeur* fail: *Primauguet* and *Albatros* are hit by gunfire from *Augusta* and *Brooklyn* and *Milan* by gunfire from the destroyer *Wilkes* (all have to be beached) and the other ships are sunk in the harbour or outside by gunfire from *Massachusetts* and *Tuscaloosa*, which ships also damage *Jean Bart*. Of the 11 submarines present in Casablanca, *Amazone* attacks *Brooklyn* on 8 Nov and *Le Tonnant* attacks *Ranger* and *Meduse* and *Antiope* attack *Massachusetts* and *Tuscaloosa* on 10 Nov, but all torpedoes are narrowly evaded. *Amphitrite*, *La Sibylle*, *Méduse*, *Oréade*, *La Psyché*, *Sidi Ferruch* and *Le Conquérant* are lost. *Le Tonnant* scuttles herself off Cadiz, *Amazone* and *Antiope* go to Dakar and the eleventh boat, *Orphée*, returns to Casablanca after the fighting. The French Navy loses, in all, 462 dead, the Army 326 and the Air Force 15; in addition, there are over 1000 wounded.

German bombers and torpedo aircraft damage and sink from 8 to 14 Nov off the North African coast the troop transports *Awatea* (13482 tons) and *Cathay* (15225 tons), the landing ship *Karanja* (9891 tons), the transports *Glenfinlas* (7572 tons) and *Leedstown* (9135 tons) and the gunboat *Ibis*. The carrier *Argus* is hit by bombs and the monitor *Roberts* is severely damaged. For successes by German and Italian submarines against the landing forces see 5–15 Nov (Mediterranean) and 8–27 Nov (Central Atlantic).

8–15 Nov   South Pacific

Japanese and US forces seek a decision in the battle for Guadalcanal. On 8 Nov US TG.67.1 (Rear-Adm Turner) sets out from Nouméa with the transports *McCawley*, *President Jackson*, *President Adams* and *Crescent City*, on which 6000 troops of the reinforced 182nd Inf Regt are embarked. Escort is provided by the cruisers *Pensacola* and *Portland* and the destroyers *Barton*, *Monssen* and *O'Bannon* (from TG.67.4). It is followed on 9 Nov from Espiritu Santo by TG.62.4 (Rear-Adm Scott) with the cruiser *Atlanta* and the destroyers *Aaron Ward*, *Fletcher*, *Lardner* and *McCalla* and the transports *Zeilin*, *Libra* and *Betelgeuse* with some 1000 troops and a construction battalion. TG.67.4 (Rear-Adm Callaghan) puts to sea from Espiritu Santo as a covering force with the cruisers *San Francisco*, *Helena* and *Juneau* and the destroyers *Cushing*, *Laffey*, *Sterett*, *Buchanan*, *Shaw*, *Gwin* and *Preston*. It joins the Turner Group on 11 Nov. During the night 11–12 Nov TF.16 (Rear-Adm Kinkaid) also puts to sea from Nouméa with a covering group consisting of the carrier *Enterprise*, the cruisers *Northampton* and *San Diego* and the destroyers *Clark*, *Anderson*, *Hughes*, *Morris*, *Austin* and *Russell*, together with TF.64 (Rear-Adm Lee), comprising the battleships *South Dakota* and *Washington* and the destroyers *Benham* and *Walke*.

On the Japanese side, the destroyers *Makinami*, *Suzukaze*, *Yugumo*, *Makigumo* and *Kazegumo* bring another 600 men and the Commander of the Japanese 38th Inf Div, Lt-Gen Sano, to Guadalcanal during the night 10–11 Nov. Air and PT boat attacks are repelled.

To protect the Japanese operation, the submarines of Group D, *I-122*, *I-175*, *I-172* and *Ro34*, are concentrated in the approaches to the N coast of Guadalcanal. *I-172* is sunk on 10 Nov by the US minesweeper *Southard*. On 11 Nov the submarines *I-7*, *I-9*, *I-21* and *I-31* fly off their aircraft to reconnoitre over Vanikoro/Santa Cruz, Espiritu Santo, Nouméa and Suva/Fiji. In the process *I-21* (Cdr* Matsumura) sinks one transport of 7176 tons. On the US side, 24 submarines are distributed in the area of the Solomons.

The Japanese 2nd Fleet (Vice-Adm Kondo) sets out from Truk on 9 Nov in order to carry out the following plan in co-operation with the 8th Fleet (Vice-Adm Mikawa) operating from Rabaul and Shortland: during the night 12–13 Nov Vice-Adm Abe is to shell Henderson Field with the battleships *Hiyei* and *Kirishima* (11th BB Sqn), screened by the 10th DD Flotilla (Rear-

Adm Kimura) comprising the cruiser *Nagara* and the destroyers *Yukikaze* and *Amatsukaze* (16th DD Div), *Akatsuki, Ikazuchi* and *Inazuma* (6th DD Div) and *Teruzuki*, together with the 4th DD Flotilla (Rear-Adm Takama) with the destroyers *Asagumo, Murasame, Samidare, Yudachi* and *Harusame* (2nd DD Div) and *Shigure, Shiratsuyu* and *Yugure* (27th DD Div). The following night (13–14 Nov) the shelling is to be repeated by a force (Rear-Adm Nishimura) consisting of the cruisers *Maya* and *Suzuya*, screened by the light cruiser *Tenryu* with the destroyers *Kazegumo, Makigumo* and *Yugumo* (10th DD Div) and *Michishio*. Vice-Adm Mikawa is to cover this operation with the cruisers *Chokai, Isuzu* and *Kinugasa* and the destroyers *Arashio* and *Asashio* (8th DD Div). At the same time Rear-Adm Tanaka with the 2nd DD Flotilla, comprising the destroyers *Hayashio, Kagero* and *Oyashio* (15th DD Div), *Kawakaze, Suzukaze* and *Umikaze* (24th DD Div), *Makinami, Naganami* and *Takanami* (31st DD Div) and *Amagiri* and *Mochizuki*, is to land 11 large transports with the bulk of the 38th Inf Div and its heavy equipment near Cape Esperance and Kokumbona. The main body of the 2nd Fleet (Vice-Adm Kondo), comprising the cruisers *Atago* (F) and *Takao*, the battleships *Kongo* (Vice-Adm Kurita, 3rd BB Sqn) and *Haruna*, the carriers *Junyo* (Rear-Adm Kakuta, 2nd Carrier Sqn) and *Hiyo*, the cruisers *Tone* and *Sendai* (Rear-Adm Hashimoto, 3rd DD Flotilla) and the destroyers *Hatsuyuki* and *Shirayuki* (11th DD Div) and *Uranami, Shikinami* and *Ayanami* (19th DD Div) takes up a covering position NE of the Solomons.

On 11 Nov TG.62.4 (Rear-Adm Scott) arrives off Lunga Point and begins at once the disembarkation from the three transports. In an attack by 12 Japanese aircraft from *Hiyo*, the transport *Zeilin* is damaged and detached with the destroyer *Lardner*. A Japanese bomber force from the 11th Air Fleet (Vice-Adm Kusaka) from Rabaul attacks Henderson Field.

In the morning of 12 Nov the transports of Rear-Adm Turner and the covering force of Rear-Adm Callaghan arrive off Guadalcanal and begin to disembark. The cruiser *Portland* is detached to TF.16 and the destroyers *Gwin* and *Preston* to TF.64. In an air attack by bombers from Rabaul, the destroyer *Buchanan* is damaged by her own AA and the cruiser *San Francisco* by a crashing Japanese aircraft. When air reconnaissance reports come in about the approaching Japanese naval forces, Adm Turner breaks off the disembarkation and withdraws the transports, escorted by the destroyers *Buch-*

anan, McCalla and *Shaw* and the minesweepers *Hovey* and *Southard*. TG.67.4, in the order the destroyers *Cushing, Laffey, Sterett* and *O'Bannon*, cruisers *San Francisco* (Rear-Adm Callaghan), *Portland, Helena* and *Atlanta* (Rear-Adm Scott) and destroyers *Aaron Ward, Barton, Monssen* and *Fletcher*, tries to intercept the approaching Japanese bombardment force of Vice-Adm Abe (see above) between Savo Island and Lunga Point. Abe, who has left the three destroyers of the 27th DD Div behind as defence to the westward, comes up against Callaghan's force in the dark on 13 Nov. In fierce engagements, at very short range, the US force is broken up. Both US admirals perish in the first minutes.

Atlanta (Capt S P Jenkins) and the destroyer *Laffey* are sunk by gunfire from *Hiyei* and torpedoes from *Akatsuki* and other destroyers, *Barton* is sunk by destroyer torpedoes and *Cushing* and *Monssen* are damaged by gunfire and blow up later. *San Francisco* (Capt Cassin Young†), *Juneau, Portland, Aaron Ward* and *Sterett* are badly damaged. On the Japanese side, *Akatsuki* sinks after being hit by gunfire from *Atlanta* and *O'Bannon* and *Yudachi*, disabled by gunfire, is sunk in the morning by *Portland*. *Hiyei* receives more than 50 shell hits and sinks in the morning after receiving two air torpedo hits from aircraft from *Enterprise* operating S of Guadalcanal and a bomb hit from a B-17, the crew having been saved. Of the Japanese submarines *I-17* and *I-26* (Cdr* Yokota), the latter attacks the returning US force, misses the flagship *San Francisco* but sinks *Juneau* (Capt Swenson†).

In order to knock out Henderson Field on 14 Nov, the Japanese cruisers *Suzuya* (Rear-Adm Hashimoto) and *Maya* shell the airfield, as planned, during the night 13–14 Nov, but with little success. The remaining ships of this force and of the Support Group (Vice-Adm Mikawa) guard the N and the W. The landing of the troops from the 11 transports, which have set out from Shortland on 12 Nov with the 2nd DD Flotilla, is postponed for 24hr to give another bombardment group under Vice-Adm Kondo an opportunity to shell Henderson Field again during the night 14–15 Nov and to provide cover for the landing. This group comprises *Atago, Takao, Sendai, Uranami, Shikinami, Ayanami, Kirishima, Nagara, Teruzuki, Inazuma, Asagumo* and *Samidare*, which join from the 1st Bombardment Group, and *Hatsuyuki* and *Shirayuki* from the carrier force.

After further reconnaissance reports, the US C-in-C South Pacific, Adm Halsey, detaches Rear-Adm Lee to Guadalcanal in

the afternoon of 13 Nov with the battleships *South Dakota* and *Washington* and the destroyers *Walke, Benham, Preston* and *Gwin*. Rear-Adm Kinkaid receives orders to remain S of Guadalcanal with the carrier *Enterprise* and the remaining ships.

Early on 14 Nov US reconnaissance aircraft sight Mikawa's and Nishimura's forces withdrawing from Guadalcanal. In several waves, Marine Corps aircraft from the carrier *Enterprise* and from Henderson Field attack. They sink *Kinugasa* and damage the cruisers *Chokai, Isuzu* and *Maya* and the destroyer *Michishio* with hits and near-misses, with the result that these ships take no further part in the operation. After sighting by reconnaissance aircraft from *Enterprise*, aircraft from the carrier and from Henderson Field and B-17 bombers from Espiritu Santo attack the Japanese landing force in several waves as it proceeds down 'The Slot'. In the first attack the transports *Canberra Maru* and *Nagara Maru* are sunk; *Sado Maru* is damaged and detached with the destroyers *Amagiri* and *Mochizuki*. Fighter protection from the carriers *Hiyo* and *Junyo* is able to shoot down some aircraft but cannot prevent the attacks. In the second attack the *Brisbane Maru*, in the third the *Arizona Maru* and *Shinanogawa Maru* and in the last the *Nako Maru* are sunk: the destroyers *Kawakaze, Makinami, Naganami* and *Suzukaze* rescue some 5000 men but 400 are lost with the ships. Rear-Adm Tanaka continues the advance with the remaining four transports, *Kinugawa Maru, Yamatsuki Maru, Hirokawa Maru* and *Yamaura Maru*, in order to beach these ships during the night 14–15 Nov on the NW corner of Guadalcanal. This, together with the landing of the rescued survivors from the destroyers, succeeds. The transports are destroyed by air attacks on 15 Nov. During the night 14–15 Nov the main body of the Japanese 2nd Fleet (Vice-Adm Kondo), comprising the heavy cruisers *Atago* and *Takao*, the battleship *Kirishima* and two escort groups with the cruiser *Nagara* and the destroyers *Teruzuki, Hatsuyuki, Shirayuki, Asagumo* and *Samidare* and the cruiser *Sendai* with the destroyers *Uranami, Shikinami* and *Ayanami*, tries to shell Henderson Field. In the process the *Sendai* group and then the other ships encounter the US force under Rear-Adm Lee (see above) as it enters 'Iron Bottom Sound'. The latter's van destroyers, *Walke, Benham* and *Preston*, at first fall victim to the Japanese torpedoes and gunfire from *Nagara*, and *Gwin* is damaged. In manoeuvring, *South Dakota* (Capt T L Gatch), with her radar out of action, comes up against *Kirishima*, *Atago* and *Takao* and is badly damaged by 42 hits in her super-structure. A torpedo attack by Rear-Adm Kimura's destroyers fails and *Ayanami* is lost. Then *Washington* (Capt G B Davis), which has remained unnoticed, approaches within 8000m with the help of radar and in 7min destroys *Kirishima* by shellfire. As she retires, she avoids the torpedo attacks of the destroyers *Kagero* and *Oyashio* detached by Rear-Adm Tanaka from the landing force.

In the next 14 days both sides carry out individual supply operations. On the Japanese side, the submarines *I-16* and *I-20* with midget submarines are deployed against the supply operations on 15 and 29 Nov. *Ha-10* torpedoes the transport *Alchiba* (6198 tons) on 29 Nov and she has to be beached. The Japanese destroyer *Hayashio* is sunk by US dive-bombers on 24 Nov when engaged in a supply mission.

8–27 Nov   Central Atlantic

On the report of the Allied landing in North Africa, all U-boats with sufficient fuel are brought at top speed from the North Atlantic to the area off Morocco ('Schlagetot' group, comprising *U572*, *U173*, *U130*, *U108*, *U103*, *U510*, *U509*, *U752* and *U511*) and off Gibraltar ('Westwall' group, comprising *U515*, *U155*, *U411*, *U564*, *U86*, *U91*, *U98*, *U218*, *U566*, *U613*, *U92*, *U413*, *U653*, *U519*, *U185* and *U263*).

In the roads of Fedala, *U173* (Lt Schweichel) attacks the convoy UGF.1 at anchor on 11–12 Nov and sinks the troop transport *Joseph Hewes* (9359 tons) and torpedoes the tanker *Winooski* (10600 tons, and the destroyer *Hambleton*. The following night *U130* (Cdr Kals) sinks the troop trans-ports *Edward Rutledge*, *Hugh L Scott* and *Tasker H Bliss* totalling 34507 tons. On 13 Nov *U411* (Lt-Cdr Spindlegger) is sunk by Hudson 'D' of No 500 Sqn RAF (Sqn Ldr Ensor) W of Gibraltar. On 15 Nov *U173* torpedoes the transport *Electra* (6200 tons) which has to be beached. *U173* is sunk the following day by the US destroyers *Woolsey*, *Swanson* and *Quick*. Attempted attacks by *U572*, *U108*, *U510*, *U511* and *U752* from 11 Nov to 18 Nov fail. *U108* is damaged by bombs on 18 Nov. Of the 'Westwall' group, *U515* (Lt-Cdr Henke) attacks the sub-marine depot ship *Hecla* (10850 tons) on 12 Nov and sinks her in many approaches; the escorting destroyer *Marne* is torpedoed. The returning transport convoy MKF.1, which is escorted, *inter alia*, by the escort carriers *Argus* and *Avenger*, the destroyers *Wrestler*, *Amazon* and *Glaisdale* (Norweg-ian) and the close escort group with the new frigate *Exe* as leader, loses on 14 Nov the troop transport *Warwick Castle* (20107 tons)

to *U413* (Lt Poel). On 15 Nov *U155* (Lt-Cdr Piening) sinks the carrier *Avenger* (Cdr Colthurst) and the troop transport *Ettrick* (11279 tons) and torpedoes the transport *Almaak* (6737 tons). On 16 Nov *U92* (Lt Oelrich) sinks one ship of 7662 tons. *U515* misses a carrier and *U218* is damaged when trying to attack a carrier force, probably by depth charges from the destroyer *Wrestler* of convoy MKF.1Y.

On 17 Nov *U566* suffers depth charge damage. On 18 Nov *U155* misses a convoy and *U613* (Cdr Köppe) and *U91* are damaged by bombs from Hudson 'V' of No 608 Sqn (Fg Off Petrie) and depth charges respectively. On 19 Nov *U413* (Lt Poel) misses the convoy KRS.2 and is damaged by Hudson 'D' of No 608 Sqn (Fg Off Wilcox) and *U98* is sunk by Hudson 'G' of the same unit. *U263* (Lt-Cdr Nölke) sinks two ships of 12376 tons from the convoy but is damaged W of Gibraltar on 24 Nov by Hudson 'Q' of No 233 Sqn (escorting convoy MKS.3) and again on 27 Nov while entering the Bay of Biscay by Hudson 'J' of No 405 Sqn. However, the U-boat reaches La Pallice on 29 Nov. On 24 Nov *U510* is also damaged and from 26 Nov the boats have to leave for the W or proceed to *U118* to refuel.

9 Nov   North Sea

The German 2nd MTB Flotilla (Lt-Cdr Feldt), comprising *S46*, *S48*, *S66*, *S70*, *S73*, *S80*, *S83*, *S101*, *S104* and *S113*, attacks a British convoy off Lowestoft, sinks a freighter 1843 tons and torpedoes a second of 1482 tons.

9 Nov   Mediterranean

The British corvette *Gardenia* sinks off Oran following a collision with the trawler *Fluellen*. Off Marsa Matruh, the mine-sweeper *Cromer* explodes after hitting a mine. The submarine *P13/Saracen* (Lt Lumby) sinks the Italian submarine *Granito* off Capo Vito, Sicily.

9–18 Nov   Mediterranean

Deployment of the British submarines of the 8th, 10th and 1st Flotillas to cover Operation 'Torch': *Ursula* and *P54/Unshaken* off Oran; *P45/Unrivalled*, *P48* and *P221/Shakespeare* off Algiers; *P211/Safari*, *P212/Sahib* and *P213/Saracen* between Sardinia and Sicily; *P44/United*, *P46/Unruffled*, *P37/Unbending*, *P35/Umbra* and *P43/Unison* N of Sicily and Messina; *Una* and *Utmost* S of Messina; and, S of the French S coast, *P51/Unseen* and *P222* and, with special missions (the landing of Gen Clay and the collecting of the French Gen Giraud), *P219/Seraph* and *P217/Sibyl*. *Traveller*, *Parthian*, *Clyde*, *Thrasher*, *Proteus* and *Porpoise* are engaged in transport journeys to Malta and then

partly deployed on the Tunisian and Libyan coasts.

In these operations, many attacks are made. *Turbulent* (Cdr Linton) sinks one ship of 1554 tons, *P211/Safari* (Cdr Bryant) sinks two ships of 2914 tons and three small craft, *P212/Sahib* (Lt Bromage) finishes off one ship of 1579 tons, *P213/Saracen* (Lt Lumby) sinks one ship of 209 tons, *Porpoise* (Cdr Bennington) sinks two ships of 11273 tons and *Proteus* torpedoes one ship of 1579 tons.

9–21 Nov   North Atlantic

The 'Kreuzotter' group is formed from the U-boats *U84*, *U522*, *U521*, *U753*, *U224* and *U383* which are left behind in the Atlantic because of their limited fuel supplies. To it are added by 17 Nov *U454*, *U606* and *U624* which have been refuelled and *U184*, *U262*, *U264* and *U611* fresh from home. On 12 Nov *U224* (Lt Kosbadt) sinks an inde-pendent of 5614 tons. On 15 Nov *U521* (Lt-Cdr Bargsten) reports the convoy ONS.144, which comprises 33 ships escorted by EG.B6 (Norwegian Lt-Cdr Monssen) with the Norwegian corvettes *Potentilla*, *Eglan-tine*, *Montbretia*, *Rose* and the British *Vervain* and the rescue ship *Perth* (HF/DF). *U521* unsuccessfully attacks and is driven off by depth charges from *Rose*; in the mist, *U611* (Lt-Cdr v Jakobs) also loses the briefly established contact. Only in the afternoon of 17 Nov do *U521* and, shortly afterwards, *U184* (Lt-Cdr Dangschat) come up. The latter leads the other boats to the scene with D/F bearings. During the night 17–18 Nov *U262*, *U264*, *U184*, *U521*, *U224*, *U383*, *U454* and *U624* attack successively. *U264* (Lt Looks) and *U184* each sink one ship of 6696 tons and 3192 tons respectively. *U624* (Lt Count Soden-Frauenhofen) sinks two ships of 10076 tons and torpedoes one more of 5432 tons which is later sunk by *U522* (Lt-Cdr Schneider). She just misses *Eglan-tine*. The other boats miss their targets and are attacked with depth charges from *Rose*, *Montbretia* and *Potentilla*. Towards morning *U262* (Lt Franke) sinks *Montbre-tia*. *U753* (Cdr v Mannstein) misses the rescue ship *Perth* with the *Rose*. Because of the expenditure of torpedoes and lack of fuel, most of the boats have to break off on 18 Nov and only *U184*, *U262*, *U264* and *U611* continue the operation. In the after-noon of 18 Nov and in the morning of 19 Nov, salvos from *U264* and *U184* miss their targets.

The escort, reinforced in the evening by the destroyers *Firedrake* and *Badger*, drives the boats off. Towards morning on 20 Nov *Potentilla* sinks *U184*, which is keeping contact, and shortly afterwards *U264* misses

Rose. In the morning the Western Local Escort Group meets the convoy and the U-boats break off the operation.

10 Nov   Bay of Biscay
The outbound *U66* (Cdr* Zapp) is damaged by Wellington 'D' of No 172 Sqn (Fg Off Dixon), using radar and Leigh Light, and has to return.

10 Nov   Mediterranean
The British sloop *Ibis* is sunk N of Algiers by Italian torpedo aircraft.

11 Nov   Bay of Biscay
The British submarine *Unbeaten* is sunk in error by British aircraft in the Bay of Biscay.

11 Nov   Indian Ocean
About 500 nautical miles SW of the Cocos Islands, the Japanese auxiliary cruisers *Aikoku Maru* (10500 tons) and *Hokoku Maru* (10438 tons) attack the Dutch tanker *Ondina* (6341 tons) travelling from Fremantle to Diego Garcia, escorted by the Indian minesweeper *Bengal* (Lt-Cdr W J Wilson). In the engagement *Bengal* succeeds in hitting the vastly better armed *Hokoku Maru* so often that the latter explodes, whereupon the second auxiliary cruiser, which has in the meantime set the tanker on fire, breaks off the engagement. *Ondina* is taken to Fremantle severely damaged.

12 Nov   Baltic
U272 is lost in a collision during a training exercise off Hela.

12 Nov–17 Dec   Arctic
Soviet mining operations off the Norwegian polar coast. On 12 Nov nine Soviet MO-IV patrol cutters lay mines off the harbours of Varangerfjord: by the end of the year they have laid 14 off Vardö, 20 off Kirkenes and 34 off Petsamofjord. There sink on these barrages *Schiff 18* (419 tons) on 19 Nov off Kirkenes, the freighter *Akka* (2646 tons) on 29 Nov off Vardö and the freighters *Hans Rickmers* (5226 tons) and *Westsee* (5911 tons) on 30 Nov off Petsamo. The latter two are partly beached. On 7 Dec the 56th MS Flotilla partly clears the barrages off Petsamo.

The submarine *K-1* and the newly operational minelaying submarines *L-20* and *L-22* lay mine barrages in Porsangerfjord in several operations. On these the patrol boats *V6116/Ubier* and *V6117/Cherusker* sink on 6 Dec. *M-121* is lost during Nov.

13 Nov–2 Dec   Central Atlantic
Convoys between US and Casablanca. UGS with 45 ships, escorted by TF.37 comprising the destroyers *Taylor*, *Strong*, *Chevalier*, *Benson*, *Davison* and *La Valette* and the tankers *Salamonie* and *Mattole*. The return convoy GUF.1 is in three parts: five transports, two freighters and a minelayer with TG.34.10 (cruiser *Philadelphia* and destroyers *Mervine*, *Cowie*, *Quick*, *Knight*, *Beatty*, *Bernadou* and *Cole*) from Safi on 13 Nov to Norfolk on 24 Nov; four transports and one tanker with TG.34.8 (battleship *Texas*, cruiser *Savannah*, destroyers *Roe*, *Ericsson*, *Livermore*, *Eberle*, *Dallas*, *Corry* and *Hobson* and carrier *Sangamon*) from Gibraltar on 15 Nov to Norfolk on 26 Nov; and ten transports, three freighters, three minelayers and two tankers with TG.34.9 (cruiser *Brooklyn*, destroyers *Boyle*, *Woolsey*, *Ludlow*, *Edison*, *Bristol*, *Wilkes*, *Swanson*, *Tillman*, *Forrest*, *Macomb*, *Quick*, *Cole*, *Kearny* and *Parker* and carrier *Chenango*).

14 Nov   Black Sea
The Soviet submarine *L-23* (Capt 3rd Class Fartushny) torpedoes the German tanker *Ossag* (2793 tons) which has been met off the Bosphorus by the Rumanian destroyers *Regele Ferdinand* and *Regina Maria*. The tanker is towed into the Bosphorus by a Turkish tug.

15 Nov   North Atlantic
The Canadian destroyer *Saguenay* is damaged beyond repair off Newfoundland in a collision with the freighter *Azara* (which sinks).

15 Nov–19 Dec   Central Atlantic
Of the U-boats again deployed off Freetown and in the area of the Cape Verde Islands, following refuelling from *U462* (Lt Vowe), *U134* (Lt-Cdr Schendel) sinks one ship of 4827 tons, *U552* (Lt-Cdr Popp) one of 3157 tons, *UD3* (Cdr* Rigele) one of 5041 tons and *U176* (Lt-Cdr Dierksen) three of 13432 tons. Between the Gulf of Guinea and the Cape Verde Islands *U161* (Lt-Cdr Achilles) sinks three ships of 16284 tons and damages one of 5161 tons and *U126* (Lt-Cdr Bauer) sinks four ships of 19672 tons.

16 Nov   Mediterranean
In escorting a German convoy from Piraeus to the Dardanelles, *UJ2102* (Lt Kleiner) sinks the Greek submarine *Triton* located by the destroyer *Hermes* (Capt Johannesson) and takes the crew prisoner.

17–18 Nov   Baltic
The Finnish motor torpedo boats *Syöksy*, *Vihuri* (Lt Kajatsalo) and *Vinha* (Lt Vuorensaari) attack the Soviet gunboat *Krasnoe Znamya* lying in the harbour at Lavansaari and sink her with torpedo hits. She is later raised and from 13 Nov 1943 to 17 Sep 1944 is repaired.

17–20 Nov   Mediterranean
Operation 'Stone Age': a British convoy of four merchant ships, escorted by the 15th Cruiser Sqn (Rear-Adm Power), comprising *Arethusa*, *Dido* and *Euryalus* and 10 destroyers, proceeds from Alexandria to Malta. Despite German air attacks in which *Arethusa* is so badly hit N of Derna on 18 Nov that she has to return, all four transports reach Malta. With this the island can be regarded as relieved.

17–21 Nov   South-West Pacific
In the Malacca Straits, the British submarine *Trusty* (Lt-Cdr King) sinks one ship of 5617 tons and, near Christmas Island, the US submarine *Searaven* (Lt-Cdr Cassedy) sinks one of 333 tons.

In the area of the Philippines, *Seal* (Lt-Cdr Hurd) and *Salmon* (Lt-Cdr McKinney) each sink one ship, of 5477 tons and 5873 tons respectively. *Stingray* (Lt-Cdr Earle) torpedoes one ship of 8360 tons.

17–23 Nov   Arctic
On 17 Nov the convoy QP.15 sets out from the Kola Inlet with 28 ships escorted by one AA ship, five minesweepers, four corvettes, one trawler and the Soviet destroyers *Baku* and *Sokrushitelny*. It is met in the Barents Sea by five British destroyers and, further W, by the British cruisers *London* and *Suffolk* and another five destroyers. Three British and one Soviet submarine take up positions off the northern Norwegian fjords against German surface ships. On 20 Nov the convoy is much dispersed in a heavy storm and parts of *Baku*'s superstructure are blown away in the sea. With a big leak in her bows and boiler rooms, the ship reaches harbour only with difficulty. *Sokrushitelny* breaks in two. The destroyers *Razumny*, *Kuibyshev* and *Uritski*, which are sent to help, are able to rescue 187 men in very heavy seas and *Sokrushitelny* sinks on 22 Nov. German air reconnaissance does not locate the convoy in the bad weather. *U625* (Lt Benker) and *U601* (Lt-Cdr Grau) each sink one ship, of 5851 tons and 3974 tons respectively, from convoy groups.

19 Nov   English Channel
The German 5th MTB Flotilla (Lt-Cdr Klug), comprising *S68*, *S77*, *S82*, *S112*, *S115* and *S116*, attacks a British convoy S of Plymouth and sinks the trawler *Ullswater* and three freighters of 3528 tons.

19 Nov   North Sea
The German MDS *Sperrbrecher 69/Ceres* is sunk off Norderney by mine.

20 Nov–10 Dec   Indian Ocean
The Japanese submarine *I-166* (Cdr Tanaka), operating SW of the Malabar Coast, sinks one ship of 5332 tons. *I-29* (Cdr* Izu) sinks two ships of 16329 tons in the Gulf of Aden but *I-27* has no success in the Gulf of Oman.

21 Nov   North Atlantic
The outgoing *U517* (Lt-Cdr Hartwig) is sunk by an Albacore of No 817 Sqn from the carrier *Victorious*.

21 Nov–6 Dec   Mediterranean
In the Bay of Naples, the British submarine
P228/Splendid (Lt-Cdr McGeogh) attacks
several convoys from 16 to 22 Nov, including on 21 Nov one of two ships and the
destroyers *Bombardiere*, *Legionario* and
Velite, the last of which is torpedoed. Off
the Tunisian coast and S of Maretimo,
P44/United, *Utmost*, *Una* and *P219/Seraph*
attack convoys without success. *Utmost* is
damaged by depth charges from the torpedo
boat *Ardente* and sunk on 25 Nov off Sicily
by the torpedo boat *Groppo*. At the beginning of Dec *Ursula* (Lt Lakin) sinks two
ships of 1962 tons off Corsica, *P35/Umbra*
(Lt-Cdr Maydon) one ship of 1097 tons off
Sousse and *P45/Unrivalled* (Lt Sprice) the
hospital ship *Città di Trapani* (1467 tons)
and one sailing ship off Tunis.
In the Aegean, the Greek submarine *Papanicolis* reports successful attacks. Off Sicily,
P217/Sibyl misses the German transport
Ankara escorted by the Italian destroyers
Granatiere and *Saetta* and the torpedo boats
Partenope and *Perseo*. Off Sardinia, *Tigris*
sinks the Italian submarine *Porfido* on 6
Dec.

23 Nov–13 Jan   Caspian Sea
Transfer of the Soviet submarines *M-120*,
and from 3 Dec of *M-32* and *M-52*, from
the Black Sea Fleet to the Caspian Flotilla.

24 Nov   English Channel
Off Ostend, the German auxiliary minesweeper *M3610* is mined and sunk.

24 Nov–3 Dec   North Atlantic
From the U-boats coming from ONS.144,
the 'Drachen' group is formed NE of Newfoundland, consisting of *U454*, *U522*, *U262*,
U611, *U623*, *U663* and *U445*. On 26 Nov
U262 (Lt Franke) and *U663* (Lt-Cdr
Schmid) each sink one ship, of 7178 tons
and 5170 tons respectively. Convoys are not
sighted.

25 Nov   Norway
The German minesweeper *M101* is lost off
Namsos following a collision with the
freighter *Levante*.

25 Nov   English Channel
Near Dieppe, the German patrol trawler
V1514 sinks after striking a mine.

26 Nov   Indian Ocean
In escorting the convoy OW.1 from Fre-
mantle to Diego Garcia with the corvettes
Cessnock and *Toowoomba*, the cruisers
Adelaide (RAN) and *Jacob van Heemskerck*
(Dutch) encounter the German blockade-
runner *Ramses* (7983 tons) proceeding from
Djakarta to France. The German ship scut-
tles herself.

26 Nov   English Channel
The German MMS *R109* is lost on a
'friendly' mine barrage off Fécamp.

27 Nov   North Atlantic
The escort forces in the North Atlantic now
comprise the Western Local Escort Force
with five RCN and the 13 RN destroyers,
25 RCN corvettes and eight RCN 'Bangor'
minesweepers and the Mid Ocean Escort
Force with seven RCN, 22 RN and two
USN destroyers, 26 RCN and 38 RN corvettes and one US Coast Guard cutter.

27 Nov   Mediterranean
Operation 'Lila': the occupation of Toulon
by II SS Armoured Corps. By order of
the C-in-C of the French Fleet, Adm de
Laborde, the French Navy is scuttled in
Toulon. Scuttled and later partly raised but
not repaired are the battleships *Provence*,
Dunkerque and *Strasbourg*, the seaplane
carrier *Commandant Teste*, the cruisers
Algérie, *Colbert*, *Dupleix*, *Foch* and *Mar-
seillaise*, the destroyer leaders *Aigle*,
Cassard, *Gerfaut*, *Guépard*, *Kersaint*, *Lynx*,
Mogador, *Tartu*, *Vauban*, *Vauquelin*,
Vautour, *Verdun* and *Volta*, the destroyers
Casque, *Mameluck*, *Bordelais*, *Le Mars* and
La Palme, the torpedo boat *La Poursuivante*,
the avisos *D'Iberville* and *Yser* and the sub-
marines *Acheron*, *Aurore*, *Caïman*, *Diamant*,
Eurydice, *Fresnel*, *Galatée*, *L'Espoir*,
Naïade, *Pascal*, *Redoutable*, *Sirène*, *Thétis*,
Vengeur and *Vénus*. Scuttled and later
refloated by the Axis, placed in repair but
not commissioned are the cruisers *Jean de
Vienne* (allocated to the Italian Navy as
FR.11) and *La Galissonnière* (*FR.12*), the
destroyer leaders *Panthère* (*FR.22*), *Valmy*
(*FR.24*) and *L'Indomptable* (German *SG9?*),
the destroyers *Siroco* (*FR.32*), *L'Adroit*
(*FR.33*), *Cyclone* (*FR.34*), *Bison* (*FR.35*),
Foudroyant (*FR.36*), *Le Hardi* (?) and
Lansquenet (later German *TA34*), the
torpedo boat *La Bayonnaise* (*FR.45*, later
German *TA13*), the avisos *Chamois* (*FR.53*)
and *L'Impetueuse* (*FR.54*, later German
SG17) and *Dédaigneuse* (*FR.56*), the sub-
marine *Henri Poincaré* and the cablelayer
Ampère (later German SG24). Captured or
scuttled and later raised, repaired and com-
missioned are the destroyer leaders *Lion*
(*FR.21*) and *Tigre* (*FR.23*), the destroyer
Trombe (*FR.31*), the torpedo boat *Baliste*
(German *TA12*), the avisos *La Curieuse*
(*FR.55*, later German *SG16*) and *Les
Esparges* (later German *M6060*) and the
netlayer *Le Gladiateur* (later German
SG18). Building, captured and completed
for the German Navy are the avisos *Matelot
Leblanc* (*SG.14*), *Rageot de la Touche*
(*SG.15*), *Amiral Sénès* (*SG.21*) and *Enseigne
Ballande* (*SG.22*).

28 Nov   Mediterranean
The British destroyer *Ithuriel* is damaged

beyond repair in a German air attack at
Bône. Off Bône, the destroyers *Quentin* and
Quiberon (RAN) sink the Italian submarine
Dessiè.

28 Nov–19 Dec   Indonesia
On 28–29 Nov the auxiliary vessel *Kuru*
and the corvettes *Armidale* and *Castlemaine* set
out for Timor from Port Darwin to bring
63 relief personnel and to evacuate 77 Portuguese refugees. On a second journey,
Armidale is sunk on 1 Dec by Japanese
torpedo aircraft; the corvette *Kalgourlie*
rescues 30 survivors. The Dutch destroyer
Tjerk Hiddes evacuates 950 people from
Timor to Port Darwin in three journeys in
the period 10–19 Dec.

29 Nov   Mediterranean
The British fast minelayer *Manxman* lays
a barrage of 156 mines near Cani in the
neighbourhood of Tunis. On 8 Dec it is
extended by another 36 mines.

29 Nov–1 Dec   Bay of Biscay
The Italian blockade-runner *Cortellazzo*
(Capt A Paladini) sets out from Bordeaux
on the way to Japan, escorted by the German
torpedo boats *T23*, *Kondor*, *Falke* and *T22*.
After the torpedo boats have left, the ship
is found on 30 Nov by a Sunderland flying
boat of No 10 Sqn RAAF and is located on
1 Dec by the destroyers *Quickmatch* (RAN)
and *Redoubt*, detached from convoy KMF.4
(SOE on the sloop *Egret*). After the crew
has left the ship, the *Cortellazo* is sunk by a
torpedo from the *Redoubt*.

29 Nov–2 Dec   Black Sea
First sortie by the Soviet Sqn (Vice-Adm
Vladimirski) against shipping on the
Rumanian/Bulgarian coast. The first group,
consisting of the cruiser *Voroshilov*, the flotilla leader *Kharkov* and the destroyer *Soobrazitelny*, is to shell the harbours of Sulina
and Burgas and the radio station at Fidonisi;
the second group, comprising the destroyers
Besposhchadny and *Boiki*, is to attack shipping targets near Capes Kaliakra and Shabla
and to shell Mangalia. On 1 Dec the
destroyers of the second group fire torpedoes at ships in the roads of Kalytch-
Kiap, but they go ashore. *Voroshilov* and
Soobrazitelny shell Fidonisi, but the cruiser
is damaged by a mine detonation in the
bow paravane of the destroyer and the force
returns.

29 Nov–11 Dec   North Atlantic
On 30 Nov the 'Draufgänger' group is
formed W of Ireland from the newly arrived
U-boats *U455*, *U221*, *U553*, *U610*, *U600*,
U604, *U569*, *U615* and *U609* to operate
against an OS convoy suspected as a result
of listening observations on 29 Nov. No
convoy is found. On 2 Dec *U604* (Lt-Cdr
Höltring) sinks one ship of 7057 tons. Two

attacks by *U435* and *U615* fail. The group is moved to the N for 6 Dec to operate against the convoys ONS.150 (EG.B4) expected according to convoy schedule, and on 7 Dec boats are directed against HX.217 from her unsuccessful patrol line (qv).

On 29 Nov the 'Panther' group is formed in the Central North Atlantic from the newly arrived U-boats *U439*, *U254*, *U758*, *U465*, *U135*, *U211* and *U524* to operate against the convoy ONS.148 (EG.B2). The group proceeds westwards to the NE of Newfoundland until 4 Dec in accordance with the day's run of an ONS convoy without finding targets. *U524* (Lt-Cdr Frhr v Steinaecker), which carries a B-Service team, listens on 4 Dec to the convoy's talk and the group is directed to the NE. At mid-day on 6 Dec *U524* sights the convoy HX.217, which comprises 33 ships escorted by EG.B6 (Cdr Heathcote) with the destroyers *Burza* (Polish) and *Fame* the and the corvettes *Vervain* (British) and *Potentilla*, *Rose* and *Eglantine* (Norwegian) and the rescue ship *Perth* fitted with HF/DF. The four U-boats which approach in the afternoon of 6 Dec lose contact in deteriorating visibility and are diverted by the destroyer *Montgomery* of the Western Local Escort Group which is firing flares on the flank. In the morning of 7 Dec *U524* again establishes contact and brings up *U254*, *U465*, *U439* and *U135* but they are driven off by the Liberator 'H' of No 120 Sqn (Sqn Ldr Bulloch). During the night 7–8 Dec *U524* sinks a ship of 8194 tons and just misses *Fame*. *U254*, *U465*, *U623* (coming with *U611* from refuelling) and *U758* are located by *Eglantine*, *Rose*, *Burza* and *Potentilla* before being able to fire and are driven off. On 8 Dec the boats of the 'Draufgänger' group—*U455*, *U221*, *U553*, *U610*, *U600*, *U604*, *U569*, *U615* and *U609*—approach; *U600* (Lt-Cdr Zurmühlen) has already sunk one independent of 6762 tons on 7 Dec. In the afternoon of 8 Dec *U610* and *U553* establish contact but after a miss on a destroyer they, with three other boats, are forced to submerge by the Liberators 'B' and 'M' of No 120 Sqn. In the evening of 8 Dec *U221* (Lt Trojer) rams *U254* (Lt-Cdr Gilardone), which sinks. Two boats are driven off by *Potentilla* and *Rose*. In the morning of 9 Dec *U455* misses one escort vessel and *U553* (Cdr Thurmann) sinks one scattered ship of 5273 tons. Two further attacks are frustrated by *Eglantine* and *Potentilla*. During 9 Dec *U553* keeps contact; in the night only *U758* (Lt-Cdr Manseck) fires, but misses *Burza*. Six other attacks are frustrated by *Potentilla*, *Rose*, *Potentilla* again, *Vervain*, *Burza* and *Rose*.

Despite strong air escort from six Hudsons of No 269 Sqn RAF, Fortresses of No 220 Sqn RAF and Catalinas of VP-84, *U628* (Lt Hasenschar) is able to keep contact until the night of 11 Dec. But all boats—*U610*, *U615* and *U623*—are driven off and *U611* is sunk by Catalina 'H' of No 84 Sqn (Lt Davis). A further operation against the strong air escort on 11 Dec has no prospect of success.

29 Nov–11 Dec   Central Atlantic
Return convoy GUF. 2 from Casablanca to Norfolk with 20 ships, escorted by TF.38 consisting of the battleship *Arkansas* and the destroyers *Plunkett*, *Gleaves*, *Benson*, *Mayo*, *Taylor*, *La Valette*, *Chevalier* and *Strong*.

29 Nov–12 Dec   Mediterranean
Flanking mine barrages are laid out from Bizerta in a north-easterly direction as far as the area W of Sicily to protect Axis supply traffic to Tunis. On 29–30 Nov the destroyer *Da Noli* (Cdr* Valdambrini) and the auxiliary ship *Barletta* in two missions lay the barrages S.91 and S.92, with 172 mines and 154 mines respectively. On 30 Nov–1 Dec the destroyers *Maestrale* (Capt Bedeschi), *Grecale*, *Mitragliere* and *Ascari* lay the barrage S.96 (224 mines). On 4–5 Dec the destroyers *Pigafetta* (Capt del Minio) *Da Noli* and the minelayer *Barletta* lay the barrage S.93 (172 mines) and the destroyers *Maestrale*, *Graecale*, *Ascari* and *Corazziere* the barrage S.97 (224 mines). On 11–12 Dec the destroyers *Pigafetta*, *Da Noli*, *Zeno*, *Mitragliere*, *Ascari*, *Corraziere* and *Graecale* lay the barrage S.94 (224 mines).

30 Nov   Pacific
Destruction of the German auxiliary cruiser *Schiff 10/Thor* (Capt Gumprich) in the harbour of Yokohama as a result of an explosion in the supply ship *Uckermark* (Cdr v Zatorski) lying alongside her. In addition to Japanese harbour craft and a freighter, the prize ship *Leuthen* is also destroyed. On her last voyage, *Schiff 10* captured or sank 10 merchant ships totalling 56037 tons.

30 Nov–1 Dec   South Pacific
Night battle of Tassafaronga. A Japanese destroyer force (Rear-Adm Tanaka), comprising *Naganami*, *Makinami*, *Oyashio*, *Kuroshio*, *Kagero*, *Kawakaze*, *Suzukaze* and *Takanami*, tries to get through to Guadalcanal with supplies. The Americans learn of the operation through their W/T interception service, whereupon Adm Halsey sends out TF.67 (Rear-Adm Wright, with the heavy cruisers *Minneapolis*, *New Orleans*, *Northampton* and *Pensacola*, the light cruiser *Honolulu* and the destroyers *Drayton*, *Fletcher*, *Maury*, *Perkins*, *Lamson* and *Lardner*) from Espiritu Santo to oppose the force. With the help of radar, Rear-Adm

Wright is able to surprise the Japanese and in the engagement to damage the destroyer *Takanami* so badly that she has later to be abandoned. Rear-Adm Tanaka then orders half of his ships to keep on for Guadalcanal in order to throw the supply containers they have brought overbroad (they are later recovered from the water) and attacks with the remaining force the superior US group with torpedoes. All four heavy cruisers are hit: *Northampton* (Capt W A Kitts) sinks from torpedoes fired by *Oyashio*, *New Orleans* loses her bow and *Minneapolis* and *Pensacola* are badly damaged.

1 Dec   English Channel
S81 (Lt Wendler) sinks the British trawler *Jasper*.

1 Dec   Baltic
Off Suursaari, the German A/S trawler *UJ1205* sinks after a collision with the minesweeper *M29*.

1–2 Dec   Mediterranean
Attack by British Force Q (Rear-Adm Harcourt), comprising the cruisers *Aurora*, *Sirius* and *Argonaut* and the destroyers *Quiberon* and *Quentin*, on the Italian convoy traffic on the route Trapani–Tunis. Of four convoys at sea totalling 13 transports, escorted by seven destroyers and 12 torpedo boats, three can be recalled after being located by British air reconnaissance. The convoy H, with four ships, the destroyers *Da Recco* (Capt Cocchia), *Camicia Nera* and *Folgore* and the torpedo boats *Clio* and *Procione*, is encountered near the Skerki Bank. The four ships and *Folgore* are sunk and *Da Recco* and *Procione* damaged; *Da Recco* is towed in by the destroyer *Pigafetta*. On the return the British force is attacked by German bombers and torpedo aircraft off Galita and loses *Quentin* by bomb hit. The Italian submarines *Nichelio*, *Asteria*, *Dandolo* and *Giada* make no contact.

On 2 Dec the British destroyers *Jervis*, *Javelin*, *Janus* and *Kelvin* surprise the Italian torpedo boat *Lupo*, which is rescuing survivors from of the freighter *Veloce* off Kerkennah, and sink it.

1–10 Dec   Black Sea
The Soviet cruiser *Krasny Krym*, the destroyers *Besposhchadny* and *Nezamozhnik* and minesweepers bring the 9th Mountain Rifle Div from Batumi to Tuapse.

1–28 Dec   Mediterranean
In the Western Mediterranean, *U375* (Lt-Cdr Könenkamp) torpedoes the British fast minelayer *Manxman* on 1 Dec and *U602* (Lt-Cdr Schüler) the destroyer *Porcupine* on 9 Dec. On 11 Dec *U443* (Lt Puttkamer) sinks the British destroyer *Blean* and on 14 Dec one ship of 1592 tons. *U565* (Lt-Cdr Franken) sinks the British destroyer *Par-*

tridge on 18 Dec and torpedoes the troop transport *Cameronia* (16297 tons) on 22 Dec. On 21 Dec the troop transport *Strathallan* (23722 tons) is sunk by *U562* (Lt Hamm). In the Eastern Mediterranean, *U617* (Lt-Cdr Brandi) attacks various convoys off the Cyrenaican coast and sinks one fleet tug (810 tons). Of the Italian submarines *Alagi*, *Bronzo*, *Galatea*, *Porfido*, *Volframio*, *Argento*, *Corallo*, *Mocenigo*, *Diaspro* and *Malachite* in the Western Mediterranean, *Mocenigo* (Lt-Cdr Longhi) torpedoes the British cruiser *Argonaut* and *Bronzo* misses one destroyer. *Porfido* and *Corallo* are sunk by the British submarine *Tigris* and the sloop *Enchantress*.

3 Dec   English Channel
The 5th MTB Flotilla (Lt-Cdr Klug), comprising *S81*, *S82*, *S115* and *S116*, attacks British convoys in the Channel and sinks one freighter (383 tons). *S115* (Lt Klocke) sinks the British escort destroyer *Penylan*.

3–11 Dec   South Pacific
The Japanese 2nd DD Flotilla under Rear-Adm Tanaka carries out supply operations from Shortland to Guadalcanal.
On 3–4 Dec the destroyers *Oyashio*, *Kuroshio*, *Kagero*, *Kawakaze*, *Suzukaze*, *Nowake* and *Arashi*, covered by the destroyers *Naganami* (Rear-Adm Tanaka), *Makinami* and *Yugure*, transport 1500 canisters with supplies to Cape Esperance and throw them overboard. But only 310 are brought ashore by the troops. During the night 7–8 Dec another attempt is made under Capt Sano with the destroyers *Oyashio*, *Kuroshio*, *Kagero*, *Kawakaze*, *Suzukaze*, *Nowake* and *Ariake* and the same covering force. On the way *Nowake* is put out of action by bomb hits and the operation has to be abandoned because of attacks by the US motor torpedo boats *PT109* (Lt J F Kennedy), *PT43*, *PT48*, *PT40*, *PT59*, *PT44*, *PT36* and *PT37*. A new attempt is made on 11–12 Dec with the destroyers *Teruzuki* (Rear-Adm Tanaka), *Oyashio*, *Kuroshio*, *Kagero*, *Tanikaze*, *Urakaze*, *Kawakaze*, *Suzukaze*, *Yugure*, *Ariake* and *Arashi*, when the seven transport destroyers throw 1200 canisters overboard. The leading destroyer, *Terezuki*, falls victim to torpedoes from the US *PT37* and *PT40* off Guadalcanal; *PT44* sinks.

3–22 Dec   North Atlantic
Continuation of the operations against the Allied supplies for 'Torch' in the area W of Gibraltar and Morocco by the 'Westwall' group, which consists of *U185*, *U515*, *U155*, *U130*, *U103* and the replenished *U106*, *U92*, *U564*, *U653*, *U519* and *U86*. *U618* and *U432* are deployed off the Moroccan harbours. On 6 Dec *U106* misses one auxiliary ship and *U155* (Lt-Cdr Piening) and

U103 (Lt Janssen) each sink one ship, of 8456 tons and 5026 tons respectively. On 7 Dec *U515* (Lt-Cdr Henke) sinks the troop transport *Ceramic* (18713 tons) and *U185* (Lt-Cdr Maus) one ship of 4576 tons. On 13 Dec *U103* torpedoes the transport *Hororata* (13945 tons). Attacks by *U519* and *U185* on 9 and 20 Dec are not successful. Off Fedala, *U432* (Lt-Cdr H O Schultze) sinks one guard boat of 310 tons and misses two transports.

4 Dec   Mediterranean
First attack on Italy by the US 9th Air Fleet: the target is the Italian Fleet in Naples. The cruiser *Attendolo* is hit and destroyed and *Montecuccolo* is badly, and *Eugenio di Savoia* and four destroyers less seriously, damaged. Then the 9th Div, comprising the battleships *Littorio*, *Roma* and *Vittorio Veneto*, is moved to La Spezia and the 3rd Div, consisting of the heavy cruisers *Gorizia* and *Trieste*, is moved from Messina to Maddalena (Sardinia). The 8th Div, comprising the cruisers *Garibaldi*, *Duca degli Abruzzi* and *Duca d'Aosta*, remains in Messina.

6 Dec   Arctic
The German patrol trawlers *V6116/Ubier* (ex-HMT *Rutlandshire*) and *V6117/Cherusker* (ex-HMT *Jasmine*) sink on mines off Horningsraag.

5–25 Dec   South Pacific
Of the Japanese submarines *I-2*, *I-3*, *I-4*, *I-5* and *I-6* employed in transport duties in the area of the Solomons, *I-3* is lost on 10 Dec in a torpedo attack by the US motor torpedo boat *PT59* and *I-4* on 20 Dec to one torpedo from the US submarine *Seadragon*. The 7th SM Flotilla, reinforced by new construction, operates from Rabaul with *Ro-101* off Milne Bay, *Ro-102* off the Jomard Channel and *Ro-103* in a transport mission.

7 Dec   Bay of Biscay
Operation 'Frankton': British canoeist raiders from the submarine *Tuna* attack German blockade runners in the Gironde.

7–28 Dec   Pacific
Off Japan, the US submarine *Kingfish* (Lt-Cdr Lowrance) sinks two ships of 9777 tons and *Halibut* (Lt-Cdr Gross) sinks three ships of 12418 tons and torpedoes two more ships of 6609 tons. *Drum* (Lt-Cdr McMahon) torpedoes the Japanese carrier *Ryuho* and lays a mine barrage off Bungo Suido on 17 Dec. *Trigger* (Lt-Cdr Benson) lays a barrage off Inubozaki on 20 Dec, sinks the destroyer *Okikaze* and three ships of 14950 tons and damages one of 5711 tons. *Sunfish* (Lt-Cdr Peterson) lays a mine barrage off Nagoya on which one ship of 750 tons sinks; in addition, one ship of 1917 tons is sunk by torpedo.

8 Dec   Mediterranean
A small German battle group (Maj-Gen Gause) occupies the coastal batteries of Bizerta and captures in the harbour the destroyer *L'Audacieux*, the torpedo boats *La Pomone*, *L'Iphigénie* and *Bombarde*, the submarines *Circé*, *Calypso*, *Dauphin*, *Requin*, *Phoque*, *Espadon*, *Saphir*, *Turquoise* and *Nautilus*, the sloops *Commandant Rivière* and *La Batailleuse* and the minelayer *Castor*. *Bombarde*, *La Pomone* and *L'Iphigenie* are commissioned into the Italian Navy as *FR.41*, *FR.42* and *FR.43* respectively and *La Batailleuse* and *Commandant Rivière* as *FR.51* and *FR.52* respectively.

The British submarine *Traveller* is sunk on a mine in the Gulf of Taranto.

8 Dec   Black Sea
In operations off the Bosphorus, the Soviet submarine *D-5* (Lt-Cdr Trofimov) sinks the small Turkish sailing ship *Koçiboglu*.

8–29 Dec   South West Pacific
In the South Asian area, the US submarine *Gar* (Lt-Cdr McGregor, D) sinks one ship of 661 tons, *Tambor* (Lt-Cdr Ambruster) sinks one of 2558 tons and *Thresher* (Lt-Cdr Millican) sinks two of 3625 tons. *Tautog* (Lt-Cdr Willingham) sinks two ships of 2871 tons and torpedoes the cruiser *Natori*. In the area of the Bismarck Archipelago, *Wahoo* (Lt-Cdr Kennedy) sinks one ship of 5355 tons, *Grouper* (Lt-Cdr McGregor) sinks one ship of 4003 tons and torpedoes one of 4861 tons, *Albacore* (Lt-Cdr Lake) sinks on 18 Dec the cruiser *Tenryu* and torpedoes one ship of 10438 tons and *Greenling* (Lt-Cdr Bruton) sinks the patrol vessel *P35* and two ships of 9118 tons and damages two of 7593 tons. *Seadragon* (Lt-Cdr Ashley) sinks the submarine *I-4* and one ship of 6187 tons and damages one ship of 8416 tons. Off Ponape and Wake, *Triton* (Lt-Cdr Kirkpatrick) sinks two ships of 5307 tons and torpedoes one of 10182 tons. *Grayback* (Lt-Cdr Saunders) sinks the submarine *I-18* and four landing craft.

9 Dec   Mediterranean
The British corvette *Marigold*, escorting convoy MKS.3Y, is sunk by Italian torpedo aircraft off Algiers.

9–18 Dec   Mediterranean
Off the Tunisian coast, the British submarine *P35/Umbra* (Lt-Cdr Maydon) sinks two ships of 3572 tons. On 12 Dec *P222* is sunk by the torpedo boat *Fortunale* when she attacks an Italian convoy off Naples. In the area of Bizerta, *P212/Sahib* (Lt Bromage) and *P46/Unruffled* (Lt Stevens) attack on 14 Dec an Italian convoy of four steamers and the torpedo boats *Ardito*, *For-*

tunale, Groppo and *Orione*: each sinks one ship, of 4959 tons and 6666 tons respectively. Off Sardinia, *P228/Splendid* (Lt-Cdr McGeogh) sinks on 15 Dec one ship of 5048 tons and on 17 Dec the destroyer *Aviere* which is escorting the German transport *Ankara* with the *Camicia Nera*. *Rorqual* (Lt-Cdr Napier) lays a mine barrage off Ischia and attacks one ship on 18 Dec. In the Aegean, *Taku* sinks one ship of 5322 tons and one sailing ship.

9–26 Dec   North Atlantic
From 9 Dec the 'Büffel' group is deployed S of Greenland on the course of convoy HX.218 (EG.B3), as decyphered by the B-Service. It consists of *U663*, *U445* and *U373*. On 13 Dec *U373* (Lt-Cdr Loeser) sights HX.218 with 54 ships, but is driven off four hours later by two destroyers. *U663* (Lt-Cdr Schmid) is attacked by depth charges from one destroyer in the night 13–14 Dec and, because she is damaged, has to start the homeward journey. In the hope that the convoy will keep to the familiar course, the 'Ungestüm' group, stationed S of Iceland from 13 Dec and comprising *U435*, *U628*, *U336*, *U591*, *U604*, *U569*, *U615* and *U524*, is sent to meet the convoy. On 14 Dec *U373* and *U445* are forced to submerge because of the strong air escort and on 15 Dec the HX.218 goes round S of the 'Ungestüm' patrol line. In the course of the search on 16 Dec *U373* sights the approaching ONS.152 (EG.C3) with 22 ships. *U524*, *U615* and *U445* come up but the boats lose contact in the deteriorating visibility and with the approach of a severe storm which reaches Force 12 on 18 Dec. The search is continued until 22 Dec but only independents and scattered ships are sighted. Of these *U591* (Lt-Cdr Zetzsche) sinks one ship of 3077 tons. The ten 'Ungestüm' boats and *U373* form a new patrol line on 25–26 Dec.

10–17 Dec   Norway
The heavy cruiser *Lützow* (Capt Stange) moves from Gotenhafen to Northern Norway (Altafjord) without incident.

10–25 Dec   Indian Ocean
After an unsuccessful operation in the Arafura Sea, the Japanese submarines *I-165* and *I-166* shell Port Gregory and the Cocos Islands respectively.

10–25 Dec   South Atlantic
The Italian submarine *Tazzoli* (Cdr* Fecia di Cossato) sinks four ships of 20480 tons off the north-east coast of Brazil. *Finzi* has to break off the operation because of a mechanical fault.

11–14 Dec   Black Sea
Sortie against the Rumanian coast by two Soviet minesweeper groups (Rear-Adm

V G Fadeev). The first group includes the minesweeper *T-407/Mina* and *T-412/ Arseni Rasskin* and the second group *T-406/Iskatel* and *T-408/Yakor*. Cover is provided by the destroyer *Soobrazitelny*. The first group attacks a German convoy between Gibrieni and Burgas comprising the steamers *Oituz* and *Zar Ferdinand*, the Rumanian torpedo boat *Smeul* and four motor minesweepers of the 3rd MMS Flotilla (Lt-Cdr Klassmann), but is driven off by the motor minesweepers feigning a motor torpedo boat attack whilst *Smeul* covers the steamers in smoke. The submarine *M-31* is lost on a mine.

11–29 Dec   South Pacific
Australian landings near Buna (Papua). To support the Australian and American troops advancing on land, the Dutch steamer *Karsik*, escorted by the corvette *Lithgow*, brings eight armoured vehicles into Oro Bay S of Buna on 10–12 and 14–16 Dec. On 14 Dec the corvettes *Ballarat*, *Broome* and *Kolac* land one battalion of 762 men and on 19 Dec another battalion of 699 men in Oro Bay. On 29 Dec the corvettes *Broome*, *Kolac* and *Whyalla* transport 615 men from Goodenough Island into Oro Bay.

Five Japanese destroyers bring 800 men from Rabaul to Cape Ward Hunt N of Buna from 12 to 14 Dec.

12 Dec   English Channel
The German MDS *Sperrbrecher 144/ Beijerland* is in action with the British destroyers *Whitshed*, *Worcester*, *Vesper*, *Brocklesby* and *Albrighton* and is sunk by torpedo fired by the Norwegian destroyer *Eskdale*.

12 Dec   Mediterranean
Italian guided torpedoes (SLCs) and frogmen, disembarked from the submarine *Ambra* (Cdr Arillo), penetrate the harbour at Algiers and badly damage the freighters *Ocean Vanquisher* (7174 tons), *Berto* (1493 tons), *Empire Centaur* (7041 tons) and *Harmattan* (4558 tons).

12 Dec   North Sea
The 4th MTB Flotilla (Lt-Cdr Bätge), comprising *S48*, *S63*, *S80*, *S110* and *S117*, attacks the British convoy FN.889 off Lowestoft and sinks five freighters totalling 7113 tons.

12–30 Dec   Central Atlantic
Supply convoys for North Africa from New York to Casablanca. UGF.3, from 12 to 24 Dec, comprises 20 ships escorted by TF.35 with the battleship *New York*, the cruiser *Philadelphia*, the destroyers *Parker*, *Mervine*, *Quick*, *Beatty*, *Cowie*, *Knight*, *Doran* and *Earle* and one tanker. UGS.3, from 12 to 30 Dec, comprises 45 ships escorted by TF.33 with the destroyers

Wainwright, *Mayrant*, *Rhind*, *Trippe* and *Rowan*.

12 Dec–3 Feb   Western Atlantic
E of the Caribbean, *U217* (Lt Reichenbach-Klinke) sinks two ships of 10576 tons; one other sinking and two torpedoings remain unclarified. *U124* and *U214* shadow a convoy on 15–16 Dec and *U124* (Lt-Cdr J Mohr) reports two tankers from it sunk (so far unidentified). On 28 Dec the boat sinks one ship from a convoy and on 9 Jan four steamers totalling 28259 tons from the convoy TB.1 (12 ships). From 3 to 23 Jan *U214* (Lt-Cdr G Reeder) and *U105* (Lt Nissen) enter the Caribbean. In all, they sink one ship of 4426 tons and three ships and one sailing ship of 20444 tons respectively. *U109* (Lt-Cdr Bleichrodt) has to return prematurely.

15 Dec   Mediterranean
The British destroyer *Petard* and the Greek destroyer *Vasilissa Olga* force the Italian submarine *Uarsciek* to surface S of Malta. The crew is unable to scuttle and the submarine is taken in tow but sinks later. Codebooks are possibly captured.

15–21 Dec   North Atlantic
The 'Raufbold' group is formed W of Ireland on 15 Dec from the U-boats coming from HX.217 and new arrivals. It consists of *U623*, *U609*, *U610*, *U600*, *U211*, *U135*, *U439*, *U410*, *U203*, *U664*, *U356*, *U409* and *U621*. On 15 Dec *U609* (Lt-Cdr Rudloff) sights the convoy ON.153 (EG.B7) with 43 ships. *U609* maintains contact until the evening of 16 Dec and brings up *U610* (Lt-Cdr Freyberg-Eisenberg-Allmendigen), *U356* (Lt Ruppelt) and *U621* (Lt Kruschka) which each sink a ship, of 9551, 6125 and 5936 tons respectively, and also *U664* (Lt Graef). During the night *U211* (Lt-Cdr Hause) torpedoes the leading destroyer *Firedrake*, which has to be scuttled by the corvette *Sunflower*. On 17 Dec *U609* keeps contact for some time in spite of heavy seas, but an attack fails in the swell. On 18–19 Dec *U621* and *U609* keep contact in turns but none of the six boats still operating comes up. *U621* sinks on 18 and 20 Dec another two scattered ships totalling 10691 tons. On 18 Dec the outbound *U563* (Lt-Cdr v Hartmann) also sinks one ship of 4906 tons W of the Bay of Biscay. On 15 Dec *U626*, which is on the way out, happens to be overtaken by the escort group of the Iceland section on ONS.152 (EG.C3) and is sunk by the US Coast Guard cutter *Ingham*.

15–25 Dec   Arctic
The British convoy JW.51A sets out for Murmansk from Loch Ewe with 16 freighters (over 100000 tons of cargo), escorted by the destroyers *Beagle* and *Boadicea*, the

corvettes *Honeysuckle* and *Oxlip*, the mine-sweeper *Seagull* and the trawlers *Lady Madelaine* and *Northern Whale*. In addition, there is a destroyer force from Seidisfjord comprising *Faulknor*, *Fury*, *Echo*, *Eclipse* and *Inglefield*. Distant cover is provided by the Home Fleet. The convoy reaches Murmansk on 25 Dec without having been located by German reconnaissance but five ships are lost in the Kola Inlet as a result of German air attacks and mines.

15–25 Dec   South Pacific
The Japanese 2nd DD Flotilla (Rear-Adm Tanaka), with the destroyers *Naganami*, *Makinami*, *Oyashio*, *Kuroshio*, *Kagero*, *Kawakaze*, *Suzukaze*, *Tanikaze*, *Urakaze*, *Yugure* and *Ariake*, and units of the 8th Fleet, including the minelayer *Tsugaru*, carry out transport missions in six operations from Rabaul and Shortland to Munda in the New Georgia Archipelago in order to construct an airfield there.

18–21 Dec   Mediterranean
In the Gulf of Hammamet, the British submarine *P211/Safari* (Cdr Bryant) sinks five vessels of 1757 tons. *P45/Unrivalled* (Lt Sprice) sinks two ships of 414 tons. Off Naples, *P42/Unbroken* (Lt Mars) torpedoes one ship of 2835 tons and *Turbulent* (Cdr Linton) sinks one ship of 5290 tons. Near Cape Bon, *P48* misses the destroyer *Lampo* in an attack on a convoy and is damaged by the torpedo boat *Perseo*. In another attempted attack on 25 Dec, the submarine is sunk by the torpedo boats *Ardente* and *Ardito*. *Ursula* (Lt Lakin) sinks on 28 Dec one ship of 4140 tons near Marettimo and is rammed and damaged two days later by a merchant ship.

19 Dec   Mediterranean
The British corvette *Snapdragon* is sunk off Benghazi in a German air attack.

20 Dec   Black Sea
The Soviet flotilla leader *Kharkov* and destroyer *Boiki* shell Yalta during the night 19–20 Dec and the destroyer *Nezamozhnik* and the patrol ship *Shkval* shell Feodosia. On the way back they encounter the returning German 1st MTB Flotilla; neither side secures a hit. The submarine *Shch-212* is sunk by air attack on 19–20 Dec N of Sinope.

21 Dec–31 Jan   South Atlantic
In Brazilian waters, *U507* (Cdr Schacht) and *U164* (Cdr Fechner) sink three ships of 14230 tons and one ship of 2608 tons respectively. On 13 and 6 Jan respectively they are sunk by Catalina flying boats of VP-83 operating as escorts.

21 Dec–25 Jan   Central Atlantic
In operations in the area of Dakar and Freetown, *U175* (Lt-Cdr Bruns) sinks one ship of 7177 tons.

22 Dec–10 Jan   Central Atlantic
Return convoy GUS.2 from Casablanca to New York, with 43 ships escorted by TF.37 comprising the destroyers *Madison*, *Lansdale*, *Davidson*, *Hilary P Jones*, *Nicholson* and *Charles F Hughes* and two minesweepers.

23 Dec   North Sea
The German MDS *Sperrbrecher 138/Friedrich Karl* sinks after striking a mine off Borkum.

24 Dec   General Situation
The High Commissioner for French North and West Africa, Admiral Darlan, is murdered in Algiers by a fanatical supporter of Gen de Gaulle.

24–31 Dec   North Atlantic
From the newly arrived U-boats the 'Spitz' group is formed on 24 Dec on the E side of the North Atlantic. It consists of *U260*, *U662*, *U123*, *U659*, *U225*, *U406*, *U440*, *U203*, *U664* and *U356*. S of the patrol line, the advancing *U664* (Lt Graef) sights on 26 Dec the convoy ONS.154 with 45 ships (Commodore Vice-Adm Egerton†), escorted by the EG.C1 (Cdr Windeyer) with the Canadian destroyer *St Laurent* and the corvettes *Battleford*, *Chilliwack*, *Kenogami*, *Napanee* and *Shediac* with the rescue ship *Toward* equipped with HF/DF. Apart from the 'Spitz' group, the 'Ungestüm' group, stationed a little further to the W and consisting of *U373*, *U435*, *U628*, *U336*, *U591*, *U615*, *U455*, *U409* and *U441*, is deployed against the convoy. In the afternoon of 26 Dec *U662* (Cdr Hermann) establishes contact and during the night 26–27 Dec *U356* (Lt Ruppelt) in two approaches sinks three ships of 13649 tons and torpedoes one of 7051 tons which *U441* (Lt-Cdr Hartmann) sinks. The latter also misses *St Laurent* and one ship. *U356*, after her second attack, is herself sunk by *St Laurent*, *Chilliwack*, *Battleford* and *Napanee*. The lost contact is re-established in the afternoon of 27 Dec by *U225* (Lt Leimkühler), which torpedoes in the night one tanker of 7087 tons which is then taken in tow by *Chilliwack*. In the morning, after an interruption of nine hours, contact is re-established by *U260* (Lt-Cdr Purkhold) which, after reconnaissance on 28 Dec, brings up by day *U336*, *U203*, *U615*, *U123*, *U406*, *U591*, *U664*, *U225* and *U440* and, after dark, *U435*, *U628* and *U662*. During the night 28–29 Dec the boats attack, sometimes repeatedly, in quick succession. After misses by *U203* and *U435*, *U591* (Lt-Cdr Zetzsche) torpedoes one ship of 5701 tons, which is later sunk by *U435* (Lt-Cdr Strelow). *U225* sinks one ship of 5273 tons and torpedoes one of 5598 tons, which is sunk by

U662. *U260* sinks one ship of 4893 tons; after a miss by *U203*, *U406* (Lt-Cdr Dieterichs) torpedoes three ships of which one of 3385 tons is sunk by *U123* (Lt v Schroeter), one of 5029 tons by *U628* (Lt Hasenschar) and one of 4871 tons by *U591*. At midnight *U225* torpedoes one ship of 4919 tons, which is sunk by *U225* and *U336* (Lt-Cdr Hunger), as well as the Commodore's ship of 7068 tons, which is sunk by *U123* and *U435*. Further attacks by *U203*, *U435*, *U628*, *U664* and (again) *U628* on escorts and merchant ships fail. When day breaks on 29 Dec the British destroyers *Milne* and *Meteor* arrive as additional escort and drive off *U260*, *U591* and *U455*. Only *U435* sinks one ship, of 5701 tons in a daylight underwater attack. In the evening of 29 Dec *U225* and *U615* repeatedly attack the auxiliary warship *Fidelity* (2456 tons), which sails with a French crew, but she is able to avoid the attacks; only in the afternoon of 30 Dec is she sunk by *U435*. *U455*, which keeps contact with the convoy until the night 30–31 Dec, is unable to bring up any other boat. The boats proceed to *U117* for replenishment.

26–27 Dec   North Atlantic
The outbound *U357* (Lt-Cdr Kellner) sights on 26 Dec NW of Ireland the convoy HX.219 with EG.B2 (Cdr Macintyre) consisting of the destroyers *Hesperus* and *Vanessa* and the corvettes *Gentian*, *Clematis*, *Heather*, *Campanula*, *Mignonette* and *Sweetbriar*. Her contact signal is located by HF/DF and *Hesperus* and *Vanessa* sink *U357* before she can send further signals and bring up the outbound *U384* and *U525*.

26–29 Dec   Black Sea
Second sortie by a Soviet minesweeping division (Rear-Adm V G Fadeye) against shipping on the Rumanian coast. With the minesweepers *T-406/Iskatel*, *T-407/Mina*, *T-408/Yakor* and *T-412/Arseni Rasskin*, it proceeds to the area between Gibrieni and Burgas. The destroyers *Besposhchadny* and *Soobrazitelny* cover the operation and make a sortie, without success, on 28 Dec into the area S of Fidonisi. Two minesweepers shell Burgas. The submarine *L-24* is lost on 30 Dec.

28 Dec   English Channel
The German MDS *Sperrbrecher 149/Goote* is sunk by mine off Den Helder.

29 Dec   North Pacific
The US fast minesweeper *Wasmuth* is sunk following the explosion of two of the ship's own depth charges during a gale off the Aleutian Islands.

28 Dec–14 Jan   Central Atlantic
Of the U-boats operating E of the Caribbean, *U105* (Lt-Cdr Nissen) sinks one

sailing vessel of 67 tons and *U217* (Lt-Cdr Reichenbach-Klinke) one ship of 7957 tons; *U124* (Lt-Cdr Mohr) sinks one independent ship of 4692 tons and on 9 Jan four ships of 23567 tons from convoy TB.1 (12 ships), which is escorted by US corvettes and PC submarine-chasers. *U109* and *U214* have no successes.

On 28 Dec convoy TM.1, comprising nine tankers with EG.B5 (Cdr Boyle) consisting of the destroyer *Havelock* and the corvettes *Pimpernel*, *Saxifrage* and *Godetia*, leaves Trinidad. Two of the tankers, departing late with *Godetia*, are sighted on 29 Dec by *U124*, but its several attack attempts are frustrated by the corvette and a Catalina from VP-53. Because there is no report of a convoy, no order to attack is given to the U-boats in the area.

Only on 3 Feb does *U514* (Lt-Cdr Auffermann) report the convoy about 1100 nautical miles NE of Trinidad en route to Gibraltar. *U514* is allowed to attack and torpedoes the tanker *British Vigilance* (8093 tons), the wreck of which is sunk on 24 Jan by the returning *U105* which also sinks an independent of 5106 tons. The BdU orders *U514* to keep contact and leads *U125* (Lt Nissen) from the E to the convoy. The 'Delphin' group with *U571*, *U620*, *U575*, *U381*, *U436* and *U442*, which have in vain searched for convoy GUS.2 (43 ships with TF.37, reported by *U182* since 29 Dec), and *U134*, *U181*, *U522* and *U511* are ordered into a patrol line across the course of the convoy for 7 Jan. Because a re-routing order from the Submarine Tracking Room, based on D/F, is not followed by convoy TM.1, the latter runs into 'Delphin' and is reported on 8 Jan by *U381* (Lt-Cdr Count Pückler).

U436 (Cdr Seibicke) attacks first, torpedoes the *Albert L Ellsworth* (8309 tons) and sinks the *Oltenia II* (6394 tons) but is damaged by a depth charge attack by *Havelock*. *U571* (Lt-Cdr Möhlmann) is driven off by *Pimpernel* and *Godetia* frustrates an attack by *U575* (Lt-Cdr Heydemann) which in a new assault in the morning of 9 Jan torpedoes the *Minister Wedel* (6833 tons) and *Norvik* (10034 tons); soon afterwards *U442* (Cdr

Hesse) torpedoes the *Empire Lytton* (9807 tons). In daylight the escorts frustrate attempts to attack by *U181* (Cdr Lüth); *U134* (Lt-Cdr Schendel) fails in its attack against the *Vanja* and is damaged by depth charges from *Godetia*. *U381* is attacked by *Harvester* and *Pimpernel*. *U620* (Lt-Cdr Stein) is able to hold the contact. In the evening of 9 Jan *U522* (Lt-Cdr Schneider) sinks the damaged *Minister Wedel* and *Norvik*, while *U442* sinks the wreck of the *Empire Lytton* and *U436* that of the *Albert L Ellsworth*. *U511* (Lt-Cdr Schneewind) sinks the independent *William Wilberforce* (5004 tons) nearby. In the evening of 10 Jan *U620* misses the rump convoy and *U522* torpedoes the *British Dominion*, which *U620* later sinks. *U571* tries attacks against the two remaining tankers, *Vanja* and *Cliona*, in the evenings of 10 and 11 Jan but the merchantman avoid these and also one by *U511* in the morning of 12 Jan. The escorts are now augmented by the destroyer *Quentin* and the corvettes *Pentstemon* and *Samphire*, sent out from Gibraltar, and by arriving aircraft. The two remaining tankers arrive at Gibraltar on 14 Jan.

30 Dec–12 Jan Central Atlantic
Return convoy GUF.3 (22 ships) from Oran, escorted by a British group with the sloop *Erne* to Gibraltar (31 Dec) and then by TF.35 with the destroyer *Parker*.

31 Dec Arctic
Operation 'Regenbogen': attack by a German naval force on the British convoy JW.51B in the Arctic. On 22 Dec the convoy JW.51B leaves Loch Ewe. It comprises 14 freighters, escorted by the destroyers *Onslow* (Capt Sherbrooke) *Oribi*, *Obedient*, *Obdurate*, *Orwell*, *Achates* and *Bulldog*, the minesweeper *Bramble*, the corvettes *Hyderabad* and *Rhododendron* and two trawlers, *Ocean Gem* and *Vizalma*, with close escort provided by the light cruisers *Sheffield* (Rear-Adm Burnett) and *Jamaica*, the destroyer *Opportune* and, from 29 Dec, the destroyer *Matchless*. Distant cover consists of the battleship *Anson* (Vice-Adm Fraser), the heavy cruiser *Cumberland* and the destroyers *Forester*, *Icarus* and *Impulsive*

with flanking cover by the submarines *Trespasser*, *Seadog*, *Unruly* and *Graph* (ex-*U570*).

On 24 Dec the convoy is located for the first time by a German reconnaissance aircraft. It is also sighted by *U354* (Lt-Cdr Herbschleb). On 30 Dec, in the afternoon, the German force puts to sea from Altafjord; it consists of the heavy cruisers *Admiral Hipper* (Capt Hartmann with the Commander Cruisers, Vice-Adm Kummetz, on board) and *Lützow* (Capt Stange) and the 5th DD Flotilla (Capt Schemmel) comprising the destroyers *Friedrich Eckoldt* (Cdr Bachmann), *Z29* (Cdr* Rechel), *Richard Beitzen* (Cdr v Davidson), *Theodor Riedel* (Cdr Riede), *Z30* (Cdr* Kaiser) and *Z31* (Cdr Alberts).

On 31 Dec the German force is directed to the area of *U354*'s contact signals. At first *Admiral Hipper* advances on the convoy in bad weather. But the convoy is skilfully defended by the destroyer group of Capt Sherbrooke and is covered by a smoke-screen. *Obedient* and *Onslow* are damaged and *Achates* is sunk. *Eckoldt*, *Beitzen* and *Z29* sink the minesweeper *Bramble*. Shortly before mid-day the British close escort intervenes in the fighting. *Admiral Hipper* receives three hits in the engagement, one of which reduces the speed of the cruiser. *Eckoldt* is sunk by *Sheffield* (Capt A W Clarke) and *Obdurate* is badly damaged by *Lützow*. Because of the confused situation, the poor visibility and the Navy Staff's W/T message ('In spite of operational orders, exercise restraint if you contact enemy of comparable strength, since it is undesirable to run excessive risks to the cruisers'), Vice-Adm Kummetz breaks off the engagement. The convoy RA.51 proceeds to the W with the escort of JW.51 without making contact with the enemy and arrives in Loch Ewe on 9 Jan 1943.

31 Dec Mediterranean
The British submarine *P311*/*Tutenkhamen* is lost on a mine off Maddalena, Sardinia.

31 Dec South Pacific
Imperial Headquarters in Tokyo decides to abandon the island of Guadalcanal.

1943

Jan–Feb   North Atlantic
Allocation of vessels to the Allied Mid Ocean and Western Local Escort Groups (convoys escorted; * denotes those attacked by U-boats): B.1: RN destroyers *Hurricane*, *Rockingham* and *Watchman*, RN corvettes *Borage*, *Dahlia*, *Meadowsweet*, *Monkshood*, *Wallflower* and *Anchusa* (ON.162, SC.119); B.2: RN destroyers *Hesperus*, *Vanessa* and *Whitehall*, RN corvettes *Campanula*, *Clematis*, *Gentian*, *Heather*, *Mignonette* and *Sweetbriar* (ON.159, SC.118*); B.3: RN destroyers *Harvester* and *Escapade*, Polish destroyers *Garland* and *Burza*, RN corvettes *Narcissus* and *Orchis*, FFN corvettes *Roselys*, *Aconit*, *Renoncule* and *Lobélia* (ON.157, SC.117, ONS.167*); B.4: RN destroyers *Highlander*, *Beverley* and *Winchelsea*, RN corvettes *Abelia*, *Anemone*, *Asphodel*, *Clover*, *Pennywort* and *Snowflake* (HX.220, ON.161, ONS.169); B.5: RN destroyers *Havelock*, *Warwick* and *Witch*, RN corvettes *Buttercup*, *Columbine*, *Godetia*, *Lavender*, *Pimpernel* and *Saxifrage* (TM.1* from Trinidad to UK, ON.168); B.6: RN destroyers *Fame*, *Ramsey* and *Viscount*, RN corvettes *Kingcup* and *Vervain*, RNoN corvettes *Potentilla*, *Acanthus*, *Eglantine* and *Rose* (SC.116, ONS.165*); B.7: RN destroyers *Chesterfield* and *Ripley*, RN corvettes *Alisma*, *Coreopsis*, *Jonquil*, *Pink*, *Sunflower* and *Loosestrife* (SC.115, ON.164, SC.120); C.1: RCN destroyers *St Laurent* and *St Croix*, RN destroyer *Burwell*, RN frigate *Itchen*, RCN corvettes *Napanee*, *Battleford*, *Kenogami*, *Shediac*, *Chilliwack*, *Sackville* and *Arvida* (HX.222, KMS.10, MKS.9); C.2: RN destroyers *Broadway* and *Sherwood*, RCN destroyer *Saguenay*, RN frigate *Lagan*, RCN corvettes *Chambly*, *Morden*, *Drumheller* and *Orillia*, RN corvettes *Polyanthus* and *Primrose* (ONS.160, HX.225); C.3: RCN destroyers *Assiniboine* and *Skeena*, RN destroyer *Burnham*, RCN corvettes *Bittersweet*, *Mayflower*, *La Malbaie*, *Eyebright* and *Agassiz* (HX.221, ON.163, HX.226); C.4: RN destroyer *Churchill*, RCN destroyer *Restigouche*, RCN corvettes *Brandon*, *Amherst*, *Collingwood*, *Sherbrooke*, *Wetaskiwin*, *Pictou* and *Galt*, RN corvette *Celandine* (ONS.158, HX.224, KMF.10B); A.3: US Coast Guard cutters *Campbell* and *Spencer*, US destroyer *Badger*, RN corvette

Dianthus, RCN corvettes *Dauphin*, *Trillium* and *Rosthern* (HX.223, ON.166*).
The Western Local Escort Groups (only RCN vessels) comprise: 24.18.1: corvettes *Arrowhead* and *Chicoutimi*, minesweeper *Digby*; 24.18.2: corvettes *Timmins*, *Buctouche*, *Kamsack* and *Edmundston*, minesweeper *Minas*; 24.18.3: corvettes *Moncton* and *Nanaimo*, minesweeper *Lachine*; 24.18.5: destroyer *Niagara*, corvette *Matapedia*, minesweeper *Granby*; 24.18.6: destroyer *Hamilton*, corvettes *Brantford* and *Dundas*, minesweeper *Gananoque*; 24.18.7: destroyer *Annapolis*, corvettes *Fennel* and *Dunvegan*, minesweeper *Cowichan*; 24.18.8: corvettes *Saskatoon* and *Quesnel*, minesweepers *Drummondville* and *Kenora*.

1 Jan   Atlantic
'Ultra' indicates an incoming blockade-runner and a Sunderland flying boat locates the *Rhakotis* (6753 tons, Capt Jakobs) en route from Japan, 200 nautical miles NW of Cape Finisterre. The ship is sunk by the cruiser *Scylla* which is directed to the scene.

1 Jan   Intelligence
Renaming of the German 'Enigma' cypher circuits, as follows: 'Heimische Gewässer' becomes 'Hydra'. (broken as 'Dolphin' and, for officers only, as 'Oyster'); 'Ausserheimische Gewässer' becomes 'Aegir' (this code, used by raiders in distant areas, is never broken because too few signals are sent); 'U-Bootübungsschlüssel' becomes 'Thetis' (never broken); 'Tokyo' becomes 'Bertok' (broken only in Sep 1943 as 'Seahorse'/'Barnacle'); 'Süd' becomes 'Hermes' (broken as 'Porpoise'); 'Kernflotte' becomes 'Neptun' (never broken); 'Östland Ostsee' becomes 'Potsdam' (broken only in Jan 1944); and 'Versorgung Fernost' becomes 'Tibet' (broken only in Aug 1943). 'Triton' remains, broken as 'Shark' since mid-Dec 1942 but up to mid-Jan 1943 with gaps and delays, then up to 8 Mar with short delays and, after a short black-out, again from 19 Mar with short delays. The introduction of a new rotor, 'Gamma', on 1 July brings about a new three-week black-out (see 1 July).

1–5 Jan   Arctic
The Soviet submarine *L-20* (Capt 3rd Class Tamman) sinks, off Kongsfjord, the steamer *Muansa* (5472 tons) proceeding in the company of *V5909*, lays a mine barrage

(cleared) off Tanafjord and disembarks agents on the coast on 5 Jan. *L-22* (Capt 3rd Class Afonin) lays a mine barrage off Honningsvaag (cleared). The Soviet steamer *Krasnyj Partizan* (2418 tons), sailing on her own to England, is sunk in the Barents Sea by *U354* (Lt-Cdr Herbschleb).

1–19 Jan   North Atlantic
In the central North Atlantic, the 'Falke' group, comprising the U-boats *U257*, *U404*, *U572*, *U71*, *U444*, *U384*, *U631*, *U333*, *U167*, *U706*, *U441*, *U525*, *U563*, *U632*, *U584*, *U607*, *U606*, *U226*, *U69*, *U201*, *U414* and *U403*, operates against the convoys ONS.158, escorted by EG.C4 with the destroyers *Churchill* (RN) and *Restigouche* (RCN) and the corvettes *Amherst*, *Brandon*, *Collingwood*, *Sherbrooke* (RCN) and *Celandine* (RN)); ON.159, escorted by EG.B2 with the destroyers *Hesperus*, *Vanessa* and *Whitehall* and the corvettes *Campanula*, *Clematis*, *Gentian*, *Heather*, *Mignonette* and *Sweetbriar*; and ONS.160, escorted by EG.C2 with the destroyer *Sherwood* (RN), the frigates *Lagan* and *Waveney* (RN) and the corvettes *Morden*, *Orillia* (RCN) and *Polyanthus* and *Primrose* (RN). The convoys are re-routed after German radio orders for the 'Falke' group are decoded via 'Ultra'. On 9 and 10 Jan *U441* (Lt-Cdr Klaus Hartmann) misses the independent *Washington Express*, *U384* (Lt v Rosenberg-Gruszczynski) sinks a ship of 6155 tons and *U632* (Lt-Cdr Karpf) sinks a straggler from convoy UGS.3 of 6773 tons.

1–31 Jan   Pacific
American submarine operations are aided by the decoding of Japanese radio traffic, especially since the break into the 'Maru' code and into the cypher used by the harbour captain at Truk in early 1943. In Jan, 57 'Ultra' intercepts led to 15 sightings, 11 attacks and four sinkings. For the American submarines arriving in their operational areas in Jan, the following successes are confirmed: Off Japan, *Porpoise* (Lt-Cdr McKnight) sinks one ship of 4999 tons, *Haddock* (Lt-Cdr Taylor) one of 10018 tons, *Finback* (Lt-Cdr Hull) one of 271 tons and *Pollack* (Lt-Cdr Lewellen) two of 8000 tons; *Drum*, *Sailfish*, *Kingfish*, *Pike* and *Searaven* have no successes. In the Central Pacific, *Whale* (Lt-Cdr Azer) sinks two ships of 13375 tons (including the *Heiyo Maru* with

the help of 'Ultra') and damages one of 5624 tons, *Wahoo* (Lt-Cdr Morton) sinks two ships of 7348 tons and damages the destroyer *Harusame* (on 24 Jan W of Wewak) and two ships of 10602 tons and *Flying Fish* (Lt-Cdr Donaho) sinks one ship of 994 tons (using 'Ultra'), damages one of 4391 tons and damages one more of 8359 tons together with *Pompano* (Lt-Cdr Thomas). In the South Pacific, *Silversides* (Lt-Cdr Burlingame) sinks four ships of 27797 tons, (including the *Toei Maru* using 'Ultra'), *Nautilus* (Lt-Cdr Brockman) sinks one ship of 1422 tons and torpedoes the destroyer *Akizuki* (on 19 Jan 270m W of Tulagi), *Guardfish* (Lt-Cdr Klakring) sinks the fast transport *No 1* (on 13 Jan) and the destroyer *Hakaze* (on 23 Jan off Kavieng), *Growler* (Lt-Cdr Gilmore) sinks one ship of 5857 tons and damages the munitions ship *Hayasaki*, *Swordfish* (Lt-Cdr Lewis) sinks one ship of 4122 tons and *Gato* (Lt-Cdr Foley) sinks three ships of 8289 tons and torpedoes a ship of 6550 tons previously damaged by aircraft; *Tuna* has no success and *Grayback* and *Greenling* are on recce missions. *Argonaut* is lost off Lae in a depth charge attack by a Japanese destroyer on 10 Jan. In the South West Pacific, *Grenadier* (Lt-Cdr Lent) sinks one sailing vessel and has three misses, *Trout* (Lt-Cdr Ramage) sinks one ship of 1911 tons and two sailing vessels and damages three ships of 37870 tons and *Grayling* (Lt-Cdr Lee) sinks one ship of 749 tons and damages one of 6032 tons. *Gudgeon* is on a guerrilla support mission.

1 Jan–8 Feb Mediterranean

Allied supply convoys for French North Africa. From the US arrive UGF and UGS convoys, escorted by US task forces, and from Great Britain come KMF and KMS convoys, escorted by British/Canadian EGs. The US convoys are taken over by British/Canadian EGs W of Gibraltar and escorted to Oran, Algiers and Bône, partly as TE convoys. The return convoys are GUF, GUS, MKF and MKS, escorted in the same way. UGS.3, comprising 39 ships escorted by TF.33 with the US destroyers *Wainwright*, *Mayrant*, *Rhind*, *Trippe* and *Rowan*, arrives on 30 Dec at Casablanca. On its way under British escort to Oran, it is attacked by *U73* (Lt Deckert), which sinks one ship of 7176 tons on 1 Jan. An attack by the Italian submarine *Dandolo* off Bougie on 1 Jan fails.

On 1 and 2 Jan, in attacks by Ju 87s of II/StG 3 (Capt Schiller) and by eight Fw 190 fighter-bombers of III/SG 10 (Capt Schröter) on the harbour at Bône, two ships of 13181 tons sink, the minesweeper

Alarm is beached after bomb hits, the cruiser *Ajax* is hit by a 500kg bomb from a Ju 87 and three ships of 18973 tons are damaged.

From the convoys, on 7 Jan *U371* (Lt-Cdr Mehl) sinks the A/S trawler *Jura* and torpedoes one ship of 7159 tons E of Algiers, which is later sunk by bombs in Algiers. Torpedo aircraft from KG 26 sink two ships of 8677 tons and damage one of 7191 tons off Bougie. In a sortie by the 3rd MTB Flotilla against the Algerian coast, *S58* (with the Flotilla Cdr, Lt-Cdr Kemnade, on board) the A/S trawler *Horatio* is sunk.

On 13 Jan *U224* is sunk by the Canadian corvette *Ville de Quebec* from the escort of convoy TE.13. In an air attack against Bône on 17 Jan, one ship of 5982 tons is damaged and on 18 Jan *U83* misses against a convoy off Oran. On 19 Jan the Italian submarine *Tritone* is sunk near Bougie by the Canadian corvette *Port Arthur* from the escort of convoy MKS.6.

On 20/21 Jan, in air attacks off the Algerian coast, one ship of 3645 tons is sunk by bombs and two of 14354 tons are damaged by torpedoes. *U453* (Lt-Cdr Frhr v Schlippenbach) sinks one ship of 5783 tons off Oran on 20 Jan but an attack by *U83* on 21 Jan to the N fails. On 20 Jan the convoy GUS.3 leaves Gibraltar escorted by TF.33 with the additional destroyer *Champlin*. Attacks by the Italian submarines *Dandolo*, *Malachite* and *Giada* W of Bône and off Oran fail on 22 and 23 Jan.

The British troop convoy KMF.6 is covered by Force H (Vice-Adm Syfret) with the battleships *Nelson* and *Rodney* and the carrier *Formidable* from Gibraltar to Algiers. On 25 Jan convoy UGF.4 (18 transports escorted by TF.34 with the battleship *Texas* and the destroyers *Buck*, *Wilkes*, *Swanson*, *Ludlow*, *Roe*, *Woolsey*, *Edison*, *Bristol* and *Butler*) arrives off Gibraltar, is taken over by the British EG with destroyers *Brilliant* and *Antelope* and the Canadian corvettes *Baddeck*, *Alberni*, *Summerside*, *Lunenburg*, *Felixtowe* and *Port Arthur* and arrives at Oran on 27 Jan. In a torpedo attack by eight SM 79s of the Italian Gruppos 105, 130 and 132 and ten He 111s of I/KG 26 on 29 Jan off Bougie, the AA ship *Pozarica* (4540 tons) and the destroyer *Avon Vale* are torpedoed; the former is a total loss on 13 Feb.

On 30 Jan the Italian submarine *Platino* (Lt-Cdr Patrelli-Campagnone) attacks convoy TE.14 and sinks the Canadian corvette *Samphire* from the escort. On 31 Jan convoy GUF.4 (30 ships), escorted by a British EG with the sloops *Erne* and *Scarborough* and supported by the French leaders *Le Terrible* and *Le Fantasque*, leaves Oran and is taken

over W of Gibraltar on 1 Feb by TF.34. On 2 Feb convoy UGS.4 (48 ships escorted by TF.38 with the destroyers *Plunkett*, *Niblack*, *Benson*, *Gleaves*, *Mayo* and *Kendrick*) is taken over W of Gibraltar by a British EG and thence taken to Oran by 3 Feb.

1 Jan–9 Feb South Pacific

Final battle for Guadalcanal. In Jan Japanese destroyers continue the supply operations and from 1 Feb carry out the evacuation of Guadalcanal ordered on 4 Jan. Participating are the 2nd DD Flotilla (Rear-Adm Koyanagi) with the cruiser *Isuzu* and the destroyers *Kuroshio*, *Oyashio*, *Kagero*, *Shiranui*, *Umikaze*, *Kawakaze*, *Suzukaze*, *Naganami* and *Makinami* and the 4th DD Flotilla (Rear-Adm Tanaka) with the cruiser *Agano* and the destroyers *Arashi*, *Hagikaze*, *Nowake*, *Maikaze*, *Akigumo*, *Yugumo*, *Makigumo*, *Kazegumo*, *Hatsukaze*, *Yukikaze*, *Amatsukaze*, *Tokitsukaze*, *Urakaze*, *Isokaze*, *Tanikaze*, *Hamakaze* and *Akizuki*. There are supply operations ('Tokyo Express') from Rabaul to Cape Esperance by night, with air support from airfields at Munda and Vila on New Georgia.

On 1–2 Jan there is a mission to Guadalcanal with 10 Japanese destroyers. B-17 bombers attack unsuccessfully but Navy SBD dive-bombers damage *Suzukaze*. An attack by PT boats from Tulagi fails. Japanese destroyers throw supply containers overboard.

On 4–5 Jan US TF.67 (Rear-Adm Ainsworth), comprising the cruisers *Nashville*, *St Louis* and *Helena* and the destroyers *Fletcher* and *O'Bannon*, shells Munda. Rear-Adm Tisdale, with the cruisers *Honolulu*, *Achilles* (RNZN, damaged by bombs), *Columbia* and *Louisville* and the destroyers *Drayton*, *Lamson* and *Nicholas*, forms a covering force SW of the Solomons. In the operation *Helena* for the first time makes successful use of proximity fuses for AA fire.

On 10–11 Jan eight Japanese destroyers undertake a mission to Guadalcanal. Following reconnaissance reports the US PT boats *PT45*, *PT39*, *PT48*, *PT115*, *PT112*, *PT43*, *PT40*, *PT59*, *PT46* and *PT36* are deployed in several groups from Tulagi. In all, six boats are able to fire 21 torpedoes; the destroyer *Hatsukaze* is lightly damaged by one hit and *PT112* and *PT43* are lost in the Japanese defensive fire.

On 14–15 Jan nine Japanese destroyers undertake a mission to Guadalcanal. On the way US Marine SBD dive-bombers from Henderson Field attack and slightly damage *Arashi*, *Urakaze*, *Tanikaze* and *Hamakaze* which, however, continue their journey.

The PT boats *PT59*, *PT38*, *PT39*, *PT115*, *PT109*, *PT45*, *PT37*, *PT40*, *PT36*, *PT48*, *PT47*, *PT46* and *PT123* are deployed from Tulagi. Seven boats fire 17 torpedoes without success.

On 19 Jan the 'Cactus Striking Force' (Capt Briscoe), comprising the destroyers *Nicholas*, *O'Bannon*, *Radford* and *De Haven*, is transferred to Tulagi and, using it as a base, repeatedly shells Japanese positions on Guadalcanal.

During the night 23–24 Jan Rear-Adm Ainsworth again shells Vila with the cruisers *Nashville* and *Helena* and the 'Cactus Striking Force.' Rear-Adm Tisdale, with *Honolulu*, *St Louis*, *Drayton*, *Lamson* and *Hughes*, is available as a covering force and 59 aircraft from the carrier *Saratoga* provide air support from the S after breaking their flight at Henderson Field.

In a supply operation, the Japanese submarine *I-1* is destroyed off Cape Esperance by the New Zealand corvettes *Kiwi* and *Moa* on 29 Jan. Important documents and cypher materials are captured.

On 30–31 Jan four and on 4–5 Feb five troop and supply transports bring reinforcements to Guadalcanal for the US Marine Corps forces. On 1 Feb the old destroyer *Stringham* and LCTs land one regiment on the west coast of Guadalcanal, covered by the 'Cactus Striking Force' composed of the destroyers *Fletcher*, *Nicholas*, *Radford* and *De Haven*. On 29–30 Jan US TF.18 (Rear-Adm Giffen), comprising the cruisers *Wichita*, *Chicago*, *Louisville*, *Montpelier*, *Cleveland* and *Columbia* and the destroyers *La Vallette*, *Waller*, *Conway*, *Frazier*, *Chevalier*, *Edwards*, *Meade* and *Taylor*, as well as the escort carriers *Chenango* and *Suwanee* some way off, approaches from the S to cover the operation and to make a sortie into the Central Solomons. In the evening of 29 Jan the force is attacked near Rennell Island by Japanese torpedo aircraft which severely damage *Chicago* and hit *Wichita* and *Louisville* with duds. In a second attack *Chicago* (Capt Davis) is sunk and *La Valette* torpedoed on 30 Jan; 1049 survivors are rescued. The carrier forces, including *Enterprise* (Rear-Adm Sherman) and *Saratoga* (Rear-Adm Ramsey), situated further to the S, and the battleship force (Rear-Adm Lee), comprising *North Carolina*, *Indiana* and *Washington*, are not able to intervene. Operation 'KE': Japanese evacuation of Guadalcanal. On 1–2 Feb 20 destroyers proceed from Rabaul to Cape Esperance. On the way 41 aircraft from Henderson Field attack and damage *Makinami* which, however, continues her journey. The 'Cactus Striking Force' with *Nicholas*, *Flet-*

cher, *Radford* and *De Haven*, which is deployed from the W, is driven off by Japanese air attacks. *De Haven* is lost by bomb hits and *Nicholas* lightly damaged by near-misses. The US PT boats *PT47*, *PT39*, *PT111*, *PT48*, *PT59*, *PT115*, *PT37*, *PT124*, *PT123*, *PT109* and *PT36* are deployed from Tulagi. Five of them are able to fire 19 torpedoes. In taking avoiding action, the destroyer *Makigumo* runs on a mine barrage laid shortly before near the Japanese route by the US minelaying destroyers *Preble*, *Montgomery* and *Tracy* and sinks. The destroyer *Kawakaze* sinks *PT111* and two others sink *PT37* and *PT123*. Nineteen Japanese destroyers take troops and return to Rabaul.

On 4–5 Feb Rear-Adm Koyanagi with the cruiser *Isuzu* and 22 destroyers proceeds to Guadalcanal and evacuates the second group of the 17th Army. The force is attacked by 64 aircraft from Henderson Field: the destroyers *Maikaze* and *Shiranui* are badly damaged and *Kuroshio* and *Hamakaze* lightly damaged but are able to continue the operation. On 7–8 Feb 18 Japanese destroyers evacuate the remainder of the troops: in the process *Isokaze* and *Hamakaze* are badly damaged in attacks by 15 aircraft. In all, 11706 men are evacuated in the period 1–9 Feb. On 9 Feb the Guadalcanal operation is ended.

2 Jan   South West Pacific

Troops of US I Corps (Lt-Gen Eichelberger) capture Buna on New Guinea. By the end of Jan the Japanese bases at Goa and Sananda also fall. With that the threat to Port Moresby is removed.

2–30 Jan   Air War/Western Europe

Mine offensive by RAF Bomber Command. For 13 nights Wellingtons, Stirlings, Halifaxes and Lancasters of Nos 3 and 4 Groups fly 538 sorties against Biscay ports, the French and Dutch coasts, the Frisian coast and up to the Kattegat; 15 aircraft are lost. The mines claim the E-boat *S 104* in the Channel on 9 Jan and the patrol trawlers *V1105* and *V2018* off Terschelling on 26 and 29 Jan respectively.

3 Jan   Mediterranean

Attack by British small battle units on Palermo. 'Chariots' (human torpedoes) are launched from the submarines *Thunderbolt* (Cdr Crouch) and *Trooper* (Lt Wraith): they penetrate the harbour and their attached charges severely damage the Italian cruiser *Ulpio Traiano* and the transport *Viminale*. The third submarine *P311* (Lt Cailey) was sunk by the Italian torpedo boat *Partenope* on 29 Dec.

3 Jan   South Atlantic

The German auxiliary cruiser *Schiff 28/Michel* (Capt v Ruckteschell) sinks the British freighter *Empire March* (7040 tons) in the South Atlantic.

4 Jan–19 Feb   Bay of Biscay

Of the US submarines deployed in the Bay of Biscay, *Shad* (Lt-Cdr MacGregor) sinks the minesweeper *M4242* on 4 Jan and torpedoes the ore transport *Nordfels* (1214 tons) on 25 Jan. *Blackfish* (Lt-Cdr Davidson) sinks the patrol boat *V408* on 19 Feb. Further successes are prevented by torpedo failures.

6–23 Jan   Mediterranean

Last Italian convoys to and from Tripoli: a few large, but mostly smaller, ships and auxiliary warships, occasionally escorted by the destroyer *Saetta*, the torpedo boats *Orione*, *Animoso* and others as well as Italian ferry barges. Against them the British Force K is deployed from Malta: on 8–9 Jan the destroyers *Nubian* and *Kelvin* sink three schooners near Kuriat and during the night 15–16 Jan they attack S of Lampedusa the steamer *D'Annunzio* (4537 tons), escorted by the torpedo boat *Perseo*. The steamer sinks; *Perseo* escapes. The same night the destroyers *Pakenham* and *Javelin* sink one auxiliary ship. During the night 18–19 Jan *Pakenham*, *Nubian* and the Greek destroyer *Vasilissa Olga* sink the transport *Stromboli* (475 tons). Early on 20 Jan *Kelvin* and *Javelin* locate N of Tripoli a convoy consisting of 10 small Italian ships (minesweepers *RD31*, *RD36*, *RD37* and *RD39*, three auxiliary minesweepers and three small vessels) and destroy it. The Malta submarines make the following sinkings off the E Tunisian coast: *Umbra* (Cdr Maydon) sinks one ship of 1523 tons and two sailing ships, *Unrivalled* (Lt Turner) sinks four sailing ships of 387 tons, *Unruffled* (Lt Stevens) sinks four ships of 2295 tons, *Unseen* (Lt Crawford) sinks three ships of 4137 tons, including one escorted by the torpedo boat *Calliope*, and *Unbroken* (Lt Mars) sinks the *Edda* (6107 tons), escorted by the torpedo boat *San Martino*. The Italian submarines *Settimo*, *Narvalo*, *Otaria* and *Santarosa* transport ammunition and fuel to Tripoli. On the return *Narvalo* is sunk by the destroyers *Pakenham* and *Hursley* from convoy ME.15 (with air support) on 14 Jan and *Santarosa* by the British *MTB260* on 19 Jan. During the night 22–23 Jan Force K, comprising the cruisers *Cleopatra* and *Euryalus* and the destroyers *Jervis*, *Javelin*, *Nubian* and *Kelvin*, shells the withdrawal routes of the German-Italian Panzer armies near Zuara. Tripoli is evacuated by the rearguards on

23 Jan after the freighters *Marco Foscarini* (6342 tons), *Assiria* (2705 tons), *Marocchino* (1524 tons), *Tevere* (8289 tons) and *Guilia* (5921 tons), which are unable to put to sea, have been scuttled on 20 Jan.

6 Jan–7 Feb   Mediterranean

In 14 operations, Italian destroyer forces, consisting of three to five units, bring back 15580 reserve troops to Tunis and Bizerta and evacuate wounded and prisoners. *Mitragliere* participates in seven operations, *Gioberti* and *Camicia Nera* in five, *Da Noli*, *Granatiere*, *Premuda*, *Zeno* and *Corazziere* in four, *Ascari*, *Pigafetta* and *Malocello* in three, *Bombardiere* and *Legionario* in two and *Bersagliere* and *Carabiniere* in one. *Bersagliere* is sunk in an air raid on Palermo on 7 Jan. On the return *Bombardiere* is sunk off Marettimo on 17 Jan by the British submarine *United* (Lt Roxburgh). British mining operations against the Italian convoy traffic of freighters and tankers are undertaken on the Italian routes inside the flanking mine barrages between the Gulf of Tunis and Sicily by the fast minelayers *Welshman* (7 and 30 Jan) and *Abdiel* (9 Jan, 3 and 7 Feb) and the minelaying submarine *Rorqual* (18 Jan). On 1 Feb, on the return from the second operation, *Welshman* is sunk by *U617* (Lt-Cdr Brandi). On 9 Jan a convoy runs on to the mine barrage laid by *Abdiel*: the destroyer *Maestrale* is damaged and *Corsaro* sinks when she comes to her assistance. The destroyer *Saetta* and the torpedo boat *Uragano* sink on the same mine barrage on 3 Feb. The corvette *Procellaria* and the torpedo boat *Prestinari* sink on 31 Jan on the mine barrage just laid by *Welshman* and the German transport *Ankara* (4768 tons) sinks on *Rorqual*'s barrage. Of the British submarines deployed near Marettimo and in the Tyrrhenian Sea, *Splendid* (Lt-Cdr McGeogh) sinks four ships of 10064 tons, including the *Emma* (7931 tons) on 16 Jan, which is escorted by the torpedo boats *Groppo*, *Uragano* and *Clio*; *Sahib* (Lt Bromage) sinks one ship of 1194 tons and *U301*; *Tribune* sinks one ship of 6673 tons; *Turbulent* (Cdr Linton) sinks three ships of 11234 tons; *Saracen* (Lt Lumby) sinks one ship of 214 tons; and *Safari* (Cdr Bryant) sinks four ships of 4137 tons. *Unbending* (Lt Stanley) torpedoes one ship. Torpedo aircraft from Malta sink three ships of 11929 tons from convoys and bombers two of 9016 tons. Apart from those named, the following Italian units take part in the escorting of the convoys: the destroyer *Lampo*, the torpedo boats *Fortunale*, *Orione*, *Ardito*, *Ardente*, *Animoso*, *Monsone*, *Ciclone*, *Cigno*, *Calliope*, *Partenope*, *Sirio*, *Pallade*, *Clio*, *Perseo*, *Castore*, *Lira*, *Libra*, *Climene*, *Dezza*, *Mon-*

tanari and *Cascino* and the corvettes *Antilope*, *Artemide*, *Gabbiano* and *Persefone*. On 12 Jan *Ardente* sinks in a collision with the destroyer *Grecale* off Sicily. Sorties by the British Force Q from Bône with the cruisers *Aurora*, *Penelope*, *Dido* and *Sirius* are largely unsuccessful. The destroyers *Lightning* and *Loyal* sink one ship S of Sardinia on 18 Jan. On 23 Jan Force Q, with the cruisers *Cleopatra* and *Euryalus* and the destroyers *Javelin*, *Jervis*, *Kelvin* and *Nubian*, bombards Zuara in Libya.

9–10 Jan   Indonesia

The Australian destroyer *Arunta* evacuates to Port Darwin 282 troops and 31 civilians from the Japanese-occupied island of Timor.

9–12 Jan   Baltic

The German battlecruiser *Scharnhorst* and heavy cruiser *Prinz Eugen*, escorted by the destroyers *Friedrich Ihn*, *Paul Jacobi* and *Z24*, start their transfer to Norway in the eastern Baltic, pass with MDSs the Belt and are located by British air reconnaissance, forewarned by 'Ultra', W of the Skagerrak. The Skl cancels the transfer and the big ships return to the Baltic, the destroyers going to Aarhus. The deployment of powerful forces from Coastal Command and of six submarines of the 9th SM Flotilla is unsuccessful.

12 Jan   North Pacific

Weak US Army forces (Brig-Gen Jones) occupy the Aleutian island of Amchitka in order to construct a fighter airfield. The operation is covered by TF.8 (Rear-Adm Kinkaid, relieved by Rear-Adm Theobald on 4 Jan). In the operations the destroyer *Worden* is lost when she goes aground.

12–19 Jan   North Atlantic

Stationed W of Ireland and S of the 'Falke' group, the 'Habicht' group, comprising *U383*, *U303*, *U624*, *U704*, *U438*, *U752*, *U613*, *U186* and *U268*, searches in vain for the re-routed convoy ONS.160 (EG.C2; see 1–19 Jan). On the way *U186* (Lt-Cdr Hesemann) sinks an independent of 7147 tons and on 17 Jan *U268* (Lt.Heydemann) sinks the whale factory ship *Vestfold* (14547 tons) with *LCT2239*, *LCT2267* and *LCT2344* on board, belonging to the convoy HX.222, which is escorted by EG.C1 with the destroyers *Chesterfield*, *Vansittart* (RN) and *St Croix* (RCN) and the corvettes *Battleford*, *Chilliwack*, *Kenogami*, *Napanee* and *Shediac* (RCN).

12–23 Jan   North Atlantic

The 'Jaguar' group, comprising *U96*, *U598*, *U266*, *U662*, *U123*, *U413*, *U594*, *U337* and *U706*, operates in the area NE of Newfoundland against convoys HX.222 (EG.C1; see 12–19 Jan) and SC.116 (EG.B6 with the

destroyers *Fame*, *Ramsey* and *Viscount*, the RN corvettes *Kingcup* and *Vervain* and the Norwegian corvettes *Potentilla*, *Acanthus*, *Eglantine* and *Rose*) which are routed clear of the U-boat group. On 15 Jan *U337* is sunk by Fortress 'G' of No 206 Sqn RAF near the convoys ONS.160 (EG.C2; see 1–19 Jan) and ON.161 (EG.B4 with the destroyers *Highlander*, *Beverley* and *Winchelsea* and the corvettes *Anemone*, *Asphodel*, *Pennywort* and *Snowflake*), which are also routed clear of 'Jaguar'. On 22 Jan *U413* (Lt-Cdr Poel) sights the convoy SC.117 escorted by EG.B3 (Cdr Tait) with the new frigate *Swale*, the Polish destroyer *Garland*, the British corvettes *Narcissus* and *Orchis* and the FFN corvettes *Roselys*, *Lobélia* and *Aconit*. *U413* sinks a straggler of 3556 tons but W/T interference prevents a punctual deployment of the other boats. The 'Jaguar' group is ordered to make a search but does not find the convoy again although on 25 Jan *U624* (Lt-Cdr Count Soden) sinks another straggler of 5112 tons.

14 Jan   Norway

The German A/S trawler *UJ1107* is sunk in a collision off Rotvaer.

14–25 Jan   General Situation

Roosevelt and Churchill meet with the military staffs of the USA and Great Britain at the Casablanca Conference. Churchill and Roosevelt demand the 'unconditional surrender' of Germany. Agreement on further operations in the Mediterranean area: a landing on Sicily after the conquest of Tunisia. Victory over the German U-boats is given top priority in the Allied conduct of the war.

14 Jan–17 Feb   Air War/Western Europe

RAF Bomber Command (Air Chief Marshal Harris) recieves orders to carry out heavy attacks on the U-boat bases at Lorient, St-Nazaire, Brest and La Pallice. First the Command flies a series of nine 'area' bombing attacks against the French port and German U-boat base of Lorient. Participating are Wellingtons, Stirlings, Halifaxes and Lancasters from Nos 1, 4 and 6 Groups: on 14/15 Jan 122 aircraft take part, on 15/16 Jan 157, on 23/24 Jan 121, on 26/27 Jan 157, on 29/30 Jan 75, on 4/5 Feb 128, on 7/8 Feb 323, on 13/14 Feb 466 and on 16/17 Feb 377; 27 aircraft are lost. During the raid of 15 Jan the A/S trawler *UJ1406* is sunk.

On 23 Jan the US 8th Air Force flies daylight raids against Lorient and Brest; in the last, the MMS *R44* is sunk.

On 29 Jan the auxiliary minesweeper *M4606* is sunk in an air attack on St Peter Port.

15–19 Jan   North Sea

The German destroyers *Friedrich Ihn*, *Paul Jacobi*, *Z24*, *Karl Galster* and *Z25* search without success for Norwegian merchant ships trying to break out from Gotenburg to Great Britain. The ships return before being intercepted.

15 Jan–19 Feb   Mediterranean

The British 'Inshore Squadron' supplies the British 8th Army as it advances through Tripolitania. In Feb alone 115137 tons of supplies are landed. Individual U-boats operate off Cyrenaica against this traffic: *U617* (Lt-Cdr Brandi) sinks four ships of 10800 tons from two convoys, apart from the fast minelayer *Welshman*. After the capture of Tripoli by the British 8th Army, combined convoys proceed to Malta and Tripoli, eg on 6–8 Feb MW.20 and XT.2 with an escort of 12 destroyers. Attacks by *U205* (Lt Bürgel) fail. On 17 Feb the boat is lost as a result of an attack by Bisley 'W' of No 15 Sqn SAAF and depth charges from the destroyer *Paladin* when she attacks TX.1; the 'Enigma' machine is later salvaged by divers. On 19 Feb *U562* is lost to a Wellington of No 38 Sqn RAF and the destroyers *Isis* and *Hursley* when attacking XT.3.

Off the Palestine coast, *U431* (Lt Schöneboom) sinks four sailing ships in Jan; *U81* (Lt Krieg) sinks five sailing ships in Feb and torpedoes one tanker of 6671 tons.

In British submarine operations in the Adriatic, *Tigris* (Lt-Cdr Colvin) sinks one ship of 5413 tons on 20 Jan and *Thunderbolt* and *Trooper* sink several sailing ships in Feb. In the Aegean the Greek submarine *Papanicolis* sinks two sailing ships in Jan.

On 16 Jan the German A/S trawler *UJ2103* (ex-Greek *Paralos*) sinks on a reef at Euboea in the Aegean.

17 Jan–8 Feb   Arctic

Convoy operation JW.52/RA.52. On 17 Jan JW.52 sets out with 14 ships (one returns), escorted by an escort group comprising the destroyer *Onslaught* (Cdr Shelby), seven other destroyers, two corvettes, one minesweeper and two trawlers. There is a covering force consisting of the cruisers *Kent*, *Glasgow* and *Bermuda* and a distant escort force (Adm Fraser) consisting of the battleships *Anson*, *Howe* and *King George V*, five cruisers and about 20 destroyers. British and Soviet submarines are in flanking formations off the Norwegian coast. The convoy is reported on 23 Jan by a Bv 138 flying boat of KF1Gr 706. On 24 Jan four or five He 115 torpedo aircraft of 1/KF1Gr 406 deployed attack the convoy unsuccessfully, losing two of their number. The U-boats ordered to the scene arc out-manoeuvred by the escort group which makes skilful use of HF/DF though *U622* (Lt-Cdr Queck) makes an unsuccessful attack on the convoy. *U625* (Lt Benker) misses *Bermuda* and *Kent*. On 25 Jan the convoy is again located by air reconnaissance but not attacked. Five Soviet destroyers meet the convoy, which enters the Kola Inlet on 27 Jan. The ice-breaker *Malygin* (1571 tons) is sunk by *U255* (Lt-Cdr Reche) and on 29 Jan the same submarine sinks the Soviet steamer *Ufa* (1892 tons).

Convoy RA.52 sets out with 11 ships and the same escort from the Kola Inlet on 29 Jan. The five Soviet destroyers initially strengthen the escort. The convoy is reported on 1 Feb SW of Bear Island by *U625* and is unsuccessfully attacked. Air reconnaissance does not find it. On 3 Feb *U255* attacks the convoy and sinks the steamer *Greylock* (7460 tons).

The Allied submarines employed in the flanking formations attack German coastal traffic during and after the operation. The Norwegian submarine *Uredd* (Sub-Lt Rören) misses the MTB tender *Adolf Lüderitz* off Aalesund on 17 Jan. On 20 Jan the Soviet destroyers *Baku* and *Razumny* under Capt 1st Class Kolchin make a sortie against the polar coast and have a brief and indecisive engagement off Syltefjord with the minelayer *Skagerrak*, which is on her way to lay a flanking mine barrage with the minesweepers *M322* and *M303* and the submarine-chasers *UJ1104* and *UJ1105*.

After several misses by the Soviet submarines *Shch-404* (Capt 2nd Class Ivanov) off Svaerholt and by *M-172* and *Shch-402* (Capt 3rd Class Kautski) in Varangerfjord, *M-171* (Capt 3rd Class Starikov) torpedoes on 29 Jan the transport *Ilona Siemers* (3243 tons) escorted by *V5906* off Kongsfjord. On 1 Feb *Shch-403* (Capt 3rd Class Shuyski) sinks the patrol boat *V6115* off Makkaur, *M-172* (Capt 3rd Class Fisanovich) *V5909* off Kiberg and *L-20* (Capt 3rd Class Tamman) the transport *Othmarschen* (7007 tons) escorted by the submarine-chasers *UJ1101* and *UJ1108* off Nordkyn. On 5 Feb the German A/S trawler *UJ1108* is sunk off Berlevaag by the Soviet submarine *Shch-422*.

17 Jan–14 Feb   Central Atlantic

After replenishing from *U463* (Cdr Wolfbauer), *U571*, *U620*, *U575*, *U381*, *U436*, *U442*, *U552*, *U511*, *U125* and *U514* form the 'Delphin' group S of the Azores to operate against US–Gibraltar convoys; from 24 Jan *U202*, *U558*, *U87*, *U264* and *U258* are added to the group. Only three stragglers from the convoy UGS.4 (48 ships escorted by TF.38 with the destroyers *Plunkett*, *Niblack*, *Benson*, *Gleaves*, *Mayo* and *Kendrick*) are sunk: the *City of Flint* (4963 tons) by *U575* (Lt-Cdr Heydemann) on 25 Jan and one Liberty Ship each by *U514* (Lt-Cdr Auffermann) and *U442* (Cdr Hesse) of 7177 and 7176 tons respectively on 27 Jan. From 22 Jan *U218*, *U521* and *U43*, and later also *U66* and *U108*, form the 'Rochen' group in the area of the Canaries. After disembarking agents, *U66* (Lt-Cdr Markworth) sinks one fishery vessel of 113 tons. On 7 Feb *U521* (Lt-Cdr Bargsten) sights the small coastal convoy Gibr.2 comprising three steamers and four A/S trawlers and having air escort; she sinks the trawler *Bredon*. The U-boats *U202*, *U558*, *U87*, *U264* and *U258* from the 'Delphin' group, which are ordered to the scene, do not arrive before the destroyer *Haydon* and the US submarine-chasers *PC471* and *PC474* join the convoy on 9 Feb. On 10 Feb *U108* is damaged by Calalina 'N' of No 202 Sqn RAF but continues its patrol. The remaining 'Delphin' boats operate W of Cape St Vincent, where *U442* and *U620* are lost to the air escort in an operation against convoy KMS.9 reported by air reconnaissance. *U442* is sunk on 12 Feb by Hudson 'F' of No 48 Sqn RAF and *U620* on 14 Feb by Catalina 'J' of No 202 Sqn RAF which also damages *U381*. The 'Rochen' group replenishes from *U118* from 10 Feb.

18–19 Jan   North Pacific

US TG.8.6 (Rear-Adm McMorris), consisting of the cruisers *Indianapolis* and *Richmond* and the destroyers *Bancroft*, *Caldwell*, *Coghlan* and *Gillespie*, bombards Attu.

18 Jan–1 Mar   South Pacific

In reconnaissance operations to Nouméa, Auckland and into the Torres Strait, the Japanese submarine *I-10* (Cdr T Yamada) sinks one ship of 7176 tons and torpedoes one of 7141 tons. *I-8* (Capt Uchino) shells Canton Island on 23 Jan. Off the Australian coast, *I-21* (Cdr* Matsumura) sinks five ships of 31437 tons. *I-18* (Cdr Muraoka) launches a midget submarine (no success) off Espiritu Santo on 25 Jan and is herself sunk on 11 Feb when she tries to attack a US force consisting of the cruiser *Helena* and the destroyers *Fletcher* and *O'Bannon*.

From Rabaul, *Ro-100*, *Ro-101*, *Ro-102* and *Ro-103* operate in the area of the Solomons and off New Guinea.

19 Jan   English Channel

The German patrol trawler *V703* sinks in a gale off Alderney.

19 Jan   Central Atlantic

The US carrier *Ranger*, acting as an aircraft transport, flies off a full complement of fighters to Accra to be transferred to the North African theatre of war.

19 Jan   Mediterranean
The Italian minesweeper *Eso* (ex-Yugoslav *Sokol*) sinks after receiving a torpedo hit from an RN aircraft E of Djerba.

19–24 Jan   Norway
The Norwegian 30th MTB flotilla, which is stationed in Lerwick (Shetlands), makes several raids with *MTB618*, *MTB619*, *MTB620*, *MTB623*, *MTB625*, *MTB626*, *MTB627* and *MTB630* on German naval communication posts in Sognefjord, on Stord and in Korsfjord. Attacks on steamers fail.

20 Jan   Mediterranean
Off Tripoli, the Italian submarine *Santarosa* is sunk while on a transport mission by the British *MTB260*.

22 Jan–3 Feb   North Atlantic
The 'Landsknecht' group is formed from the former 'Falke' boats which are short of fuel supplies. It consists of *U267*, *U465*, *U609*, *U402*, *U187*, *U262*, *U454*, *U553*, *U456*, *U614*, *U632*, *U257*, *U404*, *U584*, *U572*, *U71*, *U444*, *U384*, *U631* and *U333*. They operate without success W of Ireland and from 28 Jan most of the boats begin the return journey. *U553* is missing since then. On the way to a new formation, *U456* (Lt-Cdr Teichert) sights on 1 Feb the convoy HX.224 (58 ships), escorted by EG.C4 (Lt-Cdr Piers) consisting of the destroyers *Restigouche* (RCN) and *Churchill* (RN), the corvettes *Amherst*, *Collingwood*, *Brandon*, *Sherbrooke* (RCN) and *Celandine* (RN) and the rescue ship *Accrington*. Despite a heavy storm, *U456* keeps exemplary contact for three days and sinks two ships of 16633 tons. Of *U265*, *U614*, *U257* and *U632* (Lt-Cdr Karpf), stationed in the area, only the last sinks one straggler tanker of 8190 tons whose survivors give valuable information about the following convoy, SC.118. *U265* is sunk on 3 Feb by Fortress 'N' of No 220 Sqn RAF flying as an escort.

22 Jan–15 Feb   North Atlantic
The 'Haudegen' group is formed SE of Greenland from the U-boats of the 'Falke' group which have adequate fuel supplies. It consists of *U414*, *U606*, *U607*, *U226*, *U403*, *U525*, *U69*, *U201*, *U383*, *U303*, *U624*, *U704*, *U438*, *U752*, *U613*, *U186*, *U268*, *U358*, *U707*, *U223*, and *U466*. On the way *U358* (Lt-Cdr Manke) attacks on 22 Jan the convoy UR.59 which is proceeding to Reykjavik and sinks one ship of 1456 tons. On 26 Jan *U266* and *U383* sight escorts of convoy HX.223, which has been partly dispersed in a storm. *U466* listens to the

convoy, which consists of 24 ships escorted by EG.A3 (Cdr Heineman) with the US Coast Guard cutters *Spencer* and *Campbell* and the corvettes *Dianthus* (RN) and *Rosthern*, *Trillium* and *Dauphin* (RCN). *U358* sinks a straggler of 8221 tons and *U607* (Lt-Cdr Mengersen) torpedoes the wreck of the tanker *Kjöllborg* (8259 tons) whose back was broken in the storm and which sinks before she is hit by *U594* trying to finish her off. On 2 Feb the most northerly boat of the 'Haudegen' group sights the Greenland supply convoy SG.19 consisting of three steamers escorted by the US Coast Guard cutters *Tampa*, *Escabana* and *Comanche*. *U186*, *U268*, *U358*, *U707* and *U223* (Lt-Cdr Wächter) are directed to it and the last sinks the US Army transport *Dorchester* (5649 tons); these U-boats form the 'Nordsturm' group. The remaining 'Haudegen' boats proceed in loose formation NE of Newfoundland against the expected convoy SC.118 but they have no success because the convoy is re-routed after 'Ultra' intercepts.

23 Jan–8 Feb   Baltic/Norway
Operation 'Domino': a new attempt to transfer the German battlecruiser *Scharnhorst* and the cruiser *Prinz Eugen* from the Baltic to Norway, escorted by the destroyers *Z37* and *Erich Steinbrinck* from the E Baltic and by the destroyers *Paul Jacobi*, *Z24* and *Z25* from Kristiansand South. The Force is again sighted, on 25 Jan, by British air reconnaissance and returns into the Baltic, the destroyers making for to Kristiansand South.

The cruisers *Admiral Hipper* and *Köln* depart with the destroyers *Richard Beitzen*, *Z29* and *Z30* from Altafjord for transfer to Germany. They stop at Narvik on 25 Jan and at Trondheim from 30 Jan to 2 Feb, searching for Norwegian blockade-runners in the Skagerrak on 6 Feb and arriving at Kiel on 8 Feb.

The destroyers *Paul Jacobi*, *Erich Steinbrinck*, *Z24* and *Z25* are attacked by British torpedo aircraft while sailing from Kristiansand to Bergen. On 8 Feb the destroyers of the 8th DD Flotilla, *Z23*, *Z24*, *Z25* and *Z37*, are ordered to return to be transferred to the Biscay ports.

24–28 Jan   North Sea
On 24–25 Jan the German 2nd, 4th and 6th MTB Flotillas, with 16 boats, encounter the destroyers *Mendip* and *Windsor* while trying to attack a British convoy off Lowestoft and are driven off. From 24 to 28 Jan the German minelayers *Ostmark* and *Roland*, escorted by four vessels of the 17th PB Flotilla, lay two mine barrages off the Skagerrak.

27 Jan   Air War/Germany
Fifty-five B-17 bombers of the US 8th Air Force carry out their first daylight attack on German territory without fighter protection. The target is Wilhelmshaven.

30 Jan   North Sea
The German patrol trawler *V1102* sinks after grounding on the Bremanger reef.

30 Jan   Mediterranean
The Italian minesweeper *Unie* (ex-Yugoslav *Kobac*) is destroyed during a USAAF air attack on Bizerta.

30 Jan–4 Feb   Air War/Germany
First RAF Bomber Command raids using H2S radar, against Hamburg during the nights 30/31 Jan and 3/4 Feb, with 184 and 263 aircraft respectively. There are 16 losses.

31 Jan   General Situation
Hitler appoints the Commander U-boats, Admiral Dönitz, C-in-C of the Navy in place of the retiring Grand Admiral Raeder. Dönitz is promoted to the rank of Grand Admiral.

1 Feb   Gibraltar
U118 (Cdr Czygan) lays a mine barrage in the Straits of Gibraltar on which, on 22 Feb, the corvette *Weyburn* from convoy MKS.8 and three ships of 14064 tons are lost and the destroyer *Wivern* and two more ships of 11269 tons suffer severe damage.

1–28 Feb   Pacific
In US submarine operations, from 55 'Ultra' signals only nine lead to sightings and seven to attacks; two ships are sunk and four damaged. Off Japan, *Pickerel* (Lt-Cdr Alston) sinks two ships of 4174 tons and three sailing vessels, *Sawfish* (Lt-Cdr Sands) sinks two ships of 2517 tons and the Soviet freighter *Kola* (4994 tons) and damages two ships of 13483 tons and *Sunfish* (Lt-Cdr Peterson) sinks two ships of 6182 tons. In the Central Pacific, *Tarpon* (Lt-Cdr Wogan) sinks two ships of 27910 tons, *Halibut* (Lt-Cdr Ross) sinks the *Shinkoku Maru* (3991 tons) with help from 'Ultra' and damages one ship of 6818 tons and *Plunger* (Lt-Cdr Bass) sinks one ship of 1804 tons and damages a tanker of 14050 tons; *Runner* has misses and *Pompano* is on a recce mission. In the South Pacific, *Amberjack* is sunk off Rabaul by a Japanese torpedo boat and *Grampus* (Lt-Cdr Hutchinson) sinks the minesweeper *W-22* on 27 Feb near Kolombangara and one ship of 6442 tons but is herself sunk in the Blackett Strait by a Japanese destroyer in Mar. *Albacore* (Lt-Cdr Lake) sinks the destroyer *Oshio* on 20 Feb N of Manus and also possibly an escort vessel; *Grouper* conducts a special mission. In the South West Pacific, *Tunny* sinks one ship of 5306 tons and one sailing vessel

and damages two ships of 8278 tons but is hampered by many premature torpedo explosions and by duds. *Thresher* (Lt-Cdr Millican) sinks two ships of 10956 tons and damages the submarine *I-162*.

2–9 Feb   North Atlantic

The Commander U-boats forms on 2 Feb the 'Pfeil' group consisting of *U594*, *U413*, *U267*, *U187*, *U465*, *U402*, *U609*, *U262*, *U454*, *U89*, *U135*, *U608* and *U266* to operate against convoy SC.118 which is expected in accordance with B-Service reports and prisoners-of-war statements. On 4 Feb the convoy is reported by *U187* (Lt-Cdr Münnich), according to plan, in the middle of the patrol line. Apart from 'Pfeil', *U438*, *U624*, *U704*, *U613* and *U752* from the 'Haudegen' group and *U456* and *U614* from the HX.224 operation are directed to the scene. SC.118 consists of 61 ships with EG.B2 (Lt-Cdr Proudfoot) comprising the destroyers *Vanessa*, *Vimy* and *Beverley* and the corvettes *Campanula*, *Mignonette*, *Abelia* (British) and *Lobélia* (French), as well as the US Coast Guard cutter *Bibb*. *Bibb* and the rescue ship *Toward* locate with HF/DF the contact signal of *U187*, which is sunk by *Vimy* and *Beverley*. *U402*, *U608*, *U267* and *U609*, and *U608* again, are also located on 4 Feb and during the night and are driven off by *Vimy*, *Beverley*, *Campanula*, *Bibb*, *Lobélia* and *Mignonette*. After a change of course, *U609* establishes contact with a detached group but is attacked with depth charges by *Lobélia*, whilst *U262* (Lt Franke) sinks one ship of 2864 tons on the unprotected side but is shortly afterwards heavily attacked with depth charges by *Vimy* and *Beverley*. *Vimy* forces the contact-keeper *U609*, which has closed up, to submerge again. From the stern, *U413* (Lt-Cdr Poel) sinks one straggler of 5376 tons. In the evening of 5 Feb *U609* (Lt-Cdr Rodluff), which has come up again, is driven off by the escort, reinforced in the meantime by the US destroyers *Babbitt* and *Schenk* and the US Coast Guard cutter *Ingham* from Iceland. In the morning of 6 Feb *U465* dispatches a contact signal but is heavily bombed by Liberator 'X' of No 120 Sqn (Sqn Ldr Isted) directed to the D/F beam; the other boats are driven off. By the evening of 6 Feb *U609* again brings up *U438*, *U262*, *U456* and *U267*, but *Vimy* severely damages the last. Attempts by *U454*, *U438* and *U135* to attack are frustrated by *Lobélia*, *Abelia* and *Babbitt*. Only *U262* is able to fire, but torpedo failures prevent a success and depth charges from *Lobélia* damage the boat. After midnight *U402* (Lt-Cdr Frhr v Forstner) gets through a gap in the convoy and during the night, in the course of two approaches,

sinks six ships of 37075 tons, including the rescue ship *Toward*. A ship of 5740 tons, which has fallen behind, is sunk by *U614* (Lt-Cdr Sträter) whilst *Lobélia* (Lt-Cdr De Morsier) sinks *U609*. On 7 Feb most of the boats are forced to the rear by the defence. Only *U402* keeps contact; she is temporarily driven off at mid-day by *Bibb* but returns with *U456*. Shortly afterwards both boats are forced to submerge by *Bibb* and Fortress 'J' of No 220 Sqn RAF which also sinks *U624*. A new attempt by *U456* to attack is frustrated by *Beverley* thanks to HF/DF. Only *U402* sinks one more ship of 4265 tons during the night 7–8 Feb. An attack by *U608* on a disabled ship and the destroyer *Schenck* fails. In the morning aircraft drive off the last boats and *U135* is damaged by Liberator 'K' of No 120 Sqn RAF. On 9 Feb *U614*, trying to attack *Vimy* which is towing the damaged *Lobélia*, is badly damaged by Fortress 'L' of No 206 Sqn RAF. *U456* (Lt-Cdr Teichert) sinks one ship of 700 tons on the return journey W of the Bay of Biscay on 23 Feb.

2–28 Feb   Air War/Western Europe

RAF Bomber Command mine offensive. Over 17 nights there are 537 sorties from the Biscay ports to Brittany, along the French and Dutch coasts up to Texel, along the Frisian coast and into the Kattegat and the Western Baltic; 10 aircraft are lost. The following patrol trawlers and auxiliary minesweepers sink on mines during Feb: *V1602* on 4/5 Feb in the Skagerrak, *V1249* on 24 Feb N of Borkum, *V1405* on 25 Feb N of Walcheren and *M4453* on 25 Feb in the Bay of Biscay. On 19 Feb the transport *Ockenfels* (7574 tons) sinks off Borkum.

4–5 Feb   Mediterranean

British bombing attack on the naval base at La Spezia.

4–7 Feb   North Atlantic

The 'Hartherz' group is formed W of the Bay of Biscay with the U-boats *U183*, *U107*, *U519*, *U584*, *U572*, *U71*, *U621*, *U653*, *U628*, *U753* and *U332* to operate against the MKS and KMS convoys located by the B-Service on the Gibraltar route. No targets are sighted. *U519* is sunk on 10 Feb by Liberator 'T' (1st Lt Sandford) of the USAAF's A/S Sqn 2.

4–9 Feb   Black Sea

Following the shelling of German positions in the Novorossisk area during the night 30–31 Jan by the Soviet cruiser *Voroshilov* and the destroyers *Besposhchadny*, *Boiki* and *Soobrazitelny*, Soviet landings are made W of Novorossisk early on 4 Feb. To divert the German defence the destroyer *Boiki*

with four MO-IV patrol cutters shells Anapa during the night 3–4 Feb and four torpedo cutters cruise off Zhelezny Rog. The covering force (Vice-Adm Vladimirski), comprising the cruisers *Krasny Kavkaz* and *Krasny Krym*, the flotilla leader *Kharkov* and the destroyers *Besposhchadny* and *Soobrazitelny*, shells the main landing area towards morning. The landing force (Rear-Adm Basisty), consisting of the gunboats *Krasny Adzharistan*, *Krasnaya Gruziya* and *Krasnaya Abkhaziya*, the destroyers *Nezamozhnik* and *Zheleznyakov*, the minesweepers *T-404/Shchit*, *T-411/Zashchitnik*, *T-412/Arseni Rasskin*, *T-407/Mina* and *T-403/Gruz*, as well as the 1st Patrol Cutter Div, loses the patrol cutters *SKA-051* and *SKA-0141* on a mine barrage. In the face of heavy defensive fire only parts of the 83rd and 255th Naval Bdes and the 165th Rifle Bde are able to land and they are eliminated by 6 Feb. The other landing carried out by patrol cutters at Cape Myschako succeeds; the bulk of the forces are brought up by gunboats from 5 Feb and by 9 Feb there are 17000 troops on shore. In operations by the German 1st MTB Flotilla (Lt-Cdr Christiansen) against supplies, *T-403/Gruz* and *Krasnaya Gruzya* are sunk by the end of Feb.

4–12 Feb   Arctic

The German mining operation 'Bantos B' against the roads of Kildin is carried out unnoticed during the night 5–6 Feb by the minelayer *Brummer* (Cdr Dr Brill) and the destroyers *Theodor Riedel* and *Z31*, escorted by the minesweepers *M381* and *M361* and the A/S trawlers *UJ1102* and *UJ1101*. On the way the Soviet submarine *L-20* misses the force off Nordkyn. At the same time two Soviet submarines try out for the first time direct tactical co-operation against a target off Kongsfjord. In the evening of 5 Feb *K-3* (Capt 3rd Class Malofeyev, with the Cdr of the Submarine Bde, Rear-Adm Vinogradov, on board) and *K-22* (Capt 3rd Class Kulbakin with the Cdr of the 1st Div, Capt 2nd Class Kotelnikov, on board) attack the submarine-chasers *UJ1101* and *UJ1108* which are proceeding to the rendezvous with the minelaying force. In Force 8 winds, *K-3* sinks *UJ1108* but impedes *K-22*. Towards morning on 6 Feb *K-22* and later *L-20* miss the *Brummer* with salvos. *K-22* sinks on a flanking mine barrage. On 12 Feb *K-3* torpedoes the transport *Fechenheim* (8116 tons) in a convoy.

4–27 Feb   Indian Ocean

Convoy 'Pamphlet' with 30000 men of the 9th Australian Div proceeds from Suez to Sydney and Melbourne in the transports *Queen Mary*, *Aquitania*, *Ile de France*,

Nieuw Amsterdam and *Queen of Bermuda*. On 4 Feb it leaves Suez with anti-submarine protection in the Red Sea and Gulf of Aden provided by the destroyers *Pakenham*, *Petard*, *Isis*, *Derwent*, *Hero* and *Vasilissa Olga* (Greek). Ocean escort comprises the cruiser *Devonshire* and from Socotra also *Gambia*; the covering force in the Indian Ocean is Force A comprising the battleships *Resolution*, *Revenge* and *Warspite*, the cruiser *Mauritius* and six destroyers. Further E it is reinforced by the Dutch cruisers *Jacob van Heemskerck* and *Tromp* and two destroyers. On 18 Feb the convoy arrives in Fremantle. From there it continues with an escort consisting of the cruisers *Adelaide*, *Heemskerck* and *Tromp* and the destroyer *Tjerk Hiddes* (Dutch). The covering force S of Australia is TF.44.3 consisting of the cruiser *Australia* and the US destroyers *Bagley*, *Henley* and *Helm*. From Melbourne the Dutch ships with the exception of *Heemskerck* are detached as is the FFN destroyer *Le Triomphant*. The convoy arrives on 27 Feb without incident in Sydney.

4 Feb–6 June Bay of Biscay

First Bay offensive by No 19 Group RAF Coastal Command (Air Vice Marshal Bromet) with nine Liberators from No 224 Sqn, 16 Liberators from No 86 Sqn (transferred to Iceland from Mar), six Catalinas from No 210 Sqn, 16 Wellingtons each from Nos 304 (Polish) and 311 (Czech) Sqns, 16 Wellingtons from No 172 Sqn, nine Halifaxes from No 58 Sqn, nine Fortresses from No 59 Sqn, 16 Whitleys from No 502 Sqn, six Sunderlands each from Nos 10 and 461 Sqns RAAF and 12 Liberators (transferred from Morocco in Mar) from the USAAF's A/S Sqns 1 and 2. In addition, from Apr there are six Sunderlands from No 228 Sqn RAF and 16 Wellingtons from No 407 Sqn RCAF.

In Operation 'Gondola' (4–16 Feb) there are 312 sorties, 19 sightings and eight attacks. *U519* is sunk by USAAF Sqn 1. After 'Gondola' there are normal sorties until Mar. In the first experimental deployment of a Wellington with 10cm ASV-IV radar and Leigh Light, *U268* is sunk by aircraft 'B' from No 172 Sqn RAF. *U211*, *U508* and *U525* are damaged on, respectively, 20 Feb, 26 Feb and 3 Mar by Liberator 'C' of USAAF Sqn 1, by Liberator 'Z' of No 224 Sqn RAF and by Wellington 'M' of No 172 Sqn using Leigh Light; the last is shot down by *U333* (Lt-Cdr Cremer).

During Operation 'Enclose I' (21–28 Mar) there are 182 sorties. Few sightings are made by day because the U-boats are submerged, surfacing to charge their batteries at night.

On 21 Mar Wellington 'T' of No 172 Sqn, equipped with Leigh Light, damages the returning *U332*. On 22 Mar an ASV-IV/Leigh Light Wellington, 'G' of No 172 Sqn, sinks *U665*; *U338* (Lt-Cdr Kinzel) shoots down a Halifax of No 58 Sqn RAF. In this phase there is only one success in 27 sightings.

In Operation 'Enclose II' (6–13 Apr), *U376* is lost on 10 Apr to ASV-IV/Leigh Light Wellington 'C' of No 172 Sqn and *U465* is damaged by Catalina 'M' of No 210 Sqn RAF. Increasing night attacks with radar locating that cannot be detected by 'Metox' and the shooting down of an aircraft by *U438* lead to a change in German tactics: the boats now proceed submerged at night, charge their batteries by day and beat off aircraft with AA fire.

In Operation 'Derange' (13 Apr–6 June), as a result of the new German tactics, there is a marked increase in sightings by day with many attacks. On 26 Apr the outgoing *U566* is damaged by Wellington 'R' of No 172 Sqn; on 29 Apr the outgoing *U437* is damaged by Wellington 'H' of the same unit and *U332* is sunk by Liberator 'D' of No 224 Sqn RCAF. In the month of May there are 98 sightings and 64 attacks. On 1 May the returning *U415* is damaged in attacks by Wellington 'N' of No 172 Sqn with Leigh Light, Sunderland 'M' of No 461 Sqn RAAF (Flt Lt Smith) and Whitley 'E' of No 612 Sqn RAF. On 2 May the outgoing *U465* is sunk by Sunderland 'M' of No 461 Sqn (Flt Lt Smith). On 5 May the outgoing *U663* is sunk by Halifax 'S' of No 58 Sqn RAF (Wg Cdr Oulton) and on 6 May the outgoing *U214* is damaged by Whitley 'K' of No 10 OTU RAF. On 15 May the outgoing tanker *U463* is sunk by Halifax 'M' of No 58 Sqn (Wg Cdr Oulton) and the outgoing *U591* damaged by Whitley 'M' of No 10 Sqn RAF. On 16 May the Italian submarine *Tazzoli* is sunk by Halifax 'R' of No 58 Sqn and on 24 May the outgoing *U523* is damaged by Whitley 'J' of No 10 OTU. On 31 May the outgoing *U563* is sunk by Halifax 'R' of No 58 Sqn (Wg Cdr Oulton), Sunderland 'X' of No 228 Sqn and Sunderland 'E' of No 10 Sqn RAAF. On the same day the returning *U621* is damaged by Liberator 'Q' of No 224 Sqn RAF. On 1 June the incoming *U418* is sunk by rocket fire from Beaufighter 'B' of No 236 Sqn RAF. On 24 May *U441* (Lt-Cdr G v Hartmann) is used for the first time as an AA trap and in an engagement a Sunderland is shot down. However, the boat suffers heavy losses and damage. In addition, *U666*, *U594*, *U648*, *U662* and *U459* each shoot down one aircraft. The experience leads to

the new German tactics of group sailings in the Bay of Biscay.

5 Feb Norway

The German minelayer *Skagerrak*, escorted by the minesweepers *M322* and *M302*, lays a flanking mine barrage off Tromsö.

5 Feb–9 Mar Mediterranean

In German and Italian operations against Allied supply traffic off the Algerian coast, three torpedo aircraft on 6 Feb attack the convoy MKS.7 E of Oran, sink the Canadian corvette *Louisburg* and damage one ship of 7135 tons. Attacks by the U-boats *U407* and *U596* on the convoy escorted by six British and eight Canadian corvettes fail: *U407* misses the corvettes *Nasturtium* and *Pentstemon* though *U596* (Lt-Cdr Jahn) sinks on 7 Feb the landing vessel *LCL162*. After the escort leaves, off Algiers *U77* (Lt-Cdr O Hartmann) sinks two ships of 13742 tons. On 5 Feb the A/S trawler *Stronsay* is lost on a mine off Philippeville and the Italian *Avorio* (Lt-Cdr Fiorentini) attacks a convoy off Philippeville but is herself sunk on 8 Feb by the Canadian corvette *Regina*. After a miss by *Platino*, *Acciaio* (Lt-Cdr Beltrami) sinks the A/S trawler *Tervani* on 7 Feb. In further attacks in Feb and Mar, *U371* (Lt-Cdr Mehl) sinks one ship of 2089 tons and torpedoes one of 7176 tons, *U565* (Lt-Cdr W Franken) torpedoes two ships of 17565 tons, one of which is destroyed by aerial torpedo and *U596* (Lt-Cdr Jahn) torpedoes two ships of 14180 tons. Other attacks, by *Platino*, *U596*, *U371*, *U565*, *U458*, *U755* and *U602*, fail. *Asteria* and *U443* fall victim on 17 and 23 Feb respectively to the British destroyers *Wheatland*, *Easton*, *Lamerton* and *Bicester*; *U83* is sunk by Hudson 'V' of No 500 Sqn RAF on 4 Mar.

5 Feb–19 Apr South Atlantic/Indian Ocean

After replenishing from *U459* (Cdr v Wilamowitz-Moellendorf) in the South Atlantic, the 'Seehund' group operates off South Africa. In individual attacks the boats make the following sinkings (inclusive of successes on the way to the area and on the return): *U506* (Lt-Cdr Würdemann) sinks two ships of 9980 tons, *U516* (Cdr Wiebe) sinks four of 25586 tons, including the Dutch submarine depot ship *Colombia*, *U509* (Lt-Cdr W Witte) sinks two of 12066 tons and *U160* (Lt-Cdr Lassen) sinks three of 19353 tons. In addition, *U160* attacks on 3 Mar the convoy DN.21 (11 ships escorted by the corvette *Nigella* and the A/S trawlers *Sondra*, *Norwich City* and *Viviana*) and in three approaches sinks four ships of 25852 tons and torpedoes two more of 15224 tons before the destroyers *Quiberon* and *Relentless* arrive. Five ships of 30071 tons fall victim to *U182* (Lt-Cdr N Clausen) operating simultaneously off South Africa; but on the return the U-boat is sunk on 16 May W of Madeira by the US destroyer *Mackenzie* of TF.62 escorting convoy UGS.8. The remaining boats return after replenishing from *U117*.

The Japanese submarine *I-27* (Lt-Cdr Fukumura), operating in Mar in the Gulf of Bombay, sinks one ship of 7132 tons.

9 Feb   Mediterranean
The British corvette *Erica* sinks on a mine laid in July 1941 by the British submarine *Rorqual* off the Cyrenaican coast.

9–19 Feb   North Atlantic
After being relieved at WESTOMP on 5 and 8 Feb, the escorts of convoys ON.162 with EG.B1 (see 14–26 Feb) and ONS.163 with EG.C3, comprising the destroyers *Assiniboine* (RCN) and *Burnham* (RN), the frigate *Jed* (RN) and the corvettes *Bittersweet*, *La Malbaie* and *Eyebright*, reach St John's while the convoys go on with Western Local Escort groups to Halifax. ON.164, cscortcd by EG.B7 with the frigate *Tay*, the destroyer *Vidette* and the corvettes *Alisma*, *Pink*, *Loosestrife* and *Snowflake*, reaches WESTOMP on 13 Feb unobserved. From 9 to 15 Feb the 'Haudegen' group, comprising *U358*, *U186*, *U223*, *U69*, *U201*, *U403*, *U707*, *U606*, *U226*, *U525*, *U303*, *U607* and *U383*, is formed in a semi-circle NE of Newfoundland and waits in vain for the convoys HX.225 with EG.C2, comprising destroyers *Broadway* (RN) and *Sherwood* (RN) and the corvettes *Morden*, *Orillia* and *Pictou* (RCN) and *Polyanthus* and *Primrose* (RN), and SC.119 with EG.B1 (see 14–26 Feb). The convoy HX.226, with EG.C3 (see above but without *Assiniboine*), is routed to the W of the U-boats on 15 Feb. On that day the boats, except for *U358*, *U186*, *U223* and *U707* (the 'Taifun' group), start the journey to the supply boat *U460*. In the process *U69* (Lt-Cdr U Gräf) sights on 17 Feb convoy ONS.165, comprising 32 ships with EG.B6 (Cdr Heathcote) consisting of the destroyers *Fame* and *Viscount*, the corvettes *Vervain* and *Kingcup* and the Norwegian corvettes *Acanthus* and *Eglantine*. Directed to the contact signal located by HF/DF, *Viscount* sinks *U201* (Lt Rosenberg), which is the second boat to come up, by ramming and *Fame* sinks *U69*.

Of the former 'Haudegen' and 'Taifun' boats ordered to the scene, *U403* (Lt-Cdr Clausen) does not see the convoy again before the afternoon of 18 Feb but in two approaches sinks one ship of 5961 tons during the night 18–19 Feb. In the morning *U226* (Lt-Cdr Borchers) misses the convoy and contact is again lost. In the evening of 19 Feb *U525* (Lt-Cdr Drewitz) comes up for a short while and sinks one straggler of 3454 tons during the night of 19–20 Feb. The operation is broken off because of the proximity to land.

9 Feb–22 Mar   Mediterranean
Seven troop transport operations to Tunis and Bizerta for the German and Italian Panzer armies in Africa with the Italian destroyers *Malocello* (four trips), *Alpino* and *Pancaldo* (three each), *Pigafetta*, *Fuciliere*, *Premuda*, *Legionario* and *Ascari* (two each) and *Da Noli*, *Zeno*, *Granatiere*, *Gioberti* and *Camicia Nera* (one each) There are successive convoys with one to four freighters, escorted by one to five ships, including the destroyers *Lampo*, *Lubiana* and *Riboty*, the torpedo boats *Fortunale*, *Ciclone*, *Monsone*, *Groppo*, *Orione*, *Animoso*, *Tifone*, *Ardito*, *Calliope*, *Clio*, *Pallade*, *Sirio*, *Pegaso*, *Sagittario*, *Castore*, *Cigno*, *Libra*, *Antares*, *Cassiopea* and *Cascino* and the corvettes *Gabbiano*, *Persefone*, *Antilope*, *Artemide* and *Cicogna* as well as the German 22nd SC Flotilla with *UJ2209*, *UJ2210* and *UJ2220*. Further troop and supply transports sail, with many Italian and German naval ferry barges (the German 2nd Landing Flotilla). To counter this, the British lay mines within the German and Italian flanking barrages using the submarine *Rorqual* (24 Feb) and the fast minelayer *Abdiel* (27 Feb, 5 Mar and 8 Mar). On the two last barrages the torpedo boat *Ciclone* and one steamer of 1984 tons sink on 7 Mar and the destroyers *Malocello* and *Ascari* on 23 Mar. Torpedo aircraft from Malta sink six ships of 40048 tons and bombers four ships of 19434 tons. An attempted attack by the British *MTB61*, *MTB77* and *MTB82* on a convoy of four steamers, the torpedo boats *Monsone* and *Sirio* and the corvettes *Gabbiano* and *Antilope* S of Marettimo fails on 15–16 Feb. On 8 Mar the British destroyers *Pakenham* and *Paladin*, in a sortie towards Pantelleria, sink one ferry barge. In a sortie by the destroyers of Force Q stationed in Bône, *S55* (Lt Weber), one of the German motor torpedo boats posted as flank protection W of her own minefields, fires at and sinks the British destroyer *Lightning*. On the route between Sicily and Tunisia and in the Tyrrhenian Sea, the British submarine *Unison* (Lt Daniell) sinks three sailing ships, *Unbending* (Lt Stanley) sinks three ships of 5535 tons, *Una* (Lt Norman) sinks two ships of 7589 tons, *Unrivalled* (Lt Turner) sinks one ship of 2216 tons, *Unruffled* (Lt Stevens) sinks two ships of 5444 tons, *Unseen* (Lt Crawford) one ship of 2875 tons, *Sahib* (Lt Bromage) sinks two sailing ships, *Splendid* (Lt-Cdr McGeogh) sinks four ships of 14380 tons, *Saracen* (Lt Lumby) sinks two tugs and torpedoes one other ship, *Torbay* (Lt Clutterbuck) sinks four ships of 11552 tons and torpedoes one other, *Taurus* (Lt-Cdr Wingfield) sinks two ships of 4893 tons and three smaller ships, *Trooper* (Lt Wraith) sinks two ships of 6993 tons and two sailing ships, *Sibyl* (Lt Turner) sinks one ship of 1593 tons and the Dutch *Dolfijn* (Lt-Cdr v Oostrom) sinks the Italian submarine *Malachite* on 9 Feb and one ship of 1143 tons. In attacks on convoys, the submarine *Tigris* is sunk on 27 Feb by the German submarine-chaser *UJ2210*, *Turbulent* (Cdr Linton, VC) is sunk, probably on a mine, and *Thunderbolt* is sunk on 24 Mar by the corvette *Cicogna*.

9 Feb–16 Apr   Western Atlantic
Of the U-boats operating in the area of the Brazilian coast, *U518* (Lt-Cdr F W Wissmann) sinks three independents of 15422 tons. Off Bahia, she sights on 28 Feb the convoy BT.6 escorted by the Brazilian corvettes *Carioca* and *Caravelas* and the survey ship *Rio Branco*. In several approaches on 28 Feb and 1 Mar she fires 14 torpedoes but, because of many failures, she is able to sink only one ship of 7176 tons. Convoy BT.6, which in the meantime is escorted by a US escort group consisting of the destroyer *Borie*, the corvettes *Courage* and *Tenacity* and the submarine-chasers *PC575* and *PC592*, is attacked several times on 8–9 Mar off Cayenne by *U510* (Cdr Neitzel) which torpedoes eight ships of 54130 tons, three of which, totalling 18240 tons, sink. Off the Brazilian coast, the Italian *Barbarigo* (Lt-Cdr Rigoli) sinks three ships of 15584 tons but *Cappellini*, *Bagnolini*, *Torelli* and *Archimede*, which follow, have no success. *Archimede* is sunk on 16 Apr by a Catalina of VP-83.

E of the Antilles a Catalina of VP-53 sinks *U156* (Cdr Hartenstein†) on 8 Mar. *U68* (Lt Lauzemis) sinks two ships of 10186 tons from the convoy GAT.49 in the Western Caribbean on 13 Mar. *U183* (Cdr Schäfer) sinks one ship of 2493 tons in the Yucatan Strait and *U185* (Lt-Cdr Maus) two ships in the area of the Windward Passage on 10 Mar from the convoy KG.123 and one on 6 Apr from a GK convoy totalling, in all, 20504 tons. *U155* (Lt-Cdr Picning) sinks two ships of 7973 tons in the Gulf of Mexico.

10 Feb   Intelligence
The German B-Service introduces a separate code circuit, 'Freya', which is broken only in June 1944.

10 Feb   North Atlantic
The outgoing *U108* is damaged by Catalina 'N' of No 202 Sqn RAF and has to return.

10–14 Feb   English Channel
In attempting to break through the Channel, the auxiliary cruiser *Schiff 14/Coronel* (Capt Thienemann), escorted by the 8th MMS Flotilla (Lt-Cdr Muser), is attacked by Whirlwinds of Fighter Command and has to put in to Boulogne after being hit by bombs. After more air attacks (which, however, do no more damage), the ship returns to Dunkirk on 14 Feb and there receives orders from the Navy Staff to return to the Baltic. Thus the last attempt to bring an auxiliary cruiser into the Atlantic has failed. *Schiff 14* returns to Germany on 27 Feb.

10–25 Feb   Black Sea
In several operations, the Soviet destroyers *Zheleznyakov*, *Nezamozhnik*, *Besposhchadny* and *Soobrazitelny* bring 8037 troops from Tuapse to Gelendzhik. There are further movements with steamers and small craft along the Caucasian coast. Of the German U-boats *U24*, *U19* and *U9*, deployed against these transports, *U19* (Lt Gaude) sinks the transport *Krasny Profintern* (4648 tons) on 14 Feb. During the night 21–22 Feb the Soviet flotilla leader *Kharkov* and the destroyer *Soobrazitelny* shell German positions off the Myschako bridgehead.

11–25 Feb   Air War/Germany
RAF Bomber Command raids Wilhelmshaven: on 11–12 Feb with 177 aircraft with H2S radar (limited damage), on 18–19 Feb with 195 aircraft (most of the bombs fall in open country), on 19–20 Feb with 338 aircraft (failure) and on 24–25 Feb with 115 aircraft (little damage).

14–26 Feb   North Atlantic
The 'Ritter' group is formed in the Central North Atlantic from 14 Feb against convoy HX.226 (EG.C3; see 9–19 Feb), expected according to B-Service reports. The group consists of *U529*, *U468*, *U377*, *U225*, *U653*, *U628*, *U623*, *U753*, *U332*, *U454*, and *U603*. On 15–16 Feb convoy SC.119, escorted by EG.B1 (Cdr Bayldon) with the destroyers *Hurricane*, *Watchman* and *Rockingham*, the frigate *Kale* and the corvettes *Dahlia*, *Meadowsweet*, *Wallflower* and *Monkshood*, is routed clear to the N and passes 'Ritter' unobserved; the escorting Liberator, 'S' of No 120 Sqn RAF, sinks *U225*. Following 'Ultra' information, HX.226 makes a wide detour to the N and passes on 18 Feb also unobserved.

On 17 Feb convoy ON.166 and the following ONS.167 (EG.B3), guided by 'Ultra', are re-routed to the S of 'Ritter' while 'Ritter' and the new group 'Neptun' (see 18 Feb–3 Mar) form a long patrol line to intercept ON.166 on its old route, discovered by the B-Service. When on 18–19 Feb decyphering of reports from escorting aircraft shows a route SW of ON.166, the outgoing *U92*, *U604*, *U91* and *U600* form the 'Knappen' group to the SE of 'Ritter'. Towards mid-day on 20 Feb *U604* (Lt-Cdr Höltring) sights ON.166 comprising 40 ships and nine stragglers (Commodore Magee) and escorted by EG.A3 (Cdr Heineman) with the US Coast Guard cutters *Spencer* and *Campbell*, the RCN corvettes *Dauphin*, *Rosthern*, *Trillium* and *Chilliwack* and the RN corvette *Dianthus*.

During the night 20–21 Feb *U604* is located with radar by *Spencer* and attacked with depth charges before the groups directed to the scene arrive. In the morning of 21 Feb *U753* (Cdr v Mannstein) makes contact with a straggler (5964 tons) which is later sunk by *U603* (Lt Bertelsmann) and *U332* (Lt Hüttemann). *U623* is sunk by Liberator 'T' from No 120 Sqn RAF (Sqn Ldr Isted). In the afternoon *U91* is bombed by a flying boat which also drives off *U332*, *U454* and *U753* in co-operation with *Campbell*, *Dianthus* and *Dauphin*.

During the night 21–22 Feb *U92* (Lt-Cdr Oelrich) comes up to the convoy and in two approaches torpedoes two ships, of 9990 and 9348 tons respectively. The first is detached with *Dauphin* but later has to be sunk by her; the second is sunk by the Polish destroyer *Burza* (Cdr Pitułko) which joins the convoy from ONS.167 after *U92* and *U753* have tried to finish her off with torpedoes. At this time *Spencer* probably sinks *U529*, the loss of which becomes known only in Mar.

By day on 22 Feb *U606*, *U603* and *U628* keep contact in turn and bring up *U92*, *U358*, *U223*, *U186* and *U753* by nightfall. Most of the boats are driven off. *U753*, which is attacked with depth charges by *Rosthern* and *Trillium*, and *U606* (Lt Döhler) attack almost simultaneously. *U606* torpedoes three ships of 17260 tons, two of which sink; the third ship, of 4599 tons, is only sunk when she is finished off by *U303* (Lt-Cdr Heine). Immediately after her own attack, *U606* is assaulted with depth charges from *Chilliwack* and *Burza* and is shortly afterwards sunk by ramming from *Campbell*. The latter becomes unmanoeuvrable thanks to water pouring into the engine room and has to be taken in tow by *Burza*. During the night *U604* sinks the rescue ship *Stockport* (1683 tons) coming up from the rear. In the morning of 23 Feb *U628* (Lt Hasenschar)

and *U186* (Lt-Cdr Hesemann) attack almost simultaneously. *U628* torpedoes two ships, of 6907 tons and 6409 tons respectively, which are later sunk by *U223* (Lt-Cdr Wächter) and *U603*. *U186* sinks two ships of 11608 tons. The attacks are facilitated because only *Spencer*, *Rosthern*, *Chilliwack* and *Dianthus* continue to escort the convoy, the last of which remains behind with the disabled ships. On 23 Feb *U628* and *U707* (Lt Gretschel) keep contact and by the evening bring up *U621*, *U358*, *U653*, *U468*, *U92* and *U600*. By a sharp change of course after dark the convoy which, initially, is escorted by only three ships, shakes the boats off and no attack takes place during the night 23–24 Feb. Only two stragglers, of 7176 tons and 9382 tons, are sunk or torpedoed by *U707* and *U653* (Lt-Cdr Feiler) respectively. Not before the morning can *U600* (Lt-Cdr Zurmühlen) torpedo one ship of 4391 tons from the convoy which is now escorted by *Spencer*, *Chilliwack*, *Rosthern* and *Trillium* (the ship is later sunk by *U628*). On 24 Feb *U628* and *U603* keep contact and bring up *U621*, *U600* and *U604*, the last of which is damaged by depth charges. Air escort provided from Newfoundland drives the boats off though *U621* (Lt Kruschka) misses the *Spencer* in the evening. The escort is reinforced by the British destroyers *Mansfield* and *Witherington*. Towards morning on 25 Feb *U628*, *U92* and *U600* attack almost simultaneously: the first sinks one ship of 7264 tons but the two others miss the *Spencer*. On 25 Feb *U468* keeps contact but in the oncoming mist only *U600* and *U621* come up briefly. Contact is lost in the evening and the operation is broken off in the morning of 26 Feb.

15–27 Feb   Air War/France
Three RAF Bomber Command raids against Dunkirk with Bostons and Venturas: 23 aircraft on 15 Feb, 60 aircraft on 26 Feb and 24 aircraft on 27 Feb. Hits are scored on ships.

15 Feb–14 Mar   Arctic
The convoy JW.53 goes to sea on 15 Feb with 28 ships and a 'Through Escort Group' with the minesweepers *Jason* (Cdr Lewis) and *Halcyon*, the Hunt class destroyers, *Pytchley*, *Middleton* and *Meynell*, the corvettes *Dianella*, *Poppy* and *Bergamot* and the A/S trawlers *Lord Middleton* and *Lord Austin*. In a heavy storm six ships have to put in to Iceland and the escort carrier *Dasher* (which was to provide the air escort) and the cruiser *Sheffield* of the covering force return with considerable damage. Off Seidisfjord on 19 Feb the 'Fighting Escort

Group', comprising the cruiser *Scylla* (Capt I A P Macintyre) and the destroyers *Milne* (Capt Campbell), *Orkan* (Polish), *Orwell*, *Opportune*, *Obedient*, *Obdurate*, *Faulknor* (Capt Scott-Moncrieff), *Boadicea*, *Inglefield*, *Fury*, *Intrepid*, *Impulsive* and *Eclipse*, joins the convoy. Rear-Adm Burnett with the cruisers *Belfast* and *Cumberland* forms the covering force. Submarines of the British 9th SM Flotilla and Soviet submarines are stationed off the Norwegian coast. Of them, *K-21* (Capt 2nd Class Lunin) lays a mine barrage near Arnöy on 18 Feb, disembarks agents and on 20 Feb fires six torpedoes into Bogen Bay. *M-122*, *Shch-422*, *M-119*, *M-172* and *M-171* make attacks in the area of Varangerfjord and on 19 and 20 Feb the Soviet Naval Air Force attacks the aircraft bases at Petsamo and Kirkenes.

German air reconnaissance reports JW.53 on 23 Feb. In bad weather the convoy avoids the German U-boat concentrations by the use of HF/DF on 24 Feb. *U622* misses two destroyers. On 25 Feb 10 Ju 88s of I/KG 30 attack and damage one ship of 7058 tons; an attack by some Ju 88s and *U255* on 26 Feb has no success. The convoy is met by four Soviet destroyers and arrives with 18 ships off the Kola Inlet on 26 Feb: six ships proceed with the destroyer *Uritski* and other ships into the White Sea.

On 27 and 28 Feb Ju 87s of I/StG 5 make dive-bombing attacks on the ships of the convoy which has come into Murmansk. They badly damage three steamers of 11341 tons. In further attacks on 6 and 13 Mar with the participation of Ju 88s of I/KG 30, the steamer *Ocean Freedom* (7173 tons) is destroyed and one of 6744 tons damaged. The convoy RA.53 with 30 ships, and escorted by the same ships as JW.53, sets out from the Kola Inlet on 1 Mar. On 2 Mar it is first reported by *U255* (Lt-Cdr Reche) and shadowed, with short interruptions, for several days. On 5 Mar *U255* sinks the steamer *Executive* (4978 tons) and torpedoes the *Richard Bland* (7191 tons) which, however, continucs on hcr way. An attack by 12 Ju 88s of I/KG 30 fails in the face of heavy AA fire. Contact is lost. On 9 Mar *U586* (Lt-Cdr v d Esch) sinks the straggler *Puerto Rican* (6076 tons) from the convoy scattered in the gale. One steamer founders in the gale and *U657* misses one ship. On 10 Mar *U255* sinks the *Richard Bland*. The radar of the battleship *King George V* of the distant escort helps to collect the scattered ships.

The German battlecruiser *Scharnhorst* uses the stormy weather to proceed on 8 Mar from Gotenhafen to Bergen and on to Trond-

heim. From there she moves with *Tirpitz*, destroyers and torpedo boats on 11–12 Mar to Bogen Bay near Narvik, where the heavy cruiser *Lützow* already lies. This massing of the heavy German ships in northern Norway and the demands made by the Battle of the Atlantic on the fleet destroyers of the Home Fleet (ie formation of support groups) compel the British Admiralty to stop the Murmansk convoys for the summer of 1943. The heavy German ships move to Altafjord from 22 to 24 Mar.

16 Feb–13 Mar   Central Atlantic

From 16 Feb the 'Rochen' group, comprising *U504*, *U218*, *U521*, *U43*, *U66*, *U202*, *U558*, *U87*, *U264* and *U258*, searches for US–Gibraltar convoys S of the Azores and the 'Robbe' group, comprising *U437*, *U445*, *U410*, *U107*, *U103*, *U382*, *U569* and *U511*, N of the Azores. On 20 Feb *U264*, *U258* and *U437* are detached to accompany home the prize tanker *Hohenfriedberg/Herborg* (Capt Heidberg, 7892 tons), but the latter is located by a USAAF Liberator 500 nautical miles SW of Cape Finisterre and is sunk by the British cruiser *Sussex*. The latter avoids a salvo of four torpedoes from *U264* (Lt Looks). On 22 Feb *U522* (Lt-Cdr Schneider) reports the tanker convoy UC.1, with 33 ships escorted by EG.44 (Cdr Durnford-Slater) with the sloops *Weston*, *Folkestone*, *Gorleston* and *Totland* and the frigates *Exe* and *Ness*, and the Support Group, comprising the US destroyers *Charles F Hughes*, *Madison*, *Lansdowne* and *Hilary P Jones*. The U-boats *U382*, *U569* and the 'Rochen' group are deployed. In the morning of 23 Feb *U522* sinks one tanker of 8882 tons (but is herself sunk by *Totland*) and in the evening *U382* (Lt-Cdr Juli) torpedoes one tanker of 8252 tons with the 'Falke' acoustic homing torpedo, used for the first time. *U202* (Lt-Cdr Poser) hits three tankers, one of which (7989 tons) sinks. One tanker of 9811 tons is later sunk by *U558* (Lt-Cdr Krech) and one of 8482 tons continues her journey in the convoy. Further attacks by *U569*, *U558* and *U504* during the night 23–24 Feb and by *U521* and *U66* during the night 24–25 Feb fail. *U107* (Lt-Cdr Gelhaus) and *U66* (Lt-Cdr Markworth) each sink one independent, of 7801 tons and 4312 tons respectively. The 'Tümmler' group, replenished from *U461* from 27 Feb to 4 Mar and comprising *U504*, *U43*, *U66*, *U202* and *U558*, proceeds to the area of the Canaries. *U43* (Lt Schwantke) sinks the blockade-runner *Doggerbank* (Capt Schneidewind, 5154 tons) which turns up much earlier than expected. An operation by the 'Tümmler' group on a small southbound convoy sighted by *U43*

on 12–13 Mar fails because of the strong air escort.

17–18 Feb   North Sea

Seven motor torpedo boats of the 2nd and 4th MTB Flotillas under Lt-Cdr v Mirbach and eight boats of the 6th MTB Flotilla (Lt-Cdr Obermaier) carry out a mining operation SE of Lowestoft and NE of Great Yarmouth respectively. The southern group, after dropping its barrage, is able to escape from the corvette *Kittiwake*. Part of the northern group, in dropping its barrage, is involved in an engagement with the destroyers *Montrose* (Cdr Phipps) and *Garth* (Lt-Cdr Scartchard); *S71* is shelled to a standstill and sunk by *Garth* by gunfire and ramming.

18–19 Feb   North Pacific

US TG.8.6 (Rear-Adm McMorris), comprising the cruisers *Indianapolis* and *Raleigh* and the destroyers *Bancroft*, *Caldwell*, *Coghlan* and *Gillespie*, shells Holtz Bay and Chicago Harbor on Attu.

18 Feb–3 Mar   North Atlantic

On 18 Feb the 'Neptun' group, consisting of *U759*, *U405*, *U448*, *U359*, *U135*, *U608*, *U376*, *U566* and *U659*, is formed SW of Iceland to operate against the expected convoy HX.226 (escorted by EG.C3; see 9–19 Feb), which passes N of it on 20 Feb after being re-routed as a result of 'Ultra' interceptions. When the convoy is not located, the group moves off on 20 Feb, reinforced by *U89*, *U569* and *U377*, to the SW towards SC.120, which is escorted by EG.B7 (Cdr Gretton; see 9–19 Feb) and in addition the attached sloop *Woodpecker* (passing also to the N after being re-routed on 24–25 Feb), and towards HX.227.

HX.227's detour, however, does not go far enough to the N and the convoy is located by the most northerly 'Neptun' boat of *U759*, in the morning of 27 Feb. Radio interference prevents punctual deployment. *U759* is driven off by the escorts of the 62-ship convoy, EG.B6 (Cdr Heathcote) with the destroyers *Fame* and *Viscount*, the corvettes *Vervain* and *Kingcup* and the Norwegian corvettes *Acanthus* and *Potentilla*. *U376*, *U377*, *U608*, *U448*, *U359* and *U135* take up the pursuit but only *U405* (Cdr Hopmann) sinks a Liberty Ship (7176 tons) which has fallen behind and which has on board the MTBs *PT85* and *PT87* destined for the Soviet Union. From 28 Feb *U709* and *U634* also take part. On 1 Mar *U759* shadows an independent (7176 tons) which *U634* (Lt Dahlhaus) sinks. In the search, *U608* reports in the afternoon the approaching convoy ON.168, escorted by EG.B5 (Cdr Boyle) with the destroyers *Havelock* and *Volunteer*, the frigate *Swale* and the corvettes *Saxifrage, Godetia, Pimpernel, Buttercup* and *Lavender*, just to the N but the HF/DF-equipped *Havelock* drives her under and *U405, U359, U659* and *U448* do not find the convoys again up to 3 Mar.

21 Feb   South Pacific
Operation 'Cleanslate': the US RCTs 103 and 169 of the 43rd Inf Div (Maj-Gen Hester) land from Guadalcanal on Russell Island without encountering resistance. They are supported by three Marine Ranger BLTs. By the end of Feb a total of 9000 men are landed by LCTs.

21–22 Feb   Air War/Germany
RAF Bomber Command attacks Bremen with 143 aircraft. There is limited damage, with no losses.

21–25 Feb   North Atlantic
The outbound *U664* (Lt A Graef) sights the convoy ONS.167, escorted by EG.B3 (Cdr Tait) with the destroyers *Harvester, Escapade, Garland* (Polish) and *Burza* (Polish; detached to ON.166), the corvette *Narcissus* and the FFN corvettes *Roselys, Aconit* and *Renoncule*. In the evening of 21 Feb *U664* sinks two ships of 13466 tons from the convoy. *U758, U591, U84* and *U432*, which are running in the area to their assignments, are deployed as the 'Sturmbock' group and during the night 21–22 Feb and in the morning *U758* and *U664* make brief contact but are driven off. For 25 Feb a new 'Wildfang' patrol line is formed with the inclusion of boats returning from ON.166 and of boats replenished from *U460*; it consists of *U332, U432, U753, U226, U383, U758, U607, U664, U84, U409* and *U591*. But on 26 Feb only destroyers are seen by *U664* and *U607*.

On 25 Feb *U119* (Lt-Cdr Zech) lays a mine barrage off Reykjavik, with no known results.

23 Feb–30 May   Black Sea
German supply convoys 'Kleiner Bär 1–99' from Feodosia to Anapa to supply the Kuban bridgehead with at first two to three, then five to six MFP (naval ferry barges) of the 3rd Landing Flotilla (Cdr* Strempel) and from Apr sometimes also the 5th Landing Flotilla (Cdr Mehler). The torpedoes fired by the Soviet submarines (including *M-117, M-111* and *L-4*) against convoys 8 (22 Mar), 41 (22 Apr), 88 (18 May) and 92 (21 May) run under the flat-bottomed MFPs. In air attacks on convoy 89 (19 May) *F308* and *F367* and on convoy 99 (30 May) *F332* sink. Soviet torpedo cutters do not attack. Likewise, attempts by Soviet submarines to attack convoys off the Crimean coast are unsuccessful.

Soviet submarines and torpedo aircraft are deployed unsuccessfully W of the Crimea against German and Rumanian convoy traffic between Constanza and Sevastopol (Traffic Commander: Capt Kiderlen). From Apr patrol lines are formed with the submarines *S-33, Shch-209, M-35* and *M-112* in the open sea. On 20 Apr *S-33* (Capt 3rd Class Alexeyev) sinks the largest Rumanian transport *Suceava* (6876 tons) escorted by the Rumanian destroyer *Regina Maria* and three German motor minesweepers.

The Rumanian minelayer *Amiral Murgescu* and the German *Romania* lay several flanking barrages off Sulina and in the Bay of Odessa.

24 Feb   Baltic
The German *U649* is sunk in a collision with *U232* during exercises in the Bay of Danzig.

24 Feb   Great Britain
The British submarine *Vandal* is lost during trials in Kilbrannan Sound, cause unknown.

24 Feb   Central Atlantic
The US carrier *Ranger* flies off a complement of fighter aircraft to Accra to be transferred to North Africa.

26–28 Feb   English Channel
A group from the 5th MTB Flotilla, comprising *S65, S68, S81* and *S85*, attacks a British convoy in Lyme Bay and sinks from it the motor ship *Modavia* (4858 tons) and *LCT381* (625 tons) as well as the trawlers *Harstad* and *Lord Hailsham*.

A southbound German convoy loses the patrol boat *V1318* on a mine off Ijmuiden on 27 Feb. During the night 27–28 Feb an attempted attack by the British *MGB77, MGB79, MGB81* and *MGB111* is frustrated by defensive fire from the escorting vessels *M383, V1304, V1305, V1309, V1313, V1314* and *FlJ23. MGB79* is sunk.

26 Feb–11 Mar   North Atlantic
On 26 Feb the 'Burggraf' group, comprising *U228, U527, U230, U523, U526, U616, U435, U615* and *U332*, is formed in the Central North Atlantic and the 'Wildfang' group, comprising *U638, U89, U432, U758, U664, U84, U409* and *U591* is tranferred to the NE of Newfoundland to operate against convoys using the northern route. *U603, U91, U653, U621, U600* and *U468*, which have come after replenishing from *U462*, lengthen the 'Burggraf' group as it proceeds to the SW until 4 Mar and behind it *U634, U709, U566, U405, U359, U659* and *U448* take up waiting positions. On 5 Mar convoy ON.168, escorted by EG.B5 (Cdr Boyle) with the destroyers *Havelock* and *Volunteer*, the frigate *Swale* and the corvettes *Saxifrage, Godetia, Pimpernel, Buttercup* and *Lavender*, passes unobserved through the 'Wildfang' group in a gap formed by the unknown loss of *U529*. Convoy SC.121 passes unobserved between the 'Wildfang' and 'Burggraf' groups, but on 6 Mar *U405* (Cdr Hopmann) sights the convoy SC.121 (Commodore Birnie†) with 59 ships from which, after heavy gales, many have become stragglers. The escort is EG.A3 (Cdr Heineman), comprising the US Coast Guard cutter *Spencer*, the US destroyer *Greer*, the Canadian corvettes *Rosthern* and *Trillium*, the British corvettes *Dianthus* and *Dauphin* and the rescue ship *Melrose Abbey*. The Cdr U-boats deploys *U405, U409, U591, U230, U228, U566, U616, U448, U526, U634, U527, U659, U523, U709, U359, U332* and *U432* as the 'Westmark' group and forms the patrol line 'Ostmark' further to the E for 8 Mar from the 'Neuland' boats. It consists of *U229, U665, U641, U447, U190, U439, U530, U618* and *U642*. After *U405* is driven off, *U566* and *U230* (Lt-Cdr Siegmann) make contact during the night 6–7 Mar. *U230*, unnoticed by the escort, sinks one ship of 2868 tons. The freighter *Empire Impala* (6116 tons), which has stayed behind to recover survivors, is sunk in the morning by *U591* (Lt-Cdr Zetzsche). On 7 Mar *U228, U230, U591, U409, U526* and *U634* keep contact in spite of Force 10 winds, snow and hail showers, but they are unable to attack. In the morning of 8 Mar the gale subsides and visibility is very variable: *U527* (Lt-Cdr Uhlig) misses the convoy but *U526* (?) (Lt-Cdr Möglich) sinks one ship of 3921 tons separated from the convoy. In the evening of 8 Mar *U527, U591, U190* (Lt-Cdr Wintermeyer) and *U642* (Lt-Cdr Brünning) each sink a straggler, of 5242 tons, 5879 tons, 7015 tons and 2125 tons respectively. On 9 Mar the US Coast Guard cutters *Bibb* and *Ingham* and the US destroyer *Babbitt* arrive as reinforcement for the escort from Iceland. Liberators of No 120 Sqn RAF provide air escort and drive off the contact-keeper *U566*. Of the boats coming up by nightfall, including *U229, U409, U641, U332, U230, U405* and *U665*, two are bombed from the air and four are attacked by depth charges from *Babbitt, Rosthern* and others. An attack by *U229* (Lt Schetelig) fails. In the evening of 9 Mar *U530* (Lt-Cdr K Lange) sinks one straggler of 3058 tons. In the night *U409* (Lt Massmann) and *U405* attack almost simultaneously: they sink two ships and one ship respectively, of 9826 tons and 4665 tons. A little later *U229* sinks one ship of 4946 tons and torpedoes one more of 3670 tons. In these attacks Commodore Birnie goes down with his ship. On 10 Mar it freshens up again to Force 10 winds and, in snow and hail showers, apart from *U229*

and *U616* (Lt Koitschka) whose salvos miss, only *U523* and *U642* come briefly into contact with independents. In the afternoon the last contact-keeper, *U634*, is driven off. The partial non-functioning of the radar and W/T equipment, as a result of storm damage, greatly impedes the escort group which is further reinforced on 10 Mar by the British corvettes *Campion* and *Mallow*. Early on 11 Mar the operation is broken off.

27 Feb–1 Mar   Air War/Western Europe

On 27 Feb the US 8th AF makes a daylight attack on harbour installations in Brest. During the night 28 Feb–1 Mar 400 bombers of RAF Bomber Command attack the U-boat base at St-Nazaire. In the month of Feb 1000 tons of bombs are dropped on the U-boat pens without effect.

27 Feb–13 Mar   North Atlantic

On 27 Feb the convoy KMS.10 departs from Liverpool; it consists of 50 ships, escorted by EG.C1 (Lt-Cdr Dobson) with the RCN destroyer *St Croix* and corvettes *Shediac*, *Battleford*, *Kenogami* and *Napanee* and a support group composed of the RCN corvettes *Baddeck*, *Regina* and *Prescott* and the Bangor class minesweepers *Fort York*, *Qualicum* and *Wedgeport*. On 28 Feb the convoy XK.2 departs from Gibraltar; this consists of 20 ships, escorted by EG.38 with the RN corvettes *Coreopsis*, *Anchusa*, *Columbine* and *Jonquil*, the A/S trawler *Loch Askaig* and the supporting destroyer *Vanoc*. From 28 Feb the 'Robbe' group, comprising *U445*, *U410*, *U107*, *U103* and *U511*, operates in the area W of Gibraltar. On 1 Mar *Columbine* drives *U445* off before the convoy is sighted. On 4 Mar both convoys (which, thanks to reports from the B-Service, are expected) are located by Fw 200 Condors and in air attacks by Fw 200s and Do 217s of I/KG 40 one ship of 4765 tons from convoy XK.2 is damaged. The returning *U87* comes into contact with KMS.10 but is sunk by *St Croix* and *Shediac* before she can report its presence.

On 5 Mar the outgoing *U130* (Lt Keller), in an submerged daylight attack, sinks four ships of 16359 tons from XK.2. KMS.10, escorted also by Catalinas of No 202 Sqn RAF, is located by Fw 200s and five boats from the 'Robbe' group are sent in. *U107* is forced down by a Catalina and *U445* does not come up; however, *U410* (Lt Fenski) sinks one ship of 7133 tons and damages one of 7134 tons equipped with torpedo net defence. *U410* is slightly damaged by depth charges fired by *Shediac* and dropped from Catalinas.

On 8 Mar German agents opposite Gibraltar and the B-Service report the convoy MKS.9

leaving Gibraltar, consisting of 56 ships escorted by EG.C1 (see above); they also establish the departure of the following MKF.10A, consisting of six ships escorted by EG.44 (Cdr Farquhar) with the sloops *Egret*, *Erne* and *Fishguard* and with the frigate *Test* and the destroyers *Wheatland*, *Calpe* and *Holcombe* as support group. *U445*, *U103*, *U410* and *U107* are ordered to form a patrol line. On 9 Mar *U107* reports the convoy but contact is lost.

On 12 Mar the B-Service and Fw 200s locate the convoy OS.44 with 48 ships, escorted by EG.39 (Cdr King) with the sloops *Rochester*, *Scarborough* and *Fleetwood*, and the corvettes *Balsam*, *Coltsfoot*, *Spirea* and *Mignonette*. During the night 12–13 Mar *U107* (Lt-Cdr Gelhaus) sinks four ships of 17376 tons. On 13 Mar MKS.9 is located, also by the B-Service and Fw 200s. Efforts by *U410* and *U445* to make contact fail and the returning *U163* runs into the escort and is sunk by the corvette *Prescott*.

When new B-Service reports show the departure of convoy MKF.10B with four ships, escorted by the EG.C4 (Cdr Brewer) with the destroyers *Churchill* (RN) and *Restigouche* (RCN) and the corvettes *Amherst*, *Brandon*, *Collingwood* (RCN) and *Celandine* (RN), there are no U-boats available to follow up the information.

28 Feb   Mediterranean

The German E-boat *S35* is sunk by a mine NW of Bizerta and *S56* is damaged by a bomb in Palermo but is repaired and recommissioned. The Italian submarine *FR 111* (ex-French *Phoque*) is sunk by air attack 10 nautical miles S of Augusta during a supply mission to Lampedusa.

28 Feb–29 Mar   Air War/France

RAF Bomber Command 'area attacks' against St-Nazaire: on 28 Feb–1 Mar (437 aircraft), 22–23 Mar (357) and 28–29 Mar (323). The port area is heavily damaged and more than 60 per cent of the built-up city area is destroyed; 8 aircraft are lost.

1–31 Mar   Pacific

In US submarine operations in Mar, 24 of the 72 'Ultra' intercepts lead to sightings and 11 to attacks in which four ships are sunk and six damaged. For the US submarines which arrive in their operational areas in Mar, the following results are confirmed: In the Aleutians area, *S32* fires several duds. In Japanese waters, *Permit* (Lt-Cdr Chappel) sinks two ships of 5014 tons and one sailing vessel and damages one ship of 4645 tons and *Scamp* (Lt-Cdr Ebert) sinks one ship of 1450 tons, damages the seaplane transport *Kamikawa Maru* of 6543 tons and has several premature detonations. In the East China Sea, *Kingfish* (Lt-Cdr

Lowrance) sinks one ship of 8154 tons and one sailing vessel and damages one ship of 3883 tons and *Wahoo* (Cdr Morton) sinks nine ships of 26826 tons. In the Central Pacific, *Whale* (Lt-Cdr Burrows) sinks one ship of 6486 tons and *Finback* (Lt-Cdr Hull) and *Tunny* (Lt-Cdr Scott) sink together the *Suwa Maru* (10672 tons) with the help of 'Ultra'. *Finback* also damages the *Sanuki Maru* (7158 tons) with the help of 'Ultra' and on 9 Apr *Tunny* tries to attack a fleet carrier and an escort carrier but has seven duds and prematures. *Tuna* (Lt-Cdr de Tar) sinks one ship of 4697 tons, *Pollack* has misses and *Stingray* and *Plunger* are on reconnaissance missions. In the South Pacific, *Triton* (Lt-Cdr McKenzie) sinks two ships of 10118 tons but is herself sunk on 15 Mar by a Japanese destroyer off the Admiralties; *Grayback* (Lt-Cdr Stephan) locates with 'Ultra' support the *Noshiro Maru* of 7184 tons and torpedoes her; and *Trigger* (Lt-Cdr Benson) sinks one ship of 3103 tons and damages two of 8467 tons. *Greenling* and *Gato* are on special missions. In the South West Pacific *Tautog* (Lt-Cdr Sieglaff) lays a minefield SE of Borneo on which the destroyer *Amagiri* sinks and one ship of 6863 tons is damaged; in addition the destroyer *Isonami* (9 Apr), one ship of 5214 tons and one sailing vessel are sunk by torpedoes and gunfire. *Tambor* (Lt-Cdr Ambruster) torpedoes one ship of 691 tons and conducts a guerrilla supply mission; *Gudgeon* (Lt-Cdr Port) sinks two ships of 15421 tons and damages one of 1192 tons; and *Grayling* (Lt-Cdr Lee) sinks one ship of 4103 tons and one sailing vessel.

1 Mar   Mediterranean

The Italian destroyer *Geniere* is heavily damaged in drydock at Palermo during a USAAF air raid; she is salvaged in 1943–44 and towed to Taranto for repair. The torpedo boat *Monsone* is sunk during a USAAF air raid at Naples.

1–30 Mar   Air War/Western Europe

RAF Bomber Command mine offensive. In 19 nights 495 sorties are flown off Biscay ports, the French and Dutch coasts, and the Frisian coast and in the Kattegat; the first drops off Gdynia (4–5 Mar) and Swinemünde (1–11 Mar) are made and 17 aircraft are lost. German ships sunk are the MMS *R40* on 7 Mar and *R74* on 12 Mar off Boulogne.

2–4 Mar   South West Pacific

A Japanese force (Rear-Adm Kimura), comprising eight transports and the destroyers *Shirayuki*, *Arashio*, *Asashio*, *Tokitsukaze*, *Yukikaze*, *Uranami*, *Shikinami* and *Asagumo*, sets out from Rabaul on 28 Feb to bring 6900 troops of the Japanese 51st Div (Lt-Gen Nakano) to Lae. Reported by a Liberator early on 2 Mar NE of Dampier Strait, it is attacked 2hr later by 12 Fortresses which sink a transport and damage two. The destroyers *Yukikaze* and *Asagumo* go on ahead with 950 survivors. On 3 Mar the convoy is attacked in the Bismarck Sea by 355 American and Australian aircraft, some at very low level. The aircraft of AAF South-West Pacific (Lt-Gen Kenney) sink all transports totalling 33730 tons and the destroyers *Shirayuki*, *Arashio*, *Asashio* and *Tokitsukaze*. Japanese destroyers and the submarines *I-17* and *I-26* save 2734 men. The remainder, who do not go down with the ships, are mown down in the water by the US fighter-bombers' guns and by depth charges and machine-gun fire from the MTBs *PT66*, *PT67*, *PT68*, *PT121*, *PT128*, *PT143* and *PT150* (Lt-Cdr Atkins) to prevent the Army round Lae being re-inforced by survivors swimming to the shore. Twenty-one US aircraft are lost.

2 Mar–11 Apr   Mediterranean
Attempts by the submarines *Ascianghi* and *U593* to attack convoys near Tripoli and Alexandria fail on 2 and 3 Mar. Aircraft attack the dual convoy MW.22 and XT.4 on 5 Mar and damage one ship of 6900 tons. In further attacks on convoys off the Cyrenaican coast, *U593* (Lt-Cdr Kelbling) sinks four ships of 11581 tons on 18 Mar, 27 Mar and 11 Apr and off Palestine *U81* (Lt Krieg) sinks three ships of 454 tons.
On 19 Mar aircraft of KG 30, 54 and 77 attack Allied ships in the harbour at Tripoli and sink two ships of 8498 tons. The destroyer *Derwent* is damaged beyond repair. First use of 'circling torpedoes'. In the Aegean, the Greek submarine *Papanicolis* (Lt-Cdr Roussen) sinks three sailing ships.

3–4 Mar   Air War/Germany
RAF Bomber Command attacks Hamburg with 417 aircraft. Bombs fall mostly on the suburb of Wedel. Ten aircraft are lost.

4–8 Mar   English Channel/North Sea
The German 2nd, 4th and 6th MTB Flotillas make a sortie off Lowestoft and Great Yarmouth. On the way out *S70* is lost on a mine. They have engagements there with the British destroyers *Windsor* and *Southdown* and the corvette *Sheldrake*. On the return in the morning of 5 Mar they are attacked off Ijmuiden by Spitfire and Typhoon fighters which sink *S75*.
In an unsuccessful attack by German MTBs on a British convoy near Start Point, there is an engagement with the Polish destroyer *Krakowiak*. A further attack by German

MTBs on 7–8 Mar near the Sunk Lightship is frustrated by the British destroyer *Mackay* (Capt Jephson), *MGB20*, *MGB17* and *MGB21*. In taking avoiding action, *S114* and *S119* collide. The latter is brought to a standstill and sunk by *MGB20* after the crew has been rescued by *S114*.

5 Mar   North Sea
The German patrol trawler *V1252* is sunk following a collision with the A/A trawler *FJ27* N of Borkum.

5–8 Mar   English Channel
Operation 'Karin'. The German 8th DD Flotilla (Capt Erdmenger) with the destroyers *Z23*, *Z24*, *Z25* (returned), *Z32* and *Z37* is transferred from the North Sea through the Channel. Off Dover there is gunfire from British coastal batteries and an unsuccessful attack by British MTBs. By 6 Mar the Flotilla has reached Le Havre, by 7 Mar Cherbourg and by 8 Mar Bordeaux.

6 Mar   Norway
The German minelayer *Skagerrak* lays a flanking barrage off Bergen.

6 Mar   South Pacific
The Japanese fast patrol boat *P34/Suzuki* is heavily damaged in a collision with the target ship *Yakaze* and is towed to Truk.

6–12 Mar   Baltic/North Sea
On 6–7 Mar the minelayers *Brummer* and *Ostmark* lay the 'Karlchen' barrage N of the 'Westwall' barrage.
Operation 'Paderborn': transfer of the battlecruiser *Scharnhorst*, escorted by the destroyer *Z28* and off SW Norway also by the destroyers *Friedrich Ihn*, *Erich Steinbrinck* and *Richard Beitzen* and the torpedo boats *Greif*, *Jaguar*, *T16*, *T20* and *T21*. The ships suffer damage in severe gales. *Scharnhorst* and *Z28* arrive on 9 Mar in the Bogen Bight near Narvik. On 10–11 Mar the pocket battleship *Lützow* and destroyers *Theodor Riedel* and *Z31* are transferred from Kaafjord to Narvik and on 11–12 Mar the battleship *Tirpitz*, destroyers *Paul Jacobi* and *Karl Galster* and torpedo boats *Jaguar* and *Greif* sail from Trondheim to Narvik.

6–13 Mar   North Atlantic
On 6 Mar the 'Neuland' group, comprising *U447*, *U229*, *U665*, *U633*, *U641*, *U190*, *U530*, *U642*, *U439*, *U618*, *U757*, *U406*, *U86*, *U373*, *U441* and *U440*, is formed on the eastern side of the North Atlantic. On 7 Mar *U221* (Lt Trojer) sinks one independent of 3015 tons and *U633* is sunk by Fortress 'J' of No 220 Sqn RAF (Fg Off Knowles). After the northern boats have withdrawn as the 'Ostmark' group to SC.121 (see 26 Feb–11 Mar), *U659*, *U448*, *U608*, *U757*, *U406*, *U86*, *U373*, *U441*, *U440*, *U221*, *U444*, *U336* and *U590* are concentrated as the 'Neuland' group against

the convoy HX.228, located by the B-Service on 8 Mar. Because of the short 'black-out' of 'Ultra' data from 'Triton' (see 8–19 Mar), the movement of the 'Neuland' group on 9 Mar is not known to the STR and HX.228, re-routed to pass near the N end of the old 'Neuland' patrol line, is intercepted. At midday on 10 Mar *U336* (Lt-Cdr Hunger), stationed in the S, sights HX.228; the latter comprises 60 ships escorted by EG.B3 (Cdr Tait†) with the destroyers *Harvester*, *Escapade*, *Garland* (Polish) and *Burza* (Polish), the corvettes *Narcissus* and *Orchis* and the French corvettes *Aconit*, *Roselys* and *Renoncule*. From 5 to 14 Mar the American 6th SG (Capt Short), comprising the escort carrier *Bogue* and the destroyers *Belknap* and *Osmond Ingram*, operates with the convoy for support. Apart from the 'Neuland' group, *U333*, *U432*, *U405*, *U566* and *U359* are deployed. After *U366* is driven off, *U444* (Lt Langfeld) takes over as second contact-keeper. Of the boats which come up during the night 10–11 Mar, *U221* sinks two ships of 11977 tons, *U336*, *U86* and *U406* miss the convoy (using, in part, FAT salvos) and *U444* torpedoes one ship of 7197 tons, which is later sunk, together with another ship of 5001 tons by *U757* (Lt-Cdr Deetz). In the explosion *U757* is damaged. *U444* is sighted by *Harvester*; she submerges but has to surface after depth charge attacks and is rammed by the destroyer which for 10 minutes gets a propeller shaft stuck in the U-boat. *U444* tries, at slow speed and unable to submerge, to get away from the unmanoeuvrable destroyer but is located an hour later by the corvette *Aconit* (Lt-Cdr Levasseur) and sunk by ramming. After the repair of an engine, *Harvester* slowly follows the convoy while *Aconit* quickly closes up. In the morning, however, *Harvester*'s second shaft breaks and the stationary ship is sunk towards midday by *U432* (Lt-Cdr Eckhardt). One hour later the returning *Aconit* locates the U-boat, compels her to surface with depth charges and sinks her with gunfire and by ramming. The lost contact with the convoy is re-established towards mid-day on 11 Mar by *U228* and *U406* but the boats are driven off by the strong escort, as are, later, *U359*, *U590* and *U405*. Attempts by *U440* and *U590* to attack during the night 11–12 Mar fail and towards morning *U590*, the last contact-keeper, is driven off. The deployment of *Bogue* cannot be used to full advantage because the carrier sails in the middle of the convoy and has no freedom to manoeuvre. While this operation is running, convoy ONS.171 (39 ships escorted by EG.B1 with the destroyers *Hur-*

ricane, *Watchman* and *Rockingham*, the frigate *Kale* and the corvettes *Monkshood*, *Dahlia*, *Meadowsweet* and *Wallflower*) passes far to the N close to Cape Farewell.

6–16 Mar   South Pacific

On 6 Mar the 'Cactus Striking Force' (Capt Briscoe), consisting of the destroyers *Fletcher*, *Nicholas*, *O'Bannon*, and *Radford*, shells the Japanese airfield at Munda (New Georgia), using 1700 rounds without great success. TF.68 (Rear-Adm Merrill), comprising the cruisers *Montpelier*, *Cleveland* and *Denver* and the destroyers *Conway*, *Cony* and *Waller*, makes a sortie into Kula Gulf to shell the second Japanese airfield at Vila and encounters two Japanese destroyers, *Murasame* and *Minegumo*, which have brought supplies. They are sunk by radar-directed gunfire and torpedo salvos from the destroyer *Waller*. The US submarines *Grampus* and *Grayback* are stationed to support the operation; the former goes missing. On 16 Mar the destroyers (Cdr McInerney) *Nicholas*, *Radford*, *Strong* and *Taylor* again shell Vila.

7–10 Mar   East Mediterranean

The Italian destroyer *Sella* lays three defensive barrages with 70 mines off Rhodes.

7–14 Mar   North Atlantic

The remaining U-boats of the 'Wildfang' and 'Burggraf' groups form a new 'Raubgraf' patrol line on 7 Mar NE of Newfoundland; it comprises *U638*, *U89*, *U758*, *U664*, *U84*, *U615*, *U435*, *U603*, *U91*, *U653*, *U621*, *U600* and *U468*. The intention is to operate against convoy HX.228 but the latter is re-routed on 8 Mar to the S by a signal the B-Service decodes on 9 Mar. The convoys ON.168 (EG.B5; see 26 Feb–11 Mar) and ONS.169 (EG.B4 with the destroyers *Highlander* and *Beverley* and the corvettes *Pennywort*, *Anemone* and *Abelia*, and with the RCN corvette *Sherbrooke* attached) have many stragglers after heavy gales and are delayed. The escorts have problems because there is no possibility of refuelling at sea in the gales.

On 7 Mar the straggler *Empire Light* (6537 tons) of ON.168 is torpedoed by *U638* (Lt Bernbeck) and the Liberty Ship *Thomas Hooker* (7176 tons) of ONS.169 reports breaking up so that the corvette *Pimpernel* takes off the crew. These signals are intercepted and decoded by the B-Service. On 11 Mar *U621* (Lt Kruschka) sinks the straggler *Baron Kinnaird* (3355 tons) from ONS.169. Both wrecks are sunk on 12 Mar by *U468* (Lt Schamong) and *U653* (Lt-Cdr Feiler). On 9 Mar the 'Raubgraf' group is moved to the N to intercept convoy ON.170

which, according to the B-Service, is expected on 10 Mar. When on 11 Mar the B-Service decodes a signal from the delayed ON.169 (which has in reality already passed the 'Raubgraf' group), the group is deployed more to the W; and when on 11–12 Mar Service decodes signals to convoy HX.229A (EG.40 with the sloops *Aberdeen*, *Hastings*, *Landguard* and *Lulworth* and the frigates *Moyola* and *Waveney*) to go N close to Newfoundland, 'Raubgraf' receives orders to attack this convoy. However, on 13 Mar convoy ON.170, escorted by EG.B2 (Cdr MacIntyre) with the frigate *Whimbrel*, the destroyers *Vanessa* and *Whitehall* and the corvettes *Gentian*, *Heather* and *Sweetbriar* (*Gentian* is detached to the *Empire Light*), which could not follow the re-routing order to the W because of the escorts' fuel problems, runs on its old course into 'Raubgraf' and is reported by *U603*. But by clever use of his HF/DF on *Whimbrel* Cdr MacIntyre is able to frustrate all attempts to attack by *U603*, *U653*, *U435*, *U600* and *U468*—one of the most exemplary cases of the effective use of HF/DF.

8–19 Mar   Atlantic/Intelligence

On 8 Mar a signal from the BdU to begin using a new short signal book on 10 Mar is decoded at Bletchley Park, raising fears of a new 'black-out' because of the loss of the necessary 'cribs' to feed the 'bombs'. At this most critical time it seems to be impossible to route the convoys around the growing number of German U-boat lines so as to avoid losses of merchant ships vital to the Allied build-up in England for the invasion of Europe. However, by concentrating all available resources, the cryptanalysts at Bletchley Park are able to solve the problem using the many contact signals intercepted by convoys SC.121, HX.228, HX.229 and SC.122 and on 19 Mar the U-boat 'Triton' signals are decoded in time for them to be acted upon.

9 Mar   Indian Ocean

The German merchant ships *Drachenfels* (6342 tons), *Ehrenfels* (7752 tons) and *Braunfels* (7847 tons), lying in Mormugao (Goa), scuttle themselves.

9–16 Mar   English Channel/North Sea

On 9 Mar the British *MTB624*, *MTB622* (lost) and *MTB617* attack three German minesweepers of the 21st MS Flotilla near Terschelling, but the torpedoes are outmanoeuvred. On 10–11 Mar the Free French *MTB94* and *MTB96* attack a German convoy off Morlaix and sink *M4620*. On 11–12 Mar the British *MTB38*, *MTB35* and *MTB24* attack a German

convoy off Boulogne without success. On 15–16 Mar the Danish steamers *Maria Toft* (1922 tons) and *Agnete* (1458 tons), from a convoy escorted by the German 13th PB Flotilla, are sunk off Terschelling by the British *MTB88* and *MTB93*. During the night 13–14 Mar *S92*, *S76*, *S29*, *S86* and *S89* drop 26 UMB mines in front of a convoy off Orfordness. The motor ship *Moravia* (306 tons) is lost on them.

10 Mar   South Atlantic

The German blockade-runner *Karin* (7322 tons) scuttles herself in the South Atlantic to avoid capture by the US cruiser *Savannah* and destroyer *Eberle*.

12–14 Mar   General

The British frigate (DE) *Bayntun* is fitted with the first 'Hedgehog' and the corvette *Hadleigh Castle* with the first 'Squid' ahead-throwing A/S weapons.

12–22 Mar   Central Atlantic

Before the 'Unverzagt' group, comprising *U130*, *U515*, *U172*, *U513*, *U106* and *U167*, and the 'Wohlgemut' group, comprising *U159*, *U109*, *U524*, *U67* and *U103*, take up their patrol lines in the area of the Azores to operate against the convoy located by the B-Service, *U130* (Lt Keller) sights UGS.6—45 ships with an escort (Capt Wellborn) consisting of the US destroyers *Wainwright*, *Trippe*, *Champlin*, *Mayrant*, *Rowan*, *Rhind* and *Hobby*—but she is located by *Champlin* and sunk. In a calm sea the U-boats have difficulty in approaching the destroyers which are equipped with 10cm radar but which, without HF/DF equipment, cannot locate the W/T signals of the U-boats. *U172* (Lt-Cdr Emmermann) sinks a straggler of 5565 tons in the evening of 13 Mar. The 'Tümmler' group, consisting of *U521*, *U504*, *U43*, *U66*, *U202* and *U558*, is also deployed. On 13 Mar *U513*, *U167* and *U172* and on 14 Mar *U513*, *U167* and *U106* are driven off and *U515* is damaged by depth charges. On 15 Mar *U159* and *U524* (Lt-Cdr v Steinaecker) attempt underwater attacks by day in which *U524* sinks one ship of 8062 tons. On 16 Mar *U106* brings up nine U-boats but their attempted attacks are frustrated. Until evening *U524* and *U172* make simultaneous underwater attacks in which *Rhind* and several tankers are missed and one ship of 7191 tons is sunk. Towards the morning of 17 Mar *U558* misses the convoy. In the evening *U167* (Cdr Sturm) torpedoes one ship of 7200 tons, which is later sunk by *U521* (Lt-Cdr Bargsten). On 18 Mar strong air support is provided; *U524* still keeps contact but an attack is impossible and is therefore broken off by 19 Mar. *U524* is sunk by a Liberator of USAAF A/S Sqn 1.

13–14 Mar   Norway

In a raid by the Norwegian *MTB619* and *MTB631* off Flörö, one of three merchant ships (1249 tons) is sunk. *MTB631* is grounded near Flörö, salvaged and towed to Bergen by the minesweeper *M1*; she is later repaired and commissioned as the German *S631*.

14–20 Mar   North Atlantic

Biggest convoy operation of WW2 in a gap in the decoding of 'Triton' signals. In order to avoid the 'Raubgraf' group which is shadowing the convoy ON.170, convoys SC.122 and HX.229 are re-routed from the northern to the southern route on 13 Mar, while convoy HX.229A is routed even further to the NNW, close to Newfoundland and Greenland, where it encounters icebergs and loses the whale factory ship *Svend Foyn* (14795 tons) and two ships which have to return owing to ice damage. The W/T instructions to SC.122 and HX.229 are decoded by the German B-Service on 14 Mar and the Cdr U-boats therefore concentrates *U435*, *U603*, *U615*, *U600*, *U758*, *U664*, *U84* and *U91* from ON.170 into a narrow patrol line ('Raubgraf' group) in front of the route of SC.122 for 15 Mar. On the eastern side of the North Atlantic the 'Stürmer' group is formed to operate against SC.122: it consists of the boats coming from SC.121—*U305*, *U527*, *U666*, *U523*, *U229*, *U526*, *U642*, *U439*, *U338*, *U641*, *U665*, *U618*, *U190* and *U530*—and the new arrivals *U631*, *U598*, *U384* and *U134* on 14 Mar. The 'Dränger' group is formed to operate against HX.229 (it is assumed that this convoy will steam further to the S with the boats coming from HX.228): *U373*, *U86*, *U336*, *U440*, *U590*, *U441*, *U406*, *U608*, *U333*, *U221* and *U610*. On the Allied side, the convoys ONS.171 (EG.B1) and ON.172 (EG.C3) are routed to the N because of the assumed concentration of U-boats from the battles against SC.121 and HX.228. In the prevailing gale, SC.122 passes the 'Raubgraf' patrol line before the U-boats get to their positions and HX.229 goes round to the S. *U91* sights the destroyer *Witherington* from the WLEF, detached owing to fuel shortage, but together with *U84*, *U664* and *U758* cannot find the convoy.

In the morning of 16 Mar the homebound *U653* (Lt-Cdr Feiler) sights HX.229 with 38 ships (Commodore Mayall). Of its escort group, B4 (Lt-Cdr Luther), only the destroyer *Volunteer* and the corvettes *Anemone* and *Pennywort*, together with the destroyer *Mansfield* from the WLEF, are with the convoy, which immediately drives

off *U653*. The Cdr U-boats deploys the 'Raubgraf' group and two boats, *U228* and *U616*, just replenished from *U463*, and the 11 most southerly 'Stürmer' boats against the convoy, which is wrongly assumed to be SC.122. The 'Raubgraf' boats establish contact again in the afternoon of 16 Mar, notwithstanding a sharp detour ordered by Lt-Cdr Luther during the night 16–17 Mar, and attack in quick succession the inadequately escorted convoy HX.229. After *Mansfield* has driven off *U600* and *U615*, *U603* (Lt Bertelsmann) sinks one ship of 5214 tons; *U758* (Lt Cdr Manseck) sinks one ship of 6813 tons and torpedoes one more of 7176 tons which is later sunk by *U91* (Lt-Cdr Walkerling); *U435* (Lt-Cdr Strelow) torpedoes one ship of 7196 tons which is also later sunk by *U91*; *U91* herself, attacking simultaneously with *U435*, sinks another ship of 6366 tons; *U616* (Lt Koitschka) misses *Volunteer*; *U600* (Lt-Cdr Zurmühlen) hits three vessels with a FAT salvo, sinking the whale factory ship *Southern Princess* (12156 tons) (the other two, totalling 14839 tons, are later sunk by *U91*); and *U228* (Lt Christophersen) misses the returning *Mansfield*. During the night 16/17 Mar the 'Stürmer' boats, coming from the N, establish contact with convoy SC.122 (Commodore White), which comprises 51 ships escorted by EG.B5 (Cdr Boyle) with the destroyer *Havelock*, the frigate *Swale*, the corvettes *Pimpernel*, *Buttercup*, *Lavender* and *Saxifrage* and the rescue ship *Zamalek*, plus the US destroyer *Upshur* coming from ON.170 after having delivered the Iceland part of the convoy. The corvette *Godetia* comes up from astern after rescuing the crew of the A/S trawler *Campobello* which has foundered in the gale. *Havelock* and *Zamalek* are equipped with HF/DF and with their help the escort is able to drive off U-boats. Only *U338* (Lt-Cdr Kinzel) is able to fire: she sinks three ships of 17838 tons and torpedoes one more of 7134 tons which is later sunk by *U665* (Lt Haupt). When the Cdr U-boats learns that two convoys are located, the remaining 'Stürmer' and 'Dränger' boats are deployed.

By day on 17 Mar Liberator 'M' of No 86 Sqn RAF and then Liberator 'G' of No 120 Sqn RAF from Aldergrove come to SC.122 and, together with *Swale*, *Upshur*, *Godetia* and *Havelock*, drive off all contact-keeping boats. Only *U338* sinks one ship, of 4071 tons, in an underwater attack by day. In the case of HX.229, not all the escorts have closed up and only *Volunteer*, *Mansfield* and the newly arrived destroyer *Beverley* are with the convoy when at mid-day *U384* (Lt v Rosenberg-Gruszczynski) and *U631* (Lt

Krüger) attack almost simultaneously, each sinking one ship, of 7252 or 5158 tons respectively. In the afternoon Liberator 'J' of No 120 Sqn RAF forces down the contact-keeper *U600* and by the morning of 18 Mar the contact is lost, fortunately for the convoy since the latter is now escorted only by *Volunteer*, *Beverley*, *Anemone* and *Pennywort*. In the case of SC.122, the escorts drives off most of the many 'Stürmer' and 'Dränger' boats as they come up from both sides: only *U305* (Lt-Cdr Bahr) has any success, sinking two ships of 13045 tons after dark on 17 Mar.

The Admiralty has no ships to help the escort, especially of HX.229, in the area. Convoy ON.172 (17 ships with EG.C3, the latter consisting of the destroyer *Burnham* (RN) and the frigate *Jed* (RN) and the corvettes *Bittersweet*, *Eyebright*, *Mayflower* and *La Malbaie*) is too far off and also in an area where U-boats are expected. ON.173 (39 ships with EG.B7, consisting of the frigate *Tay*, the destroyer *Vidette* and the corvettes *Alisma*, *Loosestrife*, *Snowflake* and *Pink*) is routed N of the U-boat concentration and is too weak to risk detaching units. The southbound Gibraltar KMS.11 (62 ships with EG.C2, comprising the RN destroyers *Broadway* and *Sherwood*, the frigate *Lagan*, the RN corvettes *Primrose* and *Snowdrop*, the Canadian corvettes *Morden*, *Drumheller* and *Chambly* and the FFN sloop *Savorgnan da Brazza*) and KMF.11 (a fast convoy with nine transports accompanied by two escort groups made up of the sloops *Wren* and *Woodpecker*, the destroyers *Douglas*, *Eggesford*, *Badsworth*, *Whaddon* and *Goathland* and the Polish destroyer *Krakowiak*) have to pass the transit routes of the German U-boats and are also within range of German air attack, so that detachments are not possible. However, the Liberators of Nos 120 and 86 Sqns RAF are available and are sent out from Reykjavik and Aldergrove.

On 18 Mar, of 30 U-boats still operating, nine come close to HX.229 but are forced to submerge by the air escort, the Liberators 'L' and 'N' of No 120 Sqn RAF, and, in the evening, by Liberator 'M' from the same unit. Only *U221* (Lt Trojer), led to the scene by *U610*, is able to sink two ships, totalling 15484 tons, in an underwater attack. With SC.122, the escorting Liberators 'P' and 'E' (and later 'B', 'X' and 'L') of No 120 Sqn RAF prevent daylight attacks. In the evening of 18 Mar, and during that night, EG.B4's leader, the destroyer *Highlander* (Cdr Day), and the US destroyer *Babbitt* reach convoy HX.229, while the US Coast Guard cutter *Ingham* reaches SC.122. During the night 18–19 Mar the escorts drive off several U-boats but in an attack on HX.229 *U441* (Lt-Cdr K Hartmann) and *U608* (Lt-Cdr Struckmeier) fire salvos which miss *Highlander*; attacking SC.122, *U666* (Lt Stengel), after firing a salvo which misses, hits one ship of 5234 tons which is later sunk by *U333* (Lt Schwaff).

In the morning of 19 Mar the strong air escort drives off the U-boats from both convoys although a straggler of 5848 tons is sunk by *U527* (Lt-Cdr Uhlig) and *U523* (Lt-Cdr Pietsch). In the afternoon of 19 Mar and in the night 19–20 Mar the corvette *Abelia* and the destroyer *Vimy* join the escort of HX.229 and the last contact-keepers, *U631* with HX.229 and *U642* with SC.122, are driven off in the morning. The air escort, now including also Sunderlands of No 201 Sqn RAF and No 423 Sqn RCAF, Fortresses of No 220 Sqn RAF and Catalinas of VP-84, forces the boats to submerge and *U-384* is sunk by Fortress 'B' of No 220 Sqn RAF, *U666* is damaged by Fortress 'M' of No 220 Sqn RAF (Fg Off Knowles) and *U631* is attacked by Sunderland 'T' of No 201 Sqn RAF. The corvette *Sherbrooke* (RCN) joins HX.229.

The Cdr U-boats breaks off the operation early on 20 Mar. In all, 21 ships of 140842 tons have been sunk. The losses sustained by SC.121, HX.228, SC.122 and HX.229 amount to 20 per cent of the participating ships and lead to fears in Britain that the convoy system, the backbone of the Allied strategy against 'Fortress Europe', might have to be abandoned. However, the decision is taken to form Support Groups from destroyers of the Home Fleet: the 3rd EG with *Offa*, *Obedient*, *Oribi*, *Orwell* and *Onslaught* and the 4th EG with *Inglefield*, *Icarus*, *Eclipse* and *Fury*; in addition there is the US TU.24.4.1 with the carrier *Bogue* and the destroyers *Belknap*, *Osmond-Ingram* and *George E Badger*. The 1st, 2nd and 5th EGs are also to be formed: they will be used to support convoys in danger and force them through extended U-boat lines which cannot be circumvented.

15 Mar   South West Pacific
Formation of the 7th US Fleet (Adm Carpender): the former TF.44 becomes TF.74, comprising the cruisers *Australia*, *Hobart* and *Phoenix* and Desron 4 consisting of *Selfridge*, *Mugford*, *Patterson*, *Henley*, *Helm*, *Bagley* and *Ralph Talbot*. In Apr *Phoenix* is relieved; likewise in May Desron 4 is relieved by Desron 5 consisting of *Perkins*, *Conyngham*, *Mahan*, *Flusser*, *Drayton*, *Smith* and *Lamson* and the Australian *Arunta* and *Warramunga*. In June 1943 the destroyers, with the exception of the last three, join TF.76 (Amphibious Force).

15 Mar–2 Apr   Mediterranean
On 15 Mar *U380* (Lt-Cdr Röther) sinks one ship of 7178 tons from an MKS convoy off the Algerian coast. On 16 Mar *U77* (Lt Hartmann) sinks another ship of 5222 tons and torpedoes one of 5229 tons. On 23 Mar torpedo aircraft from KG 26 attack convoy KMF.11 N of Cape Ténès and sink the British troop transport *Windsor Castle* (19141 tons). From 25 to 27 Mar *U431*, *U77*, *U755* and *U596* attack, sometimes repeatedly, west- and eastbound convoys off the Algerian coast, but only *U431* (Lt Schöneboom) is able to sink one ship of 6415 tons. On 27 Mar torpedo aircraft from KG 26 sink one transport of 9545 tons NW of Philippeville. *U77* is lost on 28 Mar to Hudsons 'L' and 'V' of No 48 Sqn RAF and 'L' of No 233 Sqn RAF. On 30 Mar *U596* (Lt-Cdr Jahn) attacks the convoy ET.16 and sinks two ships of 16684 tons. *U755* (Lt-Cdr Göing) sinks two independents of 2075 tons but *U561* and *U375* have no success.

16 Mar   Mediterranean
The Italian torpedo boat *Medici* is sunk during a USAAF air raid on Catania.

16 Mar–14 Apr   Arctic
In Soviet operations against German supply traffic on the Norwegian polar coast, the submarine *M-104* (Lt-Cdr Lukyanov) torpedoes in Varangerfjord the steamer *Johannisberger* (4533 tons), which is beached. *K-3* (Capt 3rd Class Malofeyev), after two abortive attacks off Nordkyn against convoys with *V5902* and *V5907* on 17 and 21 Mar, is sunk by depth charges from the submarine-chaser group comprising *UJ1102*, *UJ1106* and *UJ1111*. *M-174* is badly damaged on 24 Mar on a mine in a flanking barrage. On 28–29 Mar *S-102*, *S-55* and *S-101* attack successively off Laksfjord, Tanafjord and Korsfjord respectively a German eastern convoy with *V6109* and a western convoy with *M322*, but only *S-55* (Lt-Cdr Sushkin) sinks the steamer *Ajax* (2297 tons) out of the nine steamers and the nine escorts. Operations by the destroyers *Baku*, *Grozny*, and *Gromki* on 28 and 31 Mar meet with no success. From the beginning to the middle of Apr *K-21* operates in Lopphavet, *S-56* off Tanafjord and *M-171* off Varangerfjord. Mines are laid several times in Varangerfjord by MO-IVs and torpedo-cutters, and the mine-laying submarines *L-20* and *L-22* lay barrages off the Norwegian polar coast.

17–31 Mar   Black Sea
The German U-boats *U19* (Lt Gaude) and *U24* (Lt-Cdr Petersen) operate against Soviet supply traffic on the Caucasian coast near Sukhumi and Gagry. *U19* damages one

freighter and *U24* sinks the tanker *Sovietskaya Neft* (8228 tons) in Gagry Bay on 31 Mar. In sorties by the 1st MTB Flotilla (Cdr Christiansen) and the Italian IV MAS Flotilla as far as Tuapse and off the Myschako bridgehead, *S26* and *S47* torpedo a medium-sized tanker on 17 Mar which is taken in tow to Tuapse and *S28* torpedoes a lighter wreck on 18 Mar. During the night 30–31 Mar *S72*, *S28*, *S47* and *S102* lay a mine barrage off Myschako. On 25 Mar the Soviet patrol cutter *SKA-065* (Lt Sivenko) beats off several attacks by German aircraft on a convoy and is damaged by aircraft fire.

18–23 Mar   Air War/Germany
On 18 Mar 97 B-17s and B-24s of the 8th AF attack the dockyards in Bremen-Vegesack. On 22 Mar 87 US bombers attack Wilhelmshaven; the tanker *Eurosee* (10327 tons) sinks.

18 Mar–16 June   South Pacific
In operations off the Australian East Coast, the Japanese submarine *I-26* (Cdr* Yokota) sinks two ships of 6857 tons, *I-177* (Lt-Cdr Nakagawa) sinks one ship of 8724 tons from a convoy (escorted, *inter alia*, by the Australian minesweeper *Colac*) and the hospital ship *Centaur* (3222 tons), *I-178* (Cdr Utsuki) sinks one ship of 7176 tons, *I-180* (Cdr Kusaka) sinks two ships of 4376 tons and damages two more of 7713 tons and *I-174* (Lt-Cdr Nanbu), after several misses, sinks one ship of 5551 tons from a convoy and torpedoes *LST469*. In operations off Samoa, Fiji and Nouméa, *I-25* (Cdr* M Tagami) sinks one tanker of 10763 tons, *I-19* (Lt-Cdr Kinashi) sinks two ships of 14357 tons and torpedoes one of 7181 tons and *I-17* (Lt-Cdr Harada) sinks one tanker of 10169 tons with the MTBs *PT165* and *PT173* on board. *I-32* is bombed on 16 Apr as she sets out for Samoa. *I-178* is sunk by *SC699* off Espiritu Santo on 29 May.

19 Mar   English Channel
The German auxiliary minesweeper *M3408* is lost by grounding off the Hook of Holland.

19 Mar   Baltic
The German submarine *U5* is sunk W of Pillau in a diving accident.

19 Mar   Mediterranean
The Italian destroyer *Alpino* is burnt out and sunk during an RAF air raid on La Spezia. The wreck is later transferred to Genoa.

21–30 Mar   North Atlantic
From 21 Mar the 'Seeteufel' group, consisting of *U306*, *U592*, *U188*, *U415*, *U663*, *U572*, *U564* and *U260*, is formed S of Iceland to operate against convoy ONS.1 (new series following the former ONS.171), located by the B-Service. Over the next few days *U610*, *U131*, *U526*, *U523*, *U632*, *U706*

and *U91* join the group. However, the orders are again decoded by Bletchley Park after the break of 8–19 Mar (qv).

On 24 Mar *U306* sights escorts from ONS.1—EG.B6 (Lt-Cdr Heathcote) with the destroyers *Fame* and *Viscount* and the corvettes *Vervain*, *Kingcup*, *Acanthus* (RNoN) and *Eglantine* (RNoN)—to the N of the 'Seeteufel' group, but the four northerly boats and *U168*, proceeding from the Denmark Strait, do not come up.

From 25 Mar the 'Seewolf' group, comprising *U305*, *U591*, *U631*, *U86*, *U666*, *U618*, *U336*, *U333*, *U530*, *U527*, *U440*, *U373*, *U441*, *U590*, *U641*, *U642*, *U257*, *U84* and *U615*, is formed S of 'Seeteufel' to operate against SC.123 located by German intelligence. On the way to these formations *U469* and *U169* are sunk, on 25 and 27 Mar respectively, by Fortress 'L' of No 206 Sqn RAF, in the first case while flying escort for convoy RU.67.

In the afternoon of 26 Mar *U564* (Lt Fiedler) sights convoy SC.123—EG.B2 (Cdr MacIntyre) with the sloop *Whimbrel*, the destroyers *Vanessa* and *Whitehall* and the corvettes *Gentian*, *Clematis*, *Heather* and *Sweetbriar*—and wrongly reports that it is proceeding westwards. Of the 'Seeteufel' group directed to it, *U663* and *U415* briefly establish contact with the convoy whose escort group is reinforced by the 6th SG (Capt Short) with the US escort carrier *Bogue* and the destroyers *Belknap* and *George E Badger*. Carrier aircraft force the boats to submerge.

On 27 Mar *U305* (Lt-Cdr Bahr), the northernmost boat, sights the next convoy re-routed to the N, HX.230, which comprises 45 ships and EG.B1 (Cdr Bayldon) with the destroyers *Hurricane*, *Watchman* and *Rockingham*, the frigate *Kale* and the corvettes *Dahlia*, *Meadowsweet*, *Wallflower* and *Monkshood*, reinforced by the 3rd SG (Capt McCoy) with the destroyers *Offa*, *Obedient*, *Oribi*, *Orwell*, *Onslaught* and *Icarus*, making a total of 14 vessels. Of the 22 'Seewolf' and 'Seeteufel' boats deployed, only *U305*, *U631*, *U591*, *U415* and *U610* (Lt-Cdr Frhr v Freyberg) approach the convoy for a time, the last sinking one ship of 7176 tons. Impeded by a strong south-westerly gale and driven off by the strong air escort which makes an appearance on 29 Mar, the boats are unable to register any successes. On 30 Mar *U631* is the last boat to lose contact and the operation is broken off.

While the 'Seewolf' and 'Seeteufel' groups try to get at HX.230, the following SC.124, escorted by EG.C3 with the destroyer *Burnham* (RN), the corvettes *La Malbaie*, *Eyebright*, *Bittersweet* and *Mayflower* and

the attached frigate *Jed* (RN), evades the U-boats, and ON.174, escorted by EG.B3 with the destroyers *Escapade* and *Garland* (Polish) and the corvettes *Narcissus*, *Roselys* (FFN) and *Renoncule* (FFN), is routed clear.

21 Mar–22 Apr East Mediterranean
Italian defensive mine barrages are laid out: on 21, 22 and 23 Mar and 6 Apr four barrages with 191 mines off Corsica by the minelayer *Pelagosa*; on 11 Apr one barrage of 50 mines off Naples by the destroyer *Legionario*; and on 22 Apr one barrage of 122 mines off SW Sardinia by the destroyer *Vivaldi* and the German minelayers *Brandenburg* and *Pommern*.

22 Mar Mediterranean
The British gunboat *Aphis* bombards Gabes in support of the 8th Army.

22 Mar Bay of Biscay
The returning *U665* is sunk by Wellington 'G, of No 172 Sqn with the use of Leigh Light.

22–24 Mar Norway
A German force with the battleship *Tirpitz*, the battlecruiser *Scharnhorst*, the pocket-battleship *Lützow*, the destroyers *Paul Jacobi*, *Karl Galster*, *Erich Steinbrinck*, *Theodor Riedel*, *Z28* and *Z31* and the torpedo boats *T20* and *T21*, is transferred from Narvik to Altafjord.

22 Mar–9 Apr Central Atlantic
After refuelling from returning boats, *U67*, *U159*, *U167*, *U513*, *U515*, *U123* and *U172* form the 'Seeräuber' group in the area of the Canaries to operate against the coastal convoy RS.3 (nine steamers and tugs and two corvettes) located by the B-Service. It is found on 27 Mar, and on 28 Mar *U167* (Cdr Sturm), *U159* (Lt-Cdr Witte) and *U172* (Lt-Cdr Emmermann) each sink one ship, of 4621 tons, 5449 tons and 5319 tons respectively. Strong air support results in a loss of contact on 29 Mar. From 30 Mar the boats set out for individual operations in the area of Freetown, but they have no further success. *U167* is so badly damaged on 6 Apr by Hudsons 'L' and 'W' of No 233 Sqn RAF that she has to be abandoned after the crew has been taken off. The Italian submarine *Finzi* (Lt-Cdr Rossetto) sinks two independents of 9264 tons.

23 Mar Mediterranean
The Italian submarine *Delfino* sinks off Taranto following a collision.

23 Mar–15 May Baltic
Units of the Officer Commanding Minesweepers East (Rear-Adm Böhmer) and of the Finnish Fleet (Rear-Adm Rahola) lay mine and net barrages in the Gulf of Finland. From 24 Mar until the middle

of Apr the German minelayers *Kaiser* and *Roland* and 18–24 ferry barges of the 24th Landing Flotilla lay the barrages 'Nashorn I–X' containing 7293 mines between Naissaar and Porkkala and then until 9 May the naval ferry barges of the 24th Landing Flotilla lay the barrages 'Seeigel I–V' containing 1965 mines from Suursaari to the N of Narva Bay. They are guarded by protective and explosive float barrages on the eastern side. From 22 to 28 Apr the Finnish minelayer *Ruotsinsalmi* and VMV patrol boats lay the barrages 'Rukajärvi U, R and S' containing 686 mines and 750 barrage protection floats N of Suursaari. From 28 Mar to 15 May the German Net Barrage Force (Cdr Becker) lays a double submarine net ('Walross') W of 'Nashorn'. From 24 Apr German KM boats carry out offensive mining operations on the Leningrad Sea Canal ('Brutmaschine'); and from the beginning of May Finnish motor torpedo boats and German KM boats do the same in Kronstadt Bay ('Tiger') and off Lavansaari ('Salpa'). Luftflotte 1, using 66 aircraft, drops ground mines in Kronstadt Bay on 21–22 Apr. On 30 Apr the outbound Soviet submarine *Shch-323* is lost on the 'Brutmaschine' barrage (but is later raised).

24 Mar Mediterranean
The German motor minesweeper *R10* is sunk as a result of an explosion on board the SS *Umbrino* during an air raid on Ferryville.

26 Mar Arctic
The outgoing *U339* is badly damaged by Catalina 'M' of No 190 Sqn RAF.

26 Mar Pacific
Battle of the Komandorski Islands—the one daylight battle in the old style in the Pacific War. A US striking force (Rear-Adm McMorris), consisting of the heavy cruiser *Salt Lake City*, the light cruiser *Richmond* and the destroyers *Bailey*, *Coghlan*, *Dale* and *Monaghan*, is deployed against a strongly escorted Japanese convoy for Attu. The superior Japanese force consists of the heavy cruisers *Nachi* (Vice-Adm Hosogaya) and *Maya*, the light cruisers *Abukuma* (Rear-Adm Mori) and *Tama*, the destroyers *Hatsushimo*, *Ikazuchi*, *Inazuma* and *Wakaba* and the transports *Asaka Maru* (7399 tons) and *Sakito Maru* (7126 tons). In a 3½hr engagement, *Nachi*, *Salt Lake City* and *Bailey* are damaged. Then Hosogaya breaks off the engagement in expectation of American bombers after the Japanese ships have expended most of their shells.

27 Mar Great Britain
The British escort carrier *Dasher* is destroyed on the River Clyde as a result of a petrol explosion and fire.

27–30 Mar   North Atlantic
German air reconnaissance locates convoy SL.126, with 37 ships and six escorts (EG.39?), W of the Bay of Biscay. The outbound U-boats *U267*, *U571*, *U181*, *U404* and *U662* are deployed against it. *U404* establishes contact on 28 Mar and *U662* and *U404* on 29 Mar. During the night 29–30 Mar *U404* (Lt-Cdr v Bülow) in two attacks sinks two ships of 15822 tons; *U662* (Lt-Cdr H E Müller) sinks two ships of 13011 tons and torpedoes one of 7174 tons. After losing contact, the boats continue their outward journey.

27 Mar–28 Apr   Mediterranean
Supply transports for the German and Italian armies in Tunisia with freighters escorted by the Italian destroyers *Lubiana*, *Riboty*, *Lampo* and *Mitragliere*, the torpedo boats *Fortunale*, *Tifone*, *Orione*, *Ardimentoso*, *Groppo*, *Antares*, *Sagittario*, *Cigno*, *Cassiopea*, *Clio*, *Perseo*, *Pallade*, *Libra*, *Aretusa*, *Climene*, *Cosenz*, *Dezza* and *Bassini*, the corvettes *Cicogna*, *Driade*, *Gabbiano* and *Euterpe* and the German submarine-chasers *UJ2202*, *UJ2207*, *UJ2205*, *UJ2208*, *UJ2203*, *UJ2210* and *UJ2204* and also with Italian and German naval ferry barges, partly escorted by the 3rd German MTB Flotilla. Troop transports in three operations from 16 to 18 Apr, 22 to 24 Apr and 25 to 28 Apr with the destroyers *Pigafetta* and *Pancaldo* and also the German destroyer *Hermes*. In the month of Apr a total of 2800 troops, 18690 tons of supplies, 26 guns, 46 tanks, 268 vehicles and 13 motor cycles are brought to Tunisia.
Against them there are British mining operations with the submarine *Rorqual* (Lt-Cdr Napier) on 22 Mar and 7, 21 and 30 Apr and the fast minelayer *Abdiel* on 5 and 7 Apr. In addition, there are air mining operations resulting in the sinking of one Italian ship of 1227 tons and the German *KT13*. Torpedo aircraft from Malta sink two ships of 6017 tons, bombers sink four ships of 21211 tons and the torpedo boat *Aretusa* is damaged. The destroyer *Lubiana* and three ships are lost when they run on shoals. On 27 Mar the destroyers HMS *Laforey* and the Polish *Blyskawica* shell Cape Serrat to simulate a landing.
On 1 Apr, of three steamers in a convoy escorted by the torpedo boats *Cigno*, *Cassiopea*, *Clio* and *Cosenz*, the corvette *Cicogna* and the German submarine-chasers *UJ2203*, *UJ2210* and *UJ2207*, one steamer is sunk by aerial torpedo and the two others, totalling 6912 tons, by the British *MTB266* and *MTB315*.
On 16 Apr the British destroyers *Pakenham* (Capt Stevens) and *Paladin* intercept an

Italian convoy SW of Marsala but it escapes with the torpedo boats *Tifone* and *Climene*, while the torpedo boats *Cigno* and *Cassiopea* involve the destroyers in an engagement in which *Cigno* sinks, but not before *Pakenham* is hit so severely that she has to be abandoned and scuttled by *Paladin*. *Cassiopea* is taken in tow by *Climene*.

On 28 Apr the British *MTB633*, *MTB637* and *MTB639* have no success against a convoy. The last is sunk by the escorting torpedo boat *Sagittario*. During the night 28–29 Apr the British destroyers *Laforey* (Capt Hutton) and *Tartar* attack German motor torpedo boats near Marettimo.

On the route Sicily–Tunis/Bizerta and in the Tyrrhenian Sea, the British submarine *Unison* (Lt Daniell) sinks two ships of 8240 tons, *Sahib* (Lt Bromage) sinks three ships of 4286 tons and five sailing ships, *Unseen* (Lt Crawford) torpedoes two ships, *Tribune* torpedoes one ship, *Unrivalled* (Lt Sprice) sinks two ships of 2446 tons, *Torbay* (Lt Clutterbuck) sinks one ship of 3681 tons, *Unshaken* (Lt Whitton) sinks one ship of 1227 tons, *Safari* (Cdr Bryant) sinks three ships of 7411 tons, *Unbroken* (Lt Mars) sinks two ships of 5017 tons and torpedoes one other, *Sibyl* (Lt Turner) sinks one ship of 2940 tons, *Trident* (Lt Newstead) sinks one ship of 520 tons, *Unruly* (Lt Fyfe) sinks one ship of 1256 tons, *Ultor* (Lt Hunt) sinks one ship of 2151 tons, *Taurus* (Lt-Cdr Wingfield) and *Saracen* (Lt Lumby) sink two ships of 13048 tons and *Sickle* (Lt Drummond) torpedoes one ship. *Unrivalled* also sinks the German submarine-chasers *UJ2201* and *UJ2202* in the Bay of Picarenzi on 29 Mar and *Unshaken* the torpedo boat *Climene* on 28 Apr. On 16 Apr the corvette *Gabbiano* (Cdr Ceccacci) sinks the submarine *Regent*; on 21 Apr the German destroyer *Hermes* (Cdr* Rechel) sinks the submarine *Splendid* near Capri; and on 24 Apr *Sahib* is attacked by *Giabbiano*, *Euterpe* and *Climene* near the Lipari Islands and is sunk by a Ju 88 of II/LG 1.

28 Mar   Mediterranean
The British transport *Breconshire* is sunk during an air attack on Malta.

28–29 Mar   North Sea
Seven boats of the 2nd MTB Flotilla (Cdr Feldt) unsuccessfully attack the British convoy FS.1074 off Smith's Knoll and are driven off by *MGB321* and *MGB333* and the destroyers *Blencathra* and *Windsor*. After a collision *S29* has to be abandoned.

28–29 Mar   Air War/Netherlands
RAF Bomber Command flies two daylight raids with Venturas against Rotterdam—on

28 Mar (24 aircraft, six ships hit) and 29 Mar (61 aircraft, damage caused in the city). The German transport *Ceuta* (2719 tons) is sunk.

28 Mar–11 Apr   Bay of Biscay
The Italian blockade-runner *Himalaya* (Capt Martinoli) leaves Bordeaux for the Far East, escorted by the German torpedo boats *T23*, *Falke*, *T2*, *T12* and *T18* (with distant cover provided by the destroyers *Z23*, *Z24*, *Z32* and *Z37*) from Royan and by *T19*, *T5*, *T9* and *Kondor* from Brest. When located by British air reconnaissance—forewarned by 'Ultra'—*Himalaya* and its escorts return on 30 Mar. On 30 Mar *Z23*, *Z24*, *Z32* and *Z37* depart again from the Gironde to meet the Italian blockade-runner *Pietro Orseolo* (Capt Tarchioni) coming in from the Far East 140 miles off Vigo. Attacks by Beaufort and 'Torbeau' aircraft of RAF Coastal Command are beaten off. The US submarine *Shad* (Lt-Cdr MacGregor) obtains one torpedo hit on *Orseolo*, which is, however, brought into the Gironde on 2 Apr. On 9–10 Apr a new attempt to break out by *Himalaya*, escorted by *Kondor*, *T2*, *T5*, *T22* and *T23* and covered by *Z23*, *Z24*, *Z32* and *Z37*, fails when the force is located by British air reconnaissance, again forewarned by 'Ultra'. Heavy attacks by Beaufort and 'Torbeau' aircraft are beaten off, but *Z24* has five dead and 31 wounded by cannon fire. Five aircraft are shot down by the destroyers. On 11 Apr the ships return to the Gironde.

On 10 Apr, returning from the Mediterranean, the British fast minelayer *Adventure* (Capt Bowes-Lyon) encounters, 275 nautical miles W of Vigo, the German blockade-runner *Irene/Silvaplana* (4793 tons, Capt Wendt) coming back from Eastern Asia. The ship scuttles herself.

29 Mar–1 Apr   Norway
The German minelayer *Skagerrak* lays two mine barrages in the Tromsö area.

30 Mar   Baltic
The German submarine *U416* is sunk by a mine laid by the Soviet submarine *L-3* in 1942. The boat is raised on 8 Apr and recommissioned on 4 Oct 1943.

30 Mar–2 Apr   North Atlantic/Norway
The German blockade-runner *Regensburg* (8086 tons), coming from the Far East, is intercepted by the British cruiser *Glasgow* sent to the Denmark Strait following 'Ultra' interceptions and scuttles herself; *Glasgow* rescues six survivors. On 31 Mar the

German destroyers *Paul Jacobi*, *Theodor Riedel* and *Karl Galster* depart from Altafjord to escort *Regensburg* back from the Greenland Sea but return with heavy sea damage after waiting in vain.

1 Apr   North Sea
The German patrol trawler *V1241* is sunk off Terschelling by British MTBs.

1–30 Apr   Pacific
During US submarine operations throughout Apr there are 41 'Ultra' intercepts of which 16 lead to sightings but only three to attacks, in which just one ship is damaged. In the Aleutians area, *S32* has misses. In Japanese waters, *Pickerel* (Lt-Cdr Alston) sinks two ships of 9305 tons but is herself sunk by Japanese A/S forces on 3 Apr N of Honshu, *Flying Fish* (Lt-Cdr Donaho) sinks four ships of 8917 tons and *Scorpion* (Lt-Cdr Wylie) lays a minefield at Inubo Seki on which one ship of 3295 tons is damaged, sinks three ships of 8445 tons by torpedo and sinks two sailing vessels by gunfire.

In Chinese waters, *Runner* (Lt-Cdr Burland) lays mines off Hong Kong and damages one ship of 9625 tons by torpedo, *Snook* (Lt-Cdr Triebel) lays mines off Shanghai on which two ships totalling 5940 tons sink and in addition sinks four ships of 10083 tons by torpedo and *Stingray* (Lt-Cdr Earle) lays a minefield off Wenchow, sinks by torpedo one ship of 8156 tons and damages one other of 6385 tons.

In the Central Pacific, *Haddock* (Lt-Cdr Davenport) sinks two ships of 9305 tons, including *Toyo Maru No 2* (with 'Ultra' assistance), *Porpoise* (Lt-Cdr Bennett) sinks one ship of 2023 tons, *Drum* (Lt-Cdr McMahon) sinks two ships of 10189 tons, *Pike* (Lt-Cdr McGregor) damages one ship of 3802 tons and *Seawolf* (Lt-Cdr Gross) sinks the patrol boat *P39/Tade* on 23 Apr and two ships of 4964 tons. *Drum*, *Pollack* and *Skipjack* conduct reconnaissance missions and *Tarpon* acts as marker boat for a carrier strike for the first time.

In the South Pacific, *Gato* lands coastwatchers in the Solomons. In the South West Pacific, *Trout* (Lt-Cdr Ramage) lays a minefield off Borneo, on which one ship of 5236 tons is damaged, and sinks two sailing vessels, *Gudgeon* (Lt-Cdr Port) sinks two ships of 23387 tons and conducts a guerrilla mission and *Grenadier* is sunk on 21 Apr by a Japanese A/S force off Penang.

2–3 Apr   Air War/France
RAF Bomber Command flies the last raids against St-Nazaire (55 aircraft) and Lorient (47). The city is now largely deserted by its civilian population, but no damage is inflicted on the U-boat pens.

2–23 Apr   Air War/Western Europe
RAF Bomber Command mine offensive. In 12 nights, 293 sorties, with the main effort directed against Biscay and Brittany ports and the Frisian coast, are flown; eight aircraft are lost.

On 6 Apr the auxiliary minesweeper *M4041* sinks after striking a mine in Le Verdon Roads. On 16 Apr *U526* sinks: this is probably the only loss to British mines in the Bay of Biscay in the entire period 1943–44, despite the German minesweeping forces having had to escort more than 2500 U-boats during that time. Units of the German Cdr Naval Defence Forces West (Vice-Adm Ruge; acting in his absence, Capt Hagen) have protected the U-boats against mines with minimal losses to themselves from 1940 with the 4th Escort Div (Capt Lautenschlager, with the 2nd, 6th, 24th and 40th MS Flotillas, the 8th, 10th, 26th, 28th, 42nd and 44th MS Flotillas, the 4th and 6th PB Flotillas and the 2nd Sperrbrecher Flotilla) and the 3rd Escort Div (Capt Breuning, with the 2nd and 7th PB Flotillas, the 6th Mine Detonating Flotilla and the 14th SC Flotilla).

On 26 Apr, between Dunkirk and Calais, the motor minesweeper *R114* is damaged by a mine and sinks while under tow.

2 Apr–24 May   Western Atlantic
After meeting the returning blockade-runners *Regensburg*, *Pietro Orseolo* and *Irene* for the handover of radar search receiver equipment W of the Azores (23 Mar to 6 Apr), *U161* (Lt-Cdr Achilles) and *U174* proceed to the American East Coast, but only *U161* sinks one sailing ship of 255 tons. On 25 Apr both try to approach a convoy off Halifax but *U174* is sunk by a Ventura from VP-125.

In the area of the Greater Antilles, *U176* (Lt-Cdr Dierksen) sinks two ships of 4232 tons from a convoy on 13 May and escapes from the search made by the DE *Brennan*, eight submarine-chasers and a blimp but is bombed on 15 May by an aircraft from VP-62 and sunk by the Cuban submarine-chaser *CS13*. *U129* (Cdr Witt) sinks three ships of 26950 tons but is driven off from an NG convoy on 21 Apr by the US destroyer *Swanson*.

2 Apr–15 June   Central Atlantic
From a wave of Type IX boats proceeding to the Freetown area, *U124* (Lt-Cdr J Mohr) meets convoy OS.45 on 2 Apr and, in a surprise attack, sinks two ships of 9547 tons. But she is herself sunk by ships of the 37th EG (the corvette *Stonecrop* and the sloop *Black Swan*). *U455* (Lt-Cdr Scheibe) and

U117 (Cdr Neumann) lay mine barrages off Casablanca on 10 and 11 Apr on which one ship of 3777 tons sinks and two ships of 14269 tons are damaged. The remaining boats arrive in the Freetown area during the first ten days of Apr and by the middle of May: *U515* (Lt-Cdr Henke) has sunk two ships of 6901 tons, *U123* (Lt v Schröter) the British submarine *P615* and four ships of 24200 tons and *U105* (Lt-Cdr Nissen) one ship of 4669 tons; *U126* has, at first, no success. On 30 Apr *U515* encounters the convoy TS.37 (18 ships), escorted by one corvette and three A/S trawlers, and, in three approaches, sinks by 1 May seven ships of 43255 tons from it before a support group of three destroyers comes up. After being replenished from *U460*, *U515*, *U126* and *U105* continue the operation. Several convoys are sighted but only *U126* (Lt Kietz) torpedoes two ships of 13374 tons, of which one Liberty Ship becomes a total loss. On 2 June *U105* is sunk by the French Potez flying boat *Antarès* from Dakar. Off Dakar, *U214* (Lt Count v Treuberg) lays a mine barrage on which one ship of 6507 tons is damaged.

3 Apr   Air War/France
Twelve Venturas of RAF Bomber Command fly an anti-shipping strike against Brest.

3–7 Apr   North Atlantic
The 'Löwenherz' group is formed SE of Greenland from the U-boats *U191*, *U168*, *U630*, *U635*, *U706*, *U260*, *U564*, *U592*, *U572*, *U563*, *U594*, *U584* and *U632*, coming from HX.230 and having been replenished from *U463*. On 4 Apr the returning *U530* (Lt-Cdr K Lange) sights convoy HX.231 just W of the patrol line. It consists of 61 ships with EG.B7 (Cdr Gretton) comprising the frigate *Tay*, the destroyer *Vidette* and the corvettes *Alisma*, *Pink*, *Snowflake* and *Loosestrife*. Apart from 'Löwenherz', *U229* and *U532*, which are stationed in the area, are also deployed. *U530* brings up five boats before dusk and two more during the night, when also *U635* (Lt Eckelmann) and *U630* (Lt Wickler) each sink one ship of 5529 tons and 9365 tons respectively, and *U229* (Lt Schetelig) sinks one straggler of 3406 tons. *U572*, in trying to attack, is rammed and damaged. On 5 Apr a strong air escort is provided by Liberators of No 86 Sqn RAF which forces the contact-keeper *U260* to submerge. *U563* (Lt-Cdr G v Hartmann) torpedoes one straggler of 9005 tons, which *U530* later sinks. In the afternoon *U706* (Lt-Cdr v Zitzewitz) attacks the convoy and sinks one ship of 7124 tons. During the night 5–6

Apr *U632* (Lt-Cdr Karpf) sinks at first one straggler of 7065 tons and then, in an attack on the convoy, after missing the *Alisma*, is sunk by the *Tay*. On 6 Apr *U635* is sunk by Liberator 'R' of No 86 Sqn RAF and *U594* is damaged by Liberator 'E' of No 120 Sqn RAF. Attacks by *U270* and *U134* fail. Also on 6 Apr, the 4th SG, comprising the destroyers *Inglefield*, *Fury*, *Eclipse* and *Icarus*, reaches the convoy and, together with the air escort, drives off the contact-keeping U-boats *U270*, *U229*, *U564*, *U134* and *U563* and, on the morning of 7 Apr, *U260*.

Meanwhile convoy ON.175 (EG.A3, with the US Coast Guard cutter *Spencer*, the US destroyer *Greer*, the RN corvette *Dianthus* and the RCN corvettes *Rosthern*, *Trillium* and *Dauphin*) passes by unobserved.

4 Apr   Air War/Netherlands
Twenty-four Venturas of RAF Bomber Command attack a shipyard at Rotterdam.

4–5 Apr   Air War/Germany
RAF Bomber Command raids Kiel with 577 aircraft. Decoy fires draw off the bombing and twelve aircraft are lost. The same night, 48 German bombers lay mines in the Thames estuary.

5 Apr   Air War/France
Twelve RAF Bomber Command Venturas attack a tanker in Brest harbour.

5 Apr   South Pacific
The Japanese submarine *Ro-34* is sunk 40 nautical miles off Russell Island by the US destroyers *O'Bannon* and *Strong*.

5 Apr–20 Aug   South Atlantic/ Indian Ocean
From 5 to 20 Apr the German *U180* (Cdr Musenberg) operates off South Africa and sinks one ship of 8132 tons. On 26 Apr, S of Mauritius, she transfers the Indian national-ist leader Subhas Chandra Bose to the Japanese submarine *I-29* (Cdr* Izu), which brings him to Penang. On the return journey, *U180* sinks one more ship of 5166 tons. The Italian submarine *Da Vinci* (Lt-Cdr Gazzana-Priaroggia), which in the South Atlantic, on her way out, has sunk the British troop transport *Empress of Canada* (21517 tons) and one other ship, sinks four ships off South Africa in Apr. After total sinkings of 58973 tons, she is herself sunk on the return journey near Cape Finisterre on 24 May by the British frigate *Ness* and the destroyer *Active* which are escorting convoy WS.30/KMF.15 at the time. From 26 Apr a wave of seven German Type IXD U-boats arrives off South Africa and operates there until 10 June. *U198* sinks one ship on 17 May from the convoy LMD.17 (six steamers, two A/S trawlers) and *U177* and *U178* sink two ships and one ship respect-

ively on 28 May and 1 June from CD.20 (escort: four A/S trawlers). After being replenished from their tanker *Charlotte Sch-liemann* from 21 to 26 June, the boats con-tinue their operations off Mauritius, East Africa and South Africa. *U198* sinks one ship on 1 Aug from the convoy BC.2 (four steamers, the corvettes *Freesia* and *Rockrose* and three trawlers) and *U196* one ship on 2 Aug from CB.21. *U177* repeatedly deploys the 'Bachstelze' towed helicopter. In all, the following results are achieved up to 20 Aug: *U181* (Cdr Lüth) sinks ten ships of 45332 tons, *U198* (Capt W Hartmann) sinks seven ships of 36778 tons, *U196* (Lt-Cdr Kentrat) sinks two of 12285 tons, *U177* (Lt-Cdr Gysae) sinks six of 38917 tons, *U178* (Cdr Dommes) sinks six of 32683 tons, *U195* (Lt-Cdr Buchholz) sinks two of 14391 tons and torpedoes one of 6797 tons and *U197* (Lt-Cdr Bartels) sinks three of 21267 tons and torpedoes one of 7181 tons. As a result of radio traffic located by HF/DF, Catalina flying boats 'C' of No 259 Sqn and 'N' of No 265 Sqn RAF are deployed to sink *U197* on 20 Aug. At the end of June and at the beginning of July *U511* (Lt-Cdr Schnee-wind, with the Japanese Vice-Adm Nomura on board) passes through the Indian Ocean on her way to Japan and sinks two ships of 14370 tons. *U178* goes to Penang in Aug; the remainder return to Bordeaux.
Operating from the Japanese naval base at Penang, the Japanese submarine *I-27* (Lt-Cdr Fukumura) sinks four ships of 18175 tons in the Gulf of Oman in May and June and torpedoes on 5 July one ship of 6797 tons from the convoy PA.44; in June and July *I-29* (Cdr* Izu) sinks one ship of 5643 tons in the Gulf of Aden and *I-37* (Cdr Otani) two of 15254 tons off East Africa. *I-8* (Capt Uchino), after being replenished from *I-10* on 4 July, proceeds to France. *I-10* (Capt Tonozuka) sinks one ship of 7634 tons S of Chagos.

6 Apr   Mediterranean
US bombers sink the German freighter *San Diego* (6013 tons) off Bizerta and damage the Italian transport *Rovereto* (8564 tons) so badly that she has to be beached. The German A/S trawler *UJ2202* is sunk by an airborne torpedo off Trapani.

7 Apr   Arctic
The British submarine *Tuna* sinks *U644* near Jan Mayen.

7–12 Apr   North Atlantic
On 7 Apr the 'Adler' group is formed S of Greenland with *U188*, *U257*, *U84*, *U615*, *U267*, *U404*, *U662*, *U571*, *U613* and, later, *U71*. On the same day the expected convoy SC.125 passes with EG.B6 (the destroyers *Fame* and *Viscount*, the corvettes *Vervain*

and *Kingcup* and the Norwegian corvettes *Potentilla*, *Eglantine*, *Rose* and *Acanthus*) to the W of the patrol line. *U257* sights the escort vessels but *U188*, *U257* and *U84* fail to come up and a patrol line further to the N on 8 Apr has no success. The group is, therefore, moved to the S to operate against the expected HX.232 (EG.B3). *U404* (Lt-Cdr v Bülow) reports in the afternoon of 10 Apr the convoy ON.176 (46 ships, EG.B4 with the destroyers *Highlander*, *Beverley* and *Vimy* and the corvettes *Pennywort*, *Asphodel*, *Anemone*, *Abelia* and *Clover*). Of the 'Adler' group boats deployed, *U188* (Lt-Cdr Lüdden) sinks *Beverley* in a night attack on the convoy. *U571* (Lt-Cdr Möhlmann) and *U84* (Lt-Cdr Uphoff), shadowing, encounter the convoy ONS.2 (37 ships with EG.C1, comprising the destroyers *St Laurent* and *St Croix*, the corvettes *Battle-ford*, *Kenogami*, *Napanee* and *Shediac* and, in addition, the returning 'Torch' corvettes *Camrose*, *Kitchener*, *Moosejaw* and *Ville de Quebec*) which is sailing in the vicinity. *U571* sinks one ship of 3835 tons. On 11 Apr *U615* (Lt-Cdr Kapitzky) and *U613* (Lt-Cdr Köppe) each sink one straggler, of 7177 tons and 1914 tons respectively. *U71*, *U662*, *U404* and, again, *U71*, briefly keep contact with the convoy, but all boats are driven off by the strong air and sea escort. Only *U404* makes an attack, during the night 11–12 Apr on ON.176 but this is unsuccessful. *U84*, *U662*, *U404*, *U613* and *U571* have to break off with damage and the operation is aban-doned on 12 Apr.

The convoys ON.177 (EG.C4, with the destroyers *Churchill* (RN) and *Restigouche*, the corvettes *Amherst*, *Brandon* and *Col-lingwood* and the Norwegian destroyer *St Albans*, on transfer) and ONS.3 (40th EG, with the sloops *Aberdeen*, *Hastings* and *Lul-worth* and the frigates *Moyola* and *Waveney*) also pass clear of the U-boat groups, routed following 'Ultra' intercepts.

7–18 Apr   South Pacific
Last Japanese air offensive (Operation 'I') in the Solomons under the personal command of Admiral of the Fleet Yamamoto. After the Japanese carriers *Zuikaku*, *Zuiho*, *Junyo* and *Hiyo* have brought 95 fighters, 65 dive-bombers and some torpedo aircraft to Rabaul and Buka to reinforce the 11th Air Fleet (86 fighters, 27 dive-bombers, 72 twin-engined torpedo bombers), 67 torpedo aircraft and dive-bombers with 110 fighters attack the US ships in the roads of Lunga/Guadalcanal and Tulagi on 7 Apr. They sink the US destroyer *Aaron Ward*, the tanker *Kanawha* and the New Zealand corvette *Moa*; one transport and one tanker are damaged. On

11 Apr 22 aircraft with 72 fighters attack Oro Bay near Buna (New Guinea) and on 12 Apr 43 bombers with 131 fighters attack Port Moresby. On 14 Apr a strong air force attacks Milne Bay, where two transports are sunk. US W/T intelligence decodes Japanese W/T messages about a visit by Admiral Yamamoto to Buin Airfield (Bougainville). Sixteen long-range P-38 fighters of 339 FS (Maj Mitchell) are deployed from Henderson Field, Guadalcanal. Losing one aircraft, they shoot down the two transports with Adm Yamamoto† and his Chief of Staff, Vice-Adm Ugaki (rescued), and three of the nine escorting fighters. Adm Koga succeeds as C-in-C of the Combined Fleet.

10 Apr   Mediterranean

Eighty-four American B-24 Liberators attack the Italian naval base at La Maddalena (Sardinia): the heavy cruiser *Trieste* and the motor torpedo boats *MAS 501* and *MAS 503* are sunk and the heavy cruiser *Gorizia* is severely damaged (but later towed to La Spezia).

10 Apr   Bay of Biscay

The outbound *U376* is sunk by Wellington 'C' of No 172 Sqn using a Leigh Light.

10 Apr–28 May   Mediterranean

Whilst *U303* and *U414* come into the Mediterranean from the Atlantic, *U596* and *U617* attack British naval forces unsuccessfully near Alboran (10 Apr) and the latter misses a KMF convoy (13 Apr). On 20 Apr *U565* (Lt-Cdr W Franken) sinks two ships of 9986 tons from the convoy UGS.7 (24 ships, escorted by the AA cruiser *Carlisle* and four corvettes) and an attack by *U453* fails. *U602* is sunk off Algiers on 23 Apr by Hudson 'N' of No 500 Sqn RAF. *U371* (Lt Cdr Mehl) sinks one ship of 1162 tons on 27 Apr. Of the boats coming from the Atlantic, *U410* is damaged by aircraft and *U447* is sunk E of Gibraltar. *U616* gets through but has no success; the same applies to *U375*, *U561* and *U407* operating off Algiers. On 18 May *U414* (Lt Huth) sinks one ship of 5979 tons from convoy UGS.8/KMS.14 (escorted by the destroyers *Holcombe*, *Farndale*, *Wheatland* and *Haydon*, the corvette *Pentstemon* and the trawlers *Bream* and *Prodigal*) and torpedoes one ship of 7134 tons but is herself sunk on 21 May by the US destroyer *Nields* in an attack on a US convoy; *U303* is lost to the British submarine *Sickle* off Toulon on the same day. *U755* is destroyed by aircraft off Algiers on 28 May. The Italian *Gorgo* is lost to an unknown cause, possibly in an attack by the corvette *Vetch* from convoy CTX.1 on 25 May.

11–13 Apr   North Atlantic

The 'Lerche' group, comprising *U168*, *U532*, *U706*, *U563*, *U270*, *U630*, *U584*, *U260*, *U191* and *U203*, is formed to operate against convoy HX.232, escorted by EG.B3 (Cdr Evans), with the destroyers *Escapade*, *Garland* (Polish) and *Keppel* and the corvettes *Renoncule* (FFN), *Roselys* (FFN), *Narcissus* and *Azalea* and expected on 11 Apr; the convoy, consisting of 47 ships, is located according to plan by *U584* (Lt-Cdr Deecke). During the night 11–12 Apr *U563* (Lt-Cdr v Hartmann) sinks one ship of 7117 tons and *U168* (Lt-Cdr Pich) sinks one ship of 7261 tons and torpedoes one other of 2666 tons which is later sunk by *U706* (Lt-Cdr v Zitzewitz). On 12 Apr *U530*, which also takes part in the operations on her return journey, and the contact-keepers *U584*, *U203*, *U270* and *U168* are driven off partly by the sea escort and partly by the air escort. On 13 Apr the operation is broken off and the boats proceed to *U462* for replenishment.

11–27 Apr   North Atlantic

From 11 Apr seven boats are stationed E of Newfoundland as the 'Meise' group and boats replenished from the tankers *U462* and *U463* join them to form a patrol line from 14 Apr to operate against the convoy SC.126, which comprises 38 ships escorted by EG.B5 (Cdr Boyle) with the destroyer *Havelock*, the frigate *Swale* and the corvettes *Godetia*, *Pimpernel*, *Buttercup*, *Lavender* and *Saxifrage*. Covered by the 3rd SG with the destroyers *Offa*, *Impulsive*, *Penn* and *Panther*, the convoy is routed to the S of 'Meise' and avoids the U-boats. On 19 Apr, on the way to their new positions, *U732* (Lt Carlsen) and *U108* (Lt-Cdr Wolfram) each report sinking one so-far unidentified ammunition freighter from Iceland feeder convoys.

Following B-Service reports on 20 Apr, the 'Meise' group—now comprising *U134*, *U306*, *U631*, *U203*, *U552*, *U267*, *U706*, *U415*, *U413*, *U598*, *U191*, *U438*, *U613*, *U404*, *U571*, *U381*, *U108*, *U258*, *U610*, *U257* and *U84*—is moved to a position ahead of convoy HX.234.

On 21 Apr *U306* (Lt-Cdr v Trotha) locates HX.234, escorted by EG.B4 (Cdr Day) with the destroyers *Highlander*, *Beverley* and *Vimy* and the corvettes *Pennywort*, *Anemone*, *Abelia*, *Asphodel*, *Clover* and *Rosthern*—and sinks one ship of 10218 tons during the night. In closing up, *U706* (Lt-Cdr v Zitzewitz) encounters ONS.3 (40th EG, with the sloops *Aberdeen*, *Hastings* and *Lulworth* and the frigates *Moyola* and *Waveney*). *U203*, *U415*, *U191*, *U613* and *U438* (Lt-Cdr Heinsohn) take up the

pursuit and the last also meets the following ON.178—consisting of 18 ships accompanied by EG.B1 (Cdr Bayldon) with the destroyers *Hurricane* and *Watchman*, the frigate *Kale* and the corvettes *Dahlia*, *Meadowsweet*, *Wallflower* and *Monkshood*—from which *U415* (Lt-Cdr Neide) sinks two ships of 8013 tons and *U191* (Lt-Cdr Fiehn) one of 5486 tons before contact is lost when the 3rd SG comes up to support the two convoys.

SC.127 (EG.C1; see 26 Apr–6 May) is first re-routed to the S route but the signal is decoded by the B-Service on 20 Apr and the new 'Specht' group is ordered to form a patrol line with 17 boats on 22 Apr. However, SC.127 is then ordered to circumvent this group in the gap between it and the 'Meise' group.

On 22 Apr Catalinas from VP-84 stationed in Greenland and Iceland drive the 'Meise' boats away from HX.234; only *U306* maintains contact, sinking one ship of 7176 tons in a submerged attack by day on 23 Apr. *U954* (Lt-Cdr O Loewe) torpedoes one more ship of 5313 tons before air escort is provided by Liberators of No 120 Sqn RAF and Liberator 'V' of that unit sinks *U189*.

In the search, *U732* comes across the approaching ONS.4, consisting of 41 ships accompanied by EG.B2 (Cdr MacIntyre) with the destroyers *Hesperus*, *Whitehall* and *Vanessa* and the corvettes *Clematis*, *Sweetbriar*, *Gentian* and *Heather*. This convoy and the nearby ON.179—EG.C2 under Lt-Cdr Chavasse, with the destroyer *Broadway* (RN), the frigate *Lagan* (RN), the corvettes *Amherst*, *Drumheller*, *Morden* and *Primrose* and the returning 'Torch' corvettes *Algoma* and *Calgary*—are supported by the 5th EG (Capt Abel-Smith) with the escort carrier *Biter* and the destroyers *Pathfinder*, *Obdurate* and *Opportune*. Swordfish aircraft from *Biter* force *U732* to submerge. *U191*, which takes over as contact-keeper, is located with HF/DF by *Hesperus* and sunk with 'Hedgehog'. Of the shadowing boats *U954*, *U209*, *U648*, *U108* and *U514*, only *U108* establishes contact with the convoy and only *U404* (Lt-Cdr v Bülow) with the support group. In the morning of 25 Apr *U404* fires a salvo against what is thought to be the US carrier *Ranger* but is in fact *Biter*; it misses because of a premature fuse. On the same day a Swordfish from No 811 Sqn FAA on board *Biter* sights the returning *U203*, which is sunk by *Pathfinder*. The 11 'Meise' boats stationed near HX.234 are unable to fire during the night 23–24 Apr because of hail, rain and snowstorms and because of the skilful manoeuvring of the convoy. *U306* maintains contact on 24 Apr but the strong air escort for HX.234 and ONS.5, which latter is sailing close to the N, allows only *U610* to make an unsuccessful attack, and *U710*, which is proceeding towards HX.234, is sunk by Fortress 'D' of No 206 Sqn RAF. After a miss by *U413* during the night, the remaining boats are driven off by the air escort and the reinforced sea escort, now including the 4th SG with the destroyers *Faulknor*, *Eclipse*, *Fury* and *Icarus*.

12–21 Apr   North Sea/English Channel

During the night 12–13 Apr slight damage is done to both sides in an engagement between a German convoy and the British *MGB112*, *MGB111*, *MGB75* and *MGB74*. On 13–14 Apr the German 5th MTB Flotilla (Lt-Cdr Klug), comprising *S65*, *S81*, *S82*, *S90*, *S112*, *S116* and *S121*, attacks off the Lizard Point the British convoy PW.323 (six steamers, the Norwegian destroyers *Glaisdale* and *Eskdale* and two Norwegian and three British trawlers). *S90* (Lt Stohwasser) hits the *Eskdale* with two torpedoes; she is later sunk by *S112* (Lt-Cdr Karl Müller) and *S65* (Lt Sobottka). *S121* (Lt Klocke) torpedoes the British freighter *Stanlake* (1742 tons) which is then finished off by *S90* and *S82* (Lt Dietrich). During the night 14–15 Apr the 2nd and 6th MTB Flotillas (Cdr Feldt), with *S94*, *S89*, *S92*, *S83*, *S86*, *S91*, *S114* and *S39*, carry out a mining operation off Lowestoft. There are engagements with *MGB88* and *MGB91*, the destroyer *Westminster* and the corvette *Widgeon*, in which *S83* receives a light hit. The 4th MTB Flotilla (Lt-Cdr Lützow), with *S48*, *S63*, *S88*, *S120*, *S110*, *S87* and *S122*, lays further barrages to the S. The trawler *Adonis* (1004 tons) is torpedoed and sunk. On 15 Apr there is an engagement off Cape de la Hogue between German patrol boats and submarine-chasers and the British *SGB6*, *MGB608* and *MGB615*. In an engagement off the Somme Estuary during the night 17–18 Apr the British *MGB38* and *MGB39* sink the patrol boat *V1409*. In an attack on a German convoy early on 18 Apr off Scheveningen, the British *MTB234*, *MTB241* and *MTB233* obtain shell hits, but attacks by Beaufighters off Den Helder in the afternoon have no success. On 20–21 Apr four MTBs miss a German convoy off the Hook of Holland.

12 Apr–25 May   Mediterranean

The German 3rd MTB Flotilla lays defensive mine barrages off Sousse (12–13 Apr, 2 May), off Bizerta (14 Apr, 25 Apr, 6 May) and off Porto Empedocle (16–17 May, 23 May, 25 May)—385 mines in all.

13 Apr   South Atlantic

The blockade-runner *Portland* (7132 tons, Capt Tünemann) is found by the Free French light cruiser *Georges Leygues* on the Natal–Freetown route and scuttles herself.

13–19 Apr   Air War/Italy

Two attacks by RAF Bomber Command against La Spezia: on 13–14 Apr 211 aircraft cause heavy damage and on 18–19 Apr 178 aircraft (plus eight minelaying Lancasters) are sent. Five aircraft are lost.

14 Apr–28 May   Arctic

The Soviet submarines *S-14*, *S-15*, *S-103*, *S-104*, *M-200* and *M-201* are transferred by river from Astrakhan on the Caspian Sea to the White Sea to join the Northern Fleet.

15 Apr   Norway

The German auxiliary minesweeper *M5613* sinks when she runs aground near Odderöy.

15 Apr   Air War/France

Thirteen RAF Bomber Command Venturas attack a whale factory ship in drydock at Cherbourg.

15 Apr   South Atlantic

The Italian submarine *Archimede* is sunk by two Liberators from VP-83 near San Fernando do Noronha.

15–18 Apr   North Atlantic

The outbound *U262* (Lt Franke) sights convoy HX.233 sailing on the southern route (57 ships with EG.A3 under Cdr Heinemann, with the US Coast Guard cutters *Spencer* and *Duane*, the Canadian corvettes *Wetaskiwin* and *Arvida* and the British *Dianthus*, *Bergamot* and *Bryony* and the Canadian destroyer *Skeena*, ordered up to give support). The outbound *U175*, *U628*, *U226*, *U358*, *U264*, *U382* and *U614* are deployed against the convoy. In the morning of 16 Apr the contact-keeper *U262* is driven off and only during the night 16–17 Apr does *U175* (Lt Bruns) find the convoy again. Towards morning she brings up *U382* and *U628* (Lt-Cdr Hasenschar); the latter torpedoes one ship of 7134 tons which is later sunk by *U226* (Lt-Cdr Borchers). The contact-keeper *U175* is located by HF/DF and sunk by *Spencer*. The 3rd SG (Capt McCoy), consisting of the destroyers *Offa*, *Oribi*, *Penn* and *Panther*, which comes up on 17 Apr to give support, forces *U264*, *U226* and *U382* to submerge in lengthy depth-charge pursuits.
In the evening of 17 Apr *U614* is the last boat to lose contact and on 18 Apr the operation is broken off.

16–25 Apr   Air War/Western Europe

Bombers of the 8th AF attack Lorient and Brest by day on 16 Apr. During the night 24–25 Apr 39 German bombers lay mines in the Thames Estuary.

16 Apr–5 June   Arctic

Off the Norwegian polar coast, Soviet submarines try, partly on the basis of disembarked agents' reports and air reconnaissance, to attack German supply convoys. In Varangerfjord and off Vardö, *M-172*, *M-105*, *M-171*, *M-172*, *M-104*, *M-122* (probably sunk on a flanking mine barrage), *M-105* and *M-106* are among those which operate in succession; but in spite of many attacks they and the occasional torpedo-cutters employed in small groups achieve no success. In the area between Syltefjord and Nordkyn, *Shch-422*, *S-55*, *S-101*, *S-51*, *L-22* (which lays mines off Syltefjord on 6 May), *S-56*, *S-54* and *S-102* are among those operating. Further to the W, *L-20* lays mines and *Shch-402* and *Shch-403* disembark agents on Arnöy. *Shch-422* (Capt 3rd Class Vidyaev) misses a convoy with *M361* on 19 Apr; and against the convoys, unsuccessfully attacked by *Shch-422* and *S-101* on 25 Apr and 1 May, DB-3 torpedo aircraft of the 24th Mine and Torpedo Air Regt are deployed with fighter protection from Airacobras of the 95th Fighter Regt, but they obtain no hits. On 29 Apr *S-55* (Capt 3rd Class Sushkin) sinks the steamer *Sturzsee* (708 tons) from a convoy and on 17 May *S-56* (Capt 3rd Class Shchedrin) sinks the tanker *Eurostadt* (1118 tons) and hits the *Wartheland* (5096 tons) with a torpedo which does not explode. *S-51* makes several unsuccessful attacks. *Shch-422* is damaged on 31 May by depth charges from *UJ1206* and *M343*.

17 Apr–5 May   Black Sea

Operation 'Neptun': an attack by the German V Army Corps on the Soviet Myschako bridgehead is halted on 25 Apr after initial successes. During the operation there are continual nightly sorties by the German 1st MTB Flotilla, the 3rd MMS Flotilla and the Italian IV MAS Flotilla against Soviet supply traffic: several small vessels and barges are sunk and pontoons destroyed by torpedoes from *S47*, *S51*, *S102*, *S72* and *S28*. The flotillas have frequent engagements with Soviet patrol cutters and torpedo cutters. Operations are continued after the halting of 'Neptun'. During the night 30 Apr–1 May the Soviet destroyers *Boiki* and *Besposhchadny* which try in vain to attack *U19* on the way, shell Cape Meganon and Cape Chauda, and *Zheleznyakov* and the patrol ship *Shtorm* shell Anapa. The deployment of Soviet torpedo cutters against the harbour at Anapa is unsuccessful. On 5 May *U9* (Lt Schmidt-Weichert) torpedoes the Soviet tanker *Kreml* (7666 tons).

18 Apr   Arctic

The German minelayers *Brummer* and *Ska-gerrak*, escorted by the minesweepers *M31*, *M154*, *M202* and *M251* and eight R-boats and three A/S trawlers, lay the 'Sagitta' mine barrage E of the Varanger peninsula. Unsuccessful attacks by Soviet MTBs and coastal batteries are made.

18 Apr   Air War/France

Twelve Venturas of RAF Bomber Command strike against shipping in Dieppe harbour. During one of these raids the auxiliary minesweeper *M3817* is sunk off Fécamp.

19–30 Apr   Central Pacific

Mining operations by US submarines: on 19 Apr by *Scorpion* off Kashima Nada; on 20 Apr by *Runner* off Hong Kong; on 21 Apr by *Stingray* off Wenchow; and on 30 Apr by *Snook* off Saddle Island (China).

20–21 Apr   Air War/Germany

RAF Bomber Command raids Stettin (339 aircraft) and Rostock (86 planes). There is heavy destruction in Stettin city centre and 29 aircraft are lost.

20 Apr–14 July   Norway

The German minelayer *Skagerrak* lays 21 barrages to cover the coastal routes off the NW coast of Norway.

26 Apr   North Pacific

US TG.8.6 (Rear-Adm McMorris), comprising the cruisers *Detroit*, *Richmond* and *Santa Fe* and six destroyers, shells Attu.

25 Apr–6 May   North Atlantic

While the 'Specht' group is moved NW to intercept convays ON.179 and ONS.4 (see 11–27 Apr) both the latter are re-routed following 'Ultra' data to the N of the group, to be covered by the 5th and 1st EGs with the sloops *Pelican* and *Sennen* and the frigates *Jed*, *Spey* and *Wear* coming from SC.127. Against this convoy (the existence of which has been reported by the B-Service), the new 'Amsel' group, with *U634*, *U223*, *U266*, *U377*, *U383*, *U525*, *U709*, *U448*, *U466* and *U186*, is formed in the Central North Atlantic. However, SC.127 passes to the N and also skirts round the new 'Star' group, supported by the 4th SG (see 11–27 Apr) switched from HX.234. The convoy is heard by *U377* on 28 Apr but the support group drives off the five 'Amsel' boats deployed against it. On the way *U386* (Lt Kandler) sinks one ship of 1997 tons from convoy RU.71 on 24 Apr. Meanwhile the outgoing *U107* (Lt-Cdr Gelhaus) sinks one transport of 12411 tons W of the Bay of Biscay.

On 27 Apr the 'Specht' group, now consisting of *U438*, *U662*, *U630*, *U584*, *U168*, *U203*, *U706*, *U108*, *U514*, *U270*, *U260*, *U732*, *U92*, *U628*, *U707*, *U358*, *U264*, *U614*, *U226* and *U125*, is deployed NE of Newfoundland against convoy HX.235, again reported by the B-Service, but the convoy, escorted by EG.C4 (Cdr Brewer) with the destroyers *Churchill* (RN) and *Restigouche* and the corvettes *Baddeck*, *Brandon* and *Collingwood*, is re-routed far to the S, covered by the US 6th SG (Capt Short) with the escort carrier *Bogue* and the destroyers *Belknap*, *Greene*, *Osmond-Ingram* and *Lea*. On 28 Apr the 'Star' group, comprising *U650*, *U533*, *U386*, *U528*, *U231*, *U532*, *U378*, *U381*, *U192*, *U258*, *U552*, *U954*, *U648*, *U209*, *U531* and *U413*, takes up a patrol line S of Iceland against convoy ONS.5, comprising 42 ships accompanied by EG.B7 under Commodore Capt Brook with the destroyers *Duncan* (Cdr Gretton) and *Vidette*, the frigate *Tay*, the corvettes *Sun-flower*, *Snowflake*, *Loosestrife*, *Pink*, and the trawlers *Northern Gem* and *Northern Spray*. The convoy is reported by *U650* (Lt v Witzendorff). Forced by Catalina flying boats of VP-84 to submerge several times, she brings up *U386* and *U378* by day. During the night 28–29 Apr *U386* is damaged by depth charges from *Sunflower*; *U650* and *U532* are attacked with depth charges after misses on the *Duncan* and *Snowflake* and *U532* is again attacked by *Tay* in daylight on 29 Apr. In an underwater attack by day, *U258* (Lt-Cdr v Mässenhausen) sinks one ship of 6198 tons and *U528* is damaged by Catalina 'G' of VP-84. The C-in-C Western Approaches sends the destroyer *Oribi* from SC.127 to ONS.5 for support and the 3rd SG with the destroyers *Offa* (Capt McCoy), *Impulsive*, *Penn* and *Panther* from St John's. On 30 Apr and during the night 30 Apr–1 May the weather deteriorates and, in very changeable visibility and with W/T interference, contact is lost after an unsuccessful attack by *U192* (Lt Happe) on 1 May by night. By day ONS.5 has to heave to in a heavy gale and some of the ships are separated from the convoy.

After the B-Service has located on 29 Apr the convoy SC.128 (33 ships with EG.40 comprising the sloops *Landguard*, *Lulworth* and *Hastings*, the frigates *Moyola* and *Waveney*, the corvettes *Poppy* and *Starwort* and the A/S trawler *Northern Gift*), the 'Specht' and 'Amsel' groups are formed in a semi-circle on the convoy's course. In the evening of 1 May *U628* sights smoke from the convoy, but the U-boats directed to the scene are diverted by escorts firing flares on the flank of SC.128 and the convoy avoids the U-boats by getting to the W of them.

The 'Star' and 'Specht' boats coming from ONS.5 are concentrated in a new patrol line in front of SC.128 for 4 May. It consists of *U438*, *U630*, *U662*, *U584*, *U168*, *U514*, *U270*, *U260*, *U732*, *U628*, *U707*, *U358*, *U264*, *U226*, *U125*, *U378*, *U192*, *U648*, *U533*, *U531*, *U954*, *U413*, *U381*, *U231*, *U552*, *U209*, *U650* and *U614*. But the convoy passes to the W and in the process Canso flying boat 'W' of No 5 Sqn RCAF damages *U209*, which is lost a few days later (on 8 May) possibly as a result of the damage. *U630* is lost to a still unknown cause. In the evening ONS.5, coming from the N, sails into the middle of the 'Fink' group and is reported by *U628* (Lt-Cdr Hasenschar). 'Fink' and the groups stationed further S, 'Amsel I', comprising *U638*, *U621*, *U402*, *U575*, *U504* and *U107*, and 'Amsel 2', comprising *U634*, *U223*, *U266*, *U383* and *U377* and two returning boats, are at once deployed. As refuelling was impossible on 2, 3 and 4 May because of the heavy sea, Cdr Gretton with *Duncan*, *Impulsive*, *Penn* and *Panther* is compelled to leave the convoy owing to fuel shortage. On 4 May *Tay* (Lt-Cdr Sherwood, SOE), *Vidette* (Lt Hart), *Sunflower* (Lt-Cdr Plomer), *Snowflake* (Lt-Cdr Chesterman), *Loosestrife* (Lt-Cdr Stonehouse), *Offa* (Capt McCoy) and *Oribi* (Lt-Cdr Ingram) are with the convoy which still consists of 31 ships. *Pink* (Lt Atkinson) proceeds astern with five stragglers; and another five stragglers and *Northern Spray* try to catch up. *U125* (Lt-Cdr Folkers) sinks one of them (4635 tons) in the afternoon. By day on 4 May five boats, and in the night six boats, establish contact with the convoy itself; some are driven off by *Tay*, *Offa* and *Oribi* and *U270* is damaged by depth charges from *Snowflake* and *Oribi*. Of the attacking boats, *U628* sinks one ship of 5081 tons, *U264* (Lt-Cdr Looks) two of 10147 tons and *U358* (Lt-Cdr Manke) two of 8076 tons. In addition, one straggler of 4737 tons falls victim to *U952* (Lt Curio). By day on 5 May *U192* encounters the *Pink* group; *Pink* then locates and attacks *U358* with 'Hedgehog' but the U-boat escapes. A little later *U707* (Lt Gretschel) sinks one ship of 5565 tons from the group. In the course of the day 15 boats establish contact with the convoy itself; in underwater attacks *U584* (Lt-Cdr Deecke) and *U266* (Lt-Cdr v Jessen) sink one ship and three ships respectively, of 5507 tons and 12012 tons. Disaster seems likely to occur at night when two hours before dusk mist sets in with the result that the attacking U-boats proceed headlong towards the escorts which are able to see with their radar equipment. *Sunflower* locates four boats in succession, of which *U267* (Lt-Cdr Tinschert), after a miss, is slightly damaged by gunfire. *Loosestrife* locates two boats, one of which (*U192?*) she surprises in an attempted attack and sinks with depth charges. *Vidette* drives three boats off. *Snowflake* locates almost simultaneously three boats, of which *U531* (Lt-Cdr Neckel) misses the corvette, is covered with depth charges and forced to surface. Of the ships ordered up for support, *Oribi* comes across *U125* and rams her. But the boat is at first able to get away in a rain squall before she is found by *Snowflake* which, having expended all her depth charges, sinks her by gunfire. *Sunflower* locates and rams *U533* which escapes severely damaged. *Vidette* locates a boat (probably *U531*) which has submerged again, and sinks her with 'Hedgehog'. An attempt by *Offa* to ram a U-boat which she locates just fails and *Loosestrife* makes three more depth charge attacks. Towards morning the 1st SG (Capt Brewer), comprising the sloops *Pelican* and *Sennen* and the frigates *Jed*, *Wear* and *Spey*, arrives, having been sent by C-in-C Western Approaches from St John's for support. *Pelican* locates *U438* by radar and, together with *Jed*, sinks her. *Sennen*, on the way to the separated *Pink* group, encounters *U650* and *U575*, slightly damaging the last by gunfire, but the submarines are able to escape. In the morning the operation is broken off by the Commander U-boats. This was the greatest success achieved by Type 271M radar equipment in a convoy battle.

While this big convoy operation is in progress, the convoy ON.180, escorted by EG.C3 under Cdr Medley with the destroyers *Burnham* (RN) and *Skeena* (RCN) and the corvettes *Eyebright*, *Mayflower*, *Bittersweet* and *La Malbaie*, following ONS.5, goes S of Cape Farewell further to the W to evade the U-boats behind ONS.5. The convoy HX.236, with EG.B1 under Cdr Baytdon and comprising the destroyers *Hurricane*, *Watchman* and *Rockingham*, the frigate *Kale* and the corvettes *Monkshood*, *Dahlia*, *Meadowsweet* and *Wallflower*, is diverted as HX.235 on the southern route, supported by the new 2nd SG (Capt Walker) with the sloops *Starling*, *Wren*, *Woodpecker*, *Kite* and *Wildgoose*. The convoys ON.181 (EG.B3) and ONS.6 (EG.B6), supported by the 4th SG, sail on a more direct northern route, as does ON.182 (first operation of EG.C5, under Cdr Pullen, with the destroyer *Ottawa*, the corvettes *Arvida*, *Kitchener*, *Sudbury*, *Wetaskiwin* and *Dauphin* and the RN corvette *Dianthus*, relieving the last US group, A3).

27–28 Apr English Channel
The British destroyers *Goathland* and *Albrighton* attack a German convoy 60

nautical miles NNE of Ouessant and sink the submarine-chaser *UJ1402*.

27–29 Apr Air War/Western Europe
In the heaviest RAF Bomber Command mine offensive so far, 160 aircraft lay 458 mines off Biscay and Brittany ports on 27–28 Apr and 207 lay 595 mines off Heligoland, off the Elbe estuary and in the Belts on 28–29 Apr; 23 aircraft are lost. *Inter alia*, the German passenger ship *Gneisenau* (18160 tons) sinks on British mines in the Gjedser Narrows on 2–3 May.

27 Apr–4 May Norway/Baltic
The German cruiser *Nürnberg*, escorted by the destroyer *Richard Beitzen* and the torpedo boats *Jaguar* and *Greif*, returns from Harstad to Trondheim (29 Apr) and then moves to Kiel (4 May).

29 Apr North Sea
The German patrol trawler *V807* is sunk off Terschelling by bombs dropped from Beauforts of Nos 236 and 254 Sqns RAF.

29 Apr English Channel
The German patrol trawler *V1408* is sunk by torpedo off Ijmuiden.

29 Apr Black Sea
The German motor minesweeper *R36* is lost to one of its own mines off Constantza.

29 Apr–13 May Mediterranean
Final battle for Tunis and Bizerta. In last attempts to bring supplies to Africa, the destroyers *Pancaldo* (Cdr* Ferrieri-Caputi†) and *Hermes* (German, Cdr* Rechel), each with 300 men on board, and *Lampo* (Cdr Albanese), with ammunition, are repeatedly attacked by Allied aircraft off Cape Bon on 30 Apr. *Pancaldo* and *Lampo* sink and *Hermes* is taken in tow when unable to move under her own steam. In rescue operations, fighter-bombers sink the Italian *MAS 552* and *Ms 25*. On 30 Apr the British destroyers *Nubian* and *Paladin* sink the transport *Fauna* (575 tons) off the Sicilian coast and during the night 3–4 May, in co-operation with *Petard*, the transport *Campobasso* (3566 tons) and the torpedo boat *Perseo* (Cdr Marotta) off Kelibia. The transport *Belluno* reaches Tunis with the torpedo boat *Tifone* (Cdr Baccarini) on 4 May but both are bombed there. Liberator bombers sink the transport *Sant' Antonio* (6013 tons) on 4 May off Sicily; and the escorting torpedo boats *Groppo* and *Calliope* return. The last ships to arrive off Cape Bon are the German *KT5*, *KT9* and *KT21* on 7 May, but they are so badly hit by bombs and aircraft fire that they are abandoned and lost on 9 May. After the loss of Bizerta and Tunis on 7 May organised German and Italian resistance ceases on 9 May although some individual groups hold out until 13

May. In the Tunisian harbours *Hermes*, the French destroyer *L'Audacieux*, the French submarines *Calypso*, *Nautilus*, *Turquoise* and *Circe*, 12 minesweepers, 25 freighters, nine tugs and 23 smaller craft are sunk, in some cases by air attack and in others by scuttling as block ships. Small groups attempt to break through to Sicily and Sardinia in light craft but only a few boats, including several German and Italian motor torpedo boats and MAS boats and the largest ship, the German *KT22*, break through the blockade maintained from 7 May by the British destroyers from Force K in Malta (*Nubian*, *Paladin*, *Petard* and *Jervis*—which bombards Kelibia on 7 May and again on 9 May) and Force Q from Bône (*Laforey*, *Loyal*, *Tartar* and *Blyskawica*) and the 'Hunt' destroyers *Zetland*, *Lamerton*, *Aldenham*, *Hursley*, *Kanaris* (Greek) *Dulverton*, *Lauderdale*, *Wilton* and others. They bring in some 700 prisoners.

29 Apr–27 May South Atlantic
In operations off the Brazilian coast *U154* (Lt Kusch) hits a tanker of 8917 tons with a torpedo off Recife on 8 May but the torpedo fails to explode. *U128* (Lt-Cdr Steinert) is located by land-based D/F when she transmits a W/T message. In the search which is ordered she is reported by US and Brazilian aircraft and damaged on 16 May by two Mariner flying boats of VP-72. She has to scuttle herself when the US destroyers *Moffett* and *Jouett* approach. After replenishing from *U460*, *U154* attacks convoy BT.14 (12 steamers escorted by the US destroyer *Borie*, the corvettes *Saucy*, *Tenacity* and *Courage* and the submarine-chaser *PC592*) on 27 May. She sinks one ship of 8166 tons and two ships of 15771 tons are torpedoed.

30 Apr North Atlantic
The outgoing *U227* is sunk N of the Faeroes by Hampden 'X' of No 455 Sqn RAAF.

30 Apr Intelligence
Operation 'Mincemeat'. The British submarine *Seraph* sets adrift a corpse disguised as 'Major Martin' of the Royal Marines, to be washed ashore on the Spanish coast with fake papers. The Spanish give the documents to the Germans. To what extent these documents deceive the German OKW about Allied plans is difficult to determine.

30 Apr Mediterranean
The German motor minesweeper *RA10* (ex-British *MTB314*) is sunk in an air attack off La Goulette/Tunisia.

30 Apr–9 May North Atlantic
The 'Drossel' group, comprising *U456*, *U230*, *U607*, *U436*, *U89*, *U600*, *U406*, *U659*, *U439* and *U447* operates W of Spain. On 3 May air reconnaissance locates two

convoys; one of them, an LST convoy, is briefly sighted by *U89*. *U659* and *U439*, in attempting to attack, collide and sink. On 5 May *U447* has a gun engagement with an LCT and shoots down a barrage balloon. *U456* fails to get up to a cruiser. On 6 May air reconnaissance sights the convoy SL.128 (48 ships with one sloop and four corvettes). In the morning of 7 May *U607* (Lt Jeschonnek) misses the convoy; *U456* is attacked with depth charges and *U230*, as she keeps contact, is bombed twice. *U447* is sunk by Hudsons 'X' and 'I' of No 233 Sqn RAF. *U436* and *U89* (Lt-Cdr Lohmann) attack at midday: *U89* sinks one ship of 3803 tons before bad visibility results in a loss of contact. From 9 May the group is deployed against HX.237.

1 May   Air War/Western Europe
Forty-eight B-17s of the 8th AF bombard St-Nazaire.

1 May   North Sea
Naval engagement off Terschelling. In an attack by the 31st MTB Flotilla (*MTB624*, *MTB632* and *MTB630*) and the 17th *MGB* Flotilla (*MGB605*, *MGB606*, *MGB610* and *MGB612*) on four boats of the 12th PB Flotilla (Cdr vom Hoff), *V1241* is sunk.

1–31 May   Air War/Western Europe
RAF Bomber Command mine offensive. In 12 nights, 368 sorties are flown against Biscay ports—concentrating on La Pallice and the Gironde estuary—and the Frisian coast. Nine aircraft are lost. On 25 May the German MDS *Sperrbrecher 173/Westland* is beached after hitting a mine off Ameland.

1–31 May   Pacific
In US submarine operations during the month of May there are 34 'Ultra' signals which, however, lead to only two sightings and one attack, in which latter a ship is damaged. The US submarines which arrive in their operational areas in May have the following results:
In the Aleutian area, *S41* (Lt Hartman) sinks one ship of 1036 tons, *S34* has misses and *Nautilus* and *Narwhal* conduct reconnaissance missions for the landings on Attu. In Japanese waters, *Pogy* (Lt-Cdr Wales) sinks two ships of 3423 tons and two sailing vessels and damages one ship of 6376 tons, *Wahoo* (Cdr Morton) sinks three ships of 10376 tons, *Sawfish* (Lt-Cdr Sands) sinks one ship of 2921 tons, *Trigger* (Lt-Cdr Benson) sinks two ships of 3157 tons and torpedoes the carrier *Hiyo* on 10 June off Miyake, *Tinosa* (Lt-Cdr Daspit) torpedoes one ship of 14050 tons and *Steelhead* (Lt-Cdr Weichel) lays a minefield off Erimo Seki in which one ship of 2022 tons sinks. In the Central Pacific, *Seal* (Lt-Cdr Dodge) sinks

one ship of 7354 tons, *Permit* (Lt-Cdr Chapple) sinks one ship of 8359 tons, *Plunger* (Lt-Cdr Bear) sinks two of 15428 tons, *Pollack* (Lt-Cdr Llewellen) sinks two of 8461 tons, *Whale* (Lt-Cdr Burrows) sinks one of 3580 tons, *Saury* (Lt-Cdr Dropp) sinks five of 23888 tons and *Finback* (Lt-Cdr Tyree) sinks three of 12972 tons; *Seawolf* (Lt-Cdr Gross) sinks one ship of 4739 tons and one sailing vessel and *Skipjack* and *Silversides* conduct reconnaissance missions. In the South Pacific, *Grayback* (Lt-Cdr Stephan) sinks two ships of 12270 tons and damages one of 1715 tons and the destroyer *Yuguri*, *Scamp* (Lt-Cdr Ebert) sinks one ship of 6853 tons and *Gato* conducts a special mission. In the South West Pacific, *Gar* (Lt-Cdr Quick) sinks three ships of 8261 tons and five sailing vessels, *Tautog* (Lt-Cdr Wogan) sinks two ships of 5444 tons and one sailing vessel and lands agents and *Tambor* (Lt-Cdr Ambruster) sinks two ships of 3734 tons; *Thresher* and *Trout* conduct guerrilla missions.

1 May–20 July   Mediterranean
Italian defensive mine barrages are laid out. Off the west coast of Greece, the Italian minelayers *Barletta* and *Morosini* and the German minelayers *Drache* and *Bulgaria* lay 26 barrages and the Italian minelayers *Vieste* and *Buffoluto* a further one, making a total of 3156 mines. Off the Sicilian coast, the Italian ships *Vieste* and *Vallelunga* with the barges *G53*, *G56* and *G58* lay 12 barrages of 1036 mines, and off the coast of Sardinia the Italian *Durazzo*, *Volturno*, *Buccari*, *Mazara*, *Vieste* and *Buffoluto* and a force comprising the Italian destroyer *Vivaldi* (Capt Camicia) and the German minelayers *Pommern* and *Brandenburg* lay 24 barrages with 4248 mines. In the Aegean the German minelayer *Bulgaria* lays another three barrages with 140 mines and in the Adriatic the Italian *Fasana* one barrage with 137 mines.

2–31 May   North Sea
During the nights 2–3 and 3–4 May 16 Do 217s of KG 2 lay 62 mines between the Humber and Great Yarmouth and along the convoy route between Great Yarmouth and the Thames respectively. During the night 11–12 May 20 Do 217s of KG 2 and II/KG 40 and 22 Ju 88s of KG 6 lay 26 mines on the convoy route Humber–Thames; five aircraft are lost. During the night 29–30 May, in the same estuaries, 15 Do 217s and 36 Ju 88s of KG 6 lay 62 mines; two aircraft are lost.

2 May–29 June   Mediterranean
In British submarine operations in the Western Mediterranean, sometimes in more than one mission, *Safari* (Cdr Bryant and Lt Lakin) sinks three ships of 2641 tons and

one KT ship and also torpedoes one steamer of 3069 tons, *Sportsman* (Lt Gatehouse) sinks two ships of 5110 tons, *Tactician* (Lt-Cdr Collett) sinks one ship of 385 tons, *Shakespeare* (Lt Ainslie) sinks two ships of 241 tons, *Sickle* (Lt Drummond) sinks the submarine-chaser *UJ2213* and *U303* and *Trident* (Lt Newstead) torpedoes one ship of 11718 tons. In the Central Mediterranean and Southern Adriatic, *Unrivalled* (Lt Sprice) sinks two ships of 986 tons, *Unbroken* (Lt Andrew) sinks two of 5408 tons, *Unruly* (Lt Fyfe) sinks one of 4485 tons and torpedoes one of 4000 tons, *Unruffled* (Lt Stevens) sinks one of 9895 tons, *United* (Lt Barlow) sinks two of 8649 tons, *Ultor* (Lt Hunt) sinks one of 137 tons, *Unison* (Lt Daniell) sinks one of 2998 tons and *Unshaken* (Lt Whitton) sinks one of 1425 tons; *Tactician* sinks one ship of 8034 tons and one sailing ship. In the Aegean the British *Parthian* (Lt St John) sinks one sailing ship, the Greek *Katsonis* (Lt Laskos) sinks two ships of 2908 tons and torpedoes one other and the British *Taurus* (Lt-Cdr Wingfield) and the Greek *Papanicolis* (Lt-Cdr Roussen) sink six and two caiques respectively.

3–7 May   North Sea
The German minelayers *Brummer* and *Ostmark*, escorted by the torpedo boats *Jaguar*, *Greif* and *Möwe* and 10 minesweepers, lay the 'Samuel' and 'Quersprung' mine barrages to strengthen the 'Westwall' barrage.

4 May   North Atlantic
The outgoing *U109* is sunk by Liberator 'P' of No 86 Sqn RAF flying to escort convoy HX.236 (EG.B1).

4 May–2 June   North Pacific
Operation 'Landcrab': the re-conquest of Attu by the 7th US Inf Div (Maj-Gen Brown; from 16 May Maj-Gen Landrum). In overall command is Rear-Adm Kinkaid, TF.16.

On 4 May the invasion fleet sets out from Cold Bay (Alaska). The landing plan for 8 May has to be deferred until 11 May because of the weather. On 11 May TF.51 (Rear-Adm Rockwell) with four transports and one fast transport, escorted by the destroyers *Dewey*, *Dale*, *Monaghan* and *Aylwin*, two minelayers and four minesweepers, lands 3000 men of the reinforced 17th Inf Regt. They are followed by the other units over the next few days. Fire support is provided by TG.51.1 (Rear-Adm Kingman), comprising the battleships *Nevada*, *Pennsylvania* and *Idaho*, the escort carrier *Nassau* and the destroyers *Phelps*, *Farragut*, *Hull*, *MacDonough*, *Meade*,

Edwards, *Abner Read* and *Ammen*. The southern covering force is TG.16.6 (Rear-Adm McMorris), consisting of the cruisers *Detroit*, *Raleigh*, *Richmond* and *Santa Fe* and the destroyers *Bancroft*, *Caldwell*, *Coghlan*, *Frazier* and *Gansevoort* and the northern covering force (Rear-Adm Giffen) consists of the cruisers *Wichita*, *San Francisco* and *Louisville* and the destroyers *Balch*, *Hughes*, *Mustin* and *Morris*. *Narwhal* and *Nautilus* act as marker submarines. By 2 June a total of 12000 men are landed. By 30 May the resistance of the approximately 2600 Japanese defenders (Col Yamazaki) is broken. The Japanese plan to evacuate the defenders with the 5th Fleet is abandoned on 29 May. 2379 Japanese are killed and 28 taken prisoner; the remainder are evacuated by submarines. In support operations the Japanese submarine *I-31* twice narrowly misses *Pennsylvania* and is sunk on 12 May by the destroyers *Edwards* and *Farragut* off Kiska; *I-35* unsuccessfully attacks the *Santa Fe*. On the US side there are 600 dead and 1200 wounded.

5–8 May   English Channel
Three mining operations in the Channel by the German 2nd TB Flotilla (Cdr Erdmann) with *T23*, *T2*, *T5*, *T18* and *T22*. Six boats of the 5th MTB Flotilla lay 32 mines S of Selsey Bill.

6 May–8 June   Baltic
First attempt by Soviet submarines to break out with support from the Soviet Naval Air Force and strong forces of minesweepers and torpedo cutters. *Shch-303* (Capt 3rd Class Travkin) sets out on 7 May from Kronstadt and on 11 May from Lavansaari, breaks through the 'Seeigel' barrage and tries in vain from 18 to 24 May to get through the net barrage. On the return the boat is sighted by an Ar 196 of SAGr 127 and is several times pursued by the naval ferry barges of the 24th Landing Flotilla ordered to search between the mine barrages. But she reaches Lavansaari again on 8 June through Narva Bay. Of the boats which set off on 19 and 20 May, *Shch-408* (Lt-Cdr Kuzmin) is damaged by six Finnish VMV boats and the minelayer *Riilahti* off the net barrage on 22 May; the latter is again attacked on 23 and 24 May by aircraft and by depth charges from the minelayer *Ruotsinsalmi* and on 26 May is destroyed by KFKs of the German 31st MS Flotilla. *Shch-406* (Capt 3rd Class Osipov) is several times pursued on 27, 28 and 29 May by the 24th Landing Flotilla and is sunk on 1 June near Steinskar by naval ferry barges of the 24th Landing Flotilla after bombs have been dropped by an Ar 196.

7–13 May   South Pacific
US mining operations to prevent Japanese supplies reaching New Georgia. Whilst US TF.68 (Rear-Adm Ainsworth), consisting of the cruisers *Honolulu*, *Nashville* and *St Louis* and the destroyers *O'Bannon*, *Strong*, *Chevalier* and *Taylor*, makes a sortie into Vella Gulf to divert the Japanese, a minelaying force, comprising the destroyers *Radford*, *Preble*, *Gamble* and *Breese*, lays a barrage in Blackett Strait, on which a Japanese transport destroyer force runs on 8 May and loses *Oyashio*, *Kagero* and *Kuroshio*. Only *Michishio* escapes with heavy damage from air attacks after rescuing survivors. In a second operation during the night 12–13 May Rear-Adm Ainsworth shells Vila with the cruisers *Helena*, *Honolulu* and *Nashville* and the destroyers *O'Bannon*, *Strong*, *Chevalier*, *Taylor* and *Radford*; the cruiser *St Louis* with the destroyers *Jenkins* and *Fletcher* shells Munda; and *Preble*, *Gamble* and *Breese* lay a mine barrage off Kula Gulf which is cleared by the Japanese on the following day.

8–15 May   North Atlantic
From the 'Amsel 1' and '2' boats which did not participate in the ONS.5 operation, the 'Rhein' group is formed to operate against HX.237, expected on the basis of a B-Service report. The group consists of *U709*, *U569*, *U525*, *U468*, *U448*, *U752*, *U466*, *U454*, *U359*, *U186*, *U403* and *U103*. The B-Service reports the convoy's evasive move to the S. At the southern end of 'Rhein' *U359* (Lt Förster) locates HX.237 on 9 May—46 ships escorted by EG.C2 with the destroyer *Broadway* (RN, Capt Chevasse), the frigate *Lagan* (RN) and the corvettes *Chambly*, *Drumheller*, *Morden* and *Primrose* (RN) and the rescue tug *Vizalma*—but she is immediately located by HF/DF and forced under. A patrol line formed in front of the convoy is broken through after a Swordfish from *Biter*, which reinforces EG.C2 with the 5th SG (Capt Abel-Smith, with the destroyers *Inglefield*, *Obdurate*, *Opportune* and *Pathfinder*) has forced *U454*, which is barring the way, to submerge. *U403* again establishes contact on 10 May when shadowing the rescue tug which has fallen behind. She is able to drive off a Swordfish with AA fire but is forced to submerge by one of the three destroyers of the 5th SG. Because the boats can no longer get ahead, the operation is continued only with the boats of the 'Drossel' group coming from the E—*U456*, *U230*, *U607*, *U436*, *U89*, *U600*, *U221* and *U753*. The 'Rhein' group forms with the 'Elbe' group (made up of the ONS.5 boats) the groups 'Elbe 1' (*U634*,

U575, *U584*, *U650*, *U752*, *U709*, *U569*, *U231*, *U525*, *U514*, *U468* and *U267*) and 'Elbe 2' (*U103*, *U621*, *U448*, *U466*, *U223*, *U454*, *U504*, *U402*, *U377*, *U359*, *U107*, *U383* and *U186*) to operate against the evasive move to the S made by SC.129 and likewise detected by the B-Service. Thanks to the decoding of a position by the B-Service, *U436* (Cdr Seibicke) finds convoy HX.237 in the evening of 11 May. *U403* (Lt-Cdr Clausen) and *U456* (Lt-Cdr Teichert) sink one straggler of 7138 tons and *U753* (Cdr v Mannstein) misses the convoy. After dawn on 12 May the U-boats try to keep off the Swordfish aircraft from *Biter* with their AA fire. *U230* (Lt-Cdr Siegmann) shoots one down but the U-boats are forced to submerge by the escorts summoned to the scene. *U89* is sunk by the *Broadway* directed by a Swordfish and the frigate *Lagan*. *U456*, after being damaged by a homing torpedo dropped from Liberator 'B' of No 86 Sqn on 12 May and rendered unfit to dive, sinks while attempting to dive when the destroyers *Pathfinder* and *Opportune* approach. A Swordfish of No 811 Sqn FAA from *Biter* leads *Pathfinder* to *U603*, which is slightly damaged in the ensuing attack. *U628* (Lt-Cdr Hasenschar), a returning boat, keeps contact until the morning of 13 May while from the rear *U221* (Lt Trojer) and *U603* (Lt Baltz) each sink a straggler, of 9432 tons and 4819 tons respectively. In the morning of 13 May Sunderland flying boats of No 423 Sqn RCAF provide additional air escort and Sunderland 'G' of No 423 Sqn RAF brings up the frigate *Lagan* and the corvette *Drumheller* to *U753*, which is sunk. With the convoy the corvettes *Chambly* and *Morden* drive off the other U-boats. The Cdr U-boats has to break off the operation as hopeless. At the same time the C-in-C Western Approaches orders the 5th SG to proceed at full speed to SC.129, which has been reported by *U504* (Lt Luis) in the evening of 11 May. While the escort drives off the contact-keeper located by HF/DF, *U402* (Cdr Frhr v Forstner) attacks before dark SC.129—26 ships escorted by EG.B2 with the destroyers *Hesperus* (Cdr MacIntyre), *Whitehall* and *Vanessa* and the corvettes *Gentian*, *Clematis*, *Heather*, *Sweetbriar* and *Campanula*—and sinks two ships of 7627 tons in an underwater attack. During the night 11–12 May *U383* and *U359* are driven off by *Whitehall* and *Clematis*. *Hesperus* fights a dramatic duel with *U223* (Lt-Cdr Wächter) which is forced to surface by depth charges and misses the destroyer with five torpedoes but, in spite of depth charges designed to explode just beneath the surface, gunfire and a cautious ramming, does not sink and is able to escape. In the morning of 12 May *Hesperus* sinks the contact-keeper *U186*, located by HF/DF, but in the course of the day 11 other boats establish contact and are located by HF/DF. By dusk they are all repulsed by *Hesperus*, *Whitehall*, *Sweetbriar*, *Clematis* and *Heather* and thrown off by a sharp change of course. Early on 13 May air escort is provided by Swordfish aircraft from *Biter* which has come up meantime. In the afternoon Liberators from No 86 Sqn RAF also arrive. The following day Liberator 'B' of No 86 Sqn attacks *U403*, which escapes undamaged. On 15 May *U266* is sunk by a Halifax of No 58 Sqn RAF to the rear of the convoy. The operation is broken off. On the return journey *U607* (Lt Jeschonnek) sinks a ship of 5589 tons but convoy ON.184 (EG.B4, leader destroyer *Highlander*) evades the U-boat groups.

11 May   North Atlantic

The returning *U528* is attacked near convoy OS.47 (EG.39) by Halifax 'D' of No 58 Sqn RAF and finished off by depth charges fired by the sloop *Fleetwood* and the corvette *Mignonette*.

11–23 May   North Atlantic

On 11 and 12 May the U-boat groups 'Isar' (*U304*, *U645*, *U952*, *U418*), 'Lech' (*U209*, *U202*, *U664*, *U91*) and 'Inn' (*U258*, *U381*, *U954*, *U92*) are formed SE of Cape Farewell. Of the boats proceeding to other proposed groups, *U640* (Lt Nagel) sights during the night 11–12 May the convoy ONS.7 (40 ships plus EG.B5 with the frigate *Swale*, the destroyer *Volunteer*, the corvettes *Buttercup*, *Godetia*, *Lavender* and *Saxifrage* and the rescue ship *Copeland*). Although repeatedly driven off, the boat relentlessly keeps contact until 13 May, so that *U760*, *U636*, *U340*, *U731* and *U657* can be deployed as the 'Iller' group. Then *U640* is bombed by Catalina 'G' of VP-84 and is lost.

To restore the lost contact, the Cdr U-boats forms from 15–16 May the groups 'Donau 1' (*U657*, *U760*, *U636*, *U340*, *U731*, *U304*, *U645*, *U952*, *U418*, *U258*, *U381*) and 'Donau 2' (*U954*, *U92*, *U209*, *U202*, *U664*, *U91*, *U707*, *U413*, *U952*, *U264*, *U378*, *U218*) from the above-named groups and from the 'Nahe' group setting out after replenishment. Convoy ONS.7 goes to the north end of the formation. During the night 16–17 May *U657* (Lt-Cdr Göllnitz) attacks and sinks one ship of 5196 tons but is then herself sunk by the *Swale*. On 17 and 19 May *U646* and *U273*, which are proceeding to their positions, fall victims to reconnaissance Hudsons 'J' and 'M' of No 269 Sqn

RAF S of Iceland. As a result of B-Service reports, on 17 and 18 May the evasive movements of convoys HX.238 and SC.130 are established and, in consequence, the formation is moved S and extended by the newly formed 'Oder' group in the S, consisting of *U221*, *U666*, *U558*, *U752*, *U336*, *U642*, *U603* and *U228*. But HX.238—45 ships escorted by EG.C3 with the destroyers *Burnham* (RN) and *Skeena* and the corvettes *Bittersweet*, *Eyebright*, *La Malbaie* and *Pictou* and, in the convoy the escort carrier *Fencer* on transfer—passes the patrol line. The following convoy SC.130—38 ships under Commodore Capt Forsythe with EG.B7 (Cdr Gretton) comprising the destroyers *Duncan* and *Vidette*, the frigate *Tay* and the corvettes *Snowflake*, *Sunflower*, *Pink*, *Loosestrife* and *Kitchener* (Canadian; attached until 19 May)—is reported during the night 18–19 May by *U304* (Lt Koch), which is able to bring up *U645* and *U952*. But contact is lost in the morning as the result of a sharp change in course. Air escort provided by Liberators of No 120 Sqn RAF frustrates the efforts of the U-boats. Liberator 'T' of No 120 Sqn (Ft Sgt Shores) attacks in its first approach *U731* (Lt-Cdr Techand), which remains undamaged, and forces five other boats under water, of which *U952* is badly damaged by depth charges from *Tay*. *U381* (Lt-Cdr Count v Pückler und Limpurg), is lost to an unknown cause; *U636*, which is preparing an underwater attack, is located by *Snowflake* and attacked with the help of *Duncan* as the ships cover the area several times with depth charges but she remains undamaged. Two other boats escape from *Pink* and *Sunflower* on the surface. At mid-day the 1st SG, with the frigates *Wear*, *Jed* and *Spey* and the sloop *Sennen*, comes up from the rear and sights two U-boats. One of them, *U954* (Lt Loewe) fires torpedoes as she submerges but is sunk by *Sennen* and *Jed* with 'Hedgehog'. *Duncan* frustrates an attack by *U707* which is damaged. The second Liberator, 'P' of No 120 Sqn, forces, partly in co-operation with *Vidette*, six boats under water and aircraft 'O' and 'Y' of the same unit another four and two boats respectively, three of which are bombed. Before dusk *Jed* and *Spey* drive off the last contact-keeper: only *U92* (Lt-Cdr Oelrich) makes an unsuccessful attack. In the morning the operation is broken off and Liberator 'P' sinks *U258*. From the remaining boats, *U552*, *U264*, *U378*, *U607*, *U221*, *U666*, *U752*, *U558*, *U336*, *U650*, *U642*, *U603*, *U228*, *U575*, *U621*, *U441*, *U305*, *U569*, *U468*, *U231* and *U218*, the Cdr U-boats forms the 'Mosel' group on 19 May to operate against

HX.239—42 ships escorted by EG.B3 (Cdr Evans) with the destroyers *Keppel* and *Escapade*, the frigate *Towy* and the corvettes *Orchis*, *Narcissus* and the French *Roselys*, *Lobélia* and *Renoncule*—which has been located by the B-Service. Once again an evasive movement is ordered and is detected by the B-Service, and the 'Mosel' group can be moved to the S. In the evening of 21 May ON.184, consisting of 39 ships escorted by EG.C1 with the frigate *Itchen* (RN), the destroyers *St Laurent* and *St Croix* and the corvettes *Agassiz*, *Sackville* and *Woodstock*, reaches the patrol line from the E. It is supported by the 6th SG (Capt Short) with the US escort carrier *Bogue* and the destroyers *Belknap*, *Greene*, *Osmond-Ingram* and *George E Badger*. Avenger bombers from *Bogue* damage *U231* and the destroyers *Osmond-Ingram* and *St Laurent* force two other boats to submerge. ON.184 passes through the gap. On 22 May *U468* (Lt Schamong) beats off an Avenger with AA fire. Only at midday does a report about the convoy come through from *U305* (Lt-Cdr Bahr). The southerly 'Mosel' boats are deployed but *U305* is bombed three times by Avengers and damaged. In the afternoon two Avengers of VC-9 from *Bogue* sink *U569*. Simultaneously *U218* (Lt-Cdr Becker) hears the convoy HX.239, against which the remaining 'Mosel' boats and the 'Donau' boats coming from SC.130 are deployed. But this convoy, too, has been joined by a carrier force, the 4th SG with *Archer* and the destroyers *Milne*, *Matchless*, *Eclipse* and *Fury* under Capt Scott-Moncrieff. A Swordfish from *Archer* is beaten off by *U468* and the boat escapes, as does *U218*, from the destroyers sent to attack them. *U664* and *U413* report the convoy on 23 May but no boat attacks. *U752* (Lt-Cdr Schroeter) is hit, in submerging, by a Swordfish of No 819 Sqn (*Archer*) armed with rockets; this is the first successful use of rockets in this role. She is then able to hold off three Swordfish and one Martlet fighter with her 2cm quadruple gun but has to scuttle herself when approached by the destroyers *Keppel* and *Escapade*. Both convoys have passed the U-boat concentration without loss.

11 May–26 Aug   Atlantic/Indian Ocean

Of the Italian submarines which set out as transports from Bordeaux, *Tazzoli* and *Barbarigo* are lost in the Bay of Biscay. *Cappellini* (11 May–9 July), *Giuliani* (16 May–17 June) and *Torelli* (18 June–26 Aug), which are met by the Italian colonial sloop *Eritrea*, reach Sabang and Singapore.

13 May   Mediterranean
107 US B-17 bombers drop 273 tons of bombs on harbour installations at Cagliari. The Italian submarine *Mocenigo* is sunk.

13–14 May   English Channel
The German mine barrage 'SW12' (Operation 'Stemmbogen') is laid out in the southern part of the North Sea, W of the Hook of Holland, by the 1st and 7th MS Flotillas and the 9th MMS Flotilla. On the return the British *MTB234* (Lt-Cdr P G O Dickens), *MTB244*, *MTB241* and *MTB232* attack the German force; in the engagement the leading German boat *M8* (Lt Werner Hardam†) sinks after two torpedo hits.

13 May–8 June   Black Sea
In attacks on German traffic, the Soviet torpedo cutters *TKA-115* and *TKA-125* fire torpedoes into the harbour of Anapa during the night 12–13 May. The following night the harbour is shelled by the flotilla leader *Kharkov* and by *Boiki*. During this action there is an unsuccessful engagement with the German motor torpedo boats *S51*, *S26*, and *S49*. During the night 20–21 May *Kharkov* shells Feodosia and the destroyer *Besposhchadny* Alushta. Soviet aircraft lay, in an increasing scale, air mines of British make in the Kerch Strait, which cause losses.

In German attacks on Soviet supply traffic, *S72* and *S49* torpedo two small craft on 20 May off Sochi; *U19* and *U18* have no success off Sukhumi and Poti in face of strong defence. On 22 May Ju 87s of FK I attack several convoys off Gelendzhik. The patrol cutter *SKA-041* is sunk from a convoy escorted by the minesweepers *T-407/Mina* and *T-409/Garpun*. The patrol ships *Shtorm* and *Shkval* take in tow the damaged transport *Internatsional*.

14 May   South West Pacific
The Japanese submarine *Ro-102* is sunk 5 nautical miles W of Lae by the US MTBs *PT150* and *PT152*.

14–18 May   English Channel
The RAF Coastal Command's 'shipping strike wing' with Beaufighter aircraft achieves its first successes by sinking the German minesweeper *M414* with a torpedo hit off Texel and the patrol trawler *V1106* off Borkum on 17 May. On 18 May the minesweeper *M345* is sunk off Gravelines by a Hampden of No 145 Sqn RAF and the patrol vessel *V1110* is sunk off Vlieland by an airborne torpedo.

14–29 May   Air War Germany/Western Europe
The 8th AF carries out daylight attacks on harbours: on 14 May with 108 Fortresses and 17 Liberators on Kiel (250 tons), in which the U-boats *U235*, *U236* and *U237*, being completed in the Germania yards, are sunk (but are later raised and repaired); on 15 May with 59 Fortresses on Emden; on 17 May with 119 Fortresses on the harbour installations at Lorient (250 tons) and with 35 Liberators on the docks of Bordeaux (90 tons); on 19 May with a strong force on the dockyards at Kiel; and on 21 May with many Fortresses on Wilhelmshaven (200 tons). On 29 May Fortresses and Liberators attack the U-boat bases at St-Nazaire and La Pallice with 300 tons of bombs.

14 May–8 June   Central Atlantic/Mediterranean
On 14 May convoy UGS.8A sails from New York; it consists of 80 ships, escorted by TF.66 with the US Coast Guard cutters *Bibb* and *Ingham*, the US destroyers *Babbitt*, *Greer*, *Upshur* and *Doyle* and the US minesweepers *Pioneer*, *Portent* and *Threat* with support from TG.21.3 with the escort carrier *Card* and the destroyers *Bristol*, *Ludlow* and *Woolsey*. There are no German U-boat groups in the area but some submarines are on their way from the North Atlantic to a waiting area off the Azores; one of them is attacked on 26 Jun by *Bibb* without results.

On 31 May 22 ships depart for Casablanca. The escort of 58 ships is taken over by the British destroyers *Brocklesby* and *Quantock*, the US destroyer *Bernadou*, the corvette *Pentstemon* and four A/S trawlers. On 2 June it is joined off Gibraltar by convoy KMS.15, with 71 ships, to form the largest convoy of the war so far and the first to go through the Sicilian Channel. The combined escort group in the Mediterranean comprises the US destroyers *Champlin*, *Rowan*, *Rhind* and *Niblack*, the British AA cruiser *Carlisle*, one AA ship, the British destroyers *Lauderdale* and *Quantock*, the British minesweeper *Sharpshooter* and four A/S trawlers. On 3 June the ships depart for Oran, on 4 June for Algiers (86 vessels), on 5 June for Philippeville and Bône, on 6 June for Bizerta and Tunis, on 7 June for Sousse and Sfax and on 8 June for Tripoli.

15 May   Mediterranean
The German A/S trawler *UJ2213* is sunk 15 nautical miles S of Nice by the British submarine *Sickle*.

17 May   Spain
In a large fire in the Spanish naval base of El Ferrol, the light cruisers *Miguel de Cervantes*, *Galicia* and *Mendes Nuñez* and the destroyers *Alsedo* and *Lazaga* are severely damaged.

17 May   Bay of Biscay
The outgoing *U229* is damaged by Catalina 'E' of No 190 Sqn and has to limp back, reaching Bordeaux on 7 June.

20 May   Atlantic
Formation of the US 10th Fleet under direct command of the CNO, Adm King, to conduct and co-ordinate the battle against U-boats in the Atlantic.

20 May   Mediterranean
The British minesweeper *Fantome* becomes a constructive total loss after hitting a mine off Cape Bon.

23 May–12 June   English Channel
The German 2nd MTB Flotilla (Cdr Feldt, with *S67*, *S83*, *S62*, *S94*, *S89* and *S98*), the 4th (Lt-Cdr Lützow, with *S63*, *S110*, *S122* and *S117*), the 5th (Lt-Cdr Klug, with *S90*, *S65*, *S116*, *S82*, *S112*, *S81* and *S121*) and the 6th (Lt-Cdr Obermaier, with *S79*, *S114*, *S76* and *S91*) carry out mining operations off the British south coast from Cherbourg and St Peter Port: on 23–24 May between the Isle of Wight and Portland; on 28–29 May, 30–31 May, 5–6 June and 11–12 June in Lyme Bay; and on 6–7 June off Start Point. In 77 sorties the boats lay 321 mines and 84 barrage protection floats.

24 May–5 June   North Atlantic
On 24 May the Commander U-boats decides, as a result of the heavy losses in the last convoy operations and the unsuccessful attacks made by the 'Donau' and 'Mosel' groups, to stop temporarily the battle against convoys in the North Atlantic until the situation has been clarified and new weapons become available. The boats with adequate fuel supplies are moved S to the USA–Gibraltar route and those with limited fuel supplies (*U264*, *U636*, *U731*, *U418*, *U645*, *U304*, *U664*, *U202*, *U91*, *U413*, *U378*, *U552*, *U650*, *U621* and *U575*) are distributed widely over the N Atlantic to simulate by their W/T traffic the presence of stronger groups. On 29 May *U552* is damaged by Liberator 'S' of No 59 Sqn RAF.

Turning point in the Battle of the Atlantic
The C-in-C Western Approaches deploys the 2nd SG (Capt Walker), comprising the sloops *Starling*, *Wren*, *Woodpecker*, *Cygnet*, *Wild Goose* and *Kite*, to make it possible for the convoys ONS.8 (52 ships plus EG.C4 with the destroyer *Churchill*) from 22 to 25 May and HX.240 (56 ships plus EG.C5 with the destroyer *Ottawa*) from 27 to 30 May to break through the U-boat groups suspected

on the basis of the W/T picture. But no U-boats are found. However, Liberator 'E' of No 120 Sqn sinks *U304* near HX.240 and *Starling* finds *U202* (Lt-Cdr Poser) on her third trip on 1 June and sinks her after a fifteen-hour hunt.

24 May–22 July   Western Atlantic
U190 has no success on the American East Coast. *U521* (Lt-Cdr Bargsten) is sunk on 2 June by the submarine-chaser *PC565* belonging to the escort of an NG convoy. Only *U66* (Lt-Cdr Markworth) sinks two tankers of 20368 tons and torpedoes a third of 10172 tons. One ship of 2937 tons sinks and one ship of 7176 tons is damaged on a mine barrage laid by *U119* (Cdr v Kameke) off Halifax on 1 June.

25 May   North Atlantic
The outgoing *U467* is sunk S of Iceland by Catalina 'F' of VP-84.

25–28 May   Mediterranean
In attacks by American bombers on Messina on 25 May, the Italian torpedo boat *Groppo* sinks. On 28 May the Italian torpedo boats *Angelo Bassini* and *Antares* and the corvette *FR52* sink in Livorno.

25 May–23 Aug   North Atlantic
During the time when there are no German U-boat groups operating in the N Atlantic, the following convoys run in both directions (escort groups in parentheses):—SC.131 (B6), HX.240 (C5), ON.185 (B1), ONS.9 (B2) and ON.186 (C2) depart during May; SC.132 (B5), HX.241 (B4), HX.242 (C1), SC.133 (C4), HX.243 (C2/B1), SC.134 (B2), HX.244 (C3), HX.245 (C5), ON.187 (C3), ONS.10 (B7), ON.188 (C5), ON.189 (B6), ONS.11 (B4) and ON.190 (C1) depart during June; SC.135 (B7), HX.246 (B6), SC.136 (B4), HX.247 (C1), HX.248 (C2), SC.137 (C4), HX.249 (C3), ON.191 (C2), ONS.12 (C4), ON.192 (C3), ONS.13 (B2), ON.193 (C5), ON.194 (B6) and ONS.14 (B7) depart during July; and HX.250 (C5), SC.138 (B2), SC.139 (B7), HX.251 (B6), ON.195 (C1), ONS.15 (B3), ON.196 (C2) and ON.197 (C4) depart during Aug.

26 May   Bay of Biscay
The returning *U436* is sunk W of Cape Finisterre by the British frigate *Test* and the RIN corvette *Hyderabad* escorting convoy KX.10.

26 May–21 June   North Pacific
In up to three missions, the Japanese submarines *I-7*, *I-2*, *I-5*, *I-6*, *I-9*, *I-21*, *I-24*, *I-35*, *I-168*, *I-169*, *I-171*, *I-155* and *I-157* evacuate, in all, 820 troops from Kiska to Paramushiro. In the course of the operations, *I-24* is sunk on 10 June by the submarine-chaser *PC487*, *I-9* on 11 June by the destroyer *Frazier*, *I-7* is damaged on 22 June by the destroyer *Monaghan* and is

grounded and scuttled at Kiska on 5 July, *I-2* and *I-157* are damaged when they go aground in the fog and *I-155* is damaged by heavy seas.

27 May   Mediterranean
The Free French destroyer leader *Léopard*, escorting a Malta–Alexandria convoy, runs aground NNE of Benghazi and becomes a total loss.

28 May   Mediterranean
U755 is sunk by Hudson 'M' of No 608 Sqn RAF E of Gibraltar.

28–29 May   English Channel
In a mining operation by the British 50th and 52nd ML Flotillas and by *MTB219* and *MTB221*, the covering force has an engagement near the West Dyck Bank with four patrol boats of the 13th and 14th PB Flotillas: *MGB110* sinks and *MGB108* and *MGB118* are damaged and only *MGB116* is unscathed. An attack by the British *MTB632*, *MTB629*, *MTB628* and *MTB607* fails.

30 May   Great Britain
The British submarine *Untamed* accidentally sinks off Campbeltown during an exercise. She is raised and recommissioned as *Vitality*.

31 May   Bay of Biscay
The outgoing *U440* is sunk by Sunderland 'R' of No 201 Sqn RAF.

31 May   General Situation
Grand Admiral Dönitz transfers the responsibility for all naval armaments to the Armaments Minister, Speer.

31 May–13 June   Mediterranean
Operation 'Corkscrew': British attack on Pantelleria. The cruiser *Orion* (Capt Menzies), which carried out a shelling on 12–13 May, bombards the island on 31 May accompanied by the destroyers *Petard* and *Troubridge*. On 1 June the cruiser *Penelope* (Capt Belben) repeats the shelling with the destroyers *Paladin* and *Petard*; *Penelope* is hit by the Italian coastal battery. In a sortie to the coast near Cape Spartivento, the destroyers *Jervis* and *Vasilissa Olga* (Greek) sink one Italian steamer and the torpedo boat *Castore*. During the night 2–3 June *Orion*, *Paladin* and *Troubridge* shell Pantelleria as do on 3 June the destroyers *Ilex* and *Isis*, followed on 5 June by the cruiser *Newfoundland* with the destroyers *Paladin* and *Troubridge*, and on 8 June by the cruisers *Aurora*, *Euryalus*, *Newfoundland*, *Orion* and *Penelope* and the destroyers *Jervis*, *Laforey*, *Lookout*, *Loyal*, *Nubian*, *Tartar*, *Troubridge* and *Whaddon* and *MTB73*, *MTB77* and *MTB84*. After the shellings and the dropping of 6200 tons of bombs by Allied aircraft in 5285 sorties, a landing

force (Rear-Adm McGrigor) with the 1st British Div on board appears off the island during the night 10–11 June with the headquarters ship *Largs*, the destroyers *Paladin* and *Petard* and the gunboat *Aphis*, together with a covering force comprising the British cruisers *Aurora* (Allied C-in-C Gen Eisenhower on board), *Newfoundland* (Rear-Adm Harcourt), *Orion*, *Penelope* and *Euryalus*, the destroyers *Laforey*, *Lookout*, *Loyal*, *Jervis*, *Tartar*, *Nubian*, *Troubridge* and *Whaddon* and eight MTBs. The Italian Rear-Adm Pavesi surrenders the island fortress of Pantelleria without further fighting on 11 June. On 12 June the island of Lampedusa also capitulates after a night shelling by *Aurora*, *Orion*, *Penelope* and *Newfoundland* and six destroyers. Linosa surrenders to the destroyer *Nubian* on 13 June and Lampione on 14 June. The submarine *Ultor* bombards the D/F station on Salina in the Lipari Islands.

June   Mediterranean/Intelligence
The German U-boats in the Mediterranean are allocated a separate cypher circuit, 'Medusa' which is, however, broken a short time later as 'Turtle'/'Cockle'.

1–30 June   Air War/Western Europe
RAF Bomber Command mine offensive: over 16 nights, 374 sorties are flown against Biscay ports, especially Brest, St-Nazaire, Lorient, La Pallice and the Gironde estuary, the coast of Brittany, the Dutch coast (especially off Texel) and the Frisian coast. Seven aircraft are lost. On 16 June the German MDS *Sperrbrecher 21/Nestor* sinks on a mine in the Gironde estuary.

1–30 June   Pacific
In US submarine operations there are 145 'Ultra' signals which lead to 95 sightings and 22 attacks, in which eight ships are sunk and nine damaged. For the US submarines arriving in their operational areas in June the following results are achieved. In the Aleutian area, *S30* (Lt-Cdr Stevenson) sinks one ship of 5131 tons and one sailing vessel and *S33* sinks three sailing vessels. In Japanese waters, *Salmon* (Lt-Cdr Nicholas) is on a special mission and makes two attacks with duds, *Runner* (Lt-Cdr Bourland) sinks two ships of 6273 tons and is subsequently lost to a mine off Honshu, *Sculpin* (Lt-Cdr Chappell) sinks two sailing vessels, *Gunnel* (Lt-Cdr McCain) sinks three ships of 16194 tons and damages one more of 450 tons, *Harder* (Lt-Cdr Dealey) sinks one ship of 7189 tons and damages one of 1189 tons, *Jack* (Lt-Cdr Dykers) sinks three ships of 16551 tons and *Sailfish* (Lt-Cdr Moore) sinks two ships of 6908 tons. In the East China Sea, *Snook* (Lt-Cdr Triebel) sinks

two ships of 11155 tons and damages two more of 13858 tons.

In the Central Pacific, *Greenling* (Lt-Cdr Grant) sinks one ship of 10182 tons, *Flying Fish* (Lt-Cdr Watkins) sinks one ship of 2822 tons and one sailing vessel, *Silversides* (Lt-Cdr Burlingame) lays a minefield off Kavieng (on which three ships of 7081 tons, the survey ship *Tsukushi* and the submarine-chaser *Ch-29* sink and the cruiser *Isuzu*, the destroyer *Isokaze* and two ships of 5818 tons are damaged) and sinks one ship of 5256 tons by torpedo, *Sargo* (Lt-Cdr Carmick) sinks one ship of 5226 tons, *Tunny* (Lt-Cdr Scott) sinks one ship of 1964 tons, *Growler* (Lt-Cdr Schade) sinks one ship of 5196 tons and *Porpoise* (Lt-Cdr Bennett) sinks one ship of 2718 tons and conducts a reconnaisance mission; *Seadragon* and *Hoe* have several misses and fire many duds and *Scorpion* conducts a special mission. In the South Pacific, *Guardfish* (Lt-Cdr Ward) sinks one ship of 897 tons, *Drum* (Lt-Cdr McMahon) sinks one of 5086 tons and *Peto* (Lt-Cdr Nelson) sinks one of 359 tons. In the South West Pacific, *Grayling* (Lt-Cdr Lee) sinks two sailing vessels and damages one ship of 8673 tons, *Trout* (Lt-Cdr Clark) sinks two ships of 5866 tons and two sailing vessels and carries out a guerrilla operation, *Gurnard* (Lt-Cdr Andrews) sinks one ship of 1925 tons and *Thresher* (Lt-Cdr Hull) sinks one ship of 5274 tons and on 1 July damages the destroyer *Hokaze*.

1 June–15 July   Central Atlantic

The U-boats withdrawn from the N Atlantic, *U92*, *U558*, *U953*, *U951*, *U435*, *U666*, *U336*, *U232*, *U642*, *U221*, *U603*, *U228*, *U641*, *U608*, *U211* and *U217*, are formed into the 'Trutz' group from 1 June SW of the Azores to operate against the convoy GUS.7A (45 ships plus TF.65 with the destroyers *Parker*, *Laub*, *Kendrick*, *MacKenzie*, *McLanahan*, *Boyle* and *Nields*) which set out from Gibraltar on 23 May. But the convoy is re-routed according to 'Ultra' interceptions, locates the patrol line with HF/DF and avoids it by going S. On 4 June aircraft of the US Support Group (Capt Short), comprising the escort carrier *Bogue* together with *Clemson*, *George E Badger*, *Greene* and *Osmond-Ingram*, force *U228*, *U641* and *U603* to submerge. *U641* shoots down one aircraft. *U217* is sunk on 5 June by two aircraft of VC-9 from *Bogue*. While *U488* (Lt Bartke) replenishes 14 boats of the 'Trutz' group without incident from 7 to 13 June, the *Bogue* group passes to the S with the convoy UGS.9 (74 ships plus TF.69 with the destroyers *Stevenson*, *Stockton*, *Thorn* and *Paul Jones* and the US Coast

Guard cutter *Campbell*) in an easterly direction. The outbound *U758* (Lt-Cdr Manseck) is able to hold off eight carrier aircraft with her 2cm quadruple gun (used for the first time successfully) and to inflict considerable damage on some of them. But after meeting the U-tanker, *U118*, the latter is sunk on 12 June by eight aircraft of VC-9. From 16 June the replenished 'Trutz' boats form three overlapping patrol lines in the Central Atlantic: 1 (*U608*, *U228*, *U558*, *U642*), 2 (*U641*, *U603*, *U666*, *U951*, *U953*, *U232*, *U336*, *U135*), and 3 (*U221*, *U211*, *U435*, *U193*), to operate against the expected convoy GUS.8 (which is escorted by TF.66 with the US Coast Guard cutters *Bibb* and *Ingham*, the US destroyers *Doyle*, *Hamilton*, *Upshur*, *Greer*, the US minesweepers *Pioneer*, *Threat*, *Portent*, the French destroyer *Le Malin* and the sloops *La Gracieuse* and *Cdt Delage* with Support Group 21.3 (Capt Isbell) comprising the escort carrier *Card* and the destroyers *Herbert*, *Du Pont* and *Dickerson*. The convoy avoids the patrol line, as does the UGS.10 (70 Ships with TF.61 comprising the destroyers *Livermore*, *Kearny*, *Eberle*, *Ericsson* and *McCormick* and the minesweepers *Parrott*, *Prevail* and *Pilot*, with Support Group 21.11 under Capt Fick comprising the escort carrier *Santee* and the destroyers *Overton*, *MacLeish* and *Bainbridge*) coming from the W. The outbound *U572* (Lt Kummetat) to the S is overrun and sinks the French naval tanker *Lot* (4220 tons). Whilst *U488* and *U530*, *U536*, *U170* and *U535*, which are used as temporary tankers, replenish ten medium boats and the 'Trutz' group searches further to the E, the convoy GUS.8A (43 ships with TF.69 comprising the US Coast Guard cutters *Campbell*, *Spencer*, *Duane* and the destroyers *Stevenson*, *Stockton*, *Thorn*, *Mayo*, *Tarbell* and *Paul Jones*) also passes to the S. From 29 June *U221* and *U558* go to Lisbon and *U193* and *U135* to the Canaries; the others form, from 2 July, groups 'Geier 1' (*U608*, *U633*, *U641* and *U228*), 'Geier 2' (*U211*, *U951*, *U953* and *U435*) and 'Geier 3' (*U232*, *U642* and *U336*): they proceed slowly from the area S of the Azores in the direction of Portugal. As they do so, from 7 to 9 July, *U951* and *U232* are sunk by Liberators from the 1st and 2nd A/S Sqns USAAF, *U603* is damaged by Catalina 'G' of No 202 Sqn RAF and *U435* is sunk by Wellington 'R' of No 179 Sqn RAF. *U193* is damaged by bombs near the Canaries. *U135* (Lt Luther) torpedoes on 15 July one ship of 4762 tons from the convoy OS.51 but is then sunk by the sloop *Rochester* and the corvettes *Balsam* and *Mignonette* of the 39th EG.

1 June–20 Sept   Black Sea

German supply convoys 'Hagen 1–91' with up to 13 naval ferry barges of the 1st, 3rd and 5th Landing Flotillas as well as tugs and lighters. From June there are also 'Bansin' convoys from Feodosia to Anapa. There is in addition considerable ferry traffic in the Kerch Strait to supply the German 17th Army in the Kuban bridgehead. Frequent air attacks against these convoys do little damage. Submarine attacks on the flat-bottomed naval ferry barges made by *A-3*, *L-4*, *S-31*, *Shch-215*, *M-112*, *M-117*, *M-35* and other boats are unsuccessful. Only *M-111* (Capt 3rd Class Josseliani) sinks the tugs and lighters *Dunarea* (505 tons, 18 July) and *Hainburg* (28 Aug). Torpedo cutters have no success.

In operations with several boats against the Constanza–Sevastopol route, *D-4* on 1 June misses the Italian tanker *Celeno* escorted by the Rumanian destroyer *Marasesti*, two German motor minesweepers and the submarine-chaser *Schiff 19*. On 7 July *S-33*, *Shch-201* and *Shch-203* operate against a convoy consisting of the steamers *Ardeal* and *Varna*, escorted by the Rumanian destroyers *Maresti* and *Marasesti* and the gunboats *Stihi* and *Ghigulescu*. *Shch-201* misses the convoy and *Marasesti* reports one submarine *(M-31)* sunk by depth charges. W of the Crimea *D-4* (Lt-Cdr Gremyako) sinks on 11 Aug the steamer *Boj Feddersen* (6689 tons), damaged by aircraft, and on 20 Aug the steamer *Varna* (2141 tons). Of the Italian midget submarines deployed in hunting submarines, *CB 4* (Sub-Lt Sibille) reports one submarine (*Shch-207*) sunk on 28 Aug.

Soviet submarine groups are deployed against German traffic from the Bosphorus on the basis of agents' reports. Thus, at the end of July and beginning of Aug, *L-4*, *Shch-216*, *M-117* and, later, *M-35* are deployed against the expected tanker *Firuz* (7327 tons). She is torpedoed on 6 Aug by *Shch-216* (Capt 3rd Class Karbovski) after being met by German motor minesweepers and the submarine-chaser *Xanten*. In addition, the small Turkish ships *Hudayi Bahri*, *Tayyari* and *Gurpinar* are sunk. At the end of Aug a new group operates off the Bosphorus and sinks the Turkish ships *Yilmaz* and *Verviske*. Likewise on 30 Aug *Shch-215* (Capt 3rd Class Greshilov) sinks the expected tanker *Thisbé* (1782 tons) after being met by two Rumanian destroyers and two German submarine-chasers.

During the night 20–21 Aug the Soviet patrol ships *Shtorm* and *Shkval* with four SKA patrol cutters attack Anapa airfield with rockets.

3 June   Mediterranean

The German A/S trawler *UJ2212* is sunk by an aerial torpedo between Naples and Palermo.

4 June   Norway

The Norwegian *MTB620* and *MTB626* sink the steamer *Altenfels* (8132 tons) sailing in company with *M468* in Korsfjord. The British submarine *Truculent* (Lt Alexander) sinks the outgoing *U308* N of Trondheim.

4 June   North Atlantic

On its transfer cruise to the Mediterranean, *U594* is sunk W of Gibraltar by rocket fire from Hudson 'F' of No 48 Sqn RAF.

4–6 June   English Channel

Two mining operations by the German 5th TB Flotilla (Cdr Koppenhagen), comprising *T22*, *Möwe*, *Falke*, *Greif* and *Kondor*.

5 June   South Pacific

Air battle over Russell Island. The Japanese attack with 81 aircraft from Rabaul and lose 24 machines in engagements with 101 US aircraft. US losses number seven aircraft.

5 June–11 Aug   South Atlantic

In operations in Brazilian waters, *U513* (Lt-Cdr Guggenberger) sinks four ships of 17151 tons and torpedoes one of 6003 tons, *U199* (Lt-Cdr Kraus) sinks one ship of 4161 tons and one sailing ship, *U172* (Lt-Cdr Emmermann) sinks four ships of 22946 tons and *U185* (Lt-Cdr Maus) attacks on 7 July the convoy BT.18 (20 steamers plus three Brazilian corvettes and one submarine-chaser), sinks three ships of 21413 tons and torpedoes one of 6840 tons and, later, sinks two independents of 15368 tons. *U513* falls victim on 19 July, *U591* on 30 July and *U199* on 31 July to Mariners of VP-74 and two Brazilian aircraft, Liberators of VB-107 and Venturas of VB-127 respectively. *U604* is bombed on 30 July by a Ventura from VB-129 and damaged by a Liberator from VP-107 on 3 Aug. On 11 Aug this aircraft is shot down by *U185* when taking over the crew of *U604*. *U604* is scuttled while the US destroyer *Moffett* comes up.

5 June–14 Aug   Western Atlantic

E of the Caribbean, *U572* (Lt Kummetat) sinks two sailing ships of 290 tons. *U590* (Lt Krüer) sinks one ship of 5228 tons. On 8 July *U510* (Lt Eick) attacks convoy TJ.1 (20 ships plus the US destroyer *Somers* and four US and one Brazilian submarine-chasers) and sinks two ships of 17224 tons and later one other of 1641 tons. *U590* damages a Catalina from VP-94, deployed to escort TJ.1, with AA fire but is sunk by a second Catalina from VP-94. On 21 July a Catalina with convoy TF.2 (18 steamers) sinks *U662*. On 23 July *U466* is bombed by a Liberator and on 3 Aug a Mariner from

VP-205 sinks *U572*. *U67*, *U653*, *U415*, *U406* and *U466* return without successes. In operations in the Caribbean, *U759* (Lt Friedrich) sinks two ships of 12764 tons and one sailing ship. In the area of the Windward Passage, *U159* and *U759* are sunk on 15 and 26 July respectively by Mariner flying boats of VP-32. *U134* (Lt-Cdr Brosin) shoots down blimp *K74* N of Cuba on 18 July. *U732* (Lt Carlsen) misses convoy NG.376 and is attacked by depth charges from the corvette *Brisk*. In the Caribbean, *U615* (Lt-Cdr Kapitzky) sinks one ship of 3177 tons and shoots down one Mariner from VP-205. On 6 Aug the boat wards off six aircraft (from VPB-130, VP-204 and the 10th Sqn USAAF), two of which are badly hit by AA fire, but, unable to dive, she has to scuttle herself on the approach of the US destroyer *Walker*. *U634* and *U359* are unsuccessful.

6–11 June   North Atlantic

The outgoing *U450* heavily is damaged by depth charges and gunfire from Fortress 'A' of No 220 Sqn S of Iceland on 6 June. On 11 June the outgoing *U417* is sunk by Fortress 'R' of No 206 Sqn E of Iceland.

7 June–12 July   North Atlantic

U592, *U669*, *U341*, *U271*, *U334*, *U388*, *U420* and *U667* cruise in the N Atlantic, simulating stronger U-boat formations by transmitting appropriate W/T messages and brief signals. On 8 June the outgoing *U535* is damaged S of Iceland by Hudson 'K' of No 269 Sqn RAF flying escort for convoy SC.132 (with EG.B5). On 14 June *U334* is located by the 1st SG (supporting convoy ONS.10) and sunk by the frigate *Jed* and the sloop *Pelican*. *U388* falls victim to Catalina 'I' from VP-84 based in Iceland (first use of the 'Fido' A/S homing torpedo), which aircraft also damages *U420*.

8 June   Japan

The Japanese battleship *Mutsu* sinks off Hiroshima after an internal explosion.

8 June–9 July   Mediterranean

Preparatory movements by Allied convoys for Operation 'Husky' (Sicily). From 8 June to 1 July convoys UGF.9 and UGF.9A, consisting of 25 and 11 transports respectively with the 45th Inf Div on board, proceed from Norfolk to Oran and Algiers. The escort for UGF.9 comprises TF.65 with the cruisers *Philadelphia*, *Boise* and *Birmingham* and the destroyers *Mervine*, *Davison*, *Quick*, *Beatty*, *Tillman*, *Cowie*, *Knight*, *Doran*, *Earle*, *Nelson*, *Murphy*, *Glennon*, *Jeffers*, *Maddox*, *Butler*, *Gherardi*, *Shubrick* and *Herndon*; that for UGF.9A is TF.65.5 with the cruiser *Brooklyn* and the destroyers *Buck*, *Edison*, *Wilkes*, *Nicholson*, *Swanson*, *Roe*, *Boyle*, *Parker*, *Laub*, *Kendrick*, *Nields*, *Mackenzie* and *McLan-*

ahan. From 17 to 23 June the British Force H (Vice-Adm Willis), comprising the battleships *Nelson*, *Rodney*, *Valiant* and *Warspite*, the carrier *Indomitable* and the destroyers of the 4th, 8th and 24th Flotillas (14 British, two French, one Polish and one Greek), is transferred from Scapa Flow to Gibraltar and on to Oran. From there *Valiant* and *Warspite*, together with the carrier *Formidable*, the cruisers *Aurora* and *Penelope* and six destroyers, proceed to Alexandria by 5 July. After the US battleships *Alabama* and *South Dakota* with five destroyers have arrived at Scapa Flow from Argentia at the end of June, the British battleships *Howe* and *King George V* are also moved to Gibraltar. There set out from the Clyde the convoys KMS.18A (20 June), KMS.18B (24 June), KMS.19 (25 June), KMF.18 (28 June) and KMF.19 (1 July), comprising, in all, nine troop transports, nine LSIs, six tankers, one collier and one headquarters ship. On board are the 1st Canadian Inf Div, the 1st Canadian Armoured Bde, the 40th and 41st Royal Marine Commandos and the 73rd British AA Bde. On 4 and 5 July KMS.18B loses three ships off the Algerian Coast as a result of attacks by the U-boats *U375* and *U593*.

From Alexandria and Port Said there put to sea the convoys MWS.36 (3 July), MWF.36 (5 July), MWS.37 (6 July) and MWF.37 (9 July), consisting, in all, of one headquarters ship, 29 LSIs, 60 freighters, two LSGs and five tankers. On board are the British 5th and 50th Inf Divs, the 231st Inf Bde, the 4th Armoured Bde and the 3rd Commando. On 6 July *U453* sinks one ship of 5757 tons from MWS.36 off Derna. On 7 July a part of the covering force—*Warspite*, *Valiant*, *Formidable*, *Aurora* and *Penelope* and nine destroyers—also sets out from Alexandria. These ships are to join up on 9 July in the Gulf of Sirte with *Nelson*, *Rodney*, *Indomitable*, the cruisers *Cleopatra* and *Euryalus* and eight destroyers coming from Oran. The support force, consisting of the cruisers *Newfoundland*, *Uganda*, *Mauritius* and *Orion* and six destroyers, follows from Alexandria.

From Algiers and Oran there set out the convoys NCS.1 (4 July), NCF.1 (5 July), NCS.2 (9 July) and NCF.2 (9 July) with one headquarters ship, 26 troop transports and 31 freighters. On board are the US 1st and 45th Inf Divs and elements of the 9th Inf Div which is in reserve.

The convoys TJF.1 (5 July), TJS.1 (8 July) and TJM.1 (8 July), consisting of 78 LSTs, 116 LCTs and 106 LSIs, follow from Bizerta. On board are the US 3rd Inf Div and the 2nd Armoured Div.

From Sfax there set out the convoys SBS.1 (7 July), SBM.1 (8 July) and SBF.1 (8 July), from Tripoli the MWS.36X (8 July) and from Malta the SBF.2 and SBF.3 (9 July), comprising four landing ships, one headquarters ship, 42 LSTs, 77 LCTs and 43 LCIs. On board are the British 51st Inf Div and the British 23rd Armoured Bde. With the convoy setting out from Algerian ports are the American cruisers *Brooklyn*, *Birmingham*, *Savannah*, *Boise* and *Philadelphia*, the British monitor *Abercrombie* and 48 US destroyers. The British convoys are escorted, *inter alia*, by 58 British and Allied destroyers, 36 escort vessels and 34 minesweepers.

To cover the operation, the submarines *Ultor*, *Unruly* and *Sokol* (Polish) are stationed N of the Straits of Messina and *Unshaken*, *United*, *Unbroken*, *Dzik* (Polish) and *Uproar* off Taranto.

10 June   Intelligence
The British change from 'Naval Cypher No 3' and 'Naval Cypher No 4' to the new 'Naval Cypher No 5', producing a 'black out' for the German B-Service which might have been fatal to the German U-boat war against the convoys had it not already been broken off on 24 May by the BdU on account of the heavy losses being experienced.

11 June   Indian Ocean
The Australian minesweeper-corvette *Wallaroo* is sunk in a collision off Fremantle with the SS *Gilbert Costin*.

11–13 June   Air War/Germany
Bombers of the 8th AF carry out daylight attacks on harbour installations at Wilhelmshaven and Kiel on 11 and 13 June respectively.

12 June   Western Atlantic
The US submarine *R12* sinks in a diving accident off the US East Coast.

12 June–28 July   Arctic
In attacks by German Fw 190 fighter bombers of JG 5 on shipping targets in the Kola Inlet and off the Fisherman's Peninsula and, in particular, in attacks by Soviet DB-3, Hampden and Boston torpedo bombers of the 5th Mining and Torpedo Air Div on German convoys off the coasts of the Varanger Peninsula, there are continual heavy air engagements between the escort fighters of JG 5 and Soviet fighters and the objects of their protection. These lead to losses on both sides, but ship sinkings are rare exceptions. Off the polar coast, among the Soviet submarines to operate are *M-105*, *M-106*, *Shch-422*, *S-101*, *S-51*, *S-54*, *Shch-403*, *S-56*, *L-15* (mining operations), *L-22*, *S-55* and *K-21*. Of them, *S-101* (Capt 2nd Class Egorov) makes five, *S-51* (Capt 2nd Class Kucherenko) and *M-105* (Lt-Cdr

Khrulev) two each and *S-54* (Capt 3rd Class Bratishko) one attack on convoys escorted by boats of the 61st PB Flotilla and the 12th SC Flotilla. *M-106* is sunk on 5 July near Vardö with depth charges from and ramming by *UJ1206* and *UJ1217*. *Shch-422* is lost on one of the flanking mine barrages laid out by the German minelayers *Brummer*, *Ostmark*, *Roland* and *Kaiser*. *Shch-403* (Capt 3rd Class Shuiski) misses *Brummer* laying out a mine barrage off Makkaur and *S-56* (Capt 3rd Class Shchedrin) sinks the minesweeper *M346* from a returning force off Gamvik and, on 20 July, the patrol boat *NKi09/Alane*.

12 June–2 Aug   Bay of Biscay
From the beginning of June the German U-boats pass through the Bay of Biscay in groups of two to five boats in order to be able to support each other in air attacks. Ju 88Cs of I/ZG 1 (Capt Kunkel) provide fighter protection in the inner Bay but are much inferior to the British Beaufighters of No 248 Sqn RAF and the Mosquitos of No 10 Group Fighter Command. On 12 June British aircraft sight groups of three boats for the first time. On 13 June Sunderland 'U' of No 228 Sqn RAF attacks the group consisting of *U564*, *U185*, *U415*, *U634* and *U159*, damages *U564* but is itself shot down by AA fire. On 14 June Whitley 'G' of No 10 OTU RAF sinks *U564*, accompanied by *U185*, but is also damaged by AA fire and shot down by a Ju 88. The German destroyers *Z24* and *Z32* set out to meet the submarines and to take off the survivors from *U185* and the boat sets out alone. From 14 June No 19 Group Coastal Command counters the new German tactics with Operations 'Musketry' and 'Seaslug': three times daily seven aircraft are deployed in parallel lines in the search area NW of Finisterre in order to be able to give quick support in case U-boats are sighted. Participating are Liberators of Nos 53, 86 and 224 Sqns RAF and of the 1st, 4th and 19th A/S Sqns USAAF, Catalinas of No 210 Sqn RAF and of VP-63 equipped with the magnetic locating equipment MAD, Sunderlands of Nos 226 and 228 Sqns RAF and of Nos 10 and 461 Sqns RAAF, Wellingtons of No 172 Sqn RAF and of No 426 Sqn RCAF with Leigh Lights and of No 304 (Polish) Sqn and No 311 (Czech) Sqn, Fortresses of No 59 Sqn RAF and Halifaxes of Nos 58 and 502 Sqns RAF.

On 14 June the outgoing *U68* and *U155* are damaged by gunfire from four Mosquitos of No 307 (Polish) Sqn and have to return. During a 'Musketry' patrol on 17 June Fortress 'F' of No 206 Sqn RAF damages the outgoing *U338*. On 19 June the outgoing

Italian submarine *Barbarigo* is lost, probably sunk by a USAAF aircraft. On 21 June the outgoing tanker *U462* is slightly damaged by gunfire from four Mosquitos of Nos 151 and 456 Sqns RAF and is again damaged on 2 July by Liberator 'J' of No 224 Sqn RAF and has to return. On 23 June the returning *U650* is damaged by Liberator 'K' of No 86 Sqn RAF while flying escort for convoys WS.31 and KMF.17. On 27 June the outgoing *U518* is damaged by Sunderland 'P' of No 201 Sqn RAF.

On 3 July the returning *U126* and *U154* are attacked by Wellington 'R' of No 172 Sqn RAF, which sinks *U126*; on the same day the outgoing *U386* is damaged by Liberator 'D' of No 53 Sqn RAF and *U628* is sunk by Liberator 'J' of No 224 Sqn, which is damaged by AA fire. On 5 July the returning *U535*, *U536* and *U170* are not found by the 2nd EG (which is searching on the basis of 'Ultra' information) but Liberator 'G' of No 53 Sqn RAF attacks and sinks *U535* and damages the other boats though is herself also damaged. On 7 July the outgoing *U267* is damaged by Catalina 'B' of No 210 Sqn RAF. On 8 July the outgoing 'Monsun' boat *U514* is sunk by Liberator 'R' of No 224 Sqn RAF (Sqn Ldr Bulloch) with a Mk 24 homing torpedo. On 12 July the AA-boat *U441* is damaged by gunfire from three Beaufighters of No 248 Sqn RAF and has to return with 10 dead and 13 wounded. On 13 July the outgoing *U607*, *U445* and *U613* are attacked by Halifax 'O' of No 58 Sqn RAF and Sunderland 'N' of No 228 Sqn RAF, which latter aircraft sinks *U607*. On 20 July the returning *U558* is sunk by Liberator 'F' of the 19th A/S Sqn USAAF and Halifax 'E' of No 58 Sqn RAF. On 24 July the outgoing tanker *U459* shoots down the attacking Wellington 'Q' of No 172 Sqn but the damaged boat is sunk by a Wellington of No 547 Sqn RAF. On 28 July the outgoing *U404* is sunk by Liberator 'W' of No 224 Sqn RAF and Liberator 'N' of the 4th A/S Sqn USAAF, which is also damaged. On 29 July the outgoing *U614* is sunk by Wellington 'G' of No 172 Sqn RAF.

In defensive actions, *U600*, *U462*, *U268*, *U43*, *U558*, *U459*, *U454* and *U383* each shoot down one aircraft and fighters shoot down six more. The U-tankers and damaged boats are escorted by two to four destroyers or torpedo boats: *Z24*, *Z23*, *Z32*, *T5*, *T19*, *T22*, *T24*, *T25*, *Falke*, *Greif*, *Möwe*, *Jaguar* and *Kondor* are deployed, sometimes more than once. On the British side, support groups are deployed from 20 June W of the Bay with cruiser cover against German surface ships. In the first operation, from 20 to 28 June, an aircraft leads the 2nd SG

217

(Capt Walker) to the *U650*, *U119* and *U449* group: the sloop *Starling* sinks the tanker *U119* by ramming and *Wild Goose*, *Woodpecker*, *Kite* and *Wren* sink *U449*. Cover is provided by the cruiser *Scylla*. Relief is provided in five to eight day intervals by EG.40, EG.B5 (the destroyer *Havelock*), the 2nd SG (the sloop *Wild Goose*), the 5th SG (the frigate *Nene*), EG.B1 (the destroyer *Hurricane*), a destroyer group consisting of the Canadian *Iroquois* and *Athabaskan* and the Polish *Orkan*, and EG.B5 (including the escort carrier *Archer*), with cover from the cruisers *Bermuda* and *Glasgow*. On 30 July an outbound group, consisting of the tankers *U461*, *U462* and the combat boat *U504*, is sighted by a Liberator of No 53 Sqn RAF and reported to aircraft situated in the vicinity and the 2nd SG (Capt Walker). In repeated attacks by seven aircraft, *U461* is sunk by Sunderland 'U' of No 461 Sqn, *U462* by Halifax 'S' of No 502 Sqn and *U504* by the sloops *Kite*, *Woodpecker*, *Wren* and *Wild Goose*.

On 1 Aug the outgoing *U454* is sunk by Sunderland 'B' of No 10 Sqn RAAF and the outgoing *U383* by Sunderland 'V' of No 228 Sqn RAF. On 2 Aug the outgoing *U706* is sunk by Liberator 'T' from the 4th A/S Sqn USAAF and Hampden 'A' of No 415 Sqn RCAF, and the outgoing *U106* is sunk by Sunderlands 'N' of No 228 Sqn and 'M' of 461 Sqn near the 40th EG, which picks up survivors. On 2 Aug also the outgoing *U218* is damaged by Wellington 'B' of No 547 Sqn RAF. The torpedo boats *T22*, *T24* and *T25*, which answer *U383*'s distress signal, are able to rescue survivors from *U106*.

The losses compel the Cdr U-boats to abandon the tactics of group sailings and to postpone further departures of the U-boats until they are equipped with the new Hagenuk search receiver to operate against 10cm radar. The losses of the tankers necessitate the breaking off of operations with medium boats in distant areas.

13 June   North Sea
The German patrol trawler *V1109* is sunk in an air attack with bombs and torpedoes SW of Nieuwdiep.

13 June   Greenland
The US Coast Guard cutter *Escabana* sinks at Ivigtut following an accidental explosion.

15 June   North Atlantic
The outgoing *U449* is damaged by Liberator 'F' of No 120 Sqn RAF flying escort for convoy ONS.10 (EG.B7) and has to return to France; however, she is sunk on 24 June.

15 June   English Channel
The German minesweeper *M483* is sunk S of Alderney by Whirlwinds from No 263 Sqn RAF.

15–17 June   Indian Ocean
Schiff 28/Michel (Capt Gumprich), which put to sea from Batavia on 4 June on the last operation by a German auxiliary cruiser, sinks W of Australia the Norwegian motor ship *Hoegh Silverdawn* (7715 tons) and the Norwegian tanker *Ferncastle* (9940 tons).

15 June–23 July   Black Sea
In operations against the Soviet supply traffic off the Caucasus coast, *U24* (Lt-Cdr Petersen) sinks the minesweeper *T411/Zashchitnik* near Tuapse on 15 June and *U18* (Lt Fleige) the steamer *Leningrad* near Sukhumi on 23 June and the steamer *Voroshilov* (3908 tons) on 17 July from Soviet convoys. *U19*, *U23* and *U20* have no success.

In sorties by the 1st MTB Flotilla (Cdr Christiansen), with two to five boats, there are engagements on 22–23 and 25 June with Soviet patrol cutters. On 28–29 June mines are laid near Gelendzhik. On 6–7 July *S102* is lost on a mine S of Kerch as she returns.

On 19–20 July air attacks are outmanoeuvred and on 22–23 July two steamers are torpedoed.

15 June–17 Aug   Central Atlantic
In operations in the area between the Canaries and Freetown, *U508* (Lt-Cdr Staats) sinks three ships of 21112 tons, *U618* (Lt Baberg) one ship of 5225 tons and *U757* (Lt-Cdr Deetz) one ship of 4116 tons. *U306* (Lt-Cdr v Trotha) torpedoes one ship of 5882 tons from a convoy on 16 July in several approaches. *U333*, *U571*, *U358*, *U257*, *U600*, *U382*, *U340*, *U86* and *U445* return home without successes. *U468* is sunk on 11 Aug by Hudson 'D' of No 200 Sqn RAF (Fg Off Trigg VC) which is, however, shot down by the U-boat. On 17 Aug *U403* is sunk by Hudson 'O' of No 200 Sqn RAF and Wellington 'HZ' of No 697 Sqn French AF.

16 June   Mediterranean
In the Eastern Mediterranean, the German *U97* is sunk by Hudson 'T' of No 459 Sqn RAAF.

16 June   South Pacific
Ninety-four Japanese aircraft from Rabaul and New Georgia attack ships off Guadalcanal. *LST340* and the freighter *Celeno* are damaged; a convoy is unsuccessfully attacked. Fighter aircraft from Henderson Field and ships' AA fire have great success in shooting down aircraft: only one Japanese aircraft returns.

17 June–5 July   Arctic
The Soviet ice-breakers are moved from the White Sea into the Kara Sea. On 17 June the ice-breakers *Mikoyan*, *Krassin* and the ice-breaker steamer *SKR-18/Fedor Litke* set out from Severodvinsk. They are under the orders of the Cdr of the White Sea Flotilla, Rear-Adm Kucherov, on the destroyer *Uritski* with the destroyer *Kuibyshev*, the patrol ships *SKR-28*, *SKR-30* and the British minesweepers *Britomart* and *Jason*. From 18 to 20 June cover is provided by the destroyers *Baku*, *Gremyashchi* and *Grozny*. The destroyers return on 20 June from the Kara Strait, the other escorts turn on the edge of the ice in the Kara Sea and the ice-breakers reach Dikson on 22 June. A second convoy with the ice-breakers *Admiral Lazarev* and *Montcalm*, escorted by Capt 1st Class Kolchin with *Baku*, *Gremyashchi*, *Gromki*, *Uritski*, *SKR-28*, *SKR-30* and *Britomart*, sails in the same way on 29 June to the Kara Strait in thick mist. The ice-breakers arrive in Dikson on 5 July.

19 June   Norway
The German A/S trawler *UJ1708* is sunk by a British submarine off Lister.

19 June   English Channel
The German MMS *R41* is sunk by a torpedo fired from a British MTB in the Seine Bight.

20 June   Mediterranean
King George VI arrives in Malta on board the cruiser *Aurora*, escorted by the destroyers *Lookout*, *Jervis*, *Nubian* and *Eskimo*.

21–22 June   South Pacific
Preparatory landings for Operation 'Cartwheel' (see 29 June). On 21 June the fast transports *Dent* and *Waters* land elements of the 4th Marine Raider Bn near Segi Point (New Georgia). They are followed on the next day by two companies of the 43rd US Inf Div from the fast transports *Schley* and *Crosby*.

21–28 June   North Sea
The German minelayers *Ostmark*, *Elsass* and *Brummer*, together with the destroyers *Z27* and *Z30*, lay the 'Erzengel', 'Wildschwein' and 'Steinadler' mine barrages to lengthen the 'Westwall' barrage to the N. The ships are escorted off Norway by the minesweepers *M1* and *M2* and the gunboat *K2*.

23–24 June   Air War/Mediterranean
52 RAF Bomber Command aircraft attack La Spezia on their return flight from North Africa to Britain.

23–29 June   South West Pacific
The US VII Amphibious Force (Rear-Adm Barbey), with the fast transports *Brooks*, *Gilmer*, *Sands* and *Humphreys*, 17 LSTs and

20 LCTs, 20 LCIs and four YMSs, lands the 112th US Cavalry Regt on Woodlark Island on 23–24 June and the 158th Inf Regt on Kiriwina E of New Guinea on 28–29 June. Cover and support for the operation are provided by the destroyers *Mugford*, *Helm*, *Bagley* and *Henley*.

23 June–4 July   South West Pacific
TF.74 (Vice-Adm Crutchley RAN), consisting of the cruisers *Australia* and *Hobart* and the destroyers *Arunta*, *Warramunga* and *Lamson* (US), operates in the area of the Coral Sea and the eastern Arafura Sea to cover Operation 'Cartwheel' (see 29 June).

24 June   North Atlantic
The outgoing *U194* is sunk by Liberator 'H' of No 120 Sqn RAF while escorting convoy ONS.11 (EG.B4). *U200* (Lt-Cdr Schonder), en route to the Far East, is sunk S of Iceland by Catalina 'G' of VP-84.

25 June–16 Oct   Black Sea
Re-transfer of the Soviet submarine *M120* from the Caspian Flotilla to the Black Sea Fleet.

28 June   Air War/Mediterranean
Bombers of the 8th AF drop 250 tons of bombs on St-Nazaire. US bombers drop 230 tons of bombs on Livorno. The Italian cruiser *Bari* is sunk in shallow water in Livorno harbour; the wreck is broken up by the Germans after Sept 1943.

28 June–6 Sept   Arctic
The German minelayer *Roland* lays mine barrages to cover the Norwegian coastal route: on 27–28 June off the Tanafjord, on 17–18 July off Altafjord, on 2–4 Aug off Nordkyn, on 19 Aug off Vardö, and on 6–8 Sept off Vardö ('Schlussakkord' barrage). An attack by the Soviet submarine *S-51* fails.

29 June–13 July   South Pacific
Beginning of Operation 'Cartwheel': US landings on New Georgia (Central Solomons). The Japanese submarine *Ro-103* (Lt Ichimura), which has sunk the transports *Aludra* and *Deimos* (each of 7440 tons) from a convoy returning from Guadalcanal near San Cristobal on 23 June, reports a US transport fleet on 29 June. It is, however, mistaken for a supply convoy for Guadalcanal. During the night 29–30 June US TF.36.2 (Rear-Adm Merrill), comprising the cruisers *Montpelier*, *Columbia*, *Cleveland* and *Denver* and the destroyers *Waller*, *Saufley*, *Philip*, *Renshaw* and *Pringle*, shells the Japanese base at Shortland (South Bougainville), while the minelayers *Preble*, *Gamble* and *Breese* lay a mine barrage undetected.

Early on 30 June US TF.31 (Rear-Adm

Turner), consisting of the destroyer-mine-sweepers *Talbot*, *Zane*, *Dent* and *Waters* and six transports, supported and escorted by the destroyers *Farenholt*, *Buchanan*, *McCalla*, *Ralph Talbot*, *Gwin*, *Woodworth*, *Radford* and *Jenkins*, lands the first battle group of the 43rd US Inf Div (Maj-Gen Hester) on Rendova. Air support is provided by the land-based South Pacific Air Force (Vice-Adm Fitch). The landing also succeeds without resistance at several points in South New Georgia.

The following units are alerted to cover the operation against Japanese fleet attacks: TF.36.3 (Rear-Adm De Witt) with the carrier group (Rear-Adm Ramsey), consisting of *Saratoga* and HMS *Victorious* with the AA cruisers *San Diego* and *San Juan* and the destroyers *Maury*, *Gridley*, *McCall*, *Craven*, *Fanning*, *Dunlap*, *Cummings* and *Case*, and the battleship group (Rear-Adm Davis), consisting of *Massachusetts*, *Indiana* and *North Carolina* and the destroyers *Selfridge*, *Stanly*, *Claxton*, *Dyson* and *Converse*; TF.36.4 (Rear-Adm Hill) comprising the old battleships *Maryland* and *Colorado*; and TF.36.5 (Rear-Adm McFall) comprising the escort carriers *Sangamon*, *Suwanee* and *Chenango* and the destroyers *Conway*, *Eaton*, *Lang*, *Stack*, *Sterett* and *Wilson*. In addition, 11 submarines operate in the area of the Solomons and the Bismarck Archipelago. In a Japanese air attack on the invasion fleet on 30 June the transport *McCawley* receives a torpedo hit and has to be abandoned. On 1 July the second wave with three LSTs arrives off Rendova. The Japanese submarine *Ro-101* is damaged by *Radford*. During the night 2–3 July the Japanese cruiser *Yubari* and nine destroyers shell Rendova to little effect.

During the night 4–5 July the US fast transports *Dent*, *Talbot*, *McKean*, *Waters*, *Kilty*, *Crosby* and *Schley* land three battalions of the 37th Inf Div near Bairoko in Kula Gulf to prepare an attack on Munda. Cover for the operation is provided by TF.36.1 (Rear-Adm Ainsworth), comprising the cruisers *Honolulu* and *St Louis* and the destroyers *Nicholas*, *Strong*, *O'Bannon*, *Chevalier* and *Taylor*. Simultaneously a Japanese destroyer force (Capt Orita), consisting of *Mochitsuki*, *Mikatsuki* and *Hamakaze*, lands 1200 troops near Vila in Kula Gulf. They succeed in sinking the US destroyer *Strong* with 'Long-Lance' torpedoes at great range. The destroyer's detonating depth charges damage *Chevalier*.

On 5–6 July the battle of Kula Gulf takes place. The destroyer force of Capt Orita and a second (Capt Yamashiro) consisting of

Amagiri, *Hatsuyuki*, *Nagatsuki* and *Satsuki* try to land another 2800 troops in Vila in the night, covered by Rear-Adm Akiyama with the destroyers *Niitsuki*, *Suzukaze* and *Tanikaze*. Adm Ainsworth with *Honolulu*, *Helena* and *St Louis* and the destroyers *Nicholas*, *O'Bannon*, *Radford* and *Jenkins* is deployed against the Japanese force. In the engagement the Japanese covering force sinks *Helena* with three torpedoes but itself loses *Niitsuki* in the radar-controlled fire of the US cruisers. Further attacks on both sides have no success. Of the Japanese second transport force, the damaged *Nagatsuki* runs aground and is destroyed on 6 July by US dive-bombers from Henderson Field. On 9 July four US destroyers shell Munda in the course of which attacks by some 100 Japanese aircraft are beaten off. During the night 11–12 July three cruisers and ten destroyers of US TG.36.2 (Rear-Adm Merrill) shell Munda with 3204 rounds of 6in shells and 5470 rounds of 5in shells. TF.36.1 covers the landing of supplies near Bairoko. On the way, *Taylor* sinks the Japanese submarine *Ro-107* on 12 July off Kolombangara.

On 12–13 July the battle of Kolombangara takes place. In the night a new Japanese transport force, comprising the destroyers *Satsuki*, *Mikatsuki*, *Yunagi* and *Matsukaze* (with 1200 troops), covered by Rear-Adm Izaki† with the cruiser *Jintsu* and the destroyers *Yukikaze*, *Hamakaze*, *Kiyonami* and *Yugure*, proceeds to Kula Gulf. TF.36.1 (Rear-Adm Ainsworth), consisting of the cruisers *Honolulu*, *St Louis* and HMNZS *Leander* and the destroyers of Desron 21 (Capt McInerney), comprising *Nicholas*, *O'Bannon*, *Taylor*, *Jenkins* and *Radford*, and Desron 12 (Capt Ryan), comprising *Ralph Talbot*, *Buchanan*, *Maury*, *Woodworth* and *Gwin*, is deployed against this 'Tokyo Express'. In spite of radar on the American side the Japanese sight the US force first and *Jintsu* fires her torpedoes before she is shelled to pieces by the radar-controlled fire of the US cruisers (2630 rounds fired). *Leander* (Capt S W Roskill) drops out with a torpedo hit. The Japanese destroyers of the covering force fire their torpedoes (which, however, do not hit) and escape in a rain squall. In 18 minutes they reload their torpedo tubes and attack again. *Honolulu* and *St Louis* are badly damaged by torpedo hits from Capt Shimai's destroyers and *Gwin* is sunk.

30 June   Western Atlantic
The Vichy French warships interned in Martinique and Guadeloupe (Adm George Robert) are handed over to the Free French Navy. These comprise the aircraft carrier

Béarn, the cruisers *Jeanne d'Arc* and *Emile Bertin* and some smaller vessels.

1 July   Intelligence

The Germans introduce in a second 'Greek' rotor, 'Gamma', and a new small reflector, 'C', for their 'M4' cypher machine. This leads to another short-lived 'black out' at Bletchley Park for 'Triton' up to 21 July and again from 1 to 10 Aug, and then to delays of 7 to 14 days in decoding because the first 'High Speed Bombs' from British production arrive in insufficient numbers. Only when from Aug the first of the 100 new American 'High Speed Bombs' come into service does the situation ease. From Nov 'Triton' decoding work is transferred to Op 20G in Washington to free the resources at Bletchley Park for other important work.

1–31 July   Air War/Western Europe

RAF Bomber Command mine offensive: in 15 nights, 297 sorties are flown against Biscay ports, the coast of Brittany, the Dutch coast, the Frisian coast and the Elbe estuary. Six aircraft are lost.

In July a number of German ships are lost on mines: on 8 July the MDS *Sperrbrecher 165/Corunna* at Gjedser Odde (Baltic), on 10 July the auxiliary minesweeper *M4451* off Arcachon (Bay of Biscay), on 20 July the patrol trawlers *V1014* in the Langeland Belt (Baltic) and *V805* off Terschelling, and on 23 July the minesweeper *M152* in the Gironde.

1–31 July   Pacific

During US submarine operations in the month of July there are 131 'Ultra' signals, which lead to 58 sightings and 20 attacks. Three ships are sunk and 12 are damaged.

In the Aleutians and Kuriles areas, *S35* (Lt Monroe) sinks one ship of 5490 tons, *S30* has two prematures, *S33* conducts a reconnaissance mission and *Narwhal* bombards the island of Matsuwa. In Japanese waters, *Pompano* (Lt-Cdr Thomas) sinks two ships of 24738 tons and one sailing vessel and torpedoes one ship of 6376 tons, *Permit* (Lt-Cdr Chapple) sinks two ships of 2999 tons and one sailing vessel, *Plunger* (Lt-Cdr Bass) sinks one ship of 2482 tons and damages one other of 5493 tons, *Lapon* sinks one sailing vessel and *Sturgeon* and *Skipjack* have misses and duds. Off China, *Scorpion* (Lt-Cdr Wylie) sinks two ships of 10002 tons and *Sawfish* (Lt-Cdr Sands) sinks the minelayer *Hirashima* on 27 July and one ship of 6659 tons.

In the Central Pacific, *Pogy* (Lt-Cdr Wales) sinks one ship of 7469 tons, *Spearfish* (Lt-Cdr Dempsey) damages one ship of 1580 tons and *Tinosa* (Lt-Cdr Daspit) damages

two ships of 29646 tons, one of them the 19209-ton whale factory ship *Tonan Maru No 3*, which is hit by no fewer than eight duds. (Daspit takes the last torpedo home for examination, which reveals the reasons for the failures and leads to corrections being made; first, however, on 24 July, CINCPAC has to order that the the magnetic exploders be deactivated.) *Haddock* (Lt-Cdr Davenport) sinks one ship of 5532 tons, *Pompon* (Lt-Cdr Hawk) sinks one ship of 5871 tons and damages one other of 3081 tons, *Seadragon* (Lt-Cdr Ashley), *Tunny* (Lt-Cdr Scott) and *Finback* (Lt-Cdr Tyree) together sink one ship of 10672 tons and *Finback* alone sinks the subchaser *Cha-109*, two ships of 10789 tons and one sailing vessel and torpedoes one ship of 7349 tons, *Saury* damages one destroyer by ramming, *Halibut*, *Steelhead*, *Mingo* and *Albacore* have prematures and duds in their attacks and *Seadragon*, *Sturgeon*, *S38* and *S31* conduct reconnaissance missions. In the South Pacific, *Scamp* (Lt-Cdr Ebert) sinks the submarine *I-168* and damages one ship of 18300 tons and *Guardfish* conducts a guerrilla mission. In the South West Pacific, *Tambor* (Lt-Cdr Ambruster) sinks one ship of 1972 tons, *Grouper* is damaged by one of her own prematures, *Gar* has one miss and later lands a commando party and *Trout*, *Thresher* and *Grayling* conduct special missions.

3–10 July   English Channel

From 3 to 7 July the German torpedo boats *T24* and *T25* move in several stages from the North Sea through the English Channel to the W. In the process they are unsuccessfully shelled by the Dover coastal batteries and attacked off Dunkirk on 5 July by the British *MTB240*, *MTB235* and *MTB202* and in Boulogne on 6 July by Typhoon fighter-bombers. During the night 9–10 July they form distant cover for a German convoy near Ouessant, which is screened by the 2nd MS Flotilla (Cdr Heydel), comprising *M9*, *M12*, *M10*, *M153* and *M84*. The convoy is attacked by the British destroyers *Melbreak* and *Wensleydale* and the Norwegian *Glaisdale*, which sink *M153*. In an engagement with the German torpedo boats, which then approach, *Melbreak* is badly damaged.

4 July   Air War/Western Europe

US bombers attack the U-boat base at La Pallice.

4 July–8 Sept   Mediterranean

In British submarine operations in the Western Mediterranean, the following sinkings are made, sometimes in the course of several patrols: *Saracen* (Lt Lumby) sinks two ships of 2567 tons (but is herself sunk on 14 Aug by the Italian corvette *Minerva*

off Bastia), *Safari* (Lt Lakin) sinks the minelayer *Durazzo* and one small ship, *Torbay* (Lt Clutterbuck) sinks one ship of 2609 tons, *Usurper* (Lt Mott) sinks one ship of 2536 tons, *Simoom* (Lt Milner) attacks the cruiser *Garibaldi* off La Spezia on 9 Aug (but the torpedoes miss and sink the destroyer *Gioberti*), *Sickle* (Lt Drummond) sinks the German escort vessel *SG7* (2526 tons), *Shakespeare* (Lt Ainslie) sinks the Italian submarine *Velella* on 7 Sept, *Sportsman* (Lt Gatehouse) and *Universal* (Lt Gordon) each sink one sailing ship and the Dutch *Dolfijn* (Lt-Cdr v Oostrom-Soede) sinks one ship of 7890 tons and two ferry barges. In the Central Mediterranean and Adriatic, *Rorqual* (Lt Napier) sinks one ship of 7020 tons, *Ultor* (Lt Hunt) one of 6200 tons (and the torpedo boat *Lince*), *Unrivalled* (Lt Turner) two of 170 tons, *Uproar* (Lt Kershaw) one of 1977 tons, *Unshaken* (Lt Whitton) one of 6850 tons, *Unseen* (Lt Crawford) two of 1088 tons and *Unsparing* (Lt Piper) one of 1162 tons. In the Aegean, *Rorqual* (Cdr Napier) sinks one ship of 1798 tons, *Sickle* (Lt Drummond) three sailing ships of 204 tons and *Torbay* (Lt Clutterbuck) one sailing ship of 591 tons.

5–6 July   Mediterranean

The Italian submarine *H8* is sunk during an RAF air attack against La Spezia. The German E-boat *S59* is sunk at Porto Empedocle in air attack on 6 July.

6 July–15 Aug   North Pacific

On 6 July a US task group (Rear-Adm Giffen), comprising the cruisers *Wichita*, *Portland*, *San Francisco* and *Santa Fe* and four destroyers, shells Kiska. The shelling is repeated by the destroyers *Aylwin* and *Monaghan* on five nights in the period 8–20 July. A Japanese force, which sets out on 7 July from Paramushiro, is unable, because of the weather, to carry out the evacuation from Kiska and returns on 16 July. On 15 July the submarine *Narwhal* shells Matsuwa. On 22 July TG.16.21 (Rear-Adm Giffen), comprising the cruisers *Louisville*, *San Francisco*, *Wichita* and *Santa Fe* and the destroyers *Aylwin*, *Bache*, *Hughes*, *Mustin* and *Morris*, shells Kiska and TG.16.22 (Rear-Adm Griffin), comprising the battleships *New Mexico* and *Mississippi*, the cruiser *Portland* and the destroyers *Monaghan*, *Abner Read*, *Farragut* and *Perry*, shells Little Kiska.

On 27 July a US task group, consisting of the battleships *Mississippi* and *Idaho*, the cruisers *Wichita*, *San Francisco* and *Portland* and destroyers, carries out 80 nautical miles W of Kiska a 'battle of the pips' with radar phantoms. The ships expend 518 rounds of 14in and 487 rounds of 8in shells.

A Japanese force (Rear-Adm Kimura), consisting of the cruisers *Tama*, *Abukuma* and *Kiso* and the destroyers *Ikazuchi*, *Inazuma*, *Wakaba*, *Hatsushimo*, *Asagumo*, *Hibiki*, *Yugumo*, *Kazegumo*, *Akigumo*, *Shimakaze*, *Naganami* and *Samidare* as well as the tanker *Nippon Maru* and the frigate *Kunajiri*, sets out from Paramushiro on 22 July and reaches Kiska on 28 July. *Kunajiri* and *Wakaba*, as a result of collisions on 26 July in bad weather with *Abukuma* and *Hatsushimo*, and *Tama*, because of engine trouble on 28 July, have to return. In 55 minutes the 5183-strong garrison of Kiska is taken on board and evacuated unobserved by the enemy. They arrive in Paramushiro on 1 Aug.

In preparation for the landing on Kiska, the US destroyers *Farragut* and *Hull* shell Kiska on 30 July. On 2 Aug TG.16.6 (Rear-Adm Baker), comprising the cruisers *Salt Lake City*, *Indianapolis*, *Raleigh*, *Detroit* and *Richmond* and the destroyers *Farragut*, *Meade*, *Frazier*, *Gansevoort* and *Edwards*, and TG.16.17 (Rear-Adm Kingman), comprising the battleships *Idaho* and *Tennessee* and the destroyers *Dale*, *Aylwin*, *Phelps* and *Anderson*, and on 12 Aug TG.16.6 again, shell Kiska. Aircraft drop 1310 tons of bombs in 1585 sorties.

Operation 'Cottage'. On 15 Aug the assault force, which set out from Adak on 13 Aug with 20 transports, 42 landing ships and boats and many auxiliary craft, lands 34426 men on the abandoned island of Kiska. Escort is provided by the destroyers *Farragut*, *Aylwin*, *Monaghan*, *Dewey*, *Hull*, *Dale*, *Bush*, *Daly*, *Mullany*, *Bancroft*, *Caldwell* and *Coghlan*. Preparatory shelling is undertaken by Rear-Adm Kingman with the battleships *Pennsylvania*, *Tennessee* and *Idaho*, the cruisers *Portland* and *Santa Fe* and the destroyers *Ammen*, *Abner Read* (damaged on a mine on 18 Aug), *Bache*, *Beale*, *Brownson*, *Hutchins* and *Phelps*. Air support is provided by 168 shore-based aircraft.

6 July–27 Aug Central Atlantic

From 6 to 12 July *U487* (Lt Metz) replenishes *U195*, *U382*, *U598*, *U406*, *U591*, *U604*, *U662*, *U359* and *U466* 600 nm SW of the Azores. When the proposed tanker *U462* is no longer available, *U487*, with the auxiliary tanker *U160*, is given the task of replenishing the 'Monsun' group on 14 July on its way to the Indian Ocean. However, *U514* from this group is sunk on 8 July by Liberator 'R' of No 224 Sqn RAF with a 'Fido' homing torpedo and *U506* on 12 July by a Liberator from the 1st A/S Sqn USAAF. Following 'Ultra' intercepts, the US TG.21.16 (Capt Greer), with the escort carrier *Core* and the destroyers *Barker*, *Bulmer* and *Badger*, leaves its convoy,

UGS.11 (which comprises 61 ships plus TF.62 with the destroyers *Hobby*, *Turner*, *Frankford*, *Kalk* and *McCook*, the French destroyer leader *Le Fantasque*, the escort destroyers *Evarts*, *Wyffels* and *Gillespie* and the minesweeper *Tide*). Three aircraft from *Core* encounter *U487* and sink her.
Detached from convoy GUS.19 (41 ships plus TF.61 with the destroyers *Livermore*, *Kearny*, *Eberle*, *Ericsson*, *Endicott*, *McCormick* and *Parrott* and the minesweepers *Pilot* and *Prevail*), TG.21.11 (Capt Fick), with the escort carrier *Santee* and the destroyers *Bainbridge*, *Overton* and *MacLeish*, encounters on 14 and 15 July *U160* and the 'Monsun' *U509*, which are sunk by Avengers of VC-29 from *Santee*. On 16 July the returning *U67* falls victim to an Avenger of VC-13 from *Core*. In supporting the convoy UGS.12 (79 ships plus TF.63 with the US Coast Guard cutters *Bibb* and *Ingham*, the destroyers *Whipple*, *Ford*, *Alden* and *John D Edwards* and the minesweepers *Pioneer*, *Portent* and *Threat*), TG.21.12 (Capt Dunn) with the escort carrier *Bogue* sinks on 23 July *U527* which has just been replenished by *U648*, while from the screening destroyers *Clemson*, *Osmond-Ingram* and *George E Badger* the last locates *U613* (which is on the way to a mining operation off Jacksonville) and sinks her.
On 24 July an aircraft from *Santee* damages W of Madeira *U373*, which is on the way to Port Lyautey with mines. On the return with GUS.10 (50 ships plus TF.62—as UGS.11 above without *Le Fantasque*), an Avenger of VC-29 from *Santee* sinks with 'Fido' *U43*, which is in the process of replenishing *U403*.
On 3 Aug TG.21.14 (Capt Isbell), with the escort carrier *Card* and the destroyers *Barry*, *Goff* and *Borie*, arrives to support convoy UGS.13 (82 ships plus TF.64 with the destroyers *Stevenson*, *Stockton* and *Thorn*, the escort destroyers *Hammann*, *Jacob Jones* and *Robert F. Peary* and the US Coast Guard cutters *Campbell*, *Duane* and *Spencer*) in the area S of the Azores. An Avenger damages *U66*, which is joined by *U117* on 7 Aug. Aircraft of VC-1 from *Card* attack and sink *U117* with 'Fido'. On 8 Aug *U262* and *U664* shoot down two aircraft and *U664* (Lt Graef) misses *Card* with a salvo; *U664* is sunk on 9 Aug by one of her aircraft. *Borie* outmanoeuvres an attack by *U262*. On 11 Aug *U525*, which is detached as an auxiliary tanker, is sunk by two aircraft of VC-1 from *Card* with 'Fido' N of the Azores.
U161 and *U760*, which have handed over a search receiver to the Japanese submarine *I-8*, coming from Penang, escape TG.21.15

(Capt Lyon, with the escort carrier *Croatan* and the destroyers *Paul Jones*, *Parrott* and *Belknap*), which arrives with convoy UGS.14 (67 ships plus TF.65 with the destroyers *Livermore*, *Eberle*, *Kearny*, *Ericsson*, *Mayo*, *Tarbell* and *Upshur* and the minesweepers *Pilot* and *Prevail* and two other vessels) on 12 Aug. On 21 Aug *U134* also escapes from the group but is sunk on 24 Aug by Wellington 'J' of No 179 Sqn RAF with Leigh Light when returning.
From 12 to 23 Aug *U129* and *U847*, which have helped as auxiliary tankers, succeed in replenishing four and seven boats respectively. On 23 Aug the *Core* group again comes into the supply area with convoy UGS.15 (58 ships plus TF.66 with the destroyers *Charles Lawrence*, *Baldwin*, *Harding*, *Endicott* and *McCormick* and the minesweepers *Hopping*, *Reeves*, *Symbol* and *Griffin*). *U84*, which escapes from an attack on 23 Aug, and *U185* are sunk on 24 Aug by aircraft of VC-13 from *Core*, and *Card*, which arrives as relief, sinks the auxiliary tanker *U847* with a 'Fido' on 27 Aug. *U508* avoids a 'Fido' attack.
The heavy losses necessitate a reduction in long-range operations. At the same time there is apprehension in London about the too frequent use by the US Navy of 'Ultra' information, which may arouse German suspicions about their codes being compromised.
Off the US East Coast, *U566* (Lt-Cdr Hornkohl) sinks the US gunboat *Plymouth* on 5 Aug and *U107* (Lt Simmermacher) torpedoes one ship of 7176 tons.

7 July Norway

The German A/S trawler *UJ1705* is sunk off Sognesjoen by bombs dropped by the RAF.

8 July Norway

The British Home Fleet (Adm Fraser), comprising the battleships, *Anson*, *Duke of York* and *Malaya*, the carrier *Furious*, two cruiser squadrons and three destroyer flotillas, and a US task force (Rear-Adm Hustvedt), consisting of the battleships *Alabama* and *South Dakota*, the cruisers *Augusta* and *Tuscaloosa* and five destroyers, carry out a demonstration off Norway which, however, is not detected by German air reconnaissance. The aim of diverting attention from the imminent landing in Sicily fails. When it is repeated at the end of July, some of the ships mentioned above, together with the British carriers *Illustrious* and *Unicorn*, take part. Martlet fighters shoot down five German Bv 138 reconnaissance aircraft.

8 July Black Sea

The German E-boat *S102* sinks on a Soviet mine SW of Kerch.

10 July Mediterranean

Operation 'Husky': Allied landing in Sicily (C-in-C Gen Eisenhower; Deputy and C-in-C Land Forces Gen Alexander; C-in-C Naval Forces Adm Cunningham; C-in-C Air Forces Air Chief Marshal Tedder; HQ in Malta). The British 8th Army (Gen Montgomery) is landed by the Eastern Naval Task Force (Adm Ramsay) between Syracuse and the Pachino Peninsula and the 7th US Army (Lt-Gen Patton) by the Western Naval Task Force (Vice-Adm Hewitt) near Scoglitti, Gela and Licata.

Force A (Rear-Adm Troubridge)—headquarters ship *Bulolo* with convoys MWS.36 and MWF.36 (see 16 June–9 July)—lands the British XIII Corps (Lt-Gen Dempsey) with the 3rd Royal Marine Commandos, the 5th Inf Div and the 50th Inf Div S of the Maddalena Peninsula in the sector 'Acid North' and S of Avola in the sector 'Acid South'. Beacon submarine: *Unruffled*.

Force N (Capt Lord Ashburn)—headquarters ship *Keren* with parts of the convoys MWS.36 and MWF.36—lands the British 231st Independent Bde (Brig Urquhart) on the east coast of the Pachino Peninsula in the sector 'Bark East'. Beacon submarine: *Unseen*.

Force B (Rear-Adm McGrigor)—headquarters ship *Largs* with convoys SBS.1, SBM.1 and SBF.1—lands the British 51st Inf Div (Maj-Gen Wimberley) near Cape Passero. Beacon submarine: *Unison*.

Force V (Rear-Adm Vian)—headquarters ship *Hilary* with convoys KMS.18 and MKF.18—lands the 1st Canadian Div (Maj-Gen Simmonds) on the west coast of the Pachino Peninsula. Beacon submarine: *Unrivalled*.

Troops of Forces N, B and V form XXX Corps (Lt-Gen Leese). The 1st Airborne Div lands SW of Syracuse. Support Force East (Rear-Adm Harcourt) comprises the cruisers *Newfoundland*, *Uganda*, *Mauritius* and *Orion*, the AA cruisers *Carlisle*, *Colombo* and *Delhi*, the AA ship *Palomares* and the monitors *Erebus*, and *Roberts*. In addition, there are the destroyers *Inconstant*, *Eskimo*, *Laforey*, *Lookout*, *Loyal*, *Nubian*, *Tartar*, *Arrow*, *Venomous*, *Viceroy*, *Wallace*, *Wanderer*, *Wishart*, *Woolston*, *Wrestler*, *Aldenham*, *Blencathra*, *Clare*, *Eggesford*, *Hursley*, *Hurworth*, *Lauderdale*, *Ledbury*, *Rockwood*, *Wheatland*, *Wilton*, *Atherstone*, *Cleveland*, *Hambledon*, *Mendip*, *Quantock*, *Tynedale*, *Whaddon*, *Dulverton*, *Beaufort*, *Exmoor*, *Brocklesby*, *Tetcott*, *Blankney*, *Lamerton*, *Oakley*, *Liddesdale*, *Farndale*, *Calpe*, *Easton*, *Belvoir*, *Holcombe*, *Haydon*, *Brecon*, *Brissenden* and *Puckeridge*, the Greek *Pindos*,

Adrias, *Kanaris*, *Miaoulis* and *Themistokles* and the Polish *Krakowiak* and *Slazak*; the sloops *Shoreham*, *Chanticleer*, *Crane*, *Cygnet*, *Erne*, *Pheasant* and *Whimbrel* and the Indian *Jumna* and *Sutlej*; the frigates *Bann*, *Dart*, *Plym*, *Test*, *Teviot* and *Trent*; the corvettes *Bluebell*, *Bryony*, *Camellia*, *Convolvulus*, *Delphinium*, *Dianella*, *Honeysuckle*, *Hyacinth*, *Hyderabad*, *Lotus*, *Oxlip*, *Pentstemon*, *Poppy*, *Primula*, *Rhododendron*, *Starwort*, *Vetch* and *Sakhtouris* (Greek); the cutters *Banff* and *Fishguard*; the minesweepers *Gawler*, *Lismore*, *Ipswich*, *Maryborough*, *Geraldton*, *Cairns*, *Cessnock* and *Wollongong* (all Australian) and 25 others together with the Dutch gunboats *Flores* and *Soemba*.

TF.85 (Rear-Adm Kirk)—headquarters ship *Ancon* with parts of convoys NCF.1, TJF.1 and TJM.1—lands the 45th US Inf Div (Maj-Gen Middleton) with 25800 troops on both sides of Scoglitti in the sector 'Cent'. The beacon submarine is *Seraph* and the support group and escort comprise the cruiser *Philadelphia*, the British monitor *Abercrombie* and the destroyers *Earle*, *Cowie*, *Parker*, *Laub*, *Mackenzie*, *Kendrick*, *Doran*, *Boyle*, *Champlin*, *Nields*, *Davison*, *Mervine*, *Quick*, *Tillman* and *Beatty*. On board *Ancon* is the General Commanding II US Corps, Lt-Gen Bradley.

TF.81 (Rear-Adm Hall)—headquarters ship *Samuel Chase* with parts of convoys NCF.1, TJF.1 and TJM.1—lands the 1st US Inf Div (Maj-Gen Allen) with 19250 troops near Gela in the sector 'Dime'. The beacon submarine is *Shakespeare* and the support group and escort comprise the cruisers *Boise* and *Savannah* and the destroyers *Cole*, *Shubrick*, *Jeffers*, *Nelson*, *McLanahan*, *Murphy*, *Glennon*, *Maddox*, *Dallas*, *Gherardi*, *Butler*, *Herndon* and *Bernadou*.

TF.86 (Rear-Adm Conolly)—headquarters ship *Biscayne* with convoys TJF.1, TJM.1 and TJS.1—lands the 3rd US Inf Div (Maj-Gen Truscott) and parts of the 2nd US Armoured Div with 27650 troops both sides of Licata in the sector 'Joss'. The beacon submarine is *Safari* and the support group and escort consist of the cruisers *Brooklyn* and *Birmingham* and the destroyers *Bristol*, *Buck*, *Ludlow*, *Swanson*, *Roe*, *Edison*, *Woolsey*, *Wilkes*, and *Nicholson*.

TF.80 (Flagship and reserve force, Vice-Adm Hewitt) has the headquarters ship *Monrovia* with the 18th RCT of the 1st US Inf Div and two RCTs of the 2nd Armoured Div on board transports and LSTs, escorted by the destroyers *Wainwright*, *Mayrant*, *Trippe*, *Rhind*, *Rowan*, *Plunkett*, *Niblack*,

Benson, *Gleaves* and *Ordronaux*; Lt-Gen Patton is on board *Monrovia*. The 82nd US Airborne Div is landed inland from Gela.

A covering force (Vice-Adm Willis RN), comprising the battleships *Nelson*, *Rodney*, *Warspite* and *Valiant*, the carriers *Indomitable* and *Formidable*, the cruisers *Aurora*, *Penelope*, *Cleopatra* and *Euryalus* and the destroyers *Quilliam*, *Queenborough*, *Quail*, *Isis*, *Faulknor*, *Echo*, *Intrepid*, *Raider*, *Eclipse*, *Fury*, *Inglefield*, *Ilex*, *Vasilissa Olga* (Greek), *Troubridge*, *Tyrian*, *Tumult*, *Offa* and *Piorun* (Polish), cruises in the Ionian Sea. The reserve covering group consists of the battleships *King George V* and *Howe*, the cruisers *Dido* and *Sirius* and the destroyers *Jervis*, *Panther*, *Pathfinder*, *Penn*, *Paladin* and *Petard* S of Sardinia, while the RAF and US Air Force provide 3630 aircraft.

The Italian minesweeper *Oriole* (ex-Yugoslav *Labud*) is scuttled at Augusta following bomb damage.

11 July Bay of Biscay

Three Fw 200s of KG 40, on a reconnaissance flight, sight a British troop transport convoy W of Oporto. In spite of strong AA defence, they hit the transports *California* (16792 tons) and *Duchess of York* (22021 tons), which catch fire and have to be abandoned. The third ship, *Port Fairy*, reaches Casablanca with one British destroyer. The destroyers HMCS *Iroquois*, HMS *Douglas* and the frigate HMS *Moyola* rescue all but 57 of the troops on the ships.

11 July Mediterranean

The German escort vessel *SG13* (ex-French *Cyrnos*, 3230 tons) is damaged by aerial torpedo and beached; she is salvaged and towed into La Ciotat on 23 July.

11–31 July Mediterranean

The Allied fleets support the operations of the 7th US and 8th British Armies in Sicily. On 11 July the US cruisers *Savannah* and *Boise*, with the US destroyers *Shubrick*, *Jeffers*, *Glennon*, *Butler*, *Beatty*, *Laub*, *Cowie* and *Tillman*, bring a German armoured counter-attack to a standstill near Gela. The British destroyers *Blankney* and *Brissenden* occupy Pozzallo with an improvised landing force. Within the British bridgehead the monitor *Erebus* and the cruisers *Orion*, *Uganda* and *Mauritius* support British units. As a diversionary move the British battleships *Howe* and *King George V* shell Favignana during the night 11–12 July and the cruisers *Dido* and *Sirius* Marsala on the W coast. An attempt by the British destroyers *Eskimo* and *Exmoor* and the Greek *Kanaris* to enter Augusta is beaten off by an Italian coastal battery under the personal command of the fortress commander, Rear-Adm Leonardi. Only on 12 July does Rear-Adm Troubridge, who has occupied Syracuse on 11 July, enter when the landing ship *Ulster Monarch* is able to disembark troops. On 12 July the US cruisers *Birmingham* and *Brooklyn* support the left flank of the 7th US Army. On 13 July *Erebus* shells Catania and on 16 July the British monitor *Abercrombie* and the US cruisers *Birmingham* and *Philadelphia* shell Porto Empedocle. On 17 July the British battleship *Warspite* shells Catania again and on 18 July cruiser *Mauritius* and on 19 July the cruiser *Newfoundland*, the destroyers *Laforey* and *Lookout* and the Dutch gunboat *Flores* bombard gun positions at Catania. On 21 July *Erebus* and *Newfoundland* again repeat this bombardment. As a result of German and Italian air attacks, the Allied invasion fleet loses the US destroyers *Maddox*, the US minesweeper *Sentinel* and eight transports of 54306 tons. The monitor *Erebus* and other ships are damaged by bombs. On 14 July Italian torpedo aircraft just miss the cruisers *Euryalus* and *Cleopatra* and on 16 July they hit the carrier *Indomitable*.

During the night 16–17 July, in engagements between the German 7th MTB Flotilla (Cdr Trummer) and British MTBs, five German motor torpedo boats are severely damaged. The passing Italian cruiser *Scipione Africano* sinks *MTB316* and damages *MTB260*.

The proposed massive deployment of German and Italian submarines S of Sicily fails because the available German U-boats have been operating off the Algerian coast since 22 June. In these operations *U73* (Lt Deckert) sinks one ship of 1598 tons and torpedoes one tanker of 8299 tons and *U593* (Lt-Cdr Kelbling) sinks the US *LST333* and *LST387* as well as one ship of 6054 tons from the feeder convoy KMS.18B on 5 July. Shortly beforehand, *U375* (Lt-Cdr J Könenkamp) has sunk two ships of 14296 tons from this convoy. *U371* (Lt-Cdr Mehl) torpedoes two ships of 13376 tons from a western convoy on 10 July. Attacks by *U431* and *U617* fail. Off Cyrenaica, *U453* (Lt-Cdr Frhr v Schlippenbach) torpedoes one steamer of 6894 tons and on 6 July sinks a ship of 5454 tons from the feeder convoy MWS.36. *U81* operates in the Eastern Mediterranean where she sinks one steamer of 3742 tons and four sailing ships. As a result of this, from 11 July at first only Italian submarines make attacks and only *Dandolo* (Lt-Cdr Turcio) is able to torpedo the cruiser *Cleopatra* on 16 July. Attacks by *Argo*, *Nereide*, *Beilul*, *Diaspro*, *Alagi*, *Platino*, *Nichelio* and *Ambra* fail. The Italian

Flutto is sunk by the British *MTB640*, *MTB651* and *MTB670* on 11 July and *U561* by *MTB81* on 12 July in the Straits of Messina; the Italian *Acciaio* (13 July), *Remo* (15 July) and *Micca* (29 July) by the submarines *Unruly*, *United* and *Trooper*; *U409* (12 July) by the destroyer *Inconstant*; *Nereide* (13 July) by *Echo* and *Ilex*; *Ascianghi*, after an attack on a cruiser force, by *Laforey* and *Eclipse* (23 July); and the German *U375* by the US *PC624* (30 July). The Italian *Bronzo* surfaces on 12 July off Syracuse in the middle of a British force which includes the minesweepers *Boston*, *Poole*, *Cromarty* and *Seaham* and is captured; the boat is later recommissioned as *P714*. When the German U-boats arrive, *U81* (Lt Krieg) fires torpedoes into the harbour at Syracuse on 21 July and torpedoes a steamer of 7472 tons on 22 July. On 23 July *U407* (Lt Brüller) torpedoes the cruiser *Newfoundland*.

14 July Japan
The Japanese submarine *I-179* is accidentally lost off Ino Nada.

15 July General Situation
General Morgan, Chief of the General Staff of the Supreme Cdr of the Allied Expeditionary Forces, puts a draft plan before the Joint Chiefs of Staff for an invasion of France: 'Overlord' (North West France) and 'Anvil' (Southern France).

15–17 July Arctic
The minelayer *Ostmark*, escorted by the minesweepers *M364*, *M272* and *M346* and the motor minesweepers *R56* and *R54*, lays a flanking mine barrage. In an attack by the Soviet submarine *S-56* (Capt 2nd class Shchedrin), *M346* is sunk.

17 July–13 Aug South Pacific
TF.74, comprising the Australian cruisers *Australia* and *Hobart* and the US destroyers *Jenkins*, *O'Bannon*, *Radford* and *Nicholas*, is sent from Espiritu Santo to the NW on 16 July to make good the losses in the fighting off New Georgia.

On 17 July 223 aircraft of 'Air Force Solomons' (Rear-Adm Mitscher) attack Japanese ships off Buin (Bougainville) and sink the destroyer *Hatsuyuki*. Off Rendova the Japanese submarine *Ro-106* (Lt Nakamura) sinks on 18 July the landing ship *LST342*. On 28 July *Ro-103* is lost off New Georgia to a mine.

Of the Japanese submarines sent to reconnoitre for a new attempt to reinforce New Georgia, *I-11* (Cdr* M. Tagami) attacks TF.74, torpedoing the Australian cruiser *Hobart* on 20 July and also one ship of 7176 tons; *I-17* (Lt-Cdr Harada) is sunk off Espiritu Santo on 19 Aug by two US aircraft from VS-57 and the New Zealand corvette

Tui; and *I-19* (Cdr Kinashi) destroys one ship of 7176 tons off Fiji.

During the night 19–20 July three Japanese destroyers bring supplies to Vila, while Rear-Adm Nishimura cruises off Vella Gulf with three heavy and one light cruiser and six destroyers to provide cover against US cruiser sorties. On 20 July the force loses the destroyers *Yugure* and *Kiyonami* to US torpedo aircraft and bombers from Guadalcanal and the cruiser *Kumano* is damaged. On 22 July shore-based aircraft from New Georgia sink the Japanese seaplane tender *Nisshin* which is loaded with supplies and escorted by three destroyers. On 28 July the Japanese destroyers *Ariake* and *Mikazuki* are sunk in a supply operation off Rabaul. During the night 1–2 Aug five Japanese destroyers try to reach Kolombangara. Fifteen US PT boats are deployed against them, seven of which fire their 26 torpedoes without success. *PT109* (Lt John F Kennedy) is rammed in the action by the destroyer *Amagiri* and sinks; Kennedy saves his crew with great difficulty.

On 24 July a force of US fast transports with a destroyer escort (Cdr Burke) supplies Bairoko Harbor. The destroyers shell Munda and Lailand on 25 July with little effect. The shelling is therefore repeated on 26 July to support the land operations which lead to the capture of Munda.

On 6–7 Aug there is a battle in the Vella Gulf. The US destroyer force (Cdr Moosbrugger), with *Dunlap*, *Craven*, *Maury*, *Lang*, *Sterett* and *Stack*, intercepts the Japanese group (Capt Sugiura) comprising *Hagikaze*, *Arashi*, *Kawakaze* and *Shigure*, which tries to reach Kolombangara with 900 men on board and 50 tons of supplies. Three of the Japanese destroyers sink as a result of torpedo hits by the US destroyers; only *Shigure* escapes. The survivors from the Japanese ships in the water refuse to be rescued.

18 July Mediterranean
The Italian transport submarine *Romolo* is sunk by Wellington 'B' of No 221 Sqn RAF in the Ionian Sea.

19 July Black Sea
The German motor minesweeper *R33* is sunk at Yalta during a Soviet air raid.

19 July–4 Sept Mediterranean
Italian defensive mine barrages are laid out. The Italian minelayers *Vieste* and *Vallelunga* lay seven barrages with 500 mines in the Gulf of Naples; the Italian destroyer *Vivaldi* and the German minelayers *Pommern* and *Brandenburg* lay seven barrages with 1196 mines in the Gulf of Gaeta and the Gulf of Salerno; and the Italian cruisers *Cadorna* and *Scipione Africano* with

the minelayers *Barletta* and *Morosini* lay 11 barrages with 1591 mines in the Gulf of Taranto. In the Aegean the German *Drache* and *Bulgaria* lay 15 barrages with 690 mines and in the Adriatic the Italian *Laurana* lays one barrage with 70 mines. The Italian *Buffoluto* and *Gasperi* lay two barrages with 280 mines off Acciaio (Corsica) and the German *Pommern* and *Brandenburg* three barrages of 410 mines in the Straits of Bonifacio.

20 July   Bay of Biscay
The German A/S trawler *UJ1423* is lost at Lorient following a collision with a sunken wreck.

20 July–10 Aug   Arctic
German U-boats lay the following mine barrages from 20 July to 10 Aug to interfere with Soviet traffic in the Pechora Sea: *U625* (Lt-Cdr Benker) off the Yugor Strait; *U601* (Lt-Cdr Grau) off Belusha; *U629* (Lt Bugs) in the western entrance to Pechora Bay and off Russki Savorot; *U586* (Lt-Cdr v d Esch) E of Pechora Bay; *U212* (Lt-Cdr Vogler) and *U636* (Lt-Cdr Hildebrand) off Kolguev; and *U639* (Lt Wichmann) in the Pechora Sea. A convoy of 15 river ships setting out on 25 July from the Pechora Estuary for the Ob Estuary runs on to these barrages and on 27 July it loses the minesweeper *T-904* off the Yugor Strait. On 30 July *U703* (Lt Brünner) sinks one patrol ship off Kostin Strait. The motor minesweepers *T-109* and *T-110*, delivered from Britain, are used to clear the ground mines. On 25 Aug the rescue ship *Shkval* is lost in the Yugor Strait.

21 July   South Atlantic
The German *U662* is sunk by a Mariner flying boat of VP-94 off the Amazon estuary.

21 July–16 Aug   Arctic
From 21 to 24 July the German minelayers *Ostmark* and *Kaiser*, escorted by the minesweepers *M361*, *M302*, *M364*, *M272* and the A/S trawlers *UJ1202*, *UJ1209* and *NH06*, lay a mine barrage to cover the Varanger peninsula. An attack by Soviet torpedo bombers is unsuccessful. From 10 to 12 Aug two further barrages are laid.

22 July–14 Aug   Mediterranean
On 22 July the 7th US Army captures Palermo. The US Desron 8 and the US 15th MTB Squadron enter the port. Over the next few days the PTs carry out several attacks on small convoys and German MFPs. In a German air attack off Palermo, the US destroyer *Mayrant* is damaged on 26 July. Severe damage is caused in attacks on Palermo on 31 July, 1 Aug and 4 Aug and the destroyer *Shubrick* is damaged. From 27

July the US TF.88 (Rear-Adm Davidson) supports the US troops on the N coast of Sicily. The cruisers *Philadelphia* and *Savannah* and the destroyers *Gherardi*, *Nelson*, *Jeffers*, *Murphy*, *Trippe* and *Knight* participate.

Two Italian cruiser forces, consisting of *Montecuccoli* and *Eugenio di Savoia* and *Garibaldi* and *Duca d'Aosta* respectively, which sail on 5–6 and 7–8 Aug to carry out shelling, turn away prematurely as a result of uncertainty about the enemy's position, and before TF.88 reaches the scene.

On 7–8 Aug the cruiser *Philadelphia* with three destroyers supports the landing of one BLT from two LSTs, one LCI and seven LCTs on the N coast of Sicily behind the German lines. On 10–11 Aug *Philadelphia* with six destroyers supports the landing of RCT 30. A further landing in regimental strength on 14–15 Aug encounters nothing because of the German withdrawal.

24 July–3 Aug   Air War/Germany
Four big area bombing raids by RAF Bomber Command against Hamburg, with the first use of 'Window' to disrupt German radar: on 24–25 July with 791 aircraft, on 27–28 July with 787 aircraft (causing a firestorm), on 29–30 July with 777 aircraft and on 2–3 Aug with 740 aircraft (a failure because of a thunderstorm). More than 45000 civilians are killed and great destruction in the urban parts of Hamburg is caused; 87 aircraft are lost. On 25 and 26 July daylight raids by 8th USAAF are mounted, with 252 sorties against industrial targets in the harbour area. Seventeen aircraft are lost. Limited damage is caused to the harbour and the yards, but great losses in working hours result from the evacuation of the workforce. At the Blohm & Voss yard, *U996* (fitting out) and *U1011* and *U1012* (on the slipway) are destroyed. The liner *Vaterland* (35000 tons), fitting out but used as a timber depot, is hit and burnt out and the hospital ship *Fasan* (1257 tons) is sunk and the barracks ship *General Artigas* (11254 tons) destroyed. At the Stülcken yard the escort *G1*, on the slipway, is destroyed and the barracks ship *Veendam* (14558 tons) sunk. During 8th AF raids against Kiel, the E-boats *S44* and *S137* and the old cruiser hulk *Hamburg*, used as a barracks ship, are destroyed on 25 and 27 July. At the Howaldt yard, *U396*, fitting out, is destroyed.

24 July   Air War/Norway
208 Fortresses of the 8th AF bomb the harbour installations of Trondheim. The German *U622* is sunk and the destroyer *Z28* damaged.

24 July   Mediterranean
The Italian corvette *Cicogna* is damaged beyond repair in a USAAF attack on Messina.

24/25 July   Air War/Italy
33 aircraft of RAF Bomber Command attack Leghorn on their flight back from North Africa to Great Britain.

24–25 July   English Channel
In moving from Boulogne to Ostend, *S68* and *S77* are attacked N of Dunkirk by British MGBs and MTBs, which sink *S77*. The following night *S110*, *S136*, *S81* and *S88* are moved from the Hook of Holland to Boulogne; *S88* is damaged on a mine but brought into Dunkirk.

25 July   General Situation
King Victor Emmanuel III has Mussolini arrested and appoints Marshal Badoglio the new head of government.

25 July   North Sea
The German patrol trawler *V801* is sunk W of Terschelling by an airborne torpedo.

25 July   Mediterranean
The German MMS *R186* is sunk by air attack off Spadafora in the Strait of Messina.

26 and 27 July   North Atlantic
Bombers of Air Cdr Atlantic sink the British freighters *El Argentino* (9501 tons) and *Halizones* (5298 tons) in the Atlantic NW of Lisbon and badly damage two more freighters totalling 14399 tons.

27 July   Denmark
The German minelayer *Linz*, fitting out at Copenhagen, is damaged by sabotage organised by the resistance movement.

27 July   Norway
The British *MTB345* is grounded off Aspoy near Bergen and captured by *V5301*. The crew are shot by the Gestapo on 30 July. The vessel is recommissioned as the German *SA7*.

27 July   South Pacific
The US submarine *Scamp* (Lt-Cdr Ebert) sinks the Japanese submarine *I-168* 60 nautical miles off New Hanover/New Ireland.

28 July   Caribbean
The German *U359* is sunk by an aircraft from VP-32 in the central Caribbean.

27 July–16 Sept   Baltic
New attempts by Soviet submarines to break out. With strong support from ground attack aircraft of the Naval Air Force against the German-Finnish mine guards, Soviet minesweeper forces try to penetrate the 'Seeigel-Rukajärvi' barrages to facilitate a breakthrough by the submarines. There are numerous engagements. Soviet torpedo cutters try to divert the guards. Thanks to

air attacks, the SAT *Ost* is lost on 4 Aug, the SAT *West* on 15 Sept and the Finnish escort vessel *Uisko* on 16 Sept. On 22 Aug a Finnish gunboat beats off a TKA attack and on 23 Aug the minelayer *Riilahti* is sunk by three Soviet TKAs. As a result of aircraft fire, there are casualties on board the boats of the 3rd and 25th MS Flotillas and the 3rd PB Flotilla. Freedom of movement for German and Finnish ships is temporarily impeded by Soviet mining operations with torpedo cutters and aircraft. The Soviet submarines *S-12* (Capt 3rd Class Bashchenko) and *S-9* (Capt 3rd Class Mylnikov) are lost, respectively, on German and Finnish barrages and as a result of depth charges from German MFPs of the 24th Landing Flotilla, KFKs of the 31st MS Flotilla and Finnish escort vessels.

30 July–10 Sept   Black Sea
The German U-boats *U19*, *U24*, *U23*, *U18* and *U9* operate off the Caucasian coast against Soviet supply transports. *U24* (Lt-Cdr Petersen) sinks the tanker *Emba* (7886 tons) in Sukhumi on 30 July and one tug and two motor boats on 22 Aug, *U23* (Lt Wahlen) sinks one motor minesweeper near Cape Kodor on 24 Aug and *U18* (Lt Fleige) sinks one submarine-chaser (submarine trap) on 29 Aug.

1–25 Aug   Mediterranean
Shelling to support the 8th Army in Sicily is carried out on 1 Aug by the cruisers *Aurora* and *Penelope* against Cotrone and by the cruisers *Dido*, *Euryalus* and *Sirius* and four destroyers against bridges in the Gulf of Eufemia/Calabria; on 4 Aug by the monitor *Roberts* against Taormina; on 9 Aug by *Aurora* and *Penelope* against Castellamare; on 10 Aug by the cruiser *Uganda* and the Dutch gunboat *Flores* against positions N of Reposto; on 12 Aug by *Roberts*, *Uganda* and the gunboats *Scarab* and *Soemba* (Dutch) off the E coast of Sicily; on 13 Aug by *Aurora* and *Penelope* and the destroyers *Jervis* and *Paladin* against Vibo Velentia/Calabria; on 14 Aug by *Dido* and *Sirius* and the destroyer *Panther* against Scaletta and by the gunboats *Aphis*, *Cockchafer* and *Flores* against Taormina; on 15 Aug by the destroyer *Brocklesby* and the gunboats *Aphis* and *Soemba* against targets S of Messina; on 17 Aug by *Euryalus* and *Penelope* and the destroyers *Jervis* and *Paladin* against Scalea; on 24 Aug by the destroyers *Nubian*, *Tartar* and *Tumult* against Lucri; and on 25 Aug by *Orion* against targets in Calabria.

1–31 Aug   Pacific
In US submarine operations in the month of Aug there are 68 'Ultra' signals which lead to 35 sightings and 13 attacks, with two ships sunk and eight damaged.

In the Kuriles area, *S35* conducts a special mission. In Japanese waters, *Whale* (Lt-Cdr Burrows) sinks one ship of 7148 tons, *Salmon* (Lt-Cdr Nicholas) sinks one ship of 2408 tons, *Paddle* (Lt-Cdr Rice) sinks one ship of 5248 tons and damages one more of 5486 tons, *Wahoo* (Cdr Morton) sinks two sailing vessels and damages two ships of 11076 tons, *Plunger* (Lt-Cdr Bass) sinks two ships of 8047 tons and damages one other of 5633 tons, *Tarpon* (Lt-Cdr Wogan) sinks one sailing vessel and damages one ship of 4746 tons and *Halibut* (Lt-Cdr Galantin) sinks two ships of 9943 tons and one sailing vessel and on 6 Sept torpedoes the cruiser *Nachi*. In the China-Formosa area, *Sculpin* (Lt-Cdr Chappell) sinks one ship of 3183 tons and *Seawolf* (Lt-Cdr Gross) sinks three ships of 12995 tons and three sailing vessels and on 31 Aug torpedoes the torpedo boat *Sagi*.

In the Central Pacific, *Steelhead* (Lt-Cdr Welchel) damages one ship of 5385 tons, *Pike* (Lt-Cdr McGregor) sinks one ship of 1992 tons, damages one other of 1915 tons and misses an escort carrier, *Silversides* (Lt-Cdr Burlingame) on 2 Aug torpedoes the minelayer *Tsugaru* 340 nautical miles N of Rabaul and has several prematures, *Pollack* (Lt-Cdr Llewellen) sinks two ships of 7041 tons, *Sunfish* (Lt-Cdr Peterson) sinks two ships of 5479 tons, *Swordfish* (Lt-Cdr Parker) sinks two ships of 6219 tons, *Tullibee* (Lt-Cdr Brindupke) sinks one ship of 4164 tons, *Snapper* (Lt-Cdr Clemenson) sinks one ship of 8359 tons and on 2 Sept the frigate *Mutsure* E of Truk, *Drum* (Lt-Cdr McMahon) sinks one ship of 1334 tons and damages one other of 6438 tons and *Sunfish* and *Snook* conduct reconnaissance missions. In the South West Pacific, *Grayling* (Lt-Cdr Brinker) sinks one ship of 5480 tons and conducts a guerrilla mission, *Gar* (Lt-Cdr Lantrup) sinks one ship of 995 tons, *Trout* (Lt-Cdr Clark) sinks two ships of 6910 tons and attacks one submarine with a premature and *Mingo* conducts a special reconnaissance mission.

1 Aug–6 Sept   Air War/Western Europe
RAF Bomber Command mine offensive. On 19 nights there are 686 sorties against Biscay harbours, the coasts of Brittany, the Netherlands, Frisia and Heligoland and the Elbe estuary. Ten aircraft are lost. On 1 Sept the hospital ship *Strassburg* (17001 tons) is lost on a mine at Egmond. On 6 Sept the German motor minesweeper *R94* is lost on a mine in the Channel, and on 8 Sept the auxiliary minesweepers *M3810*, *M3811* and *M3816* are lost on mines off Fécamp.

1 Aug–3 Oct   Arctic
Operation 'Wunderland II': German operations on the Siberian sea route. *U255* (Lt Harms), which on the way out has sunk on 27 July the Soviet survey ship *Akademik Shokalski* (300 tons), establishes a base on 1 Aug near Spory Navolok on the NE coast of Novaya Zemlya. Here she refuels on 4 Aug a Bv 138 flying boat which on 5, 6, 7 and 11 Aug reconnoitres as far as the Vilkitski Strait to prepare for operations against Soviet convoys by the 'Wiking' U-boat group, comprising *U302*, *U354* and *U711*, and by the cruiser *Lützow* standing ready in Altafjord. No convoys are sighted. When the flying boat is no longer available, a second operation from 4 to 6 Sept with support from *U255* and *U601* produces no result. On 21 Aug *U354* (Lt-Cdr Herbschleb) sights a convoy off Port Dikson and follows it eastwards. Only on 27 and 28 Aug are *U354* and *U302* (Lt-Cdr Sickel), which have in the meantime made a sortie into the Vilkitski Strait, able to attack in the W Siberian Sea. They torpedo the steamer *Petrovski* (3771 tons) and sink the *Dikson* (2900 tons). From 13 Aug to 25 Sept the U-boats of the 'Dachs' group carry out mining operations in the Kara Sea: *U625* (Lt-Cdr Benker) E of the Yugor Strait; *U639* (Lt Wichmann) off the Ob Estuary (sunk on the return journey on 30 Aug NW of Novaya Zemlya by the Soviet submarine *S-101* under Lt-Cdr Trofimov, with the Div Cdr, Capt 2nd Class Egorov on board); *U960* (Lt-Cdr Heinrich) E of the Matochkin Strait, where *U711* (Lt Lange) hunts a patrol ship in vain; *U636* (Lt-Cdr Hildebrand) off Dikson (on her mines the Soviet steamer *Tbilisi*, 7179 tons, sinks); *U629* (Lt Bugs) off Amderma; and *U601* (Lt-Cdr Grau) and *U960* off Dikson. *U711* explores Wardroper Island on 9 Sept and shells on 18 and 24 Sept the W/T stations at Pravdy and Blagopoluchiya. At the end of Sept *U703* (Lt Brünner), *U601* and *U960* relieve the boats of the 'Wiking' group. On 30 Sept they locate the Soviet convoy VA.18 coming from the E with the minelayer *Murman* (Capt 3rd Class Pokhmelnov), the minesweeper-trawlers *T-886*, *T-909* and *T-896* and four steamers. On 30 Sept *U960* sinks the freighter *Arkhangelsk* (2480 tons) near the Sergeya-Kirova Islands and misses the *Mossovet*. On 1 Oct *U703* sinks the *Sergei Kirov* (4146 tons); *U601* misses the *Murman* and is shelled by her. *U960* sinks *T-896* and misses *A Andreev*. As the 'Monsun' group, four to five boats from *U269*, *U277*, *U387*, *U713*, *U307*, *U355*, *U360*, *U737* and *U956* take up positions between Spitzbergen and Bear Island.

225

2 Aug North Sea
The German patrol trawler *V1108* is sunk by torpedo off Texel.

2 Aug Bay of Biscay
The German patrol trawler *V420* is sunk off the Gironde estuary in an air attack.

2–22 Aug North Atlantic
From 2 Aug the British air operation 'Derange' NW of Cape Finisterre is unsuccessful because outbound U-boats are stopped and because Spanish waters are used by homebound U-boats ('Piening' way). The deployment of long-range He 177s of II/KG 40 leads to frequent air engagements in which a total of 17 A/S aircraft and six fighters of No 19 Group RAF are lost.

3–4 Aug North Atlantic
The outgoing *U647* is lost, probably on a mine, between Iceland and the Faeroes. The outgoing U-tanker *U489* is damaged on 3 Aug by Hudson 'J' of No 269 Sqn RAF and sunk on 4 Aug W of the Faeroes by Sunderland 'G' of No 423 Sqn RCAF (Fg Off Bishop), which is shot down by the U-boat. The survivors are picked up by the destroyers *Orwell* and *Castleton*.

3–4 Aug Gibraltar
An small Italian battle unit (Cdr Notari) attacks Allied ships in Gibraltar from the *Olterra* in Algeciras with three guided torpedoes and sinks the Norwegian tanker *Thorshövdi* (9944 tons) and the American freighter *Harrison Gray Otis* (7176 tons). One freighter of 5975 tons is damaged.

3 Aug–17 Oct Pacific
The last German auxiliary cruiser, *Schiff 28/Michel* (Capt Gumprich), sights the US troop transport *Hermitage* in the area of Pitcairn Island on 3 and 7 Aug, but does not attack. On 29 Aug *Schiff 28* is able to escape undetected from the US cruiser *Trenton* W of the Chilean coast. During the night 10–11 Sept she sinks the Norwegian tanker *Indus* (9977 tons) in the middle of the Pacific halfway between the Panama Canal and Tahiti. On 22 Sept the auxiliary cruiser runs into a small convoy with the submarine-chasers *SC1042* and *SC1045* and two auxiliary vessels on the route Panama Canal–Australia, but because she overestimates the strength of the enemy she does not attack the convoy. After a sortie to the USA–Hawaii route, Gumprich begins the return journey to Japan on 7 Oct. On 17 Oct *Schiff 28* is sunk by three torpedoes from the US submarine *Tarpon* (Cdr Wogan) 90 nautical miles E of Yokohama. 116 men reach Japan in lifeboats.

4 Aug Mediterranean
The British destroyer *Arrow* is damaged beyond repair when an ammunition ship explodes in Algiers' harbour. The Italian torpedo boat *Pallade* capsizes following bomb damage sustained in a USAAF raid at Naples.

4–5 Aug North Sea
Sorties by *S39*, *S74*, *S80*, *S94*, *S89*, *S86* and *S83* of the German 2nd and 6th MTB Flotillas (Cdr Feldt and Cdr Obermaier) into the area off Harwich. The British trawler *Red Gauntlet* is sunk there by *S86* (Lt Wrampe).

5 Aug Baltic
During exercises W of Memel, the German *U34* is sunk in a collison with the tender *Lech*. The U-boat is later raised but is decommissioned.

5 Aug Mediterranean
The Italian corvette *Gazella* sinks after striking a mine off Asinara, Sardinia.

5 Aug–6 Sept Mediterranean
In submarine operations off the Sicilian east coast, *U453* and *Diaspro*, and off the north coast *U73* and *U431*, miss Allied warships. *U380* (Lt-Cdr Roether) torpedoes one ship of 7191 tons off Palermo. S of Sicily, *Argento* and *U458* are lost in attacks by the US destroyer *Buck* on 2 Aug and the escort destroyers *Easton* and *Pindos* (Greek) on 22 Aug respectively. Off Cyrenaica, *U81* misses an eastern convoy and off the Lebanese coast *U596* (Lt-Cdr Jahn) sinks four sailing ships and damages two unidentified small steamers. In attacks on convoys off the Algerian coast, *U371* (Lt-Cdr Mehl) sinks one ship of 6004 tons and *U410* (Lt Fenski) sinks two of 14436 tons. *U616* misses warships. On 6 Sept *U617* (Lt-Cdr Brandi) sinks E of Gibraltar the escort destroyer *Puckeridge*. After air attacks by Wellingtons 'J' and 'P' of No 179 Sqn RAF and pursuit by the corvette *Hyacinth*, the minesweeper *Woolongong* (RAN) and the trawler *Haarlem*, the boat has to be abandoned on the Moroccan coast on 12 Sept.

8 Aug Mediterranean
The Italian destroyer *Freccia* is sunk at Genoa in an RAF air raid.

9 Aug Norway
The German auxiliary minesweeper *M5602* is sunk following a collision off Kristiansand South.

10 Aug Mediterranean
The British submarine *Parthian* sinks after striking a mine en route from Malta to Alexandria.

11 Aug English Channel
The 4th and 5th MTB Flotillas, which are transferred to L'Abervrach for a sortie into Plymouth Sound, are attacked in two waves by British fighter-bombers: *S121* is sunk, *S117* badly damaged and four others slightly damaged. Only *S110* is undamaged.

12 Aug Baltic
The Swedish submarine *Illern* sinks after a collision with a freighter.

13 Aug Mediterranean
German He 111 torpedo bombers of KG 26 (Maj Klümper) are deployed following a reconnaissance report concerning convoy UGS.13 (75 ships escorted by the destroyer *Blankney*, the corvettes *Convolvulus*, *Saxifrage* and *Godetia* and the Australian *Geraldton*, *Cairns*, *Cessnock* and *Wollongong*). But they attack near Alboran the convoy MKS.21 (40 ships escorted by the British sloops and minesweepers *Shoreham*, *Whitehaven*, *Hythe*, *Rye* and *Romney* and the Australian corvettes *Gawler*, *Ipswich*, *Lismore* and *Maryborough*) which is proceeding in the opposite direction in the area to the N. The results ('170000 tons') are considerably exaggerated by the pilots: in fact, only the British freighter *Empire Haven* (6852 tons) and the American freighter *Francis W Pettygrove* (7176 tons) are damaged by torpedo hits.

13 Aug Mediterranean
The German MMS *R6* is sunk by bombs in Civitavecchia.

13 Aug Indonesia
First attack by the 5th USAAF from Australia with 380 heavy B-24 bombers on the oilfields of Balikpapan (Borneo).

14–24 Aug General Situation
Conference between Roosevelt and Churchill in Quebec ('Quadrant'). The main item on the agenda, apart from the imminent surrender of Italy, is 'Overlord', the invasion of France planned by the Joint Chiefs of Staff. The date: 1 May 1944. Churchill and the British delegation travel on the passenger liner *Queen Mary*, escorted by the carrier *Illustrious*, three cruisers and destroyers. The return journey is made on the battlecruiser *Renown*. In Quebec the First Sea Lord, Admiral of the Fleet Sir Dudley Pound, suffers a heart attack. His successor from 15 Oct is Adm Sir Andrew Cunningham.

15–25 Aug South Pacific
The US III Amphibious Force (Rear-Adm Wilkinson), comprising the fast transports *Stringham*, *Waters*, *Dent*, *Talbot*, *Kilty*, *Ward* and *McKean*, three LSTs and 11 LSIs, lands 4600 men from RCT 35 (25th US Div, Maj-Gen McClure) on Vella Lavella (Central Solomons). Cover and fire support is provided by the destroyers *Nicholas*, *O'Bannon*, *Taylor*, *Chevalier*, *Cony*, *Pringle*, *Waller*, *Saufley*, *Philip*, *Renshaw*, *Conway* and *Eaton*. On 17 Aug small Japanese craft land reinforcements on the north coast. The destroyers *Nicholas*, *O'Bannon*, *Taylor* and *Chevalier* (Capt

Ryan) are deployed against the covering force (Rear-Adm Ijuin), which comprises the destroyers *Sazanami*, *Hamakaze*, *Shigure* and *Isokaze*. The American force avoids 31 Japanese torpedoes but in the pursuit only slight damage is inflicted on *Hamakaze* and *Isokaze*. The submarine-chasers *Ch5* and *Ch12* are sunk.

On 25 Aug the fighting by XIV US Corps (43rd, 37th and parts of 25th Inf Divs) on New Georgia ends with the capture of Bairoko.

15 Aug–29 Oct   Arctic

In operations against German supply traffic off the Norwegian polar coast, the Soviet submarines *L-15*, *S-54*, *S-102*, *L-22* and *Shch-402* have no success in Aug. *M-104* (Lt-Cdr Lukyanov) torpedoes the steamer *Rüdesheimer* (2036 tons) on 1 Sept. *L-20* (Capt 3rd Class Tamman) is damaged after laying out a mine barrage near Sletnes on 3 Sept by *UJ1209* when she attacks a convoy. On 3 Sept *S-51* (Capt 2nd Class Kucherenko) sinks the submarine-chaser *UJ1202* off Kongsfjord. On 11 Sept *M-107* (Lt-Cdr Kofanov) sinks *UJ1217* off Syltefjord.

On 14 Sept *Shch-404* (Lt-Cdr Makarenkov) misses a convoy off Vardö. On the receipt of his report, torpedo aircraft of the 5th Mining and Torpedo Air Div are deployed with fighter protection but, thanks to JG 5, they suffer heavy losses without securing any hits. On 15 Sept the Soviet torpedo cutters *TKA-13* (Lt Shabalin) and *TKA-21* attack near Kiberg. In a repeat of this operation on 20–21 Sept, *Shch-404* and the aircraft have no success but *TKA-15* sinks the steamer *Antje Fritzen* (4330 tons). There is a similar operation on 12–13 Oct after *S-55* (Capt 3rd Class Sushkin) has sunk the mine destructor ship *Ammerland* (5381 tons) from a large German convoy in Porsangerfjord. Attacks on 13 Oct off Makkaur by *Shch-403* and off Vardö by *M-172* fail, as do air attacks off Kiberg. All three submarines are lost, probably on the flanking mine barrages laid out in the summer and autumn months by the German minelayers *Brummer*, *Ostmark*, *Kaiser* and *Roland*. Likewise, *M-174* is lost in Oct. The large submarine *K-1* goes missing from Sept, when she returned from the Kara Sea. After these losses the Soviet submarines are deployed much more cautiously.

17 Aug   Atlantic

Portugal grants the Allies the use of bases in the Azores.

17 Aug   Mediterranean

German withdrawal from Sicily (Operation 'Lehrgang') completed. The following are transported across the Strait of Messina (Capt v Liebenstein in command): 39569

German troops, including 4444 wounded; 9605 vehicles, 47 tanks, 94 guns, over 2000 tons of ammunition and fuel and about 15000 tons of other supplies; and 62000 Italian troops, 227 vehicles and 41 guns. Because of the unusually strong AA defence of the crossing area, only a few small ferrying craft are lost in spite of continual Allied air attacks.

17–23 Aug   South West Pacific

From 17 to 22 Aug the US 5th AF carries out an air offensive to neutralise the Japanese air bases in the Wewak area (New Guinea). On 22–23 Aug four destroyers of TF.74 under Capt Carter make a sortie from Milne Bay to Finschhafen to shell the area.

18 Aug   Mediterranean

The US cruisers *Philadelphia* and *Boise* and four destroyers shell Gioia-Taura and Palmi in Calabria.

20 Aug   English Channel

The German MMS *R84* is sunk by air attack and gunfire off Boulogne.

20 Aug   Baltic

The German *U670* is sunk in the Bay of Danzig following a collision with the target ship *Bolkoburg*.

22 Aug   Mediterranean

The German torpedo boat *TA12* (ex-French *Baliste*) is damaged in action with the British destroyer *Eclipse* off Cape Prasonesi/Rhodes and beached; it is subsequently destroyed in an air attack.

22 Aug–1 Sept   South Pacific

Islands are occupied without fighting for the purpose of constructing air bases. On 22 Aug an advance party of the US 2nd Marine Airborne Bn lands on Nukufetau in the Ellice Islands; on 27 Aug the remaining units and Seabees follow. On 28 Aug the 7th Marine Defence Bn occupies Nanomea. In the Solomons area, Arundel Island is occupied on 27 Aug by RCT 172 of the 43rd Inf Div to control Blackett Strait. On 1 Sept a task force (Rear-Adm Lee) comprising the LSD *Ashland* (the first use of such a ship) and the transport *Hercules* lands army troops on Baker Island. Support is provided by the destroyers *Trathen*, *Spence*, *Boyd* and *Bradford* and air cover by the carriers *Princeton* and *Belleau Wood*.

23 Aug   North Atlantic

The following escort groups are deployed for the North Atlantic convoy routes: B2 (Cdr MacIntyre) with the destroyers *Hesperus*, *Vesper* and *Vanessa* (yard), the frigate *Mourne* and the corvettes *Campanula*, *Clematis*, *Heather* (yard), *Sweetbriar* and *Gentian* (yard); B3 (Cdr Tyson) with the destroyers *Keppel* and *Escapade*, the frigate *Towy* and the corvettes *Narcissus*, *Orchis*, *Lobélia* (FFN), *Renoncule* (FFN), *Roselys*

(FFN) and *Aconit* (FFN, yard); B6 (Cdr Currie) with the destroyers *Fame* and *Vanquisher*, the frigate *Deveron* and the corvettes *Eglantine* (RNoN, yard), *Kingcup*, *Potentilla* (RNoN), *Rose* (RNoN), *Acanthus* (RNoN, yard) and *Vervain* (yard); B7 (Cdr Gretton) with the destroyers *Duncan*, *Versatile* (yard), *Vidette* and *Vansittart* (yard) and the corvettes *Loosestrife*, *Pink*, *Sunflower* and *Snowflake* (yard); C1 (Cdr Adams) with the destroyers *Assiniboine*, *Forester* (RN) and *St Laurent*, the frigate *Ettrick* (RN, detached) and the corvettes *Agassiz*, *Celandine* (RN), *Galt*, *Rimouski* (yard), *Chilliwack* (yard), *Fredericton* (yard) and *Lunenburg*; C2 (Cdr Burnett RN) with the destroyers *Gatineau* and *Icarus* (RN), the frigate *Lagan* and the corvettes *Drumheller*, *Fennel* (yard), *Kamloops*, *Polyanthus* (RN) and *Primrose* (yard); C3 (Cdr Medley RN) with the destroyers *Burnham*, *Saskatchewan* and *Skeena* and the corvettes *Bittersweet* (yard), *Eyebright* (detached), *Mayflower*, *Napanee* (yard), *Pictou*, *Sorel*, *Halifax* (yard) and *La Malbaie* (yard); C4 (Cdr McKillop RN) with the destroyers *Churchill* (RN), *Hotspur* (RN) and *Restigouche* (yard) and the corvettes *Collingwood* (yard), *Nasturtium* (RN), *Orillia* (yard), *Trillium*, *Woodstock* (yard), *Amherst* (yard) and *Brandon* (yard); and C5 (Cdr Pullen) with the destroyers *Kootenay* and *Ottawa* and the corvettes *Arvida*, *Dauphin* (yard), *Kitchener*, *Sudbury*, *Wetaskiwin*, *Dianthus* (RN, yard), *New Westminster* (yard) and *Rosthern* (yard).

For the UK–Mediterranean and Sierra Leone convoys there are B1 (Cdr Bayldon) with the destroyers *Hurricane*, *Wanderer* and *Watchman* (yard), the frigate *Glenarm* and the corvettes *Borage*, *Dahlia*, *Meadowsweet* (yard), *Wallflower* and *Monkshood*; B4 (Cdr Day) with the destroyers *Highlander*, *Walker*, *Westcott* and *Winchelsea* and the corvettes *Abelia*, *Asphodel*, *Clover* and *Pennywort*; B5 (Cdr Boyle) with the destroyers *Havelock*, *Volunteer*, *Warwick* and *Vimy* and the corvettes *Buttercup* (yard), *Godetia*, *Lavender* (yard), *Pimpernel* (yard) and *Saxifrage*; the 37th EG (A/Cdr Majendie) with the sloops *Black Swan* (yard), *Fowey*, *Stork* and *Deptford* (yard), the frigate *Johan Maurits* (RNethN) and corvettes *Campion*, *Friso* (RNethN), *Myosotis*, *Mallow* and *Stonecrop*; the 38th EG (Cdr Christie) with the frigate *Fal*, the sloops *Enchantress*, *Leith*, *Sandwich* and *Bideford* (yard) and the corvettes *Anchusa*, *Columbine*, *Violet* and *Coreopsis* (yard); the 39th EG (Cdr King) with the frigate *Tavy*, the sloops *Rochester*, *Fleetwood* (yard), *Hastings* (yard) and *Scarborough* and the corvettes *Azalea*, *Balsam*, *Geranium* and

Mignonette (yard); and the 40th EG (Cdr Dallison) with the frigates *Exe* and *Moyola*, the sloops *Bridgewater* and *Milford* and the corvettes *Armeria*, *Clarkia*, (yard), *Petunia* and *Burdock* (yard).

23–29 Aug Bay of Biscay
No 19 Group RAF Coastal Command starts a new operation, 'Percussion', in the vicinity of the Spanish coast in co-operation with support groups against the transiting German U-boats. The following units participate from airfields in SW England: Nos 59 and 86 Sqns RAF (VLR Liberator), 4th and 19th Sqns USAAF (LR Liberator), No 311 (Czech) Sqn (changing from Wellingtons to Liberators); Nos 58 and 502 Sqns RAF (Halifax); No 172 Sqn RAF and Nos 407 and 612 Sqns RCAF (Leigh Light Wellington); and No 547 Sqn. RAF and No 304 (Polish) Sqn (Wellington). Of the 'paper' strength of 169 very-long-range and long-range aircraft, 90 are operational on 23 Aug. In addition there are No 228 Sqn RAF and Nos 10 and 461 Sqns RAAF (Sunderland) and Catalinas flown by VP-63 USN (with MAD) and by No 210 Sqn RAF (with Leigh Light); of 60 aircraft, 26 are operational. Nos 143 and 248 Sqns RAF, with 23 operational Beaufighters, are also involved, while from Gibraltar there are Leigh Light Wellingtons of No 179 Sqn RAF and Catalinas of No 202 Sqn RAF, plus Hudsons of Nos 48 and 233 Sqns RAF; 29 of the 47 Gibraltar-based aircraft are operational on 23 Aug.

First the 40th EG (Cdr Dallison) with the frigates *Exe*, *Moyola* and *Waveney* and the sloops *Landguard*, *Bideford* and *Hastings* operates off Cape Finisterre and Cape Ortegal, but the returning *U510* and *U66* and the outgoing *U123* and *U518* pass; only *U134* is sunk, by Leigh Light Wellington 'J' of No 179 Sqn RAF on 24 Aug. The cruiser *Bermuda* is deployed to the W.

When the Canadian 5th SG (Cdr Birch), with the frigates *Nene* (RN) and *Tweed* (RN) and the corvettes *Calgary*, *Edmundston* and *Snowberry*, arrives to relieve the 40th EG, fourteen Do 217s of II/KG 100 and seven Ju 88Cs attack the support groups using the new Hs 293 glider bomb for the first time: *Landguard* is damaged by four near-misses and *Bideford* by one. On the same day, some 400 nautical miles W of Cape Finisterre, the outgoing *U523* runs into the combined convoy OG.92/KMS.24 (EG.B1, under Cdr Bayldon, with the destroyers *Hurricane*, *Wanderer* and *Watchman* and the corvettes *Borage*, *Dahlia*, *Meadowsweet* and *Wall-flower*) and is sunk by depth charges fired by *Wallflower* and *Wanderer*.

On 26 Aug the 5th SG is relieved by the 1st

SG (Cdr Brewer, with the sloops *Pelican* and *Egret* and the frigates *Jed*, *Rother*, *Spey* and *Evenlode*) which damages the returning *U342* with depth charges. To relieve *Bermuda* going to refuel at Plymouth, the destroyers *Grenville* and *Athabaskan* (RCN) arrive. The outgoing *U305* and *U645*, and the returning *U358*, *U571*, *U333*, *U566* and *U757*, pass unharmed.

On 28 Aug there is a second attack by 18 Do 217s against the support groups. *Athabaskan* is badly hit and *Egret* blows up. The British SGs retire to the W and the inward and outward movements of the U-boats are again facilitated.

23 Aug–4 Sept North Atlantic
Convoys pass unharmed by U-boats through the area S of Iceland on the Great Circle route, covered by aircraft of No 15 Group RAF Coastal Command flying from bases in Northern Ireland and Iceland: Nos 59 and 120 Sqns RAF (VLR Liberator); Nos 206 and 220 Sqns RAF (Fortress); No 201 Sqn RAF and Nos 422 and 423 Sqns RCAF (Sunderland); VP-84 USN (Catalina); and No 269 Sqn RAF (Hudson). Of 131 aircraft on strength, 58 are operational on 23 Aug.

From 23 to 27 Aug the Westbound ONS. 16 (EG.C3 under Cdr Medley RN with the destroyers *Saskatchewan*, *Skeena* and *Burnham* and the corvettes *Mayflower*, *Pictou* and *Sorel*) and ON.198 (EG.B2 under Cdr MacIntyre with the destroyers *Hesperus* and *Vesper*, the frigate *Mourne* and the corvettes *Campanula*, *Clematis* and *Sweetbriar*) and the eastbound HX.252 (EG.C1 under Cdr Adams with the destroyers *Assiniboine* and *Forester* and the corvettes *Agassiz*, *Celandine*, *Galt* and *Lunenburg*) pass S of Iceland. The convoy MKS.21 (EG.B4 under Cdr Day with the destroyers *Highlander*, *Walker*, *Westcott* and *Winchelsea* and the corvettes *Abelia*, *Asphodel*, *Clover* and *Pennywort*) enters the North Channel.

From 27 to 31 Aug the westbound convoy ON.199 (EG.C5 under Cdr Pullen with the destroyers *Ottawa* and *Kootenay* and the corvettes *Arvida*, *Dauphin*, *Kitchener*, *Sudbury* and *Wetaskiwin*) leaves the North Channel and passes the inbound HX.253 (EG.B3 under Cdr Evans with the frigate *Towy*, the destroyers *Keppel* and *Escapade* and the corvettes *Narcissus*, *Orchis*, *Lobélia*, *Renoncule* and *Roselys*) and SC.140 (EG.C2 under Cdr Burnett RN with the destroyers *Gatineau* and *Icarus*, the frigate *Lagan* and the corvettes *Drumheller*, *Fennel*, *Kamloops*, *Polyanthus* and *Primrose*). On the UK–Gibraltar route, convoy OS.54/KMS.25 (39th EG under Cdr King with the sloops

Rochester and *Scarborough*, the frigate *Tavy* and the corvettes *Azalea*, *Balsam* and *Geranium*) leaves the North Channel, while convoy MKS.22/SL.135 (37th EG under A/Cdr Majendie with the sloops *Fowey* and *Stork*, the corvettes *Campion*, *Friso*, *Myosotis*, *Stonecrop*, *Mallow*, *Crocus* and *Woodruff* and the new DE-frigate *Berry*) passes W of Spain, where the returning *U634* runs into it and is sunk by *Stork* and *Stonecrop*.

From 1 to 4 Sept convoys HX.253, SC.140 and MKS.22/SL.135 and the troop convoy UT.1 (Escort Group 'D' with the sloops *Dart*, *Erne*, *Fishguard*, *Banff* and *Whimbrel* and the destroyers *Clare* and *St Francis*) arrive in the North Channel, while ONS.17 (EG.B6 under Cdr Currie with the destroyers *Fame* and *Vanquisher*, the frigate *Deveron* and the corvettes *Kingcup*, *Potentilla* and *Rose*) departs W, together with the US TG.21.17 (Capt Ramsey) which includes the escort carrier *Block Island*. On 3 Sept ON.200 (EG.B7 under Cdr Gretton with the destroyers *Duncan* and *Vidette* and the corvettes *Loosestrife*, *Pink* and *Sunflower*) follows.

On 1 Sept the troop convoy MKF.22 (escorted by the battleships *Resolution* and *Revenge* and the 3rd EG under Cdr Eaden with the destroyers *Inconstant* and *Wrestler*, the sloop *Chanticleer* and the frigates *Ettrick*, *Barle*, *Usk* and *Glenarm*) leaves Gibraltar for the UK. On 4 Sept this escort damages the outbound *U515* which has to return.

23 Aug–11 Nov South Pacific
A Japanese submarine group is deployed from Truk and Rabaul in the area of the New Hebrides. On 23 Aug *I-25* reconnoitres with her aircraft over Espiritu Santo but is sunk by the destroyer *Ellet* on 3 Sept when she tries to approach a US force. On 25 Aug *Ro-35* is lost when attacked with depth charges by the US destroyer *Patterson* in the Solomons Sea. On 31 Aug *I-20* (Lt-Cdr Otsuka) torpedoes one tanker of 10872 tons but is sunk on 3 Sept by destroyer *Patterson* off the New Hebrides. *I-182* is sunk on 1 Sept by the destroyer *Wadsworth* off Esperita Santo. On 11 Sept *I-39* (Cdr Tanaka) sinks the fleet tug *Navajo*. *I-26* reconnoitres in the area of the Fiji Islands. On 15 Sept *Ro-101* is sunk by the destroyer *Saufley* and two aircraft of VP-23. A second wave of Japanese submarines operates from the middle of Sept to the beginning of Nov in the area of the New Hebrides. It comprises *I-171*, *I-39*, *I-181*, *I-32*, *I-21* and *Ro-36*, of which only *I-21* (Cdr Inada) sinks one ship of 6711 tons on 11 Nov. From the middle of Nov the submarines *Ro-104*, *Ro-105*, *Ro-*

100, Ro-109, I-38, I-16, I-6 and *I-171* are brought up chiefly for transport missions. *Ro 100* is lost on a mine off Buin/Bougainville.

24 Aug   Mediterranean
The German escort vessel *SG14* (the ex-French minesweeper *Matelot Leblanc*) is sunk by bombing S of Capri.

26 Aug   Air War/East Asia
American bombers attack the harbour of Hong Kong from bases in China.

29 Aug   Denmark
The German authorities declare a state of emergency when the Danish government rejects the German demand that it should declare a state of emergency and introduce summary courts and the death sentence for saboteurs. Strikes and sabotage break out, the Danish government resigns and the Danish Army is disarmed by German troops. The Danish Fleet (Vice-Adm Vedel) is scuttled: the coastal defence ship *Peder Skram*, the submarines *Havhesten. Havkalen, Havfruen, Havmanden, Daphne, Dryaden, Rota, Flora* and *Bellona*, the tender *Henrik Gerner*, the minesweepers *Söbjörnen, Söulven* and *Söhunden*, the patrol (ex-torpedo) boats *Hvalrossen, Saelen, Nordkoperen, Makrelen, Havhesten* and *Narhvalen*, and the minelayers *Kvintus, Sixtus, Lossen* and *Lindormen* sink in Copenhagen. The coastal defence ship *Niels Juel* is beached in Isefjord; the fishery protection vessel *Ingolf* is scuttled in the Great Belt and *Heimdall* and *Freja* are scuttled at Copenhagen. In Nyborg, Korsör and Kalundborg the crews of Danish ships are, in some cases, overwhelmed by force and the minesweepers *Sölöven, Söridderen* and *Söhesten* and the patrol boats *Springeren* and *Hajen* are among those seized. In Ulvsund the patrol boat *Havörnen* is blown up. Some of the ships are later raised, repaired and taken over by the German Navy. The patrol boat *Havkatten*, three motor minesweepers and nine small auxiliary craft escape to Sweden.

28 Aug   Mediterranean
The German escort vessel *SG10* (ex-French *Felix Henri*, 2525 tons) is sunk by the British submarine *Sickle*.

29 Aug   Indian Ocean
In operations in the Malacca Straits, the British submarine *Trident* attacks the Japanese cruiser *Kashii* off Sabang with eight torpedoes, all of which miss.

29 Aug–7 Sept   Bay of Biscay
The retreat of the British support groups to the W eases the transit of the German U-boats. From 29 to 31 Aug the German torpedo boats *T24, T22* and *T25* bring the

Japanese submarine *I-8* (Capt Uchino) into Lorient. The returning *U382, U618, U129, U262, U732* and *U600* pass close to Cape Ortegal and avoid the 'Percussion' air patrols and the 1st EG (the sloops *Pelican* and *Crane* and the frigates *Jed, Rother, Spey* and *Wear*), some of which continue for some days as group 'W' until relieved by the 5th EG (the frigates *Nene* and *Tweed* and the corvettes *Calgary, Edmundston* and *Snowberry*), covered by the cruisers *Bermuda* and *Sheffield* relieving each other for refuelling. Of the boats coming more from the W, *U86, U406* and *U760*, the last is attacked by Wellington 'C' of No 179 Sqn RAF with Leigh Light and so heavily damaged on 6–7 Sept that it has to enter El Ferrol, where the boat is interned on 9 Sept.

The outgoing boats for the 'Leuthen' group pass the Allied patrols almost unmolested: *U305, U645, U260, U338, U731, U386, U341, U229, U758, U584, U666, U641, U402* and the tanker *U460* which has to supply the 'Leuthen' boats. Only *U669*, sailing for a special operation, 'Kiebitz,' is sunk, by Wellington 'W' of No 407 Sqn RCAF with Leigh Light. The other boats proceed to their waiting areas and to the tanker.

31 Aug–1 Sept   Central Pacific
First carrier raid by the newly formed US 'Fast Carrier Task Force'. On 31 Aug–1 Sept TF.15 (Rear-Adm Pownall), comprising the carriers *Yorktown, Essex* and *Independence*, attacks Marcus Island with cover from the battleship *Indiana*, the cruisers *Nashville* and *Mobile*, the destroyers *La Valette, Stevens, Ringgold, Schroeder, Sigsbee, Thatcher, Harrison, John Rodgers, McKee, Dashiell* and *Halford* and the tanker *Guadeloupe*. In 275 sorties in six attacks, four aircraft are lost. Damage is done to shore installations but Japanese losses are slight.

31 Aug–3 Sept   Mediterranean
Operation 'Baytown': British landing in Calabria. On 31 Aug the battleships *Nelson* and *Rodney*, the cruiser *Orion* and the destroyers *Offa, Petard, Quail, Queenborough, Quilliam, Tartar, Troubridge, Tyrian* and *Piorun* (Polish) carry out the preparatory shelling of the coast between Reggio Calabria and Pessaro (Operation 'Hammer'). On 2 Sept the shelling is repeated by the battleships *Valiant* and *Warspite*, the cruisers *Orion* and *Mauritius*, some of the above-mentioned destroyers, *Faulknor* and *Loyal* and the monitors *Erebus, Roberts* and *Abercrombie*, as well as the gunboats *Aphis* and *Scarab*. On 3 Sept the British XIII Corps is transported in 22 LSTs and 270 smaller landing craft across

the Strait of Messina in face of little resistance and landed near Reggio and Villa San Giovanni. There is support from army artillery near Messina and from the guns of the monitors *Erebus, Roberts* and *Abercrombie*, the cruisers *Orion* and *Mauritius*, the gunboats *Aphis* and *Scarab* and the destroyers *Loyal, Offa, Piorun* (Polish), *Quail, Queenborough* and *Quilliam*.

1 Sept   Norway
The German patrol vessel *V5502* (the ex-Norwegian torpedo boat *Snögg*) is damaged by grounding near Bergen; she is salvaged but is sunk on 6 Sept.

1–9 Sept   South West Pacific
The US VII Amphibious Force (TF.76, Rear-Adm Barbey) sets out from Milne Bay on 1 Sept in order to land 8000 men of the Australian 9th Div (20th and 26th Bdes on 3–4 Sept and 24th Bde on 5–6 Sept) E of Lae (New Guinea). It comprises 39 LSTs, 20 LCIs, nine LCTs, 14 transports, 12 submarine-chasers and three other vessels. The landing is supported by the US destroyers *Conyngham, Flusser, Perkins, Smith, Mahan, Lamson, Mugford, Drayton* and *Reid. Reid*, as radar picket, locates an approaching Japanese bomber force early enough for it to be intercepted by US fighters. In further air attacks, *LCI339* is sunk and *LST471, LST473* and *Conyngham* damaged. On 8 Sept the destroyers *Perkins, Flusser, Smith* and *Mahan*, and on 9 Sept the fast transports *Brooks, Gilmer, Humphreys* and *Sands*, bombard Lae in support of the operation.

1–30 Sept   Pacific
In US submarine operations during Sept there are 81 'Ultra' signals which lead to 44 sightings and 13 attacks, in which five ships are sunk and three are damaged. In the Aleutians/Kuriles area, *S42* (Lt Glenn) sinks one ship of 2719 tons, *S28* (Lt Sisler) sinks one ship of 1368 tons and *Sawfish* conducts reconnaissance off the coast of Sakhalin.

In Japanese waters, *Pompano* (Lt-Cdr Thomas) sinks three ships of 8649 tons and damages one more of 3005 tons but is sunk on a mine N of Honshu, *Harder* (Lt-Cdr Dealey) sinks five ships of 15361 tons, *Spearfish* (Lt-Cdr Dempsey) torpedoes one ship of 6962 tons and *Wahoo* (Cdr Morton) sinks six ships of 17771 tons but is sunk on 11 Oct by aircraft in the La Perouse Strait. In the China/Formosa area, *Pargo* (Lt-Cdr Eddy) damages one ship of 5144 tons, *Snook* (Lt-Cdr Triebel) sinks two ships of 10370 tons and damages one other of 752 tons and *Trigger* (Lt-Cdr Donaho) sinks four ships of 34644 tons and damages one more of 6854 tons. On their way to their operational areas,

Snook and *Steelhead* are used as mark boats for carrier raids.

In the Central Pacific, *Albacore* (Lt-Cdr Hagberg) sinks one ship of 2677 tons and damages one more of 4211 tons, *Permit* (Lt-Cdr Chapple) sinks one ship of 6938 tons and damages one more of 14050 tons, *Haddock* (Lt-Cdr Davenport) torpedoes three ships of 20045 tons, including the seaplane carrier *Notoro*, *Narwhal* (Lt-Cdr Latta) sinks one ship of 4211 tons, *Gudgeon* (Lt-Cdr Post) sinks one ship of 3158 tons and damages one more of 3266 tons and, on 21 Sept, the destroyer *Oite*, *Scamp* (Lt-Cdr Ebert) sinks one ship of 8614 tons, *Cabrilla* (Lt-Cdr Hammond) torpedoes the escort carrier *Taiyo* on 24 Sept 200 nautical miles NE of Chichijima, *Pogy* (Lt-Cdr Wales) sinks one ship of 7005 tons and *Gudgeon*, *Bowfin*, *Nautilus* and *Peto* conduct special missions. In the South Pacific, *Greenling*, *Guardfish*, *Gato*, *Grouper* and *Sculpin* conduct reconnaissance. In the South West Pacific, *Bluefish* (Lt-Cdr Parker) sinks one ship of 3228 tons and the torpedo boat *Kasasagi*, *Bowfin* (Lt-Cdr Willingham) sinks one ship of 5959 tons, *Bonefish* (Lt-Cdr Hogan) sinks three ships of 24208 tons and *Billfish* and *Tuna* have prematures and duds; *Grayling* is lost between 9 and 12 Sept off Manila and *Cisco* on 28 Sept in the Sulu Sea to a Japanese freighter. *Puffer* (Lt-Cdr Selby) damages one ship of 7508 tons and is damaged by depth charges from the torpedo boat *Chidori* off Makkaur on 9–10 Oct. On 30 Sept *Barb* sails from Pearl Harbor with the first of the new Mk 18 torpedoes.

2 Sept   Arctic
The German auxiliary minesweeper *M5209* is sunk by torpedoes fired by a Soviet torpedo cutter off Kongsfjord.

2 Sept   South Pacific
The Japanese patrol boat *P35/Tsuta* is sunk at Lae (New Guinea) in a USAAF air attack.

2 Sept–19 Oct   Indonesia
Operation 'Jaywick'. The Australian motor drifter *Krait* sets out with six canoes on board from Exmouth Gulf in Australia. On 9 Sept she goes through Lombok Strait and on 18 Sept the six canoes with six limpet mines on board are launched off Singapore. *Krait* cruises for 14 days off South Borneo and the canoes carry out an attack on 21 Sept. Two ships of 7204 tons are destroyed. On 1 and 3 Oct the canoes are met and, after passing through Lombok Strait on 10 Oct, *Krait* arrives back in Exmouth Gulf on 19 Oct.

3 Sept   Arctic
The German A/S trawler *UJ1202* is sunk

off Kongsfjord by the Soviet submarine *L-20*.

3–5 Sept   English Channel
The German 5th TB Flotilla (Cdr Koppenhagen), consisting of *T25*, *Möwe*, *Kondor*, *T19* and *T27*, carries out the 'Taube' and 'Rebhuhn' mining operations in the Channel.

3–9 Sept   Mediterranean
Preparatory movements for Operation 'Avalanche' (see 9–16 Sept). The following convoys set out: from Tripoli TSS.1 (3 Sept), TSM.1, TSF.1 and TSS.2 (6 Sept) and TSS.3 (7 Sept); from Palermo TSF.1X (8 Sept); from Bizerta FSS.1 (4 Sept), FSM.1 and FSM.1X (6 Sept) and FSS.2X and FSX.3 (7 Sept); from Termini FSS.2Y (8 Sept); from Oran NSF.1 (5 Sept); and from Algiers NSF.1X (6 Sept). The convoys consist of a total of three headquarters ships, six attack transports, 15 infantry landing ships (LCIs), nine attack freighters, 94 LSTs, 131 LCIs, 66 LCTs, 21 LCSs, two fighter direction ships, three tankers, one petrol tanker, five tugs and two coastal motor boats. Three cruisers, two AA ships, two monitors, one gunboat, 31 destroyers, 21 motor torpedo boats, 36 PCs, 35 MLs, 37 minesweepers and 12 trawlers proceed with the convoys as escort. Force H (see 9 Sept) sets out from Malta on 7 Sept and, as a reserve covering force, Vice-Adm Power sets out on 7 Sept from Algiers for Augusta with the British battleships *Howe* and *King George V*. During the nights 6–7 and 8–9 Sept German bomber units make attacks on Bizerta (convoy FSS.2) and units at sea. One LST is destroyed and one LCT is damaged.

6–9 Sept   Arctic
Operation 'Sizilien' ('Zitronella'): a German task force (Adm Kummetz), comprising the battleship *Tirpitz* (Capt Meyer), the battle-cruiser *Scharnhorst* (Capt Hüffmeier) and the 4th (Capt Johannesson), 5th (Capt Wolff) and 6th (Capt Kothe) DD Flotillas, consisting of *Z27*, *Z29*, *Z30*, *Z31*, *Z33*, *Erich Steinbrinck*, *Karl Galster*, *Theodor Riedel* and *Hans Lody*, sets out to sea from Altafjord in the evening of 6 Sept to attack Allied bases on Spitzbergen. A battalion of the 349th Grenadier Regt is embarked on the destroyers. At 0300 hrs on 8 Sept Adm Kummetz detaches *Scharnhorst* and the 5th and 6th DD Flotillas which then land their troops in Grönfjord and Advent Bay. *Tirpitz* goes on with the 4th DD Flotilla to shell Barentsburg. Coastal batteries are destroyed and coal and supply dumps, water and electricity works are blown up. On 9 Sept the battle squadron returns to Altafjord.

On 19 Oct the US cruiser *Tuscaloosa* with one US and three British destroyers lands Norwegian troops in Spitzbergen to re-establish bases.

8 Sept   Baltic
The German *U983* sinks during exercises following a collision with *U988* 50 nautical miles N of Leba.

7–14 Sept   North Atlantic
On 7 Sept the Cdr U-boats cancels a refuelling stop for *U460*, which was to meet *U536* (Lt-Cdr Schauenburg) en route for Operation 'Kiebitz', the pick-up in the Bay of Chaleurs (Gulf of St Lawrence) of U-boat prisoners who have escaped from a camp in Canada. Instead, *U460* has to refuel five boats of the 'Leuthen' group further to the N from 10 to 12 Sept. However, this order is only decoded by the Allies on 13 Sept and the refuelling, involving *U260*, *U645*, *U338*, *U305* and *U386*, proceeds unhindered.

From 7 to 9 Sept the tanker convoy CU.4 (US TG.21.6 with the destroyers *Madison*, *Lansdale*, *Charles F Hughes*, *Hilary P Jones* and *Broome*) and the convoys MKF.22 (see 23 Aug–4 Sept) and HX.254 (EG.C4 under Cdr McKillop RN with the destroyers *Hotspur* and *Churchill* and the corvettes *Nasturtium*, *Collingwood*, *Orillia* and *Trillium*) enter the North Channel. ON.200 overtakes ONS.17 in the Central North Atlantic. East of Newfoundland the eastbound SC.141 (EG.B2 with the destroyers *Hesperus* and *Vesper*, the frigate *Mourne* and the corvettes *Campanula*, *Clematis* and *Sweetbriar*) and HX.255 (EG.C3 with the destroyers *Saskatchewan*, *Skeena* and *Burnham* and the corvettes *Mayflower*, *Pictou* and *Sorel*) proceed, followed and overtaken by troop convoy UT.2 (US TF.67 with the battleship *Nevada* and the destroyers *Nelson*, *Murphy*, *Glennon*, *Jeffers*, *Butler*, *Gherardi*, *Herndon*, *Cowie*, *Earle*, *Quick*, *Fitch* and *Capps* and the destroyer-escort *Weber*) on its way to the UK. In addition, the independent troop transports *Pasteur*, *Queen Mary* and *Mauretania* proceed to the W and *General Pope* to the E. On the UK–Gibraltar route, convoy KMS.25 enters the Strait of Gibraltar after parting with OS.54 which is continuing for Freetown (see 23 Aug–4 Sept). From Gibraltar there depart convoys MKS.23 (EG.B1 with the destroyers *Hurricane* and *Wanderer* and the corvettes *Borage*, *Dahlia*, *Wallflower* and *Monkshood*), and, later, convoy XK.11 (escorted by the destroyer *Warwick*, the sloop *Cygnet* and the corvette *Godetia*).

On the US–Gibraltar route there are the

convoys GUS.13 (TF.65 with the destroyers *Livermore*, *Eberle*, *Kearny*, *Ericsson*, *Swanson*, *Doran*, *Tarbell*, *Broome* and *Upshur*), supported by TG.21.15 with the escort carrier *Croatan*, the destroyers *Belknap*, *Paul Jones* and *Parrott* switching back to GUS.14; convoy UGS.16 (TF.61 with the destroyer-escorts *Evarts*, *Wyffels*, *Decker*, *Dobler*, *Smartt* and *Walter S Brown*) supported by TG.21.11 with the escort carrier *Santee* and the destroyers *Bainbridge*, *Simpson* and *MacLeish*); the returning TG.21.14 with the escort carrier *Card* and the destroyers *Borie*, *Barry* and *Dupont*; and convoy UGS.17 (TF.62 with the destroyers *Frankford*, *McCook* and *Doyle*, the destroyer-escorts *Pope*, *Pillsbury* and *Flaherty* and the minesweepers *Portent* and *Pioneer*), supported by TG.21.12 with the escort carrier *Bogue* and the destroyers *George E Badger*, *Osmond-Ingram* and *Clemson*.

On 9 Sept convoy GUS.14 (TF.66 with the destroyers *Baldwin*, *Harding*, *Endicott* and *McCormick* and the destroyer-escorts *Lawrence*, *Daniel T Griffin*, *Hopping* and *Reeves*) leaves Casablanca, picked up by TG.21.15. On 11 Sept there follows from Gibraltar convoy GUF.10 (TF.68 with the battleship *Texas* and the destroyers *Parker*, *Laub*, *MacKenzie*, *McLanahan*, *Tillman*, *Boyle*, *Champlin*, *Nields*, *Ordronaux*, *Davison*, *Mervine* and *Beatty*), picked up by TG.21.11.

8–12 Sept Mediterranean

In the afternoon of 8 Sept Gen Eisenhower announces in Algiers the conclusion of an armistice with Italy. At this point the planned German counter-measures ('Achse') come into force to disarm the main body of the Italian forces.

In accordance with the conditions of the armistice, the Italian Fleet (Adm Bergamini†) sets out from La Spezia with the battleships *Roma*, *Vittorio Veneto* and *Italia* (9th Div), the cruisers *Eugenio di Savoia* (Div Adm Oliva), *Duca D'Aosta* and *Montecuccoli* (7th Div) and the destroyers *Mitragliere*, *Fuciliere*, *Carabiniere* and *Velite* (12th Flotilla) and *Legionario*, *Oriani*, *Artigliere* and *Grecale* (14th Flotilla) and joins the cruisers *Duca degli Abruzzi*, *Garibaldi* and *Regolo* (8th Div) and the torpedo boat *Libra* coming from Genoa. The force is located by German air reconnaissance and is attacked W of the Strait of Bonifacio on the afternoon of 9 Sept by 11 Do 217s of III/KG 100, using FX 1200 radio-controlled bombs, from Istres near Marseilles. Lt Schmetz obtains a direct hit on *Roma*, which sinks. *Italia* is damaged by hits. The destroyers *Da Noli* and *Vivaldi*, coming from Castellamare, are shelled by German coastal bat-

teries in the Strait of Bonifacio and are lost on mines and by gunfire respectively; the crew of *Vivaldi* is rescued by the British submarine *Sportsman*. Of the *Regolo*, *Mitragliere*, *Fuciliere* and *Carabiniere* left behind to rescue survivors and the torpedo boats *Libra*, *Orione*, *Orsa*, *Impetuoso* and *Pegaso* summoned to the scene, *Libra* and *Orione* go to Bône and the others put into Port Mahon in the Balearics and are interned; *Pegaso* and *Impetuoso* sink after a collision just outside the harbour. The rest of the Fleet proceeds to Malta under the command of Div Adm Oliva and is met on 10 Sept by the British battleships *Warspite* and *Valiant* with the destroyers *Faulknor*, *Fury*, *Echo*, *Intrepid*, *Raider*, *Vasilissa Olga* (Greek) and *Le Terrible* (French). On 9 Sept Adm Da Zara puts to sea from Taranto with the battleships *Andrea Doria* and *Caio Duilio* (5th Div), the cruisers *Cadorna* and *Pompeo Magno* and the destroyer *Da Recco* and arrives in Malta on 10 Sept escorted by the battleship *King George V*. In addition, the battleship *Giulio Cesare*, the aircraft depot ship *Miraglia*, the destroyer *Riboty* and the torpedo boat *Sagittario* arrive in Malta from Adriatic ports. The Italian submarines (33 in all), which are either concentrated in the area off Salerno in expectation of an Allied landing at the beginning of Sept or are in Italian harbours and fit for operations, assemble in Allied harbours. By 12 Sept 11 torpedo boats, eight corvettes and smaller craft reach Palermo from harbours in the Tyrrhenian Sea.

In harbours occupied by German troops, a few ships are taken over intact by the German Navy and commissioned after short refits. These comprise the destroyers *Turbine* (Piraeus; German *TA14*) and *Crispi* (Piraeus; *TA15*); the torpedo boats *Castelfidardo* (Suda; *TA16*), *San Martino* (Piraeus; *TA17*), *Solferino* (Suda; *TA18*), *Calatafimi* (Piraeus; *TA19*), *Impavido* (Portoferraio, 16 Sept; *TA23*) and *Ardito* (Portoferraio, 16 Sept; *TA25*); the submarines *Finzi* (Bordeaux; *UIT21*), *Bagnolini* (Bordeaux; *UIT22*), *Giuliani* (Singapore; *UIT23*), *Cappellini* (Sabang; *UIT24*), *Torelli* (Singapore; *UIT25*), *S 1–9* (Baltic; *U428*, *U746*, *U747*, *U429*, *U748*, *U430*, *U749*, *U1161* and *U750*—their former designations); and the corvette *Vespa* (Pozzuoli; *UJ2221*). Most of the ships which are non-operational because they are heavily damaged or under repair are scuttled by, or made unservicable by, their crews. These include the battleship *Cavour* (Trieste); the cruisers *Bolzano* (La Spezia), *Gorizia* (La Spezia), *Taranto* (La Spezia), *Bari* (Livorno), FR 11 (ex-French *Jean de*

Vienne; Toulon) and *FR 12* (ex-French *La Galissonnière*; Toulon); the gunboat (old cruiser) *Cattaro* (ex-Yugoslav *Dalmacija*, later German *Niobe*); the destroyers *Zeno* (La Spezia), *Corazziere* (Genoa), *Maestrale* (Genoa), *Dardo* (Genoa; later German *TA31*), *Premuda* (Genoa; ex-Yugoslav *Dubrovnik*, later German *TA32*), *Sebenico* (Venice; ex-Yugoslav *Beograd*, later German *TA43*), *Pigafetta* (Fiume; later German *TA44*), *FR 21* (La Spezia; ex-French *Lion*), *FR 22* (La Spezia; ex-French *Panthère*), *FR 24* (Savona; ex-French *Valmy*), *FR 32* (Genoa; ex-French *Siroco*), *FR 33* (Toulon; ex-French *L'Adroit*), *FR 34* (Imperia; ex-French *Lansquenet*), *FR 35* (Toulon; ex-French *Bison*), *FR 36* (Toulon; ex-French *Foudroyant*) and *FR 37* (Savona; ex-French *Le Hardi*); the torpedo boats *Cascino* (La Spezia), *Ghibli* (La Spezia), *Montanari* (La Spezia), *Procione* (La Spezia), *Papa* (Genoa), *Insidioso* (Pola; later German *TA21*), *Missori* (Durazzo; later German *TA22*), *La Masa* (Naples), *Partenope* (Naples), *Audace* (Venice; later German *TA20*) and *Lira* (La Spezia; later German *TA49*); the submarines *Ambra* (La Spezia), *Aradam* (Genoa), *Sirena* (La Spezia), *Sparide* (La Spezia; later German *UIT15*), *Volframio* (La Spezia), *Murena* (La Spezia; later German *UIT16*), *Argo* (Monfalcone), *Ametista* (Ancona), *Serpente* (Ancona), *Beilul* (Monfalcone), *Nautilo* (Venice; later German *UIT19*), *FR 113* (Genoa, ex-French *Requin*), *FR ???* (Genoa; ex-French *Poincaré*), *FR 114* (Castellamare; ex-French *Espadon*), *FR 115* (Pozzuoli; ex-French *Dauphin*) and *Baiamonti* (La Spezia; ex-Yugoslav *Smeli*); the corvettes *Berenice* (Trieste), *Euterpe* (La Spezia; later German *UJ2228*), *Persefone* (La Spezia; later German *UJ2227*), *Artemide* (Livorno; later German *UJ2226*), *Antilope* (Livorno; later German *UJ6082*), *Camoscio* (Livorno; later German *UJ6081*), *FR 51* (La Spezia, ex-French *La Batailleuse*, later German *SG23*), *FR 53* (Toulon; ex-French *Chamois*), *FR 54* (Toulon; ex-French *L'Impetueuse*, later German *SG17*), *FR 55* (Toulon; ex-French *La Curieuse*, later German *SG16*) and *FR 56* (Toulon, ex-French *Dédaigneuse*); and many smaller vessels.

In addition, the following new ships are fitting out at the time and most are taken over by the Germans and commissioned: the battleship *Impero* (Trieste; abandoned); the aircraft carriers *Sparviero* (ex-passenger liner *Augustus*; Genoa; abandoned) and *Aquila* (ex-passenger liner *Roma*; Genoa; abandoned); the cruisers *Etna* and *Vesuvio* (Trieste; abandoned), *Cornelio Silla* (Genoa; abandoned), *Giulio Germanico*

(Castellamare; scuttled by the Germans), *Caio Mario* (La Spezia; sabotaged) and *Ottaviano Augusto* (Ancona; abandoned); the destroyer *Corsaro* (ex-*Squadrista*, later German *TA33*); the torpedo boats *Intrepido* (Genoa; later German *TA26*), *Arturo* (Genoa; later German *TA24*), *Auriga* (Genoa; later German *TA27*), *Rigel* (Genoa; later German *TA28*), *Eridano* (Genoa; later German *TA29*) *Dragone* (Genoa; later German *TA30*), *Stella Polare* (Fiume; later German *TA36*), *Gladio* (Trieste; later German *TA37*), *Spada* (Trieste; later German *TA38*), *Daga* (Trieste; later German *TA39*) and *Pugnale* (Trieste; later German *TA40*); the submarines *Grongo* (Muggiano; later German *UIT20*), *CM 1* (Monfalcone; later German *UIT17*) and *S 10* (Danzig; German *U1162*); and the corvettes *Egeria* (Monfalcone; German *UJ201*), *Melpomene* (Monfalcone; German *UJ202*), *Colubrina* and *Spingarda* (Venice; German *UJ205* and *UJ208*) and *Tuffetto* (Genoa; German *UJ2222*).

Of the vessels captured on the slipways, only some are taken into service by the German Navy: the torpedo boats *Lancia* (Trieste; German *TA41*), *Alabarda* (Trieste; German *TA42*), *Spica* (Fiume; German *TA45*), *Fionda* (Fiume; German *TA46*) and *Balestra* (Fiume; German *TA47*); the submarines *R 10–12* (La Spezia; German *UIT1–UIT3*), *R7–9* (Monfalcone; German *UIT4–UIT6*), *Bario*, *Litio*, *Sodio*, *Potassio*, *Rame*, *Ferro*, *Piombo* and *Zinco* (Monfalcone; German *UIT7-UIT14*) and *CM 2* (Monfalcone; German *UIT18*); and the corvettes *Tersicore* and *Euridice* (Monfalcone; German *UJ203* and *UJ204*), *Bombarda*, *Carabina* and *Scure* (Venice; German *UJ206*, *UJ207* and *UJ209*), *Marangone*, *Strolaga* and *Ardea* (Genoa; German *UJ2223*, *UJ2224* and *UJ2225*) and *Capriolo*, *Alce*, *Renna*, *Cervo*, *Daino* and *Stambecco* (Livorno; German *UJ6083*, *UJ6084*, *UJ6085*, *UJ6086*, *UJ6087* and *UJ6088*).

9 Sept Mediterranean
The German motor minesweepers *R7* and *R13* are scuttled at Salerno.

9–10 Sept Mediterranean
Informed about the Italian capitulation, the Italian torpedo boat *Aliseo* (Cdr Fecia di Cossato) leaves Bastia, but her sister-ship *Ardito* is captured by the Germans. On 10 Sept *Aliseo* and the corvette *Cormorano* attack the German vessels in the harbour with gunfire and sink the torpedo boat *TA11* and the A/S trawlers *UJ2203*, *UJ2205*, *UJ2214* and *UJ2219*.

9–11 Sept Mediterranean
In an improvised operation, 'Slapstick', the British 12th Cruiser Sqn (Commodore

Agnew), comprising *Aurora*, *Penelope*, *Sirius* and *Dido*, the fast minelayer *Abdiel* and the US cruiser *Boise*, lands the 1st British Airborne Div in Taranto. The operation is covered by Vice-Adm Power with the battleships *Howe* and *King George V*, the latter meeting the Italian ships coming from Taranto. The Italian corvette *Baionetta* goes with the cruiser *Scipione Africano* to Pescara to bring the Italian King and Government to Brindisi.

The German motor torpedo boats *S54* (Lt Klaus Degenhard Schmidt) and *S61* (Petty Officer Blömker) leave Taranto in the evening of the Italian surrender, having dropped a number of mines into the harbour undetected. The fast British minelayer *Abdiel* (2650 tons) sinks on one on 10 Sept with heavy losses among the 400 troops on board. On their way through the Adriatic the two motor torpedo boats sink the Italian gunboat *Aurora* (935 tons) off Ancona on 11 Sept and the Italian destroyer *Sella* S of Venice, and they capture the new troop transport *Leopardi* (4572 tons) with 700 troops on board. They reach Venice with their last drop of fuel and compel the local naval commander to surrender.

9–16 Sept Mediterranean
Operation 'Avalanche': landing of the 5th US Army (Lt-Gen Clark) in the Bay of Salerno. In overall command of the amphibious operation is Adm Cunningham in Malta (with the destroyer *Hambledon*) and the 'Western Naval Task Force' (TF.80) is under Vice-Adm Hewitt on board the headquarters ship *Ancon*. Attached are the AA ships *Ulster Queen* and *Palomares* and the beacon submarine is the British *Shakespeare*.

The Southern Attack Force (TF.81, Rear-Adm Hall), with the headquarters ship *Samuel Chase*, 18 transports, three tank landing ships (*Boxer*, *Bruiser* and *Thruster*), 27 LSTs, 32 LCIs, six LCTs, four LCSs, eight PCs, four SCs, nine AMs, 12 YMSs and 32 small vessels, lands VI US Corps (Maj-Gen Dawley) with the 36th Inf Div (Maj-Gen Walker) and the 45th Inf Div (Maj-Gen Middleton) off Paestum. The support group and escort (Rear-Adm Davidson) comprises the US cruisers *Philadelphia*, *Savannah* and *Brooklyn*, the British monitor *Abercrombie*, the Dutch gunboat *Flores* and the US destroyers *Wainwright*, *Trippe*, *Rhind*, *Rowan*, *Plunkett*, *Niblack*, *Benson*, *Gleaves*, *Mayo*, *Knight*, *Dallas*, *Bernadou*, *Cole*, *Woolsey*, *Ludlow*, *Bristol* and *Edison*.

The Northern Attack Force (TF.85, Commodore Oliver), with the headquarters ships *Hilary* and *Biscayne* (Rear-Adm

Conolly), eight transports, four LSIs, 90 LSTs, 96 LCIs, 84 LCTs, 23 SCs and MLs, seven minesweepers and four tugs, lands the British X Corps (Lt-Gen McCreery) with the 46th Inf Div (Maj-Gen Freeman-Attwood), the 56th Inf Div (Maj-Gen Graham), the 7th Armoured Div (Maj-Gen Erskine), the 3rd US Ranger BLT and two British Commandos. The support group and escort (Rear-Adm Harcourt) for this force consists of the British cruisers *Mauritius*, *Uganda*, *Orion* and *Delhi*, the monitor *Roberts* and the destroyers (19th Flotilla) *Laforey*, *Lookout*, *Loyal*, *Nubian* and *Tartar* and (21st Flotilla) *Mendip*, *Dulverton*, *Tetcott*, *Belvoir*, *Brocklesby*, *Quantock*, *Blackmore*, *Brecon*, *Beaufort*, *Exmoor*, *Ledbury*, *Blankney* and *Pindos* (Greek). The Support Carrier Force (TF.88, Rear-Adm Vian) consists of the cruisers *Euryalus*, *Scylla* and *Charybdis*, the light carrier *Unicorn*, the escort carriers *Battler*, *Attacker*, *Hunter* and *Stalker* and the destroyers *Slazak* (Polish), *Krakowiak* (Polish), *Cleveland*, *Holcombe*, *Atherstone*, *Liddesdale*, *Farndale*, *Calpe* and *Haydon*, while the covering force is Force H (Vice-Adm Willis), consisting of the battleships *Nelson*, *Rodney* (Rear-Adm Rivett-Carcac), *Warspite* (Rear-Adm La T Bissett) and *Valiant*, the carriers (Rear-Adm Moody) *Illustrious* and *Formidable* (Rear-Adm Talbot) and the destroyers (4th Flotilla) *Quilliam*, *Queenborough*, *Quail* and *Petard*, (24th Flotilla) *Troubridge*, *Tyrian*, *Tumult*, *Offa* and *Piorun* (Polish) and (8th Flotilla) *Faulknor*, *Intrepid*, *Eclipse*, *Inglefield*, *Fury*, *Ilex*, *Echo*, *Raider* and *Vasilissa Olga* (Greek) and the large French destroyers *Le Fantasque* and *Le Terrible*.

In an attack by German torpedo bombers during the night 8–9 Sept, *Warspite* and *Formidable* are narrowly missed.

The landing succeeds on 9 Sept against strong and increasing German resistance. But at first the disembarked troops fail to reach their target positions in spite of strong fire support from the cruisers and destroyers. The monitor *Abercrombie* is damaged by a mine and the destroyer *Laforey* by five shell hits. On 10 and 11 Sept the landing troops make only slow progress. During the night 10–11 Sept three German motor torpedo boats of the 3rd MTB Flotilla attack a US convoy and sink the destroyer *Rowan*. On 11 Sept heavy German air attacks begin, in the course of which Do 217s of II and III/KG 100 drop FX 1200 radio-controlled and Hs 293 glider bombs. On 11 Sept *Savannah* is badly damaged by a direct hit and *Philadelphia* is narrowly missed. On 13 and 14 Sept three German divisions make a strong armoured attack which compresses the Allied bridgehead and creates a serious situation. For fire support the monitor *Roberts*, the cruisers *Mauritius*, *Uganda*, *Orion*, *Aurora*, *Philadelphia* and *Boise* and the destroyers *Loyal*, *Lookout*, *Tartar*, *Nubian*, *Brecon*, *Quantock* and *Eggesford* lie off the assault area. In air attacks with FX 1200s and Hs 293s, *Uganda* is seriously damaged by hits and *Philadelphia*, *Loyal* and *Nubian* slightly damaged by near-misses. The hospital ship *Newfoundland* sinks. On 14 Sept first the cruiser *Penelope* arrives and then *Euryalus*, *Scylla* and *Charybdis*. A supply transport is heavily hit by bombs on 14 Sept and lost the next day. On 15 Sept *Valiant* and *Warspite* intervene; the latter is hit and badly damaged on 16 Sept by two radio-controlled bombs. On 16 Sept forward elements of the British 8th Army, coming up from the S, break through to the bridgehead near Salerno.

9–23 Sept   Mediterranean
After the announcement of the Italian surrender, there is fighting between the weaker German units and the stronger Italian garrison on Rhodes. The latter capitulates on 11 Sept, preventing the British occupation of the island. From 10 to 17 Sept small British battle groups and commando groups are brought by light British craft (MLs and MTBs) and Greek caiques to Casteloriso, Coo, Leros, Calino, Samos, Symi and Stampalia. From 12 to 14 Sept the Indian sloop *Sutlej*, the Greek destroyer *Kondouriotis* and the French sloops *La Moqueuse* and *Commandant Dominé* bring British troops to Casteloriso but a repetition of the operation on 16 Sept has to be abandoned. The troops which have been brought there organise themselves for defence with the help of the Italian garrisons. On 16 Sept the British 8th DD Flotilla, comprising *Faulknor*, *Echo*, *Intrepid*, *Eclipse*, *Raider* and *Vasilissa Olga*, arrives in Alexandria as a reinforcement from the Central Mediterranean. The German Admiral commanding the Aegean, Rear-Adm Lange, tries to reinforce the Aegean Islands and to take off the Italian prisoners. In attacks on these convoys the Greek submarine *Katsonis* (Lt Laskos) is rammed and sunk by the German submarine-chaser *UJ2101* (Lt-Cdr Vollheim). On 17 Sept *Echo* and *Intrepid* sink the submarine-chaser *UJ2104* off Stampalia; on 18 Sept *Faulknor*, *Eclipse* and *Vasilissa Olga* attack a convoy and damage the ships *Pluto* and *Paula*. On 23 *Eclipse* damages S of Rhodes the German torpedo boat *TA10* (ex-French *La Pomone*) and the steamer *Donizetti* with 1576 Italian prisoners on board, some of whom are rescued.

TA10 is towed into the harbour at Rhodes but sinks on 25 Sept.

9 Sept–3 Dec   Indian Ocean
The Italian submarine *Cagni* (Cdr Rosselli-Lorenzini), which, while sailing in the South Atlantic, has torpedoed the British auxiliary cruiser *Asturias* (22048 tons) on 25 July, operates without success off South Africa until 9 Sept. After the Italian surrender she enters Durban on 20 Sept. The colonial sloop *Eritrea*, sent to meet the Italian submarines, escapes from Sabang to Colombo. Of the Japanese submarines operating from Penang, *I-27* (Lt-Cdr Fukumura) sinks one ship of 5151 tons off the Indian west coast and damages another of 7176 tons with an unexploded torpedo. *I-10* (Capt Tonozuka) sinks in Sept and Oct four ships of 22906 tons in the Gulf of Aden and torpedoes one tanker of 9057 tons on 5 Oct from the convoy AP.47. After refuelling from the tanker *Brake* from 9 to 14 Sept, the German U-boats of the 'Monsun' group operate off the Indian west coast, in the Gulf of Oman, in the Gulf of Aden, off the East African Coast and round the Chagos Archipelago. By the end of Oct, *U532* (Cdr* Junker) sinks four ships of 24484 tons and torpedoes one of 5845 tons, *U188* (Lt-Cdr Lüdden) sinks one ship of 7176 tons and torpedoes one of 9977 tons, and *U168* (Lt-Cdr Pich) sinks one ship of 2183 tons and six sailing ships. Further attacks by these boats and by *U183* (Cdr Schäfer) and *U533* (Lt-Cdr Henning) are impeded by torpedo failures. *U533* is sunk on 16 Oct by Bisleys 'E' and 'H' of No 244 Sqn RAF in the Persian Gulf. The other boats go to Penang. In Oct and Nov the Japanese submarine *I-37* (Cdr Otani) reconnoitres with her aircraft the Chagos Archipelago on 4 Oct, Diego Suarez on 10 Oct, Kilindini on 17 Nov and the Seychelles on 23 Nov. She sinks two ships of 13376 tons. Off the Indian south and west coasts and the Chagos Archipelago the Japanese submarines *I-166*, *I-162* and *I-165* meet with no success in two operations in Oct and Nov. From Nov to the beginning of Dec *I-27* (Lt-Cdr Fukumura) sinks four ships of 23908 tons in the Gulf of Aden and torpedoes one ship of 7126 tons. The transport submarine *I-8*, coming from France, returns to Singapore on 28 Nov and reaches Japan. *I-34*, which sets out on a transport journey, is sunk off Penang by the British submarine *Taurus* on 13 Nov.

10–16 Sept   Black Sea
To start a major Soviet offensive against the German Kuban bridgehead, 8935 troops of the reinforced 255th Naval Inf Bde are landed in the harbour at Novorossisk under the command of Rear-Adm Kholostyakov

on 10 Sept in 129 small craft in two instalments, after 25 torpedo cutters under Capt 2nd Class Protsenko have opened the approach and eliminated the pockets of resistance. In the harbour area the Soviet units are engaged in heavy fighting with two German naval companies under Lt-Cdr Hossfeld and with reinforcements which are brought up. They are partly annihilated before the planned departures begin as part of the German withdrawal from the Kuban bridgehead. The Soviet torpedo cutters *TKA-124* and *TKA-125* and the patrol cutters *SKA-025*, *SKA-032* and *SKA-084* are lost as a result of action by the German defence.

10 Sept–5 Oct   Mediterranean
In the course of the German evacuation of Sardinia, which begins on 10 Sept, 25000 troops, 2300 vehicles and 5000 tons of supplies are brought across the Strait of Bonifacio to Corsica. After agreement with the Italian garrison, the troops proceed to Bastia and are evacuated from there by air (21107 troops and 350 tons of supplies) and by sea to Livorno and Elba (6240 troops, 1200 prisoners and 5000 tons of supplies); 15 steamers and some 120 ferry barges and other small craft are employed under Capt v Liebenstein. In a US air attack on 21 Sept five steamers are lost. The British submarine *Unseen* (Lt Crawford) sinks on 21 Sept the German minelayer *Brandenburg* and the night fighter direction ship *Kreta*; *Uproar* (Lt Herrick) sinks one ship of 731 tons and on 24 Sept, in conjunction with the Polish *Dzik* (Cdr Romanowski) and the British *Ultor* (Lt Hunt), the tanker *Champagne* (9946 tons); and *Sibyl* (Lt Turner) sinks one ship of 2910 tons and the escort *Hummer*. The minelayer *Pommern* sinks on a mine on 5 Oct. From 11 Sept contingents of French troops are transported from Algiers to Ajaccio (Corsica): on 11–13 Sept 109 men by the French submarine *Casabianca* (Cdr* D'Herminier); on 13–14 Sept 500 men and 60 tons of supplies by the French destroyers *Le Fantasque* and *Le Terrible* (Capt Perzo); on 14–16 Sept 30 men and seven tons of supplies by the submarine *Perle*; on 16–17 Sept 550 men and 60 tons of supplies by the destroyers *Le Fantasque*, *Tempête* and *L'Alcyon*; on 16–18 Sept five tons by the submarine *Aréthuse*; on 17–18 Sept a US commando unit of 400 men and 20 tons of supplies by the Italian destroyers *Legionario* and *Oriani*; on 19–21 Sept 1200 men, 110 tons of supplies, six guns and six vehicles by the cruiser *Jeanne d'Arc* and the destroyers *Le Fantasque*, *Tempête* and *L'Alcyon*; on 22–23 Sept 1500 men and 200 tons by the cruiser *Montcalm* and destroyer *Le Fan-*

233

tasque; on 23–25 Sept 350 men, 100 tons of supplies, 21 guns and 30 vehicles by the destroyers *Le Fortuné*, *L'Alcyon*, the landing ship *LST79* and the minesweepers *MMS1* and *MMS116*; on 25 Sept 850 men and 160 tons of supplies by the *Jeanne d'Arc*; on 26 Sept 750 men, 100 tons of supplies, 12 guns and 10 vehicles by the *Montcalm* and the British destroyer *Pathfinder*; on 28–30 Sept 200 men, four guns, 70 vehicles by *Le Fortuné* and *LST79* (both damaged in a German air attack, the latter sinking); and on 30 Sept–1 Oct 700 men and 170 tons of supplies by *Jeanne d'Arc* and *L'Alcyon*.

10 Sept–12 Nov   Atlantic
In operations in distant waters, *U161* (Lt-Cdr Achilles) and *U170* (Lt-Cdr Pfeffer) sink off the Brazilian coast three ships of 10770 tons and one ship of 4663 tons respectively. *U161* is sunk on 27 Sept by a flying boat of VP-74 USN. *U518* and *U123* have no success in the Gulf of Mexico and off the coast of Guiana. *U214* lays a mine barrage off Colon (Panama) on 8 Oct. *U220* (Lt Barber) lays a mine barrage off St John's on which two ships of 7199 tons are sunk. *U536* is not able to attack in the area S of Nova Scotia. On 7 Nov the returning *U123* is damaged in the Bay of Biscay by gunfire from Mosquito 'I' of No 248 Sqn RAF.

11 Sept   Black Sea
The German E-boat *S46* is lost ESE of Feodosiya in a fighter-bomber attack.

11 Sept   South West Pacific
The Japanese minesweeper *W-16* sinks on a mine S of Makassar.

12 Sept   Mediterranean
The Italian submarine *Topazio*, failing to identify herself, is sunk by Bisley 'J' of No 13 Sqn RAF off Sicily.

12 Sept   Arctic
The German A/S trawler *UJ1217* is sunk off Pylterfiord by the Soviet submarine *K-1*.

12 Sept–9 Oct   Black Sea
The German 17th Army (Gen Jaenecke), in a planned withdrawal through prepared defensive positions, evacuates the Kuban bridgehead (Operation 'Brunhild') and so prevents any break-through by the Soviet North Caucasus Front (Col-Gen Petrov) which simultaneously goes over to the attack. By using German naval ferry barges of the 1st, 3rd, 5th and 7th Landing Flotillas (Lt-Cdr Giele, Cdr* Strempel, Cdr Mehler and Cdr Stelter), Siebel ferries, engineer ferries and tugs, lighters and river tugs, 239669 troops, 16311 wounded, 27456 civilians, 115477 tons of supplies, 21230 vehicles, 27741 horse-driven vehicles, 1815 guns, 74 tanks, 74657 horses and 6255 head of cattle are transported across the Kerch

Strait under the direction of the Admiral Commanding the Black Sea, Vice-Adm Kieseritzky† and the Naval Commandant Caucasus, Capt Grattenauer. Landings made by Soviet light craft on the south coast and by the Soviet Azov Flotilla (Rear-Adm Gorshkov) on the north coast are unable to prevent the German moves. The defence of the Kerch Strait against attacks by Soviet ships is undertaken by the 1st MTB Flotilla, the 3rd MMS Flotilla and gunboats. There are frequent engagements with light Soviet forces, e.g. on 17, 20 and 24 Sept. In an attack by the 1st MTB Flotilla on Anapa on 26–27 Sept, several steamers lying alongside the pier are hit.

On 30 Sept the Soviet destroyers *Sposobny*, *Boiki* and *Besposhchadny* make an unsuccessful sortie against the German evacuation transports on the south coast of the Crimea. Off the Caucasus coast, the German *U18* (Lt Fleige) sinks on 18 Sept a small ship near Tuapse; *U20* (Lt Schöler) lays mines off Sochi on 20 Sept and sinks a lighter off Anapa on 30 Sept.

S of Evpatoria, the Soviet submarine *S-33* misses on 22 Sept the steamer *Santa Fé* escorted by the Rumanian destroyer *Regele Ferdinand*. On 28 Sept the submarine *M-113* runs on a mine W of the Crimea and reaches her base badly damaged.

12 Sept–20 Oct   Mediterranean
In U-boat operations against the Salerno bridgehead, attacks by *U565*, *U616* and again *U565* fail on 12, 15 and 24 Sept. Only *U593* (Lt-Cdr Kelbling) sinks on 21 and 25 Sept one ship of 7176 tons and the US minesweeper *Skill*. Off the Algerian coast, *U410* (Lt Fenski) sinks on 26 and 30 Sept one ship from the convoy UGS.17 (escorted by the corvettes *Gloxinia* and *Primula*, the minesweeper *Frolic* and three A/S trawlers) and two ships from a western convoy totalling 17031 tons. Off Cyrenaica, *U596* (Lt Nonn) sinks one ship of 5542 tons.

From 2 Oct T-5 torpedoes are used for the first time in the Mediterranean. Off the Algerian coast, *U223* (Lt-Cdr Wächter) sinks one ship of 4970 tons and *U371* (Lt-Cdr Mehl) from 11 to 15 Oct the British minesweeper *Hythe*, the US destroyer *Bristol* and one ship of 7176 tons from GUS.18. Attacks by *U73* and *U431* are unsuccessful. From the U-boats deployed against the Salerno bridgehead, *U616* (Lt-Koitschka) sinks the US destroyer *Buck* and two attacks fail. Likewise, four attacks by *U380* and two by *U81* fail. *U73* (Lt Deckert) sinks one ship of 4531 tons off Bône.

14 Sept   English Channel
The German auxiliary minesweeper *M3410* is lost in a torpedo attack W of Ijmuiden.

14–18 Sept   North Atlantic
In evening of 12–13 Sept Bletchley Park decodes the first signals about waiting positions and refuelling arrangements for U-boats, new developments being indicated by using the code-words 'Aphrodite' (radar-deception balloon), 'Hagenuk' (wave indicator for centimetre radar) and 'Zaunkönig' (acoustic homing torpedo). There are no route changes for convoys ON.201 (EG.C1 with the destroyers *Assiniboine* and *Forester* and the corvettes *Agassiz*, *Celandine*, *Galt* and *Lunenburg*) or HX.256 (EG.C5 with the destroyer *Kootenay* and the corvettes *Arvida*, *Kitchener*, *Sudbury*, *Eyebright* and *Wetaskiwin*).

On 14 Sept convoy UC.4 (US TG.21.6 with the destroyers *Madison*, *Lansdale*, *Charles F Hughes* and *Hilary P Jones* and destroyer-escorts *Sims* and *Donnell*) departs the North Channel on a route just N of the German waiting area, followed by convoy ONS.18 (EG.B3 under Cdr Tyson with the destroyers *Keppel* and *Escapade* and the corvettes *Narcissus*, *Orchis*, *Lobélia*, *Renoncule* and *Roselys* and including the merchant aircraft carrier *Clan MacAlpine*). On 16 Sept there follows convoy ON.202 (EG.C2 under Cdr Burnett with the destroyers *Gatineau* and *Icarus*, the frigate *Lagan* and the corvettes *Drumheller*, *Fennel* and *Polyanthus*).

On 15 Sept the Cdr U-boats orders the 'Leuthen' group to form a patrol line on 20 Sept to catch the next westbound convoys with *U238*, *U442* and *U275* coming from Norway and *U341*, *U260*, *U386*, *U338*, *U731*, *U305*, *U270*, *U645*, *U402*, *U584*, *U229*, *U666*, *U641*, *U952*, *U378*, *U758*, *U377* and *U603* from the waiting area and coming from France. On the same day TG.21.12, with the carrier *Bogue*, is ordered N to a known replenishment point but she arrives too late, the refuelling of *U536* and *U170* from *U460* having been completed on 15 Sept.

W of the Biscay, the 2nd EG (Capt Walker) with the sloops *Starling*, *Kite*, *Wild Goose*, *Woodcock* and *Wren* has some skirmishes with Ju 88 aircraft. On 16 Sept the new Canadian 9th EG (Cdr Dobson), with the destroyer *St Croix*, the frigate *Itchen* (RN) and the corvettes *Chambly*, *Morden* and *Sackville*, is ordered not to relieve the 2nd EG but to steer NW to support the convoys on the northern convoy route, which now seems to be the target of the new German operation.

14 Sept–23 Oct   North Atlantic
On the UK–Gibraltar route, the following convoys are running: SL.136/MKS.24, escorted by the 40th EG with the frigates *Exe* and *Moyola*, the sloops *Bridgewater* and

Milford and the corvettes *Armeria*, *Clarkia* and *Petunia* (3 Sept Freetown, 14 Sept meeting with MKS.24, 24 Sept Clyde); KMF.24, escorted by the 1st EG with the sloop *Pelican* and the frigates *Evenlode*, *Jed*, *Rother*, *Spey* and *Wear* (16 Sept Londonderry, 24 Sept Algiers); OS.55/KMS.27, escorted by the 37th EG with the sloops *Fowey*, *Stork* and *Hastings*, the frigate *Johan Maurits* (RNethN) and the corvettes *Campion*, *Friso* (RNethN) and *Myosotis* (16 Sept Londonderry, 28 Sept KMS.27 detached, 6 Oct Freetown); MKS.25, escorted by EG.B4 with the destroyers *Highlander*, *Walker* and *Westcott* and the corvettes *Abelia*, *Asphodel*, *Clover* and *Pennywort* (25 Sept Gibraltar, 4 Oct Londonderry); SL.137/MKS.26, escorted by the 38th EG with the sloops *Enchantress*, *Leith* and *Sandwich* and the corvettes *Anchusa*, *Columbine* and *Violet* (23 Sept Freetown, 4 Oct meeting with MKS.26, 16 Oct Londonderry); OG.94/KMS.28, escorted by EG.B2 with the destroyers *Hesperus* and *Vesper*, the frigate *Mourne* and the corvettes *Campanula*, *Clematis*, *Heather* and *Sweetbriar* (26 Sept Liverpool, 9 Oct Gibraltar); MKF.24, escorted by the 1st EG—see above (28 Sept Algier, 6 Oct Londonderry); OS.56/KMS.29, escorted by the 41st EG with the sloops *Bideford*, *Fleetwood* and *Banff*, the frigates *Odzani* and *Barle* and the corvettes *Aubrietia*, *Cyclamen* and *Stonecrop* (6 Oct Londonderry, 18 Oct KMS.28 detached, 28 Oct Freetown); and MKS.27, escorted by EG.B2—see above (14 Oct Gibraltar, 23 Oct Londonderry).

15 Sept–1 Nov   Central Atlantic
On the US–Gibraltar–Mediterranean route, the following convoys are running (US task forces only to Gibraltar): UGS.18, escorted by TF.63 with the US Coast Guard cutters *Bibb* and *Ingham*, the destroyers *Wilkes*, *Swanson* and *Roe* and the destroyer-escorts *Moore*, *J Richard Ward*, *Chase* and *Keith* (15 Sept Norfolk, 2 Oct Gibraltar, 14 Oct Port Said); GUS.15, escorted by TF.61 with the destroyers *Hobby*, *Gillespie* and *Kalk* and the destroyer-escorts *Evarts*, *Wyffels*, *Decker*, *Doffler*, *Smartt* and *Walter C Brown* and with support from TG.21.11 with the escort carrier *Santee* and the destroyers *Bainbridge*, *Simpson* and *MacLeish* (9 Sept Alexandria, 18 Sept Gibraltar, 4 Oct Norfolk); UGS.19, escorted by TF.64 with the destroyers *Stevenson*, *Stockton*, *Thorn* and *Turner*, the US Coast Guard cutter *Spencer* and the destroyer-escorts *Jacob Jones*, *Hammann*, *Robert E Peary*, *Sturtevant*, *Merak* and *Weight* and with support from TG.21.14 with the escort carrier *Card* and the destroyers *Borie*, *Goff*, *Barry* and

Dupont (25 Sept Norfolk, 12 Oct Gibraltar, 23 Oct Port Said. TG.21.14 is detached for an A/S sweep following 'Ultra'; on 4 Oct the tanker *U460* and also *U422* are sunk by two or three aircraft of VC-9 from *Card* and on 13 Oct one VC-9 aircraft from *Card* sinks *U402*); GUS.16, escorted by TF.62 with the destroyers *Frankford*, *McCook* and *Doyle*, the destroyer-escorts *Pope*, *Pillsbury* and *Flaherty* and the minesweepers *Portent* and *Pioneer* and with support from TG.21.12 with the escort carrier *Bogue* and the destroyers *George E Badger* and *Osmond-Ingram* (19 Sept Alexandria, 28 Sept Gibraltar, 15 Oct New York); UGS.20, escorted by TF.65 with the destroyers *Livermore*, *Eberle*, *Kearny* and *Ericsson*, the US Coast Guard cutters *Duane* and *Campbell* and the destroyer-escorts *Hayward*, *Farquhar* and *J R Y Blakely* and with support from TG.21.5 with the escort carrier *Core* and the destroyers *Greene*, *Goldsborough* and *Belknap* (15 Oct Norfolk, 21 Oct Gibraltar, 1 Nov Port Said. On 20 Oct two aircraft of VC-13 from *Core* sink *U378*); and GUS.17, escorted by TF.63 with the destroyers *Wilkes*, *Swanson*, *Roe*, *Schenck* and *Ward*, the US Coast Guard cutters *Bibb* and *Ingham* and the destroyer-escorts *Moore* and *Keith* (29 Sept Alexandria, 10 Oct Gibraltar, 27 Oct New York).

16–25 Sept   Air War/France
Heavy raids by the US 8th AF on Nantes and La Pallice. On 16 Sept the MMS *R19* and the torpedo boats *TA2* (ex-French *L'Agile*) and *TA4* (ex-French *L'Entreprenant*) and the MDS *Sperrbrecher 184/Bernisse*, fitting out at Nantes, are destroyed. The MDS *Sperrbrecher 16/Tulane*, repairing mine damage sustained on 8 Apr, and the auxiliary minesweeper *M4461* are destroyed by bombs at La Pallice. On 22 Sept the tanker *Jenny* (623 tons) is sunk at Nantes, where on 23 Sept the tankers *Ermland* (11232 tons) and *Wangerland* (3481 tons) and the blockade-runner *Kulmerland* (7363 tons) and on 25 Sept the tankers *Monsun* (8038 tons) and *Nordstern* (6994 tons) are also destroyed.

16 Sept   English Channel
The German patrol trawler *V1515* is sunk in air raid on Le Havre. She is later salvaged and repaired.

17–18 Sept   Air War/Western Europe
596 aircraft of Nos 5 and 8 Groups RAF and No 6 Group RCAF attack the German rocket test site at Peenemünde. There is heavy damage and 40 aircraft are lost.

17–19 Sept   Central Pacific
US air attacks on Tarawa. On 17–18 Sept 25 Liberator bombers of the 11th Bomb

Group, US 7th AF, attack Tarawa (Gilbert Islands) from Canton and Funafuti. On 18–19 Sept TF.15 (Rear-Adm Pownall), comprising the carriers *Lexington*, *Princeton* and *Belleau Wood*, covered by the cruisers *Santa Fé*, *Birmingham* and *Mobile* and the destroyers *Stevens*, *Caldwell*, *Ringgold*, *Coghlan*, *Schroeder*, *Hazelwood*, *Bradford*, *Harrison*, *John Rodgers*, *McKee*, *Bancroft* and *Dashiell* and the tanker *Guadeloupe*, carries out attacks on Tarawa. There are 190 sorties and four aircraft are lost. On 19 Sept the Liberators repeat the attack: 12 Japanese aircraft and two motor torpedo boats are destroyed.

17 Sept–9 Oct   Air War/Western Europe
RAF Bomber Command mine offensive: in 14 nights, 414 sorties are flown against French ports along the Biscay and Channel coasts, the Dutch coast, the Frisian coast, on Heligoland, in the Kattegat and, for the first time, in the Danzig Bight (29/30 Sept). Three aircraft are lost.
On 17 Sept the German auxiliary minesweepers MS *M3600* and *M3604* are lost on mines 6 nautical miles W of Ostend and on 23 Sept the MMS *R93* is lost on a mine off Dunkirk. On 13 Oct the transport *Telde* (2969 tons) is sunk off Aalborg and on 22 Oct the old torpedo boat *T157* is sunk off Neufahrwasser (Danzig).

18–23 Sept   North Atlantic
When Bletchley Park, in the morning of 18 Sept, decodes the order to the 'Leuthen' group to form a patrol line, there are problems pinpointing the end positions, which are given only by means of unknown reference points, so the evasive routing of ONS.18 and ON.202 (see 14–18 Sept) is too short. However, on 19 Sept a 'reminder' signal from the Cdr U-boats is decoded, and this gives away important tactical orders.
On 19 Oct Liberators of No 86 Sqn RAF and 10 Sqn RCAF are sent as air escorts; Liberator 'A' of No 10 Sqn RCAF sinks *U341*. The British Admiralty re-routes the convoys further to the NW. ON.202 has 38 ships and EG.C2, consisting of the destroyers *Gatineau* (Cdr Burnett) and *Icarus*, the frigate *Lagan* and the corvettes *Polyanthus*, *Drumheller* and *Kamloops*. ONS.18 has 27 ships and EG.B.3, consisting of the destroyers *Keppel* and *Escapade*, the frigate *Towy* (Cdr Evans), the corvettes *Orchis*, *Narcissus*, *Roselys*, *Lobélia* and *Renoncule* and the trawler *Northern Foam*. In the convoy there is also the merchant aircraft carrier *Macalpine*. In the morning the Canadian 9th SG, comprising the frigate *Itchen*, the destroyer *St Croix* and the cor-

vettes *Chambly*, *Sackville* and *Morden*, receives orders to join convoy ONS.18. In the evening of 19 Sept several U-boats, unbeknown to themselves, run into the escort of ONS.18: *Roselys* pursues a U-boat with depth charges and *Escapade* is badly damaged in a 'Hedgehog' attack because of a premature fuse. Early on 20 Sept *U270* (Lt-Cdr Otto) reports ON.202 but is located by HF/DF and approached by the frigate *Lagan* (Lt-Cdr Bridgeman). *U270* hits *Lagan* with a T-5 in the stern but *Gatineau* forces the U-boat to submerge. *Lagan* is taken in tow. The Cdr U-boats deploys the 'Leuthen' group. The second contact-keeper, *U238* (Lt Hepp), is located by HF/DF and driven off by *Polyanthus* but she shadows the corvette and three hours later is able to torpedo in an underwater attack two Liberty ships of 7176 tons: one sinks and the second is sunk later by *U645* (Lt-Cdr Ferro). T-5 torpedoes directed from *U645* and *U402* (Cdr Frhr v Forstner) against *Gatineau* and *Polyanthus*, which are escorting the rescue ship *Rathlin*, miss. In the morning of 20 Sept air escort is provided by Liberators of No 120 Sqn RAF. Before sufficient U-boats are assembled in the area of the convoy, *U338* (Lt-Cdr Kinzel) gives the agreed signal 'Keep on the surface for defence' when the U-boats are meant to fight their way to the convoy with their AA fire against the air escort. The single U-boat is sunk by Liberator 'F' of No 120 Sqn RAF (Flt Lt Moffatt) with an acoustic homing A/S torpedo ('Fido'). Contact is, at first, lost when *U731* is driven off. The Admiralty orders the convoys to join up under the SOE, Cdr Evans, and this is done by the evening. *U386* gains contact but is located by HF/DF and attacked with depth charges from *Keppel* and *Roselys*. A dusk attack by *U260* on steamers fails because the torpedoes do not explode. *St Croix* (Lt-Cdr Dobson), which is directed to a boat located by HF/DF, is hit by a T-5 from *U305* (Lt-Cdr Bahr) and finished off by her, while *Itchen*, which is sent for support, comes up and a T-5 explodes in her wash. During the night 20–21 Sept the U-boats try to shoot their way through to the steamers. *U229* (Lt Schetelig) misses *Icarus* with a T-5; the latter, in avoiding the torpedo, collides with *Drumheller*. *U260* (Lt-Cdr Purkhold) misses *Narcissus*; and *Polyanthus*, sent to support *St Croix*, is sunk by *U952* (Lt Curio). More T-5 firings by *U229*, *U641* (Lt Rendtel), *U270*, *U377* (Lt Kluth) and *U584* (Lt-Cdr Deecke) fail or detonate in the wash of the escorts. Towards morning on 21 Sept mist sets in and *Renoncule* and *Roselys* drive off *U377* which is still keeping listening contact.

When the mist lifts, *Macalpine* flies off her Swordfish aircraft for air escort.

In the evening of 21 Sept *U584* comes up and leads seven other boats to the area. Two boats are driven off by *Renoncule* and one boat by *Roselys*. *U584* is damaged by gunfire from *Chambly* after a T-5 failure. *U952* is almost rammed by *Northern Foam*. Towards morning *Roselys*, *Lobélia* and *Renoncule* each drive off one more boat. *U229*, which is located by HF/DF, is sunk with gunfire and ramming by *Keppel*.

The mist lifts in the afternoon of 22 Sept and Swordfish from *Macalpine* and Liberators from No 10 Sqn RCAF take over the air escort. The U-boats attack with their AA guns and partly drive the aircraft off. *U377* and *U270* are damaged. *U402* wards off a bomber. *U260* is forced to submerge by *Itchen* after being located by HF/DF; *U952* misses *Renoncule* with a T-5 and *U731* (Lt Techand) another corvette. In the dark, *Morden* sights *U666* (Lt-Cdr Engel) in front of the convoy. The latter fires two T-5s, one of which explodes just to the stern of *Morden*; the second hits and blows up *Itchen*. In the resulting confusion, *U238* sinks three ships of 15872 tons with a FAT salvo. A T-5 from *U260* explodes in the wash of the *Chambly*. Towards morning mist sets in again. After dawn the U-boats have again to defend themselves against the Liberators of No 10 Sqn RCAF, in the course of which *U422* is damaged. *U952* sinks one more ship of 6198 tons and hits a Liberty ship with an unexploded torpedo. *U758* (Lt-Cdr Manseck) finishes off one disabled ship and misses *Rathlin* and *Lobélia* which have remained behind. In the morning of 23 Sept the operation has to be broken off.

The successes reported by the U-boats (12 escorts sunk with 24 T-5 firings and three more probables) result in the effectiveness of the new torpedo being greatly overestimated.

The eastbound convoy HX.257, escorted by EG.B6 with the destroyers *Fame* and *Vanquisher*, the frigate *Devenon* and the corvettes *Kingcup*, *Potentilla* (RNoN) and *Rose* (RNoN), avoids the U-boats following ON.202/ONS.28.

20 Sept   Baltic
The German *U346* sinks off Hela in a diving accident.

21–22 Sept   Mediterranean
The British *MTB226* and *MTB228* attack the old German cruiser *Niobe* (ex *Dalmacija*) NW of Zara.

21–22 Sept   Norway
Operation 'Source' with British midget submarines against the German heavy ships in

Altafjord. Towed by the large submarines *Thrasher*, *Truculent*, *Stubborn*, *Syrtis*, *Sceptre* and *Seanymph*, the midget submarines *X5*, *X6*, *X7*, *X9*, *X10* and *X8* are to enter the fjord and attack the battleship *Tirpitz*, the battlecruiser *Scharnhorst* and the cruiser *Lützow* with ground mines. *X9* and *X8* are lost on the way, *X5* sinks, probably in a minefield in the entrance to the fjord, and *X10* has to return because of a breakdown. Only *X6* (Lt Cameron) and *X7* (Lt Plaice) succeed in getting inside *Tirpitz*'s net defences and laying the mines there. As a result of their detonation, the ship is badly damaged and out of action until Mar 1944.

On 23 Sept *Lützow* sets out for the Baltic (Operation 'Hermelin'), escorted by the destroyers *Erich Steinbrinck*, *Paul Jacobi*, *Friedrich Ihn*, *Z27* and, off SW Norway, *Z38*. She is located by British air reconnaissance on 26 and 27 Sept, but the RAF Beaufighters and Tarpon (Avenger) torpedo bombers of No 832 Sqn Fleet Air Arm sent out from the Shetlands pass by to the stern of the ship. *Lützow* reaches Gotenhafen on 1 Oct without experiencing any attack.

22 Sept–3 Oct   South West Pacific
The VII Amphibious Force (Rear-Adm Barbey), with the fast transport *Brooks*, LSTs and LSIs, lands the 20th Australian Bde on both sides of Finschhafen. Support is provided by the US destroyers *Lamson*, *Mugford*, *Drayton* and *Flusser*. The assault forces are escorted by the US destroyers *Conyngham*, *Perkins*, *Smith*, *Reid*, *Mahan* and *Henley*. On 25 Sept the Japanese submarines *I-177* and *I-176* try for the last time to supply Lae and Finschhafen. The Japanese submarines *Ro-100*, *Ro-104* and *Ro-108* are deployed against the American operation, the last sinking *Henley* on 3 Oct. Finschhafen is captured on 2 Oct.

23 Sept   Black Sea
The German MMS *R30* is sunk in a Soviet air attack off Kerch.

24–25 Sept   North Sea
Mining operation 'Probestück' by 29 German motor torpedo boats of the 2nd, 4th, 6th and 8th MTB Flotillas off Harwich and Orfordness: 120 mines are laid. In engagements, *S96* sinks the trawler *Franctireur* and is herself rammed by *ML145* and has to be abandoned. Three British MLs are damaged.

24–26 Sept   North Atlantic
En route to the Mediterranean, *U667* is damaged W of Gibraltar by Leigh Light Wellingtons 'D' and 'R' of No 179 Sqn RAF and has to return to France. On its way

back she is again attacked, by Wellington 'X' of No 179 Sqn RAF and Hudsons 'T' of No 233 and 'N' of No 48 Sqns RAF, and is again damaged but she reaches St-Nazaire on 11 Oct.

24–27 Sept   Mediterranean
In the area of Corfu, the Italian torpedo boats *Stocco* (24 Sept), *Sirtori* (25), and *Cosenz* (27) are destroyed in German air attacks.

25 Sept   North Sea
The German patrol trawler *V316* is sunk by an airborne torpedo between Den Helder and Ijmuiden.

25 Sept–7 Oct   South Pacific
From 25 Sept to 28 Oct the Japanese bring some 100 assault boats and other small craft to the northern beach of Kolombangara in order to evacuate the garrison (Maj-Gen Sasaki). Cover is provided by 11 destroyers and the submarines *Ro-105*, *Ro-106* and *Ro-109*, one of which misses the US cruiser *Columbia*. Then US destroyer forces are deployed to blockade Kolombangara: on 27–28 Sept Capt Gillan with *Charles Ausburne*, *Claxton*, *Dyson*, *Spence* and *Foote*; on 29–30 Sept Capt Walker with *Patterson*, *Foote*, *Ralph Talbot* and *McCalla*; on 1–2 Oct Capt Cooke with *Waller*, *Eaton* and *Cony* and Cdr Chandler with *Radford*, *Saufley* and *Grayson*; on 2–3 Oct Cdr Larson with *Ralph Talbot*, *Taylor* and *Perry*; and on 3–4 Oct the Chandler force. The Japanese (Rear-Adm Ijuin) are able to evacuate 9400 troops with destroyers, fast transports, assault boats etc. About a third of the small craft and 1000 men fall victim to the US destroyers. After the conclusion of the Kolombangara withdrawal, Rear-Adm Ijuin tries on 6–7 Oct to evacuate Vella Lavella with the destroyers *Fumitsuki*, *Matsukaze* and *Yunagi* (transport force) and *Akigumo*, *Isokaze*, *Kazegumo*, *Yugumo*, *Shigure* and *Samidare*. Capt Walker, with the US destroyers *Selfridge*, *Chevalier* and *O'Bannon*, is sent from the N and Cdr Larson, with *Ralph Talbot*, *Taylor* and *La Vallette*, from the S to operate against the force which is located by air reconnaissance. Off the coast of Vella Lavella there is an engagement between the Walker force and the Japanese covering group. The three US destroyers fire 14 torpedoes, one of which hits *Yugumo*. The latter's torpedo salvo, fired off first, hits *Chevalier*, which sinks after a collision with *O'Bannon*. *Selfridge* continues the engagement but is hit by one torpedo from salvos by *Samidare* and *Shigure*. But the Japanese turn away: Cdr Larson does not come up and is able only to sink the wreck of *Yugumo*.

26 Sept   Mediterranean
The German A/S trawler *UJ2218* runs

aground near Addenza in the Gulf of Genoa and is lost.

26–27 Sept   English Channel
British attack on a German convoy proceeding from Le Havre to Dunkirk. While the British *MGB108*, *MGB118* and *MGB117* try to engage the German escort vessels of the 15th PB Flotilla and the 2nd MMS Flotilla out at sea, the Dutch *MTB202*, *MTB204* and *MTB231* attack from the shore side off Fécamp and Bercq-sur-Mer and sink *V1501*, the freighter *Madali* (3019 tons) and the escort vessel *M534/Jungingen*.

26 Sept–12 Oct   East Mediterranean
German counter-attack in the Aegean. On 26 Sept Ju 88s of LG 1 sink the destroyers *Intrepid* (RN) and *Vasilissa Olga* (Greek) in the harbour at Leros and on 1 Oct the Italian *Euro*.

On 3 Oct German ships and emergency craft, escorted by the 21st SC Flotilla and supported by the Luftwaffe, carry out Operation 'Eisbär'. Troops are landed on Coo which overwhelm the garrison and take 1388 British and 3145 Italians prisoner. Owing to lack of fuel, the destroyers *Aldenham* (RN), *Pindos* and *Themistokles* (Greek) are unable to attack the invasion convoy which is located by British air reconnaissance.

On 5 Oct German bombers sink the Italian minelayer *Legnano* in Leros. On 7 Oct a convoy for Coo, reported by the British submarine *Unruly* and consisting of the freighter *Olympos* (5216 tons), seven naval ferry barges and the submarine-chaser *UJ2111*, is encountered by a British force consisting of the cruisers *Sirius* and *Penelope* and the destroyers *Faulknor* and *Fury* S of Levita and completely annihilated with the exception of one ferry barge. 1027 survivors are rescued by German ships and aircraft. The retiring British force is attacked in the Scarpanto Strait by Ju 87s of II/StG 3 and Ju 88s of LG 1 and of II/KG 51 and *Penelope* is damaged by bomb hits. On 8 Oct the British submarine *Unruly* (Lt Fyfe) sinks the German minelayer *Bulgaria* (1108 tons) loaded with supplies for Cos and misses the minelayer *Drache*. On 9 Oct the British cruiser *Carlisle* makes a sortie into the sea S of Piraeus with the destroyers *Panther* and *Rockwood* in order to intercept further German convoys. In the Scarpanto Strait, Ju 87s of II/StG 3 attack and sink *Panther* on 9 Oct; *Carlisle* is severely damaged and taken in tow by *Rockwood* to Alexandria (she is not put in service again).

27 Sept   Norway
The German patrol trawler *V5705* is lost,

to either a mine or a submarine torpedo, W of Bodö.

27 Sept   Bay of Biscay
The outgoing *U221* is sunk by Halifax 'B' of No 58 Sqn RAF but the latter is shot down by AA fire; six of the air crew are rescued by the destroyer *Mahratta*.

27 Sept–5 Oct   North Atlantic
On 27 Sept the 'Rossbach' U-boat group is formed in the Central North Atlantic to operate against convoy ON.203 located by the German B-Service. The group consists of *U389*, *U279*, *U643*, *U641*, *U731*, *U539*, *U666*, *U336*, *U758*, *U584*, *U419*, *U378*, *U952*, *U645*, *U260*, *U603*, *U275*, *U448*, *U305*, *U631* and *U402*.

The convoy avoids the patrol line by passing to the N on 28–29 Sept. Escort is provided by EG.C4 (Cdr McKillop RN) with the destroyers *Hotspur* (RN) and *Churchill* (RN) and the corvettes *Collingwood* and *Nasturtium* (RN), *Trillium* and *Orillia* (only to Iceland). The convoy is supported by the new 4th SG with the DE frigates *Blackwood*, *Burgess*, *Byard* and *Drury*.

In spite of a move by the 'Rossbach' group to the N, the following convoy reported by the B-Service, ONS.19, escorted by EG.C.3 under Cdr Medley RN with the destroyers *Saskatchewan*, *Skeena*, *Burnham* (RN) and *St-Francis* and the corvettes *Eyebright*, *Mayflower* and *Pictou*, supported by the 10th EG with the destroyers *Musketeer*, *Oribi*, *Orkan* (Polish) and *Orwell*, also passes N of the patrol line on 30 Sept, when *U279* is attacked by a Hudson of No 269 Sqn RAF. On 4 Oct *U731* and *641* are damaged by Hudson 'S' of No 269 Sqn RAF and another Hudson from the unit, while on 5 Oct Hudson 'F' of No 269 Sqn sinks *U389* with rockets. On 1 Oct convoy HX.258, escorted by EG.C1 (Cdr Adams RCN) with the destroyers *Assiniboine* and *Forester*, the frigate *Waskesiu* and the corvettes *Agassiz*, *Celandine* (RN) and *Galt* and supported by the 2nd SG (Capt Walker) with the sloops *Starling*, *Kite*, *Wild Goose*, *Woodcock* and *Wren* and the attached escort carrier *Tracker*, passes S of the patrol line. *U631* is bombed; *U448* and *U402* beat off Venturas from VB-128 USN with AA fire. In operations to protect ON.204 (EG.B1 under Cdr Bayldon with the destroyers *Hurricane* and *Wanderer*, the frigate *Glenarm* and the corvettes *Borage*, *Dahlia* and *Wallflower*, supported by the 5th EG with the frigate *Nene* and the corvettes *Calgary*, *Edmundston* and *Camrose*), *U610* and *U275* are attacked by aircraft and *U336* and *U666* by escort vessels; *U666* is damaged by depth charges. On 4 Oct Ventura 'B' of VB-128 sinks *U279* and damages *U305* and Liberator 'X' of No 120 Sqn RAF sinks *U336*. The convoy is not found.

28 Sept   South Pacific

The Japanese minelayer *Hoko* is sunk in a USAAF air attack E of Buka in the Solomons.

28 Sept–1 Nov   Central Atlantic

The U-tanker *U488* (Lt Bartke) replenishes on 28 Sept and 4 Oct the returning *U68*, *U155* and *U103* W of the Azores. *U460* (Lt-Cdr Schnoor), which replenished eight North Atlantic boats in Sept, is sighted on 4 Oct when she is replenishing *U455*, *U264* and *U422* N of the Azores by an aircraft from the escort carrier *Card* (Capt Isbell), forming TG.21.14 with the destroyers *Borie*, *Barry*, *Dupont* and *Goff*. The supply boat submerges too late and with *U422* is sunk by 12 aircraft which attack in three waves. *U264* (Lt-Cdr Looks), which covers the diving operation, is badly damaged. The convoy UGS.19 (58 ships escorted by TF.64 with the destroyers *Stevenson*, *Stockton*, *Thorn* and *Turner*, the escort destroyers *Hammann* and *Jacob Jones* and the US Coast Guard cutter *Spencer*) passes by unmolested. On 11–12 Oct the supply group, comprising *U488* and *U402*, and *U584*, *U731* and *U378*, is repeatedly sighted by aircraft from *Card*. The supply area is moved to the SE, where the AA boats *U271* and *U256* take over the protection of the tanker. On 13 Oct an aircraft from VC-9 (*Card*) sinks *U402* and *U731* is damaged. In the new area it is possible to replenish *U758*, *U378*, *U641* and *U731* before the *Core* group (TG.21.5) arrives on 20 Oct with the destroyers *Greene*, *Belknap* and *Goldsborough*. They escort convoy UGS.20 (67 ships with TF.65, comprising the destroyers *Livermore*, *Eberle*, *Kearny* and *Ericsson*, the destroyer escorts *Hayward*, *Farquhar* and *Blakeley* and the US Coast Guard cutters *Duane* and *Campbell*). Two aircraft from VC-13 (*Core*) sink *U378* and damage *U271*. To support the tanker, *U220* arrives from a mining operation and refuels *U603* and *U256* before she is sunk on 28 Oct by two aircraft of VC-1 from the escort carrier *Block Island*. While *U488* goes further to the SW to replenish *U193*, *U103*, *U530* and *U129*, individual boats meet N of the Azores for mutual replenishment and support. On 30 Oct the *Card* group with the destroyers *Borie*, *Goff* and *Barry*, which is escorting the convoy GUS.18, comes across one U-boat which escapes. On 31 Oct *U584* is sunk by two aircraft of VC-9 from *Card* but *U91* is able to submerge in time. On 1 Nov *Borie* (Lt-Cdr Hutchins), which is sent to the engagement area, encounters *U405*

(Cdr Hopmann†). In a one-hour duel involving torpedoes, gunfire and mutual rammings, as well as an attempt to board, *U405* sinks and *Borie* has to be abandoned.

29 Sept   Mediterranean

On board the British battleship *Nelson* in Malta, Gen Eisenhower for the Allies and Marshal Badoglio for Italy sign the Italian capitulation.

29–30 Sept   English Channel

The German 5th TB Flotilla, comprising *T27*, *Kondor*, *Greif*, *T19* and *T26*, carries out the mining operation 'Talsohle' in the Channel.

30 Sept–8 Oct   North Atlantic

In accordance with the Anglo-Portuguese agreement of 18 Aug, Allied air bases are established on the Azores islands of Fayal and Terceira in Operation 'Alacrity'. To transport the installations and personnel for No 247 Group RAF (Air Vice-Marshal Bromet), three small convoys (Commodore Holt) proceed to the Azores, consisting of the transport *Franconia*, tankers, freighters and small craft for local defence. Escort is provided by EG.B5, comprising the destroyers *Havelock*, *Volunteer* and *Warwick*, the corvettes *Buttercup*, *Lavender* and *Godetia* and the sloop *Lowestoft*, and the 8th SG, consisting of the escort carrier *Fencer* and the destroyers *Inconstant*, *Garland* (Polish), *Burza* (Polish), *Viscount*, *Whitehall* and *Wrestler*. On 18 Oct the first Fortress bomber arrives; it is used operationally on 19 Oct.

1 Oct   Intelligence

The German naval cypher 'Hermes' for the Mediterranean and the Black Sea is separated into several circuits: 'Hermes', for the Mediterranean (broken as 'Porpoise' since Aug 1942); 'Poseidon', for the Black Sea (broken in Oct 1943 as 'Grampus'/'Clam'); and 'Uranus', for the connection from the OKM to the Southern and South Eastern Commands (never broken).

1 Oct   Baltic

The German motor minesweeper *R205* is sunk after striking a mine in the Irben Strait.

1–31 Oct   Pacific

In US submarine operations for the month of Oct, there are 126 'Ultra' signals, which lead to 56 sightings and 19 attacks in which five ships are sunk and five damaged.

In the Aleutians/Kuriles area, *S46* has duds and *S44* is sunk off Paramushiro on 7 Oct by a Japanese destroyer. In Japanese waters, *Salmon* (Lt-Cdr Nicholas) damages one ship of 2969 tons, *Tarpon* (Lt-Cdr Wogan) sinks the German auxiliary cruiser *Schiff 28/Michel*, *Lapon* (Lt-Cdr Stone) sinks one ship of 1906 tons and damages one of 433

tons and *Seahorse* (Lt-Cdr Cutter) sinks five ships of 25431 tons and three sailing vessels.

In the China/Formosa area, 'wolf packs' of three boats each are organised for the first time: *Haddock*, *Halibut* and *Tullibee* under Cdr Brindupke and *Cero*, *Shad* and *Grayback* under Capt Momsen. From the first group, *Tullibee* (Cdr Brindupke) sinks one ship of 5866 tons, *Halibut* (Lt-Cdr Galantin) sinks one ship of 4653 tons and on 5 Oct torpedoes the carrier *Junyo* in the Bungo Channel and *Haddock* (Lt-Cdr Davenport) torpedoes one ship of 8691 tons; from the second group, *Shad* (Lt-Cdr Julihn) and *Grayback* (Lt-Cdr Moore) sink one ship of 9130 tons together, *Grayback* torpedoes two ships of 14470 tons and *Shad* misses a cruiser.

In the Central Pacific, *Peto* (Lt-Cdr Nelson) sinks two ships of 9910 tons, *Tinosa* (Lt-Cdr Daspit) and *Steelhead* (Lt-Cdr Welchel) sink together one ship of 18300 tons and *Steelhead* alone one other of 8592 tons, *Guardfish* (Lt-Cdr Ward) sinks one ship of 5460 tons, *Cero* (Lt-Cdr White) damages one ship of 15820 tons and sinks one sailing vessel, *Silversides* (Lt-Cdr Coye) sinks four ships of 15402 tons, *Flying Fish* (Lt-Cdr Donaho) sinks two ships of 7139 tons and *Seadragon*, *Mingo*, *Gato* and *Balao* have prematures and duds. *Skate* conducts the first 'planeguard' mission during a carrier strike against Wake and rescues six downed airmen. *Scamp* conducts a reconnaissance mission. In the South West Pacific, *Kingfish* (Lt-Cdr Lowrance) lays a minefield off Makassar (on which one ship of 3098 tons sinks), sinks one ship of 3365 tons by torpedo and damages one other of 14050 tons, *Gurnard* (Lt-Cdr Andrews) sinks two ships of 11468 tons, *Rasher* (Lt-Cdr Hutchinson) sinks four ships of 9143 tons and *Kingfish* and *Cabrilla* conduct guerrilla support missions.

2 Oct–27 Nov   Baltic

There is a heavy increase in Soviet air attacks on shipping in the Baltic in which the Boston bombers (supplied under Lend-Lease) of the Mining and Torpedo Div of the Naval Air Force are used with torpedoes. They also lay mines. The torpedo attacks are made especially in the area of the Irben Strait. There are many misses but on 1 Nov the steamer *Marienburg* (1322 tons) is sunk. Several German steamers are lost on mines and the Finnish ice-breaker *Sisu* is damaged. Ground-attack aircraft increasingly harass the mine guards in the Gulf of Finland. On 4 Nov the German minesweeper *M16* is severely, and *M18*, *M30*, *M459* and *M460* are slightly, damaged.

3 Oct Mediterranean

The British submarine *Usurper* is sunk by the German A/S vessel *UJ2208* in the Gulf of Genoa.

3–4 Oct English Channel

There is an engagement between the German 4th TB Flotilla (Cdr Kohlauf), comprising *T23*, *T22*, *T25*, *T26* and *T27*, and five British destroyers off Les Sept Iles.

3 Oct–25 Dec Mediterranean

In Allied submarine operations in the Western Mediterranean, the British *Ultimatum* (Lt Kett) reports an U-boat sunk on 30 Oct (but *U73* escapes undamaged) and *Ultor* (Lt Hunt) sinks one ship of 3723 tons in Oct; *Uproar* (Lt Herrick) torpedoes one ship in Nov; *Untiring* (Lt Boyd) sinks one net tender; and *Universal* (Lt Gordon) sinks one ship of 2497 tons. The French submarine *Orphée* (Lt-Cdr Dupont) sinks one tug and *Casabianca* (Lt Bellet) sinks the submarine-chaser *UJ6076* and torpedoes one ship. In Oct the Polish *Sokol* (Cdr Karnicki) sinks two small ships in the Adriatic. In the Aegean in Nov one ship is torpedoed by *Simoom* (Lt Milner) and one ship of 3160 tons by *Sickle* (Lt Drummond). One ship of 2609 tons and one dock are sunk by *Torbay* (Lt Clutterbuck). In Dec one ship of 5609 tons is sunk by *Sokol*, and one ship of 2719 tons and one of 3838 tons are sunk by, respectively, *Surf* (Lt Lambert) and *Sportsman* (Lt Gatehouse).

4 Oct Norway

A raid by the Home Fleet, reinforced by US units, is made on German shipping off Bodö (Operation 'Leader'). Covered by the British battleships *Duke of York* and *Anson*, the US cruiser *Tuscaloosa*, three British cruisers and ten British and US destroyers, the US carrier *Ranger* flies off 30 Dauntless dive-bombers and Avenger torpedo bombers and 12 fighters. They attack two German convoys and ships in the roads. They sink four steamers of 12697 tons and damage six other large ships and one ferry barge so badly that most of them have to be beached. Five aircraft are lost.

4–28 Oct North Atlantic

While the German 'Schlieffen' group is being formed, the Allied convoys avoid the concentration around convoys ON.206 and ONS.20. Convoy HX.259, escorted by EG.B3 with the frigate *Towy*, the destroyer *Keppel*, the corvettes *Narcissus*, *Orchis*, *Lobélia* (FFN), *Renoncule* (FFN) and *Roselys* (FFN) and the DE frigate *Duckworth*, crosses 4–12 Oct; ON.205, escorted by EG.C5 with the destroyer *Kootenay* and the corvettes *Arvida*, *Kitchener*, *Sudbury*, *Wetaskiwin* and *Sorel*, crosses

6–17 Oct; HX.260, escorted by EG.C4 with the destroyers *Hotspur* (RN) and *Churchill* (RN) and the corvettes *Nasturtium* (RN), *Orillia*, *Trillium* and *Woodstock*, crosses 11–19 Oct; SC.144, escorted by EG.B1 with the destroyers *Hurricane* and *Wanderer*, the frigate *Glenarm* and the corvettes *Borage*, *Dahlia* and *Wallflower*, crosses 14–25 Oct; HX.261, escorted by EG.C3 with the destroyers *Saskatchewan* and *Skeena* and the corvettes *Eyebright*, *Mayflower* and *Pictou*, crosses 16–24 Oct (and is supported 18–21 Oct by the 5th EG with the frigates *Nene* and *Tweed* and the corvettes *Calgary*, *Edmundston* and *Snowberry*); and ON.207, escorted by EG.C1 with the destroyers *Forester* (RN) and *Assiniboine*, the frigate *Ettrick* and the corvettes *Agassiz*, *Celandine* (RN) and *Galt*, crosses 19–28 Oct.

5–6 Oct Black Sea

Sortie by a Soviet destroyer force (Capt 2nd Class Negoda) on German evacuation transports off the Crimean coast. The flotilla leader *Kharkov* shells Yalta and Alushta in the night. The two destroyers *Besposhchadny* and *Sposobny* encounter, on their way to Feodosia, boats of the 1st MTB Flotilla and engage *S45*, *S28* and *S42*, and later *S51* and *S52*, without result on either side. Located in the morning by a German reconnaissance aircraft, the force, which has now joined up, is attacked by day in four sorties undertaken by Ju 87s of III/StG 3 (Maj Hamester). In the first attack, *Kharkov* (Capt 2nd Class Shevchenko) is hit and taken in tow by *Sposobny* (Capt 3rd Class Gorshenin). In the second attack, all three ships are hit: *Sposobny* tries in turn to tow the two other destroyers. In the third attack, *Besposhchadny* (Capt 3rd Class Parkhomenko) is sunk, as is, a little later, *Kharkov*. Finally, *Sposobny*, which tries to rescue the survivors, is sunk. After this loss, Stalin forbids the employment of surface ships of destroyer size upwards without his permission.

5–6 Oct Central Pacific

US TF.14 (Rear-Adm Montgomery) makes attacks on Wake. The force comprises the carriers *Essex*, *Yorktown*, *Lexington*, *Cowpens*, *Independence* and *Belleau Wood*, the cruisers *Nashville*, *Santa Fé*, *Birmingham*, *Mobile*, *New Orleans*, *Minneapolis* and *San Francisco*, the destroyers *Trathen*, *Hazelwood*, *Boyd*, *Bradford*, *Conner*, *Burns*, *Braine*, *Bullard*, *Kidd*, *Chauncey*, *Hull*, *Dale*, *Halford*, *Bancroft*, *Caldwell*, *Coghlan*, *Ringgold*, *Schroeder*, *Sigsbee*, *Harrison*, *John Rodgers*, *McKee*, *Murray* and *Dashiell* and the tankers *Cimarron* and *Kaskaskia*. In 738 sorties, 12 aircraft are lost to enemy action and 14 to accident.

The cruisers carry out a brief shelling of the island.

6–9 Oct North Atlantic

From 6 Oct the 'Rossbach' group, now comprising *U309*, *U762*, *U643*, *U641*, *U539*, *U448*, *U610*, *U419*, *U378*, *U645*, *U260*, *U603*, *U275*, *U631*, *U91*, *U731* and *U758*, is moved S to find convoys HX.259 and SC.143 reported by the B-Service. In the evening of 7 Oct *U448* sights the 3rd SG (Cdr Currie) with the destroyers *Musketeer*, *Oribi*, *Orwell* and *Orkan* (Cdr Hryniewiecki) detailed to support SC.143, which comprises 39 ships escorted by EG.C2 (Lt-Cdr Dyer) with the destroyer *Icarus* (RN) and the corvettes *Drumheller*, *Kamloops*, *Timmins* (soon detached), *Chambly*, *Morden* and *Sackville* and the merchant aircraft carrier *Rapana*. In the course of the night eight boats establish contact with the escort vessels. *U378* is driven off by aircraft. *U758* is attacked by *Orkan* after a contact signal is located by *Musketeer*'s HF/DF; a T-5, fired in defence, detonates in the wash of the destroyer. *U610* misses a destroyer with a T-5 but towards morning on 8 Oct *Orkan* is sunk by *U378* (Lt-Cdr Mäder) with a T-5. The air escort which arrives drives off the U-boats. Liberator 'R' of No 86 Sqn RAF (Flt Lt Wright) sinks *U419*, Liberators 'Z' of No 86 Sqn RAF (Fg Off Burcher) and 'T' of No 120 Sqn RAF (Fg Off Webster) sink *U643*, Liberator 'G' of No 120 Sqn damages *U762* and Sunderland 'J' of No 423 Sqn RCAF sinks *U610*. A German Bv 222 flying boat, employed for the first time over the Atlantic, sights SC.143 but the U-boats do not receive its D/F bearings; *U91* misses a destroyer with a T-5 in the evening but is driven off by aircraft with Leigh Lights (used for the first time with a North Atlantic convoy at night). In the morning of 9 Oct the operation has to be broken off. *U645* (Lt-Cdr Ferro) comes across a scattered convoy group in bad visibility and sinks one ship of 5612 tons.

7 Oct English Channel

Operation 'Gesellenprüfung'. Under the command of the 4th MTB Flotilla, Cdr Lützow, mines are sown in an extensive area S of Smith's Knoll by the 2nd, 4th, 6th and 8th MTB Flotillas with a total of 29 boats. *S62* and *S83* of the 2nd and *S93* and *S127* of the 8th Flotillas have to return because of engine trouble. The 2nd Flotilla drops 37, the 4th 44 and the 6th 40 mines (LMBs and UMBs).

8–18 Oct North Sea

The German minelayers *Ostmark* and *Roland*, escorted by the minesweepers *M426* and *M115*, lay three mine barrages, 'Lithium', 'Natrium' and 'Kalium', off the Ska-gerrak.

8–10 Oct   Black Sea

Operation 'Wiking': withdrawal of the 240 craft used to evacuate the Kuban bridgehead in four large convoys from the Kerch Strait to Sevastopol. An escort is provided by the 3rd and 30th MMS Flotillas and the 23rd SC Flotilla, with the 1st MTB Flotilla further out to the sea. The engineer assault boat *229* is sunk by air attack and the ferry barge *F474* by submarine.

9 Oct   Air War/Germany

Bombers of the US 8th AF attack Goten-hafen (Gdynia). The hospital ship *Stuttgart* (13387 tons) and the A/S trawler *UJ 1210/ KUJ13* are sunk.

12 Oct   Caribbean

The US submarine *Dorado* is sunk in error by a US aircraft S of Cuba.

12 Oct   South West Pacific

The US 5th AF, with an attack by 349 aircraft, starts the air offensive against Rabaul to isolate the base. Four aircraft are lost.

12 Oct–7 Nov   East Mediterranean

In British submarine operations against German supply traffic for Coo, *Unruly* (Lt Fyfe) sinks the transport *Marguerite* (920 tons): 350 of the 900 prisoners on board are rescued. The submarine *Trooper* is lost (cause unknown) while *Torbay* is attacked near Calino by the German submarine-trap *GA45* after sinking a sailing ship. On 15–16 Oct two attempts, by the British destroyers *Belvoir* and *Beaufort* and then by the cruiser *Phoebe* and the destroyers *Faulknor* and *Fury*, to locate a German convoy fail owing to air attacks. On 16 Oct *Torbay* sinks one of the two steamers, the *Kari* (1925 tons). During the night 16–17 Oct the destroyers *Hursley* and *Miaoulis* (Greek) find the remaining ships and sink the submarine-chaser *UJ2109* (ex-British *Widnes*) and the transport *Trapani* (1855 tons), the wreck of which is dispatched the following night by the destroyers *Penn* and *Jervis*. In addition, the ferry barge *F338* and one sailing ship are set on fire. On 19 and 20 Oct USAAF Mitchell bombers and RAF Beaufighters attack convoys N of Crete and sink, *inter alia*, the transport *Sinfra* (4470 tons) of whose 2664 prisoners (mostly Italian) 566 are rescued. The British cruiser *Aurora*, in company with the Greek destroyer *Miaoulis*, bombards targets on Rhodes. Then the emphasis of British operations is shifted to supply transports to Leros and Samos. Up to 7 Nov 2230 troops and 470 tons of supplies are transported by surface ships and 17 men and 288 tons of supplies by the British submarines *Severn* and *Rorqual* and

by the Italian *Zoea*, *Atropo*, *Corridoni* and *Menotti*. In the process, from 22 to 24 Oct, the destroyers *Hurworth* and *Eclipse* are lost on a mine barrage laid by the German mine-layer *Drache* E of Calino and the Greek destroyer *Adrias* loses her bows. In air attacks the cruiser *Sirius* and *Aurora* and the destroyer *Belvoir* are damaged. The Polish submarine *Sokol* (Cdr Karnicki) sinks five supply sailing ships and the British *Unsparing* (Lt Piper) sinks the transport *Ingeborg* (1160 tons) and the customs sloop *Nioi*. In a sortie on 7 Nov the British destroyers *Penn* and *Pathfinder* sink the German submarine-trap *GA45*.

13 Oct   General Situation

The Badoglio Government declares war on Germany.

13 Oct   Mediterranean

The British destroyers *Laforey* and *Lookout* and the Dutch gunboat *Flores* bombard positions N of the Volturno river in conjunction with the landing of tanks from four LCTs.

15–18 Oct   North Atlantic

In the evening of 15 Oct *U844* (Lt G Möller), on her way to the new 'Schlieffen' formation, reports the convoy ON.206, which comprises 65 ships escorted by EG.B6 (Cdr Currie) with the British destroyers *Fame* and *Vanquisher*, the frigate *Deveron* and the Norwegian corvettes *Rose* and *Potentilla*, as well as EG.B7 (Cdr Gretton) with the destroyers *Duncan* and *Vidette* and the corvettes *Sunflower*, *Loose-strife* and *Pink* operating as a support group. *U844* is driven off by *Vanquisher* and *Duncan*. Early on 16 Oct *U964* (Lt Hummerjohann) reports the convoy ONS.20; this consists of 52 ships escorted by the 4th SG (Cdr Paramor) with the Lend-Lease destroyer escorts *Byard*, *Bentinck*, *Berry*, *Drury*, *Bazely*, *Blackwood* and *Burgess* and A/S trawlers, with, from 18 Oct, EG.B7 as a support group. In order to bring the U-boats scattered round the two convoys up to the target the Cdr U-boats orders the submarines to fight their way through to the convoy with AA fire against the strong air escort provided in the morning by Liberators of Nos 59, 86 and 120 Sqns RAF. *U964* is sunk by Liberator 'Y' of No 86 Sqn RAF in the morning of 16 Oct; *U844* is attacked by Liberator 'L' of No 86 Sqn (which is shot down) and then sunk by Lib-erator 'S' of No 59 Sqn RAF; and *U470* is sunk by Liberators 'E' and 'Z' of No 120 Sqn and 'G' of No 59 Sqn RAF against heavy AA defence. Only *U426* (Lt-Cdr Reich) comes up in the evening of 16 Oct to convoy ONS.20 and sinks one ship of 6625 tons. EG.B7, from which *Duncan* and *Vidette* have frustrated four attempted

attacks on ON.206, is detached to support the threatened ONS.20. On the way, *Sun-flower* locates *U631* and sinks her with 'Hedgehog'. During the night 16–17 Oct six U-boats in the vicinity of ONS.20 are driven off by *Bentinck*, *Duncan*, *Vidette*, *Berry*, *Drury* and *Bazely*. In the morning of 17 Oct *U309* again reports the ONS.20 but the 'Schlieffen' group (*U762*, *U231*, *U91*, *U448*, *U267*, *U413*, *U668*, *U841*, *U426*, *U540*, *U271* and *U842*), which is deployed on the basis of her report and another from *U437*, is unable to make progress against the strong air escort. Nine U-boats are attacked: *U540* is sunk by Liberators 'D' of No 59 Sqn RAF and 'H' of No 120 Sqn RAF (WO Turnbull); *U448* and *U281* have casualties from gunfire but shoot down Sunderland 'S' of No 422 Sqn RCAF. *U608* is overrun towards evening by convoy ONS.20, which has turned sharply to the SW, and is attacked by depth charges. *U841* is sunk by *Byard*. The operation has to be broken off.

15 Oct–9 Nov   Black Sea

In operations off the Caucasian coast, the German U-boat *U9* (Lt Klapdor) reports a hit on a tanker off Sochi on 29 Oct, *U23* (Lt Wahlen) from 15 to 23 Oct reports the torpedoing of two freighters and the sinking of one fishing cutter, *U24* (Lt-Cdr Petersen) sinks a motor minesweeper and *U18* (Lt Fleige) sinks a tanker.

Soviet submarines operate chiefly W of the Crimea. Near Cape Tarkhankut the sub-marine-chaser *Schiff 19*, with three KFKs of the 23rd SC Flotilla, sinks one submarine (*Shch-203*?) on 16 Oct. One attack by *Shch-201* on 19 Oct fails. On 25 Oct and 2 Nov *M-112* (Lt Khakhanov) and *M-35* (Lt-Cdr Prokofev) sink the lighters *Tyra 5* and *No 1293* respectively off Ak Mechet. On 4 Nov *Schiff 19* sinks the Soviet submarine *A-3* off the Tendra peninsula.

17 Oct–12 Nov   Air War/Western Europe

RAF Bomber Command mine offensive. In 11 nights there are 281 sorties, mainly against the Frisian coast and the area of Texel and also against Biscay ports. Seven aircraft are lost. On 24 Oct the A/S trawler *UJ1403* sinks on a mine at Belle Isle (Biscay) but is later salvaged and recommissioned.

20 Oct–12 Nov   South Pacific

Japanese Operation 'Ro': the carrier aircraft of the Japanese 3rd Fleet (1st Carrier Sqn, comprising *Zuikaku*, *Shokaku* and *Zuiho*, and 2nd Carrier Sqn, comprising *Junyo*, *Hiyo* and *Ryuho*) are transferred from Truk to Rabaul to reinforce the latter and to carry out an air offensive from there against the Central Solomons. The carriers return to

Japan and on the way the US submarine *Halibut* torpedoes *Junyo* on 5 Nov.

The Japanese Combined Fleet (Adm Koga) is on the alert in Truk. It consists of the 1st Battle Sqn with the battleships *Yamato* and *Musashi*; the 2nd Fleet (Vice-Adm Kurita) with the 4th Cruiser Sqn consisting of *Atago*, *Takao*, *Maya* and *Chokai*, the 5th Cruiser Sqn consisting of *Myoko* and *Haguro* (transferred to Rabaul), the 2nd DD Flotilla with the cruiser *Noshiro* and the destroyers (24th DD Div) *Umikaze*, *Suzukaze* and *Michishio*, (27th DD Div) *Harusame*, *Shiratsuyu*, *Shigure* and *Samidare* (transferred to Rabaul), (31st DD Div) *Naganami*, *Makinami* and *Onami*, (32nd DD Div) *Tamanami*, *Suzunami*, *Fujinami* and *Hayanami* and the attached *Shimakaze*. The 3rd Fleet (1st and 2nd Carrier Sqns) consists of the 3rd Battle Sqn, comprising *Kongo* and *Haruna*; the 7th Cruiser Sqn comprising *Kumano*, *Suzuya* and *Mogami*; the 8th Cruiser Sqn, comprising *Chikuma* and *Tone*; and the 10th DD Flotilla comprising the cruiser *Agano* (transferred to Rabaul) and the destroyers (4th DD Div) *Nowake*, *Maikaze* and *Yamagumo*, (10th DD Div) *Akigumo*, *Kazegumo* and *Asagumo* (transferred to Rabaul), (16th DD Div) *Hatsukaze*, *Yukikaze* and *Amatsukaze*, (17th DD Div) *Urakaze*, *Isokaze*, *Tanikaze* and *Hamakaze* and (61st DD Div) *Akizuki*, *Sutsuki*, *Hatsutsuki* and *Wakatsuki* (transferred to Rabaul).

The carrier aircraft suffer heavy losses in the US carrier raids on Rabaul. They are withdrawn on 12 Nov.

20 Oct–20 Dec   West and South Atlantic

In operations in distant waters, *U516* (Lt-Cdr Tillessen) sinks six ships of 24745 tons in the Caribbean and escapes from a week-long search. *U218* lays mines off Trinidad on 27 Oct and sinks one sailing ship. Off the Brazilian coast, *U155* (Lt-Cdr Piening) and *U848* (Cdr Rollmann) each sink one ship, of 5393 tons and 4573 tons respectively. *U848* is sunk on 5 Nov by four Liberators of VB-107 USN and two Liberators of the 1st Composite Sqn USAAF from Ascension Island in a lengthy engagement. *U154* has no success. Off West Africa, *U68* (Lt-Cdr Markworth) sinks the A/S trawler *Orfasay* and three ships of 17116 tons. *U103* lays mines off Takoradi (28 Oct).

21 Oct   General Situation

The British First Sea Lord, Admiral of the Fleet Sir Dudley Pound, dies.

21 Oct   Western Atlantic

The Canadian minesweeper *Chedabucto* sinks in a collision with the SS *Lord Kelvin* in the St Lawrence river.

21 Oct   Mediterranean

After attacks against convoys E of Gibraltar which result in off-target torpedo detonations, *U431* (Lt Schöneboom) is sunk by Leigh Light Wellington 'Z' of No 179 Sqn.

22 Oct–18 Nov   Arctic

On 22 Oct the Soviet ice-breakers *Stalin* and *SKR-18/Fedor Litke* set out from Tiksi to return to the White Sea. On 26 Oct they are met in the Vilkitski Strait by the mine-layer *Murman* and the ice-breaker steamer *SKR-19/Semen Dezhnev* and brought via Dikson to the Kara Strait. There they are met by a strong escort force (Rear-Adm Kucherov) comprising the destroyers *Baku*, *Grozny*, *Gromki*, *Kuibyshev*, *Razumny* and *Razyarenny* as well as the newly arrived Lend-Lease minesweepers *T-112*, *T-113*, *T-114* and *T-115*. On the way from the Kara Strait (15 Nov) via Kolguev-North (16 Nov) into the Gorlo Strait (17 Nov), the escorts make many depth charge attacks on suspected U-boats and report two U-boats sunk and three more seriously damaged. In fact, no U-boat is in the vicinity of convoy AB.55. *U636* (Lt-Cdr Hildebrand), the last boat, lays mines off the Yugor Straits on 14 Nov and then quickly returns. The other U-boats at sea, *U387*, *U354*, *U360*, *U307* and *U277*, are stationed in the passage between Spitzbergen and Bear Island as the 'Eisenbart' group. The convoy is continually located by the German B-Service and is sighted but not attacked by a Ju 88 carrying out armed reconnaissance N of Kolguev.

23 Oct   English Channel

The German 4th TB Flotilla (Cdr Kohlauf), comprising *T23*, *T22*, *T25*, *T26* and *T27*, while providing a distant escort for a small convoy, encounters off the North Brittany coast the British cruiser *Charybdis* (Capt Voelcker), the destroyers *Grenville* and *Rocket* and the 'Hunt' destroyers *Limbourne*, *Wensleydale*, *Talybont* and *Stevenstone* which have set out from Plymouth on 22 Oct to intercept the blockade-runner *Münsterland*. *T23* (Lt-Cdr Weinlig) and *T27* (Cdr Verlohr) dispatch the cruiser with several torpedo hits and *T22* (Lt-Cdr Blöse) sinks the escort destroyer *Limbourne*.

23 Oct   Bay of Biscay

The German auxiliary minesweeper *M4451* sinks after running aground 20 nautical miles S of Ardour.

23 Oct   Mediterranean

The German minelayer *Juminda* (ex-Italian *E Gasperi*) is sunk two nautical miles W of San Stefano by British MTBs. The British minesweeper *Cromarty* sinks after striking a mine W of the Bonifacio Strait, Sardinia.

23 Oct–8 Nov   North Atlantic

On 23 Oct *U274*, which is on the way to the 'Siegfried' group, is sighted by Liberator 'Z' of No 224 Sqn RAF which is providing air escort for the convoy ON.207, which is accompanied by EG.C1 (Cdr Adams) with the destroyers *Assiniboine* and *Forester* (RN), the frigate *Ettrick* and the corvettes *Agassiz*, *Celandine* (RN) and *Galt*, supported by the 2nd SG. EG.B7 (Cdr Gretton), with the destroyers *Duncan* and *Vidette* and the corvettes *Loosestrife*, *Pink* and *Sunflower*, which is situated in the vicinity, is ordered to search for her and the destroyers *Duncan* and *Vidette* sink *U274* with 'Hedgehog'. From 24 Oct the 'Siegfried' group, comprising *U420*, *U405*, *U212*, *U91*, *U762*, *U231*, *U309*, *U608*, *U969*, *U267*, *U281*, *U413*, *U963*, *U437*, *U426*, *U842*, *U552*, *U592*, *U575*, *U226*, *U373*, *U709*, *U648* and *U967*, expects the convoy HX.262 (EG.C5 under Cdr. Pullen with the destroyers *Ottawa* and *Burnham* (RN) and the corvettes *Arvida*, *Dauphin* and *Wetaskiwin*), to whose escort has been added from ON.207 the 2nd SG (Capt Walker) with the sloops *Starling*, *Kite*, *Woodcock*, *Wild Goose* and *Magpie* and the escort carrier *Tracker*. *U413* takes several bearings with an intermediate-wave D/F on the talk of the escorts, but the boats do not come up on 25–26 Oct to the convoy, which goes round to the S of the patrol line. *U608* and *U212* are bombed and Liberator 'A' of No 10 Sqn RCAF from ON.207 sinks *U420*. The 'Siegfried' group is divided into three sections: *U967*, *U212*, *U405*, *U231*, *U608* and *U969* as section 1; *U267*, *U281*, *U413*, *U963*, *U437*, *U426*, *U552* and *U592* as section 2; and *U842*, *U575*, *U226*, *U373*, *U709* and *U648* as section 3. From 28 Oct they take up smaller patrol lines E of Newfoundland against the expected convoy SC.145 (32 ships escorted by EG.B6 (Cdr Currie with the destroyers *Fame* and *Vanquisher*, the frigate *Deveron* and the Norwegian corvettes *Eglantine*, *Potentilla* and *Rose*, supported by the 8th SG with the escort carrier *Fencer*, the destroyers *Inconstant* and the Polish *Garland* and *Burza*). *U714* transmits several wireless messages from the flank to make the convoy turn away into the formation. On 29 Oct *U405* and *U608* drive off Swordfish from *Fencer* with AA fire but the convoy passes by unnoticed. Further to the E, the approaching *U282* is located with radar by *Vidette*, which with EG.B7 has been ordered to support convoy ON.208 (EG.B3 under Cdr Evans with the frigate *Towy*, the destroyer *Keppel* and the corvettes *Narcissus*, *Orchis*, *Lobélia* (FFN), *Renoncule* (FFN) and *Roselys* (FFN)). She is sunk by the corvette *Sunflower* with 'Hedge-hog'. EG.B7 (leader *Duncan*) is detached from ON.208 to go to convoy HX.263 (4th EG under Lt-Cdr Chavasse with the DE frigates *Bentinck*, *Bazely*, *Blackwood*, *Burgess*, *Byard*, *Drury* and *Berry*). Against these convoys and ONS.21 (EG.C2 under Cdr Burnett with the destroyers *Gatineau* and *Icarus* and the corvettes *Drumheller*, *Fennel* and *Kamloops*), about which there is only indirect information, the Cdr U-boats forms on 31 Oct E of Newfoundland the groups 'Körner' (*U714*, *U212*, *U969*, *U231*, *U267*, *U281*, *U413*, *U963*, *U843*, *U586* and *U280*) and 'Jahn' (*U437*, *U426*, *U552*, *U842*, *U575*, *U226*, *U379*, *U709*, *U648* and *U608*). But only *U714* sights one aircraft on 1 Nov to the extreme N. The convoys go round the formations. The boats are there-fore divided into five sections 'Tirpitz 1–5', each of four to five boats, in order to find convoy HX.264 (EG.C1) expected from 5 Nov. Its escort is supported by the 2nd SG (Capt Walker). Aircraft from *Tracker* force *U967* to submerge on 5 Nov. In the evening *Kite* (Lt-Cdr Rysegrave) sights *U226*. Capt Walker destroys the boat on the next morning with *Woodcock* (Lt-Cdr Winner) and *Starling*. In the afternoon *Wild Goose* (Cdr Wemyss) locates *U842* and with *Star-ling* sinks her. The convoy passes undetected. On 7 Nov the operation has to be broken off since to proceed by day on the surface has become impossible because of the strong air escort. In the evening of 8 Nov the 2nd SG, which is returning to Argentia because of shortage of fuel, passes the patrol line 'Tirpitz 5' and *U648* (Lt Stahl) just misses *Tracker* (Cdr McGrath) with a FAT salvo of three and a sloop with a T-5.

24 Oct   North Atlantic
W of Spain, *U566* is sunk by Wellington 'A' of No 179 Sqn RAF with Leigh Light.

24 Oct   South Pacific
The Japanese destroyer *Mochizuki* is sunk in a USMC air attack 90 nautical miles SSW of Rabaul.

24–25 Oct   English Channel
Thirty-two German motor torpedo boats of the 2nd, 4th, 6th and 8th MTB Flotillas attack the British convoy FN.1160 off Cromer from Ijmuiden.
The convoy is escorted by the destroyers *Pytchley*, *Worcester*, *Eglinton*, *Campbell* and *Mackay*, the MGBs *MGB609*, *MGB610*, *MGB607*, *MGB603*, *MGB315* and *MGB327* and the MLs *ML250* and *ML517*. The German motor torpedo boats are reported by returning British bombers and the convoy is warned. The motor torpedo boats which approach in several groups are

driven off by *Pytchley*, *Worcester* and *Mackay*. Only *S74* (6th MTB Flotilla) is able to sink the trawler *William Stephen* which remains behind. *Mackay* rams and sinks *S63*. *MGB607* and *MGB603* encoun-ter boats of the withdrawing 4th MTB Flotilla and sink *S88* (Cdr Lützow†). In engagements with *MTB439* and *MTB442*, which also come up, the first is damaged.

25 Oct–9 Nov   North Atlantic
Attempt at a single night's short operation with support from air reconnaissance by the Air Cdr Atlantic, Lt-Gen Kessler. The convoy MKS.28 (39th EG under Cdr King with the sloops *Rochester*, *Hastings* and *Scarborough*, the frigate *Tavy*, the corvettes *Azalea*, *Balsam* and *Geranium*, the attached destroyers *Whitehall* and *Watchman* and the AA ship *Alynbank*), reported to have left Gibraltar on 23 Oct, is located by an Fw200 of III/KG 40 after it has joined SL.138 on 25 Oct. Then the 'Schill' group (*U306*, *U466*, *U262*, *U707*, *U333* and the AA U-boats *U211*, *U953* and *U441*) is formed by the Cdr U-boats on what is thought to be the probable night route of the convoy on 29–30 Oct. The Fw 200s report the convoy on 27 and 28 Nov: it has 56 ships and seven escorts. On the decisive 29 Oct the four Fw 200s deployed fly past to the N and do not find the convoy. Not before mid-day on 30 Oct does a large Bv 222 flying boat of 1(F)/SAGr 129 locate the convoy which now consists of 60 ships. Towards morning on 31 Oct the convoy passes the patrol line. *U262* (Lt Franke) sinks in an underwater attack one ship of 2968 tons; *U333* (Lt-Cdr Cremer) misses one escort vessel with a T-5; *U441* is damaged; and *U306*, after being located by HF/DF, is sunk by the destroyer *Whitehall* and the corvette *Geranium*. Because of the strong air escort, the oper-ation is broken off and the remaining boats are ordered to form a new patrol line. On 1 Nov *U953* sights an MKF convoy which is too fast for an attack. The air reconnaissance provided on 2 Nov for the expected KMS.31 has no success. On 3 Nov *U333* sights a landing ship convoy and misses an escorting destroyer with a T-5. After unsuccessful air reconnaissance on 3, 4 and 5 Nov, an Fw 200 sights on 7 Nov the convoy MKS.29A (EG.B4) but it is not found again on 8 Nov. During the night 8–9 Nov it runs into the patrol line. *U262* transmits the first report; *U466* misses a destroyer with a T-5 and is damaged by depth charges; *U707* is sunk by Fortress 'J' of No 220 Sqn RAF from the Azores which is part of the air escort pro-vided in the morning; and *U262* and *U228* miss a destroyer and straggler respectively. Although the Fw 200s report the convoy on

two more occasions, *U211*, *U333* and *U358* do not come up.

27–29 Oct   Arctic
The 'Katharina' mining operation off the Soviet Arctic coast with the destroyers *Z30*, *Z31* and *Z33* is cancelled following reports about an Allied naval force in the Barents Sea.

27 Oct–6 Nov   South Pacific
As a diversion for the imminent operation against Bougainville, 6300 men of the 8th New Zealand Bde (Brig Row) are landed on the islands of Mono and Stirling in the Treasury Archipelago, which are occupied until 6 Nov.
The 2nd US Marine Parachute Bn (Lt-Col Krulak) lands with 725 men from APDs on Choiseul but is re-embarked on 4 Nov after the failure of the diversionary exercise.
In an attack by Japanese aircraft, 12 out of 25 are shot down by the US fighter cover. The destroyer *Cony* is slightly damaged.

31 Oct   Denmark
The fishery protection vessel *Heimdal*, cap-tured and used by the Germans, is sabotaged by the Danish Resistance in Copenhagen harbour.

31 Oct   Gibraltar
The German *U732*, on its transfer cruise to the Mediterranean, is sunk off Gibraltar by the destroyer *Douglas* and the trawlers *Imperialist* and *Loch Osaig*.

31 Oct–5 Nov   North Sea/English Channel
Transfer of the German destroyers *Z27* and *ZH1* (ex-Dutch *Gerard Callenburgh*) from the German Bight, with stops at Rotterdam (2 Nov), Dunkirk (3 Nov; near-misses from British coastal batteries, with action against British MTBs the next day) and Le Havre (4 Nov), to the Gironde (5 Nov).

Nov   Intelligence
The Allies introduce the 'Combined Cypher Machine' (CCM) to service aboard war-ships.
The US intelligence organisation Op 20G takes over the decoding of the German U-boat 'Triton'/'Shark' cypher, using mass-produced 'high speed bombs'.

1 Nov   North Atlantic
During its transfer to the Mediterranean, *U340* is damaged W of Gibraltar by Wel-lington 'R' of No 179 Sqn RAF and sustains further damage from depth charge attacks by the destroyers *Active* and *Witherington* and the sloop *Fleetwood*. The CO, Lt Klaus, has to scuttle *U340* near a Spanish fishing vessel which rescues the crew, but *Fleetwood* takes the latter off into captivity.

1–13 Nov   South Pacific
The US III Amphibious Force (TF.31, Rear-Adm Wilkinson) lands 14321 men of

the 3rd Maine Div (Maj-Gen Turnage) at Cape Torokina from eight troop and four supply transports. Escort is provided by Desron 45 (Cdr Earle), comprising *Fullam, Guest, Bennett, Hudson, Anthony, Wadsworth, Terry, Braine, Conway, Sigourney* and *Renshaw*, together with four destroyer minesweepers and four large and four small minesweepers. The landing takes place without any resistance. The covering force (TF.39, Rear-Adm Merrill), with the 12th Cruiser Div, consisting of *Montpelier, Cleveland, Columbia* and *Denver*, and Desron 23 (Capt Burke), comprising *Charles F Ausburne, Dyson, Stanly, Claxton, Spence, Thatcher, Converse* and *Foote*, shells the Japanese air base at Buka on 1 Nov. Towards evening a force consisting of *Renshaw* and the minelayer destroyers *Breese, Gamble* and *Sicard* lays a mine barrage to protect the landing area to the NW. After unsuccessful air attacks from Rabaul, the Cdr of the Japanese 8th Fleet (Adm Samejima) commits the available ships to attack the US invasion fleet on 1 Nov.

Battle of Empress Augusta Bay. During the night 1–2 Nov the Japanese 5th Cruiser Sqn (Rear-Adm Omori), with the heavy cruisers *Myoko* and *Haguro*, the light cruiser *Sendai* (Rear-Adm Ijuin) with the destroyers *Shigure, Samidare* and *Shiratsuyu* and the cruiser *Agano* (Rear-Adm Osugi) with the destroyers *Naganami, Hatsukaze* and *Wakatsuki*, encounters TF.39. In avoiding a torpedo attack by US destroyers, *Samidare* and *Shiratsuyu* collide but escape. The cruiser *Sendai* sinks in the radar-controlled fire of the US cruisers. *Hatsukaze*, damaged in a collision with *Myoko*, is later sunk by the US destroyers. On the American side, *Foote* is hit by a torpedo fired by the *Sendai* force but is taken in tow, *Denver* and *Spence* are hit by gunfire and *Thatcher* is damaged in a collision with *Spence*. The remaining Japanese cruisers suffer minor damage from gunfire. On the return, the US force is attacked by Japanese carrier aircraft flown off from Rabaul, but only the *Montpelier* is hit by bombs. Rear-Adm Omori is relieved of his command for failing to carry out his mission.

From the area W of the Solomons, TF.38 (Rear-Adm Sherman) conducts carrier raids on the Japanese airfields at Buna and Buka on 1 and 2 Nov with the carriers *Saratoga* and *Princeton*, the AA cruisers *San Diego* and *San Juan* and the destroyers *Farenholt, Lardner, Woodworth, Buchanan, Lansdowne, Grayson, Sterett, Stack, Wilson* and *Edwards*.

On 3 Nov the Japanese 2nd Fleet (Vice-Adm Kurita) and elements of the 3rd Fleet set out from Truk for Rabaul: the 4th Cruiser Sqn, comprising the cruisers *Atago, Takao, Maya* and *Chokai* (which returns on 4 Nov with two destroyers as escort for a damaged tanker); the 7th Cruiser Sqn, comprising the cruisers *Suzuya, Kumano* and *Mogami*; the 8th Cruiser Sqn, comprising the cruisers *Chikuma* and *Tone*; and eight to twelve destroyers of the 2nd and 10th DD Flotillas with the cruiser *Noshiro*. They are sighted on 4 Nov N of the Bismarck Archipelago by US Liberator bombers of the US 5th AF. Against this force, *Saratoga* and *Princeton* fly off a group of 22 dive-bombers, 23 torpedo aircraft and 52 fighters after it comes into Rabaul. The Americans lose 10 aircraft but the heavy cruisers *Maya, Atago, Takao* and *Mogami* and the light cruisers *Agano, Noshiro* and the destroyer *Wakatsuki* are badly damaged, the destroyer *Fujinami* is hit by an unexploded air torpedo and the minesweeper *W-26* is damaged beyond repair. After the carrier raid, 27 Liberators, protected by 67 Lightnings, bomb the town and harbour of Rabaul. In the same evening the damaged Japanese cruisers *Atago, Chikuma, Kumano, Mogami, Suzuya* and *Tone* with five to six destroyers start the return to Truk, where they arrive on 7 Nov. During the night 6–7 Nov Japanese destroyers and one cruiser land a total of 1175 reinforcement troops near Cape Torokina and Buka. During the night 8–9 Nov a US transport force arrives with the second wave (37th Inf Div) off Cape Torokina. Twenty-six dive-bombers and 71 fighters from the air groups of the Japanese carriers moved from Rabaul and twin-engined torpedo aircraft of the 11th Air Fleet stationed there attack the transports on 8–9 Nov but only *President Jackson* is damaged. A second attack is directed against the covering force (Rear-Adm Du Bose), comprising the US cruisers *Santa Fé, Mobile* and *Birmingham* and four destroyers. *Birmingham* is damaged by torpedo and bomb hits.

To knock out the Japanese sea and air forces in Rabaul, TF.38 (see above) mounts a further carrier raid on Rabaul on 11 Nov but because of poor visibility this has little effect. A short while later the aircraft of TG.50.3 (Rear-Adm Montgomery), comprising the carriers *Essex, Bunker Hill* and *Independence*, escorted by the destroyers *Sterett, Bullard, Murray, McKee, Stack, Wilson, Edwards, Kidd* and *Chauncey*, attack from the E. They torpedo *Agano* and the destroyer *Naganami* and sink the destroyer *Suzunami*; the light cruiser *Yubari* and the destroyers *Urakaze* and *Umikaze* are slightly damaged by near-misses. Sixty-seven Japanese Navy fighters, 27 dive-bombers and 14 torpedo aircraft take off from Rabaul but these are intercepted by the fighter escort of TG.50.3 and lose 33 of their number to the fighters and AA fire without registering a hit.

During the night 12–13 Nov the third wave (21st Marines and elements of the 37th Inf Div) of US transports arrives off Cape Torokina. Cover is provided by TF.39, which is attacked at first light by several twin-engined aircraft. The cruiser *Denver* receives a torpedo hit.

On the Japanese side, the successes of the four 'sea and air battles of Bougainville' are greatly exaggerated: the pilots report the sinking of five battleships, 10 carriers, 19 cruisers, seven destroyers and nine transports as well as the damaging of 24 more ships. But of the 173 Japanese carrier aircraft committed, 121 are lost, so that, for the time being, the Japanese carrier air force ceases to be operational.

1–30 Nov   Pacific

In Japanese waters, the US submarines *Trigger* (Lt-Cdr Dornin) sinks three ships of 13262 tons, *Snapper* (Lt-Cdr Clemenson) sinks one ship of 4575 tons and *Dace* has prematures or duds. In Chinese/Formosan waters, *Sargo* (Lt-Cdr Garnett) sinks two ships of 6419 tons and *Gudgeon* (Lt-Cdr Port) sinks one ship of 6783 tons and, on 23 Nov 70 nautical miles S of Shushan, the frigate *Wakamiya*. In the Central Pacific, the submarines are distributed for Operation 'Galvanic'. Off Truk there are *Thresher* (Lt-Cdr Hull), which sinks one ship of 4872 tons, *Apogon* (Lt-Cdr Schoeni), which sinks one ship of 2962 tons and *Corvina*, which is sunk on 16 Nov by the Japanese submarine *I-179*; and E of Truk are *Sculpin* (on board Capt Cromwell†), which is sunk on 29 Nov off Truk by a Japanese destroyer, and *Searaven* (Lt-Cdr Dry), which sinks one ship of 10050 tons. There are reconnaissance positions off Kwajalein with *Seal*, off Jaluit with *Spearfish*, off Wotje with *Plunger*, off Nauru with *Paddle* and off the Gilberts with *Nautilus*. In addition, offensive patrols are undertaken, in which *Tautog* (Lt-Cdr Sieglaff) sinks the submarine-chaser *Ch-30*, *Scamp* (Lt-Cdr Ebert) sinks one ship of 6481 tons and torpedoes the cruiser *Agano*, *Drum* (Lt-Cdr McMahon) sinks two ships of 14349 tons, *Scorpion* (Lt-Cdr Wylie) torpedoes one ship of 14050 tons, *Blackfish* (Lt-Cdr Davidson) sinks one ship of 439 tons, *Albacore* (Lt-Cdr Hagberg) sinks one ship of 4704 tons, *Ray* (Lt-Cdr Harrell) sinks one ship of 2562 tons, *Raton* (Lt-Cdr Davis) sinks four ships of 21611 tons and *Gato* (Lt-Cdr Foley) sinks two ships of 8543 tons. A 'wolfpack' is formed under Cdr Warder with *Harder* (Lt-Cdr Dealey), which sinks three ships of 15270 tons and damages the submarine-chaser *Ch-20*, *Pargo* (Lt-Cdr Eddy), which sinks two ships of 7807 tons, and *Snook* (Lt-Cdr Triebel), which sinks three ships of 14314 tons.

In the South West Pacific, *Narwhal* conducts a guerrilla support mission, *Bluefish* (Lt-Cdr Porter) sinks the torpedo boat *Sanae* on 18 Nov, one ship of 10570 tons and one sailing vessel and damages one ship of 14050 tons, *Bowfin* (Lt-Cdr Griffith) sinks five ships of 26431 tons and four sailing vessels, *Crevalle* (Lt-Cdr Munson) sinks one ship of 6783 tons, *Capelin* (Lt-Cdr Marshall) sinks two ships of 5968 tons (but is lost to an A/S attack off Halmahera on 23 Nov), *Tuna* (Lt-Cdr Hardin) torpedoes one ship of 5484 tons, *Bonefish* (Lt-Cdr Hogan) sinks two ships of 7366 tons and *Cod* and *Billfish* have prematures.

In the Malacca Strait, the British *Tally Ho* (Cdr Bennington) sinks one ship of 1914 tons.

1 Nov–11 Dec   Black Sea

After an attempt to land near Cape Illy on 21 Oct has been repulsed, light forces of the Azov Flotilla (Rear-Adm Gorshkov) land elements of the 56th Soviet Army near Enikale on 1 Nov (which until 11 Nov advance to the edge of Kerch) and forces of the Novorossisk base (Rear-Adm Kholostyakov) land the 386th Naval Inf Bn near Eltigen. They are followed in the next few days by elements of the 18th Army. The bridgehead of Eltigen is blockaded by German motor minesweepers, naval ferry barges and motor torpedo boats under the Cdr of the 3rd MMS Flotilla (Lt-Cdr Klassmann). Thirty-one naval ferry barges, six motor minesweepers and five motor torpedo boats take part in 355 operations over 29 days. *F419*, *F380*, *F594*, *F306*, *F341*, *F571*, *F574*, *F573*, *F360*, *F305* and *F369* are lost on mines and, principally, in air attacks. One motor torpedo boat, four motor minesweepers and 16 naval ferry barges are damaged. On the Soviet side, in the landings and attempts to bring supplies, 12 patrol cutters, including *SKA-0192*, *SKA-0135*, *SKA-0178*, *SKA-0158*, *SKA-0105* and *SKA-0114*, the motor minesweepers *KT-173*, *KT-411*, *KT-509*, the armoured cutter *BKA-132* and approximately 150 assault boats and 40 other small craft are lost. From 4 to 11 Dec the bridgehead is compressed: 2827 prisoners are taken and about 800 troops escape to the N. About 10000 dead are counted in the Eltigen area. *SKA-01012* and *TKA-101* are sunk by the 1st MTB Flotilla.

1 Nov–9 Dec   Arctic

Resumption of the Murmansk convoys. On 28 Oct an escort group (Capt Campbell) arrives in the Kola Inlet from Scapa Flow, consisting of the destroyer *Milne* and seven more fleet destroyers, one destroyer-escort, two minesweepers (including *Harrier* with Capt Jay) and one corvette, as well as five Lend-Lease minesweepers (*T-111* to *T-115*) and six submarine-chasers (*Bo-201*, *Bo-204*, and *Bo-208* to *Bo-211*) for the Soviet Northern Fleet. The escort group sets out on 1 Nov with the convoy RA.54A (13 ships) from Archangel for Loch Ewe, where it arrives on 14 Nov without having been located by German air reconnaissance. On 15 Nov the convoy JW.54A (18 ships, the Soviet minesweepers *T-116* and *T-117* and the submarine-chasers *Bo-206*, *Bo-207* and *Bo-212*, with an escort group of eight British destroyers, one minesweeper and two corvettes) puts to sea from Loch Ewe and, only detected by the German B-Service, reaches the Kola Inlet on 24 Nov, from where some of the ships proceed with Soviet escort to Archangel. A second convoy, JW.54B (14 ships, one rescue ship, an escort group of nine destroyers, three corvettes and one minesweeper), follows unobserved from 22 Nov to 2 Dec. Four Soviet destroyers meet it off the Kola coast. On 26 Nov RA.54B (nine ships and the escort group from JW.54A) leaves Archangel. Of the German U-boat group, 'Eisenbart', which has meanwhile been reinforced (*U360*, *U713*, *U387*, *U354*, *U277*, *U307* and *U636*), only *U307* sights escort vessels briefly on 28 Nov. But she is immediately attacked with depth charges and damaged. The convoy reaches Loch Ewe on 9 Dec without loss.

To cover the operations, Vice-Adm Palliser with the British cruisers *Kent*, *Jamaica* and *Bermuda* operates in the vicinity of the convoy in the Barents Sea. Vice-Adm Moore forms the distant covering force with the battleship *Anson*, the US cruiser *Tuscaloosa* and destroyers. Allied submarines of the British 9th SM Flotilla take up covering positions off north-west Norway. The Soviet submarines *L-15* and *L-20* lay mines in the German exit routes (cleared) and *L-15* attacks a German minelaying force and two submarines-chasers unsuccessfully on 22 and 24 Nov. The Soviet submarines *M-119* and *M-200* operate off the Varanger peninsula. Off western Norway, the Norwegian submarine *Ula* (Lt Sears) sinks two ships of 2579 tons.

2 Nov   North Sea

The British fast motor transport *Master Standfast*/*MGB508* is captured off Lysekil

by the German patrol trawler *V1606*. She is later commissioned as the German MMS *RA11*.

2–3 Nov   English Channel

The German 5th MTB Flotilla (Cdr Klug), comprising *S143*, *S100*, *S112*, *S136*, *S138*, *S139*, *S140*, *S141* and *S142*, attacks the British convoy CW.221 off Hastings in the first torpedo attack since Aug 1941 in the eastern part of the Channel. *S146* sinks the freighter *Dona Isabel* (1179 tons) and *S100* and *S138* the freighters *Foam Queen* (811 tons) and *Storaa* (1967 tons). There are engagements with the British destroyer *Whitshed* and *MGB41*, *MGB42*, *ML141*, *ML230*, *ML293* and *ML464*.

3 Nov   Mediterranean

The German A/S trawler *UJ2206* is sunk in San Stefano Port by US PT boats.

3 Nov   Air War/Germany

The US 8th AF attacks Wilhemshaven with about 400 B-17s with strong fighter protection. Seven bombers are shot down.

4 Nov   Baltic

The German minesweeper *M16* is heavily damaged in a Soviet air raid on Kotka; towed to Kiel, the ship is not repaired.

4–5 Nov   English Channel/North Sea

The German 2nd (Cdr Feldt), 6th (Cdr Obermaier) and 8th (Cdr Zymalkowski) MTB Flotillas carry out with 18 boats a mining operation off Smith's Knoll and in the Humber Estuary (*S116* and *S114* have to return because of engine trouble). The 2nd MTB Flotilla drops 48, the 6th 38 and the 8th 16 mines. The 4th MTB Flotilla (Lt-Cdr Causemann), which set out with four boats, breaks off the operation because of a leak on *S48*. The 1st group of the 2nd MTB Flotilla encounters the convoy FN.1170 E of Cromer and torpedoes two ships of 7422 tons from it. The 2nd group of the 6th MTB Flotilla is attacked on the return by British aircraft and has to abandon *S74* which, after severe damage, is sunk by a torpedo from *S135*. *S61* and *S116* are damaged but are able to get away. German fighter cover is not available.

5 Nov   Mediterranean

The British and Greek destroyers *Aldenham* and *Miaoulis* bombard Kos.

5–15 Nov   South Pacific

TF.74, consisting of the Australian cruisers *Australia* and *Shropshire* and the destroyers *Ralph Talbot* and *Helm* (US) and *Arunta* and *Warramunga* (Australian), is temporarily transferred from Milne Bay to the New Hebrides to reinforce the South Pacific Forces.

6 Nov   Mediterranean
Thirty-five torpedo aircraft of KG 26 (Maj Klümper) attack the Allied convoy KMF.25A in the area E of Algiers and sink the US destroyer *Beatty* and the troop transports *Santa Elena* (9135 tons) and *Marnix van St Aldegonde* (19355 tons). The convoy is escorted by the British AA cruiser *Colombo*, 11 US destroyers (three of them radar pickets) and three British and two Greek 'Hunt' destroyers.

7 Nov   Mediterranean
The German A/S trawler *UJ2145* is sunk by an Allied submarine in the Aegean.

8 Nov   Mediterranean
The British destroyers *Grenville*, *Tumult* and *Tyrian* and the Polish *Piorun* bombard positions in the Gulf of Gaeta in support of the 5th US Army.

10–12 Nov   Bay of Biscay
The returning *U966* is heavily damaged in attacks by Wellington 'B' of No 612 Sqn RAF and Liberators 'E' of VPB-103 USN, 'E' of VPB-110 USN and 'D' of No 311 (Czech) Sqn and has to be beached and blown up near De Santafata Bay on the Spanish north coast. The outbound *U508* is sunk by Liberator 'C' of VPB-103 USN which is, however, shot down.

10–19 Nov   Central Pacific
Preparations for Operation 'Galvanic'. The 'Northern Attack Force' (TF.52) sets out from Pearl Harbor on 10 Nov and the 'Southern Attack Force' (TF.53) from the New Hebrides on 13 Nov. On 15 Nov they replenish halfway between Baker and Canton and near Funafuti respectively and they join up on 17 Nov halfway between Baker and Nanomea to proceed together. From TF.50 (fast carriers), TG.50.1 and 50.2 set out from Pearl Harbor and TG.50.3 and 50.4 from Espiritu Santo.

10–24 Nov   Mediterranean
Battle for Leros and Samos (Dodecanese). During the night 10–11 Nov the British destroyers *Petard* and *Rockwood* and the Polish *Krakowiak* shell Calino and *Faulknor* shells Coo. In the morning of 11 Nov *Rockwood* is severely damaged by an Hs 293 glider bomb in an attack by 5/KG 100. On 12 Nov the German battle group 'Müller' (the 22nd Inf Div, Lt-Gen Müller). It is transported on steamers, coastal craft and ferry barges. Escort is provided by the 9th TB Flotilla (Cdr Riede), comprising *TA15*, *TA14*, *TA17* and *TA19*, the motor torpedo boat *S55*, the 21st SC Flotilla (Cdr Dr Brandt) with five to six large and eight to ten small boats and the 12th MMS Flotilla (Lt-Cdr Mallmann and Lt Weissenborn) with ten to twelve motor minesweepers. Air

support is provided by FK X, which uses 206 aircraft on the first day. During the nights 12–13 and 13–14 Nov two British destroyer forces, consisting of *Faulknor*, *Beaufort* and *Pindos* (Greek) and *Dulverton*, *Echo* and *Belvoir* respectively, search unsuccessfully for the German transport ships. The *Faulknor* group shells targets on Leros twice. On 13 Nov Do 217s of 5/KG 100 attack the second group with Hs 293 glider bombs and sink the *Dulverton*. On 14 Nov *Echo* and *Belvoir* try to bring troop reinforcements from Samos to Leros. During the night 14–15 Nov a new British destroyer group, consisting of *Penn*, *Aldenham* and *Blencathra*, shells Leros. From 15 to 16 Nov the German torpedo boats *TA15*, *TA14* and *TA16* bring troops from Piraeus to Calino. During the night 15–16 Nov the Allied destroyers *Fury*, *Exmoor* and *Krakowiak* shell Leros and during the night 16–17 Nov *Penn* and *Aldenham* shell Coo and *Exmoor* and *Krakowiak* Samos. After heavy fighting the British commander on Leros surrenders with 3200 British and 5350 Italian troops. On 17 Nov *TA15* arrives in Leros with supplies and on 19 Nov *TA15* comes again with *TA14* and *TA19*. While the larger British ships have to leave the Aegean, light German units occupy the islands of Lisso, Patmos, Furni and Ikera on 18 Nov; 310 Italian troops are taken prisoner.
On 22 Nov the garrison of Samos capitulates after the attack by Ju 87s of II/StG 3 on the town of Tigani. After a show of strength round the island, the torpedo boats *TA15* and *TA19*, with boats of the 21st SC Flotilla, enter Vathi Bay on 23 Nov and land troops: 2500 Italian soldiers are disarmed. With that the reconquest of the Dodecanese Islands is completed.

11 Nov   Mediterranean
Sixteen Do 217s of II/KG 100, 23 He 111s of I/KG 26 and 17 Ju 88s of III/KG 26 are used against the Allied convoy KMS.31. Forty-eight aircraft attack NE of Oran and sink the transports *Birchbank* (5151 tons), *Indian Prince* (8587 tons) and *Carlier* (7217 tons). The French tanker *Nivose* (4763 tons), which is also torpedoed, sinks after a collision. Seven aircraft are lost.

11–15 Nov   North Atlantic
The boats of the 'Eisenbart' group, which are loosely stationed in groups of three E of Newfoundland (*U538*, *U391*, *U542*, *U843*, *U714*, *U424*, *U764*, *U280*, *U969*, *U212*, *U967*, *U575*, *U709*, *U282*, *U963*, *U552*, *U586*, and *U648* and *U343*), wait in vain on 11 Nov for convoy HX.264 (EG.C2) and on 14 Nov for SC.146 (EG.B3). Only *U592* sights on the return a detached convoy

group, but her attack fails. On 15 Nov the boats are ordered to withdraw eastwards. On 16 Nov *U969* and *U542* sight escorts of convoy HX.265 and *U280* is sunk by Liberator 'M' of No 86 Sqn RAF belonging to the air escort. Convoy operations by the U-boats are broken off in the Western Atlantic. The remaining 'Eisenbart' boats try to operate against convoys on the eastern side of the Atlantic in brief sorties by night and with support from air reconnaissance. This is because U-boats, on account of the enemy's air superiority, are no longer able to close up to a located convoy over great distances and only have a chance of firing their torpedoes if they are overrun by the convoy.

12 Nov   General Situation
Churchill leaves Plymouth on board the battlecruiser *Renown* in order to attend the Cairo conference ('Sextant') with Roosevelt and Chiang Kai-shek.

12 Nov–27 Dec   Black Sea
Of the German *U20*, *U18*, *U19* and *U9* deployed off the Caucasian coast, only *U18* (Lt Fleige) sinks one ship. The Soviet submarine *M-111* (Capt 3rd Class Josseliani) sinks the steamer *Theoderich* (3409 tons) near Burnas on 12 Nov, *M-117* (Lt-Cdr Kesaev) sinks *F592* from a naval ferry barge convoy on 15 Nov and *D-4* (Lt-Cdr Trofimov) sinks the steamer *Santa Fé* (4627 tons), which is escorted by the Rumanian minelayer *Amiral Murgescu*, the destroyer *Marasesti* and the German motor minesweepers *R165*, *R197* and *R209*, on 23 Nov. W of the Crimea, *L-6* (Lt-Cdr Gremyako) sinks the tanker *Wolga-Don* (965 tons), which is escorted by the Rumanian gunboats *Stihi* and *Dumitrescu* and the German *UJ2301*, *UJ2309* and *R205*, on 25 Nov. After the sinking of *F566* from a naval ferry barge convoy on 2 Dec, *D-4* is sunk on 4 Dec by the German submarine-chasers *UJ103* and *UJ102* with depth charges. Off the Rumanian coast, *S-31* (Capt 3rd Class Belorukov) sinks *F580* on 9 Dec. One or two unsuccessful attacks on convoys are made in Dec by *Shch-201*, *Shch-216*, *S-33* and *M-117*. In the process some of them are attacked with depth charges by the submarine-chasers of the 1st and 23rd SC Flotillas and damaged.

13 Nov   Mediterranean
Units of the German 71st Inf Div, embarked on the transport *Ramb III*, three Siebel ferries and many small craft, land on the Adriatic islands of Krk, Cherso and Lussino. Escort is provided by the old cruiser *Niobe*, the torpedo boat *TA21*, the coastal defence boat *Najade* and seaplanes. Several coastal sailing ships are captured.

13–21 Nov North Atlantic

On 13 Nov agents report the departure of convoy MKS.30 from Gibraltar. It joins SL.139 on 14 Nov and then consists of 66 steamers and the 40th EG (Cdr Legassick) with the frigates *Exe* and *Moyola*, the sloops *Kistna* (RIN) and *Milford*, the corvettes *Clarkia* and *Petunia* and the AMC *Ranpura*. On 15 Nov a Ju 290 of FAGr 5 (Maj H Fischer) transmits a precise report of the strength and course of the convoy, which is found again early on 16 Nov by a Bv 222 of 1 (F) SAGr 129. A patrol line, 'Schill 1', comprising *U262*, *U228*, *U515*, *U358*, *U333*, *U211* and *U600*, is formed for the night 18–19 Nov in the area of Lisbon and then, after numerous reports from the Air Cdr Atlantic on 17 and 18 Nov, moved. The 7th SG (Cdr Durnford-Slater, now SOE) with the sloops *Chanticleer*, *Crane* and *Pheasant* (F) and the DE frigates *Essington*, *Foley* and *Garlies*) is added to the escort during the afternoon of 18 Nov. In the afternoon of 18 Nov *U333* (Lt-Cdr Cremer) is attacked several times with depth charges by *Exe* and rammed, but she gets away. *U515* (Lt-Cdr Henke) is attacked by the sloops *Chanticleer* and *Crane* before she can send her contact report. She fires two T-5s; one of them hits *Chanticleer*, which is towed in a damaged state to the Azores. *U515* is shadowed by *Crane* for nearly 10hr. During the night Wellington 'F' of No 179 Sqn RAF from Gibraltar, equipped with radar and Leigh Light, locates *U211* and sinks the surprised AA U-boat. In the course of 19 Nov the 5th SG (Cdr Birch), with the British frigates *Nene* and *Tweed*, the Canadian corvettes *Calgary*, *Snowberry*, *Edmundston*, *Camrose* and *Lunenburg* and a little later the British destroyers *Winchelsea* and *Watchman* from Gibraltar, join the convoy. Fw 200s of III/KG 40 repeatedly keep contact and send bearings for the 'Schill 2' group (*U608*, *U709*, *U969*, *U343*, *U586*, *U648*, *U238*, *U86* and *U536*) formed for the night of 20 Nov. The bearings are received by five boats. At midnight *U238* (Lt Hepp) is overrun by the convoy and fires T-5s against one escort vessel; they explode in the wash of the ship. *Calgary* and *Snowberry* attack the boat with depth charges; two hours later, together with *Nene*, they force *U536* to surface and destroy her with gunfire. On 20 Nov the air reconnaissance fails, because RAF Mosquitos and Beaufighters shoot down one Fw 200 and one Ju 290 near Cape Ortegal and the radar sets of the other two machines do not work. Aircraft from Cornwall take over the air escort of the convoy and they force the seven boats of the 'Schill 3' group, earmarked for the attack

during the night 20–21 Nov, to submerge. *U618* (Lt-Cdr Baberg) and *U648* (Lt Stahl) shoot down a Sunderland of No 422 Sqn RCAF and a Liberator of No 53 Sqn RAF respectively. During the night 20–21 Nov the convoy passes the patrol line and early on 21 Nov the 4th SG, with the DE frigates *Bentinck*, *Bazely*, *Blackwood*, *Byard*, *Berry* and *Drury* and, a little later, the AA cruiser (AMC) *Prince Robert*, joins the convoy. *Essington* attacks *U967* with depth charges; *Foley* and *Crane* of the escort group sink *U538*. The U-boats no longer come up. The Air Cdr Atlantic (Lt-Gen Kessler) deploys II/KG 40 (Maj Mons) with a total of 25 long-range He 177 bombers over an area of 1400km² against the convoy, which is again located by air reconnaissance on 21 Nov. Twenty reach the target; three are shot down and two turn back. They drop 40 Hs 293 glider bombs which sink the frieghter *Marsa* (4405 tons) and damage *Delius* (6055 tons). Greater successes are thwarted by the escorts' AA fire.

14 Nov Technology

The first experimental Walter U-boat *U794* (Type Wk 202) enters service at Kiel. On 16 Nov *U792* (Type Wa 201) follows in Hamburg. Speed underwater: 26kt.

15 Nov Black Sea

The German A/S vessel *UJ102/KT40* is sunk off Eupatoriya while blowing up the wreck of a munitions transport with depth charges.

15 Nov Air War/East Asia

US bombers attack harbour installations in Hong Kong.

15 Nov–27 Dec Mediterranean

The British destroyer *Quail* and the minesweeper *Hebe* are lost on the mine barrages laid by *U453* (Lt-Cdr Frhr v Schlippenbach) off Brindisi and Bari (25 Oct, 12 Nov and 28 Nov). *U565* probably sinks the British submarine *Simoom* on 19 Nov off Kos.

In attacks in the Gulf of Taranto, *U81* (Lt Krieg) sinks one ship of 2887 tons on 18 Nov and *U596* (Lt Nonn) one of 8009 tons from the convoy HA.11 on 9 Nov. On 28 Nov *U407* (Lt Brüller) torpedoes the British cruiser *Birmingham* off Cyrenaica.

In operations against Allied convoys off the Algerian coast, *U223*, *U73* and *U616* miss their targets on 4, 7, 8 and 9 Dec, likewise *U380* on 23 and 27 Dec. From the escort of convoy KMS.34, *U223* (Lt-Cdr Wächter) torpedoes the British frigate *Cuckmere* (she is thought not worth repairing) with a T-5 on 11 Dec. Early the next day *U593* (Lt-Cdr Kelbling) sinks the British destroyer *Tynedale*. In the course of a 32 hr search by the US destroyers *Niblack*, *Wainwright* and *Benson* and the British *Calpe* and *Holcombe*, she sinks the last and damages one bomber

with AA fire before she herself is sunk. *U73* (Lt Deckert) is sunk in a similar search by the US destroyers *Niblack*, *Ludlow*, *Woolsey*, *Trippe* and *Edison* on 16 Dec after she has torpedoed a steamer of 7176 tons.

15 Nov–30 Dec Black Sea

Re-transfer of the Soviet submarine *M32* from the Caspian Flotilla to the Black Sea Fleet.

16 Nov North Pacific

The Japanese minelayer *Ukishima* is lost (cause unknown) SE of Hatsushima.

17 Nov South Pacific

The US fast transport *McKean* is sunk by a torpedo from Japanese aircraft off Empress Augusta Bay (Bougainville). The survivors are rescued by the destroyer *Sigourney* and the fast transport *Talbot*.

17–18 Nov Mediterranean

The German 11th MMS Flotilla (Lt-Cdr Freytag) with six motor minesweepers lays the 'Notung' barrage in the Ligurian Sea.

18–20 Nov Baltic

The German *U718* sinks after colliding with *U476* during exercises 20 nautical miles NE of Bornholm on 18 Nov. On 20 Nov, in another collision in the Bay of Danzig, *U768* is lost.

18 Nov–5 Dec Air War/Western Europe

RAF Bomber Command mine offensive. In nine nights, 250 sorties are flown against the Biscay coast (especially Brest) and the Brittany, Dutch and Frisian coasts. Two aircraft are lost.

On 11 Dec the patrol trawler *V602* is lost on a mine off the Charente estuary.

19–28 Nov Central Pacific

Operation 'Galvanic': US landing (Adm Spruance) on the Gilbert Islands. To prepare and isolate the landing area, TF.50 (Rear-Adm Pownall) makes carrier raids on 19 Nov. TG.50.1 (Pownall), with the carriers *Yorktown*, *Lexington* and *Cowpens*, the battleships *South Dakota* and *Washington* and the destroyers *Nicholas*, *Taylor*, *La Valette*, *Izard*, *Charrette* and *Conner*, attacks Mili; TG.50.2 (Rear-Adm Radford), with the carriers *Enterprise*, *Belleau Wood* and *Monterey*, the battleships *Massachusetts*, *North Carolina* and *Indiana* and the destroyers *Boyd*, *Bradford*, *Brown*, *Fletcher*, *Radford* and *Jenkins*, attacks Makin; TG.50.3 (Rear-Adm Montgomery), with the carriers *Essex*, *Bunker Hill* and *Independence*, the cruisers *Chester*, *Pensacola*, *Salt Lake City* and *Oakland* and the destroyers *Erben*, *Hale*, *Bullard*, *Kidd* and *Chauncey*, attacks Tarawa; and TG.50.4 (Rear-Adm Sherman), with the carriers *Saratoga* and *Princeton*, the cruisers *San Diego* and *San Juan* and the destroyers

Stack, Sterett, Wilson and *Edwards*, attacks Nauru.

On 20 Nov TF.52 (Rear-Adm Turner) lands 6472 troops from the 27th US Inf Div (Maj-Gen R Smith) on Makin from four troop transports, one supply transport and one dock ship. Escort is provided by the destroyers *Mustin, Kimberly, Burns* and *Dale,* fire support by TG.52.2 (Rear-Adm Griffin) with the battleships *New Mexico, Pennsylvania, Idaho* and *Mississipi,* the cruisers *Minneapolis, San Francisco, New Orleans* and *Baltimore* and the destroyers *Dewey, Hull, Maury, Gridley, Phelps* and *MacDonough* and air support by TG.52.3 (Rear-Adm Mullinix†) with the escort carriers *Liscombe Bay, Coral Sea* and *Corregidor* and the destroyers *Morris, Franks, Hoel* and *Hughes.* The much inferior Japanese defenders hold up the still inexperienced infantry division and the small island of Makin is only taken on 23 Nov.

On 20 Nov TF.53 (Rear-Adm Hill), with 12 troop transports, three supply transports and one dock ship, lands 18600 troops of the 2nd US Marine Div on Betio/Tarawa. Escort is provided by the destroyers *John Rodgers, Sigsbee, Heerman, Hazelwood, Harrison, McKee* and *Murray* and fire support by TG.53.4 (Rear-Adm Kingman) with the battleships *Tennessee, Maryland* and *Colorado,* the cruisers *Portland, Indianapolis, Mobile* and *Santa Fé* and the destroyers *Bailey, Frazier, Gansevoort, Meade, Anderson, Russell, Ringgold, Dashiell* and *Schroeder,* with air support from TG.53.6 (Rear-Adm Ragsdale) with the escort carriers *Suwanee, Chenango, Barnes* and *Nassau* and the destroyers *Aylwin, Farragut, Monaghan, Cotten, Cowell* and *Bancroft.* Led by the minesweepers *Pursuit* and *Requisite* and supported by the destroyers *Ringgold* and *Dashiell,* the first waves land on Betio from the lagoon. In calm waters they suffer heavy casualties at the hands of the Japanese defenders. On 23 Nov the approximately 4500 Japanese (Rear-Adm Shibasaki†) are overwhelmed. Only 17 Japanese and 129 Koreans are taken prisoner. US losses on Tarawa are 1009 dead and 2101 wounded. By 28 Nov the remaining islands of the Atoll and neighbouring Abemama are occupied. There is Japanese counter-action from the outside in the form of air attacks in which *Independence* receives a torpedo hit on 20 Nov. A Japanese submarine group is deployed. After unsuccessful attempts, *I-36* has been able to reconnoitre over Pearl Harbor on 17 Oct with her aircraft. Then Capt Iwagami, with *I-19, I-35, I-39, I-169* and *I-175,* operates without success 300 nautical miles SW of Hawaii; *I-19* is lost,

probably to an air attack, on 18 Oct. On 20 Nov this group is deployed against the invasion fleet off Makin/Tarawa. In addition, *I-40, I-176* (Lt-Cdr Yamaguchi; his boat sinks the US submarine *Corvina* on 16 Nov) and *Ro-38* set out from Truk. Of these boats, *I-175* (Lt-Cdr Tabata) sinks *Liscombe Bay* (644 dead) with three torpedoes on 23 Nov. The Japanese *I-35* is sunk on 23 Nov by the destroyers *Frazier* and *Meade* off Tarawa and on 24 Nov *Ro-38* is sunk by the destroyer *Cotten,* also off Tarawa. *I-40* is sunk on 25 Nov by *Radford* when attempting to attack off Makin, *I-39* is sunk on 26 Nov by the destroyer *Boyd* near Makin and *I-21,* which is called up from the South Pacific, is sunk on 29 Nov by aircraft from the escort carrier *Chenango.* Japanese cruisers reinforce bases in the Marshall Islands. On 19 Nov *Isuzu* and *Nagara* set out from Truk for Mili, where they arrive on 23 Nov. *Nagara* comes straight back but *Isuzu* goes on to Kwajalein and arrives there on 27 Nov. *Naka* goes to Kwajalein on 19 Nov, arriving there on 23 Nov, and thence to Maloelap, but she breaks off the operation prematurely and returns to Truk. The operation is repeated by *Nagara* which sets out on 28 Nov, reaches Maloelap on 2–3 Dec and arrives in Kwajalein on 4 Dec.

On 24 Nov the cruisers *Chokai, Suzuya* and *Chikuma* and six to eight destroyers leave Truk for Kwajalein (they arrive on 26 Nov), go from there to Eniwetok on 27–28 Nov and return on 29–30 Nov. They return to Truk from Kwajalein from 4–5 Dec to 7 Dec together with *Isuzu* and *Nagara.*

22 Nov–7 Dec   North Atlantic

The remaining 'Schill' boats (*U424, U843, U618, U600, U358, U542, U586, U262, U764, U86, U238, U648, U228, U969* and *U391*) are formed W of Spain as the 'Weddigen' group to operate against the expected combined convoy KMS.30/OG.95 (EG.B4 under Cdr Day with the destroyers *Highlander, Walker* and *Westcott* and the corvettes *Abelia, Asphodel, Clover* and *Pennywort*). During the night 22–23 Nov the 4th SG (Cdr Paramor), with the frigates (US DE type) *Byard, Bazely, Blackwood, Drury, Bentinck* and *Berry,* passes the patrol line. *U648* is sunk; *U424* and *U714* are pursued with depth charges for up to 12hr and forced under water. *U843* (Lt-Cdr Herwatz) misses one of the frigates with a T-5. The air escort deployed does not find the convoy on 23 Nov which passes further to the W. The support group remains in the area of the 'Weddigen' group. During the night 24–25 Nov eight Wellingtons of No 179 Sqn RAF from Gibraltar attack *U618*

and *U542* and bring up the frigates which damage *U618.* *U586* has to start the return journey, having been damaged. Towards morning *Bazely* and *Blackwood* sink *U600.* At mid-day on 26 Nov German air reconnaissance locates convoy MKS.31 with EG.B1 (Cdr Bayldon), which comprises the destroyers *Hurricane* and *Wanderer,* the frigate *Glenarm* and the corvettes *Borage, Dahlia, Meadowsweet* and *Wallflower,* before it joins SL.140. During the night 26–27 Nov *U764* (Lt v Bremen) misses a frigate of the 4th SG with a T-5 and is attacked with depth charges and later by a night aircraft. On 27 Nov air reconnaissance again finds the now combined MKS.31/SL.140 with 68 ships with its escort reinforced by the 4th and 2nd SGs (Capt Walker) with the sloops *Starling, Kite, Wild Goose* and *Magpie.* The 'Weddigen' group is moved accordingly. In the evening a Bv 222 of 1 (F)/SAG 129 is able to maintain contact with the convoy for five hours and to bring up six boats as a result of repeated D/F transmissions. The strong night air escort impedes the U-boats. *U391* is driven off, *U542* is sunk by Leigh Light Wellington 'F' of No 179 Sqn RAF (Fg Off McRae), *U764* shoots down a Fortress of No 220 Sqn RAF and *U262* shoots down another aircraft with AA fire. In the night *U764* and *U107* (Lt Simmermacher) unsuccessfully attack frigates of the 4th SG with two and one T-5s respectively. *U262* (Lt Franke) surfaces in the morning in the middle of the convoy and fires four torpedoes which, however, do not hit. *U238* (Lt Hepp) narrowly misses the corvette *Dahlia.* *U843* is driven off by the 2nd SG. In the morning of 29 Nov the US TG.21.12, comprising the carrier *Bogue* and the destroyers *George E Badger, Osmond-Ingram, Clemson* and *Dupont,* arrives in the operational area of the 'Weddigen' group, coming from convoy UGS.24. *U764* and *U238* are attacked by several aircraft from *Bogue* but are still able to submerge after sustaining casualties. *U86* is sunk by an aircraft of VC-19 from *Bogue.* The Cdr U-boats concentrates the remainder of the 'Weddigen' group (*U618, U238, U391, U107, U358, U228, U424* and *U843*) against convoy KMS.34/OS.60, which, however, is neither located by the air reconnaissance deployed on 30 Nov and 1 Dec nor found by the U-boats. After an unsuccessful attempt to get the group to operate with the 'Coronel' group on 6 Dec against convoy ONS.24, 'Weddigen' is disbanded on 7 Dec.

22 Nov–6 Jan   West and South Atlantic

In operations in distant waters, *U129* (Lt v

Harpe) sinks one ship of 5441 tons and misses two destroyers with T-5s between Bermuda and Cape Hatteras. In the Gulf of Mexico, *U193* (Cdr Pauckstadt) sinks one tanker of 10172 tons and, in the Caribbean, *U530* (Lt-Cdr K Lange) torpedoes one tanker of 10193 tons. Off Freetown, *U515* (Lt-Cdr Henke) sinks three ships of 20913 tons. In the South Atlantic, *U849*, which is proceeding to the Indian Ocean, is sunk on 25 Nov by a Liberator from VP-107 USN flying from Ascension Island.

In the Central Atlantic, the carrier group centred on *Bogue* (Capt Dunn), while escorting the convoy GUS.23, encounters *U219* on 12 Dec which, having replenished three boats, is replenishing the outbound *U172*. The U-tanker gets away, but *U172* is sunk by VC-19 aircraft from *Bogue* and the destroyers *George E Badger*, *Osmond-Ingram*, *Clemson* and *Du Pont*. On 20 Dec VC-19 aircraft from *Bogue* surprise *U850* on her way out to the Indian Ocean and sink her.

24–27 Nov   Mediterranean
On 24 Nov the USAAF mounts an air attack on Toulon. Of the former French ships salvaged by the Italians, the cruiser *FR 11* (ex-*Jean de Vienne*), the destroyer *Aigle*, the submarines *Naiade* and *Achéron*, the sloop *FR 53* (ex-*Chamois*) and the transport *Aude* are sunk; other vessels, including the sloop *SG 17* (ex-Italian *FR 54*, ex-French *L'Impetueuse*), are damaged. The German E-boat *S56* and the MMS *R1* are sunk, while the MMS *R3* is damaged beyond repair.

During the night 24–25 Nov 112 German bombers attack harbour installations at La Maddalena (Sardinia) and Bastia (Corsica). During the night 26–27 Nov 76 German bombers attack Naples.

25 Nov   West Pacific
Bombers of the US 14th AF attack Formosa for the first time from Chinese bases. Forty-two Japanese aircraft are destroyed at Shinchiku airfield.

25 Nov   South Pacific
Battle E of Cape St George (New Ireland). Desron 23 (Capt Burke), comprising *Charles Ausburne*, *Claxton*, *Dyson*, *Converse* and *Spence*, surprises a Japanese destroyer force (Capt Kagawa) consisting of *Amagiri*, *Yugiri* and *Uzuki*, which have troops on board for Buka (Northern Bougainville). It sinks the covering destroyers *Onami*, *Makinami* and *Yugiri* with gunfire and torpedoes. The Japanese submarine *I-177* later rescues 278 men from *Yugiri*.

On 30 Nov the destroyers under Capt Burke bombard Japanese positions near Cape Torokina.

25 Nov–11 Dec   South/Central Atlantic
On 25 Nov the Cdr U-boats sends the signal 'Kammerarrest' to U-boats in the South Atlantic which forbids attacks against single merchant ships from 1 Dec. This signal is decoded by Op 20G on 26 Nov and confirms the arrival of the first of the expected five blockade-runners known to be coming from Japan according to indications from 'Purple' and 'Bertok/Barnacle' decodes. This leads to the activation of 'barrier' patrol operations with the US TF.41 (Rear-Adm Read) comprising five TGs with one cruiser and one destroyer each and USN and Brazilian air squadrons from Natal and Récife, and air patrols of US VPBs from Ascension, beginning on 1 Dec. In addition, from Freetown and Dakar, Operation 'Freecar' is started a few days later with the British AMCs *Corfu* and *Cilicia*, the French cruiser *Suffren* and the Italian cruisers *Duca degli Abruzzi* and *Duca d'Aosta*.

The first of the German blockade-runners, *Osorno* (6951 tons; Capt Hellmann), which has left Kobe on 2 Oct and rounded the Cape of Good Hope on 15 Nov, is sighted on 8 Dec by Liberator 'B-8' from VPB-107 USN based on Ascension, but the searching TG.41.4 with the cruiser *Marblehead* and the destroyer *Winslow* intercepts only the Greek vessel *Leonidas* while the *Osorno*, disguised as the British *Prome*, escapes. A search to the NW is unsuccessful, but *U510*, going for the Indian Ocean and which has sighted *Osorno*, is reported by a Liberator from Ascension and hunted from 11 to 13 Dec by TG.41.3 with the cruiser *Memphis* and the destroyer *Somers* together with the destroyer *Jouett* from TG.41.1. When the signal from *U510* about the sighting of *Osorno* is decoded by Op 20G on 13 Dec, it seems clear that the blockade-runner has already broken the 'Barrier' and 'Freecar' patrols, which are thus suspended; thus the next blockade-runner, *Alsterufer* (2170 tons; Capt Piatek), passes the narrows unobserved. On 12 Dec the C-in-C Plymouth starts the blocking operation 'Stonewall' in the North Atlantic (see 12–22 Dec).

26 Nov   English Channel
The German 5th MTB Flotilla, consisting of nine boats, drops 54 LMB mines near St Catherine's Point.

26 Nov   Mediterranean
He 177s of II/KG 40 (Maj R Mons†) sink off Bougie the British troop transport *Rohna* (8602 tons) from the convoy KMF.26 with an Hs 293 glider bomb. There are over 1000 dead among the troops on board. Eight He 177s are shot down.

The British cruiser *Orion* and the destroyers

Paladin, *Teazer* and *Troubridge* bombard positions N of the Garigliano river.

29 Nov   Air War/Germany
The US 8th AF bombs Bremen.

29 Nov   South West Pacific
Destroyers of TG.74.2 (Capt Walker), comprising *Ralph Talbot* and *Helm* (USN) and *Arunta* and *Warramunga* (RAN), shell Japanese positions near Gasmata on the south coast of New Britain.

29 Nov   South Pacific
The US destroyer *Perkins* is lost following a collision with the Australian transport *Duntroon* off Cape Vogelkop (New Guinea).

1 Dec   Mediterranean
The British destroyers *Paladin*, *Teazer* and *Troubridge* bombard positions in the Minturno area in the Gulf of Gaeta.

1–2 Dec   English Channel
The German 5th MTB Flotilla, consisting of eight boats, attacks from Cherbourg a strongly escorted convoy located by air reconnaissance off Beachy Head. *S142* sinks the British trawler *Aventurine*.

1–31 Dec   Pacific
In Japanese waters, *Gunnel* Lt-Cdr McCain) sinks one ship of 4046 tons, *Sailfish* (Lt-Cdr Ward) sinks two ships of 9571 tons and in one attack on 30 Dec, 180 nautical miles E Hachijojima, sinks the escort carrier *Chuyo* and torpedoes the light carrier *Ryuho* (on board *Chuyo*, 20 of 21 survivors from *Sculpin* perish), *Gurnard* (Lt-Cdr Andrews) sinks four ships of 14304 tons and damages one other of 10438 tons and *Tautog* (Lt-Cdr Sieglaff) sinks three ships of 12369 tons. In the China/Formosa area, *Herring* (Lt-Cdr Johnson) sinks two ships of 10019 tons, *Flying Fish* (Lt-Cdr Risser) sinks two ships of 18784 tons and *Grayback* (Lt-Cdr Moore) sinks the destroyer *Numakaze* and three ships of 8730 tons.

In the Central Pacific, *Peto* (Lt-Cdr Nelson) sinks one ship of 2338 tons, *Aspro* (Lt-Cdr Stevenson) sinks one sailing vessel, *Pogy* (Lt-Cdr Metcalf) sinks two ships of 9910 tons and damages one more of 5969 tons, *Sawfish* (Lt-Cdr Banister) sinks one ship of 3266 tons, *Silversides* (Lt-Cdr Coye) sinks three ships of 7192 tons and *Greenling* (Lt-Cdr Grant) sinks one ship of 1936 tons; *Peto* and *Tarpon* conduct, respectively, special and reconnaissance missions. On 23 Dec *Skate* (Lt-Cdr McKinney) torpedoes the battleship *Yamato* 150 nautical rules NW of Truk.

In the South West Pacific, *Narwhal* (Lt-Cdr Latta) sinks one ship of 834 tons and conducts a guerrilla support mission, *Pompon* (Lt-Cdr Hawk) lays a minefield off Pulo Condore and sinks two sailing vessels, *Puffer* (Lt-Cdr Selby) sinks the torpedo boat

Fuyo on 20 Dec in Subic Bay and one ship of 6707 tons, *Raton* (Lt-Cdr Davis) sinks one ship of 5578 tons and damages one other of 10182 tons, *Ray* (Lt-Cdr Harrel) sinks two ships of 8704 tons, *Bluefish* (Lt-Cdr Porter) sinks two ships of 11107 tons and *Cabrilla* (Lt-Cdr Hammond) lays a minefield off Cambodia and sinks one ship of 2704 tons by torpedo. *Capelin* is lost to Japanese A/S forces N of Celebes.

2–3 Dec   Mediterranean
During the night 2–3 Dec 88 German bombers of Luftflotte 2 attack the harbour installations and ships at Bari. Thanks to bomb hits and an explosion on an ammunition ship, 18 transports totalling 71566 tons with 38000 tons of cargo are destroyed. Other ships and the harbour installations are badly damaged and there are more than 1000 dead and injured. The fire-fighting and rescue operations are impeded by a US freighter which is loaded with mustard gas shells and endangered by fires.

3 Dec–15 Jan   Indian Ocean
The Japanese submarines *Ro-110* (Lt Ebato) and *Ro-111* (Lt-Cdr Nakamura) operate in the Bay of Bengal from Penang and each sink one ship, of 4087 tons and 7934 tons respectively. In the Gulf of Oman, *I-26* (Cdr Kusaka) sinks two ships of 14352 tons and torpedoes one of 8054 tons. *I-162* cruises in the area of Addu Atoll without success. The German *U178* (Lt-Cdr Spahr) sinks one ship of 7244 tons on the Indian west coast and goes at the end of Jan to the area S of Mauritius to be replenished from the tanker *Charlotte Schliemann*.

On 16 Dec the Japanese *I-29* (Cdr Kinashi) puts to sea on a transport mission to France. From 25 Dec to 4 Jan she is replenished from the German supply ship *Bogota* and she arrives in Lorient on 11 Mar.

4 Dec   Mediterranean
The German E-boat *S511* (ex-Italian *MAS 522*), is sunk by air attack at Makronisos in the Aegean.

4–5 Dec   Mediterranean
The German 7th MTB Flotilla (Cdr Trummer) carries out the mining operation 'Ulan' with seven boats off the west coast of Italy.

4–7 Dec   North Sea
Two 'Wandschrank' mine operations with the German minelayers *Ostmark*, *Brummer* and *Elsass* and the destroyers *Hans Lody*, *Z31* and *Theodor Riedel* to block the entrance to the Skagerrak with new barrages.

4–8 Dec   Central Pacific
On 4 Dec the US 'Fast Carrier Task Force' makes a raid on Kwajalein. The following take part: TG.50.1 (Rear-Adm Pownall), comprising the carriers *Yorktown*, *Lexington* and *Cowpens*, the cruisers *Baltimore*, *San Francisco*, *New Orleans* and *Minneapolis* and the destroyers *Nicholas*, *Taylor*, *La Valette*, *Bullard*, *Kidd* and *Chauncey*; and TG.50.3 (Rear-Adm Montgomery), comprising the carriers *Essex*, *Enterprise* and *Belleau Wood*, the cruisers *Portland*, *Mobile*, *Santa Fé*, *San Juan* and *San Diego* and the destroyers *Fletcher*, *Radford*, *Jenkins*, *Erben* and *Hale*. In several attacks by the 386 carrier-based aircraft, six transport ships of 25316 tons are sunk and three ships of 17249 tons and the cruisers *Isuzu* and *Nagara* are damaged. Fifty-five Japanese aircraft are shot down and destroyed on the ground. Five US aircraft are lost.

In an attack by twin-engined torpedo aircraft, *Lexington* receives a hit. *Yorktown* carries out a diversionary raid on Wotje.

On 8 Dec TG.50.8 (Rear-Adm Lee), comprising the battleships *South Dakota*, *Washington*, *Massachusetts*, *North Carolina* and *Indiana* and the destroyers *Lang*, *Boyd*, *Charette*, *Connor*, *Burns*, *Izard*, *Stack*, *Sterett*, *Wilson*, *Bradford*, *Brown* and *Cowell*, attacks Nauru and bombards the island with 810 rounds of 16in and 3400 rounds of 5in shell. A Japanese coastal battery damages *Boyd*. Air escort is provided by the carriers *Bunker Hill* and *Monterey*.

4–23 Dec   North Atlantic
An attempt with the 'Coronel' group (*U629*, *U761*, *U672*, *U544*, *U625*, *U421*, *U734*, *U541*, *U269*, *U962*, *U543*, *U92*, *U653*, *U801*, *U667* and *U415*) to locate the convoy ONS.24 in the eastern part of the North Atlantic in a short night operation fails because the air reconnaissance flown off (two Ju 290s on 4 Dec and one Ju 290, one Fw 200 and one Bv 222 on 5 Dec) does not find the convoy, which goes round to the N of the formation. In proceeding towards HX.268, expected according to B-Service reports on 8 Dec, *U269* sights a southbound convoy, against which the boats of the 'Weddigen' group also operate and with which *U421* briefly establishes contact. On 8 Dec HX.268 also passes to the N of the patrol line without air reconnaissance having been in contact. On 11, 12 and 13 Dec the 'Coronel' boats, which are divided into three groups, search for convoy ON.214. Air reconnaissance carried out over three days with Ju 290s, Fw 200s and Bv 222s does not find it. The formation is known to the British command and the convoy avoids it

by going to the S. On 16 Dec *U284* is damaged by heavy seas and flooded and has to be scuttled on 21 Dec by *U629*. From 18 until 23 Dec *U364*, *U972*, *U981*, *U744*, *U741* and *U471* as the 'Sylt' group, *U960*, *U392*, *U302*, *U976*, *U311* and *U629* as the 'Amrum' group and *U92*, *U672*, *U544*, *U625*, *U653* and *U421* as the 'Föhr' group are stationed in the Central North Atlantic in varying formations (called 'Rügen 1–6') without success.

Convoy HX.270, with a support group that includes the carrier *Tracker*, passes on 20–22 Dec to the S of the 'Föhr' group while the US carrier group centred on *Card* closes for support. Convoys ON.216 and ONS.25 pass on 22–23 Dec between 'Föhr' and 'Amrum'; convoy MKS.33/SL.144, supported by an SG with the carrier *Fencer*, passes 'Föhr' on 22–23 Dec to the S; and convoy KMS.36/OS.62, with an SG that includes the carrier *Striker*, goes S of 'Föhr' on 23–24 Dec.

5 Dec   Indian Ocean
Heavy Japanese air attacks on dock and harbour installations in Calcutta.

9 Dec   Arctic
The German MMS *R56* is sunk in an air attack off northern Norway though is later salvaged and repaired.

11–20 Dec   Air War/Germany
On 11 Dec bombers of the 8th AF attack Emden. On 13 Dec approximately 600 bombers of the 8th AF make a daylight attack on Kiel, where the torpedo boat *T-15* and the motor minesweeper *R306* are among the vessels to sink; *U345* is heavily damaged. On 20 Dec the 8th AF attacks Bremen.

12 Dec   Norway
The German auxiliary minesweeper *M5206* sinks after a collision in Oslofjord.

12–22 Dec   North Atlantic
Following the report about the breakthrough of the first blockade-runner through the Natal–Freetown narrows, the C-in-C Plymouth, Adm Leatham, initiates Operation 'Stonewall'. The cruisers *Gambia* (RNZN) and *Glasgow* leave Plymouth and transfer to Horta in the Azores, from where they establish a continuous patrol, relieving each other for fuelling from a tanker at Horta. Nos 15 and 19 Groups RAF Coastal Command and the USN's 7th Fleet Air Wing, operating in the North Atlantic and in the Bay of Biscay, are alerted, as are the other commanders and forces at sea.

On 16–17 Dec the blockade-runner *Osorno* passes unobserved through the US–Gibraltar convoy route and on 19 Dec threads its way through the US–UK route, passing the course of convoy ON.215 (EG.C4) for a short distance and following convoy HX.270 (EG.C1, with the carrier *Tracker*) at a distance of one day while the convoy SC.149 (EG.B5) follows also at a distance of one day.

Alsterufer passes the US–Gibraltar route on 20 Dec just behind TG.21.16, which consists of the carrier *Block Island* and the destroyers *Paul Jones*, *Parrott*, *Bulmer* and *Barker*, behind the westbound convoy GUS.23 and not far from the eastbound UGS.27.

On 21–22 Dec *Osorno* changes course for the Bay of Biscay and crosses in distances of less than one day each the courses of convoys KMF.27 (escorted by the 4th SG) and MKS.33/SL.142 (EG.B4 with the carrier *Fencer*), while TG.21.15 with the carrier *Core* and four destroyers and TG.21.14 with the carrier *Card* and three destroyers try to hunt the 'Borkum' U-boat group formed by the Cdr U-boats to cover the route of the blockade-runners (see 20–26 Dec). The 'Stonewall' cruisers *Gambia* and *Glasgow* are behind *Osorno* with their patrol. *Alsterufer* remains some distance from convoy CU.9 to the E, the *Block Island* group to the SE and convoy SC.149 to the N.

12 Dec–8 Jan   Arctic

Convoy operation in the Arctic. From 12 to 22 Dec convoy JW.55A (19 ships) makes its way to the Kola Inlet (20 Dec) and to the White Sea. Of the U-boats *U277*, *U387*, *U354* and *U636* stationed E of the Bear Island Passage, only the last locates escort vessels for a short time on 18 Dec, but does not get nearer the convoy. The distant covering force, consisting of the battleship *Duke of York* (Adm Fraser, C-in-C Home Fleet), the cruiser *Jamaica* and the destroyers *Savage*, *Saumarez*, *Stord* (Norwegian) and *Scorpion*, arrives in the Kola Inlet between 16 and 18 Dec but then goes on to Akureyri (Iceland) to refuel and to meet JW.55B (19 ships) which sets out from Loch Ewe on 20 Dec. This convoy has with it an escort group (Capt McCoy) comprising the destroyers *Onslow*, *Onslaught*, *Orwell*, *Scourge*, *Impulsive* and the RCN *Haida*, *Iroquois* and *Huron*, as well as *Whitehall* and *Wrestler*, the minesweeper *Gleaner* and the corvettes *Honeysuckle* and *Oxlip*. The convoy is located by German air reconnaissance on 22 Dec, but an attack by Ju 88s on 23 Dec does not penetrate the defence. On 23 Dec convoy RA.55A, which consists of 22 ships (one has turned back) and an escort group (Capt Campbell) consisting of the destroyers *Milne*, *Meteor*, *Ashanti*, *Athabaskan* (Canadian), *Musketeer*, *Opportune*, *Virago*, *Matchless*, *Beagle* and

Westcott, the minesweeper *Seagull* and the corvettes *Dianella*, *Poppy* and *Acanthus* (Norwegian), sets out from the Kola Inlet. A cruiser covering force (Vice-Adm Burnett), with *Belfast*, *Sheffield* and *Norfolk*, operates in the Barents Sea.

On 24 Dec *U601* (Lt Hansen) from the 'Eisenbart' group (*U277*, *U387*, *U354*, *U601*, *U716*, *U957* and *U314*) is led to the scene by air reconnaissance and establishes contact with JW.55B but she, together with *U716* (Lt Dunkelberg) which fires a T-5 against a destroyer, is driven off. On 25 Dec a German task force (Rear-Adm Bey) consisting of the battlecruiser *Scharnhorst* (Capt Hintze) and the 4th DD Flotilla (Capt Johannesson) with *Z29*, *Z30*, *Z33*, *Z34* and *Z38* is deployed against JW.55B. In the morning of 26 Dec Adm Bey forms a patrol line of destroyers to search in heavy seas for the convoy. Meanwhile the British cruiser force comes up from the SE and locates *Scharnhorst* by radar. Without calling her destroyers for support, *Scharnhorst* turns and has a short engagement with the cruisers in which the *Norfolk* obtains two hits. One of those puts the top radar of *Scharnhorst* out of action and she breaks off to search for the convoy to the N. Adm Burnett takes a position between the convoy and the enemy. At midday *Scharnhorst* again meets *Belfast*, *Sheffield* and *Norfolk*, which are reinforced by the destroyers *Musketeer*, *Matchless*, *Opportune* and *Virago*. In bad visibility there is a short engagement during which *Norfolk* suffers two hits, but *Scharnhorst* mistakes the fountains from *Norfolk* for the gunfire of battleships and turns away at high speed, trying to shake off the cruisers. Coming up fast from the SW, the *Duke of York* and *Jamaica* bar *Scharnhorst*'s way. In a pursuit engagement the British ships obtain some hits with their radar-controlled fire, but once again *Scharnhorst* gets out of range until the destroyers *Savage* and *Saumarez* and *Scorpion* and *Stord* get four torpedo hits in a skilful pincer attack and bring the ship to a halt. *Scharnhorst* is battered by gunfire from *Duke of York* and *Jamaica* and from *Belfast* and *Norfolk*, which also arrive on the scene. She is also hit by another ten to eleven torpedoes from the destroyers *Musketeer*, *Opportune*, *Virago* and *Matchless*, as well as from the cruisers *Belfast* and *Jamaica*. She sinks in the evening of 26 Dec. Only 36 survivors are rescued by British destroyers, of which *Saumarez* is damaged.

JW.55B arrives in the Kola Inlet without loss on 29 Dec. Soviet ships bring some steamers into the White Sea. RA.55A arrives without loss on 1 Jan. On 31 Dec RA.55B

(eight ships with an escort group under Capt McCoy) puts to sea from the Kola Inlet and reaches Loch Ewe on 8 Jan without loss. An attack by *U957* with a T-5 fails.

Of the submarines of the British 9th SM Flotilla, concentrated as flanking cover, *Seadog* (Lt Pelly) sinks one ship of 8597 tons and the Dutch *O15* misses a convoy on 26 Dec. Of the Soviet submarines, *L-20*, *K-21* and *S-102* are deployed against *Scharnhorst* on 26 Dec. In addition, during the journeys of these convoys, *L-15*, *L-22*, *S-15* and *S-103* operate off the polar coast and *M-105* and *M-201* in Varangerfjord where Soviet torpedo cutters repeatedly try to attack. They sink *V6106* on 12 Dec.

13 Dec   Bay of Biscay

The returning *U391* is sunk by Liberator 'B' of No 53 Sqn RAF.

13–14 Dec   South West Pacific

After an attack by the US 5th AF, in which 433 tons of bombs are dropped, the VII Amphibious Force (TF.76, Rear-Adm Barbey), which has set out on 13 Dec from the Goodenough Islands with the Australian transport *Westralia*, the LSD *Carter Hall* and the fast transports *Humphreys* and *Sands*, lands 1600 men of the 112th US Cavalry RCT (Brig-Gen Cunningham) on 14 Dec in Arawe (New Britain). The operation, 'Director', is supported by the US destroyers *Reid*, *Smith*, *Lamson*, *Flusser* and *Mahan*. Escort is provided by the destroyers *Conyngham*, *Shaw*, *Drayton*, *Mugford* and *Bagley* and the covering force is TF.74, comprising the Australian cruisers *Australia* and *Shropshire* and the destroyers *Arunta* and *Warramunga*.

16 Dec–1 Jan   Air War/Western Europe

RAF Bomber Command mine offensive. In seven nights, 142 sorties are flown against the Frisian coast, the Texel area and the Dutch coast, and against some Biscay ports. Two aircraft are lost.

On 16 Dec the MMS *R54* is lost on a mine near Anholt.

18 Dec   Mediterranean

The British minesweeper *Felixtowe* is lost on a mine near Cape Ferro (Sardinia).

20–26 Dec   North Atlantic

From 20 Dec the southern boats of the 'Coronel' formation (*U801*, *U107*, *U667*, *U618*, *U270*, *U541*, *U645*, *U962*, *U415*, *U305*, *U275*, *U382* and *U641*) are moved as the 'Borkum' group to the area SW of the Bay of Biscay to operate against convoy MKS.33/SL.142, whose escort is assisted by a support group which includes the carrier *Fencer*. The deployment of five Fw 200s by day and one Bv 222 by night (20–21 Dec) and of other aircraft on 21 Dec produces no results. The Allied command deploys against the 'Borkum' group the US carrier groups of *Card* (Capt Isbell) with the destroyers *Leary*, *Schenck* and *Decatur* and *Core* with the destroyers *Greene*, *Belknap*, *George E Badger* and *Goldsborough* coming from convoy GUS.24. On 22 and 23 Dec the carrier forces are reported three times by German air reconnaissance. The Cdr U-boats orders the 'Borkum' group to operate against it in order to cover the return of the blockade-runner *Osorno*, which is located on 23 Dec by a Wildcat from *Card* in bad weather. During the night 23–24 Dec *U305* first sights the *Card* group but is driven off by *Schenck* after being located by HF/DF. *U415* (Lt-Cdr Neide) misses *Card* with a FAT salvo of three as she turns away and *Decatur* with a T-5. *Schenck* avoids a T-5 from *U645* and then sinks the boat with depth charges. *U275* (Lt Bork) gets a T-5 hit on *Leary* which is detached to support her; and *U382* (Lt Zorn) finishes off the destroyer. The *Core* group has to leave owing to fuel shortages. In the evening of 24 Dec convoy OS.62/KMS.36, coming from the N with EG.B1 and the support group with the escort carrier *Striker*, runs into the 'Borkum' formation. The destroyer leader *Hurricane* is lost in a T-5 attack by *U415*. At mid-day on 24 Dec the German 8th DD Flotilla (Capt Erdmenger), consisting of *Z27*, *Z23*, *Z24*, *Z32*, *Z37* and *ZH1* with the 4th TB Flotilla (Cdr Kohlauf) under command and comprising *T22*, *T23*, *T24*, *T25*, *T26* and *T27*, sets out from the Gironde estuary to meet *Osorno* (Capt Hellmann) in a sortie code-named Operation 'Bernau'. Although from dawn on 25 Dec Sunderland flying boats of No 201 Sqn RAF, No 422 Sqn RCAF and No 461 Sqn RAAF are in contact, Capt Erdmenger is able to meet *Osorno* at mid-day after she has shot down one flying boat. Attempted attacks by aircraft of No 19 Group Coastal Command are beaten off by Ju 88 long-range fighters of Air Cdr Atlantic and by the AA fire of the ships. In coming into the Gironde estuary on 26 Dec, *Osorno* damages her hull on the wreck of *Sperrbrecher 21* and has to be beached to save the cargo.

22 Dec   Norway
The torpedo-transport U-boat *U1062*, escorted by a destroyer, is attacked near Bergen by nine Beaufighters of Nos 144 and 404 Sqns RAF with torpedoes and gunfire but is only slightly damaged.

22 Dec   Mediterranean
The German cruiser *Niobe* (ex-Italian *Cattaro*, ex-Yugoslav *Dalmacija*, ex-

German *Niobe*), grounded on 19 Dec on Silba Island, is destroyed by the British *MTB276* and *MTB298* in the Adriatic.

22–23 Dec   Mediterranean
The torpedo boats *TA23* and *TA24* and the minelayer *Niedersachsen* carry out the mining operation 'Attacke' off the northern tip of Corsica.

23 Dec   North Sea
The British destroyer *Worcester* is damaged beyond repair after striking a mine off Smith's Knoll.

23 Dec   English Channel
Unsuccessful probing sortie by the 5th MTB Flotilla, comprising *S143*, *S136*, *S138*, *S139*, *S140*, *S141* and *S142*, against a British convoy. There are engagements with British escort forces.

23 Dec   Western Pacific
The Japanese gunboat *Nanyo* (ex-British *Lyemun*) is sunk in a USAAF air attack 35 nautical miles S of Formosa.

23 Dec–8 Jan   North Atlantic
The U-boat groups 'Sylt', 'Amrum', and 'Föhr' are divided up in sections of three ('Rügen 1–6') W of Ireland: 1 (*U364*, *U972*, *U981*), 2 (*U744*, *U545*, *U781*), 3 (*U471*, *U390*, *U546*), 4 (*U960*, *U392*, *U302*, *U976*), 5 (*U311*, *U92*, *U672*) and 6 (*U625*, *U653*, *U421*). On 22–23 Dec the westbound convoy UC.8, followed by the convoy TU.5 (escorted by TF.68 with the US battleship *Nevada*) pass between 'Rügen 2' and '3'; *U471* (Lt-Cdr Klövekorn) misses a troop transport in convoy TU.5, and is then damaged by an aircraft of RAF Coastal Command. *U653* (Lt Kandler) misses a frigate from the tanker convoy CU.9 further to the S. An attack by *U392* (Lt Schümann) on a small convoy on 26 Dec is also unsuccessful. On 30 Dec some boats establish contact with stragglers from the convoy ON.217 (EG.C5): the *Empire Housman* (7359 tons) is first missed by *U744* (Lt Blischke), then torpedoed by *U545* (Lt-Cdr Mannesmann) and later finished off by *U744*. *U731* (Lt Count Keller) misses another ship. Individual boat formations from 5 Jan with *U547*, *U545*, *U741*, *U762*, *U364*, *U972*, *U981*, *U390*, *U471*, *U392*, *U386*, *U302*, *U846*, *U311*, *U260*, *U92*, *U976*, *U757*, *U731*, *U309* and *U666* also produce no success. On 8 Jan *U757* is sunk by the convoy escorts *Bayntun* and *Camrose* from the 4th and 5th SGs.

24 Dec   Mediterranean
The large French destroyer *Le Fantasque* drives the German freighter *Nicoline*

Maersk ashore near Tortosa off the Spanish coast in the Western Mediterranean.

24–27 Dec   South West Pacific
Operation 'Dexterity'. The US VII Amphibious Force (TF.76, Rear-Adm Barbey) which sets out on 25 Dec, lands on the following day some 13000 troops of the US 1st Marine Div (Maj-Gen Rupertus) at Cape Gloucester. It consists of the transports *Westralia* and *Etamin*, the LSD *Carter Hall*, 24 LSTs, 15 LCIs, 12 LCTs, 14 LCMs, four PCs, seven SCs, three YMSs and other units. The first waves come with the fast transports *Stringham*, *Crosby*, *Kilty*, *Dent*, *Ward*, *Brooks*, *Gilmer*, *Sands*, *Humphreys* and *Noa*. Support and escort are provided by the US destroyers *Conyngham*, *Shaw*, *Drayton*, *Mugford*, *Bagley*, *Reid*, *Smith*, *Lamson*, *Flusser* and *Mahan*, with fire support and cover from TG.74.1 consisting of the Australian cruisers (Rear-Adm Crutchley) *Australia* and *Shropshire* and the destroyers *Arunta*, *Warramunga*, *Helm* and *Ralph Talbot* and TG.74.2 (Rear-Adm Berkey) comprising the US cruisers *Nashville* and *Phoenix* and the destroyers *Bush*, *Ammen*, *Bache*, *Mullany*, *Hutchins*, *Beale*, *Daly* and *Brownson*. The last is sunk in an attack by 60 Japanese aircraft; *Shaw* is badly, and *Drayton*, *Lamson*, *LST 66* and *LST 202* more lightly, damaged.
On 24 Dec the cruisers *Montpelier*, *Cleveland* and *Columbia* with four destroyers shell Buka and Buin near Bougainville as a diversion. On 27 Dec Ainsworth's task force repeats the shelling near Kieta.

25 Dec–4 Jan   South West Pacific
Japanese troops are transported from Truk to Rabaul and Kavieng. The proposed deployment of the battleship *Yamato* has to be abandoned after the torpedoing of the ship S of Truk by the US submarine *Skate* (Cdr McKinney). The operation is carried out by the cruisers *Kumano*, *Suzuya*, *Oyodo*, *Noshiro* and destroyers.
On 25 Dec US TG.50.2 (Rear-Adm Sherman), comprising the carriers *Bunker Hill* and *Monterey* and the destroyers *Bradford*, *Brown*, *Cowell*, *Bell*, *Charrette* and *Conner*, carries out a raid on Kavieng (New Ireland). One steamer of 4861 tons is sunk and the minesweepers *W21* and *W22* and one steamer are damaged. On 1 Jan the carrier aircraft locate one of the returning Japanese cruiser forces and slightly damage *Oyodo*, *Noshiro* and the destroyer *Yamagumo*. In a further raid on Kavieng on 4 Jan, the Japanese destroyer *Fumitsuki* is damaged.

26–28 Dec   Bay of Biscay
Operation 'Trave': a sortie by the 8th DD Flotilla and the 4th TB Flotilla (composition

as in operation 'Bernau' with the exception of *ZHI*, which has to remain behind with condenser trouble) into the Bay of Biscay to bring the blockade-runner *Alsterufer* (Capt Piatek) into the Gironde.

Early on 27 Dec a Sunderland flying boat sights *Alsterufer* 500 nautical miles NW of Cape Finisterre proceeding SE. The cruisers of Operation 'Stonewall' (see 12 Dec) are then deployed: from E of the position *Enterprise* (Capt Grant RCN) and from 300 nautical miles W *Glasgow* (Capt Clarke) to a position 300 nautical miles NW of Finisterre. *Gambia* (Capt William-Powlett in overall command) sets out from Fayal and *Penelope* and the fast minelayer *Ariadne* from Gibraltar. In addition, the large French destroyers *Le Fantasque* and *Le Malin* are deployed from the Azores. At 1615 hrs *Alsterufer* (2729 tons) is hit by rockets from a Liberator bomber of No 311 (Czech) Sqn and set on fire. The Halifax attack force which arrives at 1800 hrs sights the burning and sinking ship being abandoned by the crew. Four lifeboats with 74 men are picked up two days later by four Canadian corvettes. Naval Group West only learns of the loss of *Alsterufer* in the morning of 28 Dec and orders the destoyers to return. But before this the destroyers are located by Allied air reconnaissance with the result that *Glasgow* and *Enterprise* are able to find them at midday. Despite the gun superiority of the 11 destroyers and torpedo boats (25 × 15cm and 24 × 10.5cm guns against 19 × 6in and 13 × 4in guns), a pincer attack fails in the heavy seas which prevent the German ships from using their full speed. In the gun engagement, *Z27* (Cdr Günther Schultz†) with the Cdr of the 8th DD Flotilla on board (Capt Erdmenger†), *T25* (Cdr v Gartzen) and *T26* (Lt-Cdr Quedenfeld) sink. Of the rest of the force, *Z24*, *Z23*, *T24* and *T27* reach Brest, *Z32* and *Z37* the Gironde and *Z23* and *T22*, which retired to the S, St-Jean de Luz. Sixty-four survivors are rescued by British ships, 168 by an Irish steamer, six by Spanish destroyers and 55 by *U505* and *U618*.

After the engagement, *Glasgow*, *Enterprise* and *Ariadne* proceed to Plymouth, where, in spite of several German air attacks with glider bombs, they arrive on 29 Dec. *Penelope*, *Le Fantasque* and *Le Malin* return to Gibraltar. *Gambia* and the newly-arrived cruiser *Mauritius* continue the search until 1 Jan.

26 Dec–13 Jan   North Atlantic

The 'Borkum' group tries on 25 Dec and during the night 25–26 Dec to continue operations against convoy OS.62/KMS.36, but only *U305* and *U270* are able to fire T-5s (unsuccessfully) against the escorts of the support group which remain behind. On the way to a new concentration for 30 Dec against the expected convoy MKS.34/SL.143, the 'Borkum' group comprising *U270*, *U801*, *U571*, *U305*, *U275*, *U382*, *U758*, *U641* and *U377*, comes partly into contact on 29 and 30 Dec with the 6th SG (British frigates and Canadian corvettes) which is trying to rescue the survivors of the engagement on 27 Dec. *U275* and *U270* are attacked by frigates and *U275* also by aircraft. The outbound *U629* (Lt Bugs) and *U541* (Lt-Cdr K Petersen), which are also ordered to look for survivors, and *U421* (Lt Kolbus) and *U543* (Lt-Cdr Hellriegel) make, in some cases, several T-5 attacks on escort vessels, but they all fail. The convoy MKS.34/SL.143, with EG.B3, is located by German air reconnaissance on 30 and 31 Dec but passes the patrol line on 1–2 Jan. *U382* (Lt Zorn), *U275* (Lt Bork) and *U305* (Lt-Cdr Bahr) miss escort vessels with T-5s. An attempt to operate against a southbound convoy on 2–3 Jan fails because no air reconnaissance is possible on account of shortages although *U270* (Lt-Cdr Otto), which has previously been bombed, misses a destroyer with a T-5. To make the locating of the patrol lines and their avoidance more difficult, the 'Borkum' boats are divided into three small sections: 1 (*U270*, *U305* and *U382*) 2 (*U758* and *U641*) and 3 (*U377*, *U953* and *U231*). On 5, 6 and 7 Jan the boats repeatedly come into contact with the 5th SG comprising the frigates *Nene* and *Tweed* and the Canadian corvettes *Calgary*, *Snowberry*, *Edmundston* and *Camrose*) NW of Spain which is looking out for expected blockade-runners. On 5 Jan *U758* (Lt-Cdr Manseck) misses one corvette with a T-5. On 6 Jan *U270* shoots down one Fortress of No 220 Sqn RAF, but is herself damaged by it, and on 7 Jan *U305* sinks *Tweed* with a T-5. On 8 Jan one, on 9 Jan three, and on 10 and 11 Jan two Ju 290s of FAGr 5 are deployed against the expected convoy MKS.35/SL.144 but only on 9 Jan does one aircraft sight the convoy W of Portugal. In the evening of 11 Jan *U305* gets sight of the convoy. The U-boats are able with their 3.7cm AA guns to keep off the carrier aircraft of the US support group with the carrier *Block Island* (Capt Ramsey), but they are unable to press home their attack. In an attack on *U758*, rockets are unsuccessfully used by carrier aircraft. *U953* (Lt Marbach) misses the Canadian corvette *Lunenburg* of the escort group with a T-5. On 13 Jan the operation has to be broken off. A Wellington of No 172 Sqn RAF, brought to the scene by an aircraft from *Block Island*, sinks *U231*.

27 Dec   Mediterranean

The Italian submarine *Axum* runs aground on the coast of Morea during a reconnaissance sortie and is lost.

28 Dec   English Channel

A British commando operation against the Channel Island of Sark fails.

28 Dec   Arctic

The German MMS *R64* is lost to a mine off Honningsvaag.

29 Dec   Mediterranean

The Free French submarine *Protée* is sunk by the German A/S vessel *UJ2208* off Toulon.

30 Dec–30 Jan   Atlantic/Indian Ocean

The British 1st Battle Sqn, comprising the battleships *Queen Elizabeth* and *Valiant* and the battlecruiser *Renown*, sets out from Scapa Flow on 30 Dec for the Indian Ocean. The carriers *Illustrious* and *Unicorn* join them from the Clyde. They are escorted by seven destroyers. The force proceeds through the Mediterranean to Colombo, where it arrives on 30 Jan.

31 Dec   Mediterranean

The British minesweeper *Clacton* sinks on a mine off the east coast of Corsica.

1944

1–31 Jan Pacific

US submarine operations in the Pacific are being assisted more and more by 'Ultra' data, especially the breaking of the 'Maru' and 'Truk Harbour Captain' codes and also those of the Imperial Japanese Navy, allowing the departure and arrival dates of Japanese ships to be pinpointed and details of the organisation of convoys to be interpreted. To disrupt the convoy operations of the Japanese Combined Escort Fleet, the US submarine commands in the Pacific (Vice-Adm Lockwood) and in Australia (Rear-Adm Christie) employ 'wolfpacks' to some extent, mostly each of three submarines combined in response to 'Ultra' information.

In Japanese waters and the Yellow Sea, *Finback* (Lt-Cdr Tyree) sinks one ship of 10044 tons and one sampan, *Steelhead* (Lt-Cdr Welchel) sinks one ship of 6799 tons, *Seawolf* (Lt-Cdr Gross) sinks four ships of 23361 tons and, together with *Whale* (Lt-Cdr Burrows), one other of 4865 tons, *Whale* alone sinks one ship of 5869 tons, *Sturgeon* (Lt-Cdr Murphy) sinks three ships of 12270 tons, *Batfish* (Lt-Cdr Merrill) sinks one ship of 5486 tons, *Salmon* and *Archerfish* report only duds, *Snook* (Lt-Cdr Triebel) sinks five ships of 20046 tons, *Angler* (Lt-Cdr Olsen) sinks one sailing vessel and one other ship of 889 tons, *Tambor* (Lt-Cdr Kefauver) sinks four ships of 18607 tons and *Plunger* (Lt-Cdr Bass) sinks three ships of 9577 tons.

In the area of the Mandate Islands, *Balao* (Lt-Cdr Cole) torpedoes one ship of 8613 tons, *Blackfish* (Lt-Cdr Davidson) sinks one ship of 2087 tons, *Seadragon* (Lt-Cdr Ashley) torpedoes on 20 Jan the munitions ship *Irako* (9750 tons), *Albacore* (Lt-Cdr Blanchard) sinks one ship of 2629 tons and also, on 14 Jan, the destroyer *Sazanami*, *Hake* (Lt-Cdr Broach) sinks four ships of 20273 tons and one sailing vessel, *Scamp* (Lt-Cdr Ebert) sinks one ship of 9974 tons, *Guardfish* (Lt-Cdr Ward) sinks one ship of 10024 tons and, on 1 Feb off Truk, the destroyer *Umikaze*, *Seahorse* (Lt-Cdr Rutter) sinks five ships of 13712 tons, *Haddock* (Cdr Roach) torpedoes, on 19 Jan off Guam, the escort carrier *Unyo*, *Gar* (Lt-Cdr Lantrup) sinks two ships of 8994 tons, *Skipjack* (Lt-Cdr Molumphy) sinks, on 26 Jan off Ponape, the destroyer *Suzukaze* and

one ship of 6666 tons, *Dace* (Lt-Cdr Claggett) sinks one ship of 2827 tons, *Spearfish* (Lt-Cdr Williams) sinks one ship of 3560 tons and damages one other of 6345 tons and *Trigger* (Lt-Cdr Dornis) sinks one ship of 11933 tons and on 31 Jan sinks the minelayer *Nasami* and torpedoes the destroyer *Michishio*. Reconnaissance missions are undertaken by *Gato* (Cdr Foley) and *Sunfish* (Lt-Cdr Shelby) off Green Island and the Taongi and Kusaie atolls.

In the area of the South China Sea, the Malayan Archipelago and the Philippines, *Kingfish* (Lt-Cdr Jukes) sinks three ships of 14568 tons, *Rasher* (Lt-Cdr Laughon) lays a minefield off Puolo Condore and torpedoes and sinks one ship of 7251 tons, *Crevalle* (Lt-Cdr Munson) lays a minefield E of Saigon and torpedoes and sinks one ship of 2569 tons and one sailing vessel, *Thresher* (Lt-Cdr McMillan) sinks four ships of 14523 tons and one sailing vessel, *Redfin* (Lt-Cdr Austin) torpedoes the destroyer *Amatsukaze* on 16 Jan near the Spratly Islands, *Bowfin* (Lt-Cdr Griffith) lays a minefield SE of Borneo (on which one ship of 8416 tons is damaged) and on 28 Jan sinks one ship of 4408 tons by torpedo and damages the seaplane carrier *Kamoi* (17000 tons), *Flasher* (Lt-Cdr Whitaker) sinks four ships of 10578 tons, *Bonefish* Lt-Cdr Hogan) sinks one sailing vessel and torpedoes the whaling factory *Tonan Maru No 2* (19262 tons) on 9 Feb, *Tinosa* (Lt-Cdr Weiss) sinks four ships of 15484 tons and *Bluefish* (Cdr Porter) lays a minefield off E Malaya.

2 Jan North Atlantic

First Allied use of a helicopter (Sikorski R-4) in an Atlantic convoy operation.

2–5 Jan South Atlantic

From the middle of Nov 1943 US TF.41 (Rear-Adm Reid), comprising the cruisers *Omaha*, *Milwaukee*, *Cincinnati*, *Marblehead* and *Memphis* and the destroyers *Winslow*, *Moffett*, *Davis*, *Jouett* and *Somers*, operates in groups each composed of one cruiser and one destroyer from Recife (Brazil) against the German blockade-runners expected, according to 'Ultra' data concerning the closing of 'Weg Anton' for U-boat attacks, to be en route from East Asia. Two groups, made up of the French and Italian cruisers *Montcalm*, *Georges Leygues* and *Duca degli Abruzzi* and *Gloire*, *Suffren* and *Duca*

d'Aosta respectively, are deployed in turns from Freetown and Dakar. In addition, from the beginning of Jan the large French destroyers *Le Fantasque* and *Le Malin* are stationed in Horta (Azores). From Ascension, Natal and Freetown, US, Brazilian, British and French air squadrons fly reconnaissance sorties. On 1 Jan a VB-107 Liberator from Ascension Island sights the blockade-runner *Weserland* (Capt Krage). It is damaged by AA fire. On 2 Jan another is shot down and then, during the night 2–3 Jan, *Somers* sinks the blockade-runner with gunfire and rescues 133 survivors. On 4 Jan an aircraft from *Omaha* sights the blockade-runner *Rio Grande* (Capt v Allwörden, 6062 tons) which is sunk by the cruiser and the destroyer *Jouett* with gunfire. There is only one survivor. On 5 Jan the last German blockade-runner from East Asia, *Burgenland* (Capt Schütz, 7320 tons), is sighted by a US flying boat from Natal and scuttles herself when *Omaha* and *Jouett* come within sight. *Omaha*, *Jouett*, *Davis*, *Winslow*, the Brazilian corvette *Camorin* and the Brazilian steamer *Poti* recover over 2000 bales of rubber over the next few days.

2–7 Jan Air War/Western Europe

Mine offensive by RAF Bomber Command. In four nights, 129 sorties are flown against Biscay ports, especially Lorient and Brest, and the Frisian Islands, and against Swinemünde in the Baltic.

2–8 Jan Bay of Biscay

During 'Percussion' operations against the transit routes of U-boats on 2 Jan, Halifax 'A' of No 58 Sqn RAF damages the outgoing *U445*, which has to return. On 3 Jan Wellington 'L' of No 612 Sqn RAF and Liberator 'H' of No 224 Sqn RAF damage the outgoing *U373*. On 4 Jan Wellington 'B' of No 304 (Polish) Sqn RAF damages the returning *U629*. On 5 Jan Halifax 'R' of No 58 Sqn RAF damages *U415* and on 8 Jan Sunderland 'U' of No 10 Sqn RAAF sinks the returning *U426*.

2–23 Jan South West Pacific

The VII Amphibious Force (Rear-Adm Barbey) lands 2400 troops from the 126th RCT of the 32nd US Inf Div (Brig-Gen Martin) near Saidor (New Guinea) on 2 Jan from APDs, two LSTs and several LCIs. The landing craft are escorted by the

253

destroyers (Capt Carter) *Beale, Mahan, Flusser, Lamson, Drayton, Hutchins, Smith* and *Conyngham.* The covering force (Rear-Adm Crutchley RAN) comprises the cruisers *Australia* and *Shropshire,* the Australian destroyers *Arunta* and *Warramunga* and the US destroyers *Helm, Ralph Talbot, Bush, Ammen, Bache* and *Mullany* with the cruisers *Nashville* and *Phoenix.* 12000 Japanese of the 18th Army (Lt-Gen Adachi) are cut off in Sio. On 7–8 Jan the Japanese submarine *I-177* evacuates Gen Adachi. The troops try to get to Madang via Gali but they suffer repeated losses from coastal shelling near Gali by US destroyers and on 26 Jan by Rear-Adm Berkey and his US cruisers *Nashville* and *Phoenix* and destroyers *Bush, Ammen* and *Mullany* from Madang.

3 Jan   USA
The US destroyer *Turner* suffers a magazine fire and explosion at Ambrose LV, New York, and is lost.

3–13 Jan   Mediterranean
Of the German U-boats employed against Allied supply traffic from Gibraltar along the Algerian coast to Naples, *U642, U616* and *U380* attack convoys, sometimes repeatedly, without success. On 3–4 Jan *U952* and *U343* pass through the Strait of Gibraltar from the W; *U343* beats off heavy air attacks on 8 Jan with her AA guns, shooting down Wellington 'R' of No 179 Sqn RAF and damaging Catalina 'J' of No 202 Sqn RAF, but is herself damaged.

On 10 Jan 30 torpedo aircraft of Fl Div 2 in Southern France sink the freighter *Ocean Hunter* (7178 tons) from convoy KMS.37 N of Oran and torpedo the *Daniel Webster* (7176 tons), which is beached but regarded as a total loss.

5–6 Jan   Air War/Germany
On 5 Jan the US 8th AF attacks Kiel. During the night 5–6 Jan 358 aircraft of RAF Bomber Command drop 1118 tons of bombs on Stettin; 16 aircraft are lost and eight ships sunk or damaged in the harbour and yards.

5–6 Jan   English Channel
The German 5th MTB Flotilla (Lt-Cdr K Müller), comprising *S141, S100, S142, S143, S138, S136* and *S84,* attacks convoy WP.457 (SOE destroyer *Mackay*) off the British south-west coast. The boats fire a total of 23 torpedoes and sink the freighters *Polperro* (403 tons), *Underwood* (1990 tons) and *Solstad* (1408 tons) as well as the trawler *Wallasea* (545 tons).

5 Jan–5 Mar   Black Sea
In Jan there operate against Soviet coastal traffic off the Caucasus the German U-boats *U19, U20* (Lt Grafen), which torpedoes one

tanker, and *U24.* In Feb *U18* (Lt Fleige), which sinks one steamer, *U19* (Lt Ohlenburg) and *U20,* which lays mines off Poti, operate off Batum and Poti. At the beginning of Mar *U20* and *U24* are deployed against Soviet traffic from Poti to Trapezunt. On 5 Jan the German MTB *S148* is sunk N of Sulina by a mine.

Soviet submarines are, in particular, employed against German convoy traffic between the now isolated Crimea and Constanza and Odessa, which the 10th Escort Div (Capt Weyher) escorts with the 1st, 3rd and 23rd SC Flotillas, the 3rd MS Flotilla and Rumanian forces. *L-23* (Capt 3rd Class Fartushny†, with the Cdr of the Submarine Bde, Capt 1st Class Krestovski† on board) attacks a convoy SW of Evpatoria on 5 Jan and is pursued by the submarine-chasers *Schiff 19, UJ303, UJ306, UJ316, UJ312* and *UJ2301.* After engagements with naval ferry barges on 1 Jan the boat is lost, probably on 30 Jan when attacked by a Bv 138 when she returns. *L-6* (Lt-Cdr Gremyako) lays a mine barrage; *Shch-216* (Capt 3rd Class Karbovski†) attacks convoys unsuccessfully on 9 and 10 Feb and is sunk by depth charges from *UJ103* W of Evpatoria on 16 Feb. *M-112, M-35, Shch-209* and *Shch-205* have no success. During the Soviet offensive N of the lower Dnieper, Nikolaev has to be evacuated on 11 Mar after the blowing up of harbour and dockyard installations. Among the craft to be taken off are three uncompleted KT ships. From 6 to 8 Mar the Soviet 2nd Torpedo Cutter Bde (Capt 2nd Class Protsenko), comprising 10 TKAs, moves from Gelendzhik round the Crimea to Skadovsk. At the beginning of Apr six more TKAs follow.

7–29 Jan   North Atlantic
The U-boats of the 'Rügen' group—*U547, U545, U741, U981, U972* (missing from the beginning of Jan), *U364, U390, U762, U309, U731, U757, U666, U471, U392, U846, U311, U302* and *U976*—and, from the middle of Jan, the remaining 'Borkum' boats—*U305, U382, U377* and *U641*—and the newly arrived *U571, U271, U212, U592, U231* and *U238,* operate W of Ireland singly and in varying concentrations. *U386* is deployed off the North Channel, *U260* operates off Reykjavik and *U544, U763* and *U960* (Lt Heinrich) function as weather boats; the last sinks one ship of 7176 tons. On 8 Jan *U757* is sunk by the British DE *Bayntun* (4th SG) and the Canadian corvette *Camrose* (5th SG), which are part of the escort of the combined convoy OS.64/KMS.38. Various U-boats sight ships and search groups in the next few days but have no success. On its way out, *U621*

is damaged by Liberator 'A' of No 59 Sqn RAF, supporting convoy SL.144/MKS.35. *U231* is sunk by Wellington 'L' of No 172 Sqn RAF; the survivors are rescued by the 6th SG on 13 Jan. *U377* is lost on 15 Jan in an encounter with the US *Santee* carrier group. On 17 Jan *U305* is sunk by the destroyer *Wanderer* and the frigate *Glenarm.* US TG.21.12 (Capt Gallery), comprising the carrier *Guadalcanal,* the destroyer *Forrest* and the DEs *Pillsbury, Pope, Flaherty* and *Chatelain,* surprises a supply group consisting of *U516, U539* and *U544* and aircraft of VC-13 sink *U544.* In the evening of 17 Jan an He 177 sights convoy OS.65/KMS.39 (EG.B3, Cdr Evans on the frigate *Towy*). But of the U-boats directed to the scene, only *U641* gets near on 19 Jan and is sunk by the corvette *Violet.* On 19 Jan *U390* misses a steamer further to the N. Air reconnaissance provided on 20, 21 and 22 Jan cannot find the expected HX.275 and SC.151 or the westbound ON.220 (EG.C4). On 26 and 27 Jan Ju 290s of FAGr 5 repeatedly report the combined convoy OS.66/KMS.40 and ON.221. Against them are concentrated *U650, U571, U281, U271, U212* and *U592* as the 'Hinein' group and *U989, U762, U547, U390, U984, U731, U545, U386, U309, U666, U406, U283* and *U985* as the 'Stürmer' group. No 15 Group Coastal Command, reinforced by aircraft of No 19 Group, carries out massive operations against the U-boat formations in support of the convoys. *U571* and *U271* are sunk on 28 Jan by Sunderland 'D' of No 461 Sqn RAAF and Liberator 'E' of VP-103 USN flying air cover for convoys SC.151 and ON.221. On 29 Jan *U592* is damaged by Liberator 'N' of VP-102 and on its way to France is sunk on 31 Jan by the sloops *Starling* (Capt Walker), *Wild Goose* and *Magpie* of the 2nd SG. Also on its way back to France, *U364* is sunk by Wellington 'K' of No 172 Sqn RAF which, however, does not return from its 'Percussion' patrol. On 29 Jan the U-boats are summoned to France because of a false invasion alarm and are then ordered to new positions.

8 Jan   Bay of Biscay
Sunderland 'U' of No 10 Sqn RAAF sinks *U426* in the Bay of Biscay.

8–28 Jan   Mediterranean
In a British fighter-bomber attack on 8 Jan, the German escort vessel *SG20* (ex-torpedo boat *Papa*) is badly damaged by near-misses off Imperia in the Tyrrhenian Sea and runs aground. In an air attack on Savona on 20 Jan, the French destroyer *Valmy* receives two direct hits and *Le Hardi* slight damage as they lie in the harbour. In a fighter-bomber attack on a German convoy near

San Stefano on 28 Jan *R201* is sunk and *R199*, *R161* and *KT20* are damaged.

8 Jan-18 Mar   Mediterranean

Allied air attacks on Pola and Monfalcone weaken the German U-boats employed in the Eastern Mediterranean. *U81* and the refitting *UIT19* (ex-Italian *Nautilo*) are destroyed and *U596* damaged. In Feb *U453* (Lt Lührs) sinks four sailing ships off the Syrian coast, *U407* (Lt Korndörfer) torpedoes one sailing ship and one ship of 6207 tons, *U596* (Lt Nonn) misses one Italian corvette off Brindisi on 23 Feb and on 7 Mar the Italian battleship *Giulio Cesare* S of the Gulf of Taranto and *U565* (Lt Henning) misses one corvette and a cruiser off Cyrenaica at the beginning of Mar. In another patrol S of Taranto, *U453* attacks a convoy on 18 Mar but has no success.

9-23 Jan   Mediterranean

The German minelayer *Niedersachsen* (ex-Italian *Acqui*) lays on 9, 19 and 23 Jan three mine barrages off Imperia, S of Elba and N of Nettuno.

10 Jan   Mediterranean

The German MTB *S55* is damaged in an air attack and sunk when its own torpedoes explode W of Korcula in the Adriatic.

10 Jan-12 Mar   South Pacific

Last Japanese submarine operations against bases in the South Pacific. The large submarine *I-11* (Cdr Izu) reports on 11 Jan the result of a periscope reconnaissance of Funafuti but is lost before carrying out the air reconnaissance missions over the Ellice Islands and Samoa. In the area of the New Hebrides, *Ro-42* (Lt-Cdr Wada) sinks the harbour tanker *YO159* on 14 Jan and *Ro-37* is lost on 23 Jan after torpedoing the tanker *Cache* (12000 tons). *Ro-44* has no success. In Feb *Ro-106* and *Ro-109* again operate from Rabaul without success in Huon Gulf. After the evacuation of Rabaul by the fleet (the army stays there until 1945), the last boats of the 7th SM Flotilla return to Truk. *Ro-39* and *Ro-40*, which are sent at the end of Jan and the beginning of Feb to operate against the US fleets in the area of the Marshall Islands, do not return. In transport missions to Mille and Wotje, *I-175* is lost in Feb and *I-32* in Mar after a successful mission. Finally, *Ro-44* reconnoitres Majuro on 12 and 13 Mar.

11 Jan   Mediterranean

The German minesweeper *M1226* (ex-Italian *RD 9*) and the A/S vessel *UJ2143* are sunk in an air attack on Piraeus.

11 Jan-25 Feb   Indian Ocean

Reinforcement of the British Eastern Fleet (Vice-Adm Somerville), which at the end of 1943 consisted only of the battleship *Ramillies*, the escort carrier *Battler*, the 4th Cruiser Sqn (Rear-Adm Read) with *Newcastle*, *Suffolk*, *Frobisher*, *Kenya* and *Ceylon* and, for convoy duties, the cruisers *Hawkins*, *Danae* and *Emerald*, the auxiliary cruisers *Alaunia* and *Chitral*, 11 destroyers, 13 frigates, sloops and corvettes and six submarines. In Jan the 1st Battle Sqn (Vice-Adm Power) arrives with *Queen Elizabeth* and *Valiant* and the battlecruiser *Renown*, the carriers (Rear-Adm Moody) *Illustrious* and *Unicorn* and the cruisers *Sussex* and *Tromp* (Dutch) with the Dutch destroyers *Van Galen* and *Tjerk Hiddes*. In addition to the 11th DD Flotilla (Capt De Winton), comprising *Rotherham*, *Racehorse*, *Raider*, *Rapid*, *Redoubt*, *Relentless*, *Rocket* and *Roebuck* and the 16th DD Div with *Paladin*, *Penn*, *Petard* and *Pathfinder*, the 4th DD Flotilla (Capt Onslow), comprising *Quilliam*, *Quadrant*, *Quality*, *Queenborough*, *Quiberon* and *Quickmatch*, is transferred at the beginning of Mar. From Dec 1943 the 4th SM Flotilla (Capt Ionides), consisting of *Trespasser*, *Taurus*, *Truculent*, *Tally Ho*, *Tantalus*, *Tantivy*, *Sea Rover*, *Stoic*, *Stonehenge* (missing from the end of Feb) and the Dutch *K-XIV* and *O-23*, are deployed against Japanese traffic in the Malacca Strait and on the west coast of Siam as far as the Nicobar and Andaman Islands. In several operations there, *Tally Ho* (Cdr Bennington) sinks two ships of 4876 tons, on 11 Jan the cruiser *Kuma* and on 14 Feb the German U-boat *UIT23* (ex-Italian *Giuliani*) and damages on 24 Feb the torpedo boat *Kari*. *Stonehenge* (Lt Verschoyle-Campbell) sinks the auxiliary minesweeper *Wa 4* and one ship of 889 tons but then goes missing in late Feb, *Taurus* sinks a tug and a barge, *Truculent* sinks one sailing vessel, *Trespasser* sinks one ship of 3520 tons, *Tactician* sinks a coaster and *Templar* (Lt Beckley) torpedoes the cruiser *Kitakami* on 25 Feb.

11 Jan-2 May   Indian Ocean

The German U-boats of the 'Monsun' group operate in the Indian Ocean from Penang. *U532* (Cdr Junker) sinks two ships of 9457 tons and torpedoes one of 7283 tons SW of India, *U188* (Capt Lüdden) sinks seven ships of 42549 tons, partly from convoys, and seven dhows in the Gulf of Aden, *U168* (Lt-Cdr Pich) sinks two ships of 5875 tons and torpedoes one of 9804 tons off India and *U183* (Lt-Cdr Schneewind) sinks one ship of 5419 tons and torpedoes a tanker of 6993 tons in Addu Atoll. *U510* (Lt Eick), coming from France, sinks in the Gulf of Aden in Feb and Mar five ships of 31220 tons, some from convoys, and one dhow and also torpedoes one ship of 9970 tons. The operations are supported by German tankers, including the *Charlotte Schliemann* which replenishes *U178* and *U510* on 27 Jan. The British cruiser *Newcastle* and the destroyer *Relentless* and seven Catalina flying boats are deployed from Mauritius on the basis of HF/DF bearings. One of the flying boats reports the tanker and brings up *Relentless* during the night of 11-12 Feb. When she comes into sight, the tanker scuttles herself. *U532* takes off the crew and refuels from *U178* on 27 Feb.

The British carrier *Illustrious* with the cruisers *Gambia* and *Sussex* and the destroyers *Rotherham* and *Tjerk Hiddes* (Dutch) carry out Operation 'Sleuth' against suspected blockade-runners in the area SW of the Cocos Islands.

On 12 Mar *U188*, *U532* and *U168* are joined by the tanker *Brake* from Penang. But a British search group, consisting of the escort carrier *Battler*, the cruisers *Suffolk* and *Newcastle* and and destroyers *Roebuck* and *Quadrant*, is deployed against her. *Roebuck*, led to the scene by a carrier aircraft, forces the tanker to scuttle herself. *U168* takes off the crew. Of the transport U-boats, *UIT23* is sunk by the British submarine *Tally Ho* (Cdr Bennington) on 14 Feb shortly after setting out in the Malacca Strait, *UIT24* has to give her fuel to *U532* on 18 Mar and return to Penang and *UIT22* is sunk off South Africa by a Catalina flying boat on 11 Mar. The torpedo transport *U1062* reaches Penang, after refuelling from *U532* on 10 Apr. *U178* and *U188* return to Bordeaux, the other boats to Penang. Of the Japanese submarines, *I-27* (Lt-Cdr Fukumura) attacks a British convoy of five troop transports in the One and a Half Degree Channel (Maldives) on 12 Feb. The convoy is escorted by the cruiser *Hawkins* and the destroyers *Petard* and *Paladin* and is on the way from Kilindini to Colombo. The submarine sinks the transport *Khedive Ismail* (7513 tons) with over 1000 British troops on board, but is herself sunk in a counter-attack by the two destroyers.

In the Bay of Bengal, *Ro-110* (Lt Ebato), after torpedoing a steamer of 6274 tons from convoy JC.36, is sunk on 11 Feb by the Indian sloop *Jumna* and the British minesweepers *Ipswich* and *Launceston* of the escort. *I-37* (Lt-Cdr Nakagawa) makes a sortie to the African coast and sinks three ships of 19312 tons, including the *British Chivalry* on 22 Feb. With her aircraft she reconnoitres Diego Suarez (Madagascar) on 4 Mar and Kilindini on 14 Mar. She escapes from a depth charge pursuit by the British sloop *Lulworth* on 16 Mar. In Mar *I-26* (Cdr Kusaka) sinks three ships of 23591 tons, including the *Richard Hovey* on 29 Mar, off the Indian west coast and Bombay and lands agents on 25 Mar. In the central Indian Ocean, *I-166* misses one ship, *I-162* (Lt-Cdr Doi) and *I-165* (Lt-Cdr Shimizu) each sink one ship, of 7127 tons and 3916 tons respectively, and *I-8* (Cdr Ariizumi) sinks two ships of 12376 tons and one sailing ship, including the Dutch *Tjisalak*, at the end of Mar. On 1 Mar the 7th Japanese Cruiser Sqn (Rear-Adm Sakonju), comprising *Aoba*, *Chikuma* and *Tone*, sets out from the Sunda Strait to conduct mercantile warfare on the Australia–Aden route. In the area of the Sunda Strait, it is escorted by the cruisers *Kinu* and *Oi* and the destroyers *Uranami*, *Shikinami* and *Amagiri*. On 9 Mar *Tone* (Capt Mayuzumi) sinks the freighter *Behar* (7840 tons). Because the ship has sent off distress signal, Rear-Adm Sakonju breaks off the operation and returns. As a result of orders from the Cdr of the South West Area Fleet (Vice-Adm Takasu), the survivors are murdered when the *British Chivalry*, *Richard Hovey*, *Behar* and *Jean Nicolet* are sunk.

The only instance of firing on survivors by a German U-boat occurs on 13 Mar in the South Atlantic when *U852* (Lt-Cdr Eck), after dispatching the freighter *Peleus* (4695 tons), hits survivors as she tries to sink the wreckage of the ship. Another ship (5277 tons) is sunk off South Africa on 1 Apr. In Apr the boat operates off East Africa without success. As a result of HF/DF bearings on 30 Apr, a search is started with Wellingtons 'E' of No 8 and 'T' of No 621 Sqns RAF which damage *U852* so badly on 2 May that she is beached on the Somali coast and blown up.

12 Jan Air War/Italy

In an air raid against Genoa, the damaged German escort vessel *SG20* (ex-Italian torpedo boat *Papa*) capsizes. She is later salvaged but her repairs are never completed.

12 Jan–11 Feb Arctic

Convoy operation JW.56/RA.56. On 12 Jan JW.56A sets out from Loch Ewe with 20 steamers accompanied by the local escort with the minesweeper *Ready* (Capt 16th MS Flotilla), the sloop *Cygnet*, the destroyer *Inconstant* the corvettes *Borage*, *Dianella* and *Poppy* and the minesweeper *Orestes* but runs into a heavy storm on 16 Jan and has to put in to Akureyri (Iceland), where five ships stay behind with storm damage. On 21 Jan the convoy puts to sea again; it comprises 15 ships with an escort group (Capt Robson on *Hardy*) consisting of the destroyers *Hardy*, *Savage*, *Venus*, *Offa*, *Obdurate*, *Inconstant*, *Vigilant*, *Virago* and *Stord* (RNoN), the corvettes *Poppy* and *Dianella* and the minesweepers *Ready* and

Orestes. The covering force (Vice-Adm Palliser) comprises the cruisers *Kent*, *Norfolk* and *Belfast*. On 22 Jan convoy JW.56B with 16 ships follows from Loch Ewe with an escort group (Capt Campbell) consisting of the destroyers *Milne* (D3), *Musketeer*, *Opportune*, *Mahratta*, *Huron* (RCN) and *Scourge* and later *Meteor*. The close escort consists of the destroyers *Westcott* (SO), *Whitehall* and *Wrestler*, the sloop *Cygnet*, the corvettes *Rhododendron Honeysuckle* and *Oxlip* and the minesweepers *Onyx*, *Hydra* and *Seagull*. As a result of agents' reports from Iceland, the Officer Commanding U-boats Norway (Capt Peters) forms the 'Isegrim' group with ten boats in the Bear Island passage. Although the air reconnaissance provided produces no results, all the boats with the exception of the most northerly *U739* come up from mid-day on 25 Jan and attack in the dark in the afternoon and night of 25–26 Jan. *U965* (Lt Ohling), *U601* (Lt Hansen), *U360* (Lt-Cdr Becker) (four times), *U425* (Lt Bentzien) (twice), *U737* (Lt-Cdr Brasack), *U278* (Lt Franze) and *U314* (Lt-Cdr Basse) fire T-5s against escort vessels, but only the destroyer *Obdurate* is damaged, by a T-5 from *U360*. *U278*, *U360* and *U716* (Lt Dunkelberg) successively fire FAT salvos at the convoy and hit the *Penelope Barker* (7177 tons), the flagship of the convoy commodore, *Fort Bellingham* (7153 tons), and the *Andrew G Curtin* (7200 tons), all of which sink; *Fort Bellingham* is finished off by *U957* (Lt Schaar), which takes prisoners.

On 27 Jan the Soviet destroyers *Razyarenny*, *Razumny*, *Gremyashchi* and *Grozny* meet the convoy, which sails into the Kola Inlet on 28 Jan. Capt Robson meets JW.56B with six destroyers to strengthen the A/S defence. After breaking off the operation against JW.56A, the Officer Commanding U-boats again forms the 'Werwolf' group, now reinforced by *U956*, *U472*, *U313*, *U973* and *U990*, in the Bear Island passage to operate against the next convoy. JW.56B is reported at mid-day on 29 Jan by *U956* (Lt Mohs) which, by midnight, has defended herself three times with T-5s against destroyers without securing any hits. By the morning of 30 Jan *U737*, *U601* (twice), *U957* (four times), *U278*, *U472* (Lt Frhr v Forstner), *U425* (twice) and *U313* (Lt Schweiger) have fired T-5s against escort vessels, but only *U278* hits *Hardy*, which has to be sunk by *Venus*. *U737* and *U957* narrowly miss *Milne* and the Norwegian *Stord*. *U314* is sunk by the destroyers *Whitehall* and *Meteor*. No boat reaches the merchant ships. Up to early on 31 Jan *U965*,

U425 (twice), *U737*, *U956* and *U990* (Lt-Cdr Nordheimer) fire T-5s without success against escorts. *U956* also fires T-5s on the return journey on 1 Feb, the day the 16 steamers arrive in the Kola Inlet.

The combined convoy RA.56 with 37 steamers and the combined escort of the two JW convoys, consisting of 23 destroyers and corvettes (minus *Hardy*, *Virago* and *Obdurate*), which are further reinforced by three destroyers (*Verulam*, *Obedient* and *Swift*) from Scapa Flow, avoids the concentration of the remaining boats of the 'Werwolf' group (*U425*, *U957*, *U713*, *U278*, *U973*, *U990*, *U313* and *U312*). It is located by German air reconnaissance on 6 Feb but is reported on the wrong course with the result that the U-boats search in the opposite direction. The convoy arrives in Loch Ewe on 11 Feb without loss.

14–21 Jan Baltic

Break-out of the Soviet Leningrad Front (Army General Govorov) from the encirclement of the city. For this purpose the Baltic Fleet (Adm Tributs) has been transporting since 5 Nov 1943, under the command of Admiral Levchenko, the 2nd Assault Army in small craft from Leningrad to the bridgehead around Oranienburg: 44000 troops, over 200 tanks, 600 guns, 30000 tons of supplies, 2400 vehicles and 6000 horses. The guns of the fleet are employed under the command of Vice-Adm Gren to support the offensive. The ships include (1st Group, Kronstadt) the still operational turrets of the beached battleship *Petropavlovsk* (ex-*Marat*), the destroyers *Strashny* and *Silny* and the gunboat *Volga*; (2nd Group, Leningrad, Vice-Adm Rall) the battleship *Oktyabrskaya Revolutsiya*, the cruisers *Tallin* (ex-*Petropavlovsk*, ex-*Lützow*), *Maksim Gorki* and *Kirov* and the destroyers *Leningrad* and *Svirepy*; and (3rd Group, Neva, Capt 1st Class Ivanov) the destroyers *Optyny*, *Strogi*, *Stroiny* and *Grozyashchi* and the gunboats *Zeya*, *Sestroretsk* and *Oka*. In all, the ships' guns fire 24000 shells.

14 Jan–6 Feb Air War/Western Europe

Mine offensive by RAF Bomber Command. In nine nights, 219 sorties are flown against Biscay and Channel ports, especially the Gironde estuary, St-Nazaire, Brest, Cherbourg, Le Havre, the Frisian Islands, the Kiel area, the central Baltic, Oslo and Frederikstad. *U263* is sunk, probably on a mine, off La Rochelle on 20 Jan and the patrol boat *V712* is sunk off Cherbourg on 20 Jan. The German MDS *Sperrbrecher 137/Botilla Russ* sinks off St-Nazaire and the auxiliary minesweeper *M4021* at the Ile de Croix on

28 Jan. On 14 Feb *U854* is sunk 9 nautical miles N of Swinemünde.

14 Jan–25 Feb   Norway
Intensification of British submarine and air operations against German convoy traffic off the Norwegian coast. After unsuccessful submarine attacks by *Seadog* (Lt Pelly) at the beginning of Jan, there is an attack by British torpedo aircraft on two German convoys off Lister on 14 Jan: two ships of 9208 tons are sunk and *V5307* is damaged. On 20 Jan British torpedo aircraft attack a convoy near Stadlandet and damage the steamer *Emsland* (5180 tons) with the result that she has to be beached. The wreck is destroyed on 5 Feb by a torpedo from the submarine *Satyr* (Lt Weston) and by further air torpedo attacks on 11 Feb. On 20 Jan the German minelayer *Skagerrak* (1281 tons) is sunk by torpedo aircraft near Egersund. In attacks by British bombers on a convoy W of Stadlandet on 1 Feb, *UJ1702* is sunk and the steamer *Valencia* (3096 tons) badly damaged. From 7 to 13 Feb the British submarine *Taku* (Lt Pitt) sinks three ships of 13246 tons from convoys in the area of Stavanger and *Stubborn* (Lt Duff) sinks two ships of 3960 tons on 11 Feb and misses a convoy off Foldafjord on 13 Feb. On 13 Feb the Norwegian *MTB627* and *MTB653* sink two coasters totalling 2026 tons near Kristiansand North. The Norwegian submarine *Ula* (Lt Sars) misses German convoys near Egersund on 20 and 25 Feb.

15 Jan–5 Feb   Arctic
Soviet combined operation RV-1 against German convoy traffic on the polar coast with Adm Golovko in command. The air force of the Northern Fleet (Lt-Gen Andreev) makes reconnaissance flights as far as Lopphavet. There the submarine *L-22* reconnoitres. N of the German flanking mine barrages from the North Cape to Kongsfjord, the submarines *S-104*, *S-103*, *S-102*, *S-56*, *M-201* and *M-119* are alerted. On 17 Jan a torpedo aircraft, when carrying out an armed reconnaissance, reports an eastbound convoy off Tanafjord and attacks unsuccessfully. Four torpedo cutters are deployed from Pummanki without result. On 19 Jan *M-201* (Lt-Cdr Balin) misses a convoy off Tanafjord. On 20 Jan *S-56* (Capt 3rd Class Shchedrin) attacks the convoy off Sletnes and *S-102* (Capt 3rd Class Gorodnichi), which is deployed against the convoy when it is reported, also attacks it—without success. Similarly the deployment of the destroyers *Razyarenny*, *Razumny*, *Gremyashchi* and *Grozny* from 20 to 22 Jan and of the reserve submarines *S-14*, *S-15* and *M-105* leads to no result. On 23 Jan *S-*

56 misses a convoy of three steamers, the submarine-chaser *UJ1206* and the harbour patrol vessel *NKi11*, which also drive off *S-102*.
On 28 Jan *S-56* sinks the *Henrietta Schulte* (5056 tons) from a westbound convoy consisting of eight steamers escorted by *K1*, *M273*, *V5912*, *V5914*, *V5913*, *V5916*, *V6111*, *UJ1208*, *UJ1206*, *UJ1209* and *UJ1212*.

15 Jan–12 Feb   Mediterranean
The German transportation of supplies by sea along the Dalmatian coast becomes increasingly difficult and costly because of the greater use of Allied fighter-bombers from Italy. The British 24th DD Flotilla (T class) makes sorties in groups from Bari into the Central and Northern Adriatic. On 15–16 Jan *Blackmore* and *Ledbury* shell Durazzo, on 16–17 Jan *Troubridge* and *Tumult* shell Curzola and on 18–19 Jan two destroyers shell Curzola again. On 1–2 Feb *Tumult* and *Tenacious* shell Recanati and Pedaso S of Ancona and on 4–5 Feb *Tumult* and *Teazer* bombard Hvar and Curzola. On 12 Feb Curzola is again hit.

16–21 Jan   English Channel
The German 5th MTB Flotilla (Cdr Klug), comprising *S143*, *S142*, *S141*, *S100*, *S138*, *S136* and *S84*, tries unsuccessfully to attack a westbound convoy off Lizard Head during the night 16–17 Feb. After 11 torpedo misses, the boats are driven off by the escort. On 20–21 Jan the flotilla (as above but with *S137* instead of *S136*) is attacked by Beaufighters of Coastal Command when making a sortie towards Start Point. It turns away with slight damage. The British destroyers, MGBs and MTBs deployed to intercept the boats find nothing.
The 4th MTB Flotilla (Lt-Cdr Fimmen), comprising *S87*, *S99*, *S117*, *S130* and *S150*, lays 23 LMB mines off Orfordness. The same night, the German blockade-runner *Münsterland*, in trying to avoid shelling by British long-range batteries near Dover, goes ashore in fog W of Cap Blanc Nez and is destroyed by shelling. When they proceed through the channel, *T28* and *T29* avoid the British MTBs deployed against them. *T28* springs a leak in the boiler room when attacked in the Straits of Dover by two Albacore aircraft of Coastal Command.

20 Jan   Air War/Germany
During an air attack on Rostock, the German gun ferry *AF80* is sunk.

21–29 Jan   Mediterranean
Operation 'Shingle': landing by the VI US Corps (Maj-Gen Lucas) both sides of Anzio/Nettuno. On 21 Jan the ships set out from the Bay of Naples and early on 22 Jan the landing begins. TF.81, with Rear-Adm

Lowry on the headquarters ship *Biscayne*, is designated. The Southern Attack Force ('X-Ray', Lowry), comprising five LSIs, 51 LSTs, four LCG/Fs, 60 LCIs, 32 LCTs, two LCT(R)s, 23 MLs and PC/SCs and 10 other craft and the beacon submarine *Uproar*, lands the 3rd US Inf Div (Maj-Gen Truscott); support and escort are provided by the cruisers USS *Brooklyn* and HMS *Penelope*, the US destroyers *Plunkett*, *Gleaves*, *Niblack*, *Woolsey*, *Mayo*, *Trippe*, *Ludlow* and *Edison*, the British 'Hunt' destroyer *Croome*, the Greek *Themistokles* and *Kriti*, the US DEs *Herbert C Jones* and *Frederick C Davis*, the Dutch gunboats *Flores* and *Zoemba*, the British AA ship *Palomares* and 23 US minesweepers. The Northern Attack Force ('Peter', Rear-Adm Troubridge), consisting of the headquarters ship *Bulolo*, three LSIs, three large LSTs (*Boxer*, *Bruiser* and *Buster*), 30 LSTs, four LCG/Fs, 29 LCIs, 17 LCTs, one LCT(R), 17 PCs, SCs and MLs, 13 other craft and the beacon submarine *Ultor*, lands the 1st British Inf Div (Maj-Gen Penney); support and escort groups are made up of the cruisers *Orion* (Rear-Adm Mansfield) and *Spartan* (with the Soviet Rear-Adm Frolov on board), the AA ship *Ulster Queen*, the destroyers *Jervis*, *Janus*, *Laforey*, *Loyal*, *Inglefield*, *Tenacious*, *Urchin* and *Kempenfelt*, the 'Hunt' destroyers *Beaufort*, *Brecon*, *Wilton* and *Tetcott* and 16 minesweepers.
On 22 Jan 36034 troops and 3069 vehicles are landed. The minesweeper *Portent* is lost on a mine and *LCI20* as a result of a bomb hit. The AA ship *Palomares* is damaged on a mine. In an air attack on 23 Jan the destroyer *Janus* is sunk by and the destroyer *Jervis* damaged by Hs 293 glider bombs. When the supply convoy arrives on 24 Jan the hospital ship *St David* (2702 tons) is sunk in an air attack and the destroyer *Plunkett* damaged. The destroyer *Mayo* is damaged on a mine. On 26 Jan *LST422*, *LCI32* and *YMS30* are lost on mines and *LST336* is damaged by fighter-bombers. On 29 Jan the cruiser *Spartan* and the transport *Samuel Huntington* (7181 tons) fall victim to air attacks by, respectively, Do 217Ks of III/KG 100 and Ju 88s of I/LG 1 armed with bombs and glider bombs. By 29 Jan 68886 troops, 508 guns and 237 tanks have been landed.

22 Jan   Baltic
The German MMS *R75* is sunk in a collision with *U350* E of Hela.

25 Jan–10 Mar   Mediterranean
From 30 Jan the cruisers *Dido*, *Delhi*, *Brooklyn* (US), *Phoebe*, *Orion*, *Penelope*, *Mauritius* and *Philadelphia* (US) and several destroyers listed in the entry 21–29 Jan are deployed, usually in pairs, to support the

troops landed at Anzio. On 16 Feb the transport *Elihu Yale* (7176 tons) and *LCT35* are lost in bomb attacks and on 25 Feb the destroyer *Inglefield* to an Hs 293. The DE *Herbert C Jones* is damaged on 15 Feb. Many attacks are made on ships of the landing fleet by the German submarines deployed against the invasion at Anzio. On 25 Jan *U223* (Lt Gerlach) attacks a corvette and *U230* (Lt-Cdr Siegmann) a group of destroyers with T-5s and salvos—without success. On 27 Jan *Mauritius* and the destroyer *Kempenfelt* bombard roads near Formia. On 29 Jan *U223* misses a destroyer with a T-5 and the following day a landing boat and two LSTs with T-5s and salvos. On 1 Feb *U371* (Lt-Cdr Mehl) misses two destroyers with T-5s and one LST on 3 Feb, and on 2 Feb *Orion* and the Dutch gunboat *Soemba* bombard Formia. On 15 Feb *U410* (Lt Fenski) sinks a Liberty ship (7154 tons) with a T-5 and on 16 Feb *U230* sinks the British *LST418* with a T-5 and misses one submarine-chaser. On 17 Feb *U410* misses a destroyer and a patrol ship and sinks the British cruiser *Penelope* with a T-5, finishing her on 18 Feb. On 18 Feb *Mauritius* and the destroyer *Laforey* bombard Formia. On the next day *U410* misses another destroyer. On 20 Feb *U230* sinks the British *LST305* with a T-5 and *U410* the American *LST348* with a standard torpedo. On 24 Feb *U410* misses an LST and on 26 Feb *U952* (Lt Curio) a destroyer. *U616* (Lt Koitschka) misses a destroyer with a T-5 on both 2 and 6 Mar. *U952* sinks a Liberty ship of 7176 tons on 10 Mar. The US destroyers *Plunkett*, *Frederick C Davis* and *Herbert C Jones* try to interfere with the long-range control of the glider bombs by jamming.

25 Jan–16 Apr   Atlantic

In operations in distant waters, *U845* and *U539* cruise off Newfoundland until the beginning of Mar, followed by *U802* and *U856*. From the middle of Mar *U170* and *U550* cruise between Bermuda, the Bahamas and the American East Coast. In addition to some misses, *U845* (Cdr Weber) and *U802* (Lt-Cdr Schmoeckel) each sink one ship, of 7039 tons and 1621 tons respectively. On 7 Apr the US Desdiv 32 (Cdr Melson), comprising *Boyle*, *Nields*, *Ordronaux*, *Champlin* and the DE *Huse*, is deployed against *U856* when she is found and the last two sink her. On 16 Apr *U550* (Lt-Cdr Hänert) sinks a tanker of 11017 tons but is herself sunk after a T-5 miss by the DEs *Gandy*, *Joyce* and *Peterson* which are deployed against her.

On the way to the Caribbean, *U518* (Lt Offermann) misses an escort carrier SW of the Azores on 13 Feb and sinks a ship of 3401 tons in the Caribbean on 7 Mar. *U154* misses a tanker and escapes on 15 Mar from the search made by the US submarine-chaser *PC469* and, again, from the Columbian destroyer *Caldas* on 29–30 Mar. *U218* lays mines off Santa Lucia on 23 Mar and off San Juan on 1 Apr. On 7 Apr *U856* is sunk in the Caribbean by the US destroyers *Champlin* and *Huse*.

Off Freetown, *U123* misses a convoy on 10 Mar; *U66* (Lt Seehausen) sinks four ships of 19754 tons in the Gulf of Guinea and *U214* lays mines off Casablanca on 3 Apr. In the South Atlantic, *U177* is sunk on her way to the Indian Ocean on 6 Feb by a Liberator of VP-107 USN from Ascension Island. *UIT22* is damaged on 22 Feb and sunk on 11 Mar by Catalinas 'D' of No 279 Sqn RSAAF and 'P' of No 262 Sqn RSAAF and *U851* is missing from the end of Mar. In the middle of Mar US TG.21.16 (Capt Hughes), comprising the escort carrier *Block Island*, the destroyer *Corry* and the DEs *Thomas*, *Breeman*, *Bronstein* and *Bostwick*, operates SW of the Azores and, after a two-day hunt, sinks *U801* on 17 Mar and the torpedo transport *U1059* on her way to East Asia on 19 Mar. But the submarine shoots down one aircraft. The group is relieved by the beginning of Apr by TG.21.11 (Capt Dunn), comprising *Bogue*, the destroyer *Hobson* and the DEs *Haverfield*, *Janssen*, *Willis* and *Swenning*. It is followed by TG.21.12 (Capt Gallery), comprising *Guadalcanal*, the destroyer *Forrest* and the DEs *Pope*, *Pillsbury*, *Chatelain* and *Flaherty*. To it fall victim the hitherto very successful boats *U515* and *U68* on 9 and 10 Apr on their way to West Africa after *U214* (Lt-Cdr Stock) has missed one of the DEs with a T-5 on 8 Apr.

26 Jan   South West Pacific

TG.74.2 (Rear-Adm Berkey), comprising the cruisers *Phoenix* and *Boise* and the destroyers *Ammen*, *Mullany* and *Bush*, shell Madang and Alexishafen with 901 rounds of 6in and 2651 rounds of 5in shell.

26 Jan–24 Feb   Mediterranean

On 26 Jan *U455* passes through the Straits of Gibraltar to the Mediterranean. On 1 Feb 40 torpedo aircraft of the 2nd Fl Div attack the convoy UGS.30 N of Oran and sink the freighter *Edward Bates* (7176 tons). British Beaufighters, flown off from Sardinia, drive some of the torpedo aircraft away from the target. In a US air attack on Toulon on 4 Feb, *U343*, *U380* and *U642* are damaged. On 5 Feb *U969* and on 17 Feb *U967* and *U586* pass through the Straits of Gibraltar. At first the boats operate off Algeria, where *U969* (Lt Dobbert) torpedoes two ships of

14352 tons from a westbound convoy on 22 Feb. They are taken in tow but become total losses. To prevent further attempts to intrude, the US Catalina Sqn VP-63, equipped with MAD (Magnetic Anomaly Detector), is employed from Morocco from the middle of Feb and aircraft '15' and '14' locate *U761* on 24 Feb and attack and sink the boat with support from Catalina 'G' of No 202 Sqn RAF, a Ventura of VPB-127 USN and the destroyers *Anthony* and *Wishart*.

29 Jan–6 Feb   Central Pacific

TF.58 (Vice-Adm Mitscher) attacks Japanese bases in the Marshall Islands in support of Operation 'Flintlock' (see 31 Jan). TG.58.1 (Rear-Adm Reeves), consisting of the carriers *Enterprise*, *Yorktown* and *Belleau Wood*, the battleships *Massachusetts* (Rear-Adm Lee), *Indiana* (Rear-Adm Davis) and *Washington*, the cruiser *Oakland* and the destroyers *Clarence K Bronson*, *Cotten*, *Dortch*, *Gatling*, *Healy*, *Corgswell*, *Caperton*, *Ingersoll* and *Knapp*, attacks Maloelap on 29 Jan and Kwajalein on 30 and 31 Jan and up to 3 Feb. TG.58.2 (Rear-Adm Montgomery), consisting of the carriers *Essex*, *Intrepid* and *Cabot*, the battleships *South Dakota* (Rear-Adm Hanson), *Alabama* and *North Carolina*, the cruiser *San Diego* (Rear-Adm Wiltse) and the destroyers *Owen*, *Miller*, *The Sullivans*, *Stephen Potter*, *Hickox*, *Hunt*, *Lewis Hancock*, *Sterett* and *Stack*, attacks Roi from 29 to 31 Jan and from 1 to 3 Feb. TG.58.3 (Rear-Adm Sherman), consisting of the carriers *Bunker Hill*, *Monterey* and *Cowpens*, the battleships *Iowa* (Rear-Adm Hustvedt) and *New Jersey*, the cruiser *Wichita* and the destroyers *Izard*, *Charrette*, *Conner*, *Bell*, *Burns*, *Bradford*, *Brown*, *Cowell* and *Wilson*, attacks Eniwetok from 30 Jan to 2 Feb. TG.58.4 (Rear-Adm Ginder), consisting of the carriers *Saratoga*, *Princeton* and *Langley*, the cruisers *Boston* (Rear-Adm Thebaud), *Baltimore* and *San Juan* and the destroyers *Maury*, *Craven*, *Gridley*, *McCall*, *Dunlap*, *Fanning*, *Case* and *Cummings*, attacks Wotje on 29 Jan, Maloelap on 30–31 Jan and, after refuelling on 1 Feb, Eniwetok from 3 to 6 Feb. A total of 6232 sorties are flown; 22 aircraft are lost to the defences and 27 by accident. In addition, there is TG.50.15 (neutralisation group), comprising the heavy cruisers *Chester*, *Pensacola* and *Salt Lake City* and the destroyers *Erben*, *Walker*, *Hale* and *Abbott*.

To cover Operation 'Flintlock', US submarines are deployed around Truk: *Permit*, *Skipjack* (Lt-Cdr Molumphy), which sinks one ship of 6666 tons and the destroyer *Suzukaze*, and *Guardfish* (Lt-Cdr Ward), which sinks one ship of 10024 tons and the destroyer *Umikaze*. *Seal* is deployed off Ponape, *Sunfish* off Kusaie and *Searaven* off Eniwetok.

30 Jan   Baltic
The German minesweeper *M451* runs aground near Porkkala (Kallbada) and is lost.

30 Jan   Bay of Biscay
During exercises in the southern Bay of Biscay involving *Z23*, *Z32* and *Z37*, the last two collide and *Z37* is heavily damaged by a consequent torpedo explosion. Repairs to the destroyer at Bordeaux are never completed.

30–31 Jan   South West Pacific
The fast transports *Stringham*, *Talbot* and *Waters* land, with support from the US destroyers *Fullam* and *Guest*, 300 New Zealand and American troops to make an armed reconnaissance on the Green Islands and re-embark them on the following day.

31 Jan–5 Feb   English Channel
Six boats of the 5th MTB Flotilla sink the freighters *Emerald* (806 tons) and *Caleb Sprague* (1813 tons) from convoy CW.243 and the trawler *Pine* (545 tons) SE of Beachy Head on 31 Jan.

On 5 Feb there is an engagement between *T29*, *M156* and *M206* and the British destroyers *Tanatside*, *Talybont*, *Brissenden* and *Wensleydale* off the north Brittany coast. *M156* is badly damaged: she arrives in L'Abervrach and is destroyed there by Typhoons of No 266 Sqn RAF.

31 Jan–7 Feb   Central Pacific
After preparatory action by TF.58 (see 29 Jan), the 5th US Fleet (Vice-Adm Spruance) makes a landing on Kwajalein Atoll (Operation 'Flintlook'). The landing fleet is commanded by Rear-Adm Turner, the landing troops by Maj-Gen H M Smith USMC.

The Southern TF.52 (Rear-Adm Turner) with two APDs, 12 APAs, three AKAs, three LSDs, 16 LSTs and 12 LSIs lands the 7th US Inf Div (Maj-Gen Corlett) on Kwajalein; escort is provided by the destroyers *John Rodgers*, *Hazelwood*, *Haggard*, *Franks*, *Schroeder* and *Hailey*. Fire Support Group 52.8 (Rear-Adm Giffen) comprises the battleships *Idaho*, *Pennsylvania*, *New Mexico* and *Mississippi*, the cruisers *Minneapolis*, *New Orleans* and *San Francisco* and the destroyers *McKee*, *Stevens*, *Bailey*, *Frazier*, *Hall*, *Meade*, *Colahan*, *Murray*, *Harrison*, *Ringgold* and *Sigsbee*. Air Support Group 52.9 (Rear-Adm Davison) comprises the escort carriers *Manila Bay*, *Coral Sea* and *Corregidor* and the destroyers *Bancroft*, *Coghlan*, *Caldwell* and *Halligan*.

Northern Attack Force 53 (Rear-Adm Connolly), with 12 APAs, three AKAs, two LSDs and 15 LSTs, lands the 4th Marine Div (Maj-Gen Smith) on Roi; escort is provided by the destroyers *Remey*, *MacDonough*, *La Valette*, *Fletcher*, *Hughes*, *Ellet* and *Aylwin*. Fire Support Group 53.5 (Rear-Adm Oldendorf) comprises the battleships *Tennessee*, *Colorado* and *Maryland*, the cruisers *Louisville*, *Mobile*, *Santa Fé*, *Indianapolis* and *Biloxi* and the destroyers *Morris*, *Anderson*, *Mustin*, *Russell*, *Porterfield*, *Haraden*, *Hopewell*, *Johnston* and *Phelps*. Air Support Group 53.6 (Rear-Adm Ragsdale) comprises the escort carriers *Sangamon*, *Suwanee* and *Chenango* and the destroyers *Farragut*, *Monaghan* and *Dale*.

After bombardment by aircraft and, on 30 Jan, by battleships of TG.58.1, the landings are made on 31 Jan with fire support from TG.52.8 and TG.53.5. By 7 Feb 21342 troops have been landed in the S and 20104 in the N. Total losses are 372 dead and 1582 wounded. The resistance of the Japanese defenders (8675 men under Rear-Adm Akiyama) is broken by 7 Feb. There are only 265 prisoners.

On 31 Jan TG.51.2 (Rear-Adm Hill) with a battalion of the 27th US Inf Div on one APA, two APDs and one LST, escorted by the cruiser *Portland*, the escort carriers *Nassau* and *Natoma Bay* and the destroyers *Bullard*, *Black*, *Kidd* and *Chauncey*, occupies the undefended Majuro Atoll. It becomes an important base for the US Fleet. The first ships of TG.58 enter on 2 Feb.

31 Jan–20 Feb   North Atlantic
The British 2nd EG (Capt Walker), consisting of the sloops *Starling*, *Kite*, *Magpie* and *Woodpecker* and the carriers *Nairana* and *Activity*, has been sent to support the convoys proceeding W of Ireland. It sinks *U592* on 31 Jan. From 3 Feb the U-boats W of Ireland are concentrated singly and in loose formation as 'Igel 1' (*U985*, *U714*, *U283*, *U989*, *U547*, *U984*, *U212*, *U545*, *U666*, *U386*, *U549*, *U441*, *U406* and *U746*) and 'Igel 2' (*U281*, *U256*, *U650*, *U963*, *U731*, *U709* and *U91*); later they are joined by *U734* and *U546*, and by *U618*, *U238*, *U424* and *U445* respectively, to search for convoys ONS.29 and ON.223 respectively. *U846*, *U260* and *U257* are detached as weather boats. In the N, *U985* (Lt-Cdr Kessler) sinks one ship of 1735 tons from convoy RA.56 proceeding from Iceland to Loch Ewe and on 5 Feb *U256* shoots down Liberator 'T' of No 53 Sqn RAF. The 'Igel' boats are deployed against convoy SL.147/MKS.38, which is reported by Ju 290s of FAGr 5 on 6 Feb N of the Azores, and again on 7 and 8 Feb. With the convoy

is EG.B3 (Cdr Evans) with the frigates *Towy* and *La Découverte* (French), the destroyer *Burza* (Polish), the corvettes *Orchis*, *Narcissus*, *Roselys*, *Aconit* and *Renoncule*, and the A/S trawler *Northern Spray*. The 2nd SG (Capt Walker) with sloops (see above) is deployed. On 8 Feb *Wild Goose* locates *U762*, which is sunk by *Starling* and *Woodpecker*. Early on 9 Feb *U734* (Lt Blauert) and *U238* (Lt Hess) just miss *Wild Goose* and *Starling* and *Kite* and *Magpie* with T-5s and are then sunk in the course of lengthy searches. During this operation convoy UC.12 (US escort group) passes further to the N of the 'Igel' formation. On 10 Feb *U256* misses with T-5s escort vessels of HX.277 (EG.B1 and the 6th SG comprising six Canadian frigates). In the evening of 10 Feb, and during the following night, aircraft of No 15 Group Coastal Command undertake massed sorties to cover HX.277 and the outbound ON.223 (EG.B7 under Cdr Gretton on *Duncan*), the 10th SG (four frigates) and the escort carriers *Fencer* and *Striker*). Swordfish 'A' of No 842 Sqn FAA from *Fencer* sinks *U666* on 10 Feb and on 11 Feb *U424* is sunk by *Wild Goose* and *Woodpecker*. In the process *U545* and *U283* each shoot down, with the new 3.7 cm AA gun, one Leigh Light Wellington, 'N' of No 612 Sqn RAF, and an aircraft from No 407 Sqn RCAF, but they are themselves lost, *U545* to Wellington 'O' of No 612 Sqn RAF and *U283* to Wellington 'D' of No 407 Sqn RCAF. *U714* rescues the crew of *U545*. In the evening of 10 Feb, and during the night, *U731*, *U413* and *U437* repeatedly attack, further to the S, the escorts of the convoy OS.67/KMS.41 (39th EG with the carrier *Pursuer*) unsuccessfully with T-5s and shake off the hunters with 'Aphrodite' balloons with anti-radar metal foil. In the evening of 12 Feb seven He 177s of II/KG 40, which try to attack the convoy, are driven off by fighters from *Pursuer* which shoot down one He 177 and a contact-keeping Fw 200. On 13 Feb air reconnaissance sights, W of the North Channel, one of the incoming convoys, HX.277, CU.13 (US escort group) or SL.147, which is supported by the carriers *Nairana* and *Activity*. Further to the W, *U445* misses a DE of the 3rd SG (Cdr Mills on *Duckworth*) with a T-5 and is damaged in a counter-attack. On 14 Feb a Ju 290 and two Ju 88s locate, W of the North Channel, convoys ONS.29 (EG.B6 under Cdr Curry on the destroyer *Fame*, with *Vanquisher* and *Vesper*, the frigate *Deveron* and the corvettes *Kingcup*, *Vervain*, *Eglantine*, *Rose* and *Acantus*—the last three Norwegian), ON.224 (EG.C1) and OS.68/KMS.42, one of which is found again on 15 Feb by the three Ju 290s sent out in search. On 16 Feb two Ju 290s are lost. Convoy HX.278 approaches from the SW on 16 Feb with EG.B2 (Cdr Macintyre on the destroyer *Hesperus*) and the support and escort groups 2, B7 and 10 (see above). *U546* and *U984* are able to beat off the night aircraft with their 3.7 cm AA guns but do not attack. After the U-boat formations are passed, the C-in-C Western Approaches (Adm Horton) sends on 17 Feb the 2nd SG and EG.B7 to ON.224 and the 10th SG (Cdr Ormsby) with the frigates *Spey*, *Rother*, *Findhorn* and *Lossie* to ONS.29, which, together with the carrier *Striker*, is reported in the afternoon by a Ju 290. The Cdr U-boats assembles *U441*, *U546*, *U549*, *U985*, *U989*, *U406*, *U764*, *U212*, *U256*, *U709*, *U424*, *U608*, *U91*, *U603*, *U386*, *U437*, *U264*, *U963*, *U281*, *U650* and *U231* as the 'Hai' group against the convoys. But it is recognised by the British who go round it to the S. The Cdr U-boats tries to counter the evasive move, detected by the German B-Service, with massive air reconnaissance by 10 aircraft. Three aircraft find the convoy and one is shot down by fighters. During the night 18–19 Feb the convoys pass the U-boats. In the process *Spey* sinks *U406*, among whose survivors are several German radar experts, and *U386*. *Woodpecker* and *Starling* sink the first U-boat fitted with schnorkel, *U264*. *U437* and *U764* miss escorts with T-5s. *U256* (Lt Brauel) torpedoes the sloop *Woodpecker*, which sinks while under tow on 27 Feb. *U413* (Lt Poel), stationed on her own off the Scilly Isles, sinks the destroyer *Warwick* with a FAT on 20 Feb.

1 Feb Norway
The German A/S vessel *UJ1702* is sunk by bombs in an air attack W of Stadlandet.

1–29 Feb Mediterranean
In USAAF air attacks on Toulon on 4 Feb, the French netlayer *Le Gladiateur* (in repair as the German escort *SG18*) and the raised French destroyer *Vautour* are sunk and the escort vessel *SG16* (ex-sloop *La Curieuse*) is badly damaged. In attacks on Ercole and Leghorn on 14, 17 and 18 Feb, *KF458*, *R39* and *KT31* are sunk and *F770*, *R200* and the steamer *Ettore* (4270 tons) are beached after being heavily hit (*R200* is later repaired). One sailing ship is sunk by the British submarine *Ultor* (Lt Hunt) and one ship damaged; the outbound minelayer *Niedersachsen* is sunk on 15 Feb by *Upstart* (Lt Chapman) and from 27 to 29 Feb *Cesteriane* (6664 tons), escorted by *SG15*, is torpedoed and *Chieti* (3152 tons) is sunk by *Uproar* (Lt Herrick).

Mining operations by the German 10th TB

Flotilla (Cdr v Gartzen): 'Maulwurf' (1–2 Feb), 'Schlange' (3–4 Feb), 'Kobra' (16–17 Feb) and 'Delphin' (25–26 Feb). There are engagements with enemy MTBs on 14–15 Feb and on 18–19 Feb. During Operation 'Nussknacker', the shelling of Bastia (Corsica), the torpedo boat *TA23* is in action three times, *TA24* five times, *TA25* once, *TA26* twice, *TA27* four times and *TA28* three times. *SG15* makes several sorties to Capreira.

1–29 Feb Pacific
Continuation of US submarine operations with assistance from 'Ultra' data. Tankers are designated priority targets.

In Japanese waters and the East China Sea during Feb, *Gudgeon* (Lt-Cdr Post) sinks one ship of 3091 tons and five sailing vessels, *Grayback* (Lt-Cdr Moore) sinks four ships of 21594 tons but is sunk by a Japanese aircraft S of Okinawa on 27 Feb, *Trout* (Lt-Cdr Clark) sinks two ships of 18535 tons but is herself sunk by a Japanese destroyer on 29 Feb NW of the Philippines and *Sandlance* (Lt-Cdr Garrison) sinks three ships of 12756 tons, on 3 Mar the Soviet freighter *Belorossiya* (2900 tons) and on 13 Mar the cruiser *Tatsuta*. In the area of the Mandate Islands, *Pogy* (Lt-Cdr Metcalf) sinks on 10 Feb the destroyer *Minekaze* and later four more ships of 19855 tons, *Cod* (Lt-Cdr Dempsey) sinks two ships of 9831 tons, *Hoe* (Lt-Cdr McCrea) sinks one ship of 10526 tons and damages one more of 10051 tons, *Cero* (Lt-Cdr White) sinks one ship of 1086 tons and damages one of 2655 tons, *Sargo* (Lt-Cdr Garnett) sinks two ships of 11809 tons and damages one oiler of 14050 tons and *Balao* (Lt-Cdr Cole) sinks three ships of 15383 tons. *Apogon*, *Permit*, *Darter* and *Robalo* attack ships but have no success, but there are some successes by the submarines used to support Operation 'Hailstone' against Truk (see 17–23 Feb).

In the South West Pacific, the Malayan Archipelago and the Philippines, *Jack* (Lt-Cdr Dykers) sinks four ships of 20563 tons, *Puffer* (Lt-Cdr Shelby) sinks one ship of 15105 tons, *Rasher* (Lt-Cdr Laughon) sinks four ships of 20221 tons and *Ray* (Lt-Cdr Harrel) lays a minefield off Saigon on which one ship of 834 tons sinks in July 1945.

1 Feb–8 Mar Mediterranean
In British fighter-bomber attacks on Porto Lago (Delos) on 1 Feb, the submarine-chaser *UJ2124* is sunk. On 2 Feb NE of Amorgos there is an attack on a convoy with three *TA* boats and the steamer *Leda* (4573 tons), which sinks. The torpedo boat *TA14* receives a bomb hit in the engine room. On 7 Feb the Swedish Red Cross steamer *Viril*

(933 tons) is sunk in Chios. On 22 Feb the steamer *Lisa* (5343 tons), which is escorted by *TA15* and *TA17*, is sunk by an airborne torpedo N of Heraklion and on 4 Mar the steamer *Sifnos* (387 tons) is sunk in Suda Bay.

The British submarine *Sportsman* (Lt Gatehouse) sinks the steamer *Petrella* (3209 tons) on 8 Feb and the Greek *Nereus* (Lt-Cdr Panaglotes) torpedoes the *Peter* (3754 tons) on 19 Feb. Further attacks fail. *Pipinos* and *Matrozos* have no success. On 8 Mar *TA15*, while proceeding with *TA19* from Heraklion to Piraeus, is sunk by British bombers; she is raised and in repair at Piraeus when sunk by air raid (see 12 Oct 1944).

2 Feb Baltic
The German patrol vessel *V1702* sinks after colliding with *U987* during exercises.

3 Feb Air War/Germany
In an air attack by the US 8th AF on Wilhelmshaven, the accommodation ship *Monte Pasqual* (13870 tons) is burnt out and the minesweepers *M18* and *M29* are severely damaged.

4 Feb North Pacific
A US task group (Rear-Adm Baker), comprising the cruisers *Detroit* and *Raleigh* and the destroyers *Meade*, *Frazier*, *Gansevoort* and *Edwards*, bombards Paramushiro (Kuriles).

9 Feb Bay of Biscay
The returning *U193* is damaged NW of Cape Finisterre in an air attack and has to enter El Ferrol on 10 Feb to effect repairs. The boat is transferred to Lorient 19–25 Feb.

10 Feb Arctic
An Fw 200 of I/KG 40 sinks the British tanker *El Grillo* (7264 tons) off the east coast of Iceland.

10–26 Feb Air War/Western Europe
Mine offensive by RAF Bomber Command. In 14 nights, 633 sorties are flown against Biscay and Channel ports, especially Bayonne, Lorient, Cherbourg and the Frisian Islands and in the Kattegat and the western Baltic, particularly the Kiel area. Four aircraft are lost. The German MMS *R222* is sunk after hitting an air-laid mine E of Schleimünde on 21 Feb. The MDS *Sperrbrecher 10/Vigo* sinks N of Norderney on 7 Mar.

11–14 Feb Arctic
On 11–12 Feb 15 heavy Soviet bombers try to attack *Tirpitz* with 1000kg bombs. Only four aircraft find the target. A near-miss is obtained which causes slight damage.

In a Soviet air attack on Hammerfest on 14

Feb, two Norwegian coasters totalling 652 tons are lost.

11 Feb–30 May   Black Sea
Transfer of the Soviet submarines *M-202* and *M-203* from the Caspian Flotilla to the Black Sea Fleet.

12–15 Feb   English Channel/North Sea
During the night 12–13 Feb the German 2nd MTB Flotilla (Cdr Feldt), comprising *S62*, *S98*, *S80*, *S92*, *S86*, *S67* and *S83*, carries out mining operations SE of Grimsby (26 LMB mines) and the 8th MTB Flotilla (Cdr Zymalkowski), comprising *S64*, *S65*, *S68*, *S85*, *S93*, *S99*, *S127*, *S129* and *S133*, SE of the Humber (36 LMB mines). *S99* and *S65* sink the trawler *Cap d'Antifer* with torpedoes.

During the night 13–14 Feb both flotillas repeat the mining operation E of Great Yarmouth. The 2nd Flotilla (composition as before) breaks off the operation prematurely; the 8th Flotilla, with the mining boats *S85*, *S64*, *S127* and *S65*, lays a barrage. The combat force comprises *S99*, *S93*, *S133*, *S129*, and *S127*. During the night 14–15 Feb the 2nd MTB Flotilla, comprising *S89*, *S98*, *S92*, *S80* and *S67*, lays 21 LMB mines SE of Great Yarmouth. When they retire they are pursued by the British corvettes *Mallard* and *Shearwater*. The deployment of the British *MTB455*, *MTB444*, *MTB443*, *MTB441* and *MTB439* is observed by German air reconnaissance and the returning 2nd Flotilla and the 8th Flotilla, which set out as a combat group comprising *S93*, *S64*, *S117*, *S127*, *S129*, *S85*, *S133*, *S99* and *S65*, are employed against them. In an engagement with three boats of the German 34th MS Flotilla, *MTB455* and *MTB444* are damaged. *M3411* sinks after a collision when trying to avoid the enemy. In ensuing engagements, the other British MTBs and *S89* and *S133* are damaged. A sortie by 13 motor torpedo boats of the 5th and 9th Flotillas from Cherbourg against a convoy off Beachy Head is prematurely broken off when the force is located by British radar.

12–19 Feb   North Sea
Four operations in the Skagerrak by the Germans to lay defensive minefields for the northern 'Westwall' barrages: on 12–13 Feb the minelayers (Capt v Schönermark) *Brummer*, *Linz* and *Roland*, with the 6 DD Flotilla (Capt Kothe) with the destroyers *Z39*, *Z28* and *Erich Steinbrinck*, lay 'Dorothea A'; on 15–16 Feb *Brummer* and *Roland*, with the destroyers *Erich Steinbrinck* and *Hans Lody*, lay 'Dorothea B'; and on 17–

18 and 18–19 Feb *Brummer*, *Roland*, *Erich Steinbrinck* and *Hans Lody* lay 'Dorothea C' and 'D'.

13 Feb   Norway
Near Hustadvika in central Norway, the Norwegian *MTB627* and *MTB653* attack the Norwegian coasters *Irma* (1392 tons) and *Henry* (363 tons), which are in German service, and sink them.

14–18 Feb   Baltic
During exercises in the Gulf of Danzig, *U738* sinks following a collision with a steamer on 14 Feb; the boat is later raised and decommissioned. On 18 Feb *U7* is lost in a diving accident.

15–19 Feb   South Pacific
The III Amphibious Force (Rear-Adm Wilkinson) lands the 3rd New Zealand Div on Green Island (off New Ireland) on 15 Feb with nine APDs escorted by the destroyers *Fullam*, *Guest*, *Bennett*, *Hudson* and *Halford*, 12 LCIs escorted by the destroyers *Waller*, *Pringle*, *Saufley*, *Philip*, *Renshaw* and *Sigourney* and seven LSTs escorted by the destroyers *Conway*, *Eaton*, *Anthony*, *Wadsworth*, *Terry* and *Braine*. Cover to the N and E is provided by TF.39 (Rear-Adm Merrill) with the cruisers *Montpelier* and *Columbia* and five destroyers and to the S by TF.38 (Rear-Adm Ainsworth) with the cruisers *Honolulu* and *St Louis* and five destroyers.

During the night 17–18 Feb Desron 12 (Capt Simpson) shells Kavieng with 3868 rounds of 5in from the destroyers *Farenholt*, *Buchanan*, *Lansdowne*, *Lardner* and *Woodworth* and Desron 23 (Capt Burke) shells Rabaul with 6681 rounds of 5in from *Charles Ausburne*, *Dyson*, *Stanly*, *Converse* and *Spence*. During the night 22–23 Feb Desron 12 shells Kavieng again. On 24–25 Feb Desron 45 (Capt Earle) shells Rabaul with *Fullam*, *Bennett*, *Guest*, *Halford*, *Hudson*, *Anthony* and *Braine* and on 29 Feb–1 Mar Desron 22 (Capt Petersen) shells it again with *Waller*, *Philip*, *Renshaw*, *Saufley*, *Conway*, *Eaton*, *Sigourney* and *Pringle*.

17–23 Feb   Central Pacific
Operation 'Catchpole'. TF.51.11 (Rear-Adm Hill), with two APDs, eight APAs, one AKA, one LSD, nine LSTs and six LCIs, lands the reinforced 22nd Marine RCT and two battalions of the 106th Regt of the 27th US Inf Div, totalling 8000 men, on Eniwetok. Escort is provided by the destroyers *McCord*, *Trathen*, *Heerman*, *Hoel*, *Dewey*, *Hull*, *Hazelwood*, *Franks*, *Aylwin*, *Dale*, *Monaghan*, *Farragut*, *Haggard*, *Hailey* and *Johnston* and the Fire

Support Group (Rear-Adm Oldendorf) consists of the battleships *Pennsylvania*, *Colorado* and *Tennessee* and the cruisers *Indianapolis*, *Portland* and *Louisville*, with an Air Support Group (Rear-Adm Ragsdale) comprising the escort carriers *Sangamon*, *Suwanee* and *Chenango* and the destroyers *Morris*, *Hughes*, *Mustin* and *Ellet*. The landings are supported by TG.58.4 (see 29 Jan). On 17 Feb a landing takes place on Engebi and on 19 Feb on Eniwetok. By 23 Feb the resistance of the 3431 Japanese defenders (Maj-Gen Nishida) is overcome. There are only 64 prisoners. US losses are 195 dead and 521 wounded.

17–23 Feb   Central Pacific
On 12–13 Feb three groups from TF.58 (Vice-Adm Mitscher) set out from Majuro and replenish from five tankers on 15 Feb (Operation 'Hailstone'). TG.58.1 (Rear-Adm Reeves) comprises the carriers *Enterprise*, *Yorktown* and *Belleau Wood*, the cruisers *Santa Fé*, *Mobile*, *Biloxi* and *Oakland* and destroyers as on 29 Jan; TG.58.2 (Rear-Adm Montgomery) comprises the carriers *Essex*, *Intrepid* and *Cabot*, the cruisers *San Diego*, *San Francisco*, *Wichita* and *Baltimore* and destroyers as on 29 Jan but with *Stembel* and without *Sterett*; and TG.58.3 (Rear-Adm Sherman) comprises the carriers *Bunker Hill*, *Monterey* and *Cowpens*, the battleships *North Carolina*, *Massachusetts*, *South Dakota* and *Alabama* and destroyers as on 29 Jan with the addition of *Sterett* and *Lang*. In addition, TG 50.9 comprises the battleships *Iowa* and *New Jersey* (Vice-Adm Spruance), the cruisers *Minneapolis* and *New Orleans*, the carrier *Cowpens* (see above) and the destroyers *Izard*, *Charrette*, *Burns* and *Bradford*.

Early on 17 Feb there is a fighter strike on the 365 Japanese aircraft at Truk with the aircraft from the five fleet carriers. The light carriers operate against shipping. Towards evening on 17 Feb the Japanese attack with seven Kate torpedo bombers. A torpedo hit is scored on *Intrepid*, which is brought into Majuro with *Cabot*, two cruisers and four destroyers. On 18 Feb the aircraft of the remaining fleet carriers attack shipping targets: 1250 sorties are made in all and 400 tons of bombs are dropped. However, the heavy units of the Japanese Combined Fleet have recently transferred to Singapore, so only a small number of warships (though numerous auxiliaries) are sunk in the lagoon, which never again regains its importance as a base. In Truk the submarine tenders *Rio de Janeiro Maru* and *Heian Maru* as well as six tankers and 17 freighters totalling 137019 tons and about 250 aircraft are destroyed.

TG.50.9 steams round Truk to intercept fleeing ships. The training cruiser *Katori* and the destroyer *Maikaze* are sunk NW of Truk by gunfire from the US cruisers *Minneapolis* and *New Orleans* and the destroyers *Radford* and *Burns*; the cruiser *Naka* is sunk W of Truk by aircraft from the carriers *Bunker Hill* and *Cowpens*; the destroyer *Fumizuki* is sunk SW of Truk by aircraft from the carrier *Enterprise*; the destroyers *Oite* and *Tachikaze* are sunk by carrier aircraft W of Truk; and the AMCs *Aikoku Maru* and *Kiyosumi Maru* are sunk NW of Truk by carrier aircraft. Only the destroyer *Nowake* escapes the salvos of the covering battleships fired from a distance of 22 miles.

During Operation 'Hailstone', the US submarine *Seal* is stationed near Ponape and *Searaven* and *Darter* near Truk as planeguards to rescue airmen forced into the water. *Skate* (Lt-Cdr Gruner), which sinks the cruiser *Agano* on 16 Feb, *Tang* (Lt-Cdr O'Kane), which sinks one ship of 7129 tons, *Sunfish*, *Aspro* (Cdr Stevenson), which sinks the submarine *I-43*, *Burrfish*, *Dace* and *Gato* (Cdr Foley), which sinks three ships of 12903 tons and three small craft, take up positions in the exit channels from Truk.

On 20 Feb aircraft from TG.58.1 attack Jaluit; on 23 Feb TG.58.3 bombards Tinian and Rota and TG.58.2 bombards Saipan and Tinian. Japanese attempts to attack on 22 Feb fail. Of the submarines *Searaven*, *Apogon*, *Skipjack*, *Tang* and *Sunfish* (Lt-Cdr Shelby) deployed, the last two sink four ships of 14300 tons and two ships of 9437 tons respectively. 21300 tons of shipping are lost as a result of carrier aircraft action.

18–22 Feb   South Pacific
The Japanese minesweeper *W6*, which was damaged on 2 Nov 1943, is sunk by air attack on 18 Feb at Rabaul. On 22 Feb the US destroyers *Charles Ausburne*, *Dyson* and *Stanly* sink by gunfire the Japanese minelayer *Natsushima* off Kavieng.

20 Feb   Air War/Germany
The 1st Air Div of the USAAF attacks Hamburg with 432 B-17s.

20 Feb–10 Mar   Arctic
Convoy operations JW.57/RA.57. On 20 Feb convoy JW.57 sets out from Loch Ewe with 42 ships, escorted by Vice-Adm Glennie in the AA cruiser *Black Prince* with the escort carrier *Chaser*, an Ocean Escort Group (Capt Campbell on the destroyer *Milne*) and a Support Group (Cdr Tyson on the destroyer *Keppel*) with a total of 17 destroyers. The covering force is under Vice-Adm Palliser with the cruisers *Kent*, *Norfolk* and *Berwick*. The convoy is located

on 23 Feb by a Ju 88 of the Air Officer Commanding North (West) and for more than 10hr an Fw 200 maintains contact. The 'Werwolf' U-boat group (*U956*, *U674*, *U425*, *U601*, *U362*, *U739*, *U713*, *U313*, *U312* and *U990*) is deployed and, in addition, the 'Hartmut' group (*U472*, *U315*, *U673* and *U366*) sets out. On 24 Feb an Fw 200 keeps contact in spite of attacks by Martlets from *Chaser* and brings up *U425*, *U601*, *U739* and *U713*. But the last is sunk by *Keppel*. By the evening of 25 Feb the U-boats are driven off and Catalina flying boat 'M' of No 210 Sqn RAF sinks *U601*. In the evening *U990* (Lt-Cdr Nordheimer) sinks the destroyer *Mahratta* with a T-5: the destroyer *Impulsive* is able to rescue only a few of the crew. Although Fw 200s and Ju 88s still keep contact on 26 and 27 Feb, only *U956* (Lt Mohs), *U366* (Lt Langenburg) (four times), *U278* (Lt-Cdr Franze), *U312* (Lt-Cdr K H Nicolay) and *U362* (Lt Franz) are able to make unsuccessful T-5 attacks on escort vessels. On 28 Feb the convoy arrives in the Kola Inlet, observed by air reconnaissance. The remaining boats (*U739*, *U307*, *U315*, and *U472*) are formed into the 'Boreas' group to operate against the expected westbound convoy, and *U361*, *U959*, *U278*, *U973*, *U366*, *U673*, *U288* and *U354* join the formation, in some cases, after brief replenishment.

During the passage of the convoy, Operation 'Bayleaf' is carried out. The carrier *Furious* makes a raid on the Norwegian coast on 24 Feb. The battleships *Anson* and *Richelieu* (French), two cruisers and seven destroyers belong to the force. Of them, *Musketeer* and *Blyskawica* (Polish) are damaged in a collision.

On 2 Mar convoy RA.57 sets out again with 31 ships and the escort of JW.57. While Soviet destroyers, minesweepers and submarine-chasers look for submarines N of the Kola Estuary, the convoy makes a wide detour to the E, but it is located by air reconnaissance on 4 Mar. In the night *U739* (Lt Mangold) just misses the destroyer *Swift* and *U472* (Lt Frhr v Forstner), after missing with a T-5, is damaged by aircraft 'B' of No 816 Sqn FAA from *Chaser* and has to scuttle herself under gunfire from the approaching destroyer *Onslaught*. By day *U703* (Lt Brünner) is able to sink the freighter *Empire Tourist* (7062 tons) from the convoy with a FAT salvo and just misses *Milne* with a T-5. Air reconnaissance sends contact reports on 5, 6 and 7 Mar, but on 5–6 Mar only *U278*, *U288* (Lt W Meyer), *U959* (Lt Weitz) and *U673* (Lt Sauer) are able to make unsuccessful T-5 firings on destroyers. Because icing greatly impedes

the operational use of the AA guns on the U-boats, the Swordfish aircraft 'F' and 'X' of No 816 Sqn FAA, flown off from *Chaser*, are able to sink *U366* and *U973*, in spite of the difficult weather. The convoy arrives in Loch Ewe on 10 Mar.

20 Feb–1 Apr   Arctic
From 20 Feb to 3 Mar the Soviet Northern Fleet organises a new operation, RV-2, against German convoy traffic off the polar coast. The submarine *L-20* puts a raiding party ashore near Makkaur on 20 Feb, the houses are searched and four Norwegians are taken prisoner. In addition, a mine barrage is laid in Porsangerfjord on 26 Feb. *K-21* reconnoitres in Lopphavet. The operational boats of the 'S' class take up waiting positions, and *M-104*, *M-105*, *M-119* and *M-201* are put on the alert, but no German convoys are found.

On 4 Mar *S-56* makes an underwater attack, for the first time, after establishing the enemy's position by listening, but she has no success.

On 17 Mar a German eastbound convoy, with the gunboat *K-1* and four patrol boats, is located by Soviet reconnaissance. *M-201* (Lt-Cdr Balin) misses the convoy off Syltefjord. Air attacks by some 50 bombers and torpedo aircraft fail against the German fighter defence of JG 5. The torpedo cutters do not reach the convoy.

On 19 Mar the submarine *M-105* (Lt-Cdr Khrulev) misses one steamer and on 1 Apr *M-119* (Lt-Cdr Kolosov) misses a convoy. Soviet torpedo aircraft sink the patrol boat *V6109* off Busse Sound on 23 Mar.

21 Feb   Mediterranean
The German A/S vessel *UJ2208* sinks on a mine off Genoa.

21–29 Feb   English Channel
On 21 Feb 37 British Beaufighters of Coastal Command attack a German convoy near Den Helder and sink *R131*. During the night 22–23 Feb the German 2nd MTB Flotilla (Cdr Feldt), comprising *S86*, *S67*, *S128*, *S94*, *S80*, *S92* and *S135*, and the 8th Flotilla (Cdr Zymalkowski), comprising *S93*, *S64*, *S117*, *S127*, *S129*, *S85*, *S99* and *S65*, try from Ijmuiden to attack a convoy near Smith's Knoll. They are driven off by the destroyers *Garth* and *Southdown* with *MTB609* and *MTB610*. In the action *S94* and *S128* collide and have to be abandoned. During the night 24–25 Feb the 2nd Flotilla, with *S80*, *S92*, *S135*, *S86* and *S67*, and the 8th Flotilla, with the eight boats listed above, are deployed on a mining operation ESE of Great Yarmouth. In dropping the barrages, the boats come into contact with convoy FS.1371 which has been located by the B-Service. The destroyers *Vivien* and

Eglinton drive the two groups off. The motor torpedo boats fire eight FAT and G7A torpedoes. The freighter *Philipp M* (2085 tons) is sunk.

In a sortie by the same boats of the 2nd and 8th Flotillas on 25–26 Feb against a convoy near Great Yarmouth, the target is not found and the first group of the 8th is involved in an engagement with the destroyer *Meynell* but escapes.

A sortie by the 9th and 5th Flotillas, comprising *S144*, *S145*, *S146*, *S130*, *S112*, *S143*, *S139*, *S142*, *S136* and *S84*, against a CW convoy off the British south coast during the night 27–28 Feb misses the target. *S142* and *S136* are damaged in a collision.

During the night 28–29 Feb 14 boats of the 2nd and 8th Flotillas, in a sortie against a southbound convoy, are reported by a British Swordfish aircraft and they break off the operation. Similarly, a sortie of eight boats of the 5th and 9th Flotillas in the Plymouth area is prematurely detected and therefore broken off.

21–29 Feb   Mediterranean

On 21–22 Feb two British MGBs make a sortie towards Primosten. This is the first time that the base established on the island of Lissa is used for light naval forces. On 27 Feb the British destroyers *Tumult* and *Troubridge* shell Curzola.

On 28–29 Feb the large French destroyers (Capt Lancelot) *Le Terrible* and *Le Malin* make a sortie into the Northern Adriatic and find a German convoy near Isto sailing from Pola to Piraeus. It consists of the freighter *Kapitän Diederichsen* (ex-*Sebastiano Venier*, 6311 tons), the torpedo boats *TA36* and *TA37*, the submarine-chasers *UJ201* and *UJ205* and the motor minesweepers *R188*, *R190* and *R191*. *Le Terrible* sinks the freighter with gunfire and *Le Malin* damages *UJ201* by torpedo. *TA37* receives a shell hit in the engine room and is taken in tow.

22 Feb–22 Mar   North Atlantic

In changing individual positions, *U441*, *U256*, *U985*, *U603*, *U963*, *U764*, *U281*, *U437*, *U212*, *U448*, *U91*, *U262*, *U709*, *U358*, *U608* and *U962* form the 'Preussen' group W of Ireland. *U413*, *U333* and *U621* are stationed S of Ireland, in the North Channel and in the North Minch, *U546* off Iceland, and *U549*, *U552* and *U550* as weather boats. The returning *U257* on 24 Feb runs into the escort of convoy SC.153 (EG.C5 under Cdr Pullen on the destroyer *Ottawa* plus the 3rd EG with the DEs *Duckworth*, *Essington*, *Rowley*, *Berry*, *Cooke* and *Domett* and the 6th EG with the frigates *Waskesiu*, *Outremont*, *Cape Breton*, *Grou* and *Nene*) and is sunk by *Waskesiu* and

Nene. *U989* does not get to a group of the convoy stragglers. HX.279 is routed clear of 'Preussen' as is, on 26 Feb, ON.225. The 1st SG, employed to support the convoys W of Ireland and comprising the DEs *Affleck*, *Gore*, *Gould*, *Garlies*, *Balfour* and *Capel*, accounts for *U91* on 25 Feb and, after a 38hr search, *U358* (Lt-Cdr Manke) on 29–30 Feb, following the latter's sinking of *Gould* with a T-5. The DEs of the US TG.21.16 (Capt Ramsey), with the escort carrier *Block Island*, the destroyer *Corry* and the DEs *Thomas*, *Bronstein*, *Bostwick* and *Breeman*, sink *U709* and *U603* 600 nautical miles N of the Azores on 1 Mar. W of the Bay of Biscay, *U744* (Lt Blischke) sinks the landing ship *LST362* on 2 Mar. On 5 Mar the boat is found by the escort of convoy HX.280, EG.C2 (Lt-Cdr Davis) with the frigate *St Catherines*, the destroyers *Gatineau*, *Chaudière* and *Icarus* (British) and the corvettes *Chilliwack* and *Fennel*, and is sunk after firing several unsuccessful T-5s in a 30hr search with support from the British corvette *Kenilworth Castle* which is ordered to the scene. In the following days *U741*, *U625*, *U653*, *U986*, *U267*, *U672* and the schnorkel boats *U415* and *U575* (Lt Boehmer) join the 'Preussen' group. The last-mentioned sinks with a T-5 the corvette *Asphodel* from the escort of convoy SL.150/MKS.41 on 9 Mar; survivors are rescued by the corvette *Clover*. On the same day *U255* (Lt Harms) is located near convoy CU.16 (escort US TG.21.5 under Capt Kenner USCG, with the DEs *Joyce*, *Poole*, *Harveson*, *Kirkpatrick*, *Leopold* and *Peterson*) by the *Leopold*; but she is able to sink the approaching *Leopold* with a T-5. *Joyce* is narrowly missed. On 10 Mar *U845* (Cdr Weber) reports convoy SC.154 (EG.C1) but, after a lengthy search, she is sunk by the destroyers *St Laurent* and *Forester* and the Canadian frigate *Swansea* and corvette *Owensound*. T-5 attacks by *U653* and *U575* fail. Convoy HX.281 (EG.B6 with the destroyer *Fame*, the frigates *Deveron* and *Antigua* and the corvettes *Kingcup*, *Vervain*, *Eglantine*, *Rose* and *Acanthus*) passes the U-boat formations on 10 Mar without any engagement. *U625* is sunk by Sunderland 'U' of No 422 Sqn RCAF escorting convoy SC.154. *U741* and *U256*, which are ordered to help, shoot down a Wellington of No 407 Sqn RCAF. Convoy ON.227, which turns away to the S, is escorted on 12 and 13 Mar by strong air formations from Cornwall and the Azores. Nevertheless, *U311* shoots down one aircraft, a Fortress of No 206 Sqn RAF. *U575* is attacked by Wellington 'B' of No 172 Sqn and Fortresses 'J' of No 220 Sqn and 'R' of No 206 Sqn RAF and hunted

by US TG.21.11 (Capt Dunn), comprising the escort carrier *Bogue*, the destroyers *Hobson* and the DEs *Haverfield*, *Janssen*, *Willis* and *Swenning* together with the Canadian frigate *Prince Rupert* of the escort group. She is sunk after shooting down one of the carrier aircraft. On 14 Mar the sloops *Starling* and *Wild Goose* of the 2nd SG sink *U653* with help from Swordfish 'A' of No 825 Sqn FAA from the escort carrier *Vindex*. On 17 Mar *U415* is damaged by the escort of convoy CU.17, from which *U311* (Lt-Cdr Zander) sinks one tanker of 10342 tons on 19 Mar. As it is apparent that planned convoy operations are no longer possible in the North Atlantic with the available material, the Cdr U-boats dissolves the 'Preussen' group, which still consists of *U255*, *U962*, *U986*, *U672*, *U267*, *U262*, *U92*, *U741*, *U302*, *U311*, *U667* and *U437*. The boats continue to operate individually.

23–29 Feb   Mediterranean

On 23 Feb the German MMS *R187* is damaged in an air attack at Rogoznica; she is towed into Pola but sinks there. On 29 Feb *R194* is sunk by an explosion after an air attack off Corfu. During an USAAF air raid on Monfalcone, the German corvette *UJ201* (ex-Italian *Egeria*) is heavily damaged; she is neither repaired nor used again.

25–27 Feb   English Channel

During an air attack on 25 Feb, the German MMS *R52* is hit in Dieppe harbour and burns out. On 27 Feb, in an engagement between escort vessels of a German convoy S of Jersey and the British *MTB415* and *MTB431*, the German auxiliary minesweeper *M4618* is hit but reaches Jersey.

29 Feb–9 Mar   South West Pacific

A destroyer force (Rear-Adm Fechteler), which sets out on 27 Feb with TG.76.3 (Capt Carter), comprising *Reid*, *Flusser*, *Mahan*, *Drayton*, *Smith*, *Bush*, *Welles*, *Stevenson* and *Stockton*, and TG.76.2, with the APDs *Humphreys*, *Brooks* and *Sands*, lands on 29 Feb 1026 troops of the 5th Cavalry Regt (Brig-Gen Chase) in Hyäne Harbour on Los Negros (Admiralty Islands). Fire support is provided by TG.74.2 (Rear-Adm Berkey) consisting of the cruisers *Phoenix* (on board Gen MacArthur and Vice-Adm Kinkaid, the Cdr of the 7th Fleet) and *Nashville* and the destroyers *Daly*, *Hutchins*, *Bache* and *Beale*.

In the evening the ships withdraw. *Bush* and *Stockton* support the landed troops in the face of strong counter-attacks during the night 29 Feb–1 Mar. On 2 Mar the second wave of 1000 troops arrives in six LSTs and six LSMs, accompanied by Capt Dechaineux with the destroyers *Warramunga* (RAN), *Ammen* and *Mullany* and the minesweeper *Hamilton*. They are landed with support from the destroyers *Bush*, *Stockton* and *Welles* and the DMS *Long* which also come up. Because the destroyers are unable to silence the Japanese batteries in the N of Seeadler Harbour, TF.74 (Rear-Adm Crutchley), comprising the cruisers *Shropshire* (RAN), *Phoenix* and *Nashville* and the destroyers *Daly*, *Hutchins*, *Bache* and *Beale*, shells the islands of Hauwei and Norilo on 4 Mar.

On 5 Mar the third wave of 1410 troops arrives with TG.76.1 (Capt Carter), consisting of the destroyers *Flusser*, *Drayton*, *Smith*, *Wilkes*, *Swanson*, *Nicholson*, *Stevenson*, *Thorn* and *Arunta* (RAN) and the APDs *Humphreys*, *Brooks* and *Sands*. On 6 Mar *Nicholson* is damaged by the still unsilenced batteries at the entrance of Seeadler Bay. For this reason the ships of TF.74 (see above) again shell the islands on 7 Mar. They fire 64 rounds of 8in, 1144 rounds of 6in and 5in and 92 rounds of 4in. On 9 Mar the new airfield is safe.

A fourth convoy arrives on 12 Mar, consisting of six LSTs and the destroyers *Warramunga*, *Flusser*, *Reid*, *Kalk*, *Gillespie* and *Hobby*. By 30 Mar the islands off Seeadler Harbour are occupied in the face of sometimes strong resistance by the Japanese defenders (Col Ezaki).

Mar   Intelligence
The small German battle units ('Kleinkampfmittel') get a separate cypher circuit, 'Eichendorff'. This is broken in May 1944 as 'Bonito'/'Cowrie'.

1–6 Mar   North Pacific
A sortie by a US task force (Rear-Adm Baker) comprising the cruiser *Richmond* and the destroyers *Picking*, *Wickes*, *Sproston*, *Young*, *William D Porter*, *Isherwood*, *Kimberly* and *Luce* into the Sea of Okhotsk to find a Japanese convoy, reported to have set out from Attu, has to be broken off because of the weather.

1–31 Mar   Pacific
In operations partly supported by 'Ultra' information about decoded Japanese routing signals, the US submarines which arrive in their operational areas in Mar have numerous successes. Off Japan and Formosa, *Lapon* (Lt-Cdr Stones) sinks three ships of 14547 tons, *Flying Fish* (Lt-Cdr Risser) sinks three ships of 9815 tons, *Pollack* (Lt-Cdr Lewellen) sinks two ships of 4141 tons and the submarine-chaser *Ch-54* and *Barb* (Lt-Cdr Waterman) sinks one ship of 2219 tons. *Growler*, *Herring* and *Snapper* attack targets without success. In the Mandate Islands, *Nautilus* (Cdr Irvin) sinks one ship

of 6069 tons, *Picuda* (Lt-Cdr Rayborn) four ships of 19298 tons, *Tautog* (Lt-Cdr Sieglaff) three ships of 9317 tons and on 16 Mar the destroyer *Shirakumo*, *Silversides* (Lt-Cdr Coye) two ships of 2867 tons and the LST *SS-3*, *Darter* (Lt-Cdr Stovall) one ship of 2829 tons and *Stingray* (Lt-Cdr Loomis) one ship of 3943 tons. In addition there are successes during Operation 'Desecrate' against Palau (see 23 Mar–6 Apr).

In the area of the Malayan Archipelago and the Philippines, *Narwhal* (Cdr Latta) torpedoes the gunboat *Karatsu* (ex-USS *Luzon*) on 3 Mar, *Peto* (Lt-Cdr Van Leunen) sinks one ship of 4368 tons, *Bluefish* (Lt-Cdr Henderson) sinks one oiler of 19536 tons, *Bowfin* (Lt-Cdr Griffith) sinks three ships of 12744 tons, *Haddo* (Lt-Cdr Nimitz Jr) torpedoes one ship of 6197 tons and *Hake* (Lt-Cdr Broach) sinks two ships of 10289 tons.

2–8 Mar   Mediterranean
The large French destroyers *Le Terrible* and *Le Fantasque* carry out a fruitless raid into the Northern Adriatic as far as the coast of Istria on 2–4 Mar. On 7–8 Mar they bombard Zante.

2–31 Mar   Air War/Western Europe
Mine offensive by RAF Bomber Command. In 16 nights, 507 sorties are flown against the French Biscay, Brittany and Channel ports (especially Brest and Le Havre), the Dutch coast (especially off Texel), the Heligoland Bight, the Danish coasts and the western Baltic (especially off Kiel); three aircraft are lost.

The German patrol vessel *V722* is sunk on 15 Mar in the Channel area. The MDS *Sperrbrecher 163*/*Friesland* is sunk off Cuxhaven on 20 Mar. On 29 Mar the auxiliary minesweeper *M4600* is sunk off St-Malo and on 31 Mar the MDS *Sperrbrecher 141*/*Lies* is sunk off Ostend.

2 Mar–22 Apr   Norway
In submarine operations off the Norwegian coast, the British *Venturer* (Lt Launders) sinks one ship of 2526 tons off Stadlandet on 2 Mar, *Sceptre* Lt-Cdr McIntosh) sinks one ship of 8340 tons in Foldafjord on 7 Mar, *Syrtis* (Lt Jupp) sinks one ship of 241 tons off Bodö but is then sunk on a flanking mine barrage on 28 Mar, *Satyr* sinks one ship of 340 tons off Stadlandet on 24 Mar, *Terrapin* (Lt-Cdr Martin) sinks one transport and the catapult ship *Schwabenland*, totalling 14442 tons, off Egersund on 24 Mar and the Norwegian *Ula* (Lt Sars) sinks two steamers of 6040 tons and *U974* and torpedoes one ship of 7603 tons on two patrols on 4–6 and 19–22 Apr. *Unshaken* (Lt Whitton) sinks one ship of 3894 tons off

Lister on 7 Apr. In an attack by the midget submarine *X24* (Lt Shean) in the harbour at Bergen, two ships of 9492 tons are destroyed.

The submarine-chasers *UJ1703* and *UJ1704* and three Norwegian coasters are victims of British aerial torpedoes off Lindesnes on the Norwegian south-west coast.

3 Mar   Japan
The Japanese minelayer *Shirakami* sinks off Urup Island (Kuriles) following a collision with the Army transport *Nichiran Maru*.

4 Mar   South Pacific
The RAN cruiser *Shropshire* bombards Hauwei Island (Admiralties).

4–6 Mar   North Sea
The German minelayers *Brummer*, *Linz* and *Roland* and the minesweepers *M462*, *M406*, *M301* and *M426* lay the 'Grossgörschen' mine barrage in the western Skagerrak.

4–11 Mar   Air War/France
During USAAF air raids against Toulon on 4 Mar, the A/S vessel *UJ6080*/*KT42*, building there, is destroyed. On 7 Mar the cruiser *Marseillaise*, the salvaged destroyer *Gerfaut* and the destroyer *L'Indomptable* are sunk. On 11 Mar the German *U380* and *U410* are sunk and the salvaged French destroyer *Guépard* and submarines *Caïman*, *Redoutable* and *Pascal* are sunk again.

6 Mar   Arctic
U737, going out from Hammerfest, is damaged by Liberator 'B' of No 120 Sqn and has to return, reaching harbour on 12 Mar.

6–10 Mar   English Channel
During the night 6–7 Mar British MTB groups of the 53rd Flotilla make sorties against the German convoy routes off the Dutch coast. *MTB225*, *MTB241*, *MTB244* and *MTB234* have an engagement with the boats of the 34th MS Flotilla, sinking by torpedo the patrol vessel *V1304* off the Hook of Holland. One gun ferry and one patrol boat suffer damage. A sortie by *MGB617*, *MGB624*, *MGB629* and *MGB668* into the area of Terschelling on 9–10 Mar has no success.

7 Mar   Bay of Biscay
The auxiliary minesweeper *M4405* is sunk 1 nautical mile W of La Pallice in an air attack.

8 Mar   Mediterranean
The British destroyers *Tenacious* and *Troubridge* bombard targets on Korcula Island in the Adriatic.

8–28 Mar   Mediterranean
German attacks on Allied supply traffic proceeding from Gibraltar along the North African coast to Naples and Anzio. On 8 Mar a formation of German torpedo aircraft is intercepted by Beaufighters from Sardinia

before it reaches a troop convoy off Algiers. On 17 Mar *U371* (Lt-Cdr Mehl) sinks the troop transport *Dempo* (17024 tons) and one freighter of 6165 tons from the convoy SNF.17 and escapes from the intensive U-boat search. The attempts by German torpedo aircraft to attack by night the convoys KMS.44 on 19 Mar and KMS.45 on 29 Mar off the Algerian coast fail.

U-boat operations in the Western Mediterranean are very restricted as a result of losses. On 10 Mar the A/S trawler *Mull* sinks *U343* off Cagliari and the 'Hunt' destroyers *Exmoor*, *Blankney*, *Blencathra* and *Brecon* sink *U450* off Anzio. *U380* and *U410* fall victims to an air attack on Toulon on 11 Mar. On 16 Mar *U392* is located by MAD Catalinas '8', '1' and '7' from VP-63 USN when passing through the Straits of Gibraltar and sunk by the British destroyer *Vanoc* (with 'Hedgehog') and the frigate *Affleck*. On 24–25 Mar *U466* and *U421* succeed in entering the Mediterranean, but *U618* has to return after several attempts. On 29 Mar *U223* (Lt Gerlach) is found N of Sicily and sunk after a long search by the British destroyers *Tumult*, *Hambledon* and *Blencathra*, *Laforey* having been sunk first.

9–11 Mar   Bay of Biscay
To escort U-boats, the destroyers *ZH1* and *Z23* and the torpedo boats *T27* and *T29* cruise in the Bay of Biscay.

11 Mar–20 May   Baltic
German and Finnish mine barrages are laid in the Gulf of Finland. From 5 Mar the German patrol vessels take up their positions after the thawing of the ice and are attacked by Soviet aircraft for the first time on 9 Mar.

On 12 Mar the destroyers *Z25*, *Z28* and *Z39* of the 6th DD Flotilla, recently moved into the Gulf of Finland, shell Soviet positions near Hungerburg. On 13 Mar the Net Defence Force begins to lay out the 'Walross' submarine net between Nargön and Porkkala. At the same time naval ferry barges of the 24th Landing Flotilla, minesweepers and motor minesweepers again lay parts of the 'Nashorn' mine barrages, while the minelayers *Linz*, *Roland* and *Brummer*, in eight operations, and the destroyers *Z25*, *Z28*, *Z35* and *Z39*, sometimes with *M3* and *M37*, in six operations, renew the 'Seeigel' barrages under Capt Kothe. On 21 Apr *Roland* is lost on one of her own barrages. By 26 Apr the destroyers, and by 20 May the minelayers and smaller craft, have laid 7599 mines and 2795 barrage protection devices. From 12 to 20 May the Finnish minelayers *Ruotsinsalmi* and *Louhi* and smaller vessels lay out mine barrages N of Suursaari. In this period there are

frequent missions by Soviet ground-attack aircraft.

12 Mar   Bay of Biscay
The outgoing *U629* is damaged by Wellington 'C' of No 612 Sqn RAF and has to return.

13 Mar–15 May   Aegean
In submarine operations in the Aegean in Mar, the British *Ultor* (Lt Hunt) sinks one naval ferry barge, *Sportsman* (Lt Gatehouse) sinks one small motor ship and four sailing ships and torpedoes one more ship and the Greek *Pipinos* (Lt-Cdr Palles) sinks one ship of 2290 tons. In Apr the British *Ultor* sinks six sailing ships, *Sportsman* the steamer *Lüneburg* (5809 tons) and *Rorqual* (Lt-Cdr Napier) the steamer *Wilhelmsburg* (4967 tons). The Dutch *Dolfijn* (Lt-Cdr v Oostrom-Soede) sinks two sailing ships. In May the British *Ultimatum* (Lt Kett) sinks three sailing ships and destroys by gunfire five new constructions in Kalamata.

British aircraft sink *UJ2127* on 1 Apr and *UJ2141* on 15 Apr. British MTBs sink the auxiliary vessels *GR02* and *GR94* near Coo. On 8–9 Apr the German minelayer *Drache* with the torpedo boats of the 9th TB Flotilla (Cdr* Dominik), *TA17* and *TA19*, carries out a mining operation in the Aegean and beats off air attacks.

14–31 Mar   English Channel
During the night 14–15 Mar British MTBs attack two groups of the German 36th MS Flotilla (Cdr Grosse) off Gravelines and sink the leader, *M3630*, with a torpedo; the minesweeper *M10* also is sunk by *MTB353* off Dunkirk. *MTB417* sinks in the defensive fire. The withdrawing British force encounters boats of the 18th PB Flotilla (Cdr Boit) NE of Gris Nez.

During the night 15–16 Mar the 9th and 5th MTB Flotillas (Cdr v Mirbach and Cdr Klug), comprising *S144*, *S145*, *S146*, *S150* and *S100*, *S143*, *S141*, *S139*, *S84* and *S140*, try to attack the British convoy WP.492 N of Land's End. The convoy is escorted by the corvettes *Azalea* and *Primrose*. The motor torpedo boats are detected on the way by British air reconnaissance. The cruiser *Bellona* out at sea with the destroyers *Ashanti* and *Tartar* takes up a covering position and the 'Hunt' destroyers *Melbreak* and *Brissenden*, two minesweepers and MTB groups are deployed to intercept. In the engagements *S143* receives a hit in the bows and the commander is killed.

Sorties by both flotillas on 16–17 Mar against Lizard Head and on 20–21 Mar against Weymouth are broken off because the approaching boats are prematurely located by British radar. *S84* and *S139* drop out after a collision.

On 20 Mar, after beating off attacks by the British *MTB202*, *MTB212*, *MTB206* and *MTB359*, the 'Hecht' convoy with the tanker *Rekum*, escorted by the 18th PB Flotilla, runs into the fire of the British long-range guns at Dover. The tanker sinks. On 21 Mar the 10th MS Flotilla (Cdr Josephi), in escorting a 'Bromberg' convoy NE of Lezardieux, beats off attacks by British MTBs. The 4th and 5th TB Flotillas (Cdr Kohlauf and Cdr Hoffmann), comprising *T29*, *T27*, *Möwe*, *Kondor*, *Greif* and *Jaguar*, lay two barrages each of 180 EMC mines NW of Le Havre and N of Fécamp respectively on 21 and 22 Mar. Escort is provided by the 5th and 9th MTB Flotillas.

During the night 23–24 Mar the 2nd and 8th MTB Flotillas (Cdr Opdenhoff and Cdr Zymalkowski), comprising *S62*, *S67*, *S80*, *S83*, *S86* and *S92*, and *S64*, *S117*, *S85*, *S93*, *S99*, *S65*, *S133* and *S129*, make a sortie from Ijmuiden against the convoy route NE of Great Yarmouth. The 4th MTB Flotilla (Lt-Cdr Fimmen), consisting of *S169*, *S171* and *S187*, tries from the Hook of Holland to effect a diversion S of Lowestoft, but the operation is broken off because of early radar detection. When the operation is repeated on 25–26 Mar in the area of Hearty Knoll with the same units, there are engagements with British destroyers and MGBs in which *S67* and *S64* sustain slight damage.

During the nights 24–25 and 25–26 Mar the 4th and 5th TB Flotillas (see above) each lay another 180 mines (barrage 'N 24'), in the course of which there are indecisive British MTB attacks off Barfleur. The same night, Cdr Klug with *S145*, *S147*, *S150*, *S167*, *S140*, *S100*, *S143*, *S146*, *S144*, *S141* and *S138* makes a sortie in groups against a convoy near Falmouth. But the convoy escapes.

In an attack by 358 Marauder bombers on Ijmuiden on 26 Mar, *S93* and *S129* are destroyed and the patrol vessel *V1416* is sunk. During the night 27–28 Mar the boats of the 4th and 5th TB Flotillas lay a five-row protective float barrage (360 floats) to protect the mine barrages laid out and then they move to Brest via Cherbourg on 29–30 Mar.

The 2nd, 8th and 4th MTB Flotillas try during the night 27–28 Mar to ambush British MGBs and MTBs. An attempted attack by three flotillas with 13 boats near Smith's Knoll fails during the night 29–30 Mar. The following night, the three flotillas, when they are returning from a sortie against a convoy, become involved off the Dutch coast in an engagement between German escort forces and the British *MTB350*,

MTB244, *MTB245* and *MTB241*. The last boat sinks.

On Mar 29, in an attempt by *MGB40*, *MTB204*, *MGB613*, *MGB615*, *MGB611* and *MGB614* to attack a German force of three patrol boats, three gun ferries and 11 minesweeping cutters between Dieppe and Calais, *MGB611* and *MGB614* are damaged.

15 Mar   Netherlands/Intelligence
The German forces in the Netherlands are allocated a separate cypher circuit, 'Gefion'. This is broken on 18 Apr 1945 as 'Hackle'.

15–29 Mar   Mediterranean
On 15 Mar the German torpedo boat *TA20* carries out the mining operation 'Läufer' S of Ancona.

A raid by the large French destroyers *Le Terrible* and *Le Fantasque* on the Dalmatian coast on 15–16 Mar has no result. In setting out for a mining operation, the German torpedo boat *TA36* runs on an old Italian mine barrage 15 nautical miles SSW of Fiume on 18 Mar and is lost. The remainder of the force, *TA20*, *TA21*, *UJ205* and the minelayer *Kiebitz*, lay a barrage E of San Giorgio during the night 18–19 Mar; the same night, *Le Terrible* and *Le Fantasque* make a sortie from Bari to the area N of Navarino and attack a German convoy. The Siebel ferries *SF273* and *SF274* are sunk; *SF270* and the naval ferry barge *F124* are damaged and sunk on the next day by fighter-bombers.

In USAAF air attacks on Sebenico on 27 Mar, *UJ205* (ex-Italian *Colubrina*), *R188* and *R191* are destroyed and *R190* damaged. On 30 Mar the uncompleted corvettes *UJ206* (ex-Italian *Bombarda*) and *UJ207* (ex-Italian *Carabina*) are destroyed in Venice.

On 29 Mar *TA20*, with the Italian *Ms 41* and *Ms 75*, lays the mine barrage 'Brücke' E of San Giorgio.

15 Mar–20 May   Arctic
Transfer of the Soviet submarines *S-16* and *S-19* from the Caspian Flotilla by river to the White Sea and the Northern Fleet.

16 Mar   Air War/Italy
The German A/S vessel *UJ2209* is sunk during an air raid on Leghorn.

16–20 Mar   Bay of Biscay
Escort sortie by the German destroyers *Z23* and *ZH1* and the torpedo boats *T27* and *T29* in the northern Bay of Biscay on 16–17 Mar; on 19–20 Mar there is a further escort sortie in company with the torpedo boats *Greif* and *Möwe*.

16 Mar–1 May   Mediterranean
In Allied air attacks on Livorno on 16–17 Mar, *R161*, *RA256* and *UJ2209* are sunk. On 23 Mar four motor minesweepers of the 11th MMS Flotilla (Lt-Cdr Freytag) lay the 'Hütte' mine barrage off the east coast of Corsica, while *TA28* and *TA29* make a sortie towards Capreira as a diversion. On 27 Mar a convoy with six naval ferry barges is destroyed off Vado by an Allied force (Cdr Allen RN) comprising the British *MTB634*, *MGB662*, *MGB660*, *MGB659*, *LCG14*, *LCG19*, *LCG20* and the US *PT212*, *PT214*, *PT208* and *PT218*. On 30 Mar the German minelayer *Pommern* and three motor minesweepers carry out the mining operation 'Stachelschwein' NE of Capreira. From 2 to 26 Apr two boats of the 10th TB Flotilla (Cdr v Gartzen), comprising *TA23*, *TA26*, *TA27*, *TA28* and *TA29*, carry out the mining operations 'Bumerang' and 'Aphrodite' (2–3 and 3–4 Apr) near Portoferraio and S of Elba, 'Gatter' and 'Auster' (5–6 and 8–9 Apr), 'Rappen' (12–13 Apr) NW of Elba, 'Stich' and 'Öse' (15 and 18 Apr), 'Schimmel' (21–22 Apr) and 'Karo Ass' (25–26 Apr) as well as the shelling of Bastia (22–23 Apr). From 3 to 8 Apr the minelayer *Oldenburg* lays the 'Herz Dame', 'König', and 'Bube' barrages SW of La Spezia. During the operation on 25–26 Apr *TA23* runs on to a mine (laid by the Italian torpedo boat *Sirio* under Allied control) off Capreira and has to be abandoned and scuttled by *TA29*. *TA26* and *TA29* have an engagement with a US PT force consisting of *PT218*, *PT202* and *PT213*.

The British submarine *Untiring* (Lt Boyd) sinks two ships of 3337 tons and the submarine-chaser *UJ6075* from 12 Apr to 1 May.

17 Mar   Baltic
The German *U1013* is lost during exercises E of Rügen following a collision with *U286*. *U28* sinks after an accident off Neustadt and, although raised, is decommissioned.

18 Mar   Central Pacific
US TG.50.10 (Rear-Adm Lee), comprising the carrier *Lexington*, the battleships *Iowa* and *New Jersey* and the destroyers *Dewey*, *Hull*, *MacDonough*, *Phelps*, *Bancroft*, *Meade* and *Edwards*, bombards Mille. Japanese coastal batteries score 15.2cm hits on *Iowa*.

18–20 Mar   South West Pacific
During the night 18–19 Mar US TG.74.5, comprising the destroyers *Daly*, *Hutchins*, *Beale*, *Mullany* and *Ammen*, shells Wewak. As a diversionary manoeuvre, the battleships *New Mexico*, *Tennessee*, *Idaho* and *Mississipi* (Rear-Adm Griffin) shell Kavieng on 20 Mar with more than 13000 rounds of

14in and 5in. Air cover for the force is provided by the escort carriers *Manila Bay* and *Natoma Bay*. There is a screen of 15 destroyers.

On the same day, a US Amphibious Group (Commodore Reifsnider) consisting of 19 destroyers and landing craft lands four RCTs of the 4th Marine Div on Emirau (Bismarck Archipelago). Support is provided by a force comprising the cruisers *Santa Fé*, *Mobile*, *Biloxi*, *Oakland*, *Cleveland*, *Columbia* and *Montpelier*, the fleet carriers *Enterprise* and *Belleau Wood* and the escort carriers *Coral Sea* and *Corregidor*. The landing encounters no resistance. An airfield and PT base are established.

On Bougainville, the Japanese 6th Inf Div (Lt-Gen Hyakutake) with 12000 troops carries out an attack (Operation 'TA') on the US bridgehead near Cape Torokina of the reinforced 37th US Inf Div with some 27000 troops. The defence is supported from 9 to 24 Mar by Desron 22 (Capt Petersen), comprising *Pringle*, *Conway*, *Sigourney*, *Eaton*, *Renshaw* and *Saufley*. The Japanese lose 5469 dead, the Americans 263.

20 Mar   Great Britain
The British submarine *Graph* (ex-German *U570*) is wrecked on the W coast of Islay.

20 Mar   Indian Ocean
The British submarine *Stonehenge* is lost, cause unknown, in the Malacca Strait.

21 Mar–2 Apr   Indian Ocean
Operation 'Diplomat'. On 21 Mar the British Eastern Fleet (Adm Somerville) sets out from Trincomalee and Colombo with the battleships *Queen Elizabeth* and *Valiant*, the battlecruiser *Renown*, the carrier *Illustrious*, the cruisers *London*, *Gambia* (RNZN), *Ceylon* and *Cumberland* and the destroyers *Quilliam*, *Quality*, *Queenborough*, *Pathfinder*, *Van Galen* (Dutch), *Tjerk Hiddes* (Dutch), *Napier*, *Norman*, *Nepal* and *Quiberon* (the last four Australian). The fleet replenishes on 24 Mar from three tankers, escorted by the Dutch cruiser *Tromp*, and at mid-day on 27 Mar meets SW of the Cocos Islands US TG.58.5, consisting of the carrier *Saratoga* and the destroyers *Cummings*, *Dunlap* and *Fanning*. On 2 Apr the ships return together to Trincomalee. On the same day, as reinforcement for the escort carrier *Battler*, the escort carriers *Atheling*, *Begum* and *Shah* arrive and, shortly afterwards, the French battleship *Richelieu*. From Mar the 8th SM Flotilla is formed with the boats *Sea Rover*, *Sirdar*, *Spiteful*, *Stoic*, *Storm*, *Stratagem* and *Surf*. In operations in the Straits of Malacca in Mar, *Sea Rover* (Lt Angell) sinks one ship of 2005 tons and two coasters, *Surf* sinks

one tug and one barge, *Storm* sinks a coaster, *Truculent* (Lt Alexander) sinks two ships of 2110 tons and *Trespasser* and *Taurus* (Lt-Cdr Wingfield) lay mine barrages in the Malacca Strait, on which one ship of 971 tons is sunk and the Japanese submarine *I-37* is damaged on 27 Apr; in addition *Taurus* sinks one ship of 558 tons and a tug. In Apr *Storm* sinks the minesweeper *W-7* on 15 Apr and damages one more ship and *Tantalus* sinks one ship of 3165 tons and a tug and a coaster. *Sea Rover* sinks one coaster and the Dutch submarine *K-XV* sinks two sailing vessels off the NW coast of New Guinea.

22 Mar–6 May   North Atlantic
The U-boats *U267*, *U667* (schnorkel boats), *U262*, *U986*, *U741*, *U92*, *U962*, *U672*, *U311*, *U255*, *U302*, *U548*, *U385*, *U765*, *U342*, *U736* and *U473* operate individually in the North Atlantic between Ireland and Newfoundland as part of varying formations and also as weather boats. *U766*, *U821*, *U993*, *U970* and *U740*, which have also set out, are called back early to France to form the 'Landwirt' group. On 24 and 27 Mar respectively *U302* and *U970* miss escort vessels with T-5s. *U302* (Lt-Cdr Sickel) sinks two ships of 9777 tons from the convoy SC.156 escorted by EG.B5 but is then sunk by the frigate *Swale*. On 8 Apr the sloops *Crane* and *Cygnet* of the 7th SG destroy *U962*. In the middle of Apr *U385* and *U667* repeatedly miss ships; *U667* and *U993* each shoot down one aircraft. *U448* (Lt Dauter), which is returning from Iceland, tries to attack the escort carrier *Biter* on 14 Apr but is located by the Canadian frigate *Swansea* (9th SG) and sunk with the help of the British sloop *Pelican* (7th SG). *U986* falls victim on 17 Apr to the escort of a small coastal convoy consisting of the US minesweeper *Swift* and the submarine-chaser *PC619*. *U342* is sunk on 17 Apr by Canso 'S' of No 162 Sqn RCAF, *U311* is sunk on 22 Apr by the Canadian frigates *Matane* and *Swansea* and *U672* is damaged by Sunderland 'A' of No 423 Sqn RCAF on 24 Apr. On 3 May *U473* (Lt-Cdr Sternberg) misses a convoy escort with a T-5 and *U765* (Lt Wendt) torpedoes the US DE *Donnell* from a convoy (the ship is towed in but not repaired). The 2nd SG (Capt Walker), with the sloops *Starling*, *Wild Goose*, *Wren*, *Magpie* and *Whimbrel* and the escort carrier *Tracker*, and the 5th SG (Cdr Macintyre), with the DEs *Bickerton*, *Aylmer*, *Bligh*, *Kempthorne*, *Keats* and *Goodson* and the escort carrier *Vindex*, are directed to the U-boats' success report signals, located by HF/DF. After an 18hr search, *Starling*, *Wild Goose* and *Wren* compel *U473* to

surface on 5 May and sink her in a 20min gun and T-5 duel. *U765* is discovered by an aircraft from *Vindex* and, likewise after a long hunt, is forced to surface by a carpet of depth charges from *Bligh* and sunk by a second aircraft.

23 Mar   Arctic
The German patrol vessel *V6109* is sunk by torpedo off Vardö during a Soviet air attack.

23 Mar–6 Apr   Central Pacific
Operation 'Desecrate': US TF.58 (Vice-Adm Mitscher, under the overall command of Adm Spruance) carries out carrier raids on Palau, Yap and Woleai. On 23 Mar TG.58.1 (Rear-Adm Reeves), consisting of *Enterprise*, *Belleau Wood* and *Cowpens*, sets out from Espiritu Santo and on 24 Mar TG.58.2 (Rear-Adm Montgomery), consisting of *Bunker Hill*, *Hornet*, *Cabot* and *Monterey* and TG.58.3 (Rear-Adm Ginder), consisting of *Yorktown*, *Lexington*, *Princeton* and *Langley*, set out from Majuro; battleships, cruisers and destroyers are as in the Hollandia operation (see 13 Apr). On 25 Mar the force is located by Japanese reconnaissance aircraft from Truk and again on 26 Mar when it joins up and replenishes SE of Truk. As a result, the Japanese Fleet leaves Palau in anticipation of an attack. The Carrier Fleet and the 2nd Fleet have already been transferred to Tawi-Tawi. The C-inC, Adm Koga, crashes (31 Mar) on a flight to Mindanao. His successor is Adm Toyoda.

The US submarines *Gar*, *Blackfish*, *Tang* and *Archerfish* are stationed to operate against the withdrawing ships and as planeguards. *Tunny* (Lt-Cdr Scott) sinks on 23 Mar the Japanese submarine *I-42* and torpedoes one oiler of 14850 tons; on 29 Mar she torpedoes the battleship *Musashi* from a departing naval force which also includes the cruiser *Oyodo* and two destroyers. *Tullibee* (Cdr Brindupke) is hit by her own torpedo in an attack on 26 Mar on a convoy and sinks. *Bashaw* (Lt-Cdr Nichols) torpedoes one steamer of 4317 tons.

In the evening of 28 Mar Japanese aircraft try unsuccessfully to attack TF.58. On 30 Mar all three task groups attack Palau and on 31 Mar TG.58.2 and 58.3 make further attacks on Palau in which aircraft from *Lexington*, *Bunker Hill* and *Hornet* lay air mines. In all, the APD *T-31*, four submarine-chasers and 31 auxiliary warships and merchant ships of 129807 tons are sunk. Outside Palau, the torpedo boat *Wakatake* and the repair ship *Akashi* sink. TG.58.1 attacks Yap on 31 Mar. On 1 Apr all three task groups attack Woleai, where the submarine *Harder*, acting as a planeguard, saves aircraft crews. Twenty-five aircraft are lost but 26

out of 44 air crews are rescued. The Japanese submarine *I-174* is an operational loss on 3 Apr.

24 Mar   North Sea
The British submarine *Terrapin* torpedoes the German catapult ship *Schwabenland* off Egersund, Norway. The ship is beached. The tanker *Wörth* is damaged by aerial torpedoes off Listerfjord and is towed to Akers by the minesweeper *M2*.

25–27 Mar   Bay of Biscay
Mosquitos of No 248 Sqn RAF fly patrols against U-boats. *U976* is sunk on 25 Mar and *U960* damaged on 27 Mar by Mosquitos 'L' (Fg Off Turner) and 'I' (Fg Off Hilliard) of that unit while escorted by destroyers and minesweepers. The aircraft are damaged by AA fire.

27 Mar–5 Apr   Arctic
Convoy operation JW.58/RA.58. On 27 Mar convoy JW.58 with 49 ships (one returns to Iceland) sets out. With the convoy is the US cruiser *Milwaukee* on the way to be handed over to the Soviet Northern Fleet. The escort comprises the cruiser *Diadem* (Vice-Adm Dalrymple-Hamilton) with the escort carriers *Tracker* and *Activity*, one close escort group and two support groups with a total of 20 destroyers, five sloops and five corvettes. On 29 Mar *U961*, which is on the way to the Atlantic, is located by the leader of the 2nd SG, *Starling* (Capt Walker)—the group also includes the sloops *Wild Goose*, *Magpie*, *Wren* and *Whimbrel*—and sunk. On 30 Mar the C-in-C Home Fleet, Adm Fraser, puts out to sea from Scapa Flow as a covering force with the battleships *Anson* (Vice-Adm Moore) and *Duke of York*, the carriers *Furious* and *Victorious*, the escort carriers *Emperor*, *Searcher*, *Pursuer* and *Fencer*, the cruisers *Belfast*, *Royalist* (Rear-Adm Bisset), *Sheffield* and *Jamaica* and the destroyers *Milne*, *Meteor*, *Onslaught*, *Undaunted*, *Ursa*, *Verulam*, *Vigilant*, *Virago*, *Wakeful*, *Algonquin* (RCN) and *Sioux* (RCN). On 30 Mar the convoy is found by German air reconnaissance, but the Martlet fighters of *Tracker* and *Activity* shoot down one Ju 88 of 1/FAGr 22 on 30 Mar, three Fw 200s of 3/KG 40 on 31 Mar one Bv 138 of 1/SAGr 130 on 1 Apr and one Ju 88 of 1/FAGr 124 on 2 Apr. Of the three U-boat groups 'Thor' (*U278*, *U312*, *U313* and *U674*), 'Blitz' (*U277*, *U355*, *U711* and *U956*) and 'Hammer' (*U288*, *U315*, *U354* and *U968*) and the additional outbound boats *U716*, *U739*, *U360*, *U361* and *U990*, most make contact with the escort shortly after midnight on 1 Apr until the evening of 3 Apr and, in some cases, they make repeated T-5 attacks. But they are all

unsuccessful: *U968* (Lt Westphalen) attacks twice, *U674* (Lt Muhs) twice, *U278* (Lt-Cdr Franze) twice, *U313* (Lt Schweiger) once, *U711* (Lt Lange) twice, *U354* (Lt Sthamer) once, *U288* (Lt Meyer) once, *U990* (Lt-Cdr Nordheimer) once, *U739* (Lt Mangold) twice against the destroyer *Ashanti*, *U277* (Lt Lübsen) twice, *U315* (Lt Zoller) once and *U312* (Lt-Cdr K H Nicolay) once. *U355* (Lt-Cdr La Baume) is damaged on 1 Apr by rockets from Avenger 'H' of No 846 Sqn FAA from *Tracker* and sunk by the destroyer *Beagle*. On 2 Apr *Keppel* sinks *U360* (Lt-Cdr Becker) with depth charges and on 3 Apr Avenger 'G' and Wildcat 'Y' of No 846 Sqn FAA from *Tracker* and Swordfish 'C' of No 819 Sqn FAA from *Activity* sink *U288* with rockets and depth charges, after the latter has shot down a Swordfish with AA fire. On 3 Apr Capt 1st Class Kolchin sets out from the Kola Inlet with the Soviet destroyers *Razyarenny*, *Gremyashchi*, *Razumny* and *Kuibishev*, four minesweepers and four submarine-chasers and escorts the convoy on 4–5 Apr to the Kola Inlet and, later, a group of nine steamers to the White Sea.

On 3 Apr Vice-Adm Moore makes a sortie (Operation 'Tungsten') with the *Anson*, the carriers, three cruisers and five destroyers of the covering force towards northern Norway to attack the battleship *Tirpitz* in Altafjord. 41 Barracuda carrier bombers attack *Tirpitz* (Capt Meyer), with fighter protection from 21 Corsairs and 20 Hellcats, and obtain 14 hits for the loss of four aircraft. German losses are 122 dead and 316 wounded. The ship is out of action for three months. Forty Wildcat fighters provide fighter protection for the carrier force. The returning convoy RA.58 with 36 ships and the escort of JW.58 set out from the Kola Inlet on 7 Apr. Because of heavy losses in operating against JW.58, the Luftwaffe can only fly night radar reconnaissance flights and the convoy is only found on 9 Apr. Of the U-boats formed in the two groups 'Donner' and 'Keil' (*U313*, *U636*, *U703*, *U277*, *U361*, *U362*, *U711*, *U716*, *U347* and *U990*) only *U361* (Lt-Cdr Seidel), *U362* (Lt Franz) (twice), *U703* (Lt Brünner) and *U313* make unsuccessful T-5 firings against destroyers on 10 Apr. The convoy is found again by air reconnaissance early on 11 Apr but the operation has to be broken off because the U-boats are too far to the rear.

28 Mar–10 Apr   Black Sea
After the capture of Nikolaev on 28 Mar, the Soviet 4th and the 3rd Ukrainian Fronts drive the German 6th and Rumanian 3rd Armies across the Lower Bug past Odessa to the Dniester. The attempt to encircle strong German and Rumanian forces in Odessa fails because 9300 wounded, 14845 troops and 54000 tons of mobile supplies can be evacuated from Odessa by sea. Eighteen sea-going ships in 26 missions, nine towing vessels in 27 missions, 15 tugs in 33 missions and 25 naval ferry barges in 76 missions are used. Many newly built ships and lighters are taken away. The deployment of the Soviet submarines *L-6* (minelayer), *M-117*, *Shch-202*, *M-62* and others achieves no result. *S-31* attacks several convoys without success.

Of the German submarines, *U18* (Lt Fleige) and *U23* (Lt Wahlen) operate off the Caucasian coast and sink one towing convoy and one motor minesweeper respectively.

In Mar 45000 tons of supplies and the 111th Inf Div are brought to the German 17th Army on the Crimea by the sea route.

29 Mar   Mediterranean
The German gun ferry *F456* is sunk during an Allied air raid on Leghorn.

30 Mar–1 Apr   Mediterranean
On 30 Mar convoy UGS.36, with 72 merchant ships and 18 LSTs, passes through the Straits of Gibraltar. It is escorted by TF.64 (Capt Berdine USN), consisting of the US destroyers *Decatur*, *Whipple*, *Alden* and *John D Edwards*, the US DEs *Sellstrom*, *Ramsden*, *Mills*, *Rhodes*, *Savage*, *Tomich* and *Sloat* and the British 37th EG, comprising the AA cruiser *Colombo*, the Dutch frigate *Johan Maurits van Nassau*, the sloops *Black Swan*, *Amethyst* and *Deptford* and the Dutch *Friso*, the corvette *Campion* and the minesweeper *Speed* (JIG jamming transmitter for guided bombs). The U-boats deployed, *U421* and *U969*, are not able to fire on 31 Mar; one is driven off by *Tomich* and *Black Swan*.

Before dawn on 1 Apr some 20 German aircraft attack and torpedo the US freighter *Jared Ingersoll* (7191 tons) W of Algiers.

1–7 Apr   North Sea
The 'Westwall' barrages W of the Skagerrak are strengthened by two new lines, 'Katzbach A' and 'B', on 1–2 and 6–7 Apr by the minelayers *Ostmark*, *Elsass* and *Kaiser*, the destroyers *Erich Steinbrinck* and *Hans Lody* and the minesweepers *M462*, *M406*, *M301* and *M381*.

1–30 Apr   Air War/Western Europe
Mine offensive by RAF Bomber Command. In 18 nights, 782 sorties are flown against French Biscay, Brittany and Channel ports, (especially La Pallice, Lorient, Brest, Cherbourg and Le Havre), the Dutch coast (especially Den Helder and Texel), the Frisian Islands and the Heligoland Bight, the Kattegat, the Kiel area, Swinemünde and the Gulf of Danzig (particularly Gdynia and Pillau). Eighteen aircraft are lost.

The German MMS *R27* is sunk on a British air-laid mine in the sea channel off Pillau on 11 Apr, the patrol vessel *V622* is sunk off St-Nazaire on 8 Apr, the auxiliary minesweeper *M3860* is sunk in the Heligoland Bight on 17 Apr and the minesweeper *M553* (ex-Dutch *Abraham van der Hulst*) is sunk off Brüsterort on 21 Apr. On 27 Apr *U803* sinks after hitting an air-laid mine off Swinemünde.

1–30 Apr   Pacific
US submarine operations continue to be aided by the decoding, via 'Ultra', of Japanese routing signals. Destroyers and escorts are primary targets as well as the oilers. Off Japan, and in the Formosa area, *Whale* (Lt-Cdr Grady) sinks one ship of 5401 tons, *Halibut* (Lt-Cdr Galantin) sinks two ships of 5085 tons, one sailing vessel and on 27 Apr the minelayer *Kamome*, *Searaven* (Lt-Cdr Dry) sinks one vessel of 216 tons, *Tambor* (Lt-Cdr Kefauver) sinks one ship of 6442 tons and one trawler, *Guavina* (Lt-Cdr Teideman) sinks two ships of 4463 tons and one trawler, *Seadragon* (Lt-Cdr Ashley) sinks one ship of 6886 tons and one trawler and also damages one ship of 9467 tons, *Haddock* (Lt-Cdr Davenport) misses one ship (as do *Swordfish* and *Sawfish*), *Jack* (Lt-Cdr Dykers) sinks one ship of 5425 tons and one trawler and damages one ship of 6586 tons, *Sargo* (Lt-Cdr Garnett) sinks one ship of 4851 tons, *Bang* (Lt-Cdr Gallaher) sinks three ships of 10734 tons, *Tinosa* (Lt-Cdr Weiss) sinks two ships of 12876 tons and one trawler, *Parche* (Lt-Cdr Ramage) sinks two ships of 11719 tons and *Steelhead* (Lt-Cdr Welchel) sinks a trawler. *Pogy* (Lt-Cdr Metcalf) sinks the Japanese submarine *I-183* on 28 Apr.

In the Mandate area, *Seahorse* (Lt-Cdr Cutter) sinks three ships of 16694 tons and damages one more of 1915 tons (the identity of a submarine attacked on 20 Apr remains unclear), *Trigger* (Lt-Cdr Harlfinger) sinks one ship of 11738 tons and damages one of 8811 tons and, on 27 Apr, the frigate *Kasado*, *Harder* (Lt-Cdr Dealey) sinks one ship of 7061 tons and on 13 Apr the destroyer *Ikazuchi*, *Bluegill* (Lt-Cdr Barr) sinks two ships of 10667 tons and on 27 Apr the cruiser *Yubari* and *Bashaw* (Lt-Cdr Nichols) sinks two trawlers; *Scamp*, *Pampanito*, *Finback* and *Blackfish* make unsuccessful attacks. *Gudgeon* is lost on 18 Apr when attacked by Japanese aircraft off Maug Island (Marianas).

In the Malayan Archipelago and the Philippines, *Redfin* (Lt-Cdr Austin) sinks two ships of 8428 tons and on 11 Apr the destroyer *Akigumo* off Zamboanga, *Paddle* (Lt-Cdr Nowell) sinks two ships of 9732 tons, *Crevalle* (Lt-Cdr Walker) sinks two ships of 17777 tons, *Bonefish* (Lt-Cdr Edge) sinks one ship of 806 tons and damages one of 8811 tons and on 14 May sinks the destroyer *Inazuma* and *Flasher* (Lt-Cdr Whitaker) sinks two ships of 12876 tons and on 30 Apr the ex-French gunboat *Tahure*.

4 Apr–24 May   Atlantic

In operations in distant waters, *U541* and *U548* cruise between Bermuda, the Bahamas and Nova Scotia. *U541* (Lt-Cdr Petersen) misses two convoys and on 26 May halts the Portuguese steamer *Serpa Pinto* (Jewish refugees among 200 passengers) and the Greek steamer *Thetis* sailing on Swiss charter. Both are released after reference back to the Cdr U-boats. *U548* (Lt Zimmermann) sinks on 7 May the frigate *Valleyfield* from the Canadian escort group of convoy ONM.234 (three frigates and two corvettes); survivors are rescued by the Canadian *Giffard*. E of the Brazilian coast, *U129* (Lt Harpe) sinks two ships of 11965 tons in May. *U190*, *U155* and *U505* operate without success in the Gulf of Guinea and off Freetown.

SW of the Azores, *U488* (Lt-Cdr Studt) replenishes four U-boats up to the end of Apr. On their way to the Indian Ocean, the following boats pass through the Atlantic in turn: *U843* (Lt-Cdr Herwatz), which stops and releases one Portuguese and one Spanish steamer, sinks one ship of 7900 tons and is twice attacked by aircraft but escapes; *U196* (Lt-Cdr Kentrat); *U181* (Cdr* Freiwald), which sinks one ship of 5312 tons; *U537* (Lt-Cdr Schrewe); the Japanese *Ro-501* (ex-German *U1224*) (Lt-Cdr Norita); *U198* (Lt Heusinger v Waldegg); *U859* (Lt-Cdr Jebsen), which sinks one straggler of 6254 tons from the convoy SC.157 in the North Atlantic; and the Japanese *I-29* (Cdr Kinashi).

In the Central Atlantic, US task groups are employed successively against the refuelling areas and the passing U-boats. On 19 Apr the outbound *U543* evades a task group comprising the escort carrier *Tripoli* (Capt Tucker) and four DEs. On 19–20 Apr TG.21.15 (Capt Vest), comprising *Croatan* and the DEs *Frost*, *Barber*, *Snowden*, *Huse* and *Inch*, is directed to *U66* by HF/DF when she is requesting replenishment. *U488* is found at the refuelling area on 25 Apr and sunk on 26–27 Apr by the DEs. The relieving TG.21.11 (Capt Hughes), consisting of *Block Island* and the DEs *Ahrens*, *Eugene E Elmore*, *Barr* and *Buckley*, searches for *U66*, which has again been located by

HF/DF, from 1 May. On 5 May the U-boat surfaces in sight of the carrier and escapes, but is sunk on 6 May by *Buckley* in a surface attack involving gunfire, torpedoes and attempts by both ships to ram each other. The Japanese *Ro-501* falls victim to TG.22.2 (Capt Vosseler), consisting of *Bogue* and the DEs *Haverfield*, *Janssen*, *Willis*, *Francis M Robinson* and *Wilhoite*, on 13 May. The task group employed in the South Atlantic from Recife (Capt Crist), consisting of the escort carrier *Solomons* and the DEs *Straub*, *Gustafson*, *Trumpeter* and *Herzog*, attacks *U196* on 23 Apr, but she escapes.

4 Apr–9 June   Mediterranean

The German minelayer group 'West Italy' (*Oldenburg*, *Dietrich von Bern* and *Kehrwieder*) lays the 'Herz Dame', 'Herz König' and 'Herz Bube' minefields around Elba during the nights 3–8 Apr. In late May and early June three other fields are laid off La Spezia and Genoa.

6 Apr   Mediterranean

The German MMS *R192* is sunk in engagement with British MTBs off Cecina in the Tyrrhenian Sea. *U455* is lost off La Spezia when she detonates one of her own mines.

6–7 Apr   Air War/Germany

RAF Bomber Command attacks Hamburg with 33 aircraft; one aircraft is lost.

8 Apr   Baltic

The German *U2* is sunk off Pillau following a collision with the fishing vessel *Heinrich Freese*.

8–16 Apr   Black Sea

On 8 Apr the Soviet 2nd Guards Army goes over to the offensive in the Crimea against the German 50th Inf Div on the Perekop Isthmus and the Soviet 51st Army against the Rumanian 10th Div on the Sivash, whilst on 10 Apr the Soviet Coastal Army attacks the German V Army Corps on the Kerch Peninsula. After the Soviet forces break through the Rumanian 10th Div and reach the Dzhankoy junction point, the German troops have to fall back quickly on Sevastopol. 10000 troops of the V Army Corps, which has been partly driven off into the Yalta Mountains, are evacuated from the eastern side to Balaklava and Sevastopol by naval ferry barges of the 1st Landing Flotilla (Lt-Cdr Giele). On 15–16 Apr the bulk of the German and Rumanian forces reach the fortress area. The evacuation of all superfluous troops (supply forces, etc) and the Wehrmacht echelons from the Crimea to Constanza begins on 12 Apr. By 16 Apr 36000 German soldiers, 9600 Rumanian soldiers, 16000 Eastern Legionaries, 3800 prisoners-of-war and 1600 civilians are evacuated by sea on steamers and

light craft, escorted by German and Rumanian warships under the Cdr of the 10th Escort Div, Capt Weyher, and also, in part, by transport aircraft.

Deployed against the transport movements are the naval air forces of the Black Sea Fleet (Lt-Gen Ermachenkov) with about 90 aircraft of the 9th and 11th Fighter Regts and the 23rd Ground Attack Regt in the Odessa area, 93 aircraft of the 2nd Guards Mining and Torpedo Air Div and the 40th Fighter Regt in the Skadovsk area and 86 aircraft of the 11th Ground Attack Div and the 30th Reconnaissance Regt from the area N of the Crimea and later from Evpatoria, as well as 38 fighters of the 25th Fighter Regt from Kerch and later Feodosia. Up to 16 Apr they sink the motor minesweeper *R204* (11 Apr), and the naval ferry barges *F565* and *F569* and damage *R205*, *F572* and the tug *Oituz*. An attack by the 2nd TKA Bde from Skadovsk with the rocket-equipped *TKA-86* and the torpedo-cutters *TKA-14*, *TKA-85*, *TKA-94* and *TKA-104* is intercepted by the motor torpedo boats of the 1st MTB Flotilla which is stationed as flank protection. Attempted attacks by the submarines *S-31* (Capt 3rd Class Alexeyev) (twice), *A-5* (Lt-Cdr Matveyev) (twice), *Shch-215* (Capt 3rd Class Greshilov) and *L-6* (Lt-Cdr Gremyako) fail. Submarine-chasers of the 1st SC Flotilla attack several submarines with depth charges. A landing made on 13 Apr in Feodosia by light units of the Soviet Black Sea Fleet encounters no resistance: the harbour has already been abandoned.

10 Apr   Baltic

In Soviet air attacks against German ships covering the 'Seeigel' minefields, the minesweeper *M459* is sunk and the *M413* badly damaged. The latter is able to reach harbour.

10–16 Apr   Mediterranean

On 10 Apr convoy UGS.37 passes through the Straits of Gibraltar with 60 merchant ships and six LSTs escorted by TF.65 (Cdr Headden USN) comprising the US destroyers *Breckinridge*, *Blakeley*, *Biddle* and *Barney*, the US DEs *Stanton*, *Swasey*, *Price*, *Strickland*, *Forster*, *Stockdale*, *Hissem* and *Holder* and the British AA cruiser *Delhi* and frigate *Nadder*, with the US destroyer *Lansdale* and the British corvette *Jonquil* as JIG (radar-jamming) ships. The deployment of the U-boats *U421*, *U969*, and *U471* (which reaches the Mediterranean on 6 Apr) meets with no success.

During the night 11–12 Apr there is an attack in the Cape Bengut area by some 20 torpedo aircraft of the German 2nd F1 Div: *Holder* receives a hit and is brought in but not repaired and *Stanton* and *Swasey* just avoid the attacks.

Further on to Alexandria, *U407* (Lt Korndörfer) attacks the convoy off Cyrenaica and torpedoes two ships of 14386 tons: one of these sinks and one is taken in tow to Alexandria but not repaired.

10–26 Apr   Arctic

Soviet combined operation RV-3 against German convoy traffic off the Norwegian polar coast. On 10 Apr an attack by Ground Attack Regt 46 with three waves of 19 Il–2s, 16 Kittyhawks, 14 Airacobras and six Yak-1s on a German convoy fails. The torpedo-cutter *TKA-216* sinks the collier *Stör* (665 tons) off Kirkenes. *TKA-212* is lost. In Kirkenes two steamers are damaged by near-misses from low-flying aircraft. *S-104* and *M-105*, which are among the submarines, have no success. *S-54* is lost at this time, probably on a flanking mine barrage.

In an attack by torpedo cutters, including *TKA-13* and *TKA-203*, on a German convoy off Petsamofjord on 22 Apr, the torpedoes are released too early with the result that the steamers are able to avoid them. In an air attack by Ground Attack Regt 46 on the convoy on 23 Apr, the Cdr of the formation, Capt Katunin, crashes into the sea just near a ship.

10 Apr–1 May   English Channel

During the night 10–11 Apr the Norwegian *MTB715*, *MTB653*, *MTB623* and *MTB618* try to attack a German convoy off the Dutch coast but are driven off by the strong defensive fire.

A sortie by the 5th MTB Flotilla (Cdr Klug) with six boats from Cherbourg in a northerly direction on 12–13 Apr is detected early and leads to no result. Similarly, another operation with 13 boats from the 5th and 9th Flotillas against Lyme Bay on 13–14 Apr has no success.

A mining operation by the 4th and 8th Flotillas with 15 boats on 14–15 Apr is detected early from VHF talk and broken off. From 17 to 19 Apr the 5th TB Flotilla, comprising *Kondor*, *T27*, *T29 Möwe* and *Greif*, is transferred from Brest to Cherbourg as distant cover for a convoy. The German gun ferry *AF1* is sunk by an aerial bomb at Boulogne on 16 Apr.

On 18–19 Apr British fighter-bombers sink the patrol boats *V1232*, *V1236* and *V1237* from a German force off the mouth of the Ems and Terschelling.

During the night 18–19 Apr the 8th Flotilla (Cdr Zymalkowski), consisting of *S87*, *S133*, *S127*, *S64*, *S83*, *S85* and *S67*, breaks off a mining operation because of the weather and after engagements with the British destroyer *Whitshed* and MGBs. *S64*

and *S133* are damaged. In the same night the 5th Flotilla, consisting of *S112*, *S100*, *S141*, *S138*, *S140* and *S143*, lays EMC mines W of the Isle of Wight and has an engagement with the destroyer *Middleton* and MTBs, including *MTB246*. E of the Isle of Wight, the 9th Flotilla (Cdr v Mirbach), consisting of *S146*, *S147*, *S144*, *S150*, *S130*, *S145* and *S167*, lays 30 EMC mines.

During the night 19–20 Apr the 8th Flotilla again breaks off a mining operation because of the weather. The 5th and 9th Flotillas (as above but without *S140* and *S141*) make an unsuccessful sortie against a CW convoy and are driven off by the 'Hunt' destroyers *Middleton* and *La Combattante* (French, ex-*Haldon*) and pursued. In the process *S144* goes aground near Calais.

During the night 21–22 Apr the 5th TB Flotilla, comprising *Kondor*, *Möwe* and *Greif*, lays a protective barrage with 145 floats from Cherbourg. The 4th TB Flotilla, comprising *T29*, *T24* and *T27*, is transferred from Cherbourg to St-Malo. From Cherbourg the 5th MTB Flotilla, consisting of *S100*, *S112*, *S143*, *S140* and *S138*, and the 9th MTB Flotilla, consisting of *S146*, *S150*, *S145*, *S130* and *S167*, make a sortie against a WP convoy near Dungeness and Hastings. In engagements with the destroyers *Volunteer* and *Middleton* and MGBs, including *MGB214* and *MGB617* and *MTB235*, *S167* and British boats are damaged. During the night 23–24 Apr a sortie by the 4th and 8th MTB Flotillas with 11 boats towards the British south-east coast is unsuccessful. The 5th MTB Flotilla, consisting of *S100*, *S143*, *S138*, *S136*, *S140* and *S142*, attacks a CW convoy near Dungeness: Cdr v Mirbach with *S100* sinks the tug *Roode Zee* (468 tons). The 9th MTB Flotilla, consisting of *S146*, *S147*, *S145*, *S167*, *S130* and *S150*, is involved in engagements near Hastings with the destroyers *Berkeley*, *Haldon*, *Stevenstone* and *Volunteer* and MGBs and MTBs. *MTB359* is damaged. The 5th TB Flotilla, with *Kondor*, *Möwe* and *Greif*, is deployed from Cherbourg against British MTBs near Cap Barfleur. Their attacks fail. *MTB671* is sunk.

On 25 Apr the 4th TB Flotilla (Cdr Kohlauf), consisting of *T29*, *T24* and *T27*, sets out from St-Malo and lays a mine barrage NW of Les Sept Iles. During the night 25–26 Apr there is an engagement with the British cruiser *Black Prince*, the British destroyer *Ashanti* and the Canadian destroyers *Athabaskan*, *Haida* and *Huron*. *T27* is hit at the beginning of the engagement and is sent back to Morlaix. *Haida* sinks *T29* (the Flotilla Cdr, Lt-Cdr Grund,

and 135 men perish; 73 are rescued by a patrol vessel). *T24* reaches St-Malo in a damaged state.

The same night, six boats from the 5th and 9th MTB Flotillas are deployed against the concentrations located by air reconnaissance near Selsey Bill, Portsmouth and Southampton. They become involved in engagements with the destroyers *Rowley* (DE) and *La Combattante* (French), which sinks *S147*.

During the night 26–27 Apr the 5th TB Flotilla, with *Kondor*, *Greif* and *Möwe*, lays a barrage of 108 LMB mines N of Cherbourg. *T27* is transferred from Morlaix to St-Malo.

During the night 27–28 Apr the 5th and 9th MTB Flotillas, comprising *S136*, *S138*, *S140*, *S142*, *S100*, *S143* and *S150*, *S130* and *S145*, attacks a force consisting of eight US LSTs escorted by the corvette *Azalea* and the destroyer *Saladin* as it comes into Lyme Bay. *LST507* and *LST531* are sunk and *LST289* is torpedoed. When the British destroyer task force 27 (leader *Onslow*, plus *Saladin*) is deployed, it misses the German motor torpedo boats. 197 sailors and 552 troops on board perish. The same night, the 5th TB Flotilla lays another defensive barrage of 108 mines off Cherbourg. When avoiding a British fighter-bomber attack, the force runs into a British minefield: *Kondor* is damaged on a mine but brought in.

During the night 28–29 Apr, while moving from St-Malo to Brest, the torpedo boats *T24* and *T27* encounter the Canadian destroyers *Athabaskan* and *Haida* off St-Brieux. *T24* sinks *Athabaskan* with a torpedo salvo. *T27* has to be beached after an engagement with *Haida*. An attempt to get her away made by the 24th MS Flotilla fails, whereupon the minesweepers take off the crew. *T27* is further damaged by air attack on 3 May and destroyed by *MTB673* on 7 May. *T24* hits a ground mine in the morning, but is able to reach harbour. Eighty-five men are rescued from *Athabaskan*.

During the night 29–30 Apr four boats each from the 5th and 9th MTB Flotillas are deployed against targets located off Cherbourg, but they encounter nothing. When they later move to Le Havre, *S138*, *S143*, and *S100* escape from the MGBs and the destroyers *Brilliant* and *La Combattante* sent to find them.

On 30 Apr the 5th TB Flotilla, with *Möwe* and *Greif*, carries out two, and on 1 May one, defensive mining operations when the barrages 'Blitz 38, 38A and 39' are laid with 260 LMB mines.

11 Apr Air War/Germany
During an air raid against Stettin, the U-boat *U108* is sunk (it is later raised but is decommissioned) and the accommodation ship *Usambara* (8690 tons) and the training ship *Mars* are hit and burn out.

12 Apr–10 June South West Pacific
The Australian destroyer *Vendetta*, the frigates *Gascoyne* and *Barcoo* and the corvettes *Ararat*, *Benalla*, *Bendigo*, *Bowen*, *Broome*, *Bunbury*, *Bundaberg*, *Castlemaine*, *Colac*, *Cowra*, *Deloraine*, *Geelong*, *Gladstone*, *Glenelg*, *Goulbourn*, *Gympie*, *Kapunda*, *Katoomba*, *Kiama*, *Lithgow*, *Rockhampton*, *Shepparton*, *Stawell*, *Strahan*, *Townsville*, *Wagga* and *Whyalla* are employed to escort convoys between Finschhafen and the Admiralty Islands, Madang and Hollandia. In these operations, *Bundaberg*, *Stawell*, *Barcoo*, *Kapunda*, *Wagga* and *Lithgow*, on different days, shell Japanese positions between Madang and Hansa Bay and the outlying islands.

13–20 Apr North Sea
On 13 Apr the German patrol vessel *V1233* is sunk in an air attack NW of Borkum. On 16 Apr the MMS *R108* sinks off Terschelling following a collision with *R229*. On 20 Apr the German MDS *Sperrbrecher 102/Condor* is sunk by an aerial torpedo off Schiermonnikoog.

13–26 Apr Baltic
The German 'Seeigel' mine barrage in the inner Gulf of Finland is strengthened: on 13–14 Apr the minelayers (Capt Pahl) *Brummer* (Cdr Kolster), *Roland* (Cdr Wehr) and *Linz* (Cdr Dr Behlen) and the 6th DD Flotilla (Capt Kothe) with *Z28*, *Z35*, *Z39* and the attached torpedo boat *T30*, and the minesweepers *M14* and *M22*, lay the 'Seeigel 6b' barrage S of Suur Tytärsaari. On 16–17 Apr *Brummer*, *Roland*, *Linz*, *Z28*, *Z35*, *Z39* and *T30* lay the 'Seeigel 3b' barrage at Vigrund in Narva Bay, covered by the MMSs *R69* and *R73* to lay a smoke-screen to shield the ships from Soviet coastal batteries. On 19–20 Apr *Brummer*, *Roland*, *Linz*, *Z28*, *Z35* and *T30* lay 'Seeigel 7b/2' in Narva Bay. On 21–22 Apr a new operation with *Brummer*, *Roland*, *Linz*, *Z28*, *Z35*, *Z39* and *T30* and the minesweepers *M20* and *M37* is cancelled when *Roland* hits a mine, probably from a barrage laid earlier, and sinks. On 23–24 Apr *Brummer*, *Linz*, *M37*, *Z28*, *Z35*, *Z39* and *T30* lay 'Seeigel 7b/3' in Narva Bay. *M204*, *R69*, *R70*, *R72* and *R127* support the operation. On 25–26 Apr *Brummer*, *Linz*, *M20*, *M204*, *Z28*, *Z35*, *Z39* and *T30* lay 'Seeigel 8b' SW of Suur Tytärsaari, supported by *R70*, *R72*, *R119* and *R127*.

Altogether, 2831 mines and 1174 sweep detonators are laid during this operation. During Soviet minesweeping operations from 10 May to 20 Oct, 13 minesweepers, including *T-37*, *T-49* and *T-353*, are lost The MTBs *TK-46*, *TK-51*, *TK-35*, *TK-45* and *TK-90* are also lost on mines during the month of June.

13 Apr–4 May Central Pacific
Operation by US TF.58 (Vice-Adm Mitscher) to support the Hollandia landing. TF.58 sets out from Majuro on 13 Apr, is refuelled N of the Admiralty Islands on 19 Apr and begins its attacks on 21 Apr: TG.58.1 (Rear-Adm Clark), comprising *Hornet*, *Belleau Wood*, *Cowpens* and *Bataan*, makes fighter attacks on Wakde and Sarmi and shells them by night with the cruisers *Santa Fé*, *Mobile* and *Biloxi* and five destroyers of TG.58.1. On 22 Apr there is another carrier raid, followed by other raids on 23 and 24 Apr. TG.58.2 (Rear-Adm Montgomery), comprising *Bunker Hill*, *Yorktown*, *Monterey* and *Cabot*, carries out attacks on 21 Apr on Wakde and Hollandia and supports the landing in Humboldt Bay from 22 to 24 Apr. TG58.3 (Rear-Adm Reeves), comprising *Enterprise*, *Lexington*, *Princeton* and *Langley*, attacks Hollandia on 21 Apr and supports the landings near Tanahmerah Bay from 22 to 24 Apr. There is very little resistance in the air after previous attacks by the US 5th AF (Lt-Gen Kenney). Twenty-one carrier aircraft are lost. After refuelling on 27 Apr N of the Admiralty Islands, TF.58 makes a heavy attack on Truk on 29 and 30 Apr. Of 104 Japanese aircraft available, 59 are destroyed in air fights and 34 on the ground. Twenty-six US aircraft are shot down and nine lost through accident. S of Truk, the Japanese submarine *Ro-45* is sunk by TG.58.2 on 30 Apr. The US submarine *Tang* rescues 22 pilots who are shot down, some of them within the Truk lagoon.

On 30 Apr a cruiser-destroyer force (Rear-Adm Oldendorf), comprising the cruisers *Louisville*, *Portland*, *Wichita*, *Baltimore*, *Boston*, *Canberra*, *New Orleans*, *Minneapolis* and *San Francisco* and the destroyers *Bradford*, *Conner*, *Izard*, *Boyd*, *Brown*, *Cowell*, *Charrette* and *Burns*, shells the Satawan Islands group SE of Truk. On 1 May a battleship-destroyer force (Vice-Adm Lee) consisting of the battleships *Iowa*, *New Jersey*, *North Carolina*, *Indiana*, *Massachusetts*, *South Dakota* and *Alabama* and the destroyers *Miller*, *Owen*, *The Sullivans*, *Stephen Potter*, *Tingey*, *Converse*, *Thatcher*, *Pritchett*, *Cassin*, *Young* and *Bell* shells the island of Ponape. Air escort is provided by TG.58.1. This group enters Eniwetok on

4 May and TG.58.2 and TG.58.3 go to Majuro.

13 Apr–21 May Mediterranean
In operations E of Sicily, *U596* (Lt Nonn), the first boat to be fitted with schnorkel, misses an Italian corvette in the Strait of Otranto on 13 Apr and then operates without success off Taranto. *U565* cruises E of Sicily. They are relieved by *U453* (Lt Lührs) which misses a westbound convoy on 3 May. But on 18 May she attacks convoy HA.43, escorted by the Italian torpedo boats *Indomito*, *Libra*, *Fortunale* and *Monzambano* and the corvettes *Danaide* and *Urania*, and sinks one ship of 7147 tons. This is the last U-boat success in the Mediterranean. The boat is then hunted by Italian ships and, subsequently, by British destroyers. *Termagant*, *Tenacious* and *Liddesdale* sink her on 21 May.

14 Apr Indian Ocean
In Bombay, the British freighter *Fort Stikine* (7142 tons), loaded with cotton and ammunition, catches fire and explodes. As a result of the explosion and the scattered burning cotton, harbour installations and many ships are set on fire. In addition to the Dutch freighters *Generaal van der Heyden* (1215 tons), *Generaal van Swieten* (1300 tons) and *Tinombo* (872 tons), which are destroyed, three Indian warships and another 14 merchants ships of 50500 tons suffer, in some cases, severe damage. 336 people are killed and over 1000 injured.

14–26 Apr North Sea
The German minelayers *Ostmark*, *Elsass* and *Kaiser*, with the destroyers *Erich Steinbrinck* and *Hans Lody* and the minesweepers *M462*, *M406*, *M301* and *M381*, lay on 14–15 Apr the 'Leipzig' mine barrage and on 25–26 Apr the 'Ligny' barrage W of the Skagerrak.

15 Apr–10 June South West Pacific
Japanese operation 'Take-Ichi': convoy to reinforce troops on the Vogelkop Peninsula. It sets out with 20000 troops from Shanghai for Halmahera. On 26 Apr the transport *Yoshida Maru* (5425 tons) is sunk off Manila Bay by the US submarine *Jack* and on 6 May the transports *Tenshizan Maru* (6886 tons), *Taijima Maru* (6995 tons) and *Aden Maru* (5824 tons) are sunk by the US submarine *Gurnard*. Nearly half the troops embarked fail to reach Halmahera/Vogelkop.

16–24 Apr Indian Ocean
Operation 'Cockpit': carrier raid on Sabang. On 16 Apr the British Eastern Fleet sets out in two groups from Trincomalee: TF.69 (Adm Somerville) with the battleships *Queen Elizabeth*, *Valiant* and *Richelieu*, the cruisers (Rear-Adm Read) *Newcastle*, *Nigeria*, *Ceylon*, *Gambia* and *Tromp*, the

271

destroyers *Rotherham*, *Racehorse*, *Penn*, *Petard*, *Quiberon*, *Napier*, *Nepal*, *Nizam* (RAN) and *Van Galen* (Dutch); and TF.70 (Vice-Adm Power) with the battlecruiser *Renown*, the carriers (Rear-Adm Moody) *Illustrious* and *Saratoga*, the cruiser *London*, the destroyers *Quilliam*, *Quadrant*, *Queenborough*, *Cummings*, *Dunlap* and *Fanning* and the air/sea rescue submarine *Tactician*. On 18 Apr *Gambia* and *Ceylon* reinforce TF.70. On 19 Apr 46 bombers and 35 fighters fly off from the carriers to attack Sabang (northwest Sumatra) and surrounding airfields. One steamer is sunk and 24 aircraft are destroyed on the ground. One Allied fighter is lost but the pilot is rescued by the British submarine *Tactician*. When three Japanese torpedo aircraft try to attack, all the attackers are shot down by the fighter cover. The Fleet returns to Trincomalee.

17 Apr–4 May Black Sea

The Soviet Naval Air Force (see 8 Apr), the 2nd TKA Bde from Evpatoria and the 1st TKA Bde from Yalta (from 19 Apr) and the Submarine Bde (Rear-Adm Boltunov), which are jointly deployed on the basis of air reconnaissance, are used intensively against German and Rumanian transport traffic between the encircled fortress of Sevastopol (17th Army under Col-Gen Jaenecke) and Constanza. Each day there are up to eight convoys, consisting of the steamers *Oituz*, *Ardeal*, *Alba Julia*, *Budapest*, *Danubius*, *Prodromos*, *Helga*, *Ossag*, *Geiserich*, *Kassa*, *Totila*, *Teja*, *Tisza* and *Durostor*, the KT ships *KT18*, *KT25* and *KT26*, many tugs and ferry barges of the 1st, 3rd and 7th Landing Flotillas (Lt-Cdr Giele, Lt-Cdr Kuppig and Cdr Stelter). The escort, under the overall command of the Admiral Black Sea, Vice-Adm Brinkmann, is provided by the 10th Escort Div (Capt Weyher). The Rumanian naval forces are under Rear-Adm Marcellariu. The following ships are employed: the Rumanian destroyers *Regina Maria*, *Regele Ferdinand*, *Maresti*, *Marasesti*, the gunboats *Ghigulescu* and *Stihi*, the German 1st SC Flotilla (Cdr Gampert) comprising *UJ103*, *UJ104*, *UJ106*, *UJ115/Rosita* and *UJ116/Xanten*, the 3rd SC Flotilla (Lt Dr Teichmann) with the KFKs *UJ301* to *UJ307*, *UJ310*, *UJ313* to *UJ318*, the 23rd SC Flotilla (Cdr Wolters) with the KFKs *UJ2305*, *UJ2307*, *UJ2302*, *UJ2312*, *UJ2313* and *UJ2318* and the 3rd MMS Flotilla (Lt Klassmann) consisting of *R35*, *R37*, *R164*, *R165*, *R166*, *R163*, *R196*, *R197*, *R203*, *R205*, *R206*, *R207*, *R216* and *RA54*. Flanking escort is provided by the 1st MTB Flotilla (Cdr Büchting) with 13 motor torpedo boats.

On 18 Apr the Soviet submarine *M-111*

(Lt-Cdr Khomyakov) misses the steamer *Helga*. The *Alba Julia* (5700 tons) is set on fire by bombers and lost. In an attempt to attack the disabled steamer, the submarine *L-6* is destroyed by *UJ104* and *M-112* is driven off. On 22 Apr the submarines *M-62* (Lt-Cdr Malyshev) and *M-111* attack the *Ardeal* in turn without success. Bombers damage the *Ossag*, which sinks after being finished off by *M-35* (Lt-Cdr Prokofev), and *R207*. The submarine *Shch-201* (Capt 3rd Class Paramoshkin), attacks *UJ103* and is straddled with depth charges. From 26 to 28 Apr *L-4*, *Shch-202*, *Shch-201* try, sometimes repeatedly, to attack convoys. In air attacks on 28 Apr *F406* and *R37* are damaged. Torpedo cutters attempt attacks on 16, 17, 18, 24, 26 and 27 Apr. In the last, *UJ104/KT17* is torpedoed but brought into Sevastopol. In further attacks on 3–4 May the wreck of *UJ104*, *UJ2304*, the tug *Junak* and seven lighters are destroyed. The submarines *A-5* (Lt-Cdr Matveev), *M-62* and *M-111* attack three different convoys unsuccessfully. In addition to extensive supply missions, 13400 German and 29000 Rumanian troops are transported from Sevastopol during this period.

17 Apr–5 June English Channel/ North Sea/Baltic

British mining offensive to block the German sea routes to the Channel in preparation for the operation 'Neptune'. Nos 1, 3, 4, 5 and 6 Groups RAF Bomber Command drop 4000 mines in this period, including, for the first time, acoustic ground mines for low frequencies and acoustic anchor mines. The minelayers *Apollo* and *Plover* and the MTBs of the 9th, 13th, 14th, 21st and 64th MTB Flotillas and MLs of the 10th, 50th, 51st and 52nd ML Flotillas lay 3000 mines. About 100 German ships, in all, run on to these mines.

19–20 Apr Mediterranean

On 19 Apr convoy UGS.38 passes through the Straits of Gibraltar with 87 ships, escorted by TF.66 (Capt Duvall, USCG) with the US Coast Guard cutters *Taney* and *Duane* and the US DEs *Joseph E Campbell*, *Laning*, *Fechteler*, *Fiske*, *Mosley*, *Pride*, *Falgout*, *Lowe*, *Menges*, *Newell*, *Chase* and *Fessenden*; in addition, there are the Dutch AA cruiser *Heemskerck* and, as JIG ships, the US destroyer *Lansdale* and the US minesweepers *Speed* and *Sustain*. An attack by *U969* on 20 Apr fails. In the evening of 20 Apr some 60 torpedo aircraft of III/KG 26 and of I and III/KG 77 are deployed, some of which in approaching locate a Corsica–Africa convoy and sink the French freighter *El Biar* (4678 tons) from it. The others attack in the radar gap from the

African coast and sink the *Lansdale* and the freighters *Royal Star* (7900 tons) and *Paul Hamilton* (7177 tons) with torpedoes and damage the freighters *Samite* (7219 tons) and *Stephen Austin* (7176 tons). *Lowe*, *Taney* and *Heemskerck* narrowly avoid several torpedoes.

19–20 Apr Mediterranean

The minelayer *Kiebitz* and the motor minesweeper *R185* carry out the mining operation 'Hermelin' from Pola in the Adriatic.

20 Apr Air War/Italy

In an air attack against Monfalcone, the U-boat *UIT5* (ex-Italian *R 8*), fitting out, and the corvette *UJ203* (ex-Italian *Tersicore*) are destroyed.

21 Apr–6 May Arctic

An escort force (Rear-Adm McGrigor) comprising the cruiser *Diadem*, the escort carriers *Activity* and *Fencer*, the 3rd DD Flotilla with *Milne*, *Meteor*, *Marne*, *Matchless*, *Musketeer*, *Verulam*, *Ulysses* and *Virago*, the 6th SG with the Canadian frigates *Waskesiu*, *Grou*, *Cape Breton* and *Outremont* and the 8th SG with the destroyers *Keppel*, *Walker*, *Beagle*, *Westcott*, *Whitehall*, *Wrestler*, *Inconstant*, *Boadicea* and the corvette *Lotus* goes to the Kola Inlet to fetch convoy RA.59, where it arrives on 23 Apr. At the same time, on 21 Apr Vice-Adm Moore proceeds with the battleship *Anson*, the carriers *Victorious*, *Furious*, *Searcher*, *Striker*, *Emperor* and *Pursuer* and cruisers and destroyers to the northern Norwegian coast to carry out another raid on *Tirpitz*. On 24 and 25 Apr the weather prevents the aircraft from taking off. After the destroyers are refuelled the aircraft fly off on 26 Apr for an attack on shipping near Bodö. Here they find a southbound convoy and sink three German ships of 15083 tons. Six aircraft are lost to the defenders' fighters and AA fire.

After a feeder convoy of 16 steamers from the White Sea, accompanied by the Soviet destroyers *Gremyashchi* and *Gromki*, the minesweeper *T-119* and five patrol ships, arrives in the Kola Inlet on 27 Apr, convoy RA.59 puts to sea on the following day with the escort force. Initially, it is reinforced by the Soviet destroyers *Razyarenny*, *Grozny* and *Kuibyshev*, the minesweepers *T-112*, *T-114*, *T-119* and the submarine-chasers *BO-201*, *BO-204*, *BO-205*, *BO-207*, *BO-209* and *BO-212*. The US crew of the cruiser *Milwaukee/Murmansk* are distributed among the ships, as are 2300 Soviet sailors who are to man the British units (one battleship, nine destroyers and four submarines) which are to be taken over as a share of the Italian war booty in Britain. Adm Levchenko is on board the *Fencer*. The convoy is located by German air reconnaissance towards midnight on 28–29 Apr. The U-boats, which are waiting for an eastbound convoy, are deployed against RA.59 from 30 Apr as the 'Donner' group (*U277*, *U636*, *U307*, *U278*) and the 'Keil' group (*U711*, *U739*, *U674*, *U354*, *U315*, *U959*, *U313*). After a FAT salvo miss from *U307* (Lt Herrle) on the convoy, *U387* (Lt-Cdr Büchler) and *U711* (Lt Lange) repeatedly attack destroyers and steamers with T-5s and FAT salvos towards midnight on 30 Apr. *U711* sinks the *William S Thayer* (7176 tons). In the course of 1 May *U278* (Lt-Cdr Franze), *U307* and *U959* (Lt Weitz) each miss destroyers twice with T-5s. Swordfish 'C' of No 842 Sqn FAA from *Fencer* sinks *U277* on 1 May and Swordfish 'B' of No 842 Sqn FAA sinks *U959* and *U674* on 2 May, while *U307* and *U711* again miss destroyers with T-5s. Early on 3 May *U278* is attacked by two Swordfish and one Martlet but shoots down the latter and escapes.

22–28 Apr   South West Pacific
US landing operations 'Reckless' (Hollandia) and 'Persecution' (Aitape) under the overall command of Gen MacArthur and Vice-Adm Kinkaid (7th Fleet). Participating are I US Corps (Maj-Gen Eichelberger) and TF.77 (Rear-Adm Barbey). At Aitape is TG.77.1 (Barbey) with the 163rd RCT (Brig-Gen Doe) of the 41st Inf Div on three APAs, one LSD, one AKA, 16 LCIs and seven LSTs, escorted by the destroyers *Hobby*, *Nicholson*, *Wilkes*, *Grayson*, *Gillespie*, *Kalk* and *Swanson*. At Tanahmerah Bay is TG.77.2 (Rear-Adm Fechteler) with the 24th Inf Div (Maj-Gen Irving) on one APA, one LSD, one AKA, five APDs, 16 LCIs and seven LSTs, escorted by the destroyers *Reid*, *Stevenson*, *Stockton*, *Thorn*, *Roe*, *Welles*, *Radford* and *Taylor*. At Humboldt Bay is TG.77.3 (Capt Noble) with the 41st Inf Div (Maj-Gen Fuller) on nine APDs, one LSD, one AKA and seven LSTs, escorted by the destroyers *La Valette*, *Nicholas*, *O'Bannon*, *Jenkins*, *Hopewell* and *Howorth*. Air support is provided by TG.78.1 (Rear-Adm Ragsdale), comprising the escort carriers *Sangamon*, *Suwanee*, *Chenango* and *Santee* and the destroyers *Morris*, *Anderson*, *Hughes*, *Mustin*, *Russell*, *Ellet*, *Lansdowne* and *Lardner*, and TG.78.2 (Rear-Adm Davison), comprising the escort carriers *Natoma Bay*, *Coral Sea*, *Corregidor* and *Manila Bay* and the destroyers *Erben*, *Walker*, *Hale*, *Abbot*, *Bullard*, *Kidd*, *Black*, *Chauncey* and *Stembel*. Covering forces comprise TF.74 (Rear-Adm Crutchley), with the Australian cruisers *Australia* and

Shropshire, the Australian destroyers *Arunta* and *Warramunga* and the US destroyers *Ammen* and *Mullany*, and TF.75 (Rear-Adm Berkey), with the cruisers *Phoenix*, *Boise* and *Nashville* (Gen MacArthur on board) and the destroyers *Hutchins*, *Beale*, *Bache*, *Daly*, *Abner Read* and *Bush*.

The landings succeed against very slight resistance and the targets are reached by 28 Apr. Strong Japanese forces are cut off to the E.

23 Apr   Germany
The German MMS *R208* sinks while under tow by the tug *Fritz* in the Danube when it strikes an air-laid mine.

23 Apr   South West Pacific
The Japanese destroyer *Amagiri* is sunk 55 nautical miles S of Balikpapan (Borneo) after hitting a mine.

24 Apr   Mediterranean
The German MTB *S54* is damaged by a mine off Kephalonia; she is towed to Saloniki but not repaired.

26 Apr   Arctic
The German transport *KT3* is sunk W of Fuglöy (Faeroes) in a British air attack.

26 Apr–4 May   Bay of Biscay
On 26 Apr the German patrol vessel *V606* is sunk in an air attack S of Belle Isle. During air patrols, Wellington 'W' of No 612 Sqn RAF sinks the outgoing *U193* on 28 Apr. The outbound *U846* shoots down a Halifax of No 58 Sqn RAF on 2 May but is herself sunk on 4 May by Wellington 'M' of No 407 Sqn RCAF.

29 Apr–5 June   Air War/Western Europe
During a USAAF raid against Toulon on 29 Apr, *U421* is sunk.

From 30 Apr to 5 June there is an intensive mine offensive by RAF Bomber Command. In 31 nights, 1008 sorties are flown against the French Biscay, Brittany and Channel ports (especially the Gironde estuary), Brest and Dunkirk, the Belgian and Dutch coasts (especially the Schelde estuary and off Ijmuiden) the Frisian Islands, the Heligoland Bight, the Kattegat and the western Baltic up to the Pomeranian Bay. Mosquitos lay, for the first time, mines in the Kiel Canal. Eleven aircraft are lost.

The German gun ferry *AF73* is lost off Walcheren after hitting a mine on 13 May. The MMS *R179* is sunk off Le Havre on 15 May, the auxiliary minesweeper *M3238* W of Vlissingen on 17 May and the mine-sweeper *M515* W of Fehmarn on 22 May. *U618* is heavily damaged off St-Nazaire on 25 May and the MMS *R116* is sunk off Calais and the auxiliary minesweeper *M3612* off Gravelines on 29 May. The minesweeper *M13* is sunk in the Gironde

estuary on 31 May, the auxiliary mine-sweeper *M4003* off Brest on 3 June, the patrol vessel *V724* off Brest on 4 June, *V1509* and *M4031* off Le Havre and Brest respectively on 6 June and the MMS *R110* off the Hook of Holland on 10 June. The MMS *R95* is beached at Gravelines after hitting a mine and *V1510* is sunk at Cape d'Antifer on 12 June. The MMS *R50* is sunk on a German coast defence mine off Trouville on 13 June.

1 May   Air War/Mediterranean
The German transport *KT2* is sunk during an Allied air raid against Genoa. In an air attack against Venice, the corvette *UJ209* (ex-Italian *Scure*) is destroyed on the slipway at Breda.

1–31 May   Pacific
US submarines continue their operations with the assistance of decoded Japanese signals. There is greater use of 'wolfpack' tactics against convoys.

In the Kuriles, off Japan and off Formosa, *Tautog* (Lt-Cdr Baskett) sinks four ships of 16037 tons, *Skate* (Lt-Cdr Gruner) sinks one patrol boat of 31 tons, *Spearfish* (Lt-Cdr Williams) sinks one ship of 2510 tons and torpedoes the munitions ship *Mamiya* (15820 tons), *Burrfish* (Lt-Cdr Perkins) sinks the German prize-tanker *Rossbach* (5894 tons), *Silversides* (Lt-Cdr Coye) sinks six ships of 14126 tons, *Pollack* (Lt-Cdr Lewellen) sinks the destroyer *Asanagi* on 22 May, *Picuda* (Lt-Cdr Rayborn) sinks one ship of 3171 tons and, on 22 May, the gunboat *Hashidate*, *Flying Fish* (Lt-Cdr Risser) sinks two ships of 8206 tons, *Pompon* (Lt-Cdr Gimber) sinks one ship of 742 tons, *Guitarro* (Lt-Cdr Haskins) sinks one ship of 2201 tons and, on 2 June, the frigate *Awaji* and *Herring* (Lt-Cdr Zabriskie) sinks three ships of 6080 tons and, on 30 May, the frigate *Ishigaki* but is herself sunk by Japanese coastal batteries off Matsuwa (Kuriles). *Barb* (Lt-Cdr Fluckey) sinks five ships of 15471 tons and two sailing vessels and *Tilefish* has no success.

In the area of the Mandate Islands, *Sandlance* (Lt-Cdr Garrison) sinks five ships of 18328 tons, *Tuna* (Lt-Cdr Hardin) sinks one patrol vessel of 69 tons, *Hoe* (Lt Cdr McCrea) sinks, on 8 May, the frigate *Sado* and damages one ship of 10241 tons, *Sturgeon* (Lt-Cdr Murphy) sinks one ship of 1904 tons, *Bowfin* (Lt-Cdr Griffith) and *Aspro* (Cdr Stevenson) together sink one ship of 4667 tons and *Aspro* one more of 6440 tons, *Tunny* (Lt-Cdr Scott) sinks one ship of 4955 tons, *Angler* (Lt-Cdr Olsen) sinks one ship of 2105 tons, *Billfish* (Lt Cdr Farley) torpedoes one ship of 2726 tons, *Permit* (Lt-Cdr Chapple) sinks one sailing vessel and reports an attack against a submarine on 26 May which is unaccounted for and *Tambor* (Lt-Cdr Kefauver) sinks one ship of 657 tons.

In the Malayan Archipelago and the Philippines, *Pargo* (Lt-Cdr Eddy) sinks one ship of 758 tons, *Gurnard* (Lt-Cdr Andrews) sinks four ships of 29713 tons, *Cod* (Lt-Cdr Dempsey) sinks one ship of 7255 tons and, on 10 May, the torpedo boat *Karukaya*, *Rasher* (Lt-Cdr Laughon) sinks four ships of 14808 tons and reports an attack against a minelayer, *Puffer* (Lt-Cdr Selby) sinks three ships of 15597 tons, *Cero* (Lt-Cdr White) and *Ray* (Lt-Cdr Harrel) together sink one ship of 2825 tons, *Cero* one more of 6384 tons and *Ray* three of 14586 tons and *Raton* (Lt-Cdr Davis) sinks one ship of 168 tons and one sailing vessel, sinks the frigate *Iki* and damages the frigate *Matsuwa* on 24 May, and sinks the corvette *Kaibokan 15* on 6 June. *Lapon* (Lt-Cdr Stone) sinks two ships of 11253 tons and *Cabrilla* (Lt-Cdr Thompson) sinks one of 8360 tons and one sailing vessel. *Robalo*, *Narwhal* and *Perch* miss their targets.

2 May   Western Atlantic

The US destroyer *Parrott* is beached after colliding with the merchant ship *John Morton* in fog off Norfolk. She is towed to Portsmouth but not repaired.

2–3 May   Mediterranean

The British cruiser *Ajax* shells Rhodes and the French destroyers *Le Fantasque* and *Le Malin* bombard Coo.

3–5 May   Mediterranean

Convoy GUS.38, with 107 merchant ships, approaches the Straits of Gibraltar from the E, escorted by TF.66 (Capt Duval, USCG) with the US Coast Guard cutter *Taney*, 12 US DEs (see 19–20 Apr) and the British AA cruiser *Delhi*. On 3 May the DE *Menges* locates *U371* (Lt Fenski) with radar and approaches with a 'Foxer' astern, but she receives a T-5 hit. The DEs *Pride* and *Joseph E Campbell* take up the pursuit and at midday the British 'Hunt' class destroyer *Blankney*, the US minesweeper *Sustain* and the French destroyers *L'Alcyon* and *Sénégalais* also come from Oran. *U371* withdraws and submerges during the night 3–4 May but is located by *Sénégalais*. The U-boat fires T-5 torpedoes, one of which damages the approaching *Sénégalais*, and she then scuttles herself. In the meantime, the convoy proceeds. During the night 4–5 May *U967* (Lt-Cdr Brandi) is located by the DE *Laning* but she is able to sink the DE *Fechteler* with a T-5 and retire. Two more T-5s from *U967* on escorts on 26 Apr and 8 May have no success.

4 May   English Channel

The British minesweeper *Elgin* is mined 9 nautical miles E Portland. She is towed to Portsmouth but not repaired.

4 May–3 June   Arctic

British carrier attacks on northern Norway. On 6 May a British force consisting of the carriers *Furious* and *Searcher*, the cruiser *Berwick* and the destroyers *Savage*, *Wizard*, *Wakeful*, *Algonquin* (Canadian) and *Piorun* and *Blyskawica* (Polish) makes a sortie towards the Kristiansund North area: 18 Barracudas and 14 Seafires from *Furious* and 20 Wildcats from *Searcher* attack two German convoys and, with the loss of two aircraft, sink the ore steamer *Almora* (2522 tons) and the tanker *Saarburg* (7913 tons).

On 8 May a force consisting of the escort carriers *Searcher*, *Striker* and *Emperor* attacks a German convoy of five steamers and six escort vessels off Kristiansund North. Heavy damage is caused to several steamers.

On 12 May Vice-Adm Moore sets out with the battleship *Anson*, the carriers *Victorious* and *Furious* and cruisers and destroyers to make a new attack on *Tirpitz* in Altafjord. The 27 Barracudas, 28 Corsairs, four Seafires and four Wildcats flown off on 15 May have to return when off the Norwegian coast because of low clouds. A second group, consisting of the escort carriers *Emperor* and *Striker*, the cruisers *Sheffield* and *Royalist* and the destroyers *Onslow*, *Obedient*, *Ursa*, *Wakeful*, *Piorun* and *Blyskawica*, makes sorties on 14 and 15 May twice in the direction of Rörvik and Stadlandet and obtains many near-misses with carrier aircraft on German ships lying at anchor but no actual sinkings. A third sortie by Vice-Adm Moore with the carriers *Victorious* and *Furious* to attack *Tirpitz* on 28 May has to be abandoned because of the weather. The Barracudas attack a convoy off the Norwegian coast on 1 June and sink the ammunition steamer *Hans Leonhardt* (4170 tons) and set *Sperrbrecher 181* and the freighter *Florida* (5542 tons) on fire. A T-5 torpedo from *U957* on the carrier force on 30 May is not successful.

5–12 May   Black Sea

After Hitler, in spite of several requests, has rejected the idea of a timely withdrawal from Sevastopol, the Soviet 2nd Guards Army (Col-Gen Sakharov) in the northern sector on 5 May, followed in the next few days by the 51st Army (Lt-Gen Kreiser) and the Coastal Army (Gen Eremenko), attacks German and Rumanian positions of the 17th Army. Soviet troops having broken through to the Sapun Heights on 8 May, Hitler, in response to further appeals, gives the order

to withdraw the hard-pressed remnants of the 17th Army (there are still 64700 troops on 3 May). The German and Rumanian warships and transports (see 17 Apr) are able, despite continual and very strong Soviet air attacks and the massive deployment of submarines, to evacuate 37500 men by 13 May, including 25677 troops and 6011 wounded in the last three days. In the process, *UJ2310* and *UJ2315* have to be beached. As a result of attacks by Soviet air formations—see 8 Apr and the 8th Air Army (Lt-Gen Khryukin) and the 4th Air Army (Col-Gen Vershinin)—the transports *Totila* (2773 tons), *Teja* (3600 tons), *Helga* (2200 tons), *Danubius* (1489 tons) and *Prodromos* (800 tons), the minelayer *Romania* (3152 tons), the submarine-chasers *UJ2313*, *UJ2314*, *UJ310*, three auxiliary vessels, five tugs, 11 lighters and other small craft are sunk. The transports *Durostor* (1309 tons) and *Geiserich* (712 tons), which are damaged by bombs, are finished off by torpedoes from *A-5* (Lt-Cdr Matveev) and *Shch-201* (Capt 3rd Class Paramoshkin) respectively. Many attacks are made by the submarines deployed—*S-33*, *Shch-201*, *Shch-202*, *L-4*, *M-35*, *M-62*, *Shch-205* and *A-5*—but only *L-4* (Capt 3rd Class Polyakov) is able to torpedo the tanker *Friederike-Firuz* (7327 tons) from a convoy. In addition, *Shch-202* (Lt-Cdr Leonov) sinks the lighter *Elbe-5*, *M-35* (Lt-Cdr Prokofev) one barge and *S-33* (Capt 3rd Class Alexeyev) one motor yacht. Of the troops embarked on the sunken transports, 8100 cannot be rescued. In all, 130000 German and Rumanian troops are evacuated by sea and 21457 by air between 12 Apr and 13 May; 78000 are left behind as prisoners or dead.

5 May–20 July   Black Sea

German and Rumanian submarines operate against Soviet coastal traffic on the Caucasian coast. In the northern part, *Requinul* has no success in Apr–May and June–July nor *Marsouinul* in May. On 21 May the latter is damaged by depth charges. *U9* (Lt-Cdr Petersen) sinks a fishing cutter on 5 May and the minesweeper *T-411/Zashchitnik* on 11 May with a T-5 and torpedoes a tanker with one patrol vessel on 16 May. *U24* (Lt Landt-Hayen) sinks a patrol vessel on 12 May and perhaps another on 22 May. *U23* (Lt Wahlen) reports one steamer torpedoed and one tanker sunk as well as a fishing cutter and a motor gunboat. *U18* (Lt Arendt) sinks, at the end of May or the beginning of June, a tug and a motor gunboat and *U19* (Lt Ohlenburg) sinks a tug; *U20* (Lt Grafen) sinks the freighter *Pestel* (1850 tons) off Trapezunt on 19 June and four motor boats on 24 June.

6–27 May   Indian Ocean

Operation 'Transom': carrier raid on Soerabaya. On 6 May TF.65 (Adm Somerville) sets out from Trincomalee with the battleships *Queen Elizabeth*, *Valiant* and *Richelieu*, the cruisers *Newcastle*, *Nigeria* and *Tromp* and the destroyers *Rotherham*, *Racehorse*, *Penn*, *Van Galen*, *Napier*, *Nepal*, *Quiberon* and *Quickmatch* and TF.66 (Vice-Adm Power) from Colombo with the battlecruiser *Renown* (transferred to TF.65 from 7 May), the carriers (Rear-Adm Moody) *Illustrious* and *Saratoga*, the cruisers *Ceylon* and *Gambia* and the destroyers *Quilliam*, *Quadrant*, *Queenborough*, *Cummings*, *Dunlap* and *Fanning*. They replenish on 15 May in Exmouth Bay from TF.67, which comprises six fleet tankers, one water tanker and, as escort, the cruisers *London* and *Suffolk*, which went on ahead from Trincomalee on 30 Apr. The cruisers join TF.66 from 14 May. Early on 17 May, S of Java, 45 Avenger and Dauntless dive-bombers, escorted by 40 Hellcat and Corsair fighters, fly off from both carriers to attack the harbour and oil refineries at Soerabaya; 12 aircraft are destroyed on the ground and one Allied aircraft is lost. The damage inflicted on the harbour installations and ships is greatly overestimated: in fact, only one freighter of 993 tons is sunk and the patrol boat *P-36*/*Fuji* damaged beyond repair. On 18 May *Saratoga* and the three US destroyers leave the force; the remainder return to Ceylon, which they reach on 27 May.

During May, in the Straits of Malacca, the British submarine *Tantivy* sinks one junk of 150 tons, *Tally Ho!* (Cdr Bennington) lays a mine barrage on which one ship of 1945 tons is damaged, *Sea Rover* (Lt Angell) lays a minefield and sinks one ship of 1365 tons, *Tactician* lays a minefield and sinks a junk with gunfire, *Templar* (Lt Ridgway) sinks one ship of 2658 tons and *Surf* also lays a minefield.

7–8 May   North Sea

The German minelayers *Ostmark*, *Elsass* and *Kaiser*, with the minesweepers *M15* and *M29*, lay the 'Waterloo' mine barrage W of the Skagerrak.

7–20 May   Air War/Western Europe

RAF Bomber Command attacks Nantes with 99 aircraft (7–8 May) and Brest with 64 aircraft (8–9 May); two aircraft are lost. Boulogne is attacked on 11–12 with 135 aircraft and on 19–20 with 143; again, two aircraft are lost.

7 May–30 July   North Atlantic

Because of the build-up of the 'Landwirt' U-boat group in France, and of 'Mitte' in Norway as a defence against invasion, only a few weather boats operate in the North Atlantic: until the end of May *U736*, *U955*, *U385*, then *U853*, *U534* and *U857*, and, at the end of June and the beginning of July, the experimental boat for the new AA turret VI, *U673*. In spite of the regular transmission of weather reports, no losses are sustained. *U853*, *U736* and *U385* make unsuccessful attacks on escorts. *U853* (Lt-Cdr Sommer) beats off attacks on 25 May by three Swordfish aircraft armed with rockets from the merchant aircraft carriers *Ancylus* and *MacKendrick*, but she is repeatedly located by HF/DF and attacked on 17 June by aircraft from the US escort carrier *Croatan*. Nevertheless, she escapes.

From 20 to 28 May the schnorkel boats *U764*, *U441*, *U984*, *U953* and *U269* are formed into the 'Dragoner' group at the mouth of the Channel, N of Oucssant, as an exercise in repelling invasion. It has no success. From 15 June the schnorkel boat *U247* (Lt Matschulat), which sinks one trawler of 200 tons, operates in the Minches and *U719* in the North Channel. Both miss patrol vessels and *U247* misses a battleship with a salvo on 18 June. *U719* is sunk by the destroyer *Bulldog* on 26 June after a long search.

8 May   Baltic

The German patrol vessel *V1701* is sunk by Soviet aircraft in Narva Bay.

8–29 May   North Sea/English Channel

The French *MTB227*, *MTB91*, *MTB239* and *MTB92* attack a German supply convoy for the Channel Islands between Jersey and Guernsey and sink the small steamer *Bizon* (750 tons). *MTB227* is damaged by patrol boats of the 2nd PB Flotilla. On 11 May British MTBs sink *V1311* off the Hook of Holland.

On 12–13 May the Norwegian *MTB715*, *MTB627*, *MTB653* and *MTB688* try unsuccessfully to attack a convoy off the Hook of Holland. The German 5th and 9th MTB Flotillas, comprising *S100*, *S112*, *S142*, *S136*, *S141* and *S140* and *S146*, *S145*, *S130* and *S150*, are involved in engagements when they try to attack off Selsey Bill. The frigate (DE) *Stayner*, the corvette *Gentian* and *MTB96*, *MTB227*, *MTB237* and *MTB246* drive off the German motor torpedo boats. The French destroyer *La Combattante* (Cdr Patou) sinks *S141*; *S100* and *S112* arc damaged.

On 16–17 May the 2nd MTB Flotilla, consisting of *S177*, *S178*, *S189*, *S180* and *S179*, lays 20 LMB mines near Hearty Knoll and is then pursued by the destroyer *Quorn*. On 17–18 May all the German motor torpedo boat flotillas carry out mining operations: the 2nd Flotilla (Cdr Opdenhoff), consisting of *S177*, *S180*, *S179*, *S190*, *S189* and *S178*, S of Orfordness (20 LMB mines); and the 8th Flotilla (Cdr Zymalkowski), consisting of *S64*, *S87*, *S127* and *S133* (mines) and *S83*, *S117* and *S67* (torpedoes), near the Sunk Lightship (11 LMBs). The 8th is pursued by the British corvette *Sheldrake* and MGBs, including *MGB321*, but arrives in Ijmuiden without loss. The 4th Flotilla (Lt-Cdr Fimmen), consisting of *S169*, *S171*, *S188*, *S174*, *S175*, *S172* and *S187*, carries out a mining operation against a CW convoy between Folkestone and Dungeness, lays 21 LMB and 14 M-1 mines, avoids on its return British destroyers and MGB groups deployed against it and then has a brief engagement with a German convoy comprising *Von der Gröben*, the 4th MMS Flotilla and KFKs without any damage being done. The 5th Flotilla (Cdr Klug) breaks off the operation with *S100*, *S112* and *S142* because of a destroyer engagement but with *S136*, *S138* and *S140* lays 12 LMC mines near Hope Nose (Lyme Bay). The 9th Flotilla (Cdr v Mirbach), consisting of *S130*, *S168*, *S145*, *S146*, *S144* and *S150*, breaks through a destroyer group, lays 27 mines in Lyme Bay and, on the return, has another engagement with three destroyers and three MGB groups.

On 18–19 May the 9th Flotilla makes a reconnaissance sortie from Cherbourg to Le Havre and has a brief engagement with the SGBs *Grey Owl* and *Grey Wolf*. During the night 19–20 May the 5th Flotilla (see above) lays 10 BMC and 12 UMB mines near Start Point. On the return the flotilla is involved in a short engagement with the German patrol boats *V210* and *V208*, which are going to the help of *V205*. The latter is rescuing survivors from *V211*, sunk by *MTB90*, near Guernsey.

The 2nd Flotilla breaks off a mining operation near Smith's Knoll because of mist. The 8th Flotilla (see above) lays 12 UMB and 16 M-1 mines and six protective floats near Orfordness. The trawler *Wyoming* (302 tons) and the minesweeper *MMS227* sink on the barrages. On the return British Swordfish aircraft attack off Ostend: *S87* catches fire and sinks while being towed by *S83*.

The transfer of the torpedo boats *Jaguar* and *T24* from Brest to Cherbourg is abandoned when the latter hits a ground mine. *Jaguar* arrives in Cherbourg on 23 May and in the following night proceeds with *Kondor*, *Greif*, *Falke* and *Möwe* and the 6th MS Flotilla to Le Havre. On the way *Greif* sinks after fighter-bomber attacks by No 415 Sqn RAF and a collision with *Kondor*, and *Kondor* and *M84* are brought in badly damaged by ground mines. During the night 22–23 May the 5th MTB Flotilla with five boats (not *S136*) lays 20 UMB mines S of the Isle of Wight. On 23 May the German auxiliary minesweeper *M4623* is sunk off Lecardieux by British MGBs; *M39* is sunk by torpedoes from the British *MTB354* and *MTB361* off Quistreham on 24 May.

During the night 23–24 May the 9th MTB Flotilla breaks off a mining operation from Le Havre in the direction of the British south coast because of the weather. The 5th Flotilla, with five boats, carries out a mining operation off Brighton but only drops eight UMB mines because of destroyer attacks. *S112* is hit by *Vanquisher* from the escort of convoy WP.526. On 25 May the German gun ferry *AF12* capsizes after being bombed off Dunkirk. During the night 27–28 May the 9th Flotilla, with six boats, lays 24 mines along the coastal route W of Beachy Head and the 5th Flotilla with five boats lays 20 UMB mines S of the Isle of Wight. Attacks by Beaufighter bombers and destroyers are unsuccessful. On 29 May *R123* is sunk in an air attack off Le Havre.

9 May   South Pacific
End of the Allied air mining campaign. A total of 292 TBF and PY-1 sorties by the US Navy Cdr Air Solomons and the RNZAF have been flown in which 251 aircraft have dropped 251 mines in the Buin-Kahili and Faisi areas, in the Buka Passage and in Simpson Harbour of which 237 mines were magnetic and 14 acoustic. Thirteen aircraft have been lost.

9–11 May   Mediterranean
On 9 May convoy UGS.40, with 65 ships, passes through the Straits of Gibraltar, escorted by TF.60 (Cdr Sowell, USCG) with the US Coast Guard cutter *Campbell*, the US destroyers *Dallas*, *Bernadou*, *Ellis* and *Benson* and the US DEs *Evarts*, *Dobler*, *Decker*, *Smartt*, *Wyffels*, *Walter S Scott*, *Brown* and *Wilhoite*; in addition, there are the British AA cruiser *Caledon*, the French DE *Tunisien*, the French PC submarine-chaser *Cimeterre* and the JIG ships, the US minesweepers *Sustain* and *Steady*. *U967* and *U616* do not get to the convoy.

In the evening of 11 May 62 aircraft of I and III/KG 26 are deployed against the convoy. British Beaufighters flying from Sardinia intercept some of the attackers and lose two aircraft; the remainder attack in four waves in the area of Cape Bengut. The pilots believe that they have sunk a destroyer and seven freighters and damaged many

others but in fact no ship is hit and 19 aircraft are lost.

9 May–18 June   Mediterranean
From 9 to 17 May the French submarines *La Sultane* and *Curie* and the British *Ultor* make several attacks in which only some small ships are damaged. From the end of May to beginning of June *Upstart* (Lt Chapman) sinks one ship of 2954 tons, *Universal* (Lt Gordon) one escort, *Untiring* (Lt Boyd) *UJ6078* and *Ultor* (Lt Hunt) *SG11* and five small craft; and the French *Casabianca* (Lt Bellet) damages the small submarine-chaser *UJ6079*. On 11 May the British destroyer *Bicester* bombards targets in the Ardea area S of Rome; on 15 May the cruiser *Dido* bombards targets in the Gulf of Gaeta to support an Army attack.

From 11 to 28 May the German 10th TB Flotilla, consisting of *TA24*, *TA29* and *TA30*, carries out four mining operations ('Languste', 'Angel', 'Haken' and 'Widerhaken') and two reconnaissance sorties in the Ligurian Sea. On 13 May the German MMS *R215* is sunk in an attack by fighter-bombers off Chiavari. On 24 May a US group comprising *PT202*, *PT213* and *PT218* attacks a German force and sinks *UJ2223* (ex-Italian *Marangone*). *UJ2222* (ex-Italian *Tuffeto*) reaches Livorno badly damaged. On 27–28 May US PT boats sink *UJ2210*. In an engagement off the Ligurian coast between *TA29* and *TA30* and *PT304*, *PT306* and *PT307* on 31 May, both sides sustain light damage. From 2 to 14 June two boats from *TA24*, *TA26*, *TA27* and *TA30* undertake, in turn, the mining operations 'Gemse', 'Brosche', 'Tor' and 'Weide'; in the process *TA27* is sunk by USAAF fighter-bombers in Portoferraio on 9 June. The torpedo boats *TA26* and *TA30* are sunk on 14–15 June, in the mining operation 'Nadel', when they are attacked by *PT558*, *PT552* and *PT559*. On 17–18 June *TA29* and *TA24*, while laying the 'Stein' mine barrage, are involved in an engagement with the US *PT207* and the British *MTB633*, *MTB640*, *MTB655* and *MGB658*. The German hospital ship *Erlangen*, which set out on 15 June to give aid, is set on fire by Allied aircraft and has to be beached near Sestri Levante.
U230 (Lt-Cdr Siegmann) sinks the US submarine-chaser *PC558* off Palermo.

11–29 May   Arctic
Soviet combined operation 'RV-4' against German convoy traffic off the Norwegian polar coast. After a convoy is located by a Pe-2 reconnaissance plane off Svaerholt, six Il-4 torpedo aircraft of the 9th Guards Mining & Torpedo Air Regt with five fighters attack on 11 May off Makkaur and a

force of five Boston torpedo aircraft, six bombers and ten fighters off Kongsfjord, sinking *V6113*.
On 13 and 14 May Soviet air formations carry out ten attacks (217 sorties) on shipping targets in Kirkenes. The steamers *Pernambuco* (4121 tons) and *Patagonia* (5898 tons) are set on fire, *UJ1210* is damaged and a minesweeper and a patrol boat are lightly hit. German Me 109s and AA guns shoot down at least six aircraft. On 25–26 May there is a combined attack on the German eastbound convoy with the gunboat *K-1*. There are air torpedo and bomb attacks in ten waves with fighter cover, in the course of which the steamer *Solviken* (3502 tons) is sunk by torpedo and *Herta Engeline Fritzen* (3672 tons) receives a bomb hit in the bow. The submarines *S-15*, *S-56*, *S-103*, and *M-201* are deployed. *M-201* (Lt-Cdr Balin) misses the convoy off Makkaur. Shortly afterwards *S-15* (Lt-Cdr Vasilev) also misses, and survives a concentrated pursuit with depth charges from the submarine-chasers *UJ1209*, *UJ1212* and *UJ1219*.
On 29 May *S-103* (Capt 3rd Class Nechaev) attacks two German minesweepers off Laksfjord without success.

11 May–8 June   Black Sea
Transfer of the Soviet submarines *M-104*, *M-105*, *M-107* and *M-119* from the Northern Fleet to the Black Sea Fleet.

11 May–12 June   Pacific
Japanese preparations for Operation 'A-GO', the defence of the Marianas line. On 11 and 12 May elements of the 1st Mobile Fleet (Vice-Adm Ozawa) set out in two groups from Lingga Bay, where the 1st Carrier Sqn has trained its pilots, for Tawi-Tawi. They arrive there on 15 May and join up on 16 May with the elements which set out from Japan on 12 May, the 2nd and 3rd Carrier Sqns, *Musashi* and other units.
Vice-Adm Ozawa then disposes of the 2nd Fleet with the 1st Battle Sqn (Vice-Adm Ugaki) and the 3rd Battle Sqn (Vice-Adm Suzuki), comprising the battleships *Yamato*, *Musashi*, *Nagato*, *Kongo*, *Haruna* and *Fuso*, the 4th (Vice-Adm Kurita), the 5th (Rear-Adm Hashimoto) and the 7th Cruiser Sqns, consisting of the heavy cruisers *Atago*, *Takao*, *Maya*, *Chokai*, *Haguro*, *Myoko*, *Kumano*, *Suzuya*, *Tone*, *Chikuma* and *Mogami*, the 2nd DD Flotilla (Rear-Adm Hayakawa), consisting of the cruiser *Noshiro*, the 27th DD Div with the destroyers *Harusame*, *Shiratsuyu*, *Shigure*, and *Samidare*, the 31st DD Div with *Okinami*, *Kishinami*, *Naganami* and *Asashimo* and the 32nd DD Div with *Tamanami*, *Hamanami*, *Fujinami* and *Hayanami*, and the attached *Shimakaze*. In addition, there

is the 3rd Fleet with the 1st Carrier Sqn (Ozawa), comprising *Taiho*, *Zuikaku* and *Shokaku*, the 2nd Carrier Sqn (Rear-Adm Joshima), comprising *Junyo*, *Hiyo* and *Ryuho*, the 3rd Carrier Sqn (Rear-Adm Obayashi), comprising *Chitose*, *Chiyoda* and *Zuiho*, and the 10th DD Flotilla (Rear-Adm Kimura), consisting of the cruiser *Yahagi*, the 61st DD Div with the destroyers *Akizuki*, *Hatsuzuki*, *Wakatsuki* and *Shimotsuki*, the 4th DD Div with *Michishio*, *Nowake* and *Yamagumo*, the 10th DD Div with *Kazegumo* and *Asagumo* and the 17th DD Div with *Urakaze*, *Isokaze*, *Tanikaze*, *Hamakaze* and *Yukikaze*. Also are attached *Minazuki*, *Hayashimo* and *Akishimo* (the last joins later). The 1st and 2nd Supply Groups consist of nine tankers and the destroyers *Hibiki*, *Hatsushimo*, *Yunagi*, *Uzuki* and *Tsuga*.

Losses are sustained as a result of US submarine attacks when the ships exercise in the waters around Tawi-Tawi. On 22 May *Bonefish* reports the Fleet and hits *Chitose* with two unexploding torpedoes. On 24 May *Gurnard* sinks the tanker *Tatekawa Maru*, on 3 June *Puffer* the tankers *Takasaki* and *Ashizuri* and on 6–7 June *Harder* (Cdr Dealey) the destroyers *Minazuki* and *Hayanami* and, on 8 June, also *Tanikaze*. In the operations 'Kon', *Kazegumo* is sunk on 3 June by the submarine *Hake* and *Harusame* on 8 June in an air attack.

12 May   Air War/Germany
The German *U1102* is heavily damaged in a USAAF raid on Königsberg; the submarine is decommissioned and towed to Kiel. During air raid on Swinemünde, the minesweeper *M372/TS3* is sunk.

14 May   North Sea
The German minesweeper *M435* capsizes N of Ameland after an air attack by RAF Coastal Command during salvage operations by *M369*.

14–19 May   Baltic
U1234 is sunk in collision with the tug *Anton* during exercises on 14 May off Gdynia; she is later raised but decommissioned. On 19 May *U1015* is sunk following a collision with *U1014* in the Gulf of Danzig.

14–19 May   Mediterranean
U616 (Lt Koitschka) torpedoes two ships of 17854 tons from convoy GUS.39 off Cape Tenes on 14 May. While two British escorts keep the boat under water and aircraft of No 36 Sqn RAF circle the area, two US destroyer groups (Capt Converse), consisting of *Nields*, *Gleaves* and *Macomb* and *Ellyson*, *Hilary P Jones*, *Hambleton*, *Rodman* and *Emmons*, set out from Oran. After a first

depth charge attack from *Ellyson* during the night 14–15 May, contact is lost for the whole of 15 May; only in the following night does a Wellington locate the surfaced U-boat and bring the destroyers up, which sink her in the morning.

In passing through the Straits of Gibraltar, *U731* is located on 15 May by MAD Catalinas '14' and '1' of VP-63 USN and sunk by the submarine-chasers *Kilmarnock* and *Blackfly*. *U960* (Lt Heinrich), which has also broken through the Straits, attacks on 17 May the US destroyers returning from the search for *U616* and misses *Ellyson* with a salvo of three torpedoes. She is pursued by the newly deployed US destroyer group, consisting of *Woolsey*, *Benson*, *Madison*, *Niblack* and *Ludlow*, and sunk during the night 18–19 May in co-operation with two Wellingtons of No 36 Sqn RAF and a Ventura of No 500 Sqn RAF.

15–27 May   Central Pacific
US TG.58.2 (Rear-Adm Montgomery), comprising the carriers *Essex*, *Wasp* and *San Jacinto*, the cruisers *Baltimore*, *Boston*, *Canberra*, *San Diego* and *Reno*, twelve destroyers, three escort destroyers and two tankers, sets out from Majuro on 14 May and carries out heavy carrier raids on Marcus Island on 19 and 20 May and on Wake on 23 May.

16 May   Norwegian Sea
The German A/S vessel *UJ1210* is sunk by air attack off Lille Egge.

From 16 to 31 May there is an air offensive by No 18 Group RAF Coastal Command against the U-boats setting out for the Atlantic from Norway. Sunderlands of No 330 Sqn (Norwegian) and No 4 OTU RAF, Catalinas of Nos 210 and 333 (Norwegian) Sqns RAF and Liberators of No 59 Sqn RAF sight U-boats on 22 occasions and make 13 attacks. On 16 May Sunderland 'V' of No 330 (Norwegian) Sqn sinks *U240* but is herself badly damaged by AA fire and on 17 May Catalina 'C' from the same unit damages *U668* and is also hit by AA fire. On 18 May Catalina 'S' of No 210 Sqn sinks *U241* and on 21 May Sunderland 'S' from No 4 OTU damages *U995*. On 24 May *U476*, which is proceeding to northern Norway, damages Catalina 'V' of No 210 Sqn by AA fire but is herself so badly damaged that she has to be sunk by *U990* after 21 of the crew have been taken off; *U990* is herself sunk on 25 May by Liberator 'S' of No 59 Sqn RAF; *V5901* rescues 51 survivors from both both boats. On 24 May Sunderland 'R' of No 4 OTU sinks *U675*. On 26 May *U958* and *U862* are damaged by Mosquitos 'N' and 'E' of No 333 Sqn

RAF and have to return and on 27 May Liberator 'S' of No 59 Sqn sinks *U292*. In this period only the minelaying U-boat *U233* and the schnorkel boats *U719*, *U767*, *U1191*, *U988*, *U671*, *U987* and *U247* get through to the Atlantic.

17–18 May   South West Pacific
On 17 May an amphibious group (Capt Noble) with 14 destroyers, six escort destroyers, two APAs, seven LSTs, 15 LCIs and five SCs lands the 163rd RCT (Brig-Gen Doe with 7000 men) near Arara and, on the following day, on the outlying island of Wakde in order to seize the airfield there. Support is provided by TF.74 (Rear-Adm Crutchley) and TF.75 (Rear-Adm Berkey) (for composition see 22 Apr under Hollandia operation, except *Trathen* instead of the destroyer *Bush*). US losses amount to 110 men and the Japanese defenders lose 759 men with one taken prisoner.

17–26 May   Central Pacific
Destroyers of the US 5th Fleet shell the islands of Engebi in the Maloelap Atoll on 17 May, Wotje on 22 May and Mili in the Marshall Islands on 26 May.

17 May–3 Aug   Atlantic
In operations S of Nova Scotia, *U1222* (Lt-Cdr Bielfeld) and *U107* (Lt-Cdr Simmermacher) make several unsuccessful attacks on convoys and escorts in May and June.

In the area of the Azores, US task groups operate against suspected U-boat suppliers. *U549* (Lt-Cdr Krankenhagen), which is on the way to Brazil, is sighted on 28 May by an aircraft from TG.22.1 (Capt Hughes), consisting of *Block Island* and five DEs, but she is able to sink the carrier on 29 May with three torpedo hits, hit the DE *Barr* with a T-5 and just miss the DE *Eugene E Elmore* with a T-5. While the DE *Ahrens* rescues survivors, *U549* is sunk by the DEs *Eugene E Elmore* and *Robert I Paine*. The relieving TG.22.3 (Capt Gallery), consisting of *Guadalcanal* and the DEs *Chatelain*, *Pillsbury*, *Pope*, *Flaherty* and *Jenks*, after obtaining an HF/DF bearing on 1 June, looks for the homebound *U505*. The latter is forced to surface by depth charges from *Chatelain* on 4 June and, the crew having come off, she is taken over by a boarding party (Lt David) from *Pillsbury*. The Group brings the boat to Bermuda on 19 June with her important booty of codes.

Throughout June until the beginning of July the operation of the schnorkel U-boat *U543* (Lt-Cdr Hellriegel) off Freetown meets with no success. *U547* (Lt Niemeyer) sinks the A/S trawler *Birdlip* and a ship from a convoy off Liberia on 14 June and another ship on 2 July, making a total of 8371 tons.

From the beginning of June until the middle of July U-boats operate in the Caribbean: *U539* (Lt-Cdr Lauterbach-Emden) and *U516* (Lt-Cdr Tillessen) each sink one ship, of 1517 tons and 9887 tons respectively, and each torpedo one ship, of 10195 tons and 4756 tons respectively. In addition, *U539* slightly damages two tankers with near-explosions and escapes from the *Card* and *Guadalcanal* carrier groups, sent to search for U-boats in the Caribbean, both of which are sighted. The schnorkel boat *U530* has no success off Trinidad from the middle of June. TG.22.5 (Capt Vest), which relieves TG.22.3 in the area of the Azores and consists of *Croatan* and the DEs *Barber*, *Swasey*, *Snowden*, *Frost*, *Huse* and *Inch*, is directed to a HF/DF location on 10 June and the three last-named DEs sink the remaining U-tanker, *U490*, on 11 June before she is able to refuel a U-boat. The relieving TG.22.2 (Capt Vosseller), comprising *Bogue* and the DEs *Haverfield*, *Janssen*, *Willis*, *Francis M Robinson* and *Wilhoite*, searches for *U530* from 15 June, which has reported by radio having handed over search receiver equipment to the Japanese transport submarine *I-52* (Cdr Uno). On 23–24 June *I-52* is sunk by two Avengers from *Bogue* with the help of sonobuoys.

On 2 July aircraft from TG.22.4 (Capt Tague), comprising *Wake Island* and the DEs *Douglas L Howard*, *Fiske*, *Farquhar*, *J R Y Blakely* and *Hill*, sink the homebound *U543* E of the Azores in spite of strong AA fire. Further to the N, the outbound *U154* falls victim to the DEs *Frost* and *Inch* of TG.22.5. The minelayer *U233* is sunk off Halifax on 5 July by the DEs *Baker* and *Thomas* of TG.22.10, which also comprises *Card* and the DEs *Bronstein*, *Breeman* and *Bostwick*.

On the way to East Asia, *U860* (Cdr* Büchel) is sunk on 15 June by seven aircraft of VC-9 USN from TG.41.6 (Capt Crist), which includes the escort carrier *Solomons*, after she has shot down two machines. *U861* (Cdr Oesten), which follows, proceeds to the Brazilian coast but does not sight the first contingent of the Brazilian Expeditionary Force leaving Rio de Janeiro for Italy on 2 July aboard the US troop transport *General William A Mann* with the Brazilian destroyers *Marcilio Dias*, *Mariz e Barros* and *Greenhalgh*. On 20 July *U861* sinks the Brazilian transport *Vital de Oliveira* (1737 tons) and misses the submarine-chaser *Javari*. On 24 July she sinks a steamer of 7176 tons from the convoy JT.39 and escapes the search made by TG.41.6, comprising *Solomons* and the DEs *Trumpeter*, *Straub*, *Gustafson* and *Alger*, as well as *Greenhalgh* and *Mariz e Barros*. *U862* (Cdr Timm) sinks one ship of 6885 tons on 25 July.

17 May–23 Sept   Indian Ocean

In May the Japanese transport submarine *I-52* passes through the Indian Ocean on her way to Europe and at the beginning of June the damaged *U843* on her way to Penang. The Japanese *I-166* lands agents in Ceylon at the end of May and *I-165* cruises NW of Australia in June without success. *U183* (Lt-Cdr Schneewind), coming from Penang, sinks a ship of 5259 tons on 5 June NE of the Chagos Archipelago and replenishes *U537* (Lt-Cdr Schrewe) on her way from France on 25 June. The latter misses a tanker on 8 July and is hunted for several days by the destroyers *Racehorse* and *Raider*. The Japanese *I-8* (Capt Ariizumi) sinks two ships totalling 14118 tons near the Chagos Archipelago on 29 June and 2 July; in the process the survivors of the *Jean Nicolet* are murdered.

From the end of June German Type IXD2 boats arrive in the Indian Ocean from the Atlantic. Of them, *U181* (Cdr* Freiwald) sinks three ships of 19557 tons in the Arabian Sea and is hunted in vain by aircraft and the Indian sloop *Sutlej* on 15 July. *U196* (Lt-Cdr Kentrat) sinks a ship of 7118 tons near the Laccadives. *U198* (Lt Heusinger v Waldegg) sinks four ships of 22912 tons SE of Africa and Madagascar. From 4 to 6 July she is hunted together with *U859* by South African aircraft, the British destroyer *Pathfinder* and a South African A/S trawler group. One Ventura aircraft is shot down. Following two sinkings on 6–7 Aug, a submarine-hunting group, consisting of the escort carriers *Begum* and *Shah* and the frigates *Findhorn*, *Inver*, *Lossie* and *Parrett*, is deployed. On 10 Aug an Avenger of No 857 Sqn FAA from *Shah* attacks *U198*. On 12 Aug Catalina aircraft and aircraft from *Shah* bring up the Indian sloop *Godavari* and *Findhorn* and *Parret*, which sink *U198* with 'Hedgehog'. *U859* (Lt-Cdr Jebsen), after being pursued on 22–23 Aug by aircraft, the sloop *Banff* and the frigate *Tay*, proceeds to the Gulf of Aden. There she sinks two ships of 14598 tons and evades the carrier submarine-hunter group on 2 Sept. The homebound and outbound U-boats are frequently attacked by British submarines in the Strait of Malacca. On 20 June *Storm* and on 16 July *Templar* miss *U1062* which sets out twice to return to France. On 17 July *Tantalus* misses the outbound Japanese *I-166* which is shortly afterwards sunk by *Telemachus* (Cdr King). The Japanese transport submarine *I-29* arrives in Penang from France on 14 July, but when she continues her journey from Singapore she is sunk on 26 July by the US submarine *Sawfish* (Lt-Cdr Bannister). On 7 Aug *Stratagem* misses the returning *U181* and on 23 Sept *Trenchant* sinks *U859* as she arrives off Penang.

In the middle of Aug *U862* (Cdr Timm) and *U861* (Cdr Oesten) arrive in the area SE of South Africa and Madagascar. *U862* sinks four ships of 21134 tons and on 20 Aug shoots down a Catalina of No 265 Sqn RAF. She evades the carrier submarine-hunter group. *U861* sinks one ship of 7464 tons and torpedoes one ship of 8139 tons on 20 Aug from the convoy DN.68, escorted by three A/S trawlers. She also sinks another ship of 5670 tons on 5 Sept.

19 May   Baltic

The German auxiliary minesweeper *M3121/KFK165* is sunk in a Soviet air attack in the Gulf of Finland.

19 May   Air War/Italy

During an air raid on La Spezia, the German minelayer *Kehrwieder* (ex-Italian *Cotrone*) is destroyed by bomb hits.

19–31 May   Pacific

On a transport mission to Buin (Solomons), the Japanese submarine *I-16* is found on 19 May by a US destroyer escort group consisting of *George*, *Raby* and *England* which has just set out, and she is sunk by a 'Hedgehog' salvo. As it proceeds to the area NW of New Ireland, the group encounters a concentration of Japanese submarines designed to operate against Allied naval operations off the coast of New Guinea. It consists of the submarine cruisers *I-44* and *I-53* and the submarines *Ro-106*, *Ro-104*, *Ro-105*, *Ro-116*, *Ro-109*, *Ro-112*, *Ro-108*, *Ro-113*, *Ro-117* and *Ro-111*. *England* (Lt-Cdr Pendleton) sinks with 'Hedgehog' salvos *Ro-106* on 22 May, *Ro-104* on 23 May, *Ro-116* on 24 May, *Ro-108* on 26 May and *Ro-105* on 31 May. With six submarines sunk in 12 days, this is the most successful submarine-hunting operation by a single ship in WW2.

20 May   Mediterranean

The German MMS *R190* is sunk by air attack in the Strait of Otranto.

24 May   Bay of Biscay

The returning *U736* shoots down Wellington 'L' of No 612 Sqn RAF but is herself damaged by Liberator 'C' of No 224 Sqn RAF. The crippled U-boat is escorted into Lorient by five minesweepers.

25 May   Air War/Italy

During an air raid on Monfalcone, the ex-Italian submarine *Beilul*, the incomplete German *UIT4* (ex-Italian *R7*), the midget *UIT18* (ex-Italian *CM 2*) and the corvette

UJ204 (ex-Italian *Euridice*), which is fitting out, are sunk or destroyed.

25 May–13 June   South West Pacific

On 25 May the VII Amphibious Force (TF.77, Rear-Adm Fechteler on the destroyer *Sampson*) sets out from Hollandia with eight LSTs, eight LCTs in tow, 63 LVTs and 25 DUKWs as well as 15 LCIs with the first four attack waves of the 41st US Inf Div (Maj-Gen Fuller). The plan is to land them on the south coast of Biak on 27 May. Escort is provided by eight destroyers, with cover and support from TF.74 (TG.77.2, Rear-Adm Crutchley), comprising the Australian cruisers *Australia* and *Shropshire* and the destroyers *Arunta* and *Warramuga* and USS *Mullany* and *Ammen*, and by TF.75 (TG. 77.3, Rear-Adm Berkey) comprising the US cruisers *Phoenix*, *Boise* and *Nashville* and the destroyers *Hutchins*, *Daly*, *Beale*, *Bache*, *Trathen* and *Abner Read*. The approximately 10000 Japanese defenders (Col Kuzume) put up strong resistance. The Japanese attempt their reinforcement operation 'Kon'. Rear-Adm Sakonju, with the cruisers *Aoba* and *Kinu* and the destroyers *Shikinami*, *Uranami* and *Shigure*, takes 700 men on board in Zamboanga on 31 May and from Tawi-Tawi a covering force consisting of the battleship *Fuso*, the cruisers *Myoko* and *Haguro* and five destroyers proceeds to Davao. A third force, made up of the minelayers *Itsukushima* and *Tsugaru* and *LST127*, is to bring another 800 troops to Biak. On 2 June the forces put to sea but they are found by American reconnaissance aircraft and return on 3 June. The US submarine *Hake* sinks the destroyer *Kazegumo* off Davao on 8 June. On 3 June Japanese aircraft of the 23rd Naval Air Flotilla (Rear-Adm Ito) try to attack US ships but the destroyers *Reid*, *Mustin* and *Russell* beat off the attackers. A second attempt to bring 600 troops to Biak is made by Adm Sakonju with the destroyers *Shikinami*, *Uranami* and *Shigure*, escorted by the destroyers *Harusame*, *Shiratsuyu* and *Samidare*. Cover is provided by the cruisers *Aoba* and *Kinu* near Vogelkop. US air reconnaissance finds the Japanese force, whereupon Rear-Adm Crutchley, with the cruisers *Australia*, *Phoenix* and *Boise* and the US Desdivs 42, 47 and 48 (comprising *Fletcher*, *Jenkins*, *Radford*, *La Valette*, *Hutchins*, *Daly*, *Beale*, *Bache*, *Abner Read*, *Mullany*, *Trathen* and the Australian *Arunta* and *Warramunga*), is deployed against it. *Harusame* is sunk by US bombers on 8 June. In an engagement in which the US destroyers try to catch the Japanese as they retire, *Shiratsuyu* is

damaged but escapes. A third Japanese attempt to bring reinforcements to Biak is abandoned on the way because of the start of the US Marianas operation (12 June) and the ships are ordered to take part in the operation 'A-GO'. This third attempt comprises two transport groups ('A' under Rear-Adm Sakonju, with the cruisers *Aoba* and *Kinu* and the destroyers *Shikinami*, *Uranami*, *Yamagumo* and *Nowake*, and 'B', comprising the minelayers *Itsukushima* and *Tsugaru*, one LST, freighters and submarine-chasers), with cover from a task force (Vice-Adm Ugaki) composed of the battleships *Yamato* and *Musashi*, the cruisers *Myoko*, *Haguro* and *Noshiro* and the destroyers *Shimakaze*, *Okinami* and *Asagumo*.

27–28 May   Air War/France

RAF Bomber Command attacks Nantes with 104 aircraft, of which one is lost.

28 May   Air War/Italy

In an air attack on Genoa, the German minelayer *Vallelunga* is destroyed by an explosion.

30–31 May   Arctic

The German destroyers (Capt Johannesson) *Z29*, *Z31*, *Z33*, *Z34* and *Z38* form a patrol line between Bear Island and the North Cape.

In the Barents Sea, the destroyer *Milne*, on an escort mission, sinks the German *U289* from the 'Trutz' group by depth charges SW of Bear Island.

30–31 May   Mediterranean

Aircraft of the 2nd Fl Div, operating from southern France, attack the Allied convoy UGS.42 in the Western Mediterranean and sink the British freighter *Nordeflinge* (2873 tons).

June   Arctic/Intelligence

The German U-boats in the Arctic receive a separate cypher circuit, 'Niobe'; it is broken in Sept 1944 as 'Narwhal'/'Mussel'.

1 June   Norway

The German MDS *Sperrbrecher 181/Atlas* has to be beached after being hit during an air attack off Alesund.

1–23 June   Mediterranean

On 1 June 17 Baltimores, 12 Marauders and 24 Beaufighters, escorted by 13 Spitfires and four Mustangs, attack a German supply convoy of three freighters N of Crete proceeding to the island. The escort consists of the 9th TB Flotilla (Cdr* Dominik) with *TA16*, *TA17*, *TA14* and *TA19*, the 21st SC Flotilla (Cdr Dr Brandt) with four submarine-chasers and three motor minesweepers and air escort from one Ar 196 and six Ju 88s. The freighter *Sabine* (2252 tons), *UJ2101* and *UJ2105* sink after bomb hits;

the freighter *Gertrud* (1960 tons), *R211* and *TA16* reach Heraklion damaged and there on 2 June the torpedo boat is destroyed by an explosion on board *Gertrud*. On the return, the third steamer, *Tanais* (1545 tons), is sunk on 9 June by the British submarine *Vivid* (Lt Varley). After this disaster contact with Crete is maintained only by small craft sailing individually.

The British submarine *Unsparing* (Lt Piper) sinks *UJ2106* and the ferry *SF284*, and *Vampire* (Lt Taylor) sinks three sailing ships. Three more sailing ships are damaged. The submarine *Sickle* is lost on 18 June in the Antikithera Channel, probably on a mine.

1–30 June   North Atlantic

The Allied North Atlantic convoys are accompanied on the Canada–UK route by Canadian escort groups and on the UK–Gibraltar route by British escort groups, as follows: EG.C1, with the frigate *New Glasgow* and the corvettes *Chambly*, *Fredericton*, *Halifax*, *Frontenac*, *Giffard* and *Orangeville* (frigate *Chebogue* detached; corvette *Edmundston* in repair); EG.C2, with the frigates *Monnow* and *St Catherine's* and the corvettes *Chilliwack*, *Fennel*, *Morden* and *Owensound* (corvettes *Kamloops* detached, *Sackville* in repair); EG.C3, with the frigate *Prince Rupert* and the corvettes *Bittersweet*, *Napanee*, *Eyebright* (later exchanged with *Brantford*) and *Forrest Hill* (frigate *Ettrick* and corvette *Trillium* detached; corvette *La Malbaie* in repair); EG.C4, with the frigates *Montréal* and *Wentworth* and the corvettes *Brandon*, *Collingwood* and *North Bay* (corvettes *Amherst* and *Ville de Quebec* detached); EG.C5, with the frigate *Dunver* and the corvettes *Dauphin*, *New Westminster*, *Rosthern* (later *Wetaskiwin*), *Longbranch* and *Hespeler* (frigate *Nene* in repair; corvette *Algoma* detached); EG.B2, with the destroyer *Hesperus*, the DEs *Cotton* and *Gardiner* and the corvettes *Flint Castle*, *Rushen Castle* and *Tunsberg Castle* (RNoN) (frigate *Mourne* detached; corvette *Oxford Castle* in repair); EG.B3, with the frigates *Anguilla*, *Antigua* and *Towy* and the corvettes *Knaresborough Castle*, *Leeds Castle* and *Tintagel Castle* (later also *Allington Castle*; corvette *Hurst Castle* in repair); EG.B4; with the destroyer *Highlander*, the DEs *Bayntun* and *Foley*, the frigate *Helmsdale* and the corvettes *Kenilworth Castle*, *Pevensey Castle* and *Portchester Castle* (later also *Launceston Castle*; corvette *Morpeth Castle* in repair); and EG.B5, with the frigates *Ascension* and *Exe* and the corvettes *Berkeley Castle*, *Carisbrooke Castle*, *Dumbarton Castle* and

Hadleigh Castle (later also *Bamburgh Castle*; frigate *Moyola* in repair).

1–30 June   Pacific

The US submarines continue to operate with much assistance from 'Ultra' decrypts and by forming 'wolfpacks', especially during the preparatory phase of Operation 'Forager' and during the Battle of the Philippine Sea (see 11 May–12 June, 18–22 June). Apart from the successes achieved in these operations, US submarines which arrive in their operational areas in June record the following results:

Off the Kuriles, off Japan and in the Formosan area, *Pintado* (Lt-Cdr Clarey) sinks three ships of 13193 tons, *Flier* (Lt-Cdr Crowley) sinks one ship of 10380 tons and damages two of 10973 tons, *Golet* (Lt-Cdr Clark) sinks one patrol vessel of 72 tons but is sunk herself N of Honshu on 14 June by Japanese A/S forces, *Whale* (Lt-Cdr Grady) sinks one ship of 2857 tons and damages one of 4379 tons, *Swordfish* (Lt-Cdr Montross) sinks the destroyer *Matsukaze* on 9 June and also one ship of 4804 tons and three trawlers, *Batfish* (Lt-Cdr Fyfe) sinks three vessels of 1251 tons, *Bang* (Lt-Cdr Gallaher) damages two ships of 15699 tons, *Tunny* (Lt-Cdr Scott) sinks one trawler, *Tinosa* (Lt-Cdr Weiss) sinks two ships of 10687 tons and three sailing vessels, *Grouper* (Lt-Cdr Walling) sinks two ships of 3691 tons, *Parche* (Lt-Cdr Ramage) sinks one A/S vessel, *Tang* (Lt-Cdr O'Kane) sinks ten ships of 39159 tons, *Seahorse* (Lt-Cdr Cutter) sinks five ships of 17456 tons and damages on 27 June the frigate *Etorofu*, *Sealion* (Lt-Cdr Reich) sinks four ships of 7759 tons, *Archerfish* (Lt-Cdr Wright) sinks the corvette *Kaibokan 24* on 28 June, *Growler* (Lt-Cdr Schade) sinks one ship of 1920 tons, *Sturgeon* (Lt-Cdr Murphy) sinks two ships of 13951 tons, *Plaice* (Lt-Cdr Stevens) sinks two ships of 1843 tons and the subchaser *Ch-50* and *Gar* has only misses. In the Mandates area, *Shark* (Lt-Cdr Blakely) sinks four ships of 21672 tons, *Bream* (Lt-Cdr Chapple) sinks two ships of 7620 tons and *Balao* misses her targets. In the area of the Malayan Archipelago, and around the Philippines, several 'wolfpacks' operate (see 11 May–12 June and 18–22 June). *Hake* (Lt-Cdr Broach) sinks two ships of 11466 tons, *Redfin* (Lt-Cdr Austin) sinks two ships of 8169 tons, *Haddo* (Lt-Cdr Nimitz, Jr) sinks two trawlers, *Nautilus* (Lt-Cdr Irvin) sinks two sailing vessels, *Bashaw* (Lt-Cdr Nichols) sinks one ship of 6440 tons, *Jack* (Lt-Cdr Krapf) sinks three ships of 15745 tons, *Pargo* (Lt-Cdr Eddy) sinks one ship of 5236 tons and on 28 June damages the corvette *Kaibokan 10* and

Flasher (Lt-Cdr Whitaker) sinks two ships of 9636 tons and with 'wolfpack' companions *Crevalle* (Lt-Cdr Walker) and *Angler* (Lt-Cdr Olsen) sinks two more ships of 13946 tons and damages one of 6863 tons. In addition, *Flasher* torpedoes the seaplane carrier *Notoro* 1(14050 tons) on 29 June and sinks the cruiser *Oi* on 19 July. *Darter* (Lt-Cdr Stovall) sinks the minelayer *Tsugaru* on 29 June.

1 June–31 Dec   North Sea/Baltic

Air-mining offensive by the RAF against German shipping routes in the North Sea, the Skagerrak, the Kattegat and the western and southern parts of the Baltic. In a total of 1900 sorties, 1778 mines are laid in June, 708 in July, 1586 in Aug, 748 in Sept, 1133 in Oct, 750 in Nov and 1160 in Dec. Thirty-six aircraft are lost. In all, 124 ships totalling 74545 tons sink on the mines and 66 totalling 100915 tons are damaged.

2–3 June   English Channel

The German patrol vessel *V2004* is sunk off Ijmuiden by MTB torpedo and *V1810* off Boulogne by bombs on 2 June. The gun ferry *AF58* capsizes after suffering bomb hits off Boulogne.

3 June   Arctic/Greenland

A German Ju 290 transport aircraft brings back the 'Bassgeiger' weather station (26 men), which has been operating in Greenland since Aug 1943.

3 June–27 July   Norway

Continuation of the air offensive by No 18 Group RAF Coastal Command against U-boats off Norway, using Cansos of No 162 Sqn RCAF and Catalinas of No 210 Sqn, Catalinas and Mosquitos of No 333 (Norwegian) Sqn, Sunderlands of No 330 (Norwegian) Sqn, and Liberators of Nos 86, 59 and 207 Sqns RAF. On 3 June Canso 'T' of No 162 Sqn sinks the schnorkel boat *U477*.

On 6 June the outbound non-schnorkel boats *U294*, *U290*, *U958*, *U980* and *U1000* are stopped. On 8 and 10 June the boats of the 'Mitte' group, *U276*, *U397*, *U975*, *U242*, *U999*, *U677*, *U1001*, *U998*, *U1007*, *U982*, *U987*, *U745* and *U1156*, set out to form a defensive concentration off Norway; on 20–21 June there come as reliefs *U396*, *U994*, *U771*, *U317* and *U1192* and on 5 July *U319*, *U286* and *U299*. Of the outgoing schnorkel boats, *U715* is sunk on 13 June by Canso 'T' of No 162 Sqn (Wg Cdr Chapman), which is itself shot down by AA fire. *U998* is so heavily damaged on 16 June in an attack by Mosquito 'H' of No 333 Sqn that it had to be decommissioned; *U804*, on her way to be fitted with a schnorkel, is diverted to help *U998* but is herself attacked by Mosquito 'R' of No 333 Sqn RAF and

has to return because of the number of wounded on board. On 17 June *U423* is sunk by Catalina 'D' of No 333 Sqn and on 24 June *U1225* is sunk by Canso 'P' of No 162 Sqn which is itself shot down; on 30 June *U478* is sunk by Liberator 'E' of No 206 Sqn, which also fails to return. On 20 July the Type IXD2 boat *U863*, on its way to the Far East, is damaged by Mosquito 'N' of No 333 Sqn and has to return. On 25 July *U244*, escorted by another vessel, is attacked by Mosquitos 'E' and 'F' of No 333 Sqn and damaged and on 27 July *U865* is damaged by Liberator 'R' of No 86 Sqn and has to return (the aircraft is badly shot up). Off Norway, the 'Mitte' group's *U980* is sunk by Canso 'B' of No 162 Sqn, which shot down by another U-boat the next day. On 14 June *U290* is damaged by Mosquito 'H' of No 333 Sqn (Lt Johansen) and on 20 June Liberator 'K' of No 86 Sqn damages *U743*, which has to return, but is also heavily hit by AA fire. On 26 June Liberator 'N' of No 86 Sqn sinks *U317* but is itself damaged beyond repair by AA fire. On 28 June Catalina 'Q' of No 210 Sqn damages *U396* and on 15 July Liberator 'E' from No 206 Sqn sinks *U319*.

Of the 'Eismeer' U-boats en route to form the 'Trutz' group, *U347* is sunk by Catalina 'Y' of No 210 Sqn and *U361* by Liberator 'U' of No 86 Sqn on 17 July, *U742* is sunk on 18 July by Catalina 'Z' of No 210 Sqn (which has to make an emergency landing because of AA damage) and on 19 July *U968* is damaged by Liberator 'R' of No 86 Sqn, *U716* by Liberator 'F' of No 59 Sqn and *U387* by Sunderland 'O' of No 330 Sqn.

4 June   Baltic

The German minesweeper *M37* is sunk in Narva Bay after a torpedo attack by the Soviet *TKA-101*.

5 Jun-11 Dec   Black Sea

Transfer of three batches of Soviet submarines from the Pacific Fleet by rail to the Black Sea Fleet: *M-114*, *M-115* and *M-116* (5 June–8 July), *M-25*, *M-26*, *M-27* and *M-28* (30 Aug–20 Oct) and *M-23* and *M-24* (6 Oct–11 Dec).

6 June   English Channel

Operation 'Neptune' (amphibious phase of Operation 'Overlord'), the major Allied landing in Normandy. In overall command is Supreme Cdr SHAEF, Gen Eisenhower; Cdr Land Forces 21st Army Group is Gen Montgomery; Cdr Naval Forces is Adm Ramsay; and co-ordination of air forces is the responsibility of Air-Chief Marshal Tedder.

After heavy air attacks (3467 heavy bombers, 1645 medium, light and torpedo bombers, 5409 fighters and 2316 transport

aircraft are deployed), the 82nd and 101st US Airborne Divs land on the southern part of the Cotentin Peninsula and the British 6th Airborne Div SE of Caen by parachute. In the morning, supported by strong naval forces, there follow by sea the 4th US Inf Div on the east coast of the Cotentin Peninsula ('Utah'), the 1st US Inf Div near Vierville ('Omaha'), the 50th British Inf Div near Arromanches ('Gold'), the 3rd Canadian Inf Div near Courseulles ('Juno') and the 3rd British Div near Lyon-sur-Mer ('Sword'). The 'Western Naval Task Force' (Rear-Adm Kirk on the US cruiser *Augusta*) is with the 1st US Army (Lt-Gen Bradley). First, 102 US, British and Allied minesweepers clear the approaches with 16 buoy-layers. In the night Force U (Rear-Adm Moon on the headquarters ship *Bayfield*, VII US Corps, Lt-Gen Collins) with the 4th US Inf Div (Maj-Gen Barton) on the convoys U.2A, U.2B, U.1, U.3, U.3C, U.4, U.5A and U.5B and Force O (Rear-Adm Hall on the headquarters ship *Ancon*, V US Corps, Lt-Gen Gerow) with the 29th Inf Div (Maj-Gen Huebner) on the convoys O.2A, O.2B, O.1, O.3, O.3C, O.4A, O.4B and O.5 approach. The convoys for 'Utah' and 'Omaha' consist of 16 attack transports, one LSD, 106 LSTs, one LSR, 15 LCCs, 93 LCIs, 350 LCTs, 34 LCSs, 94 LCAs, 189 LCVPs, 38 LCS(S)s, 54 LCPs and, for fire support, nine LCGs, 11 LCFs, 14 LCT(R)s, two LCS(M)s and 36 LCS(S)s. The support force for 'Utah' comprises Force A (Rear-Adm Deyo) with the US battleship *Nevada*, the British monitor *Erebus*, the US cruisers *Tuscaloosa* and *Quincy*, the British cruisers *Hawkins*, *Black Prince* and *Enterprise*, the Dutch gunboat *Soemba*, the US destroyers *Hobson*, *Fitch*, *Forrest* and *Corry* (Desdiv 20) and *Butler Shubrick*, *Herndon* and *Gherardi* (Desdiv 34) and the DEs *Bates* and *Rich*. The support force for 'Omaha' is Force C (Rear-Adm Bryant), comprising the US battleships *Texas* and *Arkansas*, the British cruiser *Glasgow*, the French cruisers *Montcalm* and *Georges Leygues*, the US destroyers *McCook*, *McCormick*, *Doyle*, *Baldwin*, *Harding*, *Satterlee* and *Thompson* (Desron 18) and *Emmons* and the British 'Hunt' destroyers *Melbreak*, *Tanatside* and *Talybont*.
As escorts for the approaching 'U' and 'O' convoys, the US destroyers *Jeffers* and *Glennon* (Desron 17) and *Barton*, *O'Brien*, *Walke*, *Laffey* and *Meredith* (Desron 60) and the French corvettes *Aconit* and *Renoncule*, and the US destroyers *Frankford*, *Nelson*, *Murphy* and *Plunkett* (Desron 33), the British destroyers *Vesper* and *Vidette*, the

US DEs *Borum*, *Amesbury* and *Blessman* and the French frigates *L'Aventure* and *L'Escarmouche* are respectively deployed. The British battleship *Nelson*, the British cruiser *Bellona*, the US destroyers *Somers*, *Davis* and *Jouett* (Desdiv 18) and the French frigates *La Surprise* and *La Découverte* are available as a reserve for the 'Western Task Force'.
On 6 June 23250 troops are landed in the 'Utah' and 34250 troops in the 'Omaha' sectors.
The 'Eastern Naval Task Force' (Rear-Adm Vian on the British cruiser *Scylla*) is with the 2nd British Army (Lt-Gen Dempsey). First, 102 British and Canadian minesweepers with 27 buoy-layers clear the approaches. During the night Force G (Commodore Douglas-Pennant on the headquarters ship *Bulolo*), XXX British Corps (Lt-Gen Bucknall) with the 50th British Div on the convoys G.1 to G.13, Force J (Commodore Oliver on the headquarters ship *Hilary*) with the 3rd Canadian Div on the convoys J.1 to J.13 and Force S (Rear-Adm Talbot on the headquarters ship *Largs*), British I Corps (Lt-Gen Crocker) with the British 3rd Inf Div on the convoys S.1 to S.8, approach. The convoys for 'Gold', 'Juno' and 'Sword' consist of 37 LSIs, 130 LSTs, two LSRs, one LSD, 11 LCCs, 116 LCIs, 39 LCI(S)s, 487 LCTs, 66 LCSs, 408 LCAs, 73 LCS(S)s, 90 LCPs and 10 LCP(S)s. In addition, for fire support there are 16 LCG(L)s, 22 LCT(R)s, 14 LCS(L)s, 24 LCS(M)s, 18 LCFs, 45 LCA(H)s and 103 LCTs with armament.
The support force for 'Gold' is Force K (Capt Longley-Cook), comprising the British cruisers *Argonaut*, *Orion*, *Ajax* and *Emerald*, the Dutch gunboat *Flores*, the British destroyers (25th Flotilla) *Grenville*, *Ulster*, *Ulysses*, *Undaunted*, *Undine*, *Urania*, *Urchin*, *Ursa* and *Jervis* and the British 'Hunt' destroyers *Cattistock*, *Cottesmore*, *Pytchley* and *Krakowiak* (Polish).
The support force for 'Juno' is Force E (Rear-Adm Dalrymple-Hamilton), comprising the British cruisers *Belfast* and *Diadem* and the British destroyers *Faulknor* (8th Flotilla), *Fury* and *Kempenfelt* (27th Flotilla), *Venus*, *Vigilant*, *Algonquin* (Canadian), *Sioux* (Canadian) and the 'Hunt' destroyers *Stevenstone*, *Bleasdale*, *Glaisdale* (Norwegian) and *La Combattante* (French).
The support force for 'Sword' is Force D (Rear-Adm Patterson), comprising the British battleships *Warspite* and *Ramillies*, the monitor *Roberts*, the cruisers *Mauritius*, *Arethusa*, *Frobisher*, *Danae* and *Dragon* (Polish) and the destroyers *Saumarez* (23rd Flotilla), *Scorpion*, *Scourge*, *Serapis*, *Swift*,

Stord (Norwegian), *Svenner* (Norwegian), *Verulam*, *Virago* and *Kelvin*, and the 'Hunt' destroyers *Slazak* (Polish), *Middleton* and *Eglinton*.
Six destroyers, four sloops, eight frigates, 17 corvettes and 21 trawlers are deployed (British, Canadian, French and Norwegian) to escort the G, J and S convoys. The British battleship *Rodney* and the cruiser *Sirius* are among the ships which form the reserve for the 'Eastern Task Force'.
On 6 June 24970 troops are landed in the 'Gold' sector, 21400 troops in the 'Juno' and 28845 troops in the 'Sword'. To escort the first follow-up wave, Force B (Commodore Edgar), consisting of the US destroyers *Rodman*, *Ellyson* and *Hambleton*, the British destroyers *Boadicea*, *Volunteer* and *Vimy*, the 'Hunt' destroyers *Brissenden* and *Wensleydale* and the corvettes *Azalea*, *Bluebell* and *Kitchener* (Canadian), is deployed in the W; and in the E is Force L (Rear-Adm Parry), comprising the 'Hunt' class destroyer *Cotswold*, the escort destroyer *Vivacious*, the frigates *Chelmer* and *Halsted*, the corvettes *Clematis*, *Godetia*, *Mignonette*, *Narcissus* and *Oxlip* and three A/S trawlers, 49 LSTs, 19 LCI(L)s and 53 LCT(3)s.
The British 10th DD Flotilla, consisting of *Tartar*, *Ashanti*, *Haida* (Canadian), *Huron* (Canadian), *Blyskawica* (Polish), *Piorun* (Polish), *Eskimo* and *Javelin*, a group of frigates and eight groups of coastal forces with MTBs and MGBs, form the covering force against attacks by surface craft in the western entrance to the Channel. In the E the same role is undertaken by the 17th DD Flotilla, consisting of *Onslow*, *Onslaught*, *Offa*, *Oribi*, *Obedient*, *Orwell*, *Isis* and *Impulsive* and seven groups of coastal forces. In addition, the following belong to the escort forces: the cruisers *Despatch*, *Ceres* and *Capetown*; the destroyers *Kimberley*, *Opportune*, *Pathfinder*, *Beagle*, *Bulldog*, *Icarus*, *Campbell*, *Mackay*, *Montrose*, *Walpole*, *Windsor*, *Whitshed*, *Vanquisher*, *Versatile*, *Wanderer*, *Walker*, *Westcott*, *Wrestler*, *Caldwell*, *Leeds*, *Lincoln*, *Ramsey*, *Skate*, *Saladin* and *Sardonyx*; the 'Hunt' destroyers *Garth*, *Holderness*, *Meynell*, *Avon Vale*, *Belvoir*, *Goathland* and *La Combattante* (French); the sloops *Scarborough*, *Rochester*, *Hart*, *Kite*, *Lapwing*, *Lark*, *Magpie* and *Pheasant*; the frigates *Deveron* and *Nene* and the ex-US DEs *Cubitt*, *Dakins*, *Ekins*, *Holmes*, *Lawford*, *Retalick*, *Stayner* and *Thornborough*; and the corvettes *Puffin*, the British 'Flower' class *Armeria*, *Balsam*, *Burdock*, *Buttercup*, *Campanula*, *Celandine*, *Dianthus*, *Gentian*, *Heather*, *Honeysuckle*, *Lavender*, *Nasturtium*, *Pennywort*, *Primrose*, *Starwort*, *Sunflower* and

Wallflower, the French *Cdt Estienne D'Orves*, the Norwegian *Acanthus, Eglantine, Potentilla* and *Rose* and the Canadian *Alberni, Baddeck, Battleford, Calgary, Camrose, Drumheller, Lindsay, Louisburg, Lunenburg, Mimico, Moosejaw, Port Arthur, Prescott, Regina, Rimouski, Summerside, Trentonian* and *Woodstock*. In all, seven battleships, two monitors, 23 cruisers, three gunboats, 105 destroyers and 1073 smaller naval vessels are employed. On 6 June the German Navy has in the Channel area five torpedo boats, 34 motor torpedo boats (five others are non-operational) 163 minesweepers and motor minesweepers, 57 patrol boats and 42 gun carriers, while on the Atlantic coast from Brest to Bayonne there are available five destroyers, one torpedo boat, 146 minesweepers and motor minesweepers and 59 patrol boats.

6–13 June English Channel

German surface vessels attempt to attack the invasion fleet. During the night 5–6 June *V1509* sinks while undertaking a reconnaissance sortie from Le Havre to the W in an engagement with British covering forces. During the night of 6–7 June the 5th TB Flotilla (Cdr Hoffmann) with *T28, Möwe* and *Jaguar*, attacks ships of Force S belonging to the British Eastern Task Force off 'Sword' beach and sinks the Norwegian destroyer *Svenner*. Other torpedoes run between the battleships *Warspite* and *Ramillies* and miss the headquarters ship *Largs*. The same night, *T28, Möwe* and *Jaguar* attack unsuccessfully from Le Havre. The 5th MTB Flotilla (Cdr Klug), comprising *S136, S138, S140, S142, S100* and *S139* (*S84* returns because of engine trouble), and the 9th MTB Flotilla (Cdr v Mirbach), comprising *S130, S144, S145, S146, S150, S167* and *S168*, set out from Cherbourg. On the way out, off Cap Barfleur, *S139* and, later, *S140*, are lost on mine barrages laid earlier by the British 64th MTB Flotilla (Lt-Cdr Wilkie). *S142, S100, S150* and *S168* break through the defences of the coastal forces and sink *LST715* and one LCT off St Vaast. The other boats are driven off by the frigate *Stayner* (Lt-Cdr Hall) and *MTB448* and *MTB478*.

Off Le Havre, the 4th MMS Flotilla (Lt-Cdr Anhalt) becomes involved in an engagement with the British 55th MTB Flotilla (Lt-Cdr Bradford) and the Canadian 29th MTB Flotilla (Lt-Cdr Law). While laying the barrage 'Blitz 25' *R49* is badly damaged, as are *MTB624* and *MTB682*. The 4th MTB Flotilla (Lt-Cdr Fimmen), comprising *S169, S171, S172, S174, S173, S175, S187* and *S188*, sets out from Boulogne but finds no targets although *S172*

misses a destroyer with torpedoes.

The 2nd Flotilla (Cdr Opdenhoff), comprising *S177, S178, S179, S181* and *S189*, and the 8th Flotilla (Cdr Zymalkowski), comprising *S83, S117, S127* and *S133*, proceed from Ostend into the southern part of the North Sea on a fruitless reconnaissance sortie.

During the night 7–8 June the 2nd Flotilla is transferred from Ostend to Boulogne. The 4th Flotilla with eight boats attacks a convoy escorted by the destroyer *Beagle*; *S174, S175, S187* and *S172* report hits on landing craft. *LST376* and *LST314* are sunk. The destroyers *Saumerez, Stord, Virago* and *Isis*, which are deployed, do not come up. The 5th Flotilla, comprising *S100, S138, S84, S136* and *S142*, attacks from Cherbourg but is driven off in engagements with the frigates *Stayner* and *Retalick* (Lt-Cdr Brownrigg). *S84, S138* and *S142* are hit. The 9th Flotilla with six boats attacks a landing force, which is escorted by the British *ML903*, and sinks *LCI105* and *LCT875*. In engagements *S168* and *S145* are damaged.

During the night 8–9 June the 8th DD Flotilla (Capt v Bechtolsheim) tries to make a sortie from Brest into the invasion area with *Z32, Z24, ZH1* and *T24*, but is intercepted NW of the Ile de Bas by the British 10th DD Flotilla (Capt Jones), consisting of *Tartar, Ashanti, Haida* (Canadian) and *Huron* (Canadian), as well as *Blyskawica* (Polish), *Piorun* (Polish), *Eskimo* and *Javelin*. In the engagement, *ZH1* is sunk by torpedoes from the *Ashanti*, *Z32* is sunk after a duel with *Haida* and *Huron* is beached near the Ile de Bas and blown up. *Tartar* is severely damaged.

The same night, the 5th MTB Flotilla with five boats and the 9th Flotilla with three boats set out from Cherbourg on a mining operation. They are driven off by the US destroyers *Frankford, Baldwin* and *Hambleton*, belonging to the 'Dixie' Patrol (Capt Saunders USN), but they drop their mines. The 4th Flotilla sets out with seven boats and the 2nd with four, but the boats do not reach the mining area and return. The 5th TB Flotilla, comprising *T28, Möwe* and *Jaguar*, becomes involved in an engagement with the British 55th MTB Flotilla.

During the night 9–10 June the 5th MTB Flotilla, comprising *S84, S100, S136, S138* and *S142*, and the 9th MTB Flotilla, comprising *S130, S144, S146, S150* and *S167*, are again driven off by the US destroyers of the 'Dixie' Patrol. An attack by the torpedo boats *T28, Möwe* and *Jaguar*, setting out from Le Havre, on a destroyer patrol, consisting of *Glaisdale* (Norwegian), *Ursa* and

Krakowiak (Polish), is outmanoeuvred by the latter. The 4th MTB Flotilla, with *S188, S169, S173, S172, S187* and *S175*, goes to sea on a mining operation and lays 24 mines; on the way out and on the return there are engagements with destroyers. *S188* reports a hit on an LST and *S172* and *S187* a hit each on a steamer of 2000 tons. The 2nd Flotilla, with four boats from Boulogne, attacks a supply convoy. *S177, S178, S179* and *S189* fire FAT torpedoes and each claim to have sunk a steamer of 900 tons and 1500 tons. They put into Le Havre. The 8th Flotilla, which is being transferred from Flushing to Boulogne, returns when *S180* and *S190* hit mines.

During the night 10–11 June the 5th MTB Flotilla (Lt-Cdr Johannsen), comprising *S84, S100, S112, S136, S138* and *S142*, and the 9th MTB Flotilla, comprising *S130, S144, S146, S150* and *S167*, set out from Cherbourg. The 5th Flotilla becomes involved in an engagement with the British 35th MTB Flotilla (Lt-Cdr Cowen) and the frigate *Stayner*. *MTB448* and *S136* are lost. The frigate *Halstead* is hit in the bow by a torpedo salvo. The 9th Flotilla breaks through the defence after a short engagement with the SGBs *Grey Wolf* and *Grey Goose* and sinks the US tug *Partridge* and *LST496* and torpedoes *LST538*. Off Cherbourg, *S130* is badly damaged in a fighter-bomber attack.

The 4th MTB Flotilla, comprising *S169, S171, S173, S187, S188* and *S172* lays a barrage of 24 UMB mines W of Le Havre and escapes from an attempt at interception by the destroyers *Sioux* (Canadian) and *Krakowiak* (Polish), and by the 55th MTB Flotilla with the frigate *Duff*. The 2nd MTB Flotilla, with *S177, S179, S189* and *S178*, outmanoeuvres a destroyer patrol consisting of *Stord* (Norwegian), *Scorpion, Scourge* and *Kelvin* and attacks a supply convoy S of the Isle of Wight. The freighters *Brackenfield* (657 tons), *Ashanti* (534 tons) and *Dungrange* (621 tons) from the convoy are sunk by *S177* and *S178* (which sinks two of them). The destroyers pursue the motor torpedo boats to Boulogne.

During the night 11–12 June *S84* and *S100* and *S146* and *S144* from the 5th and 9th Flotillas respectively are transferred from Cherbourg to Le Havre and have several engagements with the destroyers of the 'Dixie' Patrol. *S150* and *S167* and *S138* and *S142* attack a destroyer force consisting of *Somers, Laffey* and *Nelson*, and in the action Cdr v Mirbach aboard *S138* torpedoes the *Nelson*. The 2nd Flotilla becomes involved in an engagement with *MTB461, MTB463* and *MTB464* of the Canadian 29th MTB

Flotilla and its frigate leader off Le Havre. *S181* and *S179* suffer damage from acoustic mine detonations as they come in. The 4th Flotilla, with *S169*, *S187*, *S173*, *S188*, *S171* and *S172*, sets out from Boulogne and is involved in an engagement with a destroyer patrol consisting of *Onslow*, *Onslaught*, *Offa* and *Oribi*. The second group is engaged by MGBs, from which *MGB17* is sunk by *S171* with gunfire.

During the night 12–13 June the motor torpedo boats *S150*, *S167*, *S138* and *S142* from Cherbourg, with support from the coastal batteries at Cap Barfleur, break through the destroyer defence of the 'Dixie' Patrol and, off Le Havre, encounter a destroyer patrol consisting of *Glaisdale* (Norwegian), *Stevenstone* and *Isis* which damage *S138*. *S100*, *S84* and *S143* (5th Flotilla) and *S169*, *S173*, *S188*, *S171* and *S172* (4th Flotilla) set out from Le Havre and become involved in fighter-bomber attacks and engagements with escort forces including the Canadian corvettes *Camrose*, *Baddeck* and *Louisburg*. *S169* returns after hitting a mine. The 2nd Flotilla sets out with four boats from Le Havre to Boulogne, escapes from the Canadian 29th MTB Flotilla but is attacked before coming in by Beaufighters of Nos 143 and 236 Sqns RAF which successively sink *S178*, *S189* and *S197* and *R97* (which comes to their assistance) and damage *S181*, *M402* and *R99*. *T28* and *Möwe* attack the destroyers *Stord* and *Scorpion* unsuccessfully off Le Havre.

6–14 June   English Channel

In air attacks and engagements with British coastal forces there are some German losses and some ships are scuttled in harbour to prevent their capture. On 6 June the gun ferries *AF62*, *AF64*, *AF67* and *AF72* are scuttled at Port-en-Bessin and Isigny. The MMS *R221* is sunk by air attack at Blainville. On 9 June the gun ferry *AF15* is damaged in air attack off Dieppe and sinks while under tow outside the harbour.

On 10 June the British 58th MTB Flotilla, comprising *MTB687*, *MTB681*, *MTB683*, *MTB666*, *MTB723* and *MTB684*, attacks the German convoy 1253 off Den Helder and sinks the patrol boats *V1314*, *V2020* and *V2021* for the loss of *MTB681*. That night, off the Hook of Holland, the Norwegian 54th MTB Flotilla (Lt-Cdr Monssen), comprising *MTB712*, *MTB715*, *MTB618*, *MTB623* and *MTB688*, attacks the German 11th MS Flotilla (Cdr Seifert), which is being transferred from Borkum and which includes *M348*, *M307*, *M347*, *M264* and *M131*. *MTB712* is damaged.

On 12 June the A/S vessel *UJ1401* and the

patrol vessel *V206* are scuttled at Caën. On 13 June, between St-Malo and Jersey, the destroyers *Piorun* (Polish) and *Ashanti* attack a German convoy and sink *M83*; *M343*, *M412*, *M422*, *M432*, *M442* and *M452* are damaged, as is *Piorun*. In trying to help the MS Flotilla, *V203* and *M4615* are damaged by fighter-bombers. On 14 June the minesweeper *M83* is torpedoed and sunk off Jersey by British MTBs.

6–30 June   English Channel

There are Allied warship losses off the Normandy beaches from mines, coastal artillery and air attack. On 5 June the US minesweeper *Osprey* sinks 30 nautical miles NW of Cap d'Antifer (Normandy) after detonating a mine and on 6 June the British destroyer *Wrestler* is mined 20 nautical miles WNW of Le Havre and damaged beyond repair. The US destroyer *Corry* is mined and sunk off 'Utah' beach and the survivors are rescued under German gunfire by the destroyers *Fitch* and *Hobson*. On 7 June the US minesweeper *Tide* is sunk by mine off 'Utah' beach.

On 8 June the US destroyer *Meredith* (ii) is mined off 'Utah' beach and sunk by a bomb that near-misses on 9 June. The British frigate *Lawford* is sunk off 'Juno' beach by German air attack, the US destroyer *Glennon* is mined and sunk by German gunfire on 9 June and the destroyer-escort *Rich* is mined while attempting to assist *Glennon*. On 10 June the French destroyer *Mistral* is damaged beyond repair 3 nautical miles off Quineville by German coastal artillery and on 13 June the British destroyer *Boadicea* is torpedoed and blown up SW of Portland Bill by German aircraft.

On 21 June the British destroyer *Fury* is mined off 'Sword' beach; she is taken in tow but breaks away in a gale and is beached, becoming a total loss. On 23 June the British cruiser *Scylla* is mined off 'Sword' beach and is a constructive total loss. On 24 June the British destroyer *Swift* is mined and sunk off 'Sword' beach, as are the trawler *Lord Austin* and *MMS8*. In addition, the Norwegian destroyer *Glaisdale* and the French frigate *La Surprise*, together with two minesweepers and three merchant ships, are damaged beyond repair.

6–30 June   Air War/Western Europe

Continuation of the mine offensive by RAF Bomber Command, though with reduced intensity. In 21 nights, 313 sorties are flown against the French Biscay, Brittany and Channel coast ports, especially Lorient, St-Nazaire, Brest and St-Malo, off Jersey, Guernsey and the Frisian Islands and in the Kattegat and the western Baltic. One

aircraft is lost. The German MMS *R51* is sunk by mine off Rouen on 15 June.

6–30 June   English Channel/Bay of Biscay

Forces deployed against the U-boat threat to 'Overlord' comprise the reinforced No 19 Group RAF Coastal Command and, under the C-in-C Western Approaches, the escort carriers *Vindex*, *Tracker* and *Activity* and three destroyer and seven frigate escort groups in overlapping patrols; the 14th EG, with the RN destroyers *Fame*, *Havelock*, *Hotspur*, *Icarus* and *Inconstant*; the 11th EG, with the Canadian destroyers *Chaudière*, *Gatineau*, *Kootenay*, *Ottawa* and *St Laurent*; the 12th EG, with the Canadian destroyers *Qu'Appelle*, *Restigouche*, *Saskatchewan* and *Skeena*; the 9th EG, with the Canadian frigates *Matane*, *Meon*, *Port Colborne*, *St John*, *Stormont* and *Swansea*; the 1st EG, with the RN DEs *Affleck*, *Balfour*, *Bentley*, *Capel*, *Garlies* and *Gore*; the 6th EG, with the Canadian frigates *Cape Breton*, *Grou*, *Outremont*, *Teme* and *Waskesiu*; the 3rd EG, with the RN DEs *Blackwood*, *Cooke*, *Domett*, *Braithwaite*, *Duckworth* and *Essington*; the 5th EG, with the RN DEs *Aylmer*, *Bickerton*, *Bligh*, *Goodson* and *Keats*; the 15th EG, with the RN DEs *Inglis*, *Lawson*, *Louis*, *Moorsom* and *Mounsey* and the attached frigate *Cam*; and the 2nd EG, with the sloops *Starling*, *Woodpecker* and *Wren* and the frigates *Loch Killin*, *Loch Fada* and *Dominica*.

From 6 June four to six of the frigate groups operate in the 'CA' area W of the Channel and the Bay of Biscay and two of the destroyer group in the entrance to the Channel.

On 6 June 17 U-boats set out from Brest, 14 from St-Nazaire, four from La Pallice and one from Lorient from the 'Landwirt' group. On 7 June the homebound *U955* is sunk in the Bay of Biscay by Sunderland 'S' of No 201 Sqn RAF, which almost collides in the dark with Sunderland 'N' of No 461 Sqn RAAF. On 7 June, of the outgoing Brest boats, *U970* is sunk by Sunderland 'R' of No 228 Sqn RAF; Wellington 'G' of No 179 Sqn RAF damages *U415*, Liberator 'L' of No 53 Sqn RAF (Flt Lt Carmichael) damages *U963* and *U256* (one of which shoots down Liberator 'B' of No 53 Sqn (Sqn Ldr Crawford) on 6 June) and on 7 June *U989* is damaged by Wellington 'C' of No 407 Sqn RCAF and Liberator 'M' of No 224 Sqn RAF, which are both, however, shot down by the U-boat. *U212* is damaged by Mosquitos 'O' and 'L' of No 248 Sqn RAF. The damaged U-boats have to return. On 8 June Liberator 'G' of No 224 Sqn RAF (Fg Off Moore) sinks *U629* and *U373* in turn and Halifax 'F' of No 502 Sqn RAF damages *U413*; and on 9 June *U740* is sunk by Liberator 'V' of No 120 Sqn RAF.

It proves impossible to enter the Channel with the non-schnorkel boats. *U766* from the Brest boats, *U228*, *U255*, *U260*, *U270*, *U281*, *U382*, *U437*, *U445*, *U608*, *U650*, *U714*, *U758*, *U985* and *U993* from the St-Nazaire boats, *U262* and *U333* from La Pallice and *U981* from Lorient are stationed in the Bay of Biscay until 15 June. Of the nine schnorkel boats, *U212* has to return twice; the others try to enter the invasion area, followed by *U767*, *U1191*, *U988*, *U671* and *U971* which come from Norway. On 7 and 8 June *U984* (Lt Sieder) fires four, *U621* (Lt Struckmann) two and *U953* (Lt Marbach) four T-5s against the four destroyers of the 12th SG but the torpedoes all detonate prematurely or in the ships' wash. Early on 9 June *U764* (Lt v Bremen) fires four T-5s during a destroyer engagement without securing a hit. Up to 11 June *U621*, *U269* (Lt Uhl) and *U275* (Lt Bork) attack destroyer groups unsuccessfully in the western entrance to the Channel. *U821* (Lt Knackfuss) is sunk in an attack by Mosquitos 'T', 'S', 'W' and 'V' of No 248 Sqn (of which one is lost) and Liberator 'K' of No 206 Sqn. On 11 June Sunderland 'U' of No 228 Sqn RAF damages *U333* but is shot down. On 12 June Liberator 'S' of No 224 Sqn damages *U441* but is shot down and on 13 June *U270* shoots down Liberator 'C' of No 53 Sqn (Sqn Ldr Crawford) but is damaged by Wellington 'Y' of No 172 Sqn RAF.

From 14 June the first U-boats reach the shipping routes simultaneously with the support groups, some of which are moved to the Channel. On 14 June *U984* misses a search group and on 15 June *U621* sinks the landing ship *LST280*, *U767* (Lt Dankleff) the frigate *Mourne* (operating with the 5th SG) and *U764* the DE *Blackwood* of the 4th SG (taken in tow but a total loss). On 18 June *U621* misses two US battleships with a salvo. *U767* is sunk by the destroyers *Fame*, *Inconstant* and *Havelock* of the 14th SG and *U441* (Lt-Cdr Hartmann) by Wellington 'A' from No 304 (Polish) Sqn. Of the schnorkel U-boats arriving in the second half of June, *U763* (Lt-Cdr Cordes) misses a search group with two T-5s during the night 22–23 June; and, after being damaged in attacks by Wellingtons 'L' of No 407 Sqn RCAF and 'D' of No 502 Sqn RAF on 20 June and by Liberator 'O' of No 311 (Czech) Sqn on 26 June, *U971* (Lt Zeplin) is sunk in the western Channel by the destroyers *Eskimo* and *Haida* after an attempted attack fails because of faulty firing. On 25 June the

DEs *Affleck* and *Balfour* sink *U1191* and *Bickerton* (Cdr Macintyre) sinks *U269*, while *U984* from the same group torpedoes *Goodson* and misses a DE. The schnorkel boat *U719* is sunk on 26 June by the destroyer *Bulldog*. On 27–29 June *U988* (Lt Dobberstein) torpedoes the corvette *Pink* (total loss) and sinks two ships of 9444 tons before she is herself sunk on 29 June by Liberator 'L' of No 224 Sqn RAF and the frigates *Essington*, *Duckworth* and *Dommett* of the 3rd SG.

On 29 June *U984* attacks convoy EMC.17 and hits four ships of 28790 tons (one ship beached and can be salvaged but the other three become total losses). *U671* (Lt-Cdr Hegewald) misses a destroyer from a search group on 30 June. After another unsuccessful attack on a search group on 2 July, the boat is damaged by depth charges and has to put in to Boulogne. The schnorkel mining U-boats *U214* and *U218* lay mines off Plymouth on 26 June and off Land's End on 1 July. One ship of 7177 tons is damaged on 6 July on the latter barrage.

By 30 June 570 Liberty ships, 788 coastal motor boats, 905 LSTs, 1442 LCTs, 180 troop transports and 372 LCIs reach the assault area in supply convoys. The convoys are escorted chiefly by British and Canadian corvettes.

7 June–2 July   English Channel

Operation 'Neptune'. In the days after the first landing, the following units are put ashore in Normandy from the follow-up convoys:

In the 'Utah' sector, the 90th US Inf Div on 7–9 June and the 9th US Inf Div on 10–13 June; in the 'Omaha' sector, the 2nd US Inf Div on 7–8 June and the 2nd US Armored Div on 10–13 June; in the 'Gold' sector, the 7th British Armoured Div on 8–10 June and the 49th Inf Div on 11–12 June; and in the 'Juno' and 'Sword' sectors, the 51st British Inf Div on 9–11 June. By 12 June 326000 troops, 104000 tons of supplies and 54000 vehicles are landed. By 2 July the figure is increased to four Corps of the 1st US Army with two Armored and 11 Inf Divs and four Corps of the 2nd British Army with three Armoured and four Inf Divs, totalling 929000 troops, 177000 vehicles and 586000 tons of supplies.

On 7 June Gen Eisenhower and Adm Ramsay visit the assault area on board the fast minelayer *Apollo*. On 12 June *PT71* brings Generals Marshall, Eisenhower, Arnold, Bradley and Hodges and Admirals King, Stark, Kirk, Moon and Wilkes to Normandy.

9 June   English Channel

As the first stage in the construction of artificial harbours off the Normandy coast, 53 old merchant ships and warships are scuttled 1500yd offshore to give a 4-mile shelter. Off the Canadian beach, the old battleships *Centurion* and *Courbet* (French), the cruisers *Durban* and *Sumatra* (Dutch) and the A/A ship *Alynbank* are scuttled.

9 June   Mediterranean

The German hospital ship *Innsbruck* sinks after receiving bomb hits during an air raid on Venice.

10–22 June   Indian Ocean

From 10 to 13 June the British carrier *Illustrious* and the escort carrier *Atheling*, with covering forces, carry out a diversionary raid on Sabang for the US Operation 'Forager' (Marianas) to tie down parts of the Japanese Fleet. On 19 June Vice-Adm Power carries out Operation 'Pedal', a carrier raid on Port Blair (Nicobars) with the carrier *Illustrious*, the battlecruiser *Renown* and the French battleship *Richelieu*, as well as the cruisers *Ceylon*, *Kenya*, *Nigeria* and *Phoebe* and eight destroyers. Eight Corsairs and 15 Barracudas attack the airfield and harbour. Two aircraft are lost.

In June, in the Straits of Malacca and to the N of it, the British submarine *Stoic* (Lt Marriott) lays a minefield on which one ship of 4556 tons is damaged, sinks with torpedoes and gunfire one ship of 1134 tons, a coaster, two junks and a landing barge and damages a junk. *Sirdar* (Lt Spender) sinks one junk and damages one motor vessel, *Tantalus* (Lt-Cdr Mackenzie) lays a mine barrage in the Malacca Strait and sinks one ship of 536 tons with gunfire, *Truculent* (Lt Alexander) lays a minefield in the Malacca Strait and sinks one ship of 3040 tons and five junks and *Storm* (Lt Young) sinks one ship of 3011 tons. The Dutch submarine *K-XIV* (Lt-Cdr v Hooff) sinks one ship of 446 tons and attacks a minelayer. The British *Sea Rover* (Lt Angell) sinks three junks, *Clyde* damages one motor vessel, *Templar* (Lt Ridgway) lays a mine barrage in the Malacca Strait, *Sturdy* (Lt Andersen) sinks five small vessels and damages one more, *Spiteful* (Lt Sherwood) sinks a sailing vessel and a junk and *Tantivy* and *Surf* (Lt Lambert) lay minefields in the Malacca Strait.

10–28 June   Arctic

Soviet combined operation (RV-5) against German convoy traffic off the polar coast. The submarine *L-20* (Cdr Tamman) lays mines near Rolvsøy and reconnoitres; *S-14*, *S-104*, *M-200* and *M-201* are in waiting positions. On 15 June the first German summer convoy from Kirkenes to Petsamo, which has a strong escort and is helped by smokescreens, is brought through without loss, in spite of attacks by Soviet torpedo cutters and aircraft. On 15 June a Soviet reconnaissance aircraft sights a German convoy of 10 steamers near Hammerfest, escorted by *M31, M35, M154, M202, M252* (the 5th MS Flotilla, Cdr Klünder) *R202, R160, R223, V6102, V6107, V6110, V6722, V6111, V6725, UJ1220, UJ1209, UJ1219, UJ1211* and *UJ1212*. It is reported on the evening of 16 June by reconnaissance aircraft in Svaerholthavet. On 17 June the German *M35, UJ1220* and *UJ1209* drive off the submarine *M-200* (Lt-Cdr Gladkov). In attacks by Il-2s of Ground Attack Regt 46, the steamer *Florianopolis* (7419 tons) is hit. Il-4 torpedo aircraft sink the steamer *Dixie* (1610 tons) S of Vardö with parachute torpedoes. The mines laid by Soviet torpedo cutters on the convoy's route off Kirkenes are cleared by motor minesweepers. Soviet bombers make attacks on the incoming convoy when the steamer *Marga Cords* (1112 tons) is damaged.

A return convoy, consisting of five steamers, six patrol boats, five submarine-chasers and two motor minesweepers, which sets out from Kirkenes on 19 June, is located by Soviet air reconnaissance S of Vardö shortly after midnight (daylight) on 20 June. The submarine *M-201* (Lt-Cdr Balin), which is shortly afterwards seen by an He 115 as she fires, is forced underwater by *UJ1209, UJ1219, UJ1220* and *UJ1222* and attacked many times with depth charges; but she escapes. An attempted attack by *M-200* or *S-14* off Syltefjord is frustrated by a Bv 138. After some steamers have left, the Soviet submarine *S-104* (Capt 2nd Class Turaev) attacks the rest of the convoy, consisting of *L M Russ* and *R159, R173, V6107, V6111, NKi08, NKi12, UJ1211* and *UJ1209*, off Tanafjord and sinks *UJ1209*. On 22 June Soviet Il-2s, Airacobras and Kittyhawks attack a small convoy near Vardö and damage the gun ferry *AF39*. On 27 and 28 June Soviet bomber formations with fighter protection carry out attacks on shipping in Kirkenes, in which the small steamer *Herta* (717 tons) and the *Florianopolis* are burnt out.

From a Kirkenes–Petsamo convoy consisting of six steamers escorted by the 7th and 21st MMS Flotillas, the *Vulkan* (989 tons) is lost by fire from coastal batteries and the *Nerissa* (992 tons) is sunk by the torpedo cutter *TKA 239* on 28 June.

10 June–early July 1944 Central Pacific

On receipt of a report from the reconnaissance aircraft flown off from *I-10* that the anchorage at Majuro is empty, the Japanese Navy deploys its available submarines in the area E of the chain of the Marianas towards which it is thought the US Fleet is proceeding. The submarines involved are *I-5, I-6, I-10, I-38, I-41, I-44, I-53, I-184, I-185, Ro-36, Ro-44, Ro-48, Ro-109, Ro-112, Ro-113, Ro-114, Ro-115* and *Ro-117*. But only *Ro-114* (Lt Ata) makes an unsuccessful attack on a battleship of the *Iowa* class (16 June), *Ro-115* (Lt Koreeda) on a tanker (19 June) and *I-6* (Lt-Cdr Fumon) on a carrier (30 June), because the main body of the American forces operates W of the Marianas. On the other hand the following boats fall victim to the American submarine hunt: *Ro-36* (13 June), *Ro-44* (15), *Ro-114* (17), *Ro-117* (17), *I-184* (19), *I-185* (22), *I-6* (30) and *I-10* (4 July).

11 June Black Sea
American air attack on Constanza.

11–17 June Central Pacific
US TF.58 (Vice-Adm Mitscher) makes carrier raids on the Marianas and Vulcan Islands in support of Operation 'Forager': TG.58.1 (Rear-Adm Clark) comprises the carriers *Hornet, Yorktown, Belleau Wood* and *Bataan*, the cruisers *Boston, Baltimore, Canberra* and *Oakland* and the destroyers *Izard, Charrette, Conner, Bell, Burns, Boyd, Bradford, Brown* and *Cowell*; TG.58.2 (Rear-Adm Montgomery) comprises the carriers *Bunker Hill, Wasp, Monterey* and *Cabot*, the cruisers *Santa Fé, Mobile, Biloxi* and *San Juan* and the destroyers *Owen, Miller, The Sullivans, Stephen Potter, Tingey, Hickox, Hunt, Lewis Hancock* and *Marshall*; TG.58.3 (Rear-Adm Reeves) comprises the carriers *Enterprise, Lexington, San Jacinto* and *Princeton*, the cruisers *Indianapolis* (Adm Spruance), *Reno, Montpelier, Cleveland* and *Birmingham* and the destroyers *Clarence K Bronson, Cotten, Dortch, Gatling, Healy, Cogswell, Caperton, Ingersoll, Knapp, Anthony, Wadsworth, Terry* and *Braine*; and TG.58.4 (Rear-Adm Harrill) consists of the carriers *Essex, Langley* and *Cowpens*, the cruisers *San Diego, Vincennes, Houston* and *Miami* and the destroyers *Lansdowne, Lardner, McCalla, Lang, Sterett, Wilson, Case, Ellet, Charles Ausburne, Stanly, Dyson, Converse, Spence* and *Thatcher*. The battle line TG.58.7 (Vice-Adm Lee), at first distributed among the other four groups, comprises the battleships *Washington, North Carolina, Iowa, New Jersey, Indiana, South Dakota* and *Alabama*, the cruisers *Wichita, Minneapolis, New Orleans* and *San Francisco* and the destroyers *Mugford, Conyngham, Patterson, Bagley, Selfridge, Halford, Guest, Bennett, Fullam, Hudson, Yarnall, Twining,* *Stockham* and *Monssen*. This task group shells Saipan on 13 June.

On 11 June all four groups first carry out a fighter strike on all the Mariana Islands, in which 36 Japanese aircraft are destroyed. TG.58.4 attacks a convoy which has just set out from Saipan and sinks the torpedo boat *Ootori*, three submarine-chasers and 10 ships of 30000 tons. On 12 and 13 June TG.58.2, 58.3 and 58.4 attack Saipan and Tinian and TG.58.1 Guam. On 14 and 15 June there are only individual sorties over the Marianas while TG.58.2 and 58.3 replenish. Rear-Adm Clark with TG.58.1 and 58.4 to the N attacks Iwo Jima, Chichijima and Hahajima in the afternoon of 15 June and on 16 June. On the way to the rendezvous of TF.58, TG.58.4 attacks the island of Pagan again on 17 June.

12 June Air War/Germany
In an air raid on Wesermünde, the patrol vessel *V1250* is sunk

13 June North Pacific
A US task group (Rear-Adm Small) consisting of two heavy and two light cruisers and nine destroyers shells Matsuwa in the Kuriles.

13 June Philippines
The US submarine *Narwhal* shells oil tanks near Bula on Ceram.

14 June Baltic
The German MMS *R73* sinks on a German mine in the 'Seeigel' barrage.

14 June Mediterranean
During rescue operations for the torpedo boats *TA26* and *TA30*, the hospital ship *Erlangen* is hit by bombs and beached. She is salvaged and towed for repairs in Genoa but is sunk during an air raid on the city on 4 Sept.

14–15 June Air War/France
During the night 14–15 June 234 Lancaster bombers of Nos 1, 3, 5 and 8 Groups RAF Bomber Command attack Le Havre; one aircraft is lost. Twenty-two Lancasters each drop one 12000lb 'Tallboy' bomb. The following boats are destroyed or sunk: the torpedo boats *Falke, Jaguar* and *Möwe* of the 5th TB Flotilla; the motor torpedo boats *S169, S171, S172, S173, S187* and *S188* of the 4th, *S66, S84, S100, S138, S142* and *S143* of the 5th and *S144, S146* and *S150* of the 9th Flotillas (the Commander of the 5th Flotilla, Lt-Cdr Johannsen†); the escort vessels *PA1* and *PA2*; the motor minesweepers *R182* and *RA9* (ex-British ML306); the minesweepers *M3801, M3802, M3822, M3855, M3873, M3874* and *M4627*; the patrol boats *V207, V1505, V1506, V1511, V1537, V1540, V1541* and *V1805*; the gun ferry *AF69*; and many

smaller auxiliary naval craft and harbour vessels.

The following night, 297 Lancasters, Halifaxes and Mosquitos of Nos 1, 4, 5, 6 and 8 Groups attack Boulogne. The following vessels are sunk: the motor minesweeper tenders *Von der Gröben*, *Brommy* and *Von der Lippe*, the motor minesweepers *R81*, *R92*, *R125*, *R129*, *R232*, *R237*, the minesweepers *M402*, *M3650*, *M3815*, the patrol boats *V1814* and *V1815*, the gun ferries *AF3* and *AF11*, three tugs and five harbour defence vessels. In addition, the motor minesweepers *R96*, *R100* and *R117* are badly damaged.

14 June–9 July   Central Pacific
Operation 'Forager': TF.52 (Vice-Adm Turner) lands V Amphibious Corps (Lt-Gen H M Smith) on Saipan. On 14 June the fire support groups begin with their preparatory shelling and support the troops on 15 June: TG.52.17 (Rear-Adm Oldendorf), comprising the battleships *Tennessee*, *California*, *Maryland* and *Colorado*, the cruisers *Indianapolis* (TF.58 until 14 June), *Louisville*, *Birmingham*, *Montpelier* and *Cleveland* and the destroyers *Remey*, *Wadleigh*, *Norman Scott*, *Mertz*, *Robinson*, *Bagley*, *Albert W Grant*, *Halsey Powell*, *Coghlan*, *Monssen*, *McDermut*, *McGowan*, *Melvin*, *McNair*, *Yarnall*, *Twining* and *Stockham*; TG.52.10 (Rear-Adm Ainsworth), comprising the battleships *Pennsylvania*, *Idaho* and *New Mexico*, the cruisers *Honolulu*, *Minneapolis*, *San Francisco*, *Wichita*, *New Orleans* and *St Louis* and the destroyers *Anthony*, *Wadsworth*, *Hudson*, *Halford*, *Terry*, *Braine*, *Guest*, *Bennett* and *Fullam* (in addition, two APDs, two DMSs and one AVD, with air support provided by TG.52.14 under Rear-Adm Bogan comprising the escort carriers *Fanshaw Bay*, *Midway*, *White Plains* and *Kalinin Bay* and the destroyers *Cassin*, *Young*, *Irwin*, *Ross*, *Porterfield*, *Callaghan* and *Longshaw*); and TG.52.11 (Rear-Adm Sallada), comprising the escort carriers *Kitkun Bay*, *Gambier Bay*, *Corregidor* and *Coral Sea* and the destroyers *Laws*, *Morrison*, *Benham*, *Bullard*, *Kidd* and *Chauncey*.

On 15 June the transport group TG.52.3 (Capt Knowles), with 13 APAs, five AKs and one LSD, lands the 2nd Marine Div (Maj-Gen Watson) and the transport group TG.52.4 (Capt Loomis), with 13 APAs, three AKAs and three LSDs, lands the 4th Marine Div (Maj-Gen Schmidt). An escort is provided by the destroyers *Newcomb*, *Bennion*, *Heywood L Edwards*, *Bryant*, *Prichett*, *Philip*, *Cony*, *Mugford*, *Selfridge*, *Ralph Talbot*, *Patterson*, *Bagley*, *Phelps*, *Shaw* and *Renshaw*.

Further waves arrive on landing ships and boats: in all, TF.52 consists of 551 ships. A total of 67451 men are landed. After heavy fighting with the Japanese defenders (Lt-Gen Saito with the reinforced 43rd Inf Div and naval units under Vice-Adm Nagumo), the island is captured on 9 July. Japanese losses are 23811 dead with 1780 prisoners and US losses 3426 dead and 13099 wounded.

During air strikes by carrier aircraft on 4 July, the Japanese minelayer *Sarushima* and the minesweeper *W25* are sunk in the Bonins.

15 June   North Sea
Beaufighter torpedo bombers of Coastal Command sink the transport *Coburg* (7900 tons) from a German convoy, the motor torpedo boat tender *Gustav Nachtigal* and the minesweeper *M103* N of the island of Schiermonnikoog.

15–21 June   Baltic
Soviet attack on the offshore islands of the Karelian isthmus. On 15 June the Finnish IV Corps has to withdraw under pressure from the 59th and 21st Soviet Armies from the Mannerheim position to Viborg. At the outset there is fire support from the battleship *Oktyabrskaya Revolutsiya*. To cover the seaward flank, the Finns use light naval forces and two submarines and call for German support. *T30* and *T31*, the 3rd MS Flotilla, the 1st MMS Flotilla and an AF Group of the 24th Landing Flotilla are employed in Viborg Bay and in Koivisto Sound. In an attack by Soviet torpedo cutters under Capt 2nd Class Osipov, *T31* is lost, and in air attacks on 20–21 June, *AF32* and the mine transport *Otter* sink and the motor minesweeper tender *Nettelbeck*, *M29*, *R119* and *R120* are damaged. Soviet landings on Koivisto are delayed but not prevented. By 23 June the islands are evacuated and occupied by the Russians who are supported, *inter alia*, by the gunboats *Volga*, *Zeya*, *Kama* and *Oka*.

16 June   Air War/Norway
In air attack on Bergen the U-boat *U998* is heavily damaged and has to be decommissioned.

16–17 June   Mediterranean
The French destroyers *Le Fantasque* and *Le Terrible* make a sortie into the Gulf of Quarnaro and sink the small tanker *Giuliana* (350 tons) in the company of the German motor minesweepers *R4*, *R8*, *R14* and *R15*, which get away.

16–29 June   English Channel
During the nights 15–16, 16–17 and 17–18 June the last three motor torpedo boats, *S130*, *S145* and *S168*, set out from Cher-

bourg, but they are driven off by destroyer patrols and the British SGB Flotilla (Lt-Cdr Baker). The Boulogne group, comprising *S177*, *S181*, *S174* and *S175*, does not find any targets on 16 June and is attacked by fighter-bombers. The following night, the group, reinforced by *S180* and *S190*, turns back after fighter-bomber attacks. *S83*, *S127* and *S133*, coming from Ostend, find no targets on 16 June and become involved in several air attacks on 17 June in which *S133* and *S83* are damaged.

During the night 16–17 June the Canadian 65th MTB Flotilla (Lt-Cdr Kirkpatrick), comprising *MTB748*, *MTB745*, *MTB726* and *MTB727*, attacks a German convoy W of the Cotentin peninsula: *MTB748* torpedoes the minesweeper *M133* which is towed into St-Malo harbour and scuttled there on 6 Aug.

During the night 18–19 June the German 2nd MTB Flotilla with six boats is transferred from Boulogne to Le Havre. In a storm, which reaches its climax during the night and lasts until 22 June, operations by light craft on both sides are impossible. The artificial harbour 'Mulberry A', off the Omaha beach-head, is made unusable because of the storm and many landing craft are driven on to the beach and destroyed. The landing of supplies is severely disrupted.

During the night 22–23 June the Canadian 65th MTB Flotilla, consisting of *MTB748*, *MTB727*, *MTB745* and *MTB743* and four British MTBs, attacks a German convoy near St Helier (Jersey) and sinks the supply ship *Hydra*. The 9th MTB Flotilla, which on 19 June went with three boats from Cherbourg to St-Malo on a transport mission, returns to Cherbourg. The 2nd Flotilla, consisting of *S177*, *S181*, *S180*, *S190*, *S174*, *S175* and *S167*, lays mines in Seine Bay. In engagements with British destroyer patrols, *S190* is hit and has to be abandoned. *S83*, *S127* and *S133* are transferred from Ostend to Boulogne. On 23 June the German MMS *R79* is sunk by rocket fire from fighter-bombers off Boulogne.

During the night 23–24 June Cherbourg is evacuated. *S130*, *S145* and *S168* proceed to St-Malo. Off Cap de la Hague, a convoy, in spite of covering fire from the 'Yorck' naval coastal battery, is attacked by two groups each of three MTBs of the British 14th MTB Flotilla (Lt Shaw) and three boats of the 35th MTB Flotilla (Lt-Cdr McCowen) and loses *AF66* and three coastal motor ships and, later, two tugs in the company of the 6th Gun Carrier Flotilla near the Channel Islands. The 2nd Flotilla (Cdr Opdenhoff) with three boats lays another barrage of 12 DM-1 mines, while three boats, forming the torpedo group, have engagements with destroyers, including *Stord* and *Venus*, and MTBs. *S175* is badly, and *S181* lightly, damaged.

During the night 24–25 June the motor torpedo boats go from St-Malo to Alderney. The 2nd Flotilla with five boats has to abandon a mining operation after fighter-bomber attacks. The three boats from Boulogne are transferred to Le Havre. On 25–26 June the new 6th MTB Flotilla (*S76*, *S90*, *S91*, *S97*, *S114*, *S132*, *S39* and *S135*) is transferred from Cuxhaven to Ijmuiden. During the night 25–26 June *S130*, *S168* and *S145* try to break through from Alderney to Dieppe. S of Selsey Bill they are involved in an engagement with the Canadian destroyers *Gatineau* and *Chaudière* which outmanoeuvre the torpedoes and force *S145* to return after being hit. The boat goes to St-Malo on 27 June.

In an attack by four British MTBs off St Helier during the night 26–27 June *M4620* is lost. The following night, the converted trawler *M4611* sinks off Jersey after an engagement at very short range with the destroyers *Eskimo* and *Huron*. After *V213* obtains hits on the destroyers, the boat escapes to Jersey. A sortie from Le Havre by the 2nd and 8th MTB Flotillas during the night 27–28 June has no success. The next night *S174*, *S177*, *S180* and *S181* lay 16 DM-1 mines and *S83*, *S167*, *S127* and *S133* cover the operation. On 28 June, in air raid on Le Havre, the damaged torpedo boat *Kondor* is destroyed and on 28–29 June the German gun ferry *AF8* is sunk by rocket fire and bombing in an air attack off Le Tréport.

17–19 June   Mediterranean

Allied coastal forces, including 37 US PT boats, land Senegalese riflemen of the French 9th Colonial Div on Elba, who occupy the island in two days after the initial resistance has been broken. Larger ships are not used because of the many German mine barrages.

18–22 June   Central Pacific

Battle of the Philippine Sea. To support the Marianas operation, the US submarines (TF.17, Vice-Adm Lockwood) are disposed from 12 June as follows: *Plunger*, *Gar*, *Archerfish*, *Plaice* and *Swordfish* in the area of Bonin Island; *Pintado*, *Pilotfish* and *Tunny* SE of Formosa; *Albacore*, *Seawolf*, *Bang*, *Finback* and *Stingray* in the area of the Marianas; *Flying Fish*, *Muskallunge*, *Seahorse*, *Pipefish* and *Cavalla* E of the Philippines; and *Growler* off Surigao Strait. From the submarines of the 7th Fleet (Rear-Adm Christie), *Hake*, *Bashaw* and *Paddle*

are positioned SE of Mindanao, *Harder*, *Haddo*, *Redfin* and *Bluefish* off Tawi-Tawi and *Jack* and *Flier* off Luzon. During the Japanese preparatory movements for Operation 'A-GO', *Harder* (Cdr Dealey) from 6 to 9 June sinks the destroyers *Minatsuki*, *Hayanami* and *Tanikaze* off Tawi-Tawi and torpedoes the *Urakaze*; *Hake* sinks the destroyer *Kazegumo* on 8 June. The fleet, which sets out from Tawi-Tawi on 13 June, is reported by *Redfin* (Lt-Cdr Austin), the passing of the carriers through the San Bernardino Strait by *Flying Fish* (Lt-Cdr Risser) on 15 June and the presence of the battleship squadron E of Mindanao by *Seahorse* (Lt-Cdr Cutter). On 16–17 June the Japanese forces, after joining up and while they refuel from two tanker groups, are twice reported by *Cavalla* (Lt-Cdr Kossler). In this way Adm Spruance receives timely warnings and can assemble (18 June) TF.58 (see 11 June) W of the Marianas to cover Operation 'Forager'. The Japanese Fleet (Vice-Adm Kurita), comprising the light carriers *Chitose*, *Chiyoda* and *Zuiho*, the battleships *Yamato*, *Musashi*, *Haruna* and *Kongo*, the cruisers *Atago*, *Takao*, *Maya* and *Chokai* and the destroyers *Naganami*, *Asashimo*, *Kishinami*, *Okinami*, *Tamanami*, *Hamakaze*, *Fujinami* and *Shimakaze* with the cruiser *Noshiro*; Carrier Group A (Vice-Adm Ozawa), comprising the carriers *Taiho*, *Shokaku* and *Zuikaku*, the cruisers *Myoko* and *Haguro* and the destroyers *Asagumo*, *Isokaze*, *Hatsutsuki*, *Wakatsuki*, *Akitsuki* and *Shimotsuki* with the cruiser *Yahagi*; and Carrier Group B (Rear-Adm Joshima) comprising the carriers *Junyo*, *Hiyo* and *Ryuho*, the battleship *Nagato*, the cruiser *Mogami* and the destroyers *Michishio*, *Nowake*, *Yamagumo*, *Shigure*, *Samidare*, *Hayashimo*, *Akashimo* and *Shiratsayu* (the last is sunk en route after a collision on 15 June). The tanker groups consist of four tankers with the destroyers *Hibiki*, *Hatsushimo*, *Yunagi* and *Tsuga* and two tankers and the destroyers *Yukikaze* and *Uzuki* respectively. Ozawa's intention is to fly off the carrier aircraft outside the range of TF.58, to touch down on Guam after the attack and then to fly back making a second attack. The Japanese reconnaissance aircraft locate parts of TF.58 in the evening of 18 June and early on 19 June. From 0800 to 1100 hrs the Japanese carriers fly off 372 aircraft in four waves but they are located with radar by the US ships at a range of up to 150km and intercepted by fighters (300 sorties) which are at once flown off. They are, in part, supported by the ships' AA fire and shoot down 242 aircraft ('Turkey Shoot'). Only a few aircraft

break through, obtaining one bomb hit on *South Dakota* and near-misses on *Indiana* and *Bunker Hill*. No more than 29 US fighters are lost. In the landing operation on Guam, US fighters attack and shoot down 30 aircraft and the 19 which land are badly damaged. Shortly after the Japanese aircraft fly off, the US submarine *Albacore* (Cdr Blanchard) attacks Group A and hits *Taiho*, which sinks after explosions. *Cavalla* sinks *Shokaku* with three torpedoes. While Ozawa refuels from the tankers on 20 June, Mitscher approaches and in the afternoon flies off 216 aircraft at great range. They encounter only 35 fighters over the Japanese ships. The carrier *Hiyo* and two tankers are sunk and *Zuikaku*, *Chiyoda*, *Haruna* and *Maya* are damaged. Twenty US aircraft are lost. In spite of lighting up the flight decks, 72 machines are lost in crash landings or coming down in the sea. Of 209 flying personnel from these aircraft, 160 are rescued. During the night 20–21 June the C-in-C of the Combined Fleet in Tokyo, Adm Toyoda, gives the order to withdraw. Adm Spruance rejects Mitscher's proposal to continue the pursuit with the fast battleships. The Japanese fleet, therefore, escapes. After refuelling on 22–23 June, three groups from TF.58 go to Eniwetok. Rear-Adm Clark makes a sortie to the N with the carriers *Hornet*, *Yorktown*, *Bataan* and *Belleau Wood* and on 24 June carries out a raid on Iwo Jima and Chichijima in which another 66 Japanese aircraft are destroyed. A Japanese attack is intercepted.

18–23 June   Black Sea

On 18 June the A/S vessel *UJ316* off Sulina and on 23 June *UJ307* and *UJ2306* off Varna sink on Soviet air laid mines.

20 June–14 Aug   Mediterranean

On 20–21 June the German torpedo boats *TA25* and *TA29* carry out a mining operation, 'Messer', in the Ligurian Sea. In an engagement with US PT boats, *TA25* sinks. The Italian destroyer *Grecale* and the motor torpedo boat *Ms 74* bring British and Italian small battle units to La Spezia, which penetrate the harbour on 22 June and destroy the heavy cruiser *Bolzano* which is being repaired. On 26 June they sink the cruiser *Gorizia*, to be used as blockship.

On 1 July the German gun ferries *KF439*, *KF503*, *KF589* and *KF620* are sunk in an Allied air raid on La Spezia. At the end of June and the beginning of July, the British submarine *Universal* (Lt Gordon) sinks the harbour patrol boat *FM06* and two blockships totalling 8752 tons, *Ultor* (Lt Hunt) one naval ferry barge and two blockships totalling 8575 tons, *Vampire* (Lt Taylor) one sailing ship and *Universal* one small submarine-chaser. At the end of July and the beginning of Aug, *Ultor* sinks the submarine-chaser *UJ2211*, *Ultimatum* one small submarine-chaser and two naval ferry barges including *F811*, *Upstart* (Lt Chapman) one small ship and *Universal* one sailing ship; the French *Curie* (Lt Chailley) torpedoes a steamer.

From 6 to 26 July *TA24*, *TA28* and *TA29* from the 10th TB Flotilla put to sea practically every night on mining operations (five), reconnaissance sorties (ten) and coastal shelling sorties (one). On 28–29 June and on 15–16, 19–20 and 25–26 July there are engagements with Allied PTs and MTBs. On 12–13 Aug *TA24* and *TA29* carry out another reconnaissance sortie.

20 June–18 Aug   Baltic
In continual attacks by Soviet ground-attack aircraft and fighter-bombers of the Baltic Fleet's Air Force (Lt-Gen Samokhin) on German patrol vessels in Narva Bay and the operational harbours in Estonia and Finland, the destroyer *Z39*, the minesweepers *M15*, *M29* and *M3112*, the ferry barge *F194* and the AA escort *FJ26* are damaged in June.

From 30 June to 1 July the Soviet MTBs *TK43*, *TK63* and *TK161* are sunk in engagements in the Narva Bay. There are 68 dead and 144 wounded. In July *M20*, *M413* (on 21 July in Narva Bay), *F237*, *F498*, *V1707* and the AA cruiser *Niobe* (ex-Dutch *Gelderland*, on 16 July at Kotka) are sunk and *M3*, *M14*, *M15*, *M19*, *M29*, *M30*, *M453*, *M460*, *M3114*, *V1705* and *F259* are damaged. There are 148 dead and 269 wounded.

In Aug the attacks slacken off somewhat. *M14*, *M443*, *M3109*, *M3128*, *M3137*, *F258*, *AF21* (on 5 Aug off Loksa) and *R67* are damaged. Throughout the period the mine barrages are repeatedly reinforced by naval barges of the 24th Landing Flotilla.

In an attempt to reinforce the 'Seeigel' barrage, the 6th TB Flotilla (Cdr Koppenhagen) runs into its own mine barrage on 17–18 Aug and loses *T22*, *T30* and *T32* with 393 men, some of whom are taken prisoner. Only *T23* returns.

22 June   Air War/France
During a USAAF air attack on Toulon, the salvaged French submarines *Sirène*, *Galatée*, *Eurydice* and *Diamant* are sunk.

22–28 June   Baltic
A German-Finnish commando operation (Steinhäger) is launched against the island of Narvi occupied by the Russians on 22 June with light craft. With support from the German 2nd TB Flotilla (Cdr Kassbaum) with *T30*, *T8* and *T10*, the 3rd MS Flotilla (Cdr Kieffer) with *M18*, *M19*, *M22*, *M15*

and *M30* and the 1st MMS Flotilla (Lt-Cdr W E Schneider) with *R67*, *R68*, *R76* and *R249*, Finnish units are to be landed by the 2nd Finnish Patrol Flotilla (Lt-Cdr Jääsalo) with nine VMV boats and the patrol vessel *Vasama* and the 1st and 2nd MTB Flotillas (Lt-Cdr Pirhonen and Lt-Cdr Salo) with four and five motor torpedo boats respectively. The operation fails because of the strong Soviet defence and inadequate co-ordination between Germans and Finns. The island is shelled on 15–16 July by three German torpedo boats, which carry out an engagement with Soviet patrol boats.

24 June   Air War/Germany
In an air attack on Wesermünde, the German MMS *R141* is sunk while under repair.

24–25 June   Mediterranean
The torpedo boat *TA34* (ex-Yugoslav *T-7*), with a Croatian crew on board, is beached and burnt out on the island of Murter on 24 June after an attack by the British *MGB659*, *MGB662* and *MTB670*. On 25 June the torpedo boat *TA22* (ex-Italian *Giuseppe Missori*) is damaged in an air attack SE of Trieste; she is not repaired.

24–28 June   North Pacific
The US TF.94 (Rear-Adm Small), comprising the cruisers *Chester*, *Pensacola* and *Concord* and the destroyers *Picking*, *Wickes*, *Sproston*, *Young*, *William D Porter*, *Isherwood*, *Kimberly*, *Luce* and *Charles J Badger*, makes a sortie to the W, protected by a weather front, and shells Paramushiro (Kuriles) on 26 June.

25 June   Mediterranean
The French destroyer *Bison*, salvaged at Toulon and in use as smokescreen platform, is rammed by a U-boat and sunk in harbour.

25–26 June   English Channel
To support the attack by VII US Corps on Cherbourg, two task forces shell German batteries W and E of the town on 25 June: Group I (Rear-Adm Deyo), with the battleship *Nevada*, the cruisers *Tuscaloosa*, *Quincy*, *Glasgow* (British) and *Enterprise* (British) and the destroyers *Ellyson*, *Emmons*, *Rodman*, *Murphy*, *Gherardi* and *Hambleton* in the W, shells the batteries near Querqueville; and Group II (Rear-Adm Barbey), with the battleships *Texas* and *Arkansas* and the destroyers *Barton*, *O'Brien*, *Laffey*, *Plunkett* and *Hobson* in the E, shells the battery 'Hamburg', which secures 28cm hits on *Texas* and *O'Brien*. *Glasgow*, *Barton* and *Laffey* are slightly damaged. The German batteries are largely destroyed. On 27 June the US destroyer *Shubrick* shells Querqueville. On 26 June the British battleship *Rodney*, the monitor *Roberts* and the cruisers *Argonaut*, *Belfast*

and *Diadem* support attacks by British units in the area of Caen.

25 June–31 Aug   English Channel
Operations by German small battle units against the Allied Operation 'Neptune'. On 25–26 June eight control and nine explosive boats ('Linsen'), towed by R-boats, try a first attack, but because of bad weather one of the explosive boats is smashed against *R46*, explodes and sinks the latter. The operation fails. On 5–6 July 26 improved one-man torpedoes ('Marder') start from Villers-sur-Mer. The operation is acclaimed but in reality only the British minesweepers *Cato* and *Magic* are sunk and the DE *Trollope* damaged while 13 'Marders' do not return. On 8–9 July 21 'Marders' start out, sinking the minesweeper *Pylades* and damaging the old cruiser *Dragon* (Polish) beyond repair (she has to be beached as a blockship in the 'Gooseberry' harbour) but no 'Marder' returns.

On 2–3 Aug there is a combined attack by 16 control and 28 explosive 'Linsen' and 58 'Marder' craft of the Small Battle Unit Flotilla 211 (Lt-Cdr Bastian); in addition, the Luftwaffe mounts an attack with the new 'Dackel' long-range circling torpedo. There is chaos at the invasion bridgehead but only the destroyer *Quorn*, the trawler *Gairsay*, *LCT764* and the transports *Fort Lac la Ronge* (7131 tons) and *Samtucky* (7219 tons) are hit and sunk or damaged, as is, again, the old cruiser *Dragon*. Six 'Marders' fall victim to Spitfires of the 2nd TAF and one is captured. On 5–6 and 6–7 Aug an unsuccessful 'Dackel' attack is mounted and on 8–9 Aug an attack by 12 control and 16 explosive 'Linsen' craft sees only eight control boats return.

On 9–10, 10–11 and 14–15 Aug there are further 'Dackel' attacks by the Luftwaffe, in which damage is caused to the freighter *Iddesleigh* (5205 tons), the cruiser *Vindictive*, the repair ship *Albatros* and one minesweeper.

During the nights 15–16 and 16–17 Aug 'Negers' are used for the last time. In the last night only 16 of 42 'Negers' of Small Battle Unit Flotilla 363 return. The French battleship *Courbet*, which has been sunk as a blockship, is hit.

It is planned to launch 53 'Marders' on 15–16 Aug but because of the weather only 14 set out, of which seven return. On 16–17 Aug 42 'Marders' are launched from Villers-sur-Mer: they sink the freighter *Fratton* (757 tons) and *LCT831* or *1062*. On 30–31 Aug the first operation using 'Biber' midget submarines is mounted: 22 craft are launched from Fécamp, but owing to the weather only 14 set out and these have no success.

26 June   Air War/Germany
The German gun ferry *AF85* is sunk in an air attack on Wesermünde.

26 June–4 Sept   Baltic
Finnish and German submarines are employed in the inner part of the Gulf of Finland because of the critical situation in Karelia. The three large Finnish boats operate from the middle of June S of Koivisto and the two small boats near Tiurinsaari. *Vesihiisi* lays mine barrages near Peninsaari on 4 and 7 July; *Vetehinen* lays a mine barrage after two sorties into Koivisto Sound on 2 July and again on 5 July. *Iku-Turso* operates on the way to Lavansaari (Aug), but, like *Vesikko* and *Saukko*, has no success. From 26 June the German *U481*, *U748* and *U1193* arrive, from 13 July *U679*, *U475*, *U479*, *U370*, *U242*, *U250* and *U348* and in Aug *U1001*, *U745* and *U717*. They generally relieve each other every two days in the positions near Koivisto and in Narva Bay. In the Koivisto area, *U679* (Lt Breckwoldt) has an engagement on 14 July with torpedo cutters. *U475* (Lt-Cdr Stöffler) damages the patrol cutter *MO-304* on 28 July. *U250* (Lt-Cdr Schmidt) sinks *MO-105* on 30 July, but is then herself sunk by depth charges from *MO-103*. The wreck is later raised (the T-5 acoustic torpedoes are recovered and shown to a British delegation, giving Stalin in 1947 the excuse for a court martial against four admirals, including the C-in-C, N G Kuznetsor and admirals Alafusov and Galler). *U370* (Lt Nielsen) damages *MO-107* on 31 July. In Narva Bay *U481* (Lt Andersen) sinks two motor minesweepers on 30 July and near Seiskari *U242* (Lt Pancke) sinks one survey ship and one lighter on 25 Aug. *U745* (Lt-Cdr v Trotha) sinks a patrol vessel in Narva Bay on 26 Aug.

28 June   Baltic
German preparations for Operation 'Tanne West' to occupy the Åland Islands in case of a Finnish capitulation. The pocket-battleship *Lützow*, with the destroyers *Z28*, *Z25*, *Z35* and *Z36*, anchors off Utö but the operation is postponed and later cancelled altogether.

28 June–27 Sept   North and West Atlantic
U858, *U804* and *U855* operate as weather boats in the North Atlantic from the end of June to the beginning of Sept. From 24 July US TG.22.6 (Capt Tague), comprising the escort carrier *Wake Island* and the DEs *Douglas L Howard*, *Fiske*, *Farquhar*, *J R Y Blakely* and *Hill*, is deployed against the weather boats detected in the radio picture.

On 2 Aug aircraft find *U804* (Lt H. Meyer) but the boat escapes after she has just missed *Douglas L Howard* with a T-5 and sunk *Fiske*. As relief, TG.22.2 (Capt Vosseller), comprising *Bogue* and the DEs *Haverfield*, *Janssen*, *Willis* and *Wilhoite* and a support group of six Canadian frigates, arrives from 4 Aug. On 15 and 18 Aug night aircraft from *Bogue* sight the approaching schnorkel boat *U802* (Lt-Cdr Schmoeckel). The boat sights the carrier on 16 Aug but does not fire. On 20 Aug six Avengers of VC-42 USN from *Bogue* sink *U1229* as she proceeds to Long Island to disembark agents. In the first half of Sept *U802* and *U541* (Lt-Cdr Petersen) penetrate into the Gulf of St Lawrence where *U541* sinks a ship of 2140 tons. On 8 and 14 Sept respectively the returning *U541* and *U802* sight TG.22.2 (*Bogue* and seven DEs) which is waiting for the boats S of Cabot Strait. But they obtain no hits with their T-5s fired at the DEs. An attack by *U541* on a convoy on 27 Sept is also unsuccessful. Off the American East Coast the schnorkel boat *U518* (Lt Offermann) torpedoes a Liberty ship of 7176 tons on 12 Sept, which, on the following day, is lost in a hurricane together with the destroyer *Warrington*, the minesweeper *YMS409* and the US Coast Guard cutters *Jackson* and *Bedloe*.

29 June   Mediterranean
The British destroyers *Tenacious*, *Terpsicore* and *Tumult* bombard a look-out station S of Valona.

30 June–1 July   Arctic
The German 4th DD Flotilla (Capt Johannesson), with the destroyers *Z29*, *Z31*, *Z33*, *Z34* and *Z38* make a sortie ('Südwind') to Bear Island.

30 June–15 July   Bay of Biscay
In Allied air attacks, the A/S vessel *UJ1408* is sunk on 30 June off Concarneau, *UJ1426* on 3 July at Lorient roads and the patrol vessel *V621* on 15 July off Belle Isle.

1–31 July   Air War/Western Europe
Continuation of mine offensive by RAF Bomber Command. In 25 nights, 180 sorties are flown against the French Biscay, Brittany and Channel ports, especially St-Nazaire, Lorient and Brest, the Belgian and Dutch coasts, the Frisian Islands, Heligoland Bight, the Elbe river, the Danish coasts, the Kattegat, the Kiel area and the western Baltic. One aircraft is lost.

The patrol vessel *V2017* is damaged off Ijmuiden on 12 July and *V713* is sunk off Brest on 19 July. On 23–24 July *U2323* is sunk off Möltenort near Kiel. The German gun ferry *AF96* is damaged beyond repair after hitting a mine off Zeebrügge on 24 July.

1–31 July   Pacific
US submarines continue their operations with assistance from 'Ultra' messages and, on occasion, form 'wolfpacks' of changing composition. The submarines which arrive in their operational areas in July achieve the following results:

In the area of the Kuriles, off Japan and in the Yellow and East China Seas, *Sunfish* (Lt-Cdr Shelby) sinks two ships of 8861 tons and two small vessels, *Pampanito* has misses, *Cobia* (Lt-Cdr Becker) sinks seven ships of 12217 tons, *Skate* (Lt-Cdr Gruner) sinks three ships of 4394 tons and on 8 July the destroyer *Usugumo*, *Tautog* (Lt-Cdr Baskett) sinks four ships of 3045 tons, *Gabilan* (Lt-Cdr Wheland) sinks the minesweeper *W25* on 17 July, *Sawfish* (Lt-Cdr Banister) sinks the submarine *I-29* on its way from Europe via Singapore to Japan, *Tilefish* (Lt-Cdr Keithley) damages the corvette *Kaibokan 17* on 18 July near Takao, *Sterlet* (Lt-Cdr Robbins) sinks three small vessels of 622 tons, *Pompon* (Lt-Cdr Gimber) sinks one ship of 2159 tons and one trawler and *Tambor* (Lt-Cdr Germershausen) sinks one ship of 2324 tons. *Snook*, *Rock* and *Shark* miss targets.

In the Mandate areas, *Guavina* (Lt-Cdr Teideman) sinks one ship of 3052 tons, *Permit* has misses, *Cod* (Lt-Cdr Atkins) sinks three small vessels of 1057 tons and *Tarpon* (Lt-Cdr Wogan) sinks four small vessels.

In the area of the Malayan Archipelago, the Philippines and the South China Sea, *Bonefish* (Lt-Cdr Edge) sinks one ship of 10026 tons and five small vessels, *Paddle* (Lt-Cdr Nowell) sinks the destroyer *Hokaze* on 6 July and *Mingo* (Lt-Cdr Staley) sinks the destroyer *Tamanami* on 8 July. *Steelhead* (Lt-Cdr Welchel) sinks two ships of 15364 tons and one small vessel and together with *Parche* (Lt-Cdr Ramage) one ship of 8990 tons, *Parche* alone sinks two ships of 14709 tons and damages one more of 7270 tons and *Hammerhead* (Lt-Cdr Martin) of this 'wolfpack' sinks one small vessel and has three misses. *Dace* (Lt-Cdr Claggett) sinks one ship of 1192 tons, *Apogon* (Lt-Cdr House) sinks one picket boat of 32 tons, *Piranha* (Lt-Cdr Ruble) sinks two ships of 12276 tons, *Sandlance* (Lt-Cdr Garrison) sinks two ships of 9643 tons, *Cabrilla* (Lt-Cdr Thompson) sinks two ships of 7884 tons, *Thresher* (Lt-Cdr McMillan) sinks two ships of 7754 tons, *Guardfish* (Lt-Cdr Ward) sinks four ships of 20428 tons, *Lapon* (Lt-Cdr Stone) sinks four ships of 7027 tons,

Ray (Lt-Cdr Kinsella) sinks five ships of 26184 tons, *Aspro* (Lt-Cdr Stevenson) sinks one ship of 2288 tons, *Crevalle* (Lt-Cdr Walker), after leaving the 'wolfpack' with *Flasher* and *Angler*, sinks one more ship of 11409 tons, *Perch* (Lt-Cdr Hills) sinks one small ship of 115 tons and *Drum* (Lt-Cdr Williamson) and *Balao* (Lt-Cdr Cole) each sink one small vessel. *Gurnard* has only misses.

2 July   South West Pacific
The US VII Amphibious Force (Rear-Adm Fechteler) lands 7100 men of the reinforced 168th Inf Regt on the island of Noemfoor. The landing is preceded by shelling from cruisers of TF.74 and 75 (Commodore Collins RAN, Rear-Adm Berkey—see 22 Apr) and 14 destroyers.

2 July–31 Aug   Mediterranean
In air attacks on German convoys near Rhodes the freighter *Agathe* (1259 tons) is sunk on 3 July. In July the British submarine *Vox* (Lt Michell) sinks the freighter *Anita* (1165 tons) and three sailing ships and *Unruly* (Lt Fyfe) sinks one small ship and misses the KT ship *Pelikan*. *Vivid* (Lt Varley) sinks the freighter *Susanne* (552 tons) and three sailing ships, *Universal* (Lt Gordon) one sailing ship and *Vigorous* one sailing ship. In Aug *Vox* sinks three sailing ships and the harbour patrol boat *GK61*, *Unswerving* (Lt Tattersall) one small ship, *Virtue* three sailing ships, *Vigorous* two sailing ships and *Vox*, again, one sailing ship. The Greek *Pipinos* (Lt-Cdr Loundras) sinks the torpedo boat *TA19* on 9 Aug off Samos and two lighters. On 10 Aug the German MMS *R34* is sunk by an aircraft (which is shot down) near Milos and on 27 Aug *R38* is mined and sunk near Paros.

3–30 July   English Channel
British MTB flotillas attack German shipping targets off the Dutch coast, between Boulogne and Le Havre and off Brittany. Among those participating off the Dutch coast are the 58th MTB Flotilla (Lt-Cdr Gemmel) and the Norwegian 54th MTB Flotilla (Lt-Cdr Monssen). During the night 3–4 July the steamer *Weserstein*, escorted by the 20th PB Flotilla (Cdr Puttfarken) consisting of *V2016*, *V2019*, *V2022*, *V1315* and *V1317*, is unsuccessfully attacked by four MTBs. The following day, when accompanied by the 26th MS Flotilla (Lt-Cdr v Lüeder), it is attacked by six MTBs, from which *MTB666* is sunk.

On 4 July the German patrol vessels *V208* and *V210* are sunk off St-Malo by MTBs with torpedoes. On 5 July the German gun ferry *AF99* is sunk by bombing off Boulogne.

During the night 8–9 July four MTBs attack a force of the 13th PB Flotilla (Cdr Fischer) comprising *V1313*, *V1301*, *V1306* and *V1310*: *MTB434* and *V1306* are sunk. On 17–18 July six MTBs attack the patrol boat *V1313* and three AF ferries and on 19–20 July the Norwegian *MTB709* and *MTB722* and the British *MTB685*, *MTB687*, *MTB729* and *MTB683* attack a German convoy: both sides sustain slight damage. On 21–22 July a force comprising *V1303* and the 34th MMS Flotilla is attacked by six MTBs: *M3413* sinks.

Off Fécamp on 1–2 July *MTB632* and *MTB650* from the 55th MTB Flotilla (Lt-Cdr Bradford) attack a force of the 10th MMS Flotilla (Lt-Cdr Nau) and sink *R180*. *MTB632* is put out of action by other minesweepers coming to the scene. The following night, *MTB629*, *MTB624*, *MTB621* and *MTB617* from the same flotilla attack a German force near Cap d'Antifer: both sides sustain slight damage. Apart from the 55th MTB Flotilla, the Canadian 29th MTB Flotilla (Lt-Cdr Law), the British 14th MTB Flotilla, the British 51st MTB Flotilla (Lt-Cdr Lyle) and, later, the 1st MTB Flotilla (Lt Mathias) and the 30th MTB Flotilla (Lt Dixon) are employed in this area, particularly against German motor torpedo boats. The 29th MTB Flotilla, comprising *MTB461*, *MTB462* and *MTB465*, has engagements on 4–5 and 13–14 July. On 8 July *MTB463* is lost in an attack on German 'Neger' one-man torpedoes.

The Canadian 65th MTB Flotilla (Lt-Cdr Kirkpatrick) is employed off Brittany. On 3–4 July, with *MTB748*, *MTB743*, *MTB735* and *MTB734*, it torpedoes the German supply steamer *Minotaure*, sinks the patrol boats *V206* and *V210* and damages *V209* and *M4622*.

On 5 July Allied destroyers begin Operation 'Dredger' against German escort vessels at the U-boat meeting points off Brest and to the S of it. During the night 5–6 July the 12th EG, comprising the Canadian destroyers *Qu'Appelle*, *Saskatchewan*, *Skeena* and *Restigouche*, attacks three patrol boats off Brest: *V715* is sunk after a courageous defence and the first two destroyers receive many small-calibre hits. The motor torpedo boats *S145* and *S112*, which are proceeding from St-Malo to Brest, rescue the survivors of *V715*.

During the night 7–8 July the destroyers *Huron* and *Tartar* of the 10th Flotilla attack boats of the 46th MS Flotilla (Lt-Cdr Zimmermann) off the Channel Islands and sink *M4605* and *M4601*. During the night 14–15 July the destroyers *Tartar*, *Haida* and *Blyskawica* make a sortie into the area of Ile

de Croix near Lorient and sink the submarine-chasers *UJ1420* and *UJ1421*. On 19–20 July the Canadian 9th EG is attacked off Brest by German aircraft with glider bombs which damage the frigate *Matane* with hits and the frigate *Meon* with near-misses.

In the eastern part of the assault area, the battleship *Rodney* supports the land operations on 7 and 11 July, the Dutch gunboat *Soemba* on 10 July, the monitor *Roberts* and the cruiser *Belfast* on 11 July, *Roberts* and the cruisers *Mauritius* and *Enterprise* on 17 and 18 July near Caen and the monitor *Erebus* and the Dutch gunboat *Flores* on 26 and 29 July.

German motor torpedo boats try often at night to make sorties into the assault area and there are many engagements. During the night 3–4 July the 8th Flotilla (Cdr Zymalkowski) sets out from Le Havre with *S83*, *S127* and *S133*, drops 12 DM-1 mines and proceeds to Dieppe. The 2nd Flotilla (Cdr Opdenhoff) with *S175*, *S176* and *S167* also drops 12 DM-1 mines but it is driven off and has to return. Then the motor torpedo boats are involved in engagements with the British frigates *Stayner* and *Thornbrough* off Cap d'Antifer which are used here as leader ships for the MTB groups.

During the night 4–5 July the 8th Flotilla, in transferring to Le Havre, has an engagement with the frigate *Trollope* and MTBs off Cap d'Antifer and has to return. The 2nd Flotilla with six boats has engagements off Le Havre with destroyers and MTBs, including *MTB 459*, *MTB462* and *MTB464* of the Canadian 29th MTB Flotilla.

During the night 5–6 July the 2nd Flotilla with six boats again has engagements with destroyers off Le Havre: *Trollope* is hit and beached, near Cap d'Antifer, becoming a constructive total loss, but the other torpedoes are outmanoeuvred. When coming in, the torpedo repair depot in Le Havre blows up: 41 torpedoes are destroyed and operations are restricted because of torpedo shortages. The 6th Flotilla (Lt-Cdr Matzen) moves some of its boats from Boulogne to Le Havre and suffers heavy fighter-bomber attacks in the process.

During the night 7–8 July the 2nd Flotilla sets out from Le Havre in two groups (*S176*, *S177* and *S182*; *S174*, *S181* and *S180*) together with *S167*, *S175* and *S168* from the 9th Flotilla (Cdr v Mirbach). The boats make several attacks on destroyers and detonations are observed. But the 'Hunt' destroyers *La Combattante* (French) and *Cattistock* and the frigate *Thornbrough*, which are involved in the engagements during the night, sustain only slight damage.

During the night 8–9 July the boats setting out from Le Havre (six of the 2nd and three of the 6th Flotillas) have to return because of the weather. The three boats of the 9th Flotilla attack targets off Dieppe without success. Because of bad visibility no further operations are possible before 15 July. The 6th Flotilla with *S132*, *S90* and *S135* has an engagement off Le Havre with the Canadian 29th MTB Flotilla, comprising *MTB459 MTB466* and *MTB464*. The 9th Flotilla, with *S175*, *S168* and *S167*, has an engage-ment off Dieppe with the boats of the British 64th MTB Flotilla (Lt-Cdr Wilkie) and the 2nd Flotilla with *S180*, *S177*, *S174* and *S182* has an engagement off Le Havre with MGBs and MTBs.

During the night 17–18 July the three boats of the 9th Flotilla set out from Dieppe but return after destroyer engagements and fighter-bomber attacks. Three boats of the 6th Flotilla set out from Le Havre and, in engagements, *S135* and *S90* damage the British *MTB361*. Of the boats of the 2nd Flotilla—*S176*, *S177*, *S182*, *S174*, *S180* and *S181*—only the first three come into contact with the enemy. *S91*, *S79* and *S114* move from Ostend to Boulogne to join the 6th Flotilla.

During the night 19–20 July sorties on the convoy routes have no success. In the night 21–22 July the torpedo boat *T28* is trans-ferred with *S132*, *S90* and *S135* from Le Havre to Boulogne and, on the way, has an engagement with the 'Hunt' destroyer *Melbreak*. The following night, the journey is continued from Boulogne to the Hook of Holland with an escort from the 8th MTB Flotilla: the destroyers *Forester* and *Stayner* with *MTB480* and *MTB484* are out-manoeuvred. *S90* and *S135*, which have come into Dieppe, are transferred to Bou-logne on 25 July with the 4th MMS Flotilla. On 24 July, in an air attack against St Peter Port, the patrol vessels *V205* and *V209* are sunk. During the night 25–26 July an oper-ation by five boats of the 2nd MTB Flotilla against destroyers off Seine Bay is broken off.

The next night, the 6th MTB Flotilla makes an attack from Boulogne on a westbound convoy off Dungeness; the 1st group, com-prising *S97*, *S114*, *S90* and *S91*, torpedoes two ships of 14217 tons and escapes from the pursuing destroyers *Obedient*, *Savage* and *Opportune* and the *MTB436*, *MTB432* and *MTB418*, the last two of which suffer slight damage. The 2nd group, comprising *S132*, *S39*, *S135* and *S79*, has engagements with *MTB229*, *MTB240* and *MTB354* and Beaufighter aircraft. The 9th Flotilla from Boulogne, comprising *S175*, *S168* and

S167, becomes involved in an engagement with the escort and has to turn back. In a sortie from Le Havre by the 2nd Flotilla, comprising *S176*, *S182*, *S174*, *S181* and *S180*, against destroyers in Seine Bay, there is an engagement with the frigate *Retalick* and an MTB group in which *MTB430* sinks as a result of ramming by *S182* and the following *MTB412* sinks on the wreck of the preceding boat. The damaged *S182* has to be blown up.

During the night 27–28 July sorties by the 2nd and 6th Flotillas have to be abandoned because of mist. The following night, *S180* and *S176* of the 2nd Flotilla fire T-5 tor-pedoes for the first time against destroyers but have no success. During the night 29–30 July *S97*, *S114* and *S91* (Petty-Officer Waldhausen, Lt Hemmer and Lt-Cdr Nolte) of the 6th Flotilla attack an eastbound convoy E of Eastbourne and with six FAT torpedoes sink the British freighter *Samwake* (7219 tons) and hit the *Fort Dear-born* (7160 tons), *Fort Kaskaskia* (7187 tons), *Ocean Volga* (7174 tons) and *Ocean Courier* (7178 tons). They escape from the frigate *Thornbrough*. During the night 30–31 July *S176*, *S180*, *S177*, *S181*, *S174*, *S132*, *S39* and *S79* attack destroyer and MTB groups, including the destroyer *Oribi*. *S174*, *S181* and *S132* fire T-5 torpedoes but they det-onate prematurely.

The torpedo boat *T28*, in spite of engage-ments with the British DE *Melbreak* on 22 July and MTB attacks, is transferred to home waters from 21 to 27 July.

3 July–27 Aug   English Channel
Operations by German schnorkel U-boats in the Channel. From 3 to 11 July *U309* (Lt Mahrholz) misses a search group and *U953* (Lt Marbach) and *U763* (Lt-Cdr Cordes) each make two attacks on convoys and sink one ship, of 1927 tons and 1499 tons respect-ively. *U390* (Lt Geissler) sinks on 5 July the A/S trawler *Ganilly* from a convoy and torpedoes one tanker of 10584 tons but is then herself sunk by the destroyer *Wanderer* and the frigate *Tavy*. *U678* (Lt Hyronimus) is sunk when attacking a convoy off Beachy Head on 6 July by the Canadian destroyers *Ottawa* and *Kootenay* and the minesweeper *Statice*. *U243*, coming from Norway, falls victim to Sunderland 'H' of No 10 Sqn RAF from the Bay Patrol on 8 July and, similarly, *U1222*, returning from Newfoundland, to Sunderland 'P' of No 201 Sqn RAF on 11 July, *U415* is lost on a mine on 14 July in Brest harbour. From another group which succeeds in getting into the Channel, *U672* has to scuttle herself on 18 July after being damaged by the DE *Balfour*. *U212* is sunk

by the DEs *Curzon* and *Ekins* on 21 July and *U741* has to put in to Le Havre. In the last 10 days of July *U309* misses a convoy and *U621* (Lt Struckmann), in four attacks, sinks the landing ship *Prince Leopold* (2938 tons) and torpedoes the troop transport *Ascanius* (10048 tons). *U275* has to put in to Boulogne in a damaged state and *U671*, which has set out from there again, is sunk on 4 Aug by the DE *Stayner* and the destroyer *Wensleydale*. The 3rd and 2nd SGs operate with aircraft from the end of July to the middle of Aug W of the entrance to the Channel against approaching U-boats and those moving from the Brittany ports. In the operation *U214* is sunk by the frigate *Cooke* on 26 July. *U333* is sunk by the sloop *Starling* (in the first use of a 'Squid' ahead-throwing weapon) and the frigate *Loch Killin* on 31 July; these ships also sink *U736* on 6 Aug. On 9 Aug *U608* is sunk by Lib-erator 'C' of No 53 Sqn supported by the sloop *Wren* of the 2nd SG. On 11 Aug *U385* is damaged by Sunderland 'P' of No 461 Sqn RAAF and sunk by *Starling*. On 12 Aug *U981*, damaged by an air-laid mine, is sunk by Halifax 'F' of No 502 Sqn RAF; 40 of her crew are rescued by *U309*. On 12 Aug *U270*, evacuating personnel from La Pallice to the Gironde, is sunk by Sunderland 'A' of No 461 Sqn RAF; 71 men of 81 are rescued by surface vessels. On 14 Aug *U618* is damaged by Liberator 'G' of No 535 Sqn RAF and sunk by the frigates *Duckworth* and *Essington* of the 3rd SG. On 18 Aug *U107* is sunk by Sunderland 'W' of No 201 Sqdn RAF. *U445* is sunk by the frigate *Louis* on 24 Aug. *U180*, which is setting out for East Asia, sinks as a result of bomb hits and a mine on 22 Aug. *U667* (Lt Lange), having sunk the Canadian corvette *Regina*, a Liberty ship of 7176 tons and the landing ships *LST921* and *LC199* on 8 and 14 Aug, is sunk on a mine as she returns off North Cornwall on 25 Aug. In the middle of Aug a new wave arrives in the Channel: of them, *U741* is sunk by the corvette *Orchis* in attacking a convoy on 15 Aug, *U621* and *U984* by the destroyers *Ottawa*, *Kootenay* and *Chaudière* of the 11th SG on 18 and 20 Aug and *U413*, after she has sunk a ship of 2360 tons, by the escort destroyers *Wensley-dale*, *Forester* and *Vidette* on 20 Aug. *U764* (Lt v Bremen), in three attacks, sinks a steamer of 638 tons. *U480* (Lt Förster) which is equipped with a rubber skin ('Alberich') against asdic, sinks in four attacks the Canadian corvette *Alberni*, the minesweeper *Loyalty* and a ship of 5712 tons and torpedoes another ship of 7134 tons. *U989* (Lt-Cdr H Rodler v Roithberg) sinks in three attacks a ship of 1791 tons and torpedoes a ship of 7176 tons. Together with *U275* and *U92*, which achieve no successes, the three boats are recalled on 27 Aug to Norway. *U218* lays a mine barrage near Start Point on 20 Aug.

4–12 July   North Sea
On 4 July the German minesweeper *M469* is torpedoed and sunk NW of Vlieland by the British *MTB458*. On 5 July the patrol vessel *V1253* is sunk by MTB torpedo off Terschelling, *V1411* is sunk off Ijmuiden and the MMS *R111* is sunk off Vlieland in an air attack by bombs and gunfire. On 8 July the minesweeper *M264* is sunk by aircraft rocket fire W of Heligoland. On 9 July *V1308* is sunk by MTB torpedo off the Hook of Holland. On 12 July *V812* is sunk by aerial torpedoes between the Elbe and the Ems.

4–21 July   Central Pacific
Preparations for the landings on Guam and Tinian. TF.58 (Vice-Adm Mitscher) carries out raids on Iwo Jima and Chichijima on 4 July with TG.58.1 (Rear-Adm Clark) and 58.4 (Rear-Adm Davison) and on Guam with TG.58.2 (Rear-Adm Reeves) and 58.3 (Rear-Adm Montgomery). Guam is also shelled by the destroyers of TG.58.3. On 5 July carrier aircraft of TG.58.1 and 58.2 make attacks on Guam (see 11 June for the composition of TF.58).

From 8 July several ships of TG.52.10 (Rear-Adm Ainsworth—see 14 June) shell Guam until 19 July with 12550 rounds of 6in to 16in shells and 16214 rounds of 5in shells. From 20 June army artillery shells Tinian from Saipan and from the beginning of June there is regular shelling by ships of TG.52.14. Air support is provided, and carrier attacks on Guam are made by aircraft of the escort carrier group TG.53.7 (Rear-Adm Ragsdale—see 21 July).

5 July   Air War/Mediterranean
USAAF attack on the harbour at Toulon with 233 B-24s. *Inter alia*, *U586* and *U642* are destroyed and *U471*, *U952* and *U969* are badly, and *U466* and *U967* slightly, damaged. Only *U230* remains operational. The A/S vessel *UJ6070* is sunk.

5–20 July   Norway
In two nights, 4–5 and 19–20 July, the German minelayer *Ostmark*, the MCMS *MRS25*, the gunboat *K2*, the minesweeper *M437* and, as escort, four vessels each of the 53rd Patrol Flotilla and the 52nd MS Flotilla lay the 'München A' and 'B' anti-submarine flanking barrages off Stadtlandet and Folla Fjord.

8–21 July   North Sea
British bombers sink the German freighters *Miranda* (736 tons) and *Tannhäuser* (1923

tons) and the Swedish steamer *Sif* (1365 tons) on 8 July SW of Heligoland.
Sortie by the British *MTB455*, *MTB457*, *MTB458*, *MTB467*, *MTB468*, *MTB469* and *MTB470* into the area off Ijmuiden. Here an engagement takes place with three German patrol boats. *V1412* is sunk and three MTBs are damaged.
On 21 July the minesweeper *M307* is sunk with aerial bombs and cannon fire N of Langeooge.

9 July   Great Britain
Capt F J Walker, the most successful U-boat hunter, dies from a stroke. He is buried at sea.

9 July   Mediterranean
The US minesweeper *Swerve* is sunk by a mine off Anzio.

9–28 July   Arctic
Soviet combined operation (RV-6) against German convoy traffic off the polar coast. The submarine *L-15* lays mines off Rolvsöy and reconnoitres. From 13 July *S14*, *S-56*, *Shch-402* and *M-200* take up waiting positions and a torpedo cutter brigade (Capt 1st Class Kuzmin) is alerted. On 10 and 13 July Soviet torpedo and ground-attack aircraft make sorties in groups and do slight damage to some ships. On 13 July a Soviet reconnaissance aircraft reports a German convoy proceeding eastwards in Mageröy Sound. In the evening of 14 July the convoy is reported in Porsangerfjord and early on 15 July *S-56* (Capt 3rd Class Shchedrin) and *M-200* (Lt-Cdr Gladkov) attack unsuccessfully with an hour's interval between them near Cape Harbaken. The torpedo cutters (Capt 2nd Class Alexeev) *TKA-12*, *TKA-13*, *TKA-238*, *TKA-239*, *TKA-240*, *TKA-241*, *TKA-242* and *TKA-243* at first pass by but are then brought to the scene by two Yak-9 reconnaissance aircraft S of Busse Sound. The escort beats off the attacks and *UJ1211* sinks *TKA-239* (which on 15 July has sunk the drifter *Hugin*). An attack by ground attack aircraft and fighter-bombers of the 14th Mixed Air Div on the incoming ships off Bökfjord causes only slight damage. In further heavy fighter-bomber attacks in the area Kirkenes-Vardö on 17, 21, 22 and 28 July, slight damage is done to the ships and only *V6307* is sunk.

11–12 July   Mediterranean
British commando troops land on the island of Hvar in the Adriatic.

11 July–19 Sept   Mediterranean
Last operations by German schnorkel U-boats in the Mediterranean. *U596* (Lt-Kolbus) sets out from Pola on 11 July, cruises off Cyrenaica, in the Strait of Otranto, off Malta and Benghazi, but makes no attacks and returns to Salamis on 1 Sept.

U407 (Lt Korndörfer) operates off Derna and Benghazi from 21 Aug to 4 Sept and *U565* (Lt Henning) N of Crete from 26 Aug to 13 Sept. There the boat is relieved from 9 Sept by *U407* (Lt Kolbus), which on 19 Sept falls victim to the British destroyers *Troubridge* and *Terpsichore* and the Polish *Garland*.

14–26 July   South West Pacific
TF.74 (Commodore Collins), comprising the Australian cruisers *Australia* and *Shropshire* and the destroyers *Arunta*, *Warramunga*, *Ammen* and *Bache* and, from 16 July, *Hutchins* and *Beale*, is employed to shell Japanese troops which try to break through to the W in the area of Aitape.

16 July   Baltic
A German MTB sinks the Soviet minesweeper *T-218* off Narva.

17 July   Norway
British carrier raid, with *Formidable*, *Indefatigable* and *Furious* under Rear-Adm McGrigor, on *Tirpitz*, lying in Kaafjord. The operation is covered by the battleship *Duke of York* (Adm Moore, new C-in-C Home Fleet) and the cruisers *Kent*, *Devonshire*, *Jamaica* and *Bellona*, together with fleet destroyers and the 20th EG. Forty-five Barracuda torpedo bombers and 50 fighters fly off from the carriers, but they are located so early that the target is completely covered in smoke and the AA defence is made fully prepared for operations. The attack is unsuccessful.

18 July   Air War/Germany
In an air attack on Kiel, the German destroyer *Paul Jacobi* is damaged by two near-misses.

18 July   English Channel
The British monitor *Roberts* and the cruisers *Mauritius* and *Enterprise* support the breakthrough of the British 2nd Army in the Caen area.

18–21 July   North Sea
On 18 July the North Coates Wing of RAF Coastal Command attacks a German convoy N of the Weser river and the island of Norderney and sinks the MMS *R139* and three merchant vessels. On 21 July a convoy of nine merchant ships with 21 escorts is attacked N of Spiekeroog by the RAF Coastal Command Beaufighter Wing: one merchant vessel and the minesweeper *M307* are sunk by bombs and cannon fire.

19–26 July   Black Sea
The Soviet submarine *Shch-209* (Lt-Cdr N V Sukhodolski), which is employed off the Bosphorus against German ships coming from Rumania, misses the Turkish steamer *Kanarya* with a torpedo on 19 July and sinks with gunfire the Turkish sailing ship *Semsi-Bahri* on 20 July and another Turkish sailing

ship on 26 July. *M-111* operates without success off Constanza. At the end of the month she is relieved by *M-113* and *M-117*. *M-113* (Lt-Cdr Volkov) tries to attack a convoy on 28 July inside the flanking mine barrages.

The German U-boats *U9* and *U24* operate off the Caucasian coast at the end of July.

20–24 July   English Channel
On 20 July the British destroyer *Isis* is (probably) mined while at anchor in Seine Bay. On 21 July the British minesweeper *Chamois* and on 24 July the destroyer *Goathland* are also mined in the Seine Bay and towed to Portsmouth; neither is repaired.

21 July–10 Aug   Central Pacific
US TF.53 (Rear-Adm Connolly) lands III Amphibious Corps (Maj-Gen Geiger) on Guam on 21 July. TG.53.1 (Rear-Adm Connolly) lands the 3rd Marine Div (Maj-Gen Turnage) W of Agana with 11 APAs, three AKAs, two LSDs and one hospital ship and sixteen LSTs, escorted by the destroyers *John Rodgers*, *Stevens*, *Harrison*, *McKee*, *Schroeder*, *Colahan*, *Stembel*, *Haggard*, *Hailey*, three DMSs and two AMs. TG.53.2 (Rear-Adm Reifsnider) lands the 1st Marine Bde and elements of the 77th Inf Div (Brig-Gen Shepherd) near Agat with 12 APAs, three AKAs, one LSD and 14 LSTs, escorted by the destroyers *Farenholt*, *Sigsbee*, *Dashiell*, *Murray*, *Johnston*, *Franks*, *Preston*, *Anthony*, *Wadsworth*, *Wedderburn*, *Black* and *Ringgold*. Fire support is provided by TG.53.5 (similar to TG.52.10 at Saipan on 14 June) under Rear-Adm Ainsworth and, in addition, the battleships *Colorado*, *Tennessee* and *California*, the cruisers *New Orleans*, *Indianapolis* and *St Louis*, the destroyers *Fullam*, *Guest*, *Monaghan*, *Dale* and *Aylwin* with air support from TG.53.7 (Rear-Adm Ragsdale), consisting of the escort carriers *Sangamon*, *Suwanee*, *Chenango*, *Corregidor* and *Coral Sea* and the destroyers *Erben*, *Walker*, *Abbot*, *Hale*, *Bullard*, *Chauncey* and *Kidd*. A total of 54891 troops are landed. They annihilate the bulk of the 19000 Japanese defenders (29th Inf Div, Lt-Gen Takashima†; 6th Expeditionary Battle Group, Maj-Gen Shigematsu†). The last Japanese island commandant is the Cdr of the 31st Army, Lt-Gen Obata†. US losses are 1290 dead, 145 missing and 5648 wounded and Japanese losses 10693 dead and 98 prisoners. The rest of the Japanese defenders retire to the jungle and fight on there in small groups, in some cases until the end of the war. (One survivor is rescued as late as 1972!) TF.58 (Vice-Adm Mitscher) attacks Guam on 21–22 July with TG.58.1, 58.2 and 58.3. From 23 July the carriers proceed to the W. From

25 to 28 July TG.58.2 and 58.3 direct attacks on Palau and TG.58.1 on Yap, Ulithi, Tais, Ngulu and Sorol. After replenishing, TG.58.1 and 58.3 attack Iwo Jima and Chichijima under Rear-Adm Clark on 4 and 5 Aug and in the operation the Japanese destroyer *Matsu* is sunk by gunfire from the destroyers *Ingersoll*, *Knapp* and *Cogswell*. On 4 Aug, off Chichijima, the transport *T-4* is sunk by aircraft of TG.58.1 and on 5 Aug *T-2* is sunk.

22–27 July   Indian Ocean
After the carriers *Victorious* and *Indomitable* arrive in Ceylon on 5 July, Operation 'Crimson' (carrier raid and bombardment of Sabang/Sumatra) is carried out. On 22 July the British Eastern Fleet (Adm Somerville) sets out from Trincomalee. Early on 25 July the carriers *Illustrious* (Rear-Adm Moody) and *Victorious*, escorted by the cruiser *Phoebe* and the destroyers *Roebuck* and *Raider*, fly off 34 Corsairs to attack the airfields round Sabang. Then the battleships *Queen Elizabeth* (Adm Somerville), *Valiant*, *Renown* (Vice-Adm Power) and *Richelieu* (French), the cruisers *Cumberland*, *Nigeria* (Rear-Adm Reid), *Kenya*, *Ceylon*, *Phoebe*, *Tromp* (RNethN) and *Gambia* (New Zealand) and the destroyers *Relentless*, *Rotherham*, *Racehorse*, *Rocket*, *Raider*, *Roebuck* and *Rapid*, come up to shell Sabang. They fire 294×15in, 134×8in, 324×6in, about 500×5in and 123×4in shells. After that *Tromp* and the destroyers *Quilliam* (Capt Onslow), *Quality* and *Quickmatch* (Australian) enter the harbour and fire eight torpedoes, 208×6in, 717×5in and 668×4in shells at close range. *Tromp* receives four hits and *Quilliam* and *Quality* one each from the coastal batteries. Thirteen Corsair fighters intercept a Japanese attack by 10 aircraft and shoot seven of them down, losing two of their own. The submarines *Templar* and *Tantivy* are employed for air–sea rescue.

In July, in the Straits of Malacca, off Sumatra and off W Thailand, the British submarine *Stratagem* (Lt Pelly) damages two small ships, *Spiteful* (Lt Sherwood) sinks one sailing vessel, *Sturdy* (Lt Andersen) sinks 10 small craft, *Porpoise* (Lt-Cdr Turner) lays a mine barrage in the Malacca Straits (on which one ship of 3029 tons, the submarine-chasers *Cha-8* and *Cha-9* and the auxiliary minesweeper *Wa-1* sink), *Spirit* (Lt Langridge) damages a tanker, *Tally Ho* (Cdr Bennington) sinks a sailing vessel and damages a steamer, *Stoic* (Lt Marriott) sinks two small steamers, *Telemachus* (Cdr King) sinks on 17 July the Japanese submarine *I-166*, *Sirdar* (Lt Spender) sinks two small vessels and *Storm*

(Lt Young) sinks one ship of 554 tons and three small vessels.

23–24 July   Air War/Germany
RAF Bomber Command raids on Kiel: 2748 tons of bombs dropped in 629 sorties. In the harbour *U239*, *U1164*, the MDS *Sperrbrecher 25*/*Ingrid Horn*, the U-boat depot ship *Erwin Wassner* and the freighter *Axel* (1540 tons) are sunk, the accommodation ship *General Osorio* (11590 tons) is burnt out and the damaged destroyer *Z39* is again hit.

24 July–1 Aug   Central Pacific
US TF.52 (Rear-Adm Hill) lands V Amphibious Corps (Maj-Gen Schmidt) on Tinian with support from army artillery from Saipan. 15614 troops of the 2nd and 4th Marine Divs (Maj-Gen Cates and Maj-Gen Watson) are landed by elements of TG.52.4 (see Saipan, 14 June) and by LSTs and smaller landing craft. Fire support is provided by TG.52.17 (Rear-Adm Oldendorf) and TG.52.10 (Rear-Adm Ainsworth—see 14 June) with the exception of a few ships and air support by TG.52.14 (Rear-Adm Bogan) and TG.52.11 (Rear-Adm Sallada—see 14 June). The Japanese defenders (elements of the 29th Inf Div, Col Ogata†) and Vice-Adm Kakuta† (1st Air Fleet) lose 6050 dead and 252 prisoners. US losses amount to 389 dead and 1816 wounded. In the shelling, the battleship *Colorado* and the destroyer *Norman Scott* are hit and damaged by a Japanese coastal battery.

25–27 July   Central Pacific
On 25 July, in a carrier air strike on Malakai (Palau), the Japanese minelayer *Sokuten* is sunk. The destroyer *Samidare* runs aground while evading the attack and is destroyed by the US submarine *Batfish*. On 27 July, in another strike, the Japanese transport *T-1* is sunk off Palau.

26 July–4 Aug   Arctic
Four submarines which are handed over by the Royal Navy to the Soviet Northern Fleet (to compensate for the share of the Italian war booty) proceed from Dundee to Murmansk under the command of Capt 1st Class Tripolski.

The first boat to set out, *V-1* (ex-*Sunfish*) (Capt 2nd Class Fisanovich), is sunk in error by Liberator 'V' of No 86 Sqn RAF on 27 July. The others, *V-2* (Capt Tripolski takes over because the commander is sick), *V-4* (Capt 3rd Class Iosseliani) and *V-3* (Capt 3rd Class Kabo), arrive between 2 and 4 Aug; they are the ex-*Unbroken*, ex-*Ursula* and ex-*Unison*.

27–31 July   South West Pacific
Operation 'Globe Trotter'. VII Amphibious Force (TF.77, Rear-Adm Fechteler),

which sets out on 27 July from Wakde with 11 destroyers, five APDs, eight LSTs, 16 LCIs, three LCI(R)s, four PCs and one ATF, lands the 6th US Div (Maj-Gen Sibert) E of Cape Sansapor off the offshore islands of Amsterdam and Middelburg on 30 July. The islands are occupied without opposition. On 31 July one BLT on landing craft with four destroyers and two PTs is landed near Sansapor W of the Cape. The operation is covered by TF.78 (Rear-Adm Berkey) comprising one heavy and two light cruisers and nine destroyers of TF.74 and TF.75. There is no coastal shelling before the landing.

28 July Baltic
The German U1166 is sunk at Eckernförde by an accidental torpedo explosion.

28–30 July Air War/Germany
In an RAF Bomber Command attack on Hamburg on 28–29 July, there are 307 sorties but 22 aircraft are lost. In a USAAF air raid on Bremen on 29 July, the torpedo boats T2 and T7 are sunk (they are later salvaged but repairs are never finished). The incomplete destroyer Z44 is sunk and the U-boats U872, U890 and U891 (the last pair fitting out) and damaged beyond repair. During another USAAF air raid on Hamburg on 30 July, the minesweeper M455 is sunk; she is later raised and repaired.

28–29 July Bay of Biscay
In an air attack on 28 July the auxiliary minesweeper M4457 is sunk off the Gironde estuary. On 29 July the patrol vessel V627 is sunk by aircraft gunfire 2 nautical miles of La Pallice.

30 July–1 Aug Baltic
The German 6th DD Flotilla, with the destroyers Z28, Z25, Z35 and Z36, transfers from Turku (Finland) to Riga preparatory to carrying out coastal bombardments in support of the Army.

31 July–1 Aug Arctic
The German battleship Tirpitz and the destroyers Z29, Z31, Z33, Z34 and Z38 sail from Altafjord for exercises in the Arctic Ocean.

31 July–2 Aug Air War/France
Two RAF Bomber Command daylight attacks are mounted on Le Havre, on 31 July with 57 aircraft and on 2 Aug with 54; one aircraft is lost. The German MTB S144 is sunk by bombs on 31 July.

Aug Mediterranean/Intelligence
German naval forces in the Aegean are allocated a separate cypher circuit, 'Athena', which is broken as 'Catfish'.

1–31 Aug Air War/Western Europe
The mine offensive by RAF Bomber

Command continues: in 25 nights, 418 sorties are flown against the Biscay and Brittany ports and during the nights 16–17, 26–27 and 29–30 Aug also against the Baltic area up to the Danzig Bight. Mosquitos lay mines in the Dortmund-Ems Canal. Eleven planes are lost.
The German auxiliary MS M4430 is sunk by mine off Le Havre and M3201 is sunk off Zeebrügge. The minesweeper M27 is sunk in the Gironde estuary on 11 Aug. U547 is damaged by mine in the Gironde but is able to continue her voyage to Germany; she is decommissioned at Stettin on 31 Dec. The minesweeper M444 is damaged by mine off Brest and sunk by air attack and the patrol vessel V605 is sunk off La Pallice on 14 Aug. The MMS R20 is sunk on a German mine off Sylt on 16 Aug. On 17–18 Aug the auxiliary MS M4207 is sunk in the Gironde and M304 and M363 are damaged. The old torpedo boat T155, wrecked by a mine off Greifswalder Oie on 21 Aug, is towed into Swinemünde but proves to be a total loss. On 19 Aug the MDS Sperrbrecher 104/Martha detonates nine mines in the Kaiserfahrt and the Stettiner Haff and on 25 Aug U1000 is damaged beyond repair in the Western Baltic and is later decommissioned at Kiel.

1–31 Aug Pacific
US submarines continue to operate to some extent in 'wolfpacks' against the convoys reported in 'Ultra' messages. The main targets are, again, oilers and destroyers or escorts. Off the Kuriles and Japan and in the Formosa area, Barbel (Lt-Cdr Keating) sinks four ships of 5463 tons, Pintado (Lt-Cdr Clarey) sinks two ships of 24663 tons and torpedoes the frigate Etorofu on 6 Aug, Croaker (Lt-Cdr Lee) sinks three ships of 8418 tons and on 7 Aug the cruiser Nagara, Sailfish (Lt-Cdr Ward) sinks three ships of 3602 tons and misses one destroyer, Greenling (Lt-Cdr Gerwick) sinks one trawler, Bowfin (Lt-Cdr Corbus) sinks three ships of 7196 tons and one trawler, Tang (Lt-Cdr O'Kane) sinks four ships of 6137 tons, Archerfish (Lt-Cdr Wright) sinks one picket boat, Ronquil (Lt-Cdr Monroe) sinks two ships of 10615 tons, Seal (Lt-Cdr Turner) sinks two ships of 6390 tons and on 8 Sept damages the destroyer Namikaze, Queenfish (Lt-Cdr Loughlin) sinks three ships of 14850 tons and on 9 Sept damages the torpedo boat Manazuru and Sealion (Lt-Cdr Reich) sinks two ships of 17834 tons and on 31 Aug the minelayer Shirataka. In company with Growler (Lt-Cdr Oakley) and Barb (Lt-Cdr Fluckey), Sealion also torpedoes one ship of 9181 tons. On 9 Sept Growler herself sinks the frigate Hirado and the destroyer Shi-

kinami; Barb sinks three ships of 15936 tons and on 16 Sept sinks the escort carrier Unyo. In the area of the Mandate Islands, Plunger has a miss and Batfish (Lt-Cdr Fyfe) sinks the minesweeper W22 on 23 Aug and the destroyer Samidare on 26 Aug.
In the area of the Malayan Archipelago and the Philippines, Puffer (Lt-Cdr Selby) sinks two ships of 5453 tons, damages one more of 4465 tons and together with Bluefish (Lt-Cdr Henderson) sinks one ship of 5135 tons; Bluefish alone sinks two ships of 29549 tons. Raton has a miss, Cero (Lt-Cdr Dissette) sinks one oiler of 14050 tons, Rasher (Lt-Cdr Munson) sinks four ships of 32667 tons and on 18 Aug the escort carrier Taiyo, Bluegill (Lt-Cdr Barr) sinks three ships of 6727 tons, one sailing vessel and on 13 Aug the submarine-chaser Ch-12 and Guitarro (Lt-Cdr Haskins) sinks four ships of 11236 tons, damages two of 886 tons and sinks on 7 Aug the frigate Kusagaki. Stingray (Lt-Cdr Loomis) sinks one trawler. Flier (Lt Cdr Crowley) is sunk on a mine in the Balabac Strait on 13 Aug. Cod (Lt-Cdr Atkins) sinks one ship of 708 tons and the landing ship T-129 on 14 Aug, Muskallunge (Lt-Cdr Russillo) sinks one ship of 7163 tons, Redfish (Lt-Cdr McGregor) sinks four ships of 30443 tons, Hardhead (Lt-Cdr McMaster) sinks on 18 Aug the cruiser Natori, Spadefish (Lt-Cdr Underwood) sinks six ships of 31542 tons and Haddo (Lt-Cdr Nimitz Jr) sinks three ships of 21013 tons, on 22 Aug the frigate Sado and on 23 Aug the destroyer Asakaze. On 22 Aug Harder (Cdr Dealey) sinks the frigates Hiburi and Matsuwa but is herself sunk on 24 Aug by Japanese minesweepers in Daval Bay (Luzon). Picuda (Lt-Cdr Donaho) sinks three ships of 9866 tons and on 25 Aug the destroyer Yunagi, Jack (Lt-Cdr Krapf) sinks one ship of 5785 tons and on 29 Aug the minesweeper W-28, Redfin (Lt-Cdr Austin) lays a mine barrage in the Api Pass (Sarawak) and sinks two small vessels and Guavina has a miss.

2 Aug Air War/Italy
The German transport KT 20 destroyed at Genoa during an air raid. The MMS RA257 (ex-Italian VAS 302) is beached after being damaged.

2–21 Aug English Channel
The British battleship Rodney shells the island of Alderney on 12 Aug, Warspite Brest on 25 Aug and Malaya the Ile de Cézembre off St-Malo on 1 Sept. The monitor Erebus shells Honfleur on 19 Sept. On 4 Aug the German gun carrier SAT-12/Glode is sunk by bombing off Walcheren. In St-Malo Roads the minesweeper M424 is damaged beyond repair in an air attack.

On 6 Aug the patrol vessel *V215* is scuttled at St-Malo.

In the area of the Channel Islands, *MTB717, MTB716, MTB720, MTB676* and *MTB677* have engagements on 5–6 Aug with German boats of the 46th MS Flotilla (Lt-Cdr Zimmermann) and the 2nd PB Flotilla (Capt Lensch). On 8–9 Aug, in an attempted attack on the boats of the two flotillas by the frigate *Maloy* with the US PT boats *PT503, PT500, PT507, PT508* and *PT509*, the last PT boat is sunk. The frigate *Borum* and *PT500* and *PT502* on 11–12 Aug and the destroyers *Onslaught* and *Saumarez*, the *Borum, PT505* and *PT498* and two British MTBs on 13–14 Aug have further engagements with the 24th MS Flotilla (Cdr* Breithaupt). In another engagement on 18–19 Aug *M432* is damaged.

In an air attack on Le Havre on 2 Aug, *S39, S114* and the tender *Planet* and four craft are sunk and *S79* and *S91* are badly damaged. In an engagement with three British MTBs off Le Havre the following night, *S180* and *S181* of the 2nd Flotilla are damaged by gunfire and *S167* and *MTB608* in collisions. The remaining operational boats of the 2nd and 6th Flotillas, *S174, S176, S177* and *S97, S132* and *S135*, undertake operations from Le Havre in the following nights in which the long-range T3D 'Dackel' torpedoes are used for the first time. On 4–5 Aug 24, on 5–6 Aug 12, on 6–7 Aug 12, on 8–9 Aug 10, on 9–10 Aug 11 and on 14–15 Aug eight 'Dackels' are fired at shipping concentrations in Seine Bay. The freighter *Iddesleigh* (5208 tons) is damaged, as are the cruiser *Frobisher*, the repair ship *Albatross* and one minesweeper. Apart from the first night, three boats are used with 'Dackels' and two to three as torpedo carriers. In addition, normal torpedo operations are carried out during the nights 11–12 and 13–14 Aug. In these operations of the escort forces and of the 2nd Escort Division (Cdr* v Blanc), there are many engagements. On 5–6 Aug the motor torpedo boats are attacked off Le Havre by *MTB475, MTB476* and *MTB474*; and *S91* is damaged by a torpedo detonation. The 14th MMS Flotilla has an engagement off Cap d'Antifer with the frigates *Thornborough* and *Retalick*. During the night 6–7 Aug the B Group of the 15th PB Flotilla has an engagement off Fécamp with *Thornborough* and the US *PT510, PT512* and *PT514*. During the night 7–8 Aug *Retalick* with four PT boats attacks the 14th MMS Flotilla and *PT520* and *PT521* are damaged. During the night 8–9 Aug boats of the 15th PB Flotilla have an engagement with two British SGBs off Fécamp in which

V241 sinks. In the next two nights there are further engagements between the 14th MMS Flotilla and the 15th PB Flotilla and MTB groups.

On 11–12 Aug the 10th MTB Flotilla (Lt-Cdr Müller), with *S183, S184, S185, S186, S191* and *S192*, is transferred from Ostend to Ijmuiden. It carries out a mining operation off Orfordness during the night 13–14 Aug, in which there is an engagement with the destroyer *Walpole*. In another operation in the night 15–16 Aug the flotilla is driven off. During the night 12–13 Aug the 4th MMS Flotilla in a mining operation off Etaples and the 38th MMS Flotilla N of Cap de la Heve have engagements with MTB groups.

The 8th MTB Flotilla (Cdr Zymalkowski), with *S193, S194, S195, S196, S197, S198, S199* and *S701*, is transferred on 14–15 Aug from Rotterdam to Boulogne. During the night 17–18 Aug boats of the flotilla attack a convoy off Dover when there is an engagement with the destroyers *Walpole* and *Opportune* and *MTB433, MTB432, MTB359, MTB353* and *MTB363*; they torpedo a freighter. During the night 20–21 Aug the destroyers *Melbreak, Watchman* and *Forester* drive the 8th Flotilla away from a convoy off Beachy Head.

During the night 18–19 Aug there are engagements near Le Tréport and Cap d'Antifer between boats of the 36th MS Flotilla and the 14th MMS Flotilla and *Melbreak* and *MTB212, MTB208, MTB209* and *MTB210*, in which *R218* is torpedoed and sunk.

In the night of 19–20 Aug the A Group of the 38th MS Flotilla beats off attacks by *MGB321, MGB322, MTB473, MTB479* and *MTB474* off Cap de la Heve and the following night two motor minesweepers of the 14th MMS Flotilla and one submarine-chaser suffer damage in engagements with *MTB471, MTB476* and *MTB477* off Cap d'Antifer.

3–5 Aug   Black Sea
With German authorization, the small Turkish motor sailing ships *Morina, Bulbul* and *Mefkure* set out from Constanza to proceed towards the Bosphorus with 913 (according to other sources 1016) Jewish refugees. They are escorted by two Rumanian KFK submarine-chasers. Near the Rumanian-Bulgarian border, the submarine-chasers turn away and the sailing ships continue their journey alone. During the night 4–5 Aug the Soviet submarine *Shch-215* (Capt 3rd Class A I Strizhak), which is employed in the operational area off Burgas against German and Axis shipping to and from the Bosphorus, encounters

Mefkure and sinks her in a gun attack. Of the approximately 320 refugees on board, only five and the Turkish crew are rescued by *Bulbul* on the following morning. *Morina* arrives in the Bosphorus in the morning of 5 Aug and *Bulbul* puts into Igneada.

At the beginning of Aug the German U-boat *U18* (Lt Fleige) sinks a steamer and a motor gunboat off Poti and damages a patrol boat and another steamer.

3–6 Aug   North Sea
The German 'Kalahari' and 'Sambesi' minelaying operations take place in the Skagerrak on 3–4 and 5–6 Aug with the minelayers *Ostmark* and *Kaiser*, the destroyers *Karl Galster, Friedrich Ihn* and *Theodor Riedel*, the minesweepers *M425, M470* and *M406* and the MDS *Sperrbrecher 23*.

4 Aug   Air War/Germany
During an air attack on Hamburg, the auxiliary minesweeper *M5607* is sunk while undergoing repairs.

4 Aug   North Atlantic
The outgoing *U300*, on its way to Reykjavik, is damaged in an attack by Canso 'F' of No 162 Sqn RCAF flying escort for convoy UR.130.

5–11 Aug   Air War/France
Nos 9 and 617 Sqns RAF Bomber Command attack the U-boat pens in Brest (5 Aug), Lorient (6), La Pallice (9) and Bordeaux (11) with 12000lb 'Tallboy' bombs. Despite some hits, no U-boats are lost.

5 Aug–4 Sept   Bay of Biscay/Brittany
After the breakthrough by the 1st US Army near Avranches on 31 July–1 Aug, Brest, Lorient and St-Nazaire are encircled by elements of the 9th US Army from 7 to 13 Aug and Nantes is taken on 13 Aug. British task forces frequently make sorties into the Bay of Biscay. On 5 Aug a force consisting of the cruiser *Bellona* and the destroyers *Tartar, Ashanti, Haida* and *Iroquois* sinks the minesweepers *M263* and *M486*, the patrol boat *V414* and the coastal launch *Otto* (217 tons) from a German convoy N of the Ile d'Yeu near St-Nazaire. The escort *SG3* (ex-French *Sans Pareil*) is damaged and shot up on 6 Aug at Les Sables d'Olonne by Beaufighters of No 236 Sqn RAF. *Haida* is slightly damaged.

On 12 Aug the 12th SG, comprising the Canadian destroyers *Assiniboine, Qu'Appelle, Skeena* and *Restigouche* and the British destroyer *Albrighton*, sinks a force of three armed trawlers S of Brest and the cruiser *Diadem* with the destroyers *Onslow* and *Piorun* sinks *Sperrbrecher 7* (7078 tons) near La Rochelle. On 14–15 Aug, off Les Sables d'Olonne, the cruiser *Mauritius* and the destroyers *Ursa* and *Iroquois* (RCN) attack a German force consisting of the torpedo boat *T24*, the aircraft repair ship *Richthofen*, *Sperrbrecher 157*, *M275* and *M385*; *Sperrbrecher 157* is sunk and *M275* badly damaged. On 20 Aug the *Diadem* force attacks the Ile d'Yeu and on 22–23 Aug *Mauritius*, *Ursa* and *Iroquois* sink *V702*, *V717*, *V720*, *V729* and *V730* off Audierne. On 4 Sept the destroyer *Blyskawica* (Polish) lands a commando group on Les Sables d'Olonne.

As a result of Allied air attacks, *M422* is destroyed at St-Malo on 4 Aug and *Sperrbrecher 146/Havik* at La Pauillac is sunk the same day. *M133* and *M206* are sunk on 6 Aug, *M271*, *M325* and *V725* in Pauillac on 5 Aug and *M366*, *M367*, *M428* and *M438* at St-Nazaire on 8 Aug by Beaufighters of Nos 236 and 404 Sqns RAF. On 9 Aug, during an air raid on Brest, the German tanker *Spichern* (9323 tons) is heavily damaged and on 31 Aug she is scuttled as a blockship. On 12 Aug Mosquitos of Nos 235 and 248 Sqns RAF sink *M370* off Royan, while off Lorient the MDS *Sperrbrecher 134/Falke* is sunk. The MDS *Sperrbrecher 16/Tulane* is sunk on 10–11 Aug at La Pallice and the patrol vessel *V410* in the Gironde estuary and the auxiliary minesweeper *M4204* at La Pallice on 12 Aug; *Sperrbecher 6/Magdeburg* is sunk on 13 Aug off Royan and *Sperrbrecher 5/Schwanheim* on 14 Aug in the Royan Roads. On 12 Aug the destroyer *Z23* is damaged at La Pallice.

On 21 Aug 19 Mosquitos of RAF Coastal Command destroy *M292* in the Gironde estuary and other aircraft the destroyer *Z23* off La Pallice. *Z24* and the torpedo boat *T24* are destroyed off Le Verdon by British bombers on 24–25 Aug.

When the harbours are evacuated the following ships are scuttled: at Nantes on 10–11 Aug the passenger steamer *Lindau* (13761 tons), the tankers *Vierlande* (14715 tons), *Monsun* (8038 tons), *Antarktis* (10711 tons), *Passat* (8998 tons), *Wilhelm A Riedemann* (10326 tons; damaged by air attack on 2 Aug) and *Wangerland* (3481 tons), the freighters *Tenerife II* (6150 tons) and *Olinda* (6068 tons) and many smaller merchant ships, the warships *Sperrbrecher 20/Kolentè*, *V623*, *M384* and the incomplete torpedo boat *TA5* (ex-French *La Farouche*), the torpedo boats *TA1*, *TA2* and *TA6* (heavily damaged in earlier air raids, now blown up) and the tankers *La Mayenne* and *La Baise* (destroyed on the stocks); at Brest on 13 Aug the patrol vessel *V723* (sunk by gunfire); on 13/14 Aug at St-Malo the patrol vessel *V727* and the auxiliary minesweeper *M4612*; on 16 Aug on the Seine and in and near Paris

the motor minesweepers *R182*, *R213*, *R217*, *RA3*, *RA4*, *RA5*, *RA6*, *RA7* and *RA8*; at Bayonne on 21 Aug the patrol vessels *V401* and *V402*; at Rochefort on 23 Aug the minesweeper *M344*; at St-Nazaire on 25 Aug the MDS *Sperrbrecher 122/Cape Hadid*; at La Rochelle on 25 Aug the auxiliary minesweeper *M4202*; on the Gironde and in Bordeaux on 25–26 Aug 21 merchant ships of 70720 tons, the destroyer *Z37*, the U-boats *U178*, *U188* and *UIT21* (ex-Italian *Finzi*), the minesweepers *M262*, *M304*, *M363* and *M4631*, the MDS *Sperrbrecher 14/Bockenheim* and the patrol vessels *V404* and *V407*; and at Brest on 28 Aug the auxiliary minesweeper and the patrol boats *V221*, *V222*, *V223*, *V224*, *V225*, *V226* and *V227*.

5 Aug–30 Sept   Arctic

Operations by German U-boats along the Siberian sea route. *U957* (Lt Schaar), *U362* (Lt Franz) *U278* (Lt-Cdr Franze), *U711* (Lt-Cdr Lange), *U739* (Lt Mangold) and *U365* (Lt-Cdr Wedemeyer) set out for the Kara Sea. On 12 Aug *U365* attacks convoy BD.5 (Capt 1st Class Shmelev), which has set out from Archangel for Dikson on 8 Aug, and torpedoes the only steamer, *Marina Raskova* (5685 tons). Because the Russians first think that they have hit a mine, the minesweepers halt, with the result that *U365* is able to sink the former US minesweepers *T-118* and *T-114* and finish off *Marina Raskova*. Only *T-116* escapes. On 26 Aug *U957* sinks the survey ship *Nord*.

From 1 to 5 Sept *U425* (Lt Bentzien), *U992* (Lt Falke), *U956* (Lt Mohs), *U968* (Lt Westphalen), *U995* (Lt-Cdr Köhntopp) and *U636* (Lt Schendel) form the 'Dachs' group and lay mine barrages in the narrows and channels in the Pechora Sea: of the results nothing is so far known. In these operations, *U425* misses a freighter on 2 Sept.

After taking on oil from *U711* and *U957*, which are returning temporarily to refuel, the other three 'Greif' boats continue their operations. In an attempt to attack a Soviet group of steamers escorted by destroyers, minesweepers and trawler patrol ships near the Krakovka Island on 5 and 6 Sept *U739* misses a destroyer. *U278* does not come up and *U362* is sunk by depth charges from the minesweeper *T-116*. From 21 to 24 Sept the U-boats of the 'Greif' group try to attack the Soviet convoy VD-1 (four transports, one *Groza* patrol ship, two *Fugas* patrol ships, three ex-US minesweepers, one trawler patrol ship and, from 23 Sept, the destroyers *Dostoyny* and *Zhestki*) on the way from the Vilkitski Strait to Dikson. On 21 Sept six successive attacks by *U711* on escort vessels fail as a result of torpedo defects. On 22 Sept *U739* and *U957* each

unsuccessfully attack a steamer. On 23 Sept *U957* sinks the patrol ship *SKR-29/Brilliant* and *U711* again reports defects when attacking three minesweepers and two steamers. On 24 Sept *U739* sinks the minesweeper *T-120*. On 24 Sept the three U-boats land a party on the island of Sterligova, which knocks out the wireless station. The boats return by 4 Oct.

6–25 Aug   Air War/France

During USAAF air raids on Toulon on 6 Aug, the German U-boats *U471*, *U952* and *U969* and the raised ex-French destroyer *Mameluck* are sunk and *U967* is damaged. On 18 Aug the raised French battleship *Strasbourg* and the cruiser *La Galissonnière* are again sunk and on 19 Aug the unserviceable U-boats *U466* and *U967* are scuttled. On 21 Aug the only serviceable U-boat, *U230*, departs but runs aground and has to be blown up. On 23 Aug the torpedo boat *TA9* (ex-French *La Bombarde*) is hit by bombs and sinks. The incomplete torpedo boat *TA13* (ex-French *La Bayonnaise*) is scuttled on 25 Aug.

8–24 Aug   Indian Ocean

On 8 Aug the floating dock in Trincomalee collapses and sinks with the battleship *Valiant*, which is badly damaged. The same day, the battleship *Howe* joins the Eastern Fleet, whose commander, Adm Somerville, is succeeded by Adm Fraser on 23 Aug. At the end of Aug the 8th SM Flotilla with the submarines of the 'S' class is transferred to Fremantle (Australia) and the 2nd SM Flotilla arrives in Ceylon.

Operation 'Boomerang': at the end of Aug the US XX Bomber Command attacks NW Sumatra with B-29 Superfortresses from Trincomalee. The British Eastern Fleet provides air rescue cover on its way. At this point the Eastern Fleet consists of the battleships *Howe*, *Richelieu* and *Queen Elizabeth*, the battlecruiser *Renown*, the carriers *Indomitable*, *Victorious* and *Illustrious*, 11 cruisers and 32 destroyers. On 24 Aug Rear-Adm Moody makes a carrier raid on Padang (south-west Sumatra) with the carriers *Victorious* and *Indomitable*, escorted by the battleship *Howe*, two cruisers and five destroyers (Operation 'Banquet').

Of the British submarines in the Malacca Strait, *Truculent* (Lt Alexander) damages the minelayer *Hatsutaka* on 3 Aug, *Terrapin* (Lt-Cdr Martin) sinks two coasters, *Trenchant* (Cdr Hezlet) sinks three small vessels, *Sturdy* (Lt Andersen) sinks two small vessels, *Statesman* (Lt Bulkeley) sinks one ship of 1983 tons, *Tally Ho* (Cdr Bennington) sinks two small vessels, *Tudor* (Lt Porter) sinks a junk, *Strongbow* sinks three small ships and nine junks and *Tantalus* (Lt Mackenzie) sinks two coasters, one tug and two junks. The Dutch *Zwaardfish* (Lt Goossens) sinks four small craft.

On 22 Aug the British submarine *Spiteful* bombards oil tanks on Christmas Island.

9 Aug Mediterranean

The German torpedo boat *TA21* (ex-Italian *Insidioso*) is badly damaged off Cape Salvore, Istria, by aircraft gunfire. She is towed in but not repaired (see 5 Nov).

9–11 Aug Norway

A British carrier force comprising *Indefatigable*, *Trumpeter* and *Nabob* (Canadian), the cruisers *Kent* and *Devonshire* and the destroyers *Myngs*, *Vigilant*, *Verulam*, *Volage*, *Virago*, *Scourge* and the Canadian *Algonquin* and *Sioux* attacks on 10 Aug the German airfield at Gossen near Kristiansund North. Six Me 110s are destroyed and three steamers damaged. The German MMS *R89* is damaged by air attack off Lepsoe and sunk after an ammunition explosion.

9–14 Aug Mediterranean

Positioning of the landing forces and convoys for Operation 'Dragoon' ('Anvil'). On 9 Aug convoy SS.1 sets out from Naples; on 10 Aug AM.1 from Oran and TM.1 from Brindisi; on 11 Aug Spec.2 from Oran, SY.1 from Naples and the 'Delta' Support Force from Taranto; on 12 Aug convoy TF.1 from Brindisi and the Carrier Force from Malta, convoys SM.1 and SF.2 and the 'Sitka' Support Force from Naples; and on 13 Aug the 'Alpha' Support Force from Malta, the 'Camel' Support Force from Palermo and the convoys SF.1 and SM.2 from Naples. Apart from the destroyers and light craft belonging to these forces, the following are additionally deployed to escort the convoys: the US destroyers *Jouett*, *Benson*, *Niblack*, *Hilary P Jones*, *Charles F Hughes*, *Frankford*, *Carmick*, *Doyle*, *McCook*, *Baldwin*, *Harding*, *Satterlee* and *Thompson*, the French *Le Fortuné*, *Forbin*, *Simoun*, *Tempête* and *L'Alcyon*, the British 'Hunt' class *Aldenham*, *Beaufort*, *Belvoir*, *Whaddon*, *Blackmore*, *Eggesford*, *Lauderdale*, *Farndale*, *Atherstone*, *Brecon*, *Calpe*, *Catterick*, *Cleveland*, *Haydon*, *Bicester*, *Liddesdale*, *Oakley* and *Zetland* and the Greek *Pindos* and *Kriti*; the US DEs *Tatum*, *Haines*, *Marsh*, *Currier*, *Frederick C Davis* and *Herbert C Jones* and the French *Marocain*, *Tunisien*, *Hova*, *Algérien* and *Somali*; the British corvettes *Aubrietia* and *Columbine*; the French sloops *Commandant Dominé*, *La Moqueuse*, *Commandant Bory*, *La Gracieuse* and *Commandant Delage*; and six PMs and six YMSs.

10 Aug Mediterranean

The German MMS *RA260* (ex-Italian *VAS 312*) runs aground at Cape Mortula as a result of a navigational error.

10 Aug–29 Mar 1945 Indian Ocean

B-29 Superfortress bombers of the US 20th AF fly 162 successful sorties from Indian bases to drop 987 mines off Palembang, Singapore and Saigon, in Camranh Bay and the Yangtze, off Pakchan, Penang and Goh Sichang and in Phan Rang Bay. No aircraft are lost but 14 are unable to drop their mines.

11 Aug Baltic

The German MMS *R70* sinks on a Soviet mine off S Pukkio in the Gulf of Finland.

11–12 Aug Air War/France

The German minesweeper *M84* is sunk in drydock at Le Havre during an air attack

11 Aug–29 Oct North Atlantic

The U-boats *U548*, *U228*, *U993*, *U650*, *U190*, *U763*, *U437*, *U547*, *U534*, *U587*, *U853*, *U256*, *U260*, *U155*, *U382*, *U673* and *U267*, which are in the Biscay harbours and not completely operational and most of which are not equipped with schnorkels, are transferred to Norway. In setting out, only *U445* is lost in the Bay of Biscay, at the hands of the British DE *Louis*. *U534* shoots down a Wellington bomber of No 172 Sqn RAF. *U123* and *U129* scuttle themselves at Lorient on 19 Aug and *U178*, *U188* and *UIT21* at Bordeaux on 20 Aug; *U766* is non-operational and is decommissioned on 21 Aug at La Pallice. Of the boats which arrive at Bergen, *U92*, *U228*, *U437* and *U993* are lost in an RAF air attack on 4 Oct. On about 17 Sept the homebound *U855* is lost, probably to a mine SE of Iceland, as is the outbound *U865*, probably to a schnorkel accident. On 18 Sept *U1228* is damaged by Liberator 'R' of No 224 Sqn RAF and has to return, while the outgoing *U867* is sunk on 19 Sept by Liberator 'Q' of No 224 Sqn RAF. The returning *U763* is damaged on 24 Sept by Liberator 'A' of No 224 Sqn RAF.

12 Aug Norway

The German minesweeper *M468* is lost on a mine W of Namsos.

13 Aug North Sea

The German minesweeper *M383* is sunk by Beaufighters of No 254 Sqn RAF in a rocket attack off Spiekeroog. The patrol vessel *V1101* is sunk N of Langeooge in an air attack.

13 Aug Air War/Italy

In an air attack on Genoa, the German minelayer *Dietrich von Bern* (ex-Italian *Mazara*) is sunk.

15 Aug Mediterranean

Operation 'Dragoon': Allied forces comprising the 7th US Army (Lt-Gen Patch) with VI US Corps (Maj-Gen Truscott) and II French Corps (Gen de Lattre de Tassigny) land on the French Mediterranean coast between Cannes and Toulon. Deployed are the Western Task Force (Vice-Adm Hewitt) with headquarters group (flagship *Catoctin*, the destroyer *Plunkett* and six minesweepers) with diversionary groups West comprising the destroyer *Endicott*, four MLs, eight PTs and 12 ASRCs and East comprising the gunboats *Aphis* and *Scarab*, four MLs, four PTs and two FDSs.

After constant air attacks by 1300 land-based aircraft, the landings begin at first light: 396 troop transport aircraft land 5000 men of the 1st Airborne Group by parachute. TF.86 ('Sitka', Rear-Adm Davidson) with five LSIs, five APDs, 24 PTs, five AMs, four MLs and one buoylayer lands the 1st Special Force on the island of Levante. Fire support is provided by the battleship *Lorraine* (French), the cruisers *Augusta* (US, flagship), *Omaha* and *Cincinnati* (US) and *Dido* and *Sirius* (British) and the destroyers *Somers* and *Gleaves* (US), *Lookout* (British) and *Themistokles* (Greek). TF.84 ('Alpha', Rear-Adm Lowry on the US Coast Guard cutter *Duane*), with one LCI, one FDS, two APAs, two APs, three AKAs, 31 LSTs, 45 LCIs, 10 LCTs, 20 LCMs, two LCGs, two LCFs, 13 LCSs, two LCCs, 27 AMs, 10 YMSs, 10 PCs, 12 SCs and 11 tugs and salvage ships, lands the 3rd US Div (Maj-Gen Daniels) in the Baie de Cavalaire. Fire support (Rear-Adm Mansfield) is provided by the battleship *Ramillies*, the cruisers *Orion*, *Aurora*, *Ajax* and *Black Prince* (British), *Quincy* (US) and *Gloire* (French) and the destroyers *Livermore*, *Eberle*, *Kearny* and *Ericsson* (US) and *Terpsichore* and *Termagant* (British). TF.85 ('Delta', Rear-Adm Rodgers on the headquarters ship *Biscayne*), with six APs, two AKAs, one LSP, one LSI, one LSG, 23 LSTs, 34 LCIs, 52 LCTS, two LCGs, two LCFs, 12 LCSs, two LCM(R)s, nine LCMs, five LCCs, 52 LCVPs, one PC, five SCs, one FT, eight AMs, 10 tugs and salvage ships, lands the 45th US Inf Div (Maj-Gen Eagles) in the Baie de Bugnon. Fire support (Rear-Adm Bryant) is provided by the battleships *Texas* and *Nevada* (US), the cruisers *Philadelphia* (US) and *Montcalm* and *Georges Leygues* (French), the large destroyers *Le Fantasque*, *Le Terrible* and *Le Malin* (French) and the destroyers *Forrest*, *Ellyson*, *Rodman*, *Emmons*, *Fitch*, *Hambleton*, *Macomb* and *Hobson* (US). TF.87 ('Camel', Rear-Adm Lewis on the headquarters ship *Bayfield*), with two APAs, three APs, three AKAs, one LSI, one LSD, one LSF, 10 LSTs, 32 LCIs, 46 LCTs, 21

LCSs, two LCGs, four LCFs, seven LCCs, 10 LCMs, 32 LCVPs, six MLs, 11 PCs, 17 SCs, 16 AMs, 12 YMSs and 10 tugs and salvage ships, lands the 36th US Div (Maj-Gen Dahlquist) both sides of Rade d'Agay. Fire support (Rear-Adm Deyo) is provided by the battleship *Arkansas*, the cruisers *Tuscaloosa*, *Brooklyn* and *Marblehead* (US), *Argonaut* (British) and *Duguay Trouin* and *Emile Bertin* (French) and the destroyers *Parker*, *Kendrick*, *Mackenzie*, *McLanahan*, *Nields*, *Ordronaux*, *Woolsey*, *Ludlow*, *Boyle* and *Champlin* (US).

Air escort in the assault area is provided by TF.88 (Rear-Adm Troubridge) with TG 88.1, comprising the escort carriers *Khedive*, *Emperor*, *Searcher*, *Pursuer* and *Attacker* (24 fighters each), the cruisers *Royalist* and *Delhi* and the destroyers *Troubridge*, *Tuscan*, *Tyrian*, *Teazer*, *Tumult* and *Wheatland* (British) and *Navarinon* (Greek); and TG 88.2 (Rear-Adm Durgin), comprising the escort carriers *Tulagi* and *Kasaan Bay* (US) and *Hunter* and *Stalker* (British), the cruisers *Colombo* and *Caledon* (British) and the destroyers *Butler*, *Gherardi*, *Herndon*, *Murphy*, *Jeffers* and *Shubrick* (US). There are also six MLs and a total of 216 fighters.

The landing is successful at all points, most of the divisions being landed on the first day. Losses are slight: *LCI588*, *LCI590*, *YMS24*, *ML563*, *PT202*, *PT218* and *BYMS2022* are lost on mines and *LST282* to a glider bomb from a German aircraft.

On the afternoon of 15 Aug Prime Minister Churchill visits the landing fleet on board the destroyer *Kimberley*. By the evening of 17 Aug 86575 troops, 12250 vehicles and 46140 tons of supplies have been landed. By 2 Sept 190565 troops, 41534 vehicles and 219205 tons of supplies have been landed; and by 25 Sept the corresponding figures are 324069 troops, 68419 vehicles and 490237 tons of supplies.

A total of 881 assault vessels with 1370 landing boats on board are deployed.

15–17 Aug   Mediterranean
US destroyers patrol off the coast of Provence. On 15 Aug *Somers* sinks the corvette *UJ6081* (ex-Italian *Camoscio*) S of Port Cros near Toulon. A boarding party recovers charts and orders before the corvette sinks. The escort vessel *SG21* (ex-French *Amiral Sénès*) is also sunk; 99 survivors are rescued.

On 17 Aug the destroyer *Endicott* with the British gunboats *Aphis* and *Scarab* sink the corvette *UJ6082* (ex-Italian *Antilope*) and the A/S vessel *UJ6073* (ex-yacht *Kemed Allah*) in the Bay of Le Ciotat; 211 survivors are rescued.

15 Aug–6 Sept   Arctic
Convoy operation JW.59/RA.59A. On 15 Aug JW.59 sets out with 33 ships, one rescue ship and 11 US SC submarine-chasers for the Soviet Northern Fleet (Lend-Lease). An escort is provided by Vice-Adm Dalrymple-Hamilton on the escort carrier *Vindex* with the *Striker*, the cruiser *Jamaica* and the 20th and 22nd EGs with seven destroyers, four sloops, two frigates and five corvettes. The Russian transfer force (Adm Levchenko and Capt 1st Class Fokin), consisting of the battleship *Arkhangelsk* (ex-British *Royal Sovereign*) and the destroyers *Zharki*, *Zhivuchi*, *Zhyuchi*, *Zhestki*, *Derzki*, *Doblestny*, *Dostoyny* and *Deyatelny*, which sets out on 17 Aug, proceeds N of the convoy. The Home Fleet (Adm Moore) operates in two groups in order to make raids on *Tirpitz* lying in Kaafjord: Rear-Adm McGrigor with the carriers *Indefatigable*, *Formidable* and *Furious*, the battleship *Duke of York*, the cruisers *Devonshire* and *Berwick* and 14 destroyers, including *Myngs*, *Vigilant*, *Sioux*, *Algonquin* (Canadian), *Stord* (Norwegian), *Kempenfelt* and *Zambesi* and, in addition, the escort carriers *Trumpeter* and *Nabob* (Canadian) with the 5th EG (Cdr Macintyre) composed of the DEs *Bickerton*, *Aylmer*, *Bligh*, *Garlies*, *Keats* and *Kempthorne*.

On 20 Aug a Ju 88 of Luftflotte 5 reports a warship force E of Jan Mayen. Early on 21 Aug the convoy reaches the patrol line of the 'Trutz' group (*U344*, *U668*, *U394*, *U363* and *U997*). *U344* (Lt-Cdr Pietsch) unsuccessfully attacks the 22nd EG with two T-5s and then sinks the sloop *Kite* with a FAT salvo. As a result of her report, a patrol line is formed for 22 Aug from *U703* and *U354*, which have just set out, and *U365* and *U711* coming from the Kara Sea. The British fleet carriers have had to break off the first attempt to attack *Tirpitz* on 20 Aug because of the weather. On 22 Aug the approach of the Barracuda and Corsair squadrons is detected in time and they are intercepted by the barrage of the heavy guns and Me 109s of JG 5 which shoot down 11 aircraft in all. The ship, which is clouded in smoke, is not hit. In the afternoon of 22 Aug the outbound *U354* (Lt Sthamer) encounters the escort carrier group which is preparing to refuel the DEs and torpedoes *Nabob* with a FAT salvo and *Bickerton* (Cdr Macintyre) with a T-5. The latter is abandoned. A second attempt to attack *Nabob* is frustrated by the Avenger bombers which take off from the listing flight deck. The carrier is taken in tow but is not repaired. Near the convoy *U363*, *U668*, *U703*, *U394* and also *U997* (after repelling three Sword-

fish and Martlets from *Vindex* and *Striker* as a well as a Soviet Catalina of the 118th Reconnaissance Regt) are compelled to submerge and are driven off. On 23 Aug only *U394*, *U711* and *U365* can occupy the planned patrol line of the 'Trutz' group: the others are too far to the rear. *U394* gets an intermediate wave bearing on the talk of the escorts. *U363* and *U703* are forced underwater near the convoy and the other boats to the rear by the air escort and surface escorts. *U711* (Lt-Cdr Lange) fires a FAT salvo at *Arkhangelsk* and a T-5 at *Zharki* but the weapons detonate prematurely. Until 24 Aug the boats try in vain to advance against the air and sea escort. *U668* (Lt v Eickstädt), *U363* (Lt-Cdr Nees) and *U997* (Lt Lehmann) each miss escorts with two T-5s and *U354* is sunk by the sloops *Mermaid* and *Peacock*, the frigate *Loch Dunvegan* and the leader of the 20th EG, the destroyer *Keppel* (Cdr Tyson). Because the convoy reaches harbour on 25 Aug, the operation is broken off and the 'Trutz' group is moved to the Bear Island Passage to operate against RA.59A. But the attacks by *U711* on a destroyer group and a Soviet submarine, which turns up, have no success. *U344* is sunk by a Swordfish from *Vindex* with rockets. The fleet carriers make another attack on *Tirpitz* on 24 Aug in which two minor hits are obtained and a fourth and unsuccessful attack on 29 Aug. In all, 247 sorties are flown in these attacks.

RA.59A sets out on 28 Aug with nine steamers and the escort of JW.59. But neither German air reconnaissance nor the U-boats of the 'Trutz' group approach it. On 2 Sept *U394* is damaged by an aircraft from *Vindex* and is sunk by the destroyers *Keppel* and *Whitehall* and the sloops *Mermaid* and *Peacock*. On 6 Sept the convoy arrives in Loch Ewe.

15 Aug–2 Sept   Air War/France
RAF Bomber Command conducts daylight raids against the French ports in the Biscay area: Brest is attacked on 15 Aug (the auxiliary MS *M4001* is sunk), on 17 Aug (79 aircraft), on 18 Aug (*M4618* sunk), on 19 Aug (*M4023* sunk), on 24 Aug (53 aircraft; *M4004* and *M4040* sunk) and on 27 Aug (27 aircraft; freighter *Oakland*, to be rebuilt as a hospital ship, sunk). On 28 Aug there is an attack with aircraft in which the German MDS *Sperrbrecher 1/Saar* and *Sperrbrecher 135/Adolph Kirsten* are destroyed. On 2 Sept there is another attack with 67 aircraft, of which two are lost. La Pallice is attacked on 18 Aug with 23 aircraft and on 19 Aug with 52. In an air attack on 20 Aug on Les Sables d'Olonne, the auxiliary MS *M4214* and the patrol vessel *V409* are sunk; and in air

attacks on the Gironde, *V413* is sunk on 24 Aug and *V411* on 26 Aug.

16–17 Aug   Air War/Germany
RAF Bomber Command attacks Stettin with 461 aircraft (five ships of 5000 tons sunk and eight of 15000 tons damaged), and Kiel with 348 aircraft. Ten aircraft are lost.

16–31 Aug   Arctic
Soviet combined operation against German convoys off the polar coast. On 17 Aug there is a heavy Soviet air attack on Kirkenes; in spite of strong fighter defence by JG 5, two steamers of 3243 tons are destroyed. On 18 Aug a convoy of six steamers, with *M251*, *M252*, *M202*, *M154*, *M35*, *M31*, *K3*, *V6102*, *V6104*, *V6111*, *V6112*, *R160*, *R202*, *UJ1224*, *UJ1219*, *UJ1220*, *UJ1222* and *UJ1211*, is located by Soviet reconnaissance aircraft. Of the submarines *S-15*, *S-51*, *S-103* and *M-201*, which are deployed from their waiting positions, only *M-201* (Lt-Cdr Balin) is able to fire at midnight (when it is light) on 18–19 Aug and sinks *V6112* off Persfjord. Then the torpedo cutters (Capt 1st Class Kuzmin) are deployed.
Three TKAs lay mines S of Busse Sound (Lt Pavlov). An advance detachment of four TKAs (Lt-Cdr Reshetko) supports the attack of the main assault group consisting of five TKAs (Capt 3rd Class Korshunevich) by putting down smokescreens. Two TKAs (Lt-Cdr Efimov) reconnoitre by night as far as Persjord. In the attack on 19 Aug *V6102* is sunk by two hits and the steamer *Colmar* (3946 tons) by one hit from either *TKA-205* or *TKA-206*. *M202* and *M31* each sink a TKA, one of which is *TKA-203*. On 23 Aug Soviet air formations make heavy attacks on Vardö and Vadsö. When, in the process, a westbound convoy is located, the submarines *S-15*, *S-51* and *S-103*, which are in waiting positions, are deployed. The attack by *S-103* (Capt 3rd Class Nechaev) off Makkaur, in which E-torpedoes are used for the first time, fails and goes unnoticed. *S-15* (Lt-Cdr Vasilev) torpedoes the steamer *Dessau* with an E-torpedo off Nordkyn on 24 Aug. The steamer is part of a convoy of five ships with *M251*, *M252*, *M202*, *M154*, *M35*, *M31*, *K3*, *V6110*, *R160*, *R202*, *UJ1219*, *UJ1211*, *UJ1220*, *UJ1224* and *UJ1222*. *Dessau* (5983 tons) is taken in tow to Mehamn. On 28 Aug *S-103* misses an eastbound convoy escorted by *K3*.

17 Aug   Air War/Italy
In an USAAF air raid on Genoa, the corvette *UJ2223* (ex-Italian *Marangone*) is sunk.

17–19 Aug   Mediterranean
On 17 Aug the German torpedo boat *TA35* (ex-Italian *Giuseppe Dezza*) is badly

damaged after hitting a mine in the Fasana Channel; the boat is not repaired. On 19 Aug the German MTB *S57* is sunk after engaging British MTBs off Dubrovnik (Korcula).

18–19 Aug   Air War/Germany
RAF Bomber Command attack against Bremen with 288 aircraft, one of which is lost. The German MCMS *Sperrbrecher 152/Fauna* is sunk by bombs shortly before she is commissioned. Eighteen other vessels are sunk and many more damaged.

19 Aug   Black Sea
The German MTBs *S26* and *S40* are sunk and *S72* damaged in Soviet air attacks in the Sulina estuary.

20 Aug   Black Sea
Sixty-two bombers and 80 fighters and ground-attack aircraft of the Soviet Black Sea Fleet, after dropping smoke bombs to counter AA fire, attack the harbour at Constanza and sink the U-boat *U9*, the MTBs *S42*, *S52* and *S131*, the MMS *R37*, the Rumanian torpedo boat *Naluca* and many smaller vessels; the Rumanian destroyers *Regele Ferdinand* and *Marasesti*, the gunboat *Stihi*, the minelayer *Dacia*, the German U-boats *U18* and *U24* and the MTBs *S28*, *S45*, *S47*, *S49*, *S51* and other vessels are damaged. On 22 Aug the MTB *S148* is lost to a mine off Bugaz.

20–21 Aug   Baltic
The German 2nd TF, comprising the heavy cruiser *Prinz Eugen*, the destroyers *Z25*, *Z28*, *Z35* and *Z36* and the torpedo boats *T23* and *T28*, is deployed against Soviet forward troops who have broken through near Tukkum in the Gulf of Riga. With support from naval guns, land communications with Army Group North, which had been cut off, are restored.

20–22 Aug   Mediterranean
German vessels on the French south coast are scuttled: the incomplete *SG22* (ex-French *Enseigne Ballande*) at Port de Bouc on 20 Aug and *SG16* (ex-French *La Curieuse*), *SG24* (ex-French *Ampère*) and *SG25* (ex-French *Les Espargues*, incomplete) at Marseilles on 22 Aug.

20 Aug–21 Oct   Norway
Intensification of British attacks on German convoy traffic on the Norwegian west coast. On 20 and 22 Aug the submarine *Satyr* (Lt-Cdr Weston) attacks two German convoys off Skudesnes and Egeröy but the salvos explode on the cliffs (a frequent cause of reported 'successes' in Norway). On 11 and 13 Sept *Venturer* (Lt Launders) attacks two convoys off Lister and with her first torpedo sinks a steamer of 678 tons.
On 11 Sept RAF Beaufighters sink *M462*

from a force of four minesweepers off southwest Norway. On 12 Sept a British force consisting of the carriers *Furious* and *Trumpeter*, the cruiser *Kent* and destroyers makes a raid on shipping near Stadlandet. Carrier aircraft sink *V5307* and damage *V5309* and *V5105*, which are beached, and the steamer *Ostland* (5374 tons). On 19 Sept Beaufighters sink two small ships in Stavfjord. On 20 Sept the submarine *Sceptre* (Lt-Cdr McIntosh) sinks one ship of 1184 tons and *M132* off Egersund. Between 26 and 27 Sept *UJ1106* and then *UJ1715* and the steamers *Cläre Hugo Stinnes* and *Knute Nelson* (total 11044 tons) sink on a mine barrage laid by the French submarine *Rubis* in the Feiestein Channel.
On 8 Oct *MTB712*, *MTB722* and *MTB711* of the Norwegian 54th MTB Flotilla attack ships N of Floröy and drive the coaster *Freikoll* (236 tons) on to the beach. On 9 Oct Beaufighters attack a convoy near Egersund and sink *UJ1711* and one ship of 1953 tons; two ships of 4170 tons are damaged as well as the gunboat *K2*. On 14–15 Oct a British force comprising the cruiser *Euryalus*, the escort carriers *Trumpeter* and *Fencer* and the destroyers *Myngs*, *Volage*, *Serapis*, *Scorpion*, *Algonquin* (RCN) and *Sioux* (RCN) carries out an air-mining operation and air raids on German shipping routes off Norway near Frohavet. On 15 Oct *V1605* is sunk by aircraft and two steamers and *V5716* are damaged and driven on to the beach. On 17 Oct the patrol boat *V6801* falls victim to Beaufighters, as do on 21 Oct two steamers and on 23 Oct *V5506* off Hjeltefjord. A British force consisting of the carrier *Implacable*, the cruiser *Bellona* and the destroyers *Venus*, *Scourge*, *Savage*, *Verulam*, *Caprice*, *Zambesi*, *Cassandra* and *Cambrian* makes carrier attacks on Sörreisa and the airfield at Bardufoss. Reconnaissance aircraft photograph *Tirpitz* anchored near Tromsö. An attempted attack by the Norwegian *MTB688*, *MTB711* and *MTB653* on a convoy near Stavfjord is frustrated by *V5101* and *V5113*.
The submarine *Viking* (Lt Banner-Martin) sinks on 14 Oct one ship of 1286 tons from a convoy and *Sceptre* sinks on 20 and 21 Oct one steamer of 2207 tons and *UJ1111* from two convoys.

21 Aug   English Channel
The British corvette *Orchis* is beached after hitting a mine off Courseulles (Normandy); she is a total loss.

22 Aug   Mediterranean
The German MMS *RA255* (ex-Italian *VAS 304*) and *RA259* (ex-Italian *VAS 311*) are sunk in the Gulf of Genoa in an engagement with British units. The German MMS

RA251 (ex-Italian *VAS 306*) is sunk in the Golfe de Juan.

23–30 Aug Black Sea

Light units of the Soviet Danube Flotilla (Rear-Adm Gorshkov) support on 23–24 Aug the crossing of the Dniester/Liman by elements of the 46th Army and in the following days they enter the Danube Estuary. Of the units of the Black Sea Fleet, the submarines *S-31*, *S-33*, *Shch-215*, *M-62*, *M-111* and *M-113* are employed on the Rumanian-Bulgarian coast but they only make two unsuccessful attacks. Of the torpedo cutters employed, *TKA-221*, *TKA-223*, *TKA-227* and *TKA-233* have a short, indecisive engagement with two submarine-chasers E of Constanza on 22 Aug. Thirty torpedo cutters and six patrol cutters take part in the capture of Constanza on 30 Aug. Minesweepers are also transferred.

23–31 Aug English Channel

Evacuation of Le Havre. During the night 23–24 Aug the 15th PB Flotilla (Cdr Rall) moves from Le Havre to Dieppe with two trawlers, one submarine-chaser and 16 KFKs and two motor minesweepers with two more in tow. Off Cap d'Antifer and Fécamp the boats are first attacked by the frigate *Thornborough* (Lt Brown), the 'Hunt' destroyer *Talybont* (Lt Holdsworth) and the MTBs (Lt Marshall) *MTB695*, *MTB694* and *MTB692*, then by the frigate *Retalick* (Lt Brownrigg), the destroyer *Melbreak* (Lt Kirby) and the MTBs (Lt Forster) *MTB212*, *MTB208* and *MTB205*. *V716* and *R229* are damaged and *R219* is sunk by fighter bombers as she comes into harbour. During the night 24–25 Aug the 15th PB Flotilla and the 38th MS Flotilla (Cdr* Palmgren) move from Dieppe to Boulogne with five trawlers, 16 drifters and three MFKs and *R117* and *F840*. The 8th Gun Carrier Flotilla carries out a supply mission to Le Havre with some units. The German ships are successively attacked by the US PT boats (Lt Saltsman) *PT250*, *PT511* and *PT514*, the frigate *Seymour* (Lt-Cdr Parry) with the MTBs (Lt Shaw) *MTB257*, *MTB256*, *MTB254* and *MTB252*, an MTB group (Lt Yock) consisting of *MTB452*, *MTB447* and *MTB453* and, also, *Talybont*, *Retalick* and *MTB205*, *MTB209* and *MTB210*. In engagements *S91* from the boats of the 6th MTB Flotilla, deployed for cover, and *M3857*, sink. *V243* is damaged and *AF103* is lost on a mine. The destroyer *Bleasdale* is the last to intervene in the engagement. The 8th MTB Flotilla, which makes a sortie against a convoy off Beachy Head, is driven off by the SGBs *Grey Wolf* and *Grey Goose*. During the night 25–26 Aug the 8th Gun Carrier Flotilla (Lt Sch-

neider) is attacked near Fécamp by *Thornborough* with an MTB group (Lt Dixon) comprising *MTB450*, *MTB481* and *MTB482*, the French destroyer *La Combattante* (Cdr Patou) with an MTB group (Lt Shaw) comprising *MTB253*, *MTB257* and *MTB254* and *Seymour* with a US PT group comprising *PT519*, *PT513* and *PT516*. *AF110*, *AF97*, *AF105* and *AF111* are lost; *AF101* and *AF109* are brought in, the latter towed by *S174*. The following night, *Retalick* with *MTB208* and *MTB210* and *Middleton* (Lt Cox) with *MTB252*, *MTB256*, *PT520*, *PT511* and *PT514* again attack boats of the 8th Gun Carrier Flotilla and the 14th MMS Flotilla. *AF13*, *AF98* and *AF108* are sunk. During the night 27–28 Aug the 14th MMS Flotilla (Lt-Cdr Nordt) with seven boats sows mines in the Seine estuary near Le Havre and proceeds with two submarine-chasers to Fécamp. Off Cap d'Antifer there are engagements with *Thornborough*, *MTB450*, *MTB447*, *MTB482* and *La Combattante*, with *MTB693*, *MTB692* and *MTB695* and *PT519* and *PT512*. *UJ1433/KUJ9* is sunk and *R231* is towed in damaged.

During the night 29–30 Aug nine motor minesweepers, six AFs, one MFL, one KFK, one submarine-chaser and one tug move from Le Havre to Fécamp. Cover is provided by boats of the 8th MTB Flotilla. Attacks by *Retalick* and the 'Hunt' destroyer *Cattistock* (Lt Keddie†) are beaten off; the latter is damaged. During the following two nights the remaining operational boats of the 2nd Escort Division (Cdr* v Blanc) are moved from Dieppe, Boulogne and Calais through the Straits of Dover to the E. On 3–4 Sept the last 13 operational motor torpedo boats are moved from the Channel area to Rotterdam and Ijmuiden: in the process *S184* is sunk by the Dover batteries. After shelling by the battleship *Warspite* and the monitor *Erebus* (the coastal guns secure two hits) on 5 and 8 Sept, there is a heavy air attack by the RAF on 11 Sept in which 807 tons of bombs are dropped. Le Havre surrenders on 12 Sept.

23 Aug–7 Oct North Atlantic

Schonorkel U-boats are employed in coastal waters. *U680* and then *U1199* (Lt Nollmann), which remains under water for 50 days, operate off the Scottish east coast. Each fires a torpedo which misses. *U482*, *U484*, *U743*, *U398*, *U296*, *U285*, *U963*, *U985*, *U953*, *U281* and *U1004* are employed in the Minches, off the Hebrides and in the North Channel for six to twelve days at a time. *U248* and *U309* have to return before they reach the North Channel because of the strong defence. From 27 Aug to 8 Sept

U482 (Lt-Cdr Count v Matuschka) attacks five convoys and sinks a tanker and the corvette *Hurst Castle* from CU.36, one ship from ONS.251 and two ships from HX.305, totalling 31611 tons. On 9 Sept, while attempting to attack convoys, *U743* is sunk near ONF.252 by the corvette *Portchester Castle* and the frigate *Helmsdale* and *U484* by the Canadian frigates *Dunver* and *Nene* and the corvettes *Hespeler* and *Huntsville* of EG.C5. The other boats return, having achieved no success. On her way into the Bristol Channel, *U247* is sunk on 1 Sept by the Canadian frigates *St John* and *Swansea* of the 9th SG. *U758*, *U262* and *U714* return without success. Off Reykjavik on 22–23 Sept, *U244* and *U979* (Lt-Cdr Meermeier) attack convoys. The latter torpedoes a ship of 5970 tons. *U772* and *U245* are stationed as weather boats in the North Atlantic.

24 Aug Air War/Netherlands

Daylight attack by No 5 Group RAF Bomber Command against the E-boat pens at Ijmuiden: the patrol vessel *V1401* and the gun ferry *AF41* are sunk (the latter is later raised and recommissioned).

24 Aug–11 Sept Black Sea

In evacuating the harbour at Constanza on 24–25 Aug, the Germans scuttle the non-operational warships, including the U-boats *U18* and *U24*, the MTBs *S28*, *S49*, *S72* and *S149* and the A/S vessels *KT39*, *UJ115/Rosita*, *UJ301* and *UJ302*. *UJ105* is lost on a mine off Varna on 25 Aug and on 26 Aug, off Kaliakra, the A/S vessels *UJ101*, *UJ102*, *UJ103/KT37*, *UJ107/KT34*, *UJ116/Xanten* and *UJ118/F368* are scuttled.

On 29–30 Aug the warships remaining in the Rumanian-Bulgarian theatre are scuttled off Varna outside Bulgarian territorial waters. Among the approximately 200 craft are the MTBs *S45*, *S47* and *S51*, the MMSs *R163*, *R164*, *R165*, *R166*, *R196*, *R197*, *R203*, *R205*, *R206*, *R207*, *R209*, *R216* and *R248*, the A/S vessels *UJ105/KT24*, *UJ2301* and *UJ2305*, the gun ferries *AF51*, *AF52*, *AF53*, *AF54* and *AF55* and ferry barges. Some of the units in the Sulina area together with vessels of the Danube flotilla, particularly ferry barges, go up the Danube under the command of Rear Admiral Zieb. The last three German U-boats in the Black Sea, *U19*, *U20* and *U23*, operate from 25 Aug in the area off Constanza. *U23* (Lt Arendt) fires a salvo into the harbour at Constanza on 1 Sept, when the damaged freighter *Oituz* (2686 tons) is hit (she is not repaired). On 2 Sept *U19* (Lt Ohlenburg) sinks the Soviet minesweeper *T-410/Vrzyv* off Constanza. When their fuel is used up, and an offer to sell them to Turkey has been rejected, the three U-boats are scuttled by their own crews near Erekli on the Turkish coast on 10 Sept.

25 Aug   North Sea
The German minesweeper *M347* is sunk by rocket fire from RAF Beaufighters off Hubert-Gat.

25–26 Aug   English Channel
The German patrol vessel *V2009* is sunk by torpedo during an attack by British MTBs off the Scheldt.

25 Aug–10 Sept   English Channel
The British battleship *Warspite* bombards Brest on 25 Aug. On 1 Sept the battleship *Malaya* bombards the German batteries on Cezembre Island off St-Malo. On 10 Sept *Warspite* and the monitor *Erebus* bombard Le Havre.

26–30 Aug   Air War/Germany
On 26–27 Aug Nos 1, 3 and 5 Groups RAF Bomber Command attack Kiel with 382 aircraft, 17 of which are shot down. The German minesweeper *M266* is sunk but later raised and repaired. In a second attack, No 5 Group sends 174 aircraft to raid Königsberg; four aircraft are lost. On 28 Aug, during a USAAF air attack on Bremen, the German MCMS *Sperrbrecher 8/Neckar* is destroyed. On 29–30 Aug Nos 1, 3, 6 (RCAF) and 8 Groups attack Stettin with 402 bombers; 23 are lost. The MMS *R193* and one merchant ship are sunk and seven merchant vessels are damaged. During a daylight raid on Kiel the liner *St Louis* is hit and burnt out.

27 Aug   English Channel
RAF Tactical Air Force Typhoons attack the British 1st Minesweeping Flotilla after being assured that there are no friendly forces in the area. The minesweepers *Britomart* and *Hussar* are sunk, *Salamander* damaged beyond repair and *Jason* and the trawler *Colsay* damaged.

28 Aug   Baltic
The German gun ferries *AF35* and *AF50* sink after hitting a mine off Kiuskeri (Viborg Bay).

28 Aug   Mediterranean
Marseille is evacuated by the Germans, who scuttle *M6062/SG12* and *M6063/SG13*.

28–29 Aug   North Sea
The German minelayer *Kaiser* lays the 'Skagerrak XXX' barrage using a new type of LMB mine.

28 Aug–24 Sept   Central Pacific
Carrier TF.38 (Vice-Adm Mitscher) sets out from Eniwetok on 28 Aug to make raids in connection with the Palau-Morotai operation. Taking part are TG. 38.1 (Rear-Adm McCain), comprising the carriers *Wasp*, *Hornet*, *Cowpens* and *Belleau Wood*, the cruisers *Wichita*, *Boston* and *Canberra* and H

destroyers; TG.38.2 (Rear-Adm Bogan), comprising the carriers *Bunker Hill*, *Intrepid*, *Cabot* and *Independence*, the battleships *Iowa* and *New Jersey* (Adm Halsey, Commander 3rd Fleet), the cruisers *Vincennes*, *Houston* and *Miami* and 18 destroyers; TG.38.3 (Rear-Adm Sherman), comprising the carriers *Lexington*, *Essex*, *Princeton* and *Langley*, the battleships *Washington*, *Indiana*, *Massachusetts* and *Alabama*, the cruisers *Santa Fé*, *Birmingham*, *Mobile* and *Reno* and 18 destroyers; and TG.38.4 (Rear-Adm Davison), comprising the carriers *Franklin*, *Enterprise* and *San Jacinto*, the cruisers *New Orleans* and *Biloxi* and 13 destroyers.

On 31 Aug, 1 Sept and 2 Sept TG.38.4 attacks Iwo Jima and Chichijima and on 1 and 2 Sept the cruisers and destroyers shell the islands. On 3 Sept TG.12.5 (Rear-Adm Smith), with the cruisers *Chester*, *Pensacola* and *Salt Lake City* and the destroyers *Dunlap*, *Fanning* and *Reid*, shells Wake. Air escort is provided by the carrier *Monterey*. On 6, 7 and 8 Sept all four task groups attack Palau with 16 carriers. On 9 and 10 Sept TG.38.1, 38.2 and 38.3 attack airfields on Mindanao with 12 carriers against very little resistance. From 12 to 14 Sept the weight of the attacks is therefore shifted to the area of the Visayas (Central Philippines). TG.38.1 attacks Mindanao again on 14 Sept and the Japanese fast transport *T-5* is sunk. In 2400 sorties over these three days more than 200 aircraft are destroyed. After replenishing, the 12 carriers make attacks on airfields on Luzon on 21 and 22 Sept, particularly in the area of Manila, and again on the Visayas on 24 Sept. On 21 Sept the destroyer *Satsuki* and the corvette *Kaibokan 5* are sunk, as are on 24 Sept the minelayer *Yaeyama*, the torpedo boat *Hayabusa* and the seaplane tender *Akitsushima*.

In these attacks over 1000 Japanese aircraft, in all, are destroyed and 150 ships of all sizes are sunk and destroyed. The Americans lose 54 aircraft in combat and 18 as a result of accidents. Adm Halsey proposes to cancel the Mindanao landing, planned for 20 Oct, and to land on Leyte on this date.

29–30 Aug   English Channel/ North Sea
The German auxiliary MS *M3600* is sunk by air attack off Berc-sur-Mer and the MDS *Sperrbrecher 176/Valeria* sunk by aerial torpedo off the Elbe. On 30 Aug the MDS *Sperrbrecher 26/Mostrand* is sunk by bombs and torpedoes during an RAF air attack on the Elbe Roads.

1 Sept   Arctic
The US Coast Guard cutter *Northland* finds

the weather observation ship *Kehdingen* when trying to establish a weather station on the ice on the east coast of Greenland. The escorting U-boat, *U703*, fires torpedoes but they explode in the ice.

1–2 Sept   Baltic
The German MTB *S80* is sunk on 1 Sept by a Soviet mine off Viborg. On 2 Sept the auxiliary minesweeper *M3144/K358* is sunk in Vergi harbour in a Soviet air attack.

1–13 Sept   Mediterranean
The Italian Adriatic coast in the area of Rimini is shelled by the British destroyers *Undine*, *Urchin*, *Loyal* and *Kimberley* and the gunboats *Aphis* and *Scarab*. The French Riviera coast is shelled by the US cruiser *Philadelphia* and the destroyers *Woolsey*, *Edison*, *Ludlow*, *Hilary P Jones* and *Madison*, the French battleship *Lorraine*, the cruisers *Montcalm*, *Emile Bertin*, *Duguay Trouin* and *Gloire* and the destroyers *Le Malin* and *Forbin*.

1–30 Sept   Pacific
US submarines continue their operations with the help of 'Ultra' information. Off the Kuriles, off Japan, in the Yellow Sea and around the Ryukyus and Formosa, *Pipefish* (Lt-Cdr Deragon) sinks two ships of 4056 tons, *Guardfish* (Lt-Cdr Ward) sinks one ship of 873 tons and damages one of 245 tons, *Searaven* (Lt-Cdr Dry) sinks one ship of 4850 tons and four trawlers and sailing vessels and damages the destroyer *Momi* on 26 Sept, *Albacore* (Lt-Cdr Blanchard) sinks two ships of 1078 tons and on 11 Sept the auxiliary submarine-chaser *Cha-165*, *Hake* (Lt-Cdr Broach) damages the destroyer *Hibiki* on 6 Sept off the Ryukyus, *Plaice* (Lt-Cdr Stevens) sinks the corvette *Kaibokan 10* on 27 Sept, *Bang* (Lt-Cdr Gallagher) sinks the corvette *Kaibokan 30* on 19 Sept, *Sunfish* (Lt-Cdr Shelby) sinks two ships of 11634 tons and damages the submarine-chaser *Cha-91*, *Finback* (Lt-Cdr Williams) sinks two ships of 1402 tons, *Apogon* (Lt-Cdr House) sinks one ship of 1999 tons and one trawler; *Skate* (Lt-Cdr Lynch) sinks two ships of 3909 tons, *Thresher* (Lt-Cdr Middleton) sinks four ships of 9278 tons, *Sea Devil* (Lt-Cdr Styles) sinks the transport submarine *I-364* on 19 Sept, *Shad* (Lt-Cdr Julihn) sinks one ship of 304 tons and on 19 Sept the cruiser *Ioshima* (ex-Chinese *Ning Hai*), *Scabbardfish* (Lt-Cdr Gunn) torpedoes the submarine depot ship *Jingei* on 19 Sept, *Tilefish* (Cdr Keithley) sinks one sailing vessel and *Barbel* (Lt-Cdr Keating) sinks one ship of 1223 tons.

In the area of the Malayan Archipelago and off the Philippines, *Paddle* (Lt-Cdr Nowell) sinks two ships of 7695 tons, *Bashaw* (Lt-Cdr Nicholas) sinks one ship of 2813 tons and damages one of 632 tons, *Pargo* (Lt-

Cdr Bell) lays a minefield in the Koti Passage (Natuna Island), sinks one ship of 599 tons and on 26 Sept sinks the minelayer *Aotaka*, *Haddo* (Lt-Cdr Nimitz) sinks the minelayer *Katsuriki*, *Pampanito* (Lt-Cdr Summers) sinks two ships of 15644 tons, *Guavina* (Lt-Cdr Teideman) sinks the fast transport *T-3*, *Flasher* (Lt-Cdr Whitaker) and *Lapon* (Lt-Cdr Baer) together sink two ships of 12895 tons (*Flasher* alone sinks two more of 12236 tons and *Lapon* alone three of 14577 tons), *Bonefish* (Lt-Cdr Edge) sinks two ships of 4632 tons and torpedoes the sea-plane carrier *Kamoi* on 27 Sept off Manila, *Aspro* (Lt-Cdr Stevenson) sinks one ship of 6886 tons and together with *Hoe* (Lt-Cdr McCrea) one more of 4026 tons and *Seawolf* is sunk by error on 3 Oct (see 15 Sept).

2–21 Sept   Baltic
On 2 Sept the Finnish Prime Minister Hackzell announces the breaking-off of diplomatic relations with Germany and demands the withdrawal of German troops from Finland. On 4 Sept the Finnish armed forces stop fighting on the whole front against the Soviet Union. From 4 to 21 Sept the following are removed by sea from Finnish Baltic harbours: 4049 German troops, 3336 wounded, 332 evacuees, 746 vehicles and 42144 tons of Wehrmacht property. 13064 tons of this is lost because of the defection of Finnish ships in Finnish or Swedish harbours. 110000 tons of Wehrmacht property has to be destroyed on the spot because it is no longer possible to get it away in time. The 3rd TB Flotilla (Cdr Verlohr) makes a reconnaissance sortie with *T18*, *T13* and *T20* to the Åland Sea as a show of force. On the return *T18* is destroyed by Soviet bombers N of Tallinn (Reval).

On 27 Sept Sweden closes her Baltic ports to German ships.

2 Sept   English Channel
The German gun ferry *AF70* is torpedoed and sunk in an engagement with British MTBs off Cape Griz Nez.

4–5 Sept   Air War/Italy
In a USAAF air raid on Genoa, 438 tons of bombs are dropped on harbour installations. The torpedo boat *TA28* (ex-Italian *Rigel*) capsizes in dock; the almost complete destroyer *TA33* (ex-Italian *Corsaro II*) and the corvette *UJ6085* (ex-Italian *Renna*) are sunk. The ex-Italian submarines *Ambra*, *UIT15* (ex-*Sparide*), *UIT16* (ex-*Murena*) and *UIT20* (ex-*Grongo*), fitting out for the German Navy, are destroyed. Many other vessels, including the German hospital ship *Er-langen*, are damaged. On 5 Sept the MMS *RA261* (ex-Italian *VAS 236*) is sunk

and the escort *SG15* (ex-French *Rageot de la Touche*) badly damaged.

4–6 Sept   Baltic
The German destroyer *Z25* makes a sortie into the Gulf of Finland to intercept Finnish vessels trying to escape to Sweden. The steamer *Najaden* is captured NW of Dagö.

5 Sept   Mediterranean
The German MMS *R12* sinks on a mine in the northern Adriatic.

5 Sept   Danube
Of the German Danube flotilla trying to move up-river, the A/S vessels *UJ106* and *UJ110* are scuttled at Prahovo.

5–11 Sept   Air War/France
Heavy daylight raids by Nos 1, 3, 5, 6 and 8 Groups RAF Bomber Command on the defences around Le Havre and the city itself: on 5 Sept with 348 aircraft, on 6 Sept with 344, on 8 Sept with 333, on 9 Sept with 272 (cancelled owing to weather), on 10 Sept with 992 and on 11 Sept with 218. Two aircraft are lost.

5–12 Sept   North Sea
On their way from Antwerp to Holland, the minesweepers *M274* and *M276* and the auxiliary minesweeper *M3631* are scuttled by their crews in the Scheldt Estuary on 5 Sept.

On 6 Sept 26 Beaufighters attack a German convoy NE of Wangerooge and sink the Swedish freighter *Rosafred* (1348 tons).

On 12 Sept British fighter-bombers attack a German convoy anchored in the roads of Den Helder.

5–30 Sept   Mediterranean
First attempt on 5 Sept to attack a French destroyer by five 'Marder' one-man torpedoes fails off San Remo. A second attack on 9–10 Sept with 14 'Marders' also fails. On 25 Sept there is a sortie by nine 'Molch' midget submarines; seven fail to return. On 30 Sept the only sortie by a 'Linsen' is made from Corsini but it is unsuccessful.

6 Sept   Baltic
The German *U1054* is damaged beyond repair following a collision with a hospital ship off Hela. The submarine is decommissioned at Kiel.

6 Sept   Air War/Germany
RAF Bomber Command attack by Nos 6 (RCAF) and 8 Groups on Emden with 181 aircraft (one of which is lost). The German MDS *Sperrbrecher 185/Hansburg* is badly damaged (it is destroyed while under repair in a subsequent attack on Wilhelmshaven).

6 Sept   Norway
The German MMS *R304* is sunk by mine off Egeröy.

6–19 Sept   Air War/Germany
On 6 Sept RAF Bomber Command drops 580 tons of bombs on Emden and on 15–16

Sept 490 bombers drop 1448 tons of bombs on Kiel. On 18–19 Sept No 5 Group RAF Bomber Command attacks Bremerhaven with 213 aircraft (two are lost).

6–19 Sept   Air War/W Europe
Mine offensive by RAF Bomber Command. In six nights, 159 sorties are flown against the Texel area, the Ems, the Weser and Elbe rivers, the Oslo area and the Kattegat. Four aircraft are lost.

The German catapult ship *Westfalen* sinks after hitting two mines in the Skagerrak. On 17 Sept the patrol vessels *V1201* and *V1202* are damaged by mines in the Heligoland area and then attacked and sunk in Mosquito sorties against assumed minesweeping forces on 17 Sept. On 26 Sept the patrol vessel *V6719* is sunk off Swinemünde and on 27 Sept the patrol vessel *V1214* is sunk off List (Sylt).

7 Sept–9 Jan   Baltic
After the loss of the Finnish harbours the German U-boats (operations leader Cdr Brandi) operate from Danzig and Goten-hafen off the entrances to the Gulf of Finland. In Sept and Oct *U717*, *U958*, *U370*, *U348*, *U475*, *U290*, *U1165* and *U481* take part. On 21 Sept *U242* and *U1001* lay mine barrages near Porkkala, on which the Finnish steamer *Rigel* (1495 tons) sinks. On 8–9 Oct *U370* sinks a motor gunboat and the Finnish tug *No 764*. *U481* (Lt Andersen) sinks three Finnish sailing ships on 15 Oct. *U1165* (Lt Homann) sinks one motor mine-sweeper and attacks a submarine convoy. *U958* (Lt-Cdr Groth) sinks two Finnish sailing ships. *U1001* (Lt Blaudow) tor-pedoes a tug on 25 Oct and *U475* (Lt-Cdr Stöffler) sinks a patrol boat. In Nov until the beginning of Dec *U475*, *U958*, *U479*, *U481*, *U679* and *U1165* are employed in the Gulf of Bothnia and in the Hangö-Tallinn area. *U679* (Lt Aust) sinks a patrol boat and the minesweeper *T-217* and is lost on 9 Jan as a result of being depth-charged by the patrol boat *MO-124*. *U481* sinks a lighter and, probably, the Finnish minelayer *Louhi*. *U637* (Lt-Cdr Riekeberg), which sets out at the end of Nov, sinks a patrol boat. *U479* is lost in late Nov on a mine laid by the Russian submarine *Lembit*.

8 Sept   English Channel
The German MMS *R235* is sunk while being transferred from Belgium to the Netherlands.

8 Sept   Air War/Mediterranean
British Beaufighters set the Italian pass-enger ship *Rex* (51062 tons) on fire in Trieste.

8–25 Sept   North Atlantic
On about 8 Sept, the outgoing *U925* is lost (cause unknown) in the area between

Iceland and the Faeroes. On about 25 Sept *U703* is lost while setting out a weather buoy in heavy seas E of Iceland.

9 Sept Norway

The German auxiliary MS *M5631/K303* is sunk by mine in Romsdalfjord.

9 Sept Mediterranean

The German A/S vessel *UJ2142* is sunk by air attack N of Crete.

10–12 Sept English Channel/ North Sea

On 10 Sept the German gun ferries *AF43* and *AF48* are sunk by air attack off Hoedekerskerke and on 11 Sept the German MMS *R80* is sunk by air attack at Hoofdplaat. On 12 Sept, during her transfer from her Dutch building yard to Germany, the unfinished torpedo boat *T61* is beached after being hit by an aerial torpedo near Den Helder.

10–28 Sept Arctic

Combined Russian operation against German convoy traffic on the Norwegian polar coast. Deployment of submarines *S-15*, *S-51*, *S-103*, *S-101* and *V-3* (using radar for the first time). On 14 and 15 Sept Russian ground-attack aircraft and fighter-bombers make attacks on Vardö and on Kiberg and Kongsfjord. The naval ferry barge *F223* and *UJ1224/KUJ10* are sunk. On 15 Sept an attack by four Russian torpedo cutters (Lt-Cdr Lozovski) and 15 Il-2 ground-attack aircraft on a German Petsamo–Kirkenes convoy is repulsed by the German escort: *TKA-214* claims one hit but *TKA-13* is sunk by the 61st PB Flotilla (Cdr Kramer). On 16 Sept, in an air attack on Kirkenes, the ammunition steamer *Wolsum* (3668 tons) explodes. On 20 Sept, in an attack by a torpedo aircraft group off the North Cape, the catapult ship *Friesenland* (5434 tons) receives a hit and has to be beached. On 21 Sept Russian aircraft sink their own submarine *Shch-402* in error. On 24 Sept a convoy located by air reconnaissance is attacked near Nordkyn by the submarine *S-56* (Capt 2nd Class Shchedrin) with a salvo of four torpedoes, but *V6105* outmanoeuvres them. Three submarine-chasers of the 12th SC Flotilla (Cdr Köplin) fight the submarine with depth charges. On 25 Sept two torpedo cutter groups (Capt 2nd Class Alexeev) attack with nine TKAs near Skalneset and Ekkeröy but they are driven off by the escort and one TKA is sunk. In simultaneous attacks by 33 Il-2 aircraft and 14 Yak-9 and 24 Kittyhawk fighter-bombers, with cover from 24 fighters, *V6101* is sunk by bomb hits, *V6105* and *F152* are damaged and beached and *V6110* and *R309* are damaged but taken in tow. On 26 Sept *S-56* unsuc-

cessfully attacks the returning minesweepers *M31* and *M251* and is damaged by depth charges.

12 Sept Norway

Operation 'Begonia': the British carriers *Furious* and *Trumpeter*, escorted by the cruiser *Devonshire* and six destroyers of the 26th Flotilla, lay mines in the Aramsund Channel.

12 Sept Mediterranean

The German escort vessel *SG19* is sunk by air attack off the Ebro estuary in the Gulf of Lions.

12 Sept Mediterranean

The German MMS *R178* is scuttled at Saloniki in the Aegean.

12–14 Sept Norway

On 12 Sept the German minesweepers *M426* and *M462* are sunk by air attack at the western entrance to Kristiansand South. The patrol vessels *V5105*, *V5307* and *V5309* are sunk off Stadlandet by air attack. On 14 Sept *V1608* is sunk by air attack off Kristiansand.

12 Sept–17 Oct Central Pacific

The US destroyer *Noa* is sunk in a collision with the destroyer *Fullam* off Palau on 12 Sept and on 13 Sept the DMS *Perry* is sunk by mine off Peleliu. On 17 Oct the DMS *Montgomery* is sunk by a mine E of Palau.

13 Sept Arctic

The German auxiliary MS *M5603* is sunk by Soviet air attack off Kiberg.

13–24 Sept Mediterranean

British offensive in the Aegean against German evacuation movements. On 13 Sept the British destroyers *Troubridge* and *Tuscan* sink the small transport *Toni* (638 tons) N of Crete. On 15 Sept the cruiser *Royalist* and the destroyer *Teazer* sink *Erpel/KT26* and the submarine-chaser *UJ2171/Heidelberg/KT4* off Cape Spatha. In Salamis the German torpedo boat *TA14* sinks in a USAAF air attack on 15 Sept and the harbour patrol boat *GD91* and the KT ship *Mannheim* are badly damaged. On 17 Sept *TA17* is damaged beyond repair in another air attack on Piraeus. In attacks by RAF Beaufighters in the Aegean from 20 to 24 Sept, the KT ship *Pelikan* is sunk off Paros, the minelayer *Drache* off Samos and the steamer *Orion* (707 tons) off Naxos.
Operation 'Odysseus': from 20 to 24 Sept the new torpedo boats *TA39* (Lt-Cdr Lange), *TA37* (Lt Winkelmann) and *TA38* (Sub-Lt Scheller) are transferred to the Aegean from Trieste through the Adriatic, the Strait of Otranto (where there is a short, indecisive engagement with the British destroyers *Belvoir* and *Whaddon*), the Gulf of Patras and the Corinth Canal. In an air attack on Piraeus/Skaramanga the last oper-

ational U-boat *U596*, the damaged *U565* and the submarine-chaser *UJ2108* are sunk.

14 Sept Air War/Germany

RAF Bomber Command's attack with Nos 4, 6 (RCAF) and 8 Groups on Wilhelmshaven is cancelled owing to weather and the aircraft are recalled.

14–15 Sept Baltic

German landing operation 'Tanne Ost' on the Finnish island of Suursaari by units of the 3rd and 25th MS Flotillas, the 13th, 21st and 24th Landing Flotillas, the 7th Gun Carrier Flotilla, the 1st MMS Flotilla and the 5th MTB Flotilla. There is strong Finnish resistance. Attacks by Russian aircraft and Finnish motor torpedo boats force the assault fleet to withdraw. The troops, which are landed, are compelled to surrender on 15 Sept (1231 prisoners including 175 wounded). On 15 Sept the German MMS *R29* is torpedoed and sunk off Suursaari by the Finnish MTB *Taisto 5*. *R76* is beached after being hit by Finnish gunfire but is salvaged.

14 Sept Mediterranean

The German A/S vessel *UJ2216* is sunk in an MTB attack off Sestri Levante.

14–24 Sept Arctic

An attempt by the schnorkel U-boat *U315* (Lt Zoller) to enter the Kola Inlet and to attack the battleship *Arkhangelsk* (ex-HMS *Royal Sovereign*) fails because of the net barrages in the inner part of the Inlet. A second attempt, by the schnorkel U-boat *U313* (Lt-Cdr Schweiger), fails from 28 Sept to 10 Oct.

15 Sept Arctic

28 Lancaster bombers of Nos 9 and No 617 Sqns RAF, operating from North Russian airfields, attack the German battleship *Tirpitz* in Altafjord with 12000lb 'Tallboy' bombs, but they score only one hit on the bows of the smoke-covered ship. The ferry steamer *Kehrwieder* is sunk.

15 Sept South West Pacific

VII Amphibious Force (TF.77), which set out from its bases (Aitape, Wakde and Hollandia) on 10 Sept, lands the 31st Inf Div (Maj-Gen Persons) and the 126th RCT (32nd Div) of XI Corps (Lt-Gen Hall) on Morotai on 15 Sept. The force comprises two groups, 'White' (Rear-Adm Barbey in overall command on the headquarters ship *Wasatch*) and 'Red' (Rear-Adm Fechteler on the destroyer *Hughes*). The landing fleet comprises two Australian APAs, five US APDs, 45 LSTs, 24 LCIs, 20 LCTs and one LSD. Support and escort is provided by 24 destroyers, four frigates, 11 LCT(R)s, six PCs, two ATFs and four YMSs and cover for the operation and pre-landing bombardment is provided by TF.75 (Rear-

Adm Berkey) with TG.75.1, comprising the US cruisers *Phoenix*, *Boise* and *Nashville* (Gen MacArthur on board) and the destroyers *Hutchins*, *Beale*, *Bache*, *Daly*, *Abner Read* and *Bush*, and TG.75.2 (Commodore Collins), comprising the Australian cruisers *Australia* and *Shropshire* the destroyers *Arunta*, *Warramunga*, *Mullany* and *Ammen*. Air support is provided by TG.77.1 (Rear-Adm T L Sprague), comprising the escort carriers *Sangamon*, *Suwanee*, *Chenango*, *Santee*, *Saginaw Bay*, *Petrof Bay* and eight destroyers. On the first day 19960 troops are landed without resistance. From 16 Sept to 3 Oct a total of 26000 combat troops and 12200 construction and ground personnel are landed. The US 5th AF (Lt-Gen Kenney) provides continuous air support from Biak, Noemfoor and Cape Sansapor. On 3 Oct the Japanese submarine *Ro-41* (Lt-Cdr Shiizuka) attacks a US carrier group consisting of the escort carriers *Fanshaw Bay* and *Midway* E of Morotai and sinks the DE *Shelton*. The other DEs, *Eversole*, *Richard M Rowell* and *Edmonds*, take up the search but they sink in error the US submarine *Seawolf* which is proceeding in the area.

15–16 Sept Air War/Germany
Nos 1, 4, 6 (RCAF) and 8 Groups RAF Bomber Command attack Kiel with 490 aircraft; six of the latter are lost.

15 Sept–5 Oct Arctic
Convoy operation JW.60/RA.60. On 15 Sept JW.60 sets out from Loch Ewe with 30 ships. The escort (Rear-Adm McGrigor) comprises the escort carriers *Campania* and *Striker*, the cruiser *Diadem* and 12 escorts of the 20th and 8th EG, including the destroyers *Keppel*, *Bulldog* and *Whitehall*, the sloop *Cygnet* and the corvettes *Allington Castle* and *Bamborough Castle*. Cover is provided by the battleship *Rodney* and the destroyers *Saumarez*, *Virago*, *Volage*, *Venus* and *Verulam*, the Canadian *Algonquin* and *Sioux* and also *Milne*, *Musketeer*, *Marne* and *Meteor*. A force consisting of the cruiser *Jamaica* and the destroyers *Orwell* and *Obedient* carries out the provisioning of Spitzbergen. The convoy is located neither by German air reconnaissance nor by the U-boat group 'Grimm' (*U278*, *U312*, *U425*, *U737*, *U921*, *U956* and *U997*) and it arrives in the Kola Inlet on 23 Sept. Some of the ships arrive with a Soviet escort in the White Sea on 25 Sept. RA.60, which sets out during the night 27–28 Sept with the escort of JW.60, avoids the 'Grimm' group and the 'Zorn' group (*U293*, *U310*, *U315*, *U363*, *U365*, *U387*, *U636*, *U668*, *U965*, *U968*, *U992* and *U995*) which has just sailed. Only *U310* (Lt Ley), which happens to be

overrun, sinks two ships of 14395 tons with FAT salvos and misses several escorts with T-5s. *U921* is sunk by Swordfish 'F' of No 813 Sqn FAA from *Campania*. On 5 Oct RA.60 arrives in Loch Ewe.

15 Sept–23 Oct Central Pacific
Operation 'Stalemate II': landing on Palau by TF.31 (Rear-Adm Wilkinson) with III Amphibious Corps (Maj-Gen Geiger). After the raids by TF.38 from 6 to 8 Sept, there begins on 13 and 14 Sept the shelling of the islands of Peleliu and Angaur, which are to be attacked, by the Fire Support Group (Rear-Adm Oldendorf), consisting of the battleships *Pennsylvania*, *Tennessee*, *Maryland*, *Mississippi* and *West Virginia*, the cruisers *Louisville*, *Portland*, *Indianapolis*, *Minneapolis*, *Honolulu* (Rear-Adm Ainsworth), *Denver* (Rear-Adm Hayler), *Columbia* and two others and 14 destroyers. Air support is provided by seven to eleven escort carriers (Rear-Adm Ofstie), which alone fly 382 sorties on the day of the landing.

On 15 Sept the Northern Attack Force lands the 1st Marine Div (Maj-Gen Rupertus) on Peleliu. The resistance of the groups of the 2nd Inf Regt of the Japanese 14th Div under Col Nakagawa with 5300 troops, who are deeply entrenched in the mountain ridges, is overcome only with difficulty. A regiment of the 81st Inf Div has to be landed. On 12 Oct the attack phase is ended, but the last 45 defenders are not overwhelmed until 25 Dec.

On 17 Sept the Southern Attack Force lands the 8th Inf Div (Maj-Gen Mueller) on the most southerly island of Angaur, which is defended by one Japanese battalion of 1600 men under Maj Goto. By 23 Oct the resistance is broken. Only 301 Japanese, in all, are taken prisoner on both islands. The bulk of the Japanese 14th Inf Div (Lt-Gen Inoue) remains isolated on the main island of Babelthuap for the rest of the war. Total US losses are 1209 dead and 6585 wounded. From 24 Sept the Kossol passage, mined in Mar, is again usable.

On 23 Sept an improvised group (Rear-Adm Blandy) lands the 323rd RCT of the 81st Inf Div (Col Watson) on Ulithi Atoll without encountering resistance. It was previously entered on 22 Sept by the Support Group, comprising the cruiser *Denver* and the destroyers *Ross* and *Bryant*. This atoll is to have great importance as a base for the rest of the war. In Mar 1945 there are 617 ships in the lagoon.

The Japanese submarines *I-44* (Lt-Cdr Kawaguchi), which makes one unsuccessful attack, *Ro-47* and *I-177* are deployed against the landing fleet. The last pair are lost on

25 Sept and 2 Oct respectively in Hedgehog attacks by the US DEs *McCoy*, *Reynolds* and *Samuel S Miles*.

16–19 Sept English Channel
On 16 Sept the German auxiliary MS *M3202* is sunk by Allied fighter-bombers off Terneuzen. On 18 Sept *M3663/K55* is sunk by fighter-bombers off the Maas estuary and *M3667/K60* is beached after suffering heavy damage. On 18–19 Sept the gun ferry *AF89* is sunk and *AF87* is damaged in an air attack off the Schelde and *AF87* is sunk in another attack on Dordrecht.

16–23 Sept Indian Ocean
Operation 'Light': the British Eastern Fleet, comprising the carriers *Victorious* and *Indomitable*, the battleship *Howe*, the cruisers *Cumberland* and *Kenya* and the destroyers *Racehorse*, *Raider*, *Rapid*, *Redoubt*, *Relentless*, *Rocket* and *Rotherham*, carries out, under Rear-Adm Moody, a carrier raid on Sigli (Northern Sumatra) and photo reconnaissance over the Nicobars.

In Sept British submarines have success in the Strait of Malacca and the western part of the Malayan Archipelago: *Strongbow* sinks eight small ships, *Sirdar* (Lt Spender) sinks one small vessel and damages two more, *Storm* (Lt Young) sinks five small craft, the Dutch *O-19* (Lt v Karnebeek) sinks one ship of 599 tons and two small vessels, *Tantivy* sinks one ship of 1799 tons, *Porpoise* (Lt-Cdr Turner) sinks one ship of 3029 tons, *Stygian* (Lt Clarabut) sinks one sailing vessel, *Spirit* (Lt Langridge) sinks four junks, *Tradewind* sinks one ship of 5065 tons and damages two small craft, *Trenchant* (Cdr Hezlet) sinks two junks and on 23 Sept off Penang sinks *U859* (she also lays a mine barrage on which two ships of 2814 tons sink), *Thorough* sinks one coaster and *Tudor* (Lt Porter) lays a mine barrage off the west coast of Thailand.

17 Sept North Sea
The German MMS *R171* sinks after hitting a wreck in the North Sea.

17–23 Sept Baltic
Under pressure from the Russian Army advancing towards Estonia, the III SS Armoured Corps pulls out to the W from the Narva position. After the evacuation of the German garrison from Suur-Tytärsaari by the 5th MTB Flotilla on 17 Sept, the island is occupied by light Soviet forces on 20 Sept. They occupy the evacuated harbours of Kunda and Loksa on 21 and 22 Sept. In the morning of 23 Sept the last German convoy leaves Tallinn with the training ship *Hansa*, (ex-AMC), four steamers, one hospital ship and 9000 men, escorted by the destroyers *Z28* and *Z25* and

the torpedo boats *T20*, *T13*, *T17* and *T19*. By then, 50000 troops in all have been transferred from Tallinn to the Baltic islands. In addition, in Aug–Sept 85000 refugees are evacuated. Covering the last transports in the entrance to the Gulf of Finland are the cruisers *Prinz Eugen* and *Lützow* and the destroyers *Z28*, *Z25*, *Z35* and *Z36*.

To block the existing routes in the Gulf of Finland, the minelayers *Brummer* and *Linz*, the torpedo boats *T23* and *T28*, the minesweepers *M18*, *M19* and *M29* and also naval ferry barges, motor torpedo boats and motor minesweepers lay several new 'Nilhorn' mine barrages.

17–28 Sept   Air War/France
Heavy daylight raids by RAF Bomber Command on Boulogne on 17 Sept (762 aircraft, 2 lost) and on Calais on 20 Sept (646), 24 Sept (188), 25 Sept (872), 26 Sept (722), 27 Sept (341) and 28 Sept (494). In total, 12 aircraft are lost in the raids on Calais.

18 Sept   Bay of Biscay
The German MTB *S145* is scuttled at Brest.

18 Sept   Mediterranean
The German gun ferries *KF461* and *KF597* are sunk in an engagement with Allied destroyers off Imperia in the Ligurian Sea.

18–19 Sept   English Channel
The German 10th MTB Flotilla (Lt-Cdr Müller) comprising *S185*, *S186*, *S191* and *S192*, with the transport group, brings ammunition and supplies to the encircled fortress of Dunkirk. In the process, the escort group, under the flotilla commander, comprising *S183*, *S200* and *S702*, runs into a patrol group consisting of the British frigate *Stayner* (Lt Turner) and *MTB724* and *MTB728* off Ostend. One of the German boats is crippled by fire from the MTBs and is sunk by *Stayner*. Then the other two boats collide and are likewise sunk.

19 Sept–6 Oct   North Sea
The German 'Klaudius', 'Kaligula' and 'Vespasian' defensive minefields are laid in the Skagerrak SW of Lindesnäs during the nights 19–20 Sept, 1–2 Oct and 5–6 Oct by the cruiser *Emden* and the minelayer *Kaiser* with the destroyers *Karl Galster*, *Richard Beitzen*, *Friedrich Ihn* and *Theodor Riedel* (*Z30* in the last operation instead of *Riedel*).

20 Sept   English Channel
The German hospital ship *Rostock* is captured and escorted to Plymouth.

20 Sept   Bay of Biscay
The Polish destroyers *Blyskawica* and *Piorun* carry out a landing on Audierne in support of French resistance fighters.

20–24 Sept   Mediterranean
On 20 Sept the German transport *Peli-kan/KT18* is beached after receiving bomb hits in Naussa Bay (Paros). On 22 Sept the German minelayer *Drache* (ex-Yugoslav *Zmaj*) is destroyed during a fighter-bomber attack in the harbour at Vathi (Samos). On 24 Sept the German A/S vessel *UJ2108* is scuttled at the Scaramagna yard in Piraeus.

21 Sept   Baltic
The German auxiliary minesweepers *M3153/K355* and *M3155/K357* are sunk by Soviet air attack at Windau.

24–28 Sept   Arctic
On 24 Sept the German patrol vessel *V5502* is sunk in an air attack off Kirkenes. On 28 Sept the gun ferry *AF25* is sunk in a Soviet air attack off Vadsö.

24 Sept–31 Oct   Mediterranean
The 'British Aegean Force' (Rear-Adm Mansfield) is employed to occupy the Aegean Islands and the Greek mainland evacuated by German troops. Taking part are the escort carriers *Hunter*, *Stalker*, *Emperor*, *Attacker*, *Searcher*, *Pursuer* and *Khedive*, the cruisers *Orion*, *Ajax*, *Royalist* (Rear-Adm Troubridge), *Black Prince*, *Argonaut*, *Aurora* and *Colombo*, the 24th DD Flotilla (Capt Firth) comprising *Troubridge*, *Termagant*, *Terpsichore*, *Teazer*, *Tuscan* and *Tumult*, the Greek *Navarinon* and the Polish *Garland*, the 'Hunt' destroyers *Brecon*, *Calpe*, *Catterick*, *Cleveland*, *Liddesdale* and *Zetland* and the Greek *Themistokles*, *Kriti*, *Pindos*, *Kanaris* and *Miaoulis*. There are many engagements with small German ships and shelling of German positions, airfields and batteries as well as landings.

On 30 Sept to 3 Oct a German convoy proceeds from Piraeus to Salonika; it consists of two steamers, escorted by *TA18* and the harbour patrol boats *GD97* and *GK92*. On 2 Oct the French submarine *Curie* (Lt Chailley) sinks the steamer *Zar Ferdinand* (1994 tons) and on 3 Oct the British *Unswerving* (Lt Tattersall) sinks the *Berta* (1810 tons). In addition, of the British submarines, *Virtue* (Lt Cairns) sinks six small craft, *Vampire* (Lt Taylor) the steamer *Peter* (3754 tons), *Vigorous* the steamer *Salomea* (751 tons), two sailing ships and the ferry *SF121* and *Vox* (Lt Michell) one sailing ship. *TA38* and *TA39* carry out a defensive mining operation off Piraeus on 5–6 Oct and sink *ML1227*. On 15 Oct the Greek minesweepers *Kasos* (*YMS74*) and *Kos* (*YMS186*), *ML870* and a tanker sink on this mine barrage.

From 6 to 13 Oct the last German ships in the Aegean are transferred from Piraeus to Salonika. In the process the torpedo boat *TA37*, *UJ210* (ex-yacht *Brigitta*) and the harbour patrol boat *GK32* are sunk on 7 Oct

in an engagement SW of Kassandra-Huk with the British destroyers *Termagant* and *Tuscan*. The minelayer *Zeus* escapes. On 9 Oct *TA38* goes aground near Makronisi; she is towed by *TA39* to Volos and sunk there in air attacks from the British escort carrier *Stalker* (No 809 Sqn) on 12 Oct together with one steamer, two supply ships, one submarine-chaser, one naval ferry barge, one SF, three KFKs, one LS boat and several motor sailing boats. The last operational ships, the steamer *Lola*, *TA39* and three motor minesweepers, are sent to Salonika after Piraeus is evacuated on 12 Oct. The non operational *TA15* and *TA17* and some small craft are scuttled. On 19 Oct the torpedo boat *TA18* is sunk off Volos in an engagement with the destroyers *Termagent* and *Tuscan*. On 29 Oct the British destroyer *Kimberley* captures the German hospital ship *Gradisca* (13870 tons) in the Aegean. On 31 Oct, because of the evacuation of Salonika by German troops, the last ships, including *S54*, *R185*, *R195*, *R210*, *R211* and three auxiliary minesweepers, *Alula*, *Otranto* and *Gallipoli*, are scuttled, *TA39* and *Lola* having sunk on mines on 16 Oct.

25 Sept   English Channel
The German minesweeper *M471* is sunk by RAF Coastal Command aircraft off Den Helden.

26 Sept–13 Nov   North Atlantic
British and Canadian support groups operate in the Shetland–Faeroes–Iceland passages against outbound German schnorkel U-boats. On 16 Oct *U1006* (Lt Voigt) is found by the Canadian frigates of the 6th SG, *Annan*, *Loch Achanalt* and *Outremont*, and, after surfacing, is sunk by *Annan* in a sharp gun and torpedo engagement. *U246* has to return on 23 Oct after being pursued with depth charges. On 24 Oct the Canadian destroyer *Skeena* of the 11th SG runs on to a shoal off Iceland and is lost in the storm.

Off Reykjavik, *U300* (Lt Hein) misses two steamers and sinks on 10 Nov three ships of 7828 tons from a convoy. *U281* has no success in the North Minch. In the North Channel, *U1004* twice misses escorts and *U483* (Lt-Cdr v Morstein) misses two steamers, one monitor and two escorts but torpedoes on 1 Nov the British DE *Whitaker*, which is taken in tow but becomes a total loss. *U1003* is not able to fire.

In the Channel, *U978* (Lt-Cdr Pulst) sinks one Liberty ship (7176 tons) and torpedoes another (7177 tons). She also dispatches the wreck of a third Liberty ship which has previously run on a mine. On 11 Nov *U1200* is sunk W of the Channel by the corvettes

Pevensey Castle, Portchester Castle, Launceston Castle and *Kenilworth Castle. U773* and *U722* carry out transport missions to St-Nazaire.

26 Sept–15 Nov   Atlantic

U245, U262 and *U518* are stationed as weather boats in the North Atlantic from the end of Sept to the middle of Oct. In Oct they are relieved by *U546* (off Dakar from 24 July to 30 Aug) and *U170* (Lt Hauber) off Freetown from 6 Sept to 5 Oct which return from their distant missions without success. The latter misses escorts of two convoys with T-5s on 28 and 31 Oct. In Nov *U396* becomes a weather boat. In the North Atlantic at the end of Oct *U1226* is lost on the way to America as the result of schnorkel trouble.

U1221 (Lt Ackermann) and *U1223* (Lt Kneip) operate from the end of Sept to the beginning of Nov off Halifax and in the Gulf of St Lawrence respectively. *U1221* misses a troop transport; *U1223* torpedoes the Canadian frigate *Magog* (not repaired) from the escort of convoy ONS.33, just misses *Toronto* on 4 Oct and torpedoes an independent of 7134 tons on 2 Nov. In spite of the deployment of a U-boat hunting group with the carrier *Core* and MAD aircraft, the boats, which are equipped with the 'Naxos' centimetre search receiver and the 'Kurier' automatic radio transmitter, are not found. *U1227* (Lt Altmeier) encounters on 4 Oct, on the way to Gibraltar, the convoy ONS.33, which is accompanied by a Canadian escort group. She torpedoes the frigate *Chebogue*, which is brought into the Bristol Channel by the corvettes *Arnprior* and *Chambly*, the frigate *Ribble* and tugs, but she remains a total loss. Off Gibraltar *U1227* misses a naval force on 25 Oct and attacks a tanker on 8 Nov from convoy UGS.58. On the way to Jakarta, *U195* and *U219* pass through the Central and South Atlantic in Sept–Oct. *U871* is sunk on 26 Sept by Fortress 'P' of No 220 Sqn RAF from the Azores; *U863* is sunk on 29 Sept by two Liberators of VB-107 USN from Ascension. The homebound *U1062* falls victim to US TG.22.1 (Capt Ruhsenberger), operating in the Central Atlantic and comprising the escort carrier *Mission Bay* and the DEs *Douglas L Howard, J R Y Blakely, Hill, Farquhar* and *Fessenden*, and is sunk on 30 Sept by depth charges from *Fessenden*.

27 Sept   North Sea

The British destroyer *Rockingham* is mined 30 nautical miles SE of Aberdeen; she sinks later while under tow.

27–28 Sept   Norway

On 27 Sept the German torpedo boat *TA7* (ex-Norwegian), fitting out at Horten, is destroyed in an explosion caused by saboteurs. The German patrol boat *NK02/Dragoner* (ex-Norwegian torpedo boat *Kjell*) is sunk by RAF Mosquitos W of Ryvingen, near Kristiansand, on 28 Sept.

29–30 Sept   Air War/Germany

No 5 Group RAF Bomber Command attacks Königsberg with 189 aircraft, of which 15 are lost.

29 Sept–24 Oct   Baltic

Russian attack on the Baltic islands. The following landing forces (Rear-Adm Svyatov) are employed: 48–55 torpedo cutters of the TKA Brigade (Capt 1st Class Oleynik), 13 patrol boats, 13 motor minesweepers, 20 harbour defence vessels, 20 tenders of the Tallinn Naval Defence Sector (Capt 1st Class Guskov) and eight armoured cutters. The assault troops consist of units of the 8th Army (Lt-Gen Starikov) with air support from the 13th Air Army (Lt-Gen Rybalchenko). On 29 Sept TKAs and 90 amphibious craft land the first advance troops on Moon Island. The Estonian 247th and 7th Divs are brought into the bridgehead and the German defenders withdraw to Ösel and blow up the bridge. On 2 Oct light forces land advance parties, and, later, the main body of the 109th Rifle Div, on Dagö, which the weak German defences evacuate by 3 Oct. On 5 Oct Soviet forces succeed in landing on Ösel. The German 218th Inf Div is unable to hold up the vastly superior Russian forces and by 20 Oct withdraws to the Sworbe peninsula. A Russian attack fails in part, as a result of coastal shelling by the German Task Force (Vice-Adm Thiele). On 22 Oct *T23* and *T28* shell Sworbe; and on 23–24 Oct the cruiser *Lützow* (Capt Knoke), with the destroyers *Z28* and *Z35* and the torpedo boats *T13, T19* and *T21*, shells Russian positions on Sworbe and near Memel. Heavy Russian air attacks, in which a bomb hit is registered on *Z28*, are beaten off.

26 Sept–29 Dec   Baltic

Escorted by the Finnish gunboat *Karjala* and the Soviet minesweeper *T-215* and smaller vessels, the Soviet submarines *Shch-310, Shch-318* and *Shch-40* (26 Sept–2 Oct), *L-3, D-2, Lembit* and *S-13* (1–5 Oct) and *Shch-309* and *S-4* (4–7 Oct) are transferred from Kronshtadt to Hangö and Abo. *M-96* is lost on a mine in Sept. *Shch-210* (Capt 3rd Class Bogorad) sails first for the Aaland Sea, then relieves *Shch-209* off Windau and sinks the training vessel *Nordstern*, the transport *Ro24/Zonnewijk* and the wreck of the training ship *Carl Zeiss* in tow (total 6946 tons). From 13 to 18 Oct *Shch-318* (Capt 3rd Class Loshkarev) off Libau has one and *Shch-407* (Capt 3rd Class

Bocharov) off Memel has two misses. *S-13* (Capt 3rd Class Marinesko) sinks the trawler *Siegfried* (563 tons) off the Gulf of Danzig and *S-4* (Capt 3rd Class Klyushkin) from 11 to 20 Oct sinks the steamers *Taunus, Terra* and *Thalatta* (total 4896 tons) off the Stolpe Bank. *Lembit* (Capt 3rd Class Matyasevich) lays mines on 11 Oct en route from Kolberg to Stolpmünde (on which the tug *Pionier 5* sinks and the steamers *Eichberg* and *Elie*, total 3760 tons, are damaged). On 13 Oct the steamer *Hilma Lau* (2414 tons) is sunk by torpedo. On 11 Oct *L-3* (Capt 3rd Class Konovalov) lays mines off Cape Arkona, on which the torpedo boat *T34* and the steamer *Spreeufer* sink and the sail training ship *Albert Leo Schlageter* is damaged; one torpedo attack misses. *D-2* (Capt 3rd Class Filov) operates without success off Kalmarsund and *Shch-307* (Lt-Cdr Kalinin) sails off Gotland and relieves *Shch-310* off Windau, where six ships are attacked without success; in addition *K-56* (Capt 3rd Class Popov) cruises 20–24 Oct off Kalmarsund and the Stolpe Bank and in the Gulf of Danzig without success.

In Nov *Shch-309* (Lt-Cdr Vetchinkin) stays for four weeks off Windau and sinks the transports *Carl Cords* and *Nordenham* totalling 5495 tons. *L-21* (Capt 3rd Class Mogilevski) cruises in the area of the Stolpe Bank and on 23 Nov lays a mine barrage which is swept without losses by the 2nd Sicherungs Flotilla. *K-52* (Capt 3rd Class Travkin) has no successes 12–21 Nov off the Gulf of Danzig; *K-51* (Capt 3rd Class Drozdov), on its way to the Pomeranian Bay on 24 Nov, sinks the Swedish steamer *Hansa* (493 tons) NW of Visby by gunfire and attacks two more vessels with gunfire.

In Dec *K-56* relieves *K-51* and misses the auxiliary cruiser *Hansa* and from 26 to 29 Dec sinks the steamer *Baltenland* (3042 tons) and the Swedish *Venersborg* (1044 tons). *K-53* (Capt 3rd Class Jaroshevich) has no success off Memel from 26 Nov to 14 Dec. On 3 Dec *Lembit* lays new mines off Brüsterort: some small vessels sink before the mines are swept by *Minenräumschiff 12. Shch-407* (Capt 3rd Class Bocharov) sinks the transport *Seeburg* (12181 tons) in the Gulf of Danzig. *S-4* (lost off Danzig on 4 Jan to depth charges from the torpedo boat *T3*), *Shch-303* (Capt 3rd Class Ignatev) off Memel and *D-2* off Windau have no successes.

Oct   France/Intelligence

The German fortresses in France are allocated a separate cypher circuit, 'Atlantik' (which is never broken).

1–2 Oct   Mediterranean

Reconnaissance expedition by the 10th TB

Flotilla (Cdr v Gartzen) with *TA24*, *TA29* and *TA32* in the western part of the Gulf of Genoa.

1–10 Oct Baltic

To drive the German troops out of Northern Finland, the Finnish III Corps puts pressure on the German units withdrawing to the NW. On 1 Oct the first elements of the Finnish 3rd Div (2900 men of the 11th Inf Regt) are landed from three steamers in Röyöttä (northern part of the Gulf of Bothnia), in order to advance to Kemi and Tornio. Strong German counter-attacks at first cause reverses until the remaining parts of the 3rd Div begin to arrive on 2 Oct and the Finnish gunboats *Uusimaa* and *Hämeen-maa* are able to support the assault troops from 6 Oct and to reinforce the AA defence. German air attacks damage several transports.

1–15 Oct North Sea

The British 11th MTB Flotilla (Lt Bourne), comprising *MTB351*, *MTB360*, *MTB349*, *MTB347* and *MTB350*, attacks off Ijmuiden during the night 30 Sept–1 Oct the German convoy 1291 (three towing convoys with new constructions and *F6*) on the way from Rotterdam to Borkum. A barrage group of three boats of the 11th MMS Flotilla (Lt-Cdr Rosenow), a mining group of four boats of the 13th MMS Flotilla (Lt-Cdr Eizinger) and the escort (Cdr Fischer), comprising *V1313*, *V1301*, *V1310*, *V1317*, *V2017*, *V2019*, *M3824*, *M3827*, *M3838*, *M3832* and *MFL675*, beat off all attacks and sink *MTB360* and *MTB347*. The convoy puts into Den Helden during the night 2–3 Oct and when it continues on its way there are air attacks off the Dutch north coast and a new 'Hansa' construction *No 922* (1923 tons) is sunk.

During the night 8–9 Oct the British 4th MTB Flotilla repeatedly attacks a German patrol boat group off the Hook of Holland. Of the boats *V1306*, *V2007* and *V1303*, the last is sunk. An attack by the 21st MTB Flotilla near Texel fails. During the night 10–11 Oct *MTB475*, *MTB473*, *MTB476*, *MTB480* and *MTB472* again attack patrol boats off the Hook of Holland and badly damage one boat. In a third attack on 15–16 Oct *V2016* is sunk.

1–31 Oct Pacific

In the Pacific, US submarines are stationed mostly in 'wolfpacks' for the impending Leyte operation and the boats achieve considerable successes, sometimes following up 'Ultra' messages in joint 'wolfpack' operations and sometimes also individually (see also 17–27 Oct).

In the Kuriles area, *Seal* (Lt-Cdr Turner) sinks two ships of 6629 tons. In Japanese waters, *Pomfret* (Cdr Acker) sinks one ship of 6962 tons and torpedoes one more of 4026 tons, *Tilefish* (Lt-Cdr Keithley) sinks one ship of 108 tons and *Besugo* (Lt-Cdr Wogan) torpedoes the destroyer *Suzutsuki* on 16 Oct and the corvette *Kaibokan 132* on 24 Oct. Operating in groups in the area of the Volcano and the Bonin Islands, *Snapper* (Lt-Cdr Walker) sinks one ship of 1990 tons and on 1 Oct the minelayer *Ajiro*, *Trepang* (Lt-Cdr Davenport) sinks one ship of 752 tons and the landing ship *T-105* and torpedoes the destroyer *Fuyutsuki* on 12 Oct, *Kingfish* (Lt-Cdr Harper) sinks two ships of 2757 tons and the landing ship *T-138* and *Tambor* (Lt-Cdr Germershausen) sinks two small vessels; *Sargo* and *Pilotfish* have only misses, as has also *Permit* in the Carolines area. SW of Kyushu, *Croaker* (Lt-Cdr Lee) sinks four ships of 10354 tons and two sailing vessels but *Perch* and *Sea Fox* have no successes; neither does *Escolar*, which goes missing in early Oct, lost possibly on a Japanese mine. E of Kyushu, *Gabilan* (Lt-Cdr Wheland) sinks a small vessel of 200 tons, *Ronquil* (Lt-Cdr Monroe) has a miss, *Burrfish* (Lt-Cdr Perkins) sinks one small vessel of 177 tons and *Besugo* (Lt-Cdr Wogan) on 16 Oct torpedoes the destroyer *Suzutsuki*. Between Kyushu and Amamioshima are stationed *Sterlet* (Lt-Cdr Robbins), *Skate* (Lt-Cdr Lynch) and *Sea Dog* (Lt-Cdr Lowrance), the last of which sinks two ships of 11148 tons. Between Okinawa and Formosa, *Salmon* (Lt-Cdr Nicholas), *Silversides* (Lt-Cdr Nichols) and *Trigger* (Lt-Cdr Connole) are stationed. *Sterlet* alone sinks one ship of 10241 tons and together with *Trigger* and *Salmon* one more of 10021 tons. *Silversides* sinks one small vessel of 97 tons.

In the Formosa Straits, *Tang* (Lt-Cdr O'Kane) sinks eight ships of 23468 tons from convoys but is then a victim of one of her own circling torpedoes. S of the Formosa Straits, *Snook* (Lt-Cdr Browne) sinks three ships of 16636 tons but *Barbero* has no success. *Shark* (Lt-Cdr Blakely), *Blackfish* (Lt-Cdr Davidson) and *Seadragon* (Lt-Cdr Ashley) operate S of Formosa. *Seadragon* sinks three ships of 13854 tons but *Shark* is lost, probably to a Japanese depth charge attack on 24 Oct. After sinking one sailing vessel and damaging one small craft on 12 Oct, *Sailfish* (Lt-Cdr Ward) torpedoes the destroyer *Harukaze* and the transport *T-111* in the Luzon Strait on 4 Nov. NW of Luzon, successes are registered by *Sawfish* (Lt-Cdr Bannister), with two ships of 13854 tons, including the seaplane carrier *Kimikawa Maru* on 23 Oct, and by *Icefish* (Cdr Peterson), with two ships of

8404 tons and, together with *Drum* (Lt-Cdr Williamson), one of 6886 tons. *Drum* herself sinks two ships of 11611 tons and damages two more of 11402 tons while *Seahorse* (Lt-Cdr Wilkins) sinks the corvette *Kaibokan 21* on 6 Oct. *Whale* (Lt-Cdr Grady) sinks two ships of 18648 tons. W of Luzon, *Cabrilla* (Lt-Cdr Thompson) sinks five ships of 26964 tons, *Aspro* (Cdr Stevenson) sinks two ships of 10912 tons and *Hoe* (Lt-Cdr McCrea) sinks one ship of 2578 tons and on 8 Oct torpedoes the corvette *Kaibokan 8*. From mid Oct groups of US submarines are stationed NE of Luzon to intercept Japanese forces during the Leyte operations: these comprise *Halibut*, *Tuna*, *Haddock*, *Pintado*, *Atule* and *Jallao* (see 17–26 Oct). W of Luzon, *Cero* sinks two sailing vessels and, SW of Luzon, *Bonefish*, *Flasher* and *Lapon* have no success, but *Baya* (Lt-Cdr Jarvis), *Hawkbill* (Lt-Cdr Scanland) and *Becuna* (Lt-Cdr Sturr) together sink two ships of 10350 tons and damage two of 14131 tons. Off Manila, *Cod* (Lt-Cdr Atkins) sinks one ship of 6886 tons and one sailing vessel and torpedoes one oiler of 14050 tons. A group consisting of *Bream* (Lt-Cdr McCallum), *Guitarro* (Lt-Cdr Haskins), *Raton* (Lt-Cdr Shea) and *Ray* (Lt-Cdr Kinsella) has much success: *Bream* torpedoes on 23 Oct the cruiser *Aoba*, *Guitarro* sinks two ships of 8729 tons, *Raton* sinks three ships and the munitions transport *Kurasaki* (total 13763 tons) and *Ray* sinks three ships of 5334 tons and the corvette *Kaibokan 7* and torpedoes an oiler of 14050 tons; *Bream*, *Guitarro* and *Ray* together sink one ship of 6806 tons and all four boats finish off the damaged cruiser *Kumano* on 14 Nov.

Blackfin is stationed N of Palawan, *Batfish* off the Sulu Strait, where she has some misses, and *Cobia* in the N Makassar Strait. S of Balikpapan, *Mingo* (Lt-Cdr Staley) sinks four trawlers and small craft and *Paddle* (Lt-Cdr Nowell) one sailing vessel, while *Bowfin* (Lt-Cdr Corbus) sinks one ship of 2219 tons off Bandjermasin.

A group comprising *Darter* (Lt-Cdr McClintock), *Dace* (Lt-Cdr Claggett), *Rock* (Lt-Cdr Flachsenhar) and *Bergall* (Lt-Cdr Hyde) operates W of Palawan. Besides successes against the Japanese Centre Force (see 17–26 Oct), *Dace* sinks two ships of 12941 tons and damages one of 5396 tons, *Rock* sinks one of 834 tons and *Bergall* sinks three of 24717 tons. Further to the W, *Angler* (Cdr Hess) sinks one ship of 2407 tons, *Bluegill* (Lt-Cdr Barr) three ships of 19631 tons and two small craft and *Hammerhead* (Lt-Cdr Martin) five ships of 25179 tons.

By contrast, there is only one Japanese submarine, *I-12* (Cdr Kudo), in the Pacific engaged on distant operations between Hawaii and the American West Coast. She sinks one Liberty ship of 7176 tons and goes missing at the end of Oct.

3–30 Oct   Air War/Netherlands
Heavy air attacks by Nos 1, 3, 4 and 8 Groups RAF Bomber Command on German defensive positions, and on the dykes at Walcheren to cause a breach and flood the island. On 3 Oct 359 aircraft are sent, on 7 Oct 123, on 11 Oct 63, on 17 Oct 49, on 21 Oct 75, on 23 Oct 112 (of No 5 Group), on 28 Oct 277, on 29 Oct 358 and on 30 Oct 110. Eight aircraft are lost altogether.

4 Oct   Arctic
Crew members of the US ice-breaker *Eastwind* destroy a German weather station on the island of Lille Koldewey off the north-east coast of Greenland.

4 Oct   Air War/Norway
Nov 6 and 8 Groups RAF Bomber Command attack the U-boat pens at Bergen with 140 aircraft (1 lost). Seven hits are achieved, *U228* and *U993* being sunk and *U92* and *U437* being damaged beyond repair. The catapult ship *Schwabenland* and three other ships of 11708 tons are damaged.

4 Oct   Air War/Italy
In an air attack on Genoa, the U-boat *UIT1* (ex-Italian *R 10*), building, is destroyed.

4–6 Oct   Baltic
German minelaying operation 'Krokodil Süd', to block the southern exit of the Moonsund, with MTBs of the 5th Flotilla and the minelayers *Brummer* and *Linz* with the minesweepers *M17*, *M18* and *M29*.

4–29 Oct   Air War/Western Europe
Mine offensive by RAF Bomber Command. In nine nights 250 sorties are flown against the Dutch coast off Texel, the Heligoland Bight, the Weser and Elbe rivers, the Oslo area, the Danish coasts, the Kattegat and the western Baltic. On 5–6 Oct Mosquitos lay mines in the Kiel Canal; six aircraft are lost. On 8 Oct *U763* is damaged by a mine in the Skagerrak; she is later lost in an air attack while undergoing repairs at Königsberg. On 14 Oct, in the Bay of Biscay, the A/S vessel *UJ1411* sinks on a mine from an earlier drop off St-Nazaire. On 18 Oct the minesweeper *RA2* (ex-French *Ch45*) is sunk by a mine NE of Ostend. On 20 Oct the destroyer *Z30* is damaged in Oslofjord and on 23 Oct *U985* is damaged off southern Norway by mine and decommissioned.

4 Oct–5 Jan   Indian Ocean
The first group of East Asian U-boats sets out with raw materials from Jakarta to return to Norway. *U168* is sunk on 6 Oct N of Java by the Dutch submarine *Zvaardfish*; *U181* (Cdr* Freiwald) sets out on 19 Oct,

sinks a tanker of 10198 tons in the Central Indian Ocean on 2 Nov but, when off South Africa, has to return because of damage to her propeller shaft and puts in again on 5 Jan. *U537* is sunk N of Bali by the US submarine *Flounder* on 9 Nov. *U196* is missing in the Sunda Strait since setting out on 30 Nov. On 28 Nov *U843* sets out and reaches the Atlantic on 28 Dec after being replenished from *U195* coming from France. *U195* and *U219* arrive in Jakarta from there in Dec.

When transferring from Singapore to Penang, the Japanese submarines *Ro-113* and *Ro-115* are missed by the British submarine *Strongbow* on 12 Oct. On 24 Oct *Stygian* misses one of the two boats as they set out for the Bay of Bengal. *Ro-113* (Lt Harada) sinks one ship of 3827 tons on 5 Nov. Neither the shore-based aircraft sent to search nor TF.66 with the escort carriers *Begum* and *Shah* can find the Japanese submarines. The British submarine *Tally Ho* misses one of them as she comes into harbour on 8 Nov. In a second operation, *Ro-113* is bombed on 3–4 Dec by a Liberator of No 222 Sqn RAF, but on 17–18 and 18–19 Dec she attacks two ships off Madras, which just get away, and the boat arrives again off Penang on 28 Dec where the British submarine *Thule* misses her with six torpedoes. *Ro-115* cruises without success off the east coast of Ceylon and is hunted on 22 Dec by the sloop *Flamingo*.

5 Oct   Mediterranean
The British cruiser *Aurora* and the destroyer *Catterick* bombard Levitha Island in the Aegean and land a party, to whom the island surrenders.

5–7 Oct   Air War/Germany
On 5 Oct Nos 1 and 5 Groups RAF Bomber Command attack Wilhelmshaven with 227 aircraft (of which one is lost). On 6–7 Oct Nos 1 and 5 Groups attack Bremen with 253 aircraft, causing damage to the Deschimag yard.

5 Oct–1 Nov   English Channel
Operations by German small battle units. On 5–6 Oct there is an attempt to use 'Linsen' craft from Flushing for attacking Allied minesweepers in the Schelde estuary and to send some groups to supply Dunkirk. Both operations fail because of bad weather and the Allied defences and 36 'Linsen' are lost or have to be abandoned. On 31 Oct–1 Nov a second attempt to use 'Linsens' fails. Flushing has to be evacuated.

6–15 Oct   Baltic
After the Russian break-through to the Baltic between Libau and Memel from 6 to 10 Oct, the heavy cruisers *Prinz Eugen* (Capt Reinicke) and *Lützow* (Capt Knoke) and the

6th DD Flotilla (Capt Kothe), comprising *Z25*, *Z35* and *Z36*, shell Soviet assembly positions near Memel on 10–12 and 13–15 Oct. AA defence and submarine defence is provided by the 3rd TB Flotilla, consisting of *T21*, *T13*, *T16* and *T20*. Russian air attacks are beaten off.

On 15 Oct, off Gdynia, the German cruiser *Leipzig* is almost cut in two in a collision in fog with *Prinz Eugen*.

6–17 Oct   Central Pacific
Adm Halsey (Cd 3rd Fleet) operates with TF.38 off Formosa and Luzon to eliminate the Japanese air forces. TF.38 (Vice-Adm Mitscher) sets out with three groups from Ultithi on 6 Oct. TG.38.4 joins them on 7 Oct coming from the area W of Palau. On 8 Oct the warships are refuelled from eight fleet tankers. On the same day TG.30.2 (Rear-Adm Smith) shells Marcus Island with the cruisers *Chester*, *Pensacola* and *Salt Lake City* and the destroyers *Dunlap*, *Fanning*, *Case*, *Cummings*, *Cassin* and *Downes*. On 9 Oct TF.38 proceeds to the NW. TG.38.1 (Vice-Adm McCain) comprises the carriers *Wasp*, *Hornet*, *Monterey* and *Cowpens*, the cruisers *Wichita*, *Boston*, *Canberra* and *Houston* and the destroyers *Izard*, *Charrette*, *Conner*, *Bell*, *Burns*, *Cogswell*, *Caperton*, *Ingersoll*, *Knapp*, *Boyd*, *Cowell*, *McCalla*, *Grayson*, *Brown* and *Woodworth*. TG.38.2 (Rear-Adm Bogan) comprises the carriers *Intrepid*, *Hancock*, *Bunker Hill*, *Cabot* and *Independence*, the battleships *Iowa* and *New Jersey* (Adm Halsey), the cruisers *Vincennes*, *Miami*, *San Diego* and *Oakland* and the destroyers *Owen*, *Miller*, *The Sullivans*, *Stephen Potter*, *Tingey*, *Hickox*, *Hunt*, *Lewis Hancock*, *Marshall*, *Halsey Powell*, *Cushing*, *Colahan*, *Uhlmann*, *Benham*, *Stockham*, *Wedderburn*, *Twining* and *Yarnall*. TG.38.3 (Rear-Adm Sherman) comprises the carriers *Essex*, *Lexington*, *Princeton* and *Langley*, the battleships *Washington* (Vice-Adm Lee), *Massachusetts*, *South Dakota* and *Alabama*, the cruisers *Santa Fé*, *Mobile*, *Birmingham* and *Reno* and the destroyers *Clarence K Bronson*, *Cotten*, *Dortch*, *Gatling*, *Healy*, *Porterfield*, *Callaghan*, *Cassin Young*, *Irwin*, *Preston*, *Laws*, *Longshaw*, *Morrison* and *Prichett*. TG.38.4 (Rear-Adm Davison) comprises the carriers *Franklin*, *Enterprise*, *San Jacinto* and *Belleau Wood*, the cruisers *New Orleans* and *Biloxi* and the destroyers *Maury*, *Gridley*, *Helm*, *McCall*, *Mugford*, *Bagley*, *Patterson*, *Ralph Talbot*, *Wilkes*, *Nicholson* and *Swanson*.

Air battle off Formosa. On 10 Oct one group flies off to attack Amamioshima, two groups to attack Okinawa and one group to attack Sakishima Gunto. In all, 1936 sorties are flown. The Americans lose 21 aircraft but the submarine depot ship *Jingei*, the mine-layer *Takashima* and the escort *Kali* (ex-Manchurian *Hai Wei*), three smaller ships and four steamers are destroyed in Okinawa. The 2nd Japanese Air Fleet (Vice-Adm Fukudome), which has 400 aircraft, loses 30 machines in air combat and on the ground. Attempts to attack the carrier groups, which have been located by air reconnaissance, fail because the formations fail to find the targets.

On 11 Oct TG.38.1 and 38.4 fly 61 sorties against the airfield of Aparri from NE of Luzon: 15 Japanese aircraft are destroyed there. TG.38.2 and 38.3 refuel to the E from 12 fleet tankers of TG.30.8 (Capt Acuff), comprising 34 tankers, 17 destroyers and 26 DEs, and they take over 61 replacement aircraft in turns from the escort carriers *Altamaha*, *Barnes*, *Sitkoh Bay*, *Cape Esperance*, *Nassau*, *Kwajalein*, *Shipley Bay*, *Steamer Bay*, *Nehenta Bay*, *Sargent Bay* and *Rudyerd Bay*, which are employed as replenishment carriers, during Oct.

On 12 and 13 Oct all four task groups make continual attacks on airfields and installations on Formosa. On 12 Oct there are 1378 sorties and on 13 Oct 974 sorties. Forty-eight planes are lost, but many Japanese aircraft are destroyed in the air and on the ground. The 2nd Japanese Air Fleet tries to make attacks from Formosa on the two southern task groups, but these are intercepted. 'T' force flies 56 sorties from Kyushu on 12 Oct and 30 sorties on 13 Oct and on both days 52 aircraft fly from Okinawa. The carrier *Franklin* narrowly misses torpedoes; one of the four attacking aircraft crashes in flames on the deck and causes slight damage. When it is getting dark, *Canberra* is hit by a torpedo and badly damaged.

Early on 14 Oct TG.38.1 makes another attack on Formosa: 246 sorties and 23 aircraft are lost. TG.38.4 attacks Aparri. From bases in China B-29s attack targets in Formosa and Okinawa in 109 sorties. The 2nd Japanese Air Fleet flies a total of 419 sorties from Formosa, Okinawa and Kyushu against the US Fleet: 225 aircraft return without having found their targets. In an attack on TG.38.1, *Houston* is torpedoed in the evening. *Canberra* is taken in tow by *Wichita* and *Houston* by *Boston*: TG.30.3 (Rear-Adm DuBose) forms a covering force with the cruisers *Santa Fé* and *Mobile*, the carriers *Cowpens* and *Cabot* and the destroyers *Charrette*, *Conner*, *Bell*, *Burns*, *Cogswell*, *Caperton*, *Ingersoll*, *Knapp*, *Boyd*, *Cowell*, *Miller*, *The Sullivans* and *Stephen Potter*. On 15 Oct units of the 2nd Japanese

Air Fleet fly 199 sorties against TF.38 as it retires; *Houston* is again hit by a torpedo. TG.38.4 makes attacks on airfields N of Manila on Luzon, in the course of which there are fierce air battles with 50 fighters of the 1st Japanese Air Fleet (Vice-Adm Teraoka) and attacks by 130 Japanese aircraft on TG.38.4. But the attacks are repelled and 32 machines are shot down.

In all, from 12 to 15 Oct, in 881 sorties and with 321 losses to themselves, the Japanese pilots claim to have sunk 11 carriers, two battleships and one cruiser and to have damaged eight carriers, two battleships, one cruiser and 13 other ships. Submarine group A, comprising *I-26*, *I-45*, *I-53*, *I-54* and *I-56*, and the 2nd Striking Force (Vice-Adm Shima), consisting of the cruisers *Nachi*, *Ashigara* and *Abukuma* and the destroyers *Akebono*, *Ushio*, *Kasumi*, *Shiranuhi*, *Wakaba*, *Hatsushimo*, *Hatsuharu* and *Suzutsuki*, are deployed against the damaged ships. The last-named is torpedoed by the US submarine *Besugo* on 15 Oct. *Skate* reports the force, whereupon TG.38.2 and 38.3 make a sortie to the N on 16 Oct, followed by TG.38.1 which is, at the time, replenishing. The Japanese torpedo boat *Hato* is sunk by carrier aircraft in the South China Sea, W of Luzon, on 16 Oct. On 16 and 17 Oct the 2nd Japanese Air Fleet flies another 107 sorties against TF.38 without finding targets. Twenty-four aircraft are lost. From Luzon, aircraft of the 1st Air Fleet vainly try to find TG.38.4, which, after replenishing on 16 Oct, again attacks central and southern Luzon on 17 Oct. On 17 Oct the carrier groups in the N have to return because of the beginning of the Leyte operation. Adm Shima puts into Amamioshima, when reconnaissance reports on 16 Oct that there are still 13 carriers, seven battleships and ten cruisers intact.

7 Oct   North Sea
The German gun ferry *AF76* is sunk by air attack off Terschelling; it is later raised and repaired.

7–11 Oct   Mediterranean
Coastal shelling of the Rivera by the French cruiser *Emile Bertin*, the destroyer *Le Fortuné* and the US destroyers *Eberle*, *Jouett* and *Gleaves*.

7–26 Oct   Arctic
The withdrawal of XIX Mountain Corps on the Murmansk front, which is being prepared, coincides with the offensive by the 14th Soviet Army (Col-Gen Shcherbakov) with the 99th, 131st and 31st Rifle Corps and the 126th and 127th Light Rifle Corps (seven rifle divs, one armoured brigade and four rifle brigades) from the southern flank, supported by the air divisions of the 7th Air

Army. To interrupt the main supply routes from the N, ships of the Northern Fleet (Adm Golovko) land naval infantry units repeatedly in the rear of the German 6th Mountain Div, which, however, is able with elements of the 2nd Mountain Div to avoid the threatening encirclement. On 10 Oct 2837 men of the 63rd Naval Rifle Bde (Col Krylov) land in 10 BO, eight MO and 12 TKA cutters (Capt 1st Class Zyuzin) in Maativuono Bay opposite the Fisherman's Peninsula, on 12 Oct 660 men in seven TKA and six MO cutters at the entrance of Petsamofjord, on 18 Oct 485 men in six MO cutters near Jakobselv, on 23 Oct 600 men of the 12th Naval Bde (Col Rassokhin) in six MO and four TKA cutters at Jarfjord, and on 25 Oct 835 men in 15 TKA and four BO cutters and two motor boats at Bökfjord. On the following day they, with units of the 131st Rifle Corps, occupy Kirkenes which, in the meantime, has been evacuated by the Germans.

To cover and support the landings, the air regiments of the Northern Fleet and six destroyers (*Gremyashchi* and *Gromki* for artillery support and four for cover against German attacks) are deployed. Of them, the destroyers *Baku*, *Gremyashchi*, *Razumny* and *Razyarenny* shell Vardö and Vadsö on 26 Oct.

The submarines *L-20* (mining operation), *S-51*, *V-2*, *S-104*, *M-171* (mining operation), *S-102*, *S-14*, *V-4* and *S-101* are deployed off the Norwegian polar coast against the expected German evacuation by sea. In 13 attacks the boats claim 18 successes; in fact, only one steamer (1730 tons) and *UJ1220* are lost in an attack by *S-104* (Capt 2nd Class Turaev) on 12 Oct, *UJ1219* in one by *V-4* (Capt 3rd Class Iosseliani) on 20 Oct through torpedo fire and one small Norwegian cutter on a mine laid by *M-171*.

In two attacks by a total of 10 torpedo cutters only two minesweepers are lost, *M303* on 11 Oct to *TKA-205* and *TKA-219* and *M31* on 21 Oct to *TKA-215*, instead of the 10 vessels claimed, and *R311* is damaged. Three TKAs are lost.

Fourteen major air attacks are mounted by the 5th Mining and Torpedo Div, the 6th Fighter Div and the 14th Ground Attack Div (all under Maj-Gen Preobrazhenski).

On 14 Oct the German repair ship *Südmeer* (8133 tons) is sunk by Soviet torpedo aircraft off Porsanger Fjord. On 15 Oct the patrol vessel *V6704* is scuttled at Vadsö. On 16 Oct the MMS *R301* is sunk by torpedo during an air attack off Vardö and *V6707* is sunk by bombs at Kirkenes. On 17 Oct *V6107* is sunk by bombs in Varanger Fjord, as is *V6801* is off Hogsteinen. On 21 Oct the German gun ferries *AF6* and *AF57* are sunk by Soviet air attack off Kirkenes and the MMS *R151* is sunk by air attack off Vardö. On 23 Oct *V6311* is sunk by air attack off Sylte Fjord, on 24 Oct *V6111* is sunk by aerial torpedo off Kors Fjord and on 25 Oct the MMS *R250* is sunk by air attack off Bassfjord.

However, the bulk of the German evacuation convoys reach their destinations. Over 40000 tons of supplies are taken away by sea. The evacuation and retreat is covered and supported by the German 4th DD Flotilla with the destroyers *Z29*, *Z31*, *Z33*, *Z34* and *Z38* from 21–31 Oct.

8 Oct   English Channel
The British minesweeper *Mulgrave* is sunk by mine off Normandy; she is beached and later salvaged but not repaired.

10 Oct   Baltic
The German *U2331* is sunk in an accident off Gdynia; she is raised but decommissioned.

11–12 Oct   Mediterranean
On 11 Oct four MGBs of the 57th Flotilla destroy two German coastal convoys off Vir in the Adriatic. The British destroyer *Loyal* is badly damaged by an acoustic mine in the Tyrrhenian Sea. Because of severe shock damage, she is a constructive total loss.

15 Oct   Mediterranean
Operation 'Manna': the re-occupation of Athens by a force under Rear-Adm Mansfield with the cruisers *Ajax*, *Aurora*, *Black Prince*, *Orion* and *Sirius* and the landing ships *Prince David* (RCN), *Prince Henry* (RCN), *Bruiser* and *Thruster*.

15–16 Oct   Arctic/Greenland
The German weather observation ship *WBS 11/Externsteine*, in the ice on the Greenland east coast, is compelled to surrender by the US Coast Guard ice-breakers *Eastwind* and *Southwind*.

15–19 Oct   Indian Ocean
Operation 'Millet'. As a diversion for the imminent US landing on Leyte, the British Eastern Fleet sets out from Trincomalee on 15 Oct with TF.63 (Vice-Adm Power) in three groups: TG.63.1, comprising the battlecruiser *Renown* (flagship) and the destroyers (4th Flotilla) *Quilliam*, *Queenborough* and *Quiberon* (RAN); TG.63.2, comprising the cruisers *London*, *Cumberland* and *Suffolk* and the destroyers *Relentless*, *Raider*, *Norman* (RAN) and *Van Galen* (Dutch); and TG.63.3, comprising the carriers *Indomitable* and *Victorious*, the cruiser (fighter direction ship) *Phoebe* and the destroyers *Whelp*, *Wakeful*, *Wessex* and *Wager*. On 17 and 19 Oct the carriers make attacks on the Nicobar Islands. On 17 Oct TG.63.2 shells the islands and in the night

London, *Norman* and *Van Galen* repeat the shelling. On 18 Oct *Renown*, *Suffolk*, *Raider*, *Quilliam* and *Queenborough* shell the islands. But the diversion does not succeed because Operation 'Sho' has already begun. On 19 Oct, however, the Japanese try to attack with 12 torpedo aircraft. Seven Japanese aircraft are shot down by the fighter cover for a loss of three.

In Oct, in the Strait of Malacca and in the western part of the Indonesian Sea, *Tally Ho* (Cdr Bennington) sinks one small craft and the auxiliary submarine-chaser *Cha-135*, *Sea Rover* (Lt Angell) damages two small craft, the Dutch *Zwaardfish* (Lt-Cdr Goossens) sinks on 6 Oct the German *U168*, on 17 Oct sinks the minelayer *Itsukushima* and damages the minelayer *Wakataka* and in addition sinks three small craft, *Statesman* (Lt Bulkeley) sinks two small coasters, *Sturdy* (Lt Andersen) sinks two coasters of 329 tons and 12 small craft, *Subtle* sinks two small craft, *Strongbow* sinks one ship of 1185 tons, *Stygian* (Lt Clarabut) sinks eight small craft, *Tantivy* sinks 21 small craft and damages one more, *Stoic* (Lt Marriott) sinks five small vessels, *Trenchant* (Cdr Hezlet) sinks one ship of 984 tons, *Shalimar* damages five small landing craft, *Storm* (Lt Young) sinks 11 junks, *Terrapin* (Lt Brunner) sinks the minesweeper *W-5*, one ship of 872 tons and three sailing vessels and *Tradewind* lays a mine barrage in the Mergui Archipelago on which one ship of 593 tons sinks and sinks with gunfire one coaster and seven junks.

15 Oct–4 Nov   Air War/Western Europe
RAF Bomber Command, with 506 aircraft, drops 2198 tons of bombs on Wilhelmshaven during night attacks on 15–16 Oct (*U777* is sunk) and 867 tons of bombs on Bremerhaven on 18–19 Oct. In daylight attacks on 17 Oct, 3400 tons of bombs are dropped on encircled Boulogne and on 20 Oct 3365 tons of bombs on Calais.

The US 8th AF, in daylight attacks, drops 1656 tons of bombs on fuel dumps and oil refineries in Hamburg on 25 Oct and 1030 tons of bombs on the harbour of Hamburg on 4 Nov. In this action the destroyer *Erich Steinbrinck* and the new U-boat *U2557* are badly damaged and *Sperrbrecher 30* and the freighters *Hermann Fritzen* (3845 tons) and *Signal* (3176 tons) are sunk. The accommodation ship *Veendam* (15450 tons) is burnt out.

17–26 Oct   South West Pacific
Battle for Leyte. On 16–17 Oct the preparatory air attacks begin: from Morotai long-range P-38 fighters of the US 5th AF (Lt-Gen Kenney) make fighter sorties and

B-24 bombers of the 13th and 5th AFs from Sansapor and Biak make attacks on airfields on Mindanao. On 16 and 17 Oct aircraft from the escort carriers of TG.77.4 (Rear-Adm T L Sprague) make attacks on Leyte, Cebu and North Mindanao. There take part TU.1 (Sprague), consisting of the escort carriers *Sangamon*, *Suwanee*, *Chenango*, *Santee*, *Saginaw Bay* and *Petrof Bay*, the destroyers *McCord*, *Trathen* and *Hazelwood* and the DEs *Edmonds*, *Richard S Bull*, *Richard M Rowell*, *Eversole* and *Coolbaugh*; TU.2 (Rear-Adm Stump), consisting of the escort carriers *Natoma Bay*, *Manila Bay*, *Marcus Island*, *Kadashan Bay*, *Savo Island* and *Ommaney Bay*, the destroyers *Haggard*, *Franks* and *Hailey* and the DEs *Richard W Suesens*, *Abercrombie*, *Oberrender*, *Le-Ray Wilson* and *Walter C Wann*; and TU.3 (Rear-Adm C A F Sprague), consisting of the escort carriers *Fanshaw Bay*, *St Lo*, *White Plains*, *Kalinin Bay*, *Kitkun Bay* and *Gambier Bay*, the destroyers *Hoel*, *Heerman* and *Johnston* and the DEs *Dennis*, *John C Butler*, *Raymond* and *Samuel B Roberts*. The covering force is TG.77.3 (Rear-Adm Berkey), comprising the cruisers *Phoenix*, *Boise*, *Australia* (RAN) and *Shropshire* (RAN) with the destroyers *Hutchins*, *Bache*, *Beale*, *Daly*, *Killen*, *Arunta* (RAN) and *Warramunga* (RAN). It enters Leyte Gulf early on 17 Oct with the minesweeping and survey force (TG.77.5) and is reported by Japanese coastal guards. Imperial headquarters then puts Operation 'Sho-1' into force and the Japanese fleet movements begin. In the north, US TF.38 (Vice-Adm Mitscher) begins with attacks to neutralise the Japanese 1st Air Fleet (Vice-Adm Teraoka) and the 4th Army Air Fleet on Luzon. On 17 Oct TG.38.4 (Rear-Adm Davison) attacks Luzon with the carriers *Franklin*, *Enterprise*, *San Jacinto* and *Belleau Wood*, the battleships *Washington* and *Alabama*, the cruisers *Wichita* and *New Orleans* and 15 destroyers. On 18 Oct, apart from TG.38.4, TG.38.2, comprising the carriers *Intrepid*, *Hancock*, *Bunker Hill*, *Cabot* and *Independence*, the battleships *Iowa* and *New Jersey*, the cruisers *Biloxi*, *Vincennes* and *Miami* and 16 destroyers, and TG.38.3 (Rear-Adm Sherman), comprising the carriers *Lexington*, *Essex*, *Princeton* and *Langley*, the battleships *Massachusetts* and *Indiana* and the cruisers *Santa Fé*, *Birmingham*, *Mobile* and *Reno* and 12 destroyers, also attack targets in Luzon. The Japanese minelayer *Maeshima* is sunk. Counterattacks by 100 Japanese aircraft on TF.38 and by 25 aircraft on TF.77 do not get through. The US 5th AF and the escort carriers make further attacks on 18 and 19

Oct on Mindanao and the Leyte area respectively. The units of the Japanese 2nd Naval Air Fleet which are still operational are transferred to Luzon, where Vice-Adm Onishi assumes command of the 1st Air Fleet.

With massive air escort from aircraft of all carrier groups and the US 5th AF, the 7th US Fleet (Vice-Adm Kinkaid) enters Leyte Gulf with the 6th US Army (Lt-Gen Krueger). The landings begin early on 20 Oct, with X Corps (Maj-Gen Sibert) in the N and XXIV Corps (Maj-Gen Hodges) in the S. From N to S, the following forces are landed: TG.78.2 (Rear-Adm Fechteler) lands the 1st Cavalry Div (Maj-Gen Mudge) on eight APAs, two AKAs, two LSDs, 14 LSTs and nine LSMs. TG.78.1 (Rear-Adm Barbey) lands the 24th Inf Div (Maj-Gen Irving) on eight APAs, four AKAs, three LSDs, 12 LSTs and smaller craft. Fire support is provided by TF.78, comprising the battleships (Rear-Adm Weyler) *Mississippi*, *Maryland* and *West Virginia* and TG.77.3 (Rear-Adm Berkey—see above). In the S, TF.79 (Vice-Adm Wilkinson) with TG.79.2 (Rear-Adm Boyle) lands the 96th Inf Div (Maj-Gen Bradley) on 14 APAs, four AKAs, four LSDs and 24 LSTs and TG.79.1 (Rear-Adm Connolly) the 7th Inf Div (Maj-Gen Arnold) on 13 APAs, four AKAs, one LSD and 31 LSTs. Fire support in the S is provided by Rear-Adm Oldendorf with the battleships *Tennessee*, *California* and *Pennsylvania* and the cruisers *Louisville*, *Portland*, *Minneapolis*, *Honolulu*, *Denver* and *Columbia* (for destroyers see Battle of Surigao Strait).

Resistance to the landings is at first slight. The Japanese 16th Inf Div retires to prepared hill positions to await the arrival of the 30th and 102nd Inf Divs via Ormoc which are to attack with the Air Force and Fleet.

As a result of Japanese air attacks, the cruiser *Honolulu* is torpedoed in the evening of 20 Oct and on 21 Oct a Japanese aircraft crashes on *Australia*. Both cruisers have to be towed away badly damaged.

On 21 Oct the aircraft of TG.77.4 support the land operations while those of TG.38.2 and 38.3 make attacks on the western Vizayan Islands. TG.38.1 and 38.4 replenish. On 22 Oct the escort carriers stand by E of Leyte Gulf. TG.38.2 and 38.3 go for replenishment. TG.38.4, which is proceeding with 'Cripdiv' (see 6 Oct) to Ulithi, is recalled on 22 Oct. TG.38.1 (with the carrier *Hancock*) goes on to Ulithi.

After receiving reports of the US landings, the C-in-C Combined Fleet (Adm Toyoda) orders the Japanese task forces to set out.

On 22 Oct the Centre Force (Vice-Adm Kurita) puts to sea from Brunei (Borneo) with the battleships *Yamato*, *Musashi*, *Nagato*, *Kongo* and *Haruna*, the cruisers *Atago*, *Takao*, *Chokai*, *Maya*, *Myoko*, *Haguro*, *Kumano*, *Suzuya*, *Chikuma* and *Tone*, the cruisers *Noshiro* and *Yahagi* (the destroyer leaders), and the destroyers *Shimakaze*, *Hayashimo*, *Akishimo*, *Kishinami*, *Okinami*, *Naganami*, *Asashimo*, *Hamanami*, *Fujinami*, *Nowake*, *Kiyoshimo*, *Urakaze*, *Yukikaze*, *Hamakaze* and *Isokaze*. It is followed by the Southern Force (Vice-Adm Nishimura) with the battleships *Fuso* and *Yamashiro*, the cruiser *Mogami* and the destroyers *Michishio*, *Asagumo*, *Yamagumo* and *Shigure*. The 2nd Striking Force (Vice-Adm Shima), comprising the cruisers *Nachi* and *Ashigara* and the destroyers *Akebono*, *Ushio*, *Kasumi*, *Shiranuhi*, *Wakaba*, *Hatsushimo* and *Hatsuharu*, is to join it in the Sulu Sea. A transport unit (Vice-Adm Sakonju) composed of the cruisers *Aoba* and *Kinu*, the destroyer *Uranami* and four fast transports, which is to bring troop reinforcements from Manila to Ormoc, is attacked on 23 Oct W of Manila Bay by the US submarine *Bream* (Lt-Cdr McCallum) which torpedoes the *Aoba*. From the N, Vice-Adm Ozawa advances with a diversionary force which is to draw TF.38 on to itself. It consists of the carriers *Zuikaku*, *Zuiho*, *Chiyoda* and *Chitose*, the carrier/battleships (Rear-Adm Matsuda) *Ise* and *Hyuga*, the cruisers *Isuzu*, *Tama* and *Oyodo*, the destroyers *Hatsutsuki*, *Akitsuki*, *Wakatsuki* and *Shimotsuki*, the escort destroyers *Maki*, *Kiri*, *Kuwa* and *Sugi* and a supply force comprising two tankers, the destroyer *Akikaze* and the corvettes *Kaibokan 22, 29, 31, 33, 43* and *132*.

Shortly after midnight on 23 Oct the US submarines *Dace* (Lt-Cdr Claggett) and *Darter* (Lt-Cdr McClintock) locate Kurita's force N of Salawan and report it. In a torpedo attack, *Dace* sinks *Maya* and *Darter* sinks *Atago*. *Darter* also torpedoes *Takao*, which has to return with two destroyers. A second attempt by *Darter* to attack fails; the boat runs on a reef and has to be destroyed by gunfire from the submarine *Nautilus*. As a result of the submarines' reports, Adm Halsey comes up with TG.38.3 (Rear-Adm Sherman), comprising *Lexington* (Vice-Adm Mitscher), *Essex*, *Princeton* and *Langley*, E of Luzon, TG.38.2 (Rear-Adm Bogan and Adm Halsey), comprising *Intrepid*, *Cabot* and *Independence*, E of the San Bernardino Strait and TG.38.4 (Rear-Adm Davison), comprising *Franklin*, *Enterprise*, *San Jacinto* and *Belleau Wood*, E of Samar. Early on 24 Oct Japanese aircraft

from Luzon attack TG.38.1 but are intercepted. Only one machine gets through, hitting *Princeton*, which is burnt out and has to be abandoned. In attempts to save the ship, the cruiser *Birmingham* is badly damaged by explosions on board *Princeton*.

Battle in the Sibuyan Sea. On 24 Oct four waves of American carrier aircraft attack the Japanese Centre Force. The first wave, consisting of 21 fighters, 12 dive-bombers and 12 torpedo aircraft from *Intrepid* and *Cabot*, obtains one torpedo hit on *Myoko*, which is damaged and has to return, and one bomb and one torpedo hit on *Musashi* (Rear-Adm Inoguchi†). The second wave of 19 fighters, 12 bombers and 11 torpedo aircraft from the same carriers obtains four more bomb and torpedo hits on *Musashi*. The third wave of 16 fighters, 20 bombers and 32 torpedo aircraft from *Essex* and *Lexington* obtains another four bomb and two torpedo hits on *Musashi* and two bomb hits with little effect on *Yamato*. The almost simultaneously attacking waves from the *Franklin* and *Enterprise* and the *Intrepid* and *Cabot* with 42 fighters, 33 dive-bombers and 21 torpedo aircraft cause *Musashi* to sink after some ten bomb and six torpedo hits. The other battleships receive hits which do not affect their fighting capacity. In all, 30 US aircraft are lost. From the N, a Japanese reconnaissance plane locates TG.38.3 and Ozawa flies off the 76 operational aircraft from his four carriers but they do not find their targets and fly on to Luzon. Only 25 aircraft remain on the carriers. Adm Halsey orders the Task Groups of TF.38 to concentrate and recalls TG.38.1, which is on the way to Ulithi, in order to attack the Japanese carriers located in the afternoon in the N.

Battle of Surigao Strait. In the S the advancing Japanese forces of Nishimura and Shima are located by US air reconnaissance on 24 Oct and the *Wakaba* is sunk by aircraft from *Franklin*. Rear-Adm Oldendorf forms 13 groups each of three PT boats in the southern approaches to Surigao Strait. The attacks are largely beaten off or outmanoeuvred: only *PT137* (Lt Kovar) is able to torpedo *Abukuma*. In the southern approach to the Surigao Strait, the Nishimura force is repeatedly attacked by US destroyer groups. *Remey*, *McGowan* and *Melvin* obtain a hit on *Fuso* from the E and *Monssen* and *McDermut* several hits from the W on the destroyer *Yamagumo*, which sinks, *Michishio*, which is brought to a standstill, and *Asagumo*, which returns with her bows blown off. A hit is also obtained on *Yamashiro*. This is followed by attacks from *Hutchins*, *Daly* and *Bache*, which sink

Michishio and hit *Fuso* so that she later sinks. Shortly afterwards, *Arunta* (RAN), *Killen* and *Beale* attack with guns and torpedoes. There follow attacks by *Robinson*, *Halford* and *Bryant* from the NE, by *Edwards*, *Leutze* and *Bennion* from the NW and by *Newcomb*, *Leary* and *Albert W Grant*, which is damaged by the fire from the heavy US ships. From the NW the cruisers *Boise*, *Phoenix* and *Shropshire* (RAN) open fire and from the NE the cruisers *Columbia*, *Denver*, *Minneapolis*, *Portland* and *Louisville* and, finally, the battleships *West Virginia*, *California*, *Tennessee*, *Maryland* and *Mississippi*. *Pennsylvania* is unable to fire because other American ships obstruct her. *Yamashiro* is sunk by torpedoes from *McDermut*, *Shigure* escapes undamaged and *Mogami* turns away heavily damaged but collides with the approaching *Nachi*. Shima returns and on the way the destroyer *Asagumo* is sunk by gunfire from *Denver*; in the morning of 25 Oct *Mogami* has to be abandoned following air attacks.

Battle of Samar. The Japanese Kurita force passes through the San Bernardino Strait after dark on 24 Oct, unobserved by US air reconnaissance, and by dawn on 25 Oct is E of Samar where it encounters TG.77.4.3 (Rear-Adm C A F Sprague—see above), which is mistaken for fleet carriers. Making skilful use of rain squalls, the force flies off its aircraft and tries, with cover from torpedo attacks from the destroyers and DEs and from smokescreens, to escape towards Leyte Gulf. One of the torpedo salvos from *Hoel* and *Johnston* hits *Kumano*, which is brought to a standstill; *Suzuya* tries to give help. The Japanese ships are repeatedly forced to take evasive action in the face of further torpedo attacks and air attacks by aircraft from TG.77.4.2 (Rear-Adm Stump) until finally *Tone* and *Chikuma*, followed by *Haguro* and *Chokai*, are able to come up the weather side and bring the carriers under effective fire, in which *Yamato* and *Nagato* join from the N. *Hoel*, *Johnston*, *Samuel B Roberts* and *Gambier Bay* sink. While *Haruna* and *Kongo* try to attack TG.77.4.2, which has in the meantime been sighted, its aircraft hit the *Chikuma* and *Chokai* so heavily that they sink, *Chokai* by a coup de grâce from *Fujinami*. *Tone* and *Haguro* have already approached to within less than 10000m from the remaining escort carriers, but Adm Kurita breaks off the attack under the weight of the air attacks (in which *Suzuya* is torpedoed and has to be sunk by *Okinami*) and turns away to the San Bernardino Strait. At that moment, six Japanese kamikaze aircraft (Sub-Lt Saki) attack TG.77.4.3 and sink the carrier *St Lo*

and damage *Kalini Bay*, *Kitkun Bay* and *White Plains*; only *Fanshaw Bay* remains undamaged. From Mindanao, a kamikaze formation of five aircraft attacks TG.77.4.1 and damages *Sangamon*, *Suwanee* and *Santee*: the last is later torpedoed by the Japanese submarine *I-56* (Cdr Morinaga). *I-54*, in trying to attack this task group, is sunk by the DE *Richard M Rowell*. TG.38.1 (Vice-Adm McCain), which has been recalled from Ulithi and which comprises the carriers *Wasp*, *Hornet*, *Hancock*, *Monterey* and *Cowpens*, the cruisers *Chester*, *Pensacola*, *Salt Lake City*, *Boston*, *San Diego* and *Oakland* and 20 destroyers, flies off early on 25 Oct two waves totalling 147 aircraft against Kurita's withdrawing force. They cause damage.

Battle off Cape Engaño. In the meantime the three other groups of TF.38 have advanced during the night 24–25 Oct at high speed to the N to find the Ozawa force. At dawn TF.34 (Vice-Adm Lee) is formed from the battleships *Iowa*, *New Jersey* (Adm Halsey), *Washington*, *Alabama*, *Massachusetts* and *Indiana*, the cruisers *Santa Fé*, *Mobile*, *New Orleans* and *Wichita* and ten destroyers, to engage the Japanese ships with gunfire. In the course of the day the US carriers fly off their aircraft in six waves (in all, 326 dive-bombers and torpedo aircraft and 201 fighters) to attack.

The light carrier *Chitose* is set on fire by aircraft from *Essex* and *Lexington* and sinks and the fleet carrier *Zuikaku* is torpedoed by aircraft from *Intrepid*, *San Jacinto*, *Lexington* and *Cowpens* and sinks. The light carrier *Zuiho* is sunk by aircraft from *Essex* and *Langley* and the light carrier *Chiyoda* and the destroyer *Hatsutsuki* are damaged by aircraft from *Lexington* and *Franklin* and sunk by gunfire from the cruisers *Santa Fé*, *Wichita*, *New Orleans* and *Mobile*. The battleship *Hyuga* escapes in spite of 34 near-misses. The battleship *Ise* escapes from an attack by the US submarine *Halibut* which, with *Tuna*, *Haddock*, *Pintado*, *Atule* and *Jallao*, forms a patrol line along the withdrawal route of Ozawa's force. *Halibut* (Cdr Galantin) sinks the destroyer *Akizuki* and *Jallao* (Lt-Cdr Icenhower) is able to sink the damaged cruiser *Tama*.

As a result of Rear-Adm Sprague's reports, Adm Halsey has been speeding to the S since mid-day with the six battleships, the cruisers *Biloxi*, *Vincennes* and *Miami* and eight destroyers, while TG.38.2 follows as air escort. In order to find the Kurita force before it reaches the San Bernardino Strait, Adm Halsey proceeds towards it in the evening at high speed with the fastest battleships, *Iowa* and *New Jersey*, and eight

destroyers. But Kurita has already passed through it; only the destroyer *Nowake*, left behind to rescue survivors, is sunk, by the destroyer *Owen*.

On 26 Oct TG.38.1 and 38.2, which have arrived E of the San Bernardino Strait, again attack the Kurita force as it returns through the Sibuyan Sea and they sink, partly in co-operation with B-24s from the US 5th AF from Biak and Morotai, the cruisers *Kinu* (by TG.77.4) and *Noshiro* (by the carriers *Wasp* and *Hornet*) and the destroyers *Uranami* (by TG.77.4) and *Hayashimo* (by *Wasp* and *Hornet*) which, in part, belong to the transport unit. Off the south coast of Panay, B-24s of the 13th USAAF sink the cruiser *Abukuma*, already disabled by *PT137*.

A new Japanese kamikaze attack with five aircraft from Cebu on TG.77.1 damages *Suwanee*.

18 Oct   South West Pacific
The Australian minesweeper *Geelong* is lost off the coast of New Guinea in a collision with the steamer *York*.

19 Oct   Norway
The German *U957* is badly damaged in a collision with a transport off the Lofoten Islands and has to be decommissioned.

20 Oct–10 Nov   Arctic
Convoy operation JW.61/RA.61. On 20 Oct JW.61, consisting of 29 steamers and six Lend-Lease submarine-chasers for the Soviet Northern Fleet, sets out from Loch Ewe. The escort (Vice-Adm Dalrymple-Hamilton) comprises the escort carriers *Vindex*, *Nairana* and *Tracker*, the cruiser *Dido*, the 17th DD Flotilla, consisting of *Onslow*, *Opportune*, *Orwell*, *Offa*, *Obedient* and *Oribi*, and the DEs of the 21st EG, comprising *Conn*, *Byron*, *Fitzroy*, *Deane*, *Redmill* and *Rupert*, and of the 24th EG, comprising *Louis*, *Inglis*, *Lawson*, *Loring*, *Narborough* and *Mounsey*, as well as the destroyer *Walker*, the sloops *Lark* and *Lapwing* and the corvettes *Camellia*, *Oxlip* and *Rhododendron* of the 8th and 20th EGs. The convoy passes through the concentration of the 'Panther' U-boat group (*U293*, *U295*, *U310*, *U315*, *U363*, *U365*, *U387*, *U425*, *U636*, *U668*, *U737*, *U771*, *U956*, *U965*, *U968*, *U992*, *U995*, *U997* and *U1163*). On 26–27 Oct *U1163*, (Lt Balduhn), *U956* (Lt Mohs), *U365* (Lt-Cdr Wedemeyer), *U995* (Lt Hess) and *U295* (Lt Wieboldt) vainly attack escort vessels with T-5s—sometimes repeatedly. On 28 Oct the convoy, met by Russian destroyers, minesweepers and submarine-chasers, arrives off the Kola Inlet. Russian escorts bring some of the steamers into the White Sea on 30 Oct. From 29 Oct to 6 Nov the special

convoy JW.61A, consisting of two large transports with 11000 liberated Russian prisoners of war, proceeds from Britain to Murmansk accompanied by the escort carrier *Campania*, the cruiser *Berwick*, the destroyers *Saumarez*, *Cassandra*, *Scourge*, *Serapis*, *Cambrian* and *Caprice* and the 3rd EG with the DEs *Duckworth*, *Berry*, *Cooke*, *Domett*, *Essington* and *Rowley*.

Soviet destroyers and minesweepers bring the feeder convoy DB.10 from the White Sea to the Kola Inlet from 30 Oct to 1 Nov. There *U310* (Lt Ley) and *U295* try in vain to attack the escorts with T-5s. On 2 Nov RA.61, with 33 ships and the escort of JW.61 together with the 3rd E.G, sets out. Off the Kola Inlet *U295* hits the DE *Mounsey* with a T-5. The boats of the 'Panther' group are unable to get to the convoy against the strong escort. But bad radar conditions frustrate the attacks against the U-boats near the convoy. It reaches Loch Ewe without loss on 9 Nov. From 5 to 8 Nov further attacks by the German U-boats *U997* (Lt Lehmann), *U956* and *U771* (Lt Block) on Soviet escort vessels have no success. *U771*, returning submerged, is sunk by the British submarine *Venturer* in an underwater attack.

20 Oct–29 Nov   Arctic

Soviet convoy operation AB.15: the icebreakers *Josif Stalin* and *Severny Veter* return from the eastern part of the Siberian sea route through the West Siberian and Kara Sea, escorted by a destroyer, five ex-US minesweepers and five ex-US submarine-chasers. The convoy is under the orders of Rear-Adm Bogolepov and under the overall command of the Cdr White Sea Flotilla, Vice-Adm Panteleev. In the Kara Sea, 10 U-boat attacks are claimed; but, in fact, there has been no U-boat in the Kara Sea since 2 Oct. After passing through the Kara Strait, the escort is reinforced with seven destroyers. The Gorlo Strait is reached in Force 9 winds.

The U-boat attacks and engagements claimed near Kanin Nos on 24 Oct with the convoy DB.9 and the minesweeper T-116, the patrol ship *SKR-20*, the submarine-chaser *MO-251* and the destroyer *Doblestny* and on 1 Nov with the convoy DB.10 and the minesweepers *T-111* and *T-113* and the destroyer *Derzki* must also be based on faulty observation, since all German U-boats were deployed with the 'Panther' group in the operation against the convoys JW.61 and RA.61.

23 Oct   Norway

The German patrol boat *V5506/Zick* (ex-Norwegian torpedo boat *Trygg*) is beached after receiving a bomb hit at Hjeltefjord.

24 Oct–4 Nov   Norway

Operation 'Hardy': aircraft from the British escort carriers *Campania* and *Trumpeter*, escorted by the cruiser *Devonshire* and the destroyers *Saumarez*, *Serapis*, *Scorpion*, *Savage*, *Zambesi* and *Zephyr*, lay mines in Lepsorev and Harrhamsfjord near Aalesund and attack W/T stations on Vigra and Hanoy. Two small Norwegian ships are set on fire and driven ashore.

Operation 'Athletic': from 26 to 28 Oct another force (Rear-Adm Moore), consisting of the carrier *Implacable* escorted by the cruiser *Mauritius* and the destroyers *Myngs*, *Venus*, *Verulam*, *Volage*, *Algonquin* (RCN) and *Sioux* (RCN), makes attacks on Bodö/Sandnessjoen, in which the naval ferry barges *F235* and *F236* are damaged, on Rörvik, in which the patrol vessel *V5722* and the aircraft depot ship *Karl Meyer* are destroyed, and on Lodingen and Kristiansund North, in which the minesweeper *M433*, *Minenräumschiff 26* and two steamers are destroyed and *U1060* is damaged by a Firefly of No 1771 Sqn FAA. On 30 Oct *U1061* is damaged by Liberator 'A' of No 224 Sqn RAF and Leigh Light Wellington 'R' of No 407 Sqn RCAF. On 4 Nov *U1060*, which is beached after the attack of 27 Oct, is destroyed by Liberators 'Y' and 'H' of No 311 (Czech) Sqn RAF and Halifaxes 'D' and 'T' of No 502 Sqn RAF.

25 Oct   Iceland

The Canadian destroyer *Skeena* is wrecked in a gale at Reykjavik.

25 Oct   Air War/Italy

In an USAAF air raid on Genoa, the German destroyer *TA31* (ex-Italian *Dardo*) is damaged beyond repair.

25–26 Oct   Mediterranean

The British cruiser *Aurora* and the destroyers *Tetcott* and *Tyrian* bombard Milos.

25–31 Oct   Baltic

On 25 Oct the German the auxiliary minesweeper *M3117/K163* is sunk by Soviet air attack in the eastern Baltic. On 31 Oct the German troop evacuation transport *Bremerhaven* is sunk by Soviet air attack N of Hela; 410 are dead.

26 Oct   North Atlantic

The Norwegian corvette *Rose* is sunk in collision with the DE *Manners* in convoy ON.260 540 nautical miles E of Cape Race.

27 Oct–12 Nov   Air War/Norway

A raid by No 5 Group RAF Bomber Command against the U-boat pens and harbour installations at Bergen has to be abandoned because of the weather: only 47 aircraft drop their bombs and three are lost.

27 Oct–27 Nov   South West Pacific

TF.38 (Vice-Adm Mitscher) continues to support the Leyte fighting. On 27 Oct Gen MacArthur calls for support for Leyte from TF.38 because the USAAF can only employ inadequate forces on Tacloban. TG.38.3 (Rear-Adm Sherman), with the carriers *Essex*, *Lexington* and *Langley*, flies fighter protection for Leyte. An attack by *Essex* hits a small Japanese supply convoy and the destroyers *Fujinami* and *Shiranuhi* are sunk. On 28 Oct TG.38.4 (Rear-Adm Davison), with *Franklin*, *Enterprise*, *San Jacinto* and *Belleau Wood*, and TG.38.2 (Rear-Adm Bogan), with *Intrepid*, *Hancock*, *Cabot* and *Independence*, take over the support role. TG.38.4 wards off a Japanese air attack by 44 aircraft, 13 of which are shot down at a cost of four American. The Japanese submarine *I-46* (Lt-Cdr Kawaguchi) tries to attack the group but is located and sunk by the destroyers *Helm* and *Gridley*. *I-26* (Lt-Cdr Nishiuchi) must also have been lost about this time. During the night 28–29 Oct *I-45* (Lt-Cdr Kawashima) sinks the DE *Eversole*, which is proceeding to an escort carrier group, but the submarine is herself sunk by the DE *Whitehurst* belonging to a tanker group in the vicinity. In addition, *I-53*, *I-56* (which makes several unsuccessful attacks and torpedoes *LST695*), *I-38* and *I-41* operate E of Leyte and *Ro-43*, *Ro-46*, *Ro-109* and *Ro-112* E of Luzon. On 29 Oct TG.38.2 attacks airfields in the area of Manila; while losing 11 of its own aircraft, it shoots down 71 Japanese and destroys 13 on the ground. Only one Japanese kamikaze pilot out of 13 lightly hits the *Intrepid*. On 30 Oct TG.38.4 covers Leyte and is attacked by six Japanese kamikazes, which severely damage *Franklin* and *Belleau Wood*. TF.38 proceeds to Ulithi: TG.38.1 arrives on 29 Oct, TG.38.3 on 30 Oct and TG.38.2 and 38.4 on 2 Nov. Vice-Adm Mitscher hands over command to Vice-Adm McCain. Rear-Adm Montgomery takes over TG.38.1.

In Leyte Gulf, Japanese aircraft and kamikaze pilots direct their attacks against ships used to support the 6th Army. On 27 Nov the battleship *California* is damaged by aircraft fire. On 28 Nov 12 kamikazes from Luzon and three from Cebu attack, and one damages the cruiser *Denver*. On 1 Nov seven kamikazes attack in Leyte Gulf and sink the destroyer *Abner Read* and damage the destroyers *Anderson*, *Claxton* and *Ammen*; *Killen* and *Bush* receive bomb hits. On 2 Nov Japanese bombers attack the airfield at Tacloban and sink the escort vessel *PCER848* and damage a transport. On Leyte, the Japanese defenders (the 16th Inf Div, Lt-Gen Makino†) are reinforced by units of the 35th Army (Lt-Gen Suzuki), elements of the 102nd and 1st Inf Divs as well as smaller contingents which are landed in Ormoc. TF.38 has to intervene again. To support the ships in Leyte Gulf, TG.34.5 is sent on 1 Nov with the battleships *New Jersey* and *Iowa*, the cruisers *Biloxi*, *Vincennes* and *Miami* and six destroyers and TG.38.2. But it is recalled on 2 Nov to attack Luzon with TF.38 (three groups but not 38.4). On the way the cruiser *Reno* is torpedoed on 3 Nov by the Japanese submarine *I-41* (Lt-Cdr Kondo); she is detached to Ulithi with four destroyers.

On 5 and 6 Nov TG.38.1, with *Wasp*, *Hornet*, *Monterey* and *Cowpens*, TG.38.2 with *Intrepid*, *Hancock*, *Cabot* and *Independence*, and TG.38.3, with *Lexington*, *Langley* and the new *Ticonderoga*, attack Luzon. The Americans lose 25 aircraft but over 400 Japanese aircraft are destroyed. In addition, the cruiser *Nachi* is sunk in Manila Bay by aircraft from *Lexington* and on the west coast of Luzon the cruiser *Kumano* is hit by no fewer than nine torpedoes out of 23 fired by a submarine group (Cdr Chapple) consisting of *Guitarro*, *Bream*, *Raton* and *Ray*. The cruiser can, however, be beached. Twelve Japanese kamikaze aircraft attack TG.38.3 and badly damage *Lexington*. Five more kamikazes are no longer able to find the retiring TF.38 on 7 Nov.

In spite of frequent air attacks by the US 5th AF, Japanese convoys bring troops and supplies to Ormoc at the beginning of Nov. On 9 Nov a convoy with 2000 troops of the 26th Inf Div is attacked by 30 B-25s but is able to land most of the troops. On the next day the corvette *Kaibokan 11* and two steamers of the returning convoy are sunk. TF.38 (Rear-Adm Sherman) makes heavy attacks on the reinforcement transports on 11 Nov (347 sorties) with TG.38.1 (*Hornet*, *Monterey* and *Cowpens*), TG.38.3 (*Essex*, *Ticonderoga* and *Langley*) and TG.38.4 (*Enterprise* and *San Jacinto*). Eleven US aircraft are lost; but the Japanese destroyers *Hamanami*, *Naganami*, *Shimakaze* and *Wakatsuki*, the minesweeper *W30* and five transports are sunk. Of the 10000 troops embarked on the ships, only a fraction reach the shore. A Japanese attempt to find TF.38 with 11 kamikazes fails. On the same day, a task force (Rear-Adm Smith) comprising the cruisers *Chester*, *Pensacola* and *Salt Lake City* and destroyers shells Iwo Jima.

After replenishing on 12 Nov, the three Task Groups of TF.38 make new attacks on 13 and 14 Nov on the Luzon area, particularly on ships in Manila Bay. From 14 Nov *Wasp*, which has returned from Guam with a new Air Group, is again there with

Vice-Adm McCain. The Japanese cruiser *Kiso*, the destroyers *Akebono*, *Akishimo*, *Hatsuharu* and *Okinami* and 10 steamers are sunk and the destroyer *Ushio* and five steamers damaged. Kamikaze attacks with four aircraft each are intercepted. After further replenishment on 16 Nov and the relief of TG.38.3 by 38.2 (*Intrepid*, *Hancock*, *Cabot* and *Independence*), the carriers again attack Luzon and ships in Manila Bay on 19 Nov. The cruiser *Isuzu* is damaged and two steamers and one submarine-chaser sunk. Four kamikaze aircraft are intercepted. When she tries to approach TG.38.2 the Japanese submarine *I-41* is found by a submarine-hunter group with the escort carrier *Anzio* and sunk. The 'Kikusui' group, which set out from Japan on 8 Nov, tries on 20 Nov to use 'Kaiten' one-man torpedoes for the first time. But in approaching the Kossol Passage (Palau), *I-37* is sunk on 19 Nov by the DEs *McCoy*, *Reynolds* and *Conklin*. *I-36* (Lt-Cdr Teramoto) and *I-47* (Lt-Cdr Orita) launch one and four 'Kaiten' respectively off Ulithi on 20 Nov. One of them (Sub-Lt Nishida) destroys the tanker *Mississinewa* (11316 tons); two others, in trying to attack the cruisers *Mobile* and *Biloxi*, are destroyed by gunfire close to the ships, one by the destroyer *Case* and one by a USMC aircraft. Their success is greatly exaggerated in Japan.

After two replenishments, on 20 and 23 Nov, TG.38.2 (Rear-Adm Bogan) and 38.3 (Rear-Adm Sherman) again attack Luzon on 25 Nov. There take part four fleet carriers, three light carriers, six battleships, five light cruisers and destroyers. The cruiser *Kumano*, the former Chinese small cruiser *Yasoshima* (ex-*Ping Hei*), the landing ships *T6* and *T10* and three steamers are sunk. A Japanese submarine group consisting of *Ro-41*, *Ro-43*, *Ro-49*, *Ro-50*, *Ro-109* and *Ro-112* tries to approach the carriers but only *Ro-50* (Lt-Cdr Kimura) fires a salvo, which misses. Twenty-five Kamikaze aircraft have, however, more success: *Intrepid* and *Cabot* are severely, and *Hancock* and *Essex* slightly, damaged. TF.38 proceeds to Ulithi, TG.4 arriving on 23 Nov, TG.1 on 25 Nov and TG.2 and 3 on 27 Nov.

In the meantime, frequent air and kamikaze attacks are made on the ships in Leyte Gulf. On 12 Nov two repair ships and on 17 Nov and again on 23 Nov a troop transport are hit.

28 Oct   South West Pacific
The British submarine *Trenchant* launches 'Chariots' against shipping in Phuket Harbour, Thailand. The naval auxiliary *Sumatra Maru* (984 tons) is sunk.

29 Oct–12 Nov   Norway
On 29 Oct there is an unsuccessful attack by 32 Lancaster bombers of Nos 9 and 617 Sqns from Lossiemouth (Scotland) on *Tirpitz* at her new anchorage near Tromsö. On 12 Nov 21 Lancasters from the same units attack *Tirpitz* (Capt Weber†) again as she lies off Tromsö and, as a result of several hits by 12000lb 'Tallboy' bombs, the ship capsizes. Twenty-eight officers and 874 men of the ship's crew perish; 880 are rescued.

31 Oct   Mediterranean
The German MMSs *R185* and *R195* are scuttled at Saloniki.

Nov   North Sea/Intelligence
The German naval forces in the North Sea are allocated a separate cypher circuit, 'Barbara' (which is never broken).

1 Nov   Baltic
The German *U262* is damaged beyond repair in a collision with *U664* off Gdynia.

1 Nov   North Sea
Operation 'Infatuate': landing by the 152nd Bde of the 52nd British Inf Div (Maj-Gen Hakewell-Smith), the 4th Commandos, the 10th Inter-Allied Commandos and the 4th Special Service Bde (RM Cdos 41, 47 and 48) on the island of Walcheren in the Scheldt estuary. The island, which is defended by the German 70th Inf Div, (Lt-Gen Daser), bars the approach to Antwerp with its coastal batteries. The island is shelled by the battleship *Warspite* and the monitors *Erebus* and *Roberts*. In the operation, which ends with the surrender of the German garrison on 8 Nov, the following landing craft are lost: the LCTs *789*, *839*, *1133* and *7011*, the LCGs *1*, *2*, *101* and *102*, the LCFs *37* and *38*, 10 LCAs, one LCI, two LCPs and three LCSs.

1–20 Nov   Mediterranean
The British escort destroyers *Wheatland* and *Avon Vale*, sent to lay an ambush, sink the German torpedo boat *TA20* and the corvettes *UJ202* and *UJ208* S of Lussino in the Adriatic on 1 Nov.

On 3 Nov the minelayer *Kiebitz*, escorted by the torpedo boats *TA40*, *TA44* and *TA45*, carries out a mining operation in the Northern Adriatic. Fighter-bomber attacks are held off. In a US air attack on Fiume, the torpedo boat *TA21*, *Kiebitz* and the escort vessel *G104* are sunk. From Mar to Nov 1944 *Kiebitz* has laid about 5000 mines in the Adriatic, sometimes supported by the minelayer *Fasana*.

On 20 Nov a group of boats from the 3rd MTB Flotilla sinks two motor sailing ships off Ancona.

1–27 Nov   Norway
Attacks on German shipping. On 1 Nov the Norwegian *MTB712* and *MTB709* sink the

German patrol boats *V5525* and *V5531* in Sognefjord.

Operation 'Counterblast'. In the night 12–13 Nov, assisted by 'Ultra' intelligence, a British naval force (Rear-Adm McGrigor) consisting of the heavy cruiser *Kent*, the light cruiser *Bellona* and the destroyers *Myngs*, *Verulam*, *Zambesi* and *Algonquin* (Canadian) attacks the German convoy KS.357 off Listerfjord (SE of Egersund). Of the four freighters of the convoy, *Greif* (996 tons) and *Cornouailles* (3324 tons) sink, as do, of the six escort vessels, the minesweepers *M427* and *M416* and the submarine-chasers *UJ1221*, *UJ1223* and *UJ1713*. In the rescue operations in the morning of 13 Nov the motor minesweeper *R32* is lost in air attacks.

On 13 Nov the Norwegian *MTB688* and *MTB627* attack a German convoy in the southern exit of Krakhelle Sound (Sognefjord). Four torpedoes are outmanoeuvred by the two steamers. The escorting *UJ1430* (slightly damaged), *UJ1432* and *V1512* drive the boats off.

In a raid by aircraft from the escort carrier *Pursuer*, escorted by the cruiser *Euryalus* and the destroyers *Caesar*, *Nubian*, *Venus* and *Zephyr*, on 14 Nov off Trondheim, *V6413* is sunk.

On 20 Nov 8 Avengers of No 856 Sqn FAA from the carrier *Premier*, escorted by 16 Wildcats of No 881 Sqn FAA from *Pursuer*, lay mines at Haugesund. The ships are escorted by the cruiser *Diadem* and the destroyers *Onslaught*, *Scorpion*, *Scourge* and *Zealous*.

On 27 Nov aircraft from the British carrier *Implacable* attack a southbound German convoy off Mosjöen (N of Namsos) and destroy the Norwegian freighters *Rigel* (3828 tons)—of 2721 men, including 2248 Russian prisoners, only 415 are rescued—and *Korsnes* (1795 tons), as well as the German freighter *Spree* (2867 tons) which is lying at anchor. The carrier is escorted by the light cruiser *Dido* and the destroyers *Myngs*, *Scourge*, *Zephyr*, *Scorpion*, *Sioux* (Canadian) and *Algonquin* (Canadian). On 27–28 Nov the Norwegian *MTB715* and *MTB623* unsuccessfully attack off Sognefjord a patrol boat force consisting of *V5514*, *V5527* and *RA203*. A second group, comprising *MTB717* and *MTB627*, attacks a German convoy and torpedoes the steamer *Welheim* (5455 tons) which has to be beached. The escort vessels *V5303*, *V5312* and *R312* obtain hits on the MTBs.

1–30 Nov Pacific

US submarine operations continue with assistance from 'Ultra' information (which leads sometimes to the formation of 'wolf-packs'). In the Kuriles–Hokkaido area, *Skipjack* (Lt-Cdr Molumphy?) sinks one picket boat and *Albacore* (Lt-Cdr Blanchard) is lost on 7 Nov on a Japanese mine N of Hokkaido. Off Honshu, *Greenling* (Lt-Cdr Gerwick) sinks two ships of 1916 tons and on 10 Nov the patrol boat *P-46/Yugao*, *Scamp* (Cdr Hollingsworth) is sunk off Tokyo Bay on 16 Nov by Japanese A/S forces, *Scabbardfish* (Lt-Cdr Gunn) sinks two ships of 1280 tons and the submarine *I-365* and on 22 Nov damages the frigate *Oki* and *Archerfish* (Lt-Cdr Enright) sinks off Shionomisaki on 29 Nov the carrier *Shinano* (which, at 59000 tons, is the biggest warship to be sunk by a submarine in WW2) On 10 Nov a group under Cdr Klakring sails from Saipan on an anti-picket boat sweep SE of Japan to clear the way for a carrier strike. Participating are *Silversides*, *Saury*, *Trigger*, *Tambor*, *Ronquil*, *Burrfish* and *Sterlet*. *Silversides* (Lt-Cdr Coye) sinks one picket, *Saury* (Lt-Cdr Waugh) sinks one and damages one, *Tambor* sinks one picket and *Ronquil* and *Burrfish* together sink one, but because of the fierce resistance put up by the well-armed boats damage is inflicted on *Tambor* and *Burrfish*, while *Ronquil* is damaged by her own gunfire.

South of Kyushu and in the Yellow Sea a 'wolfpack' operates, with *Queenfish* (Cdr Loughlin, pack leader), *Barb* (Cdr Fluckey) and *Picuda* (Lt-Cdr Shepard) and then another with *Spadefish* (Cdr Underwood, pack leader), *Peto* (Lt-Cdr Caldwell) and *Sunfish* (Lt-Cdr Shelby): *Queenfish* sinks five ships of 14415 tons and damages one of 4667 tons, *Peto* sinks three ships of 9196 tons, *Barb* sinks two ships of 15261 tons and three sailing vessels (and one ship of 5396 tons with *Spadefish*), *Spadefish* alone sinks two ships of 4060 tons and on 17 Nov the escort carrier *Shinyo* (ex-German liner *Scharnhorst*), *Picuda* sinks three ships of 21659 tons and damages one of 6925 tons and *Sunfish* sinks three ships of 16179 tons. In addition, in this area *Billfish* sinks one sailing vessel and *Sea Fox* has one miss.

In the Formosa Strait and E of Formosa, a 'wolfpack' with *Redfish* (Cdr McGregor, pack leader), *Shad* and *Bang* (Lt-Cdr Gallaher) operates. *Redfish* sinks one ship of 2552 tons and two sailing vessels, on 9 Dec together with *Sea Devil* (Lt-Cdr Styles) damages the carrier *Junyo* beyond repair and alone on 19 Dec sinks the carrier *Unryu*, *Bang* sinks two ships of 5223 tons and one sailing vessel and *Sealion* (Lt-Cdr Reich) on 21 Nov sinks the battleship *Kongo* and the escorting destroyer *Urakaze* off Keelong.

In the South China Sea, a 'wolfpack' with *Parche* (Cdr Ramage as pack leader), *Pomfret* (Cdr Hess) and *Sailfish* (Lt-Cdr Ward) operates. *Pomfret* sinks three ships of 13976 tons and together with *Atule* (Lt-Cdr Maurer) the patrol vessel *P-38/Yomogi* and *Atule* alone sinks two ships of 24241 tons and on 20 Nov the minesweeper *W-38*. W of Luzon, *Blackfin* (Lt-Cdr Laird) sinks two ships of 3065 tons, *Pintado* (Lt-Cdr Clarey) misses a carrier but sinks on 3 Nov the destroyer *Akikaze*, *Gunnel* (Lt-Cdr O'Neill) sinks one ship of 5623 tons and on 8 and 17 Nov the torpedo boats *Sagi* and *Hiyodori*, *Growler* is sunk on 8 Nov by Japanese naval ships, *Haddo* (Lt-Cdr Lynch) sinks one ship of 856 tons and damages one of 1189 tons and sinks on 25 Nov the frigate *Shimushu*, *Hake* (Lt-Cdr Hayler) torpedoes the cruiser *Isuzu* off Corregidor on 19 Nov and *Gar* has a miss.

Also the South China Sea there is a 'wolfpack' with *Flounder* (Cdr Stevens as pack leader), *Guavina* (Lt-Cdr Teideman) and *Bashaw* (Lt-Cdr Nichols). On its way to rendezvous with the group, *Flounder* sinks on 10 Nov the German *U537* in the Java Sea and later, together with her pack-mates, one ship of 5698 tons and *Guavina* sinks two other ships of 4620 tons. *Gurnard* (Cdr Cage) lays a minefield at Tanjong Patoe and sinks one ship of 6923 tons. In the area around Hainan and off the Indo-Chinese coast, *Haddock* has some misses, *Barbel* (Lt-Cdr Keating) sinks two ships of 8801 tons and *Pampanito* (Lt-Cdr Fenno) sinks two ships of 6439 tons. N of Palawan and Sarawak, *Hardhead* (Cdr Greenup) sinks one ship of 5266 tons and on 25 Nov the corvette *Kaibokan 38*, *Redfin* (Lt-Cdr Austin) sinks one ship of 5226 tons, *Besugo* (Lt-Cdr Wogan) sinks the landing ship *T-151*, *Mingo* (Lt-Cdr Staley) sinks one ship of 9486 tons and *Pargo* (Lt-Cdr Bell) sinks one ship of 5226 tons. Off NW Borneo, *Jack* (Lt-Cdr Fuhrmann) sinks two ships of 12455 tons and *Cavalla* (Lt-Cdr Kossler) sinks on 25 Nov the destroyer *Shimotsuki*. Off Makassar, *Barbero* (Lt-Cdr Hartman) sinks three ships of 9126 tons and the submarine-chaser *Ch-30*.

2–16 Nov North Sea

S175, *S207* and *S167* of the 9th German MTB flotilla sink the British tanker *Rio Bravo* (1141 tons) off Ostend and the Navy trawler *Colsay* (554 tons) off Nieuport on 2 Nov. The same night, there is an engagement between British MTBs and German patrol boats.

On 15–16 Nov British MTBs and the frigates *Retalick* and *Thornborough* locate six German motor torpedo boats of the 9th Flotilla in the Scheldt estuary which have come out on a mining operation and, in

315

the ensuing engagement, damage *S168* and compel the German boats to return.

2–22 Nov   Indian Ocean
On 2 Nov the British submarine *Shalimar* bombards targets on the Nicobar Islands. On 22 Nov the submarine *Stratagem* (Lt Pelly) is sunk by a Japanese destroyer in the Malacca Strait.

3–5 Nov   English Channel
The German gun ferries *AF44* and *AF92* are sunk in air attacks off Zijpe.

4–5 Nov   Air War/Italy
In an air attack on La Spezia on 4 Nov, the German torpedo boat *TA49* (ex-Italian *Lira*), fitting out, is wrecked.

6–17 Nov   Arctic
The German 4th DD Flotilla, with the destroyers *Z33*, *Z31*, *Z34* and *Z38*, covers the retreat from Tanafjord.

6–28 Nov   Air War/Western Europe
Mine offensive by RAF Bomber Command. In seven nights, 126 sorties are flown against Heligoland Bight, the Elbe river, the Danish and Norwegian coasts (especially in the Oslo and Kattegat area) and the western Baltic; two aircraft are lost. The German minesweeper *M584* is sunk by mine in the Kattegat on 30 Nov, as is the gun ferry *AF4* in the Ems river on 1 Dec.

9 Nov   Norway
The German MTB *S203* is sunk following a collision with the MMS *R220* but is salvaged and repaired.

10 Nov   English Channel
The British minesweeper *Hydra* is damaged beyond repair off Ostend and is towed into Sheerness.

10 Nov   South Pacific
The US ammunition ship *Mount Hood* blows up at Manus in the Admiralty Islands.

11 Nov   Baltic
The German patrol vessel *V1802* is sunk by Soviet air attack off Memel.

11 Nov   Mediterranean
The German hospital ship *Tübingen* is sunk by bombs and rocket fire from Allied aircraft off Cape Promontore.

11 Nov   Central Pacific
The Japanese minesweeper *W-22* sinks on a mine at Babelthuap.

12 Nov   Air War/Italy
The German transport *KT35* is destroyed in an air raid on Genoa. *KT36* is beached while attempting to evade an air attack off Moneglia.

12 Nov–4 Dec   Mediterranean
The British destroyer *Kimberley* bombards a German battery on Alimnia in the Dodecanese on 12 Nov and destroys two landing barges in Livadia Bay on 14 Nov. On 29 Nov the British minesweeper *MMS101* is mined and sunk in the Gulf of Salonika. On 4 Dec the cruiser *Aurora* and the destroyers *Marne*, *Meteor* and *Musketeer* bombard shipping targets at Rhodes.

14 Nov   South West Pacific
The Japanese escort *Heiyo* (ex-British minesweeper *Herald*) sinks on a mine in the Java Sea.

14–17 Nov   Mediterranean
The British destroyers *Brocklesby* and *Wheatland* bombard Bar in the northern Adriatic on 14 Nov; on 17 Nov the bombardment is repeated by the destroyers *Eggesford* and *Lauderdale*.

15 Nov   South West Pacific
The British fast minelayer *Ariadne*, with the US destroyers *Shaw* and *Caldwell*, the DE *Willmarth* and 20 landing craft, transports a regiment of the 31st US Inf Div from Morotai to Pegun Island in the Mapia Group for the purpose of erecting a weather station and a Loran station. The 200 Japanese on the island are overwhelmed by the US troops who land after shelling by the destroyers.

15 Nov–9 Jan   North Atlantic/English Channel
Operations by German schnorkel U-boats. On the way out to the North Atlantic *U322* is bombed on 24 Nov W of the Shetlands by Sunderland 'G' of No 330 (Norwegian) Sqn and sunk on 25 Nov by the frigate *Ascension* of the 5th SG. *U650* is lost from unknown causes in the 'Northern Transit Area' at the beginning of Dec.
In the area of Reykjavik, *U979* (Lt-Cdr Meermeier) from 23 Nov to 1 Dec misses one trawler, one convoy and one frigate. N of Scotland *U296* and *U775* (Lt Taschenmacher) operate from the end of Nov until the middle of Dec. *U775* sinks the DE *Bullen* with a T-5 on 6 Dec. *U1009* has to return owing to schnorkel trouble. *U1020*, *U297* and *U312* are employed round Scapa Flow against British carrier groups: on 6 Dec *U297* is sunk by the frigate *Loch Insh* and the DE *Goodall*. *U312* is damaged on 28 Dec when she goes aground in Hoxa Sound; *U1020* (Lt Eberlein) torpedoes the destroyer *Zephyr* on 31 Dec but is lost, probably in mid-Jan, in an attack by the destroyer *Onslaught* and a Polish destroyer. *U482* cruises in the North Channel and *U1202* (Lt-Cdr Thomsen) sinks a Liberty ship (7176 tons) in a convoy in the Bristol Channel. *U400* is sunk on 17 Dec by the frigate *Nyasaland* (18th EG) SW of Ireland when she tries to attack a convoy.
In the Channel, *U991* (Lt-Cdr Balke), in addition to three unsuccessful attacks, reports the sinking of a Liberty ship on 15 Dec. The same day, *U680* misses a trawler.

U772 (Lt-Cdr Rademacher), after a miss, sinks three ships of 10970 tons from two convoys and torpedoes two ships of 14367 tons on 29 Dec from the convoy TBC.1, one of which becomes a total loss. On 30 Dec the boat is sunk by Leigh Light Wellington 'L' of No 407 Sqn RCAF. *U486* (Lt G Meyer) sinks one ship of 6142 tons on 18 Dec, misses a destroyer on 21 Dec and sinks on 24 Dec the troop transport *Leopoldville* (11509 tons) which is escorted by the destroyers *Anthony* and *Brilliant* and three other escorts; 819 men drown. On 26 Dec the DE *Capel* is sunk and the DE *Affleck* damaged in a T-5 attack on the 1st SG; *Affleck* is never repaired. *U1209* runs on rocks off SW Ireland and is lost on 18 Dec. *U485*, the last boat to enter the Channel in 1944, misses a destroyer. The transport U-boats *U773* and *U722* return from St-Nazaire. During the preparations for the Ardennes offensive, *U1053*, *U870*, *U1232* and *U1009* are used as weather boats in the North Atlantic. As she departs for Gibraltar, *U870* (Cdr Hechler) meets a convoy on 20 Dec and from it sinks *LST359* and torpedoes *Fogg*, one of four US DEs. On the way out, in the North Atlantic, *U877* meets convoy HX.327 (EG.C3) on 27 Dec and is sunk by the Canadian corvettes *St Thomas* and *Edmundston*. When the weather boats are located by DF, a hunter group, equipped with the new DAQ HF/DF and consisting of the US DEs *Otter*, *Hubbard* and *Varian*, is deployed against them, but, at first, it has no success.

Off Cabot Strait, *U1228* (Lt Marienfeld) on 24 Nov sinks the corvette *Shawinigan* sailing on her own; in the Gulf of St Lawrence *U1230* (Lt-Cdr Hilbig) sinks one ship of 5458 tons; and *U1231* (Capt Lessing) misses two escort vessels and a steamer. *U806* (Lt-Cdr Hornbostel) sinks one ship of 7219 tons from an HX convoy off Halifax and, from three convoys forming up, the minesweeper *Clayoquot* on 24 Dec. The corvettes *Fennel* and *Transcona* are narrowly missed by T-5s.

16–19 Nov   Baltic
The German gun ferry *AF22* is sunk off Sventoi/Irbenstrait and *AF26* off Windava on 16 Nov; *AF18* capsizes off Sworbe after receiving bomb hits on 19 Nov during a Soviet air attack.

17–20 Nov   Norway
On 17 Nov the German minelayer *NKi01* (ex-Norwegian *Glommen*) is sunk by bombs in Trondheim Fjord. On 20 Nov the patrol vessel *V5107* is sunk by MTB torpedo N of Lagemen.

17–23 Nov   Indian Ocean
Operation 'Outflank'. A task force from the British Eastern Fleet under Rear-Adm Vian, consisting of the carriers *Indomitable* and *Illustrious*, the cruisers *Newcastle*, *Argonaut* and *Black Prince* and the destroyers *Kempenfelt*, *Whirlwind*, *Wrangler*, *Wessex* and *Wakeful*, sets out from Trincomalee on 17 Nov. After replenishing on 18 Nov from the tanker *Wave King* with the destroyers *Wager* and *Whelp*, the force flies off 27 Avenger bombers and 28 Corsair and Hellcat fighters early on 20 Nov to attack Pangkalan Brandan (NW Sumatra) but, because of the weather, they have to be diverted to the S to the oil installations of Belawan Deli. In the afternoon there is an attack on airfields near Sabang. There are no losses. The force returns on 23 Nov.

18–19 Nov   Mediterranean
An attempt to attack Allied traffic off the coast at San Remo in the Ligurian Sea with 15 'Marders' fails.

18–24 Nov   Baltic
Soviet offensive against the Sworbe Peninsula. On 18 Nov the Soviet 8th Army goes over to the attack with support from strong artillery and air formations and fire support from the gunboats *Volga*, *Bureja*, *Zeya* and 11 armoured cutters on the eastern side. On 18 Nov German minesweepers have engagements with Soviet ships on the eastern side of Sworbe: *M328* sinks one armoured cutter and on 21 Nov the minesweeper *T207/Shpil*. On 19 Nov *TKA-193* reports one minesweeper hit. From the W the torpedo boats *T23* and *T28* intervene in the fighting and on 19 Nov they, too, proceed to the eastern side in spite of heavy air attacks. On 20–21 Nov the task force (Vice-Adm Thiele), comprising the cruiser *Prinz Eugen* (Capt Reinicke), the 6th DD Flotilla with *Z25*, *Z35*, *Z36* and *Z43*, and the 3rd TB Flotilla (Cdr Verlohr) with *T21*, *T13*, *T16* and *T19*, intervenes from the W. On 22, 23 and 24 Nov the pocket-battleship *Admiral Scheer* (Capt Thienemann), with *Z25* and *Z35* and the 2nd TB Flotilla (Cdr Paul) comprising *T3*, *T12*, *T5*, *T9*, *T13* and *T16*, relieves the force. Several air attacks are repelled. *Lützow*, which is approaching as a relief for 24 Nov, has to return because the evacuation is completed during the night 23–24 Nov. 4694 men are transported by naval ferry barges. On the east coast on 20–21 Nov, *M328*, *M423*, *V1713* and *V302* have engagements with gunboats, armoured cutters and torpedo cutters.

18 Nov–15 Feb   Australia
The German U-boat *U862* (Cdr Timm) proceeds from Djakarta to the W and S of Australia to the Adelaide area, where on 9 Dec she has to break off an attack on the Greek steamer *Ilissos* when an aircraft approaches. A search by the Australian corvettes *Burnie*, *Lismore* and *Maryborough* on 10 Dec leads to no result. On 24 Dec *U862* sinks the US freighter *Robert J Walker* (7180 tons) in three approaches off Sydney. The ships deployed in the search, the US submarine-chaser *PC597*, the Australian destroyer *Quickmatch*, the corvettes *Ballarat*, *Goulbourn*, *Kalgoorlie* and *Whyalla*, the trawlers *Kiama* and *Yandra* and the British destroyers from Melbourne, *Quilliam*, *Quadrant* and *Quality*, do not find the U-boat but rescue survivors. Liberator bombers of the RAAF, deployed following DF bearings on a W/T message, do not find the U-boat on 29, 30 and 31 Jan SW of Fremantle. On 5–6 Feb *U862* sinks the US freighter *Peter Sylvester* (7176 tons) in three approaches 820 nautical miles W of Fremantle. The attack only becomes known when a steamer finds survivors. The ships deployed from Fremantle, the US frigate *Corpus Christi* and the Australian corvette *Dubbo*, find other boats. A planned search from 11 to 20 Feb for two missing boats with aircraft, with the British escort carriers *Slinger* and *Speaker*, which are in the course of being transferred, and with the US frigate *Hutchinson* and the Australian corvettes *Warnambool* and *Castlemaine*, leads to no result. Only on 28 Feb does the passing British escort carrier *Activity* find a boat. On 10 Mar the US submarine *Rock*, returning from a patrol in enemy waters, finds the last boat, which has covered 1100 nautical miles in 32 days. All 143 survivors are rescued.

20 Nov   Mediterranean
British MTBs, in an attack on a German convoy off Sestri-Levante (SE of Genoa), sink the submarine-chaser *UJ2207*.

21 Nov   North Sea
The German gun ferry *AF86* is sunk by fighter-bombers off Ameland.

21 Nov   North Pacific
A task group under Rear-Adm McCrea with two light cruisers and nine destroyers shells Matsuwa in the Kuriles.

22–23 Nov   Air War/Norway
An attack by No 5 Group RAF Bomber Command against the U-boat pens at Trondheim with 178 aircraft is abandoned because of the smokescreen which covers the target. Three aircraft are lost.

22–23 Nov   Indian Ocean
Reorganisation of the British Eastern Fleet: Vice-Adm Power forms the British East Indies Fleet with the battleship *Queen Elizabeth*, the battlecruiser *Renown*, five escort carriers, eight cruisers and 24 destroyers. The modern ships form the British Pacific Fleet under Adm Fraser and include the battleships *King George V* (Vice-Adm Rawlings) and *Howe*, the carriers *Indefatigable* (Rear-Adm Vian), *Illustrious*, *Victorious* and *Indomitable*, the cruisers *Swiftsure*, *Argonaut*, *Black Prince*, *Ceylon*, *Newfoundland* and the New Zealand *Gambia* and *Achilles* and three destroyer flotillas (the 4th with 'Q' class, the 25th with 'U' class and the 27th with 'W' class).

In the Malacca Strait and the western parts of the Malayan Archipelago in the month of Nov, *Tantalus* (Lt-Cdr Mackenzie) sinks one ship of 1918 tons and a small coaster and damages the submarine-chaser *Ch-1*, *Spirit* (Lt Langridge) sinks one small tanker and damages one ship, *Thorough* lays a minefield (in the Malacca Strait) and sinks three coasters and three junks, *Tudor* (Lt Porter) sinks one coaster, the Dutch *O-19* (Lt-Cdr v Karnebeek) sinks one small steamer, *Tally Ho* (Cdr Bennington) sinks the auxiliary minelayer *Wa-4* of 288 tons and 10 junks, *Stratagem* (Lt Pelly) sinks one ship of 1945 tons, *Spark* (Lt Kent) sinks two sailing vessels, *Sturdy* (Lt Andersen) sinks two coasters and six sailing vessels, *Supreme* sinks seven junks, *Stygian* (Lt Clarabut) sinks two coasters and one small landing craft and *Strongbow* sinks three junks and one tug in company with a barge.

24 Nov–5 Dec   Baltic
To block the exit of the Irben Strait, the German minelayers *Linz* and *Brummer* together with the minesweepers *M17*, *M155* and *M203* lay the 'Nordlicht I', 'II' and 'IV' barrages during the nights 24–25 and 29–30 Nov and 4–5 Dec.

25 Nov   South West Pacific
The Japanese minesweeper *W-18* is sunk in an attack by aircraft from the US 14th AF off Hainan Island.

27 Nov–6 Dec   South West Pacific
Japanese attempt to counter-attack on Leyte. Airbone commando troops are to knock out the US airfields and kamikazes are to hit the ships in order to weaken support for the US troops. TG.77.2 (Rear-Adm Weyler) is in Leyte Gulf with the battleships *Maryland*, *West Virginia*, *Colorado* and *New Mexico*, the cruisers *Columbia*, *Denver*, *Montpelier* and *St Louis* and 16 destroyers. The air landing on 27 Nov fails; bombers and five kamikazes damage *Colorado*, *Montpelier* and *St Louis* and *Maryland* just avoids an aerial torpedo but is hit, together with the destroyers *Saufley* and *Aulick*, by kamikazes on 29 Nov. A second attempt is made on 5–6 Dec: three kamikazes damage the destroyers *Mugford* and *Drayton*. The air landings, in which para-

troops are used, are to some extent more successful; for two days there is hard fighting for the airfield at Burauen. In the same period, US destroyers make sorties into Ormoc Gulf, first with *Waller*, *Saufley*, *Renshaw* and *Pringle* on 27 Nov which sink one Japanese midget submarine, then by *Waller*, *Renshaw*, *Cony* and *Conner* on 29–30 Nov and by *Conway*, *Cony*, *Eaton* and *Sigourney* on 1–2 Dec, but they are unsuccessful. On 3 Dec *Allen M Sumner*, *Moale* and *Cooper* intercept two Japanese destroyer-escorts with reinforcements for Ormoc. They sink *Kuwa*, but *Take* sinks *Cooper* with a torpedo and escapes. *Moale* is damaged by gunfire.

27 Nov–14 Dec   Arctic

Convoy operation JW.62/RA.62 in the Arctic. JW.62 has 30 merchant ships, escorted by the 8th and 20th EGs including the destroyers *Keppel*, *Beagle*, *Bulldog*, and *Westcott*, the sloops *Cygnet*, *Lapwing* and *Lark*, the corvettes *Allington Castle* and *Bamborough Castle* and the Norwegian corvettes *Tunsberg Castle* and *Eglantine* which are being transferred to Murmansk. The covering force comprises the cruiser *Bellona*, the 1st Div of the 7th DD Flotilla (*Caesar*, *Cassandra*, *Caprice* and *Cambrian*) and the 17th DD Flotilla (*Onslow*, *Orwell*, *Obedient*, *Offa*, *Onslaught* and *Oribi*) and as support groups there are the escort carriers *Campania* and *Nairana* with the frigates *Tavy*, *Tortola*, *Bahamas* and *Somaliland* and the Canadian 9th EG with the frigates *St John*, *Stormont*, *Monnow*, *Loch Alvie*, *Nene* and *Port Colborne*.

On 27 Nov the convoy is located by German air reconnaissance. A fighter from *Nairana* shoots down the contact-keeper. The U-boat groups 'Stock' (*U313*, *U315*, *U293*, *U363*, *U299*, *U365*, *U286*, *U318*, *U995* and *U992*) and 'Grube' (*U295*, *U1163*, *U387*, *U997*, *U668*, *U310* and *U965*) are deployed W of Bear Island and off the Kola coast. On 1 Dec the 'Stock' group is moved to the Kola coast because it is assumed that the convoy has passed the Bear Island passage. The convoy makes a diversion whilst the support groups make sorties against the suspected U-boat concentration—without result. On 2 Dec *U995* and *U363* (Lt-Cdr Nees) attack the Soviet coastal convoy PK.20 (Kirkenes–Kola), consisting of three steamers and four large and two small submarine-chasers. *U363* sinks the steamer *Proletari* (1123 tons). On 3 Dec *U1163* (Lt Balduhn) sinks on the eastern Kola coast the steamer *Revolutsioner* (433 tons) from the Soviet convoy KB.35 (Kola–White Sea), comprising two steamers and two former trawler patrol boats, *T-38* and *SKR-20*. On

4 Dec *U363*, *U992* (Lt Falke) and *U995* (Lt Hess) make unsuccessful attacks on a Soviet coastal convoy off the Kola Inlet escorted by ex-US minesweepers. On 4–5 Dec in attacks on a Soviet coastal convoy in the entrance to the White Sea *U997* (Lt Lehmann) misses steamers and sinks the submarine-chaser *BO-226* (ex-US *SC1485*); *U295* (Lt Wieboldt) misses the destroyers *Deyatelny* and *Zhivuchi* with T-5s near Jokanga and is pursued by them. From 5 to 7 Dec *U293* (Lt-Cdr Klingspor), *U992*, *U995*, *U365* (Lt Todenhagen), *U318* (Lt Will), *U997* and *U1163* (Lt Balduhn) attack, sometimes repeatedly, Soviet A/S groups as well as escorts and ships of the incoming JW.62. But only on 7 Dec is the submarine-chaser *BO-229* (ex-US *SC1477*), belonging to a Soviet anti-submarine group (Capt 3rd Class Gritsyuk) comprising *BO-227*, *BO-228*, *BO-229* and *BO-150*, sunk by *U997*. JW.62 comes into harbour without loss. Before the return convoy RA.62 sets out with 28 ships and the escort of JW.62 on 9 Dec, the Allied support groups and a Soviet destroyer force (Rear-Adm Fokin) composed of *Baku*, *Gremyashchi*, *Razumny*, *Derzki*, *Doblestny* and *Zhivuchi* try to drive off the U-boats from the entrance to the Kola Inlet. In the process *U997* misses *Zhivuchi* and *Razumny* with T-5s on 9 Dec. *U387* is sunk by depth charges from the corvette *Bamborough Castle* (according to Soviet claims, by ramming from *Zhivuchi*). Only *U365* is able to establish contact with the convoy and to torpedo the destroyer *Cassandra* on 11 Dec after an unsuccessful attack on a tanker the day before. On 13 Dec the boat, while keeping contact with great determination, is sunk by Swordfish 'L' and 'Q' of No 813 Sqn FAA from the *Campania*.

An attempt by German torpedo aircraft of I/KG 26 (Maj Sölter) to attack the convoy SW of Bear Island is unsuccessful and results in the loss of two Ju 88s. The Norwegian corvette *Tunsberg Castle* runs on a mine of the German flanking barrage near Makkaur on 12 Dec and sinks.

28 Nov   Baltic

In a Soviet air raid against Libau, the German torpedo boat *T10* is damaged; she is transferred to Gdynia for repairs (see 18–19 Dec). *U80* is lost in a diving accident off Pillau.

28–29 Nov   North Sea

The first Allied convoy, consisting of 18 ships, arrives in Antwerp on 28 Nov. On 29 Nov German motor torpedo boats make an unsuccessful attempt to attack another Allied convoy proceeding to Antwerp.

30 Nov   English Channel

The British DE *Duff* is mined NW of Ostend; the ship is returned to Harwich but is laid up and not repaired.

30 Nov   Great Britain

The last British battleship, *Vanguard*, is launched.

1 Dec   North Sea

AF10 is sunk by air attack off the Frisian coast.

1–31 Dec   Pacific

US submarines continue their operations with the help of 'Ultra' information, often working together in 'wolfpacks' against Japanese convoys. In the Kuriles area, *Apogon* has a miss. Off Honshu, *Tilefish* (Lt-Cdr Kaithley) sinks on 19 Dec the torpedo boat *Chidori*. S of Kyushu, *Sea Devil* (Lt-Cdr Styles) sinks two ships of 16326 tons and damages the carrier *Junyo* (see 1–30 Nov), *Plaice* (Lt-Cdr Stevens) damages the DE *Maki* on 9 Dec and *Whale* (Lt-Cdr Grady) sinks two trawlers and two sailing vessels. In the Tsushima Strait, *Sea Owl* (Lt-Cdr Bennett) torpedoes the auxiliary submarine-chaser *Cha-135* and *Finback* (Lt-Cdr Williams) sinks one ship of 2111 tons off the Bonins. N of Luzon a 'wolfpack' operates with *Trepang* (Cdr Davenport, pack leader), *Razorback* (Lt-Cdr Brown) and *Segundo* (Lt-Cdr Fulp). *Trepang* sinks four ships of 13573 tons, *Razorback* sinks the torpedo boat *Kuretake* on 30 Dec and, together with *Segundo*, one ship of 6933 tons and *Segundo* alone sinks two ships of 7009 tons. In the same area, *Pintado* (Lt-Cdr Deragon) sinks the landing ship *T-104* and the fast transport *T-12* on 13 Dec and *Blenny* sinks two ships of 4203 tons and on 14 Dec the corvette *Kaibokan 28*. W of Luzon, *Hawkbill* (Lt-Cdr Scanland) sinks on 15 Dec the torpedo boat *Momo* and one barge.

In the NW part of the South China Sea, a 'wolfpack' with *Pampanito* (Cdr Fenno, pack leader), *Searaven* (Cdr Dry), *Sea Cat* (Cdr McGregor) and *Pipefish* (Cdr Deragon) operates. They have several misses and only *Pipefish* sinks, on 13 Dec, the corvette *Kaibokan 64*. Elsewhere in the South China Sea, *Flasher* (Lt-Cdr Grider) sinks four ships of 38668 tons and on 4 Dec the destroyer *Kishinami*, *Hammerhead* (Lt-Cdr Martin) and *Paddle* (Lt-Cdr Nowell) together sink one ship of 2854 tons and *Sealion* (Lt-Cdr Putnam) sinks the munitions transport *Mamiya* (15820 tons). Off Indo-China, *Dace* (Lt-Cdr Clagett) lays a minefield off Pulo Gambier and sinks one ship of 6925 tons and the munitions transport *Nozaki* of 640 tons. E of Malaya, *Bergall* (Lt-Cdr Hyde) torpedoes on 13 Dec the cruiser *Myoko* (which is never repaired). In the Java Sea, *Hoe* has one miss.

5–9 Dec Mediterranean
The British cruiser *Caledon*, the escort destroyer *Easton* and the corvette *La Malouine* with the Greek destroyer *Navarinon* and the corvette *Sakhtouris* shell ELAS positions near Piraeus and Salamis. On 21 Dec the cruiser *Ajax* shells ELAS positions near Piraeus.

6 Dec Arctic
The German gun ferry *AF27* is sunk off Kvaenangenfjord in a gale; she is later raised and recommissioned.

7 Dec Baltic
The German patrol vessel *V1606* is sunk by airborne torpedo off Steinort.

7–15 Dec South West Pacific
Following a sortie by the destroyers *Nicholas*, *O'Bannon*, *Fletcher* and *La Valette* during the night 6–7 Dec, TG.78.3 (Rear-Adm Struble), with eight APDs, 27 LCIs, 12 LSMs and four LSTs and a minesweeper group, lands the 77th US Inf Div (Maj-Gen Bruce) S of Ormoc early on 7 Dec. Cover and support are provided by the destroyers *Hughes*, *Barton*, *Walke*, *Laffey*, *O'Brien*, *Flusser*, *Lamson*, *Edwards*, *Smith*, *Reid*, *Conyngham* and *Mahan*. After the successful landing which encounters no strong resistance, 21 Japanese kamikaze pilots attack and sink the destroyer *Mahan*, the APD *Ward* and *LST737*. The destroyer *Lamson* and the APD *Liddle* are badly damaged. A Japanese attempt to land a reinforced regiment near Ormoc with the escort destroyers *Ume* and *Sugi* and the APD *T-11* is frustrated by aircraft from Tacloban: the APD sinks and the destroyers are damaged. On 8 Dec three transports are sunk W of Leyte. On 10 Dec *Hughes* is damaged in Leyte Gulf by kamikazes. On 11 Dec the destroyer *Reid* is sunk by two kamikazes W of the Surigao Strait and the destroyer *Coghlan*, from a supply convoy, has an engagement with the Japanese destroyers *Uzuki* and *Yuzuki*, which are sunk by *PT492* and *PT490* and by aircraft which also badly hit a troop convoy near Palompon. On 8 Dec the Japanese midget submarine *Ha-81* fails to secure a hit off Ormoc.

7–14 Dec Norway
Operation 'Urbane'. During the RA.62 convoy operation (see 27 Nov–14 Dec), a British carrier force (Rear-Adm McGrigor) with the fleet carrier *Implacable* and the escort carriers *Premier* and *Trumpeter*, escorted by the cruiser *Diadem* and the destroyers *Zambesi*, *Savage*, *Vigilant*, *Zealous*, *Serapis*, *Stord* (RNoN), *Sioux* (RCN) and *Algonquin* (RCN) operates off west Norway. On 7 Dec twelve Avengers

from No 856 Sqn FAA (*Premier*), escorted by 14 Wildcats from No 881 Sqn (*Trumpeter*) lay mines in the Salhusstrommen. On 8 Dec twelve Fireflies of No 1771 Sqn from *Implacable*, escorted by nine Wildcats of No 881 Sqn from *Trumpeter*, sink two merchant ships off Stavanger.

On 14 Dec the cruisers *Diadem* and *Mauritius*, with four destroyers, attack shipping off Stadtlandet. German reconnaissance aircraft come upon a force comprising *Premier*, *Trumpeter*, the cruiser *Devonshire* and the destroyers *Zealous*, *Serapis*, *Savage*, *Zephyr*, *Algonquin* and *Sioux*. Thirty torpedo aircraft of II/KG 26 (Capt R Schmidt) try in vain to find the British ships and two Ju 88s fail to return.

8 Dec Norway
The Norwegian *MTB717* and *MTB653* attack a German convoy off Korsfjord, consisting of two steamers and the patrol boats *V5113* and *V5114*, and sink the freighter *Ditmar Koel*.

8 Dec–3 Jan North Atlantic
Allied escort groups on the North Atlantic route from St John's to the North or South Western Approaches comprise, in the order of their convoy escort runs, EG.B1, with the DE *Inman* and the corvettes *Dianella*, *Lotus*, *Poppy* and *Tintagel Castle* and with the corvette *Clover* detached and the frigate *Chelmer* (SO) and the corvette *Starwort* non-operational; EG.B3, with the frigate *Exe* (SO) and the corvettes *Borage* and *Flint Castle* and with the frigate *Gardiner* and corvettes *Geranium* and *Vervain* detached and the corvette *Pimpernel* non-operational; EG.C5, with the RCN frigates *Runnymede* (SO) and *St Stephen* and the RCN corvettes *Eyebright*, *Hespeler*, *Long Branch* and *New Westminster* and with the RCN corvette *Huntsville* detached; EG.C1, with the RCN frigates *Hallowell* and *Royal Mount* and the RCN corvettes *Arnprior* (SO), *Chambly*, *Frontenac* and *Orangeville* and with the corvettes *Giffard* and *Fennel* detached; and EG.C8, with the RCN frigates *Stonetown* (SO) and *Poundmaker* and the RCN corvettes *Edmundston*, *Guelph*, *Humberstone* and *Leaside*.

From the North or South Western Approaches to St John's the escort groups comprise EG.C7, with the RCN frigate *Lanark* (SO) and the RCN corvettes *Coppercliff*, *Hawkesbury*, *Owen Sound* and *Parry Sound* and with the RCN frigate *Cape de la Madeleine* and RCN corvette *Collingwood* detached; EG.C.4, with the RCN frigate *Glace Bay* and the RCN corvettes *Beauharnais*, *Atholl*, *Bowmanville*, *North Bay*, *Petrolia* and *Whitby* and with the RCN frigate *Wentworth* (SO) non-operational;

EG.C6, with the RCN frigates *East View* (SO) and *Lauzon* and the RCN corvettes *Cobourg*, *St Lambert* and *Tillsonburg* and with the RCN corvettes *Brandon* and *Peterborough* detached; EG.C2, with the RCN corvettes *Asbestos*, *Kamloops*, *Kincardine* and *Norsyd* and with the RCN frigates *Longueuil* (SO) and *Capilano* detached; EG.B2, with the destroyer *Highlander* (SO), the DE *Manners* and the corvettes *Acanthus* (RNoN), *Morpeth Castle*, *Sweetbriar*, *Columbine* and *Primrose*; and EG.C3, with the RCN frigates *Kokanee* (SO) and *Sea Cliff* and the RCN corvettes *St Thomas* and *Trillium* and with the RCN corvettes *Stellarton* detached and *Forrest Hill* and *Rivière du Loup* non-operational. Support groups off the South West Approaches are the 30th EG with the corvettes *Caistor Castle*, *Kenilworth Castle*, *Launceston Castle*, *Pevensey Castle* and *Portchester Castle* (the last under refit in Dec) and the 31st EG with the corvettes *Berkeley Castle*, *Carisbrooke Castle*, *Dumbarton Castle*, *Hadleigh Castle* and *Lancaster Castle*.

8 Dec–5 Jan Central Pacific
A US task group (Rear-Adm Smith), consisting of the cruisers *Chester*, *Pensacola* and *Salt Lake City* and destroyers, bombards Iwo Jima on 8 Dec. On 24 and 27 Dec and on 5 Jan the shelling is repeated. On 5 Jan one of the five destroyers, *David W Taylor*, is damaged on a mine.

11–12 Dec Baltic
The 6th DD Flotilla (Capt Kothe†) carries out an offensive mining operation in the Gulf of Finland with *Z35*, *Z36*, *Z43*, *T23* and *T28*. In the course of the operation *Z35* (Cdr Bätge†) and *Z36* (Cdr Frhr v Hansen†) run on to other German mines and sink NE of Reval. More than 630 crewman are dead. Russian MTBs rescue some survivors from *Z35*.

11–24 Dec Indian Ocean
In 13 days the newly formed British TF.64 (Capt Bush), comprising the British destroyers *Napier* and *Nepal*, minesweepers, landing boats and the Indian ML flotillas 55 and 56 with *HDML1275*, *HDML1303*, *ML438*, *ML439*, *ML440*, *ML441*, *ML447*, *ML847* and *ML855*, bombards the neighbourhood of St Martin's Island on the Arakan coast to support the coastal flank of British XV Corps at the Burma front.

Operation 'Robson'. On 17 and 20 Dec TF.67 (Rear-Adm Vian), with the carriers *Indomitable* and *Illustrious*, the cruisers *Argonaut*, *Black Prince* and *Newcastle* and the destroyers *Kempenfelt* (D27), *Wager*, *Wakeful*, *Wessex*, *Whelp*, *Whirlwind* and *Wrangler*, attacks the oil, harbour and railway installations of Belawan-Deli in Northern Sumatra and makes an unsuccessful attack on installations at Medan, Sumatra.

In the area of the Malacca Strait and in the western part of the Malayan Archipelago, the British submarine *Shalimar* sinks 11 small craft, *Sea Rover* (Lt Angell) sinks one coaster, *Porpoise* (Lt-Cdr Turner) lays a mine barrage off Penang and sinks one junk, *Subtle* sinks three junks, *Spiteful* Lt Sherwood) sinks a coaster, *Stoic* (Lt Marriott) sinks one ship of 1986 tons, *Thule* (Lt Mars) lays a minefield in the Malacca Strait and sinks 13 junks, two barges and five sailing vessels, *Trenchant* (Cdr Hezlet) and *Terrapin* (Lt Brunner) jointly sink two ships of 1053 tons, three coasters, a trawler, five junks and two landing craft and damage three small craft, *Tudor* (Lt Porter) sinks five junks and two sailing craft, *Sirdar* (Lt Spender) sinks a coaster, *Statesman* (Lt Bulkeley) sinks six barges and one junk, *Sea Scout* sinks two coasters, *Thorough* lays a minefield in the Malacca Strait and sinks three junks and *Shakespeare* sinks one ship of 2515 tons.

11–22 Dec   Central Pacific

On 11 Dec TF.38 (Vice-Adm McCain) sets out from Ulithi. It consists of TG.38.1 (Rear-Adm Montgomery), comprising the carriers *Yorktown*, *Wasp*, *Cowpens* and *Monterey*, the battleships *Massachusetts* and *Alabama*, the cruisers *San Francisco*, *Baltimore*, *New Orleans* and *San Diego* and 18 destroyers; TG.38.2 (Rear-Adm Bogan), comprising the carriers *Lexington*, *Hancock*, *Hornet*, *Independence* and *Cabot*, the battleships *New Jersey*, *Iowa* and *Wisconsin*, the cruisers *Pasadena*, *Astoria*, *Vincennes*, *Miami* and *San Juan* and 20 destroyers; and TG.38.3 (Rear-Adm Sherman), comprising the carriers *Essex*, *Ticonderoga*, *Langley* and *San Jacinto*, the battleships *North Carolina*, *Washington* and *South Dakota*, the cruisers *Mobile*, *Biloxi*, *Santa Fé* and *Oakland* and 18 destroyers.

After replenishing from the tanker group (Capt Acuff) on 13 Dec, the carriers make continual air attacks on the airfields of Luzon in support of the Mindoro operation from 14 to 16 Dec. On 15 Dec the corvette *Kaibokan 54* is sunk. In all, there are 1427 fighter and 244 bomber sorties. Twenty-seven aircraft are lost in combat and 38 by accident. About 170 Japanese aircraft are destroyed, as well as four steamers and one landing ship.

On the way to replenishment, TF.38 runs into a typhoon on 18 Dec. The destroyer *Spence* sinks and the carriers *Cowpens*, *Monterey* and *Cabot* and the destroyers *Dyson*,

Hickox, *Benham* and *Maddox* are damaged. Of the supply group, the destroyers *Hull* and *Monaghan* sink and the escort carriers *Altamaha*, *Nehenta Bay*, *Cape Esperance* and *Kwajalein*, the destroyers *Aylwin* (Capt Acuff), *Dewey* and *Buchanan*, the DEs *Melvin R Newman*, *Tabberer* (which rescues 55 men from *Monaghan*) and *Waterman*, the tanker *Nantahala* and one tug are damaged; 146 aircraft are lost. Owing to the search for survivors, the attacks on Luzon planned for 19 to 21 Dec have to be abandoned. TF.38 returns to Ulithi.

12 Dec   Baltic

The German *U416* is sunk at the entrance to Pillau in a collision with the minesweeper *M203*.

12–15 Dec   Air War/Netherlands

On 12 Dec the German MTB *S198* is sunk while sheltering off Ijmuiden during an air attack. An attack by 17 aircraft from No 617 Sqn RAF Bomber Command against the E-boat pens at Ijmuiden fails on 15 Dec because smoke covers the target.

13–14 Dec   Air War/Norway

Attack by No 5 Group RAF Bomber Command is made against ships in Oslofjord. The main target, the cruiser *Köln*, is only damaged by near-misses and the destroyer *Karl Galster* escapes undamaged.

13–31 Dec   Air War/Western Europe

Mine offensive by RAF Bomber Command. In 11 nights, 260 sorties are flown against the Danish and Norwegian coasts, especially around the Oslo area and in the Kattegat, Heligoland Bight, the Elbe river, the Skagerrak and the Baltic up to the Danzig Bay. Four aircraft are lost.

The German *U2342*, in a convoy of 10 U-boats escorted by the minesweeper *M502*, is sunk off Swinemünde. The German minelayer *Elsass* is sunk on a air laid mine E of Samsö on 3 Jan.

14 Dec   Baltic

In a Soviet air attack on the harbour of Libau, the transports *Erika Schünemann* (1177 tons) and *Minna Cords* (951 tons) and the tanker *Inka* (427 tons) are sunk. Several other ships are damaged.

14 Dec   Mediterranean

The British destroyer *Aldenham* is mined 45 nautical miles SE of Pola and sunk; 63 men are rescued by the destroyer *Atherstone*.

15–24 Dec   South West Pacific

TG.78.3 (Rear-Adm Struble), comprising the cruiser *Nashville*, eight APDs, 30 LSTs, 12 LSMs, 31 LCIs, 10 large and seven small minesweepers and 14 small craft, lands the Western Visayas task force (Brig-Gen Dunckel)—the 503rd Parachute Regt and

the 19th RCT of the 24th Div—on Mindoro. The escort consists of the destroyers *Barton*, *Walke*, *Laffey*, *O'Brien*, *Allen M Summer*, *Moale*, *Ingraham*, *Dashiell*, *Paul Hamilton*, *Bush*, *Stanly*, *Lowry* and *Howorth*; the covering force comprises (Rear-Adm Berkey) the cruisers *Phoenix*, *Boise* and *Shropshire* (RAN) and the destroyers *Fletcher*, *La Valette*, *O'Bannon*, *Hopewell*, *Radford*, *Arunta* (RAN) and *Warramunga* (RAN); and the distant covering force is TF.77.12 (Rear-Adm Ruddock), comprising the battleships *West Virginia*, *Colorado* and *New Mexico*, the cruisers *Denver*, *Columbia* and *Montpelier*, the escort carriers *Natoma Bay*, *Manila Bay*, *Marcus Island*, *Kadashan Bay*, *Savo Island* and *Ommaney Bay* and the destroyers *Waller*, *Renshaw*, *Conway*, *Cony*, *Eaton*, *Robinson*, *Corner*, *Sigourney*, *Bennion*, *Remey*, *Mertz*, *McDermut*, *Patterson*, *Haraden*, *Twiggs*, *Stembel*, *Ralph Talbot* and *Braine*. On the way, the flagship *Nashville* is badly damaged by a kamikaze attack on 13 Dec. There are many casualties among the command staff. The destroyer *Haraden* is damaged. Following a successful landing on 15 Dec there are further kamikaze attacks; *LST738* and *LST472* have to be abandoned after hits and the carrier *Marcus Island* and the destroyers *Paul Hamilton* and *Howorth* are slightly damaged.

Over the following days there are further kamikaze attacks. On 21 Dec *LST460* and *LST479* are sunk; the destroyers *Charles Ausburne*, *Converse* and *Foote* rescue most of the troops. On 22 Dec the destroyer *Newcomb* is narrowly missed and *Bryant* is damaged. On 18 Dec the Japanese midget submarine *Ha-76* misses with a torpedo.

16–27   Dec Norway

The German destroyers *Z31* and *Z29* lay a mine barrage off Honningsvaag on 16 Dec. On 27 Dec the operation is repeated by *Z31* and *Z33*.

16–31 Dec   British Coastal Waters

Against the German schnorkel U-boats operating in the British coastal waters and in the English Channel, escort groups operate in overlapping patrols. From Londonderry, in the Shetland–Faeroes narrows, off the Hebrides, in the Irish Sea, W of Ireland and in St George's Channel are the 6th EG, with the RCN frigates *New Waterford* (SO), *Annan*, *Grou*, *Loch Morlich*, *Loch Achanalt* and *Teme* and with the RCN frigate *Waskesiu* detached and the RCN frigates *Cape Breton* and *Outremont* under repair or refit; the 25th EG, with the RCN frigates *Orkney* (SO), *La Hulloise*, *Sainte Thérèse* and *Thetford Mines* and with the RCN frigate *Joliette* under repair; and the

26th EG with the RCN frigates *Beacon Hill* (SO), *Jonquière*, *Montréal*, *New Glasgow* and *Ribble*.

From Belfast, in the area of the western entrance to the English Channel, are the 1st EG, with the DEs *Affleck* (SO, damaged by torpedo from *U486*), *Bentley*, *Capel* (sunk by *U486*), *Garlies* and *Gore*; and the 3rd EG, with the DEs *Duckworth* (SO), *Berry*, *Cooke*, *Domett*, *Essington* and *Rowley*.

From Liverpool, in the same area and in the Channel, are the 2nd EG, with the sloop *Wild Goose* (SO) and the frigates *Dominica*, *Labuan*, *Loch Fada* and *Loch Ruthven* and with the frigate *Tobago* under repair; and the 14th EG, with the destroyers *Duncan*, *Havelock*, *Icarus* and *Inconstant* and with the destroyers *Fame* (SO), *Assiniboine* (RCN), *Forester* and *Hotspur* under refit or repair. From Greenock, in the same area, is the 18th EG, with the DEs *Balfour* (SO) and *Hoste* and the frigates *Loch Fyne*, *Towy*, *Zanzibar* and *Nyasaland* (detached after sinking *U400* on 17 Dec).

From Plymouth, operating in the Channel area, are the 10th EG, with the DEs *Bayntun*, *Braithwaite* and *Foley* and the frigates *Helmsdale* and *Loch Eck* and with the frigate *Loch Dunvegan* under repair; the 17th EG, with the DEs *Burges*, *Cranstoun* and *Moorsom* and the frigates *Ascension*, *Loch Killin* and *Loch Lomond*; and the 21st EG, with the DEs *Conn* (SO), *Byron*, *Deane*, *Fitzroy*, *Redmill* and *Rupert*.

From Rosyth, off northern Scotland, is the 4th EG, with the DEs *Byard* (SO), *Bazely*, *Bentinck*, *Calder*, *Drury* and *Pasley*.

On the UK–Gibraltar route are the 5th EG, with the DEs *Aylmer*, *Bligh*, *Grindall*, *Keats*, *Kempthorne* and *Tyler*; the 15th EG, with the DEs *Louis* (SO), *Inglis*, *Lawson* and *Narborough* and with the DEs *Loring* and *Mounsey* under repair; and the 19th EG, with the destroyer *Hesperus* (SO) and the frigates *Anguilla*, *Antigua*, *Cotton*, *Goodall* and *Loch Insh*.

On the UK–Murmansk run are the 7th EG, with the destroyers *Keppel* (SO) and *Whitehall*, the sloops *Cygnet* and *Lapwing* and the corvettes *Allington Castle*, *Bamborough Castle* and *Honeysuckle* and with the destroyer *Bulldog* in repair (the group is with convoys JW.62/RA.62 and JW.63 and RA.63); the 8th EG, with the destroyers *Beagle*, *Walker* and *Westcott*, the sloop *Lark* and the corvettes *Alnwick Castle*, *Bluebell*, *Oxlip* and *Rhododendron* (with convoys JW.62/RA.62 and JW.63/RA.63); the 9th EG, with the RCN frigates *St John* (SO), *Monnow*, *Nene*, *Port Colborne*, *Stormont* and *Swansea* and with the frigate *Loch Alvie*

under repair; and the 20th EG, with the frigates *Bahamas*, *Papua*, *Pitcairn*, *Somaliland*, *Tavy* and *Tortola* (with convoy JW.62/RA.62).

Detached from the Western Approaches Command for operations in Canadian waters are the 11th EG, with the RCN destroyers *Gatineau*, *Kootenay* and *Restigouche* and with the destroyers *Qu'Appelle* (SO), *Chaudière*, *Ottawa*, *St Laurent* and *Saskatchewan* under refit or repair; the 16th EG, with the RCN frigates *Antigonish* (SO), *Charlottetown*, *Springhill* and *Stettler* and with the RCN frigate *Toronto* under repair and the RCN frigate *Magog* damaged beyond repair; and the 27th EG, with the RCN frigates *Meon* (SO), *Coaticook*, *Ettrick*, *La Salle* and *Levis*.

18 Dec   Norway
The German *U737* is sunk in the Vestfjord following a collision with the minesweeper depot ship *MRS25*.

18–19 Dec   Air War/Germany
No 5 Group RAF Bomber Command, with 236 aircraft, drops 824 tons of bombs on Gotenhafen: the training ship *Schleswig-Holstein*, the target ship *Zähringen*, the torpedo boat *T10*, the U-boat depot ship *Waldemar Kophamel* and the freighters *Warthe* (4922 tons), *Leverkusen* (1273 tons), *Theresia L M Russ* (1694 tons) and *Heinz Horn* (3994 tons) and the tanker *Blexen* (715 tons) are sunk. Four aircraft are lost.

21 Dec   Norway
UJ1113, *UJ1116*, *R402* and the steamer *Weichselland* (3654 tons), from a German convoy, run on a mine barrage laid by the French submarine *Rubis* (Cdr Rousselot) in the Feiestein Channel (19 Dec) and sink. This is the last operation by the most successful mining submarine of the Second World War: she has sunk 15 ships of 25770 tons and eight small warships.

22–25 Dec   North Sea
In German MTB activity on the Thames–Antwerp convoy route 22–23 Dec, the 8th MTB Flotilla with five boats, the 6th with *S212*, *S222*, *S705*, *S211*, *S704* and *S223* and the 9th with *S130*, *S167*, *S168*, *S175* and *S207* and, from the 10th Flotilla, *S185* and *S192*, drop 58 LMBs and 15 UMBs. The two boats of the 10th Flotilla go down in a surprise attack by the British DD *Walpole*, the frigates *Torrington* and *Curzon* and the corvette *Kittywake*: *S185* (Lt Klaus-Degenhard Schmidt†) and *S192* (Sub-Lt Holz†) sink with all hands. The British freighter *Empire Path* (6140 tons) sinks on mines in these barrages. The 2nd Flotilla, with six boats, operates against a convoy without success.

On 24–25 Dec the 8th Flotilla tries to operate on the convoy route to Antwerp but is frustrated by the British DEs *Ekins* and *Thornborough*, the frigate *Caicos* and the corvette *Shearwater*. Seventeen boats of the 2nd, 6th and 9th Flotillas drop 39 LMBs and 12 UMBs on the Thames–Antwerp convoy route.

22–27 Dec   English Channel
Operations by German small battle units. On 22–23 Dec 18 'Biber' midget submarines sail from Poortershavn and Hellevoetsluis against the Schelde traffic. Attacked by Allied MTBs, most are lost and only the freighter *Alan-a-Dale* (4700 tons) is sunk. On 23–24 and 24–25 Dec 11 and three 'Bibers' set out but fail to return, having had no success. On 27 Dec there is an accident in which 11 'Bibers' are destroyed.

23–26 Dec   Norway
In operations by the Norwegian 54th MTB Flotilla (Lt Herlofsen), *MTB722* and *MTB712* attack a German force in Bömlofjord in the evening of 23 Dec and sink the minesweeper *M489*. Early on 26 Dec the *MTB717* and *MTB627* attack a convoy of two steamers and *V5102* and *V5114* near Fröysjoen and sink the tanker *Buvi*.

24 Dec   Central Pacific
The US destroyer *Case* sinks the Japanese fast transports *T-7* and *T-8* with gunfire off Chichi Jima, Bonin Islands.

25 Dec   English Channel
The British DE *Dakins* is mined 14 nautical miles NW of Ostend; she returns to base but is not repaired.

26 Dec   South West Pacific
A Japanese force which set out from Camranh Bay (Indo-China) on 24 Dec shells the US bridgehead on Mindoro. It consists of the destroyer *Kasumi* (Rear-Adm Kimura), the heavy cruiser *Ashigara*, the light cruiser *Oyodo* and the destroyers *Kiyoshimo*, *Asashimo*, *Kaya*, *Sugi* and *Kashi*. One transport is sunk. The Japanese force turns away and escapes after American air attacks and the sinking of the *Kiyoshimo* by *PT223*. This is the last Japanese naval sortie into the area of the Philippines.

26–30 Dec   South West Pacific
Japanese aircraft destroy in Philippine waters the American transports *Hobart Baker* (7176 tons), *John Burke* (7180 tons) and *James H Breasted* (7212 tons) and the tanker *Porcupine* (7218 tons); they damage several other ships.

28 Dec–1 Jan   Air War/Norway
On 28 Dec the German mine depot ship *La France* (ex-Norwegian) is sunk off Skudesnes by rocket fire from aircraft. During the night 28–29 Dec No 5 Group RAF Bomber Command, with 68 aircraft, tries to

attack a large German ship in Oslofjord but the attack fails. Only *U735* is hit and sunk by one aircraft. During the night 31 Dec–1 Jan a second attack with 28 aircraft is made against cruisers in Oslofjord without success. One aircraft is lost.

29–30 Dec   Arctic

After several unsuccessful attacks on Soviet coastal convoys on the Kola coast, *U995* (Lt Hess) sinks one small and so far unidentified steamer. *U956* (Lt Mohs) torpedoes the steamer *Tbilisi* (7176 tons) from the convoy KP.24 off Kola Bay. The steamer is beached.

29–30 Dec   Air War/Netherlands

On 29 and 30 Dec 16 and 13 Lancasters respectively, from No 617 Sqn RAF Bomber Command, mount sorties against the E-boat pens at Rotterdam and Ijmuiden but the second attack has to be abandoned because of the weather.

30 Dec–2 Jan   South West Pacific

In USAAF attacks on shipping at San Fernando, Luzon, on 30 Dec and 2 Jan, the Japanese corvettes *Kaibokan 20* and *Kaibokan 138* are sunk.

30 Dec–21 Jan   Arctic

Convoy operation JW.63/RA.63. On 30 Dec JW.63 sets out from Loch Ewe with 35 ships escorted by the escort carrier *Vindex* (Vice-Adm Dalrymple-Hamilton), the cruiser *Diadem* and the destroyers *Zambesi*, *Myngs*, *Zebra*, *Algonquin* (RCN), *Sioux* (RCN), *Savage*, *Serapis*, *Scourge*, *Scorpion* and *Stord* (Norwegian) from the Home Fleet and, from the 8th and 20th EGs, the destroyers *Keppel*, *Westcott* and *Walker*, the sloops *Cygnet*, *Lapwing* and *Lark* and the corvettes *Alnwick Castle*, *Allington Castle* and *Bamborough Castle*. The German U-boats of the 'Stier' group, *U299*, *U956*, *U995* and *U997*, are stationed in Bear Island Passage and *U293*, *U310* and *U636* N of Kola. On 8 Jan the ships of the convoy arrive in the Kola Inlet and the White Sea unobserved. The convoy in the opposite direction, RA.63, sets out from the Kola Inlet on 11 Jan with 30 ships and the same escort as JW.63; it arrives in Loch Ewe on 21 Jan without being found by German air reconnaissance.

30 Dec–25 Jan   Central and South West Pacific

Operations by the 3rd Fleet (Adm Halsey) in support of the landings on Luzon. On 30 Dec TF.38 (Vice-Adm McCain) sets out from Ulithi. The Force is made up of TG.38.1 (Rear-Adm Radford), with the carriers *Yorktown*, *Wasp*, *Cabot* and *Cowpens*, the battleships *South Dakota* (Vice-Adm Lee) and *Massachusetts*, the cruisers *San* Francisco, *Baltimore*, *Boston* and *San Diego*, the destroyers (Desron 61) *De Haven*, *Mansfield*, *Lyman K Swenson*, *Collett*, *Maddox*, *Blue*, *Brush*, *Taussig* and *Samuel N Moore* and (Desron 53) *Cushing*, *Colahan*, *Benham*, *Yarnall*, *Stockham*, *Wedderburn*, *Twining* and *Uhlmann*; TG.38.2 (Rear-Adm Bogan), with the carriers *Lexington*, *Hancock* and *Hornet*, the battleships *New Jersey* and *Wisconsin*, the cruisers *Pasadena*, *Astoria*, *Wilkes-Barre* and *San Juan* and the destroyers (Desron 52) *Owen*, *Miller*, *The Sullivans*, *Stephen Potter*, *Tingey*, *Hickox*, *Hunt*, *Lewis Hancock* and *Marshall*, (Desron 62) *Adult*, *English*, *Charles S Sperry*, *Waldron*, *Haynsworth*, *John W Weeks* and *Hank* and (Desdiv 102) *Capps*, *David W Taylor*, *Evans* and *John D Henley*; and TG.38.3 (Rear-Adm Sherman), with the carriers *Essex*, *Ticonderoga*, *Langley* and *San Jacinto*, the battleships *Washington* and *North Carolina*, the cruisers *Santa Fé*, *Vincennes*, *Miami*, *Biloxi* and *Flint* and the destroyers (Desron 50) *Clarence K Bronson*, *Cotten*, *Dortch*, *Gatling*, *Healy*, *Cogswell*, *Caperton*, *Ingersoll* and *Knapp* and (Desron 55) *Porterfield*, *Callaghan*, *Cassin*, *Young*, *Preston*, *Laws*, *Longshaw*, *Prichett* and *Halsey Powell*. Night TG.38.5 (Rear-Adm Gardner) comprises the carriers *Enterprise* and *Independence* and the destroyers (Desron 47) *McCord*, *Trathen*, *Hazelwood*, *Haggard*, *Franks* and *Buchanan*. By day it operates with TG.38.2.

After refuelling on 2 Jan, carrier raids are made by TG.38.1 on 3 and 4 Jan on North Formosa, by TG.38.2 on South Formosa and the Pescadores and by TG.38.3 on Central Formosa and the Southern Ryukyu Islands. The operation is considerably impeded by the weather and in part abandoned. Some 100 Japanese aircraft are destroyed for a loss of 22 American planes. The Japanese minesweeper *W-41* is sunk. After refuelling on 5 Jan, 757 sorties are made on 6 and 7 Jan by the carrier aircraft against kamikaze airfields in preparation for the Lingayen landing and to ensure air superiority over Luzon: 75–80 Japanese aircraft are destroyed for the loss of 28 American. After refuelling on 8 Jan, a new attack is made on Formosa and the Ryukyu Islands, particularly Okinawa, on 9 Jan. The Americans lose 10 aircraft but the destroyer *Hamakaze*, the corvette *Kaibokan 3*, one submarine-chaser and five tankers and freighters are sunk and the frigates *Yashiro* and *Miyake*, four corvettes, one minesweeper, two submarine-chasers and three merchant ships are damaged. Simultaneously, B-29s attack Formosa from China.

On 10 Jan TF.38 enters the South China Sea and refuels until 11 Jan from the fast supply group (Capt Acuff) consisting of the tankers *Manatee*, *Monongahela*, *Patuxent*, *Neosho*, *Chikaskia*, *Niobrara*, *Pamanset* and *Caliente*, the escort carriers *Nehenta Bay*, *Rudyerd Bay*, *Cape Esperance* and *Altamaha* and the destroyers *Dale*, *Welles*, *Thatcher*, *Dyson*, *Hobby*, *Farragut*, *MacDonough*, *Thorn* and *Weaver*. On 12 Jan TG.38.5 flies off its aircraft at night and early in the day all task groups attack the coast and harbours of Indo-China with the main assault by TG.38.2 on Camranh Bay, where large Japanese warships are thought to be. The sortie towards the coast made by *New Jersey*, *Wisconsin*, *Baltimore*, *Boston*, *Pasadena*, *Astoria*, *Wilkes-Barre* and destroyers has no success. In 1465 air sorties, in which 23 American aircraft are lost, 29 merchant ships from Japanese convoys totalling 116000 tons, the training cruiser *Kashii*, which is sailing as convoy flagship, the frigate *Chiburi*, the corvettes *Kaibokan 23*, *Kaibokan 51*, *Kaibokan 17*, *Kaibokan 19*, *Kaibokan 35* and *Kaibokan 43*, the submarine-chasers *Ch-31* and *Ch-43*, the patrol vessel *P103* (ex-US minesweeper *Finch*), the minesweeper *W-101* (ex-British *Taitam*) and one landing ship are sunk. In addition, more frigates, corvettes, minesweepers, landing ships and submarine-chasers are damaged. In Camranh Bay the French cruiser *Lamotte-Picquet* is destroyed.

After further refuelling on 13 and 14 Jan, impeded by strong monsoon winds, the carrier groups make fighter sorties and attacks on S Formosa, the Pescadores and the Chinese province of Fukien on 15 Jan. The Japanese destroyers *Hatakaze* and *Tsuga*, the landing ship *T-14*, one transport and one tanker are sunk. Twelve aircraft are lost. On 16 Jan targets are attacked on the South China coast between Hong Kong and Hainan. The Americans lose 27 aircraft but two ships are sunk and five escort vessels damaged. The forces are greatly hindered by bad weather. The refuelling W of Luzon, which began on 17 Jan, has to be interrupted on 18 Jan because of the heavy seas. When it is completed on 19 Jan the force returns through the Luzon Strait on the orders of the C-in-C Pacific.

On 21 Jan there is a new attack on Formosa. In 1164 sorties, 104 Japanese aircraft are destroyed and 10 merchant ships sunk and the destroyers *Harukaze*, *Kashi* and *Sugi* and two landing ships are damaged. In Japanese air attacks, a single aircraft scores a bomb hit on *Langley* and a single kamikaze fighter hits *Ticonderoga*. An attack by seven kamikazes and six fighters from the S is intercepted by the fighter cover from *Cowpens*. In a second attack by eight kamikazes (the 'Niitaka' group) of the 1st Air Fleet and five fighters from the N, each gets one hit on *Ticonderoga* and *Maddox*. A returning American bomber loses a bomb when landing on *Hancock*, which is damaged. In all, there are 205 dead and 351 injured on the ships. *Ticonderoga* withdraws, escorted by two cruisers and three destroyers.

22 Jan the carrier aircraft make 682 sorties against the Ryukyu Islands with the emphasis on Okinawa.

After refuelling on 23 Jan the task force returns to Ulithi, arriving there on 25 Jan. In this operation a total of 300000 tons of shipping are sunk and 615 Japanese aircraft destroyed. The American losses are 201 aircraft and 167 pilots.

31 Dec   Air War/Germany

Bombers of the US 8th AF attack Hamburg.

In the harbour *U906*, the minesweeper *M445* and the freighters *Faro* (2621 tons), *Mannheim* (897 tons) and *Rival* (809 tons) are sunk. *U908* (building) is destroyed and *U2530*, *U2532* and *U2537* (building) are badly damaged.

31 Dec   Mediterranean

An attempt to attack Allied traffic off Ville Franche with five 'Marders' fails.

1945

1–10 Jan English Channel

First use of German 'Seehund' two-man submarines. On 1 Jan 17 boats are sent out but only two return: one each is sunk by the destroyer *Cowdray* and the frigate *Ekins* and only the trawler *Hayburn Wyke* is sunk on the Allied side. On 3 Jan there is a sortie by eight 'Seehunds' but it fails because of bad weather. On 6 Jan two 'Seehunds' fail because of engine troubles. On 10 Jan five 'Seehunds' leave for Margate and the Kentish coast but have no success while a sortie by 12 'Molchs' is postponed because of the weather.

1–31 Jan Pacific

US submarines continue their operations with assistance from 'Ultra' decrypts and sometimes hunt in 'wolfpacks'. Of the submarines arriving in Jan S of Honshu, *Threadfin* (Lt-Cdr Foote) sinks two ships of 1945 tons and, S of Kyushu, *Piranha* (Lt-Cdr Ruble) has two misses, *Tautog* (Cdr Baskett) sinks two ships of 1900 tons and the fast transport *T-15* and damages one ship of 10000 tons and *Silversides* (Lt-Cdr Nichols) sinks one ship of 4536 tons. N of Iwo Jima and the Bonins, *Sennet* (Lt-Cdr Porter) sinks two pickets and *Kingfish* (Lt-Cdr Harper) sinks three ships of 4344 tons. SW of Iwo Jima, *Spearfish* (Lt-Cdr Williams) sinks one sailing vessel and a 'wolfpack' W of Iwo Jima comprising *Queenfish* (Cdr Loughlin, pack leader), *Picuda* (Lt-Cdr Shepard) and *Barb* (Cdr Fluckey) sinks three ships of 19002 tons and damages one more of 10045 tons. *Queenfish* alone sinks two ships of 9373 tons and one coaster, *Picuda* one ship of 5497 tons and *Barb* one of 5244 tons. Off the Ryukyu Islands, *Puffer* (Lt-Cdr Dwyer) sinks the corvette *Kaibokan 42* on 10 Jan and damages *Kaibokan 30*. *Parche* (Lt-Cdr McCrory) sinks one ship of 984 tons and *Swordfish* is sunk off Okinawa by Japanese surface forces.
In the Yellow Sea and off Shanghai, *Balao* (Lt-Cdr Ramirezdearalland) sinks one ship of 5244 tons, *Atule* (Lt-Cdr Maurer) one of 6888 tons and *Spot* (Cdr Post) two of 405 tons and six small vessels.
Off Formosa, *Aspro* ((Lt-Cdr Stevenson) finishes off one ship of 8170 tons which has been damaged in an air strike and *Spadefish* (Lt-Cdr Underwood) sinks three ships of 12523 tons and on 28 Jan the frigate *Kume*.

S of Hong Kong, *Blackfish* sinks 14 sailing vessels; off Hainan *Sea Robin* (Lt-Cdr Stimson) sinks one ship of 5135 tons; off the Indo-Chinese coast, *Boarfish* (Cdr Gross) sinks two ships of 13858 tons (one damaged by air) and *Pargo* (Lt Cdr Bell) torpedoes the frigate *Manju* on 30 Jan and sinks the destroyer *Nokaze* on 20 Feb; off the Malayan coast, *Cobia* (Lt-Cdr Becker) sinks on 14 Jan the minelayer *Yurishima* and *Blackfin* (Cdr Kitch) sinks the destroyer *Shigure* on 24 Jan and damages one ship of 5135 tons; and, off Penang, *Besugo* (Lt-Cdr Wogan) sinks one ship of 10020 tons and on 2 Feb the corvette *Kaibokan 144*.
In the Java Sea, *Becuna* (Lt-Cdr Sturr) sinks one coaster and *Cavalla* (Lt-Cdr Kossler) sinks two ships of 1880 tons; and, off Bali, *Bergall* (Lt-Cdr Hyde) sinks on 27 Jan the auxiliary minesweeper *Wa-102* (ex-Dutch *Fakfak*), damages on 30 Jan the munitions transport *Arasaki* (920 tons) and sinks on 7 Feb the corvette *Kaibokan 53* and damages one ship of 10238 tons.

2–4 Jan Indian Ocean

Operation 'Lightning'. TF.64 (Rear-Adm Martin) sets out on 2 Jan from Chittagong with the Australian destroyers *Napier* and *Nepal*, the British sloop *Shoreham*, two LCIs and several MLs and lands some 1000 men of the British 3rd Commando Bde (Brig Hardy), embarked on three ships, on the north-west tip of the Akyab peninsula. Then the Indian 74th Bde is brought over from the mainland when the Indian sloops *Narbada* and *Jumna* and *ML387* and *ML829* are deployed for support. Because the Japanese have evacuated Akyab, TF.61 (Rear-Adm Read), comprising the cruisers *Newcastle*, *Nigeria* and *Phoebe* (Fighter Direction Ship) and the destroyers *Pathfinder*, *Raider* and *Rapid*, does not need to intervene.
Operation 'Lentil'. TF.63 (Rear-Adm Vian, 1st Carrier Sqn), comprising the carriers *Indomitable*, *Victorious* and *Indefatigable*, the cruisers *Suffolk*, *Ceylon*, *Argonaut* and *Black Prince* and the destroyers *Kempenfelt*, *Whelp*, *Wager*, *Grenville*, *Urania*, *Undaunted*, *Undine* and *Ursa*, makes a raid on the oil refineries of Pankalan Brandan (Sumatra) on 4 Jan with Avenger bombers and cover from Hellcat and Corsair fighters. One aircraft is lost.

2–8 Jan South West Pacific

The US landing fleets proceed from Leyte Gulf through the Surigao Strait, the Sulu Sea and the Mindoro Strait to Lingayen Gulf.
On 2 Jan TG.77.6 (Minesweeping and Survey Group), comprising 68 minesweepers, sets out escorted by the US destroyers (Desdiv 48) *Bush*, *Halford*, *Stanly* and *Stembel*, the Australian sloop *Warrego* and the Australian frigate *Gascoyne*.
On 3 Jan there follows the Fire Support Group, TG.77.2 (Vice-Adm Oldendorf), divided into Unit 1 (San Fabian, Rear-Adm Weyler), comprising the battleships *Mississippi*, *West Virginia* and *New Mexico*, the Australian cruisers *Australia* and *Shropshire*, the US cruiser *Minneapolis* and the US destroyers (Desron 60) *Allen M Sumner*, *Lowry*, *Laffey*, *O'Brien*, *Barton*, *Moale*, *Ingraham* and *Walke*; and Unit 2 (Lingayen, Vice-Adm Oldendorf), comprising the battleships *California*, *Pennsylvania* and *Colorado*, the cruisers *Louisville*, *Portland* and *Columbia* and the US destroyers (Desron 56) *Leutze*, *Heywood L Edwards*, *Kimberly*, *Newcomb*, *Richard P Leary*, *William D Porter*, *Bennion*, *Bryant* and *Izard* and the Australian *Arunta* and *Warramunga*. In addition there are Escort Carrier Group 77.4 (Rear-Adm Durgin) with Unit 1 (Lingayen, Rear-Adm Durgin), comprising the escort carriers *Makin Island*, *Lunga Point*, *Bismarck Sea*, *Salamaua* and *Hoggatt Bay*, the destroyers (Desron 6) *Maury*, *Gridley*, *Bagley*, *Helm*, *Ralph Talbot*, *Patterson* and *McCall* and the DEs *Edmonds* and *Howard D Clark*, and Unit 2 (San Fabian, Rear-Adm Stump), comprising the escort carriers *Natoma Bay*, *Manila Bay*, *Wake Island*, *Steamer Bay*, *Savo Island* and *Ommaney Bay* and the destroyers (Desron 51) *Hall*, *Halligan*, *Bell*, *Burns*, *Paul Hamilton*, *Twiggs* and *Abbot* and the Hunter Killer Group (Capt Cronin) with the escort carrier *Tulagi* and the DEs *Stafford*, *William Seiverling*, *Ulvert M Moore*, *Kendall C Campbell* and *Goss*. There also follows a group of UDTs (underwater demolition teams) on 10 fast transports (APDs).
On 4 Jan the San Fabian Attack Force, TF.78 (Vice-Adm Barbey), with I Corps

(Maj-Gen Swift) and the headquarters ship *Blue Ridge*, sets out from Leyte. TG.78.1 (Vice-Adm Barbey) has the 43rd Inf Div (Maj-Gen Wing) on eight APAs, two APs, three AKs, three LSDs, 21 LSTs, 10 LSMs, 13 LCIs, six LCTS and 19 support LCIs escorted by the destroyers (Desron 23) *Charles Ausburne*, *Drayton*, *Shaw*, *Russell*, *Jenkins*, *La Valette*, *Converse*, *Foote*, *Braine* and the DEs *Charles J Kimmel* and *Thomas F Nickel*. TG.78.2 (Rear-Adm Fechteler) has the 6th Inf Div (Maj-Gen Patrick) on eight APAs, three APs, one AKA, three AKs, two LSDs, one LSV and 30 LSTs, 10 LSMs, three LCIs, six LCTs and nine support LCIs escorted by (Desron 2) *Morris*, *Lang*, *Stack*, *Sterett*, *Mustin*, *Dashiell* and *Wilson* and the DEs *Day*, *Hodges*, *Peiffer* and *Tinsman*. Air escort is provided by the escort carriers *Kadashan Bay* and *Marcus Island* with the destroyers *Charette* and *Conner*.

On 5 Jan the Lingayen Attack Force, TF.79 (Vice-Adm Wilkinson), with XIV Corps (Maj-Gen Griswold) and headquarters ship *Mount Olympus*, puts to sea from Leyte. TG.79.1 (Rear-Adm Kiland) has the 37th Inf Div (Maj-Gen Beightler) on nine APAs and three Australian LSIs, one AP, three AKs, one LSD, one LSV and 19 LSTs, 18 LSMs, six LCTs and 22 support LCIs escorted by the destroyers (Desron 22) *Waller*, *Saufley*, *Philip*, *Renshaw*, *Cony* and *Robinson* and the DEs *Abercrombie*, *Le Ray Wilson* and *Gilligan*. TG.79.2 (Rear-Adm Royal) has the 40th Inf Div (Maj-Gen Brush) on 10 APAs, two APs, three AKAs, three LSDs, one LSV and 19 LSTs, 31 LSMs, six LCTs and 21 support LCIs escorted by the destroyers (Desdiv 48 and 44) *Bush*, *Halford*, *Conway*, *Eaton*, *Sigourney* and *Stembel* and the DEs *Walter C Wann*, *Richard W Suesens*, *Oberrender* and also the destroyers (Desron 49), *Picking*, *Isherwood*, *Luce*, *Sproston*, *Wickes*, *Young* and *Charles J Badger*. Air escort (Rear-Adm Ofstie) is provided by the escort carriers *Kitkun Bay* and *Shamrock Bay* with the DEs *John C Butler* and *O'Flaherty*.

From 3 Jan the movements are partly detected by Japanese coast guard stations and air reconnaissance and the two-men submarines stationed in Cebu, and kamikaze pilots of the 1st Air Fleet (Vice-Adm Onishi) are deployed against them. On 3 Jan the midget submarine *Ha-84* misses three ships and kamikazes damage the tanker *Cowanesque*. On 4 Jan the escort carrier *Ommaney Bay* is so badly damaged by kamikaze from Sarangani W of Panay that she has to be sunk by the destroyer *Burns*. On 5 Jan the midget submarines *Ha-69*, *Ha-81*

and *Ha-82* unsuccessfully attack TF.78 in the Sulu Sea. Of the flagship group—TG.77.1 with the headquarters ship *Wasatch* (7th Fleet, Adm Kinkaid, and the Cdr of the 6th Army, Lt-Gen Krueger), the cruiser *Boise* (C-in-C South-West Pacific, Gen MacArthur) and the destroyers *Smith*, *Frazier*, *Coghlan* and *Edwards*—and the close covering group (Rear-Adm Berkey), comprising the cruisers *Phoenix*, *Montpelier* and *Denver* and the destroyers (Desron 21) *Nicholas*, *Fletcher*, *Radford*, *O'Bannon*, *Taylor* and *Hopewell*, the midget submarines narrowly miss *Boise*. The attacking submarine *Ha-82* is sunk by *Taylor*. Off Manila *Bennion*, with *Warrego* and *Gascoyne* from the minesweeping group, encounters the Japanese destroyers *Momi* and *Hinoki* which have set out from Manila Bay. The latter escapes, but *Momi* is damaged by *Bennion* and sunk by aircraft. On 5 Jan three groups of 16, 4 and 15 kamikazes take off from Mabalacat (Luzon) against TF.77. The cruisers *Louisville* and *Australia*, the escort carrier *Manila Bay*, the DE *Stafford*, the tender *Orca*, the tug *Apache* and *LCI(G) 70* are damaged by hits and the escort carrier *Savo Island* and the destroyers *Arunta* and *Helm* by near-misses. There are 54 dead and 168 injured.

On 6 Jan a total of 29 kamikaze aircraft with 15 escort fighters take off from various airfields and attack TG.77.2 as it enters Lingayen Gulf to shell the assault area. The minesweeper *Long* is sunk; the battleships *New Mexico* (Capt Fleming† and the British Lt-Gen Lumsden† as observer) and *California*, the cruisers *Australia*, *Columbia* and *Louisville* (Rear-Adm Chandler†), the destroyers *Walke*, *Allen M Sumner* and *O'Brien* and the minesweepers *Brooks* and *Southard* are all damaged by hits (*Brooks* is not repaired) and the cruiser *Minneapolis* and the destroyers *Richard P Leary*, *Newcomb* and *Barton* by near-misses. There are 156 dead and 452 injured. The US escort carriers fly 126 sorties to provide fighter protection. During the night 6–7 Jan individual Japanese torpedo aircraft attack and sink the minesweeper *Hovey*. There are 22 dead and 24 injured.

On 7 Jan individual bombers attack and sink the minesweeper *Palmer* (28 dead and 38 injured) and just miss *Boise* in Mindoro Strait. *LST 912* and the transport *Callaway* are damaged by the seven kamikazes which take off: there are 33 dead and 22 injured. During the night 7–8 Jan, in the last surface engagement of the Pacific war, the destroyers *Charles Ausburne*, *Braine*, *Shaw* and *Russell* sink the Japanese escort destroyer *Hinoki* which has come out again.

On 8 Jan several kamikazes from Clark Field attack the 7th US Fleet off Lingayen Gulf, in the course of which the escort carriers *Kadashan Bay* and *Kitkun Bay* and the cruiser *Australia* are damaged. There are 17 dead and 36 injured.

3 Jan   Norway
The German destroyers *Z31* and *Z33* lay a mine barrage off Hammerfest.

4–5 Jan   Air War/France
Nos 1, 5 and 8 Groups RAF Bomber Command attack the German-occupied harbour at Royan with 354 aircraft. 700 French civilians and 40 German soldiers die.

4–27 Jan   North Atlantic
Either side of the Pentland Firth (Orkneys), the German U-boats *U278* and *U313* operate against British carrier groups but are only able to fire on steamers and patrol boats—and then without success. *U905* and *U764*, which set out for the area W of Britain, have to return because of schnorkel trouble. In the North Channel, *U1009* misses a patrol boat and a destroyer. Off the Clyde, *U482* (Lt-Cdr Count Matuschka) attacks a convoy and torpedoes the escort carrier *Thane* (not repaired) and one ship of 7429 tons but she is sunk on 16 Jan after a lengthy search by the ships of the 22nd EG, the sloops *Peacock*, *Hart*, *Starling* and *Amethyst* and the frigate *Loch Craggie*. In St George's Channel and in the Irish Sea, *U1055* (Lt R Meyer) sinks from 9 to 15 Jan four ships of 19418 tons, including one from convoy ON.277. *U285* returns home without success. From 20 Jan *U1172* (Lt Kuhlmann), which sinks two ships of 2751 tons, *U825* (Lt Stoelker) and *U1051* (Lt v Holleben) operate simultaneously in this area. Apart from the 22nd EG, five other escort groups are deployed against these boats. On 26 Jan the 4th and 5th EGs hunt *U1051*, which, after torpedoing the DE *Manners* (not repaired), is sunk by the DEs *Aylmer*, *Calder* and *Bentinck*. On 27 Jan the two other boats torpedo two ships of 15360 tons from convoy HX.322; *U1172* is then sunk by the DEs *Tyler*, *Keats* and *Bligh* of the 5th EG. *U325* operates without success in the Channel. *U1199* (Lt-Cdr Nollmann) torpedoes one ship of 7176 tons from Thames–Bristol convoy BC.43 off Wolf Rock on 21 Jan and is sunk by the destroyer *Icarus* and the corvette *Mignonette* of the escort.

U1009, *U248*, *U1230* and *U1231* are stationed in turn as weather boats in the North Atlantic. A US DE-hunter group, consisting of *Hubbard*, *Hayter*, *Otter* (Cdr Bowling) and *Varian*, is deployed against the boats which are located by HF/DF. *U248* falls victim to the group on 16 Jan.

W of Gibraltar, *U870* (Cdr Hechler) attacks the convoy GUS.63 on 3 Jan and sinks one ship of 7207 tons. On 7 Jan she attacks an eastbound convoy and on 8 Jan a westbound convoy, both unsuccessfully. On 9 Jan she sinks the French submarine-chaser *L'Enjoue* and on 10 Jan one ship of 4637 tons from an eastbound convoy.

Off Halifax, *U1232* (Capt Dobratz) misses a destroyer and a passenger steamer and sinks five ships of 26804 tons from three convoys (one of them is a Liberty ship which is taken in tow but becomes a total loss).

5 Jan   Central Pacific

A US task group (Rear-Adm Smith) comprising the cruisers *Chester*, *Pensacola* and *Salt Lake City* and the destroyers *Dunlap*, *Fanning*, *Cummings*, *Ellet*, *Roe*, and *David W Taylor* shells Iwo Jima, Hahajima and Chichijima; *Taylor* is damaged on a mine. At the same time there is an attack by B-29s of the US 21st Bomb Group.

5 Jan   North Pacific

A US task group (Rear-Adm McCrea) consisting of the cruisers *Raleigh*, *Detroit* and *Richmond* and nine destroyers shells Suribachi Wan near Paramushiro in the Kuriles.

5–8 Jan   Arctic

The German U-boats *U295*, *U716* and *U739* each set out with two 'Biber' midget submarines attached to their superstructures. The intention is to enter the Kola Inlet and to make attacks with them on the Soviet battleship *Arkhangelsk* and Allied escort vessels. The operation has to be abandoned because of trouble with the midget submarines.

6 Jan   English Channel

The British destroyer *Walpole* is mined off Flushing; she is towed to Sheerness but is damaged beyond repair.

6–29 Jan   Air War/Western Europe

Mine offensive by RAF Bomber Command. In six nights, 159 sorties are flown against the Baltic area, especially off Flensburg, Kiel and Swinemünde, and against the Kattegat and the Oslo area. Six aircraft are lost. The German escort vessel *F5* is sunk by mine in the Central Baltic on 29 Jan, the German hospital ship *Berlin* (15286 tons) is sunk on 31 Jan off Swinemünde after hitting three mines and *U3520* is sunk by a mine off Bülk, Kiel Bay.

6 Jan–10 May   Indian Ocean/ Atlantic

The last German East Asian U-boats return. *U510* (Lt-Cdr Eick), which sets out from Jakarta on 6 Jan, has, after sinking the steamer *Point Pleasant Park* (7136 tons) on

23 Feb in the Indian Ocean, to put in to St-Nazaire on 24 Apr because of fuel shortage. *U532* (Cdr* Junker) sets out on 13 Jan and sinks in Mar the freighter *Baron Jedburgh* (3656 tons) and the tanker *Oklahoma* (9298 tons) in the Atlantic and puts in to Liverpool on 10 May after the surrender where she is inspected by the C-in-C Western Approaches, Adm Horton. *U843* (Lt-Cdr Herwatz) and *U861* (Cdr Oesten) arrive in Bergen in Apr. *U195* has to return after developing a defect and replenishing *U532*. The last boat to set out, *U183*, is sunk on 23 Apr by the US submarine *Besugo*.

7 Jan–12 Mar   Baltic/Courland

At first from the Gulf of Danzig, and later from the Western Baltic, regular German convoys proceed to Libau and Windau to supply the Army Group Courland. For escort, the minesweepers of the 1st, 3rd and 25th and, later, the 12th and 2nd MS Flotillas are employed out at sea, and off the Lithuanian coast KFKs of the 31st MS Flotilla as submarine-hunters, those of the 14th Defence Flotilla as mining escort and those of the 1st MMS Flotilla and the 7th Gun Carrier Flotilla as defence against the Soviet torpedo cutters stationed in Polangen.

Soviet submarines operating against this traffic claim some successes. In the area W of Libau, *Shch-307* (Lt-Cdr Kalinin) torpedoes a ship on 17 Jan, probably the steamer *Steinburg* (1319 tons). Then *Shch-309* (Capt 3rd Class Vetchinkin) on 23 Feb sinks the transport *Göttingen* (6267 tons) and is heavily attacked by the escorting *M801*. SW of Libau, *Shch-310* (Lt-Cdr Bogorad) has several misses in Jan and *Shch-318* (Capt 3rd Class Loshkarev) sinks the freighters *Hiddensee* and *Ammnerland* (total 3096 tons) on 4 and 10 Feb respectively. On mines laid by *L-3* (Capt 3rd Class Konovalov) off Brüsterort, some small boats sink and on 29 Jan the freighter *Henry Lütgens* (1141 tons) is sunk by torpedo. On 9 Mar *Shch-303* (Lt-Cdr Ignatev), off Libau, torpedoes the freighter *Borbek* (6062 tons), which is later sunk by aircraft. Other claims of successes by Soviet submarines cannot be corroborated. Soviet aircraft make several attacks on harbours and lay mines, on which the auxiliary minesweepers *M3137* and *M3138* sink on 12 and 23 May respectively. But the evacuation of eight of the 35 Army Group Courland divisions to East Prussia and Pomerania takes place without substantial losses.

9 Jan   Baltic

The German auxiliary minesweeper *M3145/K333* is sunk by mine in the Irben Strait.

9–17 Jan   South West Pacific

Operation 'Mike I': landing in Lingayen Gulf. The US TF.78 and 79, with support from TG.77.2 (fire support) and TG.77.4 (escort carriers), land I US Corps in Lingayen Gulf (for composition see 2 Jan). The landing of about 70000 troops on the first day succeeds against slight resistance because the Japanese defence (14th Army Group, Gen Yamashita) in the Lingayen area has withdrawn the 23rd Inf Div (Lt-Gen Nishiyama) and the 58th Bde to the mountains. Only from 11 Jan onwards are there major engagements on shore.

The Japanese react with kamikaze attacks by the 1st Naval Air Fleet and the 4th Army Air Fleet. On 9 Jan nine kamikazes set off with seven escorting fighters. The battleship *Mississippi* and the cruisers *Columbia* and *Australia* are damaged by hits and the DE *Hodges* by near-misses. During the night 9–10 Jan some 70 Japanese explosive boats attack from San Juan, but they sink only *LCI(M) 974* and *LCI(G) 365* and damage the transport *War Hawk*, *LST 925* and *LST 1028*.

On 11 Jan more explosive boats attack and damage *LST 610*. A bomber attacks the destroyer *Wickes* and kamikaze pilots the DE *Le Ray Wilson* and the transport *Du Page*. During 9–10 Jan there are 114 dead and 377 injured.

On 11 Jan Amphibious Group 3 (Rear-Adm Conolly), with the headquarters ship *Appalachian*, arrives with the 25th Inf Div (Maj-Gen Mullins), the 158th RCT and the 13th Armored Group on 13 APDs, 17 APAs, three APs, seven AKAs, eight AKs, 10 Liberty ships and 50 LSTs escorted by the destroyers (Desron 54) *Remey*, *McNair*, *Norman Scott*, *Melvin*, *Mertz*, *McGowan*, *McDermut*, *Monssen* and the DEs *Greenwood* and *Loeser*. Air escort (Rear-Adm Henderson) is provided by the escort carriers *Saginaw Bay* and *Petrof Bay* and the DEs *Richard S Bull* and *Richard M Rowell*. Of the Japanese submarines *Ro-43*, *Ro-46*, *Ro-50*, *Ro-55*, *Ro-109* and *Ro-49*, *Ro-49* (Lt Sugayoshi) makes an unsuccessful attack on a battleship and *Ro-46* (Lt-Cdr Suzuki) on transports. Kamikaze pilots attack approaching and departing transports and escort vessels: the APD *Belknap*, the APA *Zeilin* and *LST 700*, as well as the DEs *Gilligan* and *Richard W Suesens*, are damaged (*Belknap* is not repaired). There are 50 dead and 107 injured. Four Liberty ships and one LST from a supply convoy are damaged by six kamikazes in the area of Bataan: 129 dead and 23 injured. On 13 Jan, in a final kamikaze attack on the landing fleets, a hit is obtained on the escort carrier

327

Salamaua: 15 are killed and 88 injured. Because of the loss of all operational aircraft and the withdrawal of the remaining units of the 1st Naval Air Fleet, there is an end to the planned attacks. From 14 to 27 Jan four more supply convoys arrive for the US invasion forces. From 17 Jan the units of the 6th US Army are no longer dependent on naval support and the last formations are withdrawn. The escort carriers have flown a total of 6152 sorties from 6 to 17 Jan, including 1416 for close support. They lose only two of their aircraft.

9–31 Jan   Indian Ocean
In the Malacca Straits and in the western part of the Malayan Archipelago, the Dutch *O-19* (Lt-Cdr v Kernebeek) lays a minefield in the W Java Sea on which one ship of 935 tons is sunk, the British *Strongbow* sinks a junk, *Porpoise* (Lt-Cdr Turner) lays a mine barrage in the Malacca Straits on which one ship of 340 tons and the auxiliary submarine-chaser *Cha-57* sink and is then lost, probably on a Japanese mine, *Stygian* sinks seven small craft, *Shalimar* sinks nine and damages three coasters and small craft, *Supreme* damages one coaster of 302 tons and two other coasters, *Spirit* (Lt Langridge) sinks one coaster and one small craft, *Thrasher* sinks 11 junks, *Subtle* sinks a coaster and four junks, *Tantalus* (Lt-Cdr Mackenzie) sinks a coaster, a tug with three barges and a junk and *Rorqual* lays two mine barrages off the W coast of Thailand and off the Andaman Islands.

10 Jan   Norway
The German minesweeper *M322*, on fire, is beached off Lepsoey.

10 Jan   Mediterranean
German explosive boats ('Linsen') unsuccessfully attack the French destroyer *Le Fortuné* off San Remo.

11–12 Jan   Norway
A British cruiser squadron consisting of the cruisers *Norfolk* (Rear-Adm McGrigor) and *Bellona* and the destroyers *Onslow*, *Orwell* and *Onslaught* attacks a German convoy off Egersund. Shell hits are obtained on some freighters, including *Bahia Camarones* (8551 tons) and *Charlotte* (4404 tons), which are badly damaged and have to be abandoned. In an engagement with the convoy escort, the minesweeper *M273* is sunk. An unsuccessful attempt to attack is made by *U427*. The squadron withdraws under fighter cover from the escort carriers *Trumpeter* and *Premier*, which frustrate an attack by Ju 88 torpedo aircraft from II/KG 26.

11–21 Jan   Central Pacific
Japanese submarine cruisers try to attack American naval bases with 'Kaiten' torpedoes (Operation 'Kongo'). *I-36* (Lt-Cdr

Teramoto) launches four 'Kaitens' off Ulithi. One detonates a few yards from the side of the ammunition ship *Mazama* and another possibly sinks the landing craft *LCI 600*. *I-47* (Lt-Cdr Orita) launches four 'Kaitens' in the roads of Hollandia: there are two detonations in the vicinity of the transport *Pontus H Ross* (7247 tons) and one torpedo fails to explode. Attempted attacks by *I-53* in the Kossol Passage in Palau, by *I-56* on Manus in the Admiralty Islands and by *I-58* on Apra Harbor on Guam have no success. Also unsuccessful is an attempted attack by *I-48* on Ulithi on 20 Jan: this boat is sunk on 21 Jan by the US DEs *Conklin*, *Corbesier* and *Raby*.

11 Jan–19 Mar   Baltic
Last operations by German U-boats in the Baltic off the Gulf of Finland. On 11 Jan *U745* (Lt-Cdr v Trotha) sinks a patrol boat off Revalstein and on 16 Jan *U290* (Lt Herglotz) misses a vessel off Baltischport (Paldiski). *U242*, *U348* and *U1001* return at the end of Jan from reconnaissance operations into the southern part of the Gulf of Bothnia and the central Gulf of Finland and are then sent to the W.
At the beginning of Feb *U745*, *U475*, *U370* and *U676* are still operating, but *U745* is lost, probably on a mine, on 4 Feb and *U676* on 19 Feb. *U475* is the last boat to return to Danzig on 17 Mar. On 19 Mar all German U-boats are withdrawn for operations in the W.

12 Jan   Air War/Norway
Thirty-three aircraft from Nos 9 and 617 Sqns RAF Bomber Command attack the German U-boat pens and harbour installations at Bergen; four aircraft are lost. *U775* and *U864* are damaged and the minesweeper *M1* and the freighter *Ilona Siemers* are sunk by 12000lb 'Tallboy' bombs.

12 Jan   Mediterranean
The British minesweeper *Regulus* is sunk by mine in the southern Corfu Channel.

12 Jan   Indian Ocean
The British TF.64 (Rear-Adm Martin), with several transports and landing craft, the Australian destroyer *Napier*, the Indian sloops *Narbada* and *Jumna* and *HMDL1248* and *ML854*, lands units of the 3rd British Commando Bde near Myebon between Akyab and Ramree (Burma). The cruiser *Phoebe* acts as fighter direction ship.

13–14 Jan   North Sea
The German 'Titus I' defensive mine barrage is laid by the cruiser *Nürnberg* (Capt Griessler), the minelayer *Linz* (Cdr* Abel), the destroyers *Friedrich Ihn* and *Theodor Riedel*, the torpedo boats *T19* and *T20*, and seven boats of the 8th MMS Flotilla. Several British air attacks are driven off.

13–15 Jan   North Sea
S176, *S210*, *S174* and *S209* of the 2nd MTB Flotilla lay mines off Cromer and British FN and FS convoys lose two ships of 8871 tons on these mines. Two other ships are damaged. *S221*, *S180*, *S181* and *S177* have to return owing to engine trouble. *S180* sinks on a German mine off Texel. *S127*, *S48*, *S92* and *S85* of the 5th MTB Flotilla also lay mines off the British East Coast. *S98* and *S67* have to return because of engine trouble. During the night 14–15 Jan six German MTB flotillas operate off the British East Coast and the Scheldt estuary. The 2nd Flotilla (Cdr Opdenhoff), with *S221*, *S174*, *S209* and *S181*, and the 5th Flotilla (Lt-Cdr Holzapfel), with *S98*, *S67*, *S92* and *S48*, penetrate as far as the swept channels off the Humber. The 5th Flotilla is engaged by the British destroyer *Farndale*. The 9th Flotilla (Cdr v Mirbach), with *S206*, *S168*, *S130* and *S175*, operates in the Scheldt estuary and is engaged by the British DE *Seymour* and coastal forces. The 6th Flotilla (Lt-Cdr Matzen), with *S221*, *S222*, *S705*, *S211* and *S223*, attacks a convoy W of the Scheldt and fires six torpedoes. *S222* and *S705* report hits with FAT torpedoes. The flotilla is driven off by the British DE *Curzon* and the destroyer *Cotswold* off Westkapelle. The 4th Flotilla (Cdr Fimmen), with *S205*, *S204* and *S219*, operates off Margate and is engaged by the corvette *Guillemot*. The 8th Flotilla (Cdr Zymalkowski), with *S194*, *S196*, *S197*, *S199* and *S701*, proceeds to within four miles of Tongue Sand Fort and attacks a convoy of landing ships with eight FAT and LUT torpedoes. *LST 45* is hit by a LUT torpedo. Gunfire from the fort drives off the boats.

15 Jan   Norway
The German patrol vessel *V5304* is sunk by rocket fire in an air attack off Lervik.

15 Jan   Mediterranean
The Italian squadron consisting of the light cruiser *Attilio Regolo*, the destroyers *Carabiniere*, *Fuciliere* and *Mitragliere*, the torpedo boat *Orsa* and the naval ferry barges *Mz 785*, *Mz 780* and *Mz 800*, which has been lying at anchor in Port Mahon (Balearics) and interned by Spain since 8 Sept 1943, sets out for Malta.

15 Jan   Mediterranean
The French cruisers *Montcalm* (Rear-Adm Jaujard) and *Georges Leygues* shell German positions near San Remo (Riviera).

15–24 Jan   Arctic
The German U-boats *U293*, *U295*, *U636*, *U956*, *U968* and *U997* operate against Soviet coastal traffic off the Kola coast. On 16 Jan the Soviet convoy KB.1, with six Allied freighters and four tankers, proceeds

from the Kola Inlet to the White Sea. The escort (Capt 1st Class Rumyantsev) consists of the flotilla leader *Baku* and the destroyers *Deyatelny* (Lt-Cdr Kravchenko), *Derzki*, *Doblestny*, *Zhivuchi*, *Dostoiny* and three others as a covering group and six Pe-3 bombers as air escort. *U286* (Lt Dietrich) comes up and sinks *Deyatelny* with a T-5.

On 20 Jan a convoy of two steamers, the destroyer *Uritski*, two minesweepers, nine BO submarine-chasers, four TKAs and a Norwegian group with the corvette *Eglantine* and the trawlers *Karmøy*, *Tromøy* and *Jelöy*, together with the Soviet destroyers *Razumny* and *Razyarenny* as a covering force, sets out from Kola for Liinahamari. *U293* (Lt-Cdr Klingspor) torpedoes *Razyarenny*, which is with difficulty taken in tow by the minesweeper *T-117*.

On 21 and 24 Jan the destroyers *Derzki*, *Zhivuchi*, *Doblestny* and *Dostoiny* look for U-boats located between Jokanga and Kola. *U636* misses a search group on 23 Jan and is hunted by six BO and two MO submarine-chasers and two TKAs. On 26 Jan the Soviet submarines *V-2* and *V-3* are deployed in the U-boat hunt.

15 Jan–24 Feb   Baltic

Soviet attack on East Prussia. On 15 Jan the Soviet 2nd White Russian Front goes over to the attack from the Narev bridgehead near Pultusk with support from the 4th Air Army. Forward troops of the 5th Guards Armoured Army pass Elbing and reach the Frisches Haff coast near Tolkemit on 27 Jan; they sever contact between the 4th Army in E Prussia and the 2nd Army in W Prussia. On 16 Jan the 3rd White Russian Front, with support from the 1st Air Army, attacks to the N of Gumbinnen in the direction of Königsberg; the 43rd Army of the Soviet 1st Baltic Front attacks from Tilsit and passes N of Königsberg along the Kurisches Haff. In order to assemble forces to build up a defensive position on Samland, XXVIII German Corps is transferred over the ice from the Memel bridgehead to the Kurische Nehrung (24–28 Jan) and refugees and wounded are evacuated in ships, including the ferry ship *Deutschland* (2972 tons). The Soviet 1st Baltic Front, which from 26 Jan pursues them, is not able to hold up the evacuation. The Soviet 39th and 43rd Armies have advanced in the meantime into the western Samland between Königsberg and Cranz and have severed land communications between Pillau and Königsberg. In support of the XXVIII Corps attack from the Cranz bridgehead to the SW in an attempt to restore contact, the German TF.2 (Vice-Adm Thiele), comprising the cruiser *Prinz Eugen* (Capt Reinicke), the

destroyers *Z25* (Cdr* Gohrbandt) and *Paul Jacobi* (Cdr Bülter) and the torpedo boats *T23* (Lt-Cdr Weinlig), *T33* (Lt-Cdr Priebe), *T1*, *T12* and *T35*, shells land targets near the German advance on 29 and 30 Jan. Gun carriers, including *Polaris* and *Joost*, shell forward Soviet armour from the Königsberg Sea Canal. In support of the counter-attack by the rest of the German 3rd Army from the Fischhausen area, which is designed to secure a continuous front in W Samland, *Z25*, *T28* (Lt-Cdr Temming) and *T33* repeatedly intervene in the fighting from 2 to 5 Feb. The pocket-battleship *Admiral Scheer* (Capt Thienemann) stands by at sea with the torpedo boats *T23*, *T35* (Lt-Cdr Buch) and *T36* (Lt-Cdr Hering). An attempted attack on *T36* by the Soviet submarine *L-3* (Capt 3rd Class Konovalov), which has previously laid mines near Brüsterort, fails on 4 Feb. The SAT *Polaris* is lost by a bomb hit on 5 Feb.

In support of the German 4th Army near Frauenburg against the advancing Soviet 48th and 3rd Armies, the cruiser *Lützow* (Capt Knoke) and *T8* (Lt-Cdr Strömer), *T28* and *T33* are employed on 8 Feb and *Admiral Scheer* with *Z34* (Cdr Hetz), *T23*, *T28* and *T36* on 9 and 10 Feb.

After bringing up the 93rd Inf Div by sea from Courland from 11 to 13 Feb, the reinforced Samland army detachment makes an attack from 18 to 24 Feb to restore land communications between Pillau/ Fischhausen and Königsberg. In support of the attack *Admiral Scheer*, *Z38* (Cdr Frhr v Lyncker), *Z43*, *T28* and *T35* shell concentrations of the Soviet 39th Army near Peyse and Gross-Heydekrug on the South Coast of Samland on 18 and 19 Feb. On 20 Feb the torpedo boats go into the Sea Canal and continue the shelling from there. On 23 Feb *Z43* (Capt Wenninger), *Z38* and *T28* again intervene in the land fighting, which restores the land access to Königsberg.

16 Jan   Mediterranean

The German MTB *S33* is sunk by a torpedo fired by the British *MTB698* off the West coast of the island of Unije in the Adriatic.

16–17 Jan   Mediterranean

A last attempt to attack Allied traffic off La Spezia with 30 'Linsens' fails.

16 Jan–4 Feb   Indian Ocean

Operation 'Matador'. TF.64 (Rear-Adm Martin on the destroyer *Napier*), with four personnel carriers, two LSIs, two APs, one AK, 55 LCs and 20 MLs, lands the British 4th and the Indian 71st Bdes in the northern part of Ramree Island (off Arakan, Burma). A bombardment force consisting of the battleship *Queen Elizabeth* (Rear-Adm

Walker), the cruiser *Phoebe* (FDS), the destroyers *Rapid* and *Raider*, the sloops *Flamingo*, *Kistna* (RIN) and *Redpole* and the forgate *Spey* supports the operation with preparatory fire on the assault areas. Air escort is provided by the escort carrier *Ameer* with the destroyer *Norman* (RAN). An attack by 18 Japanese aircraft is beaten off. On 22 Jan the sloops *Jumna* (RIN) and *Narbada* (RIN) and *ML416*, *ML843*, *ML854*, *ML885* and *ML892* land the 42 and 44 RM Commandos and the 1st and 5th Army Commandos at Kangaw, Burma.

Operation 'Sankey'. A task force which sets out from Akyab on 24 Jan comprising the destroyers *Norman* and *Raider* and the frigates *Spey* and *Teviot*, and TF.65 (Rear-Adm Read), consisting of the cruisers *Newcastle*, *Nigeria* and *Kenya* and the destroyers *Paladin* and *Rapid*, lands on 26 Jan 500 marines transported on the cruisers on Cheduba Island S of Ramree. The C-in-C Eastern Fleet, Adm Power, observes the operation from the destroyer *Nepal* (RAN). Air escort is provided by the escort carrier *Ameer* and the FDS cruiser *Phoebe*. Before the landing takes place, the assault area is shelled by *Norman*, *Raider*, *Paladin* and *Rapid*. The Indian 36th Bde follows on the next day.

Operation 'Crocodile'. The destroyers *Norman* and *Raider* with four LCs put 120 men ashore on the island of Sagu S of Ramree on 30 Jan. The operations are supported by the destroyers *Nepal* and *Pathfinder* until 4 Feb.

Operation 'Meridian'. The British Pacific Fleet, as TF.63, sails from Trincomalee for transfer to the Pacific on 16 Jan. It comprises the battleship *King George V* (Vice-Adm Rawlings), the carriers (Rear-Adm Vian) *Indomitable* (Capt Eccles), *Illustrious* (Capt Lambe), *Victorious* (Capt Denny) and *Indefatigable* (Capt Graham), the cruisers *Argonaut*, *Black Prince* and *Euryalus* and the destroyers *Grenville*, *Undine*, *Ursa*, *Undaunted*, *Kempenfelt*, *Wakeful*, *Whirlwind*, *Wager* and *Whelp*. Later it is joined by the cruiser *Ceylon* and the destroyer *Wessex*. On 20 Jan these ships meet TF.69, comprising the tankers *Echodale*, *Wave King* and *Empire Salvage* and the destroyer *Urchin*, which set out on 13 Jan, and the tanker *Arndale*, which set out from Fremantle on 15 Jan, for refuelling. Reconnaissance and air–sea rescue are assigned for the submarines *Sturdy*, *Tantivy* and *Tantalus*. On 21–22 and 22–23 Jan the weather off Sumatra prevents the carrier aircraft being flown off. On 24 Jan 43 Avenger bombers, 12 Firefly fighter-bombers with rockets and 50 Hellcat, Corsair and Seafire fighters fly off from the four carriers SW of Sumatra to make a successful attack on the oil refinery at Pladjoe N of Palembang. The defence is taken by surprise. Only about 20 fighters of the Japanese Army Air Force take off and 14 of them are shot down; thirty-eight are destroyed on the ground. The British lose seven aircraft to enemy action and 25 as a result of crash landings.

After replenishing on 26–27 Jan, TF.63 returns on 2–29 Jan and early on 29 Jan flies off 48 Avengers, 10 Fireflies, 24 Corsairs and 16 Hellcats, which make a raid on the oil refineries at Soengi-Gerong near Palembang. In air engagements 30 Japanese aircraft are shot down, while 38 are destroyed on the ground. Sixteen Allied aircraft do not return but some of the crews are rescued. An attempted Japanese attack on TF.63 with 12 bombers is intercepted by the fighter cover and all the bombers are shot down by the fighters or by the AA fire.

After again refuelling from the tankers on 30 Jan, TF.63 proceeds to Fremantle, where it arrives on 4 Feb.

16 Jan–9 Feb Norway
In operations off Norway, the Norwegian submarine *Utsira* (Lt-Cdr Valvatne) sinks the patrol boat *V6408* off Trondheim on 16 Jan. The British *Venturer* (Lt Launders) sinks the small steamer *Stockholm* (618 tons) on 22 Jan off Stavanger, *U864* on 9 Feb and the minesweeper *M381* on 12 Feb.

17 Jan Air War/Germany
In a USAAF air raid on Hamburg, *U2515* and *U2532*, together with the repair ships *Hiev* and *Griep* and *U2537*, are destroyed, *U2523* is sunk but later raised and decommissioned and *U2530* is again damaged. *U2534* is sunk but raised and repaired. In a raid on Wilhelmshaven in Jan, *U382* is damaged beyond repair.

17 Jan Baltic
The German minesweeper *M305* ices up and capsizes in a gale off Brüsterort.

17 Jan North Sea
The German patrol vessel *V1417* is sunk by air attack off Terschelling.

17 Jan Mediterranean
The German MTBs *S58* and *S60* are scuttled after being damaged by gunfire from British MGBs and running aground on the W coast of Unije on 10 Jan.

21 Jan Baltic
The German gun ferry *AF30* is sunk by grounding off Hela. It is raised and repaired in Mar.

21–30 Jan English Channel
On 21–24 Jan there is an operation with 26 'Seehunds' against Ramsgate, North Foreland and Lowestoft. Seven return prematurely, there is only one unsuccessful attack

in the Thames estuary, on 22 Jan, and the last boat is scuttled on 24 Jan. On 29–30 Jan 15 'Bibers' sortie from the Hook of Holland for the Schelde. They meet with no success, some returning with ice damage. Of the 10 'Seehund' boats which leave Ijmuiden for Margate, only two reach their destinations: they make an unsuccessful attack.

22 Jan Norway
The German destroyers *Z31*, *Z34* and *Z38* lay mines in Laafjord, Mageröyfjord and Breisund.

22–23 Jan North Sea
Three boats of the German 9th MTB Flotilla attack an Allied convoy N of Dunkirk. *S168* and *S175* sink the British freighter *Halo* (2365 tons) and are damaged in action with two British MTB groups. Five boats of the 6th Flotilla and four boats of the 4th are intercepted N and NE of Ostend and are driven off by MTB groups. The 8th Flotilla (Cdr Zymalkowski), with *S194*, *S196*, *S197*, *S199* and *S701*, reaches the Thames NE of the North Foreland and is engaged by the British escort vessels *Seymour* and *Guillemot* and MTBs. The German boats fire two T-5 torpedoes and eight other torpedoes, all of which miss. *S199* (Lt Quistorp) is heavy damaged by ramming from *S701* and has to be scuttled near Tongue Sand Fort. The British *MTB495* collides with *S701* (Lt Toermer). Both boats are brought in but *S701* is out of service until the end of the war.

23–30 Jan North Sea
Mining operations by German motor torpedo boat flotillas. During the night 23–24 Jan *S98*, *S48* and *S85* of the 5th Flotilla lay mines off East Dudgeon. *S127*, *S92* and *S67* are attacked by aircraft and have to return. During the night 24–25 Jan *S221*, *S181* and *S177* of the 2nd, *S206*, *S175* and *S703* of the 4th and 9th and *S211*, *S222*, *S704* and *S223* of the 6th Flotilla lay mines along the coastal routes off Orfordness. During the night 29–30 Jan *S221*, *S174*, *S209*, *S181* and *S177* of the 2nd Flotilla lay mines off the Humber. The 5th Flotilla has to return owing to bad weather.

24 Jan Air War/Germany
U763 is sunk during a Soviet air raid on Königsberg.

24 Jan–13 Feb Central Pacific
Preparatory bombardment of Iwo Jima. On 24 and 29 Jan and on 12 Feb B-29s of the US 20th AF and, each day from 31 Jan to 13 Feb, B-24s of the 7th AF, attack Iwo Jima and drop approximately 6800 tons of bombs. On 25 Jan a US task force (Rear-Adm Badger) comprising the battleship *Indiana*, the 5th Cruiser Div (Rear-Adm Smith) with *Chester*, *Pensacola* and *Salt*

Lake City and eight destroyers bombards the island with 203 16in and 1354 8in shells.

24 Jan–17 Feb South West Pacific
Landings in West Luzon. On 27 Jan the 32nd Inf Div and the 1st Cavalry Div are landed in Lingayen Gulf as reinforcements for the 6th US Army on Luzon. On the way, the Japanese midget submarines *Ha-76*, *Ha-81* and *Ha-84* try, unsuccessfully, to attack the convoys in the Mindoro Sea on 24–25 Jan.

Operation 'Mike VII': Amphibious Group 9 (Rear-Adm Struble) lands the 38th Inf Div (Maj-Gen Hall) and the 134th RCT of XI Corps (Maj-Gen Siebert) near Zambales N of Subic Bay on 29 Jan. About 30000 troops are landed in one day from 22 transports and 35 LSTs. Air support is provided by the US 5th AF (Lt-Gen Kenney) and escort by 14 destroyers (Desron 49) and DEs, 11 minesweepers and 19 YMSs. Fire support is provided by TG.74.2 (Rear-Adm Riggs), comprising the cruiser *Denver* and two destroyers. On 30 Jan four APDs and the LSV *Monitor* land one BLT of the 38th Inf Div on Gamble Island in Subic Bay. Distant cover for both operations is provided by TG.74.3 (Rear-Adm Berkey,) comprising the cruisers *Boise*, *Phoenix* and *Shropshire* (RAN) and four destroyers. In Japanese counter-measures the submarine *Ro-46* (Lt-Cdr Tokunaga) torpedoes the APA *Cavalier* (7800 tons).

Operation 'Mike VI': Amphibious Group 8 (Rear-Adm Fechteler) lands the 11th Airborne Div (Maj-Gen Swing) on four APDs, 35 LCIs and eight LSMs near Nasugbu SW of Manila Bay on 31 Jan. It is escorted by six destroyers (Desron 5) and three DEs. Fire support is provided by TG.74.2 (Rear-Adm Riggs), comprising the cruiser *Denver* and the destroyers *Claxton* and *Dyson*. On 31 Jan the Japanese submarine *Ro-115* is sunk by the US destroyers *O'Bannon*, *Jenkins* and *Bell* and the DE *Ulvert M Moore* in the vicinity of the distant covering force, TG.74.3. In an explosive boat attack, the US submarine-chaser *PC1129* is sunk. The destroyer *Claxton* and the DE *Lough* beat off further attacks. *Lough* and the destroyer *Conyngham* sink the two US motor torpedo boats, *PT77* and *PT79*, in error on 1 Feb. W of Luzon, the Japanese submarine *Ro-55* is severely damaged by the DE *Thomason* on 7 Feb and is probably sunk on the return by the US submarine *Batfish* on 11 Feb. The submarine *Ro-50* (Lt-Cdr Kimura), which is deployed SW of Leyte, after missing a target on 1 Feb, sinks the US *LST 577* from a supply convoy on 7 Feb. On 13 Feb the midget submarine *Ha-69* has two

misses W of Mindanao. On 13 Feb US motor torpedo boats enter Manila Bay for the first time since 1942. On the same day minesweepers begin clearing operations in the entrance to Manila Bay. TG.74.3 (Rear-Adm Berkey), comprising the cruisers *Boise* and *Phoenix* and the destroyers *Fletcher*, *Hopewell*, *La Valette* and *Radford* (Desron 21), shells the assault area on the southern tip of Bataan and Corregidor. In the process, *La Valette* and *Radford* are damaged by mines. On 14 Feb the shelling is repeated. Reinforcements from the reserve force (Commodore Farncomb, RAN) arrive, consisting of the cruisers *Shropshire* (RAN), *Minneapolis* and *Portland* and six destroyers. Amphibious Group 9 (Rear-Adm Struble) lands the 151st RCT and the 34th RCT from the 38th Inf Div, totalling 5300 troops, from 62 landing craft at the southern tip of Bataan on 15 Feb. On 16 Feb the 503rd Parachute RCT is dropped on Corregidor. Landing boats land one battalion of the 34th RCT on Corregidor. Support is provided by the destroyers of Desron 49, including *Picking*, *Young* and *Wickes*. Since 22 Jan aircraft of the US 5th AF have dropped 3200 tons of bombs on the rock island.
An attack by the Japanese submarine *Ro-109* (Lt Masuzawa) on 17 Feb on a convoy and its escort is not successful.

25–26 Jan   South West Pacific
American aircraft drop mines off Singapore and Saigon and in Camranh Bay. Among other ships, the battleship *Ise* is damaged on these mines on 5 Feb and the frigate *Nomi* on 11 Feb.

25 Jan–10 Mar   Baltic
With the Soviet attack threatening E Prussia and Danzig, there begins the greatest evacuation operation in history. Overall responsibility for the operations is with the German Naval High Command East (Adm Kummetz); in the area of the Gulf of Danzig–Courland is the 9th Escort Div (Cdr* v Blanc) and in the area W of Rixhöft as far as the Danish islands is the 10th Escort Div (Rear-Adm Bütow and, from Feb, Cdr* Heydel). The shipping is directed by the Wehrmacht Naval Transport Cdr (Rear-Adm Engelhardt).
It is chiefly the large passenger ships which are employed and which, until then, have been used as accommodation ships in Pillau, Gotenhafen and Danzig , e.g. *Cap Arcona* (27561 tons), *Robert Ley* (27288 tons), *Wilhelm Gustloff* (25484 tons), *Hamburg* (22117 tons), *Hansa* (21131 tons), *Deutschland* (21046 tons), *Potsdam* (17528 tons), *Pretoria* (16662 tons), *Berlin* (15286 tons), *General Steuben* (14660 tons), *Monte Rosa* (13882 tons), *Antonio Delfino* (13589 tons),

Winrich von Kniprode (10123 tons) and *Ubena* (9554 tons); also employed are the freighters *Moltkefels* (7862 tons), *Wangoni* (7848 tons), *Neidenfels* (7838 tons), *Lappland* (7650 tons), *Vega* (7287 tons), *Volta* (7258 tons), *Göttingen* (6267 tons), *Sachsenwald* (6261 tons), *Kanonier* (6257 tons), *Duala* (6133 tons), *Vale* (5950 tons), *Wiegand* (5869 tons), *Urundi* (5791 tons), *Tübingen* (5493 tons), *Albert Jensen* (5446 tons), *Brake* (5347 tons), *Tanga* (5346 tons), *Mathias Stinnes* (5337 tons), *Goya* (5230 tons), *Mendoza* (5193 tons), *Cometa* (5125 tons), *Eberhard Essberger* (5064 tons) and many other ships of less than 5000 tons. Auxiliary warships and escort vessels are also used chiefly to evacuate refugees. To protect the convoys, the 1st, 3rd and 25th MS Flotillas (Cdr Pinkepank, Cdr Dr Kieffer and Lt-Cdr Vogeler and, from Feb, Lt-Cdr v Haxthausen) of the 9th Escort Div are employed in the area Gulf of Danzig–Courland, each with some six operational boats, as are the 1st and 17th MMS Flotillas (Lt-Cdr Hoff, Cdr Zaage and, from Mar, Lt-Cdr Voss), each with 7–10 motor minesweepers, the 3rd and 17th PB Flotillas (Cdr Böttger and Cdr Dittmer) with 6–8 converted trawlers, the 3rd and 14th Defence Flotillas (Cdr Leonhardt and, from Mar, Cdr* Palmgren and Cdr Petersen) with many small fishery vessels and KFKs, the 31st MS Flotilla (Lt-Cdr Prater) with four KFK groups, the 3rd SC Flotilla (Lt-Cdr Dr Teichmann) with many small fishery vessels, the 13th and 24th Landing Flotillas (Cdr Wassmuth and Cdr* Brauneis) with naval ferry barges and the 3rd and 7th Gun Garrier Flotillas (Cdr Dr Schröder and Cdr Dr Sonnemann) with SATs, LATs and AFs. In the area between the Gulf of Danzing and the Pomeranian Bay the newly formed 12th and 2nd MS Flotillas (Lt-Cdr Ostertag and Lt-Cdr Rosenow) with the modern Type 43 minesweepers of the 10th Escort Div are employed, as are the 15th MMS Flotillas (Lt-Cdr Mergelmeyer) with the new motor minesweepers, the 2nd Defence Flotilla (Lt-Cdr Dr Reimann) with many small fishery vessels and KFKs, the 36th MS Flotilla (Cdr Reinhold) with converted drifters, the KFK Training Flotilla and the newly formed 6th SC Flotilla (from Mar, Lt-Cdr Bittkow), as well as the 11th Landing Flotilla (Cdr Wiegand) with naval ferry barges for transport purposes. In the Western Baltic the 1st Defence Flotilla from Kiel is used for mine defence (Capt G Schulz).
On 25 Jan the *Robert Ley*, *Pretoria*, *Ubena* and others set out as the first ships from Pillau with a total of 7100 refugees. At the

end of Jan more ships follow until by 28 Jan 62000 refugees have been taken by ship. The cruiser *Emden* brings refugees and the sarcophagus of the Reich President Hindenburg from Pillau. The main obstacle to the evacuation is the British air mining offensive by the RAF in the Western Baltic and as far as the Pomeranian Coast. This causes frequent blockages of the compulsory routes within the 20-mile line and considerable delays while the 1st and 2nd Defence Flotillas search for mines. In the month of Jan 668 mines are dropped in 159 sorties and on them a total of 18 ships of 42673 tons sink and eight of 9177 tons are damaged; in Feb 1354 mines are dropped in 291 sorties and 23 ships of 25642 tons sink and 13 of 13490 tons are damaged; and in Mar 1198 mines are dropped in 270 sorties and 26 ships of 69449 tons sink and 11 ships of 48557 tons are damaged. Mines are concentrated in the area off Swinemünde, where on 29 Jan the escort vessel *F5* sinks, as do on 30 Jan the U-boat tender *Memel* (1057 tons), on 31 Jan the hospital ship *Berlin* (15286 tons) and from 12 to 17 Feb the transports *Ditmar Koel* (670 tons), *Dieter H Stinnes* (2545 tons) and *Consul Cords* (951 tons) and *Minenräumschiff 11* (5095 tons), and where the transport *Drechtdijk* (9338 tons) is damaged. On 18 Feb *Tolina* is sunk by the Soviet *TKA-181*. Off Warnemünde between 24 Feb and 5 Mar the transports *Ellen Larsen* (1938 tons), *Erika Fritzen* (4169 tons) and *Rixhöft* (5378 tons), and *R177* and *Hansa* (21131 tons) are lost and the tanker *Jaspis* (6049 tons) and the freighter *Irene Oldendorf* (1923 tons) are damaged. On 6–7 Mar, off Sassnitz, the *Hamburg* (22117 tons) runs on to mines.
The destroyer *Z28* is sunk in Sassnitz in an a RAF air raid on 6 Mar. 191 Lancasters and seven Mosquitos attack Sassnitz and sink the submarine-chasers *UJ1109*, *UJ1118*, *UJ1119* and the hospital ship *Robert Möhring* (3344 tons). For the rest, the danger from the air at this period is still slight because the Soviet Air Force is largely involved in land operations. As a result, considerable feats of evacuation can be recorded at this time. Each of the large passenger ships takes between 5000 and 9000 evacuees at a time and the freighters anything up to 5000, according to their size. Initially, the defence against Soviet submarines operating in the Baltic is completely inadequate because no effective A/S vessels are available until the second half of Feb when the 11th and 12th SC Flotillas are moved to the area. In this period the Soviet submarines concentrate their activities on the route to Courland (see 7 Jan–12 Mar),

but some large boats operate along the deep-water route off the Gulf of Danzig and around the Stolpe Bank. *Lembit* and *L-21* lay mines off Kolberg and Hela, but the losses are difficult to attribute because of the presence also of British air-laid mines. On 28 Jan *K-51* (Capt 3rd Class Drozdov) sinks near Bornholm the Danish *Viborg* (2028 tons). In the area of the Stolpe Bank, *S-13* (Capt 3rd Class Marinesko) sinks the unescorted liner *Wilhelm Gustloff* (25484 tons) with three hits on 30 Jan; of the more than 6000 passengers on board, 564 are rescued by *T36*, 252 by *Löwe*, 37 by *M341*, 15 by *TS2*, seven by *TF19*, one by *V1703* and 28 by *Göttingen*. The cruiser *Admiral Hipper*, with 1500 wounded on board, has to leave because of the danger of submarines. The fully laden *Cap Arkona* is missed on the following day. On 10 Feb *S-13* sinks the liner *General Steuben* (14660 tons), the latter escorted by *T196* and *TF10*. The escorts rescue only about 300 of the more than 3000 passengers on board because of the bitter cold. From 24 Feb to 7 Mar *K-52* (Capt 3rd Class Travkin) claims one torpedo boat and five ships along the deep-water route from Libau to Swinemünde but these successes cannot be corroborated.

26 Jan–11 Mar British Coastal Waters/Atlantic

In operations by German U-boats in the North Sea, *U245* (Cdr Schumann-Hindenberg) sinks one ship of 7240 tons and torpedoes one of 2628 tons from convoys in the Thames Estuary. In the first operations by the new Type XXIII boats off the British East Coast, *U2324* (Lt Hass) misses one ship and *U2322* (Lt Heckel) sinks one ship of 1317 tons. In the area of Moray Firth *U309*, in attempting to attack convoy WN.74, is found by the Canadian 9th EG and sunk by the frigate *St John*. On 16 Feb *U1279* is lost to an unknown cause. On 3 Feb an unknown U-boat is attacked and on 14 Feb *U989* and on 17 Feb *U1278* fall victim to the 10th EG (Cdr Burnett), employed N of the Shetlands and comprising the DEs *Bayntun* and *Braithwaite* and the frigates *Loch Eck* and *Loch Dunvegan* which are supporting EN and WN convoys. The 9th EG is summoned to the scene but does not need to intervene. In the area off the North Minch, *U1104* attacks several steamers and convoys without success. *U1014*, which has penetrated into the North Channel, is sunk on 4 Feb by the 23rd EG, comprising the frigates *Loch Scavaig*, *Loch Shin*, *Nyasaland* and *Papua*. *U1064* (Cdr Schneidewind) sinks one ship of 1564 tons from a convoy. *U483* (Lt-Cdr v

Morstein), after missing a corvette, is badly damaged by depth charges, but gets away. *U1019* (Lt Rinck) is attacked W of the North Channel by a Liberator with the help of sonobuoys and 'Fido' homing torpedoes, but escapes. *U963*, *U1058* and *U1276* operate without success in the Irish Sea. *U1276* (Lt-Cdr Wendt) attacks the convoy HX.337 on 20 Feb and sinks the Canadian corvette *Vervain* but is herself sunk by the sloop *Amethyst* of the 22nd EG. *U1208* is lost in the Channel, probably on a mine. *U1302* (Lt-Cdr W Herwatz) sinks four ships of 10312 tons, including two ships from the convoy SC.167, and torpedoes one ship of 6991 tons, but is sunk after a long search by the Canadian frigates *La Hulloise*, *Strathadam* and *Thetford Mines* of the 25th EG on 7 Mar. *U775* cruises in the same area but gets away.

In the English Channel, *U1017* (Lt Riecken) makes several unsuccessful attacks on escorts off Cherbourg and sinks two ships of 10604 tons, including one from the convoy TBC.60 on 6 Feb. *U244* (Lt Fischer) reports a torpedoing near the Channel Islands. On 22 Feb *U1004* (Lt Hinz) sinks the Canadian corvette *Trentonian* and one ship of 1313 tons from the convoy BTC.76; *U480* (Lt Förster) sinks one ship of 1644 tons from BTC.78 on 24 Feb but is sunk by the frigates *Duckworth* and *Rowley*. *U1203* (Lt Seeger) sinks one ship of 580 tons and misses several escorts and convoys. *U1018* (Lt-Cdr Burmeister) sinks one ship of 1317 tons from BTC.81 on 27 Feb but is hunted by the 2nd EG and sunk by the frigate *Loch Fada*. Directed by the report from Liberator 'H' of VPB-112 USN (escorting convoy ONA.287), the 2nd EG, consisting of the frigates *Labuan* and *Loch Fada* and the sloop *Wild Goose*, also sinks *U327* on the same day. On 24 Feb *U927* is sunk on her way to the Channel by Warwick 'K' of No 179 Sqn RAF. *U868* and *U275* are employed on supply missions to St-Nazaire.

Off Gibraltar, *U300* (Lt Hein) torpedoes two ships of 16727 tons (one is a total loss) from a convoy on 17 Feb but, after a T-5 miss, is sunk on 22 Feb by the minesweepers *Recruit*, *Invade* (US) and *Pincher* (British). *U869* (Lt-Cdr Neuerburg) tries to attack convoy GUS.74 on 28 Feb but is located and sunk by the US frigate *Knoxville*, the DEs *Fowler* and *Francis M Robinson* and the French A/S vessels *L'Indiscret* and *Le Résolu*. *U1233* (Cdr Kuhn), which makes a sortie into the Gulf of Maine (via Bermuda), misses several targets. *U907* has no success off Reykjavik. *U1022* (Lt-Cdr Ernst) sinks one ship of 1349 tons from UR.155 on 28 Feb and one tug of 328 tons on 3 Mar.

28 Jan Norway
When the 4th DD Flotilla (Capt v Wangenheim), comprising *Z31*, *Z34* and *Z38*, tries to move from Norwegian waters into the Baltic, it is intercepted off Bergen by the British cruisers *Diadem* (Vice-Adm Dalrymple-Hamilton) and *Mauritius*. In an engagement *Z31* is damaged. The flotilla returns to Bergen, from where *Z34* and *Z38* put to sea again the next evening and, in spite of British air attacks, reach Kiel on 1 Feb, after putting into Stavanger.

The German MMS *R57* is sunk in a collision with *U1163* in Trondheim Fjord.

30 Jan Norway
Raid on the Stadlandet area by the British escort carriers *Campania* and *Nairana* with the heavy cruiser *Berwick* and destroyers.

31 Jan Norway
The German minesweeper *M382* is torpedoed and sunk by the Norwegian *MTB715* off Ravnefjord, N of Molde.

31 Jan South China Sea
The Japanese DE *Ume* is sunk by US 14th AF aircraft based in China.

Feb Mediterranean/Intelligence
Separate cypher circuits are introduced for the German naval forces in the southern Adriatic ('Albanien') and for the Aegean islands ('Aegaeis').

1–28 Feb Pacific
US submarines continue to strangle the Japanese supply shipping along the coasts, using information from 'Ultra' and coast watchers.

In the area S of Honshu, a 'wolfpack' with *Lagarto* (Cdr Latta, pack leader), *Haddock* (Cdr Brockman) and *Sennet* (Lt-Cdr Porter) conducts an anti-picket strike, sinks two pickets and damages one more. Then *Lagarto* sinks on 24 Feb the submarine *I-371* and *Sennet* on 16 Feb the minelayer *Nariu*. *Bowfin* (Cdr Tyree) sinks three small vessels and the corvette *Kaibokan 56* on 17 Feb, *Trepang* (Lt-Cdr Faust) sinks four ships of 2515 tons and *Piper* (Cdr McMahon) sinks one vessel of 111 tons. S of Kyushu, *Tilefish* (Lt-Cdr Schlech) sinks two small vessels and the minesweeper *W-15* on 5 Mar. N of the Bonin Islands, *Ronquil* (Lt-Cdr Monroe) damages one ship of 1924 tons. In the Yellow Sea, *Gato* (Lt-Cdr Farrell) sinks one ship of 2325 tons and on 14 Feb the corvette *Kaibokan 9*. *Sea Cat* has two misses. In the East China Sea, *Spikefish* (Lt-Cdr Managhan) has a miss. N of Formosa, *Scabbardfish* (Lt-Cdr Gunn) sinks one vessel of 137 tons and *Rasher* has a miss. S of Formosa, *Batfish* (Lt-Cdr Fyfe) damages one landing craft and sinks on 9 Feb one unidentified submarine and on 11 and 12 Feb the submarines *Ro-112* and *Ro-*

OF I-41
N. PHILIPPINES

113. Piranha (Lt-Cdr Ruble) sinks one sailing vessel. NE of Luzon, *Archerfish* misses a submarine.

Around Hainan and off the Indo-Chinese coast, *Bashaw* (Lt-Cdr Nichols) and *Flasher* (Cdr Grider) sink together three small vessels and *Bashaw* alone sinks two ships of 15255 tons and damages one small craft, while *Flasher* sinks one ship of 850 tons. *Hoe* (Lt-Cdr Refo) sinks on 25 Feb the frigate *Shonan*. *Guitarro* has a miss, *Hammerhead* (Lt-Cdr Smith) sinks on 23 Feb the frigate *Yaku*, *Becuna* (Lt-Cdr Sturr) sinks one ship of 1945 tons and *Blenny* (Lt-Cdr Hazzard) sinks four ships of 12611 tons.

In the Gulf of Thailand, *Ray* (Lt-Cdr Kinsella) damages the corvette *Kaibokan 61* on 9 Feb, and off the Malayan coast, *Hardhead* (Cdr Greenup) sinks one ship of 834 tons, *Pampanito* (Lt-Cdr Summers) sinks two ships of 10410 tons and *Guavina* (Cdr Lockwood) sinks two ships of 15565 tons. In the Java Sea, *Cobia* (Lt-Cdr Becker) sinks two small craft and, S of Bali, *Hawksbill* (Lt-Cdr Scanland) sinks one ship of 5396 tons, two landing craft and one small vessel and the submarine-chasers *Kusen-Tokumu Tei Cha-130* and *Cha-114*.

1-28 Feb Indian Ocean
British submarines operate in the Malacca Straits and the western part of the Malayan Archipelago and achieve a number of successes. *Spark* sinks two coasters, a tug and a barge, *Tantivy* sinks two coasters and a tug and *Statesman* sinks two junks, *Tradewind* sinks one ship of 834 tons, *Thorough* sinks two coasters, one landing craft, one barge and 18 junks, *Statesman* sinks seven coasters, one tug, two barges and a trawler, *Sea Scout* sinks eight junks, *Terrapin* (Lt Brunner) sinks five coasters and three junks and *Trenchant* (Cdr Hezlet) sinks six coasters, one tug, three barges, one junk and, together with *Terrapin*, the submarine-chaser *Tokumu Tei Ch-8*. The Dutch *Zwaardfish* (Lt-Cdr Goossens) has a miss.

3-5 Feb Baltic
On 3 Feb the German torpedo recovery boat *TFA4* (ex-Danish torpedo boat *Glenten*) is sunk off Pillau by Soviet coastal gunfire. On 5 Feb the German gun carrier *SAT15/ Polaris* and the A/S vessel *UJ307/K543* is sunk by Soviet air attack off Pillau.

3-8 Feb Air War/Netherlands
On 3 Feb 36 Lancasters of Nos 9 and 617 Sqns RAF Bomber Command attack the E-boat and midget U-boat pens at Ijmuiden and Poortershaven. The attack is repeated on 8 Feb by 15 Lancasters of No 617 Sqn against the pens at Ijmuiden with 'Tallboy' bombs.

3-13 Feb Arctic
Convoy operation JW.64 to Murmansk with 26 ships, escorted by the escort carriers *Campania* (Rear-Adm McGrigor) and *Nairana*, the cruiser *Bellona* and 17 escort vessels including the destroyers *Onslow*, *Orwell*, *Onslaught*, *Sioux*, *Serapis* and *Zealous* and vessels of the 8th and 20th EGs. On 6 Feb the convoy is located by weather aircraft and reported. The 'Rasmus' U-boat group (*U286, U307, U425, U636, U711, U716, U739* and *U968*) is deployed in the Bear Island Passage and the boats *U293, U318, U992* and *U995* off the Kola Inlet. On 7 Feb KG 26, with 48 Ju 88s, tries to attack but misses the convoy; seven aircraft are lost. On 8-9 Feb temporary contact is established by reconnaissance aircraft. On 10 Feb an attack by II/KG 26 with 14 and by III/KG 26 with 18 torpedo aircraft fails to get through the fighter and AA defence. Five Ju 88s are shot down. The U-boats are unable to attack in face of the escort and are moved to the area off the Kola Inlet. When the convoy enters the Kola Inlet, *U992* (Lt Falke) torpedoes the corvette *Denbigh Castle* on 13 Feb; the corvette is taken in tow by the Soviet salvage ship *Burevestnik* but has to be written off as a total loss.

U995 misses the Norwegian steamer *Idefjord* in the harbour at Kirkenes on 9 Feb.

3-26 Feb Air War/Western Europe
Mine offensive by RAF Bomber Command. In ten nights, 302 sorties are flown against the Heligoland Bight, the Elbe river, the Danish coast and the Kattegat, the Oslo area, Kiel Bay, Pomeranian Bay and the Danzig area. Eight aircraft are lost.

The German ice-breaker *Pollux* (4500 tons) is beached after hitting a mine off Pillau on 7-8 Feb. On 9 Feb *U923* is sunk in Kiel Bay. On 12 Feb the patrol vessel *V1106* is sunk off Otterndorf/Elbe, and on 14 Feb *V1104* off Osteröey. *U1273* is sunk in Oslofjord on 17 Feb and the MMS *R177* off Stolpmünde on 28 Feb.

5-23 Feb English Channel
Operations by German small battle units. On 5 Feb eight, on 10 Feb ten and on 12 Feb five 'Seehunds' depart and sink on 12 Feb the tanker *Liseta* (2628 tons) from convoy TAM.80 off the North Foreland. At least two boats are lost and several beached. On 16 Feb four 'Seehunds', together with 15 'Linsens', sortie against the Schelde traffic but fail to score successes. On 20 Feb three 'Seehunds' depart for Ramsgate, on 21 Feb four for the South Falls and one more on 23 Feb. They sink *LST364* from convoy TAM.87 and the cable ship *Alert*

(941 tons) E of Ramsgate. All boats return. 'Molchs' are sunk by *ML588* and *ML901*.

6 Feb Mediterranean
The German MTBs *S36* and *S61* collide during an engagement off Pola and are towed into that port. The boats are not repaired.

10 Feb-4 Mar Central Pacific
First major carrier raid on Tokyo and support for the landing on Iwo Jima by TF.58 (Vice-Adm Mitscher). On the approach route the submarines *Sterlet*, *Pomfret*, *Piper*, *Trepang*, *Bowfin* and *Sennet*, *Lagarto* and *Haddock* are deployed to sink Japanese patrol boats. On 10 Feb TF.58 sets out from Ulithi. It comprises TG.58.1 (Rear-Adm Clark), with the carriers *Hornet*, *Wasp*, *Bennington* and *Belleau Wood*, the battleships *Massachusetts* and *Indiana*, the cruisers *Vincennes*, *Miami* and *San Juan* and 15 destroyers of Desrons 61 and 25; TG.58.2 (Rear-Adm Davison), with the carriers *Lexington*, *Hancock* and *San Jacinto*, the battleships *Wisconsin* and *Missouri*, the cruisers *San Francisco* and *Boston* and 19 destroyers of Desrons 62 and 52 and Desdiv 92; TG.58.3 (Rear-Adm Sherman), with the carriers *Essex*, *Bunker Hill* and *Cowpens*, the battleships *South Dakota* and *New Jersey*, the battlecruiser *Alaska*, the cruisers *Indianapolis* (Adm Spruance, 5th Fleet), *Pasadena*, *Wilkes Barre* and *Astoria* and 14 destroyers of Desrons 55 and 50; TG.58.4 (Rear-Adm Radford), with the carriers *Yorktown*, *Randolph*, *Langley* and *Cabot*, the battleships *Washington* and *North Carolina*, the cruisers *Santa Fé*, *Biloxi* and *San Diego* and 17 destroyers of Desrons 47 and 48; and TG.58.5 (Night Group, Rear-Adm Gardner), with the carriers *Enterprise* and *Saratoga*, the cruisers *Baltimore* and *Flint* and 12 destroyers of Desron 54 and Desdiv 53. By day TG.58.5 operates mostly with TG.58.2

Four patrol boats having been sunk by the submarines, six more are sunk by a patrol line of destroyers advancing in front of the task force and consisting of *Haynsworth*, *Barton*, *Ingraham*, *Moale*, *Dortch* and *Waldron*. The approach thus succeeds. On 16 Feb, 125 nautical miles SE of Tokyo, the carriers fly off, first, fighters to eliminate the enemy fighter defence in the air and on the ground, then bombers which are to attack, in particular, aircraft factories in the Tokyo area. The attacks are greatly impeded by the weather. On 17 Feb there are further attacks on shipping targets in the area of Yokohama, when the transport *Yamashio Maru* (10602 tons) is sunk and the frigate *Amakusa* and the corvette *Kaibokan 47* are damaged. Including fighter protection, 2761 sorties are flown in all; 60 aircraft are lost in combat and 28 due to accident. On 18 Feb the destroyers are replenished and TG.58.4 makes raids to neutralise Hahajima and Chichijima. TG.58.1 and 58.5 are detached for replenishment. TG.58.2 and 58.3 from 19 to 22 Feb and TG.58.1, 58.4 and 58.5 from 20 Feb support the landing on Iwo Jima from the W. On 23 Feb TF.58 assembles and until 24 Feb replenishes from the tanker group (Rear-Adm Beary). On 25 and 26 Feb further carrier raids on the Tokyo area are badly impeded by the weather and some are broken off prematurely. On 27 Feb there is an operation partly in support of Iwo Jima, on 28 Feb replenishment and on 1 Mar a carrier raid on Okinawa in which the Japanese torpedo boat *Manazuru* and the minesweeper *Tsubame* are destroyed. The ships return on 2 Mar and arrive in Ulithi on 4 Mar.

TU.58.1.22 (Rear-Adm Whiting), consisting of the cruisers *Vicksburgh*, *Miami*, *Vincennes* and *San Diego* and 15 destroyers, shells Okino-Daito Jima (Ryukyu Islands) on 2 Mar.

11 Feb   Indian Ocean

The British destroyer *Pathfinder* is damaged by near-misses in an attack by Japanese Army aircraft S of Akyab; she is towed to Chittagong but not repaired.

12 Feb   Mediterranean

Attack by explosive motor boats against ships in Split harbour. The British A/A cruiser *Delhi* is heavily damaged and not repaired.

13–18 Feb   Baltic

On 13 Feb the German minesweeper *M421* is sunk off Kolberg on a German minefield. On 18 Feb *U2344* sinks in a collision with *U2336* off Heiligendamm.

14–28 Feb   Arctic

Convoy operation RA.64. The U-boats *U286*, *U310*, *U318*, *U425*, *U636*, *U711*, *U739*, *U968*, *U992* and *U995* are stationed N of the Kola coast. On 14 Feb *U968* (Lt Westphalen), *U711* (Lt-Cdr Lange) and *U992* attack the Soviet convoy BK.3 coming from the White Sea off the Kola Inlet. The convoy is escorted by a strong group of Soviet destroyers. The U-boats sink the tanker *Norfjell* (8129 tons) and the freighter *Horace Gray* (7200 tons) from the convoy. On 16 Feb *U286* (Lt Dietrich) unsuccessfully attacks another coastal convoy further to the E.

From 14 to 16 Feb the destroyers *Sioux*, *Zambesi* and *Zest* evacuate the Norwegian inhabitants of the island of Söröy who are distributed among the convoy RA.64.

On 16 Feb groups of Soviet destroyers, minesweepers, submarine-chasers, torpedo cutters and aircraft and a part of the British escort force (Rear-Adm McGrigor), comprising the escort carriers *Nairana* and *Campania*, the cruiser *Bellona* and 16 escort vessels, including the destroyers *Onslow*, *Orwell*, *Onslaught*, *Serapis* and *Zealous* and the destroyer *Whitehall*, the sloop *Lark* and the corvettes *Alnwick Castle* and *Bluebell* from the 8th and 20th EGs, all try to drive the German U-boats away from the entrance to the Kola Inlet. The sloop *Lark* and the corvette *Alnwick Castle* sink *U425* on 17 Feb. The outbound convoy of 34 ships is attacked by *U968* and *U711*: the first torpedoes the sloop *Lark* and the freighter *Thomas Scott* (7176 tons). The Soviet submarine-chaser *MO-434* rescues part of the crew of *Lark*, which is beached, and the Soviet destroyer *Zhestki* takes the freighter in tow, but she becomes a total loss. *U711* sinks the corvette *Bluebell*. Contact is lost on 18 Feb. *U286*, *U711*, *U716*, *U307*, *U968* and *U992* are moved to the Bear Island Passage but are unable to establish contact. On 20 Feb the convoy is again located by German air reconnaissance. KG 26 (Lt-Col Stemmler) is deployed against the convoy with 40 Ju 88 torpedo aircraft. Six aircraft are shot down by the fighter cover and no successes are achieved. The pilots believe they have sunk two cruisers, two destroyers and at least eight freighters. *U307*, *U716* and *U286*, which are directed to the supposedly disabled ships, find no targets. The British air escort drives off the U-boats. In a second attack 8/KG 26 (Capt Prinz) sinks the straggler *Henry Bacon* (7177 tons) on 23 Feb; this is the last ship to be sunk by German aircraft in the Second World War.

15 Feb   Norway

The German *U1053* is sunk during a deep diving trial off Bergen.

15 Feb–9 Mar   North Sea

The German defensive minelaying operation 'Titus II', with the minelayers *Ostmark*, *Lothringen* and *Linz*, the destroyer *Friedrich Ihn* and the torpedo boats *T20* and *T17*, is cancelled on both 16 and 17 Feb. On 8 Mar mines are laid by the same force that laid the 'Augustus' field but with *Karl Galster* instead of *Friedrich Ihn*.

16 Feb   Indian Ocean

The assault on Ruywa, Burma, is supported by the sloops *Flamingo* and *Narbada* (RIN).

16–18 Feb   North Pacific

A US task group comprising Crudiv 1 and nine destroyers shells Kurabu Zaki and Paramushiro in the Kuriles on 16 and 18 Feb.

16–19 Feb   Central Pacific

Preparation for the landing on Iwo Jima. On 16 Feb US TF. 54 (Rear-Adm Rodgers),

comprising the battleships *Tennessee*, *Idaho*, *Nevada*, *Texas*, *New York* and *Arkansas*, the cruisers *Chester*, *Salt Lake City*, *Pensacola*, *Tuscaloosa* and *Vicksburgh* and 16 destroyers of Desron 51 and Desdivs 91 and 112, arrives and begins shelling the designated areas in preparation for the assault. TF.52 (Support Force, Rear-Adm Blandy), with the Minesweeper Group 52.3, the Frogman Group 52.4 and the LCI Support Group 52.5, and the escort carrier group 52.2 (Rear-Adm Durgin), comprising the escort carriers *Sargent Bay*, *Natoma Bay*, *Wake Island*, *Petrof Bay*, *Steamer Bay*, *Makin Island*, *Lunga Point*, *Bismarck Sea*, *Saginaw1 Bay* and *Rudyerd Bay* with their destroyer and DE escort, provide air cover and fly 158 attack sorties. The effect of the shelling is slight because of inadequate observation in poor weather. A repetition on 17 Feb in better weather is more successful. Japanese coastal batteries obtain one hit on *Tennessee* and six on *Pensacola*. The UDTs (underwater demolition teams), after being disembarked by the APDs *Bull*, *Bates*, *Barr* and *Blessman*, begin the work of removing underwater obstacles. All 12 LCIs used for support are hit by the Japanese coastal batteries and nine are put out of action. The escort carriers fly 226 sorties, some with napalm bombs. Forty-two B-24s of the US 7th AF make attacks. On 18 Feb the shelling is continued, as are the air attacks (28 sorties). Including the air escort, the escort carrier aircraft fly 612 sorties in all and lose three of their number.

The US DMS *Gamble* is damaged beyond repair by a Japanese naval aircraft on 18 Feb.

17–18 Feb   Air War/Germany

Six Mosquitos of RAF Bomber Command attack Bremen using the 'Oboe' navigation system.

17–22 Feb   Mediterranean

British air attack on the harbour of Trieste: the damaged Italian battleship *Conte di Cavour* and the unfinished *Impero* are sunk and the destroyer *TA44* (ex-Italian *Pigafetta*) and the torpedo boat *TA41* (ex-Italian *Lancia*) are wrecked on 17 Feb.

In an air raid on 20 Feb, the German minelayer *Laurana* and the torpedo boat *TA48* (ex-Yugoslav *T3*) are sunk and the torpedo boat *TA40* (ex-Italian *Pugnale*) is damaged beyond repair. In an attack on Fiume, the torpedo boat *TA46* (ex-Italian *Fionda*) is badly damaged. On 22 Feb the MMS *R4* is sunk at Albona in an air attack.

17 Feb–2 Mar   North Sea

Operations by German motor torpedo boat flotillas. During the night 17–18 Feb the 2nd and 5th Flotillas lay mines off the

Humber. On these mines the French destroyer *La Combattante* and the trawler *Aquarius* (187 tons) are sunk and two ships are damaged. The 9th Flotilla lays a mine barrage off the south-east coast of Britain. An operation off the Scheldt during the night 20–21 Feb has no success.

During the night 21–22 Feb six flotillas are dispatched to the British East Coast with 22 boats in all. NE of Great James the 5th Flotilla and the 2nd Flotilla attack the British convoy FS.1734 and report seven and four torpedo hits respectively The British freighters *Goodwood* (2780 tons) and *Blacktoft* (1109 tons) are sunk. The freighter *Skjold* (1345 tons) is damaged by gunfire from the 2nd Flotilla. The 8th Flotilla attacks a landing ship convoy in the Thames Estuary and sinks *LCP707. S193* is sunk by the escorts. The 4th, 6th and 9th Flotillas have no success. On the return journey, *S167* of the 9th Flotilla sinks in a collision. In the next two nights the flotillas lay mines on the Thames–Scheldt convoy route. On these mine barrages the freighters *Auretta* (4571 tons), *Sampa* (7219 tons), *Robert L Vann* (7176 tons) and one trawler sink.

During the night 1–2 Mar *S220* of the 4th Flotilla is sunk in an engagement with the British DE *Seymour*.

18 Feb   Norway
The German MDS *Sperrbrecher 139/Flamingo* strikes a mine W of Lindesnes and is sunk during salvage operations.

19 Feb–16 Mar   Central Pacific
Operation 'Detachment': landing on Iwo Jima. US TF.51 (Vice-Adm Turner) lands V Amphibious Corps (Lt-Gen H M Smith). TF.51 consists of TF.52, 53, 54 and 56—495 ships. On 19 Feb TF.54 (for composition see 16 Feb), reinforced by the battleships *North Carolina* and *Washington*, the cruisers *Indianapolis* (Adm Spruance, Cdr 5th Fleet), *Santa Fé* and *Biloxi* and 10 destroyers from two Desdivs of TF.58, carries out a heavy preparatory bombardment of the assault areas. This is interspersed with air attacks from the carrier aircraft of TG.58.2 and 58.3 (see 10 Feb) and extended further inland and speeded up with the assault.

The landing is made by TF.53 (Rear-Adm Hill): in the N the 4th Marine Div (Maj-Gen Cates) is landed by TG.53.2 (Commodore Flanagan) on 15 APAs, six AKAs, two LSDs, 19 LSTs and 12 LSMs and in the S the 5th Marine Div (Maj-Gen Rockey) by TG.53.1 (Commodore McGovern) on 15 APAs, six AKAs, one LSD, 19 LSTs and 16 LSMs. One destroyer squadron is available for each as an escort. A further transport squadron has the 3rd Marine Div ready

for combat on board as a reserve. Part of it has to be used on the first day. Some 30000 men are landed on the first day. There is strong resistance from the well-prepared Japanese defenders (Cdr: Lt-Gen Kuribayashi, GOC 109th Inf Div) with flanking fire from entrenched positions on Mount Suribachi (taken on 23 Feb) and the northern mountain terrain on the assault area. Carrier aircraft fly 606 sorties on the first day with 274 tons of bombs, 2254 rockets and over 100 napalm bombs.

The only Japanese counter-action from outside comes from a kamikaze attack with 32 aircraft on 21 Feb, when the escort carrier *Bismarck Sea* is sunk and the fleet carrier *Saratoga*, the escort carrier *Lunga Point*, the transport *Keokuk* and *LST 477* and *LST 809* are damaged. There are 242 dead and 191 injured. Apart from the submarine *Ro-43*, the 'Kaiten'-carrying submarines *I-368*, *I-370* and *I-44* are deployed as the 'Chihaya' group and, later, *I-36* and *I-58* as the 'Kamitake' group. Of the carrier/DE groups *Tulagi* and *Anzio*, used as hunter-killer groups, the latter sinks on 25–26 Feb *Ro-43* and *I-368* and the DE *Finnegan* of a convoy escort sinks *I-370*. Only *Ro-43* (Lt Tsukigata) makes an attack on an escort and torpedoes the destroyer *Renshaw* on 21 Feb. By 16 Mar Japanese defenders on Iwo Jima are overcome. They lose 20703 dead and 216 prisoners. The US Marine Corps loses 5931 dead and missing and there are 17272 wounded.

19 Feb–7 Apr   South West Pacific
Control is gained of the passage through the San Bernardino Strait between Samar and Luzon (Philippines). On 19–20 Feb groups of LCMs, with support from Marine Corps aircraft from Leyte, land company and battalion battle groups of the 182nd RCT on the NW tip of Samar and the offshore islands of Dalupiri, Capul and Biri. The landing on Biri is at first repulsed by the Japanese defenders but then succeeds on the far side of the island. On 21 Feb the midget submarine *Ha-84* has a miss.

On 3 Mar elements of the 132nd RCT of the Americal Div are landed with LCMs on the islands of Ticao and Burias W of the San Bernardino Strait.

On 1 Apr a US assault group (Capt McGee), consisting of three APDs, five LSTs, four LSMs, nine LCIs and six support LCIs and SCs, lands the 158th RCT (Brig-Gen MacNider) near Legaspi (south Luzon). Fire cover is provided by the destroyers *Bailey* and *Bancroft* and the DEs *Day* and *Holt*.

On 3 Apr elements of the 108th RCT of the 40th Inf Div are landed in the capital of the

island of Masbate, which has been occupied by Philippine guerrillas since 29 Mar.

20 Feb   Air War/Germany
In an air raid on Hamburg, the already damaged *U2530* is hit again.

22 Feb–4 Mar   Indian Ocean
On 22 and 23 Feb light assault craft, supported by the Indian sloops *Narbada* and *Jumna*, land 6635 men of the 3rd Commando Bde and other British and Indian Army units on the banks of the Myebon River near Kangaw.

Operation 'Stacey'. From 24 Feb to 4 Mar the escort carriers *Empress* and *Ameer* with the cruiser *Kenya* (Vice-Adm Walker), the destroyers *Virago*, *Vigilant*, and *Volage* and the frigates *Spey*, *Swale*, *Plym* and *Trent* carry out air photo reconnaissance of the Kra Peninsula, of the NE coast of Sumatra, of Penang and of the Simalur and Banjak Islands. They also make raids on Japanese shipping in the Andaman Sea. On 24–25 Feb the destroyers *Rapid*, *Rocket*, *Roebuck* and *Rotherham* shell the Andaman Islands and again on 3 Mar. In a sortie towards the coast near Tavoy, coastal craft are sunk on 1–2 Mar and a Japanese air attack is beaten off on 1 Mar.

23–24 Feb   Air War/Norway
Eighty-three of RAF Bomber Command aircraft attack shipping installations at Horten; one is lost. The torpedo boat *TA8* (ex-Norwegian), fitting out there, is badly damaged.

24 Feb   Air War/Germany
In a USAAF air raid on Bremen, *U3007* is sunk and *U3052* is destroyed on the slipway.

24 Feb–5 Mar   South West Pacific/China
In sorties made by B-29s of the US 20th AF from India, Singapore is attacked on 24 Feb, the Johore Straits (Singapore) are mined during the night 27–28 Feb and the River Yangtse in China is mined on 4–5 Mar.

26 Feb–18 Mar   Baltic
Soviet attack on Eastern Pomerania. On 26 Feb the armies of the Soviet 1st White Russian Front start an attack from the area E of Stargard in the direction of the Stettiner Haff and Kolberg. From the area of Friedland, part of the 2nd White Russian Front advances in the direction of Köslin, which is taken by the 3rd Guards Cavalry Corps on 5 Mar. In the W, the 2nd Guards Armoured Army reaches the Stettiner Haff on 3 Mar, the 1st Guards Armoured Army and the Polish 1st Army the area near Kolberg and the 3rd Assault Army the crossing to Wollin near Dievenov. To cover the bridgehead opposite Wollin, TF.2, comprising the pocket battleship *Admiral Scheer*, the

destroyers *Z38*, *Z31* (Cdr Paul) and *Paul Jacobi* and the torpedo boat *T36*, is employed. From 11 to 18 Mar *Z43*, *Z34* and *T33* support the approximately 2500–3000 defenders of Kolberg, which has been encircled since 7 Mar, so as to make possible the evacuation of about 75000 isolated refugees with the help of naval ferry barges of the 11th Landing Flotilla and support from the 5th Gun Carrier Flotilla. In the roads, some of them are embarked on the transports *Westpreussen* (2870 tons) and *Winrich von Kniprode* (10123 tons) and warships. During the night 17–18 Mar the evacuation of some 75000 refugees, soldiers and wounded is completed.

28 Feb   South West Pacific
Operation 'Victor III'. US Amphibious Group 8 (Rear-Adm Fechteler, TG.78.2), with, as headquarters ship, the US Coast Guard cutter *Spencer*, lands 8000 men of the reinforced 186th RCT (41st Inf Div, Brig-Gen Haney) on Palawan (Philippines). The assault group consists of four APDs, the LSD *Rushmore*, 19 LSTs, 20 LSMs, 10 LSIs and 14 support LCIs, one PC and three SCs, with escort by the destroyers (Desron 5) *Flusser*, *Conyngham*, *Smith*, *Drayton* and *Shaw*. A minesweeper group comprises four YMSs. The preparatory bombardment and support are provided by TG.74.2 (Rear-Adm Riggs), comprising the cruisers *Denver*, *Montpelier* and *Cleveland* and the destroyers (Desron 21) *Fletcher*, *O'Bannon*, *Jenkins* and *Abbot*. Air escort and support are provided by the US 5th AF (Maj-Gen Whitehead) and 13th AF (Brig-Gen Wurtsmith).

On 1 Mar the first supply convoy arrives with 19 LSTs and an escort consisting of the destroyers *Waller*, *Sigourney* and *McCalla*. A base for PT Squadrons 20 and 23 is set up by the motor torpedo boat depot ship *Willoughby*.

1–31 Mar   Air War/Western Europe
Mine offensive by the RAF Bomber Command. In 15 nights, 243 sorties are flown against the Norwegian and Danish coasts, especially off Oslo and in the Kattegat, the Heligoland Bight, the Jade, the Weser and Elbe, the Kiel area, Flensburg, Eckernförde and the Baltic, especially the area off Sassnitz. Mosquitos drop mines into the Kiel Canal. Seven aircraft are lost.

On 5 Mar *U3519* is lost on a mine off Warnemünde. The evacuation transport *Hansa* (21131 tons) sunk near the Giedser lightvessel on 6 Mar. On 7 Mar the transport *Hamburg* (22117 tons) is sunk off Sassnitz. The training ship *Hugo Zeye* sinks NW of Fehmarn on 14 Mar and on 15 Mar the ice-breaker *Castor* (5150 tons) sinks off Warnemünde. On 21 Mar the auxiliary minesweeper *M3827* is sunk at the northern entrance to the Sund.

1–31 Mar   Pacific
Allied submarines continue their operations against Japanese shipping along the coasts. S of Honshu, *Sterlet* (Lt-Cdr Lewis) sinks one ship of 1148 tons, *Bowfin* and *Bluefish* have only misses, and *Ronquil* (Lt-Cdr Monroe) sinks a small vessel. S of Kyushu, *Haddock* has misses, *Tirante* (Cdr Street) sinks six ships of 11336 tons and on 14 Mar the frigate *Nomi* and the corvette *Kaibokan 31* and damages on 9 Mar the corvette *Kaibokan 102* and *Threadfin* (Lt-Cdr Foote) sinks on 28 Mar the frigate *Mikura*. In the Ryukyu area, *Plaice* has a miss, *Springer* (Cdr Kefauver) on 18 Mar sinks the fast transport *T-18* and damages the minesweeper *W-17* and *Trigger* sinks two ships of 2576 tons but is herself sunk on 28 Mar in the East China Sea by Japanese surface forces. In the Yellow Sea, *Balao* (Cdr Worthington) sinks five ships of 11886 tons and *Tench* (Lt-Cdr Baskett) sinks two trawlers. In the East China Sea, *Razorback* (Lt-Cdr Brown) sinks four small vessels, *Sea Cat* has only misses, *Kete* (Lt Cdr Ackermann) sinks three ships of 6881 tons but is herself sunk at the end of Mar (possibly by a Japanese submarine on its way back), *Segundo* (Lt-Cdr Fulp) sinks one ship of 3087 tons and *Spadefish* (Cdr Germershausen) sinks three ships of 4343 tons and two sailing vessels. In the Formosa Strait, *Spot* (Lt-Cdr Post) sinks two ships of 6178 tons and three small vessels.

Off the coast of Indo-China, *Baya* (Lt-Cdr Jarvis) sinks two ships of 5761 tons, *Blueback* (Lt-Cdr Clemenson) sinks five small vessels, *Rock* has only a miss, *Bluegill* (Lt-Cdr Barr) sinks one ship of 5542 tons and *Hammerhead* (Lt-Cdr Smith) sinks the corvettes *Kaibokan 84* on 29 Mar and, probably, *Kaibokan 18* and *Kaibokan 130*. Off Malaya, *Sealion* (Lt-Cdr Putnam) sinks one ship of 1458 tons; W of Borneo *Perch* has a miss; and in the Java Sea *Sea Robin* (Cdr Stimson) sinks four ships of 4690 tons and two small vessels and, together with *Bream* (Lt-Cdr McCallum), one more small craft (*Bream* alone sinks two small vessels).

Of the British submarines in the Malaccan Strait and in the Malayan Archipelago, *Supreme* sinks one coaster and five junks, *Clyde* sinks one ship of 233 tons and one junk, *Sturdy* sinks two landing craft, *Sea Dog* sinks three coasters, *Scythian* sinks eight junks, *Subtle* sinks eight junks, *Spirit* sinks one coaster, *Thrasher* sinks five junks, *Torbay* sinks one coaster, *Selene* sinks four junks, *Stygian* sinks five coasters and the auxiliary minesweeper *W-104* and damages the minelayer *Wakataka* on 27 Mar and also the auxiliary submarine-chasers *Cha-130* and *Cha-104*, *Rorqual* sinks three coasters and three junks, *Thule* sinks eight junks and *Spark* sinks two coasters.

2 Mar   Baltic
The German minesweeper *M575* capsizes and sinks in the Öresund.

2 Mar   Mediterranean
A British raiding force of 500 men, supported by the destroyer *Liddesdale*, captures the island of Piskopi NW of Rhodes.

3 Mar–6 Apr   British Coastal Waters/Atlantic
On the Scottish east coast, *U714* (Lt-Cdr Schwebke) sinks in Mar the Norwegian minesweeping trawler *Nordhav* and one ship of 1226 tons but is then sunk by the new South African frigate *Natal* on 14 Mar. Off St Abb's, the new Type XXIII Boat *U2321* (Lt Barschkies) sinks one ship of 1406 tons. *U778* off the Moray Firth, *U978* off the Pentland Firth, *U1105* off Cape Wrath and *U1108* off the North Minch have no success. The last has to return when she goes aground. As a result of air patrols with Liberators of Nos 86, 120 and 224 Sqns RAF, U-boats are attacked in the Shetland–Faeroes Passage and the North Channel but the assessments are now in doubt in some cases. *U296* is lost in early Mar, probably on a mine. The attack by Liberator 'B' of No 86 Sqn RAF on 20 Mar may not have been on *U905*, which must have been lost earlier, while the attack by Liberator 'M' of No 120 Sqn RAF was on *U1003*, which escaped damage, not on *U296*. *U1106* is sunk by Liberator 'O' of No 224 Sqn RAF on 29 Mar. At the beginning of Apr *U249* is bombed and forced to return.

In the area of the Hebrides and the North Minch, *U722* (Lt Reimers) sinks on 16 Mar one ship of 2190 tons from the convoy RU.156 and *U965* misses one ship. On 21 Mar *U1003* collides under water with the frigate *New Glasgow* of the Canadian 26th EG which, with *Beacon Hill*, *Jonquière*, *Ribble* and *Sussexvale*, is looking for U-boats. The Canadian frigates *Strathadam*, *La Hulloise* and *Thetford Mines*, of the 25th EG, are brought up take part in the search: the last-named finds the survivors of the U-boat which has in the meantime been scuttled. The 21st EG, with the DEs *Conn*, *Rupert* and *Deane* in the N and *Fitzroy*, *Redmill* and *Byron* in the S, has meanwhile been deployed against the U-boats in the area of the Minches and to it *U965* and *U722* fall victim on 27 Mar. *U1021* is probably mined off Trevose Head on 14 Mar.

In the southern part of the Irish Sea, *U1019* operates without success in Mar and *U260* and *U1169* are lost on British mine barrages on 12 Mar and 5 Apr respectively. *U681*, having missed a patrol vessel, is bombed by Liberator 'N' of VPB-103 USN on 11 Mar and is beached on the Irish coast. Wellington 'Y' of No 304 (Polish) Sqn RAF sinks *U321* W of the Channel on 2 Apr.

Of the transport boats returning from St-Nazaire, *U868* goes to Norway and *U275* (Lt Wehrkamp) into the Channel, where she sinks one ship of 4934 tons from convoy ONA.289 but is lost on a submarine mine barrage off Beachy Head on 10 Mar. On the way to St-Nazaire, *U878* (Lt-Cdr Rodig) sinks the Canadian minesweeper *Guysborough* on 17 Mar. *U683* is lost to an unknown cause; the 2nd EG, comprising the frigate *Loch Ruthven* and the sloop *Wild Goose*, attacks the wreck of *U247* W of the Channel by error on 12 Mar.

SW of Ireland and in the Channel, *U1202* (Lt-Cdr Thomsen) attacks an escort carrier group and two convoys. *U399* (Lt Buhse) sinks two ships of 7546 tons from convoys, *U315* (Lt Zoller) sinks one ship of 6996 tons from convoy TBC.103, and *U1195* (Lt-Cdr Cordes) sinks one ship of 7176 tons from a convoy on 21 Mar (torpedoed but a total loss). *U1002* and *U953* operate without success in, and W of, the Channel. Support groups are deployed against these U-boats: the 3rd EG with its leader, the DE *Duckworth*, sinks *U399* and *U246* (Lt-Cdr Raabe) on 26 and 29 Mar respectively after the latter has torpedoed the frigate *Teme* (not repaired) from a Canadian search group which is with convoy BTC.111. On 6 Apr *U1195* attacks convoy VWP.16 in the Channel and sinks the troop transport *Cuba* (11420 tons) but is herself sunk by the escorting destroyer *Watchman*.

Off Iceland, *U773* cruises without success. *U1064* is temporarily employed as a weather boat.

Off the Canadian Atlantic coast, *U866* (Lt Rogowski) repeatedly attacks convoys. Directed to the HF/DF bearings of the boat, the US DEs *Lowe*, *Pride*, *Menges* and *Mosley* sink her on 18 Mar. The Canadian 16th EG does not come up in time.

4 Mar Air War/Germany
U3508 is destroyed in an air raid on Wilhelmshaven.

6–7 Mar Air War/Germany
No 5 Group RAF Bomber Command attacks Sassnitz harbour with 198 aircraft (one is lost). The German destroyer *Z28* and the evacuation transport *Robert Möhring* are sunk; 353 die. The A/S vessels *UJ1109* and *UJ1119* are also sunk.

6–26 Mar English Channel
Operations by German small battle units. On 6 Mar, during preparations for a 'Biber' operation, 14 of the craft are destroyed and nine damaged when a torpedo is released accidentally. On 6 Mar five, on 9 Mar three and on 11 and 16 Mar one 'Seehund' each set off for the North Foreland. *MTB675* sinks one, the frigate *Torrington* two and Beaufighter 'F' of No 254 Sqn RAF one.

On 6 Mar four, on 9, 11 and 16 Mar one each and on 19 Mar two 'Seehunds' set off for the coastal waters of East Anglia. One of the craft sinks the freighter *Taber Park* (2878 tons) from convoy FS.1753 but one 'Seehund' is sunk by *MTB394* SE of Great Yarmouth.

On 11–12 Mar a combined operation is launched against traffic bound for Antwerp. S-boats, 15 'Bibers', 14 'Molchs' and 27 'Linsens' depart from Rotterdam and Hellevoetsluis but 13 'Bibers', 9 'Molchs' and 16 'Linsens' do not return; 12 can be accounted for by Allied forces.

On 22 Mar 12 'Linsens' are sent to Ostend but have no success. On 23–24 Mar 16 'Bibers' try to attack Schelde traffic but have no success; three are sunk by the frigate *Retalick*.

On 24 and 26 Oct four 'Seehunds' sail for the East Anglian coast and six for the Thames. They sink the coaster *Jim* (833 tons) and the steamer *Newlands* (1556 tons) but four boats fail to return. One is sunk by Beaufighter 'Q' of No 254 Sqn, one by the corvette *Puffin* (which is damaged beyond repair by the exploding warhead); one is sunk by *HDML1471* and one by *ML586*.

7 Mar Air War/Norway
In an air attack on Lysekiel, the patrol vessels *V1610* and *V1612* are sunk.

7 Mar–15 Apr Baltic
On 7 Mar the Soviet 2nd White Russian Front launches an attack from the Köslin–Vistula line near Marienwerder on the Gotenhafen–Danzig area. The German 2nd Army is thrown back to the Rixhöft–Neustadt–Karthaus line, where it is temporarily able to stabilise the front with support from naval guns and so gain valuable time to evacuate refugees. From 10 Mar the cruiser *Prinz Eugen* (Capt Reinicke) takes part in the operation and from 15 Mar the old battleship *Schlesien* (Capt H-E Busch), the SATs *Soemba*, *Joost* and *Ostsee* and the gunnery training vessel *Drache*. On 21 Mar *Schlesien* has to withdraw because of lack of ammunition but her place is taken on 23 Mar by the cruiser *Lützow* (Capt Knoke) with *Z31* and *Z34*. From 25 Mar the cruiser *Leipzig* (Cdr Bach), which has had orders to be made seaworthy, also takes part in the shelling of land targets.

The Soviet naval air force, in particular the 9th Ground Attack Div (Lt-Col Slepenko) and the 8th Mining and Torpedo Div (Col Kurochkin), flies 2023 sorties against embarkation operations in Danzig and Gotenhafen and off Hela. Destroyers, torpedo boats, minesweepers and small auxiliary warships form an AA barrage to protect the transports but on 12 Mar the transport *Gerrit Fritzen* (1761 tons), *M3137/K181* and *UJ303* are sunk and on 18 Mar the MMS *R227* and the transport *Orion* (1722 tons) near Scholpin; the *Ellen* (565 tons) is damaged, as is the *Lisa Essberger* (1172 tons) in the roads of Gotenhafen on 19 Mar. On 22 Mar the *Frankfurt* (1186 tons) sinks, as do on 26 Mar the *Bille* (665 tons) and the *Weser* (999 tons). But before the fall of Gotenhafen on 28 Mar and of Danzig on 30 Mar several large transports and numerous smaller ships are still able to proceed to the W crowded with refugees. For example, on 23 Mar *Deutschland* has 11145 on board and on 28 Mar 11295 and *Potsdam* over 9000. Losses are caused by a mine barrage laid off Hela on 8 Mar by the Soviet submarine *L-21* (Capt 3rd Class Mogilevski with the Div Cdr, Capt 1st Class Orel, on board). On 14 Mar the torpedo boats *T3* (Lt-Cdr v Diest†) and *T5* (Lt Wätjen) sink on this as does, later, probably *U367*; on 9 Apr *Z43* is damaged. But mine barrages laid by *Lembit* and *L-3* apparently have no success. In the area of the Stolpe Bank, the Soviet submarine *K-53* (Capt 3rd Class Yaroshevich) sinks the freighter *Margarethe Cords* (1912 tons) on 17 Mar. *L-21* sinks the patrol boat *V2022* on 22 Mar and the tug *Erni*; after unsuccessful attacks, she is hunted off Kolberg in the next few days by *F8* and *TS4*. *Shch-303* (Lt-Cdr Ignatev) torpedoes the *Bohus* (6002 tons), which is later sunk by aircraft.

In Gotenhafen on 27 Mar, before the evacuation, the wreck of the battlecruiser *Gneisenau* is sunk as a block ship. During the night 4–5 Apr the rest of the VII Armoured Corps, comprising 8000 troops, and about 30000 refugees from the Oxhöfter Kämpe bridgehead are brought to Hela in 25 KFKs, 27 MFPs, five SATs and five other ships in Operation 'Walpurgisnacht'. The operations and the embarkations off Hela are covered in the following days by the cruiser *Lützow*, the destroyers *Z38*, *Z31* and *Paul Jacobi*, the torpedo boat *T36* and the SATs *Ostsee*, *Soemba* and *Robert Müller 6* etc. Among the transports proceeding to the W are the *Pretoria* (7000 refugees), *Deutschland* (10000), *Cap Arcona* (9000) and *Eberhart*

Essberger (4750). By 10 Apr 157270 wounded have been evacuated from Hela alone since 21 Mar, while from the still-unoccupied ports in the Gulf of Danzig, Pillau, Kahlberg, Schiewenhorst and Oxhöft, 264887 people are evacuated to Hela in small craft and naval ferry barges in Apr. From 7 to 13 Apr a sharp increase in Soviet air operations against the embarkations is apparent. In the process, the transport *Flensburg* (5450 tons), the supply ship *Franken* (10850 tons)—which, together with her sister ship *Dithmarschen*, has replenished the units of the fleet—the aircraft repair ship *Hans Albrecht Wedel*, *UJ301*, the transports *Albert Jensen* (5446 tons), *Moltkefels* (7862 tons), *Wiegand* (5869 tons) and *Karlsruhe* (897 tons), the hospital ship *Posen* (1069 tons), *UJ1102* and *R69* are lost. From 9 Apr Soviet torpedo cutters are transferred to Neufahrwasser and from 10 Apr are reported to have made 10 sorties. On 10 Apr the freighter *Neuwerk* (804 tons) is sunk.

The embarkations off Hela continue under the AA cover of the warships but on 8 Apr, because of lack of fuel and ammunition, the cruiser *Lützow* with *Z38* and *Z31* (damaged by bomb hits) are withdrawn; and on 10 Apr *Z39* and *T33* have to bring *Z43*, damaged by mines and bombs, to the W. For AA defence, *Z34*, *Paul Jacobi*, *T33*, *M203* and the SATs *Soemba*, *Ostsee*, *Nienburg*, *Robert Müller 6* and *AF21* remain behind. On 15 Apr the destroyers *Z34*, *Paul Jacobi* and *Z39*, the torpedo boats *T23*, *T28*, *T33* and *T36* and minesweepers withdraw with a convoy that consists of the steamers *Matthias Stinnes*, *Eberhart Essberger*, *Pretoria* and *Askari* with about 20000 refugees. *Z34* (Cdr Hetz), which returns, is torpedoed by the Soviet *TKA-131* and *TKA141* under Lt Korotkevich and Lt-Cdr Solodovnikov respectively; *T36* and *M204* bring the ship to Swinemünde.

8 Mar   South China Sea
The Japanese corvette *Kaibokan 69* is damaged in a USAAF air attack off Hainan and sunk while under tow on 16 Mar.

8–9 Mar   Air War/Germany
Nos 4, 6 (RCAF) and 8 Groups RAF Bomber Command attack with 312 aircraft the harbour area of Hamburg. One aircraft is lost and the liner *Robert Ley* damaged.

8–9 Mar   English Channel
The minesweepers *M412*, *M432*, *M442* and *M452*, of the 24th MS Flotilla (Lt-Cdr Mohr) carry out a raid on the harbour of Granville with three gun carriers and six smaller vessels from the Channel Islands. The US patrol boat *PC564* is overwhelmed. Assault troops are landed: they blow up

harbour installations and four freighters of 3612 tons, liberate 67 German prisoners and capture the collier *Eskwood* (791 tons). *M412* runs aground in shallow water and has to be blown up.

10 Mar   Indo-China
The French sloops *Amiral Charner* and *Marne* are scuttled at My Tho to avoid their capture by the Japanese.

10–12 Mar   Baltic
On 10 Mar the German A/S vessel *UJ302* sinks after icing up in the eastern Baltic. On 12 Mar *UJ303* and *UJ305* are lost in a heavy gale.

10 Mar–9 Apr   South West Pacific
Operation 'Victor IV'. A US amphibious group (Rear-Adm Royal, TG.78.1), with the headquarters ship *Rocky Mount*, lands the bulk of the 41st Inf Div (Maj-Gen Doe) near Zamboanga (south-west tip of Mindanao, the Philippines). The transport group comprises four APDs, one LSD, 23 LSTs, 21 LSMs, 32 LCIs and 17 support LCIs, two PCs and two SCs. The minesweeping group comprises 11 YMSs with the Australian sloop *Warrego* and the escort consists of the destroyers (Desron 22) *Waller*, *Saufley*, *Philip*, *Sigourney*, *Robinson*, *McCalla*, *Bancroft* and *Bailey* and the DEs *Rudderow* and *Chaffee*. Preparatory bombardment and fire support is provided by TG.74.3 (Rear-Adm Berkey), comprising the cruisers *Phoenix* and *Boise* and the destroyers (Desron 21) *Fletcher*, *Nicholas*, *Taylor*, *Jenkins* and *Abbot*. Air support is provided by elements of the US 5th AF (Maj-Gen Whitehead) and 13th AF (Brig-Gen Wurtsmith).

Elements of these units land on the Basilan Islands on 16 Mar, on Tawi-Tawi on 2 Apr and on Jolo on 9 Apr. The midget submarines *Ha-79*, *84* and *78* miss with their torpedoes.

11 Mar   Air War/Germany
The German submarine depot ship *Wilhelm Bauer* is hit by bombs and gunfire during a British air attack and is burnt out at Warnemünde; she sinks on 8 Apr. *U758* is damaged at Kiel by air attack. In Hamburg, *U682* and the already damaged *U2530* and *U2547* (fitting out) are sunk and *U2549* and *U2550* are newly damaged in a USAAF air attack.

11–12 Mar   Air War/Germany
B-24s of the US 8th AF drop 709 tons of bombs on Kiel on 11 Mar: in the harbour, the minesweepers *M266*, *M804* and *M805* and a small tanker are sunk. B-17s of the same formation drop 861 tons of bombs on Bremen.

In Hamburg, American bombers sink *U2515* and six merchant ships totalling 17201 tons.

B-17s and B-24s of the 8th AF drop 1435 tons of bombs on Swinemünde on 12 Mar. In the harbour and in the Burmeister yards the (in some cases uncompleted) motor minesweepers *R243*, *R272*, *R273*, *R274*, *R275* and *R276*, 20 KFKs (*KFK 677*, *679*, *680* and *683-699*), the passenger ship *Cordillera* (12655 tons), the patrol boat *V2003*, four freighters and one tug are destroyed.

11–12 Mar   Norway
On 11 Mar the German minesweeper *M2* is sunk by aircraft rocket fire in Fedjefjord. On 12 Mar the minesweeper depot ship *Paris* is sunk off Haugesund by British MTBs.

11–21 Mar   Arctic
Operation against convoy JW.65 in the Arctic. On 11 Mar the convoy sets out from the Clyde with 24 merchant ships escorted by the escort carriers *Campania* (Vice-Adm Dalrymple-Hamilton) and *Trumpeter*, the cruiser *Diadem* and 19 destroyers, sloops, frigates and corvettes. On 13 Mar the B-Service learns of its departure. *U307*, *U312*, *U363*, *U968*, *U716*, and *U997* are stationed in the Bear Island Passage as the 'Hagen' group and *U995* off the Kola Inlet. Later, *U711* joins 'Hagen' and *U313* and *U992* proceed to the Kola Inlet. Air reconnaissance from 14 to 17 Mar produces no results. From 17 Mar all the U-boats are moved to the entrance to the Kola Inlet and are stationed in two lines of six and seven boats. At 0900 hrs on 20 Mar the convoy passes through the first line in a snowstorm. *U995* (Lt Hess), having sunk the Soviet submarine-chaser *BO223* on 3 Mar, torpedoes the steamer *Horace Bushnell* (7176 tons) which is a total loss. When the second line is passed at mid-day, *U716* (Lt Thimme) misses one escort and, in attacks by *U313* (Lt-Cdr Schweiger) and *U968* (Lt Westphalen), the latter sinks the sloop *Lapwing* and the steamer *Thomas Donaldson* (7217 tons). An attempt, after the convoy has come in, to operate with the U-boats against the carriers, suspected to be in the Barents Sea, fails.

13 Mar   Bay of Biscay
The German A/S vessel *UJ1414* is sunk at Lorient by gunfire.

13 Mar   South China Sea
The Japanese corvette *Kaibokan 66* is sunk by USAAF air attack off Amoy.

13 Mar   Indian Ocean
Operation 'Turret': amphibious attack against Letpan, E of Ramree Island, Burma, with the covering destroyers *Eskimo* and

Roebuck and the sloops *Cauvery* (RIN) and *Jumna* (RIN).

14–23 Mar   Central Pacific

US TF.58 (Vice-Adm Mitscher) makes a raid on Japan. On 14 Mar TF.58 sets out from Ulithi (on 11 Mar the carrier *Randolph* was damaged by a kamikaze in Ulithi). TG.58.1 (Rear-Adm Clark) comprises the carriers *Hornet*, *Wasp*, *Bennington*, *Belleau Wood* and *San Jacinto*, the battleships *Massachusetts* and *Indiana*, the cruisers *Baltimore*, *Pittsburgh*, *Vincennes*, *Miami*, *Vicksburgh* and *San Juan* and the destroyers (Desron 61) *De Haven*, *Mansfield*, *Lyman K Swenson*, *Collett*, *Maddox*, *Blue*, *Brush*, *Taussig* and *Samuel N Moore*, (Desdiv 106) *Wedderburn*, *Twining* and *Stockham* and (Desron 25) *John Rodgers*, *Harrison*, *McKee*, *Murray*, *Sigsbee*, *Ringgold*, *Schroeder* and *Dashiell*; TG.58.2 (Rear-Adm Davison) comprises the carriers *Enterprise* and *Franklin*, the cruiser *Santa Fé* and the destroyers (Desron 52) *Owen*, *Miller*, *Stephen Potter*, *Tingey*, *Hickox*, *Hunt*, *Lewis Hancock* and *Marshall*; TG.58.3 (Rear-Adm Sherman) comprises the carriers *Essex*, *Bunker Hill*, *Hancock*, *Cabot* and *Bataan*, the battleships *Washington*, *North Carolina* and *South Dakota* (Vice-Adm Lee), the cruisers *Indianapolis* (Adm Spruance, 5th Fleet), *Pasadena*, *Springfield*, *Astoria* and *Wilkes-Barre* and the destroyers (Desron 62) *Ault*, *English*, *Charles S Sperry*, *Waldron*, *Haynsworth*, *Wallace L Lind*, *John W Weeks*, *Hank* and *Borie* and (Desron 48) *Erben Walker*, *Hale*, *Stembel*, *Black*, *Bullard*, *Kidd* and *Chauncey*; and TG.58.4 (Rear-Adm Radford) comprises the carriers *Yorktown*, *Intrepid*, *Langley* and *Independence*, the battleships *Wisconsin*, *Missouri* and *New Jersey*, the battlecruisers *Alaska* and *Guam*, the cruisers *St Louis*, *Flint*, *Oakland* and *San Diego*, the destroyers (Desron 54) *Remey*, *Norman Scott*, *Mertz*, *Monssen*, *McGowan*, *McNair* and *Melvin*, (Desron 47) *McCord*, *Trathen*, *Hazelwood*, *Heerman*, *Haggard*, *Franks* and *Hailey* and (Desdiv 105) *Cushing*, *Colahan*, *Uhlmann* and *Benham*.

After refuelling on 16 Mar, a strong attack is made early on 18 Mar by the carrier groups on Kyushu, largely concentrating on airfields. Under the command of the Japanese 5th Air Fleet (Vice-Adm Ugaki), 48 kamikaze aircraft set off for the US carrier groups. Eighteen do not find their targets and return. The main attack is directed against TG.58.4. *Intrepid* is set on fire by a kamikaze which crashes near the ship, but she is able to extinguish the fire, and *Yorktown* and *Enterprise* are slightly damaged.

On 19 Mar the carrier attacks are concentrated on the Japanese bases in the Inland Sea, especially Kure. There the Japanese carriers *Amagi*, *Katsuragi*, *Ryuho*, *Hosho* and *Kaiyo* and the new *Ikoma*, the battleships *Yamato*, *Hyuga* and *Haruna*, the cruisers *Tone* and *Oyodo* and the new submarines *I-400*, *I-205* and *Ro-67* are damaged. A Japanese bomber formation of the 5th Air Fleet obtains a hit on *Wasp*, which is set on fire, and has 101 dead and 269 injured, but which brings the flames under control after 15min, and two hits on the *Franklin*, which is set on fire and suffers heavy damage as the result of bomb and ammunition explosions and has 724 dead and 265 injured. 1700 survivors are rescued by the cruisers *Santa Fé* and *Pittsburgh*. Capt Gehres is able to get the very badly damaged ship under control again and, later, to bring her into the dockyard under her own steam. Thirty-nine kamikaze pilots (of whom 20 return) inflict less damage on the *Enterprise*, while *Essex* is damaged by her own AA fire. On 20 Mar the destroyers are replenished. During this there is an attack by 20 Japanese kamikaze bombers, one of which just misses *Hancock* and hits the destroyer *Halsey Powell*. Another damages the planeguard submarine *Devilfish*. On 21 Mar Japanese reconnaissance aircraft maintain contact with TF.58: 18 twin-engine bombers with 'Oka' bombs (manned rocket bombs, called 'Baka' by the Americans) and 55 kamikazes (45 of which return) with 15 escort fighters (three of which return) set off. The bomber force is located and intercepted by 150 fighters which shoot all bar one aircraft down.

On 22 Mar TF.58 proceeds to the tanker group and is refuelled. In the process, the task groups, as a result of the losses, are distributed in three new groups: TG.58.1 comprises *Hornet*, *Bennington*, *Belleau Wood*, *San Jacinto*, *Massachusetts*, *Indiana*, *Vincennes*, *Miami*, *Vicksburgh* and *San Juan*; TG.58.3 comprises *Essex*, *Bunker Hill*, *Hancock* (later *Shangri-La*), *Bataan*, *South Dakota*, *New Jersey*, *Pasadena*, *Springfield*, *Astoria* and *Wilkes-Barre*; and TG.58.4 comprises *Yorktown*, *Intrepid*, *Enterprise*, *Langley*, *Wisconsin*, *Missouri*, *Alaska*, *Guam*, and *San Diego*.

The damaged *Wasp* and *Franklin* are accompanied to Ulithi by *Independence*, *Washington*, *North Carolina*, *Baltimore*, *Pittsburgh*, *Santa Fé*, *Flint* and *Oakland*.

14 Mar–20 Apr   British Coastal Waters

German schnorkel U-boats operate individually (and mostly submerged) in the coastal waters around Great Britain.

Because they keep radio silence and are ordered to their operational areas by written orders before their departure or by means of radio signals in individual codes, it is difficult for the Submarine Tracking Room to fix their positions and the RAF Coastal Command Groups and the escort forces are dependent on visual sightings and attack reports. The following escort groups operate.

From Portsmouth, mostly in the Channel, are the 14th EG, with the destroyers *Havelock* (SO), *Assiniboine* (RCN), *Duncan*, *Hesperus*, *Hotspur*, *Icarus* and *Inconstant* (the destroyer *Forester* is on trials and *Fame* and the RCN *Saskatchewan* are under repair); the 1st EG, with the DEs *Balfour*, *Bentley*, *Garlies*, *Gore*, *Hoste* and *Stockham*; the 26th EG, with the RCN frigates *Beacon Hill* (SO), *Jonquière*, *Ribble* and *Sussexvale* (the frigate *New Glasgow* is under repair after ramming *U1024*); the 9th EG, with the RCN frigates *Loch Alvie*, *Matane*, *Monnow* and *Nene* (the frigate *St Pierre* is detached and *St John* (SO), *Port Colborne*, *Stormont* and *Swansea* are in repair or refit).

From Plymouth, operating in the Channel and the South Western Approaches, are the 2nd EG with the sloop *Wild Goose* (SO) and the frigates *Dominica*, *Labuan*, *Loch Fada*, *Loch Ruthven* and *Tobago*; the 3rd EG, with the DEs *Duckworth* (SO), *Berry*, *Cooke*, *Domett*, *Essington* and *Rowley*; and the 6th EG, with the RCN frigates *New Waterford* (SO), *Annan*, *Loch Achanalt* and *Loch Morlich* (the frigate *Waskesiu* is detached, *Cape Breton*, *Grou* and *Outremont* are in repair and *Teme* has been damaged beyond repair by *U246*).

From Rosyth, in the area N of Scotland, are the 17th EG, with the DEs *Burgess*, *Cranstoun* and *Moorsom* and the frigates *Ascension*, *Loch Killin* and *Loch Lomond*; and the 30th EG, with the corvettes *Caistor Castle*, *Kenilworth Castle*, *Launceston Castle* and *Pevensey Castle* (*Portchester Castle* is detached but on the way to join).

From Londonderry, operating in the North Western Approaches and the Irish Sea, are the 21st EG, with the DEs *Conn* (SO), *Byron*, *Deane*, *Fitzroy*, *Redmill* (damaged beyond repair by *U1105* on 27 Apr) and *Rupert*; the 15th EG, with the DE *Mounsey* (the DE *Dacres* is on trials and *Louis* (SO), *Inglis*, *Lawson* and *Loring* are under repair); the 5th EG, with the DEs *Aylmer*, *Bligh*, *Grindall*, *Keats*, *Kempthorne* and *Tyler*; and the 4th EG, with the DEs *Bazely*, *Bentinck*, *Calder*, *Drury* and *Pasley* (*Byard* is under repair). In Liverpool, the 12th EG is working up after repairs and comprises the sloops *Black Swan* and *Mermaid* and the frigates *Loch Tarbert*, *Barbados* and *Cayman*.

The following groups operate from Greenock as escorts for Murmansk or Gibraltar convoys. The 7th EG, with the corvettes *Allington Castle*, *Alnwick Castle*, *Bamborough Castle*, *Farnham Castle*, *Honeysuckle* and *Oxlip* (convoys JW.65/RA.65 and JW.66/RA.66; the sloop *Cygnet* is working up and the corvette *Rhododendron* in repair); the 8th EG, with the frigates *Aire* and *Loch Moro* (the frigate *Natal* (SAN) is working up and the frigates *Loch Achray* and *Loch Glendhu* are in repair); the 18th EG (with the frigates *Towy* (SO), *Good Hope* (SAN), *Loch Fyne*, *Perim*, *St Helena* and *Zanzibar* all in refit up to early Apr); the 19th EG, with the frigates *Loch Shin* (SO), *Anguilla* and *Loch Insh* and the DEs *Cotton* and *Goodall*, the last being sunk on 29 Apr by *U968* (convoy JW.66/RA.66; the frigate *Antigua* is in repair); the 20th EG (with the frigates *Bahamas*, *Pitcairn*, *Sarawak*, *Somaliland*, *Tavy* and *Tortola* all under refit or repair to early Apr); the 22nd EG, with the sloops *Hart* (SO), *Amethyst*, *Magpie*, *Peacock* and *Wren* and the frigate *Loch Craggie*; and the 31st EG, with the corvettes *Berkeley Castle*, *Carisbrooke Castle*, *Dumbarton Castle*, *Hadleigh Castle* and *Lancaster Castle*. From the Western Approaches Command, detached to Canada, are the 11th EG, with the RCN destroyer *Kootenay* (the destroyers *Qu'appelle* (SO), *Chaudière*, *Gatineau* and *Ottawa* are under repair or refit); the 27th EG, with the RCN frigates *Meon* (SO), *Coaticock*, *Dunver*, *Ettrick* and *Levis* (the frigate *La Salle* is in repair); and the 28th EG, with the RCN frigates *Sainte Thérèse* (SO), *Buckingham*, *Fort Erie*, *Incharron* and *Prestonian*.

15 Mar   North Pacific
A US task group (Rear-Adm McCrea) consisting of Crudiv 1 and seven destroyers shells Matsuwa (Kuriles).

16 Mar   North Sea
The German A/S vessel *UJ1105* is sunk by air attack in the Skagerrak.

16 Mar   Air War/Italy
In an air attack on Monfalcone, the German MMS *R14* and the incomplete U-boats *UIT6* (ex-Italian *R 9*), *UIT7* (ex-Italian *Bario*), *UIT8* (ex-Italian *Litio*) and *UIT9* (ex-Italian *Sodio*) are sunk or destroyed.

17–18 Mar   North Sea
A German defensive minefield is laid in the western Skagerrak by the minelayers *Ostmark* and *Lothringen* accompanied by the destroyers *Friedrich Ihn* and the torpedo boats *T17*, *T19* and *T20*.

17–19 Mar   Indian Ocean
The British destroyers *Saumarez* (D26) *Rapid* and *Volage* bombard Sigli in Sumatra on 17 Mar and Port Blair, Andaman Islands, on 19 Mar.

17–26 Mar   North Sea
German motor torpedo boat flotillas operate off the British East Coast and the Scheldt. During the night 17–18 Mar the 2nd Flotilla carries out a mining operation off Smith's Knoll. A torpedo operation by the 6th and 9th Flotillas off Margate has to be broken off owing to fog.

During the night 18–19 Mar the 6th Flotilla (Lt-Cdr Matzen) lays mines on the East Coast and attacks the British convoy FS.1759 off Lowestoft. The motor torpedo boats report seven hits and sink the freighters *Crichtoun* (1097 tons) and *Rogate* (2871 tons). The 2nd, 4th, 6th and 9th Flotillas operate with mines and torpedoes on the Thames–Scheldt route. The mining operation is successful. *LST80*, the freighters *Samselbu* (7253 tons), *Empire Blessing* (7062 tons) and one trawler sink; and the Liberty ship *Hadley F Brown* (7176 tons) is damaged. The 8th Flotilla is temporarily out of action following an air attack on its base at Ijmuiden on 14 Mar.

On 21–22 Mar the 2nd and 5th Flotillas make a sortie against traffic between the Thames and the Scheldt. Engine trouble on *S210* necessitates the breaking-off of the operation. On the return *S181* is sunk NW of Texel by British Mosquito bombers and the 2nd Flotilla commander, Cdr Opdenhoff†, perishes. Seven boats are damaged.

On 22–23 Mar the 6th and 4th Flotillas lay mines on the Thames–Scheldt traffic route. On 25–26 Mar the operation is repeated by the 4th, 9th and 6th Flotillas, but only the 9th lays its mines. The 4th and 6th Flotillas are driven off by the destroyers *Arendal* (Norwegian) and *Krakowiak* (Polish) and the DE *Riou*. During these operations, the freighters *Eleftheria* (7247 tons), *Charles D McIver* (7176 tons), one trawler and two small warships, *ML466* and *LCP 840*, are lost on the mines.

The 5th and 8th Flotillas are transferred to the Baltic and Norway.

18 Mar   Mediterranean
The 10th TB Flotilla (Cdr Burkart) carries out an offensive mining operation in the Ligurian Sea with *TA24*, *TA29* and *TA32*. NW of Corsica there is an engagement with the British destroyers *Meteor* and *Lookout*. *TA24* and *TA29* are sunk. The British destroyers and coastal forces rescue 244 survivors, including the flotilla commander.

18–29 Mar   South West Pacific
Operation 'Victor I': US Amphibious Group 9 (Rear-Adm Struble, TG.74.3), with, as headquarters ship, the US Coast Guard cutter *Ingham*, lands 14000 men of the 40th Inf Div (Maj-Gen Brush) by 22 Mar on the south coast of Panay. The transport group consists of 16 LSTs, 20 LSMs, 13 LCIs and eight support LCIs. The minesweeping group comprises YMSs with the Australian sloop *Warrego* and the escort comprises the destroyers (Desron 23) *Charles Ausburne*, *Thatcher*, *Claxton*, *Converse* and *Dyson*. Fire support is provided by TG.74.2 (Rear-Adm Riggs) with the cruiser *Cleveland* and the destroyers (Desdiv 44) *Conway*, *Stevens* and *Eaton*.

On 29 Mar forces of the 185th RCT, which have been standing by, land on the northwest coast of Negros. On 8 Apr the 503rd Parachute RCT follows.

18 Mar–1 May   Baltic
On 18 Mar the Soviet armies begin their sixth major offensive against the Army Group Courland. This, like the previous ones, has to be broken off after about 10 days.

On 26–27 Mar Soviet torpedo bombers attack a convoy off Libau and sink the small tanker *Sassnitz*, as well as *R145* and *R260*. Eight fighters from JG 54 then drive off the aircraft, allowing the remaining motor minesweepers to retire. At the scene of the incident, three motor torpedo boats of the German 5th MTB Flotilla (Lt-Cdr Holzapfel) surprise a group of nine Soviet torpedo cutters the following night and in fierce engagements *TKA-166*, *TKA-181* and *TKA-199* are destroyed and 15 prisoners are taken including the Cdr of the Russian 2nd TKA Div.

In Apr the Russian submarine *Shch-310* (Capt 3rd Class Bogorad) is among those to operate off Libau: on 10 Apr she sinks the freighter *Ilmenau* (1201 tons) and on 16 Apr, probably, the *Cap Guir* (1536 tons). *L-3* (Capt 3rd Class Konovalov) claims to have sunk one ship on 1 May (unclarified). The German freighter *Huelva* (1923 tons) is lost on 24 Apr as a result of air attack.

19 Mar   China
The Japanese river gunboat *Suma* is sunk by a US air-laid mine near Kiangying on the Yangtse.

19–26 Mar   Indian Ocean
Destroyer raids by the British Eastern Fleet in the area of the Andamans. In a coastal shelling on 19 Mar, the destroyer *Rapid* is hit by a Japanese gun battery.

On 26 Mar a destroyer division of four ships attacks a Japanese convoy comprising two steamers and the submarine-chasers *Ch-63* and *Ch-34*. The first salvo of ten torpedoes misses. Then a Liberator bomber sinks one of the steamers and in a second approach the destroyers sink the second submarine-chaser with 16 torpedoes, one of which hits, and the two remaining ships with gunfire.

19–29 Mar Baltic

From 19 to 25 Mar the Soviet 3rd White Russian front compresses the pocket of the German 4th Army S of Königsberg on the Frisches Haff. These troops have been supplied by ferry barges across the Haff since Jan. Now 11365 wounded, 324 troops and 14520 refugees from among them are evacuated to Pillau; and, in the last night, on 25 Mar, as many as 5830 troops and 2830 wounded are evacuated.

Because of the situation near Danzig/Gotenhafen, the embarkations at Pillau are considerably interrupted from 8 to 28 Mar and in air attacks individual ships are lost, for example *Meteor* (3717 tons) on 9 Mar and *Jersbek* (2804 tons) on 30 Mar.

19 Mar–12 Apr Norway

In Allied submarine operations off Norway, the British *Venturer* (Lt Launders) sinks the freighter *Sirius* (998 tons) off Namsos on 19 Mar, the Norwegian *Utsira* (Lt-Cdr Valvatne) the freighter *Torridal* (1501 tons) off Follafjord on 5 Apr and the British *Tapir* (Lt-Cdr Roxburgh) the outbound *U486* on 12 Apr.

19 Mar–24 Apr North Atlantic

The Allied North Atlantic convoys are escorted from St John's to the South Western Approaches (HX and SC convoys) by the following escort groups: EG.C3, with the RCN frigates *Kokanee* (SO) and *Sea Cliff* and the RCN corvettes *St Thomas*, *Stellarton* and *Trillium* (the RCN corvette *Rivière du Loup* joins the convoy from the East) and with the RCN corvette *Forrest Hill* detached; EG.B3, with the frigate *Exe* (SO), the DE *Gardiner* and the corvette *Geranium*, with the RCN corvette *Charlock*, attached, the corvette *Flint Castle* detached and the corvettes *Borage* and *Pimpernel* in repair; EG.C5, with the RCN frigates *Runnymede* (SO) and *St Stephen* and the RCN corvettes *Belleville*, *Huntsville*, *Lachute* and *West York* and with the RCN corvettes *Hespeler* and *Long Branch* in repair; EG.C2, with the RCN frigates *Longueuil* (SO) and *Capilano* and the RCN corvettes *Asbestos*, *Kamloops*, *Kinkardine*, *Smith's Falls* and *North Bay* and with the RCN corvette *Norsyd* in repair; EG.C1, with the RCN frigates *Hallowell* (SO) and *Royal Mount* and the RCN corvettes *Arnprior*, *Fennel* and *Orangeville* and with the RCN corvette *Chambly* detached and *Frontenac* and *Giffard* in repair; and EG.C7, with the RCN

frigate *Lanark* (SO) and the RCN corvettes *Coppercliff*, *Hawkesbury*, *Merittonia* and *Barry Sound* and with the RCN corvette *Amherst* following and the RCN frigate *Cape de la Madeleine* and the corvette *Owen Sound* in repair.

The ON and ONS convoys are escorted from the South Western Approaches to St John's by EG.C9, with the RCN frigates *Penetang* (SO) and *Victoriaville* and the RCN corvettes *Fredericton*, *Thorlock* and *Fergus* and with the corvette *Halifax* detached; EG.C4, with the RCN frigate *Glace Bay* (SO) and the corvettes *Beauharnais*, *Bowmanville*, *Petrolia* and *Whitby* and with the corvette *Atholl* detached and the frigate *Wentworth* in repair; EG.C6, with the RCN frigates *East View* (SO) and *Lauzon* and the corvettes *Cobourg*, *Lambert*, *Tillsonburg* and *Peterborough*; EG.C8, with the RCN frigates *Stonetown* (SO) and *Poundmaker* and the corvettes *Humberstone*, *Leaside* and *Edmundston* and with the corvette *Guelph* detached; EG.B2, with the destroyer *Highlander* (SO) and the corvettes *Acanthus* (RNoN), *Nordkyn* (RNoN), *Buttercup*, *Primrose* and *Morpeth Castle* and with the corvette *Sweetbriar* detached; and EG.B1, with the frigate *Chelmer* (SO), the DE *Inman* and the corvettes *Dianella*, *Poppy*, *Starwort* and *Tintagel Castle* and with the corvette *Lotus* in repair.

20 Mar Air War/Germany

B-17s of the 8th USAAF drop 777 tons of bombs on Hamburg.

In an attack on Bremen on 21 Mar the destroyer *Z51*, which is being fitted out, sinks.

20–22 Mar Air War/Germany

In an air raid on 20 Mar on Kiel, the German minesweepers *M15*, *M16*, *M18*, *M19* and *M522* are sunk by bombs. On 21 Mar Nos 1 and 8 Groups RAF Bomber Command attack Bremen with 139 aircraft. During the night 21–22 Mar No 5 Group attacks Hamburg with 159 aircraft and the German MMS *R239* is bombed and sunk.

21 Mar English Channel

The German MTB *S203* is sunk in an air attack off Texel after hitting a mine.

21 Mar Mediterranean

In an air raid on Venice, the German torpedo boat *TA42* (ex-Italian *Alabarda*) is sunk.

23–31 Mar Central Pacific

Preparatory phase of the landing on Okinawa. On 23 Mar TF.58 (for composition see 14 Mar) increases the air attacks with all three task groups in preparation for the landings. The attacks are continued on 24 and 25 Mar.

On 24 Mar TG.58.1, in 112 sorties, makes

an attack on a convoy sighted S of Kyushu, all of whose eight ships are destroyed, including the torpedo boat *Tomozuru* and the corvette *Kaibokan 68*. The battleships *New Jersey*, *Wisconsin* and *Missouri* (Rear-Adm Denfeld) with five destroyers and *Massachusetts* and *Indiana* (Vice-Adm Lee) with six destroyers shell Okinawa on 24 Mar. On 27–28 Mar TF.58 replenishes, in the course of which the destroyer *Murray* is damaged by a single Japanese aircraft. On 28 Mar the corvette *Kaibokan 33* is sunk. On 29 Mar TG.58.4 again attacks Okinawa and TG.58.3 and 58.1 attack the northern Ryukyu islands and Kyushu. On 30–31 Mar TG.58.1 replenishes, while TG.58.3 and 58.4 make further attacks on the Okinawa area and to the N of it.

The British Pacific Fleet (Vice-Adm Rawlings), which sets out from Ulithi on 23 Mar, replenishes on 25 Mar and, as TF.57 (Vice-Adm Vian), attacks on 26 and 27 Mar the Sakishima-Gunto group of islands of the southern Ryukyus in order to neutralise the airfields there. The British task force consists of the carriers *Indomitable*, *Victorious*, *Illustrious* and *Indefatigable*, the battleships *King George V* and *Howe*, the cruisers *Swiftsure*, *Gambia* (RNZN), *Black Prince*, *Argonaut* and *Euryalus* and the destroyers *Grenville*, *Ulster*, *Undine*, *Urania*, *Undaunted*, *Quickmatch*, *Quiberon*, *Queenborough*, *Kempenfelt*, *Whirlwind* and *Wager*. From 28 to 30 Mar TF.57 replenishes from a supply group consisting of the escort carriers *Striker* and *Speaker*, the sloops *Crane* and *Pheasant*, the frigate *Findhorn*, three tankers and the destroyers *Quality* and *Whelp* which relieve *Kempenfelt* and *Whirlwind*. On 31 Mar the attacks to neutralise Sakishima-Gunto are resumed.

From 24 to 25 Mar the units of TF.52 (Rear-Adm Blandy) and of TF.54 (Rear-Adm Deyo) arrive off Okinawa. Three escort carrier groups (TG.52.1, Rear-Adm Durgin) support the air attacks made by TF.58 and 57 and take over their roles when they are being replenished. Taking part are Group 1 (Rear-Adm Durgin), comprising the escort carriers *Makin Island*, *Fanshaw Bay*, *Lunga Point*, *Sangamon*, *Natoma Bay*, *Savo Island* and *Anzio*, the destroyers (Desdiv 120) *Ingraham*, *Hart*, *Boyd*, *Bradford*, *Patterson* and *Bagley* and the DEs *Lawrence C Taylor*, *Melvin R Newman*, *Oliver Mitchell*, *Robert F Keller*, *Tabberer*, *Richard M Rowell*, *Richard S Bull*, *Dennis*, *Sederstrom*, *Fleming* and *O'Flaherty*; Group 2 (Rear-Adm Stump), comprising the escort carriers *Saginaw Bay*, *Sargent Bay*, *Marcus Island*, *Petrof Bay*, *Tulagi* and *Wake Island*, the destroyers (Desdiv 91) *Capps*, *Lowry*,

Evans and *John D Henley* and the DEs *William Seiverling*, *Ulvert M Moore*, *Kendall C Campbell*, *Goss*, *Tisdale* and *Eisele*; and Group 3 (Rear-Adm Sample), comprising the escort carriers *Suwanee*, *Chenango*, *Santee* and *Steamer Bay*, the destroyers (Desron 58) *Metcalf*, *Drexler*, *Fullam*, *Guest* and *Helm* and the DEs *Edmonds* and *John C Butler*. On 24 Mar the minesweeping group (TG.52.2, Rear-Adm Sharp on the minelayer *Terror*) begins the work of sweeping with three groups of fast minesweepers (consisting of *Forrest*, *Hobson*, *Macomb*, *Dorsey* and *Hopkins*; *Ellyson*, *Hambleton*, *Rodman* and *Emmons*; and *Butler*, *Gherardi*, *Jeffers* and *Harding*), seven groups of 36 fleet minesweepers and four groups each of six YMSs. Each has one fast minelayer allocated for temporary support from the following: *Gwin*, *Lindsey*, *Aaron Ward*, *Adams*, *Tolman*, *Henry A Wiley*, *Shea*, *Tracy*, *J William Ditter*, *Robert H Smith*, *Shannon*, *Thomas E Fraser*, *Henry F Bauer* and *Breese*.

On 25 Mar the UDTs arrive on 10 APDs and begin clearing the assault beaches of underwater obstacles. The cruisers *San Francisco* and *Minneapolis* and three destroyers shell the assault areas on Kerama Retto on 25 Mar and, supported by the battleship *Arkansas*, before the assault on 26 Mar. On 26 Mar the Western Islands Attack Group (TG.51.1, Rear-Adm Kiland), with headquarters ship *Mount McKinley*, lands the 77th Inf Div (Maj-Gen Bruce) on Kerama Retto against slight resistance. The transport squadron consists of 13 APAs, six AKAs, 28 LSTs, 11 LSMs and eight support vessels and the escort (Capt Moosbrugger) the headquarters ship *Biscayne*, the destroyers (Desron 49) *Picking*, *Sproston*, *Wickes*, *William D Porter*, *Isherwood*, *Kimberly*, *Luce*, *Charles J. Badger* and the DEs *Scribner*, *Kinzer*, *Richard W Suesens*, *Abercrombie*, *Oberrender*, *Riddle*, *Swearer* and *Stern*.

On 26 Mar the Fire Support Group (TF.54, Rear-Adm Deyo) begins the shelling of Okinawa. Group 1 comprises the battleships *Texas* and *Maryland*, the cruiser *Tuscaloosa* and the destroyers (Desdiv 110) *Laws*, *Longshaw*, *Morrison* and *Prichett*; Group 2 comprises the battleships *Arkansas* and *Colorado*, the cruisers *San Francisco* and *Minneapolis* and the destroyers (Desdiv 51) *Hall*, *Halligan*, *Paul Hamilton*, *Laffey* and *Twiggs*; Group 3 comprises the battleships *Tennessee* and *Nevada*, the cruisers *Wichita* and *Birmingham* and the destroyers (Desron 60) *Mannert L Abele*, *Zellars*, *Bryant*, *Barton* and *O'Brien*; Group 4 comprises the battleships *Idaho* and *West Virginia*, the

cruisers *Pensacola*, *Portland* and *Biloxi* and the destroyers (Desron 55) *Porterfield*, *Callaghan*, *Irwin*, *Cassin Young* and *Preston*; Group 5 comprises the battleships *New Mexico* and *New York*, the cruisers *Indianapolis* (Adm Spruance, 5th Fleet) and *Salt Lake City* and the destroyers (Desron 56) *Newcomb*, *Heywood L Edwards*, *Leutze*, *Richard P Leary* and *Bennion*; and Group 6 comprises the DEs *Samuel S Miles*, *Wesson*, *Foreman*, *Whitehurst*, *England*, *Witter*, *Bowers* and *Willmarth*. There are also 53 support landing craft with rocket-launchers. Once the US intention to attack Okinawa is recognised, the Japanese submarines *I-8*, *Ro-41*, *Ro-49* and *Ro-56* are deployed to attack with torpedoes. *Ro-41* encounters TG.58.4 on 22 Mar and is sunk by the destroyer *Haggard* on 23 Mar. *Ro-49* (Lt-Cdr Go) misses the cruisers *Wichita* and *St Louis* on 25 Mar and *Ro-56* misses *Pensacola* on 27 Mar. *I-8* is detected by aircraft on 30 Mar and sunk by the destroyers *Morrison* and *Stockton*. On 25 Mar Operation 'Tengo' (the defence of Okinawa and South Japan) is put into force by Japanese Imperial Headquarters. The air formations of the 3rd and 10th Naval Air Fleets are put under the operational command of the 5th Air Fleet (Vice-Adm Ugaki) which operates from Kyushu. The remains of the 1st Air Fleet operate from Formosa. At dawn on 25 Mar the first kamikaze attack is made with 25 aircraft (three return): the destroyer *Kimberly*, the minelayer *Robert H Smith* and the fast transports *Gilmer* and *Knudsen* (bomb hits) are damaged. In the evening of 26 Mar eleven kamikazes attack. Hits are obtained on the battleship *Nevada*, the cruiser *Biloxi*, the destroyers *O'Brien*, *Porterfield* and *Callaghan*, the DE *Foreman* and the minesweeper *Skirmish*. The destroyer *Halligan* is beached after receiving a torpedo hit (from *Ro-49*?). With TG.58.1, the destroyer *Murray* is hit with bombs from dive-bombers. On 27 Mar TF.54 continues the shelling. There is an attack by 15 kamikazes: the minelayer *Adams* and the minesweeper *Southard* are damaged. On 27 Mar there is an unsuccessful attempt by explosive boats to approach TF.51 off Kerama Retto. On 28 Mar there is renewed shelling: the minesweeper *Skylark* is sunk while searching for mines. The AKA *Wyandot* is damaged by bomb hits. During the night 28–29 Mar there are individual attacks by aircraft from Okinawa: *LSM(R) 188* is badly hit. As a result, airfields are shelled on 29 Mar and TF.52 makes attacks on airfields and bases for explosive boats and midget submarines. On 30 Mar, after further shelling of Okinawa, there is an attack by four kami-

kazes in the evening: the flagship of the 5th Fleet, *Indianapolis*, is hit. Adm Spruance transfers to the battleship *New Mexico*. On 31 Mar there are kamikaze attacks in which the minelayer *Adams*, the APA *Hinsdale* and *LST724* and *LST884* are hit.

23–31 Mar   Arctic
Operation against convoy RA.65 in the Arctic. On 23 Mar 25 merchant ships, escorted as JW.65, set out from the Kola Inlet. Some of the U-boats have only just again concentrated off the Inlet. *U313* and *U968* respectively hear and sight the convoy and the escort carriers but are not able to attack. An attempt to put a patrol line in front of the convoy with *U307*, *U310*, *U313*, *U363*, *U668*, *U711*, *U716*, *U968* and *U992* produces no results on 25 Mar. Attempts by the Luftwaffe up to 27 Mar to establish contact with the convoy so as to be able to launch a torpedo attack fail and the operation is abandoned. The convoy arrives on 31 Mar in Scapa Flow.

On 22 and 31 Mar *U711* (Lt-Cdr Lange) and *U312* (Lt v Gaza) each torpedo one armed trawler off the Kola Coast.

23 Mar–14 Apr   Baltic
The Soviet submarines *Lembit* (Capt 3rd Class Matiyasevich) and *L-3* (Capt 3rd Class Konovalov) lay mines off Rixhöft and Brüsterort. Several patrol vessels are probably lost here, but the Soviet claims cannot be wholly substantiated.

26 Mar–26 Apr   South West Pacific
Operation 'Victor II': US Amphibious Group 8 (Capt A T Sprague, TG.78.2), with, as headquarters ship, the US Coast Guard cutter *Spencer*, lands 14000 men of the Americal Div (Maj-Gen Arnold) near Cebu (Philippines). The transport group consists of four APDs, 20 LSTs, 11 LSMs, 15 LCIs, nine support LCIs and two PCs. The minesweeping group comprises eight YMSs. Escort is provided by the destroyers (Desron 5) *Flusser*, *Shaw*, *Conyngham*, *Smith* and *Drayton* and fire support by TG.74.3 (Rear-Adm Berkey) comprising the cruisers *Phoenix*, *Boise* and *Hobart* (Australian) and the destroyers (Desron 21) *Fletcher*, *Nicholas*, *Taylor*, *Jenkins* and *Abbot*. Air support is provided by the US 13th AF (Maj-Gen Wurtsmith).

Elements of these forces land a battalion of the 164th Regt on Bohol on 11 Apr and the 164th RCT near Sibulan in SE Negros on 26 Apr.

On 1 Apr another transport division of VII Amphibious Force (Capt McGee), consisting of the destroyers *Bailey* and *Bancroft*, the DEs *Day* and *Holt*, three APDs, nine LCIs, five LSTs and four LSMs, lands the US 158th RCT on Legaspi (South Luzon).

On 2 Apr one BLT of the 163rd RCT is landed on the Sulu Archipelago by another group of VII Amphibious Force (Capt Murphy). The destroyer *Shaw* runs aground on 2 Apr off Leyte and is lost.

27 Mar   Air War/Germany
One hundred and fifteen aircraft of No 5 Group RAF Bomber Command attack the U-boat pens at Bremen Farge and 20 Lancasters from No 617 Sqn RAF Bomber Command drop 'Grand Slam' bombs on the pens. Two hits are scored.

27 Mar   Air War/Italy
In an USAAF air raid on Venice, the German corvette *UJ205* (ex-Italian *Colubrina*) is sunk.

27 Mar–14 Aug   Pacific
B-29 bombers of the 21st Bomb Group USAAF fly from Tinian on mining sorties. Of 1529 aircraft airborne, 102 return and 1427 drop 12135 mines (4921 magnetic, 3507 acoustic, 2959 pressure-magnetic and 748 low-frequency) in the Shimonoseki Strait and off Kure-Hiroshima, Sasebo, Fukuoka-Karatsu, Harima-Nada, Kobe-Osaka, Hiuchi Nada, Nagoya, Tokyo-Yokohama, Niigata-Sakata, Maizuru-Tsuruga, Nanao-Fushiki, Hagi, Yuya, Senzuki, Sakai and Funakawa in the Japanese Islands and off Fusan, Rashin, Reisui, Masan, Seishin, Konan, Genzan, Geijits Wan and Hamada in Korea. Fifteen aircraft are lost.

28 Mar   South West Pacific
In a USAAF air attack off Macassar (Celebes), the Japanese minesweeper *W-11* is sunk.

30–31 Mar   Air War/Germany
B-24s of the US 8th AF drop 916 tons of bombs on harbour installations at Wilhelmshaven: the cruiser *Köln*, the U-boats *U96*, *U429* and *U3508*, the escort vessel *F6/Königin Luise* the motor torpedo boat *S186*, the minesweepers *M329* and *M3430*, the U-boat tender *Weichsel*, two tugs and four freighters totalling 11259 tons are sunk.

B-17s of the 8th AF drop 1103 tons of bombs on Bremen. *U72*, *U430*, *U870*, *U882* and *U3036* and the incomplete *U884*, *U3045* and *U3046* are sunk and *U3042* and *U3043* are destroyed on the slipway.

On 31 Mar–1 Apr Nos 1, 6 (RCAF) and 8 Groups RAF Bomber Command, with 469 aircraft, attack Hamburg, especially the Blohm & Voss yard. Eleven aircraft are lost. *U348*, *U350*, *U747*, *U1131* and *U1167* are lost to bomb hits and *U2340* is destroyed.

1–5 Apr   Central Pacific
Operation 'Iceberg': TF.51 (Vice-Adm Turner) with a total of 1213 ships, including 603 landing craft, lands the 10th US Army (Lt-Gen Buckner) on Okinawa: 451866

men, including three reserve divisions, are embarked. The assault areas are previously shelled intensively by TF.54 (see 23 Mar) and continually bombarded by TF.58 (see 14 Mar) and TF.52 (see 23 Mar).

The Northern Attack Force (TF.53, Rear-Adm Reifsnider), with the headquarters ship *Panamint*, lands III Amphibious Corps (Maj-Gen Geiger), of which TG.53.1 (Commodore Knowles) brings the 6th Marine Div (Maj-Gen Shepherd) on 16 APAs, six AKAs, one LSD and the LSV *Catskill* and TG.53.2 (Commodore Moyer) the 1st Marine Div (Maj-Gen del Valle) on 15 APAs, six AKAs, two LSDs and the LSV *Monitor*. Also divided among both divisions are 46 LSTs, five LSMs and 16 LCTs, as well as 18 leader vessels (PCSs, PCs and SCs). The escort is TG.53.6 with the destroyers (Desdiv 4) *Morris*, *Mustin*, *Lang*, *Stack* and *Sterett* and (Desdiv 90) *Pringle*, *Hutchins*, *Massey*, *Russell*, *Wilson*, *Stanly*, *Howorth* and *Hugh W Hadley*, the DEs *Gendreau*, *Fieberling*, *William C Cole*, *Paul G Baker* and *Bebas*, two APDs, two PCEs and one SC.

The Southern Attack Force (TF.55, Rear-Adm Hall), with the headquarters ship *Teton*, lands XXIV Corps (Maj-Gen Hodge), of which TG.55.1 (Commodore Carlson) brings the 7th Inf Div (Maj-Gen Arnold) on 16 APAs, seven AKAs, one LSD and the LSV *Ozark* and, in addition, 30 LSTs, 22 LSMs and two LCIs, and TG.55.2 (Commodore Richardson) the 96th Inf Div (Maj-Gen Bradley) on 16 APAs, six AKAs, two LSDs, 23 LSTs, five LSMs, one LCI and six support LCSs. Nineteen leader vessels and 17 more support landing craft are allocated and the escort is TG.55.6 with the destroyers (Desdiv 48) *Anthony*, *Bache* and *Bush*, (Desron 45) *Bennett*, *Hudson*, *Hyman*, *Purdy*, *Beale*, *Wadsworth* and *Ammen* and (Desron 66) *Putnam* and *Rooks*, the DEs *Crouter*, *Carlson*, *Damon M Cummings*, *Vammen*, *O'Neill* and *Walter C Wann*, one APD, one PCE and two SCs.

The landing goes according to plan against, initially, slight resistance, because the Japanese 32nd Army (Lt-Gen Ushijama) is firmly entrenched in the southern mountain terrain and has made preparations for long-drawn-out fighting. The troops on shore are daily supported by battleships, cruisers and destroyers of TF.54, by aircraft of the escort carriers of TF.52 (564 aircraft to begin with) and by TF.58 from which two groups are continually in the operational area while the third is being replenished. On 2 Apr the Japanese corvette *Kaibokan 186* and the fast transport *T-17* are sunk.

The British TF.57 carries out daily neu-

tralisation raids on the Sakishima-Gunto island group from 31 Mar to 2 Apr. While it is being replenished on 3, 4 and 5 Apr, it is relieved by the Escort Carrier Group of Rear-Adm Sample (see 23 Mar).

In the evening of 1 Apr there are kamikaze and Oka bomb attacks on the landing fleet and the support force. The battleship *West Virginia* and the transports *Alpine*, *Achernar* and *Tyrrell* are hit; and the destroyer *Prichett*, the minesweeper *Skirmish* and the transport *Elmore* are damaged by bombs from dive-bombers and high-level bombers and the DE *Vammen* on a mine. The British carrier *Indomitable* and the destroyer *Ulster* are hit in kamikaze attacks by the Japanese 1st Air Fleet. The latter is towed to Leyte by the cruiser *Gambia*.

In the evening of 2 Apr there is a kamikaze attack (14 machines) on the transports with the re-embarked 77th Inf Div; the APAs *Chilton*, *Henrico*, *Goodhue* and *Telfair* are badly hit. The APD *Dickerson* is seriously damaged and has to be scuttled on 4 Apr. Bombers hit the destroyer *Prichett* and the DE *Foreman*. Early on 3 Apr *LST599* is damaged by kamikaze and at dusk the escort carrier *Wake Island*, the minesweeper *Hambleton*, the DE *Foreman* and *LCT876*. The destroyer *Sproston* is damaged in a dive-bombing attack.

On 4 Apr there are no kamikaze sorties because of heavy storms. Many LSTs are damaged on the beaches. On 5 Apr the battleship *Nevada* receives five hits from a Japanese coastal battery when shelling targets on shore.

1–30 Apr   Pacific and Indian Ocean
Allied submarines operate against Japanese coastal traffic along the Asiatic coasts, partly in 'wolfpacks' aided by 'Ultra' data. East of Hokkaido and Northern Honshu, *Cabrilla* has one miss, *Parche* (Lt-Cdr McCrory) sinks two ships of 567 tons and one small craft and on 9 Apr the minesweeper *W-3* and *Sunfish* (Cdr Reed) sinks three ships of 4671 tons and on 16 Apr the corvette *Kaibokan 73*. S of Honshu, *Sea Dog* (Cdr Hydeman) sinks one ship of 530 tons and *Sennet* (Cdr Porter) sinks one ship of 1901 tons and on 19 Apr the auxiliary submarine-chaser *Cha-97* and damages the repair ship *Hashima* on 28 Apr and the corvette *Kaibokan 50* on 1 May. *Cero* (Lt-Cdr Berthrong) sinks five ships of 9015 tons and damages one small craft and *Rasher* sinks two small vessels. S of Kyushu, *Crevalle* (Lt-Cdr Steinmetz) sinks one small craft and damages one trawler and on 10 Apr the frigate *Ikuna*, *Seahorse* (Lt-Cdr Wilkins) sinks one sailing vessel and *Silversides* (Lt-

Cdr Nichols) sinks two picket boats of 449 tons. E of the Bonin Islands, *Tunny* sinks one picket boat. W of Kyushu, *Trepang* (Lt-Cdr Faust) sinks one ship of 4667 tons and one sailing vessel, on 28 Apr the landing ship *T-146* and on 4 May the minesweeper *W-20*; *Springer* (Cdr Kefauver) sinks on 28 Apr the submarine-chaser *Ch-17*, on 2 May the frigate *Ojika* and on 3 May the corvette *Kaibokan 25*.

Off Okinawa, *Sea Owl* (Cdr Bennet) on 18 Apr sinks the submarine *Ro-46*. In the Yellow Sea, *Sea Devil* (Lt-Cdr Styles) sinks four ships of 10413 tons and damages one of 6800 tons, *Trutta* (Cdr Smith) sinks three small craft and damages one more and *Picuda* misses a destroyer. In the East China Sea, *Cod* (Lt-Cdr Adkins) on 25 Apr sinks the minesweeper *W-41*.

In the Formosa Strait, *Sea Fox* (Lt-Cdr Klinker) has a miss and *Queenfish* (Cdr Loughlin) sinks one ship of 11249 tons. *Snook* is sunk E of Formosa by Japanese forces on 8 Apr.

In the Gulf of Siam, *Hardhead* (Cdr Greenup) lays a minefield at Pulo Obi and sinks by torpedo one ship of 6886 tons and by gunfire two small craft and the British *Tradewind* sinks one ship of 1116 tons, one tug and two junks. Off Lingga, *Guitarro* (Lt-Cdr Haskins) lays a minefield in the Berhala Strait on which one ship of 2345 tons sinks and on 7 May the munitions transport *Hayasaki* (920 tons) is damaged.

In the Sunda Sea, *Besugo* (Cdr Miller) on 6 Apr sinks the minesweeper *W-12* and on 23 Apr the German *U183* and one vessel of 199 tons, the British *Sea Scout* sinks one coaster, the Dutch *Zwaardfish* (Lt-Cdr Goossens) damages two small craft and the British *Sleuth* and *Solent* sink the auxiliary minesweepers *Wa-1* and *Wa-3*, one landing craft and one coaster and damage one other coaster. In the Sunda Strait, the Dutch *O-19* (Lt-Cdr v Kernebeek) lays a mine barrage, sinks one ship of 676 tons and misses the cruiser *Haguro*. In the Java Sea, *Gabilan* (Cdr Parham) sinks one ship of 762 tons and one small craft and together with *Charr* (Cdr Boyle) on 7 Apr the cruiser *Isuzu*; *Charr* alone also lays a minefield at Pulo Obi. *Bream* (Lt-Cdr McCallum) lays a minefield at Pulo Obi and sinks with torpedo one ship of 1230 tons.

In the Malacca Strait, the British *Statesman* (Lt Bulkeley) sinks seven landing craft, 10 junks, one sailing vessel and three barges. Off the Nicobar Islands, the British *Thorough* sinks two coasters, three landing craft and one auxiliary gunboat and W of Sumatra the Dutch *O-24* sinks one small craft.

2 Apr Baltic
The German MMS *R256* is sunk in an air attack E of Bornholm after colliding with the torpedo boat *T11*. In Apr *UJ1101* is lost in the eastern Baltic from an unknown cause.

3–4 Apr Air War/Germany
About 700 bombers of the US 8th AF drop 2200 tons of bombs on the harbour installations in Kiel. The U-boats *U237*, *U749*, *U1221*, *U2542*, *U3003* and *U3505*, the minesweeper *M802*, the mine transport *Irben*, the MMSs *R59*, *R72*, *R119* and *R261*, the passenger ship *New York* (22337 tons), the hospital ship *Monte Olivia* (13750 tons) and the tanker *Mexphalte* (2578 tons) are sunk or destroyed or burn out.

3–6 Apr South China Sea
In USAAF attacks against Japanese shipping along the Chinese coast on 3 Apr, the frigate *Manju* is destroyed at Hong Kong. On 5 Apr the corvette *Kaibokan 1* and on 6 Apr the destroyer *Amatsukaze* and the corvette *Kaibokan 134* are sunk in the area of Amoy.

4 Apr Japan
The Japanese frigate *Mokutu* is sunk by an air-laid mine in the Shimonoseki Strait.

4–28 Apr Air War/Western Europe
Mine offensive by RAF Bomber Command. In five nights, 271 sorties are flown, mainly over the Kattegat, the Belts and Kiel Bay but also the Oslo area. Three aircraft are lost. The German MMS *R126* is sunk by mine in the Great Belt on 14 Apr, the MCMS *Sperrbrecher 167/Malmedy* in the Heligoland Bight on 27 Apr and *U1007* off Wismar on 2 May.

5 Apr Air War/Germany
U677 is destroyed in a USAAF air raid on Hamburg.

5–30 Apr English Channel
Last operations by German small battle units. There are 36 'Seehund' sorties. Off the East Anglian coast and the Thames Estuary, the cable ship *Monarch* (1150 tons) is sunk off Orfordness but three 'Seehunds' are sunk by Beaufighter 'U' of No 236 Sqn RAF on 12 Mar, by the destroyer *Garth* on 14 Mar and by the corvette *Sheldrake* on 29 Mar. In operations against Scheldt traffic, the small US oiler *YO17* (800 tons) from convoy TAC.90 is sunk but one 'Seehund' is sunk by Beaufighter 'B' of No 236 Sqn and one by shore batteries, and one is stranded. Of the 17 boats sailing for the Dover/Dungeness area on 11 Apr, one boat attacks convoy UC.638 and damages the *Port Wandham* (8580 tons) but is sunk by MTB632. On 12 Apr one boat is sunk by air attack and on 13 Apr one more by Barracuda 'L' of No 810 Sqn FAA. From 17

Apr the freighter *Samida* (7219 tons) is sunk and the Liberty ship *Solomon Juneau* (7176 tons) from convoy TBC.123 is damaged but one 'Seehund' is sunk by *ML102* and one by Beaufighter 'W' of No 254 Sqn. The last 'Seehund' sorties are supply missions to Dunkirk on 28 Apr and 2 May.

'Biber' sorties take place on 9 Apr with five boats, on 11 Apr with two and on 21 Apr with six to lay mines. However, their success is unclear and most of the craft are sunk. 'Linsens' are used for supply runs to Dunkirk but many are sunk by the frigate *Ekins*.

5 Apr–4 May British Coastal Waters
In U-boat operations off the British East Coast, *U2324* (Lt-Cdr v Rappard) sinks one ship of 1150 tons off the Thames and *U245* (Cdr Schuman-Hindenberg) two ships of 9847 tons from convoy TAM.142; *U2329* (Lt Schlott) torpedoes one ship of 7209 tons off Lowestoft and Orfordness; *U2326* (Lt Jobst) misses one ship; and *U2322* (Lt Heckel) reports the sinking of an unknown ship. *U975* (Lt-Cdr Brauel) and *U637* (Lt-Cdr Riekeberg) lay mines off Hartlepool and Newcastle respectively. Off the Firth of Forth, *U1274* (Lt Fitting) sinks one ship of 8966 tons from convoy FS.1784 but is herself sunk by the destroyer *Viceroy* of the escort on 16 Apr. *U1206* has to be abandoned on 14 Apr because of a diving problem and *U398* is missing off the Scottish east coast. *U287* cruises E of the Orkneys without success.

On the way to their operational areas W of Britain, *U396* and *U1017* are lost in attacks by Liberators 'V' of No 186 and 'Q' of No 120 Sqns RAF on 23 and 29 Apr respectively. In the area of the Hebrides and the North Channel, *U218* (Lt-Cdr Stock) lays a mine barrage in the Clyde. *U636* is sunk by the DEs *Bazely*, *Drury* and *Bentinck* of the 4th EG on 21 Apr and *U293* (Lt-Cdr Klingspor) or *U956* (Lt-Cdr Mohs) sinks one ship of 878 tons. *U1105* (Lt Schwartz) torpedoes the DE *Redmill* and avoids sonar detection by her pursuers thanks to her 'Alberich' skin. *U1305* has no success.

In the Irish Sea, *U1024* (Lt-Cdr Gutteck) unsuccessfully attacks a corvette on 5 Apr and sinks one ship on 7 Apr and one on 12 Apr from convoys which together total 14376 tons but she is then forced to surface by a 'Squid' from the frigate *Loch Glendhu* of the 8th EG. The abandoned boat is boarded by the frigate *Loch More* and taken in tow but she sinks. Valuable documents are captured. *U825* has no success nor has *U1052*. *U242* is discovered on 30 Apr by Sunderland 'H' of No 201 Sqn RAF as she uses her schnorkel. The aircraft summons the 14th EG, whose destroyers *Hesperus* and *Havelock* sink the U-boat. On 8 Apr, SW of Ireland, *U1001* is sunk by the DEs of the 21st EG, *Fitzroy* and *Byron*, on 8 Apr, and *U774* by the DEs of the 4th EG, *Calder* and *Bentinck*, also on 8 Apr. On 10 Apr the transport *U878*, which is returning from St-Nazaire, tries to attack convoy ON.295 and, in doing so, is sunk by the destroyer *Vanquisher* and the corvette *Tintagel Castle*. On 15 Apr *U285* falls victim to the DEs *Grindall* and *Keats* of the 5th EG and *U325* and *U326* are regarded as missing in this area.

In the Channel, *U1063*, in attacking a convoy escorted by the 17th EG, is sunk by the frigate *Loch Killin* on 15 Apr. *U1107*, (Lt-Cdr Parduhn) which is equipped with an 'Alberich' skin, sinks two ships of 15209 tons from convoy HX.348 and escapes from the escort. But on 25 Apr she is sunk by Liberator 'K' of VPB-103 USN with a Mk 44 homing torpedo. *U1055* is located near Ouessant on 30 Apr by Catalina 'R' of VP-63 using MAD and is sunk with a 'Retrobomb'. *U776* and *U249* have no success near Ouessant and off the Scillies respectively. *U255* (Cdr Piening) from St-Nazaire lays a mine barrage off Les Sables d'Olonne.

5 Apr–5 May   North and West Atlantic

U1009 is employed as a weather boat in the North Atlantic. *U979* (Lt-Cdr Meermeier) operates off Reykjavik and sinks at the beginning of May a trawler of 348 tons and torpedoes a tanker of 6386 tons. *U541* is sent to Gibraltar as is *U485* from St-Nazaire. The Type IXC boats operate off the American and Canadian east coasts. *U857* (Lt-Cdr Premauer) torpedoes a tanker of 8537 tons in the Gulf of Maine on 5 Apr and is found on 7 Apr and destroyed by a search group consisting of the US frigates *Knoxville* and *Eugene* and the DEs *Gustafson* and *Micka*. *U548* (Lt Krempl) sinks a ship of 6959 tons off Cape Hatteras and, five days later, on 19 Apr, is sunk by a search group, TG.22.10, comprising the DEs *Buckley*, *Reuben James*, *Scroggins* and *Jack W Wilke*. *U190* (Lt Reith) sinks the Canadian minesweeper *Esquimalt* off Halifax on 16 Apr and escapes. *U879* (Lt-Cdr Manchen) sinks one tanker of 8300 tons in the Gulf of Maine and torpedoes one ship of 6825 tons. In trying to attack the convoy KN.382, she is located by the frigate *Natchez* on 29 Apr and sunk by her and the DEs of TG.02.10, *Coffman*, *Bostwick* and *Thomas*.

With the U-boats *U805*, *U518*, *U880*, *U858*, *U1235* and *U546*, which set out more or less simultaneously in the middle of Mar,

the Cdr U-boats forms a 'Seewolf' group in the North Atlantic on 14 Apr. The intention is to comb the Great Circle route for convoys in a westward direction. The movements are detected by 'Ultra' and the operation 'Teardrop' is organised to deal with it; two carrier groups form search lines N of the Azores on what is known to be the U-boat course to counter what is, at first, thought to be a German attempt to operate V2 rockets from towed launching containers. In the N is TG.22.2 (Capt Ruhseeberger), comprising the escort carrier *Mission Bay* and the DEs *Douglas L Howard*, *J R Y Blakely*, *Hill*, *Fessenden*, *Farquhar*, *Pride*, *Menges* and *Mosley*, and in the S is TG.22.5 (Capt Craig), comprising the escort carrier *Croatan* and the DEs *Frost*, *Huse*, *Inch*, *Stanton*, *Swasey*, *Carter*, *Neal A Scott*, *Muir* and *Sutton*. In spite of bad weather, *U1235* and *U880* are located with sonar on 15 and 16 Apr by TG.22.5 and sunk by the DEs *Stanton* and *Frost* with 'Hedgehog'. *U805* is sighted by an aircraft from the Azores, but she twice escapes lengthy searches. On 22 Apr *Carter* and *Neal A Scott* of the group also sink *U518* before two other carrier groups relieve the first two: in the N, TG.22.4 (Capt Purvis), comprising the escort carrier *Core* and the DEs *Moore*, *Sloat*, *Tomich* and *J Richard Ward*, in the S TG.22.3 (Capt Dufec), comprising the escort carrier *Bogue* and the DEs *Haverfield*, *Willis*, *Wilhoite* and *Swenning* and, in front, a search line (TG.22.7), consisting of the DEs *Pillsbury*, *Keith*, *Otterstetter*, *Pope*, *Flaherty*, *Chatelain*, *Frederick C Davis*, *Neunzer*, *Hubbard*, *Varian*, *Otter*, *Hayter*, *Janssen* and *Cockrill*. On 24 Apr an aircraft from *Bogue* sights *U546*. Hunted by nine DEs, Lt-Cdr Just is able first to sink *Frederick C Davis* with a T-5, in spite of 'Foxers' being put out. After almost six hours, *U546* is forced to surface, just misses *Flaherty* with another T-5 and then sinks. Only *U858* and *U805* get to the American coast, as well as *U853* and *U530*, sailing on their own, and *U889* and *U881* behind them. The last, in trying to attack the carrier group of *Mission Bay*, which has again set out, is sunk on 6 May by *Farquhar*. *U853* (Lt Frömsdorf) probably sinks the submarine-chaser *Eagle 56* on 23 Apr and is, after sinking a collier of 5353 tons, sunk on 5 May by the frigate *Moberly*, the destroyer *Ericsson* and the DEs *Atherton* and *Amick*.

6–7 Apr   Air War/Netherlands

On 6 Apr an attack by 55 aircraft of RAF Bomber Command on Ijmuiden's shipping installations is abandoned because of the weather. On 7 Apr 15 Lancasters of No 617 Sqn RAF attack E-boat pens.

6–8 Apr   North Sea

The German 2nd MTB Flotilla (Lt-Cdr Wendler) carries out a mining operation in the Humber Estuary on 6–7 Apr with *S174*, *S176*, *S177*, *S209*, *S210* and *S221*. As it withdraws, there is an engagement with British MTBs. *S176* sinks *MTB494* by ramming and has to be abandoned. *S177* sinks after being rammed by *MTB5001*, which is also lost. This is the last operation by the 2nd MTB Flotilla.

The following night, 7–8 Apr, the 4th and 6th MTB Flotillas (Cdr Fimmen and Lt-Cdr Matzen), with *S205*, *S204*, *S219*, *S202*, *S703* and *S304*, and *S222*, *S705*, *S211*, *S223*, *S704*, *S212* and *S706*, lay mines along the Thames–Scheldt convoy route. In engagements with British MTBs, the 4th MTB Flotilla loses *S202* and *S703* after a collision. *S223* of the 6th MTB Flotilla sinks off Ostend after hitting a mine. The 9th MTB Flotilla (Cdr v Mirbach), with *S206*, *S168*, *S130*, *S175*, *S207* and *S214*, has to break off an operation in which small battle units with 'Linsens' are to be transported to the Scheldt because of bad weather.

6–10 Apr   Central Pacific

Big Japanese attack on the US landing fleet off Okinawa. On 6–7 Apr the 'Kikusui 1' kamikaze attack takes place, concentrating on the landing fleet round Okinawa and the radar picket destroyers stationed at 16 points round the island. There are weaker attacks on TG.58.1 and 58.3 NE of Okinawa and on TF.57 S of Okinawa. The escort carriers of TF.52 E of Okinawa are not attacked. On 6 Apr 198 kamikaze pilots set off from Kyushu, 41 of which return. Fifty-five are shot down by the fighter cover and 35 by the AA defence. Twenty-seven ships are hit, some of them more than once. The picket destroyers *Bush* and *Colhoun*, the destroyer-minesweeper *Emmons*, *LST 447* and the ammunition transports *Hobbs Victory* and *Logan Victory* (each 7607 tons) sink. The destroyers *Leutze*, *Newcomb* and *Morris* and the DE *Witter* are damaged beyond repair and the minesweepers *Rodman* and *Defense* and the destroyer *Mullany* suffer severe damage which keeps them out of action for the rest of the war. Medium damage is inflicted on the destroyers *Howorth*, *Hyman* and *Haynsworth* (TF.58) and the DE *Fieberling*. The carriers *Illustrious* (TF.57) and *San Jacinto* (TF.58), the destroyers *Bennett*, *Hutchins* and *Harrison* (TF.58) and the minesweepers *Facility*, *Ransom*, *Devastator*, *YMS 311* and *YMS 321* are slightly damaged. On 7 Apr 54 kamikaze pilots of the 5th Naval Air Fleet set out from Kyushu, and, in addition, some 125 army kamikaze pilots are employed on 6–7 Apr.

Of the 54 naval kamikazes, 24 return and some 30 are shot down on 7 May by the fighter cover and AA defence. The battleship *Maryland* and the picket destroyer *Bennett* receive serious hits, the carrier *Hancock* (TF.58) and the DE *Wesson* sustain medium damage and the destroyer *Long-shaw* and the minesweeper *YMS 81* receive minor damage. The motor gunboat *PGM 18* and the minesweeper *YMS 103* are lost on mines.

On 6 Apr a Japanese Task Force (Vice-Adm Ito†) sets out from Tokuyama in the Inland Sea. It consists of the battleship *Yamato* (Rear-Adm Ariaga†), the cruiser *Yahagi* (Capt Hara with the Cdr of the 2nd DD Flotilla, Rear-Adm Komura, on board) and the 17th, 21st and 41st DD Divs comprising *Isokaze*, *Hamakaze* and *Yukikaze*, *Asashimo*, *Kasumi* and *Hatsushimo*, and *Fuyutsuki* and *Suzutsuki*. But, shortly afterwards, it is reported by a B-29 and, after passing through the Bungo Channel, by the US submarine *Threadfin* and, a little later, by *Hackleback*.

Early on 7 Apr flying boats from Kerama Retto and reconnaissance aircraft from TG.58.1 and 58.3, assembled S of Amamioshima, establish contact SW of Kyushu. TG.58.4, which provides the fighter cover over Okinawa, tries to close in at high speed. At 1000 hrs the main attack force of 280 aircraft sets off from TG.58.1 and 58.3. *Hamakaze* and *Yahagi* are sunk and *Yamato* receives two bomb and one torpedo hits. In the second attack with approximately 100 aircraft from 1400 hrs, the destroyers *Isokaze*, *Asashimo* and *Kasumi* sink first, then, after nine more torpedo and three bomb hits, *Yamato*, and with her perish 2498 sailors. The remaining destroyers return, some of them badly damaged. In all, the Japanese Navy loses 3665 dead. Of the 386 US aircraft deployed, only 10 fail to return.

On 8 and 9 Apr there follow only individual kamikaze attacks, in which the picket destroyers *Gregory* and *Sterett* and the minesweeper *YMS 92* are damaged. On 8–9 Apr explosive boats attempt attacks from Okinawa, in the course of which the destroyer *Charles J Badger* and the transport *Starr* are damaged. As a result of kamikaze attacks, the US Fleet loses 466 dead and has 579 injured in the period 6 to 10 Apr. The Japanese submarines *Ro-49* and *Ro-56* are lost on 4 and 9 Apr respectively to depth charges from the destroyer *Hudson* and the destroyers *Monssen* and *Mertz*.

6–25 Apr   Baltic
On 6 Apr the attack by the Soviet 3rd White Russian Front, supported by strong air

forces, begins against Königsberg, whose defenders are overwhelmed on 9 Apr and have to surrender on the following day. In the harbour the hull of the cruiser *Seydlitz* is blown up. The Soviet armies continue the attack towards the W and on 15 Apr break through the front in Samland. Some 70000 refugees are trapped in Pillau; some of them are brought across to the Frische Nehrung and others are evacuated by sea. In the process the freighters *Mendoza* (5193 tons), *Vale* (5950 tons) and *Weserstein* (1923 tons) are lost as a result of air attacks between 8 and 11 Apr. On 16 Apr the SATs of the 7th Gun Carrier Flotilla (Lt-Cdr Eggers), *Soemba*, *Nienburg*, *Ostsee*, *Robert Müller 6*, *Kemphan* and the gunnery training vessel *Drache* arrive to support the defensive battle near Fischhausen. On 18 Apr *Drache* is sunk in an air attack and *Robert Müller 6* is damaged and then sunk by the submarine *L-3* (Capt 3rd Class Konovalov) which is summoned to the scene.

During the last night, 24–25 Apr, the naval ferry barges bring another 19200 refugees and troops across. In all, 141000 wounded and 451000 refugees are evacuated through Pillau from 25 Jan.

7–12 Apr   Mediterranean
Allied warships shell German bases and traffic routes along the Riviera. Participating are the French cruisers *Gloire* and *Duguay-Trouin*, the destroyers *Tigre*, *Tempête* and *Trombe*, the British destroyers *Meteor* and *Musketeer* and the US destroyer *Mackenzie*.

8 Apr   Baltic
The German fleet oiler *Franken* (11115 tons) and the A/S vessel *UJ301* are sunk by Soviet air attack off Hela.

8–10 Apr   Air War/Germany
On 8 Apr the US 8th AF attacks Hamburg, followed during the night 8–9 Apr by 440 aircraft of RAF Bomber Command which drop 1491 tons of bombs and on 9 Apr by 40 of No 5 Group and 17 Lancatsers of No 617 Sqn RAF with 'Grand Slam' and 'Tall-boy' bombs. Five aircraft are lost. *U677*, *U747*, *U982*, *U2509*, *U2514* and the already damaged *U2550* are sunk or destroyed. During the night 9–10 Apr 591 aircraft of Nos 1, 3 and 8 Groups RAF attack Kiel and drop 2634 tons of bombs on harbour installations. The pocket-battleship *Admiral Scheer* capsizes, the heavy cruiser *Admiral Hipper* and the light cruiser *Emden* are badly damaged, the torpedo boat *T1*, the U-boats *U1131*, *U1227* and *U2516* are sunk or damaged and the minesweeper *M504* and three merchant ships of 2787 tons are destroyed.

On 9 Apr 34 Mosquito bombers of Nos 143,

235 and 248 Sqns RAF Coastal Command sink *U804*, *U843* and *U1065* in the Kattegat.

8–14 Apr   Central Pacific
On 8 Apr TF.58 (Vice-Adm Mitscher) resumes support for the Okinawa operations. After the return of TG.58.2, TF.58 is composed of TG.58.1 (Rear-Adm Clark) with the carriers *Hornet*, *Bennington*, *Belleau Wood* and *San Jacinto*, the battleships *Massachusetts* and *Indiana*, the cruisers *Vincennes*, *Miami*, *Vicksburgh* and *San Juan* and destroyers of Desrons 25 and 61; TG.58.2 (Rear-Adm Bogan) with the carriers *Randolph*, *Enterprise* and *Independence*, the battleships *Washington* and *North Carolina*, the cruisers *Baltimore*, *Pittsburgh*, *Flint* and *Oakland* and destroyers of Desrons 52 and 53; TG.58.3 (Rear-Adm Sherman) with the carriers *Essex*, *Bunker Hill* and *Bataan*, the battleships *New Jersey* and *South Dakota*, the cruisers *Pasadena*, *Springfield*, *Astoria* and *Wilkes-Barre* and destroyers of Desrons 45, 62 and 48; and TG.58.4 (Rear-Adm Radford) with the carriers *Yorktown*, *Intrepid* and *Langley*, the battleships *Wisconsin* and *Missouri*, the battlecruisers *Alaska* and *Guam*, the cruiser *San Diego* and the destroyers of Desrons 47 and 54. At least two task groups are daily in the operational area with one group replenishing and another either coming up or withdrawing. While the British TF.57 is replenishing on 8 and 9 Apr, the escort carrier group of Rear-Adm Sample, comprising *Suwanee*, *Chenango*, *Santee* and *Rudyerd Bay*, takes over the neutralisation of the Sakishima-Gunto Islands. From 11 to 13 Apr TF.57, reinforced by the cruisers *Uganda* and *Gambia* and the destroyers *Ursa*, *Urchin* and *Whirlwind*, daily attacks airfields and installations on North Formosa. On 14 and 15 Apr the force replenishes again when the carrier *Formidable* relieves *Illustrious* and the destroyers *Kempenfelt*, *Wessex*, *Urania* and *Quality*. In this period TG.52.1 (Rear-Adm Sample) continues the operations against Sakishima-Gunto.

On 11 Apr 64 Kamikazes (34 of which return) fly off to attack TF.58. The battleship *Missouri*, the carrier *Enterprise*, the destroyers *Kidd* and *Bullard* and, off Okinawa, the DE *Samuel S Miles* are hit.

On 12 Apr 83 naval and about 60 army kamikaze pilots set off on Operation 'Kikusui 2' with strong fighter cover to attack the landing fleet with nine Oka bombers. The picket destroyer *Mannert L Abele* is sunk and *Stanly* damaged by Oka bombs. The picket boat *LCS(L) 33* is sunk and *LCS(L) 57* damaged by kamikazes. Also damaged are the picket destroyers *Purdy*, *Cassin*

Young and *Jeffers* (DMS) and, in the area between Okinawa and Kerama Retto, the battleships *Tennessee* and *Idaho*, the destroyer *Zellars*, the minesweepers *Lindsey* and *LSM 189* (the last three ships are out of action until the end of the war), the DEs *Rall*, *Whitehurst*, *Riddle* and *Walter C Wann* and the minesweeper *Gladiator*. In lighter attacks on 13 Apr the DE *Connolly* is damaged.

On 14 Apr 35 of 76 kamikazes which set off and seven Oka bombers attack again. They first damage the battleship *New York* and the destroyers *Dashiell*, *Hunt* and *Sigsbee*. The last-named is out of action until the end of the war.

Of the 'Tatara' group of submarines which sets out with 'Kaiten' torpedoes, *I-47* and *I-58* return without success. *I-44* is sunk on 10 Apr by the DE *Fieberling* and *I-56* is sunk on 17 Apr by the destroyers *Heerman*, *McCord*, *Collett*, *Mertz* and *Uhlmann* and aircraft of the carrier *Bataan* when she tries to attack TF.58.

8–18 Apr   Indian Ocean
Operation 'Sunfish'. Sortie by a part of the British Eastern Fleet, TF.63 (Vice-Adm Walker), consisting of the battleships *Queen Elizabeth* and *Richelieu* (French), the heavy cruisers *London* and *Cumberland* and the destroyers *Saumarez*, *Vigilant*, *Verulam*, *Virago* and *Venus*, towards the N coast of Sumatra. On 11 Apr Sabang is shelled. The escort carriers *Emperor* and *Khedive* provide air escort and on 11 Apr attack Port Blair and Emmahaven when the submarine-chaser *Ch-7* and one small freighter are sunk. On 14–15 Apr the carrier aircraft carry out photographic reconnaissance over Penang, Port Swetenham and Port Dickson. On 16 Apr they again attack Emmahaven and Padang.

10 Apr   Baltic
British aircraft sink the torpedo boat *T13* SE of Laesö in the Skagerrak and damage *T16*, which latter is finally destroyed in an RAF air raid on Frederikshaven.

11 Apr   Norway
In an attack by the Dallachy Wing, RAF Coastal Command, on the area of Fedjefjord, the German minesweeper *M2* is sunk.

11 Apr   Baltic
The German hospital ship *Posen* (1104 tons), the training vessel *TS10/M376* and the A/S vessel *UJ1102* are sunk in air attacks by Soviet bombers off Hela.

12 Apr   General Situation
Death of President Roosevelt.

12 Apr   Mediterranean
The British cruiser *Orion* shells San Remo.

12–16 Apr   North Sea/English Channel
Twelve German motor torpedo boats of the 4th, 6th and 9th Flotillas lay mines in the area Nore–Flushing–Channel. In doing so, they are engaged by the British DE *Ekins* and the escort destroyer *Hambledon* and British MTBs. The motor torpedo boats are attacked by aircraft of RAF Coastal Command on their return. On these mines the tanker *Gold Shell* (8208 tons) sinks and the freighters *Conakrian* (4876 tons), *Benjamin H Bristow* and *Horace Binney* (7191 tons each) are damaged.

On 16 Apr *Ekins* is damaged beyond repair by two mines 13 nautical miles NW of Ostend.

13 Apr   Mediterranean
In an engagement with the British *MTB670* and *MTB697*, the German torpedo boat *TA45* (ex-Italian *Spica*) is sunk in the Morlacca Channel.

13–16 Apr   Air War/Germany
Nos 3, 6 (RCAF) and 8 Groups RAF Bomber Command, with 481 aircraft, attack Kiel and drop 1905 tons of bombs on harbour installations; two aircraft are lost. The German minelayer *Brummer* (ex-Norwegian *Olav Tryggvason*) is damaged beyond repair.

On 13 Apr an attack by 34 Lancasters of Nos 9 and 617 Sqns RAF on the cruisers *Lützow* and *Prinz Eugen* at Swinemünde has to be abandoned because of cloud cover. On 15 Apr 20 Lancasters again have to turn back, but on 16 Apr 18 Lancasters of No 617 Sqn succeed in sinking *Lützow* with one 'Tallboy' hit and several near-misses in the Kaiserfahrt.

14 Apr   North Sea
The German *U235* is sunk in error by the German torpedo boat *T17* in a depth charge attack.

14–20 Apr   Bay of Biscay
From 14 to 16 Apr aircraft of the US 8th AF, in three attacks on Royan and other German bases in the Gironde estuary, drop 2962 tons, 2551 tons and 1290 tons respectively. From 15 to 20 Apr, following the heavy air attacks, the final battle for the German fortress 'Gironde-Nord' (Royan) takes place. Operation 'Vénérable': after shelling by a French naval force (Vice-Adm Rue) comprising the battleship *Lorraine*, the cruiser *Duquesne*, the destroyers *Basque*, *Le Fortuné* and *L'Alcyon*, the DE *Hova*, the frigates *L'Aventure*, *La Découverte* and *La Surprise* and the sloop *Amiral Mouchez*, a land attack is made by the 10th French Div (Maj-Gen de Larminat) and the 66th US Div (Maj-Gen Kramer). On 20 Apr the last pockets of German resistance capitulate.

15 Apr   Air War/Germany
In a USAAF air attack on Kiel, *U103* is sunk by bomb hits.

15 Apr   Norway
The German minesweeper *M368* is damaged in a collision with a U-boat off Norway and sinks on a mine off Kindesnes.

15–18 Apr   Baltic
The German harbour defence boats *NO 31* and *NO 37* desert to Sweden and sink when towed into harbour at Göteborg. On 16 Apr *NO 21* (ex-Norwegian torpedo boat *Örn*) deserts from Oslo to Sweden. On 18 Apr *KFK298* deserts from Pillau to Karlskrona.

15–26 Apr   Central Pacific
US TF.58 continues the operations off Okinawa with four groups. On 15–16 Apr one group provides fighter protection over Okinawa, two groups make fighter sorties against Kyushu and the fourth replenishes. The British TF.57 makes attacks on Sakishima-Gunto on 16–17 Apr. The US escort carrier groups TG.52.1.1, 2 and 3 relieve each other in overlapping operations off Okinawa. The battleships, cruisers and destroyers of TF.54 continue to support the land fighting from off Okinawa.

After weaker attacks by 10 kamikazes (eight of which return) on 15 Apr, when the destroyer *Wilson* and the tanker *Taluga* are slightly damaged, the Japanese 5th Air Fleet begins the mass attack 'Kikusui 3' with 126 kamikazes (42 of which return) and six Oka bombers on 16 Apr. On 17 Apr 49 are employed, of which 30 return. In attacks on TF.58, the carrier *Intrepid* is badly damaged and the battleship *Missouri* and the destroyer *Benham* (17 Apr) less seriously damaged. After *Intrepid* drops out, TG.58.2 is broken up and its ships are distributed among TG.58.1, 3 and 4.

The attacks are concentrated on the landing fleet, particularly the picket destroyers. *Laffey* (Cdr Becton) is attacked by 22 aircraft: seven are shot down by fighters and nine by AA defence. There are six kamikaze hits and four bomb hits, resulting in 31 dead and 72 wounded; nevertheless, it is possible to bring the badly damaged ship into harbour. *Pringle* sinks, *Bryant* and the minelayer *Harding* are damaged beyond repair and the minesweeper *Hobson* is so badly damaged that she is out of action for the rest of the war. The DE *Bowers* and the picket boats *LCS(L) 116* and *LCS 51* sustain lesser damage.

On 16 Apr an Amphibious Group (Rear-Adm Reifsnider) lands the 77th Inf Div on the small offshore island of Ie Shima, which is taken by 21 Apr after offering strong resistance. Later, the 77th Inf Div is brought to Okinawa as a reserve. On 18–19

347

Apr two groups of TF.58 and two escort carrier groups make strong attacks in 650 sorties on the positions of the Japanese 62nd and 63rd Divs in the first Shuri line. After heavy artillery preparatory fire from the 27th Army Artillery Battery and TF.54, comprising the battleships *Texas, Arkansas, Colorado, Idaho, New Mexico* and *New York*, six cruisers and eight destroyers, as well as the battleships *North Carolina* and *South Dakota* and the destroyers of Desron 48 from TF.58, XXIV Corps attacks with the 27th, 96th and 7th Inf Divs early on 19 Apr. But the attack brings little result. After heavy fighting and strong support from TF.54 and carrier aircraft, the Japanese finally pull out from the first line on 23 Apr and withdraw to the second Shuri position. On 22 Apr 35 kamikaze aircraft (three of which return) attack TF.58, when the destroyers *Hudson* and *Wadsworth* are damaged, and the landing fleet. The minesweeper *Swallow* and picket boat *LCS 15* are sunk and the destroyer *Isherwood*, the minelayer *Shea* and the minesweepers *Ransom* and *Gladiator* are damaged.

After replenishment on 18–19 Apr the British TF.57 makes another attack on Sakishima-Gunto on 20 Apr and then returns to Leyte. From 21 Apr the escort carrier group TG.52.1.3, comprising *Suwanee, Sangamon, Chenango* and *Santee*, takes over the task of neutralising the Ryukyu Islands and northern Formosa. An escort carrier group carries out a raid on 25 Apr on the Okino-Daito-Shima group of islands E of Okinawa.

16 Apr Baltic

The German *U78*, used as a transformer station, is sunk in Pillau by Soviet Army artillery.

16 Apr Mediterranean

The German MMS *R15* is sunk in the northern Adriatic Sea by a torpedo fired by a British MTB.

16–25 Apr Arctic

Convoy operation JW.66. On 16 Apr JW.66 sets out from the Clyde with 22 merchant ships. The escort (Rear-Adm Cunningham-Graham) consists of the escort carriers *Vindex* and *Premier*, the cruiser *Diadem*, the Home Fleet destroyers *Zephyr, Zest, Zealous, Zodiac, Stord* (Norwegian), *Offa, Haida* (RCN), *Huron* (RCN) and *Iroquois* (RCN), the 8th EG, consisting of the sloop *Cygnet* and the corvettes *Alnwick Castle, Bamborough Castle, Farnham Castle, Honeysuckle, Rhododendron, Oxlip* and *Lotus*, and, as support group, the 19th EG, consisting of the frigates *Loch Insh, Loch Shin* and *Anguilla* and the DEs *Cotton* and *Goodall*. The German B-Service learns of the con-

voy's departure and *U286, U295, U307, U313, U363* and *U481* are stationed W of Bear Island as the 'Faust' group. Air reconnaissance is unable to locate the convoy up to 21 Apr. The U-boats are therefore moved to positions off the Kola estuary. In addition, *U318, U427, U711, U992, U278, U294, U312, U716, U968* and *U997* set out for the operational area. Some boats come into contact on 21 and 22 Apr with the Soviet coastal convoy PK.9 from Petsamo to Kola: this consists of two steamers and is escorted by the destroyers *Karl Libknecht* (Capt 1st Class Rumyantsev), *Derzki, Zhestki* and *Dostoiny*, two minesweepers, six BO submarine-chasers, including *BO-131, BO-225* and *BO-228*, four TKAs and a Norwegian group comprising the corvette *Eglantine* and the trawlers *Karmöy, Jelöy* and *Tromöy*. *U997* (Lt Lehmann) sinks the Soviet steamer *Onega* (1603 tons) and torpedoes the Norwegian steamer *Idefjord* (4287 tons) which is taken in tow. Further attacks by *U997, U481* and *U294* are frustrated by the escort vessels, which avoid several T-5s. *U481* (Lt-Cdr Andersen) also claims to have sunk a trawler on 19 Apr. Only *U711* (Lt-Cdr Lange), which has penetrated furthest into the Kola Inlet, is able to fire, unsuccessfully, at JW.66, which reaches harbour on 25 Apr. She also claims to have sunk a small steamer on 19 Apr. On 22 Apr, with Russian permission, the British minelayer *Apollo* and the destroyers *Obedient, Opportune* and *Orwell* lay a deep minefield (276 mines) as a protection against German U-boats from Syet Navolok to Kildin.

During the convoy operation a British force comprising the escort carriers *Queen* and *Searcher* and escort vessels carries out operations off the Norwegian coast. On 20 Apr mines are laid, on 26 Apr an air attack on a convoy fails because it is beaten off by Me 109 fighters and on 28 Apr a fighter sortie is made.

16 Apr–4 May Baltic

Continuation of the evacuation from the embarkation points in the Lower Vistula to Hela and from there to the W. On 16 Apr a convoy with eight ships and escort vessels leaves Hela, where the aircraft repair ship *Boelcke* sinks in an air attack. In the night the convoy is attacked off Rixhöft by the Soviet submarine *L-3* (Capt 3rd Class Konovalov); she sinks the transport *Goya* (5230 tons). Only 165 of the 6385 persons on board can be rescued.

In air attacks on 19 and 20 Apr the steamer *Altengamme* (5897 tons) is lost off Sassnitz and *V215* and *Königsberg* (180 tons) off Hela. On 25 Apr the *Emily Sauber* (2435

tons) falls victim to one of the attacks made by Soviet torpedo cutters from Neufahrwasser. Attacks by the submarine *K-52* (Capt 3rd Class Travkin) from 21 to 27 Apr and then by *K-53* (Capt 3rd Class Yaroshevich) on the Stolpe Bank do not, as far as is known, have any success.

On 20 Apr the *Eberhard Essberger* sets out from Hela with 6200 persons and the *Lappland* leaves for the W on 21 Apr with 7700. On 21 Apr a total of 28000 refugees are embarked and on 28 Apr seven steamers evacuate 24000 individuals. The total for Apr is 387000. Two claims by the Soviet submarine *K-56* (Capt 3rd Class Popov) NE of the Pomeranian Bay cannot be substantiated.

On 25 Apr the uncompleted aircraft carrier *Graf Zeppelin* and four steamers and small craft are blown up in Stettin before the Soviet 2nd Assault Army advances across the Lower Oder via Anklam towards Stralsund. The latter is reached on 1 May and the 19th Army crosses to Wollin near Dievenow and advances on Swinemünde. The old battleship *Schlesien*, which is sent on 2 May into the Greifswalder Bodden to protect the Wolgast Bridge to Usedom, runs on to a British air ground mine near Greifwalder Oie and is towed back to Swinemünde (see 3–9 May). On 4 May the wreck, together with the *Lützow*, is blown up. So, too, are other ships, left behind in the harbour. The Cdr Destroyers (Vice-Adm Kreisch) with five steamers, the destroyers *Z38, Z39, Z34* and *Z43, T33, T36*, the tender *Jagd*, the auxiliary cruiser *Orion* and the AA ship *Hummel* with 35000 persons on board, sets out for Copenhagen.

17 Apr North Sea

The German patrol vessel *V1207* is sunk in an air attack off Heligoland.

17 Apr Mediterranean

German motor torpedo boats engage Allied destroyers off San Remo. The French destroyer *Trombe* is torpedoed.

17–22 Apr South West Pacific

Operation 'Victor V': US Amphibious Group 8 (Rear-Adm Noble) with the headquarters ship *Wasatch* lands X Corps (Maj-Gen Siebert) with the 24th Inf Div (Maj-Gen Woodruff) and the 31st Inf Div (Maj-Gen Martin) on the coast of Moro Gulf, West Mindanao (Philippines). The transport group 'Green' comprises three APDs, 51 LSTs, 13 LMSs, seven LCTs, 22 LCIs, eight Liberty ships and 16 support LCIs and two PCs. The minesweeper group comprises five YMSs. Escort is provided by the destroyers (Desron 23) *Charles Ausburne, Braine, Robinson* and *Aulick* and (from Desron 5) *Flusser* and *Conyngham* and the

DEs *Jobb* and *Albert T Harris*. The transport group 'Red' (Capt Zurmuehlen) with the US Coast Guard cutter *Spencer* comprises 20 LSTs, three LSMs, two APDs, five LCIs and seven support LCIs, as well as two SCs and two YMSs. The escort consists of the destroyers *Dyson* and *McCalla* and fire support is provided by TG.74.2 (Rear-Adm Riggs), comprising the cruisers *Montpelier*, *Denver* and *Cleveland* and the destroyers (Desron 22) *Conway*, *Eaton*, *Stevens*, *Young*, *Cony* and *Sigourney*.

18–19 Apr   Air War/Germany
On 18 Apr 969 aircraft of RAF Bomber Command attack the island of Heligoland and drop 4994 tons of bombs. This is followed on 19 Apr by an attack by 36 Lancasters of Nos 9 and 617 Sqns with 'Tallboy' bombs. The island is devastated.

18–28 Apr   Baltic
The Soviet submarine *K-52* (Capt 3rd Class Travkin) claim six successes along the deep waterway but these cannot be substantiated.

19 Apr   Baltic
Twenty-two Mosquitos of Nos 143, 235, 248 and 333 Sqns RAF attack U-boats in the Kattegat during their transfer from Kiel to Norway. *U251* is sunk, as is the escorting minesweeper *M403*, but *U2502* and *U2335* reach Kristiansand.

19 Apr   Mediterranean
Italian small battle units, transported by the destroyer *Grecale* and the motor torpedo boat *Ms 72*, sink in Genoa the almost completed aircraft carrier *Aquila* (23350 tons) to prevent her being used as a block ship.

21 Apr   English Channel
The British DE *Retalick* engages German 'Linsens' 28 nautical miles of SW Ostend and sinks four.

21 Apr   Baltic
The German minelayer *Ostmark* (ex-French *Côte d'Argent*) is sunk W of Anholt in an RAF air attack.

21–24 Apr   Air War/Germany
During the night 21–22 Apr 107 Mosquitos of RAF Bomber Command attack Kiel. Two aircraft are lost. On 22 Apr Nos 1, 3, 6 (RCAF) and 8 Groups RAF Bomber Command attack Bremen with 767 aircraft but because of the cloud cover only 195 of these are able to drop 969 tons of bombs. Two aircraft are lost. On 23–24 Apr 60 Mosquitos of RAF Bomber Command attack Kiel and on 25 Apr, in a USAAF air raid on Bremerhaven, *U1197* is damaged beyond repair.

23–24 Apr   Baltic
RAF Coastal Command attacks German shipping in the Kattegat: the freighters *Tübingen* (5543 tons) and *Ingerseks* (4969 tons) are sunk and three ships are damaged.

23–25 Apr   Mediterranean
The French cruisers *Montcalm* and *Duguay Trouin* and the British destroyer *Lookout* shell German bases on the Italian Riviera. With negotiations about a capitulation of the German forces in Northern Italy in progress, the German Naval Command orders the scuttling of the ships in the harbours still under German control. Only some of the ships are in an operational state, many being in repair or under construction. In Genoa the following ships are scuttled on 24 Apr: the destroyers *TA31* (ex-Italian *Dardo*, damaged), *TA32* (ex-Italian *Premuda*, ex-Yugoslav *Dubrovnik*), *TA34* (ex-French *FR 34*, ex-French *Lansquenet*, in repair) and the Italian *FR 32* (ex-French *Siroco*, laid up) and *FR 24* (ex-French *Valmy*, laid up); the wreck of the destroyer *Alpino*; the damaged torpedo boat *Ghibli*; the corvettes *UJ2221* (ex-Italian *Vespa*), *UJ2224* (ex-Italian *Strolaga*), *UJ6083* (ex-Italian *Capriolo*), *UJ6084* (ex-Italian *Alce*), *UJ2225*, *UJ2226*, *UJ2227*, *UJ2228* and *UJ6086* (ex-Italian *Ardea*, *Artemide*, *Persefone*, *Euterpe* and *Cervo*, building or refitting), *UJ2231* (ex-Italian *FR 51*, ex-French *La Batailleuse*, refitting); the U-boats *UIT2* and *UIT3* (ex-Italian *R 11* and *R 12*, fitting out); the MMSs *R162*, *R189*, *R198*, *R199* and *R212*; the MMSs *RA253*, *RA254*, *RA258*, *RA264*, *RA262* (ex-Italian *VAS 307*, *VAS 301*, *VAS 309*, *VAS 310* and *VAS 239*), *RA265–268* (ex-*VAS 313–316*), *RD101*, *RD111*, *RD112* (ready) and *RD102–RD110* (building); and the Italian *MAS 549*, *MAS 561*, *MAS 558*, *MAS 557* and *MAS 505*. The vessels of the RSI, *VAS 252*, *VAS 253* and *VAS 263*, are also scuttled. At Oneglia on 25 Apr the old torpedo boat *SG20* (ex-Italian *Papa*) is scuttled, as are, in Imperia, the Italian destroyer *FR 37* (ex-French *Le Hardi*) and torpedo boats *MAS 544* and *MAS 551*.

25 Apr   Air War/Germany
RAF Bomber Command drops 2176 tons of bombs on the coastal fortifications of Wangerooge.

25–26 Apr   Air War/Norway
One hundred and nineteen aircraft of RAF Bomber Command attack the yards at Tonsberg.

26 Apr   North Sea
The German patrol vessel *V1114* is sunk by air attack in the Heligoland Bight.

26 Apr   Mediterranean
The German escort vessel *SG15/UJ2229* (ex-French *Rageot de la Touche*) is sunk off Genoa by the British submarine *Universal*.

27 Apr   Germany
Bremen is taken by British troops.

27 Apr–1 May   South West Pacific
Operation 'Oboe I': landing on Tarakan (Borneo). On 27 Apr US TG.74.3 (Rear-Adm Berkey), comprising the cruisers *Phoenix*, *Boise* and the Australian *Hobart*, as well as the US destroyers (Desron 21) *Taylor*, *Nicholas*, *O'Bannon*, *Fletcher*, *Jenkins* and the Australian *Warramunga*, begins the preparatory shelling of the assault area in the S of Tarakan. It is continued on 28 and 29 Apr. On 30 Apr a battalion lands on the small offshore island of Sadan. On 1 May Amphibious Group 6 (Rear-Adm Royal), with the headquarters ship *Rocky Mount*, lands 18000 men of the reinforced 26th Australian Bde (Brig Whitehead) on Tarakan. The transport group comprises two Australian LSIs, one US AKA, one LSD and 45 LSTs and the escort comprises the destroyers *Waller* (Desron 22), *Philip*, *Bailey*, *Bancroft*, *Caldwell*, *Drayton* and *Smith*, the DEs *Formoe* and *Charles E Brannon*, the Australian frigates *Burdekin*, *Barcoo* and *Hawkesbury* and 21 PTs. The destroyer *Jenkins* is damaged by Japanese mines on 30 Apr, the minesweeper *YMS 481* sinks as a result of coastal shelling on 2 May and *YMS 334* and *YMS 364* are damaged by shelling and *YMS 363* on a mine.

27 Apr–2 May   Central Pacific
TG.58.3 and 58.4 continue to relieve each other in overlapping operations off Okinawa. TG.58.1 goes to Ulithi from 28 Apr to 8 May. Off Sakishima-Gunto, TG.52.1.3 is relieved on 28 Apr by TG.52.1.1 comprising the escort carriers *Makin Island*, *Fanshaw Bay*, *Lunga Point* and *Salamaua*.

From 27 to 30 Apr, with the main effort on 28 Apr, approximately 65 Japanese Navy and 60 Army aircraft from Kyushu carry out the kamikaze operation 'Kikusui 4'. In the process, the destroyer *Hutchins* and the APD *Rathburne* are damaged beyond repair. *Ralph Talbot* is damaged on 27 Apr, *Wadsworth*, *Daly*, *Twiggs* and *Bennion* on 28 Apr, *Hazelwood* and *Haggard* on 29 Apr, *Bennion* again on 30 Apr, the DE *England* on 27 Apr, the minesweeper *Butler*, the hospital ship *Comfort* and the casualty transport *Pinkney* on 28 Apr, the minelayers *Shannon* and *Harry F Bauer* on 29 Apr and *Terror* on 30 Apr. *Haggard*, *Rathburne* and *Pinkney* are out of action for the rest of the war.

Of the Japanese submarines, *Ro-109* is sunk on 25 Apr by the DE *Horace A Bass*. The 'Kaiten' group 'Amatake' makes unsuccessful attacks: on 29 Apr *I-36* (Cdr Sugamasa) on the destroyer *Ringgold* and on 1, 2 and 6 May *I-47* (Cdr Orita) on convoys.

27 Apr–7 May   Indian Ocean

Operation 'Dracula': landing near Rangoon. From 27 to 30 Apr the British Assault Force 'W' (Rear-Adm B C S Martin), with the headquarters ship *Largs*, sets out in six convoys from Akyab and Kyaukpyu. The 26th Indian Div is embarked on the LSHs *Waveney* and *Nith*, the LSIs *Glenroy*, *Persimmon*, *Prins Albert* and *Silvio*, the LSE *Barpeta*, 45 LSTs and 110 small landing craft. Escort for the landing group is provided by the Indian sloops *Cauvery*, *Narbada*, *Godavari*, *Kistna*, *Sutlej* and *Hindustan*. There are also 22 minesweepers from the 7th and 37th MS Flotillas. The landing force is covered by the 21st Carrier Sqn, consisting of the cruisers *Phoebe* and *Royalist* (Commodore Oliver), the escort carriers *Hunter*, *Stalker*, *Emperor* and *Khedive*, the destroyers *Saumarez*, *Venus*, *Virago* and *Vigilant*, eight frigates and two sloops. On 1 May the landing is made without resistance. Rangoon, which has been evacuated by the Japanese, is occupied on 3 May.

Operation 'Bishop'. A covering group, TF.63 (Vice-Adm Walker), comprising the battleships *Queen Elizabeth* and *Richelieu*, the escort carriers *Shah* and *Empress*, the cruisers *Cumberland*, *Suffolk*, *Ceylon* and *Tromp* and the destroyers *Rotherham*, *Tartar*, *Nubian*, *Penn* and *Verulam*, makes air attacks and shells Car Nicobar and Port Blair. TF.62, comprising the destroyers *Roebuck*, *Racehorse* and *Redoubt*, shells Martaban on 30 Apr and Car Nicobar on 1 May. In the process, a convoy of nine ships is destroyed on 30 Apr. On 5 and 6 May the 21st Carrier Sqn, with the destroyers *Virago*, *Tartar* and *Nubian*, makes raids on Japanese bases between Mergui and Victoria Point. On 6 May TF.63 shells Port Blair in the Andaman Islands with battleships, cruisers and the destroyers *Rotherham*, *Saumarez*, *Venus*, *Vigilant* and *Verulam*. On 9 May the forces return to Trincomalee.

28 Apr   Air War/Germany

In air raids on Kiel *U56* is sunk and in raids on Wesermünde *U1223* is sunk.

29 Apr–1 May   Bay of Biscay

Operation 'Jupiter': French troops land on the island of Oleron in the Gironde estuary with support from a French naval force (Vice-Adm Rue) comprising the cruiser *Duquesne*, the destroyers *Le Fortuné*, *L'Alcyon* and *Basque* and light units. On 1 May the last German troops surrender.

29 Apr–2 May   Mediterranean

On 29 Apr the British 56th Div takes Venice, on 30 Apr Tito partisans force their way into Trieste and on 1 May New Zealand and Yugoslav troops meet near Monfalcone NW of Trieste. On 1 May the remaining German ships in Trieste are scuttled. They include the torpedo boats *TA41* (ex-Italian *Lancia*) and *TA43* (ex-Italian *Sebenico*) and the non-operational *TA40* (ex-Italian *Pugnale*) and *TA22* (ex-Italian *Missori*). On 2 May the MMSs *R6*, *R8* and *R10* are scuttled in the Tagliamento estuary.

29 Apr–2 May   Arctic

Last convoy battle of WW2. It involves RA.66, comprising 24 merchant ships and the escort of JW.66 (see 16–25 Apr), which arrives in the Clyde on 8 May. On 29 Apr, before the departure of the convoy, Allied escort vessels, supported by Soviet submarine-chasers and minesweepers, are sent to the area off the Kola Inlet to drive off the German U-boats *U278*, *U286*, *U307*, *U312*, *U313*, *U318*, *U363*, *U427*, *U481*, *U711*, *U716*, *U968*, *U992* and *U997* stationed there. *U307* (Lt Krüger) and *U286* (Lt Dietrich) are sunk by the frigates *Loch Insh*, *Loch Shin*, *Anguilla* and *Cotton* of the 19th EG. *U968* (Lt Westphalen) just misses the corvette *Alnwick Castle* and sinks the frigate *Goodall*. *U427* (Lt Gudenus) just misses the Canadian destroyers *Haida* and *Iroquois* and has to endure a long and severe pursuit during which 678 depth charge explosions are counted and *U313* (Lt-Cdr Schweiger) gets involved in an engagement with Soviet submarine-chasers, but both boats get away. As a result of these actions, the U-boats are driven off and do not approach the convoy. Air reconnaissance is unable to keep contact with the convoy and the operation has to be broken off.

29 Apr–4 May   South West Pacific

US Amphibious Group 9 (TG.78.3, Rear-Adm Struble) lands the US 185th RCT (Maj-Gen Brush) near Padan Point on Los Negros on 29 Apr in LSMs with cover from destroyers.

On 3–4 May TG.78.2 (Rear-Adm Noble) lands a battle group of 1000 men near Santa Cruz in the Gulf of Davao after preparatory fire from the cruiser *Denver*.

30 Apr   North Sea

The German minesweeper *M455* is sunk in an RAF raid on Cuxhaven.

1 May   Mediterranean

Raid on Rhodes by the destroyers *Kimberley* (British), *Catterick* (British) and *Kriti* (Greek).

1 May   Mediterranean

The Italian submarine *Argo* is scuttled at Monfalcone.

1–2 May   Baltic

The German gun ferry *SAT16/Westflandern* is sunk by air attack off Nexö in the Kattegat. The patrol vessel *V2001* is sunk by air attack in the central Baltic.

1–4 May   Germany

In German harbours which are in danger of being occupied, the following U-boats are scuttled.

At Wilhelmshaven: *U3006* (Type XXI) on 1 May, *U8*, *U14*, *U17*, *U60*, *U61*, *U62*, *U137*, *U139*, *U140*, *U141*, *U142*, *U146*, *U148*, *U151* and *U152* (Type VII), *U71*, *U552* and *U554* (Type VII) and *U3504* (Type XXI) on 2 May and *U339* and *U708* (Type VII) on 3 May.

At Bremerhaven/Wesermünde: *U3009* (Type XXI) on 1 May, *U120* and *U121* (Type II) on 2 May and *U822* and *U828* (Type VII), *U1232* (Type IX) and *U3001*, *U3509* and the incomplete *U3047*, *U3050* and *U3051* (Type XXI) on 3 May.

At Vegesack: *U704* (Type VII) on 3 May.

At Nordenham: *U323* (Type VII) on 3 May.

At Bremen: *U72* (Type VII, damaged in air attack) on 2 May.

At Hamburg: *U3004* and *U3506* (Type XXI), *U2327* and *U2370* (Type XXIII) and the damaged *U2549* (Type XXI) on 2 May and *U2501*, *U2504*, *U2505* and *U3502* (Type XXI) and *U2332* and *U2371* (Type XXIII) on 3 May.

In the Kiel Canal: *U428* and *U748* (Type VII) on 3 May.

At Kiel: *U3525* (Type XXI, damaged by air attack) on 1 May, *UA* (ex-Turkish *Batiray*) on 2 May and *U11*, *U57*, *U58* and the damaged *U59* (Type II), *U52*, *U446*, *U475*, *U560*, *U903*, *U922*, *U924*, *U958*, *U1166*, *U1192*, *U1205* and the incomplete *U1027* and *U1031* (Type VII), the damaged *U1227* (Type IX), *U795* (Walter Type Wa 202), *U2508*, *U2519*, *2520*, *U2539*, *U2543*, *U2545*, *U2546*, *U2548*, *U2552*, *U3005*, *U3010*, *U3029*, *U3031*, *U3038*, *U3039*, *U3040*, *U3518* and *U3530* (Type XXI), *U2330* and *U4705* (Type XXIII), *UC2* (ex-Norwegian *B6*), *UD1* (ex-Dutch *O-8*), *UD2* (ex-Dutch *O-12*) and *UD4* (ex-Dutch *O-26*) on 3 May and *U4709*, *U4711* and *U4712* (Type XXII) on 4 May.

At Heikendorf: *UB* (ex-British *Seal*) on 2 May.

At Laboe: *U2355* (Type XXIII) on 3 May.

At Travemünde/Neustadt: *U316* (Type VII) and *U2510*, *U2526*, *U2527*, *U2528*, *U2531*, *U3002*, *U3016*, *U3018*, *U3019*, *U3020*, *U3021*, *U3521* and *U3522* (Type XXI) on 2 May and *U1170* and the decommissioned *U1196* (Type VII) and *U2533*, *U2535*, *U2536*, *U3011*, *U3012*, *U3013*, *U3023*, *U3025*, *U3026*, *U3027*, *U3037*, *U3501*, *U3511*, *U3513*, *U3516* and *U3517* (Type XXI) on 3 May.

At Warnemünde: *U612* and *U1308* (Type VII) on 2 May and *U929* (Type VII) on 3 May.

At Eckernförde: *U2512* (Type XXI) on 3 May.

At Wassersleben/Flensburg: the damaged *U717* (Type VII) on 2 May.

1–31 May Pacific/Indian Ocean

Allied submarine operations. Off the Kuriles, *Sea Poacher* (Lt-Cdr Gambacorta) sinks one trawler and four small craft, *Plaice* (Lt-Cdr Stevens) sinks one vessel of 11 tons, three trawlers and three small craft and *Piper* has one miss. Off the Laperouse Strait, *Sterlet* (Lt-Cdr Lewis) sinks two ships of 4155 tons. Off Hokkaido, *Bowfin* (Cdr Tyree) sinks two ships of 3599 tons, *Sandlance* sinks one ship of 220 tons and *Tench* (Lt-Cdr Baskett) sinks five ships of 5161 tons, three trawlers and one small craft. North of the Bonin Islands, *Tigrone* sinks one small craft of 19 tons.

In the East China Sea and the Yellow Sea, *Lionfish* sinks one sailing vessel, *Raton* (Lt-Cdr Shea) sinks three ships of 5759 tons, *Shad* (Lt-Cdr Mehlhop) sinks two ships of 5308 tons and damages one ship of 1398 tons and one small craft, *Balao* sinks one sailing vessel, *Ray* (Lt-Cdr Kinsella) sinks one trawler and 18 other small vessels, *Billfish* (Lt-Cdr Farley) sinks two ships of 3211 tons and three sailing vessels and *Segundo* (Lt-Cdr Fulp) sinks one ship of 1591 tons and 10 small vessels.

In the Gulf of Thailand on 4 May, *Lagarto* is sunk by a Japanese minelayer. *Hammerhead* (Cdr Smith) sinks two ships of 6845 tons, the British *Supreme* sinks two coasters and one junk and *Cobia* (Lt-Cdr Bekker) sinks two ships of 6834 tons. E of Malaya, *Hawkbill* (Lt-Cdr Scanland) sinks on 16 May the minelayer *Hatsutaka* and one auxiliary minesweeper and *Bullhead* (Lt-Cdr Griffith) sinks four small craft. In the Malacca Strait, the British *Statesman* (Lt Bulkeley) sinks four small craft, *Scythian* sinks two small craft, *Sibyl* sinks five junks and *Sea Dog* sinks two small craft. W of Thailand, the British *Clyde* sinks one junk. In the Sunda Strait, the US *Blenny* (Lt-Cdr Hazzard) sinks two vessels of 601 tons and one small landing craft. In the Java Sea, the Dutch *K-XIV* sinks one junk, the British *Rorqual* lays a minefield in the approaches to Batavia and sinks one coaster, the US *Baya* (Lt-Cdr Jarvis) sinks two ships of 2637 tons, the British *Trump* sinks two coasters and three small vessels and damages one more, the British *Terrapin* sinks two small craft, the US *Bergall* (Lt-Cdr Hyde) sinks one small vessel, two tugs and three barges, *Blueback* (Lt-Cdr Clemenson) sinks the submarine-chaser *Ch-2* and two small craft and damages two other submarine-chasers, the British *Trenchant* (Cdr Hezlet) sinks on

25 May the auxiliary minesweeper *Wa-105* and on 8 June the cruiser *Ashigara*, the British *Thorough* sinks one ship of 1000 tons and three coasters, one trawler and one sailing vessel, the US *Lamprey* damages one subchaser and *Boarfish* and *Croaker* have only misses. In the Sunda Sea, the British *Tiptoe* sinks one ship of 982 tons and two coasters and the US *Chub* (Cdr Rhymes) sinks one ship of 377 tons and on 21 May the minesweeper *W-34*.

2 May Baltic

The German minesweeper *M387/TS2* is scuttled at Lübeck.

2 May Germany

End of the fighting for Berlin. The 6th British Airborne Div meets units of the 70th Soviet Army near Wismar.

2 May Japan

In the Sea of Japan, the Japanese frigate *Mikura* is lost, probably on a mine.

2–3 May Air War/Germany

Last attack by RAF Bomber Command against Kiel with 179 Mosquitos of Nos 5 and 100 Groups: 174 tons of bombs are dropped.

2–6 May Baltic/North Sea

Mass RAF attacks on shipping concentrations in the Western Baltic and on U-boats (approximately 60) proceeding to Norway.

On 2 May Typhoons of the 2nd Tactical Air Force sink off Lübeck Bay the steamer *Florida* (5542 tons) and *U1007* and 33 Mosquitos of Nos 143, 248, 235, 404 and 333 Sqns, No 18 Group Coastal Command, sink *M293* and *U2359* in the Kattegat.

On 3 May Typhoons of Nos 83 and 84 Groups of the 2nd TAF sink off Lübeck Bay the steamers *Cap Arcona* (27561 tons) and *Thielbek* (2815 tons), full of concentration camp detainees (some 5000), as well as the steamers *Deutschland* (21046 tons), *Dwarssee* (552 tons) and *Erna Gaulke* (400 tons); off the Bay of Kiel the steamers *Inster* (4713 tons), *Irmtraud Cords* (2814 tons) and *Wolgast* (164 tons); and south of the Belt entrances the escort boat *F3* and the U-boats *U1210*, *U3028*, *U3030* and *U3032*; *U746* is damaged. In the area of the Belts, Beaufighters of No 16 Group Coastal Command (13 from No 236 Sqn RAF and 17 from No 254 Sqn RAF) sink the steamer *Pallas* (627 tons) and the U-boat *U2524* with rocket and cannon fire. Mosquitos of No 18 Group sink the minesweeper *M301* in the Kattegat. *U3505* is sunk at Kiel.

On 4 May Typhoons of the 2nd TAF sink in the Southern Baltic the steamer *Ostwind*, the motor torpedo boat *S103* and the U-boats *U2521* and *U904* and damage *U733*

and *U876*. Beaufighters of No 16 Group (12 from No 236 Sqn RAF and 10 from No 254 Sqn RAF, with a Mustang escort) sink in the Belts the minesweeper *M36* and the U-boats *U236*, *U2338*, and *U2503* (*U393* is damaged and beached) and Mosquitos of No 18 Group sink in the Kattegat the motor ships *Else Hugo Stinnes* (3291 tons) and *Ernst Hugo Stinnes* (3295 tons) and the gunboat *K1*.

On 5–6 May Liberators of No 18 Group RAF Coastal Command attack in the Kattegat U-boats on transfer to Norway. On 5 May aircraft 'L' of No 311 (Czech) Sqn sinks *U3523*, 'K' of No 206 Sqn damages *U3503*, 'T' of No 224 Sqn sinks *U579*, 'G' of No 86 Sqn sinks *U534* and 'S' of No 224 Sqn sinks *U2365* and on 6 May 'G' of No 86 Sqn sinks *U2534* and 'K' of No 86 Sqn sinks *U1008*.

3 May Baltic

The German tender *Hai/F3*, the torpedo boats *T8* and *T9* and the evacuation transport *Der Deutsche* are sunk by British air attack in the Kiel Bight. The incomplete *U474* is sunk at Kiel and the MTB *S201* sunk by bombs at the E-boat base there. The target ships *Bolkoburg*, *Swakopmund* and *Wega* are sunk by air attack off Fehmarn. The destroyer *Z43* is scuttled in the Geltinger Bight and the torpedo boats *T8* and *T9* are scuttled in the Strande Bight. The German fast tug *Herold* (ex-*S18*) is sunk by air attack off Laland.

3 May Germany

The British XII Corps occupies Hamburg. Fifty-nine medium and large ships, 19 floating docks and about 600 small craft are sunk or scuttled in the harbour.

3 May Mediterranean

The last seven German E-boats in the Mediterranean, *S30*, *S36*, *S61*, *S151*, *S152*, *S155* and *S156*, proceed from Pola to Ancona to surrender to the Allies.

3–9 May Baltic

Last evacuations from Hela to the west. From 1 to 8 May small craft and naval ferry barges of the 13th Landing Flotilla (Cdr Wassmuth) bring approximately 150000 refugees and troops from the landing stages of the Lower Vistula to Hela. On 3 May the transports *Sachsenwald* and *Weserstrom* proceed to the W with 8550 refugees and the torpedo boats *T36* and *T108* each with 150. The freighters *Linz*, *Ceuta* and *Pompeji* and the auxiliary cruiser *Hansa*, which after the surrender comes into force in NW Germany and Denmark are outside territorial waters, proceed to Hela on 5 May with the destroyers *Hans Lody* (Cdr* Haun), *Friedrich Ihn* (Cdr Richter-Oldekop), *Theodor Riedel* (Cdr Blöse) and *Z25* (Cdr

Gohrbandt) and the torpedo boats *T17* (Lt-Cdr Liermann), *T19* (Lt-Cdr Frhr v Luttitz), *T23* (Lt-Cdr Weinlig), *T28* (Lt-Cdr Temming) and *T35* (Lt-Cdr Buch). There, together with *V2002*, *M453*, *V303* and the training vessel *Nautik*, they embark 45000 refugees. After beating off Soviet torpedo cutter attacks from Kolberg, the ships arrive off Copenhagen on 6 May, where the fast warships are unloaded in the roads in order to set out again. Together with the destroyers *Z38* (Cdr Frhr v Lyncker) and *Z39* (Cdr Loerke) and the torpedo boat *T33* (Lt-Cdr Priebe) coming from Swinemünde, *Karl Galster*, *Friedrich Ihn*, *Hans Lody*, *Theodor Riedel*, *Z25*, *T17*, *T19*, *T23* and *T28* put in to Hela again on 7 May and, until early on 8 May before the beginning of the Armistice, take on board 20000 soldiers and refugees who are disembarked in Glücksburg on 9 May. The same night, the freighters *Weserberg* and *Paloma* set out with 5730 refugees. The small pleasure steamer *Rugard*, with 1500 refugees, wards off an attempt by three Soviet torpedo cutters to capture her on 8 May. In all, some 1420000 refugees are evacuated by sea from the area of the Gulf of Danzig and Pomerania between 25 Jan and 8 May. In this figure the short-distance evacuations within the Gulf of Danzig are not taken into account: they can be reckoned to have included 600000 refugees.

3–29 May   Central Pacific

Continuation of the Okinawa operations. From 3 to 9 May TG.58.3 with the carriers *Essex*, *Bunker Hill*, *Shangri-La* and *Bataan* and TG.58.4 with *Yorktown*, *Intrepid*, *Enterprise* and *Langley* operate off Okinawa on an overlapping basis. Constant replenishment is provided by the supply group of the 5th Fleet under Rear-Adm Beary on the cruiser *Detroit*. The supply units consist of tankers, ammunition ships, freighters and spare parts transports, as well as the escort carriers *Attu*, *Admiralty Islands*, *Bougainville* and *Windham Bay*, employed as aircraft transports. Escort is provided by the escort carriers *Shamrock Bay* and *Makassar Strait*, 11 destroyers and 24 DEs. On 7 May the Japanese minelayer *Nuwashima* is sunk. On 10 May TG.58.1, with the carriers *Hornet*, *Bennington*, *Randolph*, *Belleau Wood* and *San Jacinto*, relieves TG.58.4, which goes to Ulithi. The night operating carrier *Enterprise* remains with TF.58. On 11 May *Bunker Hill* (Capt Seitz) is badly damaged by kamikaze hits: there are 392 dead and 264 injured. Vice-Adm Mitscher transfers to *Enterprise* and attacks on 12–13 May Kyushu and the kamikaze airfields there with TG.58.1 and 58.3. Early on 14

May, when returning, *Enterprise* is also badly hit. Vice-Adm Mitscher transfers yet again, this time to *Randolph*. The British TF.57 (Vice-Adm Rawlings/Vice-Adm Vian) sets out again from Leyte. It comprises the carriers *Indomitable*, *Victorious*, *Formidable* and *Indefatigable*, the battleships *King George V* and *Howe*, the cruisers *Swiftsure*, *Uganda* (RCN), *Gambia* (RNZN), *Euryalus* and *Black Prince* and the destroyers *Grenville*, *Ursa*, *Urchin*, *Undine*, *Urania*, *Undaunted*, *Quilliam*, *Queenborough*, *Quiberon*, *Quickmatch*, *Quality*, *Kempenfelt*, *Whirlwind* and *Wessex*. After replenishing on 3 and 4 May, it makes a carrier raid on the Sakishima-Gunto group. The battleships, the cruisers and the first seven destroyers shell the islands and airfields. In the operation *Formidable* is hit by a kamikaze and *Indomitable* sustains slight damage. After repairs in the night, new attacks are made on 5 May. On 6–7 May there is further replenishment by a British supply group consisting of tankers, ammunition ships, the transport/escort carriers *Ruler*, *Striker*, *Chaser* and *Speaker* and an escort of the destroyers *Napier*, *Nepal*, *Norman* and *Nizam*, the sloops *Crane*, *Whimbrel*, *Pheasant* and *Woodcock*, the frigates *Avon*, *Parret* and *Findhorn*, the Australian minesweeper corvettes *Whyalla*, *Ballarat*, *Bendigo* etc. While TF.57 replenishes on 3, 6–7, 10–11, 14–15, 18–19 and 22–23 May, attacks on Sakishima-Gunto are made by US air escort carriers of TG.52.1.3 (*Sangamon*, *Suwanee*, *Chenango* and *Santee*). On 3 May *Sangamon* is damaged beyond repair by kamikaze aircraft. On 9, 12–13, 16–17, 20–21 and 24–25 May, TF.57 makes attacks. On 9 May damage is inflicted on the *Victorious* and *Formidable* by kamikaze hits. The destroyers *Napier*, *Nepal*, *Troubridge*, *Tenacious* and *Termagant* operate temporarily with TF.57 as relief for other destroyers. *Quilliam* is severely damaged in a collision on 20 May. The New Zealand cruiser *Achilles* joins TF.57 on 23 May. *Formidable* is detached before the last attacks.

Japanese kamikaze attacks as part of 'Kikusui 5' on 3 and 4 May with 75 naval and 50 army aircraft sink the destroyers *Little*, *Luce* and *Morrison* on picket stations and the boats *LSM(R) 195*, *LSM(R) 190* and *LSM(R) 194*. The destroyer *Aaron Ward* is damaged beyond repair and the destroyer *Ingraham* and, after an Oka bomb hit, the minelayer *Shea* are put out of action until the end of the war. Lesser damage is sustained by the destroyers and destroyer/minesweepers *Macomb*, *Bache*, *Lowry*, *Massey*, *Gwin* and *Cowell* and *LCS(L) 25*.

With the support group off Okinawa, the cruiser *Birmingham* (Rear-Adm Deyo) is damaged on 3 May, the minesweepers *Gayety*, *Hopkins*, *YMS 327* and *YMS 331* on 4 May and the tenders *St George* and *Pathfinder* on 5 May. On 9 May the DEs *Oberrender* and *England* are damaged beyond repair. In all, there are 605 dead and 806 injured.

On 10 May new mass attacks ('Kikusui 6') begin with 70 naval and 80 army kamikaze aircraft. On the picket stations from 10 to 13 May, the destroyers *Evans* and *Hugh W Hadley* and *LCS(L) 88* are damaged beyond repair and the *Bache* and the DE *Bright* are put out of action until the end of the war. The carrier *Bunker Hill* is heavily damaged by two kamikazes. Off Okinawa, the battleship *New Mexico* is badly hit on 12 May but remains in action until 28 May. On 17 May the destroyer *Douglas H Fox* is put out of action until the end of the war by a kamikaze hit. On 18 May the destroyer *Longshaw* is stranded off Okinawa and severely damaged by Japanese gunfire from the shore and the APD *Sims* is damaged, and on 20 May *LST 808* is sunk and the destroyer *Thatcher* and the APD *Chase* are damaged beyond repair and the DE *John C Butler* slightly damaged. In all, there are 227 dead and 370 injured.

A further wave ('Kikusui 7') with 65 Navy and 100 Army kamikazes attacks on 24–25 May. On the picket stations the destroyer *Stormes* is severely, and *LCS(L) 121* slightly, damaged; but the mass of the aircraft fly round the radar pickets and attack the ships off Okinawa, in the course of which the APDs *Barry* and *Bates* and *LSM 135* are sunk, the APD *Roper* and the minesweepers *Butler* and *Spectacle* are damaged beyond repair and the DE *O'Neill* is severely, and the DE *William C Cole* and the APD *Sims* and one Liberty ship are slightly, damaged. On 26 May individual kamikazes damage the destroyer/minesweeper *Forrest*, the submarine-chaser *PC 1603* and the tender *Dutton*.

On 27–28 May there follows 'Kikusui 8' with 60 Navy and 50 Army aircraft. On the picket stations, the destroyer *Drexler* sinks and the *Braine* is severely, and the *Anthony* slightly, damaged. Also slightly damaged are *LCS(L) 52* and *LCS(L) 119*. Off Okinawa the minesweeper *Southard*, the APDs *Loy*, *Rednour* and the transport *Sandoval* receive hits. On 29 May the destroyer *Shubrick* and the APD *Tatum* are damaged, the former beyond repair.

Repair ships restore a large number of the damaged ships in the roads at Kerama Retto. In the second half of May TF.58 continues its sorties against Okinawa. On 24 May two task groups make another raid on the kamikaze airfields on Kyushu, particularly Kanoya, where a group of Oka bombers, which is ready to take off, is surprised on the ground and destroyed.

On 27–28 May Adm Spruance's command is transferred to Adm Halsey; the 5th Fleet becomes the 3rd Fleet; Vice-Adm McCain relieves Vice-Adm Mitscher; and TF.58 becomes TF.38.

4 May   Germany
Signing of the surrender of German troops in NW Germany, Denmark and Holland.

4 May   Baltic
The German MMS *R104* is sunk in the Kiel Canal.

4 May   Norway
Operation 'Judgement': raid by a British task force (Vice-Adm McGrigor) comprising the escort carriers *Searcher*, *Queen* and *Trumpeter*, the cruisers *Norfolk* and *Diadem* and the destroyers *Carysfort*, *Opportune*, *Savage*, *Scourge* and *Zambesi*, together with *Obedient* and *Orwell* which are returning from Murmansk, on German shipping W of Narvik and on the base at Kilbotn near Narvik. *U711*, the depot ship *Black Watch* and one trawler are sunk.

4–5 May   Baltic
The U-boats in Flensburger Förde scuttle themselves after the announcement of the imminent capitulation in the NW German area, in accordance with the 'Regenbogen' order issued earlier but contrary to the terms of the surrender which forbid the sinking or damaging of ships.

In the inner Flensburger Förde: *U750*, *U827*, *U999* and the incomplete *U1025*, *U1026*, *U1028*, *U1029* and *U1030* (Type VII) and *U2540* (Type XXI).

At Solitüde: *U2551* (Type XXI).

At Kupfermühlen Bay: *U29*, *U30*, *U46*, *U290*, *U382*, *U1132*, *U1161*, *U1303* and *U1304* (Type VII).

At Hörup Haff: *U351* (Type VII, damaged by bomb hit), *U1234* (Type IX) and *U2354*, *U4701*, *U4702* and *U4704* (Type XXIII).

At Wassersleben Bay: *U3033* and *U3034* (Type XXI).

At Holnis: *U393* (Type VII, damaged by bomb hit).

At Geltinger Bay: *U267*, *U349*, *U370*, *U397*, *U721*, the damaged *U746*, *U1056*, *U1101*, *U1162*, *U1168*, *U1193*, *U1204*, *U1207* and *U1306* (Type VII), *U794* (Walter Type Wa 201), *U2507*, *U2517*, *U2522*, *U2525*, *U2541*, *U3015*, *U3022*, *U3044*, *U3510*, *U3524*, *U3526* and *U3529* (Type XXI) and *U2333*, *U2339*, *U2343*, *U2346*, *U2347*, *U2349*, *U2357*, *U2358*, *U2360*, *U2362*, *U2364*, *U2366*, *U2368*,

U2369, *U4703*, *U4707* and *U4710* (Type XXIII).

At Flensburg: *U2540* (Type XXI).

At Schleimünde: *U2367* (Type XXIII, damaged in collision).

At Eckernförde: *U1405* (Walter Type XVII).

In the Lübeck Bay: *U1016* (Type VII).

At Cuxhaven: *U1406* and *U1407* (Walter Type XVII).

In the outer Weser off Wesermünde: *U38* (Type IX) and *U3501*, *U3527* and *U3528* (Type XXI).

Off Aarhus: *U2544* (Type XXI).

4–5 May   Atlantic/British Coastal Waters
When the U-boat war ends, the following German boats are in their operational areas:

In the Arctic: *U278*, *U313*, *U318*, *U968*, *U992* and *U1165*.

In the North Sea: *U2336* and *U287*.

W of the North Channel: *U293*, *U1105*, and *U1305*.

In the Irish Sea: *U825*, *U956* and *U1023*.

In the English Channel and its western entrance: *U249* and *U776*.

Off Reykjavik: *U979*.

In the North Atlantic *U1009* (as weather boat):

Off the Canadian coast: *U190*, *U805* and *U889*.

Off the US East Coast: *U530*, *U853*, *U858* and *U881*.

On a supply mission to St-Nazaire in the Bay of Biscay: *U516*.

Outbound:

To the North Sea: *U2324* and *U2326*.

To the area W of Britain: *U244*, *U764*, *U901*, *U977*, *U320*, *U1010*, *U1057*, *U1058*, *U1109*, *U1272* and *U2511* (4 May: mock attack on British cruiser).

To Gibraltar: *U485* and *U541*.

To the US coast: *U802*, *U1228* and *U1231*.

To the Caribbean: *U873*.

In addition, *U963* is on her way to a mining operation off Portland.

To East Asia: *U234*.

Homebound:

From France: *U255*.

From the North Sea: *U2322*.

From the North Atlantic: *U826*.

From a mining operation in the Clyde: *U218*.

From East Asia: *U510*, *U532*.

5–6 May   North Atlantic
U853 (Lt Frömsdorf†) sinks off Block Island (RI) the US freighter *Black Point* (5353 tons)—the last U-boat success off America—and is then destroyed by the US DE *Atherton* and the frigate *Moberley*.

6 May   Baltic
The German MTB *S226* is scuttled after being damaged in an air attack E of Fehmarn.

6 May–7 June   Northern Europe
Occupation of ports in the Northern area. On 6 May a British force (Capt Williams) comprising the cruisers *Birmingham* and *Dido* and the destroyers *Zealous*, *Zephyr*, *Zest* and *Zodiac* puts to sea, passes through the German mine barrages off the Skagerrak and reaches Copenhagen on 9 May where the German cruisers *Prinz Eugen* and *Nürnberg* are surrendered. The Flag Officer Denmark, Vice-Adm Vesey-Holt, takes over the command. The operation is covered by Vice-Adm McGrigor's Task Force, comprising the escort carriers *Searcher* and *Trumpeter*, the cruiser *Norfolk* and the destroyers *Carysfort*, *Zambesi*, *Obedient*, *Opportune* and *Orwell*.

On 12 May the future Flag Officer Norway (Rear-Adm Ritchie) puts to sea with the cruiser *Devonshire*, the fast minelayers *Apollo* (Crown Prince Olaf of Norway on board) and *Ariadne* and the destroyers *Iroquois* (RCN), *Savage*, *Scourge* and *Arendal* (Norwegian) and enters Oslo on 13 May. On 15 May the corvette *Buttercup* follows with parts of the Norwegian naval staff.

On 14 May the destroyers *Valorous* and *Venomous*, accompanied by six minesweepers, enter Kristiansand South and the destroyers *Wolsey* and *Wolfhound* enter Stavanger. On 15 May the destroyers *Woolston* and *Vivacious*, the Norwegian corvette *Acanthus* and British and Norwegian minesweepers enter Bergen; on 16 May the destroyers *Mackay* and *Viceroy* with nine minesweepers (Capt Ruck-Keene) enter Trondheim.

On 13 May the Norwegian destroyer *Stord* (with Rear-Adm Danielsen, as Sector Cdr Northern Norway on board) and the British destroyer *Broadway* set out from Rosyth. On 16 May they meet the German Arctic U-boats which are being transferred to Trondheim off Vestfjord and hand them over to the escort of convoy JW.67, the 9th EG (see 12–31 May) which is ordered up. The two destroyers arrive in Tromsö in the evening of 16 May. From there *Stord* lands a Norwegian weather station on Bear Island on 25–26 May. On 26 May the Norwegian Bde in Scotland arrives in Tromsö from Britain on board the transport *Largs Bay*.

The destroyers *Zealous* and *Zodiac* are transferred from Copenhagen to Kiel. In Copenhagen *Birmingham*, *Zest* and *Zephyr* are relieved from 13 May by the cruiser *Devonshire* and the destroyers *Iroquois* and *Savage* which, together with the *Dido*, take the German cruisers *Prinz Eugen* and *Nürnberg* to Wilhelmshaven from 24 to 26 May. Vice-Adm McGrigor arrives in Bergen with the cruiser *Norfolk* and the 30th EG and the cruiser *Berwick* with the destroyers *Haida* (RCN) and *Huron* (RCN) and the 5th EG arrive in Trondheim to take over and transfer the U-boats (29–31 May).

The British Flag Officer Wilhelmshaven (Rear-Adm Muirhead) embarks a company of Scots Guards on boats of the German 7th MS Flotilla on 11 May and occupies Heligoland.

On 13 May Rear-Adm Breuning, who has arrived from Holland in a motor torpedo boat, signs in Felixstowe the surrender of the naval forces stationed in Holland.

On 14 May the German minesweeper *M607* arrives in the Firth of Forth with documents on the German mine barrages in the Skagerrak and Kattegat. The first British warships to arrive in Wilhelmshaven are the destroyers *Southdown* and *Brocklesby* and in Cuxhaven the fast minelayer *Adventure*.

On 8 May the destroyers *Beagle* and *Bulldog* proceed to St Peter Port in Guernsey to receive the surrender of the Channel Islands. The destroyer *Faulknor* and the frigate (DE) *Narborough* escort six minesweepers and two patrol boats to Britain on 17 May.

7 May   Baltic

The German minesweeper *M22* is sunk near Achterwehr in the Kiel Channel. The MTBs *S301* and *S191* sink after colliding in Fehmarnsund.

7 May   Norway

Catalina 'X' of No 210 Sqn RAF (Flt Lt Murray) sinks *U320* (Lt Emmrich) off Bergen. This is the last U-boat sunk in the fighting.

7 May   North Sea/Irish Sea

Last successes by German U-boats in WW2: *U1023* (Lt Schroeteler) sinks the Norwegian minesweeper *NYMS 382* in the Irish Sea and *U2336* (Lt Klusmeyer) sinks the freighters *Avondale Park* (2878 tons) and *Sneland* (1791 tons) off the Firth of Forth.

7 May   General Situation

Signing of the unconditional surrender of the German Wehrmacht in Gen Eisenhower's headquarters in Reims. It comes into force early on 8 May.

7 May   Germany

Canadian, Polish and British troops occupy Emden, Wilhelmshaven and Cuxhaven.

7 May   Sea of Japan

The Japanese minesweeper *W29* is sunk by mine off Kinzurusaki, W Honshu.

8 May   Baltic

The German MMS *R88* is scuttled in the Kiel Canal; also scuttled are *U37* and *U2538* off Sonderburg, *U3503* off Gothenburg and in *U2365* in the Kattegat.

Sixty-five small craft of the German Navy set out from Libau for the W in four convoys with approximately 14400 persons, as do 61 craft from Windau in two convoys with approximately 11300 troops. Only some of the slowest units, with about 300 men on board, are captured by the Soviets on 9 May.

8–9 May   Mediterranean

Surrender of the German garrisons in Crete, Milos, Rhodes, Leros, Coo and some smaller islands in the Dodecanese.

9 May   English Channel

The British minesweeper *Prompt* is damaged by mine 12 nautical miles NW of Ostend; she is towed to Southend but not repaired.

9 May   Bay of Biscay

Surrender of the German bases at Lorient, La Rochelle and St-Nazaire, as well as those Channel Islands still occupied by German troops.

9–17 May   Atlantic

German U-boats at sea put in to Allied harbours in accordance with instructions:
9 May: *U249* Portland (Channel).
10 May: *U1105*, *U1009* and *U1305* Loch Eriboll, *U1058* Lough Foyle, *U825* Portland, *U1023* Weymouth, *U532* Liverpool and *U510* St-Nazaire.
11 May: *U826* Loch Eriboll and *U293* Loch Ailsh.
12 May: *U802* Loch Eriboll and *U889* St John's (Newfoundland).
13 May: *U956* Loch Eriboll, *U1228* Portsmouth (USA) and *U858* the Delaware estuary.
14 May: *U764* and *U1010* Loch Eriboll, *U244*, *U516* and *U1231* Lough Foyle, *U485* and *U541* Gibraltar, *U2326* Dundee and *U805* and *U234* Portsmouth (USA).
16 May: *U255* Lough Foyle, *U776* Portland and *U190* St John's.
17 May: *U873* Portsmouth (USA).
Of these boats *U1058* and *U1305* become Soviet war booty, *U1105*, *U805*, *U1228*, *U858*, *U873* and *U234* US war booty and *U190* British war booty. In addition, *U510* and *U2326* are handed over to France. The remaining boats are sunk (Operation 'Deadlight').

9–23 May   South West Pacific

In support of the 6th Australian Div (Maj-Gen Stevens), which is advancing from Aitape (New Guinea) along the coast eastwards to the centre of Japanese resistance put up by the remains of the 18th Army in

Wewak, the Wewak Support Force operates off the coast with the Australian sloop *Swan* and the minesweeper-corvettes *Colac*, *Dubbo* and *Deloraine*. On 9–10 May the cruisers *Newfoundland* and *Hobart* (RAN, Commodore Farncomb) and the Australian destroyers *Arunta* and *Warramunga* arrive in support and shell Wewak. On 11 May 623 men of a BLT are landed by one LCM, nine LCIs and two support LCIs in Dove Bay E of Wewak. They capture the Wewak peninsula and by 23 May the Japanese pockets of resistance in the Wewak area have been overcome.

10 May   Baltic

The German E-boat depot ship *Carl Peters* is sunk by mine in Geltinger Bay.

10 May   South West Pacific

Part of Amphibious Group 9 (Rear-Adm Struble, TG.78.3) lands the 108th RCT of the 40th Inf Div in Macalajar Bay in northern Mindanao on 10 May.

10–16 May   Indian Ocean

On 10 May the Japanese cruiser *Haguro* and the destroyer *Kamikaze* set out from Singapore to evacuate Japanese troops from the Nicobars and Andamans. The ships are reported in the Malacca Strait by the British submarines *Statesman* and *Subtle*. Thereupon TF.61 (Vice-Adm Walker), comprising the battleships *Queen Elizabeth* and *Richelieu*, the cruisers *Cumberland* and *Tromp* (Dutch) and the 21st Carrier Sqn (Commodore Oliver) with the cruiser *Royalist* and the escort carriers *Hunter*, *Khedive*, *Shah* and *Emperor* and eight destroyers, sets out from Trincomalee to intercept the Japanese force in the Eleven Degrees Channel. On 11 May the escort carriers launch an attack with Hellcat fighters on Car Nicobar and are sighted by a Japanese reconnaissance aircraft. *Haguro* and *Kamikaze* return.

While TF.61 proceeds to the area NW of Sumatra, TF.62, comprising the cruiser *Nigeria* and the destroyers *Roebuck*, *Racehorse* and *Redoubt*, sets out from Trincomalee on 13 May. On 14 May Adm Walker detaches the *Cumberland* with the 21st Carrier Sqn and the 26th DD Flotilla (Capt Power), consisting of *Saumarez*, *Verulam*, *Vigilant*, *Venus* and *Virago*, into the area W of the Six Degrees Channel. On 15 May a reconnaissance aircraft flown off from *Shah* sights the Japanese ships, which have set out again, NE of Sabang, but they return at once. After the breakdown of the catapult on *Shah*, only three Avenger bombers are able to fly off from the crowded flight deck of *Emperor* and they have no success. During the night 15–16 May Capt Power, with the 26th DD Flotilla, approaches the two Japanese ships in the Malacca Straits SW of Penang and deploys his five destroyers in a classical night pincer attack. *Saumarez* receives three heavy hits in an engagement; then *Haguro*, after strenuous manoeuvring, is hit by torpedo salvos and sinks. *Kamikaze* escapes with only slight damage. Then *Hunter* and *Khedive* make attacks on the Andaman Islands.

11 May   English Channel
Surrender of the German garrison in Dunkirk.

12–31 May   Arctic
Last convoy pair, JW.67/RA.67, from the Clyde to the Kola Inlet and back, each with 23 ships. The escort includes the escort carrier *Queen* and the destroyers *Onslow* and *Obdurate*; in addition, there is the 4th EG with the DEs *Bentinck*, *Drury*, *Bazely*, *Pasley* and *Byard* and the Canadian 9th EG with the frigates *Loch Alvie*, *Monnow*, *Nene*, *St Pierre* and *Matane*. JW.67 arrives in the Kola Inlet on 20 May and RA.67 sets out on 23 May.

On the way out, the 9th EG is detached on 16 May in order to halt the Arctic U-boats proceeding from Vestfjord to Trondheim and to accompany them to Loch Eriboll on 19 May. The U-boats include *U278*, *U294*, *U295*, *U312*, *U313*, *U318*, *U363*, *U427*, *U481*, *U668*, *U968*, *U992*, *U997* and *U1165*. The last boat, *U716*, follows later. All boats are sunk in Operation 'Deadlight'.

14 May   South West Pacific
The 6th Australian Division is landed at Wewak and captures the airfield. Support is provided by the cruisers *Newfoundland* and *Hobart* (RAN), the destroyers *Arunta* (RAN) and *Warramunga* (RAN), the RAN sloops *Swan* and *Warrego* and the RAN minesweepers *Colac* and *Dubbo*.

14 May   Baltic
The torpedo recovery vessel *TFA3* (ex-Danish *Dragen*) is sunk by mine in the Geltinger Bight.

16 May   North Sea
The German U-boat *U287* is lost on a mine in the Elbe river at Altenbruch.

16 May   China
End of the air mining offensive from the China Theatre, which started on 16 Oct 1943. B-24s of the US 14th AF have flown 255 sorties, with 209 aircraft dropping 976 mines and B-29s of the 20th AF have flown 22 sorties, laying 263 mines and losing four aircraft (altogether, 825 mines magnetic, 182 acoustic and 232 contact). The targets were Haiphong, Hong Kong, Takao, Shanghai, Yulinkan (Hainan), Canton, Kiirun Ko and the Yangtse.

16 May–15 June   Indian Ocean
The Indian sloops *Cauvery*, *Narbada*, *Godavari*, *Kistna*, *Sutlej* and *Hindustan*, supported at first by the cruiser *Phoebe* and later by *Ceylon*, patrol between the Mergui Archipelago and Port Blair in the Andaman Sea to prevent the evacuation of Japanese troops and their supply.

On 5 June the 10th DD Flotilla, comprising the British destroyers *Tartar*, *Eskimo*, *Nubian*, *Penn* and *Paladin*, sets out from Trincomalee to intercept shipping between the Nicobars and Sabang. Following a report by the submarine *Trident*, the first three destroyers are directed on 12 June to a convoy and sink the submarine-chaser *Ch-57* and the freighter *Kuroshio Maru*. *Penn* and *Paladin* sink a landing boat off SW Sumatra.

17 May   Central Pacific
The US TU.12.5.3 (Rear-Adm C A F Sprague), comprising the carrier *Ticonderoga* and the destroyers *Rowe*, *Smaller* and *Stoddart*, makes a raid on the Japanese-occupied Marshall Islands, Taroa and Maloelap.

19 May   Indian Ocean
The British submarine *Terrapin* is damaged beyond repair by Japanese A/S ships firing depth charges.

19 May   North Pacific
US Desdiv 114 shells Paramushiro (Kuriles).

20 May   North Atlantic
The German U-boat *U963* is scuttled off the Portuguese coast near Nazare following the cancellation of a minelaying sortie off Portland.

24 May   North Sea
U979, returning from an operation off Iceland, is beached on the island of Amrum.

27 May–28 June   Pacific
The Japanese 'Todoroki' submarine group, with 'Kaiten' torpedoes, is used in the open sea against shipping coming from Leyte, Guam, Saipan and other bases to Okinawa. On 27–28 May *I-367* (Lt Taketomi) attacks a convoy with two 'Kaiten', one of which damages the US DE *Gilligan*. On 30 May an aircraft of the 'hunter-killer' escort carrier *Anzio* sinks *I-361*. *I-36* (Cdr Sugamasa) attacks on 22 June a convoy E of the Marianas with torpedoes and damages the LST repair ship *Endymion*. On 27–28 June she misses a tanker with one 'Kaiten' and just misses the transport *Antares* with two. On 28 June *I-165* is sunk by an aircraft in a search in the area of the Marianas. *I-53* and *I-363* return without success.

29–31 May   Norway
German U-boats in Norwegian harbours are sent to British assembly areas. From Trondheim on 29 May: *U483*, *U773*, *U775*, *U953*, *U957*, *U978*, *U994*, *U1019*, *U1064* and *U1203* (Type VIIC) and *U861* (Type IXD).

From Bergen: On 29 May *U907*, *U991*, *U1052*, *U298* and *U299* (Type VIIC); on 30 May *U245*, *U328*, *U928*, *U930*, *U1002*, *U1004*, *U1005*, *U1022*, *U1057*, *U1104*, *U1271*, *U1272*, *U1301* and *U1307* (Type VIIC), *U218* (Type VIID), *U1061* (Type VIIF), *U539* and *U868* (Type IXC), *U875* (Type IXD), *U2506*, *U2511* and *U3514* (Type XXI), *U2328* (Type XXIII) and *UD5* (ex-Dutch *O27*); and on 31 May *U778* (Type VIIC).

From Stavanger: on 29 May *U637*, *U901* and *U1171* (Type VIIC); and on 31 May *U3035* (Type XXI) and *U2322*, *U2324*, *U2329*, *U2345* and *U2348* (Type XXIII).

From Kristiansand South: on 29 May *U281*, *U299*, *U369*, *U712*, *U985* and *U1163* (Type VIIC), *U2529* (Type XXI) and *U2321*, *U2325*, *U2334*, *U2335*, *U2337*, *U2350*, *U2353*, *U2354*, *U2361* and *U2363* (Type XXIII).

From Horten: on 29 May *U975* and *U1108* (Type VIIC), *U170* (Type IXC), *U874* (Type IXD) and *U2502*, *U2513*, *U2518*, *U3017*, *U3041* and *U3515* (Type XXI); and 31 May *U1109* (Type VIIC).

Of these U-boats, *U1057*, *U1064*, *U2529*, *U3035*, *U3041*, *U3515* and *U2353* become Soviet war booty, *U2513* US war booty and *U712*, *U953*, *U1108*, *U1171*, *U3017* and *U2334* British war booty; in addition, *U2518* and *U2326* are handed over to France. The other boats are sunk by British forces W of the Hebrides in the period 25 Nov–7 Jan as part of Operation 'Deadlight'. For the time being, the Type VIIC *U926* and *U1202* (Bergen) and *U995* (Trondheim) and the Type XXIII *U4706* (Kristiansand) remain in Norway; they are later allocated to that country as booty. In addition, *U324* and *U1275* (Bergen), *U310* and *U315* (Trondheim) and *U975* (Horten)—all Type VIIC—are later scrapped.

29 May–13 June   Central Pacific
The US Fast Carrier Task Force continues operations E of Okinawa as TF.38 under Adm Halsey on board the battleship *Missouri* and Vice-Adm McCain on the carrier *Shangri-La*. TG.38.2 (Rear-Adm Sherman) goes to Leyte on 29 May. TG.38.1 (Rear-Adm Clark) and 38.4 (Rear-Adm Radford) alternate in providing fighter cover for Okinawa. On 2 and 3 June TG.38.1 remains off Okinawa, while TG.38.4 makes a fighter raid on kamikaze airfields on Kyushu from the carriers *Shangri-La*, *Ticonderoga*, *Yorktown*, *Langley* and *Independence*. On 4 June replenishment from the Logistic Support

Force (Rear-Adm Beary) is interrupted because of an approaching typhoon. On 5 June TG.38.1 runs into the centre of the whirlwind and almost all ships, the carriers *Hornet*, *Bennington*, *Belleau Wood* and *San Jacinto*, the battleships *Massachusetts*, *Indiana* and *Alabama*, the cruisers *Pittsburgh* (100ft of her bows torn off), *Baltimore*, *Quincy*, *Atlanta*, *Duluth* and *San Juan* and the destroyers (Desron 61) *De Haven*, *Maddox*, *Blue*, *Brush*, *Taussig* and *Samuel N Moore* and (Desron 25) *John Rodgers*, *McKee*, *Schroeder*, *Dashiell* and *Stockham* of Desdiv 106 are more or less badly damaged. TG.38.4 is able to retire to the N: only the fleet flagship *Missouri* is slightly damaged. Of the supply group, the flagship, the cruiser *Detroit*, the escort carriers *Windham Bay*, *Salamaua*, *Bougainville* and *Attu*, the DEs *Donaldson*, *Conklin* and *Hilbert*, the tankers *Lackawanna* and *Millicoma* and the ammunition transport *Shasta* are damaged. Most of the ships continue their operations. On 6 June refuelling takes place. With TG.38.1 the new carrier *Bon Homme Richard* relieves *Bennington* and in place of the *Pittsburgh* and *Baltimore* come *Topeka* and *Oklahoma City*. On 7 and 8 June TG.38.1 makes sorties over Okinawa. On 9 June it makes experimental sorties with napalm bombs on Okino-Daito-Shima, which is also shelled by the battlecruisers *Alaska* and *Guam* and five destroyers under Rear-Adm Low. TG.38.4 makes another raid on Kanoya (Kyushu) on 8 June. On 10 June the battleships (Rear-Adm Shafroth) *Massachusetts*, *Alabama* and *Indiana* and five destroyers shell Minamioshima. Then TF.38 returns to Leyte, where it arrives on 13 June. Thus end three months of uninterrupted operations by the carrier fleet.

1–30 June   Pacific/Indian Ocean

Continuation of the Allied submarine operations against the Japanese supply traffic along the Asiatic coasts. In the Kuriles area, *Dace* (Lt-Cdr Cole) sinks one ship of 1391 tons, one trawler and one lugger, *Apogon* (Lt-Cdr House) sinks one ship of 2636 tons and one small craft and on 2 July damages the auxiliary submarine-chasers *Cha-58* and *Cha-65*, *Cabezon* (Cdr Lautrup) sinks one ship of 2631 tons and *Barb* (Cdr Fluckey) sinks three ships of 4167 tons, two trawlers, 13 small craft and on 18 July the corvette *Kaibokan 112*. E of the Tsugaru Straits, *Piranha* (Cdr Irvine) sinks two ships of 7012 tons and three small craft and on 22 June damages the corvette *Kaibokan 196* and *Parche* (Lt-Cdr McCrory) sinks three ships of 10571 tons and ten small craft. E of Honshu, *Guardfish* (Cdr Ward) sinks one trawler and, S of Honshu, *Trepang* (Lt-Cdr

Faust) sinks one ship of 606 tons and one small craft. W of Kyushu, *Tirante* (Cdr Street) sinks four ships of 3521 tons and ten small craft.

In the East China Sea, *Haddo* (Lt-Cdr Lynch) sinks two ships of 5326 tons, two small craft and on 1 July the corvette *Kaibokan 72* and *Dentuda* (Cdr McCain Jr) sinks two small vessels of 176 tons. In the Yellow Sea, *Sea Cat* (Cdr McGregor) sinks one sailing vessel, *Paddle* (Lt-Cdr Nowell) sinks seven small vessels, *Ronquil* (Lt-Cdr Monroe) has a miss, *Sea Devil* (Lt-Cdr McGivern) sinks one ship of 2211 tons and three trawlers and *Sea Owl* (Cdr Bennett) sinks on 9 June the corvette *Kaibokan 41* and then one sailing vessel.

In Operation 'Barney', a 'wolfpack' under the name 'Hydeman's Hellcats' leaves Guam on 27 May, proceeds through the Korean Strait using sonar detection equipment to evade the mined areas and enters the Sea of Japan. Participating are *Sea Dog* (Cdr Hydeman, pack leader), *Crevalle* (Cdr Steinmetz), *Spadefish* (Cdr W J Germershausen), *Tunny* (Cdr Pierce), *Skate* (Cdr Lynch), *Bonefish* (Cdr Edge), *Flying Fish* (Cdr Risser), *Bowfin* (Cdr Tyree) and *Tinosa* (Cdr Latham). From 9 to 20 June *Sea Dog* sinks seven ships of 7928 tons and one small craft and damages one ship of 1045 tons, *Crevalle* sinks three ships of 6643 tons and two small craft and torpedoes on 22 June the frigate *Kasado*, *Spadefish* sinks five ships of 8638 tons and four small vessels and on 13 June the Soviet ship *Transbalt* of 11439 tons, *Tunny* has no success, *Skate* sinks on 10 June the submarine *I-122* and in addition four ships of 7816 tons, *Bonefish* sinks two ships of 5326 tons but is herself sunk on 18 June in Toyama Wan (Honshu) by Japanese surface craft, *Flying Fish* sinks two ships of 4113 tons and 12 small vessels, *Bowfin* sinks two ships of 2785 tons and one sailing vessel and *Tinosa* sinks four ships of 6690 tons. The group passes the La Perouse Strait on 24 June and returns to Pearl Harbor on 4 July.

In the Gulf of Thailand, *Tambor* (Lt-Cdr W T Germershausen) sinks one ship of 1248 tons and the British *Selene* sinks four coasters and two small craft; W of Thailand, the US *Thresher* sinks three junks; N of Sumatra, the British *Statesman* (Lt Bulkeley) sinks one junk and damages the submarine depot ship *Komahashi* of 1125 tons; in the Malacca Strait, *Trident* sinks two landing craft and one junk, *Vivid* sinks one junk and *Torbay* sinks one coaster and two junks; and, in the Bangka Strait, the US *Caiman* (Cdr Azer) sinks two sailing vessels, the British *Stygian* (Lt Clarabut) sinks a

coaster and the British *Solent* sinks two landing craft.

In the Java Sea, the Dutch *K-XIV* sinks two small craft, the British *Taciturn* sinks the auxiliary submarine-chaser *Cha-105* and the hulk of the former Dutch submarine *K-XVIII* as well as a small sailing vessel and the US *Hardhead* (Cdr Greenup) sinks three small craft and the submarine-chasers *Cha-113* and *Cha-42*. In the Sunda Strait, the US *Kraken* (Lt-Cdr Henry) sinks two small craft and damages one more and *Baya* (Lt-Cdr Jarvis) sinks on 16 July the torpedo boat *Kari* and two trawlers and together with *Capitaine* (Lt-Cdr Friedrich) one submarine-chaser.

3 June   North Atlantic

The German U-boat *U1277* is scuttled off Oporto, Portugal.

3–8 June   Indonesia

The Japanese cruiser *Ashigara* (Vice-Adm Hashimoto) sets out from Singapore with the destroyer *Kamikaze* for Batavia, where she takes 1200 Japanese troops on board. When she sails on 7 June she is reported by a US submarine. The British submarine *Trenchant* (Cdr Hezlet), which is deployed, attacks the ships with eight torpedoes in the Bangka Strait. They narrowly miss *Kamikaze* but sink *Ashigara* with five hits.

3–22 June   Central Pacific

Last phase in the fighting for Okinawa. On 3 June elements of TF.53 (Rear-Adm Reifsnider) land marines on the island of Ineya Shima and on 9 June on Aguni Shima.

From 3 to 7 June 20 Japanese Navy and 30 Army aircraft carry out the kamikaze operation 'Kikusui 9'. In this action off Okinawa, the battleship *Mississippi*, the cruiser *Louisville*, the escort carrier *Natoma Bay*, the destroyer *Anthony* and the destroyer/minelayers *Harry F Bauer* and *J William Ditter* and the picket boat *LCI(L) 90* receive hits. The last two are damaged beyond repair.

A single kamikaze aircraft sinks the destroyer *William D Porter* on 10 June. On 11 June the picket boat *LCS(L) 122* is damaged and on 16 June a single torpedo aircraft sinks the destroyer *Twiggs*.

In the final fighting in the S of Okinawa, the Cdr of the US 10th Army, Lt-Gen Buckner, is killed on 18 June. Maj-Gen Geiger takes over the command temporarily.

From 21 to 22 June 30 Navy and 15 Army aircraft make the last co-ordinated Japanese kamikaze attack, 'Kikusui 10', off Okinawa and Kerama Retto. In this attack the DE *Halloran*, the aircraft tenders *Curtiss* and *Kenneth Whiting*, the minesweeper *Ellyson*,

LST 534 and the picket boats *LSM 59* and *LSM 213* are damaged.

7–20 June South West Pacific

Operation 'Oboe VI': landing in Brunei Bay (Borneo). On 7 June five fleet minesweepers and 12 YMSs begin to search for mines: in the process the minesweeper *Salute* is sunk on 8 June. By 12 June 102 mines are cleared. Cover for the minesweepers and shelling of the assault areas are undertaken by TG. 74.3 (Rear-Adm Berkey), comprising the cruisers *Phoenix*, *Nashville*, *Boise* (Gen MacArthur on board) and the Australian *Hobart* and the destroyers *Killen*, *Albert W Grant*, *Conner*, *Charette*, *Bell*, *Burns* and the Australian *Arunta*. On 8–9 June the shelling is continued. On 10 June Amphibious Group 6 (Rear-Adm Royal, TG. 78.1), with the headquarters ships *Rocky Mount* and the US Coast Guard cutter *Spencer*, lands 29361 men of the Australian 9th Inf Div (Maj-Gen Wootten) in Brunei Bay. The transport group comprises three Australian LSIs, one US LSD, two AKAs, nine APDs, 35 LSTs, 21 LSMs and 55 LCIs; the escort comprises the destroyers *Robinson* (Desron 22), *Saufley*, *Waller*, *Philip* and *Frazier* (Desron 14) and *Bancroft*, *Bailey*, *Edwards*, *Caldwell* and *McCalla*, the DEs *Douglas A Munro*, *Charles E Brannon*, *Albert T Harris*, *Dufilho*, *Jobb* and *Day* and the Australian frigates *Hawkesbury*, *Barcoo* and *Lachlan*.

On 20 June elements of these forces land one BLT near Luton (Sarawak/Borneo) which occupies the oilfield of Miri by 25 June.

10–11 June North Pacific

A US task group (Rear-Adm Brown) bombards Matsuwa (Kuriles) with the cruisers *Richmond* and *Concord* and five destroyers.

12–17 June Central Pacific

Operation 'Inmate': the British TG.111.2 (Rear-Adm Brind) makes a carrier raid on Truk. On 12 June the carrier *Implacable*, the escort carrier *Ruler*, the cruisers *Swiftsure*, *Newfoundland*, *Uganda* and *Achilles* and the destroyers *Troubridge*, *Tenacious*, *Termagant*, *Terpsichore* and *Teazer* set out from Manus. Early on 14 June *Implacable* makes an attack with 21 Avengers, 11 Fireflies and 48 Seafires (partly CAP). During the night 14–15 June *Uganda*, *Achilles* and *Tenacious* shell the island of Dublon, *Newfoundland* and *Troubridge* shell Uman and *Swiftsure* and *Teazer* shell Moen. On 15 June aircraft from *Implacable* make further attacks. In all, there are 113 attacks and 103 CAP sorties. On 17 June the force returns to Manus.

14 June Baltic

The U-boat tender *Donau* and the torpedo recovery vessels *TFA1*, *2*, *5* and *6* (ex-Danish torpedo boats *Högen*, *Örnen*, *Hvalen*

and *Laxen*) are destroyed when an ammunition dump explodes.

15 June–9 July South West Pacific

Operation 'Oboe II': landing in Balikpapan (Borneo). On 15 June three fleet minesweepers and 38 YMSs begin mine clearance in the extensive Japanese minefields in the waters round Balikpapan which were also sown with air mines by the USAAF. Eighteen US air magnetic mines and nine Japanese anchor mines are cleared. *YMS 50* is lost on 18 June, *YMS 39* and *YMS 365* on 26 June and *YMS 84* on 9 July. *YMS 368*, *YMS 47* and *YMS 314* are damaged. *YMS 335*, *YMS 10*, *YMS 364* and *YMS 49* and the destroyer *Smith* are damaged by Japanese coastal guns. Cover and gun support for the minesweepers is provided by elements of TG.74.2 (Rear-Adm Riggs) with the cruisers *Denver* and *Montpelier* and four destroyers. On 24 June the UDTs begin their work. On 25 June there is an unsuccessful Japanese air torpedo attack. It leads to a request for escort carriers.

The shelling of the assault areas is continued from 25 to 30 June by TG.74.2, comprising the cruisers *Denver*, *Montpelier*, *Columbia*, *Cleveland* and *Tromp* (Dutch) and the destroyers *Conway* (Desron 44), *Eaton*, *Cony*, *Stevens*, *Albert W Grant*, *Killen* and *Arunta* (RAN), by TG.74.3 (Rear-Adm Berkey), comprising the cruisers *Nashville* and *Phoenix* and the destroyers *Charette* (Desdiv 102), *Bell*, *Conner* and *Burns*, and by TG.74.1 (Commodore Farncomb RAN), comprising the cruisers *Shropshire* and *Hobart* (RAN) and the US destroyers *Hart* and *Metcalfe*. Gen MacArthur is on board *Cleveland* and Vice-Adm Barbey (Cdr Amphibious Forces, 7th Fleet) on *Phoenix*. After renewed heavy shelling (in all, 38052 rounds of 3in to 8in shells from 15 June), 33446 troops of the reinforced Australian 7th Inf Div (Maj-Gen Milford) of I Corps are landed in Balikpapan on 1 July. The landing is effected by TG.78.2 (Rear-Adm Noble) with the three Australian LSIs, *Manoora*, *Kanimbla* and *Westralia*, the headquarters ship *Wasatch*, one US AKA, one LSD, five APDs, 35 LSTs, 22 LSMs and 50 LCIs, escorted by the US destroyers *Flusser* (Desron 5), *Drayton*, *Conyngham* and *Smith*, *Frazier* (Desron 14) and *Bailey* and *Robinson* (Desron 22), *Saufley*, *Waller* and *Philip* and the DEs *Chaffee*, *Edwin A Howard*, *Key*, *Leland E Thomas* and *Rutherford*. Air support is provided by the US 5th and 13th AF and, from 1 to 3 July, by an escort carrier group (Rear-Adm Sample) comprising *Suwanee*, *Gilbert Islands* and *Block Island*, the destroyer *Helm* and the

DEs *Cloves*, *Mitchell*, *Kyne*, *Lamons* and *Donaldson*. By 3 July the airfield at Sepinggan is taken and on 4 July the oilfields are taken. On 5 July one battalion of the Australian 9th Inf Bde is brought across Balikpapan Bay to the W bank near Penadjam; part of it is landed on 9 July further to the N near Djinabora. Small Dutch units land on 7 July N of the Sumbir river near Kariango and Teloktebang.

20 June Indian Ocean

Operation 'Balsam'. Aircraft from the escort carriers *Stalker*, *Khedive* and *Ameer* of the British East Indies Fleet attack airfields in Northern Sumatra and Japanese shipping in the Malacca Straits. The escort comprises the cruisers *Suffolk* and *Royalist* and five destroyers.

20 June Central Pacific

The US TG.12.4 (Rear-Adm Jennings), comprising the carriers *Hancock*, *Lexington* and *Cowpens* and five destroyers, makes a carrier raid on the island of Wake on the way to join TF.38.

21 June Pacific

End of the ground fighting on Okinawa; suicides of the commander of the Japanese defending forces, Lt-Gen Ushijama (Cdr 32nd Army) and of his Chief of Staff, Maj-Gen Cho.

Japanese losses are approximately 130000 dead and 42000 civilians; 10755 Japanese are taken prisoner. The US Army loses 7613 dead and missing and has 31807 wounded, the Navy 4907 dead and missing and 4824 injured. Thirty-six American ships are sunk and 368 damaged. According to American reports, the Japanese lose 7830 aircraft to the Americans' 763.

21–30 June North Sea

The U-boats which are still in the northern Germany/Denmark area and are operational are transferred from Wilhelmshaven to Britain:

On 21 June *U155*, *U883*, *U1230* and *U1233* (Type IXC), *U3008* (Type XXI) and *U2336*, *U2341*, *U2351* and *U2356* (Type XXIII); on 22 June *U806* (Type IXC); on 23 June *U368*, *U1102*, *U1103*, *U1110*, *U1194* and *U1201* (Type VIIC); on 24 June *U291*, *U680*, *U720*, *U779*, *U1197* and *U1198* (Type VIIC); and on 30 June *U143*, *U145*, *U149* and *U150* (Type IID) and *U739* (Type VIIC). These boats are sunk in Operation 'Deadlight' with the exception of *U3008* which becomes US war booty.

25 June–7 July North Pacific

Operations by US TF.92 (Rear-Adm Brown) from Attu. From 25 to 22 July it makes a sortie with the cruisers *Richmond* and *Concord* and the destroyers *Bearss* (Desdiv 114), *John Hood*, *Jarvis* and *Porter* into the Sea of Okhotsk. On 26 June they encounter a Japanese convoy SW of Paramushiro and sink one ship. Others are damaged. The cruiser *Trenton* and the destroyers *Anderson* and *Hughes* operate E of the Kuriles.

From 3 to 7 July five of the above-named make a new raid into the Sea of Okhotsk and shell Shitsuka on southern Sakhalin on 5 July.

26 June–11 July   Japan

On 26 June the escort destroyer *Enoki* is mined sunk off Fukui Island in the Inland Sea. On 30 June the escort destroyer *Nara* is severely damaged by mine WSW of Shimonoseki (she is towed into harbour but not repaired) and on 11 July the escort destroyer *Sakura* is sunk by mine in Osaka harbour.

27 June   South West Pacific

End of organised Japanese resistance on Luzon. Individual pockets of resistance hold out until the end of the war.

1–18 July   Central Pacific

The air mining offensive in the Central Pacific Theatre, which began on 30 Dec 1943, ends on 1 July. Aircraft from Fleet Air Wing 1 USN have flown 188 sorties, aircraft from Task Force 58/38 84 sorties and B-24s of the US 7th AF 129 sorties; a total of 345 of aircraft have dropped 662 mines (575 magnetic, 34 acoustic, 33 pressure-magnetic and 20 low-frequency) for the loss of three machines. The targets were Jaluit, Maloelap, Wotje, Mille, Palau, Truk, the Bonins and SW Korea.

Attack by TF.38 (Adm Halsey, Vice-Adm McCain) on Japan. On 1 July TF.38 sets out from Leyte. TG.38.1 (Rear-Adm T L Sprague) comprises the carriers *Bennington*, *Lexington*, *Hancock*, *Belleau Wood* and *San Jacinto*, the battleships *Indiana*, *Massachussetts* and *Alabama*, the cruisers *Topeka*, *Duluth*, *Dayton*, *Atlanta* and *San Diego* and the destroyers (Desron 61) *De Haven*, *Mansfield*, *Lyman K Swenson*, *Collett*, *Maddox*, *Blue*, *Brush* and *Taussig*, (Desron 25) *John Rodgers*, *Harrison*, *McKee*, *Murray*, *Ringgold*, *Schroeder* and *Dashiell* and (Desdiv 100) *Caperton*, *Cogswell*, *Ingersoll* and *Knapp*. TG.38.3 (Rear-Adm Bogan) comprises the carriers *Ticonderoga*, *Randolph*, *Essex*, *Monterey* and *Bataan*, the battleships *South Dakota* and *North Carolina*, the cruisers *Pasadena*, *Springfield*, *Wilkes-Barre*, *Astoria* and *Oakland* and the destroyers (Desron 48) *Erben*, *Walker*, *Hale*, *Abbot*, *Stembel*, *Bullard*, *Black*, *Chauncey* and *Heerman* and (Desron 62) *English*, *Charles S Sperry*, *Ault*, *Waldron*, *John W Weeks*, *Hank*, *Wallace L Lind* and *Borie*. TG.38.4 (Rear-Adm Radford) comprises

the carriers *Yorktown*, *Shangri-La* (Vice-Adm McCain), *Bon Homme Richard*, *Independence* and *Cowpens*, the battleships *Iowa*, *Missouri* (Adm Halsey) and *Wisconsin*, the cruisers *Quincy*, *Chicago*, *Boston*, *St Paul* and *San Juan* and the destroyers (Desron 53) *Cushing*, *Colahan*, *Uhlmann*, *Benham*, *Stockham* and *Wedderburn*, (Desron 54) *Remey*, *Norman Scott*, *Mertz*, *Monssen*, *McGowan*, *McNair* and *Melvin* and (Desdiv 113) *Rowe*, *Smalley*, *Stoddard*, *Watts*, *Wren* and the radar picket *Frank Knox*.

After replenishing on 7 and 8 July, the carriers attack the Tokyo area on 10 July with 1022 aircraft, concentrating on air bases. Then the three task groups proceed to the N and replenish on 12 July E of the Tsugaru Strait. The attack on 13 July is postponed because of the weather. On 14 July 1391 aircraft set off for targets in N Honshu and S Hokkaido and ferry traffic in the Tsugaru Strait. The attacks are repeated on 15 July. In the operations, the escort destroyer *Tachibana*, the corvettes *Kaibokan W65, 74* and *219*, the minesweeper *Sokaitei 24* and the submarine-chaser *Kusentai Ch28* are sunk in addition to 37 ferry ships, transports and patrol craft, totalling 48717 tons. The escort destroyer *Yanagi*, the frigates *Iwo*, *Fukue* and *Kasado*, the corvettes *Kaibokan 215*, *205, 55, 47* and *221*, the submarine-chasers *Kusen T-T Cha-72, 81* and *47* and 28 ferry ships, transports and patrol ships totalling 49965 tons are damaged. On 14 July TG.34.8 (Rear-Adm Shafroth), with the battleships *South Dakota*, *Indiana* and *Massachussets*, the cruisers *Quincy* and *Chicago* and nine destroyers of Desron 48, shells, for the first time, targets on the Japanese main islands, the steel and iron works at Kamaishi. In all, 802 rounds of 16in, 728 rounds of 8in and 825 rounds of 5in are fired. On 14 and 15 July TG.35.1 (Rear-Adm Jones), with the cruisers *Pasadena*, *Springfield*, *Wilkes-Barre* and *Astoria* and six destroyers of Desron 53, carries out a raid on shipping off the east coast of N Honshu but finds no targets. On 15 July TG.34.1 (Rear-Adm Badger), with the battleships *Iowa*, *Missouri* and *Wisconsin*, the cruisers *Dayton* and *Atlanta* and seven destroyers of Desron 54 and *Frank Knox*, shells the iron and steel works at Muroran (860 rounds of 16in). On 16 July the destroyers are refuelled and the British TF.37 (Vice-Adm Rawlings and Vice-Adm Vian) joins the force with the carriers *Formidable*, *Victorious* and *Implacable*, the battleship *King George V*, the cruisers *Newfoundland*, *Achilles* (RNZN), *Uganda* (RCN), *Euryalus*, *Gambia* (RNZN) and *Black Prince* and the destroyers *Quiberon*, *Quickmatch*, *Quality*, *Quadrant*,

Troubridge, *Tenacious*, *Termagant*, *Teazer*, *Terpsichore*, *Grenville*, *Undaunted*, *Undine*, *Urania*, *Urchin* and *Ulysses*.

On 17–18 July the US and British carriers make heavy raids on the Tokyo-Yokohama area. After eliminating the fighter and AA defence, aircraft from *Yorktown* put the Japanese battleship *Nagato* out of action. In addition, the escort destroyer *Yaezakura*, the submarine *I-372*, the submarine-chaser *Kusen T-T 225* and the motor torpedo boat *PT28* are sunk, the training cruiser *Kasuga* is badly hit and the destroyer *Yakaze*, one landing ship, one submarine-chaser and one motor torpedo boat are damaged. During the night 17–18 July TG.34.1 (Rear-Adm Badger), with the battleships *Iowa*, *Missouri*, *Wisconsin*, *North Carolina* and *Alabama*, the cruisers *Dayton* and *Atlanta* and eight destroyers and the British battleship *King George V* and the destroyers *Quality* and *Quiberon*, shells industrial targets in the Hitachi area NE of Tokyo. The US battleships fire 1238 rounds of 16in, the cruisers 292 rounds of 6in and *King George V* 267 rounds of 14in. During the night 18–19 July, after an uneventful sortie against shipping targets, TG.35.2 (Rear-Adm Holden), with the cruisers *Topeka*, *Duluth*, *Atlanta* and *Dayton* and eight destroyers of Desron 62, and TG.35.3 (Rear-Adm Jones), with the cruisers *Pasadena*, *Springfield*, *Astoria*, *Wilkes-Barre* and six destroyers, shells targets near Cape Nojima SE of Tokyo. Because of a threatening typhoon, the groups withdraw on 19 July to replenish on the following day. The carrier *Indefatigable* with the destroyers *Barfleur*, *Wrangler* and *Wakeful* joins TF.37 on 20 July.

1–31 July   Pacific/Indian Ocean

Allied submarines continue to operate against the diminishing Japanese coastal shipping. In the area E of Honshu, *Runner* (Lt-Cdr Bass) sinks on 10 July the minesweeper *W-27*, *Moray* (Cdr Burrows) sinks one ship of 361 tons, *Kingfish* (Lt-Cdr Harper) sinks three small vessels, *Sea Poacher* (Lt-Cdr Gambacorta) sinks one ship of 334 tons and five small craft, *Aspro* (Lt-Cdr Stevenson) sinks one tug and *Thornback* (Cdr Abrahamson) damages the subchaser *Ch-42* on 31 July and sinks one small vessel. S of Honshu, *Steelhead* (Lt-Cdr Welchel) sinks three small craft, *Carp* (Lt-Cdr Hunnicut) sinks eleven small vessels and *Peto* (Lt-Cdr Caldwell) sinks one sailing vessel. S of Kyushu, *Quillback* (Lt-Cdr Nicholson) sinks one small craft and *Lionfish* (Lt-Cdr Spruance) misses one submarine.

In the Sea of Japan, *Sennet* (Lt-Cdr Clark)

sinks four ships of 13102 tons. In the East China Sea, *Queenfish* (Lt-Cdr Loughlin) sinks one small vessel. In the Yellow Sea, *Trutta* (Cdr Smith) sinks 16 sailing vessels, *Sea Robin* (Lt-Cdr Stimson) sinks one ship of 1224 tons and on 5 July the subchaser *Cha-85* and four small craft, *Spot* (Cdr Post) sinks two small craft, *Threadfin* (Lt Cdr Foote) sinks on 20 July the minesweeper *W39* and five small vessels, *Pomfret* (Cdr Hess) sinks five small vessels, *Pogy* (Lt-Cdr Bowers) sinks two ships of 4668 tons and *Tench* (Cdr Sieglaff) sinks 15 small vessels of different types.

In the Gulf of Thailand, the British *Sea Scout* sinks one coaster and ten small vessels, the British *Supreme* sinks three coasters and three small craft, the US *Hammerhead* (Lt-Cdr Smith) sinks two ships of 1734 tons and the US *Bugara* (Cdr Schade) sinks 56 small craft. E of Malaya, *Brill* has misses, *Bumper* (Cdr Williams) sinks one ship of 1189 tons and five small vessels, *Hawkbill* (Lt-Cdr Scanland) sinks five small craft and *Cod* (Lt-Cdr Adkins) sinks 25 small craft. E of Singapore, *Bluefish* (Lt-Cdr Forbes) sinks on 8 July the submarine-chaser *Cha-50* and on 15 July the submarine *I-351* and one small craft. *Lizardfish* (Cdr Butler) sinks the submarine-chaser *Ch37*.

In the Malacca Strait, the British *Sibyl* sinks eleven small craft, *Seadog* sinks ten small craft (in part together with *Shalimar* which sinks in addition eight craft) and *Thrasher* sinks six small vessels. N of Sumatra, *Vigorous* sinks one coaster. In the Sunda Strait, the US *Blueback* (Lt-Cdr Clementson) sinks two small craft and the British *Tiptoe* sinks five small craft, one of them in company with *Trump*. In the Java Sea, the US *Blenny* (Lt-Cdr Hazzard) sinks on 16 July the gunboat *Nankai* (ex-Dutch *Regulus*) and 64 small vessels, the British *Thule* sinks three coasters and damages one more, *Trenchant* (Cdr Hezlet) sinks four small craft, *Tudor* sinks five coasters, *Stubborn* sinks on 25 July the patrol boat *P-2/Nadakaze* and three small craft and damages one other, the US *Chub* (Cdr Rhymes) sinks seven small craft and the Dutch *O-21* sinks two coasters and one small craft.

2 July North Pacific
The US submarine *Barb* (Cdr Fluckey) bombards with rockets Japanese installations on Kaihyo Island on the east coast of Karafuto (Kuriles). This is the first rocket operation by submarines.

5–10 July Indian Ocean
Operation 'Collie'. Preparatory to the planned landing on the Malayan north-west coast (Operation 'Zipper') near Port Swettenham and Port Dickson, British mine-

sweepers of the 6th, 7th and 37th Flotillas clear 167 mines off the coast and in the area of the Nicobars. The operation is covered by the cruiser *Nigeria* and the destroyers *Roebuck*, *Eskimo* and *Vigilant*, which also shell Nancowry. Air escort is provided by the escort carriers *Ameer* and *Emperor*, which also make carrier raids on North Sumatran airfields with the escort carriers *Stalker* and *Empress*.

10 July South Atlantic
The German U-boat *U530* enters Mar del Plata in Argentina after its operation off the US East Coast.

10 July Indian Ocean
End of the Allied air mining offensive by the air forces in the India-Burma theatre, which started on 22 Feb 1943. RAF B-24 Liberators have flown 697 sorties with 631 aircraft, dropping 3235 mines, and US 10th AF B-24s have flown 121 sorties with 100 aircraft, laying 404 mines. B-25s of the 10th AF have flown 46 sorties with 43 aircraft, laying 101 mines, 14th AF B-24s have flown 24 sorties with 23 aircraft, laying 116 mines, and 20th B-29s have flown 154 sorties with 140 aircraft, laying 724 mines. A total of nine aircraft have been lost. The mines comprised 4192 magnetic, 246 acoustic, 36 drifting contact and 106 dummies, dropped on 37 targets along the coasts of Burma, Thailand, Malaya, the Andamans, Sumatra and Indo-China.

12 July North Pacific
A US task group comprising the cruisers *Richmond* and *Concord* and five destroyers shells Suribachi Point in the Kuriles.

12 July South West Pacific
Allied landing near Andus, Borneo. Australian troops take Maradi in West Borneo.

16 July–12 Aug Central Pacific
US TF.95 (Vice-Adm Oldendorf) operates from Okinawa to support troops on the island and to provide air warning (radar picket stations). It also makes sorties against shipping in the East China Sea. TG.95.1 (Vice-Adm Oldendorf) comprises the battleships *Tennessee* and *Pennsylvania*. It frequently operates in company with TG.95.3. TG.95.2 (Rear-Adm Low) comprises the battlecruisers *Alaska* and *Guam* and the cruisers *Cleveland*, *Columbia*, *Denver* and *Montpelier*. TG.95.3 comprises TU.1, with the escort carriers *Lunga Point*, *Makin Island* and *Cape Gloucester*, and TU.2, with the battleships *California* and *Nevada* and the cruisers *Salt Lake City*, *Chester*, *Wichita* and *St Louis*. There are also 18 destroyers. TG.95.7 comprises the battleships *Arkansas* and *Texas* and the cruisers *Portland*, *Mobile* and *Vicksburgh* (the two last join TF.38 after the Wake Raid).

In addition, the destroyers of Desrons 23, 45, 49 and 55 are employed as part of TF.95 and are sometimes allocated to the TGs or the radar picket stations. They include from Desron 23 *Charles Ausburne*, *Claxton*, *Dyson*, *Converse* and *Thatcher*, from 49 *Picking*, *Wickes* and *Harridan*, from 55 *Porterfield*, *Callaghan*, *Cassin Young*, *Irwin*, *Preston* and *Laws*, from Desdiv 92 *Boyd*, *Bradford*, *Brown* and *Cowell* and from Desron 24 *Ammen*, *Beale*, *Daly* etc. Drawing on these forces, TG.95.2 (Rear-Adm Low) makes a raid with two battleships, four light cruisers and eight destroyers on shipping in the East China Sea and in the Yellow Sea from 16 to 23 July. But it has only limited success. On 19 July the destroyer *Thatcher* is damaged beyond repair by kamikaze aircraft off Okinawa.

From 26 to 28 July TF.95 (Vice-Adm Oldendorf), comprising the battlecruisers *Alaska* and *Guam*, the battleships *Nevada*, *Tennessee* and *California*, the cruisers *Cleveland*, *Columbia*, *Denver* and *Montpelier*, the escort carriers *Makin Island*, *Lunga Point* and *Cape Gloucester* and 18 destroyers, makes a raid into the area of the Yangtse estuary off Shanghai with little effect. In this period minesweeping operations in the area SE of Okinawa and in the East China Sea are also covered. In radar picket operations, the destroyer *Callaghan* is sunk on 28 July by kamikaze pilots and the destroyer *Cassin Young* is damaged on 29 July.

From 1 to 7 Aug TF.95 carries out three anti-shipping strikes in the East China Sea. On 5–6 Aug Rear-Adm Litch makes a raid on the Tinghai area (China) with the escort carriers *Cape Gloucester*, *Fanshaw Bay*, *Lunga Point* and *Makin Island*. Cover is provided by four battleships, four cruisers, seven destroyers and three DEs. On 12 Aug the battleship *Pennsylvania* receives an air torpedo hit off Okinawa.

16 July–13 Aug Central Pacific
Last Japanese submarine operation with 'Kaiten' torpedoes. From the 'Tamon' group which sets out on 16 July, *I-47* (Lt-Cdr Suzuki) attacks a convoy with torpedoes in the Philippine Sea on 21 July and damages the transport *Marathon* (7607 tons). *I-53* (Lt-Cdr Oba) launches on 24 July two 'Kaitens' on a convoy, one of which sinks the US DE *Underhill*. A second attack with two 'Kaitens' on 4 Aug E of Formosa does not achieve anything. *I-58* (Cdr Hashimoto) launches a 'Kaiten' on 27–28 July against a force on the Guam–Leyte route and probably damages the destroyer *Lowry*. On 29–30 July she sinks with two hits from a salvo of six the unescorted heavy cruiser

Indianapolis (Capt McVay) E of Luzon. The cruiser has brought parts of the atomic bombs from San Francisco to Tinian and is proceeding to Leyte. Of the cruiser's crew of 1199, only 316 are rescued by American flying boats and destroyers between 2 and 8 Aug. On 10 Aug *I-58* launches two 'Kaitens' on a convoy. The DE *Johnnie Hutchins* avoids them but a search with two hunter-killer groups, comprising the DEs *Kendall C Campbell*, *Douglas A Munro*, *Rolf*, *William Seiverling* and *George A Johnson*, *Connolly*, *Metiver* and *Witter*, fails to find *I-58*. On 12 Aug the submarine launches two more 'Kaitens' against the LSD *Oakhill* and the DE *Thomas F Nickel* which graze the targets but detonate after being deflected.

I-366 (Lt Tokioka) reports on the evening of 11 Aug an attack with three 'Kaitens' on a convoy 500 nautical miles N of Palau. *I-367* returns without success. *I-373* is sunk on the way out by the US submarine *Spikefish*.

In the middle of July the 1st SM Div (Capt Ariizumi) sets out from Japan for Truk with the 'aircraft carrier submarine cruisers' *I-400* (Cdr Kusaka), *I-401* (Lt-Cdr Nambu), *I-14* (Cdr Shimizu) and *I-13* (Cdr Ohashi). The last is sunk on 16 July by the hunter-killer group, comprising the escort carrier *Anzio* and five DEs, by an aircraft and by the DEs *Lawrence C Taylor* and *Robert F Keller*. The others put to sea from Truk in the middle of Aug with their eight aircraft on board to make a kamikaze aircraft attack on Ulithi. But the attack is broken off because of the cease-fire and on their return to Japan the submarines are captured between 27 and 29 Aug.

18 July–9 Aug   Central Pacific
Raids by US task groups on Wake, chiefly with units which, after being repaired on the US West Coast, are proceeding via Pearl Harbor to join TF.38. Taking part in the carrier raid on 18 July are the carrier *Wasp*, the cruisers *Oklahoma City*, *Amsterdam*, *Tuscon* and *Flint* and, probably, the destroyers *Samuel N Moore*, *Twining*, *Wadleigh* and *Franks* and the new radar picket destroyers *Highbee*, *Southerland* and *Benner* which join TF.38 on 21–22 July. On 1 Aug the carrier *Cabot* and on 6 Aug the carrier *Intrepid* make a carrier raid. With them sail respectively the destroyers *Walke*, *O'Brien*, *Lowry*, *Allen M Summer*, *Moale* and *Robert K Huntington* from Desron 60, and the cruisers *Mobile* and *Vicksburgh* and the destroyers *Clarence K Bronson*, *Cotten*, *Dortch*, *Gatling* and *Healy* from Desron 50. They join TF.38 just before and just after the Aug raids. On 1 Aug TG.95.1 also shells the island using the battleships *Tennessee*

and *Pennsylvania*: the latter is hit by coastal guns. On 9 Aug a task group comprising, *inter alia*, the battleship *Pennsylvania*, cruisers and destroyers carries out another shelling of Wake.

In the area of the Marianas, the escort carrier *Vella Gulf* makes raids on 24 and 26 July on the islands of Pagan and Rota.

21–22 July   Central Pacific
The greatest supply operation of the war at sea. The US TG.30.8 (Rear-Adm Beary), comprising the command cruiser *Detroit*, the escort carriers *Chenango*, *Thetis Bay*, *Hollandia*, *Roi*, *Munda* and *Gilbert Islands*, 15 tankers, five ammunition transports and four freighters for supplies, replenishes TF.38 and elements of British TF.37 with about 60000 tons of oil, 6369 tons of ammunition, 1635 tons of supplies, 99 aircraft and 412 reserve personnel.

21 July–13 Aug   North Pacific
Sorties by US TF.92 (Rear-Adm Brown) from Attu against the North Kuriles from 21 to 23 July and from 11 to 13 Aug. On 22 July the cruisers *Pensacola*, *Richmond* and *Concord* and the destroyers (Desdiv 114) *Bearss*, *John Hood*, *Jarvis*, *Porter*, *Anderson*, *Hughes* and *McDermut* shell Suribachi on Paramushiro. On 12 Aug the same force shells Matsuwa and Paramushiro. *McDermut* is hit by coastal battery fire.

24–26 July   Indian Ocean
British minesweepers clear the minefields around Phuket Island off the west coast of the Kra Isthmus; in the operation the minesweeper *Squirrel* is sunk. The operation is covered by Vice-Adm Walker with the battleship *Nelson*, the cruiser *Sussex*, the escort carriers *Ameer* and *Empress* and four destroyers. The carriers make raids on the Kra Isthmus and the ships shell shore installations. On 26 July there is the first kamikaze attack on the British East Indies Fleet, when the carrier *Ameer* is damaged and the minesweeper *Vestal* is sunk.

24–30 July   Central Pacific
The US TF.38 continues its attacks on Japan with three task groups (see 1 July) and the British TF.37. On 24 July the carrier aircraft make 1747 sorties against harbours and bases in the Inland Sea, particularly Kure and Kobe. The Japanese carrier *Amagi* and the cruiser *Oyodo* are sunk. The battleships *Ise*, *Hyuga* and *Haruna*, the training cruiser *Iwate* and the heavy cruiser *Aoba* are so badly damaged that they settle on the bottom. Also damaged are the carriers *Katsuragi*, *Ryuho* and *Hosho*, the escort carrier *Kaiyo*, the cruiser *Kitakami*, the destroyer *Yoitsuki*, the escort destroyers *Hagi*, *Kaba* and *Tsubaki*, the target ship *Settsu*, the corvettes *Kaibokan 190* and *Kai-*

bokan 4 and one landing ship. Fifteen merchant ships and auxiliary warships totalling 22326 tons are sunk. During the night 24–25 July TG.35.3 (Rear-Adm Jones), comprising the cruisers *Pasadena*, *Springfield*, *Wilkes-Barre* and *Astoria* and six destroyers from Desron 53, shells the seaplane station off Kushimoto and the airfield near Shionomisaki in S Honshu. After replenishing from TG.30.8, the aircraft of TF.38 and TF.37 again attack the harbours of the Inland Sea on 28 July. In addition to the ships already hit and partly destroyed on 24 July, the cruiser *Tone*, the training cruiser *Izumo* and the escort destroyer *Nashi* are destroyed and the unfinished large submarine *I-404* wrecked. The frigate *Habushi*, the torpedo boat *Asagao*, the corvettes *Kaibokan 6*, *Kaibokan 30*, *Kaibokan 44*, *Kaibokan 45* and *Kaibokan 190*, the submarine *I-205*, the submarine-chaser *Kusentai Ch14* and the submarine depot ship *Komahashi* are badly damaged. Eight auxiliary ships and transports totalling 6059 tons sink.

After the destroyers have refuelled, the carrier groups attack the harbours of Kobe, Nagoya and Maizuru on 30 July. There the frigate *Okinawa*, the corvette *Kaibokan 2*, the minelayer *Tojima*, the submarine-chaser *Kusentai Ch26* and seven ships of 10834 tons are sunk and the destroyer *Yukikaze*, the frigate *Takane*, the submarines *I-202* and *I-153*, the submarine depot ship *Chogei*, the submarine-chaser *Kusen T-T Cha-182* and two ships of 7516 tons are badly damaged.

TG.34.8 (Rear-Adm Shafroth), comprising the battleships *South Dakota*, *Indiana* and *Massachusetts*, the cruisers *Quincy*, *Chicago*, *St Paul* and *Boston*, the nine destroyers of Desron 48 and the radar picket destroyer *Southerland*, as well as a British group comprising the battleship *King George V* and the destroyers *Undine*, *Ulysses* and *Urania*, shells in the night 29–30 July works and aircraft factories near Hamamatsu (S Honshu). The seven destroyers of Desron 25 under Capt Ludewig make a sortie during the night 30–31 July into Suruga Bay S of Tokyo and shell Shimizu. Then TF.38 and TF.37 (the cruiser *Argonaut* relieves *Uganda* on 27 July) withdraw to the SE to replenish (1–8 Aug).

29 July   South West Pacific
End of the Allied air mining campaign, which started on 22 Apr 1943. RAAF Catalinas have flown 1215 sorties in which 1128 aircraft have laid 2498 mines (49 different targets) along the New Guinean coasts and the Admiralties. There have also been four sorties by B-24 bombers of the US 5th AF, with 24 mines dropped. Of the total, 1933

mines were magnetic, 465 acoustic and 124 magnetic-acoustic; 11 aircraft were lost.

30 July   Indian Ocean

The midget submarines *XE-3* (Lt Fraser) and *XE-1* (Lt Smart), which are towed by the British submarines *Stygian* and *Spark* into the entrance to Singapore harbour, damage the Japanese cruiser *Takao* with fixed explosive charges so badly that she sinks to the bottom. *Myoko* is undamaged.

30 July–23 Aug   Central Pacific

Japanese losses to mines. On 30 July the destroyer *Hatsushimo* is sunk WNW of Maizuru; on 9 Aug the frigate *Ikara* is sunk in the Koguchi Channel and in the same area on 10 Aug the corvette *Kaibokan 63* is sunk; on 17 Aug the corvette *Kaibokan 46* is sunk off Mokpo in the Yellow Sea and on 23 Aug the corvette *Kaibokan 75* is lost, probably on a mine, off Hokkaido.

1–15 Aug   Pacific/Indian Ocean

In their last operations, Allied submarines achieve further successes against Japanese shipping. Off the Kuriles, *Razorback* (Lt-Cdr Brown) sinks seven trawlers and one other small craft and *Muskallunge* sinks two trawlers and, off the Tsugaru Strait, *Atule* (Cdr Maurer) sinks on 13 Aug the corvette *Kaibokan 6* and damages *Kaibokan 16*. E of Honshu, *Gato* (Lt-Cdr Farell) sinks on 3 Aug the submarine chaser *Ch-42* and *Balao* (Lt-Cdr Worthington) sinks two small craft. S of Kyushu, *Piper* sinks two small vessels and, in the Sea of Japan, *Pargo* (Lt-Cdr Bell) sinks one ship of 5455 tons, *Jallao* (Lt-Cdr Icenhower) sinks one ship of 5794 tons and *Torsk* (Lt-Cdr Llewellen) sinks one ship of 873 tons and one small vessel and on 14 Aug the corvettes *Kaibokan 47* and *Kaibokan 13*. In the Yellow Sea, *Billfish* (Lt-Cdr Farley) sinks one ship of 1081 tons and one small vessel and *Argonaut* (Lt-Cdr Schmidt) sinks one small vessel. In the East China Sea, *Spikefish* (Lt-Cdr Managhan) sinks a trawler and on 14 Aug the submarine *I-373*.

In the Gulf of Thailand, the British *Solent* sinks one patrol boat and, together with *Sleuth*, 15 junks and *Sea Scout* sinks one patrol vessel. E of Malaya, the US *Carbonero* (Cdr Murphy) sinks eight small vessels and, off Singapore, the US *Lamprey* (Cdr Nelson) sinks two small craft. In the Malacca Strait, the British *Spur* sinks 11 junks and *Statesman* sinks one coaster and five junks. W of Sumatra, the US *Ray* (Cdr Kinsella) sinks 35 small craft and, in the Bangka Strait, the US *Icefish* (Lt-Cdr Peterson) sinks one small vessel.

In the Java Sea, the British *Thorough* sinks six small craft, the US *Caiman* (Cdr Azer) sinks four sailing vessels, the British *Taci-*turn sinks two sailing vessels, the US *Bullhead* is lost off Bali in an attack by Japanese aircraft and the British *Trump* sinks two coasters.

6–9 Aug   Japan

On 6 Aug B-29 'Enola Gay' (Col Tibbets), of the 509th Composite Group (20th AF), drops the first atomic bomb on Hiroshima: 80 per cent of the city is destroyed. There are at least 92167 dead and 37425 injured among the city's population.

On 9 Aug a B-29 (Maj Sweeney) drops the second atomic bomb on Nagasaki. There are at least 40000 dead and 60000 injured among the civilian population.

7–9 Aug   Japan/Korea

In USAAF air attacks, the Japanese corvette *Kaibokan 39* is sunk on 7 Aug off Kuche and the fast transport *T-21* on 9 Aug off Tsuwajima.

8–10 Aug   North Pacific

Soviet mining operations. On 8 Aug, S of Askold Island, the minelayer *Astrakhan* and the escort vessel *Zarnitsa*, escorted by two TKAs and two MOs, and on 9 Aug the minelayer *Teodor*, lay 465 mines in the Tartar Straits. *Nette* and *Argun* and the minesweepers *T-12*, *Cheka* and *Provodnik* lay 760 mines and 160 sweep detonators. On 9 Aug, off the Vladimir-Olga base, the minesweeper *Sokol* and the escort vessel *Burun*, escorted by the submarine-chasers *BO-319*, *BO-320* and *MO-30*, lay 72 mines and again in the night 9–10 Aug 56 mines and 45 sweep detonators. On 10 Aug the minelayer *Gizhiga*, protected by two *M*-type submarines, lays 199 mines in Sakhalin Bay. A defensive minefield is also laid off Petropavlovsk with 236 mines.

9–12 Aug   Pacific

The Soviet Union declares war on Japan. The Soviet Pacific Fleet (Adm Yumashev) consists of two modern cruisers, *Kalinin* and the *Kaganovich*; one flotilla leader, *Tbilisi*; 10 modern destroyers, *Rastoropny*, *Razyashchi*, *Rezvy*, *Ryany*, *Revnostny*, *Redki*, *Rekordny*, *Rezki*, *Retivy* and *Vnushitelny*; two old destroyers, *Stalin* and *Voikov*; eight patrol ships and torpedo boats of Soviet construction and 11 US Lend-Lease frigates; 10 Soviet minelayers; eight Soviet and 18 ex-US deep-sea minesweepers; 18 ex-US coastal minesweepers; 49 submarine-chasers including 20 ex-US Type SC; 204 torpedo cutters including 45 ex-US PT boats; and 78 submarines of Soviet construction. It employs almost exclusively old and ex-US Lend-Lease ships in support of the land operations and landings.

On 9 Aug MBR-2 flying boats and Il-4 bombers attack Unegi and Najin. After dawn Yak-9 fighters and Il-2 ground attack aircraft of the 2nd Mining and Torpedo Air Div, the 10th dive-bomber Div and the 12th Ground Attack Div (Lt-Gen Lemeshko) attack the harbours again and also Chongjin. On 10 Aug the attacks are repeated. In 552 air sorties and attacks by TKAs of the 1st Torpedo Cutter Bde (Capt 2nd Class Kukht), the frigate *Yashiro*, the corvette *Kaibokan 87* and 16 merchant ships of 57325 tons are sunk or damaged.

To cover the coast of Amur Province, the submarines *L-14*, *L-17*, *Sh-122*, *Sh-123*, *Sh-102*, *Sh-104*, *Sh-126*, *Sh-127*, *Sh-134* and *Sh-135* take up positions in the Sea of Japan. *Sh-109* and *Sh-117* are stationed off W Sakhalin.

9–15 Aug   Central Pacific

After replenishing on 2–3 Aug, TF.38 moves N with the British TF.37. Passing typhoons prevent further attacks on targets in Japan for several days. After the destroyers have refuelled, TG.38.1, 38.3 and 38.4 and TF.37 make sorties against N Honshu and Hokkaido on 9 Aug. The following alterations have been made in the composition of the task groups since 1 July (see that entry): TG.38.1—the cruisers *Oklahoma City* and *Amsterdam*, the destroyer *Samuel N Moore*, the radar picket destroyer *Highbee* and the carrier *Cabot*; TG.38.3—the carrier *Wasp*, the cruisers *Tuscon* and *Flint*, the destroyers of Desron 60, the radar picket destroyers *Benner* and *Southerland*; and TG 38.4—the destroyers *Wadleigh*, *Franks* and *Twining*. TF.37 (Vice-Adm Rawlings and Vice-Adm Vian) consists of the carriers *Victorious*, *Indefatigable*, *Formidable* and *Implacable*, the battleships *Duke of York* (Adm Fraser, C-in-C British Pacific Fleet) and *King George V*, the cruisers *Achilles* (RNZN), *Gambia* (RNZN), *Newfoundland*, *Uganda* (RCN), *Black Prince* and *Euryalus*, the destroyers *Quickmatch*, *Quadrant*, *Quiberon* and *Quality* (all four RAN) and *Grenville*, *Urania*, *Undine*, *Undaunted*, *Urchin*, *Troubridge*, *Tenacious*, *Termagant*, *Ulysses*, *Teazer*, *Barfleur*, *Wrangler* and *Wakeful*.

On 9 Aug the four carrier groups make attacks on airfields and shipping targets in N Honshu and Hokkaido: 251 aircraft are destroyed. A lone Japanese aircraft damages the destroyer *Borie*. TG.34.8 (Rear-Adm Shafroth), with the battleships *Alabama*, *Indiana* and *Massachusetts*, the cruisers *Quincy*, *Boston*, *St Paul* and *Chicago* and seven US destroyers of Desron 48, together with a British group comprising the cruisers *Gambia* and *Newfoundland* and the destroyers *Terpsichore*, *Termagant* and *Tenacious*, shells Kamaishi on Honshu. Aircraft from the battleships *South Dakota* and *Indiana* serve as artillery spotters.

On 10 Aug there is another carrier raid on shipping targets, airfields and railways in N Honshu. On 9–10 Aug the frigates *Amakusa* and *Inagi*, the escort *Ohama* the minesweepers *Sokaitei W1* and *Sokaitei W33* and nine ships of 6425 tons are sunk and the minelayer *Tokiwa* and the escort destoyer *Yanagi* are badly damaged, as are five ships of 14178 tons.

On 11 and 12 Aug the ships are replenished by TG.30.8 (Rear-Adm Beary). The British TF.37 returns with most of its ships to Manus. *Indefatigable*, *King George V*, *Gambia*, *Newfoundland* and the destroyers *Barfleur*, *Napier* (RAN), *Nizam* (RAN), *Wakeful*, *Wrangler*, *Troubridge*, *Termagant*, *Tenacious* and *Teazer* form TG.38.5.

On 13 Aug the five groups make new attacks on the Tokyo area: 254 Japanese aircraft are destroyed on the ground and the fighter cover shoots down a further 18.

On 14 Aug the destroyers are refuelled. Early on 15 Aug a new wave of attacks from the carriers begins on Tokyo before orders from the C-in-C Pacific, Adm of the Fleet Nimitz, are received to stop hostilities. Fierce air engagements develop because the order does not reach all the attacking formations in the air. The last Japanese kamikaze pilots, including the Cdr of the 5th Air Fleet, Vice-Adm Ugaki†, fly off from Tokyo.

10–18 Aug Korea

In Soviet air attacks on 10 Aug, the Japanese corvette *Kaibokan 82* is sunk SSW of Kumsudan, NE Korea, on 15 Aug the frigate *Kanju* is sunk off Wonsan and on 18 Aug the corvette *Kaibokan 213* is sunk off Pusan.

11–12 Aug North Pacific

The US TF.92 (Rear-Adm Brown), comprising the cruisers *Richmond* and *Concord* and 12 destroyers, shells Japanese installations in the Kuriles.

12–21 Aug Pacific

Soviet landing operations on the east coast of Korea in support of the advance by the 25th Army. On 12 Aug a force (Rear-Adm Ivanovski) comprising the frigates *EK-7* and *EK-9*, the minesweeper *T-271*, two patrol boats and eight torpedo cutters, including *TKA-567* and *TKA-578*, lands 879 men of the reiforced 75th Naval Inf Bn in Unggi (Yuki) in NE Korea, which has, in the meantime, been evacuated by the Japanese and reached shortly before by the Soviet 303rd Rifle Div by the land route. On the same day, patrol and torpedo cutters land an advance party of 163 men in Najin (Rashin), which remains in the harbour area until the arrival of the landing force (Capt

1st Class Poltavski) with the reinforced 358th Naval Inf Bn (617 men) and it is possible on 15 Aug to establish contact with the forward troops of the 25th Army. Taking part are the headquarters ship, flotilla leader *Tbilisi*, out at sea, the landing force, comprising the frigate *EK-5*, the minesweepers *T-279* and *T-281*, the patrol boats *BO-303*, *BO-305*, *MO-8*, *MO-16*, four coastal patrol boats and two torpedo cutters. On 14–15 Aug *T-279*, one TKA, the transports *Suchan*, *Kamchatneft* and the tanker *No 1* are lost or badly damaged on air mines laid beforehand by US Army aircraft.

On 13 Aug the frigate *EK-2* and the minesweeper *T-278* land an advance party of 260 men near Chongjin (Seishin) which is only able to hold out with difficulty and with losses, as a result of Japanese counterattacks, until the landing force (Adm Yumashev) arrives on 15 Aug. This force consists of the old destroyer *Voikov*, the frigates *EK-1*, *EK-3*, *EK-8*, *EK-9*, *EK-7*, the minesweepers *T-275*, *T-280*, *T-272*, *T-273*, *T-274*, *T-276*, 18 torpedo cutters, the patrol ships *Metel*, *Vyuga*, the patrol cutters *BO-304*, *BO-306*, *BO-307*, *BO-317*, two MO cutters, the LCI landing boats *DS-31*, *DS-32*, *DS-33*, *DS-38*, *DS-39*, *DS-40*, *DS-41*, *DS-42*, *DS-44*, *DS-45*, the LCT *TDS-01* and seven transports and 5000 men of the 13th Naval Inf Bde embarked on them. On 16 Aug the transports *Nogin*, *Navastroy* and *Dalstroy* run on to mines, On 19 Aug the reinforced 77th Naval Inf Bn with 650 men is landed near Cape Odaejin (Odentsin) by a force (Capt 1st Class Studenichnikov) comprising the patrol ship *Metel* and six TKAs.

On 21 Aug a force (Rear-Adm Frolov) consisting of the destroyer *Voikov*, the frigate *EK-3*, the minesweepers *T-277*, *T-282* and six TKAs lands a battle group of 2000 men in Wonsan, whose garrison offers no resistance and surrenders on 22 Aug.

16–25 Aug Pacific

The Soviet North Pacific Flotilla (Vice-Adm Andreev), which comprises nine submarines, one patrol ship, six (and later six more) minesweepers and 24 torpedo cutters, carries out landings on S Sakhalin.

On 16 Aug a force consisting of the patrol ship *Zarnitsa*, the minelayer *Okean*, the patrol cutters *MO-27*, *MO-29*, *MO-33*, *MO-34*, 14 torpedo cutters, the minesweepers *T-522*, *T-524*, *T-590*, *T-591*, two lighters, the patrol cutters *BO-310*, *BO-314* and five more torpedo cutters lands 1554 men of a naval landing unit against slight resistance near Toro behind the 88th Japanese Div.

On 20 Aug a force under Capt 1st Class Leonov, comprising *Zarnitsa*, *Okean*, the patrol-cutters *BO-302*, *BO-314*, *MO-25*, *MO-31*, *MO-32*, *MO-35*, *MO-63*, the minesweepers *T-588*, *T-593*, *T-591*, *T-522*, three transports and two auxiliary ships, as well as the *TKA-631*, *TKA-641*, *TKA-645*, *TKA-646* and the submarine *Shch-118*, lands the 113th Rifle Bde near Maoka.

On 25 Aug *Okean*, *T-522*, *T-524*, *T-599*, *T-600*, *T-601*, *T-602*, *T-603*, *T-604*, four BO patrol cutters and six TKAs, coming from Maoka, put a landing party ashore in Chonto and Otomari.

17 Aug South Atlantic

The German U-boat *U977* enters Mar del Plata, Argentina, after its voyage from Norway.

18–25 Aug North Pacific

Forces of the Naval Defence Sector Petropavlovsk (Capt 1st Class Ponomarev) carry out landings on the northern Kurile Islands. On 18 Aug a force consisting of the minelayer *Okhotsk*, the patrol ships *Kirov* and *Dzerzhinski*, nine MO patrol cutters, the minesweepers *Vekha*, *T-155*, *T-156*, *T-525*, the motor minesweepers *T-334* and one other, the survey ships *Polyarny* and *Lebed*, 14 transports and 15 landing vessels lands two rifle regiments and a reinforced artillery regiment on Shimushu, the most northerly of the Kurile Islands. After strong initial resistance by the elements of the Japanese 91st Div stationed on Shimushu, the Japanese capitulate on 19 and 20 Aug. In the operations *T-152* is lost.

On 23 Aug Soviet units, without encountering resistance, are landed on Paramushiro and on 25 Aug on Onekotan, Harumukotan and Sjasikotan.

19–27 Aug North Pacific

The Soviet submarines *L-12* (Lt-Cdr Shelgantsev) and *L-19* (Capt 3rd Class Kononenko) operate in the Sea of Japan and attack Japanese transports. On 22 Aug each claim one sinking. *L-19* is then lost, to an unknown cause.

19 Aug–20 Sept China

Japanese surrender in China. On 19 Aug the Chinese Generalissimo Chiang Kai-shek orders all Red Chinese troops to remain in their positions in North China and the Japanese Expeditionary Army to surrender only to the Nationalist troops. On the instructions of Mao Tse-tung the order is ignored by the Red Chinese troops. After the evacuation of Kalgan (NW of Peking) by the Japanese, Red Chinese troops occupy the city on 20 Aug. On 24 Aug troops of the Red Chinese 18th Army Group (Gen Chu-Teh) occupy the harbours of Chefoo and Wei Hai Wei. Then the Japanese troops are ordered to remain in their positions until the arrival of the Nationalist Chinese troops and to defend themselves against Red Chinese attacks.

On 25 Aug the new Nationalist Chinese 6th Army occupies Nanking and there on 9 Sept the Cdr of the Japanese China Area Army, Gen Okamura, signs the capitulation of Japanese forces in China in the presence of representatives of Chiang Kai-shek.

On 10 Sept the Nationalist Chinese 94th Army occupies Shanghai and the US TF.95 and a British carrier group (see 27 Aug–16 Sept) operate off the Yangtse estuary. A few days later the Nationalist Chinese 3rd Army reaches Hankow.

On 9 Sept the Nationalist Chinese General Li establishes an advance headquarters for Marshal Chiang Kai-shek in Peking, which is held by Japanese troops and where on 17 Sept the first Nationalist Chinese units arrive by air in US transport aircraft.

On 24 Sept Chiang Kai-shek requests the USA to land troops in Shanghai, Nanking, Peking and Tientsin. On 21 Sept US and British warships (see above) arrive in Shanghai.

22 Aug   Central Pacific

The garrison of the Atoll Mili (Marshall Islands) is the first Japanese garrison in the Pacific to capitulate: it does so on board the DE *Levy*.

25–31 Aug   Japan

From 25 Aug carrier aircraft of TF.38 carry out daily patrol flights over Japan to control shipping, rail and road movements and to locate prisoner-of-war camps. On 28 Aug the first advance parties land to secure Atsugi airfield near Tokyo. On 30 Aug the airborne landing of the 11th US Airborne Div (Maj-Gen Swing) begins at Atsugi. The 187th Parachute RCT occupies and secures the airport and the 188th Parachute RCT the harbour of Yokohama. On 31 Aug the 511th Airborne RCT follows. In the afternoon of 30 Aug the Commander of the US 8th Army, Lt-Gen Eichelberger, and the Supreme Allied Commander, Gen of the Army Douglas MacArthur, land at Atsugi. On 29–30 Aug the 4th RCT of the 6th Marine Div lands in Yokosuka, whose naval base is surrendered to the US 3rd Fleet on board the cruiser *San Diego*.

26 Aug–3 Sept   North Pacific

Soviet units occupy the Kurile Islands. On 26 Aug units land on Matsuwa, on 27 Aug on Shinshiru and on 28 Aug on Urup and Etorofu. From 1 to 3 Sept units of the North Pacific Fleet occupy the southern Kurile islands of Kunajiri, Shikotan and Taraku.

27 Aug   South West Pacific

The Japanese forces on Morotai and Halmahera under Lt-Gen Ishii surrender to the US 93rd Inf Div.

27 Aug   Japan

The 3rd US Fleet (Adm Halsey) arrives in Sagami Bay. Taking part is TF.38 (Vice-Adm McCain), comprising:

TF.38.1 (Rear-Adm T L Sprague), with the carriers *Bennington*, *Lexington*, *Hancock* and *Belleau Wood*, the battleships *Alabama* and *Indiana*, the cruisers *Topeka*, *Duluth*, *Atlanta*, *Dayton* and *San Juan*, the destroyers (Desron 61) *De Haven*, *Mansfield*, *Lyman K Swenson*, *Collett*, *Maddox*, *Blue*, *Brush*, *Taussig* and *Samuel N Moore* and (Desron 48) *Erben*, *Hale*, *Black*, *Bullard*, *Chauncey* and *Heerman* and the radar picket destroyers *Highbee*, *Perkins* and *Frank Knox*.

TG.38.2 (Rear-Adm Ballentine), with the carriers *Randolph*, *Intrepid*, *Antietam* and *Cabot*, the battleship *Wisconsin*, the cruisers *Oklahoma City*, *Amsterdam*, *Mobile*, *Vicksburgh* and *Tucson*, the destroyers (Desron 60) *Walke*, *O'Brien*, *Lowry*, *Allen M Sumner*, *Moale*, *Robert K Huntington* and *Bristol* and (Desron 57) *Rowe*, *Smalley*, *Stoddard*, *Watts*, *Wren*, *Wadleigh*, *Norman Scott*, *Franks* and *Barton* and the radar picket destroyers *Rogers* and *Duncan*.

TG.38.3 (Rear-Adm C A F Sprague), with the carriers *Ticonderoga*, *Wasp*, *Monterey* and *Bataan*, the battleships *South Dakota* and *North Carolina*, the cruisers *Pasadena*, *Springfield*, *Wilkes-Barre* and *Oakland*, the destroyers (Desron 62) *English*, *Charles S Sperry*, *Ault*, *Waldron*, *John W Weeks*, *Hank*, *Wallace L Lind* and *Borie* and (Desron 25) *John Rodgers*, *Harrison*, *McKee*, *Murray*, *Kimberly*, *Ringgold*, *Schroeder* and *Dashiell* and the radar picket destroyers *Benner* and *Southerland*.

TG.38.4 (Rear-Adm Radford), with the carriers *Yorktown*, *Shangri-La*, *Bon Homme Richard*, *Independence* and *Cowpens*, the battleships *Iowa* and *Missouri*, the cruisers *Quincy*, *Boston*, *St Paul*, *Chicago*, *San Diego* and *Flint*, the destroyers (Desron 50) *Clarence K Bronson*, *Cotten*, *Dortch*, *Gatling*, *Healy*, *Cogswell*, *Caperton*, *Ingersoll* and *Knapp* and (Desron 53) *Cushing*, *Colahan*, *Halsey*, *Powell*, *Uhlmann*, *Benham*, *Yarnall*, *Twining*, *Stockham* and *Wedderburn* and the radar picket destroyers *Chevalier*, *Myles C Fox* and *Hawkins*.

The British TG.38.5 (Vice-Adm Rawlings), with the carrier *Indefatigable*, the battleships *Duke of York* (Adm Fraser) and *King George V*, the cruisers *Newfoundland* and *Gambia* (RNZN) and the destroyers *Barfleur*, *Teazer*, *Tenacious*, *Termagant*, *Terpsichore*, *Napier* (RAN) and *Nizam* (RAN).

The Commonwealth ships are joined on 31 Aug by the Australian TG.70.9, coming from Leyte and comprising the cruisers *Shropshire* and *Hobart* and the destroyers *Bataan* and *Warramunga* as well as the minesweepers *Ipswich*, *Ballarat* and *Cessnock*.

In addition, US TG.32.9 is present, with the old battleships *New Mexico*, *Mississippi*, *Idaho*, *Colorado* and *West Virginia* and the destroyers (Desron 21) *Nicholas*, *O'Bannon*, *Taylor*, *Terry*, *Ross* and *Hopewell*. The supply fleet is TG.30.8, comprising the cruiser *Detroit*, the escort carriers *Thetis Bay*, *Hollandia*, *Roi*, *Munda* and *Gilbert Islands*, the destroyers *Wilkes*, *Nicholson*, *Woodworth*, *Buchanan*, *Lansdowne*, *Lardner*, *Gillespie*, *Kalk*, *Stevenson*, *Stockton* and *Thorn* and the DEs *Griswold*, *Carlson*, *Reynolds*, *Mitchell*, *Donaldson*, *William C Miller*, *Cabana*, *Dionne*, *Canfield*, *Deede*, *Elden*, *Lake*, *Lyman*, *Crowley*, *Le Ray Wilson*, *Joseph E Connolly*, *Willmarth*, *Bangust*, *Waterman*, *Weaver*, *Hilbert*, *Lamons*, *Kyne* and *McClelland*.

Of the Pacific submarines, *Archerfish*, *Cavalla*, *Gato*, *Haddo*, *Hake*, *Muskallunge*, *Pilotfish*, *Razorback*, *Runner*, *Segundo*, *Seacat* and *Tigrone* arrive with the depot ship *Proteus*. There also take part a large number of minesweeping vessels and supply ships. The Japanese destroyer *Hatsuzakura* brings Japanese representatives to *Missouri*, where they receive instructions for the surrender ceremony. Pilots bring the ships to their anchorages. On 29 Aug the C-in-C Pacific, Fleet Adm Nimitz, arrives and embarks on the battleship *South Dakota*.

27 Aug–12 Sept   Indian Ocean

On 27 Aug a British task group (Vice-Adm Walker) comprising the battleship *Nelson*, the cruiser *Ceylon*, the escort carriers *Hunter* and *Attacker*, three destroyers and two LSIs sets out from Rangoon for Penang where it arrives on 28 Aug. Commodore Poland with the cruiser *London* and a destroyer anchors off Sabang. Japanese delegations bring documents concerning mine barrages and give assurances of their peaceful intentions. On 29 Aug the C-in-C East Indies Fleet, Adm Power, arrives with the cruiser *Cleopatra* off Sabang and on 1 Sept off Penang. On 31 Aug Vice-Adm Hirose surrenders on behalf of the forces on Sumatra on board *London* and on 2 Sept Vice-Adm Uzumi for the Penang area on board *Nelson*. After minesweepers have cleared the approaches, marines are landed on 2 and 3 Sept in Sabang and on the island of Penang. Spitfire fighters are flown into Penang.

The 6th, 7th and 37th MS Flotillas clear the Straits of Malacca. On 2 Sept Adm Power goes with *Cleopatra* and the Indian sloop *Bengal*, behind the 6th MS Flotilla, to Singapore where he arrives on 2 Sept. On 4 Sept the cruiser *Sussex* follows with the 7th MS Flotilla, one destroyer and a convoy with the headquarters ship *Kedah* from Bombay with the 5th Indian Div, XV Corps HQ and the British 3rd Commando Bde on board. After Lt-Gen Itagaki and Vice-Adm Fukudome have surrendered on board *Sussex* on behalf of the Japanese forces in the Singapore and Johore area on 4 Sept, British-Indian forces land. The 3rd Commando Bde remains embarked and proceeds to Hong Kong (see below). On 9 Sept the planned Operation 'Zipper' begins with the landing of the 25th Indian Div (Maj-Gen Wood) near Morib, 18 nautical miles S of Port Swettenham and the 23rd Indian Div (Maj-Gen Hawthorn) near Sepang, 8 nautical miles N of Port Dickson. Over 100000 troops are landed in three days. The covering force comprises the battleships *Nelson* and *Richelieu*, the cruisers *Nigeria*, *Ceylon*, and *Cleopatra*, 15 destroyers and the 21st Carrier Sqn consisting of the cruiser *Royalist*, the escort carriers *Hunter*, *Stalker*, *Archer*, *Khedive*, *Emperor* and *Pursuer* and, as a Spitfire transport, the *Trumpeter*.

On 12 Sept Lt-Gen Itagaki and Vice-Adm Fukudome, representing the indisposed Japanese C-in-C South East Asia, Field-Marshal Terauchi, sign the surrender of all Japanese forces in South-East Asia in the presence of the Allied C-in-C South East Asia, Adm Lord Mountbatten.

27 Aug–16 Sept South China Sea

On 27 Aug the British TG.111.2 (Rear-Adm Harcourt) sets out from Subic Bay to occupy Hong Kong. The force consists of the carriers *Indomitable* and *Venerable*, the cruisers *Swiftsure*, *Euryalus* and *Black Prince*, the destroyers *Kempenfelt*, *Ursa*, *Quadrant* and *Whirlwind*, the Canadian auxiliary cruiser *Prince Robert*, the 8th SM Flotilla with the depot ship *Maidstone* and eight submarines and the Australian minesweepers *Mildura*, *Castlemaine*, *Bathurst*, *Broome*, *Fremantle*, *Strahan* and *Wagga*. On 29 Aug it meets there a task group (Rear-Adm Daniel) originally earmarked for Singapore and consisting of the battleship *Anson* and the carrier *Vengeance* and two destroyers. On 29 Aug the minesweepers begin the clearance work. On 30 Aug *Kempenfelt*, *Swiftsure* (with Rear-Adm Harcourt), *Ursa*, *Euryalus*, *Prince Robert*, *Mildura* and *Bathurst* come in. As they do so, three Japanese explosive boats are seen to be setting out from the small battle unit base. Aircraft of the *Indomitable* and *Venerable* then attack the anchorage in Lamma Bay and destroy the boats.

On 11 Sept the convoy with the 3rd Commando Bde and the escort carrier *Smiter* with an RAF contingent on board arrive from Singapore. On 14 Sept the C-in-C British Pacific Fleet, Adm Fraser, arrives with the battleship *Duke of York*. On 16 Sept the Japanese Maj-Gen Okada and Vice-Adm Fujita surrender on behalf of the Japanese forces in the Hong Kong area in the presence of Rear-Adm Harcourt.

On 27 Aug a British task group (Rear-Adm Servaes) is formed from the carrier *Colossus*, the cruisers *Bermuda* and *Argonaut* and the destroyers *Tyrian*, *Tumult*, *Tuscan* and *Quiberon*, in order to occupy the Shanghai area with elements from US TF.95 (see above).

28 Aug–1 Oct Japan

Mine clearance in Japanese waters. Under the orders of the Cdr Minesweeping Craft Pacific, Rear-Adm Struble, minesweeping forces begin on 28 Aug with the work of clearing the important sea lanes for the occupation of Japan.

From 28 Aug to 4 Sept 23 DMSs and AMs clear the approaches and anchorages of Yokohama, Yokosuka and Tokyo Bay. Seventy-four Japanese and three US mines are cleared. The same force then clears Japanese barrages off Sendai and Chosi (Hondo).

From 1 to 8 Sept a minesweeping force clears the approaches to Kagoshima (Kyushu), then on 9 Sept those to Sasebo and on 10 Sept those to Nagasaki. The force loses five YMSs in the typhoon 'Louisa' on 16 Sept. On 8 Sept US minesweepers begin clearance work in the Tsugaru Strait.

On 11 Sept 27 minesweepers begin to clear a passage through the Kii Channel to the Inland Sea and the entrances to Kobe and Osaka. In the course of the work, some Japanese minesweepers are also used for the first time.

From 22 Sept 32 US and 33 Japanese minesweepers begin to create a passage through the Bungo Channel to Kure and Hiroshima. For the first time mine destructor ships are used against pressure mines, including *LST 553*, *LST 768* and three US and four Japanese transports, as well as two old Japanese destroyers which are lost.

From 28 Sept a passage is cleared through the Ise Channel to Nagoya.

30 Aug Central Pacific

Surrender of the Japanese garrison of Marcus Island on board the destroyer *Bagley*.

30 Aug North Pacific

The US TF.92 (Rear-Adm Brown), comprising the cruisers *Richmond* and *Concord*, the headquarters ship *Panamint*, the destroyers *Bearss*, *John Hood*, *Jarvis*, *And-*

erson, *Hughes*, *Porter* and *Izard* and the DEs *Sellstrom*, *Ramsden*, *Mills*, *Rhodes*, *Richey* and *Savage*, and the escort carrier group (Rear-Adm Martin) comprising *Hoggatt Bay*, *Kitkun Bay*, *Nehenta Bay*, *Fanshaw Bay*, *Manila Bay* and *Savo Island* and the destroyers *Guest*, *Hudson*, *Halford*, *Fullam*, *Stanly*, *Wainwright*, *Bennion*, *Killen* and *Albert W Grant*, arrives off Ominato (northern tip of Honshu) and accepts the surrender of the Japanese bases.

2 Sept Japan

Signing of the overall Japanese surrender on board the American battleship *Missouri* in Sagami Bay. The Foreign Minister Shigemitsu and the Chief of the Army General Staff, Gen Umezu, sign for Japan. Gen MacArthur accepts the surrender on behalf of the Allies. Fleet Admiral Nimitz signs for the USA, Gen Hsu Yung-chang for China, Adm Sir Bruce Fraser for Great Britain, Lt-Gen Derevyanko for the Soviet Union, Gen Sir Thomas Blamey for Australia, Col Moore-Cosgrove for Canada, Gen Leclerc for France, Adm Helferich for Holland and Air Vice Marshal Isitt for New Zealand.

2 Sept–1 Oct Central Pacific

On 2 Sept the US Commandant of Peleliu, Brig-Gen Rogers, accepts the surrender of the Japanese forces on Pagan (Palau Islands) under Lt-Gen Inoue. On the same day the garrison of the Mariana island of Rota surrenders. On 3 Sept the Japanese C-in-C on the Philippines, Gen Yamashita, accompanied by Vice-Adm Okochi, signs in Baguio the surrender of the Japanese forces on the Philippines in the presence of the Cdr of the US Army Force West Pacific (Gen Styler) and the Cdr of the 32nd Div (Maj-Gen Gill).

On board *Portland*, Vice-Adm Murray accepts the surrender of the Japanese island fortress of Truk and the islands in the area of the Central Carolines. On board the destroyer *Dunlap* off Chichijima, Commodore Magruder accepts the surrender of the Bonin Islands by Lt-Gen Tachibana. Brig-Gen Sanderson, on board the DE *Levy*, accepts the surrender of the island garrison of Wake.

On 4 Sept the islands of Jaluit (Carolines) and Aguijan (Marianas) surrender and on 5 Sept those of Yap and Ulithi; on 7 Sept the Kusaie island group (Carolines) is surrendered and on Okinawa the commander of the 10th US Army, Gen Stilwell, accepts the surrender of the remaining forces on the Ryukyu Islands; on 9 Sept the island of Formosa is surrendered; and on 10 Sept the Marshall Islands of Wotje and Maloelap, and on 11 Sept Ponape, are surrendered. On 14 Sept Brig-Gen Stevenson on board the

Australian frigate *Diamantine* accepts the surrender of the garrison of Nauru (Capt Saeda) and on 1 Oct the surrender of Ocean Island (Cdr Suzuki). On 19 Sept the last major garrison, that of Woleai (Carolines), surrenders.

2 Sept–22 Oct Japan

Operation 'Blacklist': the occupation of Japan. The occupation is carried out in the area to the N of, and inclusive of, Tokyo by the 3rd Amphibious Force (Vice-Adm Wilkinson with the headquarters ship *Mount Olympus*) and the US 8th Army (Lt-Gen Eichelberger) and, to the S, by the 5th Amphibious Force (Vice-Adm Hill with the headquarters ship *Auburn*) and the US 6th Army (Gen Krueger).

In the area of the 8th Army, XI Corps (Lt-Gen Hall) occupies the Tokyo area, XIV Corps (Maj-Gen Griswold) the area of N Honshu (with the exception of Ominato) and IX Corps (Maj-Gen Ryder) the area of the Tsugaru Strait and Hokkaido. In XI Corps's zone, TF.33 lands on 2 Sept the 1st Cavalry Div (Maj-Gen Chase) in Yokohama and on 3 Sept the 112th Cav RCT is landed in Tateyama to secure Tokyo Bay. On 5 Sept the first reconnaissance of Tokyo is made and on 8 Sept the 1st Cav Div marches in. The flags are raised in the presence of Gen MacArthur, the Allied Supreme Commander in Japan. After the completion of the airlift of the 11th Airborne Div (Maj-Gen Swing) on 6 Sept, the 27th Inf Div (Maj-Gen Griner) is flown to Atsugi from Okinawa from 7 to 14 Sept. From 8 to 10 Sept TF.35 lands the Americal Div in Yokohama. On 14 Sept the 43rd Inf Div (Maj-Gen Wing) follows but is withdrawn to return to the USA on 27 Sept.

XIV Corps begins the occupation of N Honshu in Sendai on 15 Sept. It is allocated the 11th Airborne Div which comes to Sendai by land and the 27th Inf Div which comes to Niigata. As relief, the 97th Inf Div (Maj-Gen Kramer) arrives in the Tokyo area on 20 Sept.

In the IX Corps zone on 6 Sept the North Pacific Force (Vice-Adm Fletcher, relieved by Rear-Adm Denebrinck in the middle of Sept) lands advance detachments of the Marine Corps in Ominato (northern tip of Honshu). On 8 Sept minesweeping forces begin clearing the Tsugaru Strait. From 25 to 27 Sept an Amphibious Group lands the 81st Inf Div (Maj-Gen Mueller) in Aomori in the Tsushima Strait and on 4 Oct the 306th RCT is landed in Otaru on Hokkaido. The bulk of 77th Inf Div (Maj-Gen Bruce) follows on 15 Oct to Otaru and from there to Sapporo. From 7 Oct IX Corps establishes its HQ in Sapporo.

In the area of the 6th Army, V Amphibious Corps (Lt-Gen H Schmidt) occupies Kyushu, X Corps (Maj-Gen Siebert) Shikoku and S Honshu and I Corps (Maj-Gen Swift) Honshu from the Kii Channel as far as the line Shizuoka–Takaoka.

In the zone of V Amphibious Corps, the 127th RCT of the 32nd Inf Div (Maj-Gen Gill) is brought by air on 4 Sept to Kanoya (southern tip of Kyushu). Amphibious Group 4 (Rear-Adm Reifsnider) lands the 5th Marine Div (Maj-Gen Bourke) in Sasebo on 22 Oct. On 22 Sept the 2nd Marine Div (Maj-Gen Hunt) follows to Nagasaki. On 15 Oct the rest of the 32nd Inf Div is landed in Shimonoseki and proceeds to Saga in central Kyushu. The operations are covered by a group under Rear-Adm Deyo.

In the zone of I Corps, Amphibious Group 8 (Rear-Adm Noble) lands the 33rd Inf Div (Maj-Gen Clarkson) in Kobe on 25 Sept, the 98th Inf Div (Maj-Gen Harper) in Wakayama on 27 Sept and the 25th Inf Div (Maj-Gen Mullins) in Nagoya on 2 Oct. The HQ of 6th Army is established in Kyoto and that of I Corps in Osaka.

In the zone of X Corps (HQ Kure) the 24th Inf Div (Maj-Gen Woodruff) is landed by an amphibious group (Commodore Ryan) in Matsuyama (Shikoku) on 7 Oct and the 41st Inf Div (Maj-Gen Doe) by Amphibious Group 11 (Rear-Adm Rogers) in Kure on 22 Sept.

5 Sept–17 Oct Korea

The occupation of Korea is carried out by the US 7th Fleet (Adm Kinkaid) and XXIV Corps (Lt-Gen Hodge). On 5 Sept an amphibious group (Commodore Brittain) comprising 18 APAs, one AKA, several APDs, a minesweeping group and a covering group sets out from Okinawa with the US 7th Inf Div (Maj-Gen Arnold). In overall command is the 7th Amphibious Force (Vice-Adm Barbey on the headquarters ship *Catoctin*). On 8 Sept there is a landing at Inchon and from there the capital, Seoul, is occupied after moving by land.

On 9 Sept the Japanese Governor-General Abe, the Cdr of the 17th Area Army, Lt-Gen Kotsuki, and Vice-Adm Yamaguchi sign in the governmental palace in Seoul, and in the presence of Gen Hodge and Adm Kinkaid, the surrender of the Japanese forces in Korea S of the 38th Parallel. The plan to bring a BLT on 20 Sept by sea to Pusan cannot be carried out because of the mining of the harbour. On 22 Sept an amphibious group (Commodore Palmer) lands the 40th Inf Div (Brig-Gen Meyers) at Inchon and on 23 Sept a BLT of this Div is brought by land to Pusan. On 17 Oct the

6th Inf Div (Maj-Gen Hurdis) follows to Inchon with the same amphibious group (Commodore Palmer).

Air escort for this operation and that of VII Amphibious Force off northern China (see 26 Sept–31 Oct) is provided by TF.72, comprising the carriers *Antietam*, *Intrepid* (relieved by *Boxer* from 11 Oct) and *Cabot*, cruisers and destroyers.

6–13 Sept South West Pacific

Acts of surrender in the area of the Bismarck Archipelago and New Guinea. On 6 Sept a British force comprising the carrier *Glory*, the Australian destroyer *Vendetta*, the sloops *Hart* and *Amethyst* and the Australian minesweeper corvettes *Kiama*, *Dubbo*, *Lithgow*, *Townsville*, tug *Reserve* and two MLs arrives off Rabaul. On board *Glory* the Cdr of the Japanese 8th Area Army, Gen Imamura, and the Cdr of the South East Area Fleet, Vice-Adm Kusaka, sign in the presence of the Cdr of the Australian 1st Army, Lt-Gen Sturdee, the surrender of the Japanese forces in the area of the Bismarck Islands, New Guinea and the Solomons (a total of 139000 men). On 8 Sept the Cdr of the Japanese 17th Army, Lt-Gen Kanda, and Vice-Adm Samejima sign on board the Australian frigate *Diamantine* off Cape Torokina the surrender of the forces on Bougainville. On 10 Sept, on board *ML 805*, the Japanese Rear-Adm Sato signs, in the presence of the Cdr of the Australian 6th Div, Maj-Gen Robertson, the surrender of the Wewak offshore islands. On 13 Sept the surrender of the Japanese 18th Army is signed by Lt-Gen Adachi in the presence of Gen Robertson on the airfield of Wom near Wewak. On 19 Sept Lt-Gen Ito and Rear-Adm Tamura surrender the forces on New Ireland in the presence of Maj-Gen Eather on board the Australian sloop *Swan* in Nabuto Bay.

6–9 Sept Central Pacific/Japan

US troops begin to return to the USA. On 6 Sept TF.11 (Vice-Adm Sherman), comprising the battleships *New Mexico*, *Idaho*, *Mississippi* and *North Carolina*, the carriers *Monterey* and *Bataan* and a Desron, sets out from Tokyo for the USA via Okinawa with 'high priority returns'. On 9 Sept Operation 'Magic Carpet' begins with the formations of TF.16.12 (Rear-Adm Kendall), consisting initially of eight escort carriers. The force expands to 369 warships by Dec, including six battleships, 18 cruisers, 11 fleet carriers, 46 escort carriers and 12 hospital ships. In some cases they make several trips. By Mar 1946 1307859 personnel are brought back. The highest single quota is taken by the carrier *Saratoga*, with 29204. In the same period transports carry 1815535 personnel.

8–21 Sept   Dutch East Indies

Acts of surrender by the Japanese forces in the area of Eastern Indonesia. On 8 Sept the Japanese Vice-Adm Kamada signs on board the Australian frigate *Burdekin*, in the presence of the Cdr 7th Australian Div, Maj-Gen Milford, the surrender of the Japanese forces in the area of Balikpapan. On 9 Sept the Japanese Maj-Gen Yamamura signs on board the Australian minesweeper *Kapunda*, in the presence of Brig-Gen Eastick, the surrender of the Japanese forces in the area of Kuching (Brunei) in northwest Borneo. On the same day the Cdr of the Japanese 2nd Army, Lt-Gen Teshima, signs in Morotai, in the presence of the Cdr of the Australian Army, Gen Blamey, the surrender of the Japanese forces in the Dutch East Indies. On 10 Sept the Australian minesweeper *Glenelg* arrives with three ships off Ambon and the minesweeper *Latrobe* off Ceram. On 14 Sept Menado (Celebes) is surrendered to the minesweeper *Glenelg*. On 15 Sept the Australian frigates *Burdekin* and *Gascoyne* arrive in Bandjermasin. On 21 Sept the Australian frigate *Barcoo* is the first to occupy Makassar (Celebes) with four ships.

9–10 Sept   Central Pacific

On 9–10 Sept typhoon 'Louisa', whose centre passes 15 nautical miles E of Okinawa and which brings wind speeds of 100kt and, in gusts, up to 120kt, causes great damage to US ships off Okinawa. Twelve ships sink, 222 ships and craft are driven aground and 32 more are damaged. By 19 Nov 79 units are salvaged and made seaworthy, 132 are in the course of being repaired and 53 are abandoned as unserviceable.

11 Sept–3 Oct   Indonesia

On 11 Sept the Australian survey ship *Moresby* arrives off Koepang (Timor) with the minesweepers *Horsham*, *Benalla*, *Parkes*, *Katoomba*, *Warrnambool* and *Gladstone* and the Dutch minesweeper *Abraham Crijnssen*: it is surrendered by the Japanese Col Kaida to Brig-Gen Dyke.

On 27 Sept the Portuguese sloops *Bartolomeo Dias* and *Gonçalves Zarco* and, two days later, the transport *Angola*, arrive in Dili to re-occupy the Portuguese part of the island.

On 3 Oct the commander of the Japanese 48th Div, Lt-Gen Yamada, surrenders all Japanese forces on Timor in the presence of Brig-Gen Dyke.

15 Sept–1 Nov   Indonesia

On 15 Sept the British cruiser *Cumberland* (Rear-Adm Patterson) arrives off Jakarta with one frigate and four Australian minesweepers. On 16 Sept there follow another frigate, two minesweepers and four landing craft and the Dutch cruiser *Tromp*. Because of disturbances on shore between Indonesian Nationalists and the Japanese, a British battalion is not landed in Batavia before 29 Sept. On 3 Oct a Brigade Group is landed. On 6 Oct advance detachments of the 23rd Indian Div and the HQ of XV Corps arrive and on 10 Oct the 23rd Div.

On 10 Oct elements of the 26th Indian Div land on Sumatra. On 19 Oct the troop transport *Glenroy* brings a BLT to Semarang to crush an uprising. On 25 Oct the transport *Waveney* lands the 49th Indian Bde in Soerabaya. On 1 Nov the Indian 5th Div follows with a convoy under the command of the headquarters ship *Bulolo*. A covering force is provided by the British cruiser *Sussex* with the destroyers *Caesar*, *Carron* and *Cavalier*.

26 Sept   Indian Ocean

The Indian sloop *Narbada* arrives in Port Blair (Andamans) and accepts the surrender of the local Japanese garrison under Vice-Adm Hara.

26 Sept–31 Oct   China

The US VII Amphibious Force (Vice-Adm Barbey) receives orders to land the III Amphibious Corps (Maj-Gen Rockey) in the area Tientsin/Chinwangtao and on the Shantung peninsula.

On 26 Sept an amphibious force (Commodore Brittain) sets out from Okinawa with the 1st Marine Div (Maj-Gen Peck). On 30 Sept the troops are disembarked in the Peiho Estuary: a BLT occupies the Taku forts and the remainder are transported by LCI, LCM and LCT to Tientsin. The 1st RCT and the 11th RCT remain there; the 5th RCT goes to Peking and a BLT of the 7th RCT goes later to Chinwangtao. On 6 Oct the approximately 50000 Japanese troops in this area under Gen Uchida surrender to Maj-Gen Rockey in Tientsin. US Marines

protect traffic communications and the coal mines against attacks by Red Chinese units and prepare for the repatriation of the Japanese.

On 4 Oct the Amphibious Group (Commodore Short) arrives off Chefoo (Shantung) from Guam with the 6th Marine Div (Maj-Gen Shepherd). Red Chinese troops are in occupation of Chefoo and deny a landing to the commander of the covering group, Rear-Adm Settle, on the cruiser *Louisville* on 4 Oct and Vice-Adm Barbey who has in the meantime arrived in his flagship *Catoctin* on 7 Oct. The convoy is then re-routed to Tsingtao which the Japanese Maj-Gen Nagano still holds with 10000 troops. On 10 Oct the 6th Marine Div is landed here and Gen Nagano surrenders to Gen Shepherd. In all, some 53000 US Marines are landed in North China.

Subsequently, VII Amphibious Force receives orders to transport the Nationalist Chinese 13th Army from Kowloon to Hulutao in Manchuria and then the 52nd Army (each of 30000 troops) from Haiphong (Indo-China) to Yingkow in Manchuria. Although Marshal Malinovski has agreed with the Nationalist Chinese commander, Gen Tu Li-ming, to allow the landing in Soviet-occupied harbours, the Soviet troops evacuate the harbours when the landing fleets arrive and hand them over to Red Chinese troops who prevent a landing. The Nationalist Chinese have therefore to be disembarked further S in Chinwangtao which in the meantime has been occupied by a BLT of the 1st Marine Div.

3–20 Oct   Indo-China

On 3 Oct the first French troops under Gen Leclerc arrive in Saigon on board the troop transports *Queen Emma* and *Queen Beatrix*. They are escorted, *inter alia*, by the battleship *Richelieu* and the large destroyer *Le Triomphant*.

From 15 to 20 Oct more French ships arrive, including the carrier *Béarn*, the cruisers *Gloire* and *Suffren*, the destroyer *Le Fantasque*, the DEs *Somali* and *Sénégalais*, the sloops *Annamite* and *Gazelle* and the transport *Quercy*.

30 Nov   Western Atlantic

The RCN corvette *Merittonia* is wrecked off the coast of Nova Scotia.

INDEXES

Notes on the Use of the Index

By cross-reference to the various indexes it is possible to trace the activities of individual ships, personnel, forces etc. throughout the war. It should be noted that where a person or vessel or unit is listed on a particular page, that name or number may occur more than once on the page, possibly under a separate date heading. Further notes concerning the use of the index and abbreviations used will be found under the respective index headings. The only abbreviations standard throughout the index are those relating to countries, viz:

Index of Warships

This index contains the active warships and the auxiliaries, most of which latter were originally classified as merchant ships but were taken over by the navies concerned and put into war service. Ships transferred from one navy to another are listed with both their old and their new names.

In general, the abbreviations used to denote the ship type follow US Navy practice. These abbreviations are explained in the general list at the beginning of the book.

Small warships of the Japanese Navy appear as follows:

Aux ML *Fusetsu-Tokumu-Tei*
MTB *Gyorei-Tei*
APD *Ishokaitei* see under 'P' (old DD)
APD *Itto-Yuso-Kan* see under 'P'
Corvette *Kaibokan*
Midget SM *Kaiten*
SC *Kusentai* see under 'Ch'
Aux SC *Kusen-Tokumu-Tei* see under 'Cha'

LST *Nito-Yuso-Kan* see under 'T'
MS *Sokaitei* see under 'W'
Aux MS *Sokai-Tokumu-Tei* see under 'Wa'

Soviet warships have been given an additional abbreviation denoting the area where the vessel served during the war:

(B) Baltic,
(BS) Black Sea,
(N) Arctic (Northern),
(P) Pacific

Finally, special abbreviations are used to designate small and auxiliary warships of the Soviet Navy:

BK/BKA *Bronekater* Armoured cutter
BO *Bolshoi ochotnik* Submarine Chaser
MO *Maly ochotnik* Small submarine chaser
SKR *Storoshevoy korabl* Patrol vessel
T/TShch *Tralshchik* Minesweeper
TK/TKA *Torpedny kater* Motor torpedo boat

INDEX OF WARSHIPS

Index of Merchant Ships

We have placed the different types of merchant ship in this section under broad categories, not distinguishing between the various types of propulsion used nor between the different categories of vessel of a particular type. Thus all cargo carrying vessels, irrespective of type or size, have been listed as freighters, while all passenger carrying vessels (except ferries which are listed as such) have been placed under the broad category of liner. The only category which might cause some confusion is CRS, which were small cross-channel type passenger vessels. These were fitted out with sick bays, dormitories and a medical staff not normally found on warships sailing with the close escort of convoys, nor on merchant ships. They were employed mainly on the Arctic convoys, where they were used for the express purpose of staying behind to rescue seamen from damaged and sinking ships. Note also that several entries in this index are cross-referenced to the Warships Index.

CRS Convoy Rescue Ship
F Freighter
F(C) Freighter fitted with catapult for flying off aircraft
FV Fishing Vessel
L Liner
SV Sailing Vessel
T Tanker
WFS Whale Factory Ship
WV Whalercatcher
Y Yacht

Index of Naval Forces

Index of Armies

Index of Air Forces

Index of Personnel

Note that, for this index only, the abbreviation 'LCdr' is employed to denote Lieutenant-Commander.

Miscellaneous Index

Convoys – Mine Barrages – Operations